STREET ATLAS
Lancashire

Contents

III   *Key to map symbols*

IV-V   *Key to map pages*

VI   *Administrative and post code boundaries*

1   *Street maps (including parts of north Lancashire, pages 220-236, at reduced scale)*

239   *Index of hospitals, railway stations, schools, shopping centres, street names and universities*

PHILIP'S

First edition published 1997 by

Ordnance Survey®
Romsey Road
Maybush
Southampton SO16 4GU

and

George Philip Ltd.
an imprint of Reed Books
Michelin House, 81 Fulham Road, London SW3 6RB
and Auckland, Melbourne, Singapore and Toronto

ISBN 0-540-06440-8 (hardback)
ISBN 0-540-06441-6 (wire-o)

© Crown copyright 1997

© Reed International Books Ltd 1997

Printed and bound in Spain by Cayfosa

To the best of the Publishers´ knowledge, the
information in this atlas was correct at the time of
going to press. No responsibility can be accepted
for any errors or their consequences.

The representation in this atlas of a road, track or
path is no evidence of the existence of a right of way.

**The mapping between pages 1 and 238 (inclusive)
in this atlas is derived from Ordnance Survey®
OSCAR® and Land-Line® data, and Landranger®
mapping.**

Ordnance Survey, OSCAR, Land-Line and Landranger
are registered trade marks of Ordnance Survey, the
National Mapping Agency of Great Britain.

Key to map symbols

(22a)	**Motorway** (with junction number)
	Primary routes (dual carriageway and single)
	A roads (dual carriageway and single)
	B roads (dual carriageway and single)
	Minor through road (dual carriageway and single)
	Minor roads
	Roads under construction
	Railways
	Tramway, miniature railway
	Rural track, private road or narrow road in urban area
	Gate or obstruction to traffic (restrictions may not apply at all times or to all vehicles)
	All paths, bridleways, byway open to all traffic, road used as a public path
	The representation in this atlas of a road, track or path is no evidence of the existence of a right of way
226	**Adjoining page indicators** (The colour of the arrow indicates the scale of the adjoining page – see scales below.)
85	
204 / 199	**Adjoining page indicator** showing the pages adjoining the top and bottom halves of the current page

Acad	**Academy**	Mon	**Monument**
Cemy	**Cemetery**	Mus	**Museum**
C Ctr	**Civic Centre**	Obsy	**Observatory**
CH	**Club House**	Pal	**Royal Palace**
Coll	**College**	PH	**Public House**
Ex H	**Exhibition Hall**	Resr	**Reservoir**
Ind Est	**Industrial Estate**	Ret Pk	**Retail Park**
Inst	**Institute**	Sch	**School**
Ct	**Law Court**	Sh Ctr	**Shopping Centre**
L Ctr	**Leisure Centre**	Sta	**Station**
LC	**Level Crossing**	TH	**Town Hall/House**
Liby	**Library**	Trad Est	**Trading Estate**
Mkt	**Market**	Univ	**University**
Meml	**Memorial**	YH	**Youth Hostel**

	British Rail station
	Private railway station
	Bus, coach station
◆	**Ambulance station**
◆	**Coastguard station**
◆	**Fire station**
◆	**Police station**
✚	**Casualty entrance to hospital**
✝	**Church, place of worship**
H	**Hospital**
i	**Information centre**
P	**Parking**
PO	**Post Office**
Queen Elizabeth's Gram Sch	**Important buildings, schools, colleges, universities and hospitals**
	County boundaries
River Lune	**Water name**
	Stream
	River or canal (minor and major)
	Water
	Tidal water
	Woods
	Houses

■ The dark grey border on the inside edge of some pages indicates that the mapping does not continue onto the adjacent page

■ The small numbers around the edges of the maps identify the 1 kilometre National Grid lines

The scale of the maps on pages numbered in blue is 5.52 cm to 1 km (3½ inches to 1 mile)

0	¼	½	¾	1 mile
0	250m	500m	750m	1 Kilometre

The scale of the maps on pages numbered in green is 2.78 cm to 1 km (1¾ inches to 1 mile)

0	¼	½	¾	1 mile
0	250m	500m	750m	1 Kilometre

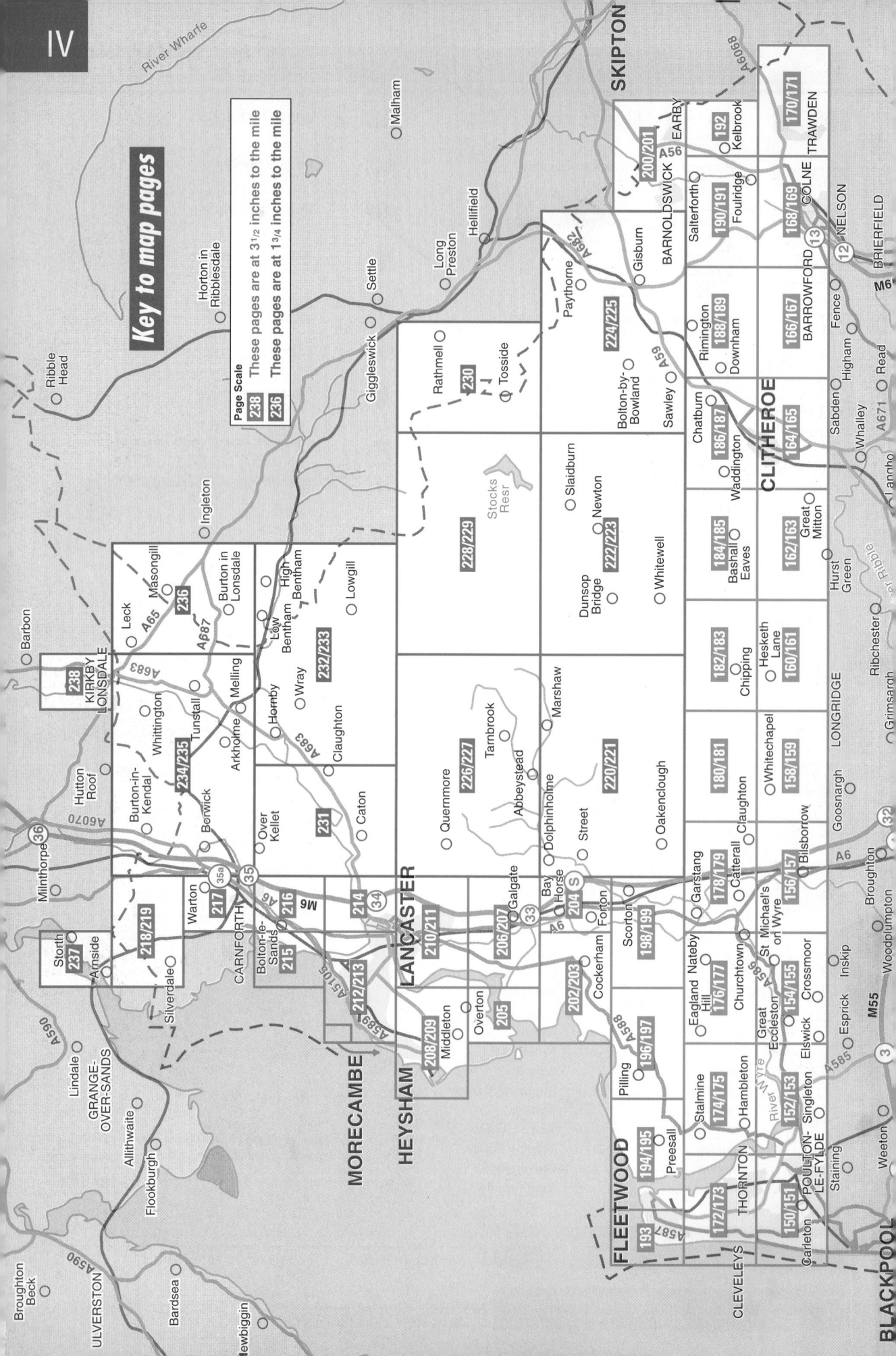

IV

Key to map pages

Page Scale
238 ☐ These pages are at 3½ inches to the mile
236 ☐ These pages are at 1¾ inches to the mile

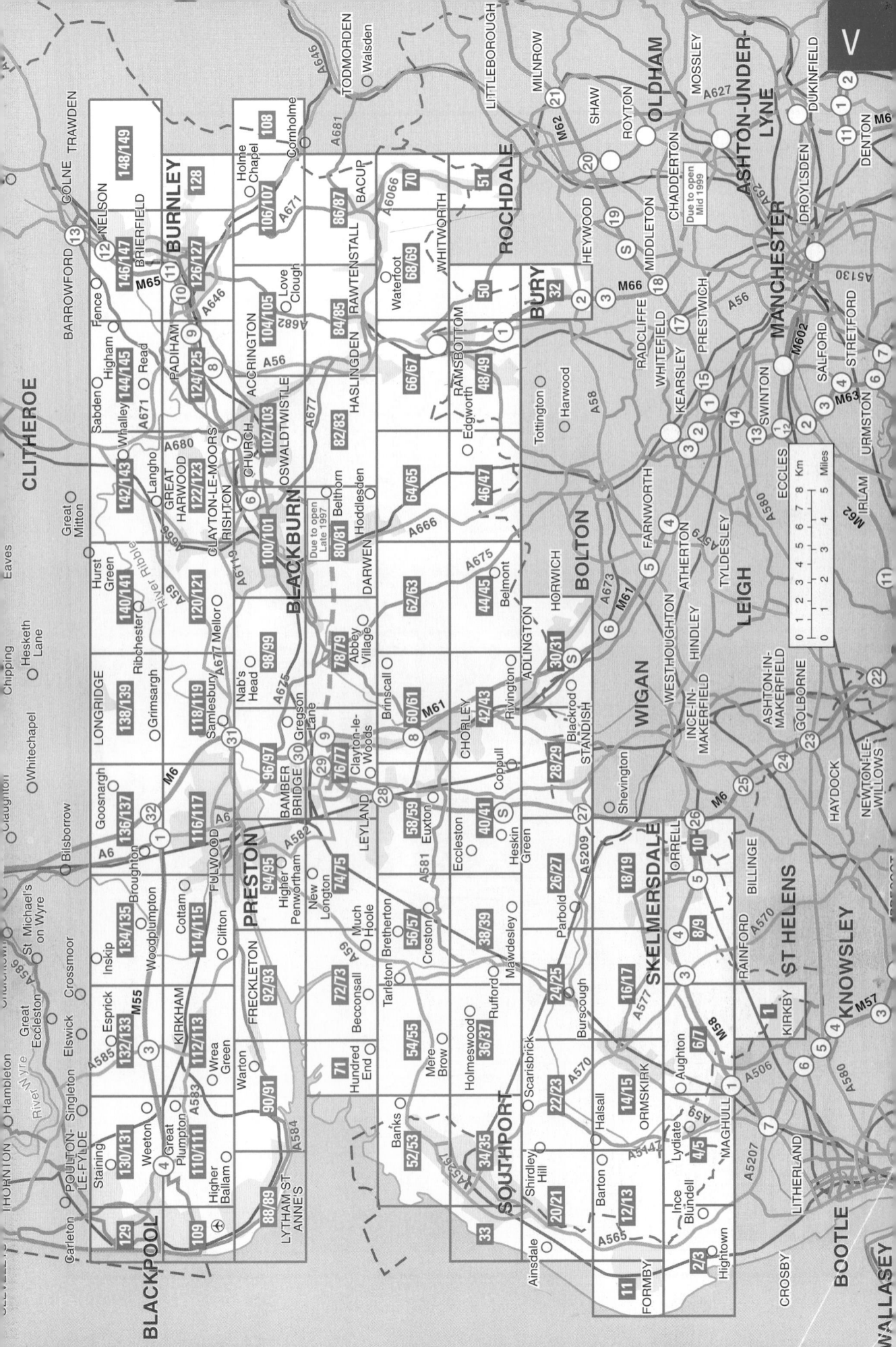

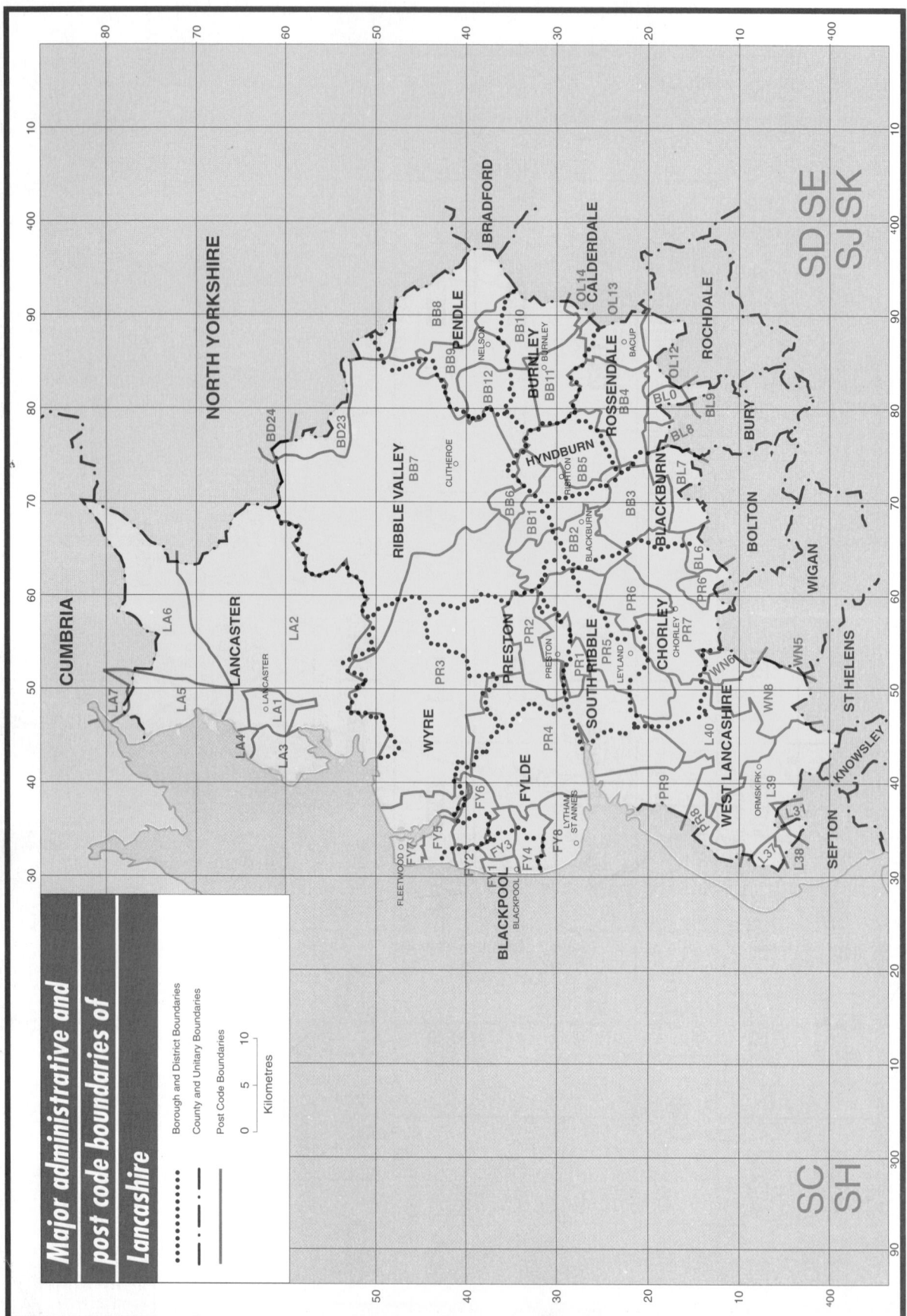

Major administrative and post code boundaries of Lancashire

Borough and District Boundaries
County and Unitary Boundaries
Post Code Boundaries

0   5   10
Kilometres

A B C D E F

Brookfield
Farm

Voces
Farm

Walkden House
Farm

8

Hesketh's
Shroggs

Sewage
Works

Barrow Nook
Hall

Grayson's
Farm

HALL LA

Simonswood Brook

New Bridge
Farm

7

SINFACRE LA

Wood House
Farm

High Barn
Farm

Abram's
Farm

Hall's
Folly

STOPGATE LA

SIDING LA

01

SHEVINGTON'S
LA

Wild Goose
Slack

6

Gate House
Bridge

SIMONSWOOD IND PK

Timber
Yard

CALDER CL

MOOR LA

PINGWOOD LA

Woodwards
Plantation

5

Woods
Farm

HEADBOLT LA

Bridge
Farm

1 LAPFORD WLK
2 BYTON WLK
3 LINSDALE CRES
4 WHITBURN RD
5 KENBURY CL

Southead

Spencer's House
Farm

DALE LA

Eccleston
House

NORTH PERIMETER RD

00

Simonswood
Moss

4

BRAMCOTE RD
BRAMCOTE CRES
LAPFORD CRES

SHACKLADY RD
RANTLAND
FALSTONE CL
ROUGHWOOD DR

WARRENHOUSE
RD

Ashcroft's
Plantation

DEROT RD

Works

OAKLEE
GR
FOSCOTE

JARBETT RD

WATTS LA

CHANGFORD

BROOK HEY DR

A3
1 WINGATE RD
2 BROOK HEY WLK
3 WINGATE WLK
4 KENNELWOOD AVE
5 JADE CL
6 QUERNMORE WLK
7 CHANGFORD GN
8 BIRBECK WLK
9 FAIRTHORN WLK
10 HARLESTON WLK
11 BURWELL CL
12 KENMAY WAY

NORTH MERSEY
BSNS CTR

WOODWARD RD

MOSS END WAY

MARL RD

HAMMOND RD

BRADMAN RD

3

Northwood

QUERNMORE RD

CLORAIN
CL

BIRBECK RD

CLORAIN RD
DARMOND RD

MOSS LA

ASHCROFT RD

SANDERLING RD

HARLESTON
WLK

QUARRYSIDE DR

SIMONSWOOD LA

1 OLD ROUGH LA
2 RETFORD RD
3 BRECHIN RD
4 LIFTON RD
5 SIMONSWOOD WLK
6 COLWALL WLK

COURTYARD
WORKS

NEWSTET RD

BIRCHILL RD

STOCKPIT RD

DRAWWELL RD

ACORNFIELD RD

PERIMETER RD

Top House
Farm

99

BOUNDARY LA

2

Sch

MINSTEAD AVE

COLWALL
CL

Playing
Field

KIRKBY BANK RD

Orchard
Works

CRANSTOCK RD

WYLLIN RD

MINTOR RD

GLESSIDE RD

ARBOUR LA

LEES RD

WEBBER RD

YARDLEY RD

Kirkby Moss

MADRYN AVE

ORMSIDE CRES

1 WESTHEAD WLK
2 WESTHEAD CL
3 PARK BROW DR
4 CLIEVES RD

ACORN
BSNS CTR

YARDLEY
CTR

Charley
Wood

BARNMILL
HOBBS
HARRISON

WESTHEAD AVE

KIRKBY

A5208

COUNTY RD

CUSSON RD

CHARLEY WOOD RD

GORES RD

A5208

BROOM LA

MOSSLAWN RD

DELFBY CRES

RUSHDEN RD

DULAS
CRAWAR
CROSLAND RD

1

42 A B 43 C 44 D E F 98

A B C D E F

8
7
05
6
5
04
4
03
3
2
1
02

27 A B 28 C D 29 E F

Mount Pleasant
ALEXANDRA RD
ALBERT RD
ELSWORTH CL
ST LUKE'S CHURCH RD
STAPLETON RD
Marsh Farm
Range High Sch
PARK CL
HOGGS HILL LA
Sewage Works
Works
Raven Meols Hills
Nature Reserve
Sefton Coastal Path
Cambrai Cottage
Grange Farm
GRANGE RD
Altcar Training Camp
LC
DANGER AREA
Battery Cottage
River Alt
Sefton Coastal Path
Altcar Rifle Range
DANGER AREA
ST GEORGE'S RD
DANGER AREA
MARK RD
HESTER CL
ST STEPHEN'S RD
LAKE WAY
LOWER ALT RD
ALT RD
SCHOOL RD
PO
NORTHOLMES
RATHBONE RD
RIVERSIDE
WESTWAY
VILLAGE WAY
SANDILANDS
SANDILANDS DR
BLUNDELL AVE
THE ROUND
EVANS'DE
WIGNALLS MEADOW
SARHILLS
OLD ACRE
LARKHILL LA
BRIARY
MOORHOUSES
THORNBECK AVE
WITHINS FIELD
BLUNDELL GR
ALTON CL
WHITLEY
BRENTWOOD CL
LANGLEY CL
BLUNDELL RD
RICHMOND CL
OAKFIELD
MAYFAIR CL
Formby Bank
Liverpool Bay
Sefton Coastal Path

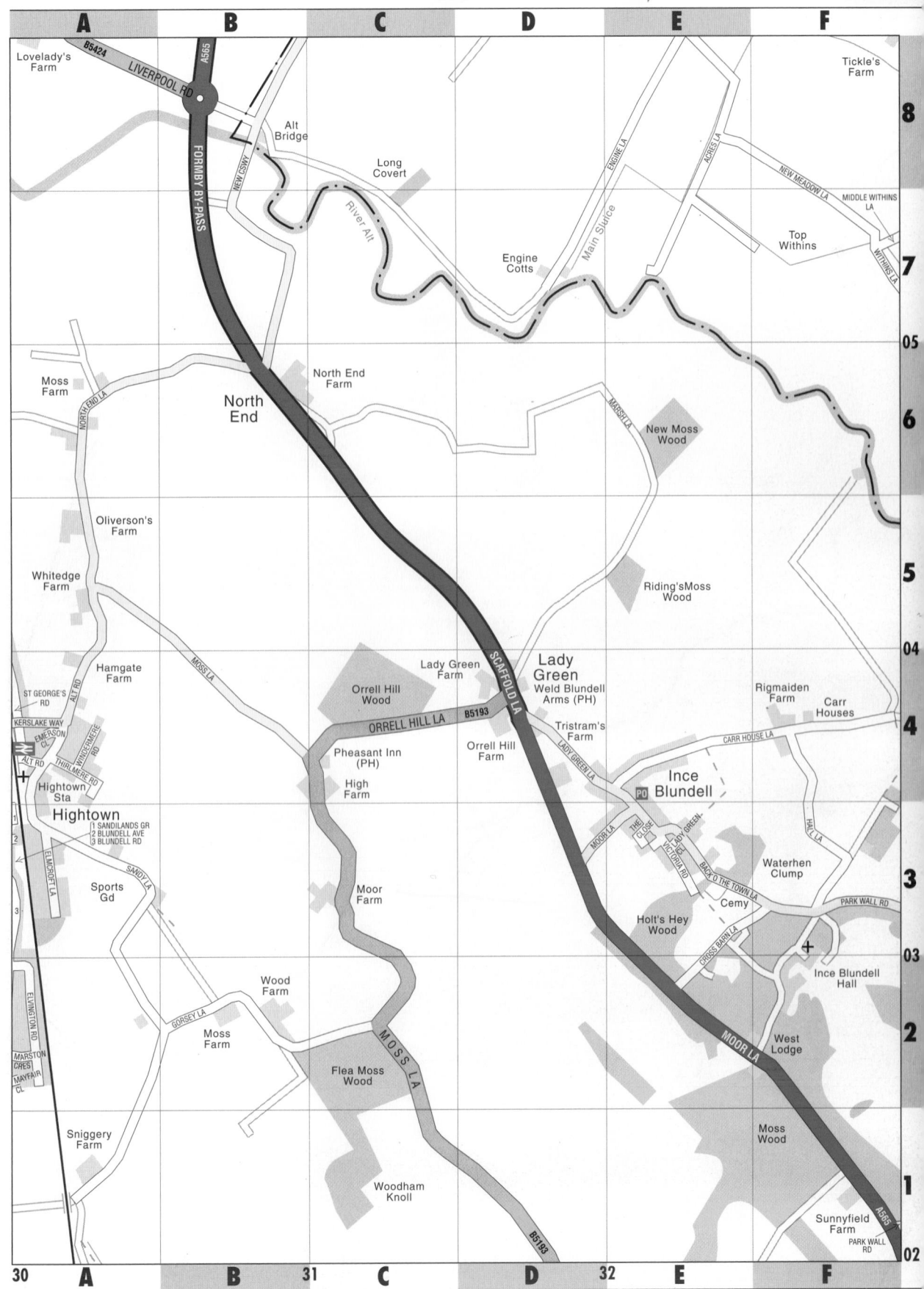

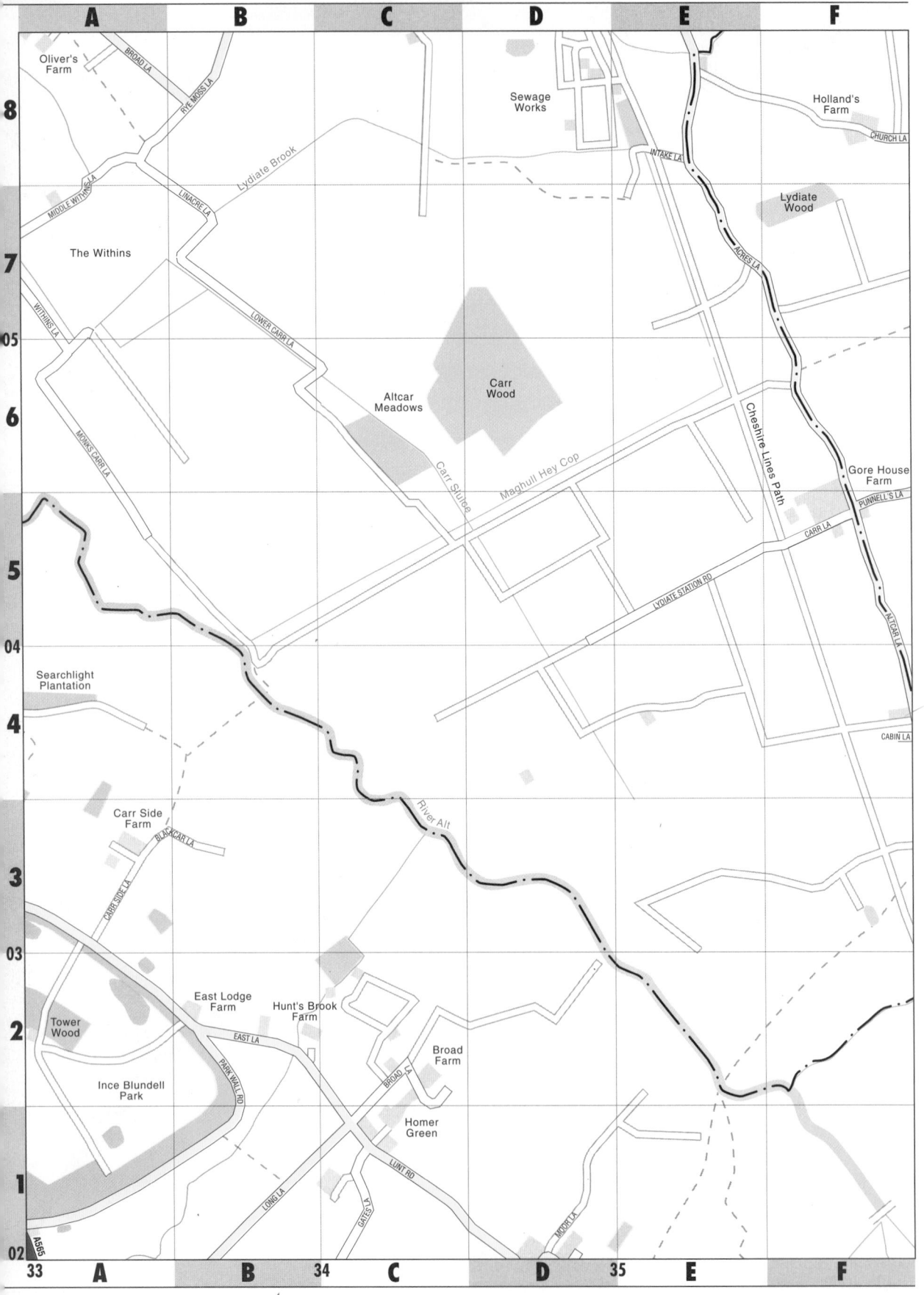

A B C D E F

8

05

7

6

5

04

4

03

3

02

2

1

02

33 A B 34 C D 35 E F

Oliver's Farm
BROAD LA
RYE MOSS LA
Sewage Works
Holland's Farm
CHURCH LA
MIDDLE WITHINS LA
LINACRE LA
Lydiate Brook
INTAKE LA
Lydiate Wood
ACRES LA
The Withins
WITHINS LA
LOWER CARR LA
Altcar Meadows
Carr Wood
Cheshire Lines Path
MONKS CARR LA
Carr Sluice
Maghull Hey Cop
Gore House Farm
PUNNELL'S LA
CARR LA
LYDIATE STATION RD
ALTCAR LA
Searchlight Plantation
CABIN LA
River Alt
Carr Side Farm
BLACKCAR LA
CARR SIDE LA
Tower Wood
East Lodge Farm
Hunt's Brook Farm
EAST LA
PARK WALL RD
Broad Farm
BROAD LA
Ince Blundell Park
Homer Green
LONG LA
GATES LA
LUNT RD
MOOR LA
A565

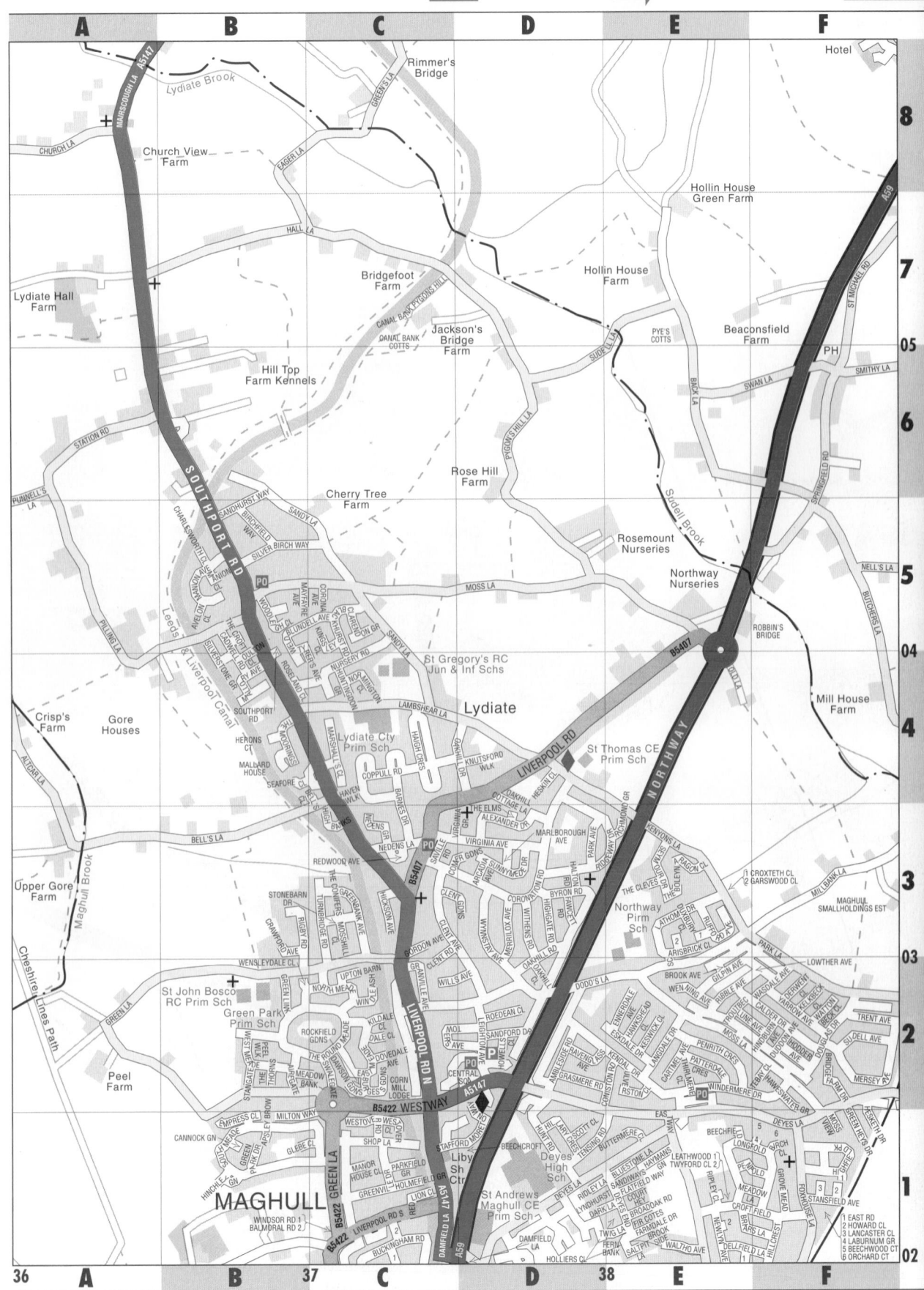

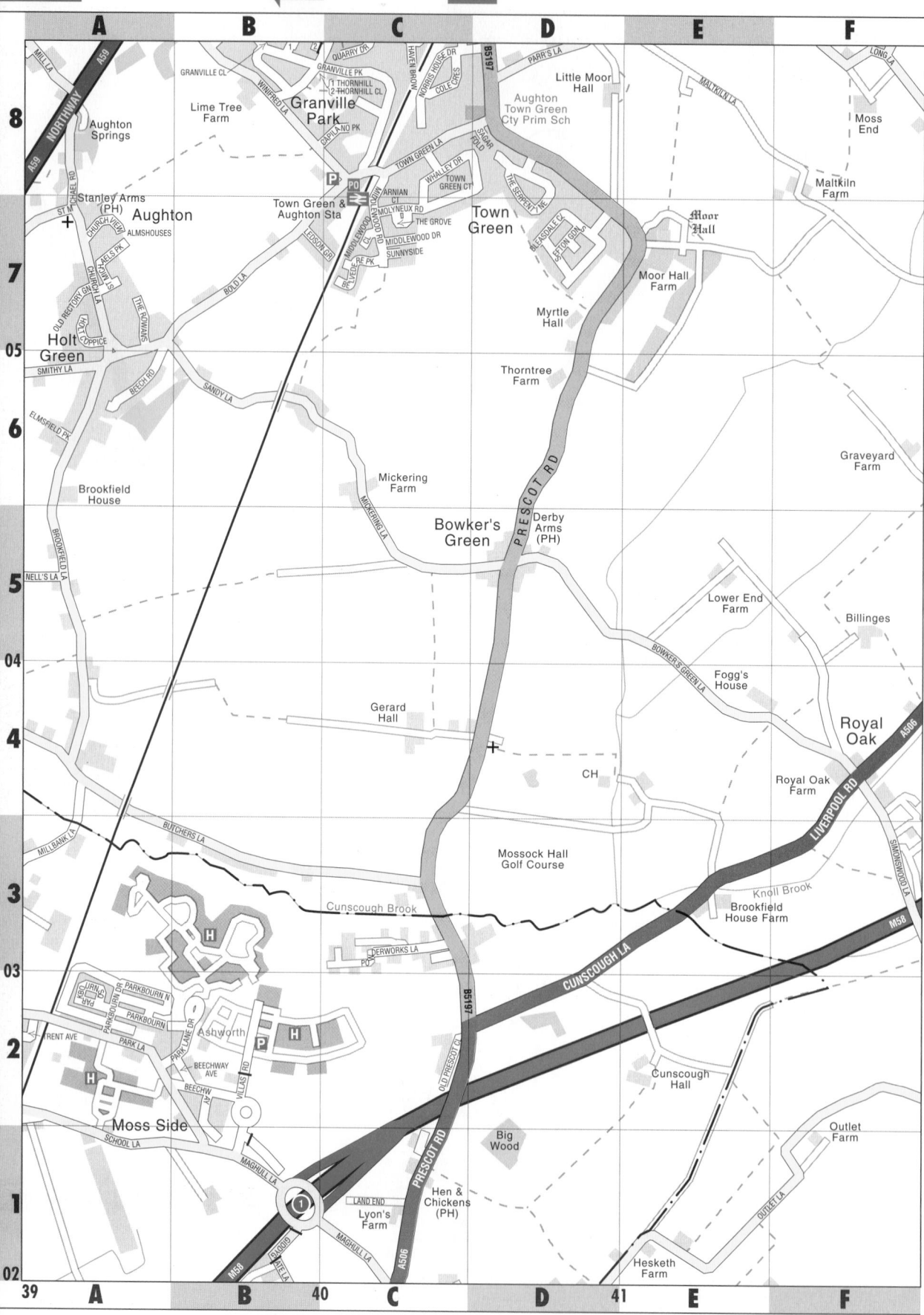

A B C D E F

8

7

05

6

5

04

4

3

03

2

1

02

A59 NORTHWAY

MILL LA
Aughton Springs
Aughton
ST MICHAEL RD
CHURCH VIEW
WELS PK
CHURCH LA
OLD RECTORY GN
VICH
COPPICE
Holt Green
SMITHY LA
ELMSFIELD PK
THE ROWANS
SANDY LA
BEECH RD
NELL'S LA
BROOKFIELD LA

GRANVILLE CL
Lime Tree Farm
WINIFRED LA
QUARRY DR
GRANVILLE PK
Granville Park
1 THORNHILL
2 THORNHILL CL
CAPILA-NO PK
TOWN GREEN LA
P
PO
LEDSON GR
BOLD LA
MINOR
BC
RE PK
MINSLEWOOD
Town Green & Aughton Sta

NORRIS HOUSE DR
COLE CRES
HAVEN BROW
B5197
Brookfield House
Mickering Farm
MICKERING LA

PARR'S LA
Little Moor Hall
Aughton Town Green Cty Prim Sch
SAGAR FIELD
WHALLEY DR
TOWN GREEN CT
ARNIAN CI
MOLYNEUX RD
THE GROVE
MIDDLEWOOD DR
SUNNYSIDE
Town Green
THE SERPENTINE
BLEASDALE CI
SEFTON GDN
Myrtle Hall
Thorntree Farm
Bowker's Green
PRESCOT RD
Derby Arms (PH)

MALTKILN LA
Moss End
Maltkiln Farm
Moor Hall
Moor Hall Farm
Graveyard Farm
Lower End Farm
Billinges
BOWKER'S GREEN LA
Fogg's House
Royal Oak
A506
Royal Oak Farm
LIVERPOOL RD
SIMONSWOOD LA
M58

Gerard Hall
CH
Mossock Hall Golf Course
Knoll Brook
Brookfield House Farm

BUTCHERS LA
MILL BANK LA
Cunscough Brook
DERWORKS LA
PO
H
PARKBOURN N
PARKBOURN DR
PARKBOURN
Ashworth
H
P
Moss Side
SCHOOL LA
BEECHWAY AVE
BEECHW
VILLAS RD
PARK LANE DR
PARK LA
TRENT AVE
H
MAGHULL LA
B5197
OLD PRESCOT CL
CUNSCOUGH LA
Cunscough Hall
Big Wood
Outlet Farm
OUTLET LA

1
PRESCOT RD
A506
MAGHULL LA
LAND END
Lyon's Farm
Hen & Chickens (PH)
Hesketh Farm
M58
GATE LA
COLI

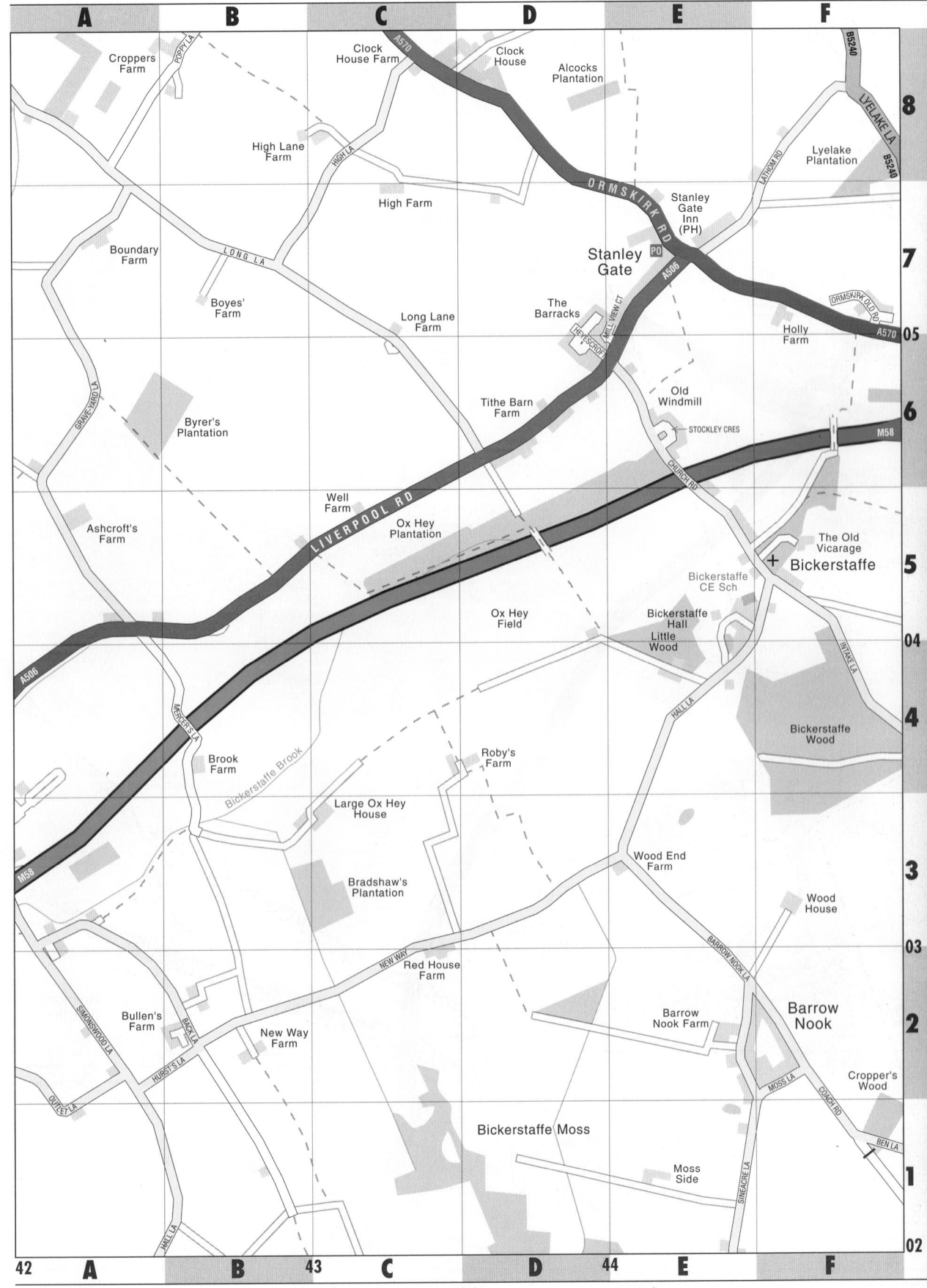

7
17

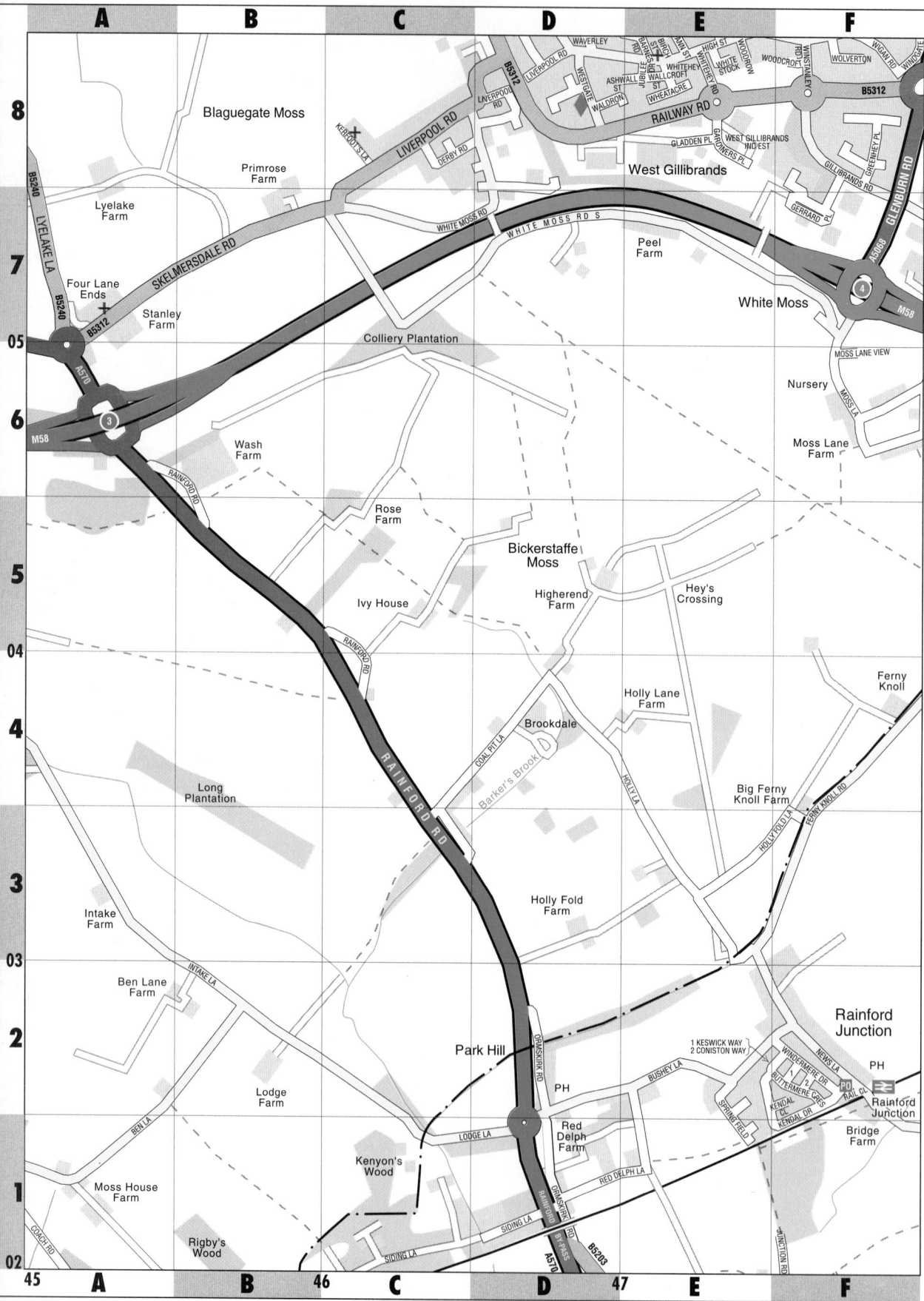

A B C D E F

8

Blaguegate Moss

Primrose
Farm

B5312
LIVERPOOL RD

Liverpool Rd

WAVERLEY

BIRCH ST

BACK BIRCH ST
MAIN ST

WHITEHEY RD

HIGH ST
WHITE STOCK

WOODROW

WOODCROFT

WINSTANLEY RD

WOLVERTON

WOLVERTON

WIGAN RD

WINDGATE

ASHWALL ST
WALLCROFT

WHEATACRE

WALDRON

WESTGATE

RAILWAY RD

GLADDEN PL

GROMERS PL

WEST GILLIBRANDS
IND EST

GERRARD PL

GILLIBRANDS RD

GREENHEY PL

B5312

Lyelake
Farm

7

B5240
LYELAKE LA

SKELMERSDALE RD

WHITE MOSS RD

WHITE MOSS RD S

West Gillibrands

Peel
Farm

GLENBURN RD
A5068

Four Lane
Ends

B5240
B5312

Stanley
Farm

Colliery Plantation

White Moss

4
M58

05

A570

MOSS LANE VIEW

6

M58

3

RAINFORD RD

Wash
Farm

Nursery

MOSS LA

Moss Lane
Farm

Rose
Farm

Bickerstaffe
Moss

Higherend
Farm

Hey's
Crossing

Ivy House

RAINFORD RD

04

Ferny
Knoll

Holly Lane
Farm

Long
Plantation

COAL PIT LA

Brookdale

Barker's Brook

HOLLY LA

Big Ferny
Knoll Farm

HOLLYFORD LA

FERNY KNOLL RD

RAINFORD RD

4

3

Intake
Farm

Holly Fold
Farm

03

Ben Lane
Farm

INTAKE LA

Rainford
Junction

2

Park Hill

ORMSKIRK RD

PH

BUSHEY LA

1 KESWICK WAY
2 CONISTON WAY

WINDERMERE DR

NEWS LA

BUTTERMERE CRES

KENDAL CL

KENDAL DR

RAIL 2

PO

PH

Rainford
Junction

Lodge
Farm

LODGE LA

Red
Delph
Farm

SPRING FIELD

Bridge
Farm

Kenyon's
Wood

RED DELPH LA

1

Moss House
Farm

GRIMSHAW RD

SIDING LA

JUNCTION RD

COACH RD

Rigby's
Wood

SIDING LA

RAINFORD BY-PASS

A570

B5203

02

45

A B 46 C D 47 E F

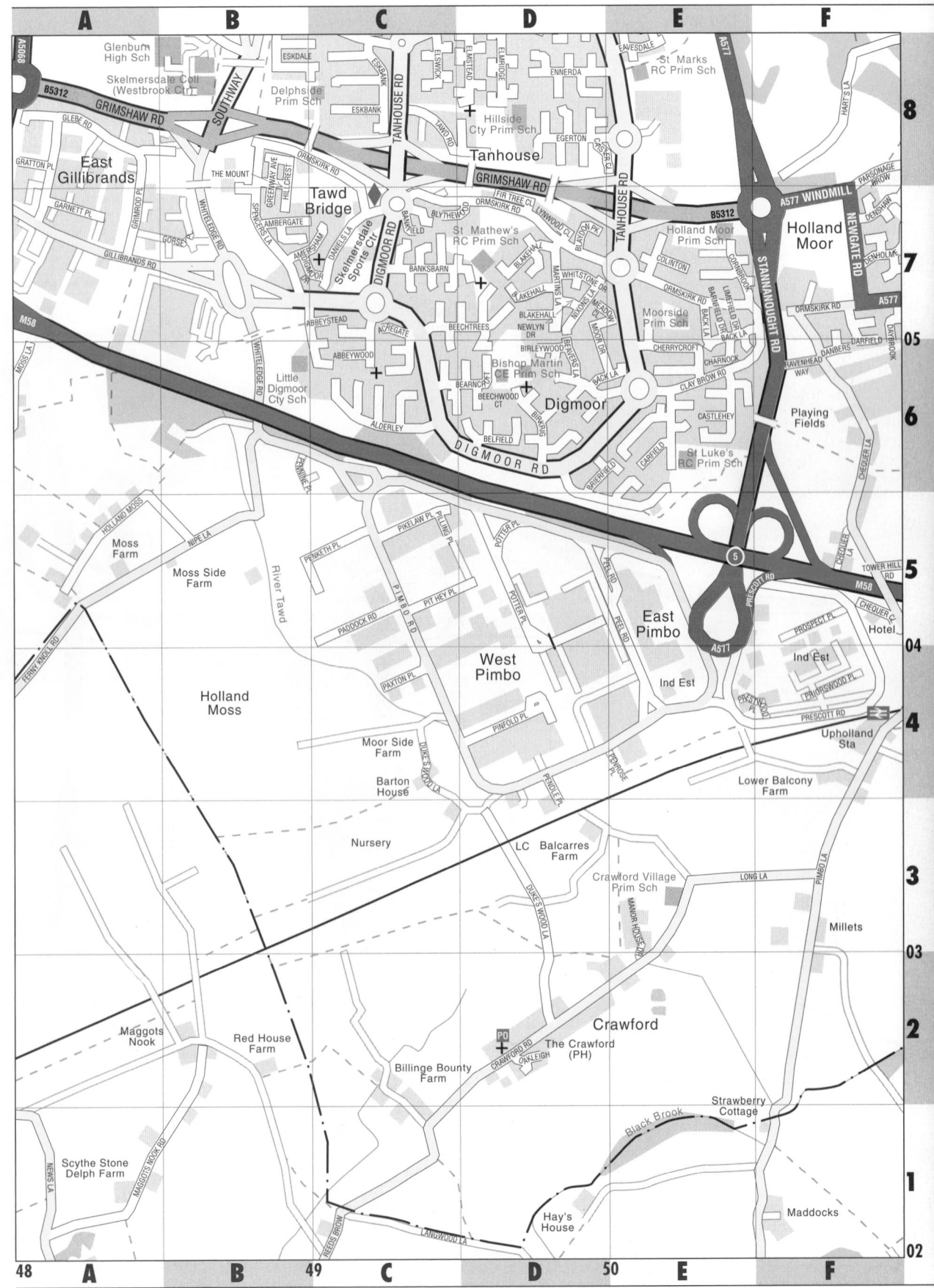

A B C D E F

8
7
09
6
5
08
4
3
07
2
1
06

Cloven-le-Dale
LC
Woodvale Airfield

Fisherman's Path

LC

LITTLE BREWERY LA
Clarence House Sch
OLD TOWN LA
BREWERY LA

Formby Hills

ST ANNE'S CL
KENTON CL
YORK CL
PARDISE LA
WEST LA
STANLEY RD
ST ANNE'S RD
ST ANNE'S PATH

FISHERMAN'S CL
RIMER'S AVE
ARGARMEOLS RD
CANTERBURY LA
WRIGLEY'S CL
WRIGLEY'S

Freshfield Caravan Pk

MERSEY AVE
STANLAWE RD
GREGSON'S AVE
CUMMINS AVE
FRED BARNES
MAYFIELD CT
TIMMS LA
GREEN LA
CRICKET PATH

MONTAGU RD
ARGARMEOLS GR
QUEENS AVE
THE BIRCHES

Picnic Area

CH
VICTORIA WAY
GOLF RD
LC
Freshfield Sta
LOWSWOOD
GRANGE LA
Freshfield
GORES LA
DEAN'S CT
BORROWDALE

Golf Links

SHIREBURN RD
FAIRHOS CT
SAMWYS CT
TOWER END
FAIRWS CT

VICTORIA RD
COLLEGE PATH
DERBY RD
PIERCEFIELD RD
PO

BADGERS PLACE

FIRS CRES
FIRS CL
FIRS LINK
COLLEGE CL
VICARAGE RD
VICARAGE RD
HAZEBANK GDNS
FRESHFIELD CT
OLD TOWN LA
BRECON RD
GRANGE RD
FRIARS RD
LODGE
BYRON RD
GRABURN RD

SQUIRREL GN
BIRCH GN
ST PETER'S CL
LARCH CL
OAKFIELD DR
COLLEGE CL
HOLMWOOD RD
LENTON GDNS
VAUGHAN CL
ST GEORGE'S RD
Formby High Sch
WILLOW LA
OLD MILL LA
FORMBY GDNS
ALDER CL
DEVON CRES

Sandfield Farm

GORSE WAY
PROCTOR RD
DUNES DR
LARKHILL LA
HARINGTON RD
BEECH DR
WOOD GDNS
BARKFIELD LA
LONG LA
CLIFDEN RD
HALL LA
DAVENHAM RD

BLUNDELL AVE
WICKS CRES
WICKS GREEN CL
WARREN GN
NELD CL
BARKFIELD AVE
FRESHFIELD RD
COPPICE LEYS
LONSDALE RD
FORMBY
Holy Trinity CE Prim Sch
THE GALLERY
PAGE CT
FURNESS AVE
SCHOOL AVE
SCHOOL LA
THE CLOISTERS
PO

WICKS GREEN CL
SPRUCE WAY
RICE CRES
HARINGTON GN
HOLMWOOD CL
WICKS GDNS
ROSEMARY LA
FURNESS AVE
MICHAELS CL
CHAPEL LA
SUMNER RD
CROPTON RD
TREE TOPS LA

St Jerome's RC Prim Sch
DENHURST CL
HAZLEHURST CL
FOXHILL CL
GREENLOON'S DR
GREENLOON'S DR
Woodlands Prim Sch
GRASMERE AVE
WOODLANDS RD
BUTTERMERE CL
EMERDALE CL
WICKS LA
TARN RD
HEYWOOD CL
LENSEY CL
BROWNS LA
DUKES WAY
PHILLIP'S LA
ELBOW LA

SPRUCE WAY
KIRKLAKE RD
KIRK LA
BANK AVE
KIRKDALE DR
COTTAGE
ELMDALE
COTTON CL
FEWRFELT
THISTLE CL
CONISTON RD
MERE AVE
LANGDALE
ESKDALE
ESKDALE RD
RYDAL AVE
BRIDGE ST
MARSH BROWS
ASHURST
DUKE ST
Liby
Formby Sta
PHILLIP'S LA
MEADOW CROFT
DICKINSON CL
ROBINSON GRN

Formby Bridge
FORMBY BRIDGE
P
RAVENSCROFT
WALKER CL
GLENDALE
BIRKEY LA

CHURCH WAY
SPRINGFIELD
St Luke's Dr
BUSHBY'S PK
BROOKS RD
WM
BROOKS RD
CHINDIT CL
SEFTON RD
CROFT
QUEEN'S RD
FORMBY ST
KING'S CL
KING'S RD
DICKINSON CL
RAVEN MEOLS LA

CHURCH GN
BUSHBY'S LA
LIME TREE WAY
TRAP HILL
MAPLE CL
PINEWOOD CL
SEALAND AVE
SEALAND AVE
MEOLS CL
Eccles Crossing
NURSERY DR
HARBREY LA

P
LIFEBOAT RD
Shorrocks Hill
ST LUKE'S CHURCH RD
CHESTNUT WAY
ELM DR
St Luke's Ave Sch
JUBILEE RD
ELSON RD
ANDREWS WYCRT
PO
ANDREWS WY
FOSTON RD
BUCKINGHAM RD
KENSINGTON RD
SANDRINGHAM RD
WINDSOR RD
PARK AVE
PARK WAY
CASTLE DR
OSBORNE
MARINA RD
Bill's La
KENT RD
ASHCROFT RD

Formby Point Caravan Pk

BEECHWOOD DR
SYCAMORE GR
ASPEN GR
CEDAR DR
MAYFIELD AVE
CHESTNUT GR
GEORGIAN PL
CARR'S CRES
CARR'S CRES W
FUNCHAL AVE
ELSON RD
CRESCENT AVE
HAMPTON RD
BALMORAL AVE
EDINBURGH RD
LANCASTER RD
HOGGS HILL LA
ALTCAR LA
BELVEDERE DR
Sewage Works

Sefton Coastal Path

ALEXANDRA RD
ELMSWOOD RD
BUNGALOW
SANDHURST CL
MELDRETH CL
HEYDON CL
BURWELL CL
ORWELL CL
STAPLETON RD
STAPLETON RD
HADSTOCK AVE
CAMBRIDGE RD
BARTON RD
KEW RD
SUTTON RD
ANDREW CL
ECCLES HEYS RD

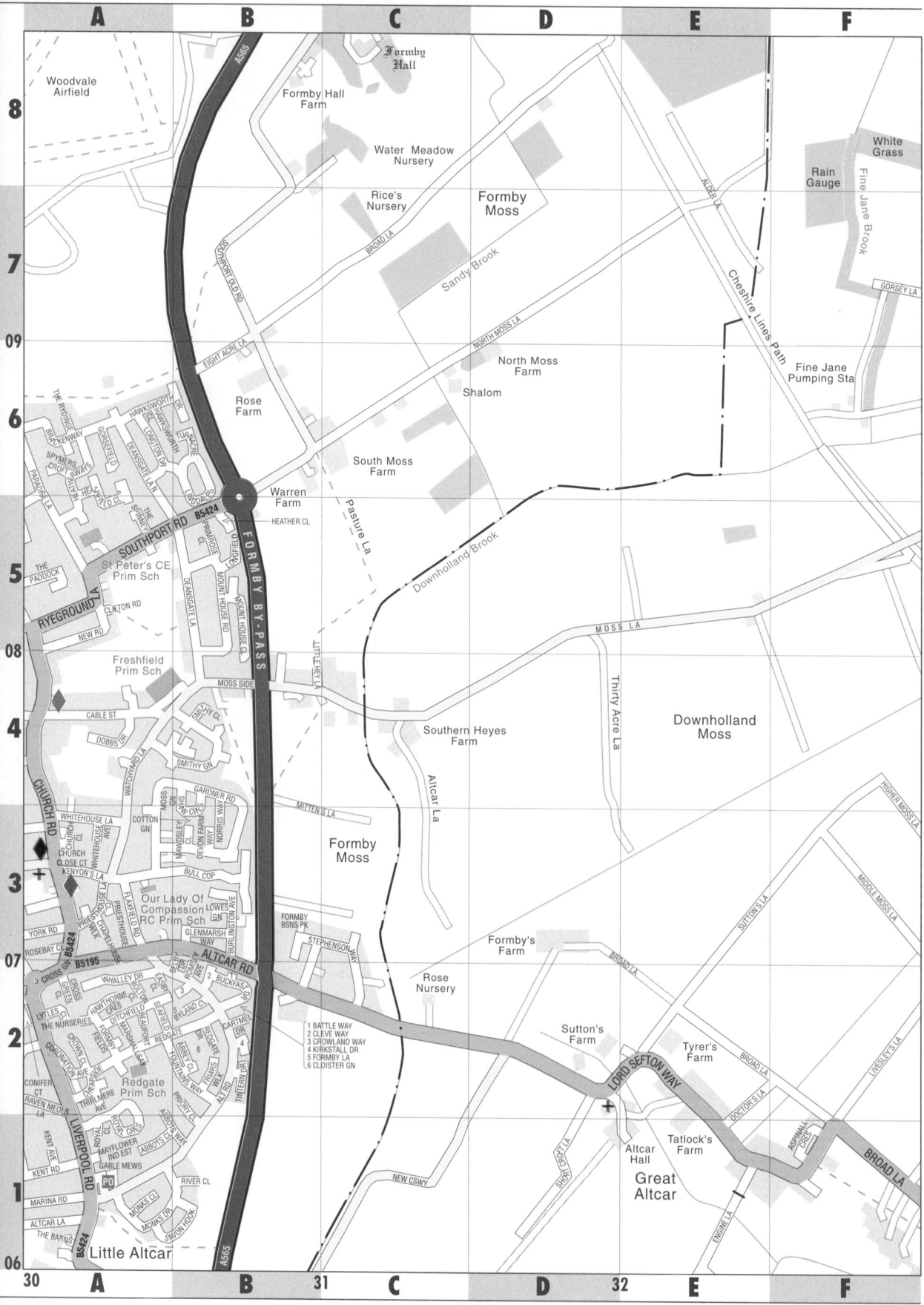

11
20

A B C D E F

8

Woodvale
Airfield

Formby
Hall

Formby Hall
Farm

Water Meadow
Nursery

Rice's
Nursery

Formby
Moss

White
Grass

7

Broad La

Sandy Brook

Rain
Gauge

Fine Jane Brook

GORSEY LA

09

Cheshire Lines Path

EIGHT ACRE LA

North Moss La

North Moss
Farm

Fine Jane
Pumping Sta

6

Rose
Farm

Shalom

South Moss
Farm

Warren
Farm

B5424

HEATHER CL

SOUTHPORT OLD RD

5

SOUTHPORT RD

St Peter's CE
Prim Sch

Pasture La

Downholland Brook

RYEGROUND LA

CLIFTON RD

NEW RD

08

DEANSGATE LA

MOUNT HOUSE RD

MOUNT HOUSE CL

MOSS SIDE

MOSS LA

Freshfield
Prim Sch

LITTLE HEY LA

4

CABLE ST

DOBBS DR

SMITHY CL

SMITHY GN

Southern Heyes
Farm

Thirty Acre La

Downholland
Moss

FORMBY BY-PASS

WATCHYARD LA

GARDNER RD

MITTEN'S LA

Altcar La

HIGHER MOSS LA

3

WHITEHOUSE LA

CHURCH RD

COTTON
GN

NORRIS WAY

DEVON FARM
WAY

BULL COP

Formby
Moss

MIDDLE MOSS LA

Our Lady Of
Compassion
RC Prim Sch

LOWES
LGN

FLAXFIELD RD

BURLINGTON AVE

FORMBY
BSNS PK

SUTTON'S LA

YORK RD

ROSEBAY CL

B5424

GLENMARSH
WAY

STEPHENSON WAY

Formby's
Farm

BROAD LA

07

CROSS GN

B5195

ALTCAR RD

Rose
Nursery

2

WHALLEY DR

BUCKFAST

1 BATTLE WAY
2 CLEVE WAY
3 CROWLAND WAY
4 KIRKSTALL DR
5 FORMBY LA
6 CLOISTER GN

Sutton's
Farm

Tyrer's
Farm

BROAD LA

LORD SEFTON WAY

DOCTOR'S LA

LIVESLEY'S LA

CARTMEL

BYLAND

ABBEY CL

PRIORY CL

TINTERN DR

ALT RD

Redgate
Prim Sch

LIVERPOOL RD

MAYFLOWER
IND EST

GABLE MEWS

ABBOTS CL

RIVER CL

Tatlock's
Farm

ASPINALL CRES

BROAD LA

KENT AVE

KENT RD

MARINA RD

ALTCAR LA

THE BARNS

MONKS CL

MONKS DR

SAVON HOOK

NEW CSWY

SHORT LA

Altcar
Hall

Great
Altcar

ENGINE LA

1

B5424

Little Altcar

A565

06

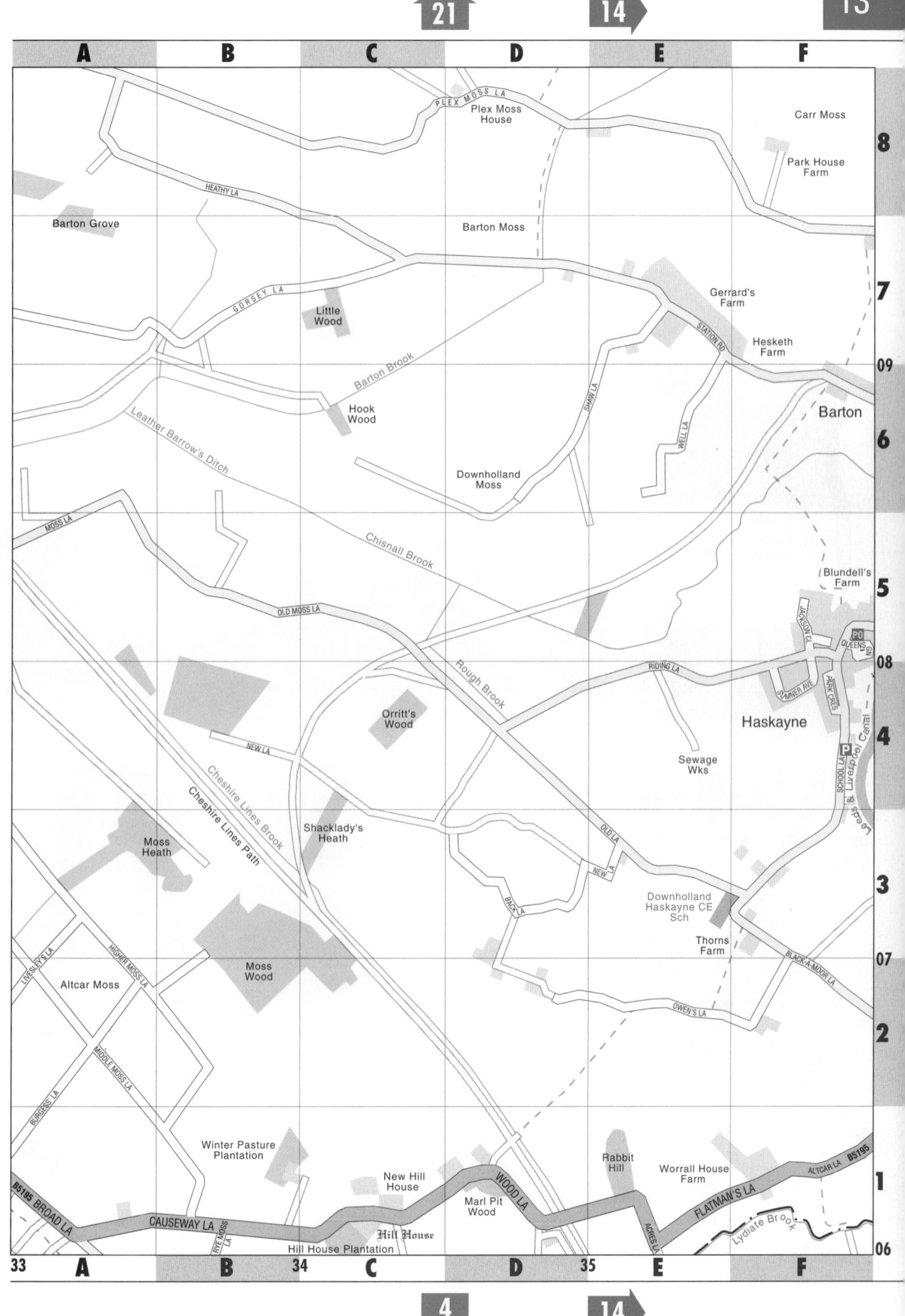

A B C D E F

8
7
09
6
5
08
4
3
07
2
1
06

PLEX MOSS LA
Plex Moss House
Carr Moss
Park House Farm
HEATHY LA
Barton Grove
Barton Moss
Gerrard's Farm
GORSEY LA
STATION RD
Little Wood
Hesketh Farm
Barton Brook
Barton
Leather Barrow's Ditch
Hook Wood
SHAW LA
WELL LA
Downholland Moss
MOSS LA
Chisnall Brook
Blundell's Farm
JACKSON CL
PO
QUEENS
OLD MOSS LA
Rough Brook
RIDING LA
SOMNER AVE
PARK CRES
Orritt's Wood
Haskayne
NEW LA
Sewage Wks
SCHOOL LA
Leeds & Liverpool Canal
P
Cheshire Lines Brook
Shacklady's Heath
OLD LA
Cheshire Lines Path
Downholland Haskayne CE Sch
Moss Heath
BACK LA
NEW LA
Thorns Farm
BLACK-A-MOOR LA
LIXSEY'S LA
HIGHER MOSS LA
Altcar Moss
Moss Wood
OWEN'S LA
MIDDLE MOSS LA
BURGESS LA
Winter Pasture Plantation
Rabbit Hill
Worrall House Farm
ALTCAR LA
B5195
B5195 BROAD LA
New Hill House
WOOD LA
FLATMAN'S LA
CAUSEWAY LA
RYE MOSS LA
Marl Pit Wood
ACRES LA
Lydiate Brook
Hill House
Hill House Plantation

33 A B 34 C D 35 E F 06

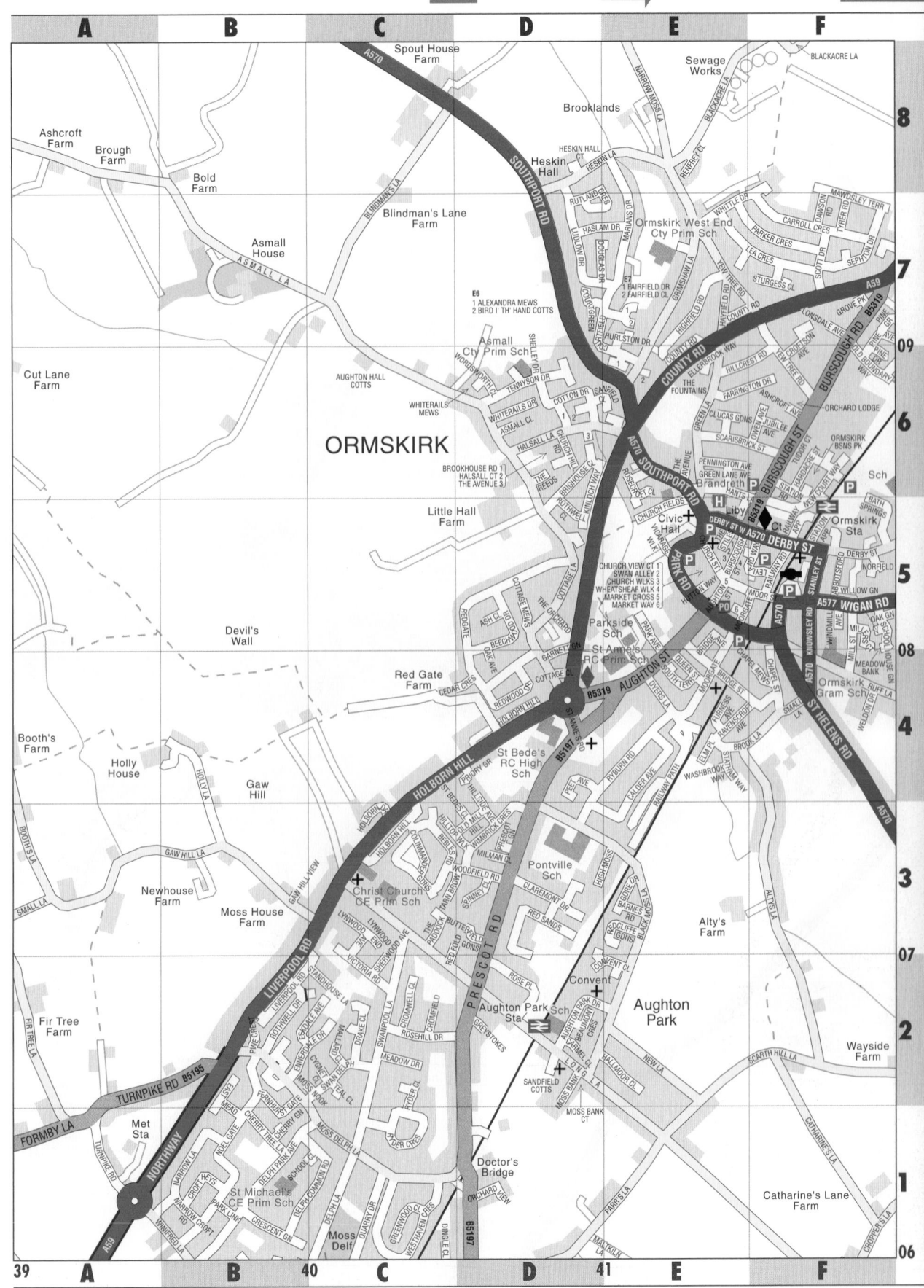

ORMSKIRK

Heyes Farm

A59

HIGH LA

Sycamore House Farm

Abbey Farm

Burscough Priory

Jump's Farm

Bullen's Wood

Timbobbin Farm

ABBEY LA

MILL DAM LA

BLYTHE LA

LADY ALICE'S DR

Needless Inn Farm

Bath Lodge

Grove Farm

A59

SANDY LA

Robinsons Farm

CRANES LA

Mains Wood

Brooklands Ave

Ave

Dark Lane Farm

DARK LA

LATHOM LA

CH

New Park Brook

Bath Farm

Leas Farm

New Park Ormskirk Golf Course

Nursery Ave

Waterworks Rd

Pengle Dr

Hettings House

Charlesbye Mews

Lady's Wlk

Leveldale

New Park Wood

CASTLE LA

Halsall's Lodge

Greetby Hill

Delph Rd

Charlesbye Cl

Charlesbye Ave

Ormskirk CE Prim Sch

Derby Hill Cres

Tower Hill

Edgley Dr

Taylor Ave

Thompson Ave

Crosshall High Sch

Cross Hall Farm

Otterheads Farm

Derby Hill Rd

Latham Ave

Sunny Fields

A577

WIGAN RD

PO

Mawdsley's Farm

Birchenholt

Sefton Brook

H

Hall Brow Cl

Lincoln Way

CROSSHALL BROW

PO

Ormond Ave

HALTON GREENACRE MEADOW

DICK'S LA

Ormskirk & District General

Milton Dr

Normanhurst

Beech Meadow

Westhead

HOLLY CL

Lathom St James CE Prim Sch

WIGAN RD

Dingle Heyes Farm

A570

Woodlands Cl

Ruff La

The Ruff

Threlfalls Farm

Ruff Farm

Wellfield

SCHOOL LA

Brighouse Green

B5240

PLOUGH LA

Dicket's Brook

Edge Hill Coll of HE

VICARAGE CL

ST JAMES CL

BEWCASTLE DR

WARLAM CL

WELLFIELD LA

VICARAGE LA

A577 DICKET'S LA

ST HELENS RD

Slack House Cotts

SCARTH HILL LA

B5240

Slack House Farm

Scarth Hill

Turner's Farm

Westhead Farm

SCARTH HILL LA

Wtr Twr

Delph Farm

WHITELEYS LA

Goose Brook

LYELAKE LA

Brookdale Farm

POPPY LA

Scarth Hill Farm

Fosters Farm

Stuart's Farm

ORMSKIRK RD

CROPPER'S LA

White House Farm

A570

B5240

Wiswall's Farm

Grapel's Farm

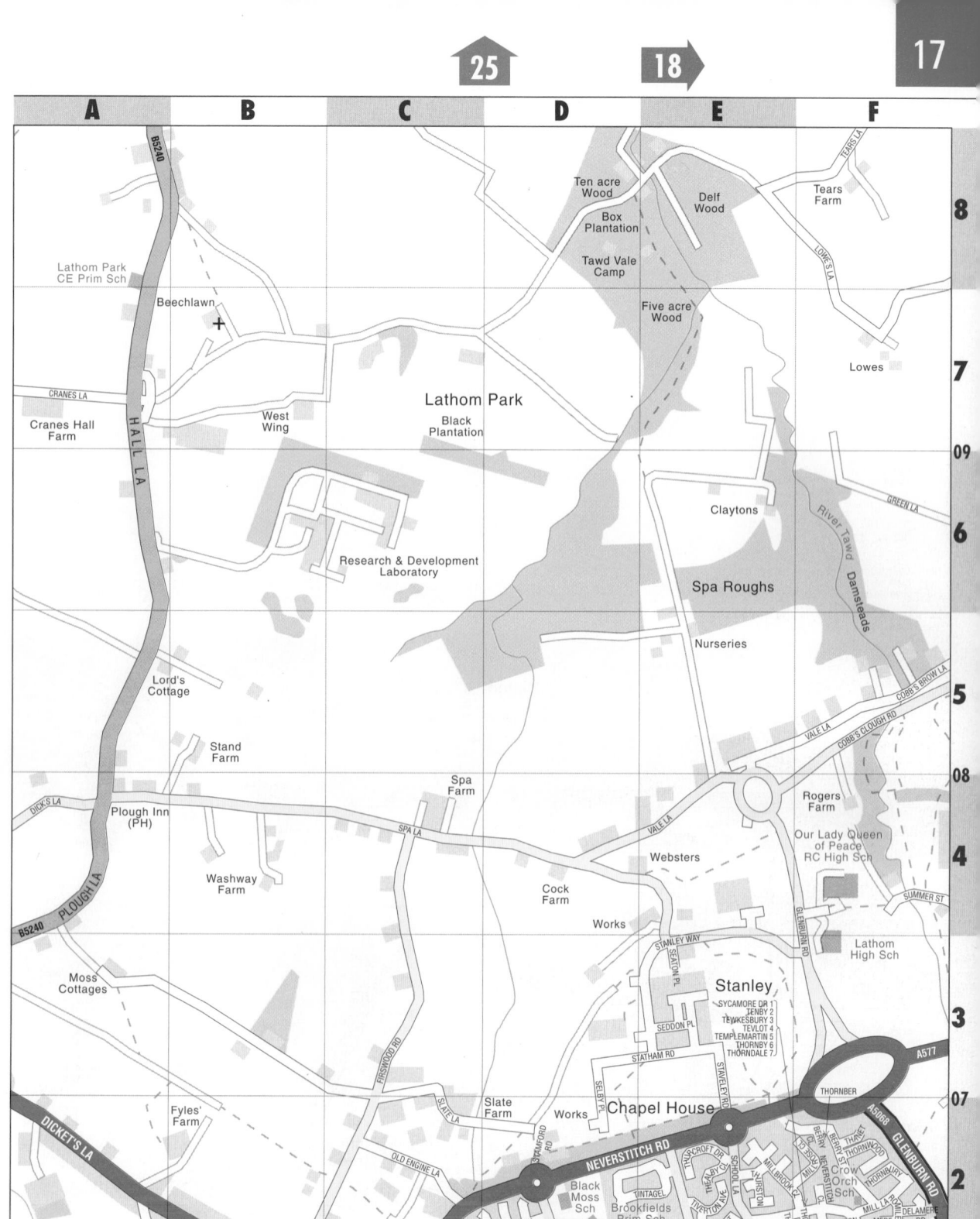

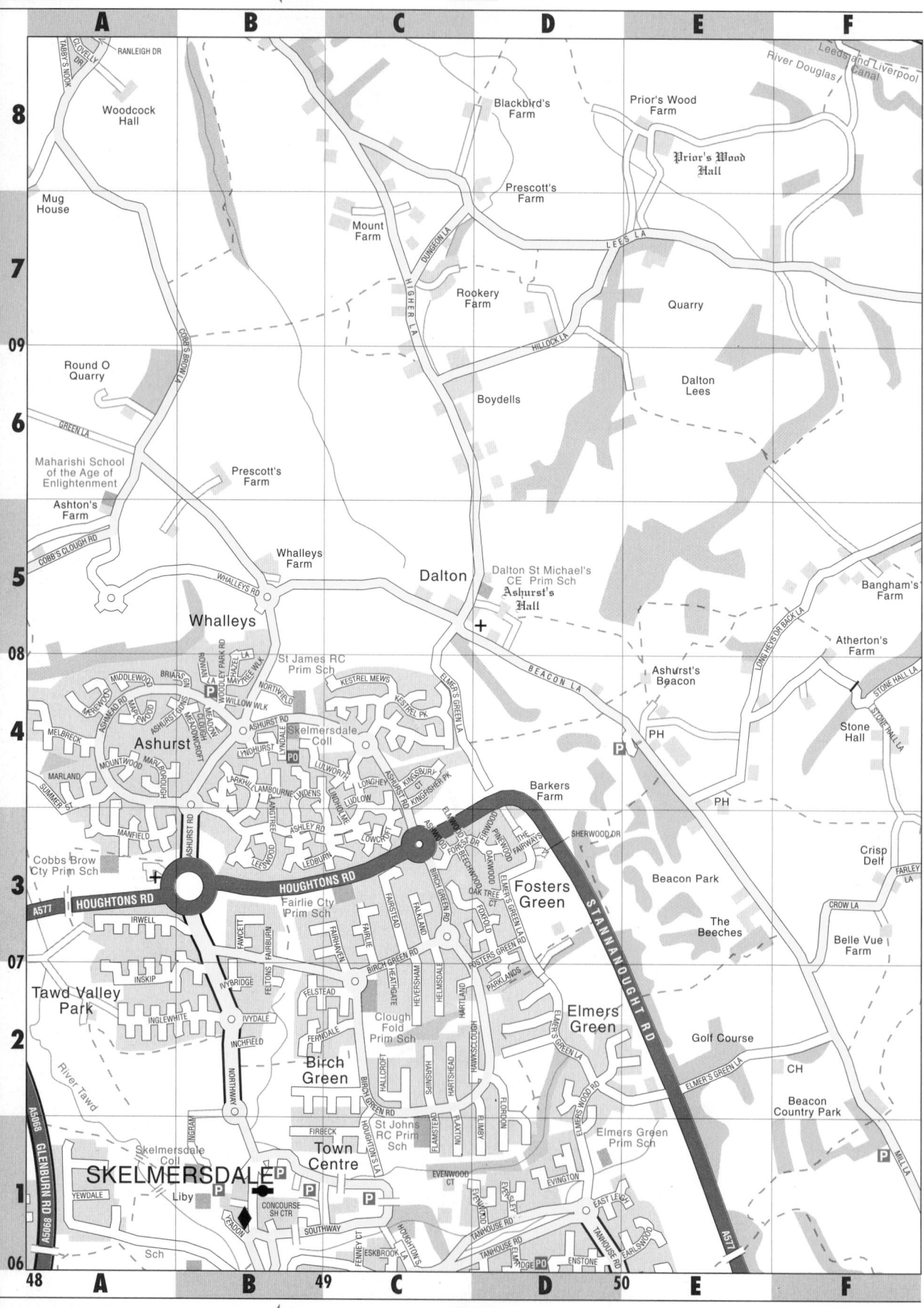

17
26

A B C D E F

8

7

09

6

5

08

4

3

07

2

1

06

48 A B 49 C D 50 E F

17
9

Woodcock Hall

Mug House

Round O Quarry

Maharishi School of the Age of Enlightenment

Ashton's Farm

Prescott's Farm

Whalleys Farm

Whalleys

Ashurst

Tawd Valley Park

Cobbs Brow Cty Prim Sch

SKELMERSDALE

Skelmersdale Coll

Town Centre

Birch Green

Blackbird's Farm

Prescott's Farm

Mount Farm

Rookery Farm

Boydells

Dalton

Dalton St Michael's CE Prim Sch

Ashurst's Hall

St James RC Prim Sch

Skelmersdale Coll

Kestrel Mews

Barkers Farm

Fosters Green

Fairlie Cty Prim Sch

Clough Fold Prim Sch

St Johns RC Prim Sch

Elmers Green

Elmers Green Prim Sch

Prior's Wood Farm

Prior's Wood Hall

Quarry

Dalton Lees

Ashurst's Beacon

Beacon Park

The Beeches

Golf Course

Beacon Country Park

Bangham's Farm

Atherton's Farm

Stone Hall

Crisp Delf

Belle Vue Farm

RIVER Douglas

Leeds and Liverpool Canal

HOUGHTONS RD
A577

STANNANOUGHT RD

GLENBURN RD B5069

A5068

River Tawd

RANLEIGH DR

CLOVELLY

TABBY'S NOOK

COBB'S BROW LA

GREEN LA

COBB'S CLOUGH RD

WHALLEYS RD

HIGHER LA

DUNGEON LA

LEES LA

HILLOCK LA

BEACON LA

LONGHEYS DR BACK LA

STONE HALL LA

FARLEY LA

CROW LA

ELMER'S GREEN LA

ASHURST RD

NORTHWAY

MELLA

River Douglas

A B C D E F

8

Hillside
Golf Links

Recn
Gd

ARUNDEL RD
HALSALL RD
A5267
FARNBOROUGH RD
DUNBAR CRES
A565
WATERLOO RD
A5267 LIVERPOOL RD
Sch
CENTRAL AVE

7

Birkdale
Hills

Dunes

Sefton Coastal Path

Howes
House

Southport & Ainsdale
Golf Links

Birkdale
High Sch

WINDY HARBOUR RD
St Mary's
GDNS
ALMA
CT
CARR LA
Recn
Gd
LEYBOURNE AVE RANELAGH DR
NIXON'S LA

13

Ainsdale
High Sch

Cemy

Anderson's
Farm

6

Railway
Cottages

MICKLETON DR

CHILTERN RD

Recn
Gd

Cemy

Halsall
Moss

5

Ainsdale

Ainsdale
Sta

Sherwood
House

Liby

Allot
Gdns

White Otter
Farm

12

Shoreside
Cty Prim Sch

Ainsdale
CE Prim Sch

4

Dunes

Merefield
Sch

Hill House
Farm

Sewage
Works

3

Big Ball's
Hill

West End
Lodge

Segar's
Farm

Woodvale
Prim Sch

Plex
Moss

11

Woodvale

Cheshire Lines Path

St John Stone
RC Prim Sch

MEADOW LA

2

Woodvale
Airfield

Headbolt
Farm

WOODVALE RD

1

FORMBY BY-PASS
A565

Liverpool
Old Rd

Motel

Caravan
Park

Golf
Course

PLEX MOSS LA

Gettern
Farm

10

30 A B 31 C D 32 E F

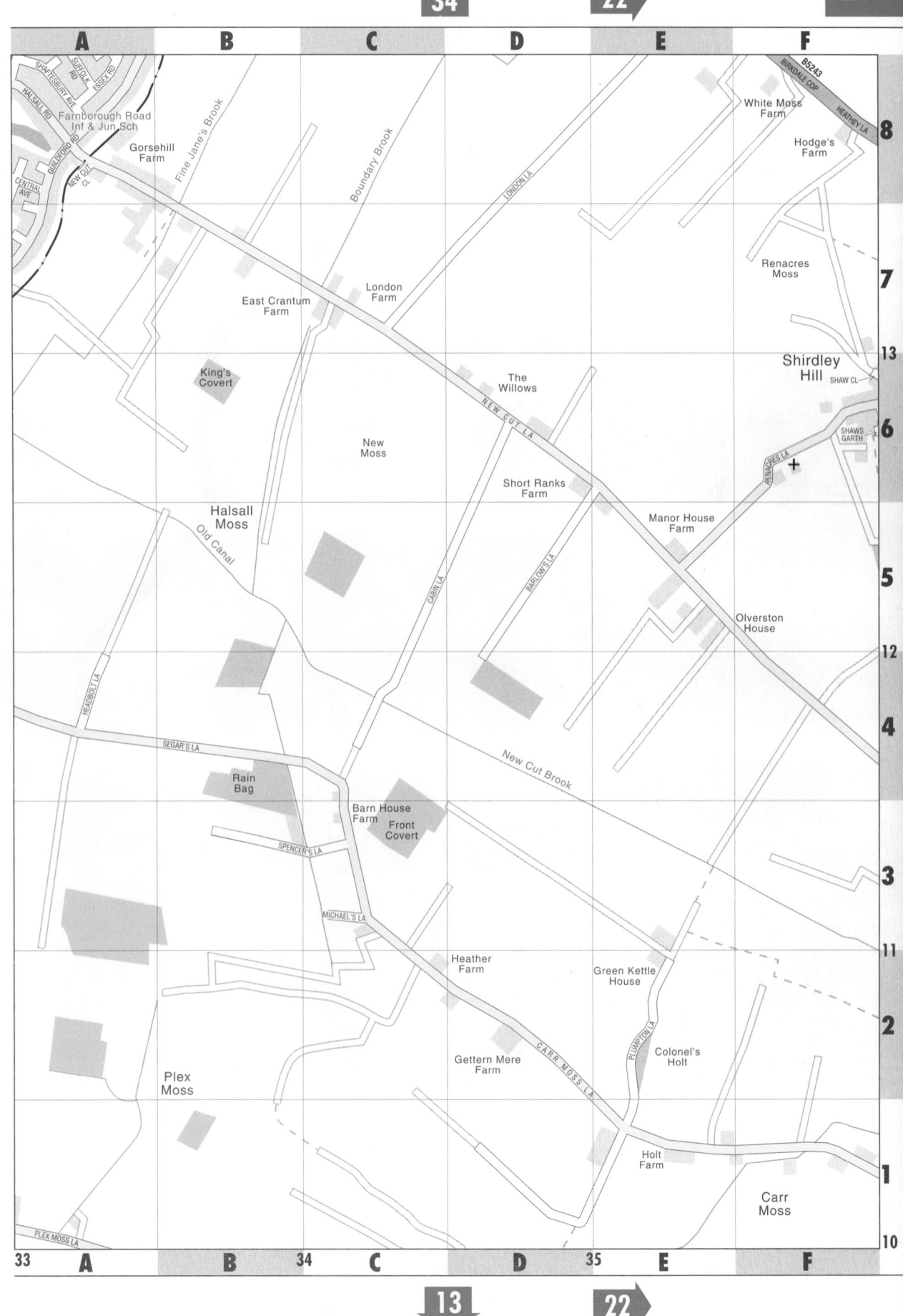

A B C D E F

8

White Moss Farm
Hodge's Farm
B5243
BIRKDALE COP
HEATHEY LA

Farnborough Road
Inf & Jun Sch
SHAFTESBURY AVE
SUFFOLK RD
ESSEX RD
HALSALL RD
GUILDFORD RD
CENTRAL AVE
NEW CUT CL

Gorsehill Farm

Fine Jane's Brook

Boundary Brook

London LA

Renacres Moss

7

East Crantum Farm
London Farm

13

Shirdley Hill
SHAW CL

King's Covert

The Willows

NEW CUT LA

SHAWS GARTH

6

New Moss

Short Ranks Farm

Manor House Farm

RENACRES LA

Halsall Moss

Old Canal

CABIN LA

BARLOWS LA

Olverston House

5

HEADBOLT LA

12

SEGAR'S LA

New Cut Brook

4

Rain Bag

Barn House Farm
Front Covert

SPENCER'S LA

3

MICHAEL'S LA

Heather Farm

Green Kettle House

11

PLUMPTON LA

Gettern Mere Farm

CARR MOSS LA

Colonel's Holt

2

Plex Moss

Holt Farm

1

Carr Moss

PLEX MOSS LA

10

33 A 34 B C 34 D 35 E F

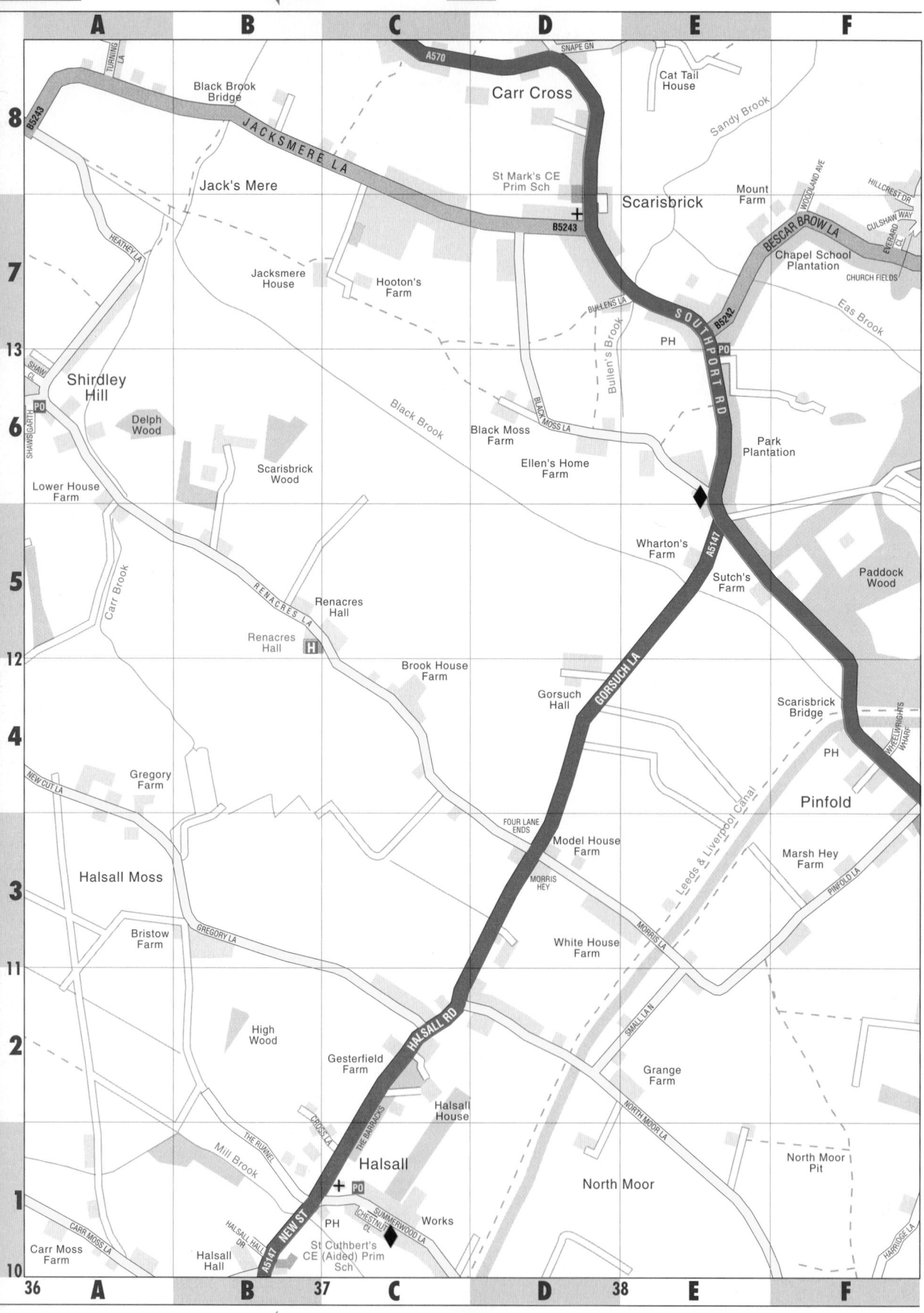

A B C D E F

8

7

13

6

5

12

4

3

11

2

1

10

36 A 37 B C 38 D E F

Turning La
B5243
Black Brook Bridge
Jacksmere La
Jack's Mere
Jacksmere House
Hooton's Farm
Heathey La
Shirdley Hill
Shaw Cl
PO
Delph Wood
Lower House Farm
Scarisbrick Wood
Carr Brook
Renacres La
Renacres Hall
Renacres Hall H
Brook House Farm
Gregory Farm
New Cut La
Halsall Moss
Bristow Farm
Gregory La
High Wood
Mill Brook
The Runnel
Cross La
Gesterfield Farm
Halsall Rd
Halsall House
The Barracks
Halsall
PO
New St
Halsall Halt Dr
A5147
PH
Chestnut Cl
Summerwood La
St Cuthbert's CE (Aided) Prim Sch
Works
Halsall Hall
Carr Moss La
Carr Moss Farm

A570
Snape Gn
Carr Cross
Cat Tail House
Sandy Brook
St Mark's CE Prim Sch
Scarisbrick
Mount Farm
Woodland Ave
Hillcrest Dr
Culshaw Way
Everband Cl
B5243
Bescar Brow La
Chapel School Plantation
Church Fields
Bullens La
Southport Rd
B5242
PO
PH
Black Brook
Black Moss La
Black Moss Farm
Ellen's Home Farm
Eas Brook
Park Plantation
Wharton's Farm
A5147
Sutch's Farm
Paddock Wood
Gorsuch La
Gorsuch Hall
Scarisbrick Bridge
Leeds & Liverpool Canal
Wheelwrights Wharf
PH
Pinfold
Four Lane Ends
Model House Farm
Morris Hey
Morris La
White House Farm
Marsh Hey Farm
Pinfold La
Small La
Grange Farm
North Moor La
North Moor
North Moor Pit
Harridge La

A | B | C | D | E | F

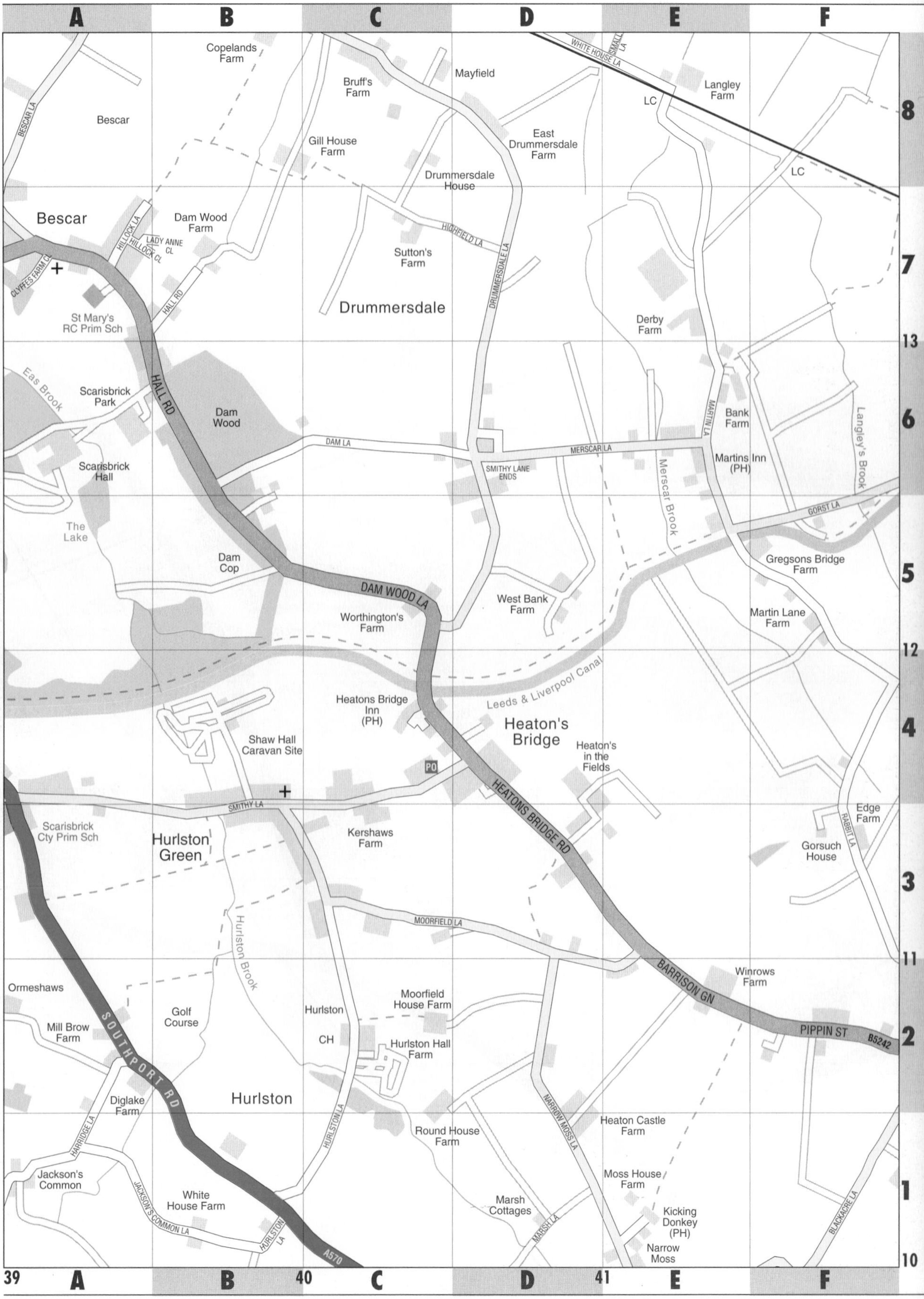

8

WHITE HOUSE LA
SMALL LA

Copelands Farm

Bescar

Mayfield

Bruff's Farm

Langley Farm

LC

Gill House Farm

East Drummersdale Farm

Bescar

Dam Wood Farm

HILLOCK LA
LADY ANNE CL
HILLOCK CL

Drummersdale House

LC

HIGHFIELD LA

7

CLYFFES FARM CL

+

St Mary's RC Prim Sch

HALL RD

Sutton's Farm

Drummersdale

DRUMMERSDALE LA

Derby Farm

13

Eas Brook

Scarisbrick Park

Dam Wood

MARTIN LA

Bank Farm

6

DAM LA

MERSCAR LA

Scarisbrick Hall

SMITHY LANE ENDS

Martins Inn (PH)

GORST LA

The Lake

Dam Cop

Merscar Brook

Gregsons Bridge Farm

5

DAM WOOD LA

West Bank Farm

Langley's Brook

Worthington's Farm

Martin Lane Farm

12

Leeds & Liverpool Canal

Heatons Bridge Inn (PH)

Heaton's Bridge

4

Shaw Hall Caravan Site

Heaton's in the Fields

Edge Farm

+

PO

SMITHY LA

HEATONS BRIDGE RD

Gorsuch House

RABBIT LA

Scarisbrick Cty Prim Sch

Hurlston Green

Kershaws Farm

3

Hurlston Brook

MOORFIELD LA

BARRISON GN

11

Ormeshaws

Winrows Farm

Golf Course

Moorfield House Farm

SOUTHPORT RD

PIPPIN ST

B5242

Mill Brow Farm

Hurlston CH

2

HURLSTON LA

Hurlston Hall Farm

NARROW MOSS LA

Heaton Castle Farm

Diglake Farm

Hurlston

Round House Farm

Moss House Farm

BLACKMORE LA

HARRIDGE LA

Jackson's Common

White House Farm

Marsh Cottages

Kicking Donkey (PH)

1

JACKSON'S COMMON LA

HURLSTON LA

A570

MARSH LA

Narrow Moss

10

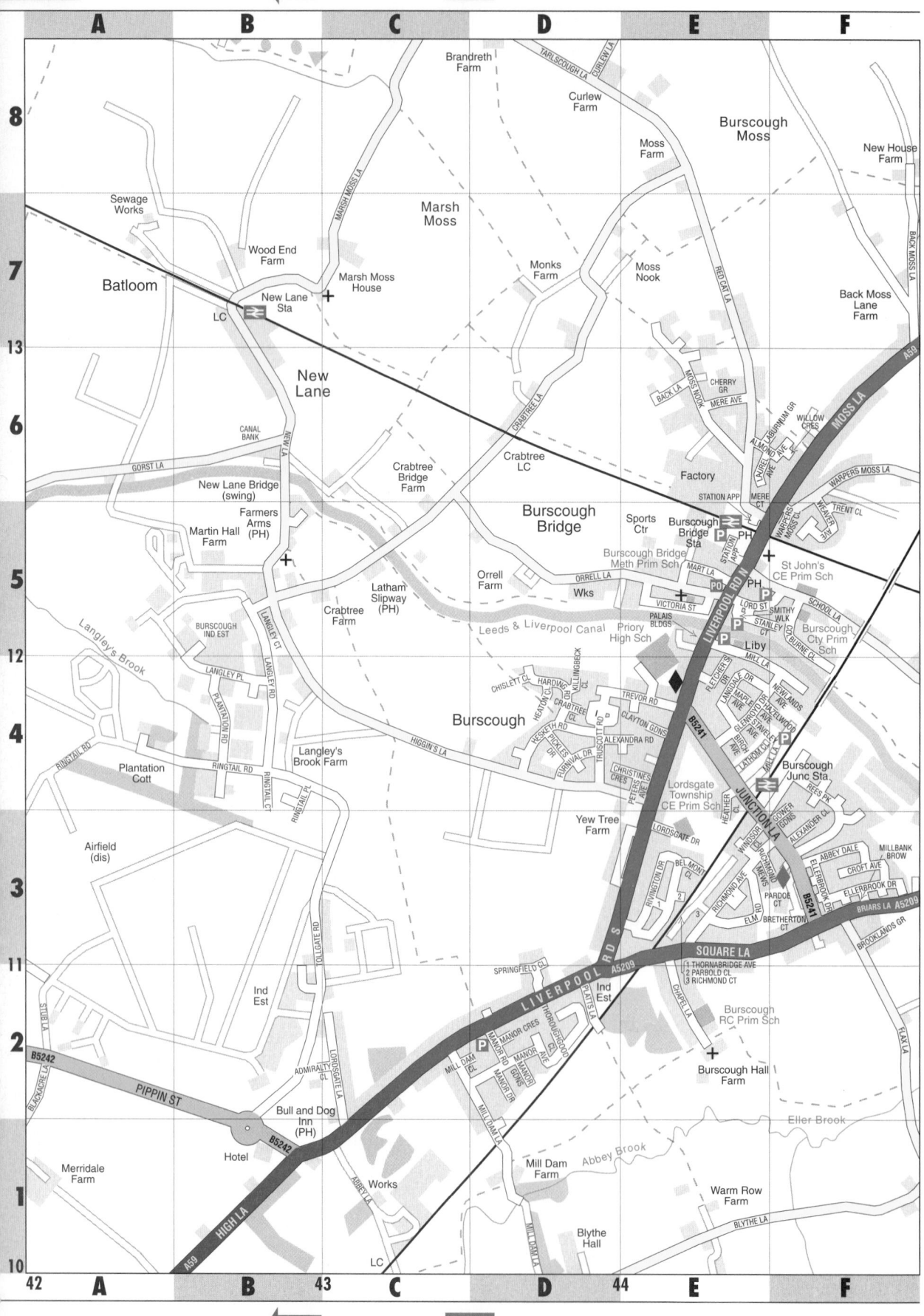

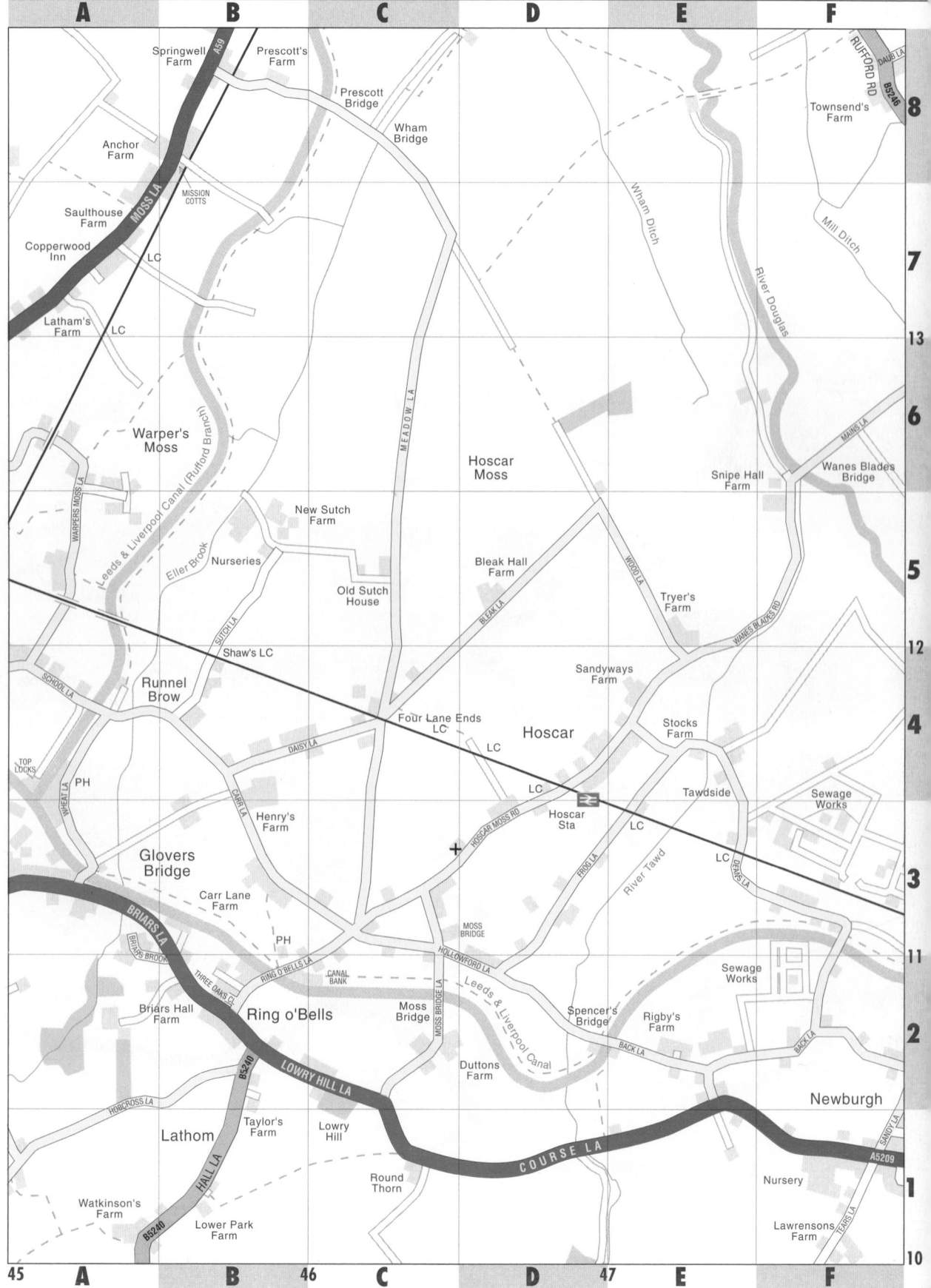

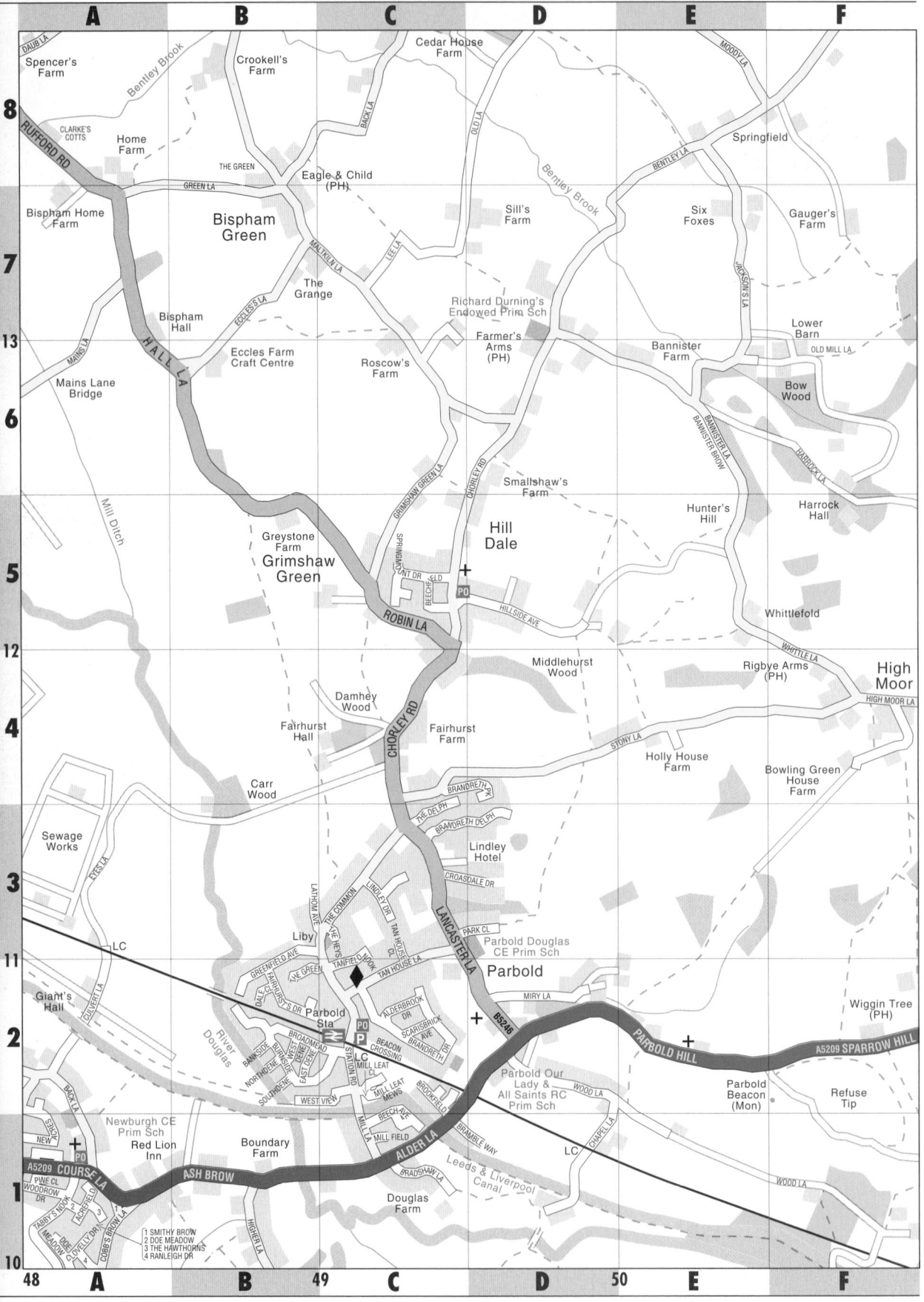

A   B   C   D   E   F

8

7

13

6

5

12

4

3

11

2

1

10

RUFFORD RD

Spencer's Farm

DAUB LA

Clarke's Cotts

Home Farm

THE GREEN

Crookell's Farm

Cedar House Farm

BACK LA

OLD LA

MOODY LA

Springfield

Gauger's Farm

Eagle & Child (PH)

GREEN LA

Bispham Green

BENTLEY LA

Sill's Farm

Six Foxes

Lower Barn

Bentley Brook

Bispham Home Farm

HALL LA

MAINS LA

ECCLES LA

MALKEN LA

LEE LA

The Grange

Bispham Hall

Richard Durning's Endowed Prim Sch

Bannister Farm

OLD MILL LA

Mains Lane Bridge

Eccles Farm Craft Centre

Roscow's Farm

Farmer's Arms (PH)

JACKSON'S LA

BANNISTER BROW

Bow Wood

HARROCK LA

Mill Ditch

GRIMSHAW GREEN LA

CHORLEY RD

Smallshaw's Farm

Hunter's Hill

Harrock Hall

Greystone Farm

Grimshaw Green

SPRINGMOUNT DR

BEECHFIELD

Hill Dale

PO

BANNISTER LA

Whittlefold

ROBIN LA

HILLSIDE AVE

WHITTLE LA

Rigbye Arms (PH)

High Moor

Damhey Wood

Middlehurst Wood

HIGH MOOR LA

Fairhurst Hall

CHORLEY RD

Fairhurst Farm

STONY LA

Holly House Farm

Bowling Green House Farm

Carr Wood

BRANDRETH PK

THE DELPH

BRANDRETH DELPH

Lindley Hotel

CROASDALE DR

Sewage Works

EYES LA

LC

LATHOM AVE

INGLEY DR

THE COMMON

TAN HOUSE LA

PARK CL

LANCASTER LA

Parbold Douglas CE Prim Sch

Liby

THE HEYS

TANFIELD

TAN HOUSE LA

Parbold

Giant's Hall

COLVERT LA

GREENFIELD AVE

THE GREEN

FAIRHURST'S DR

DALE CL

ALDERBROOK DR

SCARISBRICK AVE

MIRY LA

Wiggin Tree (PH)

River Douglas

Parbold Sta

PO

P

BEACON CROSSING

BRANDRETH

B5246

PARBOLD HILL

A5209 SPARROW HILL

BANKSIDE

BROADMEAD

STATION RD

EAST DENE

NORTHDENE

MILL LEAT CL

WEST VIEW

MILL LEAT MEWS

BROOKFIELD

Parbold Our Lady & All Saints RC Prim Sch

WOOD LA

Parbold Beacon (Mon)

Refuse Tip

SOUTHDENE

MILL LA

BEECH AVE

CHAPEL LA

Newburgh CE Prim Sch

PWE CL

WOODROW DR

PO

Red Lion Inn

Boundary Farm

ASH BROW

MILL FIELD

ALDER LA

BRAMBLE WAY

LC

A5209 COURSE LA

BACK LA

PERCY ST

NEW

TABBY'S NOOK

CLOVELLY DR

COBB'S BROW LA

HIGHER LA

Douglas Farm

BRADSHAW LA

Leeds & Liverpool Canal

WOOD LA

MC ADAM DR

1 SMITHY BROW
2 DOE MEADOW
3 THE HAWTHORNS
4 RANLEIGH DR

48   A   B   49   C   D   50   E   F

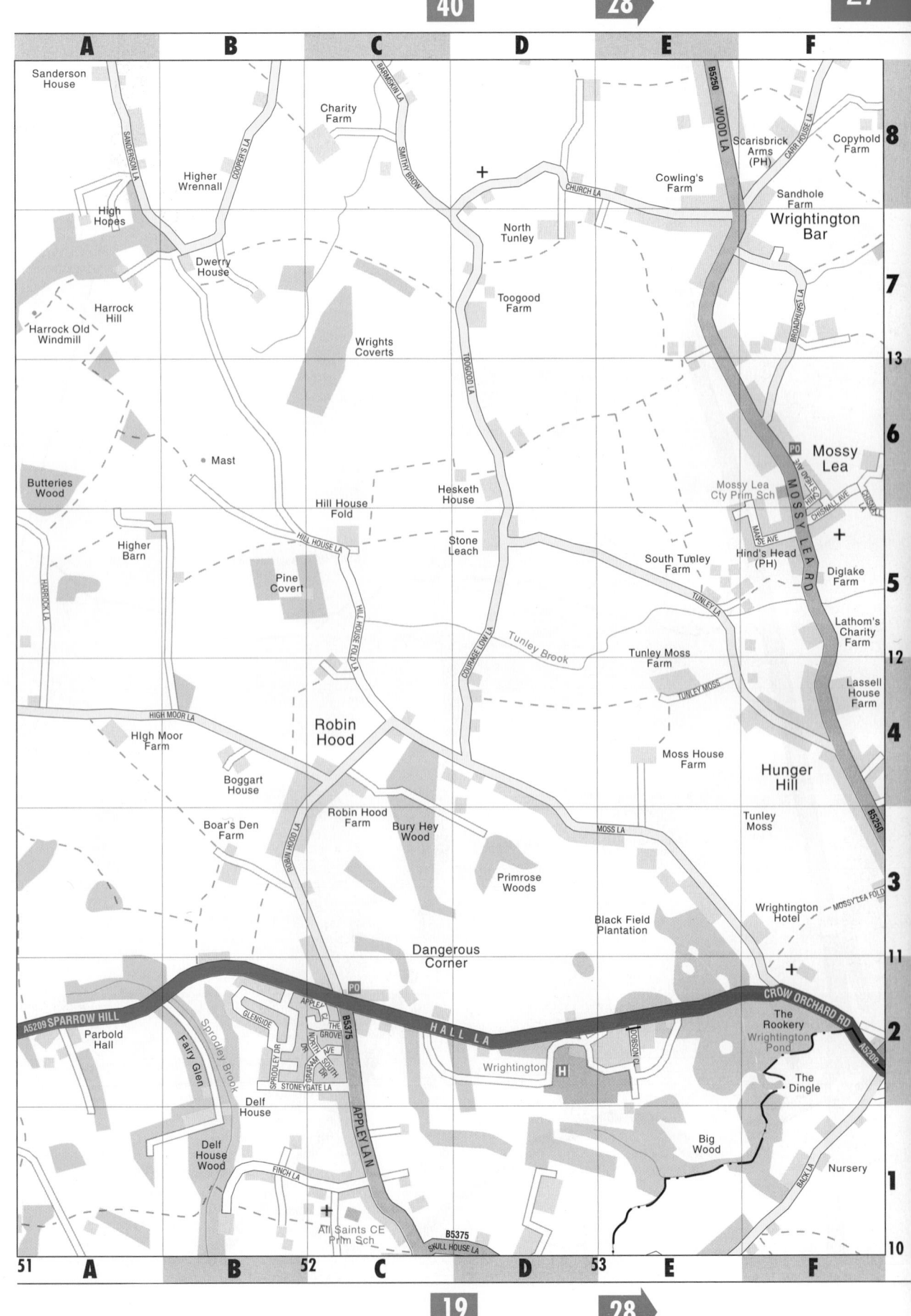

Sanderson House
Charity Farm
Scarisbrick Arms (PH)
Copyhold Farm
High Hopes
Higher Wrennall
Cowling's Farm
Sandhole Farm
Wrightington Bar
Dwerry House
North Tunley
Harrock Hill
Harrock Old Windmill
Toogood Farm
Wrights Coverts
Mossy Lea
Butteries Wood
Mast
Hesketh House
Mossy Lea Cty Prim Sch
Higher Barn
Hill House Fold
Stone Leach
Hind's Head (PH)
Diglake Farm
South Tunley Farm
Pine Covert
Lathom's Charity Farm
Tunley Brook
Tunley Moss Farm
Lassell House Farm
High Moor Farm
Robin Hood
Tunley Moss
Moss House Farm
Hunger Hill
Boggart House
Tunley Moss
Boar's Den Farm
Robin Hood Farm
Bury Hey Wood
Moss La
Primrose Woods
Wrightington Hotel
Mossy Lea Fold
Black Field Plantation
Dangerous Corner
The Rookery
Wrightington Pond
Parbold Hall
Sparrow Hill
Fairy Glen
Sprodley Brook
Glenside
The Grove
Appley
Hall La
Wrightington
The Dingle
Delf House
Stoneygate La
Appley La N
Delf House Wood
Finch La
Big Wood
Nursery
Back La
All Saints CE Prim Sch
B5375
Skull House La

Sanderson La
Cooper's La
Barrison La
Smithy Brow
Church La
Wood La
Carr House La
Broadhurst La
Toogood La
Chorley Rd
Chisnall Ave
Mosse Ave
Mossy Lea Rd
Chisnall La
Hill House La
Hill House Fold La
Courage Low La
Tunley La
High Moor La
Robin Hood La
Dobson Cl
B5250
A5209
Crow Orchard Rd

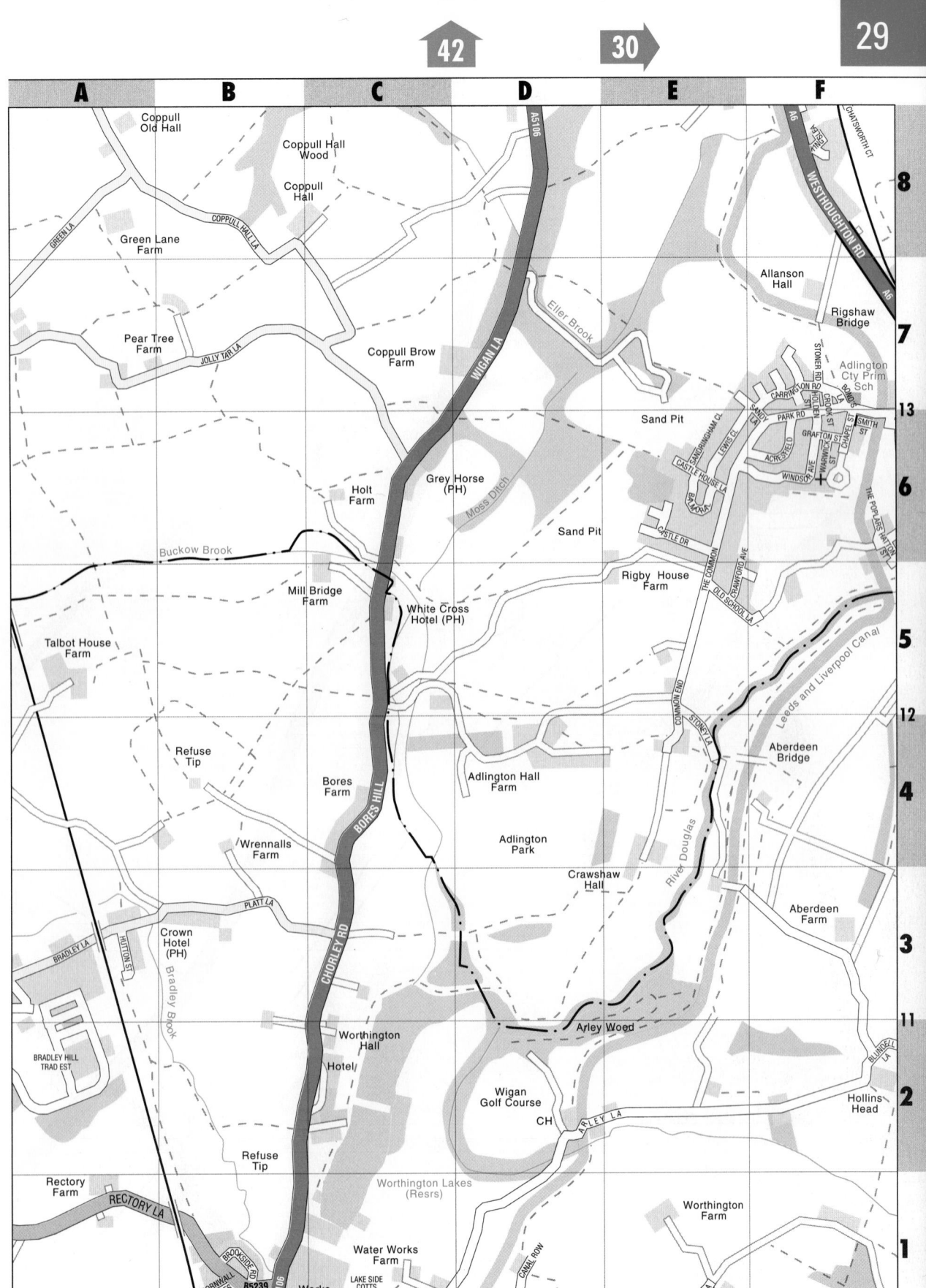

Coppull Old Hall
Coppull Hall Wood
Coppull Hall
Green Lane Farm
Coppull Hall La
Green La
Pear Tree Farm
Jolly Tar La
Coppull Brow Farm
Wigan La
A5106
Eller Brook
Westhoughton Rd
A6
Chatsworth Ct
Allanson Hall
Rigshaw Bridge
Adlington Cty Prim Sch
Stoner Rd
Roller La
Carrington Rd
Park Rd
Crook St
Smith St
Sandbirmingham Cl
Lewis Cl
Grafton St
Compel St
Castle House La
Acre Sf Rd
Warm Rd
Windsor
The Poplars Hatton
Holt Farm
Grey Horse (PH)
Moss Ditch
Sand Pit
Sand Pit
Castle Dr
Rigby House Farm
The Common
Old School La
Crawford Ave
Leeds and Liverpool Canal
Buckow Brook
Mill Bridge Farm
White Cross Hotel (PH)
Talbot House Farm
Common End
Stoney La
Aberdeen Bridge
Refuse Tip
Bores Farm
Adlington Hall Farm
River Douglas
Aberdeen Farm
Bores Hill
Wrennalls Farm
Adlington Park
Crawshaw Hall
Bradley La
Hutton St
Platt La
Crown Hotel (PH)
Bradley Brook
Chorley Rd
Worthington Hall
Hotel
Arley Wood
Blundell La
Hollins Head
Bradley Hill Trad Est
Wigan Golf Course
CH
Arley La
Refuse Tip
Rectory Farm
Rectory La
Worthington Lakes (Resrs)
Worthington Farm
Brookside Rd
Cornwall Cres
Dorset Rd
Sussex Cl
Essex Cl
Wessex Cl
Devon Dr
B5239
A5106
Works
Water Works Farm
Lake Side Cotts
Mayfair Cotts
Canal Row
Pennington La
Pennington La
Pennington Farm

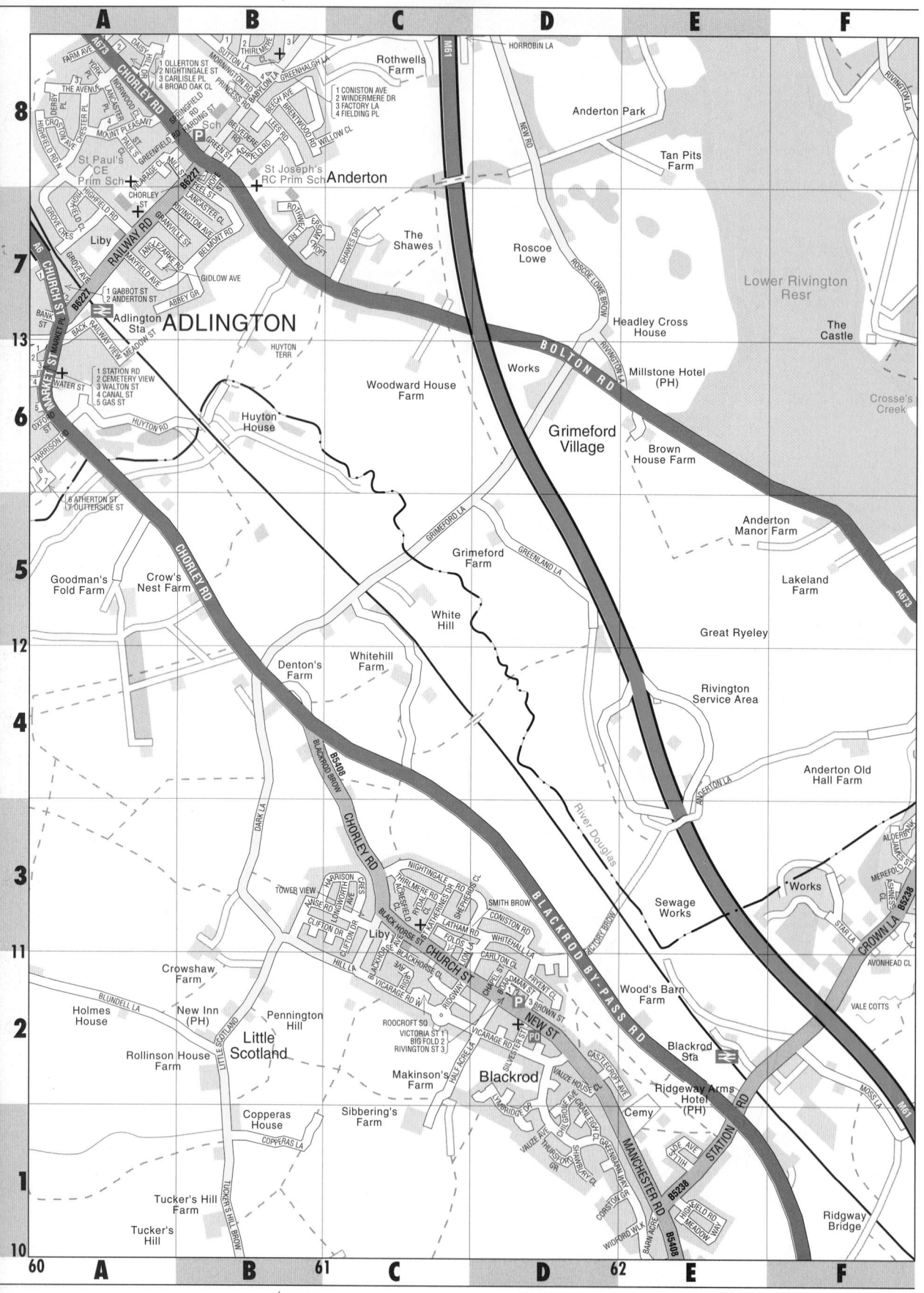

B4
1 DICKINSON CT
2 PETER MARTIN ST
3 WRIGHT ST W
4 JULIA MEWS
5 WHITTON MEWS
6 MOTTRAM MEWS
7 FLOCKTON CT
8 CROXTON WLK
9 BEATRICE MEWS
10 HARCOURT MEWS
11 ABRAHAM ST
12 SPRING GDNS
13 RAWLINSON ST
14 ABBOTT ST
15 ROBINSON ST
16 BACK RAWLINSON ST

E1
1 SYCAMORE WLK
2 ROWAN AVE
3 FIR TREE WAY
4 BIRCH TREE WAY
5 CHERRY TREE WAY
6 ELM GR
7 ARROWSMITH CT
8 ASH GR
9 OAK AVE

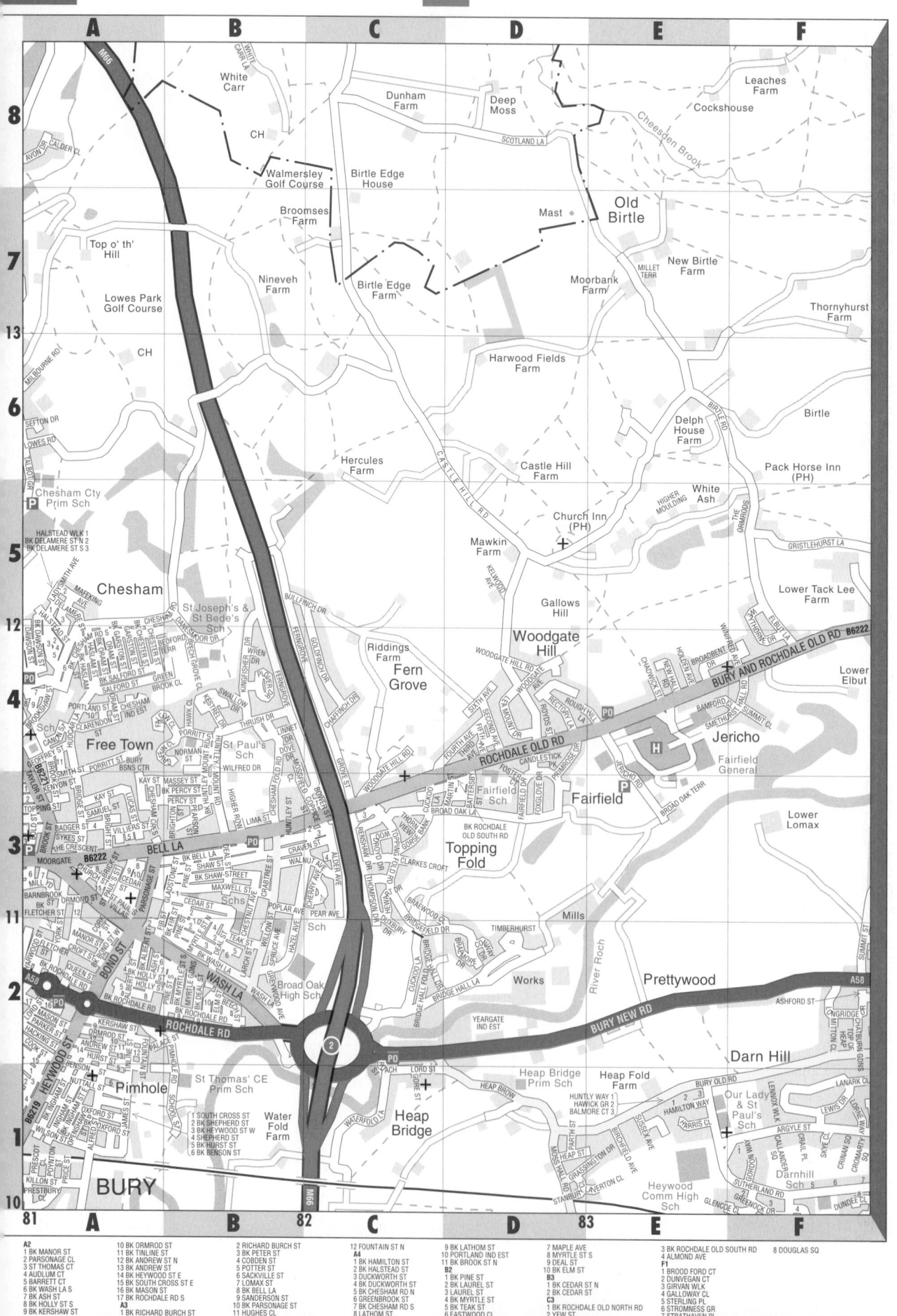

A2
1 BK MANOR ST
2 PARSONAGE CL
3 ST THOMAS ST
4 AUDLIM CT
5 BARRETT CT
6 BK WASH LA S
7 BK ASH ST
8 BK HOLLY ST
9 BK KERSHAW ST

10 BK ORMROD ST
11 BK TINLINE ST
12 BK ANDREW ST
13 BK ANDREW ST
14 BK HEYWOOD ST E
15 BK SOUTH CROSS ST E
16 BK MASON ST
17 BK ROCHDALE RD S

A3
1 BK RICHARD BURCH ST

2 RICHARD BURCH ST
3 BK PETER ST
4 COBDEN ST
5 POTTER ST
6 SACKVILLE ST
7 LOMAX ST
8 BK BELL LA
9 SANDERSON ST
10 BK PARSONAGE ST
11 HUGHES CL

12 FOUNTAIN ST N

A4
1 BK HAMILTON ST
2 BK HALSTEAD ST
3 DUCKWORTH ST
4 BK DUCKWORTH ST
5 GREENBROOK ST
6 EASTWOOD CL

9 BK LATHOM ST
10 PORTLAND IND EST
11 BK BROOK ST N

B2
1 BK PINE ST
2 BK LAUREL ST
3 LAUREL ST
4 BK MYRTLE ST
5 BK TEAK ST
6 YEW ST

7 MAPLE AVE
8 MYRTLE ST S
9 DEAL ST
10 BK ELM ST

B3
1 BK CEDAR ST N
2 BK CEDAR ST

C3
1 BK ROCHDALE OLD NORTH RD

3 BK ROCHDALE OLD SOUTH RD
4 ALMOND AVE

F1
1 BROOD FORD CT
2 DUNVEGAN CT
3 GIRVAN WLK
4 GALLOWAY CL
5 STERLING PL
6 STROMNESS GR
7 STRATHAVEN PL

8 DOUGLAS SQ

34

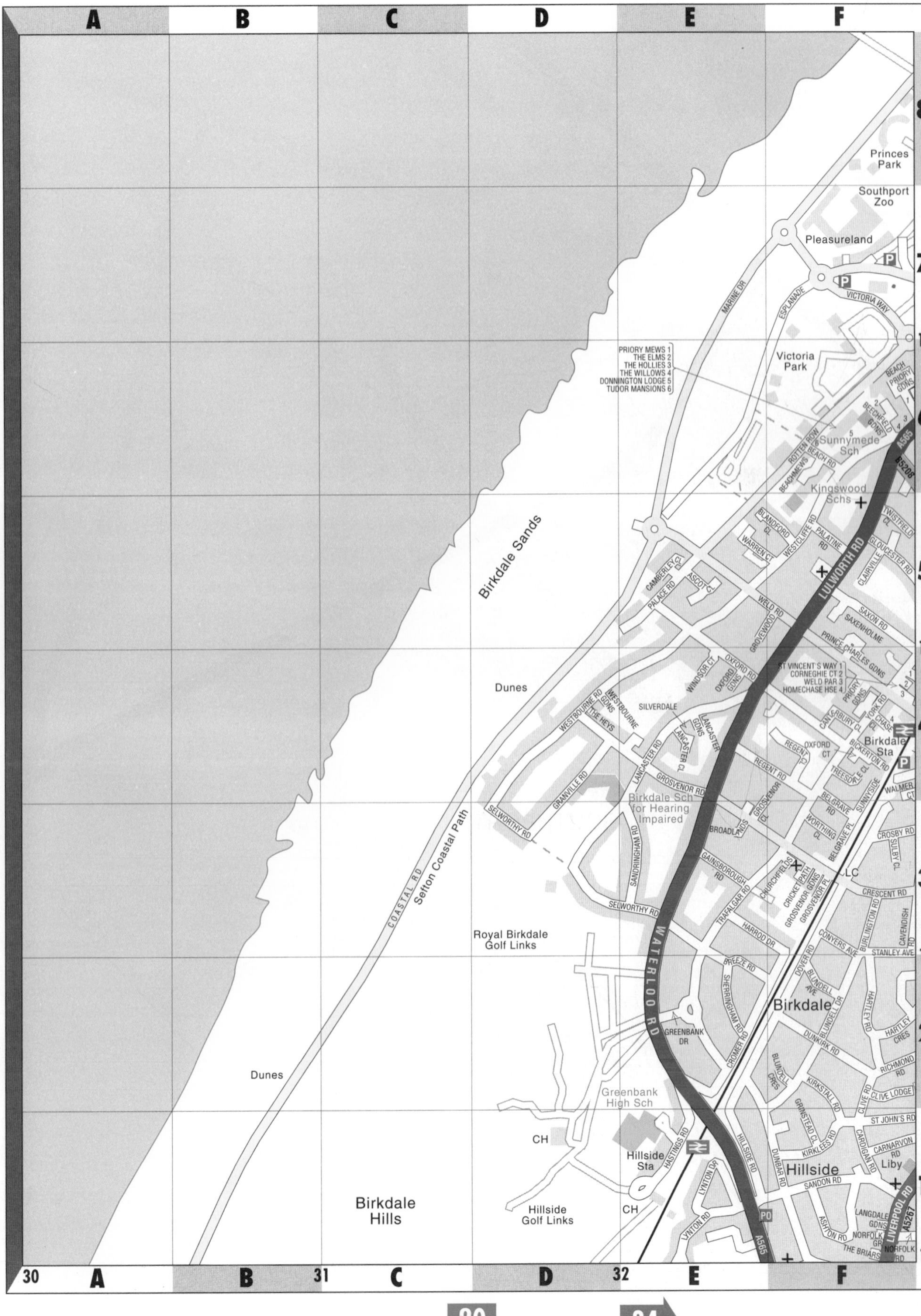
A
B
C
D
E
F
8
7
17
6
5
16
4
3
15
2
1
14
30
31
32
Princes Park
Southport Zoo
Pleasureland
MARINE DR
ESPLANADE
VICTORIA WAY
Victoria Park
PRIORY MEWS 1
THE ELMS 2
THE HOLLIES 3
THE WILLOWS 4
DONNINGTON LODGE 5
TUDOR MANSIONS 6
BEACH PRIORY GDNS
BEECHFIELD GDNS
Sunnymede Sch
ROTTEN ROW
BEACH RD
BEACHMEWS
A565
B5208
Kingswood Schs
Birkdale Sands
BLANDFORD CL
WARREN CT
WESTCLIFFE RD
PALATINE RD
LULWORTH RD
TWISTFIELD CL
GLOUCESTER RD
CLAIRVILLE
CAMBERLEY CL
PALACE RD
ASCOT CL
WELD RD
GROVEWOOD
SAXON RD
SAXENHOLME
PRINCE CHARLES GDNS
ST VINCENT'S WAY 1
CORNEGHIE CT 2
WELD PAR 3
HOMECHASE HSE 4
Dunes
WINDSOR CT
OXFORD RD
OXFORD GDNS
PRIORY GDNS
YORK RD
CHASE CL
CANTERBURY CL
WESTBOURNE RD
WESTBOURNE GDNS
THE HEYS
SILVERDALE
LANCASTER GDNS
LANCASTER CL
LANCASTER RD
Birkdale Sta
REGENT RD
OXFORD CT
BICKERTON RD
TRESCO CL
GRANVILLE RD
GROSVENOR RD
Birkdale Sch for Hearing Impaired
GROSVENOR CL
BELGRAVE RD
SUNNYSIDE
WALMER CT
SELWORTHY RD
BROADLANDS
WORTHING CL
BELGRAVE PL
CROSBY RD
SULBY CL
SANDRINGHAM RD
GAINSBOROUGH RD
CHURCHFIELDS
CRICKET PATH
GROSVENOR GDNS
GROSVENOR PL
LC
CRESCENT RD
COASTAL RD
Sefton Coastal Path
TRAFALGAR RD
HARROD DR
BURLINGTON RD
CAVENDISH RD
CONYERS AVE
STANLEY AVE
Royal Birkdale Golf Links
WATERLOO RD
BREEZE RD
SHERRINGHAM RD
DOVER RD
BLUNDELL AVE
Birkdale
HARTLEY RD
HARTLEY CRES
BLUNDELL DR
GREENBANK DR
CROMER RD
DUNKIRK RD
RICHMOND RD
BLUNDELL CRES
KIRKSTALL RD
CLIVE RD
CLIVE LODGE
Dunes
Greenbank High Sch
GRINSTEAD CL
ST JOHN'S RD
CH
HASTINGS RD
KIRKLEES RD
CARDIGAN RD
CARNARVON RD
Hillside Sta
HILLSIDE RD
DUNBAR RD
Hillside
Liby
LYNTON DR
SANDON RD
Birkdale Hills
Hillside Golf Links
CH
LYNTON RD
PO
LANGDALE GDNS
ASHTON RD
NORFOLK GR
NORFOLK RD
THE BRIARS
LIVERPOOL RD
A5267

20

34

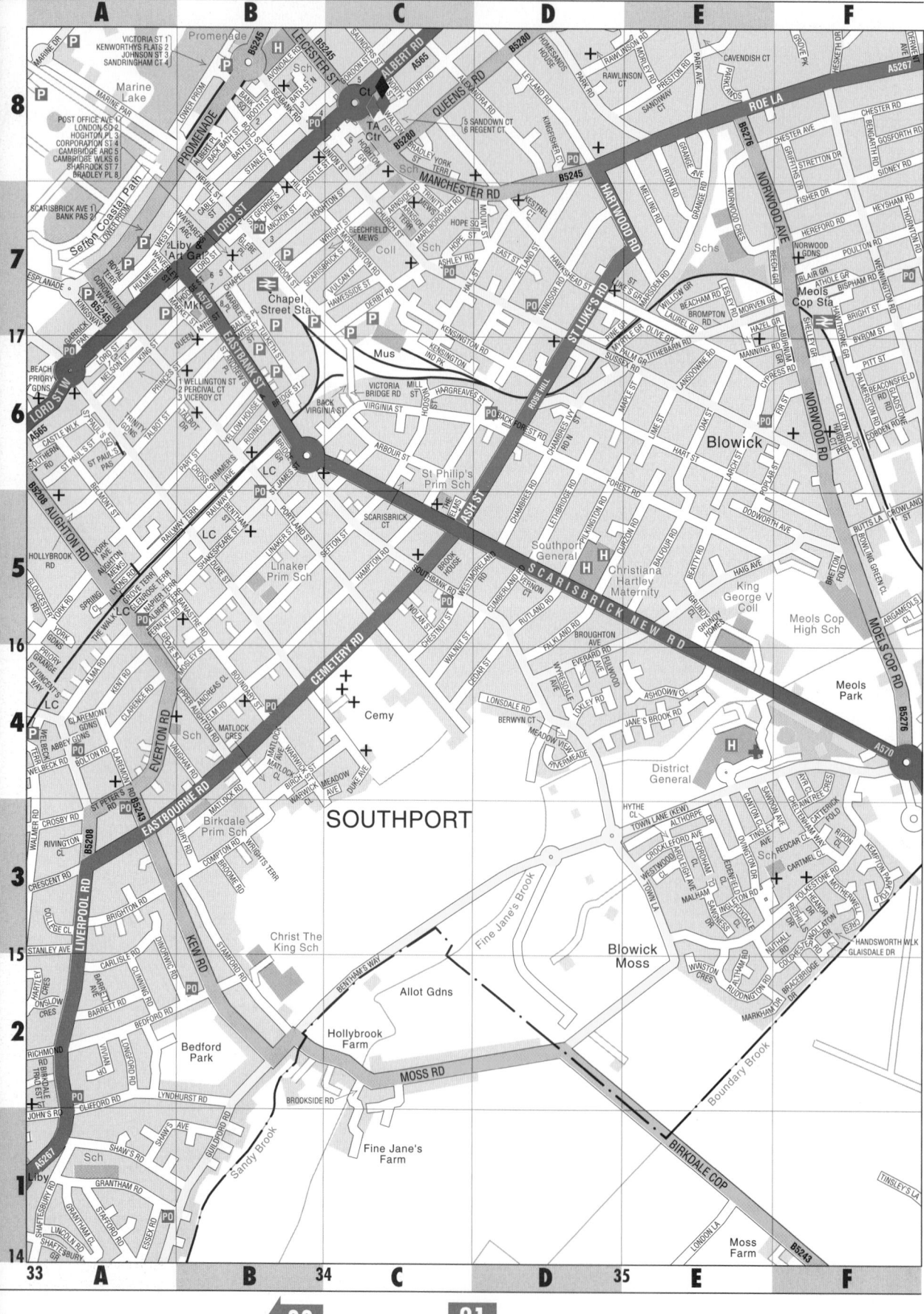

A B C D E F

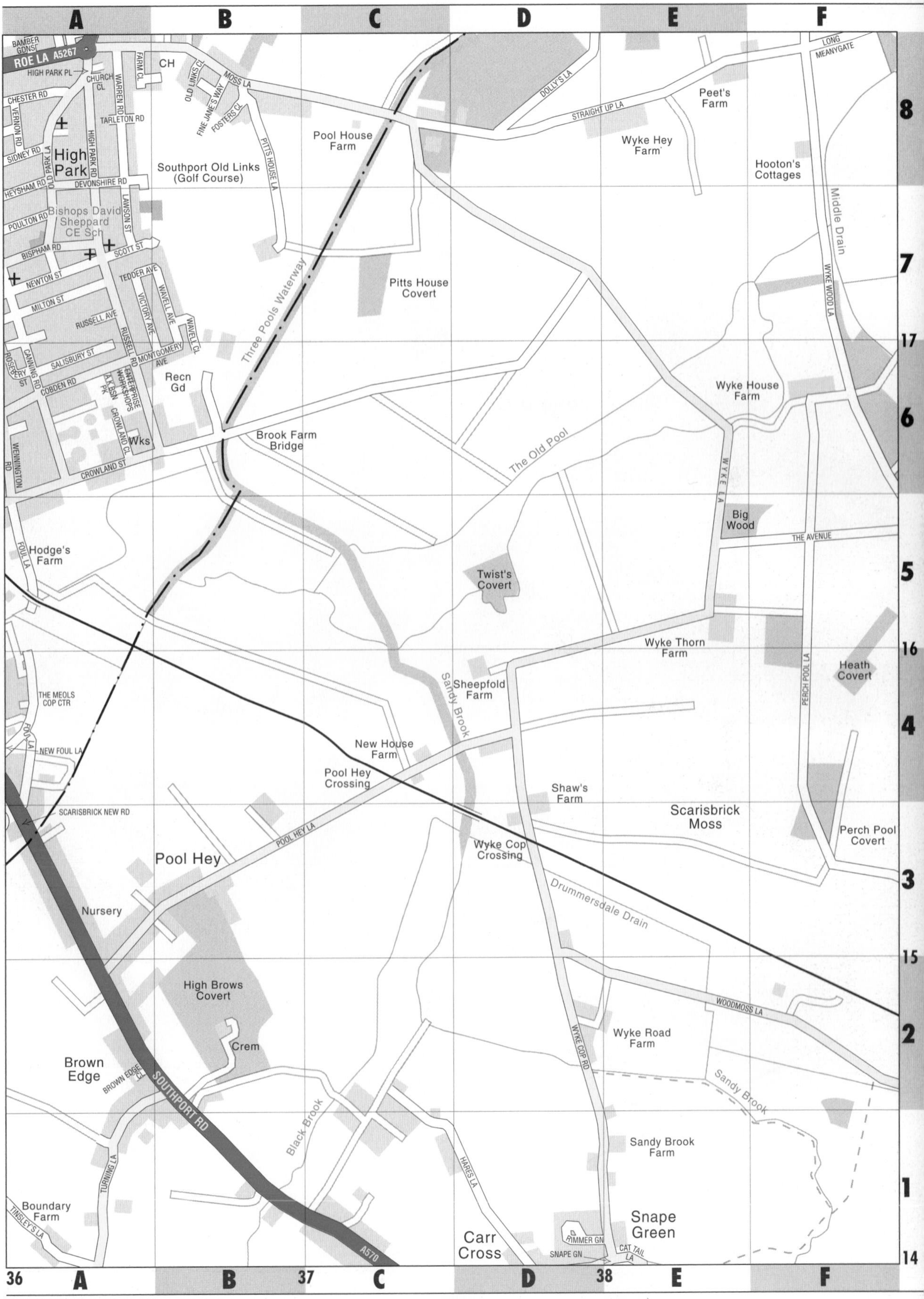

ROE LA A5267
BAMBER GDNS
High Park Pl
CH
Old Links Cl
Moss La
Peet's
Farm
Long
Meanygate
Chester Rd
Vernon St
Church Cl
Warren Rd
Farm Cl
Fine Jane's Way
Fosters Cl
Pool House
Farm
Straight Up La
Dolly's La
Wyke Hey
Farm
High Park Rd
Tarleton Rd
Southport Old Links
(Golf Course)
Hooton's
Cottages
High Park
Sidney Rd
Heysham Rd
Devonshire Rd
Pitts House La
Middle Drain
Poulton Rd
Bishops David
Sheppard
CE Sch
Lawson St
Bispham Rd
Scott St
Pitts House
Covert
Wyke Wood La
Newton St
Tedder Ave
Milton St
Wavell Ave
Wyke House
Farm
Russell Ave
Victory Ave
Russell Rd
Salisbury St
Montgomery Ave
Wavell Cl
Canning Rd
Cobden Rd
Recn
Gd
Cowley Rd
Enterprise
Workshops
J.K.K. Esh
Crowland Cl
Wks
The Old Pool
Wyke La
Big
Wood
The Avenue
Wennington Rd
Crowland St
Brook Farm
Bridge
Foul La
Hodge's
Farm
Twist's
Covert
Heath
Covert
Wyke Thorn
Farm
Perch Pool La
The Meols
Cop Ctr
Sheepfold
Farm
Foul La
New Foul La
New House
Farm
Scarisbrick New Rd
Pool Hey
Crossing
Shaw's
Farm
Scarisbrick
Moss
Perch Pool
Covert
Pool Hey La
Pool Hey
Wyke Cop
Crossing
Drummersdale Drain
Nursery
Sandy Brook
Woodmoss La
High Brows
Covert
Wyke Road
Farm
Brown
Edge
Crem
Brown Edge Cl
Southport Rd
Black Brook
Wyke Cop Rd
Sandy Brook
Sandy Brook
Farm
Snape
Green
Turning La
Boundary
Farm
Tinsley's La
A570
Hares La
Carr
Cross
Rimmer Gn
Snape Gn
Cat Tail La

8 7 17 6 5 16 4 3 15 2 1 14

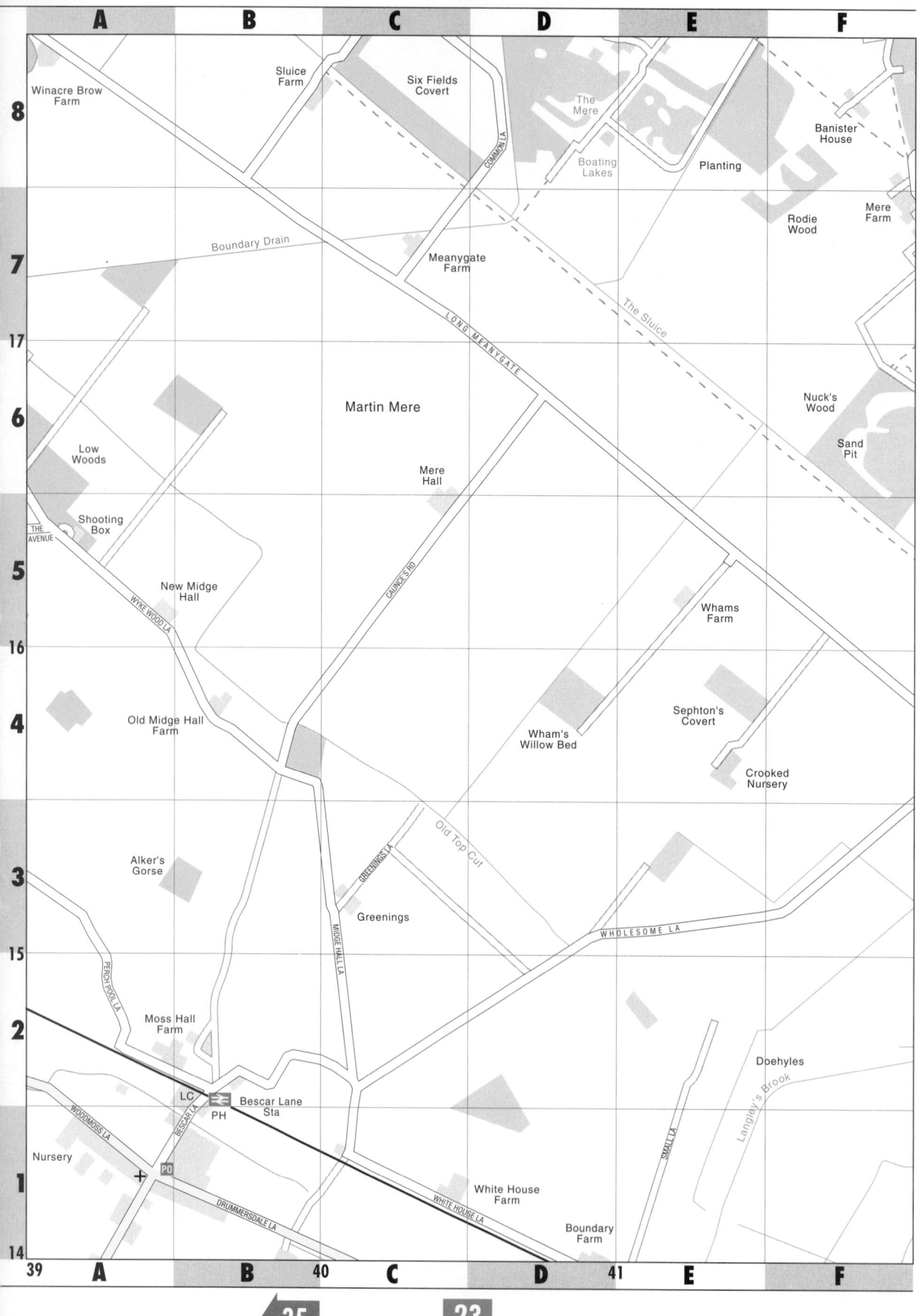

A B C D E F

8

Winacre Brow Farm

Sluice Farm

Six Fields Covert

The Mere

Boating Lakes

Planting

Banister House

COMMON LA

7

Boundary Drain

Meanygate Farm

Rodie Wood

Mere Farm

The Sluice

LONG MEANYGATE

17

6

Martin Mere

Nuck's Wood

Sand Pit

Low Woods

Mere Hall

Shooting Box

CAUNCE'S RD

THE AVENUE

New Midge Hall

5

Whams Farm

WYKE WOOD LA

16

Sephton's Covert

4

Old Midge Hall Farm

Wham's Willow Bed

Crooked Nursery

Old Top Cut

3

Alker's Gorse

GREENINGS LA

Greenings

WHOLESOME LA

MIDGE HALL LA

15

PERCH POOL LA

Moss Hall Farm

2

Doehyles

Langley's Brook

LC

BESCAR LA

Bescar Lane Sta

PH

WOODMOSS LA

SMALL LA

Nursery

PO

1

White House Farm

DRUMMERSDALE LA

WHITE HOUSE LA

Boundary Farm

14

39 A B 40 C D 41 E F

A B C D E F

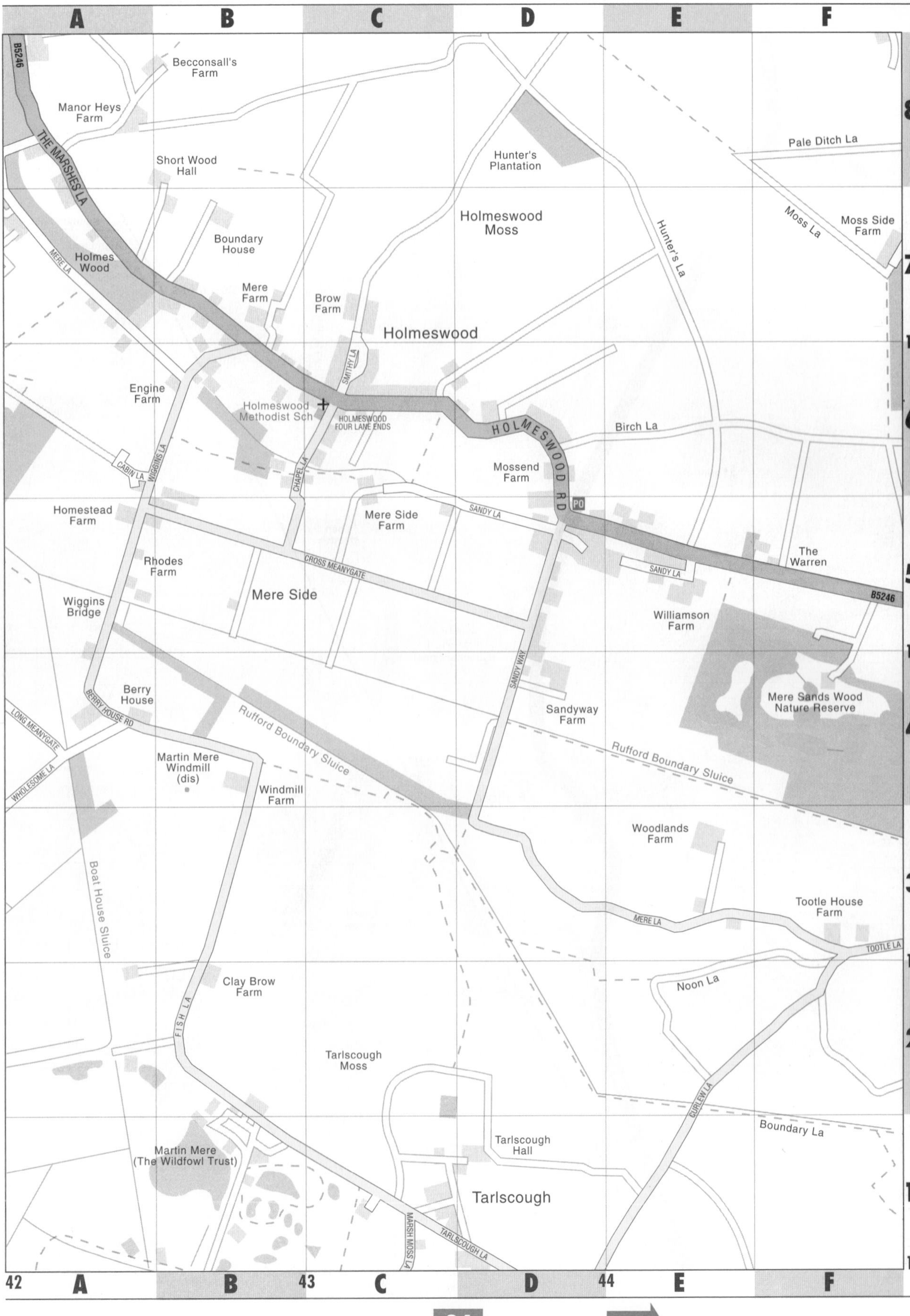

8

B5246

Becconsall's
Farm

Manor Heys
Farm

THE MARSHES LA

Short Wood
Hall

Hunter's
Plantation

Pale Ditch La

Holmeswood
Moss

Moss La

Moss Side
Farm

7

MERE LA

Holmes
Wood

Boundary
House

Mere
Farm

Brow
Farm

Holmeswood

Hunter's La

17

SMITHY LA

Engine
Farm

Holmeswood
Methodist Sch

HOLMESWOOD
FOUR LANE ENDS

HOLMESWOOD RD

Birch La

6

CABIN LA

WIGGINS LA

CHAPEL LA

Mossend
Farm

SANDY LA

PO

Homestead
Farm

Mere Side
Farm

CROSS MEANYGATE

SANDY LA

The
Warren

5

B5246

Rhodes
Farm

Mere Side

Williamson
Farm

16

Wiggins
Bridge

BERRY HOUSE RD

Berry
House

Rufford Boundary Sluice

SANDY WAY

Sandyway
Farm

Rufford Boundary Sluice

Mere Sands Wood
Nature Reserve

4

LONG MEANYGATE

Martin Mere
Windmill
(dis)

Windmill
Farm

WHOLESOME LA

Woodlands
Farm

MERE LA

Tootle House
Farm

3

Boat House Sluice

FISH LA

Clay Brow
Farm

TOOTLE LA

15

Noon La

2

Tarlscough
Moss

CURLEW LA

Boundary La

Martin Mere
(The Wildfowl Trust)

Tarlscough
Hall

1

MARSH MOSS LA

TARLSCOUGH LA

Tarlscough

14

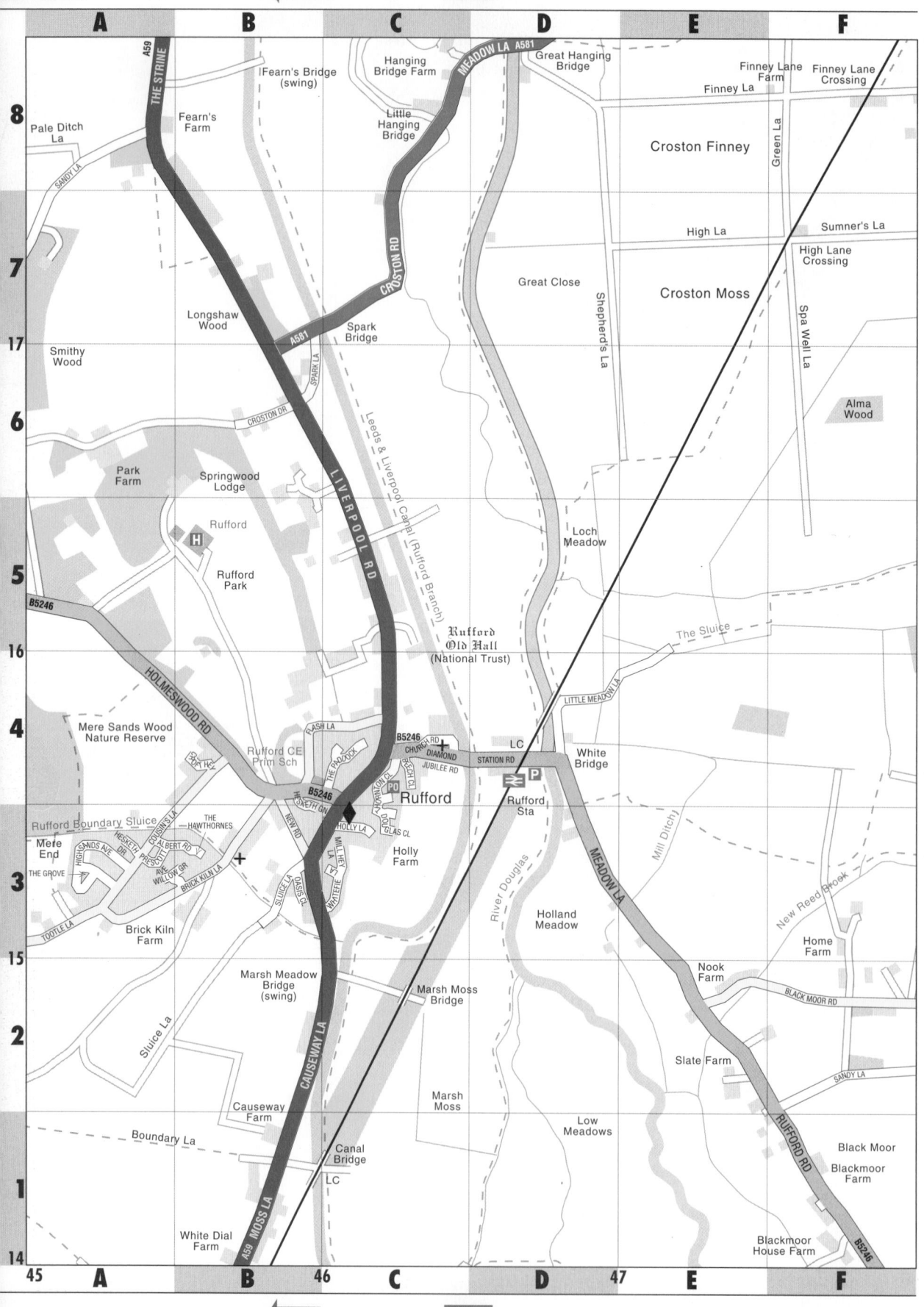

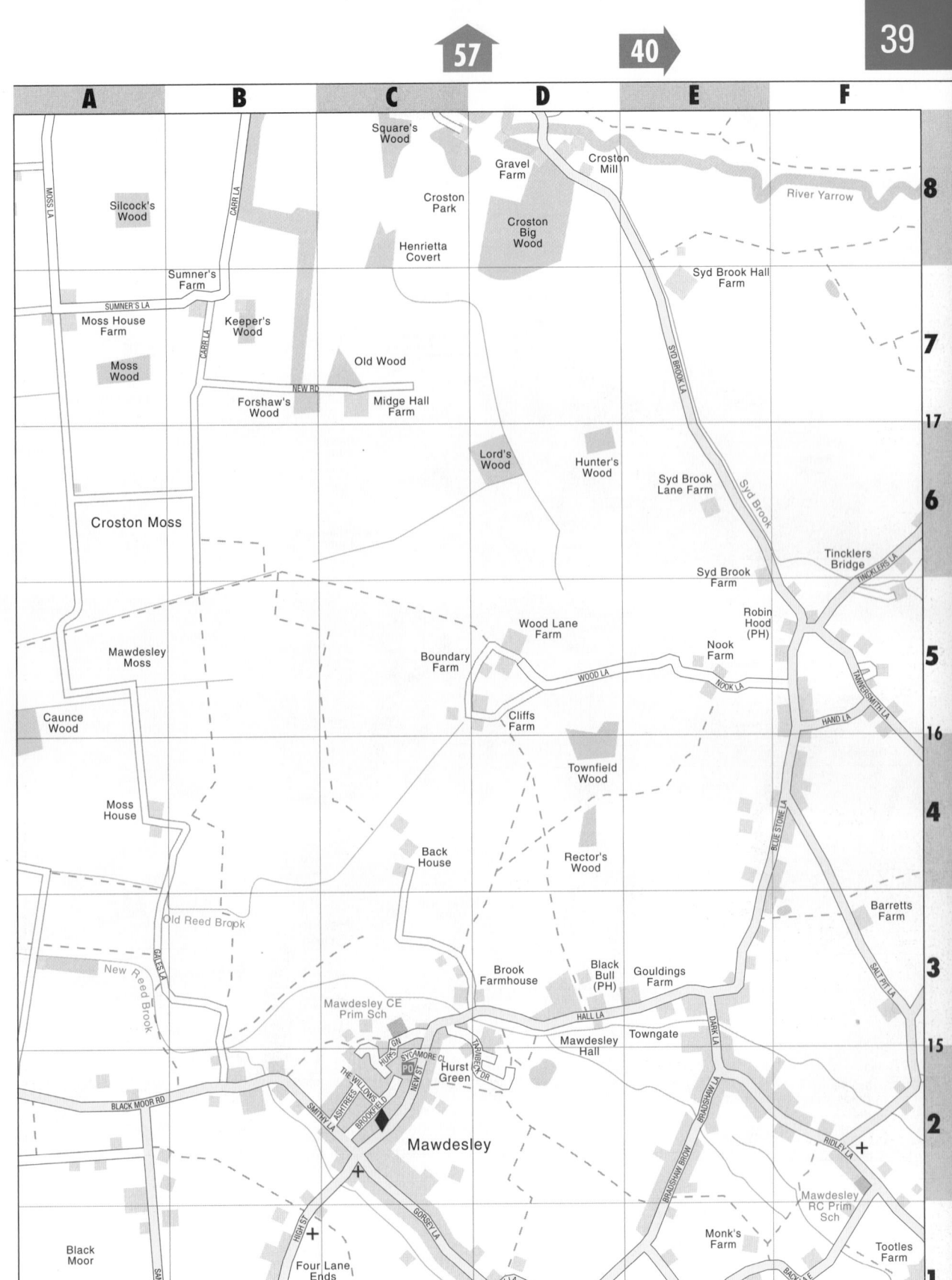

57

40

A B C D E F

Square's
Wood

Gravel
Farm

Croston
Mill

River Yarrow 8

Silcock's
Wood

Croston
Park

Croston
Big
Wood

Syd Brook Hall
Farm

Sumner's
Farm

MOSS LA

CARR LA

SUMNER'S LA

Henrietta
Covert

7

Moss House
Farm

Keeper's
Wood

CARR LA

Old Wood

Moss
Wood

NEW RD

Forshaw's
Wood

Midge Hall
Farm

17

Lord's
Wood

Hunter's
Wood

Syd Brook
Lane Farm

SYD BROOK LA

Syd Brook 6

Croston Moss

Tincklers
Bridge

TINCKLERS LA

Syd Brook
Farm

Mawdesley
Moss

Wood Lane
Farm

Robin
Hood
(PH)

5

Boundary
Farm

WOOD LA

Nook
Farm

NOOK LA

TANNER SMITH LA

Caunce
Wood

Cliffs
Farm

HAND LA

16

Townfield
Wood

Moss
House

BLUE STONE LA

4

Back
House

Rector's
Wood

Barretts
Farm

Old Reed Brook

GALES LA

Brook
Farmhouse

Black
Bull
(PH)

Gouldings
Farm

SALT PIT LA

New Reed Brook

Mawdesley CE
Prim Sch

HALL LA

Mawdesley
Hall

Towngate

DARK LA

15

BLACK MOOR RD

SMITH LA

ASH TREES

HURST GN

SYCAMORE CL

PO

NEW ST

BROOKFIELD

TARBECK DR

Hurst
Green

BRADSHAW LA

BRADSHAW BROW

Mawdesley

Mawdesley
RC Prim
Sch

RIDLEY LA +

2

THE WILLOWS

Black
Moor

HIGH ST +

Four Lane
Ends

GORSEY LA

BACK LA

BACK LA E

Monk's
Farm

House
Farm

Tootles
Farm

SANDY LA

Joy Bank
Farm

SCHOOL LA

OLD LA

MOOD LA

BENTLEY LA

1

DAUB LA

14

26

40

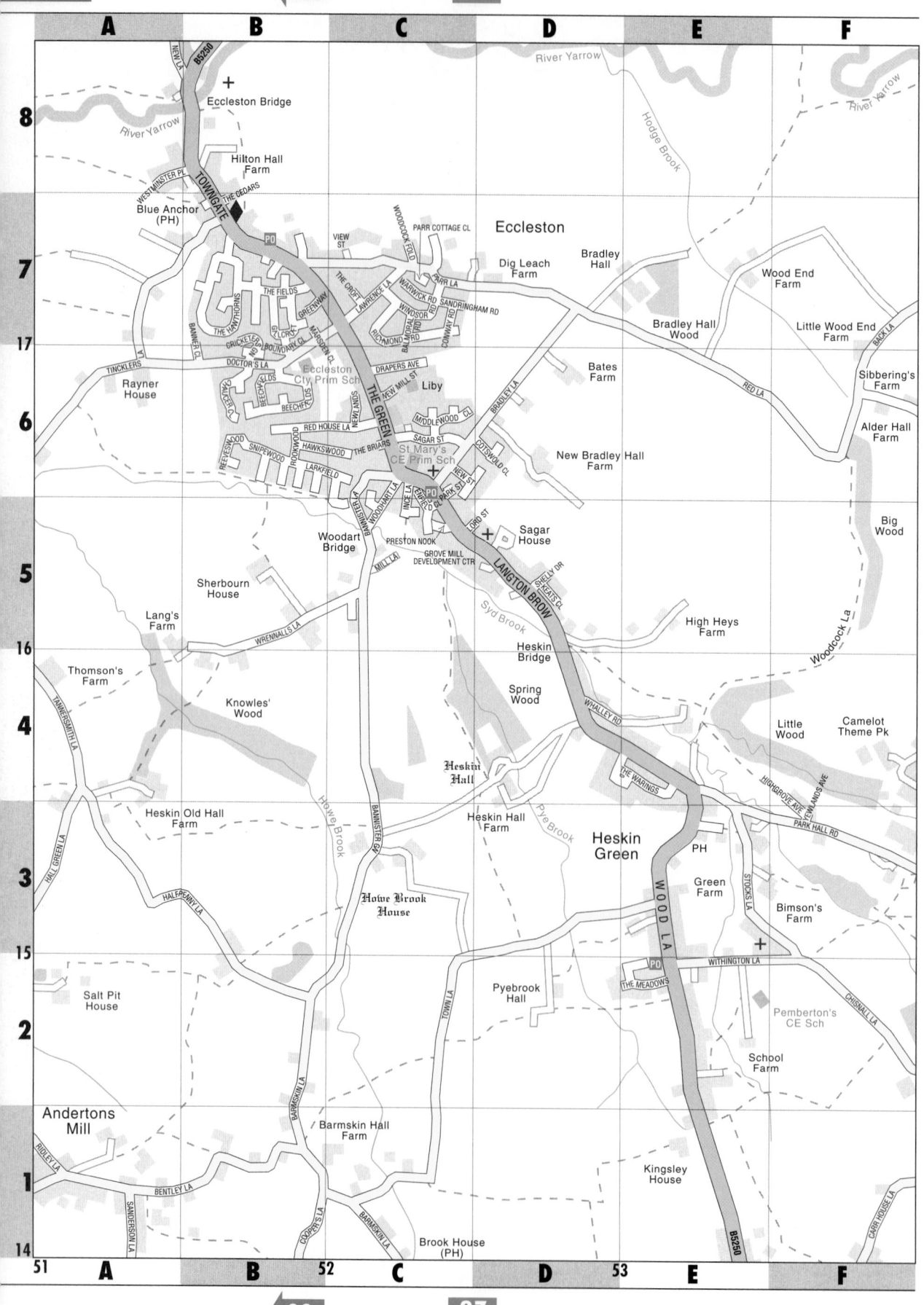

A B C D E F

8

Eccleston Bridge

River Yarrow

Hilton Hall Farm

WESTMINSTER PL

Blue Anchor (PH)

THE CEDARS

PO

Eccleston

River Yarrow

Hodge Brook

Bradley Hall

Wood End Farm

7

THE FIELDS

THE HAWTHORNS

THE CROFT

GREENWAY

LAWRENCE LA

PARR LA

VIEW ST

WOODOCK FOLD

PARR COTTAGE CL

WARWICK RD

SANDRINGHAM RD

WINDSOR

RICHMOND

BALMORAL

CONWAY RD

Dig Leach Farm

Bradley Hall Wood

Little Wood End Farm

BACK LA

17

TINCKLERS

Rayner House

CRICKETER'S

BOUNDARY CL

DOCTOR'S LA

THE FIELDS

BANNER CL

MARSDEN CL

SIDNEY AVE

CALDER

BEECHER CL

REEVES WOOD

Eccleston Cty Prim Sch

DRAPERS AVE

NEW MILL ST

Liby

Bates Farm

RED LA

Sibbering's Farm

6

SNIPEWOOD

LARKFIELD

HAWKSWOOD

RED HOUSE LA

THE BRIARS

THE GREEN

MIDDLEWOOD CL

SAGAR ST

St Mary's CE Prim Sch

BRADLEY LA

COTSWOLD CL

New Bradley Hall Farm

Alder Hall Farm

Big Wood

5

Woodart Bridge

BENNING

WOODART LA

MILL LA

INCE LA

Preston Nook

PO

PARK RD

GROVE MILL DEVELOPMENT CTR

LORD ST

NEW ST

Sagar House

LANGTON BROW

SHELLY DR

KEATS CL

High Heys Farm

Woodcock La

Sherbourn House

Syd Brook

16

Lang's Farm

WRENNALLS LA

Heskin Bridge

WHALLEY RD

Little Wood

Camelot Theme Pk

4

Thomson's Farm

Knowles' Wood

Spring Wood

THE WARINGS

HIGHGROVE AVE

YEWLANDS AVE

PARK HALL RD

Howe Brook

3

HALFPENNY LA

Heskin Old Hall Farm

BANNISTER GN

Heskin Hall

Heskin Hall Farm

Pye Brook

Heskin Green

PH

Green Farm

STOCKS LA

Bimson's Farm

CHISNALL LA

WOOD LA

15

Salt Pit House

HALL GREEN LA

TANNERSMITH LA

Howe Brook House

TOWN LA

Pyebrook Hall

PO

THE MEADOWS

WITHINGTON LA

Pemberton's CE Sch

2

Andertons Mill

RIDLEY LA

BARMSKIN LA

Barmskin Hall Farm

School Farm

1

BENTLEY LA

SANDERSON LA

COOPER'S LA

BARMSKIN LA

Brook House (PH)

Kingsley House

CARR HOUSE LA

B5250

14

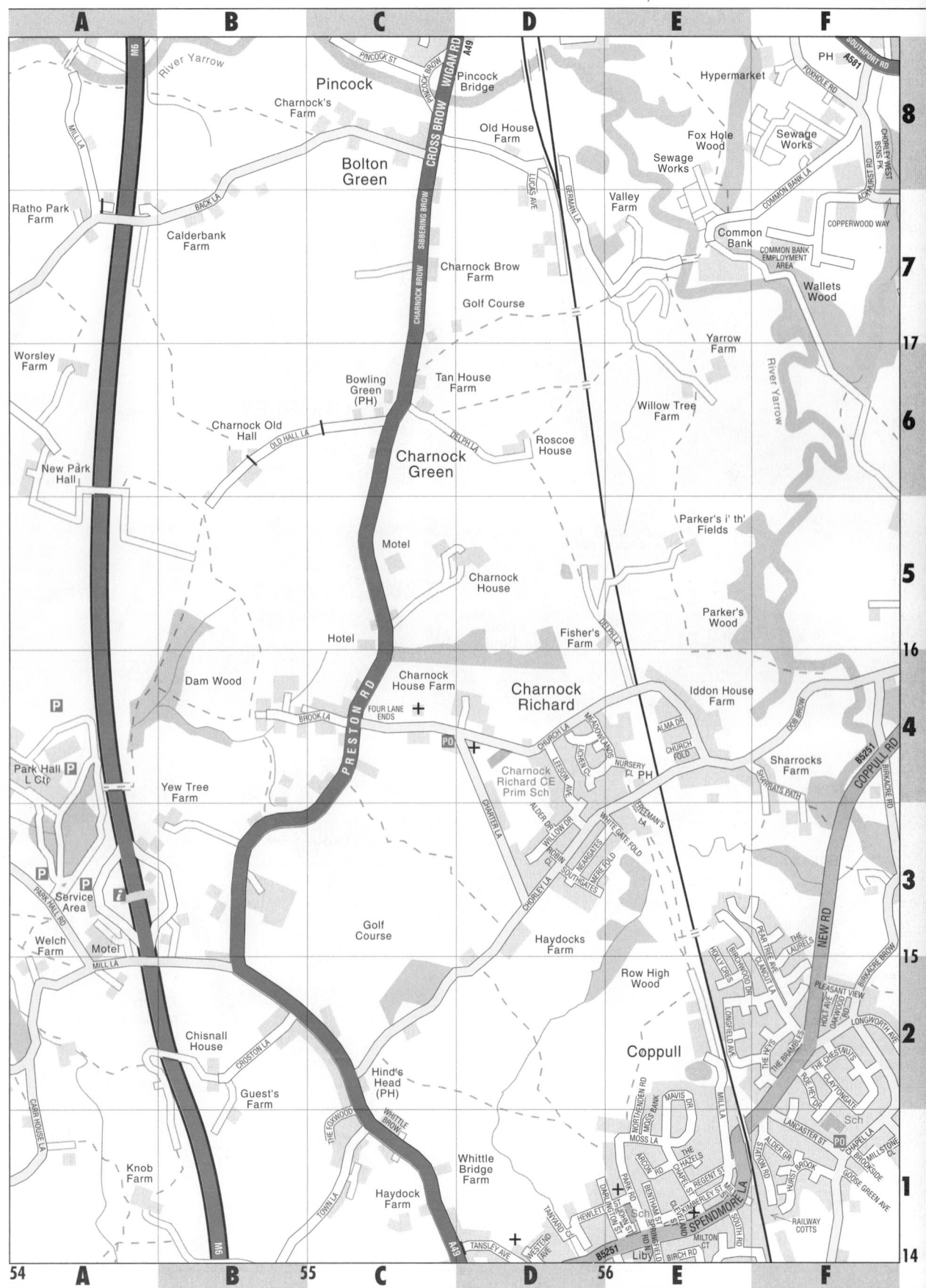

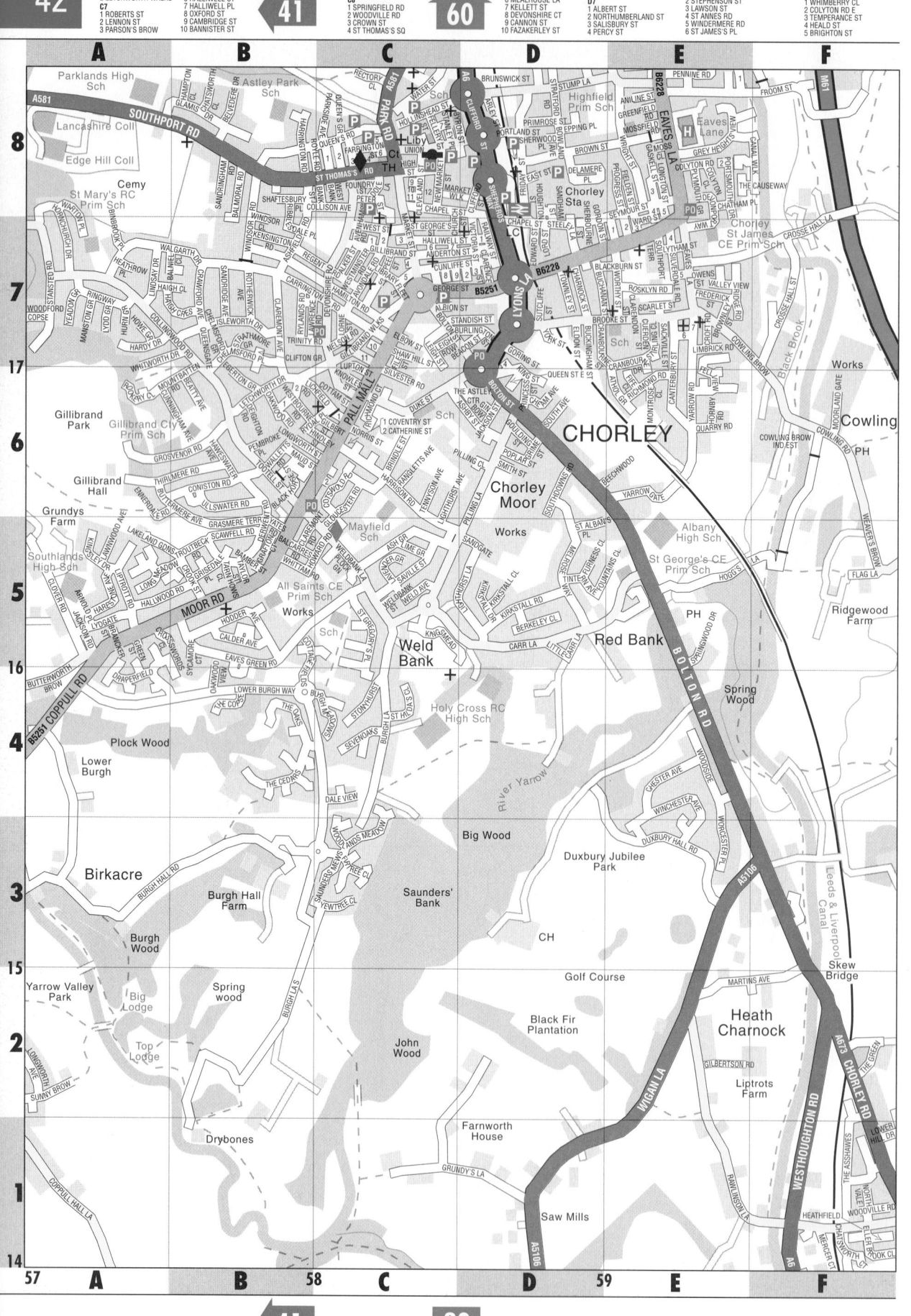

43
62

A   B   C   D   E   F

8

Devil's Ditch

Black Lower
Hill

Counting
Hill

High Shores

Anglezarke Moor

Redmond's
Edge

Limestone Clough

Rushy Brow

Standing Stones
Hill

7

Limestone Brook

White Ledge
Hill

Spitlers Edge

17

Lead Mines Clough

6

Holts Flat

Higher
Anshaw

Sam Pasture

Will
Narr

5

River Yorrow

Hordern
Pasture

16

RIVINGTON RD

4

DEAN HEAD LA

Hordern
Stoops

Wilcock's
Farm

Moor
Bottom

3

Sparks
Bridge

Moses
Cocker's

Shore

Bradleys

SHEEP HOUSE LA

15

BELMONT RD

Noon Hill Slack

Winter
Hill
Masts

2

Noon Hill

HALL LA

Rivington Hall
Barn

Catter
Nab

Rivington
Moor

1

Brere's Meadow
Pit

14

43
31

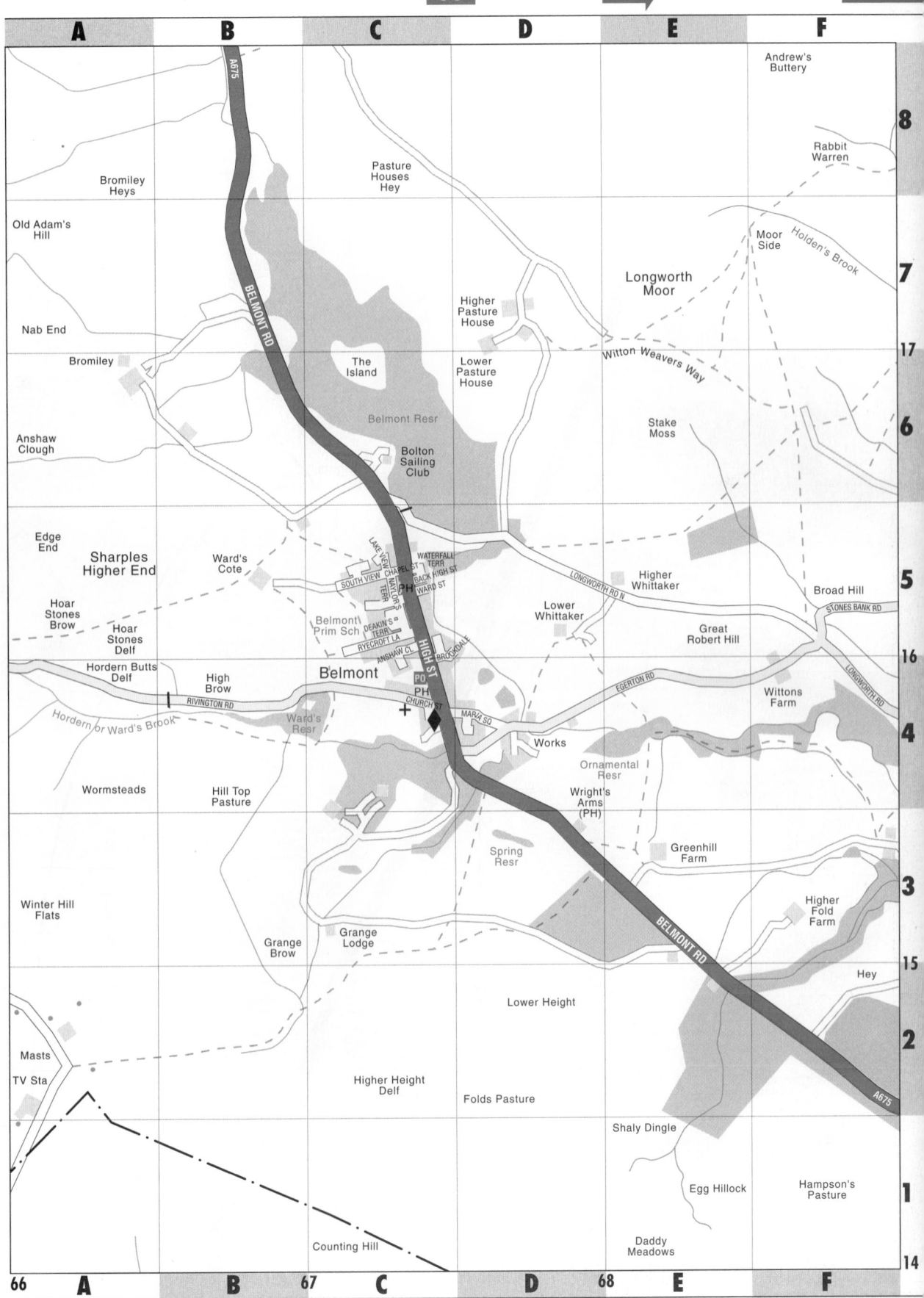

A   B   C   D   E   F

Andrew's
Buttery

8

Rabbit
Warren

Bromiley
Heys

Old Adam's
Hill

Moor
Side

Holden's Brook

7

Longworth
Moor

Nab End

17

Bromiley

The
Island

Higher
Pasture
House

Witton Weavers Way

Anshaw
Clough

Belmont Resr

Lower
Pasture
House

Stake
Moss

6

Bolton
Sailing
Club

Edge
End

Sharples
Higher End

Ward's
Cote

WATERFALL
TERR

Higher
Whittaker

Broad Hill

5

LAKE VIEW
CHAPEL ST
NAYLOR'S
TERR
SOUTH VIEW
TERR
PH
BACK HIGH ST
WARD ST

LONGWORTH RO N

STONES BANK RD

Hoar
Stones
Brow

Lower
Whittaker

LONGWORTH RD

Hoar
Stones
Delf

Belmont
Prim Sch

DEAKIN'S
TERR
RYECROFT LA

Great
Robert Hill

16

Hordern Butts
Delf

High
Brow

ANSHAW CL

HIGH ST

BROADDALE

Belmont

PO
PH
CHURCH ST

EGERTON RD

Wittons
Farm

RIVINGTON RD

Hordern or Ward's Brook

Ward's
Resr

MARIA SQ

Works

4

Wormsteads

Hill Top
Pasture

Ornamental
Resr

Wright's
Arms
(PH)

Winter Hill
Flats

Spring
Resr

Greenhill
Farm

BELMONT RD

Higher
Fold
Farm

3

Grange
Brow

Grange
Lodge

15

Hey

Masts

Lower Height

2

TV Sta

Higher Height
Delf

Folds Pasture

A675

Shaly Dingle

1

Egg Hillock

Hampson's
Pasture

Counting Hill

Daddy
Meadows

14

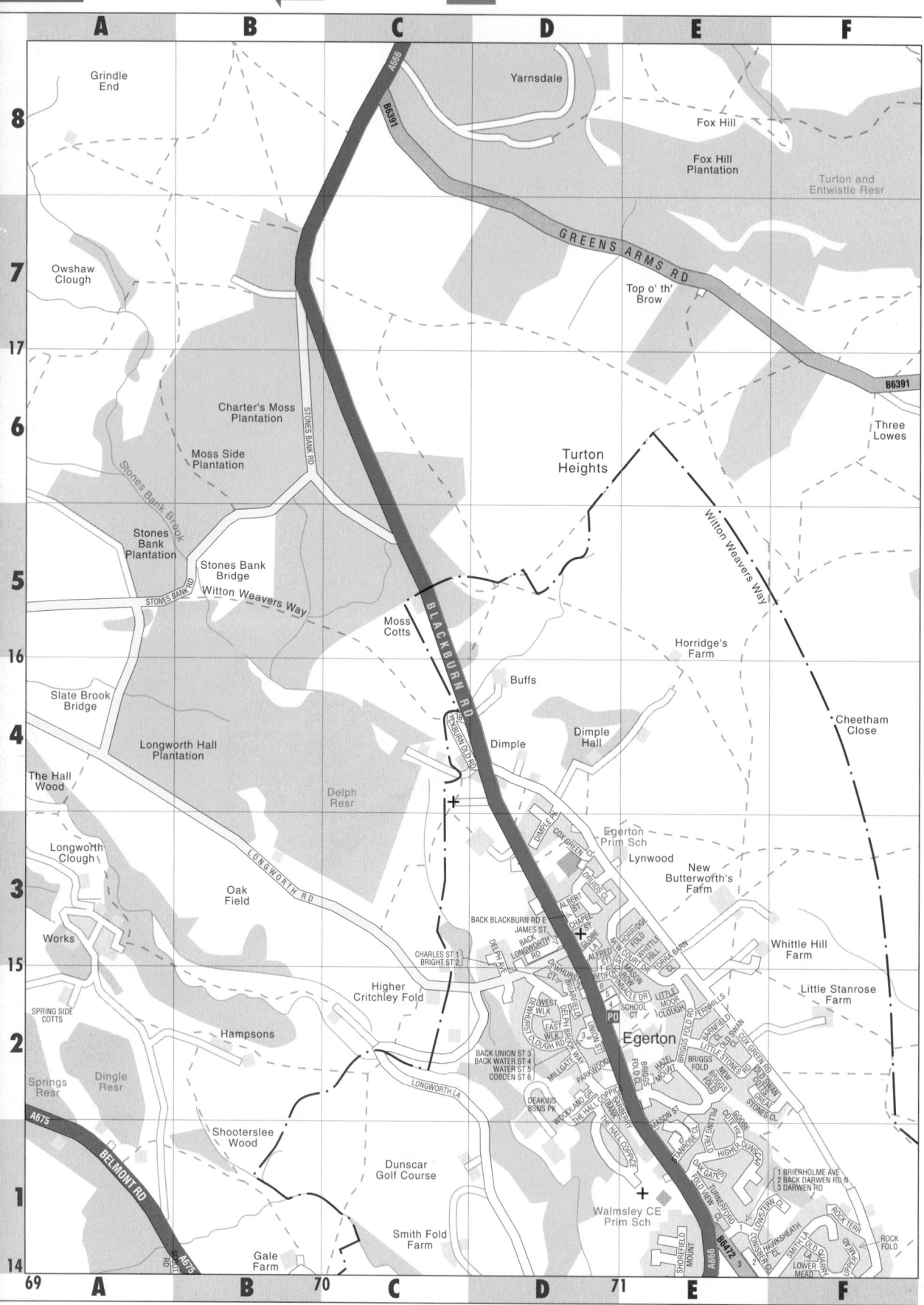

A B C D E F

8

7

17

6

5

16

4

15

3

2

1

14

Grindle End

Owshaw Clough

Charter's Moss Plantation

Moss Side Plantation

Stones Bank Brook

Stones Bank Plantation

Stones Bank Bridge

Witton Weavers Way

STONES BANK RD

Slate Brook Bridge

The Hall Wood

Longworth Hall Plantation

Longworth Clough

Oak Field

Works

LONGWORTH RD

Delph Resr

Spring Side Cotts

Hampsons

Springs Resr

Dingle Resr

Shooterslee Wood

BELMONT RD

A675

A675 SOUTH RD

Gale Farm

Dunscar Golf Course

Smith Fold Farm

Higher Critchley Fold

LONGWORTH LA

CHARLES ST 1
BRIGHT ST 2

DELPH LANE

Yarnsdale

Fox Hill

Fox Hill Plantation

Turton and Entwistle Resr

GREENS ARMS RD

Top o' th' Brow

B6391

Three Lowes

Turton Heights

Witton Weavers Way

Horridge's Farm

Cheetham Close

A666

B6391

BLACKBURN RD

Moss Cotts

Buffs

Dimple

Dimple Hall

BLACKBURN OLD RD

Egerton Prim Sch

Lynwood

New Butterworth's Farm

Whittle Hill Farm

Little Stanrose Farm

Egerton

Walmsley CE Prim Sch

A666

B6472

1 BRIERHOLME AVE
2 BACK DARWEN RD N
3 DARWEN RD

ROCK FOLD

SHOREFIELD MOUNT

69 A 70 B C 71 D E F

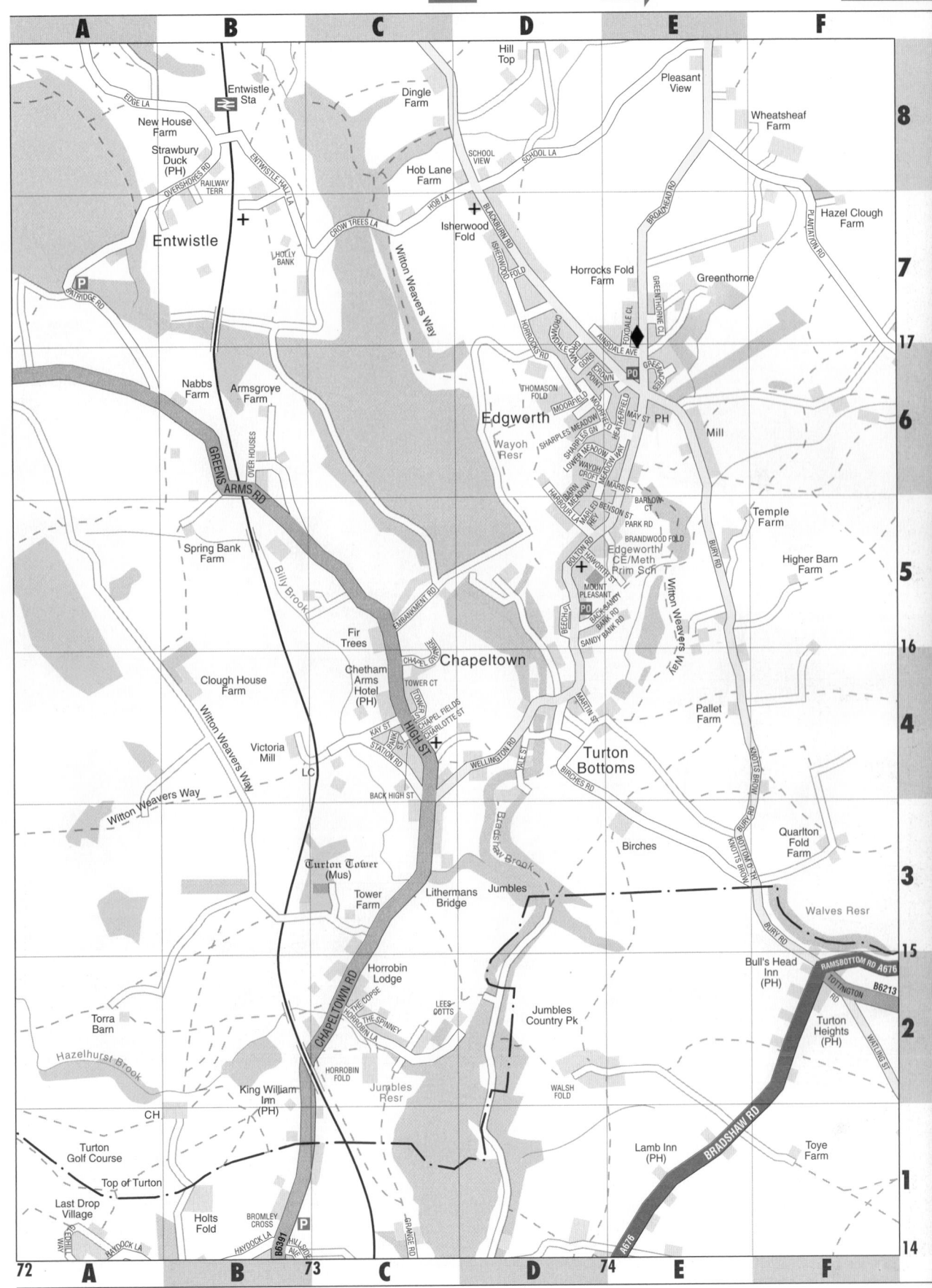

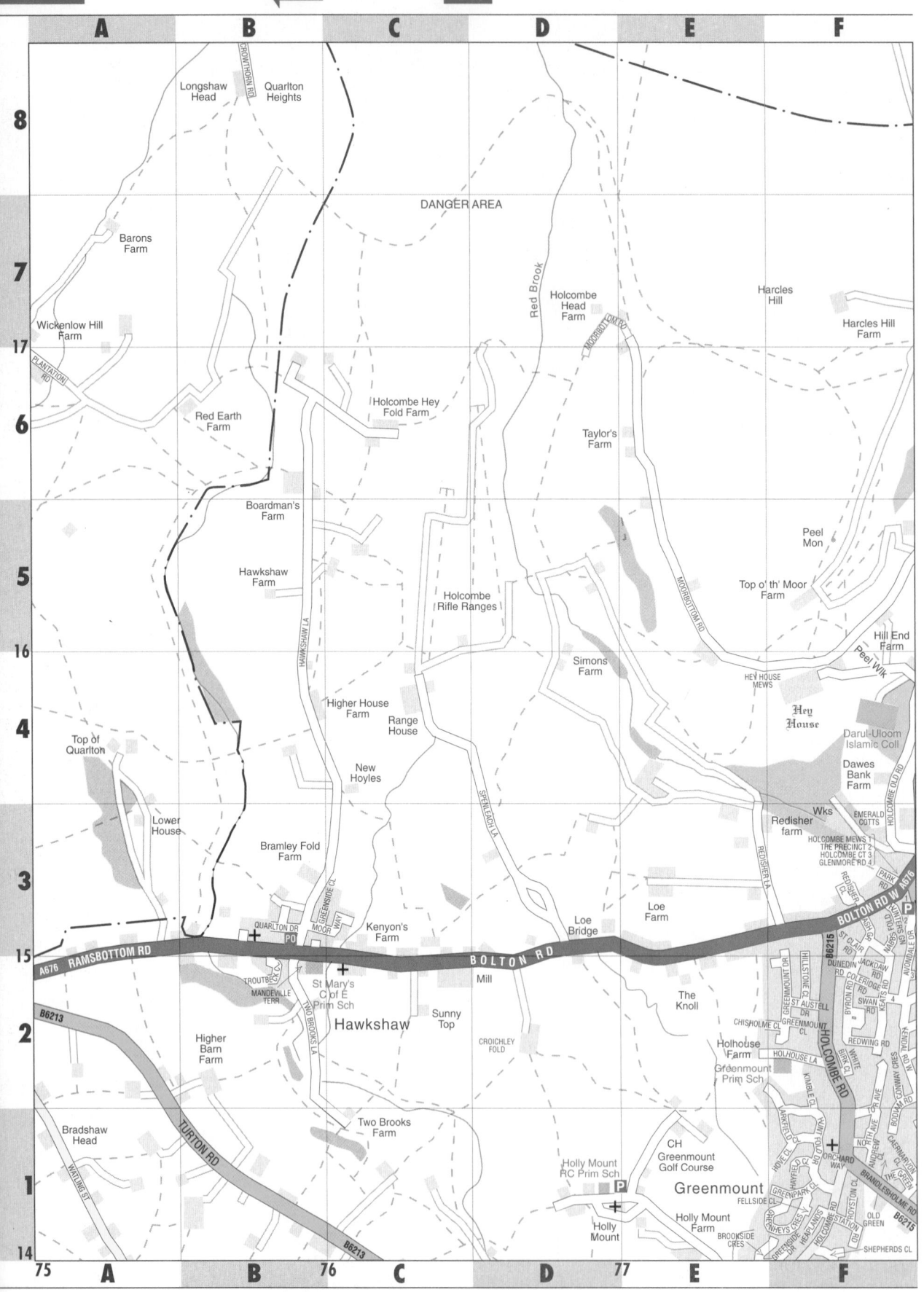

A   B   C   D   E   F

8

Longshaw Head   Quarlton Heights

7

Barons Farm

DANGER AREA

Red Brook

Holcombe Head Farm

Harcles Hill

Harcles Hill Farm

Wickenlow Hill Farm

17

6

Red Earth Farm

Holcombe Hey Fold Farm

Taylor's Farm

Peel Mon

Boardman's Farm

Hawkshaw Farm

Holcombe Rifle Ranges

Top o' th' Moor Farm

Peel Wik

Hill End Farm

5

16

Simons Farm

Hey House Mews

Higher House Farm

Range House

Hey House

Darul-Uloom Islamic Coll

Dawes Bank Farm

4

Top of Quarlton

New Hoyles

Wks

Redisher farm

Emerald Cotts

Holcombe Mews 1
THE PRECINCT 2
HOLCOMBE CT 3
GLENMORE RD 4

Lower House

Bramley Fold Farm

Loe Farm

Loe Bridge

BOLTON RD W A676

P

3

Kenyon's Farm

QUARLTON DR   PO

GREENSIDE CL

MOOR WAY

BOLTON RD

The Knoll

ST CLAIR

DUNEDIN RD

COLERIDGE RD

JACKDAW RD

SWAN RD

AVONDALE CIR

B6215

15

A676   RAMSBOTTOM RD

Troutbeck

MANDEVILLE TERR

St Mary's C of E Prim Sch

TWO BROOKS LA

Mill

Sunny Top

CROICHLEY FOLD

Holhouse Farm

HOLHOUSE LA

Greenmount Prim Sch

BYRON RD

GREENMOUNT DR

HILLSTONE CL

ST AUSTELL DR

CHISHOLME CL

GREENMOUNT CL

WHITE

REDWING RD

BIRK CL

BODKIN

CONWAY RD

WYNDHAM AVE

NORA

CAERNARVON RD

HOLCOMBE RD

B6213

2

Higher Barn Farm

Hawkshaw

Bradshaw Head

WATLING ST

TURTON RD

Two Brooks Farm

CH Greenmount Golf Course

Holly Mount RC Prim Sch

P

Greenmount

Holly Mount

Holly Mount Farm

ORCHARD WAY

FELLSIDE CL

LARKFIELD CL

KNOLL CL

ROYTON CL

WAYFIELD

GREENPARK RD

FAIRHOLME

PRINHEYS CRES

GREENSIDE

HEADLANDS

THE GREEN

BRANDLESHOLME RD

THE AVENUE

NORTON AVE

KIMBLE CL

HEADLANDS

STATION RD

OLD GREEN

B6215

BROOKSIDE CRES

SHEPHERDS CL

1

14

75   A   B   76   C   D   77   E   F

B6213

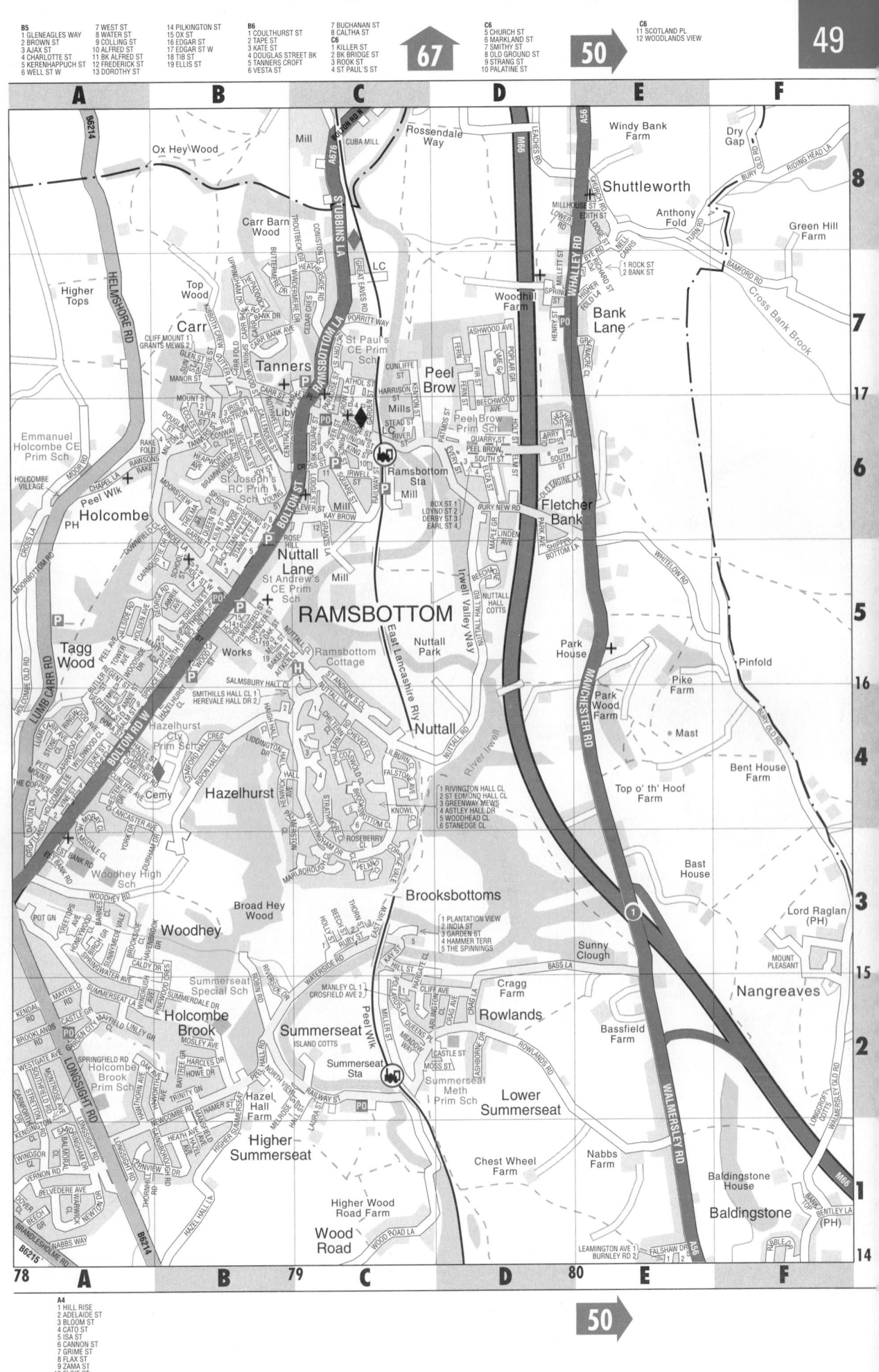

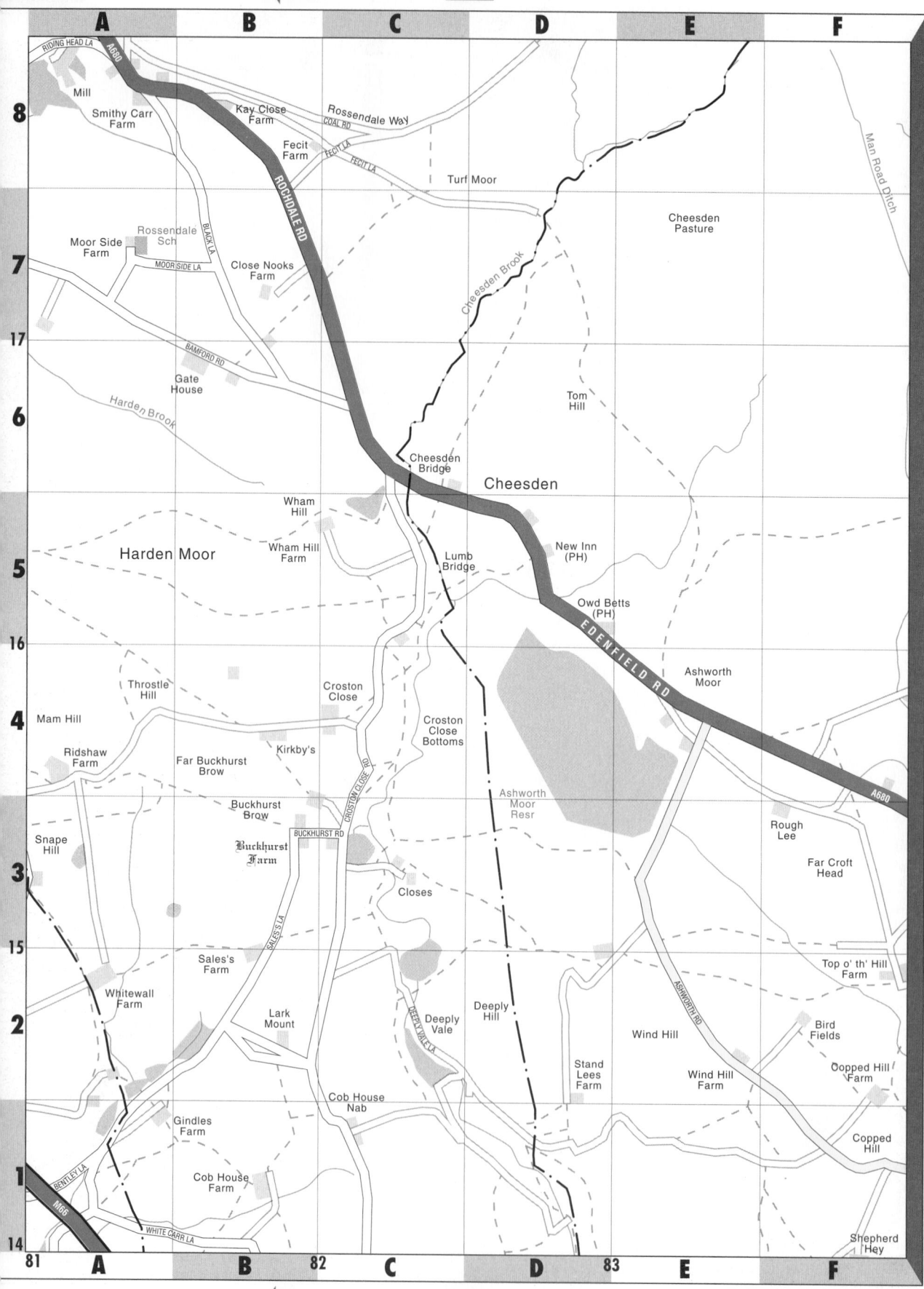

A   B   C   D   E   F

8

RIDING HEAD LA
A680
Mill
Smithy Carr
Farm
Kay Close
Farm
Rossendale Way
COAL RD
Fecit
Farm
FECIT LA
Turf Moor
Cheesden
Pasture
Man Road Ditch

7

Moor Side
Farm
Rossendale
Sch
BLACK LA
MOOR SIDE LA
Close Nooks
Farm
ROCHDALE RD
Cheesden Brook

17

BAMFORD RD
Gate
House
Harden Brook
Tom
Hill

6

Cheesden
Bridge
Cheesden

Wham
Hill
Wham Hill
Farm
Lumb
Bridge
New Inn
(PH)

Harden Moor

5

Owd Betts
(PH)
EDENFIELD RD
Ashworth
Moor

16

Throstle
Hill
Croston
Close
Croston
Close
Bottoms
A680

4

Mam Hill
Kirkby's
Ridshaw
Farm
Far Buckhurst
Brow
Ashworth
Moor
Resr
Rough
Lee

Buckhurst
Brow
CROSTON CLOSE RD
BUCKHURST RD
Far Croft
Head

3

Snape
Hill
Buckhurst
Farm
Closes
Top o' th' Hill
Farm

15

Whitewall
Farm
Sales's
Farm
SALES LA
Deeply
Vale
DEEPLY VALE LA
Deeply
Hill
Wind Hill
Bird
Fields

2

Lark
Mount
Stand
Lees
Farm
Wind Hill
Farm
ASHWORTH RD
Copped Hill
Farm

Gindles
Farm
Cob House
Nab
Copped
Hill

1

BENTLEY LA
M66
Cob House
Farm
WHITE CARR LA
Shepherd
Hey

14

81   A   B   82   C   D   83   E   F

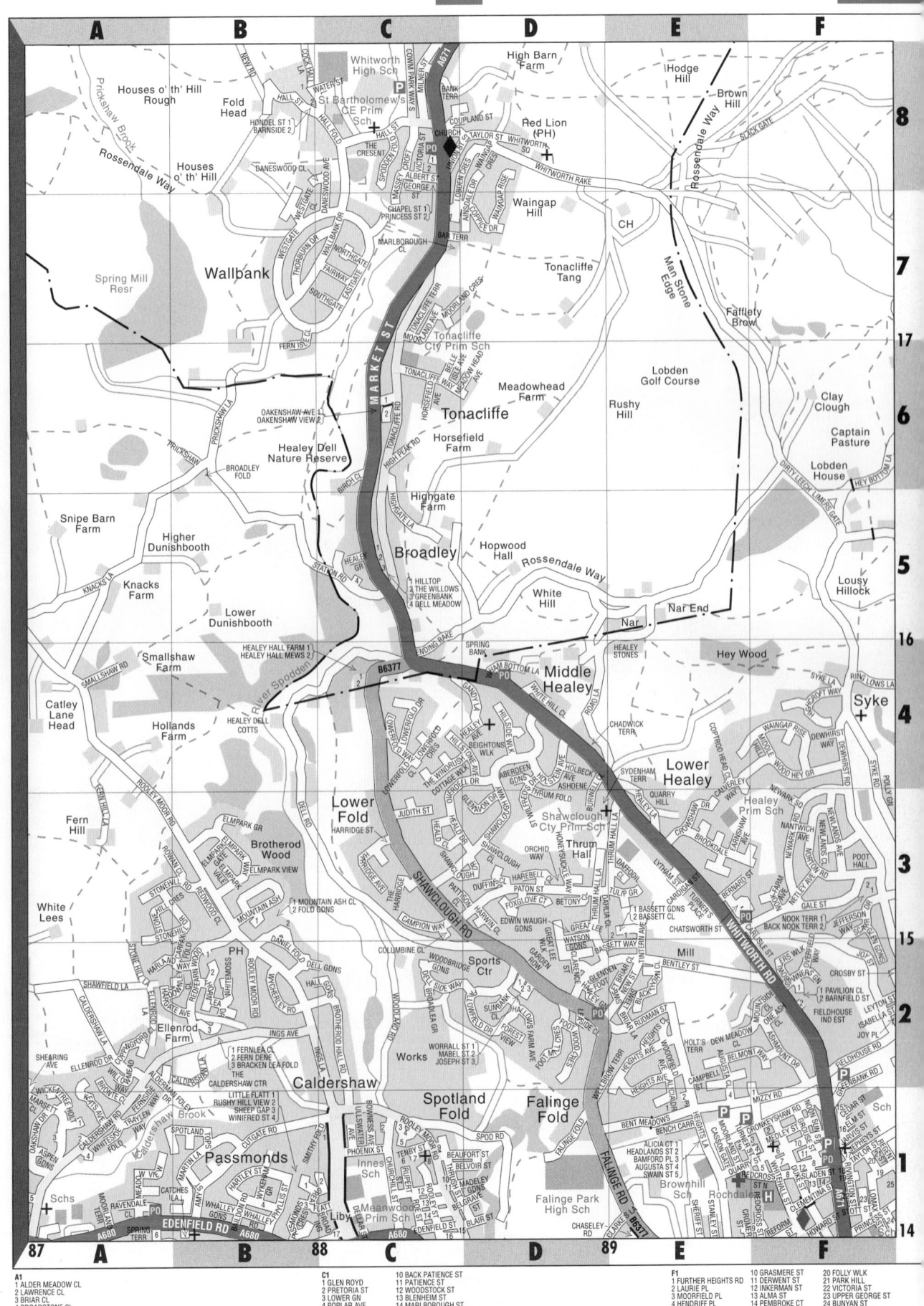

A B C D E F

8

7

21

6 — Wks

Marshside — Marshside Marsh

P

5

Sefton Coastal Path

20 — Stanley High Sch

4 — Marshside

PREBAL CL · SALWICK CL · PILLING CL · ELSWICK RD · GARSTANG RD · FRECKLETON RD · CATON · FYLDE RD · ST ANNES RD · WILLOWHEY · LYTHAM RD · MARSHSIDE RD

Southport Sands — MARINE DR

Bank Nook

FLEETWOOD RD · ST MICHAEL'S RD · FLEETWOOD CL · GRANBY CL · PAUL'S LA · KNOB HALL LA · COTTYS BROW · CROSTON'S BROW

3 — FLEETWOOD RD

Hesketh Golf Links

THRELFALLS CL · RADNOR DR · LONGACRE · CLENGERS BROW · BAKER'S LA · DENBIGH AVE · EDEN AVE

19 — BELLIS AVE · KINGS AVE · CHURCHILL AVE · THRELFALL'S LA · HESKETH RD

CH — COCKLE DICK'S LA · BRAEMAR AVE · THE LAWNS · EMMANUEL RD · BRADSHAW AVE · CAMBRIDGE GDNS · CAMBRIDGE AVE

2 — COCKLE DICK'S LA · MAPLEWOOD · A565

Municipal Golf Links — CAMBRIDGE RD

FAIRWAY — HESKETH RD

PROMENADE · ALBANY RD · LATHOM RD · KNOWSLEY RD · AVONDALE RD N · LEYLAND RD · PARK RD W · FLEETWOOD RD · CLIFF RD · ARGYLE CT · ARGYLE RD · HOWARD CT · ALBERT CT · GRANVILLE CT · BROCKLEBANK RD · CAMBRIDGE CT · GRIFFON HOUSE · BERESFORD GDNS · COUDRAY RD · SILVERTHORNE DR · BERESFORD DR · KINGS KEY RD

CH

PARK CRES

1 — Marine Lake

Sefton Coastal Path

Hesketh Park — H — Hesketh Park

SAUNDERS ST · IRVING ST · AVONDALE RD S · ALEXANDRA RD · GORDON ST · GORDON AVE · ALBERT RD · PARK RD · POPLAR BANK · BRENTWOOD · LINDLEY RD · PARK AVE · ALLERTON RD · RAWLINSON RD · PRESTON RD · HENLEY CT · HENLEY DR · SANDREY'S DR · HESKETH DR · KINLOSS DR · HILBRE DR · MONTROSE DR · CARISBROOKE DR · CHURCHGATE · CRESCENT DR · ROOKERY RD

18 — Leicester St — B5245 — A565 — PO — B5280 — PO

33 A B 34 C D 35 E F

54

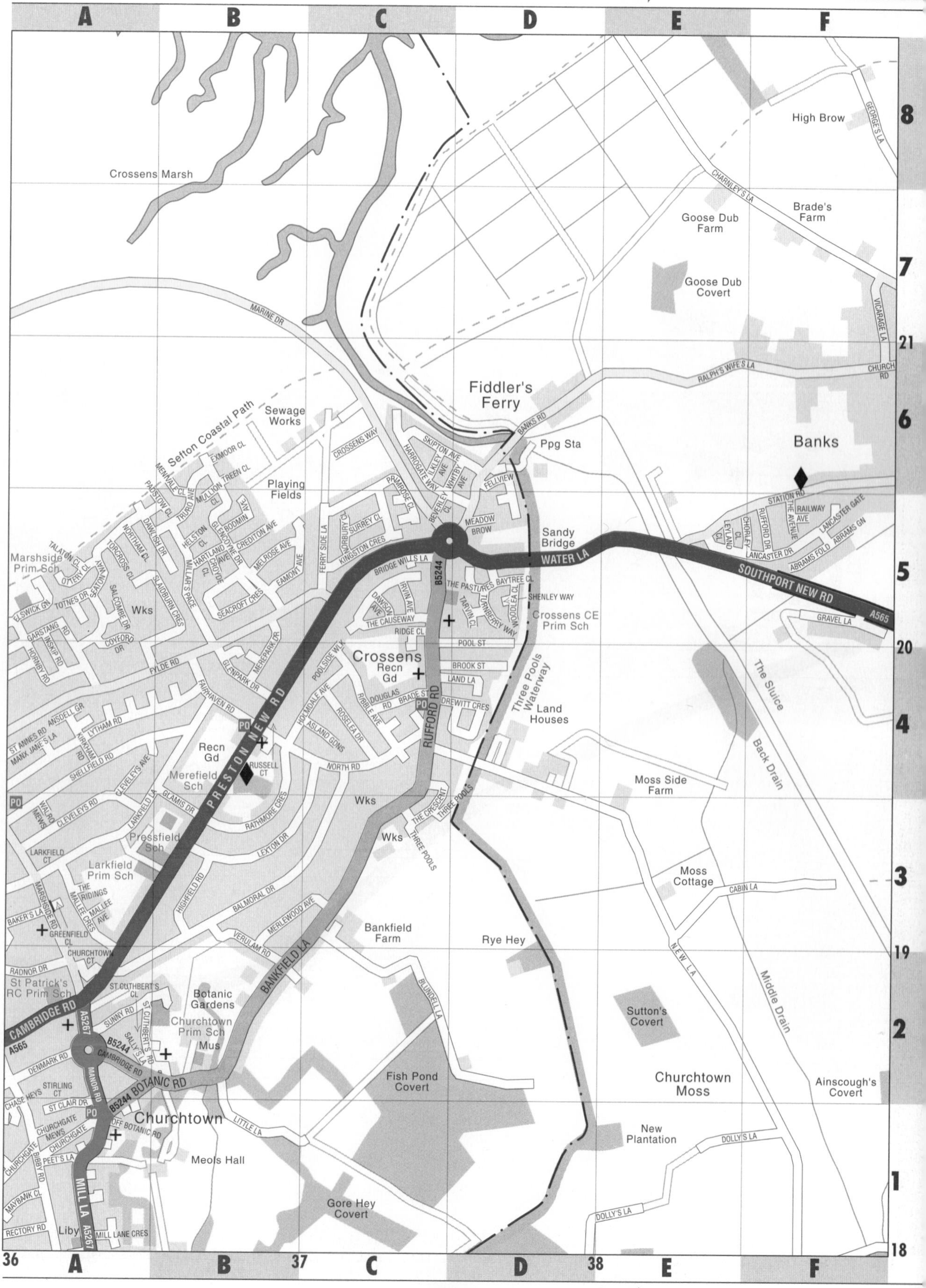

A
B
C
D
E
F
8
7
21
6
5
20
4
3
19
2
1
18
36
37
38
Crossens Marsh
High Brow
GEORGE'S LA
CHARNLEY'S LA
Brade's Farm
Goose Dub Farm
Goose Dub Covert
VICARAGE LA
MARINE DR
RALPH'S WIFE'S LA
CHURCH RD
Fiddler's Ferry
Sewage Works
Sefton Coastal Path
BANKS RD
Ppg Sta
Banks
CROSSENS WAY
SKIPTON AVE
HARROGATE WAY
ILKLEY AVE
WHITBY AVE
EXMOOR CL
MENIVALE CL
TREEN CL
MULLION CL
Playing Fields
PADSTOW CL
TRURO AVE
BODMIN
PRIMROSE CL
BEVERLEY CL
FELLVIEW
STATION RD
RAILWAY AVE
LANCASTER GATE
THE AVENUE
RUFFORD DR
CHORLEY CL
LEYLAND CL
LANCASTER DR
ABRAMS FOLD
ABRAMS GN
NORTHAM CL
DAWLISH DR
HELSTON CL
HARTLAND AVE
GLENEAGLES DR
CREDITON AVE
SURREY CL
NORBURY CL
FERRY SIDE LA
KINGSTON CRES
MEADOW BROW
Sandy Bridge
WATER LA
SOUTHPORT NEW RD
TALATON CL
OTTERY CL
TORCROSS CL
SEATON WAY
SLAIDBURN CRES
MILLAR'S PACE
MELROSE AVE
EAMONT AVE
BRIDGE WILLS LA
B5244
THE PASTURES
BAYTREE CL
SHENLEY WAY
Marshside Prim Sch
ELSWICK GN
TOTNES DR
SALCOMBE DR
Wks
SEACROFT CRES
DAWSON AVE
IRVIN AVE
THE CAUSEWAY
TARVIN CL
TURNBERRY WAY
WOODLEA CL
Crossens CE Prim Sch
GRAVEL LA
A565
GARSTANG RD
INSKIP RD
HORNBY RD
COWFORD DR
RIDGE CL
POOL ST
FYLDE RD
GLENPARK DR
MEREPARK DR
POOLSIDE WLK
Crossens
Recn Gd
BROOK ST
LAND LA
The Sluice
FAIRHAVEN RD
HOLMDALE AVE
DOUGLAS RD
BRADE ST
DREWITT CRES
Three Pools Waterway
ANSDELL GR
LYTHAM RD
ST ANNES RD
MANX JANE'S LA
KIRKHAM RD
PO
RIBBLE AVE
ROSELEA DR
ASLAND GDNS
RUFFORD RD
Land Houses
Back Drain
SHELLFIELD RD
CLEVELEYS AVE
Recn Gd
PRESTON NEW RD
RUSSELL CT
Merefield Sch
NORTH RD
Moss Side Farm
WALRO MEWS
CLEVELEYS RD
LARKFIELD LA
GLAMIS DR
RATHMORE CRES
Wks
THE CRESCENT
THREE POOLS
Pressfield Sch
LARKFIELD CT
LEXTON DR
Wks
Larkfield Prim Sch
THE RIDINGS
MALLEE CRES
MALLEE AVE
MARSHSIDE RD
HIGHFIELD RD
Moss Cottage
CABIN LA
BAKER'S LA
GREENFIELD CL
BALMORAL DR
MERLEWOOD AVE
Bankfield Farm
Rye Hey
CHURCHTOWN CT
VERULAM RD
RADNOR DR
NEW LA
St Patrick's RC Prim Sch
ST CUTHBERT'S CL
BANKFIELD LA
Botanic Gardens
BLUNDELL LA
Middle Drain
CAMBRIDGE RD
A5267
SUNNY RD
ST CUTHBERT'S RD
SALLY'S LA
Churchtown Prim Sch
Sutton's Covert
A565
B5244
Mus
DENMARK RD
CAMBRIDGE RD
Fish Pond Covert
Churchtown Moss
Ainscough's Covert
CHASE HEYS
STIRLING CT
MANOR RD
BOTANIC RD
ST CLAIR DR
CHURCHGATE MEWS
CHURCHGATE
PO
Churchtown
OFF BOTANIC RD
LITTLE LA
New Plantation
DOLLY'S LA
PEET'S LA
BIBBY RD
Meols Hall
MAYBANK CL
MILL LA
Gore Hey Covert
DOLLY'S LA
RECTORY RD
Liby
A5267
MILL LANE CRES

35

54

Tinsley's Farm

Far Banks

Gore Hall Farm

Boundary Farm

Heath Farm

Brookfield's Farm

New House Farm

New House Farm

Bank View Farm

LITTLE LA

GORSEY LA

Wright's Plantation

Banks Meth Prim Sch

Moss Edge Farm

MOSS LA

Nursery

Nursery

Holmes Moss

St Stephens' CE Prim Sch

PO

CHURCH RD

LONG LA

Sugar Stubbs Coverts

Brand Heald

BOUNDARY LA

P

MEOLS CT

STATION RD

Greaves Hall

H

Little Runner

Moss Side Farm

GRAVEL LA

THE CLOSE

A565

Gravel Farm

Jump's Farm

Hollywood Farm

GREEN LA

Woodend Farm

Sugar Stubbs

SUGAR STUBBS LA

Wright's Farm

MOSS SIDE LA

Caravan Park

GRAVEL LA

SOUTHPORT NEW RD

Tarleton Runner

Runner Plantations

DALWEB IND PK

GRAVEL LA

Long Ditch Bridge

Boundary Farm

BOBBINERS LA

GRAVEL LA

Gravel Farm

MERE LA

Riverside Caravan Site

Legh House Farm

A565

LONGFOLD

Ring Ditch

Tarleton Mere Brow CE Prim Sch

PO

B5246

THE GRAVEL

CINDER LA

B5246

Back Drain

The Sluice

COMMON LA

Mere Brow

Mere Meanygate

TABBY NOOK

Caravan Site

72
56

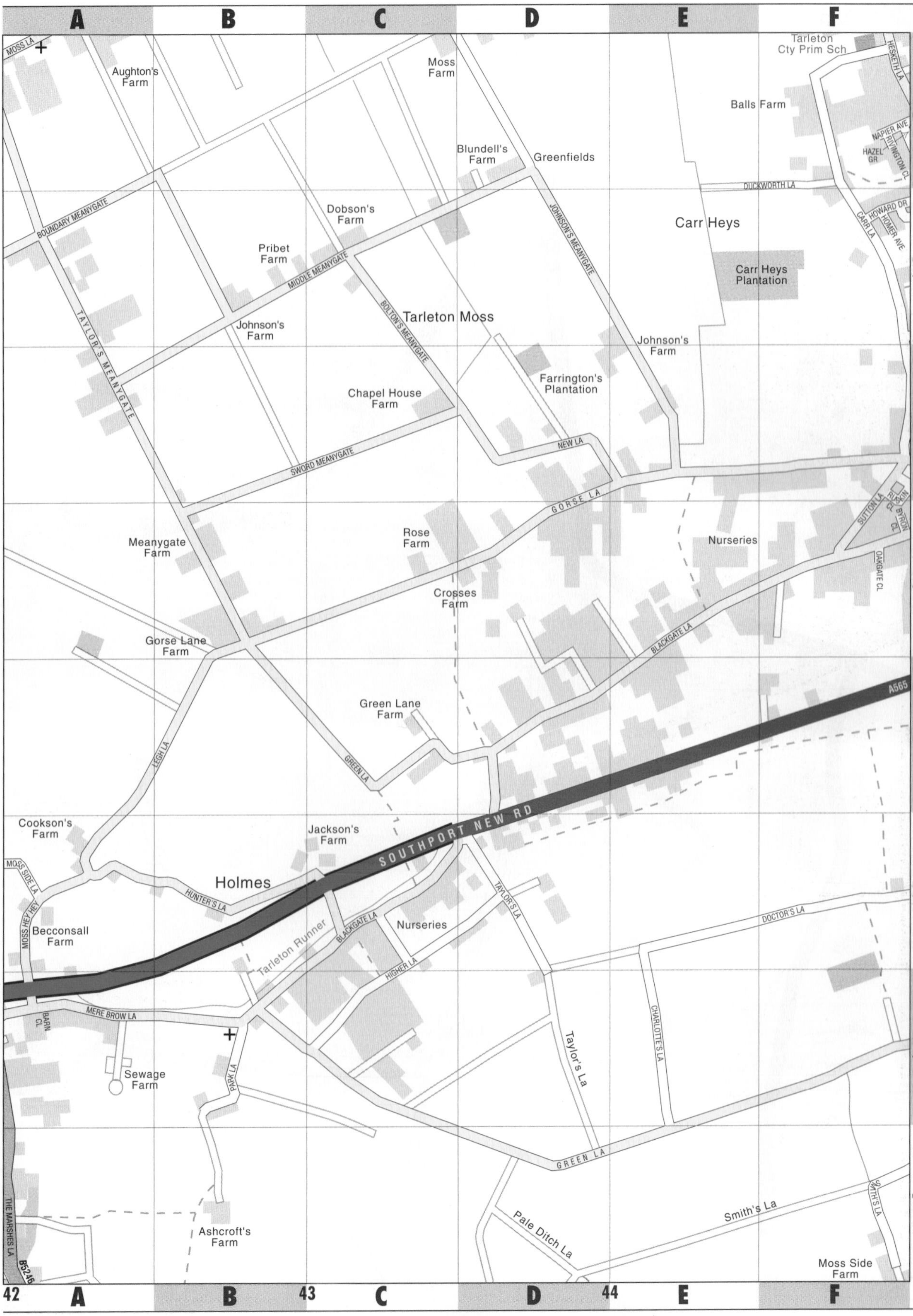
A
B
C
D
E
F
MOSS LA
Aughton's Farm
Moss Farm
Tarleton Cty Prim Sch
HESKETH LA
Balls Farm
NAPIER AVE
RIVINGTON CL
HAZEL GR
Blundell's Farm
Greenfields
DUCKWORTH LA
BOUNDARY MEANYGATE
Dobson's Farm
JOHNSON'S MEANYGATE
Carr Heys
CARR LA
HOWARD DR
HOMER AVE
Pribet Farm
MIDDLE MEANYGATE
Carr Heys Plantation
TAYLOR'S MEANYGATE
BOLTON'S MEANYGATE
Tarleton Moss
Johnson's Farm
Johnson's Farm
Farrington's Plantation
Chapel House Farm
NEW LA
SWORD MEANYGATE
GORSE LA
SUTTON LA
BYRON CL
Rose Farm
Nurseries
Meanygate Farm
OAKGATE CL
Crosses Farm
Gorse Lane Farm
BLACKGATE LA
A565
Green Lane Farm
LEGH LA
GREEN LA
SOUTHPORT NEW RD
Cookson's Farm
Jackson's Farm
MOSS SIDE LA
Holmes
HUNTER'S LA
TAYLOR'S LA
MOSS HEY HEY
Becconsall Farm
BLACKGATE LA
Nurseries
DOCTOR'S LA
Tarleton Runner
HIGHER LA
MERE BROW LA
BARN CL
CHARLOTTE'S LA
Taylor's La
Sewage Farm
PARK LA
GREEN LA
Pale Ditch La
Smith's La
SMITH'S LA
THE MARSHES LA
Ashcroft's Farm
B5246
Moss Side Farm
8
7
21
6
5
20
4
3
19
2
1
18
42
43
44

37
56

55
73

A B C D E F

8

7

21

6

5

20

4

3

19

2

1

18

Marsdens Farm

Mill Hill

Mill Hill Farm

HAULDERS LA

LIVERPOOL OLD RD

A59

Carrs

Carr House Bridge

Carr House

B5247

Long Fold

CORAL LEACH COTTS

Brook House Farm

NORTH RD

Finches Farm

SPENCERS DR
RIVER VIEW
POWIS DR
AVONDALE DR
HILLCREST DR
SUTTON AVE
HILLCREST DR
HEALEY GR
CRESTWAY

HAIG AVE

THE BEECHES
MEOLSGATE AVE
FIRBANK AVE
THE SPINNEY
OAKLANDS AVE
WILLOW HEY

Tarleton Cty High Sch

Tarleton

KEARSLEY AVE
FLETCHER AVE
MAYOR
HUNTER AVE
LATHAM CRES

PLOX BROW

Plocks Farm

The Windmill

CARR HOUSE LA

B5248

POMPIAN BROW

Bretherton

Bretherton Endowed CE Prim Sch

B5247

BAMFORDS OLD
SARAH LA

SOUTH RD

BACK LA

LIBY
BAMBERS
RE CT
MARK
SQ
GORSE
GORSE LA
THE CLIPS
ERS
PRIORY CL
PD
COPE LA
WAVERLEY DR
CHURCH RD
CHURCH WALK
Tarleton CE Prim Sch
CHURCH VIEW
CHAPEL MEADOWS
BARRONWOOD CT

River Asland or Douglas

Canal Bridge

BANK BRIDGE

Tarleton Bridge

Bank Hall

Ashcroft's Farm

Hudsons Farm

WINDGATE

A59

SOUTHPORT NEW RD

A565

Ram's Head (PH)

Cuerden Farm

Back Lane

Leeds and Liverpool Canal

Rufford Branch

River Douglas

Glynwood

Odd House

BROAD MEADOW LA

EYES LA

Bretherton Eyes

River Lostock

LIVERPOOL RD

A59

DOCTOR'S LA

Nursery

Bank's Farm

GREEN LA

Green Lane Farm

SMITH'S LA

Manor Farm

THE STRINE

Strine Brook

White Dial Farm

OLD GREEN RD
LOCK LA

Moor Farm

Sollom

SOLLOM LA

Red Bridge Farm

Red Bridge

Sollom Lane

Isle of Man Farm

MEADOW LA

River Yarrow

A581

A581

Cottage Lane

Green Lane

45 A 46 C D 47 E F
B C D E F

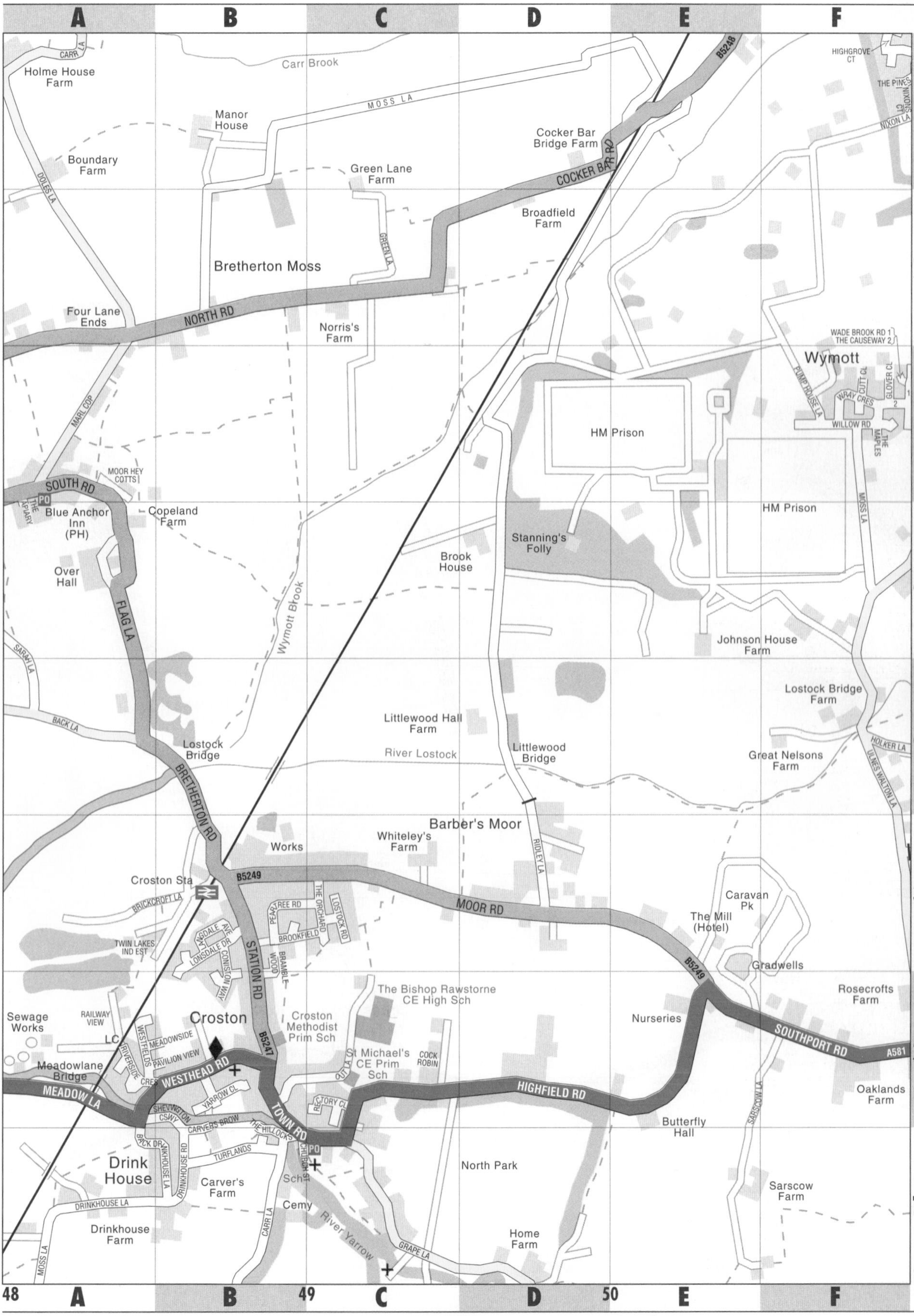

	A	B	C	D	E	F

Holme House Farm

Carr Brook

MOSS LA

Manor House

Boundary Farm

Green Lane Farm

Cocker Bar Bridge Farm

COCKER BAR RD

B5248

HIGHGROVE CT

THE PINES

NIXON LA

8

Bretherton Moss

GREEN LA

Broadfield Farm

7

Four Lane Ends

NORTH RD

Norris's Farm

Wymott

WADE BROOK RD 1
THE CAUSEWAY 2

21

DOLES LA

MARL COP

MOOR HEY COTTS

SOUTH RD

PO

THE APIARY

Blue Anchor Inn (PH)

Copeland Farm

HM Prison

PUMPHOUSE LA
WYMAY COTTS
WYMAY CRES
GLOVER CT
WILLOW RD
THE MAPLES

6

Over Hall

FLAG LA

Brook House

Stanning's Folly

HM Prison

MOSS LA

5

Wymott Brook

Johnson House Farm

20

SARAH LA

BACK LA

Lostock Bridge

BRETHERTON RD

Littlewood Hall Farm

River Lostock

Littlewood Bridge

Lostock Bridge Farm

Great Nelsons Farm

HOLKER LA
ULNES WALTON LA

4

Barber's Moor

Works

Whiteley's Farm

RIDLEY LA

Caravan Pk

The Mill (Hotel)

Gradwells

3

Croston Sta

BRICKCROFT LA

B5249

PEAR TREE RD
THE ORCHARD
LOSTOCK RD
BROOKFIELD
BRAMBLE WOOD

MOOR RD

B5249

Rosecrofts Farm

19

TWIN LAKES IND EST

LONGSDALE DR
COLESDALE
CONISTON WAY

STATION RD

B5247

The Bishop Rawstorne CE High Sch

Nurseries

SOUTHPORT RD

A581

2

Sewage Works

RAILWAY VIEW

LC

WESTFIELDS
MEADOWSIDE
RIVERSIDE
PAVILION VIEW
CRES

Croston

Croston Methodist Prim Sch

St Michael's CE Prim Sch

COCK ROBIN

SARSCOW LA

Oaklands Farm

Meadowlane Bridge

MEADOW LA

WESTHEAD RD

SHEVINGTON CSWY
CARVERS BROW

YARROW CL

TOWN RD

THE HILLOCKS
CHURCH RD
RECTORY CT

HIGHFIELD RD

Butterfly Hall

Drink House

BACK DR
DRINKHOUSE LA
DRINKHOUSE RD
TURFLANDS

Carver's Farm

Cemy

CARR LA

Sch
PO

North Park

Home Farm

Sarscow Farm

1

Drinkhouse Farm

MOSS LA

DRINKHOUSE LA

River Yarrow

GRAPE LA

18

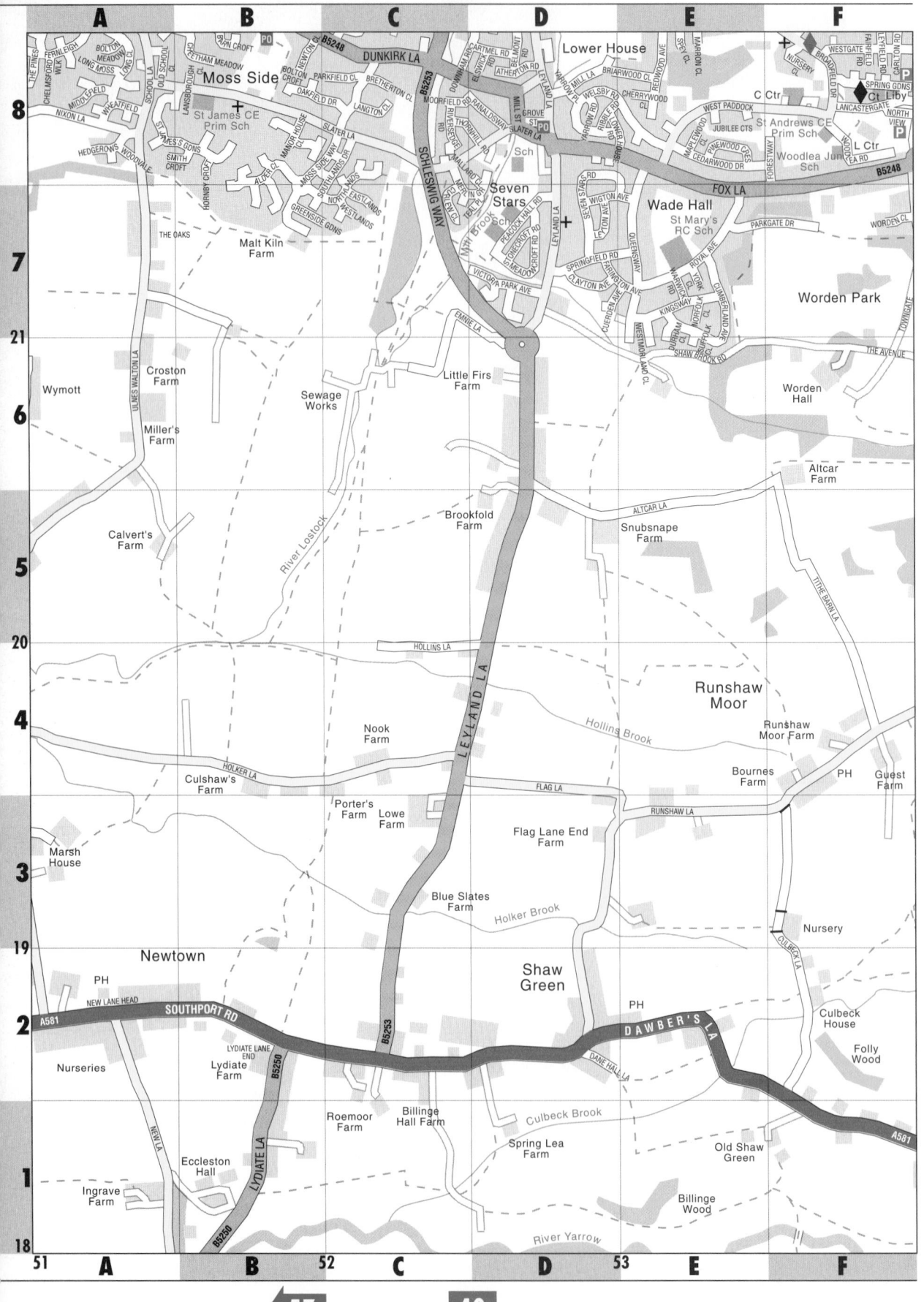

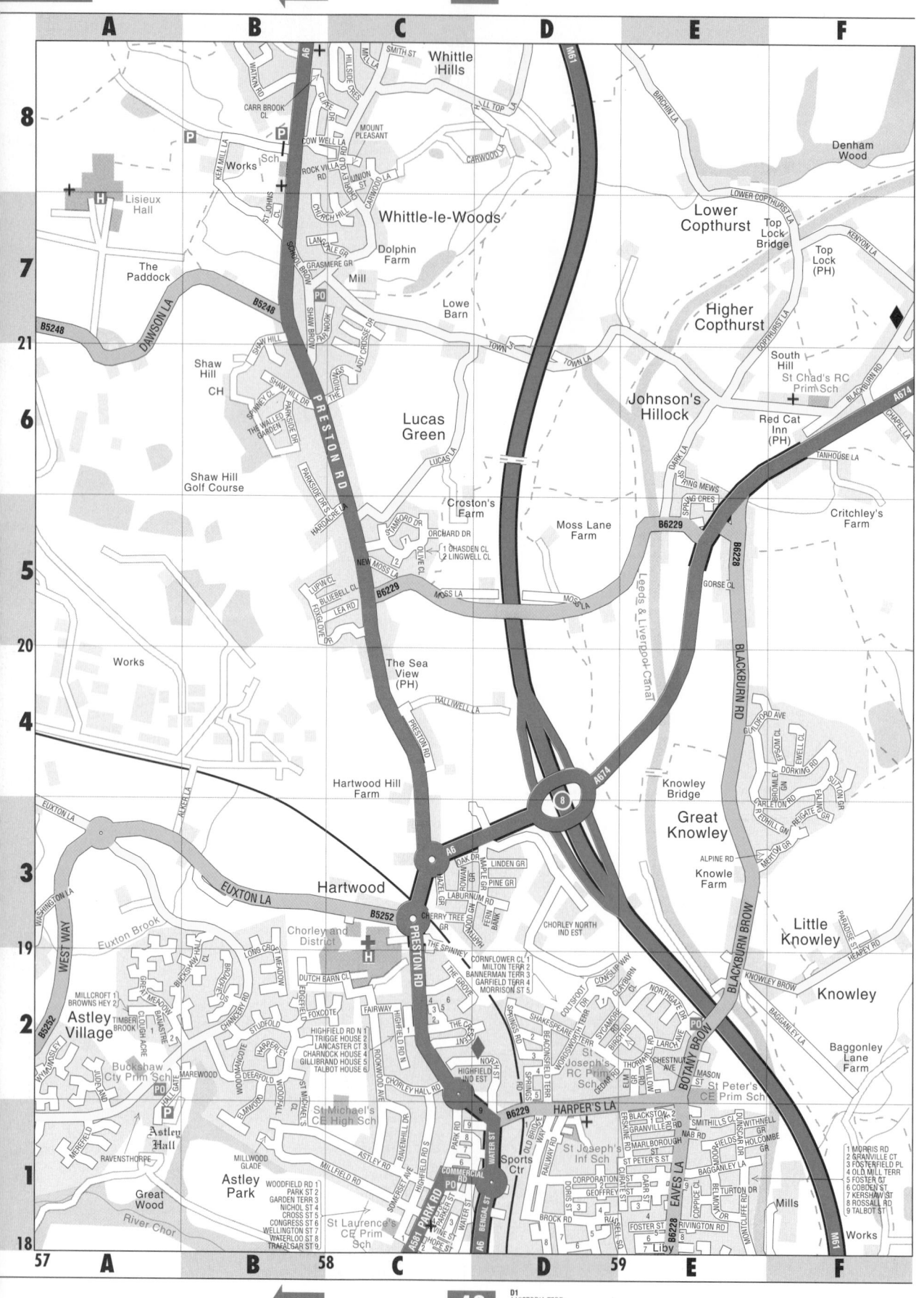

D1
1 VICTORIA TERR
2 VICARAGE ST
3 WESTWELL RD
4 INGLE MEWS
5 RUSSELL SQ W
6 WHINFIELD AVE
7 MAYFIELD AVE
8 BRIERCLIFFE RD
9 PRESTON ST

Whins Farm

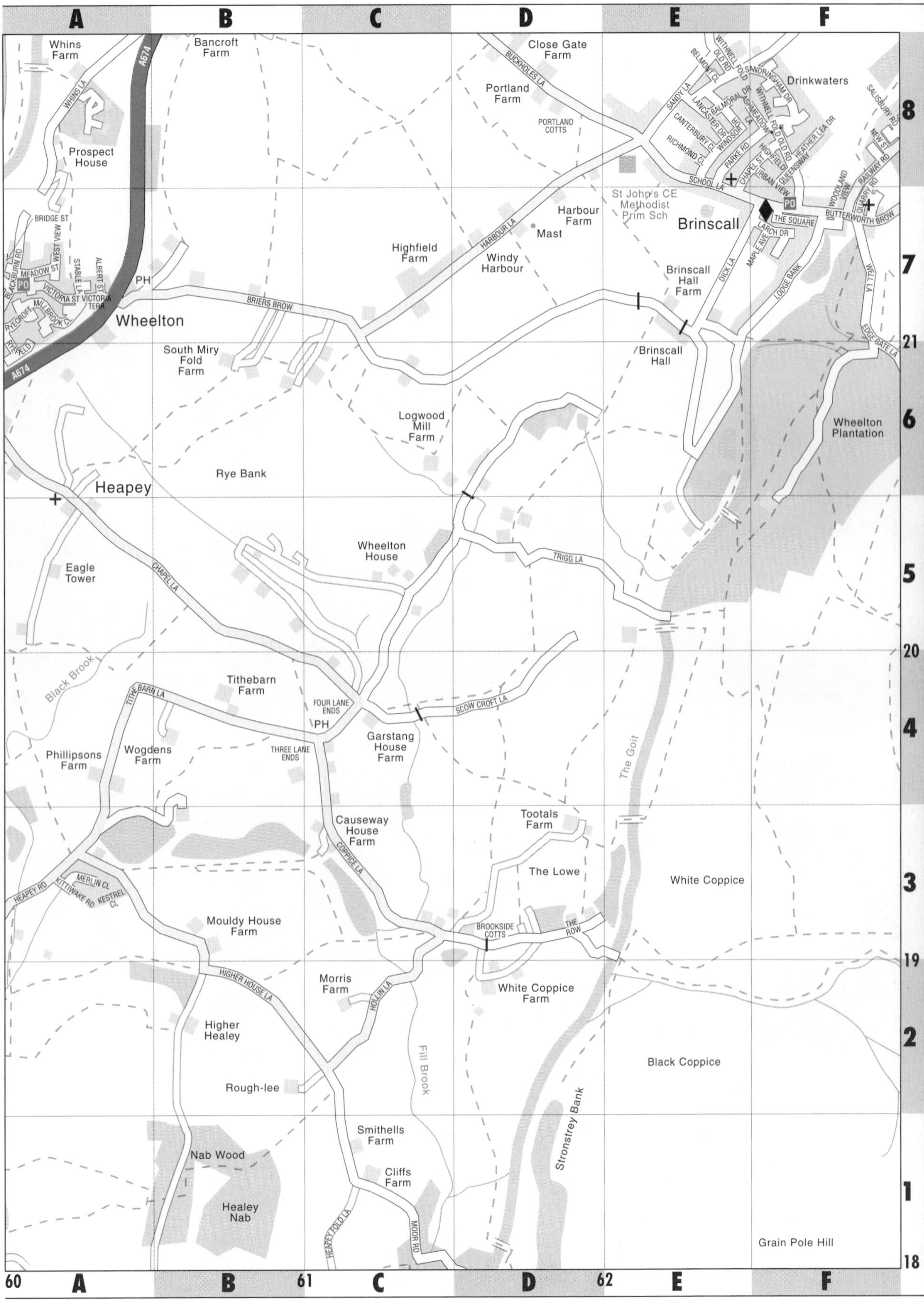

A674

Bancroft Farm

Close Gate Farm

BUCKHOLES LA

Portland Farm

PORTLAND COTTS

WITHNELL FOLD OLD RD
BELMONT DR
SANDY LA
LANCASTER DR
BALMORAL DR
WINDSOR
CANTERBURY CL
SANDRINGHAM DR
WITHNELL FOLD RD
ASHWORTH DR
Drinkwaters
SALISBURY RD
NEW ST

RICHMOND CL

Prospect House

8

WHINS LA

BRIDGE ST

Harbour Farm
Mast

St John's CE Methodist Prim Sch

SCHOOL LA
PARKE RD
CHAPEL ST
URBAN VIEW
HIGHFIELD
QUEENSWAY
WOODLAND VIEW
PO
BUTTERWORTH BROW
HEATHER LEA DR
RAILWAY RD

Brinscall

THE SQUARE

MAPLE AVE
LARCH DR
DICK LA
LODGE BANK
EDGE GATE LA
WELL LA

7

WEST VIEW ST
MEADOW ST
STABLE LA
ALBERT ST
VICTORIA TERR
BLACKBURN RD
PO
MILLBROOK
PH

Highfield Farm

HARBOUR LA

Windy Harbour

Brinscall Hall Farm

Wheelton

RYECROFT
FIELD ST
FIFIELD CL

A674

South Miry Fold Farm

BRIERS BROW

Brinscall Hall

21

Logwood Mill Farm

Wheelton Plantation

6

Rye Bank

Heapey

Eagle Tower

CHAPEL LA

Wheelton House

TRIGG LA

5

Black Brook

TITHE BARN LA

Tithebarn Farm

FOUR LANE ENDS
PH

SCOW CROFT LA

The Goit

20

Phillipsons Farm

Wogdens Farm

THREE LANE ENDS

Garstang House Farm

4

Causeway House Farm

COPPICE LA

Tootals Farm

The Lowe

White Coppice

3

HEAPEY RD
MERLIN CL
KITTIWAKE RD
KESTREL CL

Mouldy House Farm

BROOKSIDE COTTS

THE ROW

19

HIGHER HOUSE LA

Morris Farm

HOLLIN LA

White Coppice Farm

Higher Healey

2

Fill Brook

Black Coppice

Rough-lee

Smithells Farm

Stronstrey Bank

Nab Wood

Cliffs Farm

1

HEAPEY FOLD LA

MOOR RD

Healey Nab

Grain Pole Hill

18

A   **B**   **C**   **D**   **E**   **F**

MOUNT PLEASANT

Norcross Farm

COLE LA

A675

NORCROSS BROW

TWIST MOOR LA

RAILWAY RD

PROSPECT TERR

DERBY ST

CHURCHILL RD

BUTTERWORTH BROW

HARTINGTON RD

RODDLESWORTH LA

BOLTON RD

Roddlesworth

8

7

21

EDGE GATE LA

Watsons

Roddlesworth
Moor

MILL LA

6

Solomon's
Temple

Hatch Brook

Withnell Moor

Green Hill

River Roddlesworth

5

Cold Within
Hill

Calf Hey
Bridge

20

Wet Meadows

Ferney Slacks

Brown Hill

BELMONT RD

A675

4

Heapey
Moor

Wheelton Moor

Brown
Hill

3

Drinkwaters

Great Hill

19

Black Brook

2

Adam's
Delf

Black Hill
Upper

1

Bromiley Pastures

18

A   B   C   D   E   F

Sunnyhurst Hey Resr

SNIDDLE HILL LA
Sniddle Hill Farm
TURN LA

INVERNESS RD
WESTLAND AVE
BELGRAVE RD
MANOR RD
GRANVILLE RD
LIME RD
EAST PK AVE
ARLINGTON RD
RADCLIFFE RD

Ryal Farm

Royal Arms (PH)
P
HOLLINSHEAD TERR

Jubilee Tower

Belgrave

8

Tockholes No 2 Plantation

Higher Wenshead

Darwen Hill

Stepback Brook

7

Height Side

21

New Barn

TOCKHOLES RD

6

Green Lowe Farm House

DUCKSHAW RD

Duckshaw Clough

Picnic Area
P

MILL LA

Darwen Moor

Duckshaw Brook

Duckshaw Farm

5

Slipper Lowe

20

Thorny Bank Plantation

Cartridge Hill

Brown Lowe

Whitehall Farm

4

Piccadilly

Conyries Plantation

Black Hill

BELMONT RD

CROOKFIELD RD

Turn Lowe

Wilding Fields

3

Witton Weavers Way

19

Little Hill

Green Lowe

2

Old Man's Hill

Hulton Pasture

Lower Pasture Barn

1

Turton Moor

A6675

Long Lands

18

66   A   B   67   C   D   68   E   F

64

A8
1 HESSE ST
2 BUFF ST
3 CLEMENT ST
4 BECKETT ST
5 STANSFIELD ST
6 SPRINGFIELD FLATS
7 ALICE ST
8 JEPSON ST
9 COBDEN ST
10 RADFIELD AVE
11 HILLSIDE AVE

◀ **63**

▲ **81**

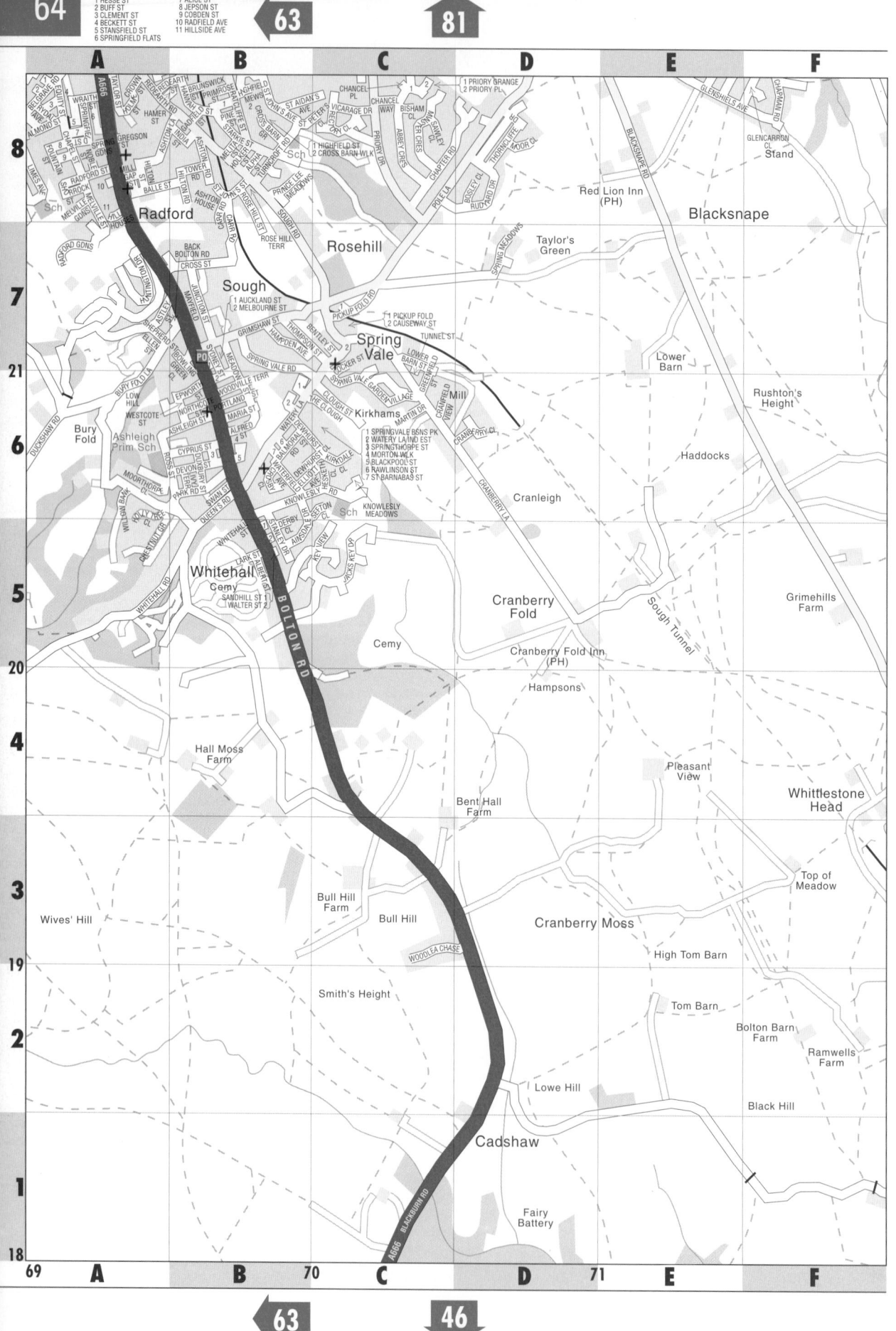

Radford

Rosehill

Sough

Spring Vale

Kirkhams

Whitehall

Cemy

Blacksnape

Red Lion Inn (PH)

Taylor's Green

Lower Barn

Rushton's Height

Haddocks

Cranleigh

Cranberry Fold

Sough Tunnel

Grimehills Farm

Cranberry Fold Inn (PH)

Hampsons

Hall Moss Farm

Pleasant View

Whittlestone Head

Bent Hall Farm

Top of Meadow

Bull Hill Farm

Bull Hill

Cranberry Moss

High Tom Barn

Wives' Hill

Smith's Height

Tom Barn

Bolton Barn Farm

Ramwells Farm

Lowe Hill

Black Hill

Cadshaw

Fairy Battery

Bury Fold

Moorthorpe

Ashleigh Prim. Sch

Westcote

Low Hill

1 Priory Grange
2 Priory Pl

1 Pickup Fold
2 Causeway St

1 Auckland St
2 Melbourne St

1 Springvale Bsns Pk
2 Watery La Ind Est
3 Springthorpe St
4 Morton Wlk
5 Blackpool St
6 Rawlinson St
7 St Barnabas St

1 Highfield St
2 Cross Barn Wlk

BOLTON RD

BLACKBURN RD

A666

	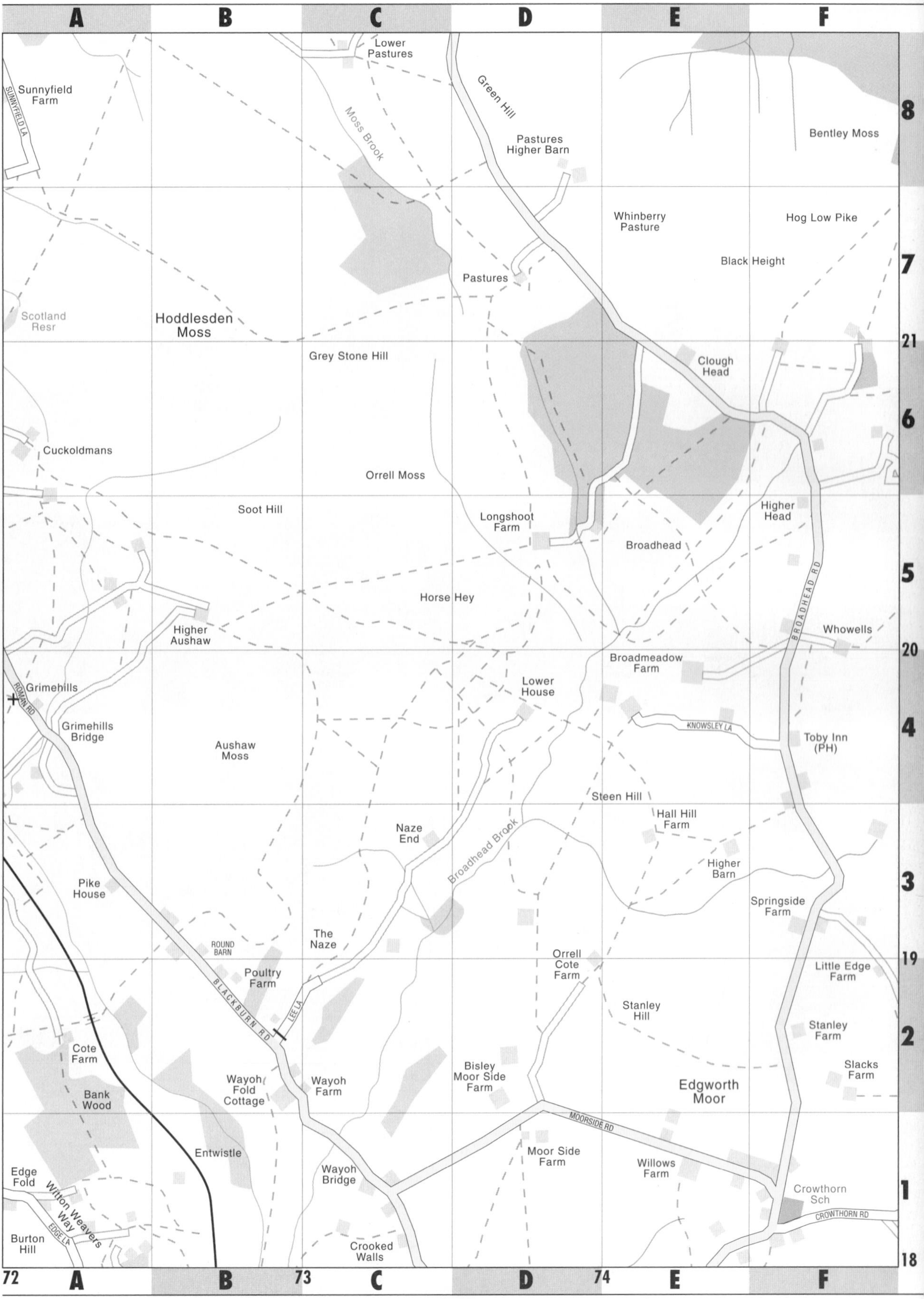 A	B	C	D	E	F	

Sunnyfield Farm

SUNNYFIELD LA

Lower Pastures

Green Hill

Bentley Moss

8

Moss Brook

Pastures Higher Barn

Whinberry Pasture

Hog Low Pike

Scotland Resr

Hoddlesden Moss

Pastures

Black Height

7

21

Grey Stone Hill

Clough Head

Cuckoldmans

6

Orrell Moss

Higher Head

Soot Hill

Longshoot Farm

Broadhead

BROADHEAD RD

Horse Hey

Broadmeadow Farm

Whowells

5

Higher Aushaw

20

Grimehills

Lower House

ROMAN RD

Grimehills Bridge

KNOWSLEY LA

Toby Inn (PH)

4

Aushaw Moss

Steen Hill

Hall Hill Farm

Pike House

Naze End

Broadhead Brook

Higher Barn

Springside Farm

3

ROUND BARN

The Naze

Orrell Cote Farm

Little Edge Farm

19

BLACKBURN RD

Poultry Farm

LEE LA

Stanley Hill

Stanley Farm

2

Cote Farm

Slacks Farm

Bank Wood

Wayoh Fold Cottage

Wayoh Farm

Bisley Moor Side Farm

Edgworth Moor

MOORSIDE RD

Edge Fold

Entwistle

Moor Side Farm

Willows Farm

Crowthorn Sch

1

WITTON WEAVERS WAY

EDGE LA

Wayoh Bridge

CROWTHORN RD

Burton Hill

Crooked Walls

18

72	A		B	73	C		D	74	E		F	

82 →
66 →
47
66 →

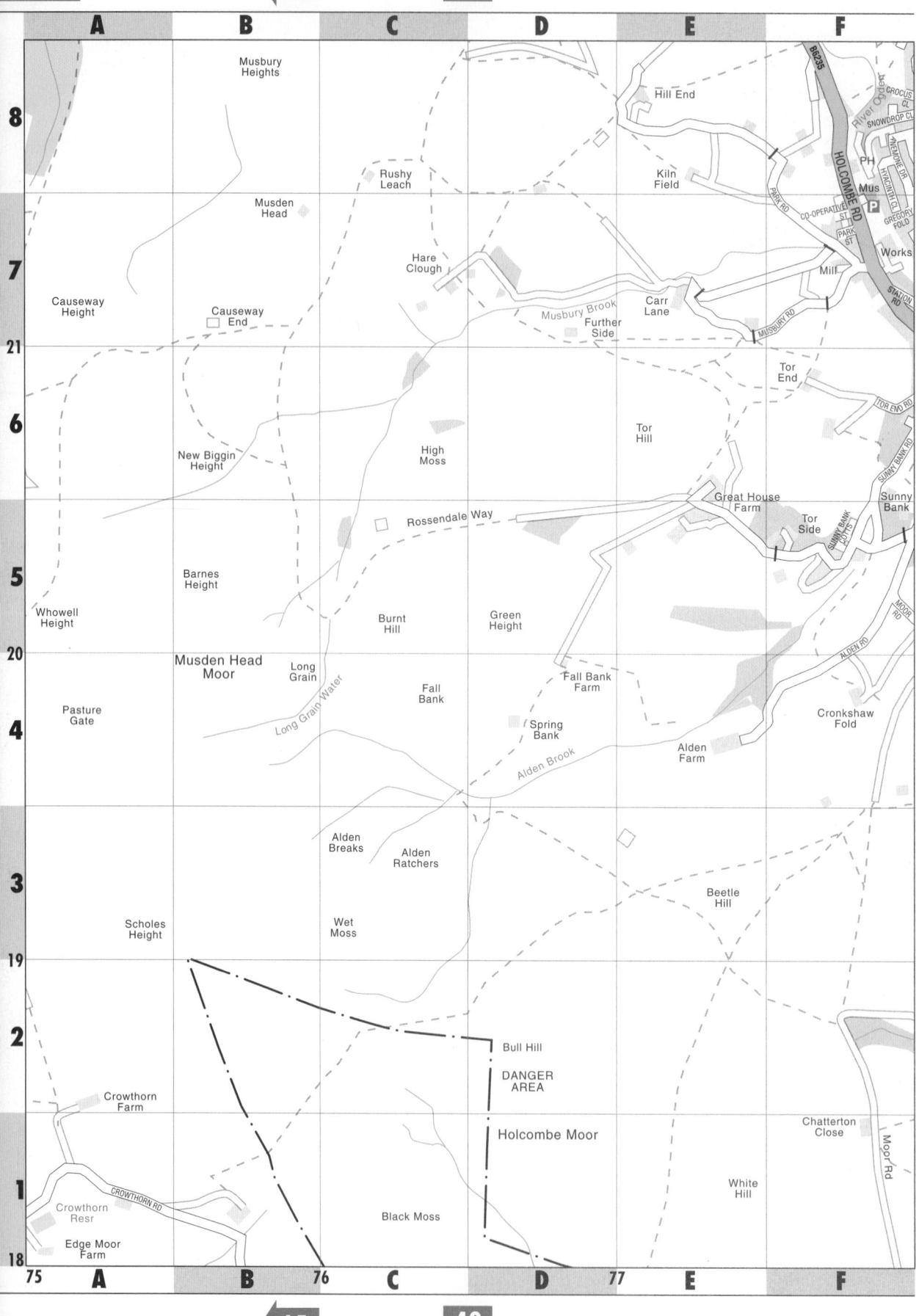

A B C D E F

8

7

21

6

5

20

4

3

19

2

1

18

75 A B 76 C D 77 E F

Musbury
Heights

Musden
Head

Rushy
Leach

Hill End

Kiln
Field

Hare
Clough

Musbury Brook

Further
Side

Carr
Lane

Mill

Works

Causeway
Height

Causeway
End

Tor
End

Tor
Hill

Tor
End Rd

New Biggin
Height

High
Moss

Great House
Farm

Tor
Side

Sunny
Bank

Rossendale Way

Barnes
Height

Whowell
Height

Burnt
Hill

Green
Height

Musden Head
Moor

Long
Grain

Long Grain Water

Fall
Bank

Fall Bank
Farm

Cronkshaw
Fold

Pasture
Gate

Spring
Bank

Alden Brook

Alden
Farm

Alden
Breaks

Alden
Ratchers

Beetle
Hill

Scholes
Height

Wet
Moss

Bull Hill

DANGER
AREA

Crowthorn
Farm

Holcombe Moor

Chatterton
Close

Crowthorn Rd

Crowthorn
Resr

Black Moss

White
Hill

Edge Moor
Farm

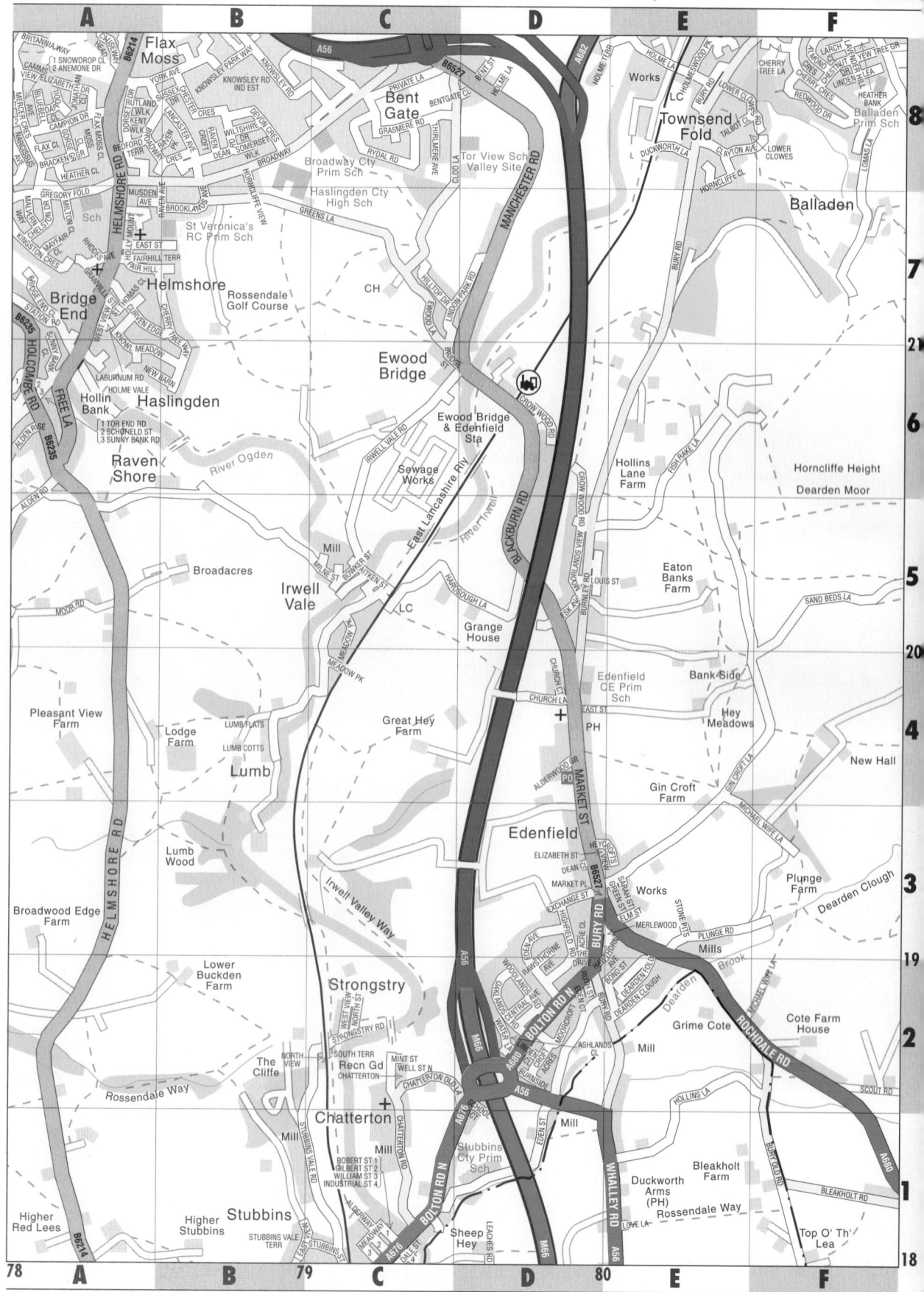

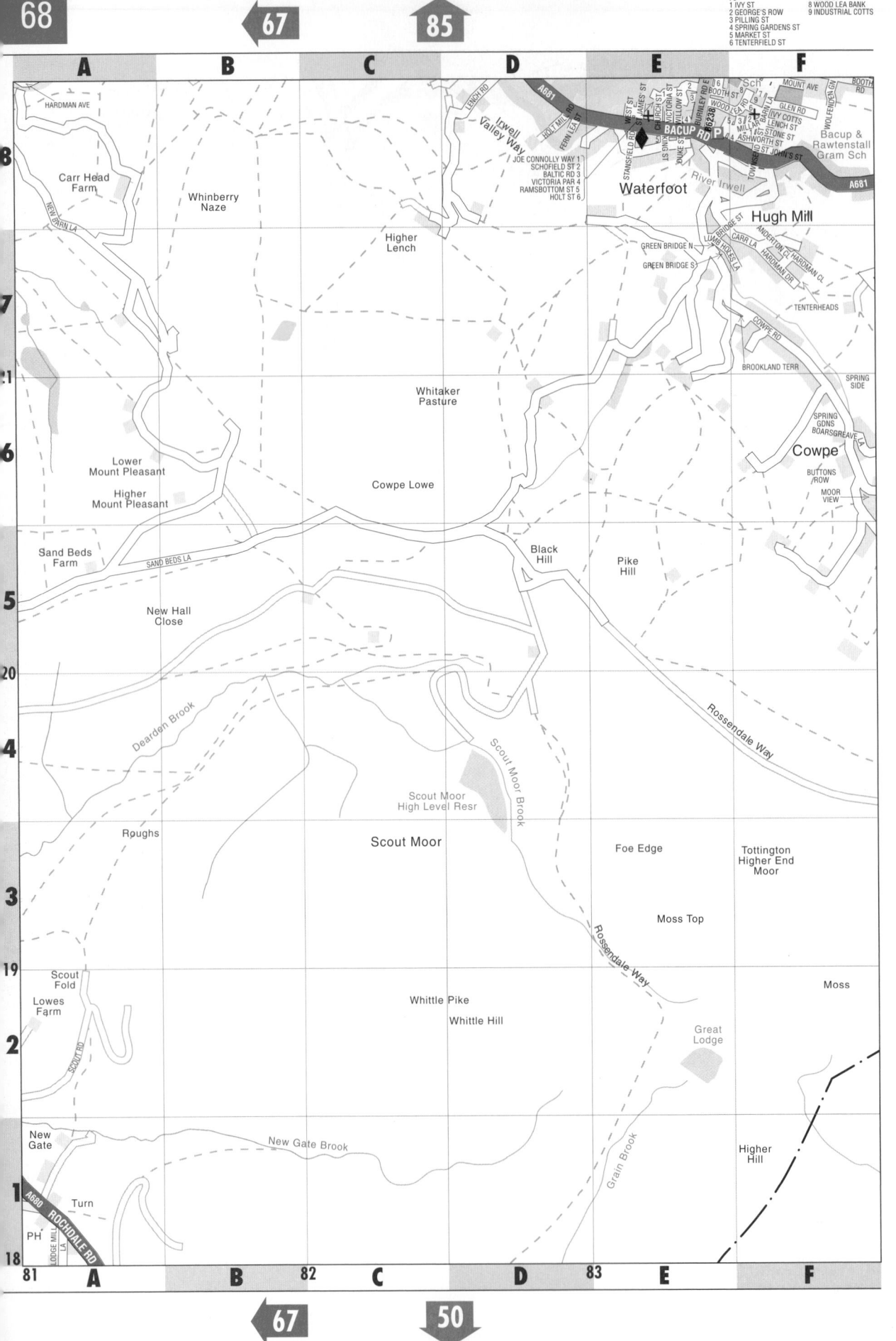

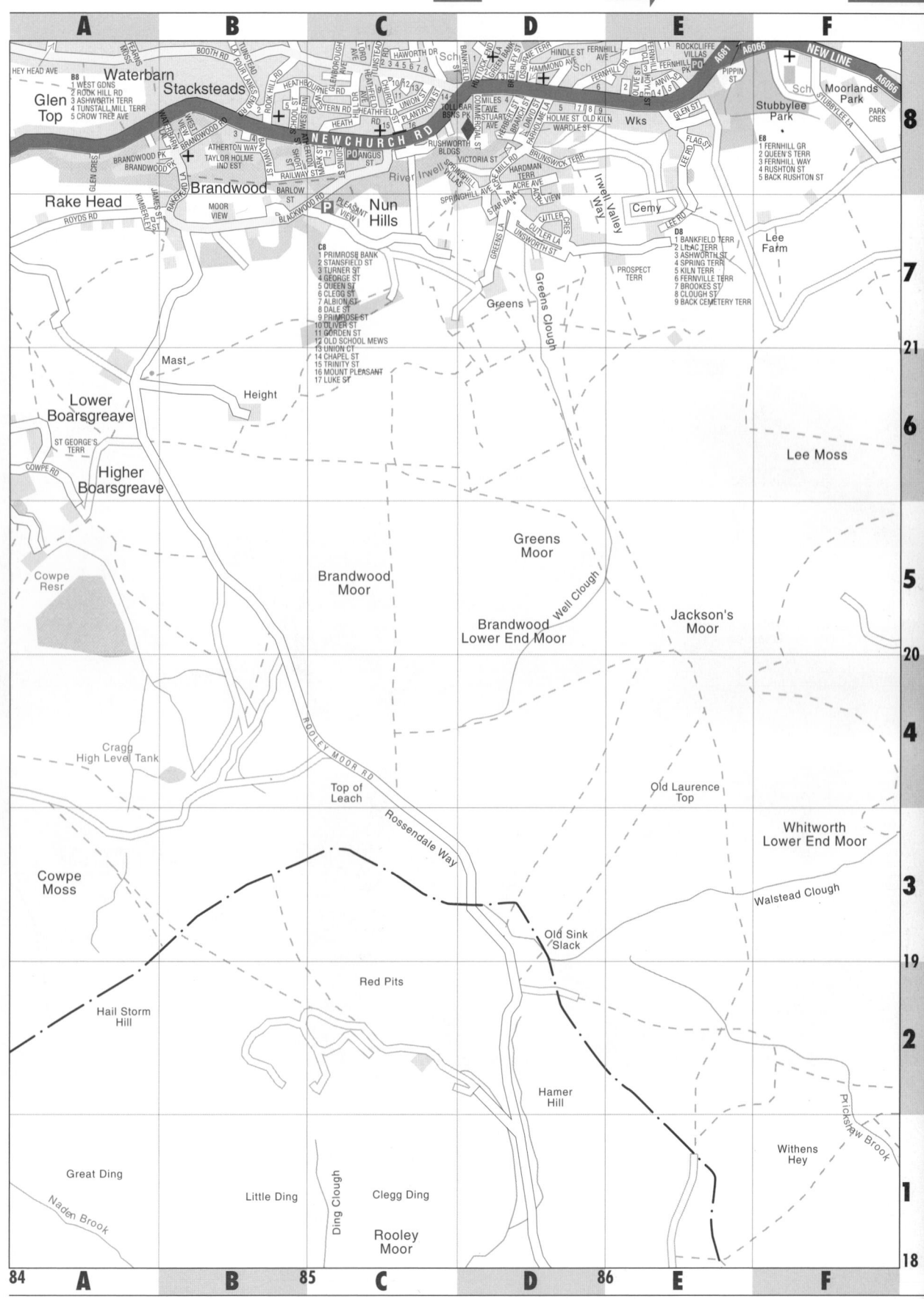

HEY HEAD AVE
B8
1 WEST GDNS
2 ROOK HILL RD
3 ASHWORTH TERR
4 TUNSTALL MILL TERR
5 CROW TREE AVE

Waterbarn
Stacksteads

Glen Top

Brandwood

Rake Head

MOOR VIEW

Nun Hills

PLEASANT VIEW

BRANDWOOD PK
BRANDWOOD

TAYLOR HOLME IND EST
ATHERTON WAY

BARLOW ST

BLACKWOOD RD

NEWCHURCH RD

River Irwell

RUSHWORTH BLDGS

VICTORIA ST

Brunswick Terr

HARDMAN TERR

ACRE AVE

SPRINGHILL AVE

STAR BANK

C8
1 PRIMROSE BANK
2 STANSFIELD ST
3 TURNER ST
4 GEORGE ST
5 QUEEN ST
6 CLEGG ST
7 ALBION ST
8 DALE ST
9 PRIMROSE ST
10 OLIVER ST
11 GORDEN ST
12 OLD SCHOOL MEWS
13 UNION CT
14 CHAPEL ST
15 TRINITY ST
16 MOUNT PLEASANT
17 LUKE ST

GREENS LA

CUTLER LA

UNSWORTH ST

Greens

Greens Clough

NEW LINE

A6066

A682

Moorlands Park

Stubbylee Park

PARK CRES

E8
1 FERNHILL GR
2 QUEEN'S TERR
3 FERNHILL WAY
4 RUSHTON ST
5 BACK RUSHTON ST

GLEN ST

Cemy

Irwell Valley Way

PROSPECT TERR

D8
1 BANKFIELD TERR
2 LILAC TERR
3 ASHWORTH ST
4 SPRING TERR
5 KILN TERR
6 FERNVILLE TERR
7 BROOKES ST
8 CLOUGH ST
9 BACK CEMETERY TERR

LEE RD

Lee Farm

Lower Boarsgreave

ST GEORGE'S TERR

COWPE RD

Higher Boarsgreave

Mast

Height

Cowpe Resr

Brandwood Moor

Greens Moor

Well Clough

Brandwood Lower End Moor

Jackson's Moor

Lee Moss

Cragg
High Level Tank

ROOLEY MOOR RD

Top of Leach

Rossendale Way

Old Laurence Top

Whitworth Lower End Moor

Walstead Clough

Cowpe Moss

Old Sink Slack

Hail Storm Hill

Red Pits

Hamer Hill

Withens Hey

Prickshaw Brook

Great Ding

Naden Brook

Little Ding

Ding Clough

Clegg Ding

Rooley Moor

8
7
21
6
5
20
4
3
19
2
1
18

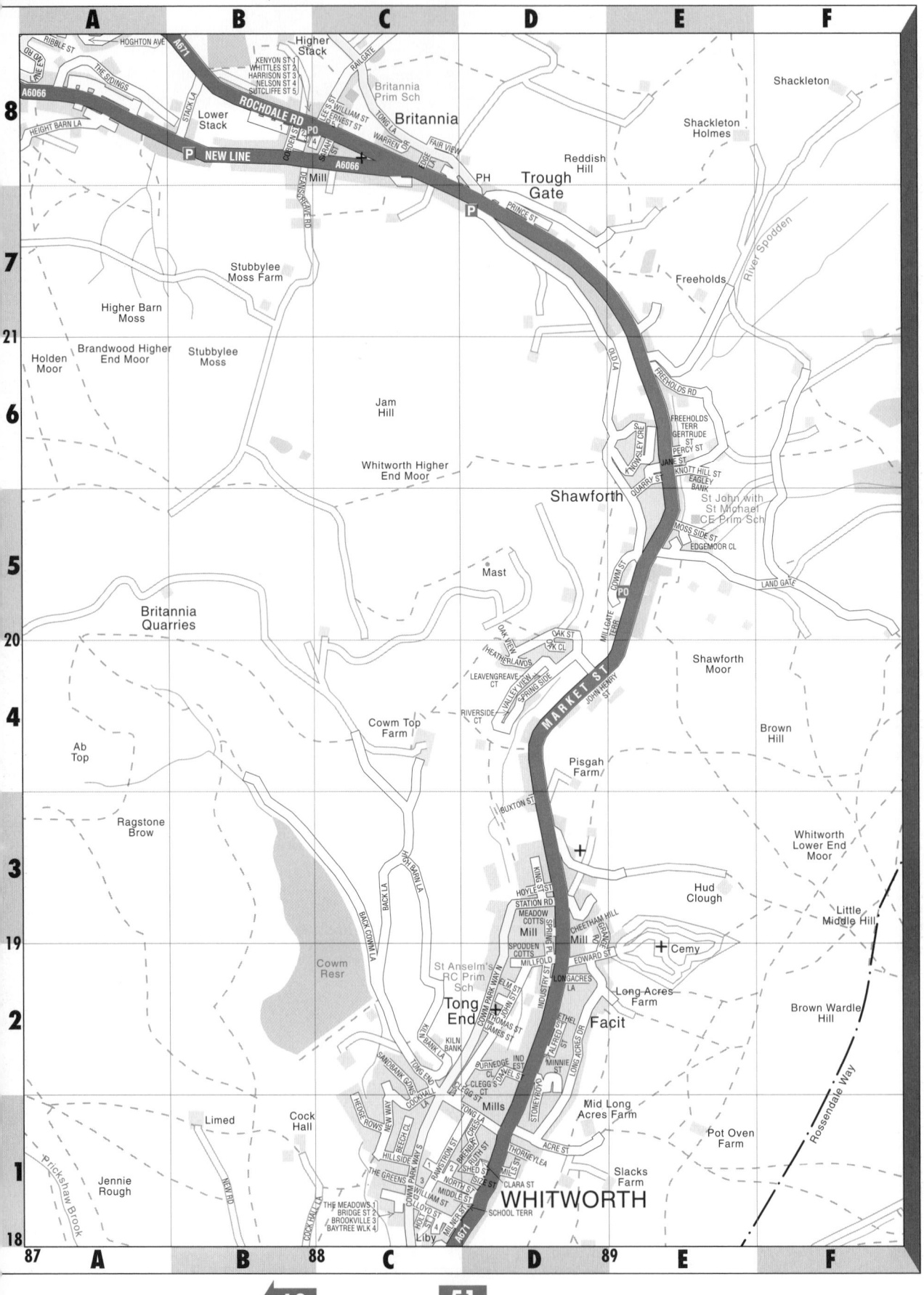

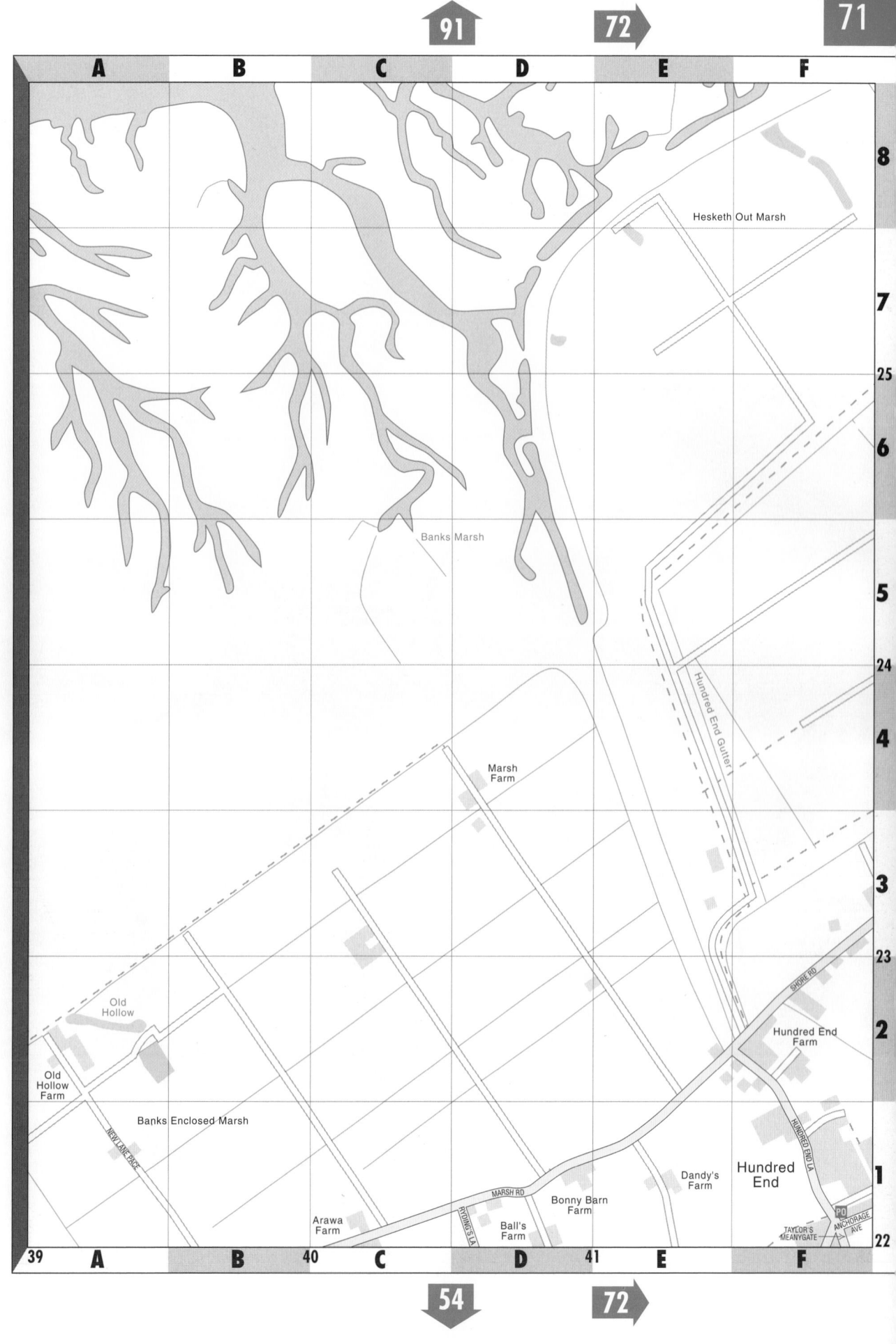

91
72

A B C D E F

8

Hesketh Out Marsh

7

25

6

Banks Marsh

5

Hundred End Gutter

24

4

Marsh Farm

3

23

SHORE RD

Old Hollow

2

Hundred End Farm

Old Hollow Farm

HUNDRED END LA

Banks Enclosed Marsh

Dandy's Farm

Hundred End

1

NEW LANE PACE

Arawa Farm

MARSH RD

RIDING'S LA

Bonny Barn Farm

Ball's Farm

PO

TAYLOR'S MEANYGATE

ANCHORAGE AVE

22

39 A B 40 C D 41 E F

54
72

A   B   C   D   E   F

8 Hesketh Out Marsh

Ribble Bank Farm

7 Westgate Farm

25

6 Hesketh New Marsh   Anchorage Farm

GUIDE RD

5 Carr Heys Watercourse

Hesketh Old Marsh

DIB RD

24 Hesketh-with-Becconsall All Saints CE Sch

MARSH RD

THE BROW

ROSE GDNS

MEADOW LA

New Farm

4 SCHOOL FOLD

BELSFIELD DR

RIBBLE

Hesketh Bank

GREENFIELD

LANGDALE AVE

GLEN PARK DR

DELTA PARK AVE

CHAPEL RD

R CHAPEL GDNS

HAZELWOOD DR

FAIRWINDS AVE

SHORE RD

THE WALK

Bank Farm

Wright's Farm

CROPPER GDNS

CHANDLERS CROFT

THE GLEN

NEWARTH LA

STATION RD

XDALE

BECCONSALL LA

3 New Manor Farm

PARDOE CL

CHARLES CL

ORCHARD CL

23 Ribble View Farm

Hesketh

PH

D AVE

SIDNEY AVE

CUMBIN

SIDNEY AVE

CHERRY VALE

MEADWAY

WOODLEA

GRANVILLE AVE

BOUNDARY LA

PO

MILL LA

ASTLAND GDNS

2

Kingsfold Christian Sch

Becconsall

SMITH AVE

GREENWAYS

MOSS LA

1 Nurseries

Millers Farm

Nurseries

Hesketh Moss

JOHNSON'S MEANYGATE

FERMOR RD

BOUNDARY MEANYGATE

HESKETH LA

CULWOOD AVE

DOUGLAS AVE

ANCHORAGE AVE

Pear Tree Farm

NURSERY DR

22

42   A   B   43   C   D   44   E   F

River Asland or Douglas

A B C D E F

8

Nurseries

GRANGE LA
MARSH LA
BACK LA

Hall Pool
Bridge

Hall Pool

MANORCROFT 1
ORCHARD LA 2
BROOKWAY 3

ASPENDALE CL
MEADOWAY
LONGACRE
3
2
1

PO
TUSON
CROFT
BROOK
HEY

Ribble Way

Dolphin Inn
(PH)

Tarra Carr Gutter

SEDGEFIELD
CHRISTLETON
DALE AVE
THE MALT KILNS
ASH LEA
BIRKDALE AVE
STONEFIELD
FORMBY CRES
WOODLANDS WAY

BENTLEY PARK
RD

7

Marsh
Farm

Mast

Sewage
Works

Nursery

MEADOW HEAD LA
MEREFIELD
TOWNFIELD
MERESIDE CL
DRUMACRE LA W

LIVERPOOL RD

HALL LA

25

Hall Green

HIGHFIELD DR

6

HALL CARR LA

TRANMOOR

HIGHER
FURLONG

Little
Hoole
Marsh

Odd
House

Hall Carr
Farm

FAIRVIEW CL

OLD MILL
CT

LIVERPOOL OLD RD

5

River Asland or Douglas

Marsh House
Farm

Walmer Bridge

SCHOOL ST

SEA VIEW
WALMER
GN

Lower Marsh
House

STATION RD

PO

24

Marsh
Farm

Sewage
Works

LANGTON BY-PASS
A59

Lane Ends
Farm

KNOLL LA

4

Becconsall Marsh

Balls
Farm

PINE AVE

MARLFIELD

LONG
MEADOW
MARLFIELD
OLDFIELD

Becconsall
Hall

Ravenskerne

Rakes Brook

BROOK LA
THORNFIELD
BIRCHFIELD

FELTON
WAY
ACRE RD
COPPER BEECH

SOUTHFIELD
GDNS

3

BECCONSALL LA

FIR TREE CL
WEST CROFT

LIVERPOOL OLD RD

SWALLOW
FIELD

Much Hoole

GREEN HEY
GREAT HEY
MIDDLE HEY

BARNFIELD

23

KIRK HEAD

Much Hoole Marsh
House

Lane House
Farm

PARK AVE

NORTHALL

WINSOME
WAY

MOSS HOUSE LA

Hunger Hill
Farm

2

Goose
Green

HAUNDERS LA

NORTHERN AVE

SMITHY LA

Marsh
Farm

Rose & Crown
(PH)

TOWN LA

Much Hoole
Town

Hoole CE
Prim Sch

Church
Farm

PO

Manor
House

Carr Brook

1

Nursery

NURSERY
DR

Dobson's
Farm

LUNDS LA

A59

22

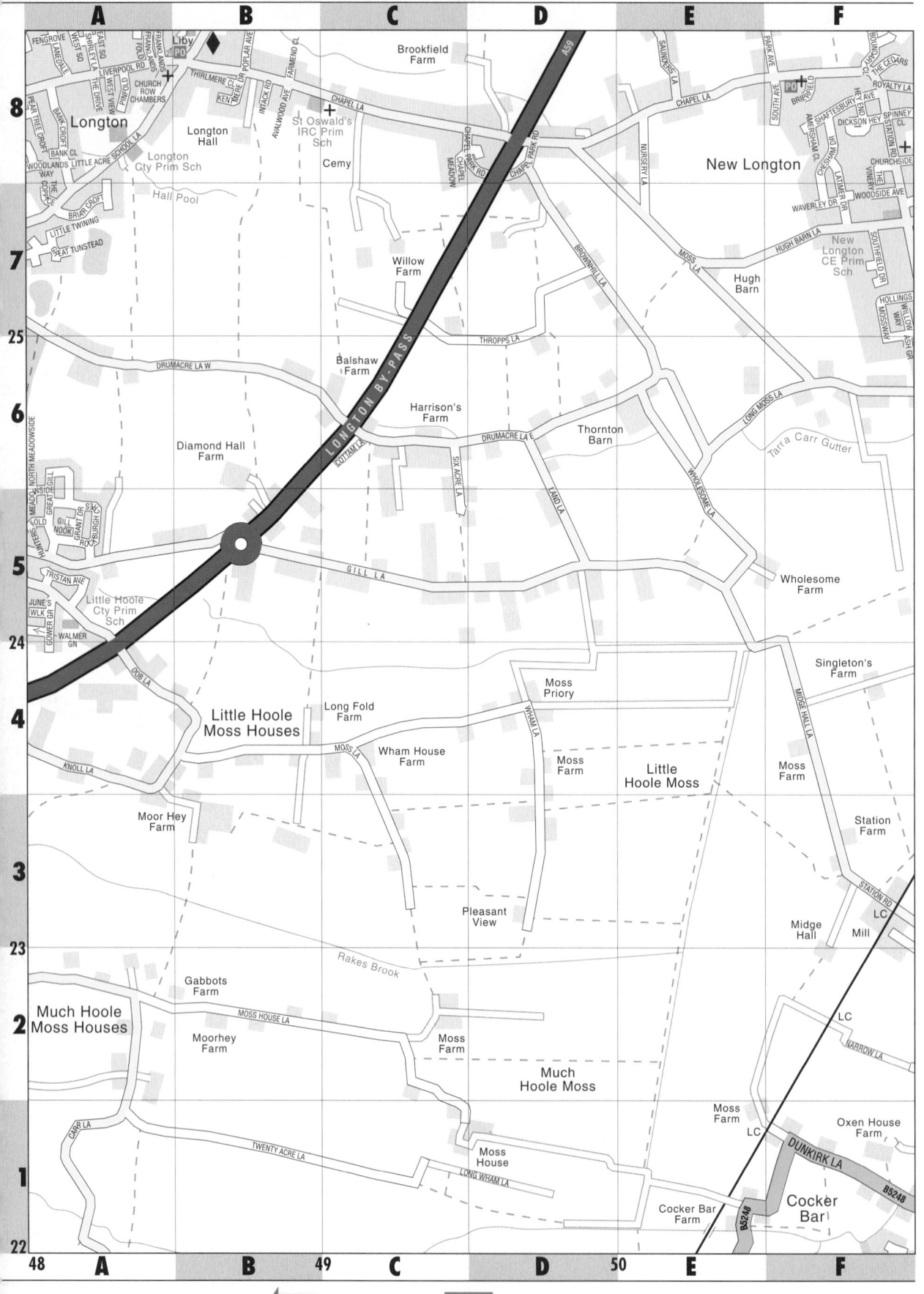

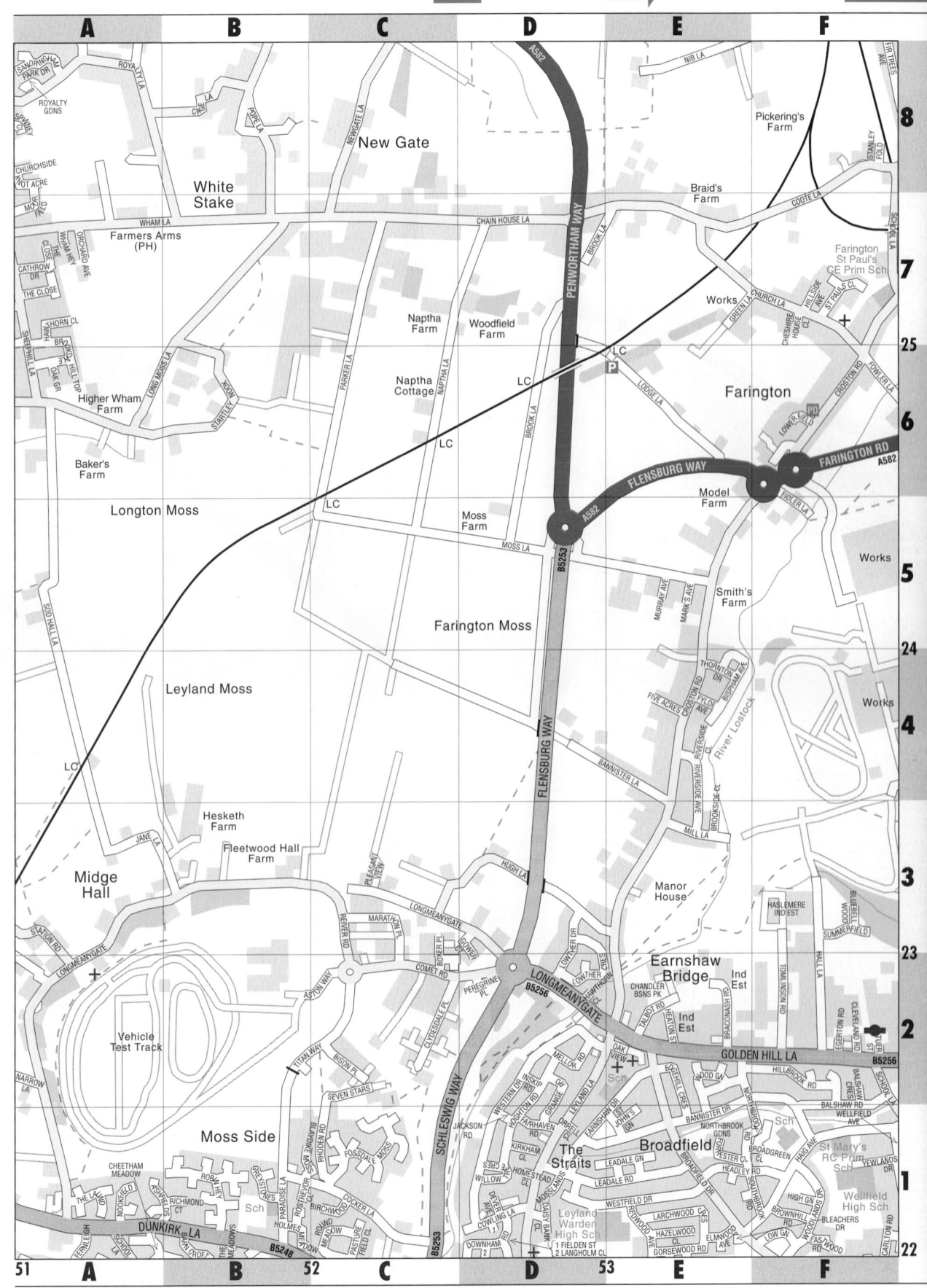

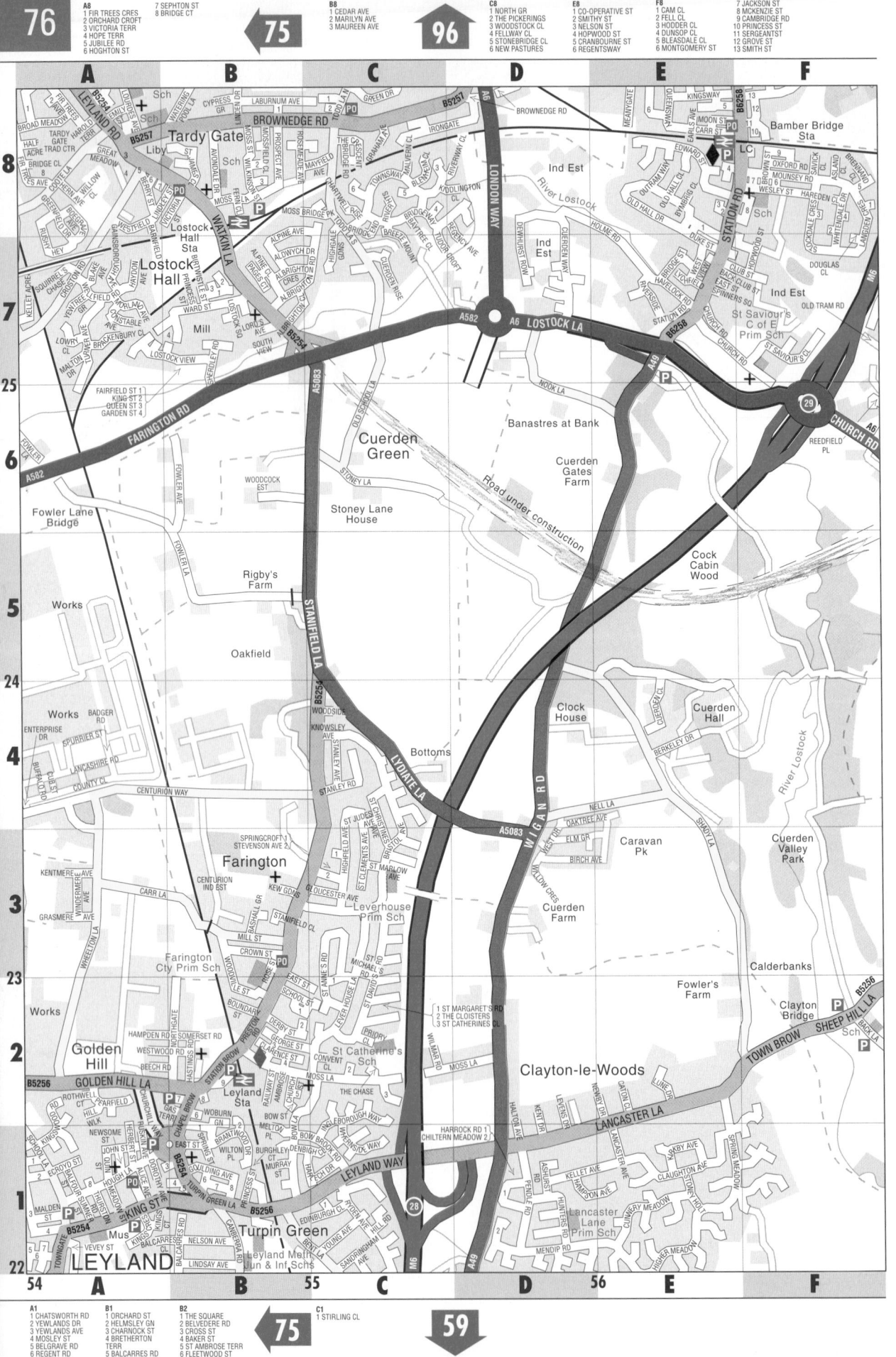

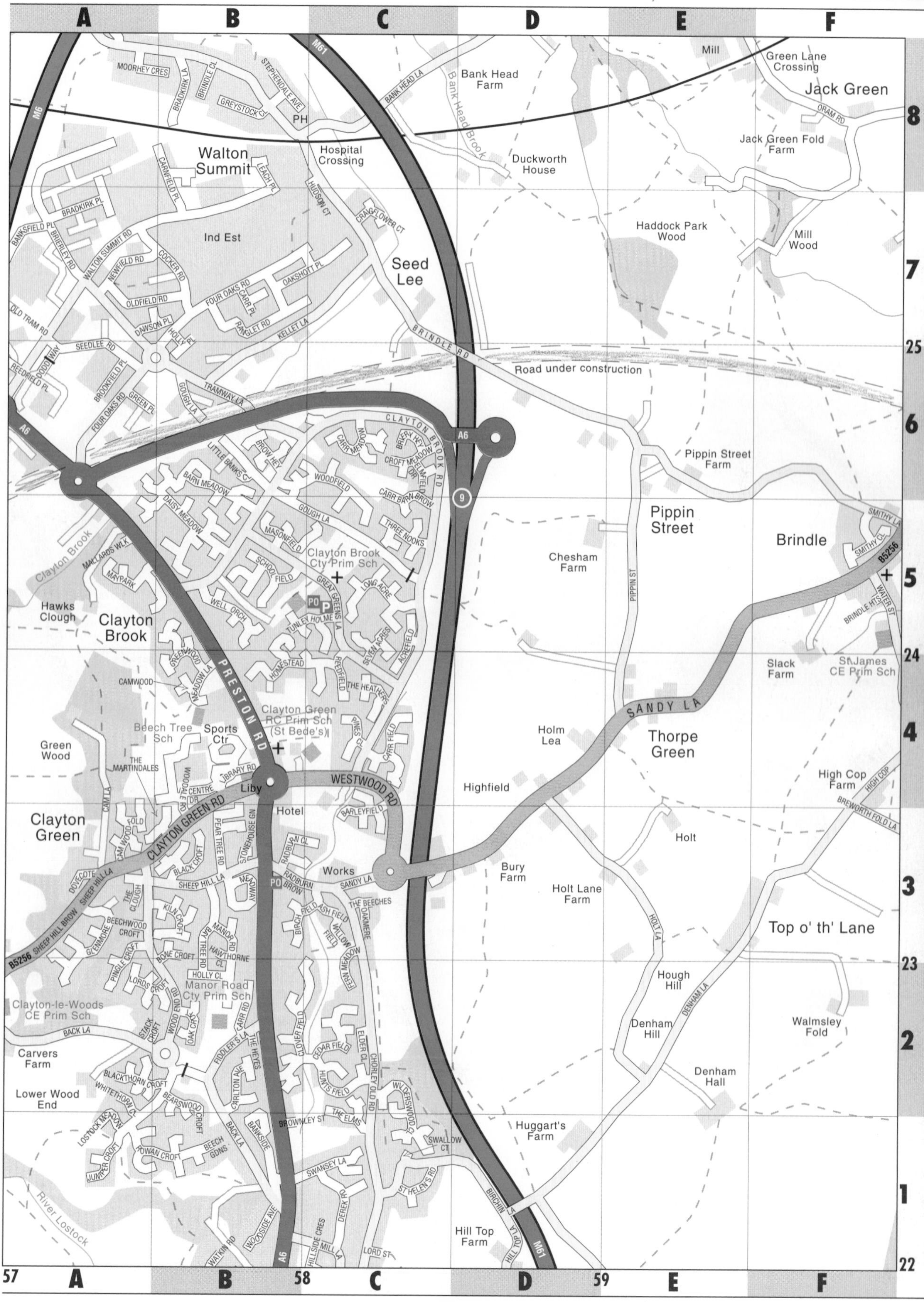

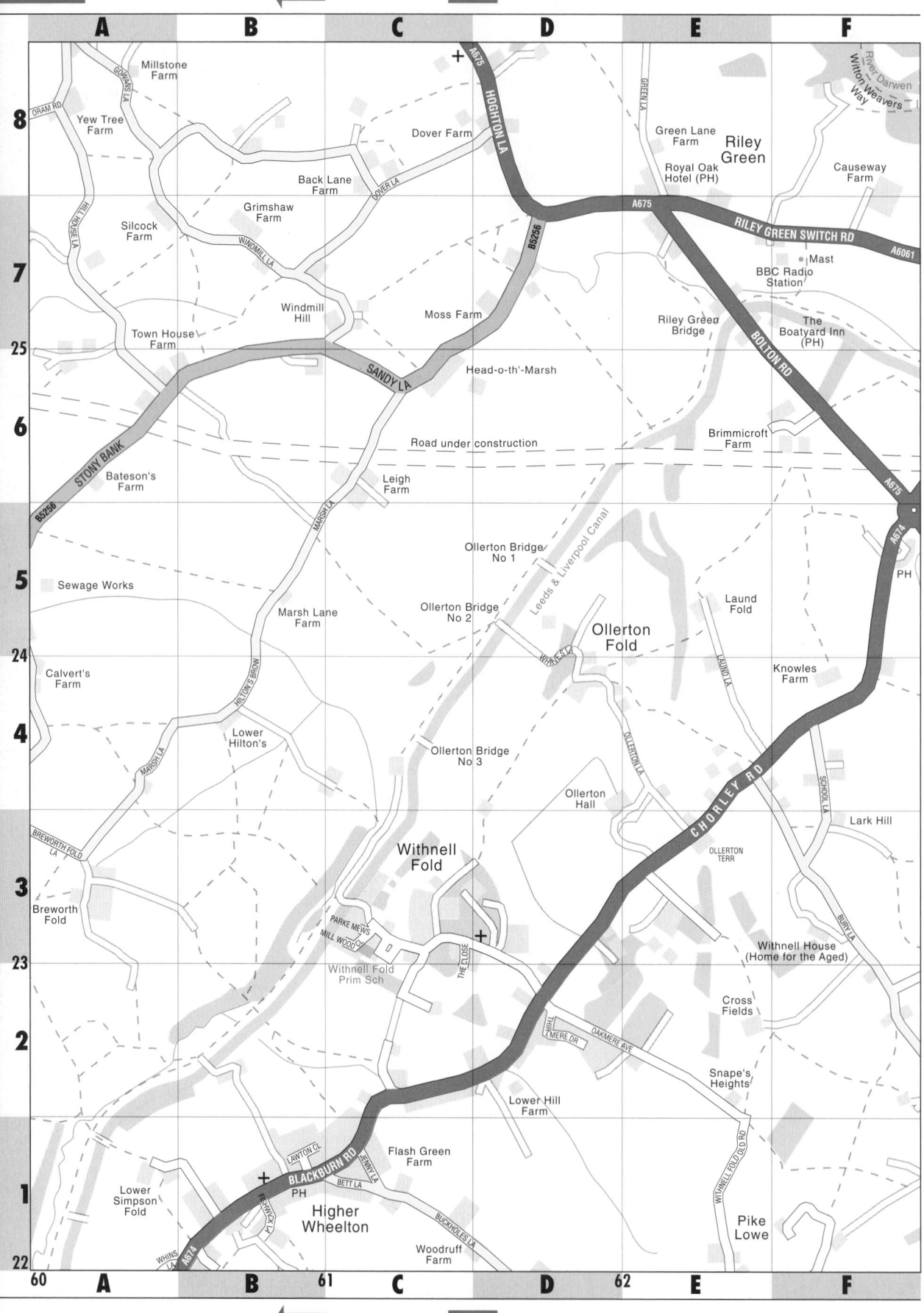

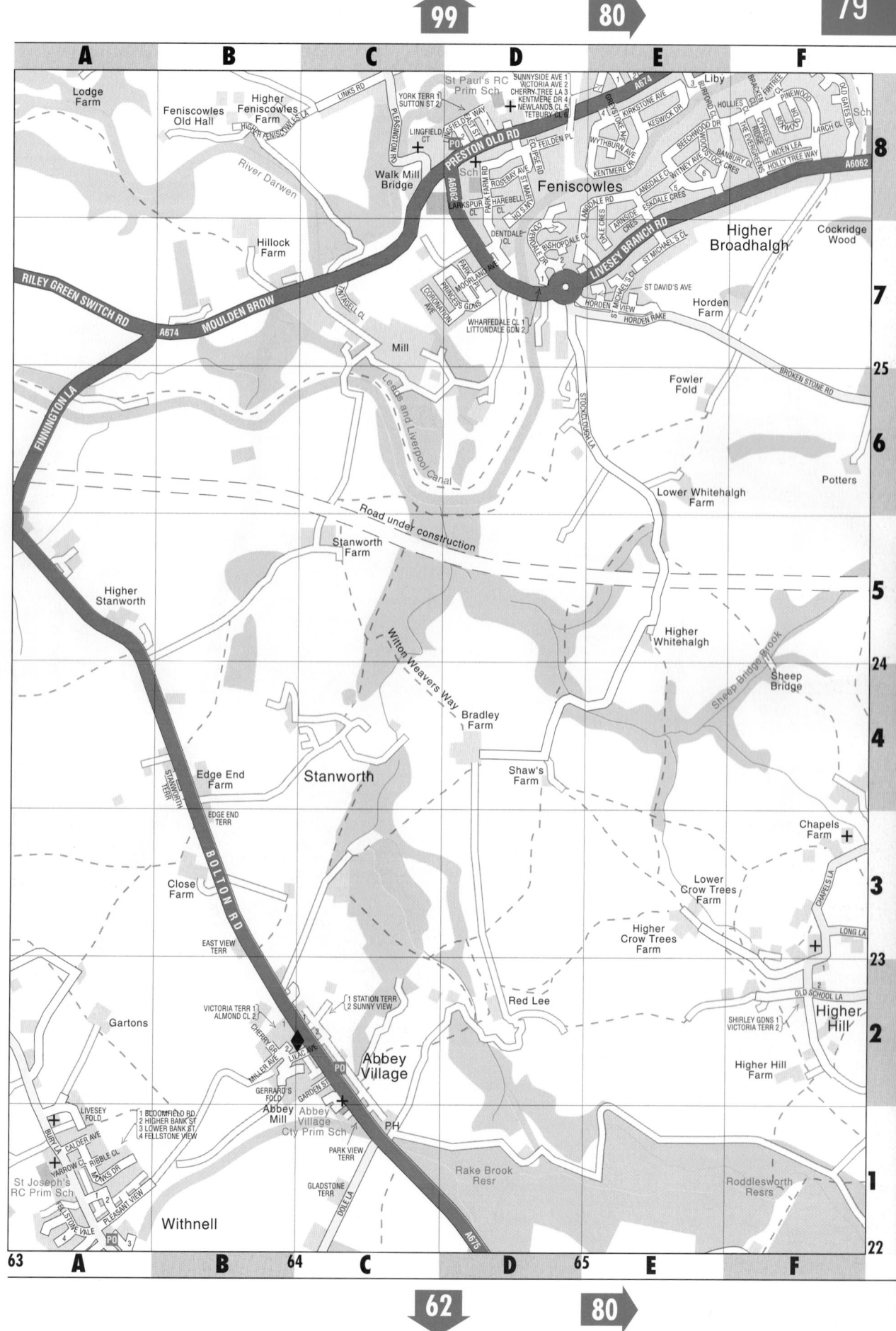

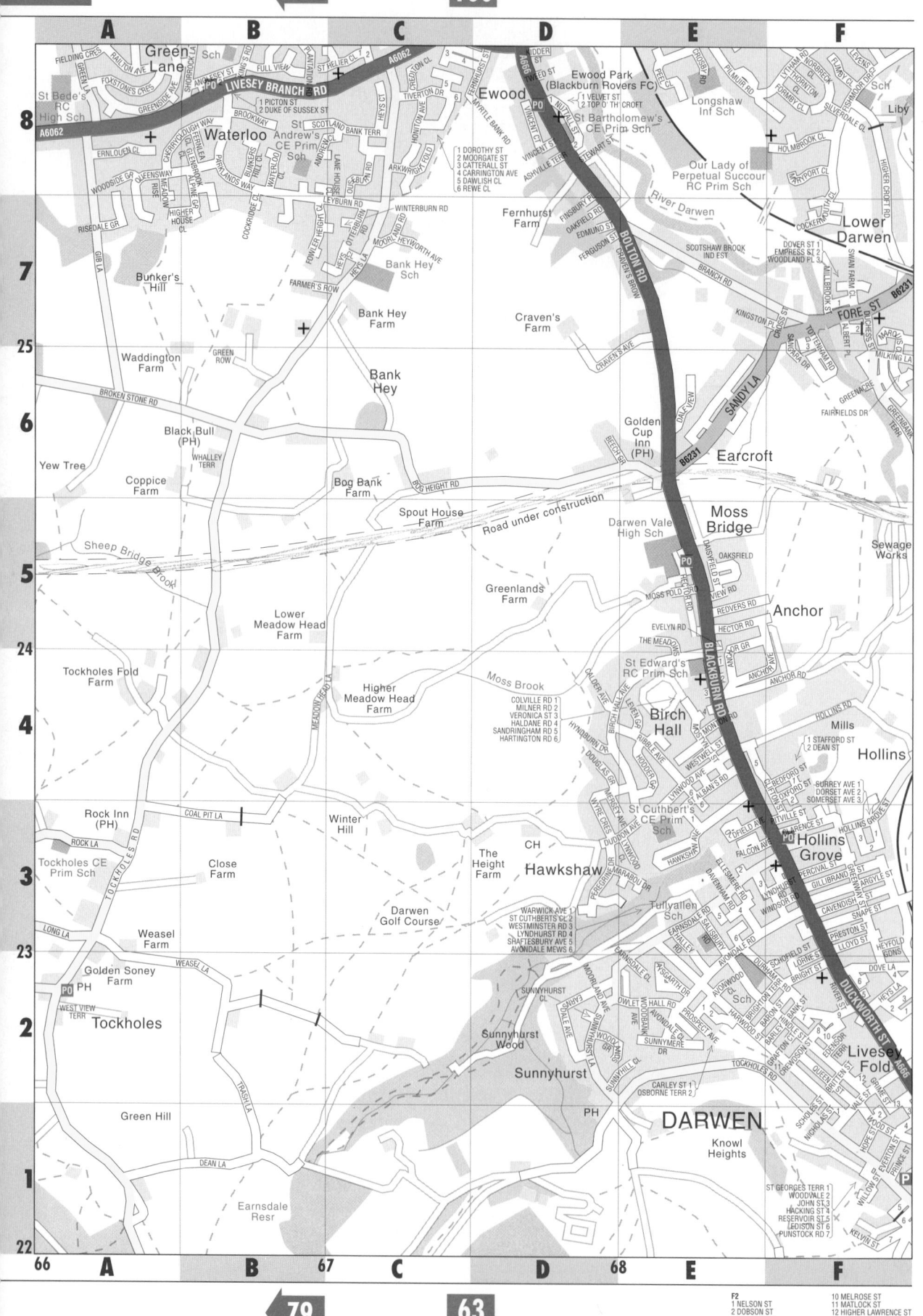

F2
1 NELSON ST
2 DOBSON ST
3 FRANCES ST
4 BROUGHTON ST
5 FINCH ST
6 DERWENT ST
7 ALEXANDRA VIEW
8 ALEXANDRA RD
9 WOOD STREET LIVESEY FOLD
10 MELROSE ST
11 MATLOCK ST
12 HIGHER LAWRENCE ST
13 ROBERT ST

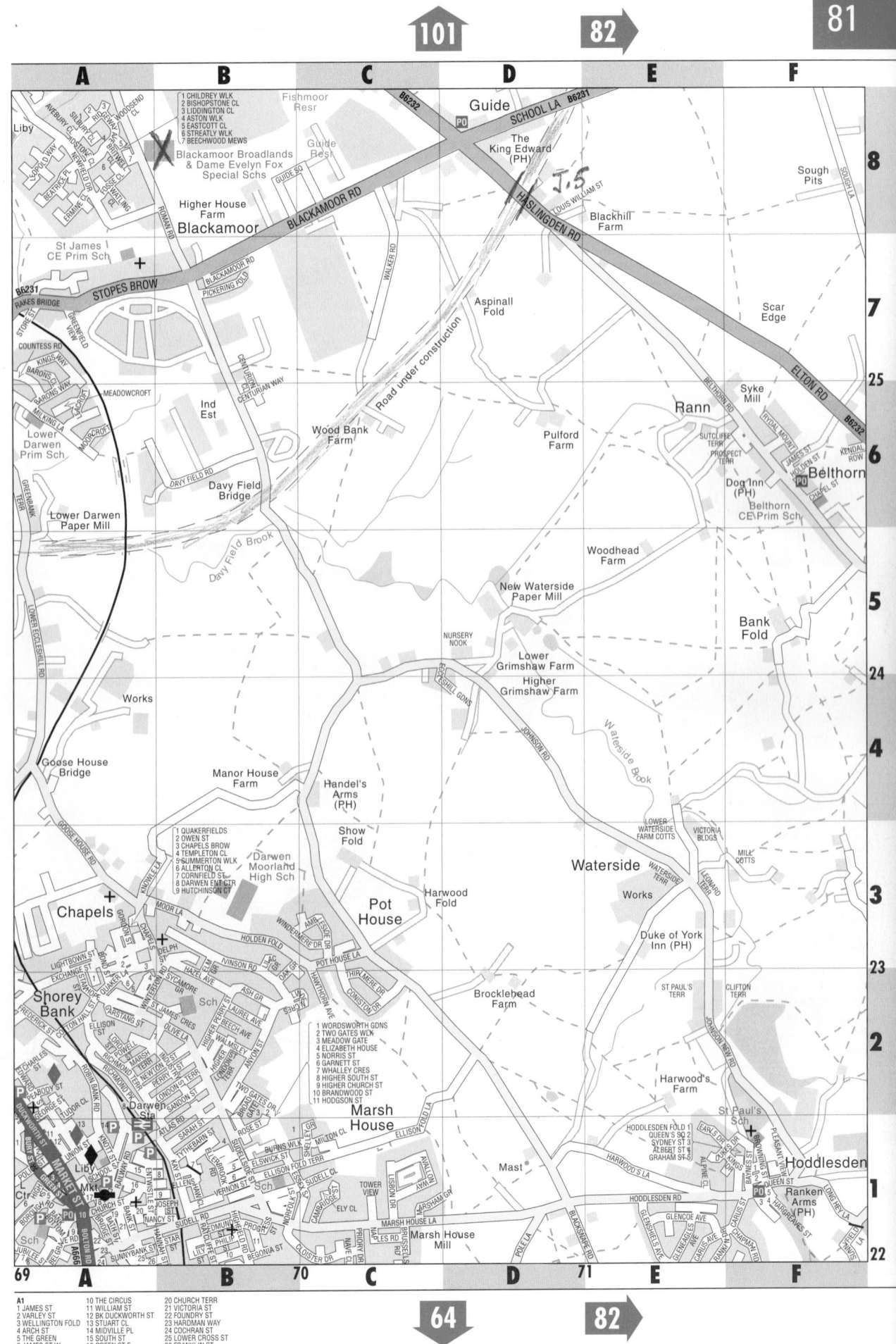

A1
1 JAMES ST
2 VARLEY ST
3 WELLINGTON FOLD
4 ARCH ST
5 THE GREEN
6 JAMES ST W
7 ASHWORTH TERR
8 HESSE ST
9 BELGRAVE SQ
10 THE CIRCUS
11 WILLIAM ST
12 BK DUCKWORTH ST
13 STUART CL
14 MIDVILLE PL
15 SOUTH ST
16 GREEN ST E
17 CROFT ST
18 PARLIAMENT ST
19 CHURCH BANK ST
20 CHURCH TERR
21 VICTORIA ST
22 FOUNDRY ST
23 HARDMAN WAY
24 COCHRAN ST
25 LOWER CROSS ST
26 FRANKLIN ST

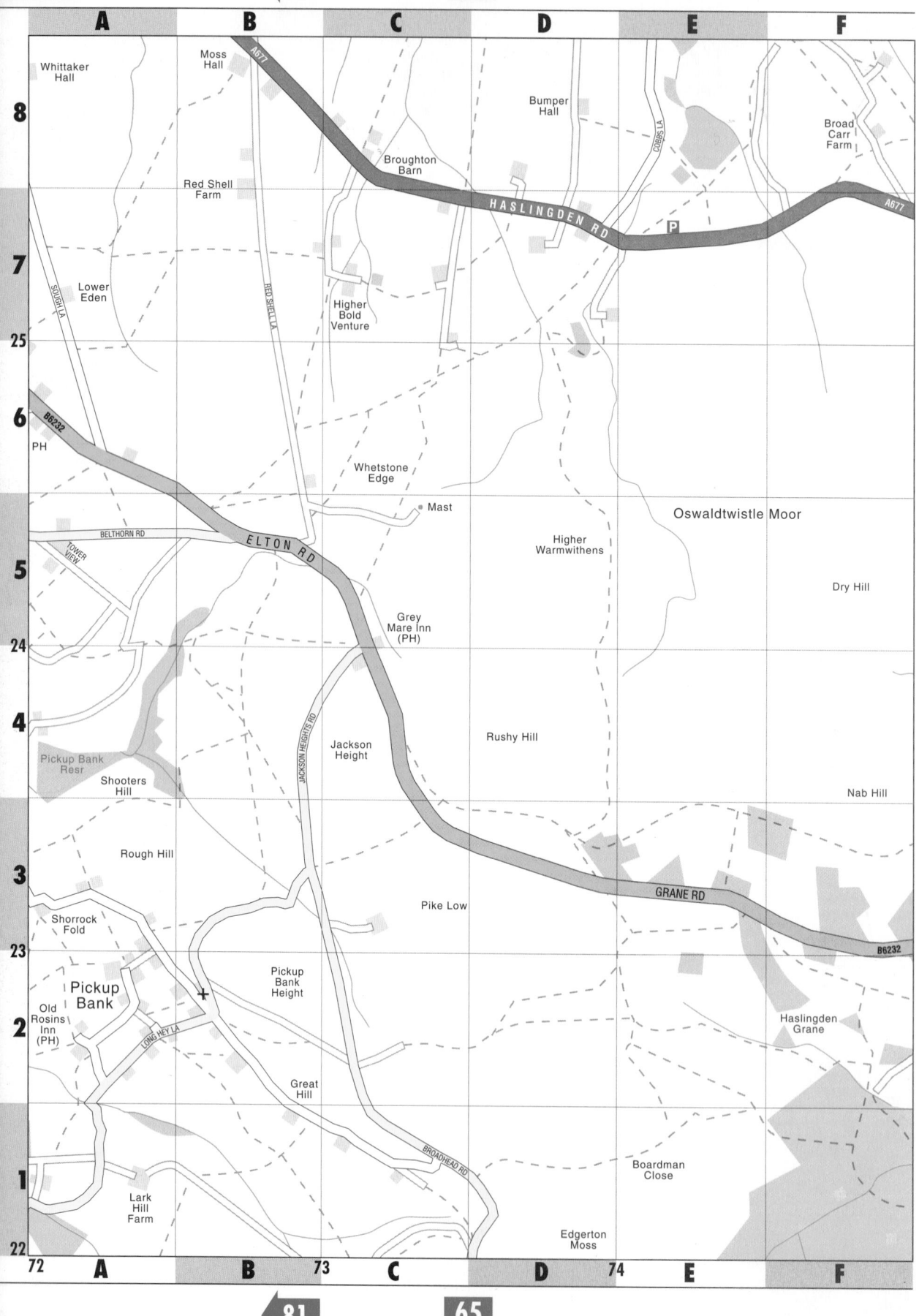

A B C D E F

8
7
25
6
5
24
4
3
23
2
1
22

Whittaker Hall

Moss Hall

Bumper Hall

Broad Carr Farm

Red Shell Farm

Broughton Barn

HASLINGDEN RD

A677

COBBS LA

A677

P

Lower Eden

SOUGH LA

RED SHELL LA

Higher Bold Venture

PH

B6232

Whetstone Edge

Mast

Oswaldtwistle Moor

BELTHORN RD

ELTON RD

TOWER VIEW

Higher Warmwithens

Dry Hill

Grey Mare Inn (PH)

Pickup Bank Resr

Shooters Hill

JACKSON HEIGHTS RD

Jackson Height

Rushy Hill

Nab Hill

Rough Hill

GRANE RD

B6232

Shorrock Fold

Pike Low

Pickup Bank Height

Haslingden Grane

Pickup Bank

Old Rosins Inn (PH)

LONG HEY LA

Great Hill

Boardman Close

1
Lark Hill Farm

BROADHEAD RD

Edgerton Moss

72 A 73 B C 73 D 74 E F

103
84

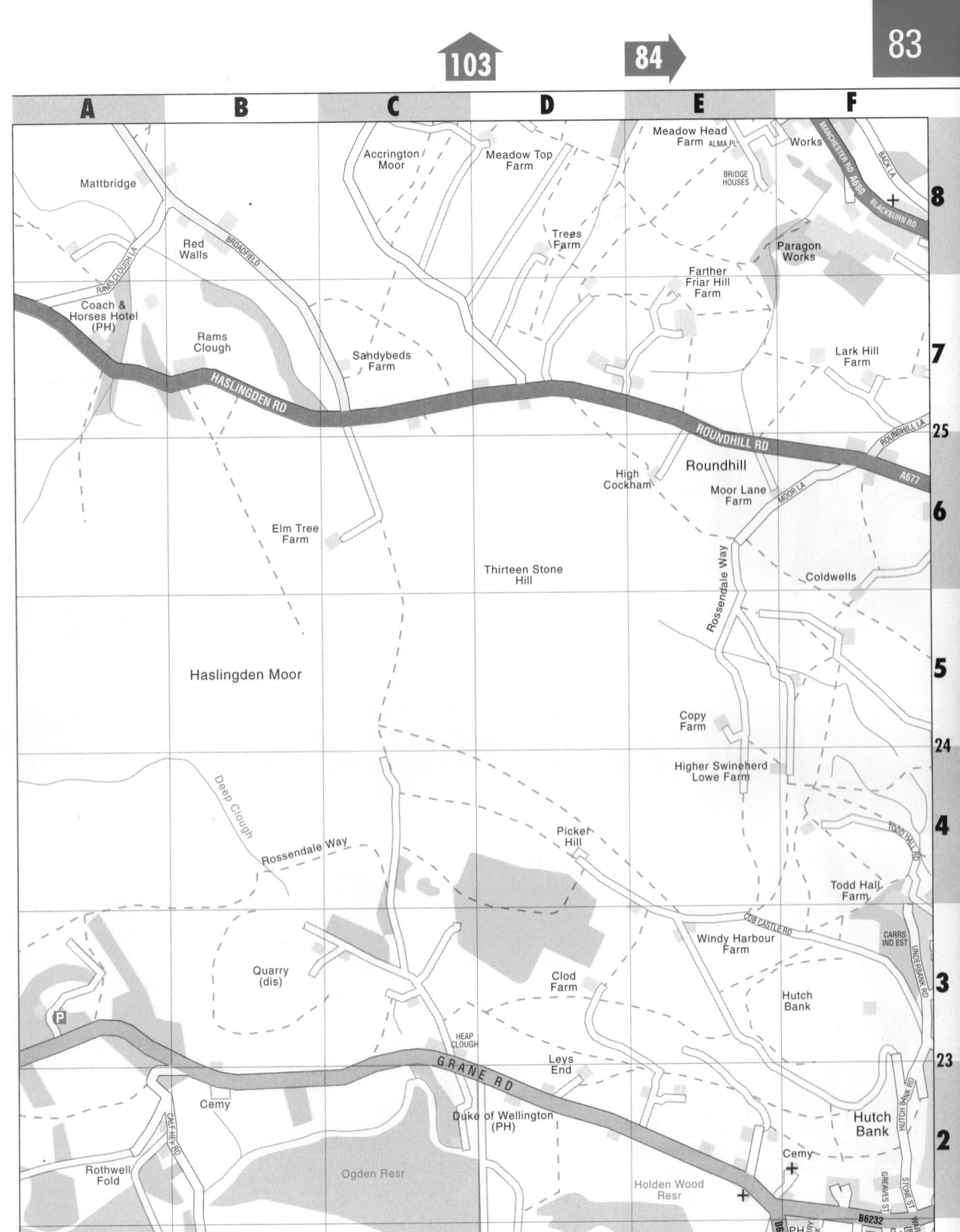

66
84

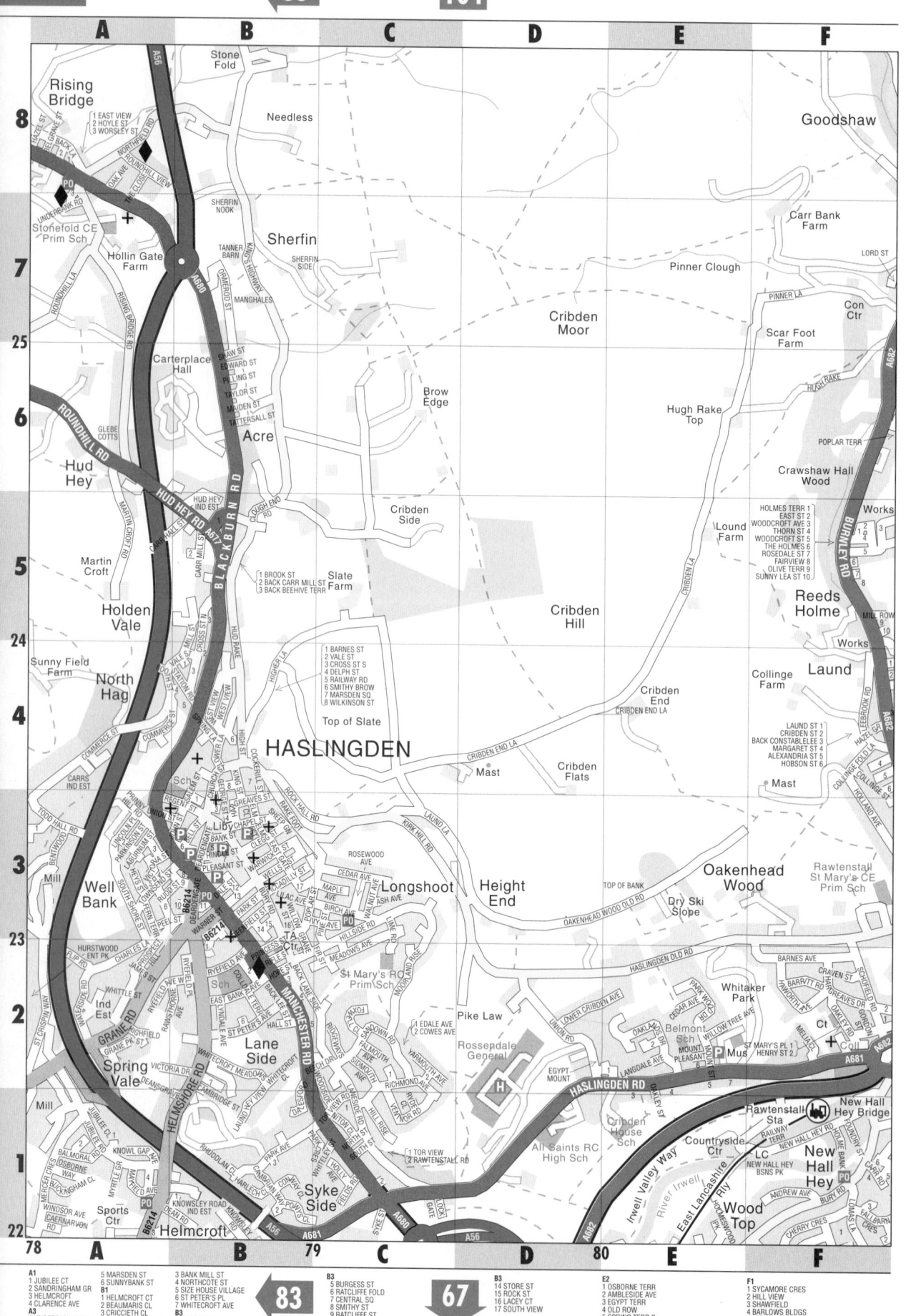

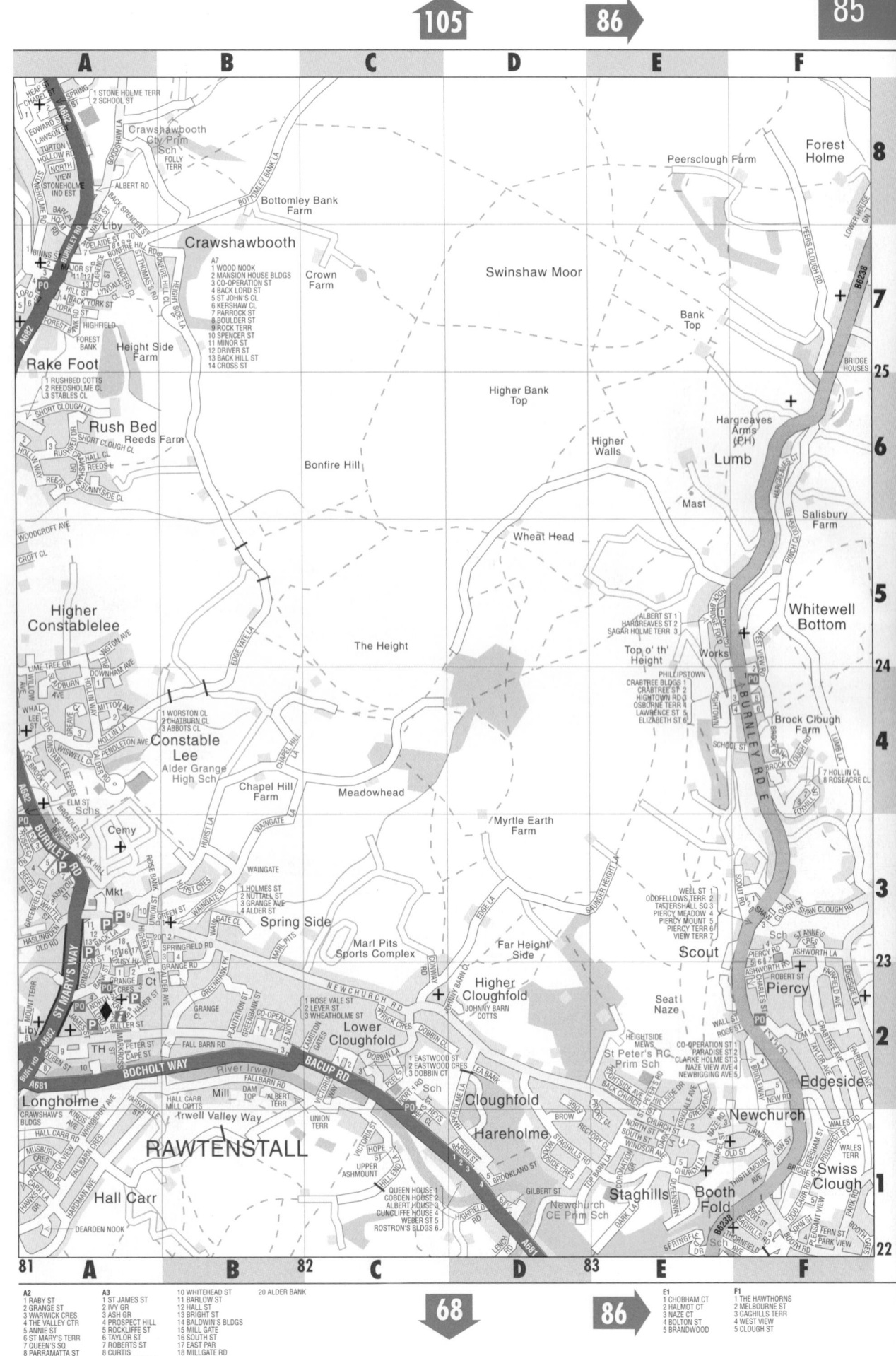

Forest Holme

Peersclough Farm

8

Crawshawbooth Cty Prim Sch

1 STONE HOLME TERR
2 SCHOOL ST

FOLLY TERR

Bottomley Bank Farm

Swinshaw Moor

Liby

Crawshawbooth

A7
1 WOOD NOOK
2 MANSION HOUSE BLDGS
3 CO-OPERATION ST
4 BACK LORD ST
5 ST JOHN'S CL
6 KERSHAW CL
7 PARROCK ST
8 BOULDER ST
9 ROCK TERR
10 SPENCER ST
11 MINOR ST
12 DRIVER ST
13 BACK HILL ST
14 CROSS ST

14 BACK YORK ST

Crown Farm

LOWER HOUSE GILL

B6238

BRIDGE HOUSES

25

Rake Foot

Height Side Farm

Higher Bank Top

Hargreaves Arms (PH)

7

1 RUSHBED COTTS
2 REEDSHOLME CL
3 STABLES CL

Rush Bed
Reeds Farm

Higher Walls

Lumb

6

Bonfire Hill

Wheat Head

Mast

Salisbury Farm

Higher Constablelee

The Height

1 ALBERT ST 1
HARGREAVES ST 2
SAGAR HOLME TERR 3

Whitewell Bottom

5

1 WORSTON CL
2 CHATBURN CL
3 ABBOTS CL

Top o' th' Height

Works

24

Constable Lee

Alder Grange High Sch

PHILLIPSTOWN
CRABTREE BLDGS 1
CRABTREE ST 2
HIGHTOWN RD 3
OSBORNE TERR 4
LAWRENCE ST 5
ELIZABETH ST 6

Brock Clough Farm

BURNLEY RD E

Chapel Hill Farm

Meadowhead

7 HOLLIN CL
8 ROSEACRE CL

4

Cemy

Myrtle Earth Farm

Schs

Mkt

WELL ST 1
ODDFELLOWS TERR 2
TATTERSHALL SQ 3
PIERCY MEADOW 4
PIERCY MOUNT 5
PIERCY TERR 6
VIEW TERR 7

ST ANNE'S CRES

3

BURNLEY RD

Waingate

1 HOLMES ST
2 NUTTALL ST
3 GRANGE AVE
4 ALDER ST

Spring Side

Far Height Side

Scout

Piercy

23

Marl Pits Sports Complex

Higher Cloughfold

Seat Naze

ROBERT ST

1 EASTWOOD ST
2 EASTWOOD CRES
3 DOBBIN CT

JOHNNY BARN COTTS

CO-OPERATION ST 1
PARADISE ST 2
CLARKE HOLME ST 3
NAZE VIEW AVE 4
NEWBIGGING AVE 5

Edgeside

2

BOCHOLT WAY

BACUP RD

1 ROSE VALE ST
2 LEVER ST
3 WHEATHOLME ST

Lower Cloughfold

St Peter's RC Prim Sch

Newchurch

Longholme

CRAWSHAW'S BLDGS

Mill

Cloughfold

Swiss Clough

1

Irwell Valley Way

RAWTENSTALL

Hareholme

Staghills

Booth Fold

QUEEN HOUSE 1
COBDEN HOUSE 2
ALBERT HOUSE 3
CUNCLIFFE HOUSE 4
WEBER ST 5
ROSTRON'S BLDGS 6

Newchurch CE Prim Sch

B6238

Hall Carr

DEARDEN NOOK

22

A2
1 RABY ST
2 GRANGE ST
3 WARWICK CRES
4 THE VALLEY CTR
5 ANNIE ST
6 ST MARY'S TERR
7 QUEEN'S SQ
8 PARRAMATTA ST
9 LONGHOLME RD

A3
1 ST JAMES ST
2 IVY GR
3 ASH GR
4 PROSPECT HILL
5 ROCKLIFFE ST
6 TAYLOR ST
7 ROBERTS ST
8 CURTIS
9 CRANKSHAW ST

10 WHITEHEAD ST
11 BARLOW ST
12 HALL ST
13 BRIGHT ST
14 BALDWIN'S BLDGS
15 MILL GATE
16 SOUTH ST
17 EAST PAR
18 MILLGATE RD
19 GRANGE TERR

20 ALDER BANK

E1
1 CHOBHAM CT
2 HALMOT CT
3 NAZE CT
4 BOLTON ST
5 BRANDWOOD

F1
1 THE HAWTHORNS
2 MELBOURNE ST
3 GAGHILLS TERR
4 WEST VIEW
5 CLOUGH ST

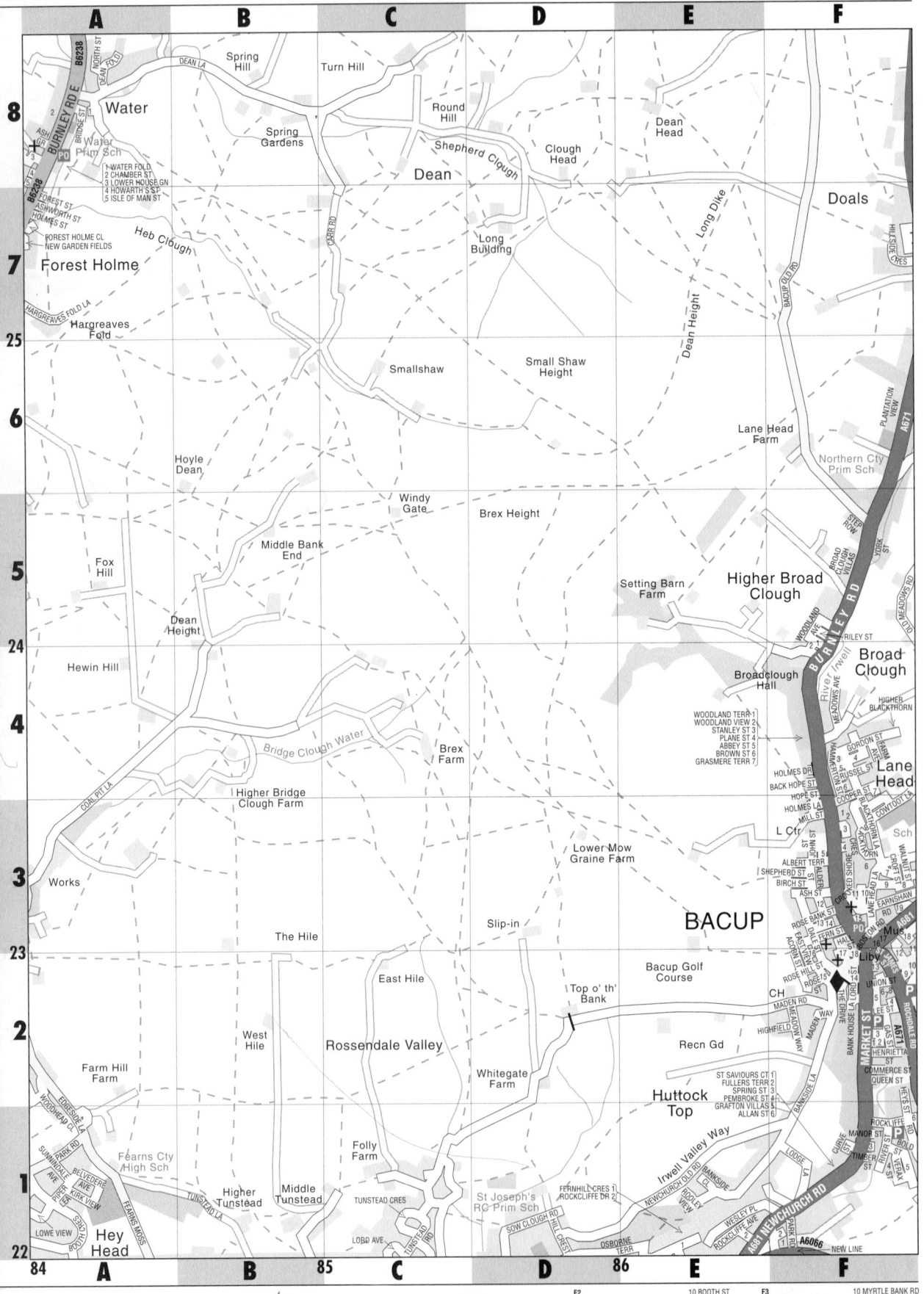

A   B   C   D   E   F

8   Water
Spring Hill
Turn Hill
Round Hill
Dean Head
Doals
Spring Gardens
Shepherd Clough
Clough Head
Dean
Water Prim Sch
1-WATER FOLD
2 CHAMBER ST
3 LOWER HOUSE GN
4 HOWARTH S ST
5 ISLE OF MAN ST
FOREST ST
ASHWORTH ST
HOLMES ST
FOREST HOLME CL
NEW GARDEN FIELDS

7   Forest Holme
Heb Clough
Long Building
Long Dike

25 Hargreaves Fold
Smallshaw
Small Shaw Height
Dean Height
Lane Head Farm
Northern Cty Prim Sch

6   Hoyle Dean
Windy Gate
Brex Height
Higher Broad Clough

5   Fox Hill
Middle Bank End
Setting Barn Farm
Broadclough Hall
Broad Clough

24 Dean Height
WOODLAND TERR 1
WOODLAND VIEW 2
STANLEY ST 3
PLANE ST 4
ABBEY ST 5
BROWN ST 6
GRASMERE TERR 7
Higher Blackthorn
Lane Head

4   Hewin Hill
Bridge Clough Water
Brex Farm
HOLMES DR
BACK HOPE ST
HOPE ST
HOLMES LA
MILL ST

3   Works
Higher Bridge Clough Farm
Lower Mow Graine Farm
L Ctr
ALBERT TERR
SHEPHERD ST
BIRCH ST
ASH ST
BACUP
ROSE BANK ST
Mus

23 The Hile
Slip-in
Bacup Golf Course
CH
Liby
P

2   West Hile
Rossendale Valley
Top o' th' Bank
East Hile
Recn Gd
Highfield
MADEN RD
MADEN WAY
ST SAVIOURS CT 1
FULLERS TERR 2
SPRING ST 3
PEMBROKE ST 4
GRAFTON VILLAS 5
ALLAN ST 6
Henrietta
COMMERCE ST
Queen St
P

Farm Hill Farm
Whitegate Farm
Huttock Top
Irwell Valley Way
ROCKLIFFE
P

1   Fearns Cty High Sch
Higher Tunstead
Middle Tunstead
Folly Farm
St Joseph's RC Prim Sch
FERNHILL CRES 1
ROCKCLIFFE DR 2
WESLEY PL
ROCKCLIFFE AVE

22 Hey Head
LOBD AVE
SOW CLOUGH LA
OSBORNE TERR
NEW LINE
A6066

84 A   85 B   C   D   86 E   F

F2
1 FOUNDRY ST
2 HENRIETTA STREET IND EST
3 FORGE ST
4 INDUSTRIAL PL
5 KING ST
6 AUSTIN ST
7 IRWELL ST
8 KERSHAW ST
9 LUMB SCAR
10 BOOTH ST
11 PICKUP ST
12 IRWELL TERR
13 TOWER ST
14 BANK ST
15 THISTLE ST
16 LILY ST
17 PRINCESS ST
18 MAITLAND ST
F3
1 UNDERBANK HOUSE
2 MOWGRAIN VIEW
3 UNDERBANK CL
4 LAUREL ST
5 BACK ST JOHN ST
6 ST JOHN'S CT
7 STANLEY MOUNT
8 BENTLEY ST
9 HIGHER CROSS ROW
10 MYRTLE BANK RD
11 WATERSIDE TERR
12 DAISY BANK
13 BAKER ST
14 GOOSE HILL ST
15 HARCOURT ST
16 ST JAMES SQ
17 YORKSHIRE ST
18 HAMMERTON GN
19 EARNSHAW ROW

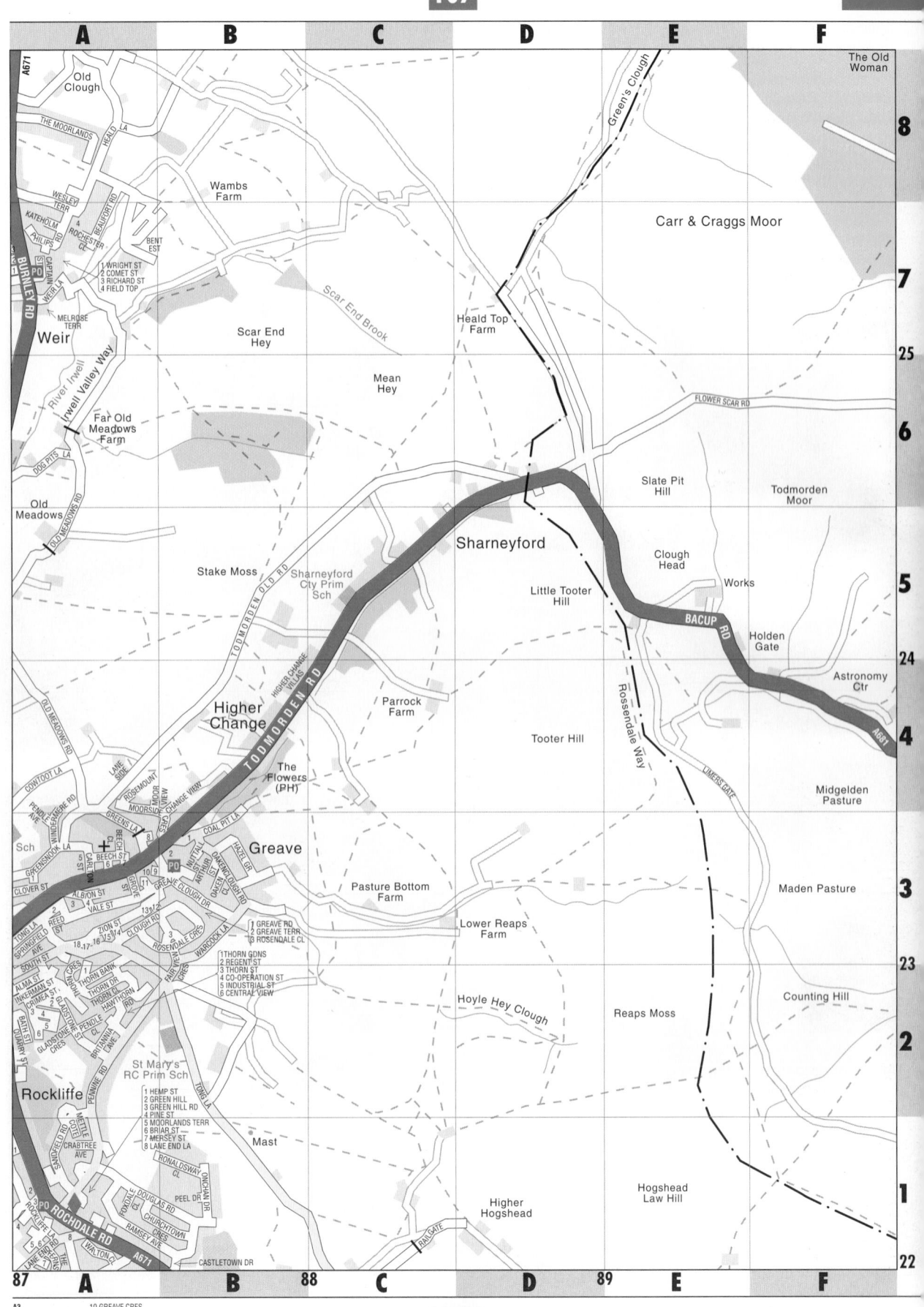

109

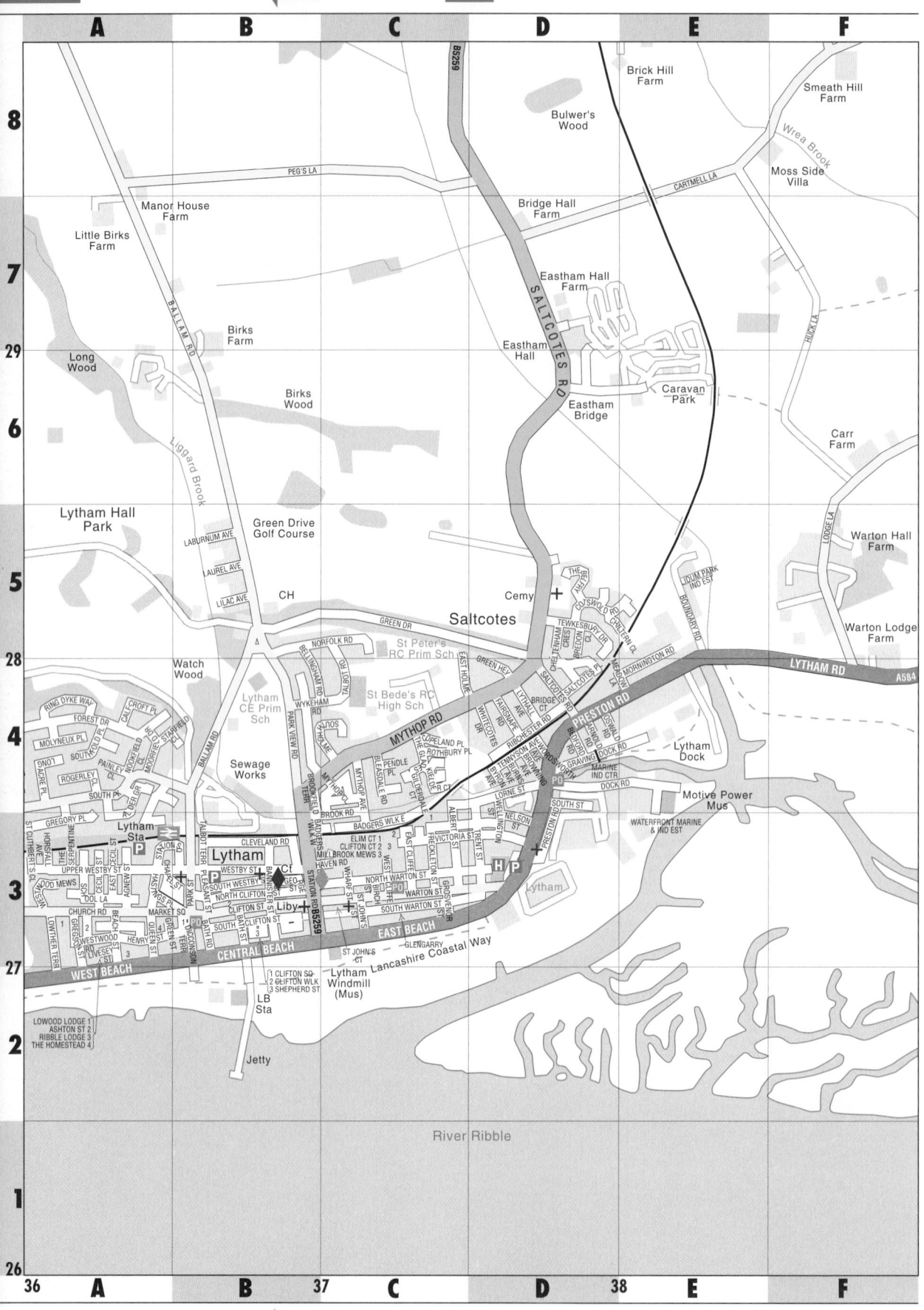

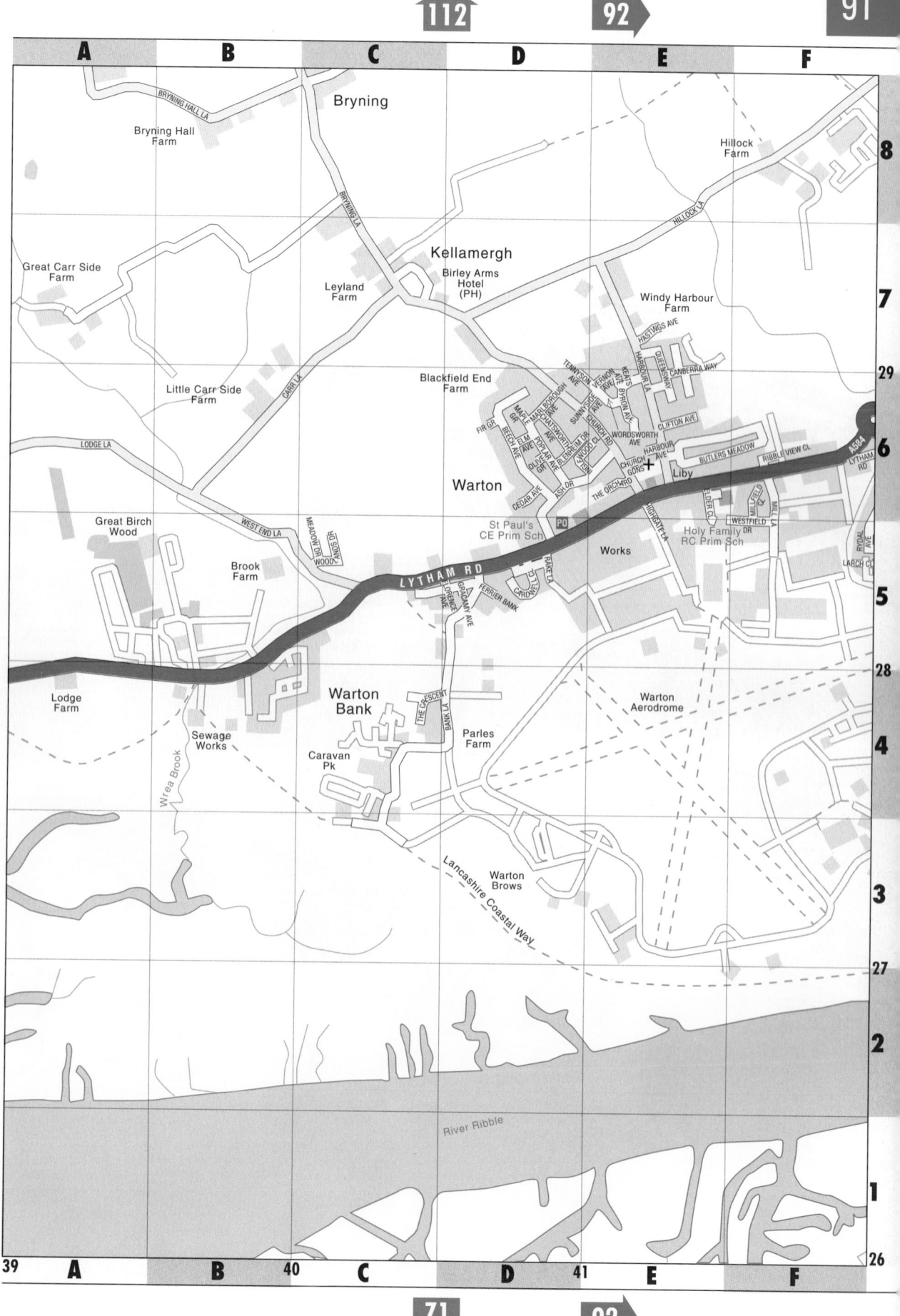

A B C D E F

8
7
29
6
5
28
4
3
27
2
1
26

Bryning

Bryning Hall Farm

BRYNING HALL LA

Great Carr Side Farm

Little Carr Side Farm

Leyland Farm

CARR LA

BRYNING LA

Kellamergh

Birley Arms Hotel (PH)

Blackfield End Farm

Hillock Farm

HILLOCK LA

Windy Harbour Farm

HASTINGS AVE

QUEENSWAY

CANBERRA WAY

TENNYSON AVE
VERNON AVE
HARBOUR LA
BYRON AVE

MARLBOROUGH AVE
SUNNY DR
CHURCH RD
CLIFTON AVE

FIR GR
MAPLE GR
KEATS AVE
WORDSWORTH AVE

ELM GR
POPLAR AVE
B. BARNEM LA
WILDOOT CL DR
HARBOUR AVE

BEECH AVE
OLIVER AVE
CHATSWORTH

LODGE LA

LODGE LA

CEDAR AVE

ASH DR

THE ORCHARD
CHURCH GDNS
Liby

BUTLERS MEADOW

RIBBLE VIEW CL.

A584
LYTHAM RD

Warton

St Paul's CE Prim Sch

PO

Works

Holy Family RC Prim Sch

DR

WESTFIELD

ELDER CL
MILLFIELD
MILL LA

RYDAL AVE
LARCH CL.

Great Birch Wood

WEST END LA

MEADOW DR
WOODS GR

Brook Farm

LYTHAM RD

FERRIER BANK

CD TOWN
FAKE LA
CD TOWN
CROWD
HIGHGATE LA

Lodge Farm

Sewage Works

Warton Bank

THE CRESCENT
BANK LA
FLORENCE AVE
NORMANDY AVE

Caravan Pk

Parles Farm

Warton Aerodrome

Wrea Brook

Warton Brows

Lancashire Coastal Way

River Ribble

A B C D E F

8

Nurseries

Strike Farm

Strike La

Strike Lane Cty Prim Sch

Marbank Farm

Lower House Farm

Nursery

Toll House Bridge

A584

Halfpenny Hall Bridge

Newton Marsh

7

Raker House Farm

Freckleton

Freckleton CE Prim Sch

PRESTON NEW RD

Dow Brook

Middle Pool

29

St Ives Ave

PH

PO

Liby

Green Acres

Marquis Dr

Tarnbrick

Marsh Dr

MARSH GATES

1 CLOVER DR
2 SPRING HILL
3 FOXGLOVE WAY
4 FERNDALE CL

1
2
3
HILL TOP CL

Freckleton Marsh

6

Sedgeley

Langdale Mews CL

East Way

Derwent Cl

Derwent Cl

Douglas Dr

Blackfield Rd

Clifton Pl

Further Ends Rd

Wades Croft

Cookson Cl

Green La

Croft Butts La

Richardson Cl

Preston Old Rd

Astley

Naze La

Rigby St

Bunker St

Summit Dr

1 QUERNMORE IND EST
2 MASON CL
3 CROFT MANOR
4 ANSBRO AVE

Grange Farm

Grange Farm Cotts

Rowstorne Sports Ctr

Kimberly Cl

Green La

5

Rydal Ave

Calder Ave

Rydal Ave

Willow Cl

Willow Dr

1 POPLAR DR
2 LARCH CL
3 BEECH DR

Caravan Pk

Stoney La

Naze La E

THE CRESCENT

28

Cherry La

Naze Lane Ind Est

Freckleton Pool

4

Bush La

Pool La

Bottoms Farm

Pool Stream

3

Naze Mount

Lancashire Coastal Way

27

River Ribble

2

1

River Asland or Douglas

26

42 A 43 B C 44 D E F

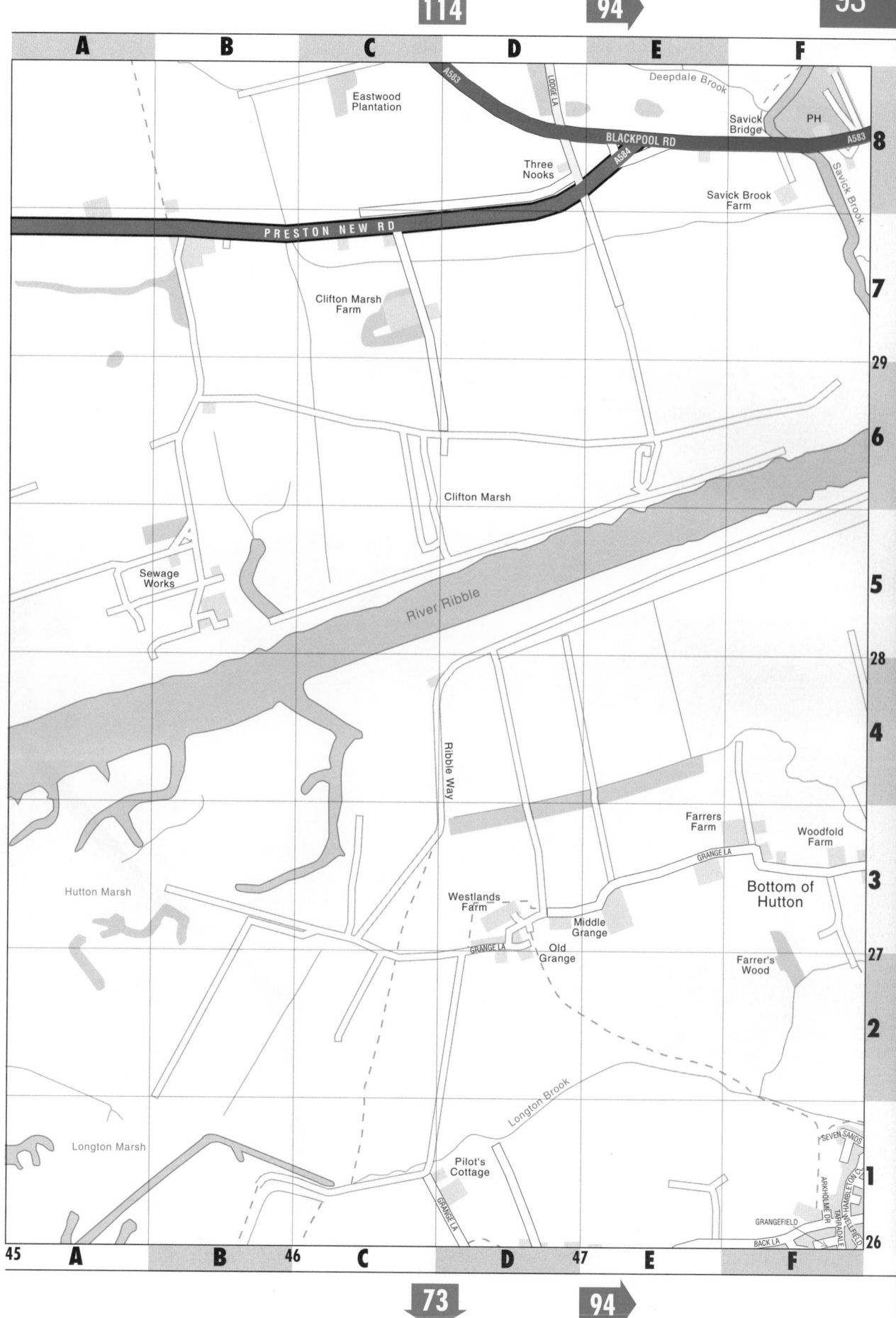

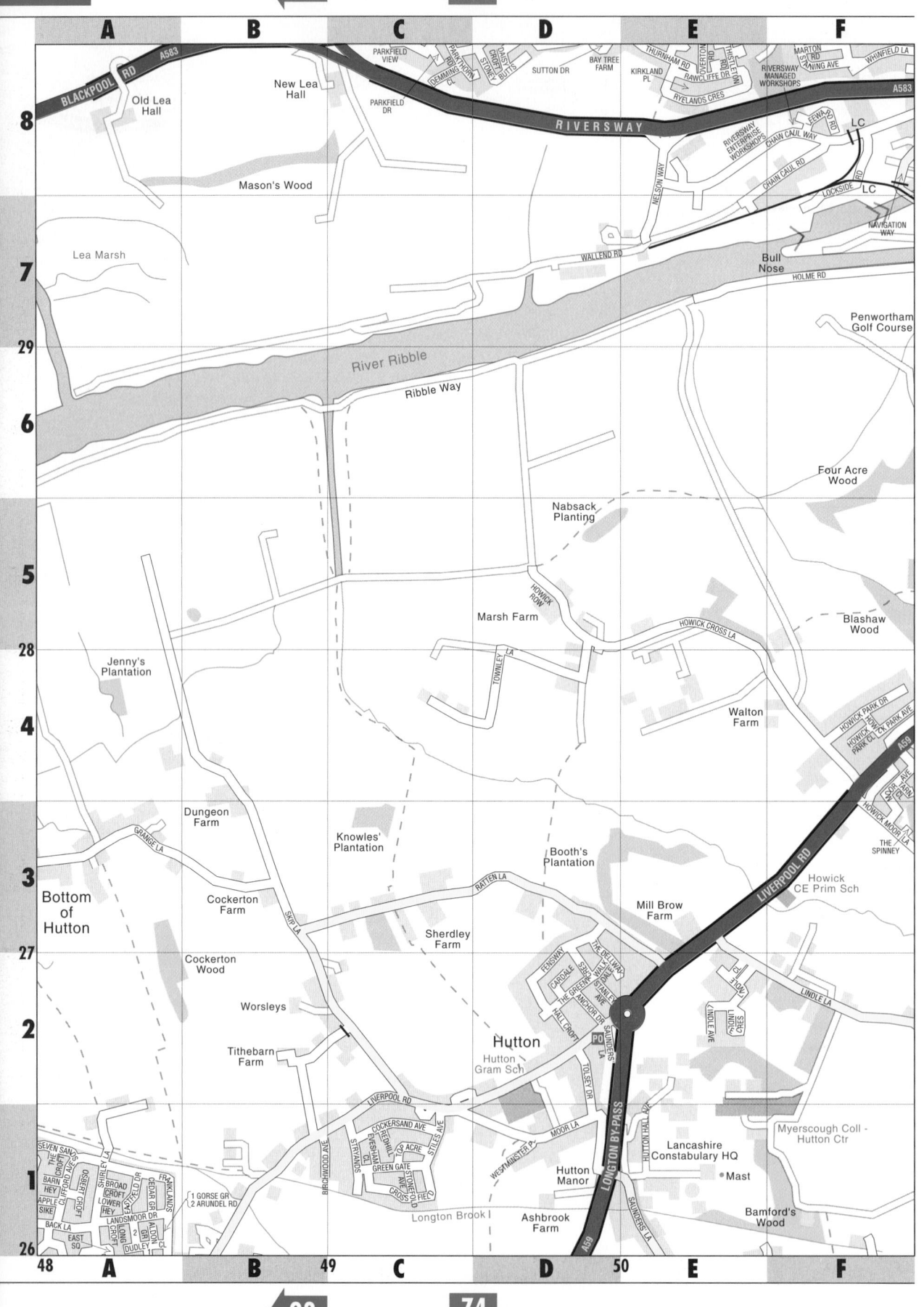

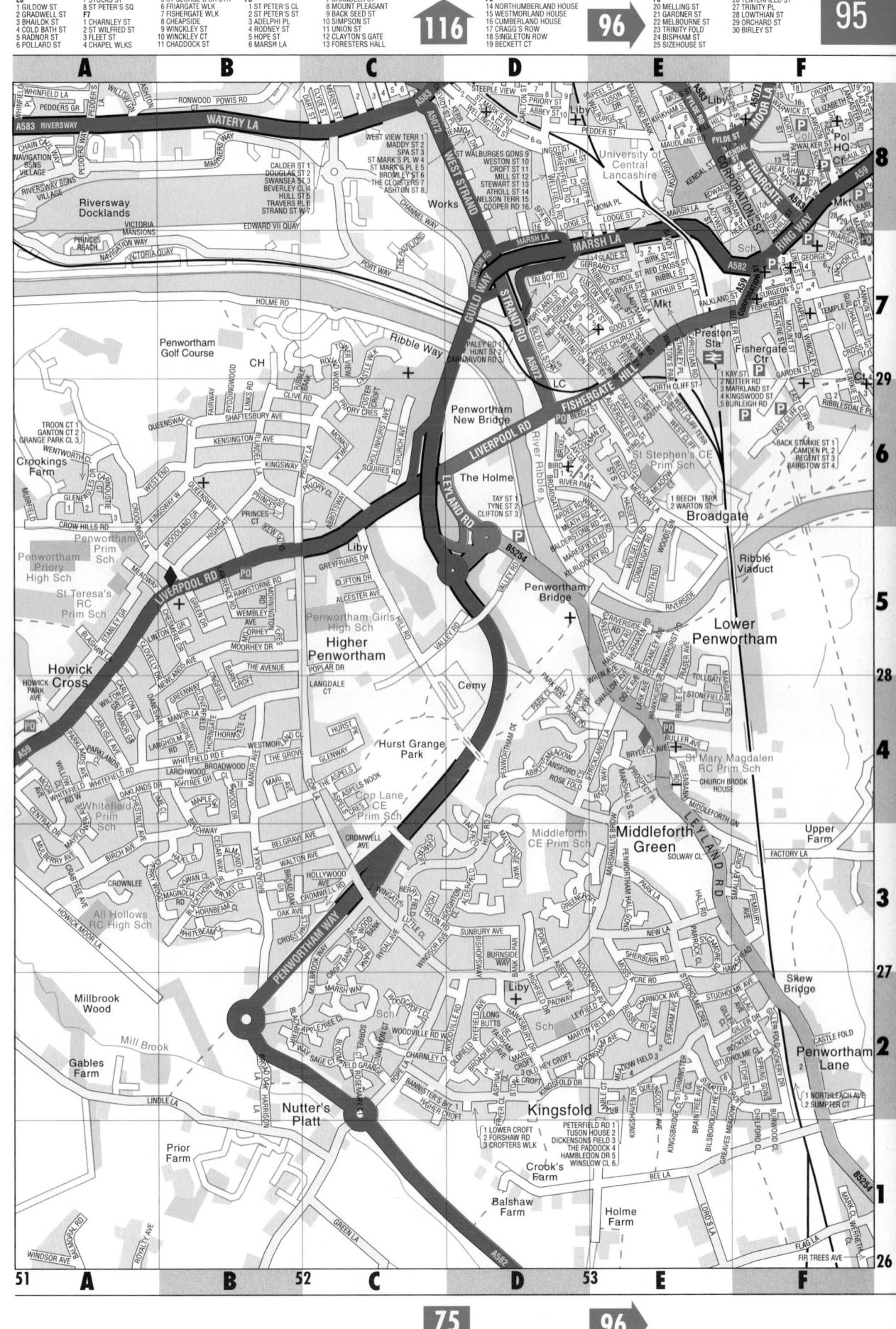

E8	7 STOCKS ST	5 ST GEORGE'S SH CTR	**F8**	7 CHANDLER ST	**F8**	26 TENTERFIELD ST
1 GILDOW ST	8 ST PETER'S SQ	6 FRIARGATE WLK	1 ST PETER'S CL	8 MOUNT PLEASANT	14 NORTHUMBERLAND HOUSE	27 TRINITY PL
2 GRADWELL ST	**F7**	7 FISHERGATE WLK	2 ST PETER'S ST	9 BACK SEED ST	15 WESTMORLAND HOUSE	28 LOWTHIAN ST
3 BHAILOK ST	1 CHARNLEY ST	8 CHEAPSIDE	3 ADELPHI PL	10 SIMPSON ST	16 CUMBERLAND HOUSE	29 ORCHARD ST
4 COLD BATH ST	2 ST WILFRED ST	9 WINCKLEY ST	4 RODNEY ST	11 UNION ST	17 CRAGG'S ROW	30 BIRLEY ST
5 RADNOR ST	3 FLEET ST	10 WINCKLEY CT	5 HOPE ST	12 CLAYTON'S GATE	18 SINGLETON ROW	
6 POLLARD ST	4 CHAPEL WLKS	11 CHADDOCK ST	6 MARSH LA	13 FORESTERS HALL	19 BECKETT CT	

116 ▲   **96** ▶

F8
20 MELLING ST
21 GARDNER ST
22 MELBOURNE ST
23 TRINITY FOLD
24 BISPHAM ST
25 SIZEHOUSE ST

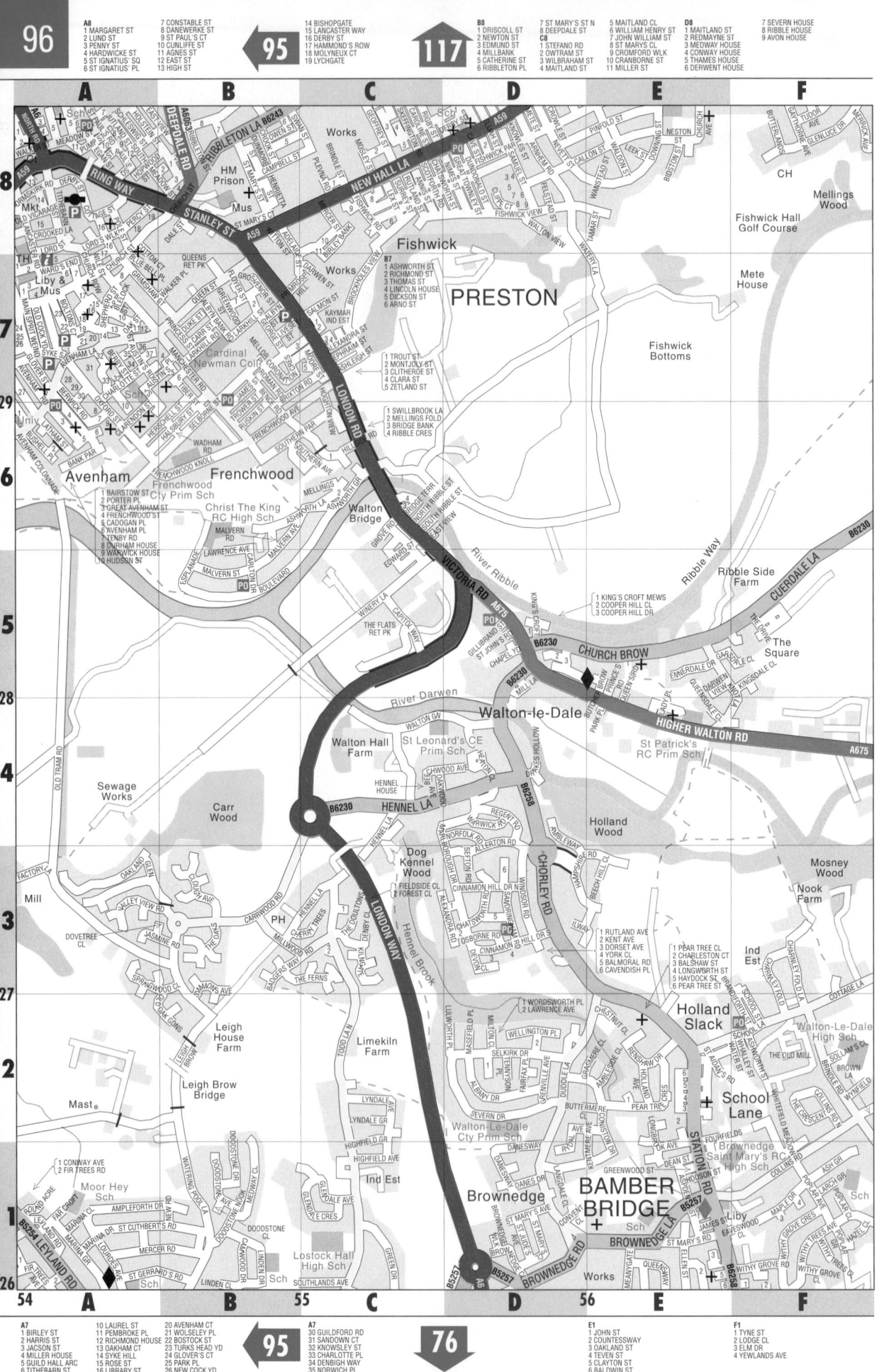

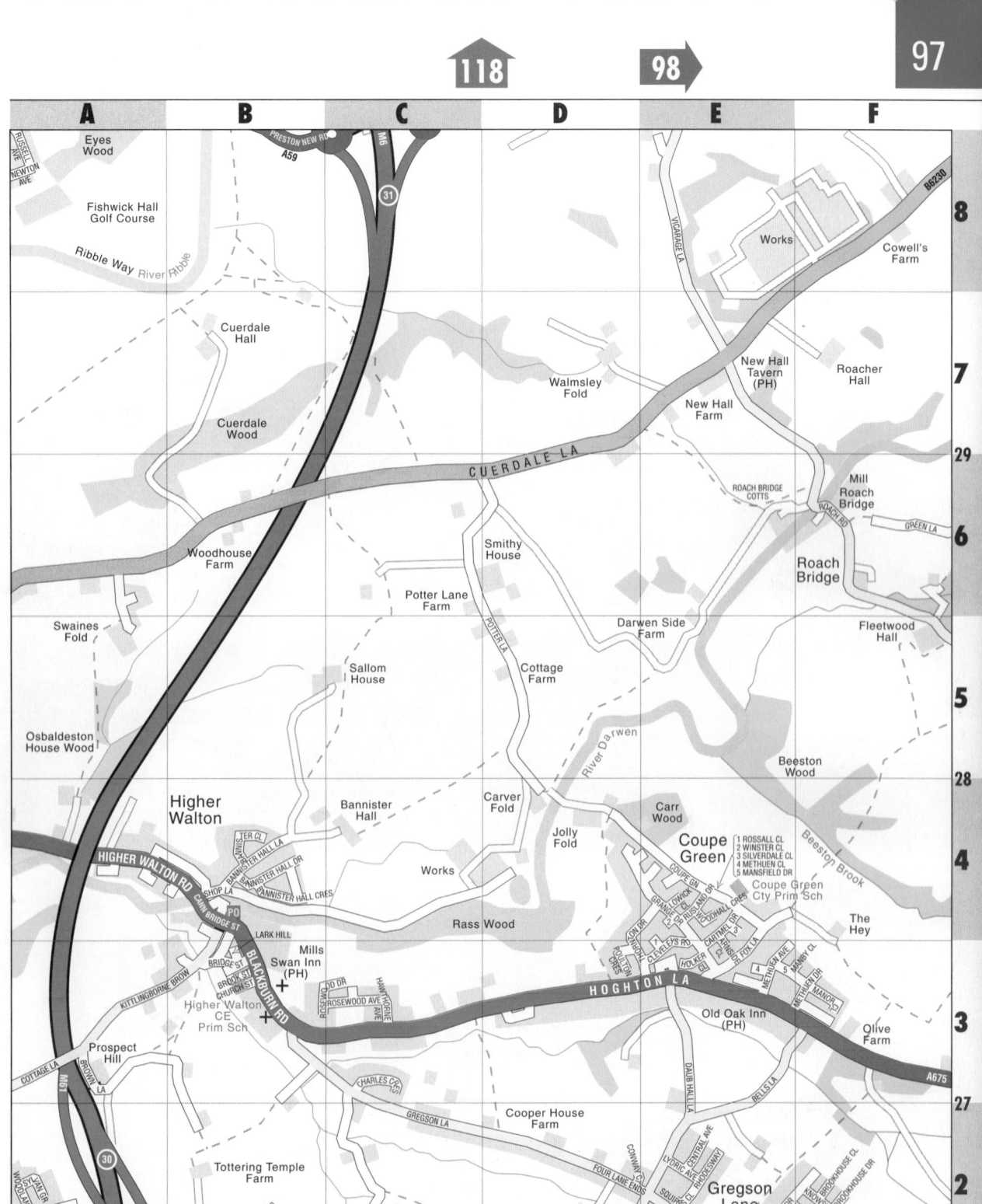

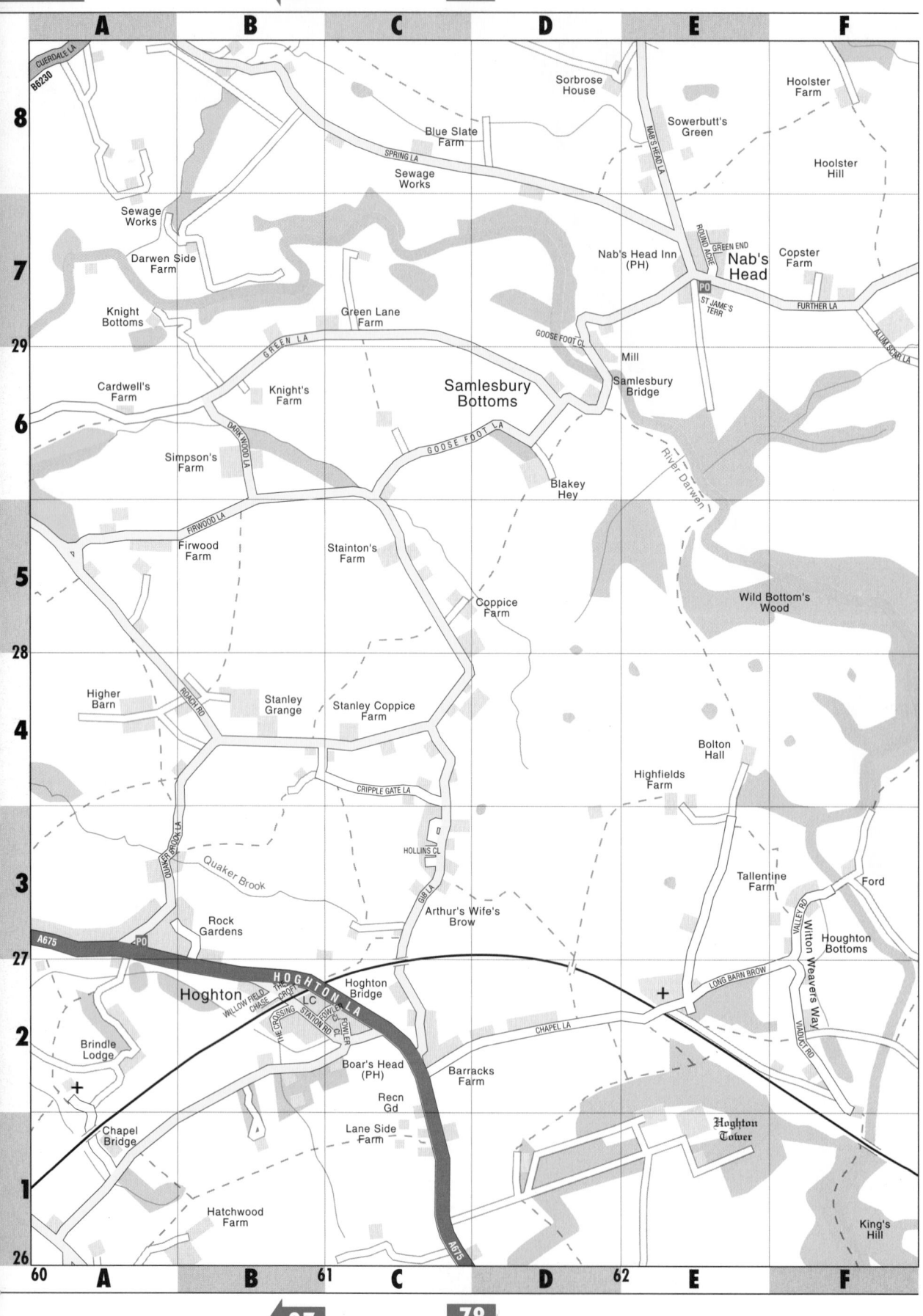

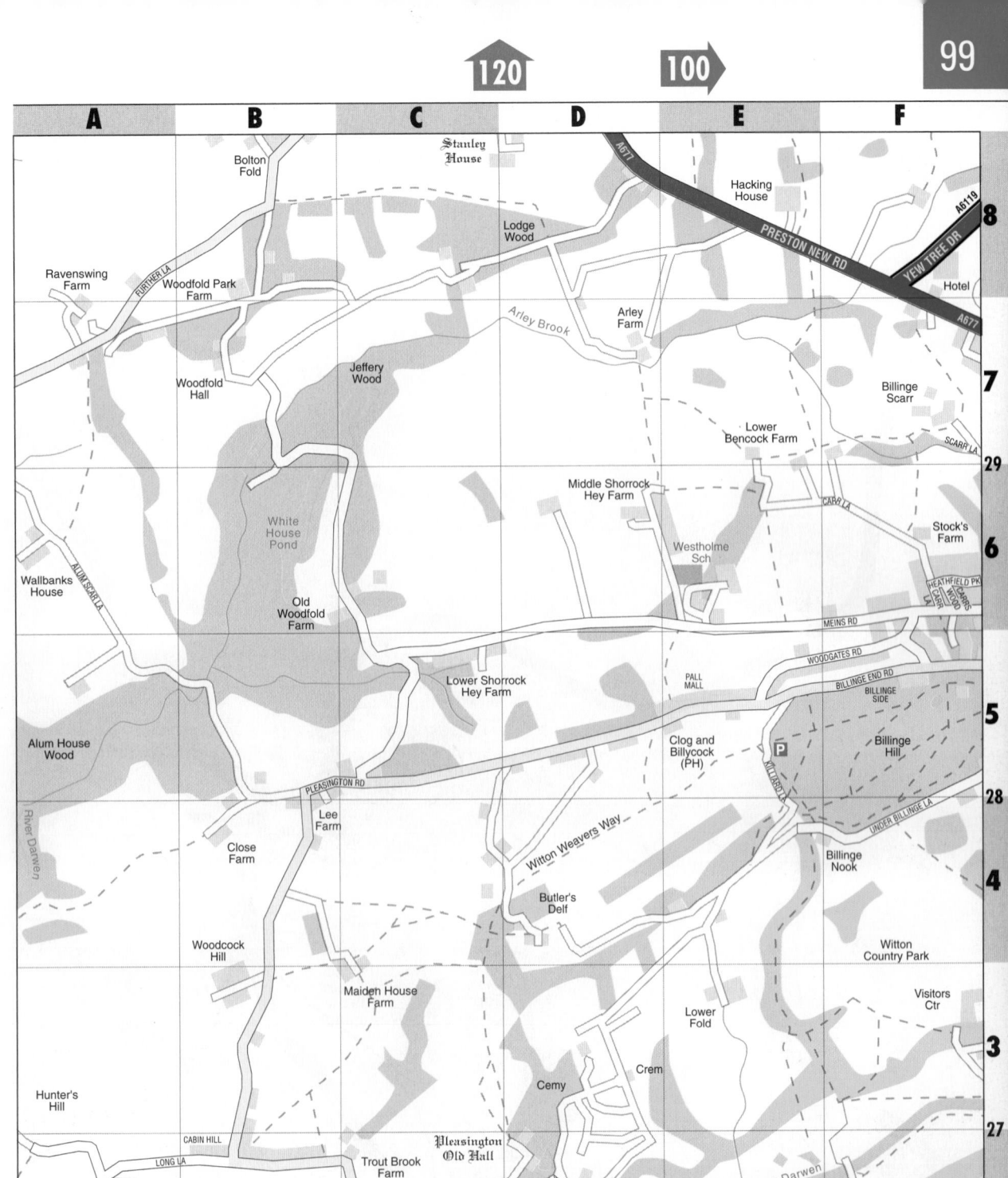

Stanley House
Bolton Fold
Hacking House
PRESTON NEW RD
A677
A6119
YEW TREE DR
Hotel
A677

Ravenswing Farm
FURTHER LA
Woodfold Park Farm
Lodge Wood
Arley Brook
Arley Farm
8

Woodfold Hall
Jeffery Wood
Lower Bencock Farm
Billinge Scarr
SCARR LA
7
29

Wallbanks House
ALUM SCAR LA
White House Pond
Middle Shorrock Hey Farm
Westholme Sch
CARR LA
Stock's Farm
HEATHFIELD PK
CARR WOOD
6

Old Woodfold Farm
MEINS RD
WOODGATES RD
BILLINGE END RD
BILLINGE SIDE
Billinge Hill

Alum House Wood
Lower Shorrock Hey Farm
PALL MALL
Clog and Billycock (PH)
P
KILLBRD LA
5
28

River Darwen
PLEASINGTON RD
Lee Farm
Witton Weavers Way
Billinge Nook
UNDER BILLINGE LA
4

Close Farm
Butler's Delf
Witton Country Park
Visitors Ctr

Woodcock Hill
Maiden House Farm
Lower Fold
3
27

Hunter's Hill
CABIN HILL
LONG LA
Crem
Cemy
River Darwen
BILLINGE VIEW
TOWER RD
A674

Higher Park Farm
Pleasington Old Hall
Trout Brook Farm
SANDY LA
OLD HALL LA
OLD HALL LA
TOWER RD
Butler's Bridge
HILLCREST RD
GEDDES ST
2

Throstle Nest Brow
PRIORY CT
PH
REGENTS CL
Witton Weavers Way
CHERRY TREE TERR 1
HUNTERS LODGE 2
GLADSTONE TERR 3
Cherry Tree Sta
WOOD VIEW
GREEN LA

Brownlands Farm
Pleasington Sta
PR BOWDEN AVE
WOODNOOK RD
Tongue Hill
Pleasington
Playing Fields
PRESTON OLD RD
PO
Leeds and Liverpool Canal
1

Pleasington Golf Course
BROWNLOW TERR
CH
PO
ROSE HILL RD
Cherry Tree
LIVESEY HALL CL
THE CRESCNT
St Francis CE Prim Sch
Lbry
WOODLANDS AVE
SPRINGFIELD AVE
A674
OLD GATES DR
26

99

121

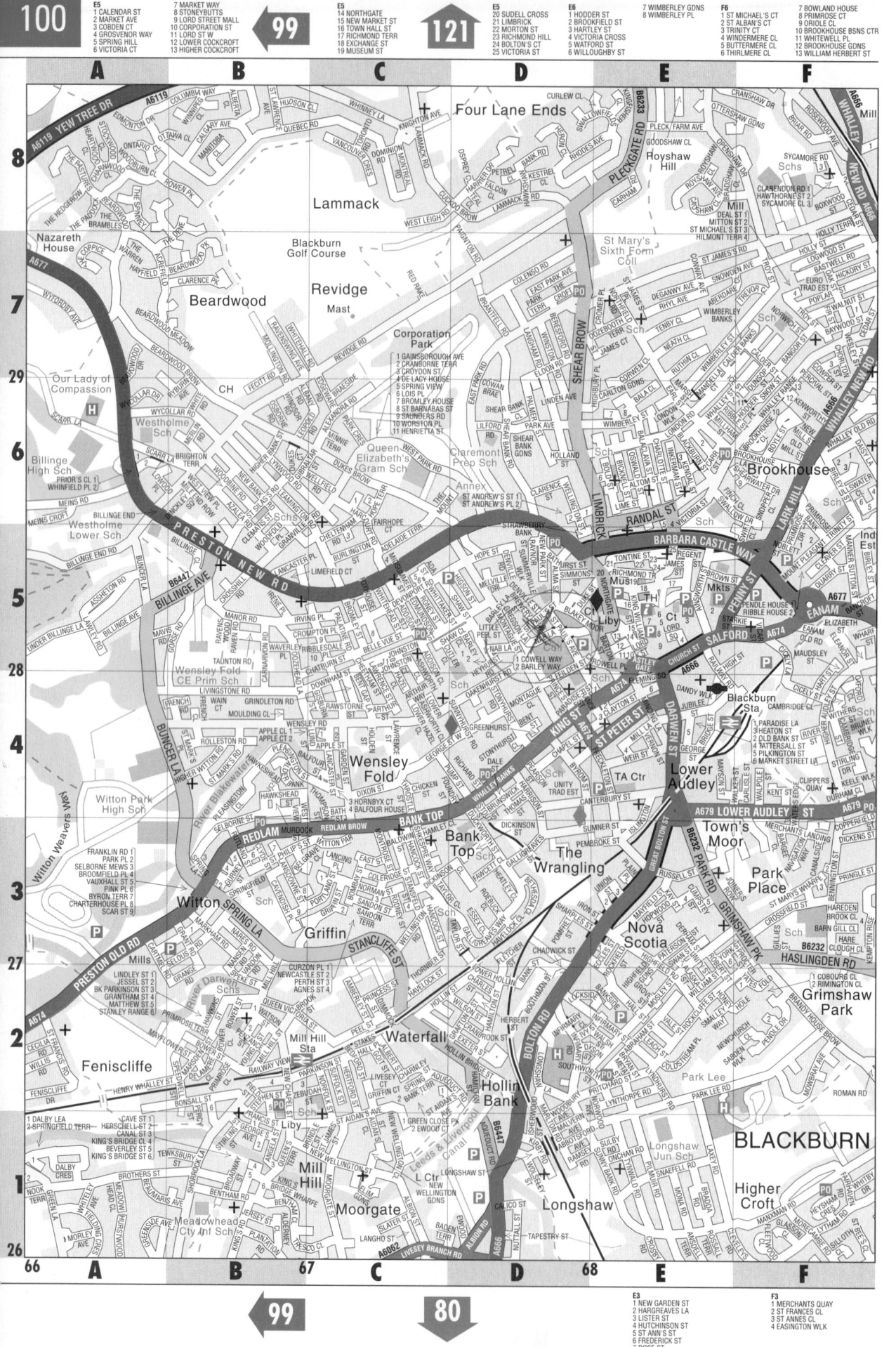

E5
1 CALENDAR ST
2 MARKET AVE
3 COBDEN CT
4 GROSVENOR WAY
5 SPRING HILL
6 VICTORIA CT

7 MARKET WAY
8 STONEYBUTTS
9 LORD STREET MALL
10 CORPORATION ST
11 LORD ST W
12 LOWER COCKCROFT
13 HIGHER COCKCROFT

E5
14 NORTHGATE
15 NEW MARKET ST
16 TOWN HALL ST
17 RICHMOND TERR
18 EXCHANGE ST
19 MUSEUM ST

E5
20 SUDELL CROSS
21 LIMBRICK
22 MORTON HILL
23 RICHMOND HILL
24 BOLTON'S CT
25 VICTORIA ST

E6
1 HODDER ST
2 BROOKFIELD ST
3 HARTLEY ST
4 VICTORIA CROSS
5 WATFORD ST
6 WILLOUGHBY ST

7 WIMBERLEY GDNS
8 WIMBERLEY PL

F6
1 ST MICHAEL'S CT
2 ST ALBAN'S CT
3 TRINITY CT
4 WINDERMERE CL
5 BUTTERMERE CL
6 THIRLMERE CL

7 BOWLAND HOUSE
8 PRIMROSE CT
9 ORIOLE CT
10 BROOKHOUSE BSNS CTR
11 WHITEWELL PL
12 BROOKHOUSE GDNS
13 WILLIAM HERBERT ST

E3
1 NEW GARDEN ST
2 HARGREAVES LA
3 LISTER ST
4 HUTCHINSON ST
5 ST ANN'S ST
6 FREDERICK ST
7 ROSE ST

F3
1 MERCHANTS QUAY
2 ST FRANCES CL
3 ST ANNES CL
4 EASINGTON WLK

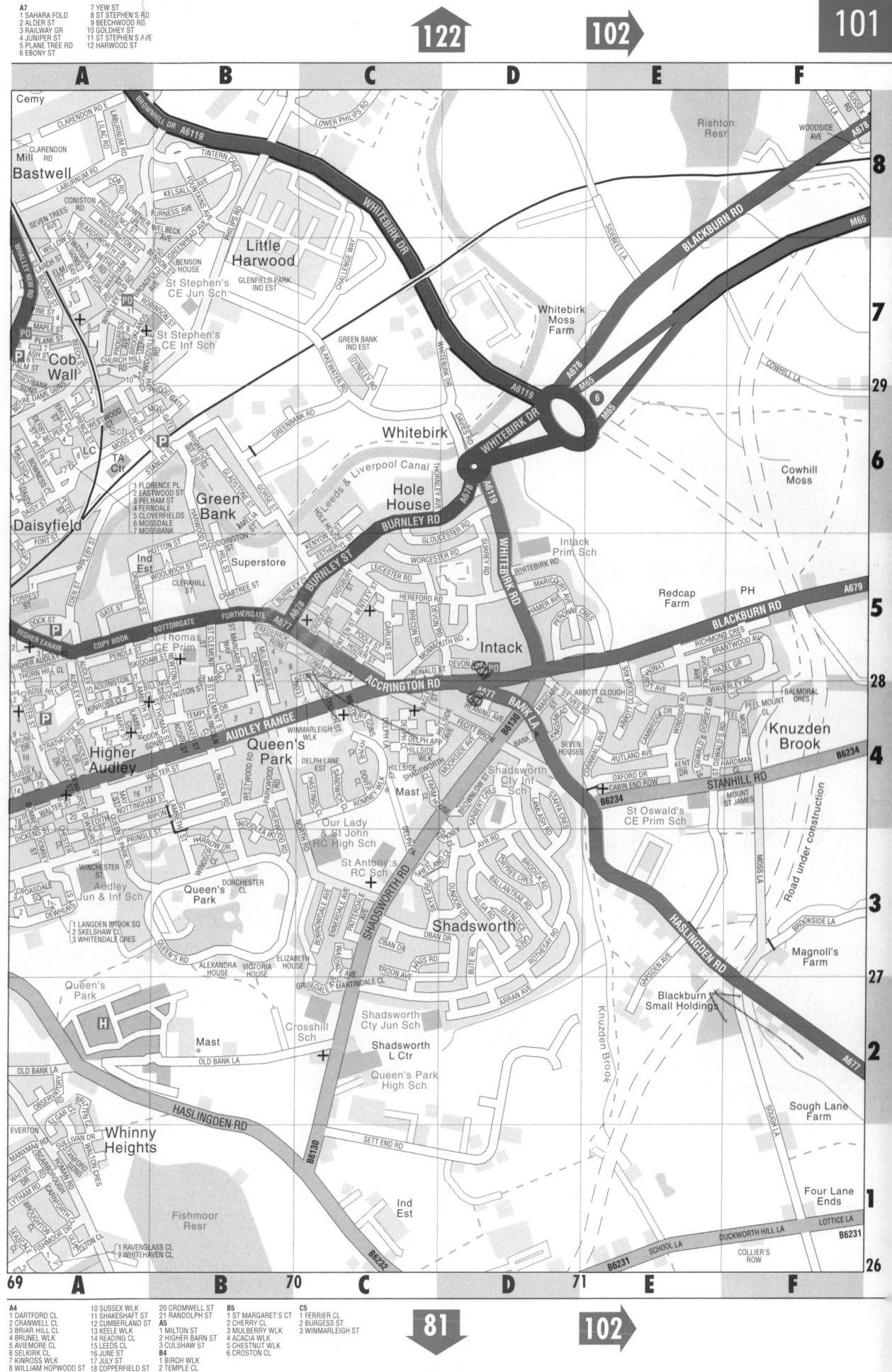

A7
1 SAHARA FOLD
2 ALDER ST
3 RAILWAY GR
4 JUNIPER ST
5 PLANE TREE RD
6 EBONY ST
7 YEW ST
8 ST STEPHEN'S RD
9 BEECHWOOD RC
10 GOLDHEY ST
11 ST STEPHEN'S AVE
12 HARWOOD ST

A4
1 DARTFORD CL
2 CRANWELL CL
3 BRIAR HILL CL
4 BRUNEL WLK
5 AVIEMORE CL
6 SELKIRK CL
7 KINROSS WLK
8 WILLIAM HOPWOOD ST
9 BRISTOL CL
10 SUSSEX WLK
11 SHAKESHAFT ST
12 CUMBERLAND ST
13 KEELE WLK
14 READING CL
15 LEEDS CL
16 JUNE ST
17 JULY ST
18 COPPERFIELD ST
19 DORRITT ST
20 CROMWELL ST
21 RANDOLPH ST
A5
1 MILTON ST
2 HIGHER BARN ST
3 CULSHAW ST
B4
1 BIRCH WLK
2 TEMPLE CL
3 CLEMENTS CL
B5
1 ST MARGARET'S CT
2 CHERRY CL
3 MULBERRY WLK
4 ACACIA WLK
5 CHESTNUT WLK
6 CROSTON CL
C5
1 FERRIER CL
2 BURGESS ST
3 WINMARLEIGH ST

A B C D E F

OSWALDTWISTLE

CHURCH

Rishton Sta
Moor Side Farm
1 GLOUCESTER RD
2 THE ESPLANADE
Willis Farm
Shaw Brook
Rishton Golf Course
Park Plantation
Cowhill Fold
Accrington & District Golf Course
Wolfenden Farm
Plowtalgh Farm
Peel Bank
St Nicholas CE Prim Sch
QUEENSWAY 1
CORNWALL PL 2
DORSET PL 3
SUSSEX CL 4
Cote Holme
Alleytroyds
Works

E6
1 FLORENCE ST
2 ALBERT ST
3 EDMUNDSON ST
4 GRIMSHAW ST
5 PRINCESS ST
6 ERNEST ST
7 COMMERCIAL ST
8 EDWARD ST
9 BANK ST
10 LION CT

West End
Foxhill Bank
Church & Oswaldtwistle Sta
Spring Hill
Sports Ctr

E5
1 JACKSON ST
2 DEVON PL
3 PARSONAGE ST
4 SADLER ST
5 ST ANNES CL
6 BLACKPOOL ST
7 CLAYTON ST

SPREAD EAGLE ST 1
WHAM BROOK CL 2
TURNPIKE WAY 3
ANGLIAN CL 4

West End Cty Prim Sch
Higher Stanhill
Knuzden Hall
Knuzden Moss
Stanhill
Little Moor End
White Ash Estate
Dunnyshop
1 ST ANDREW'S CL
2 ST ANDREW'S CT
3 KAY ST
4 BENT ST
5 COOPERS CL
6 PEEL ST
7 THOMAS ST
8 HIGHER PEEL ST
9 SMITHY BRIDGE ST 10
Hippings Meth Prim Sch
Brook Side
Bury Meadow Farm
Works
BROADFIELD ST 1
MELROSE AVE 2
THE MEADOWS 3
Broadfield
Broadfield Sch
Old Field Farm
Duckworth Hall
Greenfield Terr
Britannia Cotts
Britannia Inn (PH)
Britannia Poultry Farm
Duckworth Hill
Town Bent
Town Bent Farm
Hoyle Bottom
Cockerley Fold
Ye Olde Brown Cow Inn (PH)

72 A 73 C D 74 E F

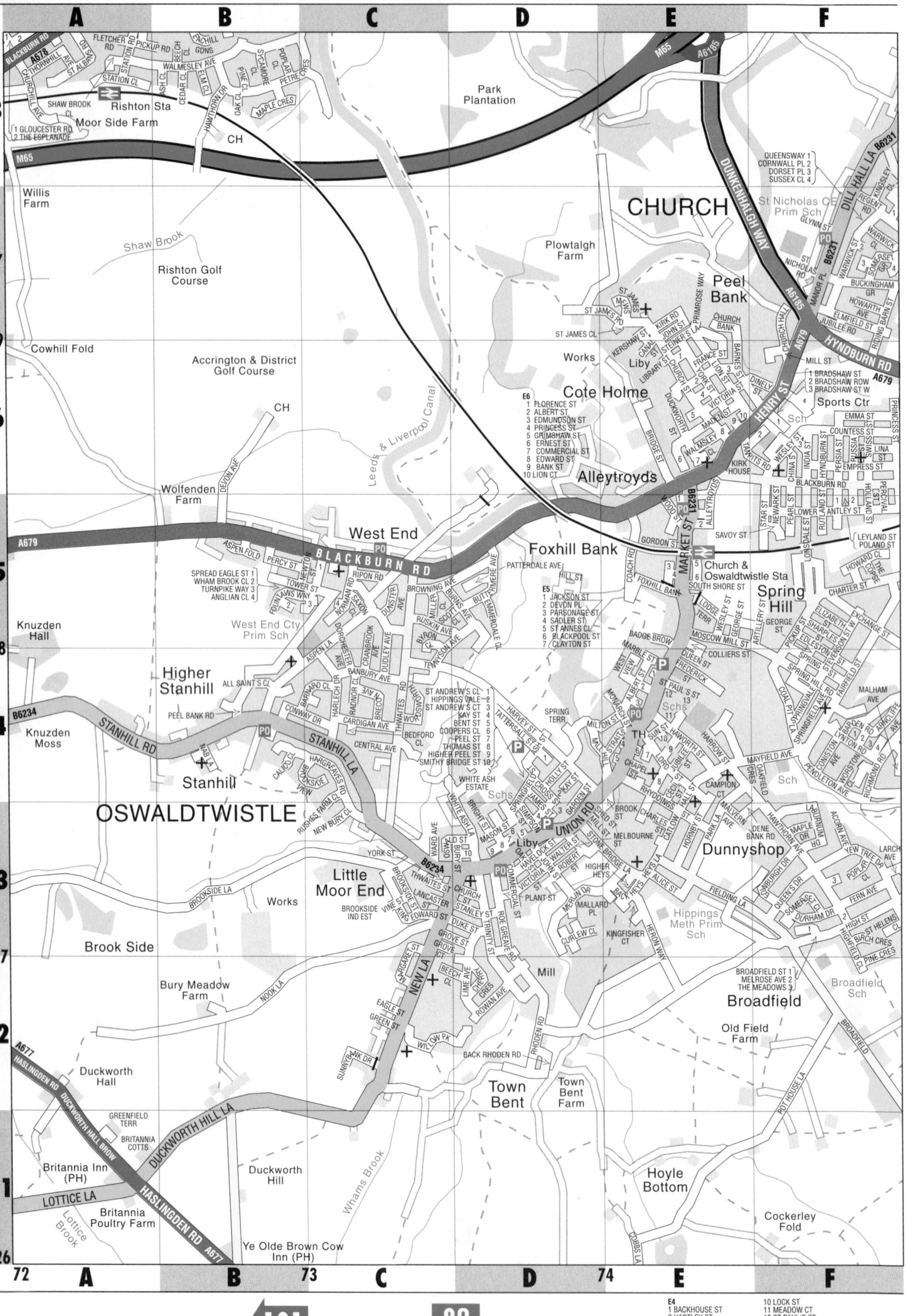

E4
1 BACKHOUSE ST
2 HARTLEY ST
3 HODGSON ST
4 DALE ST
5 SPRING ST
6 MOUNT PLEASANT ST
7 OFF MOUNT PLEASANT ST
8 WATSON ST
9 PADDOCK ST
10 LOCK ST
11 MEADOW CT
12 ST PAUL'S CT
13 WORSLEY CT
F4
1 GAYLE WAY
2 BURNSALL RD
3 REETH WAY
4 BUCKDEN RD

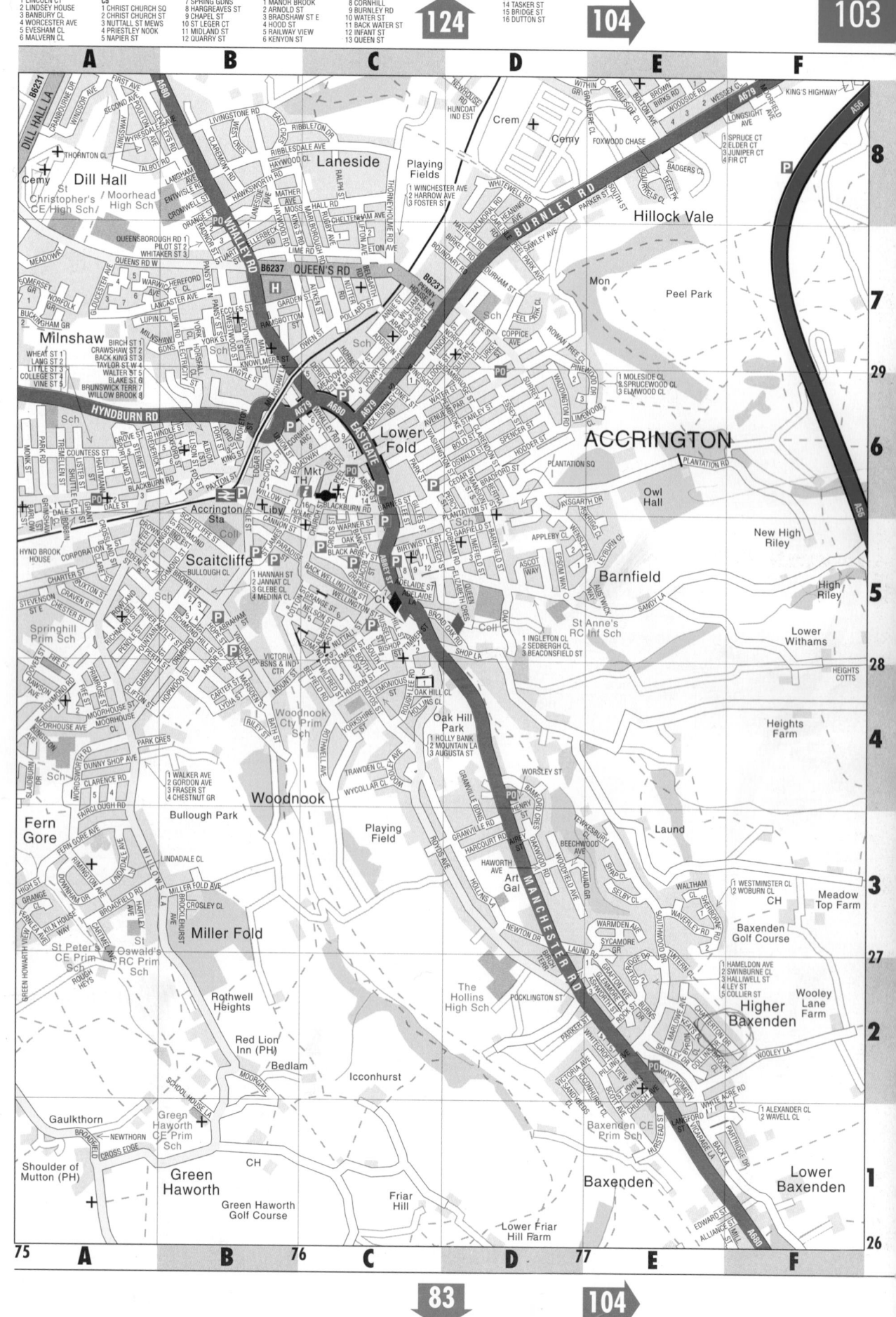

← 103
125

A B C D E F

8

Cronker
Plantation

Thorny
Bank

Thorny Bank
Wood

Hameldon
Scouts

7

Snipe Rake

Hameldon Common

Hapton Park

Windy
Harbour

Great Slack

Park Scout

29

Moleside Moor

Great Hameldon

Great Hill

6

Moleside End
Farm

King's Highway

Burnley Way

Masts

SANDY LA

New Laithe
Height

5

West
Farm

A56

Great Clough

Heights
Farm

28

Higher
Hey

Higher Moor

Snipe Hole

Great
Clough

4

Mitchell's House
Resrs

3

Black
Moss

KING'S HIGHWAY

Higher
Withens

Rossendale Way

Rough Hill
Farm

Works

27

Hen Heads
Farm

Goodshaw Hill

SLIVEN CLOUGH RD

Goodshaw
Fold

LOVE CLOUGH RD

2

SPRINGBANK
GDNS

GOODSHAW FOLD RD

New Barn

Limy Water

1

GOODSHAW LA

Lane Top
Farm

Fair Banks

Gin Clough

Pewit
Hall

A56

Cross Edge
Farm

26

78 A B 79 C D 80 E F

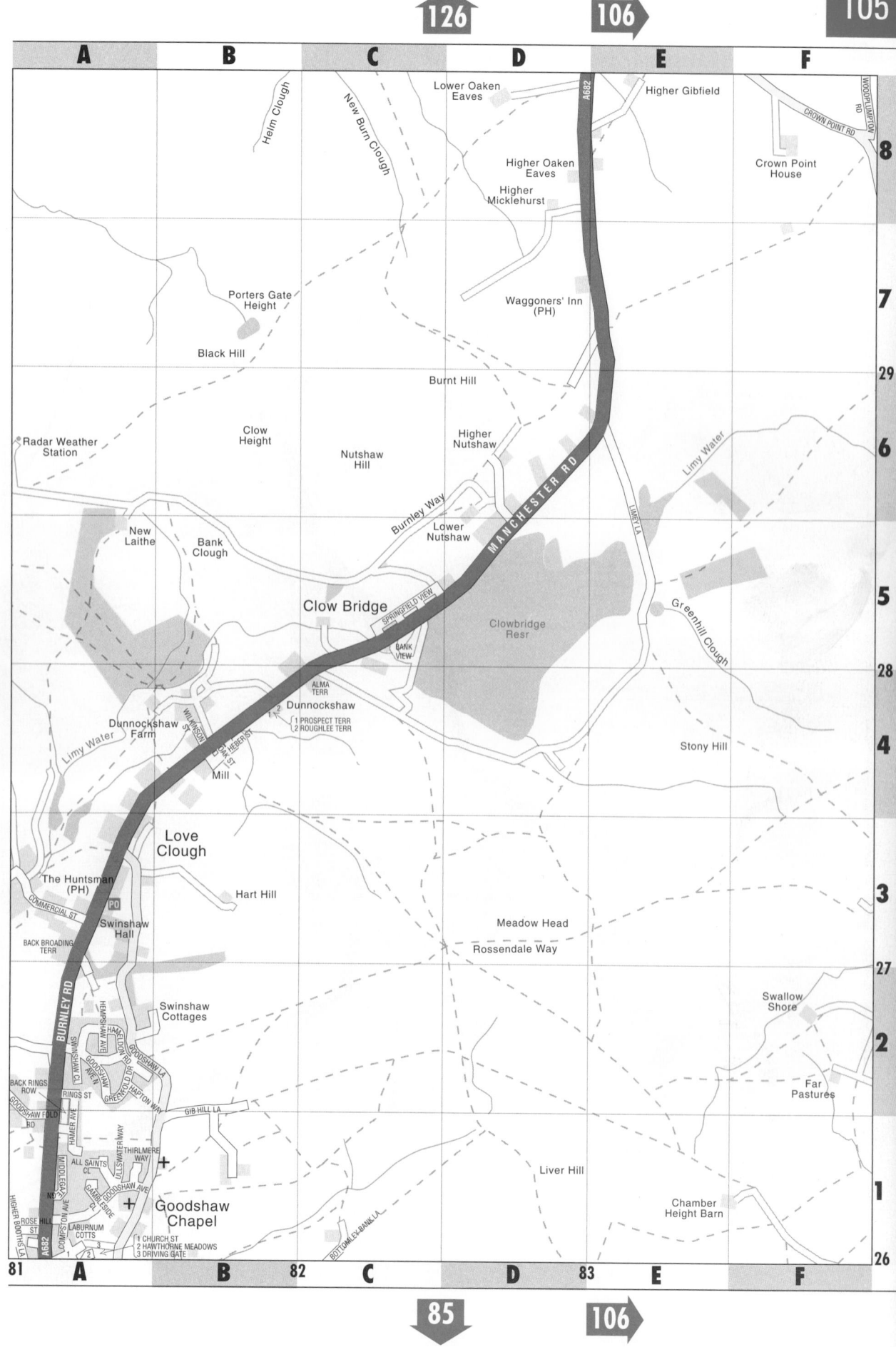

Lower Oaken Eaves
Higher Gibfield
Crown Point House
WOODTOP LUMP TOP
CROWN POINT RD
A682
Higher Oaken Eaves
Higher Micklehurst
Waggoners' Inn (PH)
Helm Clough
New Burn Clough
Porters Gate Height
Black Hill
Burnt Hill
Clow Height
Nutshaw Hill
Higher Nutshaw
MANCHESTER RD
Limy Water
Radar Weather Station
Burnley Way
Lower Nutshaw
LIMY LA
New Laithe
Bank Clough
Clow Bridge
SPRINGFIELD VIEW
BANK VIEW
Clowbridge Resr
Greenhill Clough
ALMA TERR
Dunnockshaw
1 PROSPECT TERR
2 ROUGHLEE TERR
Stony Hill
Dunnockshaw Farm
WM WINSON ST
OAK ST
JOHN HEBER ST
Limy Water
Mill
Love Clough
Hart Hill
Meadow Head
Rossendale Way
Swallow Shore
The Huntsman (PH)
COMMERCIAL ST
PO
Swinshaw Hall
BACK BROADING TERR
BURNLEY RD
Swinshaw Cottages
Far Pastures
HEMPSHAW AVE
GOODSHAW AVE
HASELDON CL DR
GREENFIELD CL DR
HAPTON WAY
BACK RINGS ROW
RINGS ST
GOODSHAW FOLD RD
HAMER AVE
GIB HILL LA
Liver Hill
MIDDLESIDE CL
GOODSHAW AVE
ALL SAINTS CL
ULLSWATER WAY
THIRLMERE WAY
GARNET ESIDE
Chamber Height Barn
HIGHER BOOTHS LA
ROSE HILL ST
A682
COMPSTON AVE
LABURNUM COTTS
Goodshaw Chapel
1 CHURCH ST
2 HAWTHORNE MEADOWS
3 DRIVING GATE
BOTTOMLEY BANK LA

← 105
127

A B C D E F

8

Walk Mill

Burnley Way

Sagar Fold

RUSH HEY BANK

Everage Clough

Dixon Hill

HANE ROW

Towneley Arms (PH)

Buck Clough

Dyneley Knoll

Crown Point

CROWN POINT RD

Spring Gardens

Dyneley Farm

Burnley Way

LONGFIELD TERR

Co-operative Bldgs

PH

PO

A646

BURNLEY RD

River Calder

Calf Banks Wood

HONEY HOLME LA

A646

29

7

BACUP RD

STONE HOUSE FOLD

P

6

Easden Clough

Dodbottom Wood

Stone House Edge

Long Shay

Quarry

5

28

White Hill

Cow Side

Black Clough

4

Red Moss

B6238

Deerplay Moor

BURNLEY RD

Deerplay Hill Syke

Bent Hill Rough

Bent Hill

Deerplay Hill

3

27

Windy Bank

Clough Bottom Resr

Clough Bottom

BURNLEY RD

Mon

Irwell Spring

2

Near Pastures

BURNLEY RD E

Whitewell Brook

Croft Farm

Deerplay Inn (PH)

Rossendale Way

Irwell Valley Way

A671

BACUP OLD RD

1

GRAVER WEIR TERR

TERRA COTTA BLDGS

Meadows Farm

Nabb Farm

Clifton

HARROW STILES LA

Height End

EAST BANK

B6238

26

84 A B 85 C D 86 E F

← 105
86 ↓

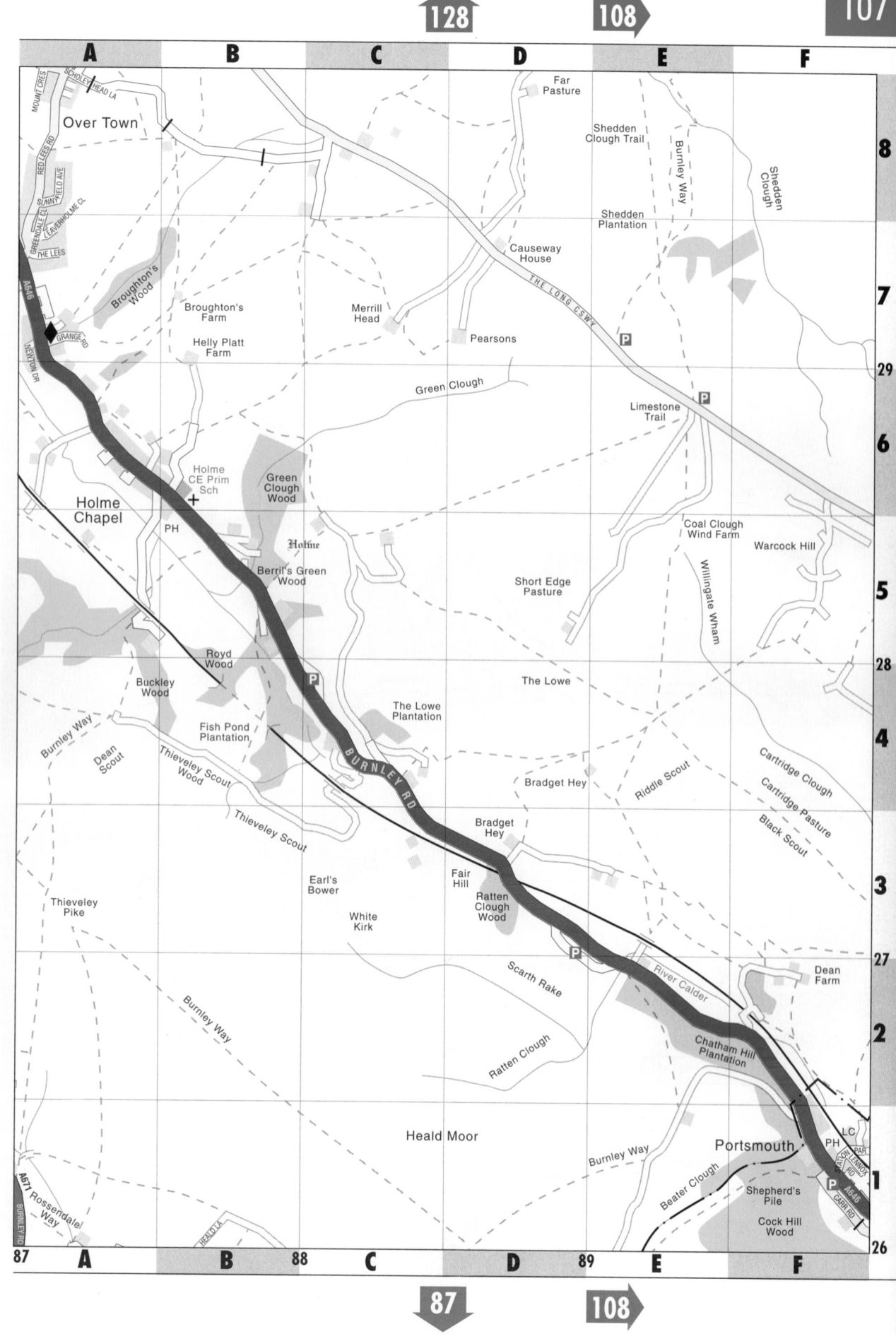

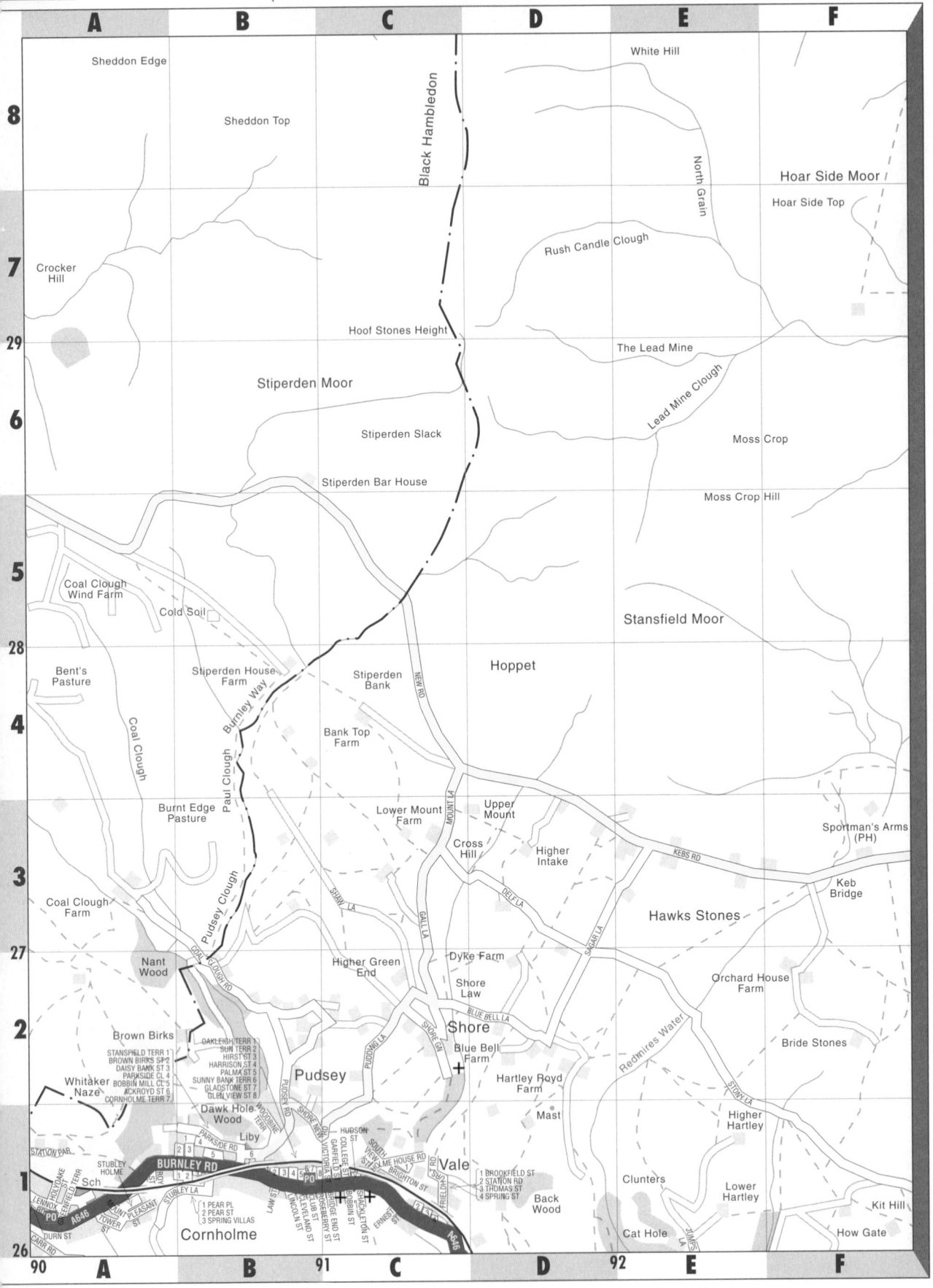

Sheddon Edge

Sheddon Top

Black Hambledon

White Hill

North Grain

Hoar Side Moor

Hoar Side Top

Crocker Hill

Rush Candle Clough

Hoof Stones Height

The Lead Mine

Stiperden Moor

Lead Mine Clough

Moss Crop

Stiperden Slack

Stiperden Bar House

Moss Crop Hill

Coal Clough Wind Farm

Cold Soil

Stansfield Moor

Bent's Pasture

Stiperden House Farm

Stiperden Bank

Hoppet

Burnley Way

NEW RD

Coal Clough

Bank Top Farm

Paul Clough

Burnt Edge Pasture

Lower Mount Farm

Upper Mount

MOUNT LA

Sportman's Arms (PH)

Cross Hill

Higher Intake

KEBS RD

Keb Bridge

Coal Clough Farm

Pudsey Clough

SHAW LA

GALL LA

DELF LA

Hawks Stones

SUGAR LA

Nant Wood

COAL CLOUGH RD

Higher Green End

DyKe Farm

Shore Law

Orchard House Farm

Redmires Water

Brown Birks

OAKLEIGH TERR 1
SUN TERR 2
HIRST ST 3
HARRISON ST 4
PALMA ST 5
SUNNY BANK TERR 6
GLADSTONE ST 7
GLEN VIEW ST 8

BLUE BELL LA

Shore

Bride Stones

STANSFIELD TERR 1
BROWN BIRKS SF 2
DAISY BANK ST 3
PARKSIDE CL 4
BOBBIN MILL CL 5
ACKROYD ST 6
CORNHOLME TERR 7

PUDDING LA

SHORE GN

Blue Bell Farm

STONY LA

Whitaker Naze

Pudsey

Hartley Royd Farm

Higher Hartley

Dawk Hole Wood

Liby

PUDSEY RD

SHORE RD

Mast

HUDSON ST

SOUTH VIEW

CALDERDALE WAY

GARFIELD ST

SME HOUSE RD

STATION PAR

PARKSIDE RD

WOODBINE TERR

BURNLEY RD

STUBLEY HOLME

Sch

HOLDAKE ST

LENNOX ST

PO

DURN ST

A646

CARR RD

MOUNT PLEASANT

STUBLEY LA

1 PEAR PL
2 PEAR ST
3 SPRING VILLAS

LAW ST

LINCOLN ST

CLEVELAND ST

CLUB ST

PO

GREEN END ST

BIRBIN ST

SHACKLETON ST

VICTORIA ST

ERNEST ST

BRIGHTON ST

Vale

1 BROOKFIELD ST
2 STANON RD
3 THOMAS ST
4 SPRING ST

SOUTHROYD

A646

Cornholme

Back Wood

Clunters

Lower Hartley

Kit Hill

Cat Hole

JUMPS

How Gate

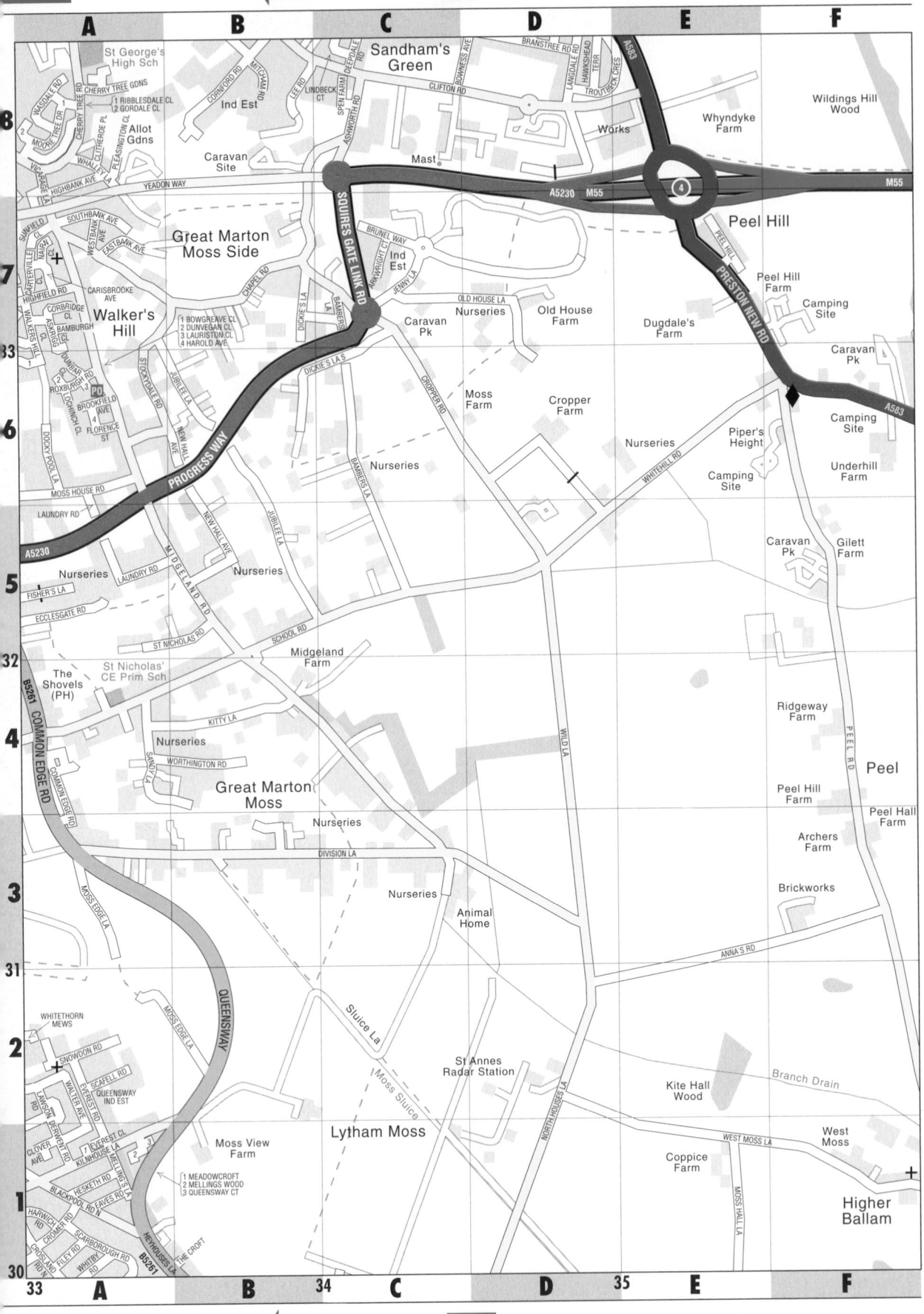

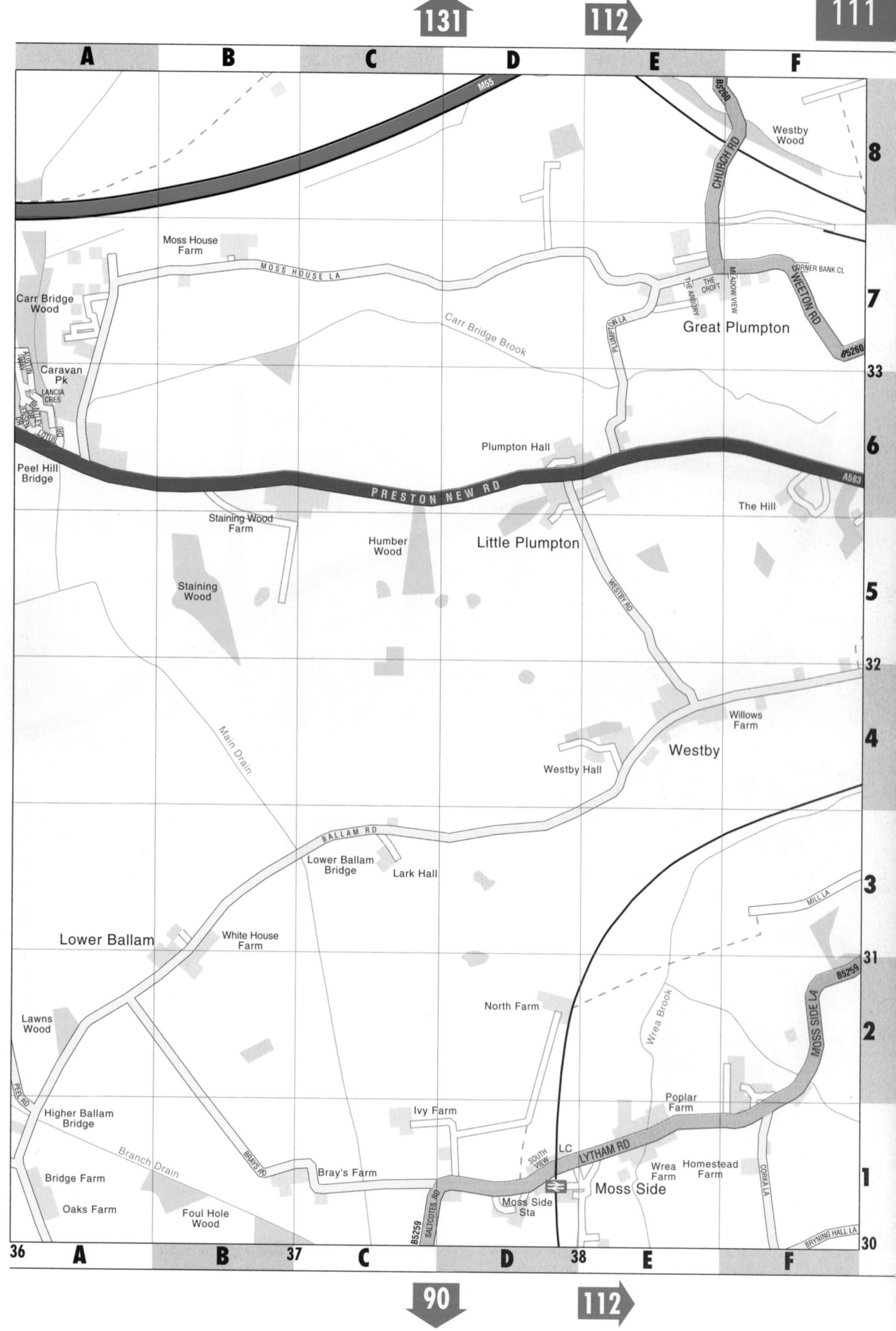

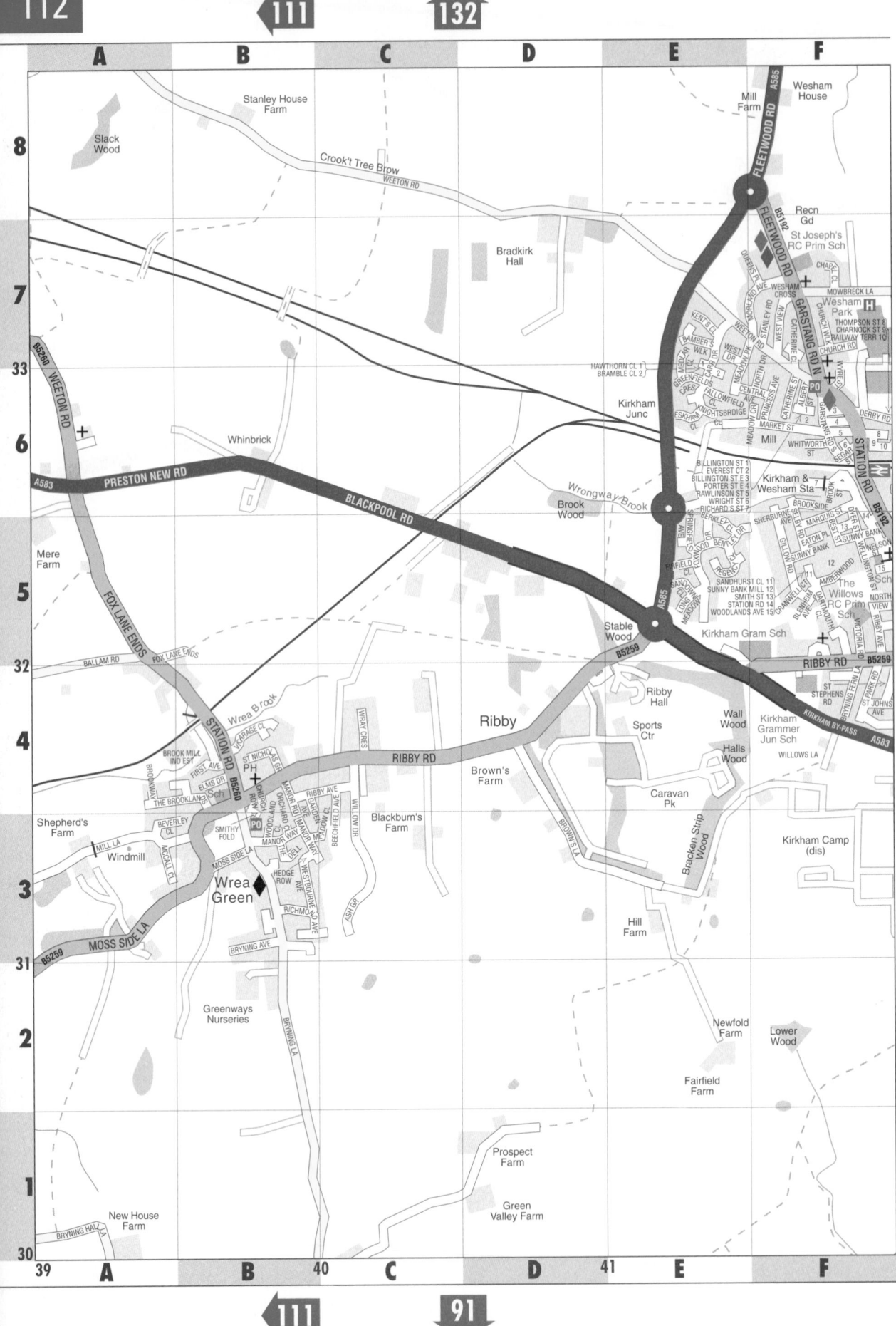

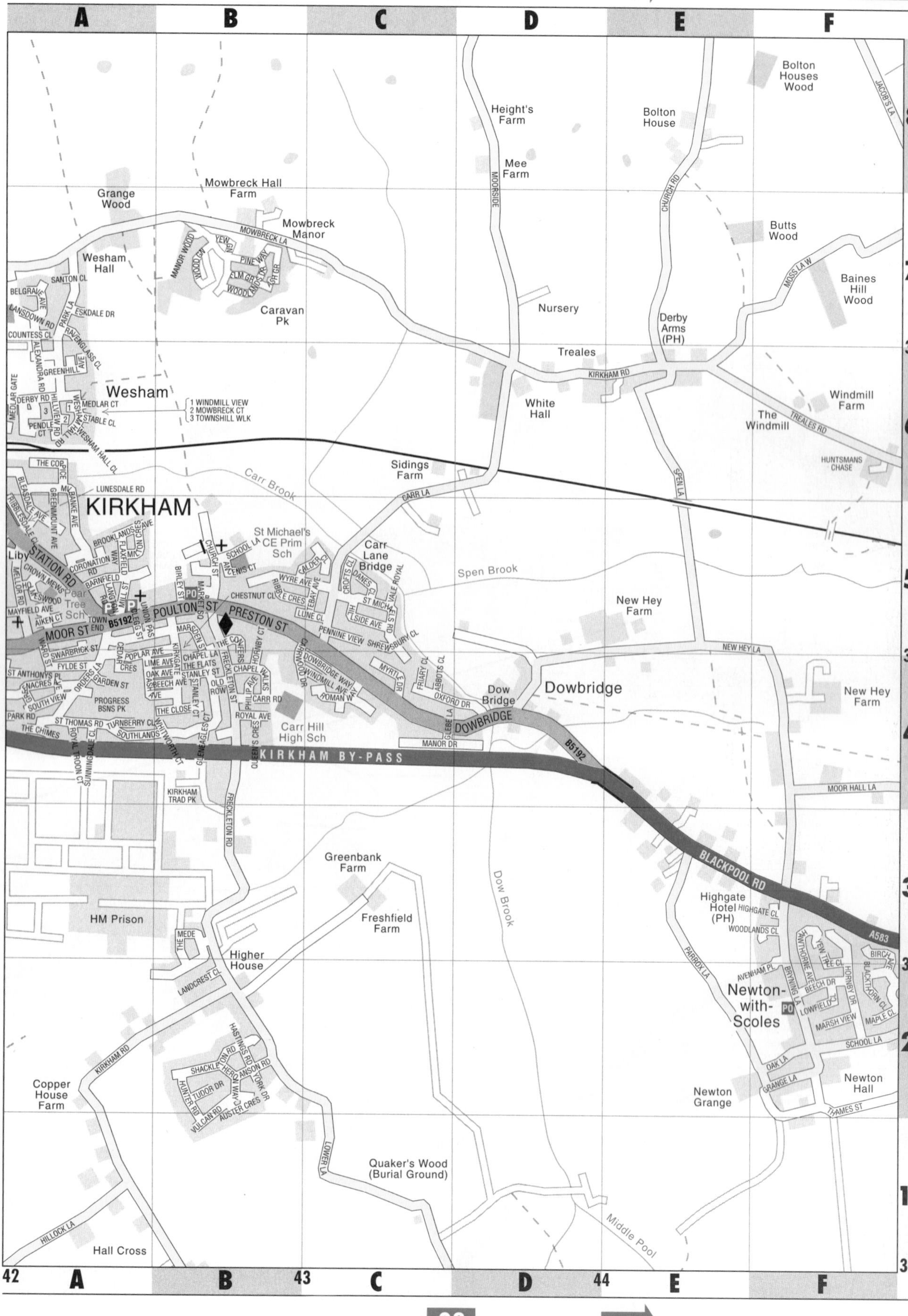

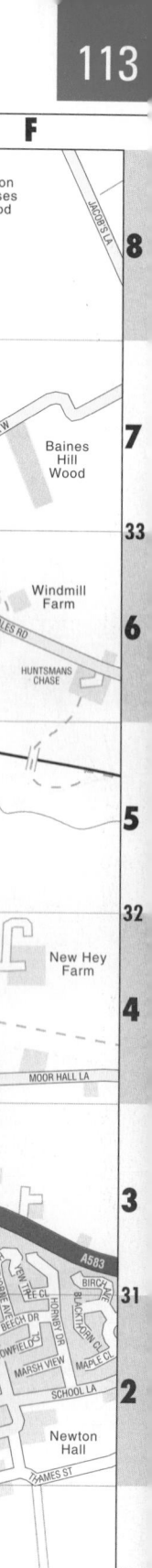

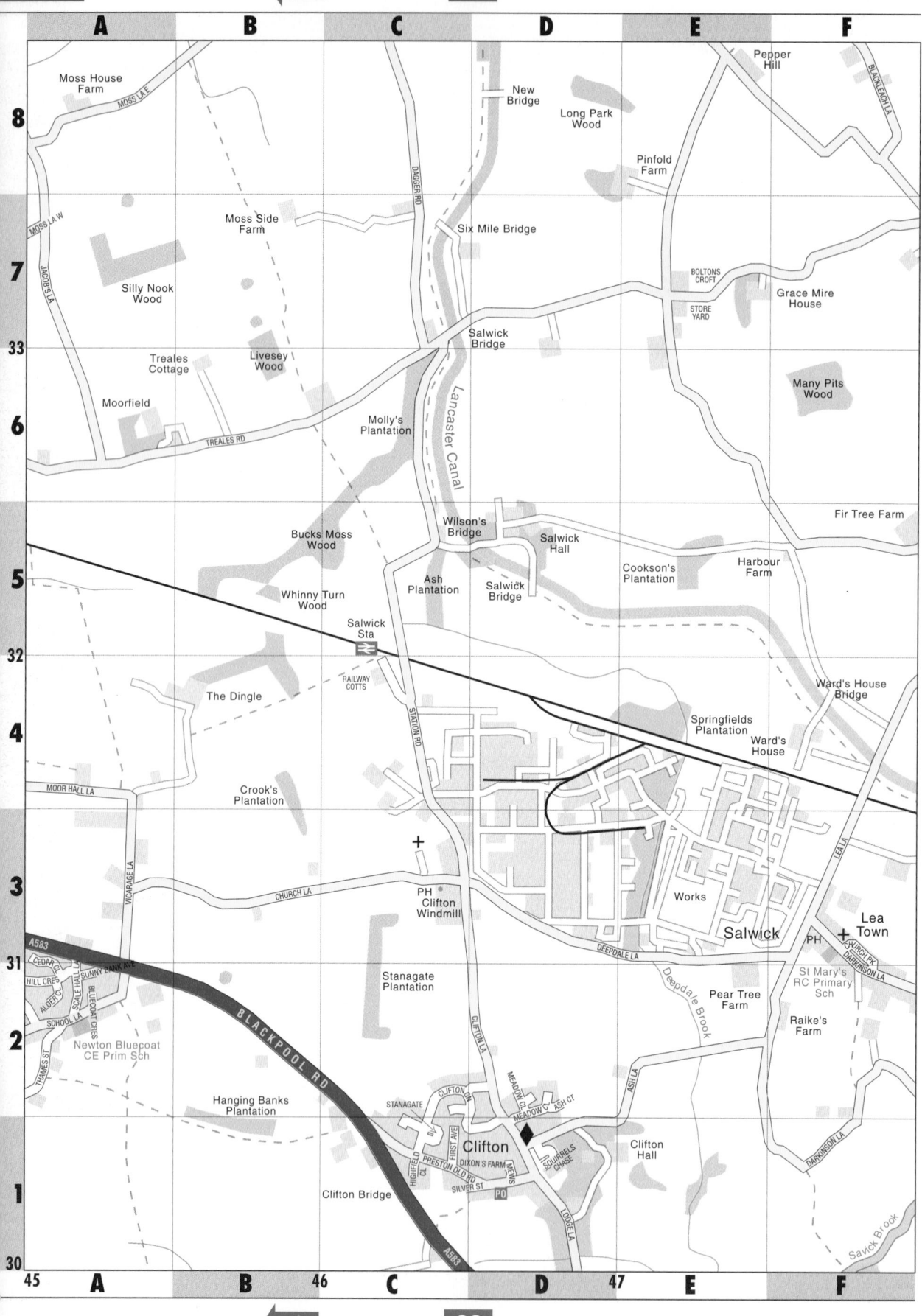

A **B** **C** **D** **E** **F**

8

Moss House Farm

MOSS LA E

New Bridge

Long Park Wood

Pepper Hill

BLACKLEACH LA

MOSS LA W

JACOB'S LA

7

Moss Side Farm

Silly Nook Wood

DAGGER RD

Six Mile Bridge

Pinfold Farm

BOLTONS CROFT

Grace Mire House

STORE YARD

33

Treales Cottage

Livesey Wood

Salwick Bridge

Many Pits Wood

6

Moorfield

TREALES RD

Molly's Plantation

Lancaster Canal

5

Bucks Moss Wood

Whinny Turn Wood

Wilson's Bridge

Salwick Hall

Ash Plantation

Salwick Bridge

Cookson's Plantation

Harbour Farm

Fir Tree Farm

Salwick Sta

32

The Dingle

RAILWAY COTTS

STATION RD

Ward's House Bridge

4

MOOR HALL LA

Crook's Plantation

Springfields Plantation

Ward's House

VICARAGE LA

3

CHURCH LA

PH Clifton Windmill

Works

Salwick

LEA LA

Lea Town

CHURCH PK

PH

DARKINSON LA

31

A583

CEDAR

HILL CRES

ALDER

SCHOOL LA

FIFTH

SUNNY BANK AVE

BLUECOAT CRES

Stanagate Plantation

Deepdale Brook

Pear Tree Farm

St Mary's RC Primary Sch

Raike's Farm

2

THAMES ST

Newton Bluecoat CE Prim Sch

BLACKPOOL RD

CLIFTON LA

Hanging Banks Plantation

STANAGATE

CLIFTON

MEADOW LA

MEADOW C

ASH CT

ASH LA

Clifton Hall

1

Clifton Bridge

HIGHFIELD CL

PRESTON OLD RD

SILVER ST

Clifton

DIXON'S FARM

SKEW BRIDGE

SQUIRRELS CHASE

PO

LODGE LA

A583

Savick Brook

30

45 **A** **B** **46** **C** **D** **47** **E** **F**

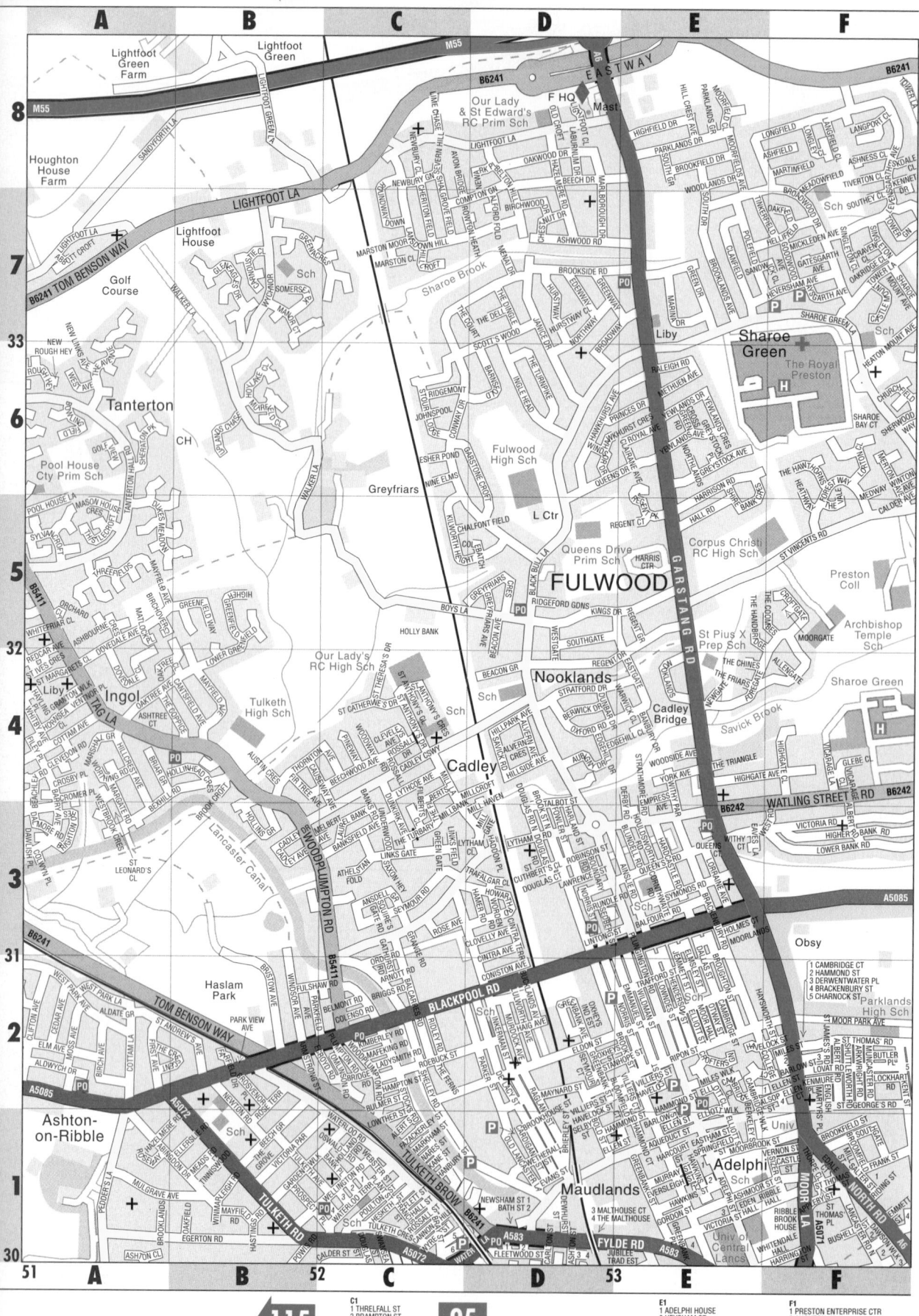

C1
1 THRELFALL ST
2 BRAMPTON ST
3 ELTON ST
4 BRUNSWICK PL
5 PECHELL ST
6 BLANCHE ST

E1
1 ADELPHI HOUSE
2 HEYSHAM ST
3 DERWENT HALL
4 TOWN BROOK HOUSE

F1
1 PRESTON ENTERPRISE CTR
2 AUGHTON WLK
3 BECKETT CT
4 HANOVER ST

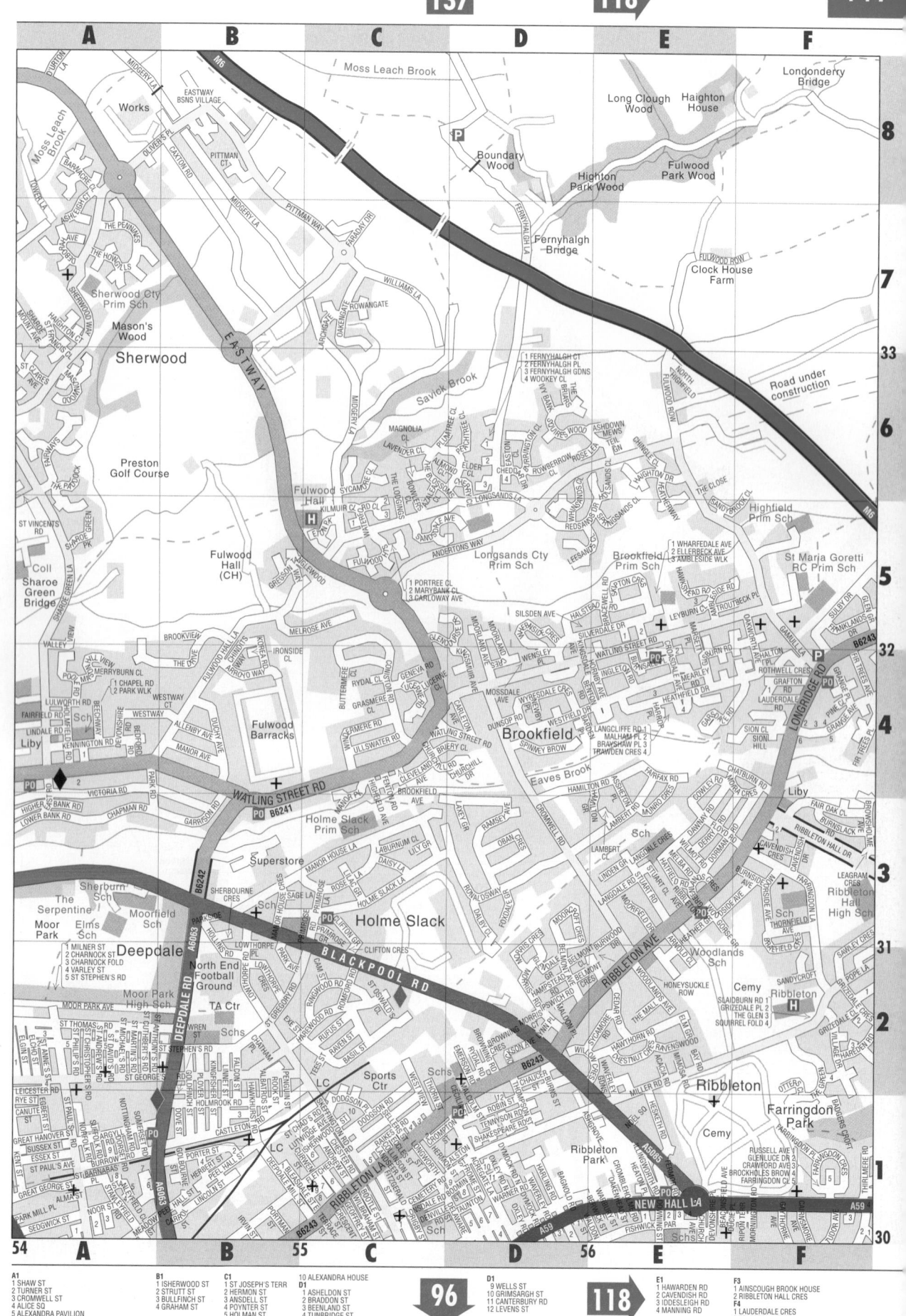

A1
1 SHAW ST
2 TURNER ST
3 CROMWELL ST
4 ALICE SQ
5 ALEXANDRA PAVILION
6 ELIZABETH SQ
7 ALBERT TERR
8 EDWARD SQ
9 STAFFORD RD

B1
1 ISHERWOOD ST
2 STRUTT ST
3 BULLFINCH ST
4 GRAHAM ST

C1
1 ST JOSEPH'S TERR
2 HERMON ST
3 ANSDELL ST
4 POYNTER ST
5 HOLMAN ST
6 GILLETT ST
7 CURWEN ST
8 WIGNALL ST
9 ST LUKE'S PL

10 ALEXANDRA HOUSE
D1
1 ASHELDON ST
2 BRADDON ST
3 BEENLAND ST
4 TUNBRIDGE ST
5 SALISBURY ST
6 CALVERLEY ST
7 TUNBRIDGE PL
8 TRURO PL

D1
9 WELLS ST
10 GRIMSARGH ST
11 CANTERBURY RD
12 LEVENS ST

E1
1 HAWARDEN RD
2 CAVENDISH RD
3 IDDESLEIGH RD
4 MANNING RD

F3
1 AINSCOUGH BROOK HOUSE
2 RIBBLETON HALL CRES
F4
1 LAUDERDALE CRES
2 EDLESTON LODGE
3 LEICESTER LODGE
4 HOLLAND LODGE
5 ROTHWELL LODGE
6 SHERBORNE LODGE

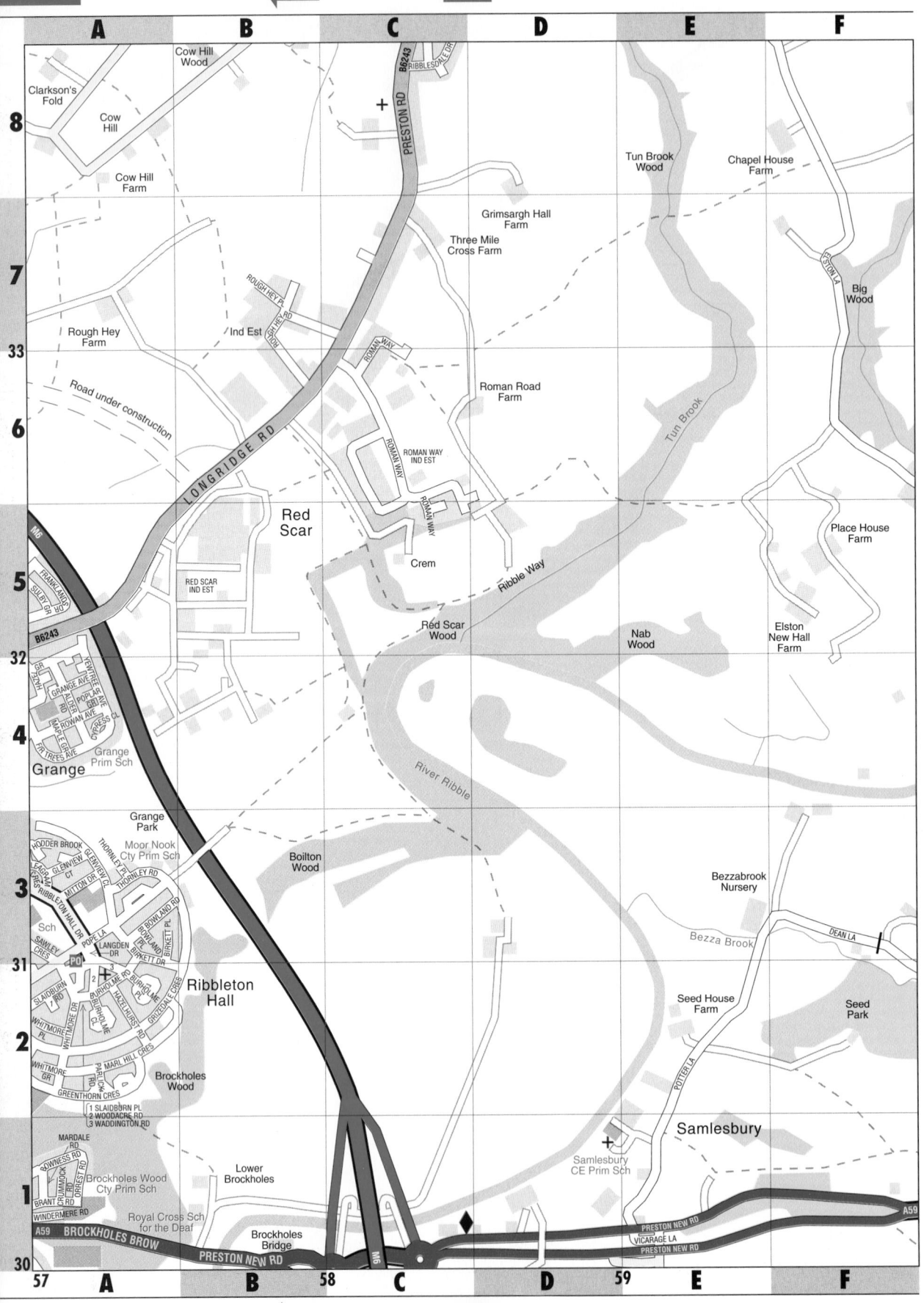

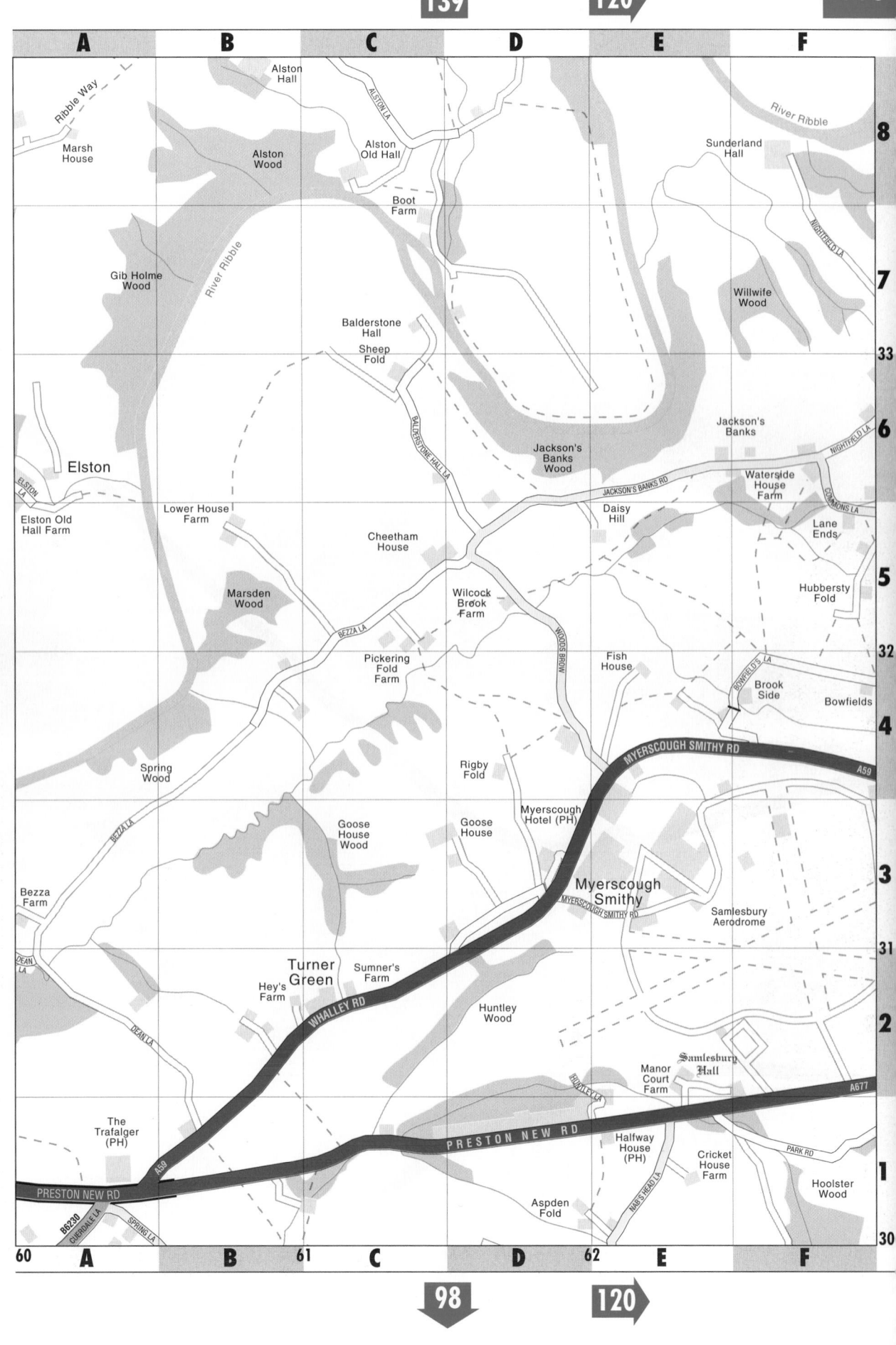

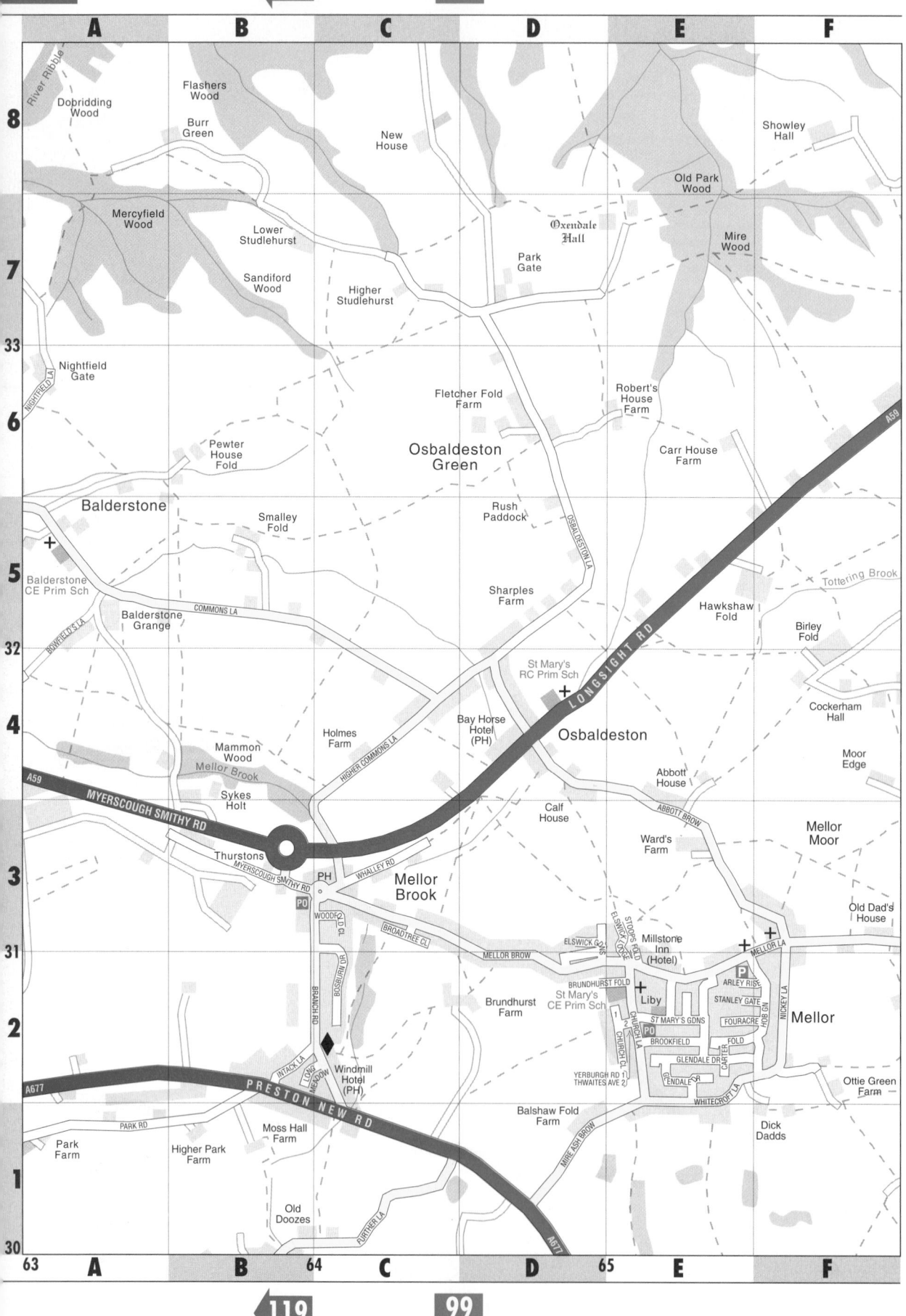

A   B   C   D   E   F

8

River Ribble

Dobridding Wood

Flashers Wood

Burr Green

New House

Showley Hall

Mercyfield Wood

Lower Studlehurst

Old Park Wood

7

Sandiford Wood

Higher Studlehurst

Park Gate

Oxendale Hall

Mire Wood

33

Nightfield Gate

Fletcher Fold Farm

Robert's House Farm

6

Pewter House Fold

Osbaldeston Green

Carr House Farm

A59

Balderstone

Smalley Fold

Rush Paddock

Tottering Brook

5

Balderstone CE Prim Sch

Sharples Farm

Hawkshaw Fold

Birley Fold

Nightfield La

Commons La

Balderstone Grange

32

Bowefield's La

St Mary's RC Prim Sch

Cockerham Hall

4

Mammon Wood

Holmes Farm

Bay Horse Hotel (PH)

Osbaldeston

Abbott House

Moor Edge

Mellor Brook

Higher Commons La

Osbaldeston La

Longsight Rd

Abbott Brow

Ward's Farm

Mellor Moor

Sykes Holt

Calf House

A59

Myerscough Smithy Rd

3

Thurstons

Myerscough Smithy Rd

Whalley Rd

Mellor Brook

Old Dad's House

PH

PO

Woodfd Cl

Broadtree Cl

Mellor Brow

Elswick Gdns

Stoops Fold

Millstone Inn (Hotel)

Arley Rise

Mellor La

Nickey La

31

Bosburn Dr

Brownhill Rd

Brundhurst Fold

St Mary's CE Prim Sch

Liby

P

Stanley Gate

Fouracre Fold

Mellor

2

Brundhurst Farm

St Mary's Gdns

PO

Brookfield

Glendale Dr

Carter Fold

Hob Gn

Intack La

Low Meadow

Windmill Hotel (PH)

Church La

Church Cl

Yerburgh Rd 1

Thwaites Ave 2

Glendale Cr

Whitecroft La

Ottie Green Farm

A677

Park Rd

Preston New Rd

Balshaw Fold Farm

Dick Dadds

1

Park Farm

Higher Park Farm

Moss Hall Farm

Mire Ash Brow

A677

30

Old Doozes

Further La

A **B** **C** **D** **E** **F**

8

Dewhurst House

Langho Colony

RIBCHESTER RD

White Holme

Eden Holme

Oakes Bridge

OAKS BAR

Oaks Farm

ALBANY DR

Copster Green

7

Brook Cottage

LONGSIGHT RD

OAKS BROW

Low Farm

Clayton-Le-Dale

LOVELY HALL LA

Lovely Hall

Ashes Farm

Mire Fold

Nook House

33

Royal Oak Inn (PH)

Salesbury CE Prim Sch

1 CHURCH VIEW
2 HAZELMOOR

THE HAZELS

VICARAGE LA

DURHAM RD

SHETLAND

BERKSHIRE DR

SHROPSHIRE CL

ELY CL

A666

PETER'S CROFT

6

SHOWLEY RD

Harwood Fold

PH

PO

ST PETER'S CL

RYDER ST

RIBCHESTER RD

Clayton Hey Fold Farm

Salesbury

SHOWLEY CT

BEECH CL

MAPLE CL

KNOWSLEY RD W

COMMERSET AVE

THE HAWTHORNS

GROSVENOR LODGE

WHALLEY RD

VALLEY CL

B6245

CH
FAIRWAYS CT

HOLLOWHEAD LA

5

Showley Fold

Tottering Brook

Blue Slate Farm

Midge Hall

Showley Brook

Ramsgreave Wood

Bottoms Farm

KNOWSLEY RD

BROOKLYN RD

WOODCREST

MAYPOR CRES

BEAVER CL

HOLLOWHEAD AVE

HOLLOWHEAD CL

WILESHIRE BANKS

32

Hagg's Hall

Mountain Ash Farm

CLIFTON GR

STATION CL

Wardfall

SACCARY LA

Cunliffe Moss Farm

Ramsgreave Hall Farm

Ramsgreave and Wilpshire Sta

RAMSGREAVE RD

ISLE OF MAN

WAVERLEY AVE

PARIS

WALDEN CL

4

PRIMROSE WLK

Primrose Hill

ZECHARIAH BROW

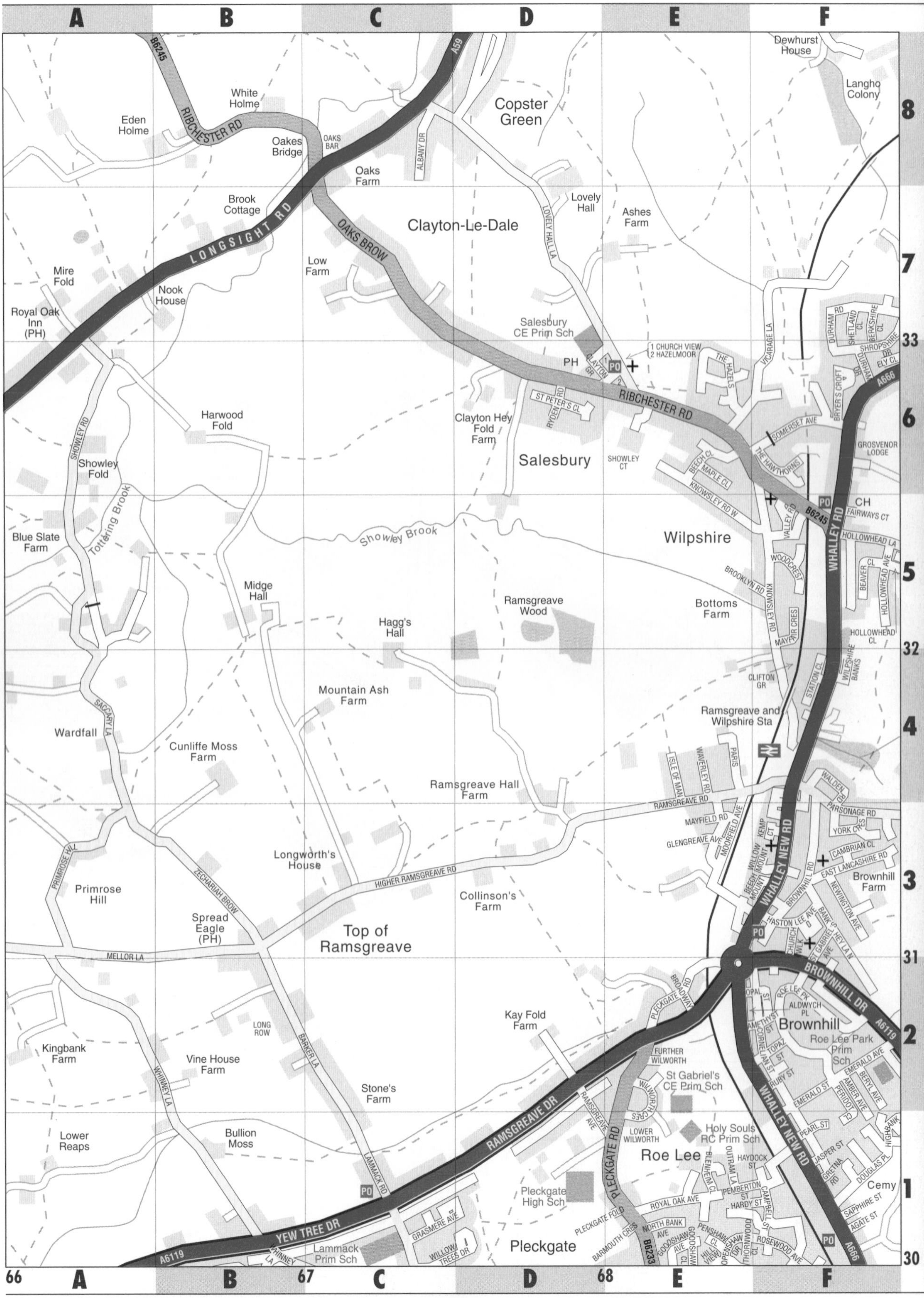

Longworth's House

HIGHER RAMSGREAVE RD

Collinson's Farm

MAYFIELD RD

GLENGREAVE AVE

MOORFIELD AVE

KEMP ST

WILLOW

BEECH

PARSONAGE RD

YORK CRES

EAST LANCASHIRE RD

CAMBRIAN CL

Brownhill Farm

NEWINGTON AVE

3

Spread Eagle (PH)

MELLOR LA

BARKER LA

Top of Ramsgreave

PLECKGATE RD

HASTEN LEE AVE

WHALLEY NEW RD

CHURCH

BANK OF HEYS LA

PO

31

LONG ROW

Kay Fold Farm

BROADWAY

OLD WAY

BROWNHILL DR

A6119

Brownhill

Kingbank Farm

Vine House Farm

WHINNEY LA

FURTHER WILWORTH

St Gabriel's CE Prim Sch

WILWORTH CRES

Holy Souls RC Prim Sch

LOWER WILWORTH

Roe Lee Park Prim Sch

OPAL

ALDWYCH PL

AMETHYST

OPAL ST

RUBY ST

EMERALD AVE

EMERALD ST

AMBER ST

PERIDOT

ROE LEE PK

2

Lower Reaps

Bullion Moss

Stone's Farm

LAMMACK RD

RAMSGREAVE DR

Roe Lee

BLENHEIM

OUTRAM LA

BARMOUTH CRES

ROYAL OAK AVE

NORTH BANK AVE

HAYDOCK

PEMBERTON

HARDY ST

CAMPBELL ST

PEARL ST

JASPER ST

GRETNA

DOUGLAS PL

HIGH BANK

SAPPHIRE ST

AGATE ST

Cemy

1

YEW TREE DR

A6119

CHINNEY

Lammack Prim Sch

GRASMERE AVE

WILLOW TREES DR

Pleckgate High Sch

Pleckgate

PLECKGATE FOLD

PENSHAW

GOODSHAW CL

THORNWOOD

ROSEWOOD AVE

B6233

PO

A666

30

66 **A** 67 **B** **C** 68 **D** **E** **F**

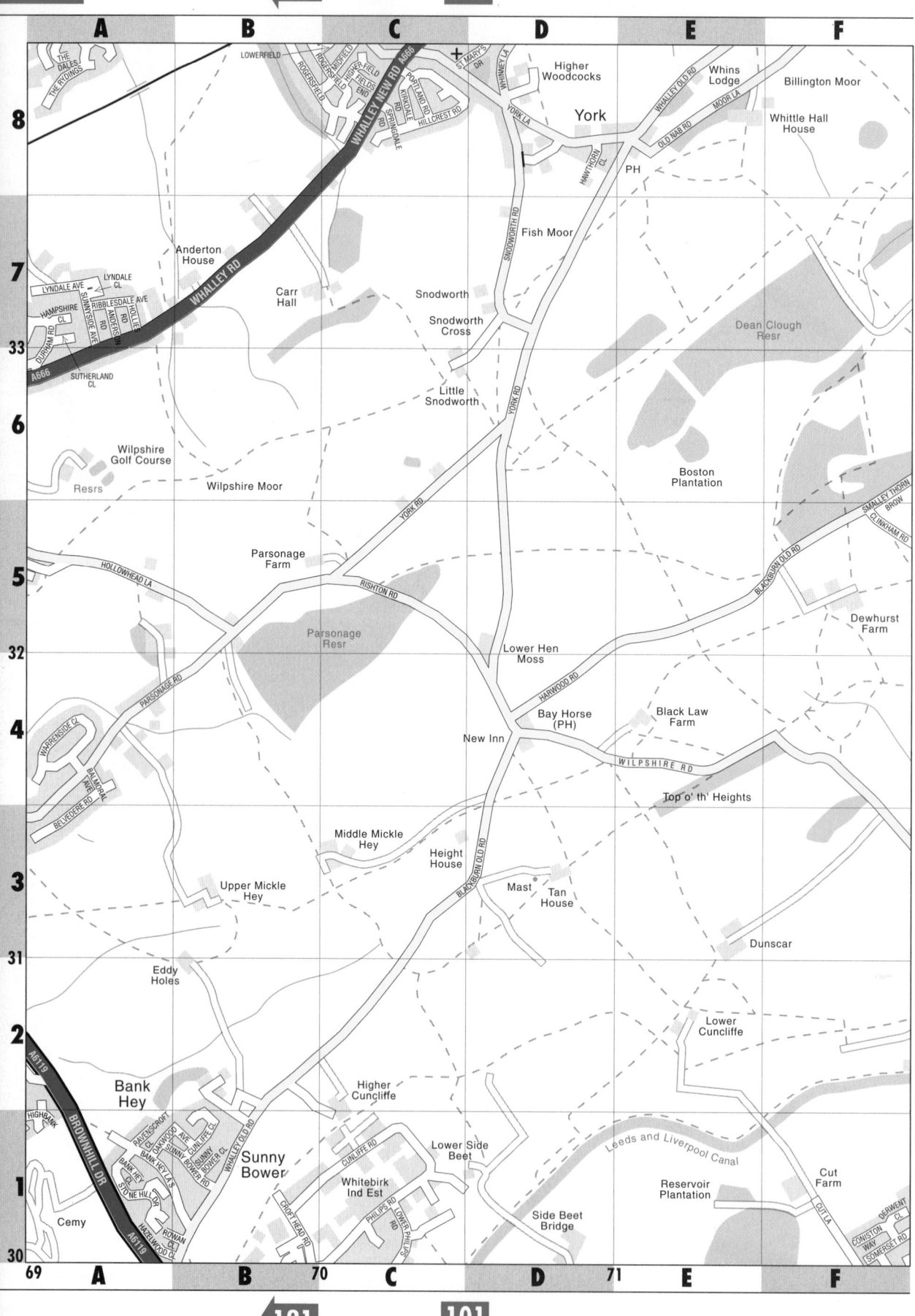

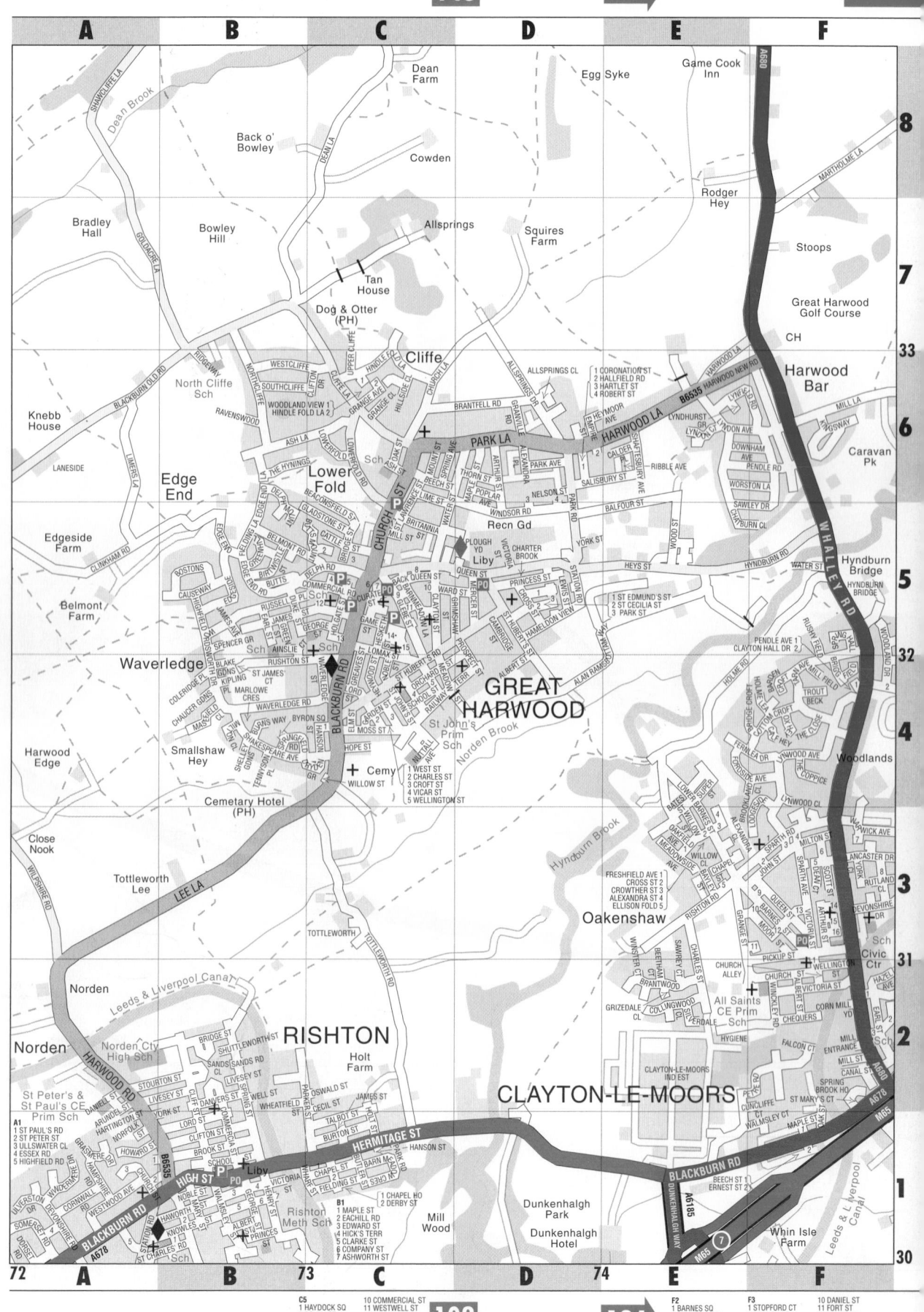

CH Great Harwood Golf Course
Harwood Bar
Caravan Pk
Hyndburn Bridge

GREAT HARWOOD

Woodlands

Oakenshaw

CLAYTON-LE-MOORS

RISHTON

Norden

Waverledge

Lower Fold

Cliffe

C5
1 HAYDOCK SQ
2 DELPH CT
3 SOUTH VIEW
4 BRIDGE ST
5 EDWARD ST
6 TOWN HALL SQ
7 TOWN HALL ST
8 JOINERS ALLEY
9 LOYND ST
10 COMMERCIAL ST
11 WESTWELL ST
12 KING ST
13 NOWELL ST
14 WALMSLEY ST
15 SEGAR ST

F2
1 BARNES SQ
2 GRIMSHAW ST
3 TALBOT AVE
4 KING ST

F3
1 STOPFORD CT
2 BRANCH RD
3 FRANCIS ST
4 ANN ST
5 JACKSON ST
6 DRYDEN ST
7 NORFOLK CL
8 GLOUCESTER AVE
9 ALMA ST
10 DANIEL ST
11 FORT ST
12 JAMES ST
13 GEORGE ST
14 NEW CHURCH CL
15 BACK ARTHUR ST
16 MERCER ST

A1
1 ST PAUL'S RD
2 ST PETER ST
3 ULLSWATER CL
4 ESSEX RD
5 HIGHFIELD RD

B1
1 MAPLE ST
2 EACHILL RD
3 EDWARD ST
4 HICK'S TERR
5 CLARKE ST
6 COMPANY ST
7 ASHWORTH ST

1 CHAPEL HO
2 DERBY ST

1 WEST ST
2 CHARLES ST
3 CROFT ST
4 VICAR ST
5 WELLINGTON ST

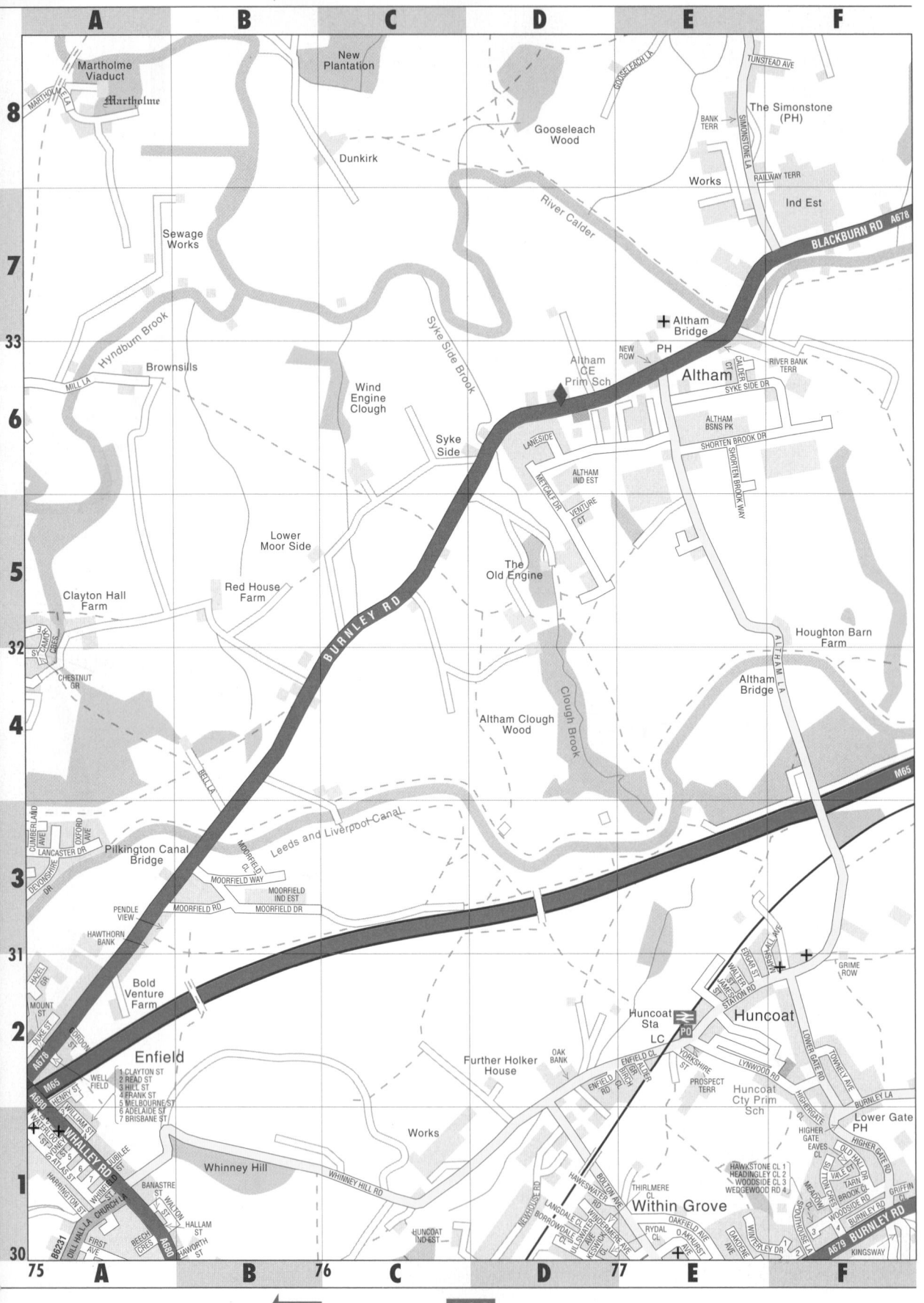

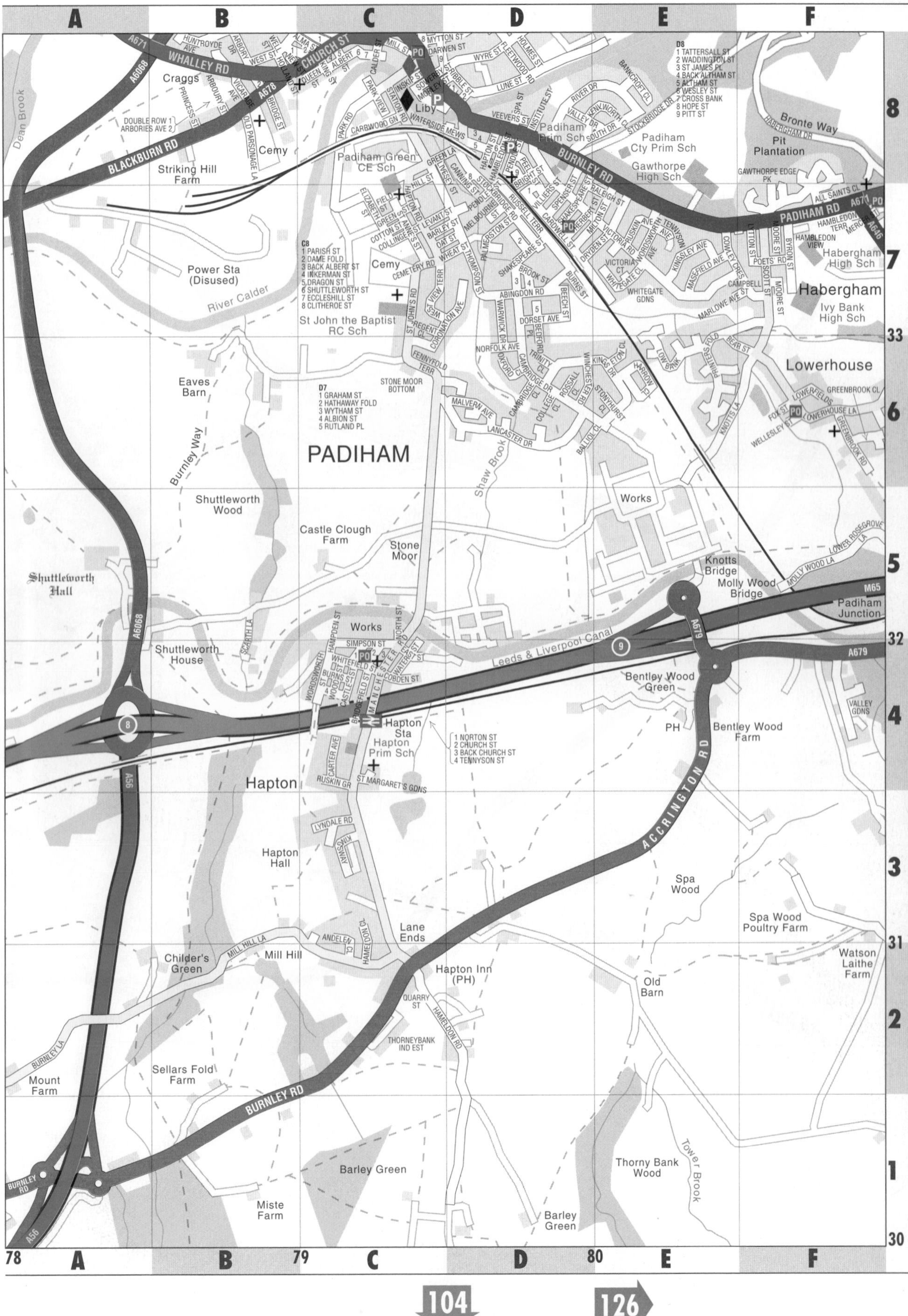

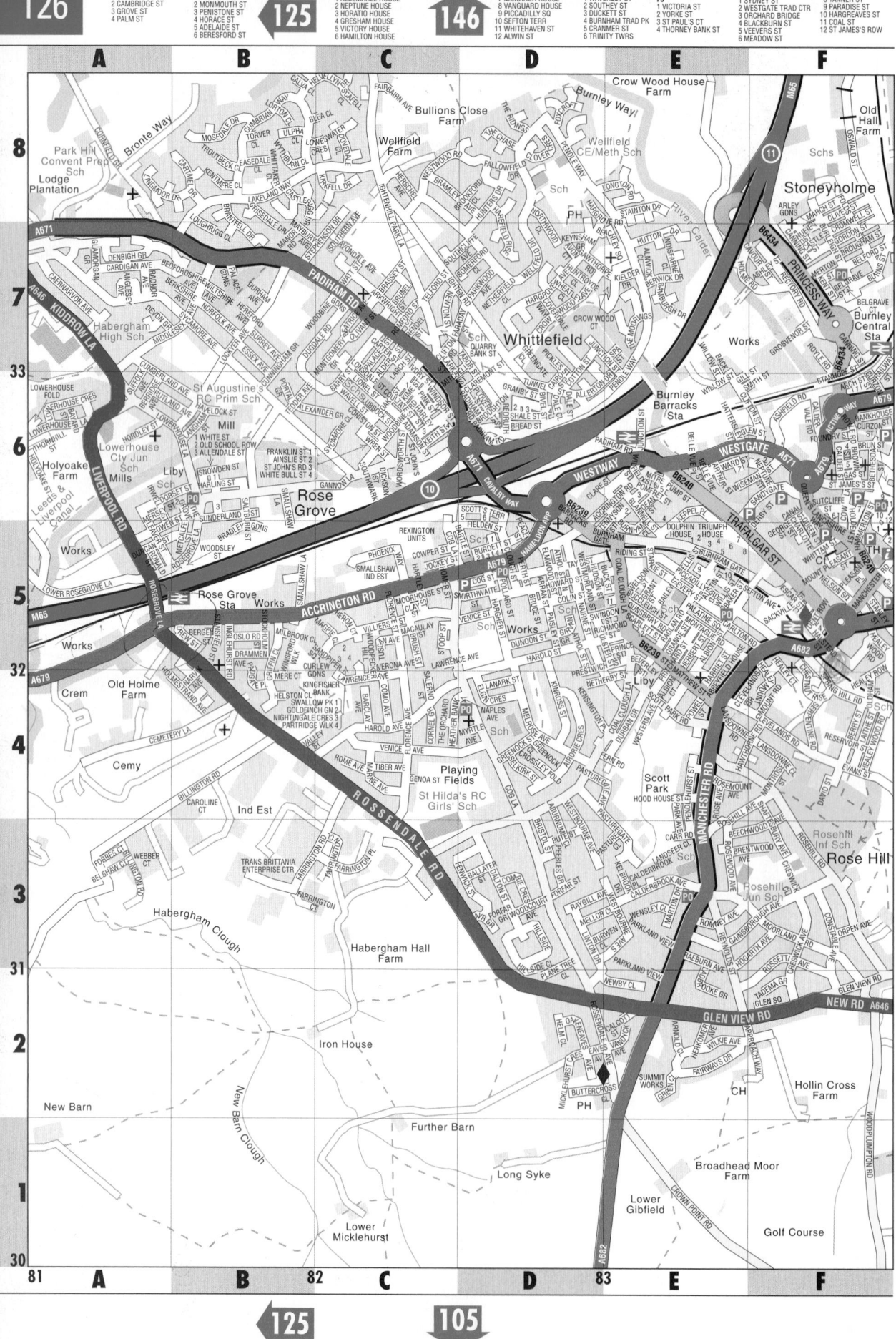

D5	D6	E5	E5	E6	7 HOPWOOD ST	F6	7 FREE TRADE ST
1 HARCOURT ST	1 PLOVER VIEW	1 ALBEMARLE HOUSE	7 MONARCH HOUSE	1 WAVERLEY ST		1 SYDNEY ST	8 TANNER ST
2 CAMBRIDGE ST	2 MONMOUTH ST	2 NEPTUNE HOUSE	8 VANGUARD HOUSE	2 SOUTHEY ST	F5	2 WESTGATE TRAD CTR	9 PARADISE ST
3 GROVE ST	3 PENISTONE ST	3 HORATIO HOUSE	9 PICCADILLY SQ	3 DUCKETT ST	1 VICTORIA ST	3 ORCHARD BRIDGE	10 HARGREAVES ST
4 PALM ST	4 HORACE ST	4 GRESHAM HOUSE	10 SEFTON TERR	4 BURNHAM TRAD PK	2 YORKE ST	4 BLACKBURN ST	11 COAL ST
	5 ADELAIDE ST	5 VICTORY HOUSE	11 WHITEHAVEN ST	5 CRANMER ST	3 ST PAUL'S CT	5 WEEVERS ST	12 ST JAMES'S ROW
	6 BERESFORD ST	6 HAMILTON HOUSE	12 ALWIN ST	6 TRINITY TWRS	4 THORNEY BANK ST	6 MEADOW ST	

← **125**   **146**

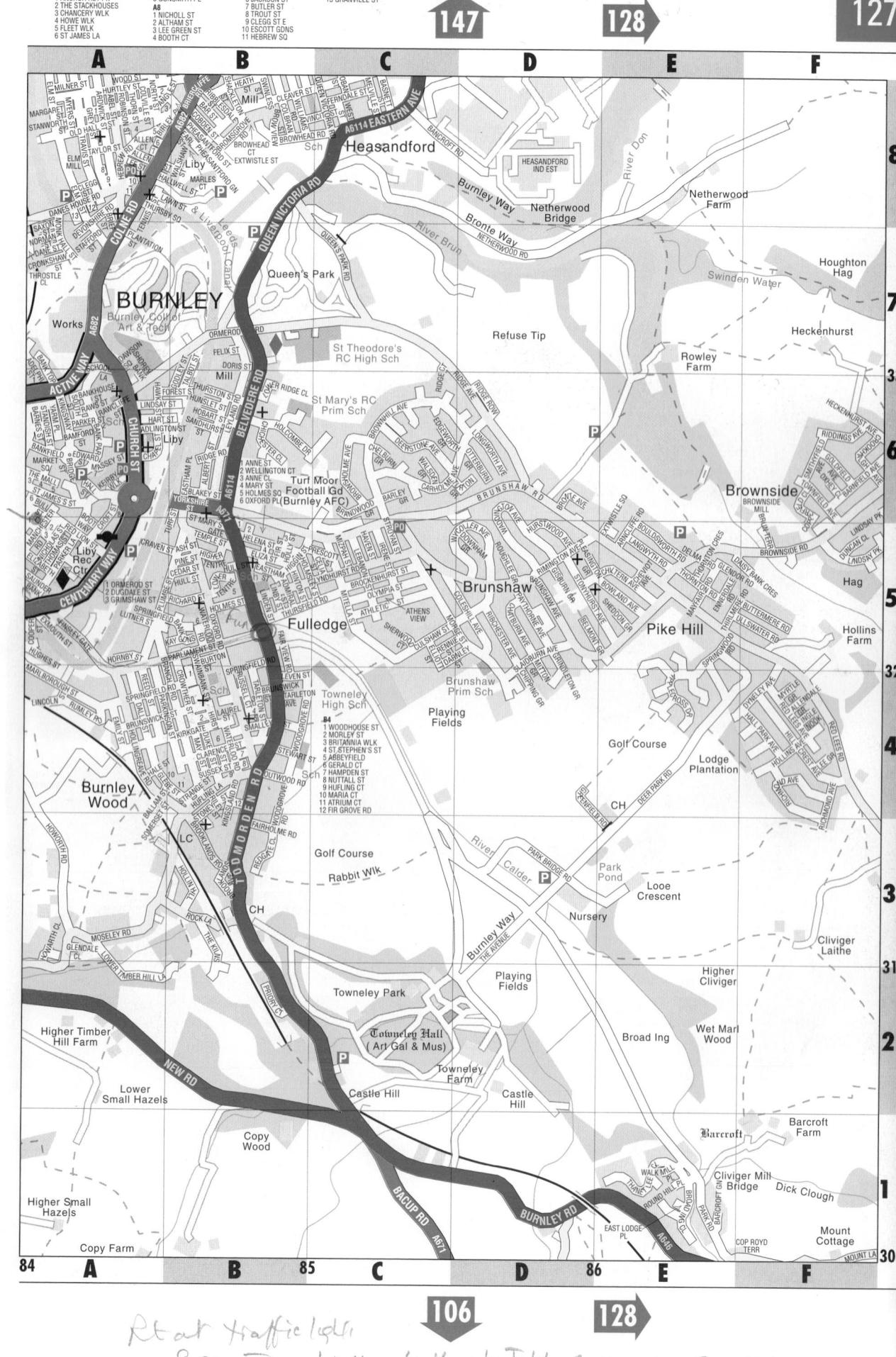

147

128

A6
1 ANCHOR RET PK
2 THE STACKHOUSES
3 CHANCERY WLK
4 HOWE WLK
5 FLEET WLK
6 ST JAMES LA

7 BURNLEY BSNS CTR
8 GUNSMITH PL

A8
1 NICHOLL ST
2 ALTHAM ST
3 LEE GREEN ST
4 BOOTH CT

5 BARRETT ST
6 JACKSON ST
7 BUTLER ST
8 TROUT ST
9 CLEGG ST E
10 ESCOTT GDNS
11 HEBREW SQ

12 BOND ST
13 GRANVILLE ST

Heasandford

Heasandford
IND EST

River Don

Netherwood
Farm

Netherwood

Burnley Way

Bronte Way

Netherwood
Bridge

River Brun

NETHERWOOD RD

Swinden Water

Houghton
Hag

Queen's Park

Refuse Tip

Rowley
Farm

Heckenhurst

BURNLEY

Burnley Coll of
Art & Tech

Works

St Theodore's
RC High Sch

St Mary's RC
Prim Sch

Brownside

Brownside
Mill

Turf Moor
Football Gd
(Burnley AFC)

Brunshaw

Pike Hill

Brownside Rd

Fulledge

Brunshaw
Prim Sch

Hollins
Farm

Hag

Townely
High Sch

B4
1 WOODHOUSE ST
2 MORLEY ST
3 BRITANNIA WLK
4 ST STEPHEN'S ST
5 ABBEYFIELD
6 GERALD CT
7 HAMPDEN ST
8 NUTTALL ST
9 HUFLING CT
10 MARIA CT
11 ATRIUM CT
12 FIR GROVE RD

Playing
Fields

Golf Course

Lodge
Plantation

Burnley
Wood

LC

CH

Golf Course

Rabbit Wlk

River
Calder

Park Bridge Rd

Park
Pond

Looe
Crescent

Nursery

Cliviger
Laithe

Higher
Cliviger

Burnley Way
THE AVENUE

Playing
Fields

Higher Timber
Hill Farm

NEW RD

Townely Park

Broad Ing

Wet Marl
Wood

Lower
Small Hazels

Townely Hall
(Art Gal & Mus)

Townely
Farm

Castle Hill

Castle
Hill

Barcroft

Barcroft
Farm

Copy
Wood

BACUP RD

BURNLEY RD

Cliviger Mill
Bridge

Dick Clough

Higher Small
Hazels

EAST LODGE
PL

COP ROYD
TERR

Mount
Cottage

Copy Farm

[handwritten notes at bottom:] Rt at traffic lights
See Town Hall   left at T.H carry on Car Pk + Huk

A B C D E F

8

Extwistle
Hill

Houghton's
Farm

Lee
Green

Roggerham
Gate Inn
(PH)

Holden
Clough

Extwistle Hall

Lee Green
Resr

Burnley Way

Swinden
Bottom

Swinden
Bridge

Ing
Hey

Twist
Castle

Delf Hill

Twist Hill

Swinden Water

Bronte Way

Swinden
Resrs

Extwistle Moor

7

Houghton
Hag

Wood
Hey
Farm

High
Halstead

Works

Stepping
Stones

Hell Clough

Lower
Bottin
Farm

Higher
Bottin
Farm
House

Swinden

Swinden Water

33

Higher
Cote

Extwistle Rd

Ring
Stones

6

Mill

Wasnop Edge

Ben Edge

Worsthorne
Prim Sch

Brownside Rd

Heckenhurst Ave

Halsted St

Gordon St

Showfield Ct

Crowther Ct

Langfield

Inch Field

Slipper Hill

Hameldon
Pasture

Lindsay Pk

Water St

Hope St

Smith St

Gorple Gn

The Crescent

Annarly Fold

Stanworth St

North St

GORPLE RD

Hurstwood Brook

Smallshaw Clough

5

Old Hall
Farm

Worsthorne

Stoneycroft

Raven St

Wallhurst Cl

Oak La

Wallhurst Cl

Hallstreams La

PH

Saville
Green

Brown
Edge

1 CLEGG ST
2 CHAPEL ST
3 HIGGIN ST
4 THE SQUARE
5 WHITTAM CT
6 CROSS ST
7 CHURCH SQ

32

Ormerod St

Brown
Edge

4

Salterford
Bridge

Hurstwood La

Burnley Way

Hurstwood
Resr

Pike
Stones

Salterford La

River Brun

Hurstwood

Spensy Clough

3

Ormerod
House

Gin
Wood

Hurstwood
Hall

Cant Clough
Farm

Hindle
Banks

Higher Red
Lees

P

31

Newfield
Farm

Brown
Hill

Rock Water
(Bird Conservation Centre)

Cant Clough Resr

Foxstones La

Red Lees Rd

Round
Hill

Rough
Wood

Rock Water

Cant Clough Beck

2

Crow
Holes

Near
Pasture

Middle
Pasture

Farside
Farm

PH

Shedden
Heys

Worsthorne
Moor

1

Greencliff La

The Long Cswy

School La

30

Mereclough

Mosley
Height

87 A B 88 C D 89 E F

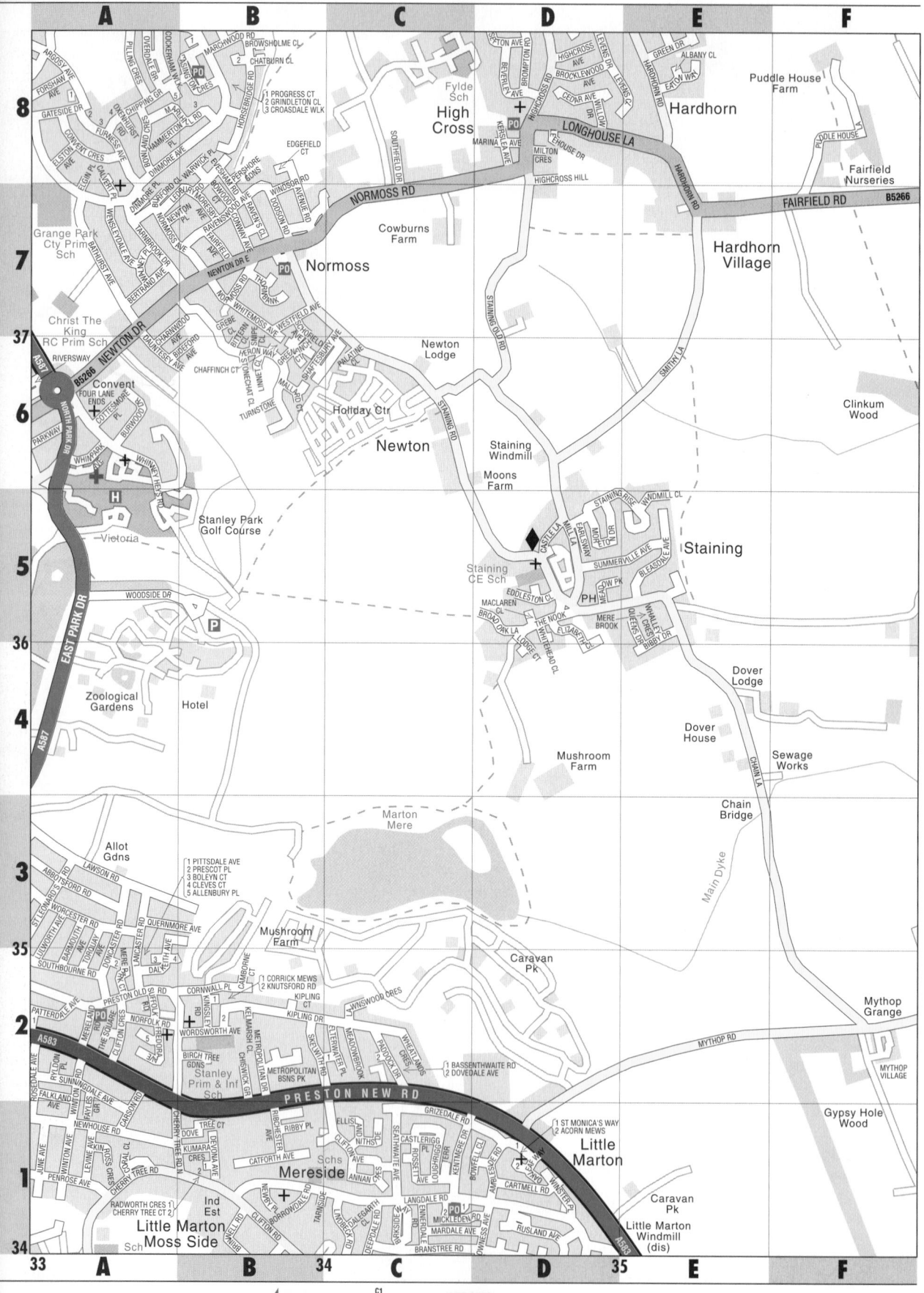

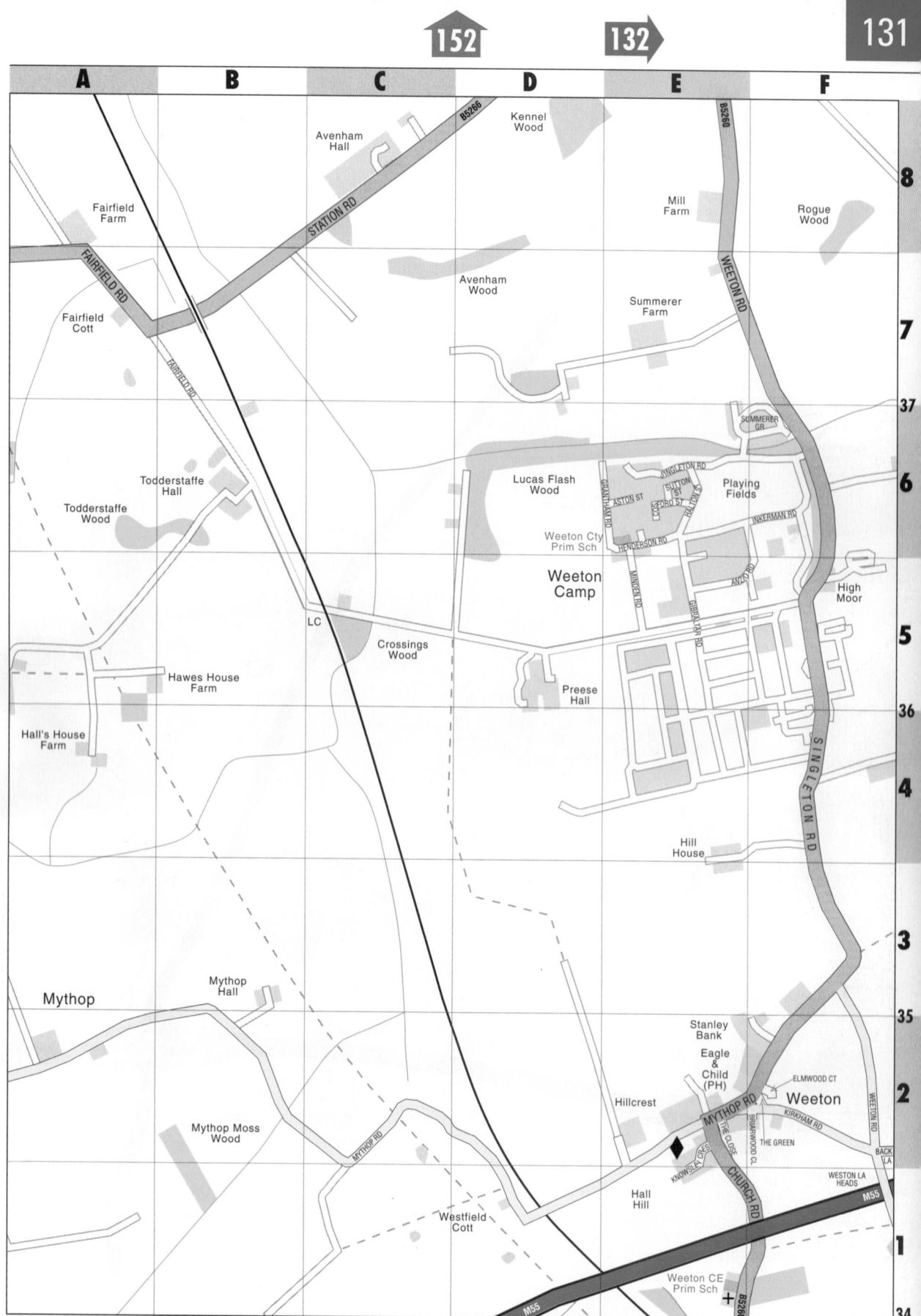

8

7

37

6

5

36

4

3

35

2

1

34

Fairfield Farm

Fairfield Cott

Todderstaffe Wood

Todderstaffe Hall

Hawes House Farm

Hall's House Farm

Mythop

Mythop Hall

Mythop Moss Wood

Westfield Cott

Hall Hill

Hillcrest

FAIRFIELD RD

STATION RD

B5266

Avenham Hall

Kennel Wood

Avenham Wood

Mill Farm

Rogue Wood

B5260

WEETON RD

Summerer Farm

SUMMERER GR

Lucas Flash Wood

SINGLETON RD

SUTTON ST

ASTON ST

SEFORD ST

COO

HALTON ST

GRANTHAM RD

Playing Fields

INKERMAN RD

Weeton Cty Prim Sch

HENDERSON RD

Weeton Camp

MINDEN RD

ANZIO RD

GIBRALTAR RD

High Moor

LC

Crossings Wood

Preese Hall

Hill House

SINGLETON RD

Stanley Bank

Eagle & Child (PH)

ELMWOOD CT

Weeton

MYTHOP RD

KIRKHAM RD

WEETON RD

THE CLOSE

BRIARWOOD CL

THE GREEN

BACK LA

KNOWSLEY CRES

CHURCH RD

WESTON LA HEADS

M55

Weeton CE Prim Sch

B5260

MYTHOP RD

A　　B　　C　　D　　E　　F

8

Inskip

Lower Slip Inn Farm

Inskip CE Sch

B5269

WEST DR

MANOR RD

NELSON GDNS

SCHOOL LA

SOUTH DR

HIGHFIELD AVE

WENTWORTH AVE

MILL CL

DERBY CRES

Stavens Pool Bridge

SUNNINGDALE PL

Dead Dam Bridge

Laytus Farm

The Derby Arms (PH)

Carr House Green Common

WOODS LA

Woodplumpton Brook

7

PRESTON RD

PO

Lower House

37

Higham Side

Walker House Farm

Higham Nook

HIGHAM SIDE RD

Woodsfold

Woodsfold Bridge

6

Airfield (disused)

Old Woodsfold Farm

New Woodsfold Farm

LEWTH LA

B5269

Inskip Wood

GREEN LA

Raikes Farm

JANE LA

5

Moss Farm

Wolf's Farm

Brades Farm

MOSS LA

Running Pump (PH)

CATFORTH RD

INSKIP RD

Wks

36

Pointer Wood

Pop Hall Farm

CHAPEL LA

SQUARE LA

Catforth

4

Moss House

MILLER LA

Poultry Farm

SQUARE LA

Bay Horse (PH)

PO

Sanderson's Wood

BAY HORSE LA

Hale Hall

Melling's Farm

WILLACY LA

Red Lion Farm

BENSON LA

BENSON LA

3

Willacy Lane End

SALWICK RD

ROOTS LA

35

Stanley Lodge

Locking Stoops

Blundell's Wood

Lancaster Canal

Roots Bridge

2

M55

BLUE MOOR

Kellet's Bridge

Moss Farm

Blackleach

BLACKLEACH LA

1

Stud Farm

Brook Wood

Stanley Grange

DAGGER RD

M55

MOSS LA E

34

45　　A　　46　　B　　46　　C　　D　　47　　E　　F

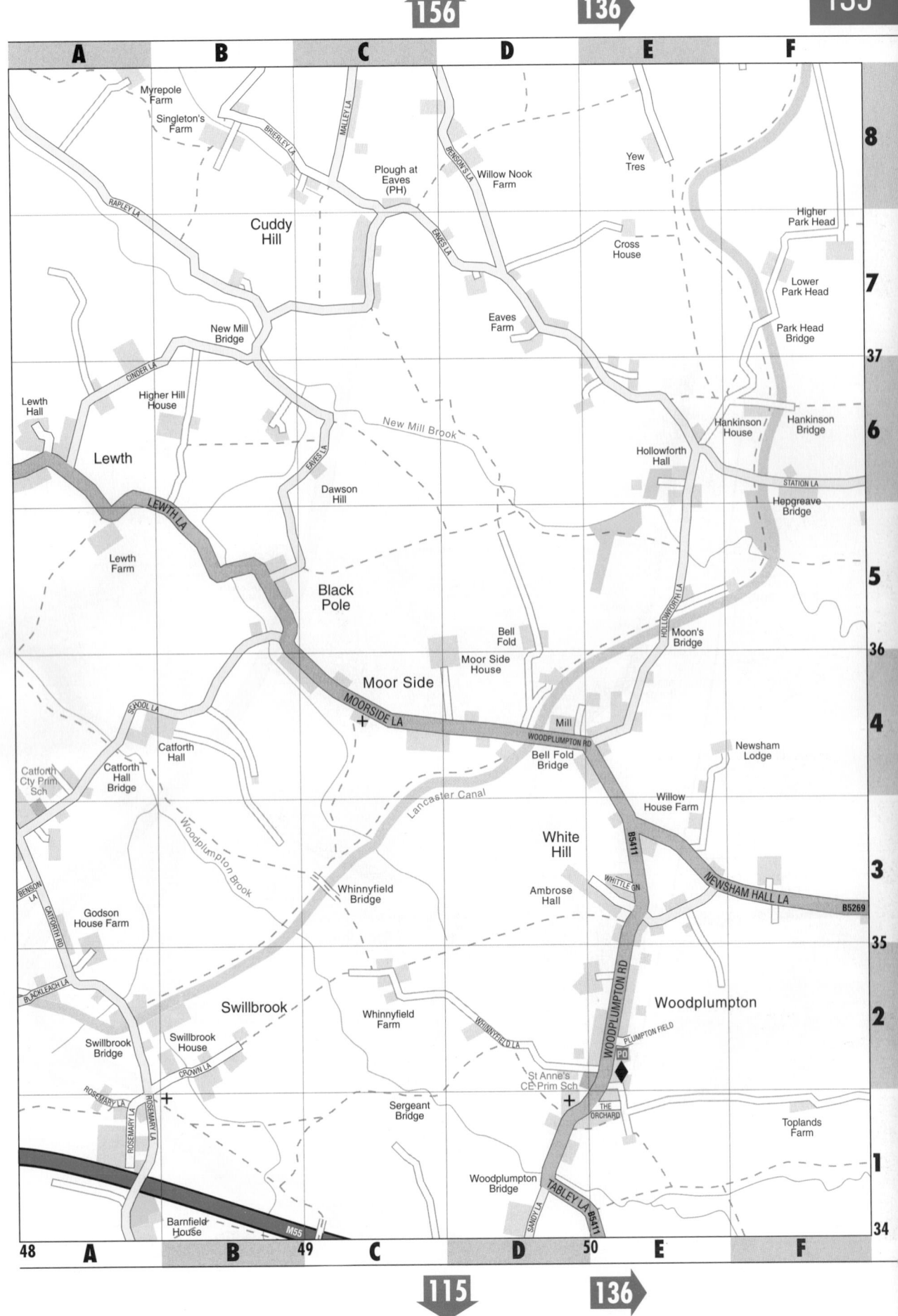

A B C D E F

8

7

37

6

37

36

35

34

Myrepole Farm
Singleton's Farm
BRIERLEY LA
MALLEY LA
Plough at Eaves (PH)
BENSON ST LA
Willow Nook Farm
Yew Tres
RAPLEY LA
Cuddy Hill
Higher Park Head
Cross House
Lower Park Head
EAVES LA
Eaves Farm
Park Head Bridge
New Mill Bridge
CINDER LA
Higher Hill House
Lewth Hall
Hankinson House
Hankinson Bridge
Lewth
EAVES LA
New Mill Brook
Hollowforth Hall
STATION LA
LEWTH LA
Dawson Hill
Hepgreave Bridge
Lewth Farm
Black Pole
Bell Fold
HOLLOWFORTH LA
Moon's Bridge
Moor Side House
Moor Side
MOORSIDE LA
Mill
WOODPLUMPTON RD
Newsham Lodge
SCHOOL LA
Catforth Hall
Bell Fold Bridge
Catforth Cty Prim Sch
Catforth Hall Bridge
Lancaster Canal
White Hill
Willow House Farm
B5411
WHITTLE GN
Newsham Hall La
B5269
Woodplumpton Brook
Whinnyfield Bridge
Ambrose Hall
BENSON LA
CATFORTH RD
Godson House Farm
BLACKLEACH LA
Woodplumpton
WOODPLUMPTON RD
Swillbrook
Whinnyfield Farm
PLUMPTON FIELD
PO
Swillbrook Bridge
Swillbrook House
CROWN LA
WHINNYFIELD LA
St Anne's CE Prim Sch
ROSEMARY LA
ROSEMARY LA
Sergeant Bridge
THE ORCHARD
Toplands Farm
Barnfield House
M55
Woodplumpton Bridge
SANDY LA
TABLEY LA
B5411

135
157

A   B   C   D   E   F

8

LONG CROFT
ST LAWRENCE'S AVE
SOUTH GR
GREEN DR
ASH BANK CL
MOSSLEA GR
HOLMSWOOD CRES
MOSSLEA DR
FORBES LA
JEPPS LA
Blacow House Farm
Barton Brook
Cross House Farm
Westfield
BARTON LA

7

THE CONIFERS
ALISA CL
JEPPS AVE
ST HELIER'S PL
St Lawrence CE Prim Sch
Hotel
Hill Top

Barton

Bell Fold Farm

Goosnargh La

37

Barton House

6

Helme Wood

Benson's House

WOODLANDS CRES
WOODLANDS WAY
Newsham St Mary's & St Andrews RC Sch
Barton & Broughton Sta
THORNTREES AVE

Tunsteads

Almond's Farm

B5269

STATION LA
ST MICHAEL'S PL

Newsham

5

Black Fir Wood

GARSTANG RD

Barton Hall

Dean Brook

36

Garden Wood

Cardwell Bridge

4

Sewage Wks

Barton Brook Bridge

Hoole's Farm

WHITTINGHAM LA

PUDDING PIE NOOK LA

LANGLEY LA

M6

Crow Hall
Newsham Hall
Yates's Farm

3

STANLEY CROFT
SUNNINGDALE
ASHFORD CRES
MERE CL
WEST CRES
NORTHWAY
STONE PARK RD
WENTWORTH DR
GREENWAY
FAIRWAYS AVE
KINGSWAY CT
KINGSBURY AVE
PINEWOOD
WILLOW TREE AVE
Old Hall

B5269
NEWSHAM HALL LA
LOW CROFT
NORMANDY RD
MOSS HOUSE RD
WOODPLUMPTON LA
VICTORIA CT
DOWNING CT
FRINGLE WOOD
Burlingtons (PH)
Broughton
M6

35

Crow Hall Bridge
SANDYGATE LA
ARNSIDE RD
PO

2

Hodder Viaduct
BROADFIELD
MOORCROFT
Broughton Cty High Sch
Bank Hall Farm
Hotel
M55

Bailey's Bridge
Broughton in Amounderness CE Prim Sch

CHURCH LA

Broughton House
A6
Grange Farm

1

Broughton Bridge
D'URTON LA
HIGHRIGG DR

Sandpit
Blundel Brook Bridge
Woodplumpton Brook
1
M55

34
M55
EASTWAY
B6241

135
116

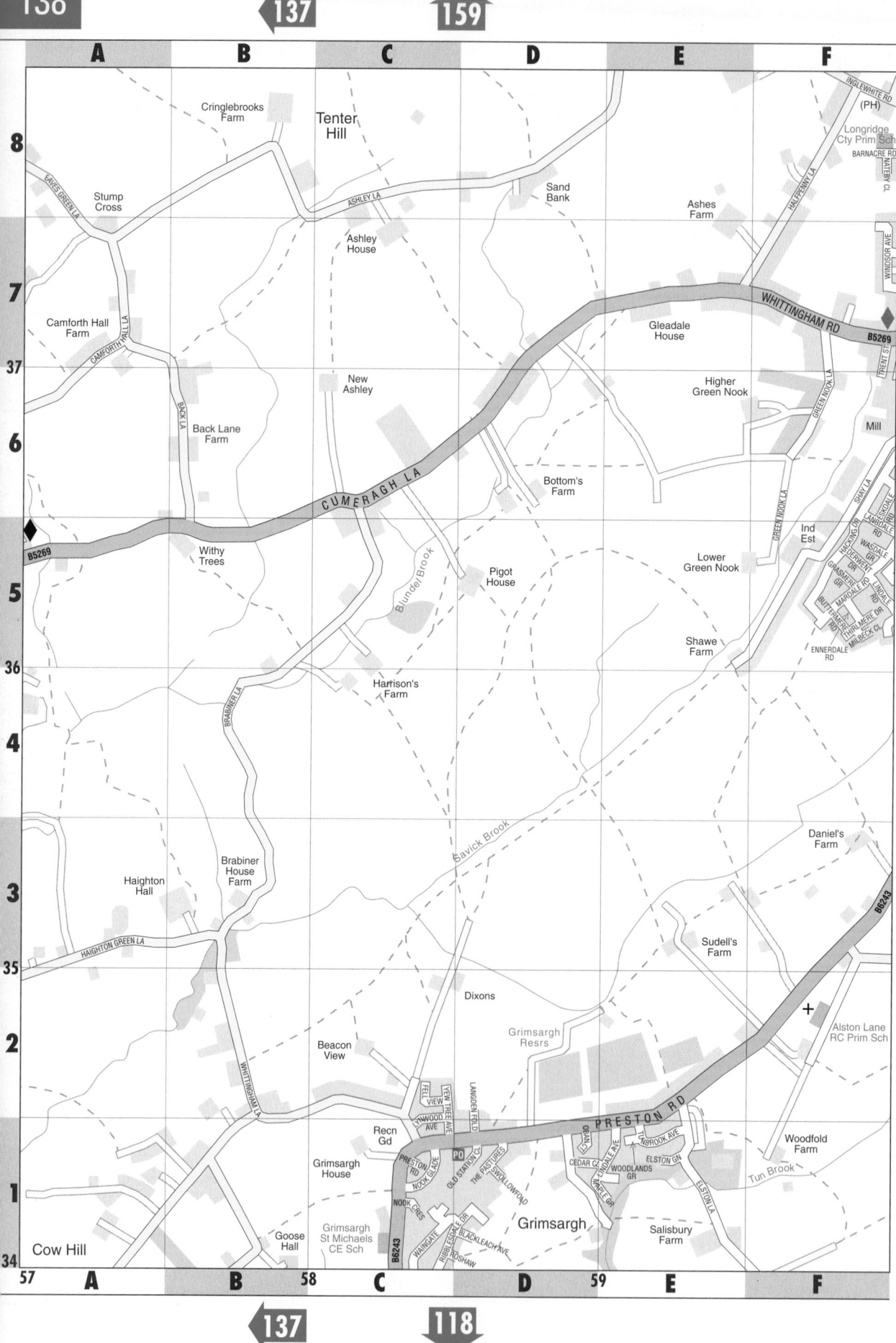

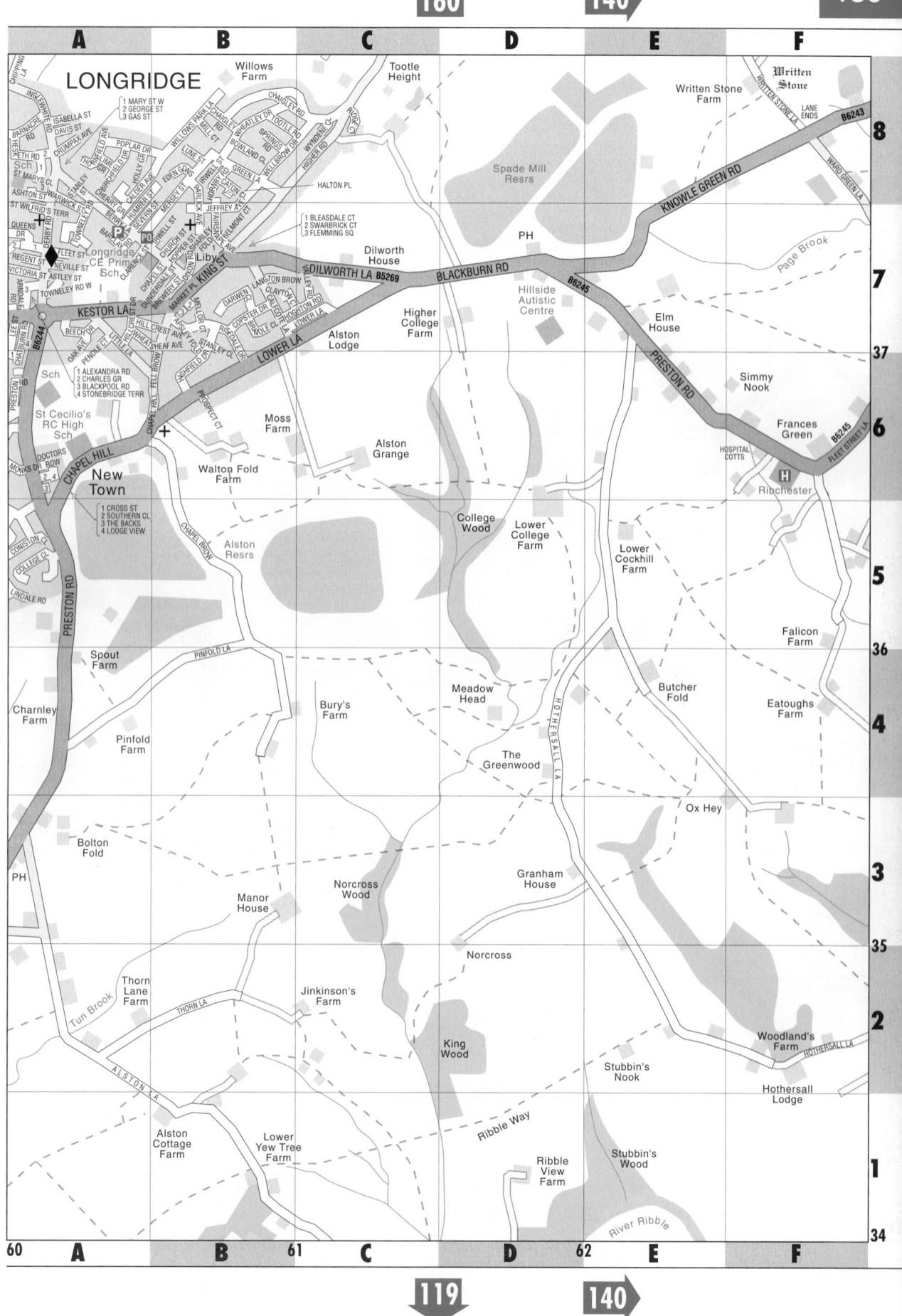

LONGRIDGE

1 MARY ST W
2 GEORGE ST
3 GAS ST

Willows
Farm

Tootle
Height

Written
Stone

Written Stone
Farm

LANE
ENDS

B6243

8

Spade Mill
Resrs

Page Brook

HALTON PL

1 BLEASDALE CT
2 SWARBRICK CT
3 FLEMMING SQ

Dilworth
House

PH

Longridge
CE Primary
Sch

Liby

KING ST

DILWORTH LA   B5269   BLACKBURN RD

B6245

Hillside
Autistic
Centre

Elm
House

KNOWLE GREEN RD

7

37

KESTOR LA

LOWER LA

Alston
Lodge

Higher
College
Farm

Simmy
Nook

Frances
Green

B6245

FLEET STREET LA

6

B6244

PRESTON RD

1 ALEXANDRA RD
2 CHARLES GR
3 BLACKPOOL RD
4 STONEBRIDGE TERR

Sch

St Cecilio's
RC High
Sch

DOCTORS
ROW

Moss
Farm

Alston
Grange

HOSPITAL
COTTS

H

Ribchester

CHAPEL HILL

New
Town

1 CROSS ST
2 SOUTHERN CL
3 THE BACKS
4 LODGE VIEW

Walton Fold
Farm

College
Wood

Lower
College
Farm

Lower
Cockhill
Farm

5

CONISTON CL

COLLEGE CL

LINDALE RD

CHAPEL BROW

Alston
Resrs

Falicon
Farm

36

PRESTON RD

Spout
Farm

PINFOLD LA

Meadow
Head

Butcher
Fold

Eatoughs
Farm

4

Charnley
Farm

Pinfold
Farm

Bury's
Farm

HOTHERSALL LA

The
Greenwood

Bolton
Fold

Ox Hey

3

PH

Manor
House

Norcross
Wood

Granham
House

35

Norcross

Thorn
Lane
Farm

THORN LA

Jinkinson's
Farm

King
Wood

Stubbin's
Nook

Woodland's
Farm

HOTHERSALL LA

2

ALSTON LA

Tun Brook

Hothersall
Lodge

Alston
Cottage
Farm

Lower
Yew Tree
Farm

Ribble Way

Ribble
View
Farm

Stubbin's
Wood

1

River Ribble

34

139
161

A **B** **C** **D** **E** **F**

8

KNOWLE GREEN RD
B6243
Mill House
CLAY HILL LA
Seed Green
Moor House
B6243
Moor Cock Farm
DEAN BROW
B6243
HUNTINGDON HALL RD
Pope's Farm

7

Springs Farm
WARD GREEN LA
MILL HOUSE LA
GREEN MOOR LA
Kellets
COW GREEN LA
Scott House
Cox Farm
Old Buckley
OLD BUCKLEY LA
Davies Gate Wood
Duddel Hill
Duddel Wood
DUDDEL BROOK

37

Ward Hall
WARD GREEN CROSS
Cross Keys Inn (PH)
B6245
FLEET STREET LA

6

WOOD'S BROW
Buckley Gate
Buckley Hall
Buckley Wood
Phillip's Farm
STONYGATE LA
Stydd Wood

5

Lord's Farm
PRESTON RD
Pinfold Farm
Ashmoor House
Oak Bank
Cherry Yate
Stydd Manor
Little Stydd Wood

36

Higher Alston
Dale Hey Farm
Boyce's Farm
✝

4

Eatoughs Wood
Singleton House
Boyce's Brook
New House
CHESTER BROOK
EASTGATE
Stydd ✝
STYDD LA
GALLOWS LA

3

Parsonage Wood
Parsonage Farm
MANOR AVE
◆
CHURCH ST
CHURCH ST
Ribchester
SUNNYSIDE AVE
PARSONAGE AVE
FORT AVE
P
PO
RIBBLESDALE RD
CLAYTONHALGH
PH
Stone Bridge
BLACKBURN RD
B6245
Little Town

35

Hothersall Wood
Red Bank
WATER ST
CHURCH ST
GREENSIDE
P
✝
Mus
✝
Ribchester CE Prim Sch

2

Hothersall Hall
HOTHERSALL LA
Boat House
Lower Barn Farm
BREMETENNACVM ROMAN FORT
Anchor Hill
Lower Madgell Bank

River Ribble
Ribble Way
Osbaldeston Hall
Catterall

1

34

63 **A** **B** 64 **C** **D** 65 **E** **F**

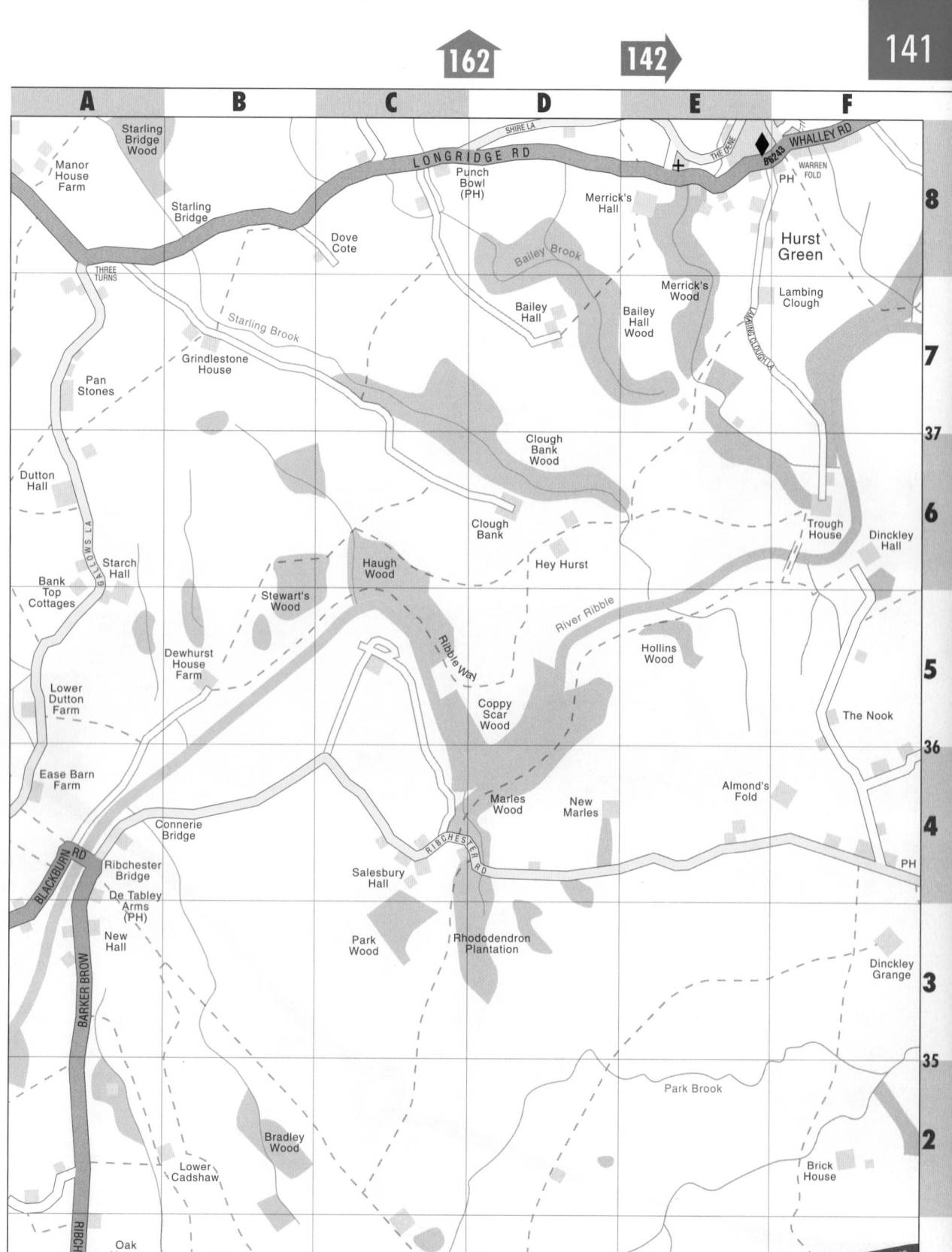

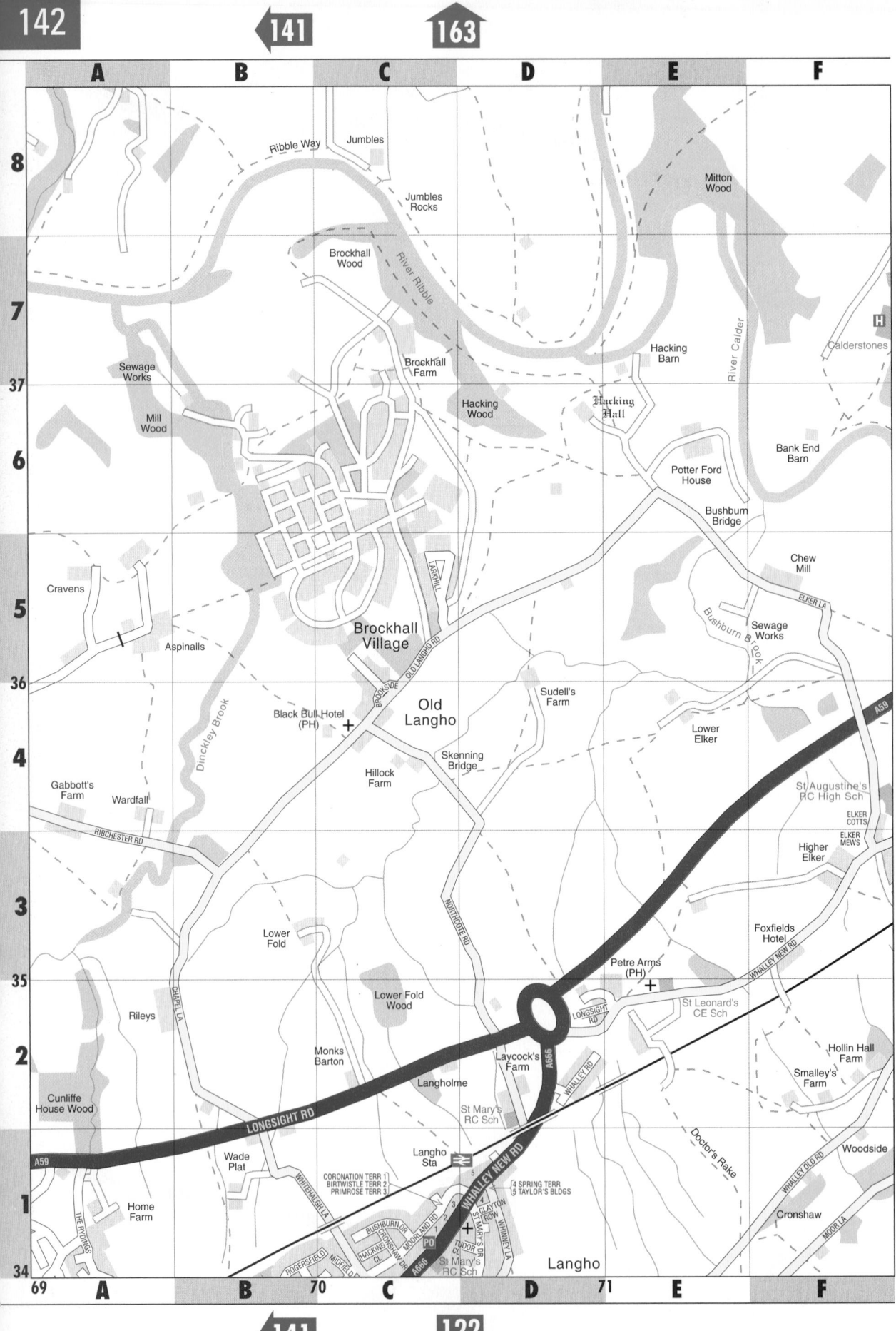

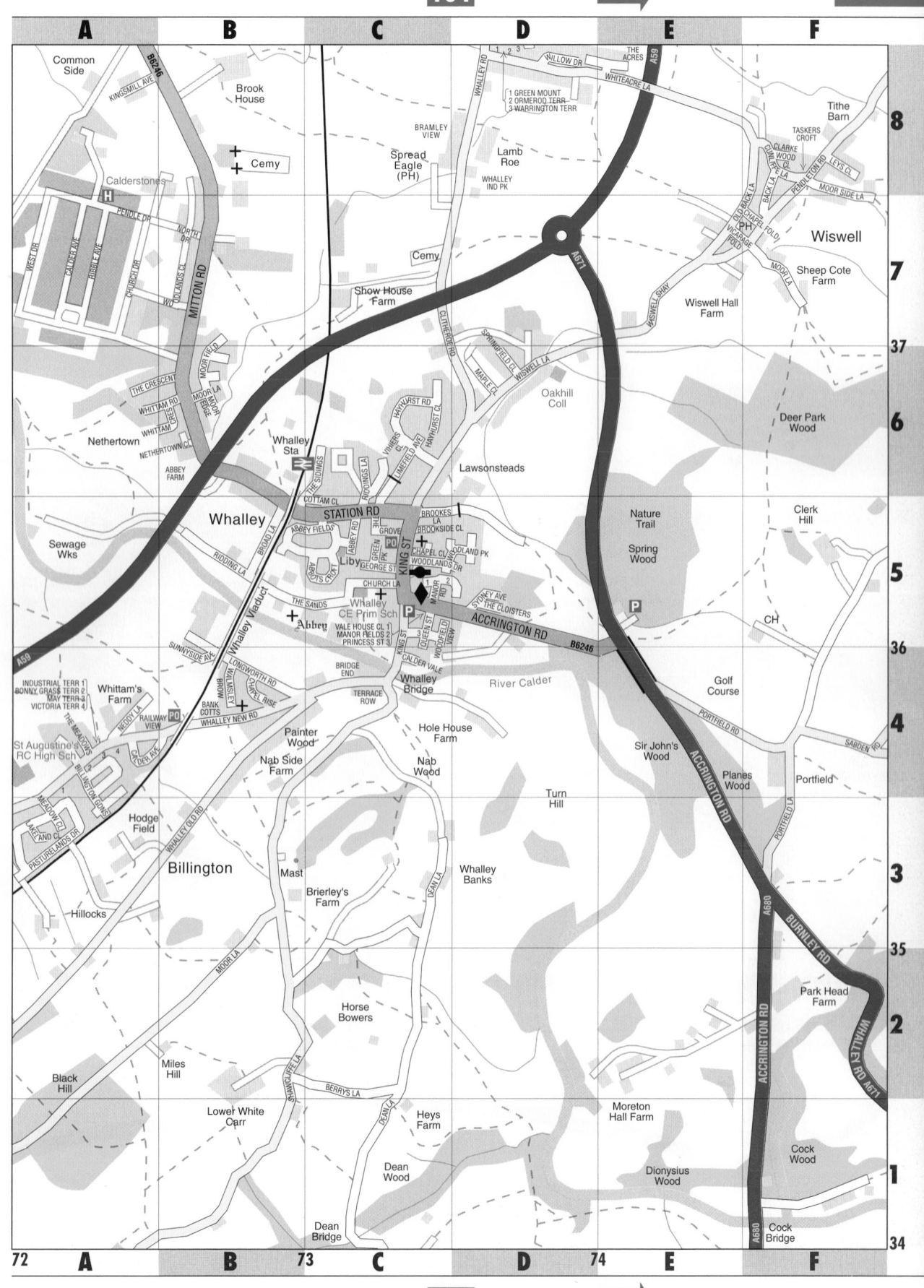

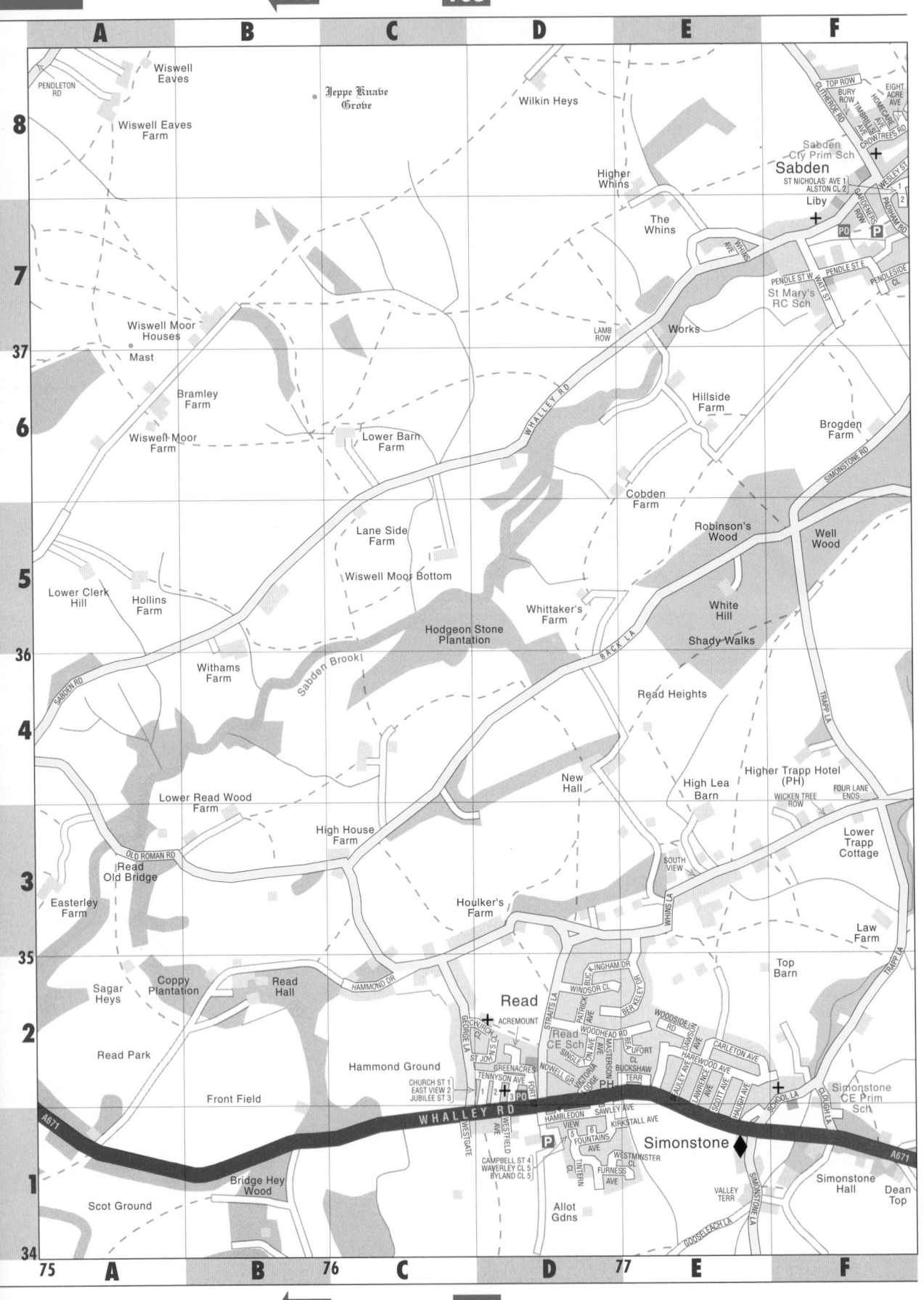

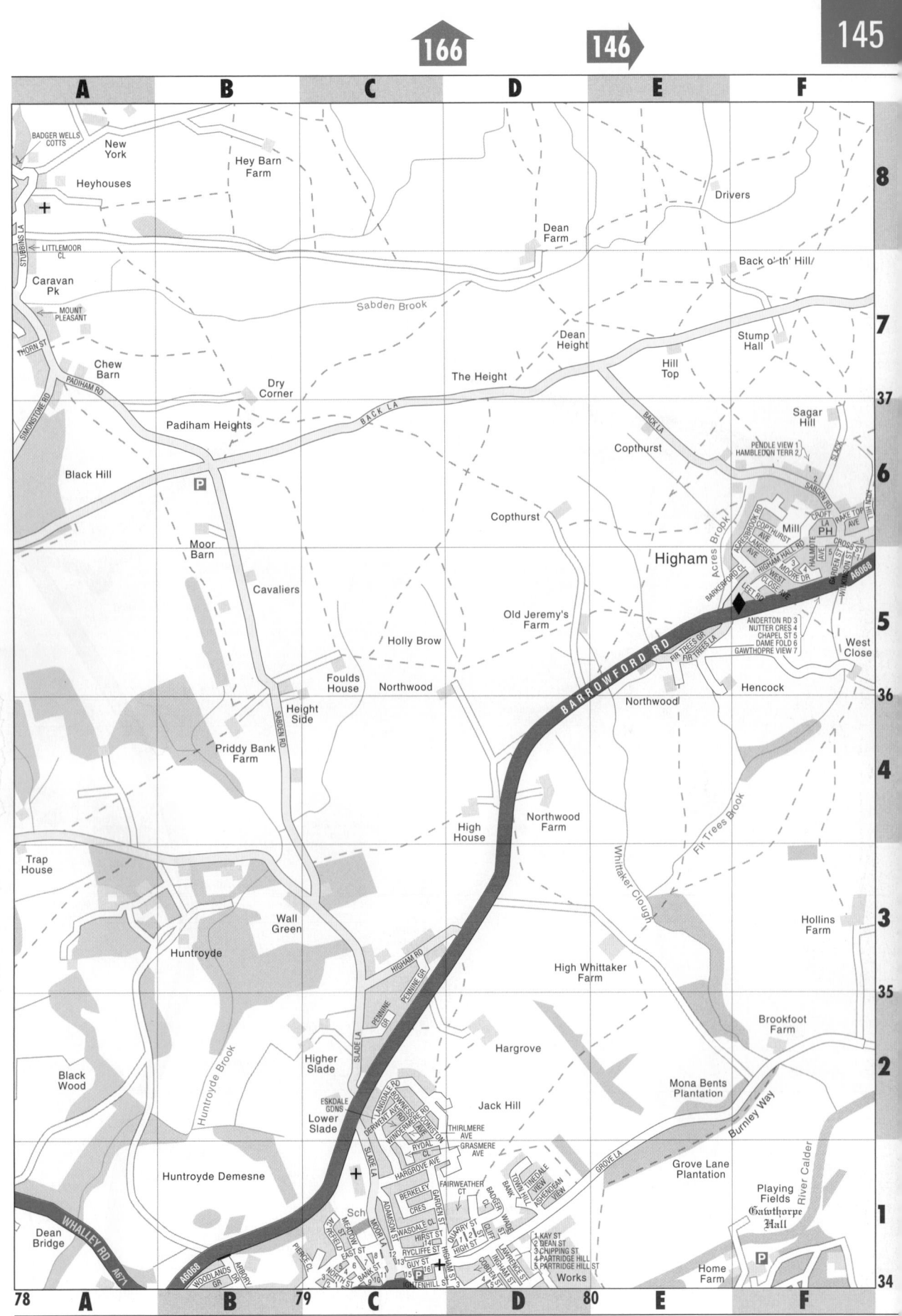

166 146

A B C D E F

8

7

37

6

5

36

4

35

3

2

1

34

BADGER WELLS COTTS
New York
Heyhouses
LITTLEMOOR CL
STUBBINS LA
Caravan Pk
MOUNT PLEASANT
THORN ST
Chew Barn
PADIHAM RD
SIMONSTONE RD
Black Hill
Padiham Heights
Moor Barn
Cavaliers
SABDEN RD
Height Side
Priddy Bank Farm
Trap House
Wall Green
Huntroyde
Black Wood
Huntroyde Brook
Huntroyde Demesne
Dean Bridge
WHALLEY RD
A6071
A6068
WOODLANDS GR
ARBORY
PIERCE CL
MEADOW
ENFIELD
EAST ST
NORTH ST
BANK ST
MOOR LA
Sch
HIGHAM RD
LANSDALE RD
DERWENT AV
BOWNESS RD
WINDERMERE RD
ESKDALE GDNS
Lower Slade
Higher Slade
SLADE LA
HIGHAM RD
PENNINE GR
PENNINE GR

Hey Barn Farm
Dry Corner
BACK LA
Holly Brow
Foulds House
Northwood
High House
Hargrove
Jack Hill
RYDAL CL
THIRLMERE AVE
GRASMERE AVE
HARGROVE AVE
BERKELEY CRES
ADAMSON'S
WASDALE CL
GUY ST
RYCLIFFE ST
HIRST ST
QUARRY ST
HIGH ST
GARDEN ST
FAIRWEATHER CT

Dean Farm
Sabden Brook
Dean Height
The Height
Old Jeremy's Farm
Northwood
Northwood Farm
High Whittaker Farm
High Whittaker
Whittaker Clough
FIR TREES GR
FIR TREES LA
BARROWFORD RD
Fir Trees Brook
GROVE LA
Grove Lane Plantation
BADGER WALK
BANK HILL
TOWN HILL
TREEDALE VIEW
ASHENDEAN VIEW
1 KAY ST
2 DEAN ST
3 CHIPPING ST
4 PARTRIDGE HILL
5 PARTRIDGE HILL ST
Works

Drivers
Back o' th' Hill
Stump Hall
Hill Top
Sagar Hill
Copthurst
Mill PH
Higham
Copthurst
BACK LA
SLADE
SARDEN RD
CROFT LA
RAKE TOP
AYLESBROOK AVE
COPTHURST AVE
HIGHAM HALL RD
LANESIDE AVE
WEST CLOSE AVE
MOORE DR
THALMUTE AVE
LEET RD
BARKERFORD RD
PENDLE VIEW 1
HAMBLEDON TERR 2
ANDERTON RD 3
NUTTER CRES 4
CHAPEL ST 5
DAME FOLD 6
GAWTHORPE VIEW 7
West Close
Hencock
Hollins Farm
Brookfoot Farm
Mona Bents Plantation
BURNLEY WAY
River Calder
Playing Fields
Gawthorpe Hall
Home Farm
Acres Brook

78 79 80

C1
1 THE MEWS
2 CHAPEL WLK
3 SPRING GARDENS TERR
4 HALL HILL ST
5 CROSSHILLS
6 ST GILES ST
7 ST LEONARD'S ST
8 CLAYBANK
9 HAVELOCK ST
10 CHURCH LA
11 GAWTHORPE ST
12 BARBON ST
13 JOHN O' GAUNT ST
14 COPTHURST ST
15 FACTORY LA
16 HABERGHAM ST

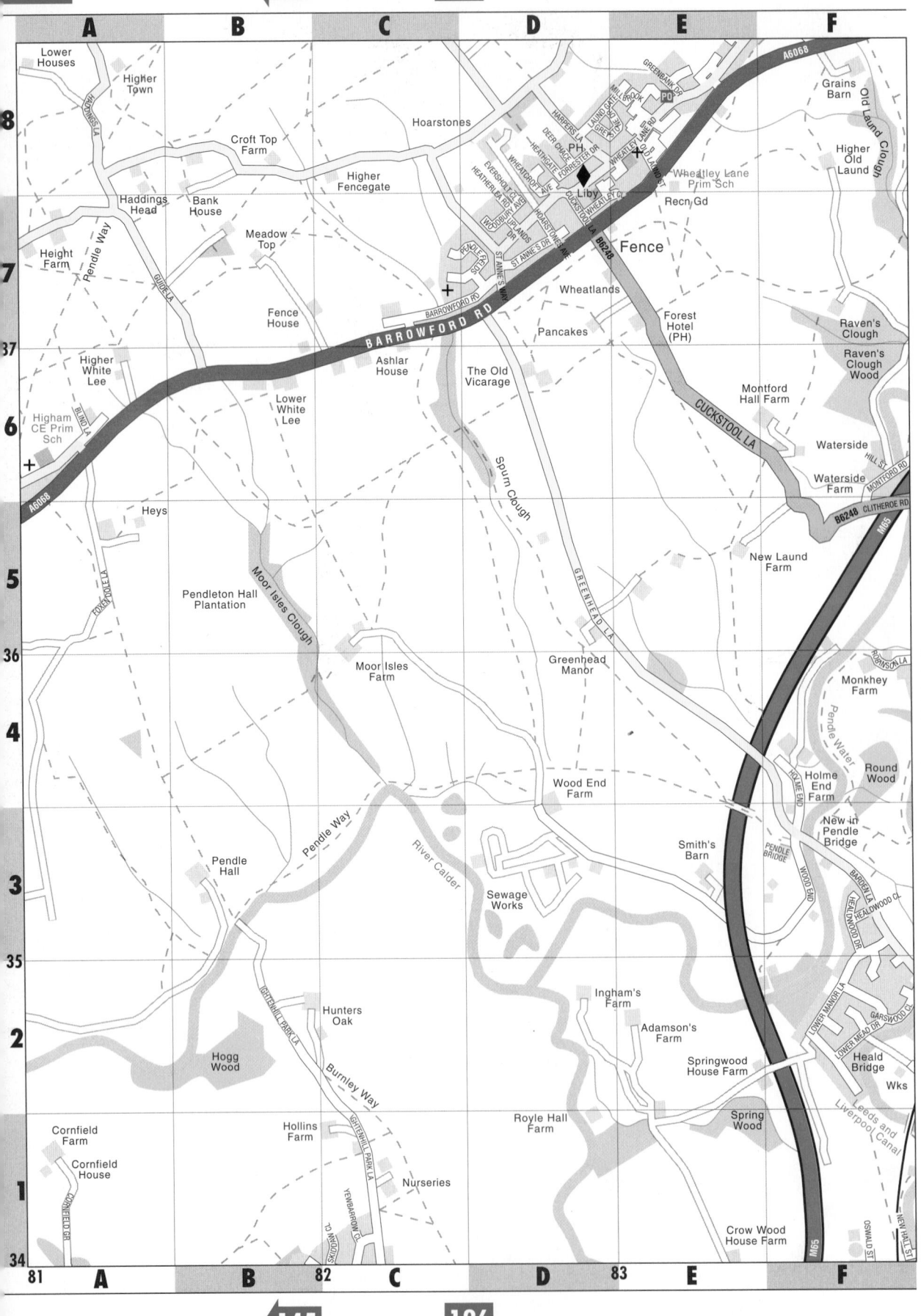

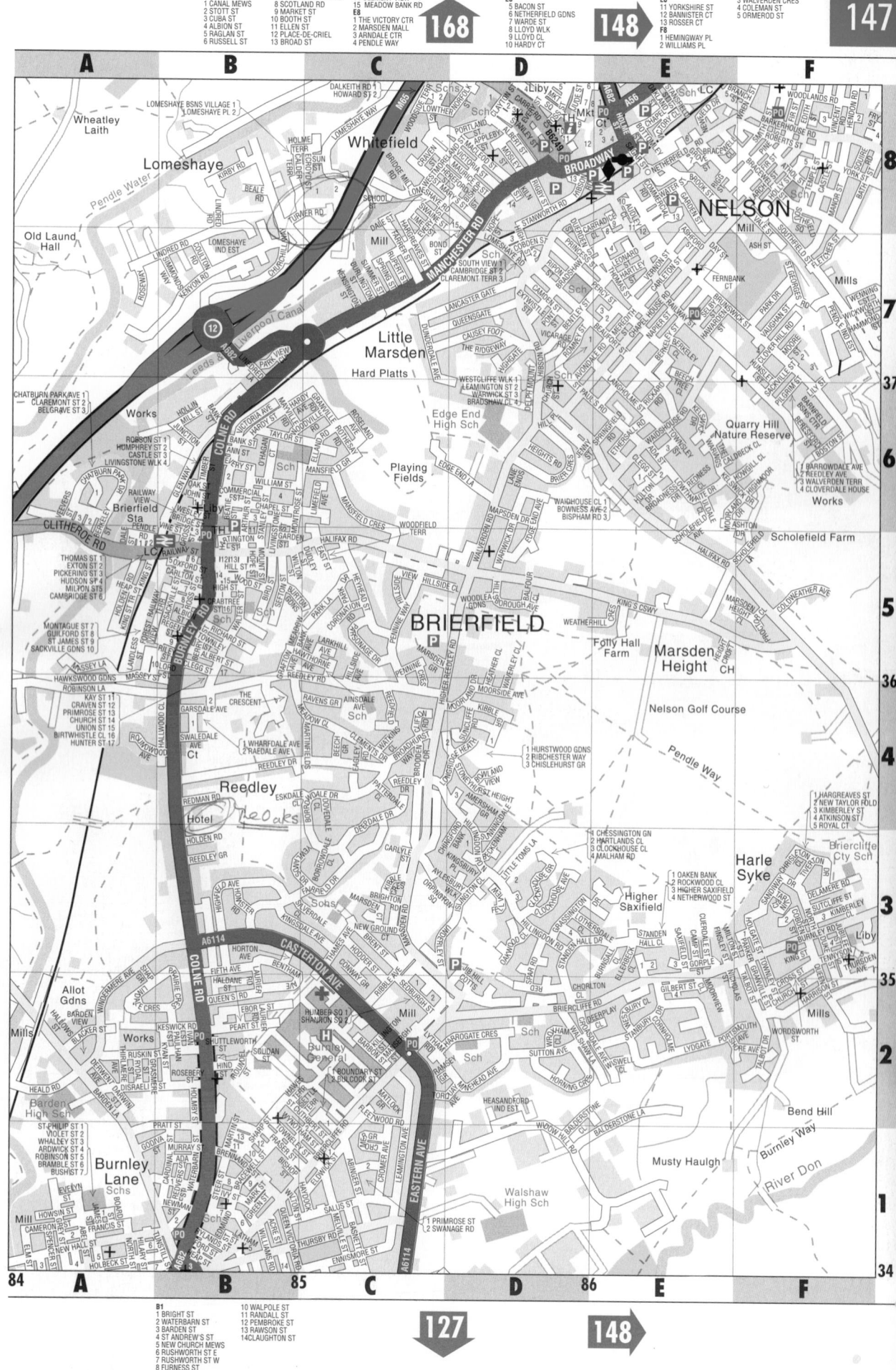

D8
1 CANAL MEWS
2 STOTT ST
3 CUBA ST
4 ALBION ST
5 RAGLAN ST
6 RUSSELL ST

7 BACK SCOTLAND RD
8 SCOTLAND RD
9 MARKET ST
10 BOOTH ST
11 ELLEN ST
12 PLACE-DE-CRIEL
13 BROAD ST

14 CLEMENT VIEW
15 MEADOW BANK RD

E8
1 THE VICTORY CTR
2 MARSDEN MALL
3 ARNDALE CTR
4 PENDLE WAY

E8
5 BACON ST
6 NETHERFIELD GDNS
7 WARDE ST
8 MARSDEN ST
9 LLOYD WLK
9 LLOYD CL
10 HARDY CT

E8
11 YORKSHIRE ST
12 BANNISTER CT
13 ROSSER ST

F8
1 HEMINGWAY PL
2 WILLIAMS PL

3 WALVERDEN CRES
4 COLEMAN ST
5 ORMEROD ST

168

148

147

B1
1 BRIGHT ST
2 WATERBARN ST
3 BARDEN ST
4 ST ANDREW'S ST
5 NEW CHURCH MEWS
6 RUSHWORTH ST E
7 RUSHWORTH ST W
8 FURNESS ST
9 RENSHAW ST

10 WALPOLE ST
11 RANDALL ST
12 PEMBROKE ST
13 RAWSON ST
14 CLAUGHTON ST

127

148

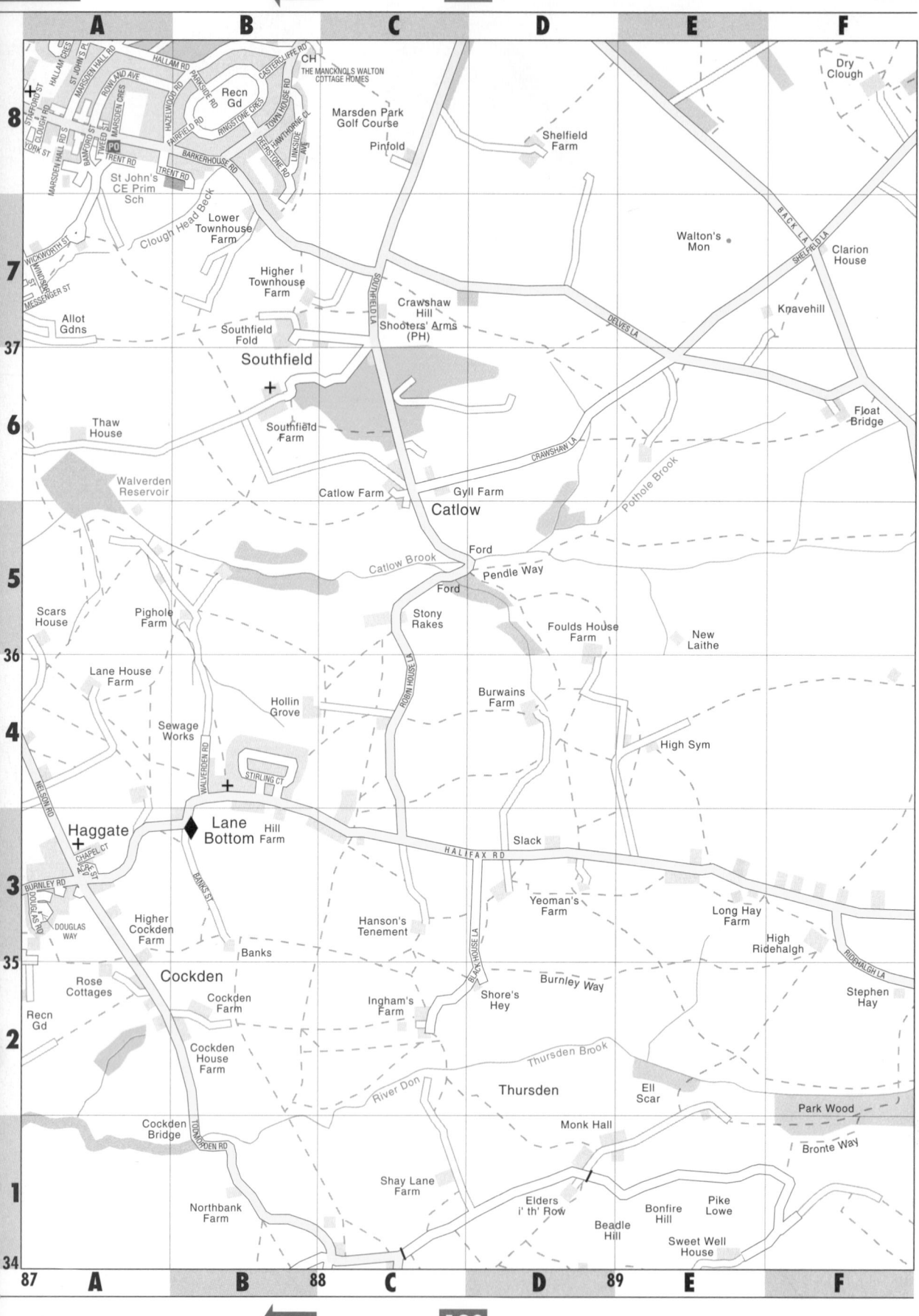

A B C D E F

8

7

37

6

5

36

4

3

35

2

1

34

Map labels:

Hallam Cres · Hallam Rd · Marsden Hall Rd · Rowland Ave · Stafford St · Tweed St · Clough St · York St · Wickworth St · Winnard St · Messenger St · Allot Gdns · Thaw House · Scars House · Nelson Rd · Burnley Rd · Douglas Rd · Douglas Way · Chapel Ct · Haggate · Rose Cottages · Recn Gd

Marsden Hall Rd S Pt · Hazelwood Rd · Fairfield Rd · Bamford St · St John's Rd · PO · Trent Rd · St John's CE Prim Sch · Barkerhouse Rd · Parkside Rd · Ringstone Cres · Recn Gd · Castercliffe Rd · Town House Rd · Deerstone Rd · Hawthorne Cl · Linkside Rd · CH · THE MANCKNOLS WALTON COTTAGE HOMES

Lower Townhouse Farm · Higher Townhouse Farm · Southfield Fold · Southfield · Southfield Farm · Clough Head Beck

Pinfold · Marsden Park Golf Course · Southfield La · Crawshaw Hill Shooters' Arms (PH) · Shelfield Farm · Walton's Mon · Delves La · Back La · Shelfield La · Dry Clough · Clarion House · Knavehill · Float Bridge

Catlow Farm · Gyll Farm · Catlow · Crawshaw La · Pothole Brook

Walverden Reservoir · Pighole Farm · Catlow Brook · Ford · Ford · Pendle Way · Stony Rakes · Foulds House Farm · New Laithe

Lane House Farm · Hollin Grove · Robin House La · Burwains Farm · High Sym

Sewage Works · Walverden Rd · Stirling Ct · Lane Bottom · Hill Farm · Halifax Rd · Slack · High Ridehalgh · Ridehalgh La

Higher Cockden Farm · Banks St · Banks · Hanson's Tenement · Black House La · Yeoman's Farm · Long Hay Farm

Cockden · Cockden Farm · Ingham's Farm · Burnley Way · Shore's Hey · Stephen Hay

Recn Gd · Cockden House Farm · Thursden Brook · River Don · Thursden · Ell Scar · Park Wood

Cockden Bridge · Todmorden Rd · Northbank Farm · Shay Lane Farm · Monk Hall · Bronte Way · Elders i' th' Row · Beadle Hill · Bonfire Hill · Pike Lowe · Sweet Well House

170

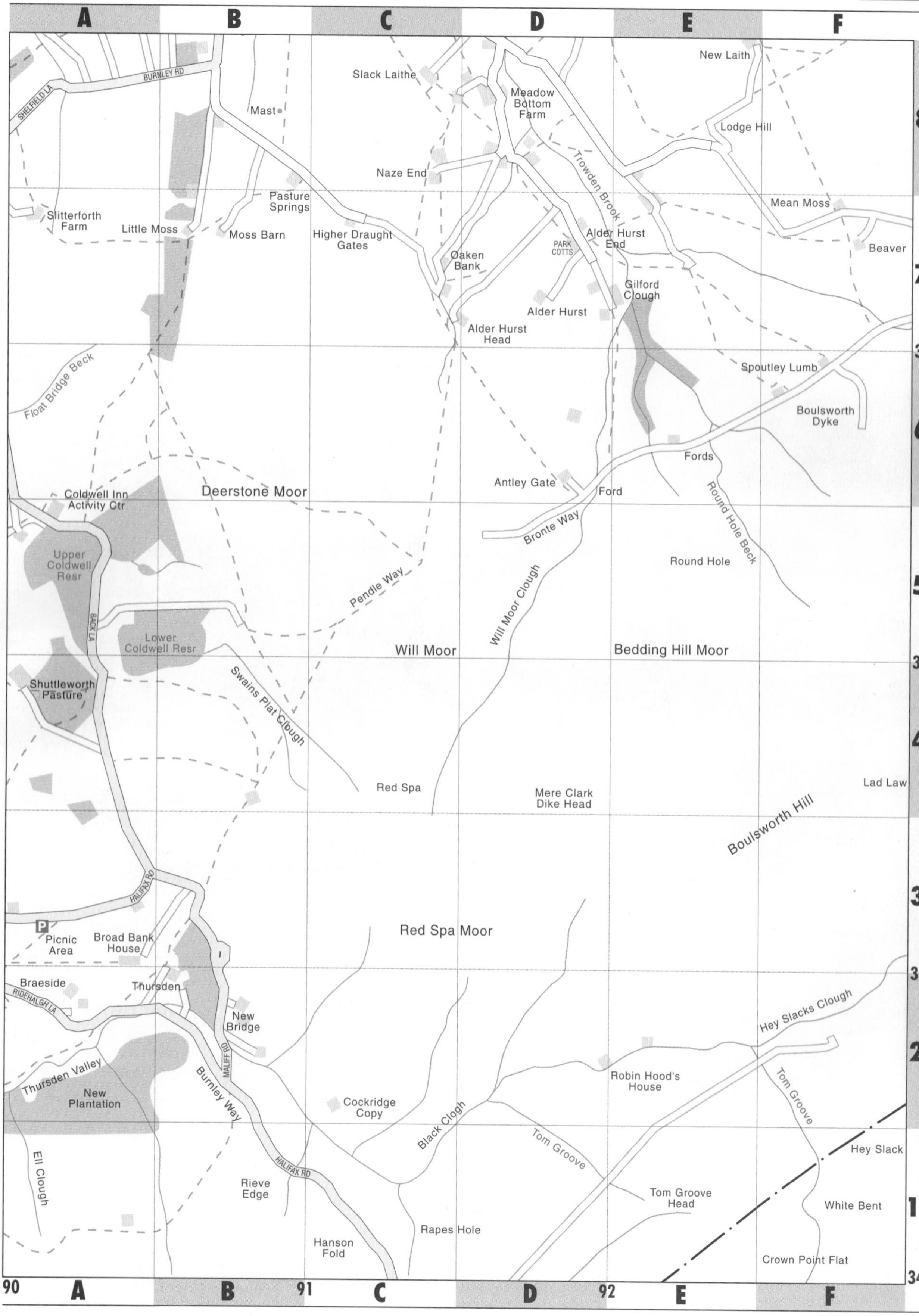

A B C D E F
BURNLEY RD
SHELFIELD LA
Slack Laithe
New Laith
Mast
Meadow Bottom Farm
Lodge Hill
Naze End
Trowden Brook
Pasture Springs
Mean Moss
Slitterforth Farm
Little Moss
Moss Barn
Higher Draught Gates
Alder Hurst End
PARK COTTS
Beaver
Oaken Bank
Gilford Clough
Alder Hurst
Alder Hurst Head
Spoutley Lumb
Float Bridge Beck
Boulsworth Dyke
Fords
Antley Gate
Ford
Round Hole Beck
Deerstone Moor
Coldwell Inn Activity Ctr
Bronte Way
Upper Coldwell Resr
Round Hole
Will Moor Clough
Pendle Way
BACK LA
Lower Coldwell Resr
Will Moor
Bedding Hill Moor
Shuttleworth Pasture
Swains Plat Clough
Red Spa
Mere Clark Dike Head
Lad Law
Boulsworth Hill
HALIFAX RD
P
Picnic Area
Broad Bank House
Red Spa Moor
Braeside
Thursden
RIDEHALGH LA
New Bridge
Hey Slacks Clough
MALIFF RD
Thursden Valley
Burnley Way
Robin Hood's House
Tom Groove
New Plantation
Cockridge Copy
Black Clough
Tom Groove
Hey Slack
Ell Clough
HALIFAX RD
Rieve Edge
Tom Groove Head
White Bent
Rapes Hole
Hanson Fold
Crown Point Flat
8 7 37 6 5 36 4 3 35 2 1 34
90 A B 91 C D 92 E F

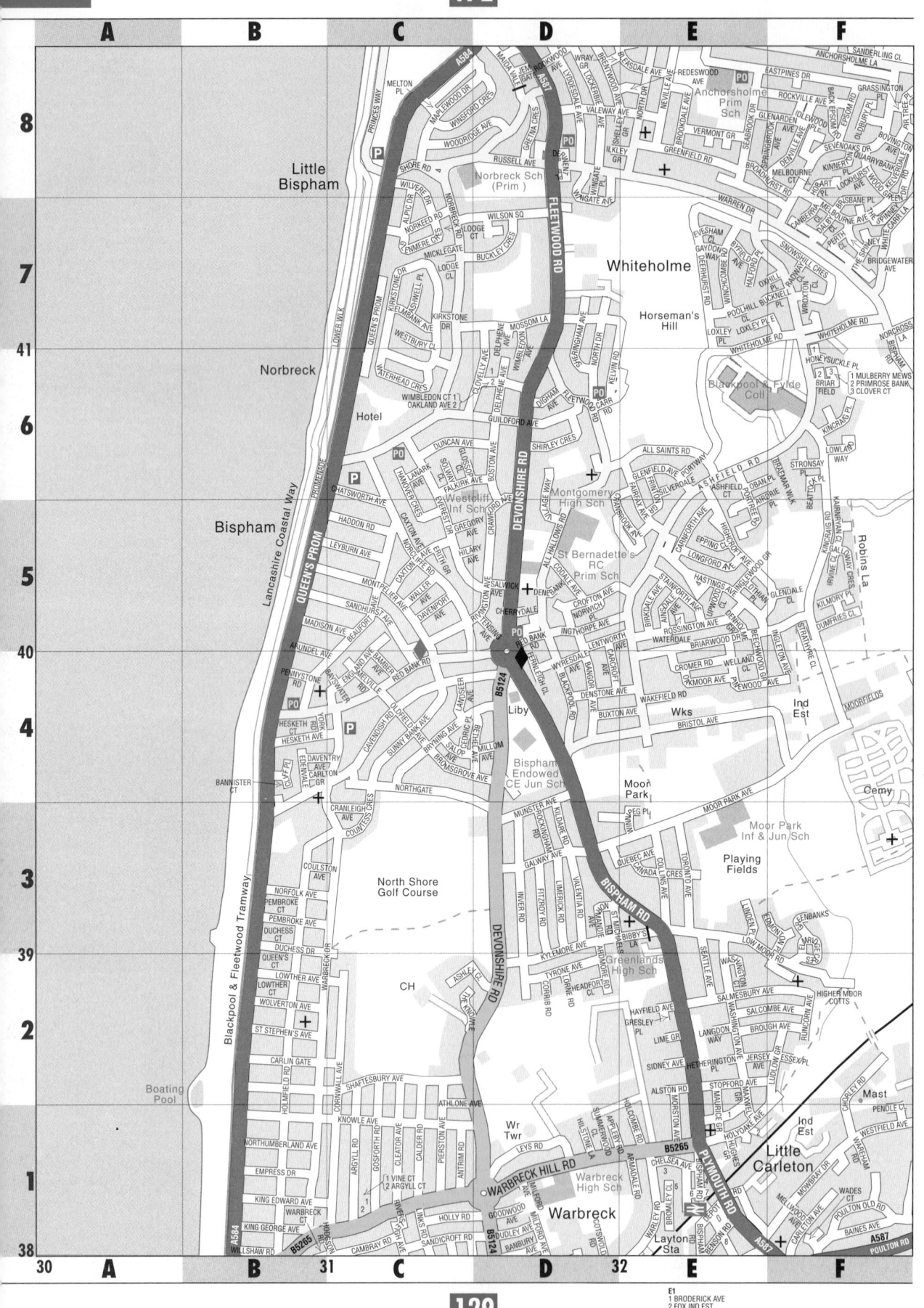

E1
1 BRODERICK AVE
2 FOX IND EST
3 CHELSEA CT
4 CHELSEA MEWS
5 BROMLEY CT
6 PEARL AVE
7 HENLEY CT
8 DELAWARE RD

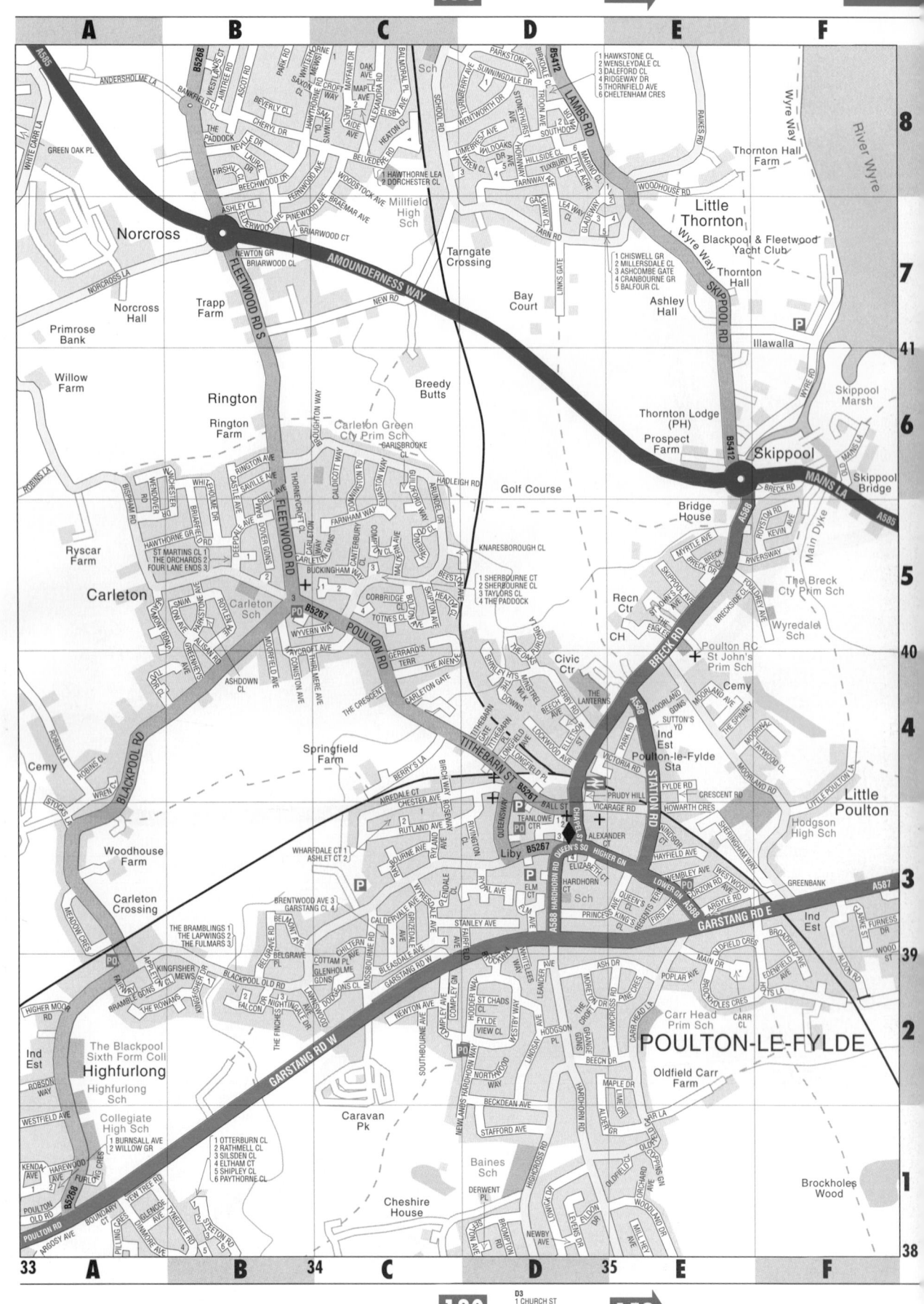

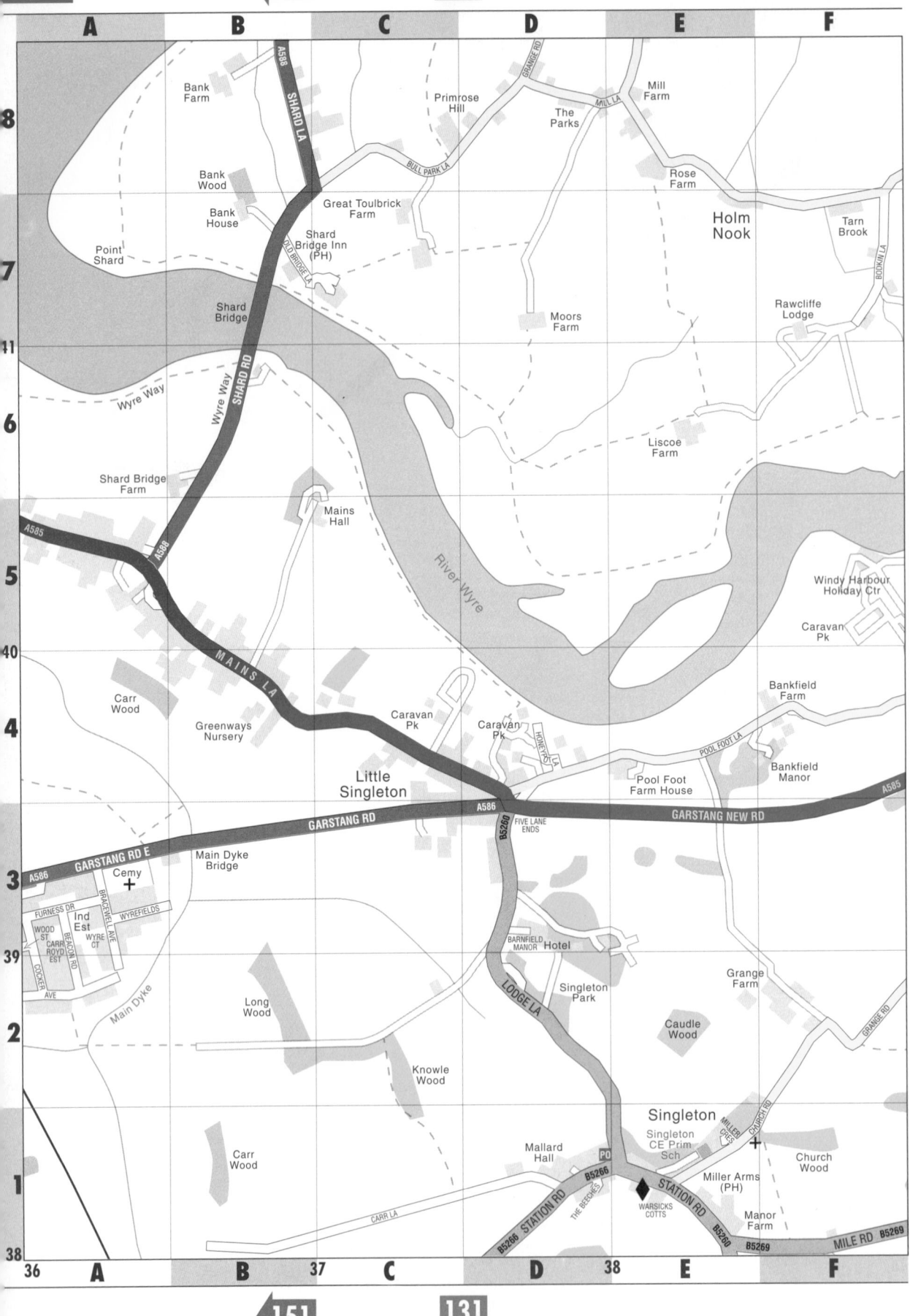

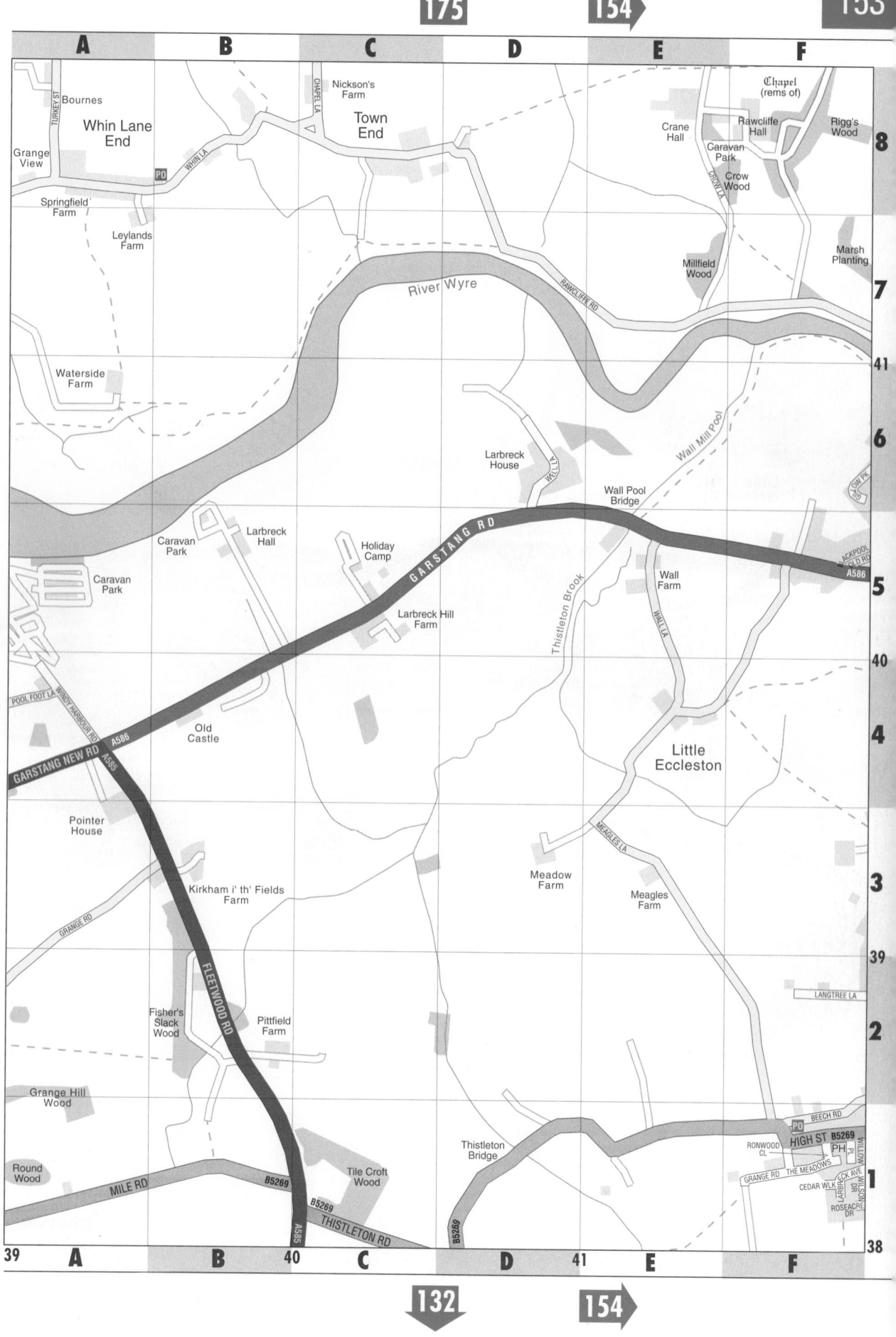

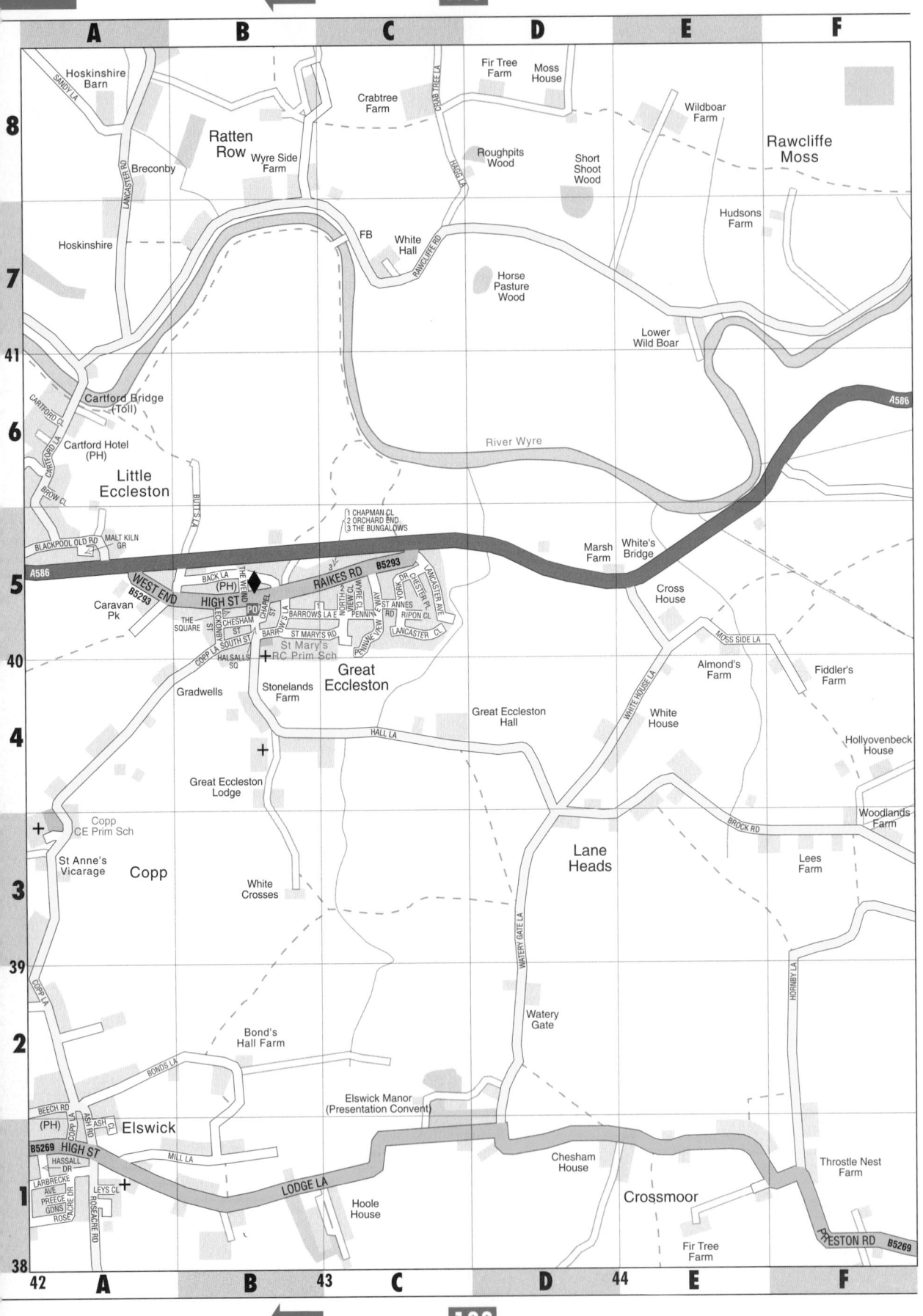

A   B   C   D   E   F

8

7

41

6

5

40

4

3

39

2

1

38

42   A   B   43   C   D   44   E   F

Hoskinshire Barn

SANDY LA

Ratten Row

Crabtree Farm

Fir Tree Farm

Moss House

CRAB TREE LA

Wyre Side Farm

Roughpits Wood

Short Shoot Wood

Wildboar Farm

Rawcliffe Moss

LANCASTER RD

Breconby

FB

White Hall

RAWCLIFFE RD

HAGG LA

Horse Pasture Wood

Hudsons Farm

Hoskinshire

Lower Wild Boar

A586

Cartford Bridge (Toll)

River Wyre

CARTFORD CL

Cartford Hotel (PH)

Little Eccleston

BUTT'S LA

BROW CL

CARTFORD LA

MALT KILN GR

Blackpool Old Rd

1 CHAPMAN CL
2 ORCHARD END
3 THE BUNGALOWS

Marsh Farm

White's Bridge

A586

West End

(PH)

BACK LA

B5293

HIGH ST

RAIKES RD

B5293

LANCASTER AVE

Cross House

B5293

PO

Caravan Pk

THE SQUARE

CHESHAM ST

SOUTH ST

CORP LA

LECKONBY ST

CHAPEL ST

WYRE ST

BARR

BARROWS LA E

WYRE ST

DR CHESTER PK

ST ANNES RD

RIPON CL

PENNINE VIEW

PENNINE VIEW

LANCASTER CL

MOSS SIDE LA

Almond's Farm

Fiddler's Farm

HALSALLS SQ

ST MARY'S RD

St Mary's RC Prim Sch

Great Eccleston

Great Eccleston Hall

WHITE HOUSE LA

White House

Hollyovenbeck House

Gradwells

Stonelands Farm

HALL LA

Woodlands Farm

Great Eccleston Lodge

BROCK RD

Copp CE Prim Sch

Copp

St Anne's Vicarage

White Crosses

Lane Heads

Lees Farm

CORP LA

WATERY GATE LA

Bond's Hall Farm

BONDS LA

Watery Gate

HORNBY LA

ASH RD

Elswick Manor (Presentation Convent)

LARBRECK AVE

BEECH RD

(PH)

ASH RD

Elswick

MILL LA

Chesham House

Throstle Nest Farm

B5269

HIGH ST

HASSALL DR

LEYS CL

LODGE LA

Hoole House

Crossmoor

PRESTON RD

B5269

PREECE GDNS

ROSE

ROSACRE RD

Fir Tree Farm

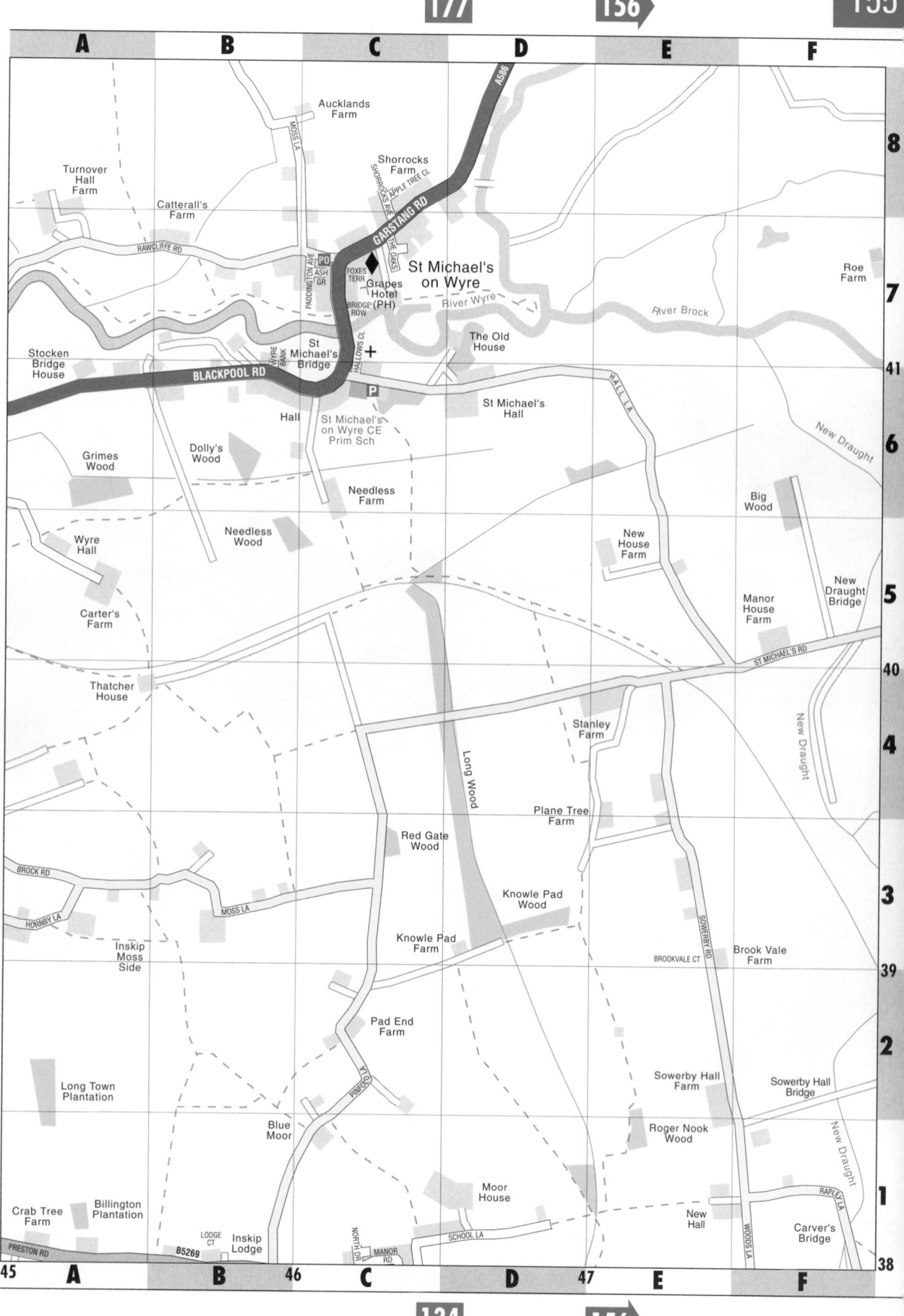

A   B   C   D   E   F

Aucklands Farm

MOSS LA

Shorrocks Farm

APPLE TREE CL

SHORROCKS AVE

GARSTANG RD

A586

Turnover Hall Farm

Catterall's Farm

RAWCLIFFE RD

PADDINGTON AVE

THE OAKS

P.O.

ASH GR

FOXES TERR

BRIDGE ROW

Grapes Hotel (PH)

St Michael's on Wyre

River Wyre

River Brock

Roe Farm

Stocken Bridge House

WYRE BANK

St Michael's Bridge

HALLOWS CL

The Old House

BLACKPOOL RD

P

Hall

St Michael's on Wyre CE Prim Sch

St Michael's Hall

HALL LA

New Draught

41

Grimes Wood

Dolly's Wood

Needless Farm

Big Wood

6

Needless Wood

New House Farm

New Draught Bridge

Wyre Hall

Manor House Farm

5

Carter's Farm

ST MICHAEL'S RD

40

Thatcher House

New Draught

Stanley Farm

4

Long Wood

Plane Tree Farm

BROCK RD

MOSS LA

Red Gate Wood

Knowle Pad Wood

SOWERBY RD

Brook Vale Farm

3

HORNBY LA

Inskip Moss Side

Knowle Pad Farm

BROOKVALE CT

39

Pad End Farm

2

PINFOLD LA

Long Town Plantation

Sowerby Hall Farm

Sowerby Hall Bridge

New Draught

Blue Moor

Roger Nook Wood

RAPLEY LA

Crab Tree Farm

Billington Plantation

Moor House

New Hall

WOODS LA

Carver's Bridge

1

PRESTON RD

LODGE CT

B5269

Inskip Lodge

NORTH DR

MANOR RD

SCHOOL LA

38

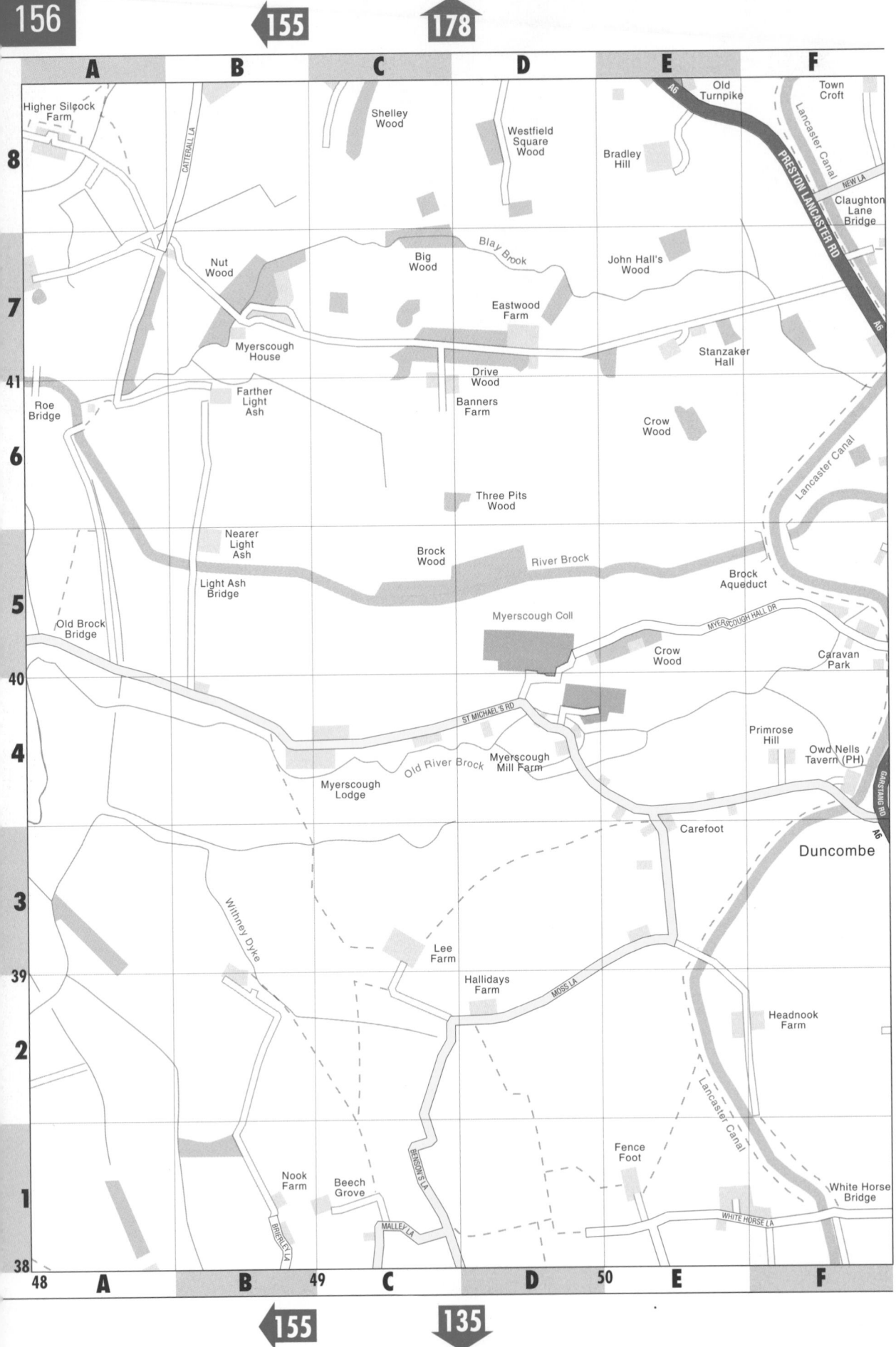

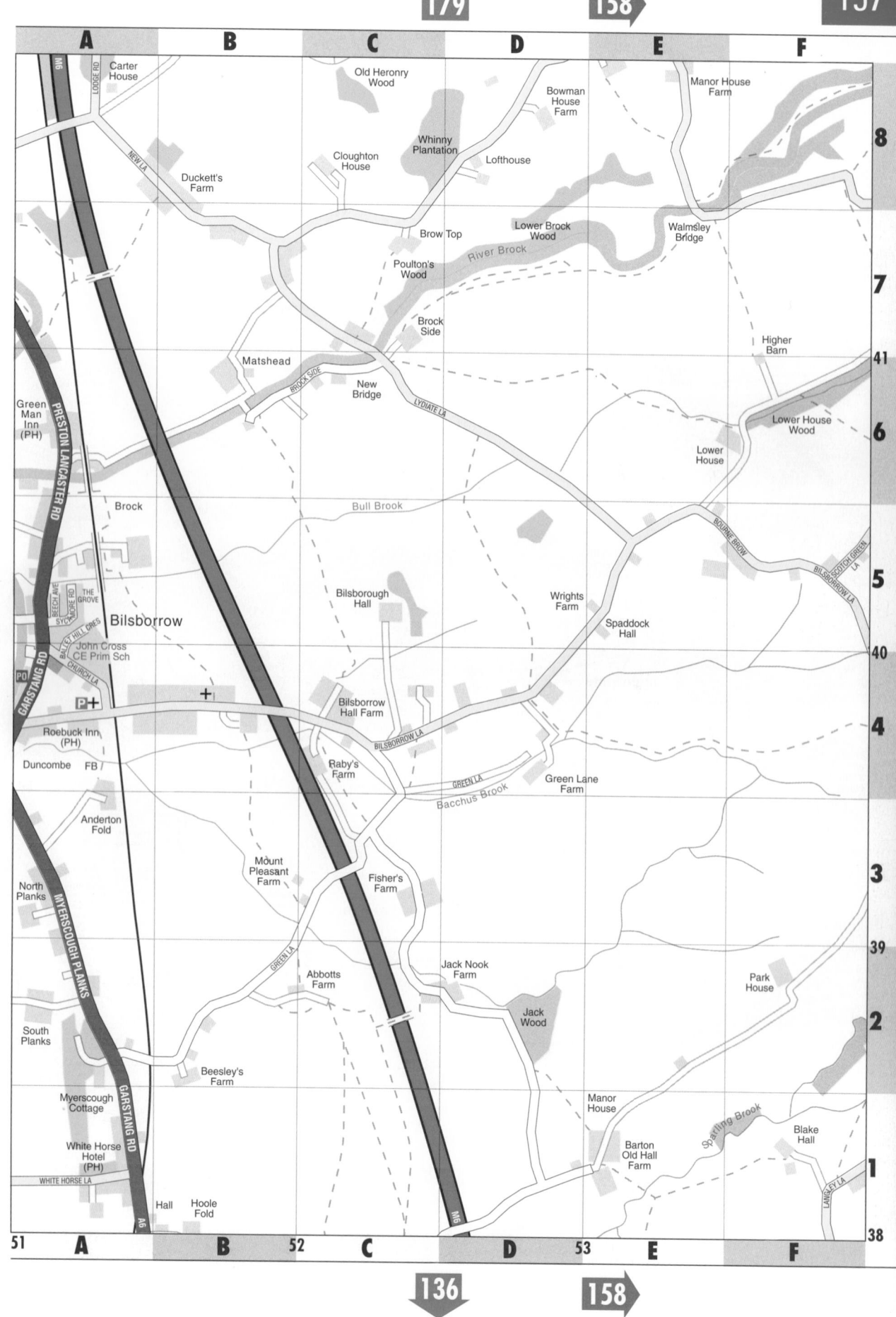

157
180

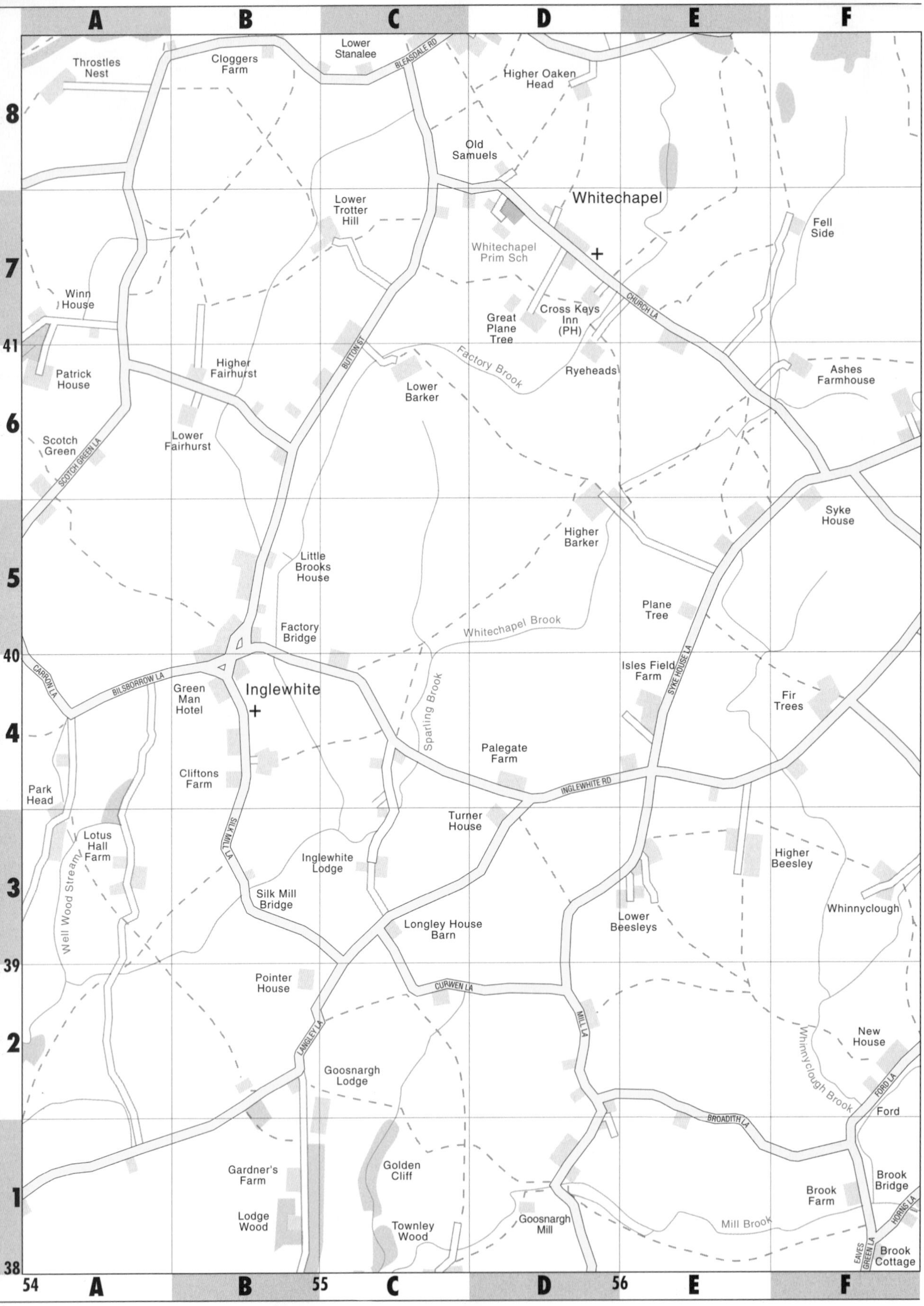

A B C D E F

8

Throstles Nest
Cloggers Farm
Lower Stanalee
BLEASDALE RD
Higher Oaken Head

Old Samuels

7

Whitechapel

Lower Trotter Hill

Whitechapel Prim Sch

Fell Side

CHURCH LA

Winn House

41

Patrick House

BUTTON ST

Great Plane Tree

Cross Keys Inn (PH)

Ryeheads

Ashes Farmhouse

Higher Fairhurst

Lower Barker

Factory Brook

6

Scotch Green

SCOTCH GREEN LA

Lower Fairhurst

Syke House

Higher Barker

5

Little Brooks House

Whitechapel Brook

Plane Tree

40

Factory Bridge

CARRON LA

BILSBORROW LA

Green Man Hotel

Inglewhite

Spatling Brook

Isles Field Farm

SYKE HOUSE LA

Fir Trees

4

Park Head

Cliftons Farm

Palegate Farm

INGLEWHITE RD

Lotus Hall Farm

Well Wood Stream

SILK MILL LA

Turner House

Higher Beesley

Whinnyclough

3

Inglewhite Lodge

Silk Mill Bridge

Longley House Barn

Lower Beesleys

39

Pointer House

CURWEN LA

MILL LA

Whinnyclough Brook

New House

2

LANGLEY LA

Goosnargh Lodge

BROADITH LA

FORD LA

Ford

1

Gardner's Farm

Golden Cliff

Brook Farm

Brook Bridge

Lodge Wood

Townley Wood

Goosnargh Mill

Mill Brook

EAVES GREEN LA

HORNS LA

Brook Cottage

38

54 A 55 B C 56 D E F

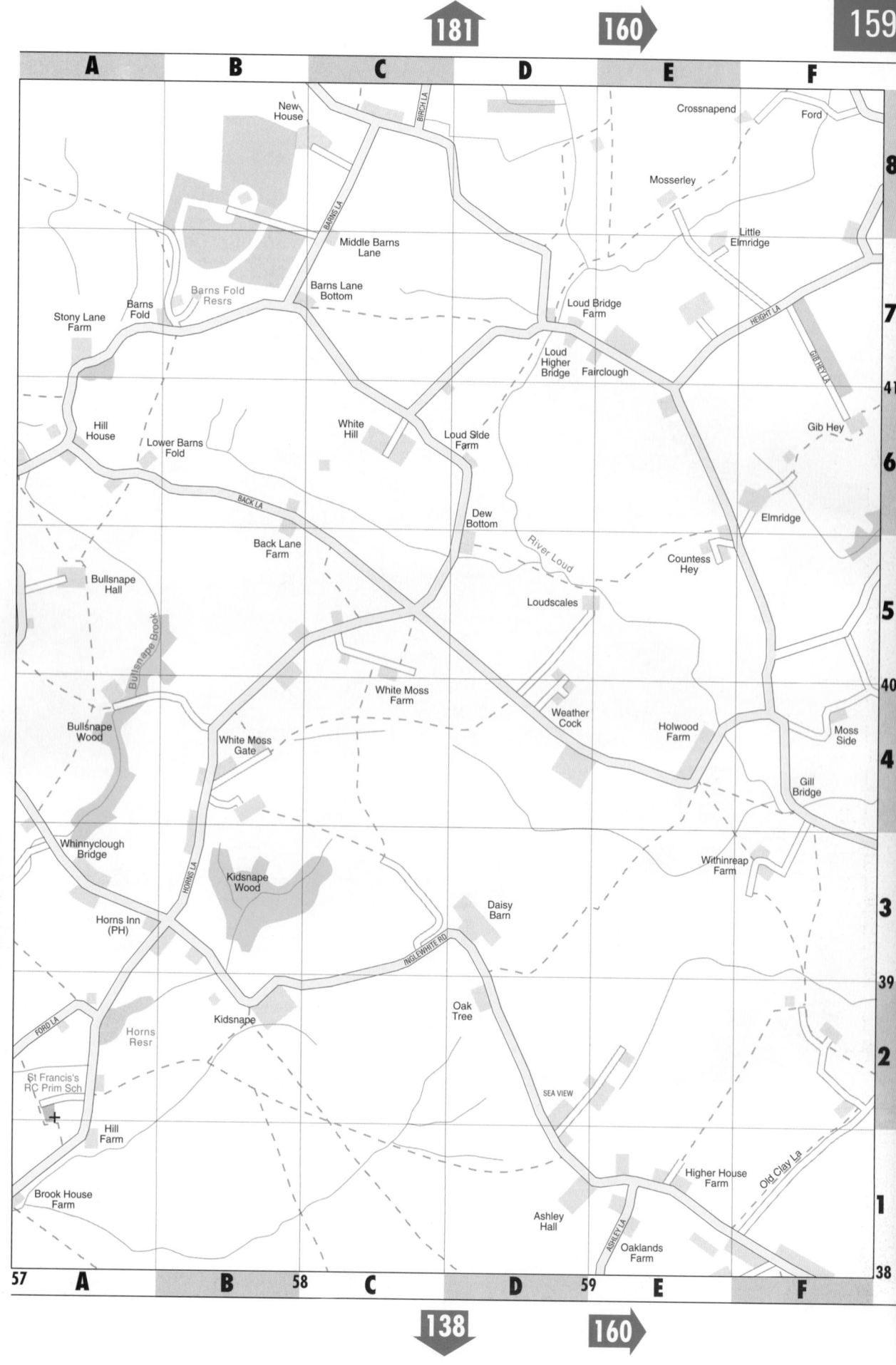

A B C D E F

8
7
41
6
5
40
4
3
39
2
1
38

New House
Crossnapend
Ford
Mosserley
Little Elmridge
BARNS LA
BIRCH LA
HEIGHT LA
GILL HEY LA
Middle Barns Lane
Barns Lane Bottom
Barns Fold Resrs
Barns Fold
Loud Bridge Farm
Stony Lane Farm
Loud Higher Bridge
Fairclough
Hill House
Lower Barns Fold
White Hill
Loud Side Farm
Gib Hey
BACK LA
Back Lane Farm
Dew Bottom
River Loud
Elmridge
Countess Hey
Bullsnape Hall
Loudscales
Bullsnape Brook
White Moss Farm
Weather Cock
Holwood Farm
Moss Side
Bullsnape Wood
White Moss Gate
Gill Bridge
Whinnyclough Bridge
Kidsnape Wood
Withinreap Farm
HORNS LA
Horns Inn (PH)
Daisy Barn
INGLEWHITE RD
FORD LA
Oak Tree
Horns Resr
Kidsnape
39
St Francis's RC Prim Sch
SEA VIEW
Hill Farm
Higher House Farm
Old Clay La
Brook House Farm
Ashley Hall
ASHLEY LA
Oaklands Farm

159
182

A B C D E F

8

7

41

6

5

40

4

3

39

2

1

38

Old Vicarage
PARSONAGE LA
Higher Parsonage
PARKINSON'S LA
Astley House
CUTLER LA
Fields Farm
Sandy Bank Farm
Pale Farm
Folly
Dobson's Hall
Wallclough
MILL LA
Higher Chipping House
Hesketh Lane
LONGRIDGE RD
Loud Side
Leach House
Dog and Partridge (PH)
HESKETH LA
Lanshaw Bridge
SCHOOL LA
Hesketh End
Crow Trees Farm
JUDD HOLMES LA
Judd Holmes
Loud Lower Bridge
ARBOUR LANE END
Black Moss House
Rose Grove
Arbour Farm
Elmridge Wood
Lyme House Farm
Black Moss
Black Moss Wood
Knott
River Loud
HOPE LA
FOUR ACRE LA
Lea House Bridge
Dale House
Clap Gate
Woodhill
LONGRIDGE RD
ELM BROW
Elm Wood
Wheatley Farm
Turnley's
Blackmoss House
Bradleys Farm
Moss Gate Farm
Derby Arms (PH)
White Fold
Longridge Golf Course
Priest Hill
Little Town
Oaks Barn
CH
BIRKS BROW
Higher Birks
Higher Cockleach
Curtis House
Sharple's House
Hill Top
FORTY ACRE LA
COCKLEACH LANE ENDS
LORD'S LA
Old Rhodes
Stone Croft
OLD CLITHEROE RD
Hills
Lower Cockleach
Jenkinsons
Dilworth Brows
Billingtons
Resrs
Beacon Fell Caravan Pk
Cottam House Farm
CHIPPING LA
Nook Fold
WRITTEN STONE LA
Tootle Height

60 A B 61 C D 62 E F

A B C D E F

8

River Loud

Park Wood

Bradley Hall
Plantation

Head of
Moor

Bradley
Hall

BRADLEY
CT

Weed Acre
Farm

Mocking
Brook
Wood

Rams
Clough
Wood

7

Thornley
Hall

CLOUGH LA

Rams Clough

Spire Hill

ROCK BROW

Woodstraw
House

41

FOUR ACRE LA

6

West House
Barn

Meg
Hall

Thornley Hall Fell

Giles
Farm

Moor Game
Hall

5

FORTY ACRE LA

P

Cardwell
House

Jeffrey
Hill

Gannow
Fell

Lennox
Farm

40

Fell
House

Plantation
Farm

4

Myers's
Farm

Longridge
Fell

Forty
Acre
Farm

Low Hill
Wood

3

Cuckoo
Hall

Cowley
Brook
Farm

OLD CLITHEROE RD

Hougher
Fall
Farm

Low Mill
House

HUNTINGDON HALL RD

High
House

Newdrop
Inn
(PH)

Goodshaw
House

39

Cutler's
Hill

2

Hoardsell

Dutton
Manor

Lane
Ends

Moor
Hey

Squire
House

Knowle
Green

Longfield

Hall's Arms
(PH)

NEW ROW

Moor
Nook

1

Moss
Gate

KNOWLE GREEN RD B6243

GREEN MOOR LA

STONYGATE LA

TOP OF FAWNA RD

B6243

38

63   A   B   64   C   D   65   E   F

A   B   C   D   E   F

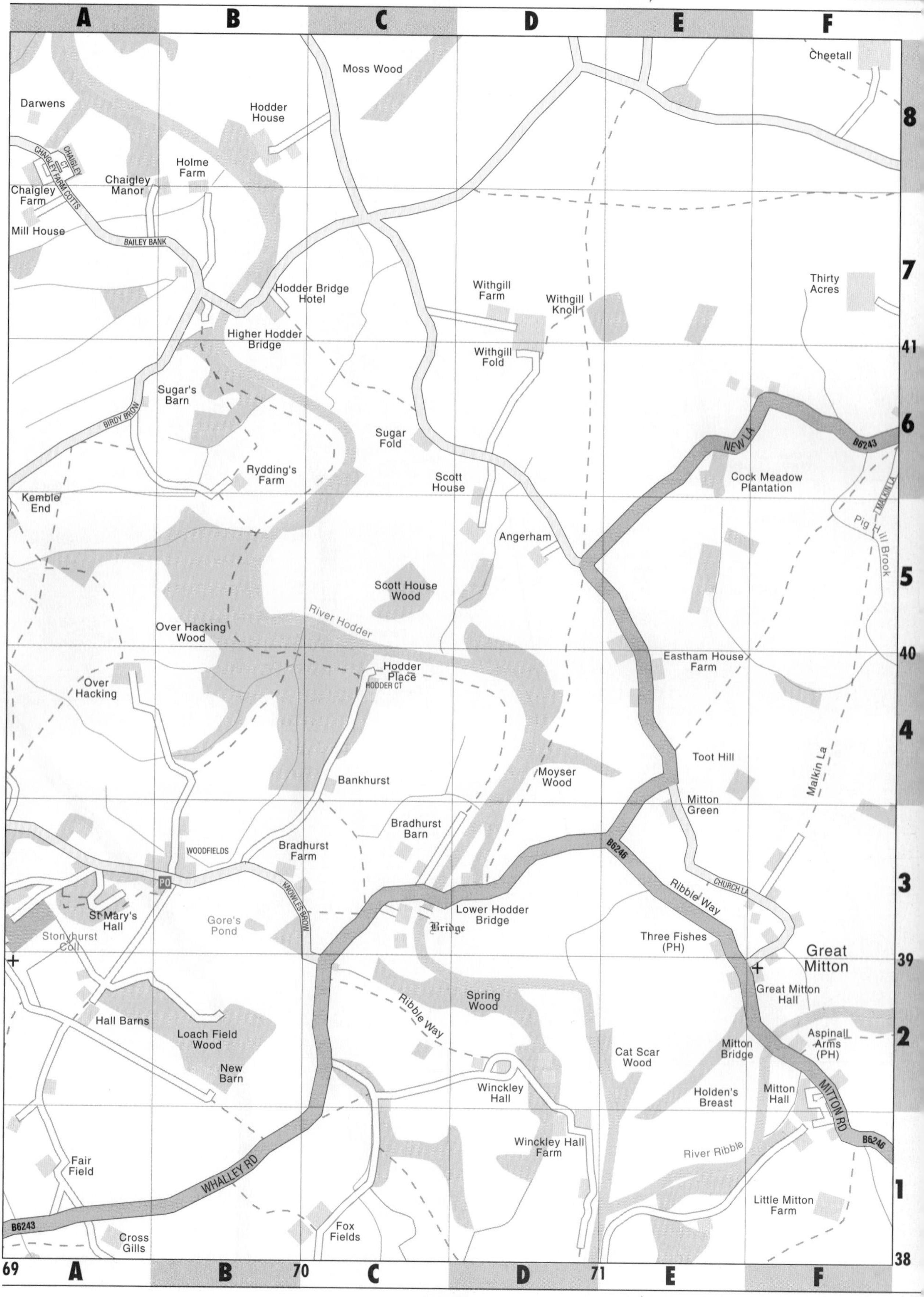

8

Cheetall

Darwens

CHAIGLEY CTS

CHAIGLEY FARM CTS

Chaigley
Manor

Holme
Farm

Hodder
House

Moss Wood

Chaigley
Farm

Mill House

BAILEY BANK

7

Hodder Bridge
Hotel

Withgill
Farm

Withgill
Knoll

Thirty
Acres

Higher Hodder
Bridge

41

Sugar's
Barn

BIRDY BROOK

Withgill
Fold

NEW LA

B6243

6

Rydding's
Farm

Sugar
Fold

Cock Meadow
Plantation

Kemble
End

Scott
House

Angerham

Pig Hill Brook

TRINNICKLE BROOK

5

Scott House
Wood

Over Hacking
Wood

River Hodder

40

Over
Hacking

Hodder
Place

HODDER CT

Eastham House
Farm

4

Bankhurst

Moyser
Wood

Toot Hill

Malkin La

Bradhurst
Barn

Mitton
Green

Woodfields

Bradhurst
Farm

B6246

Mitton
Green

3

PO

KNOWLES BROW

Lower Hodder
Bridge

Ribble Way

CHURCH LA

St Mary's
Hall

Gore's
Pond

Bridge

Three Fishes
(PH)

Great
Mitton

Stonyhurst
Coll

39

Great Mitton
Hall

Hall Barns

Loach Field
Wood

Ribble Way

Spring
Wood

Aspinall
Arms
(PH)

Mitton
Bridge

2

New
Barn

Cat Scar
Wood

Holden's
Breast

Mitton
Hall

MITTON RD

Winckley
Hall

B6246

Fair
Field

WHALLEY RD

Winckley Hall
Farm

River Ribble

Little Mitton
Farm

1

B6243

Cross
Gills

Fox
Fields

38

69   A   B   70   C   D   71   E   F

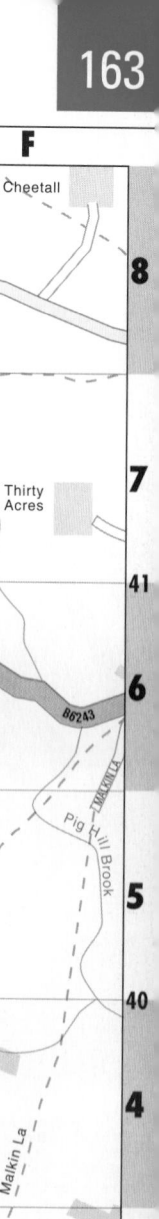

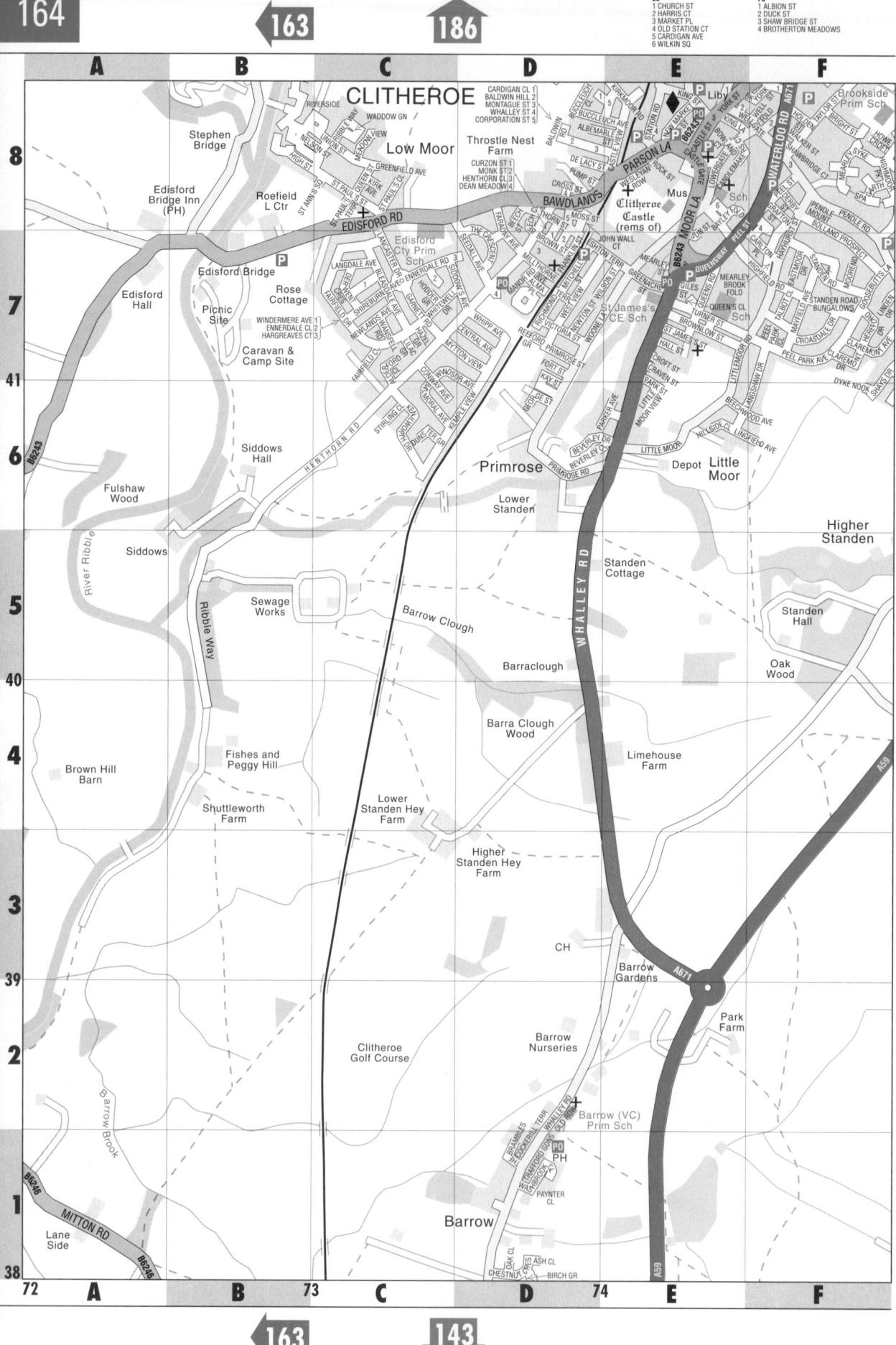

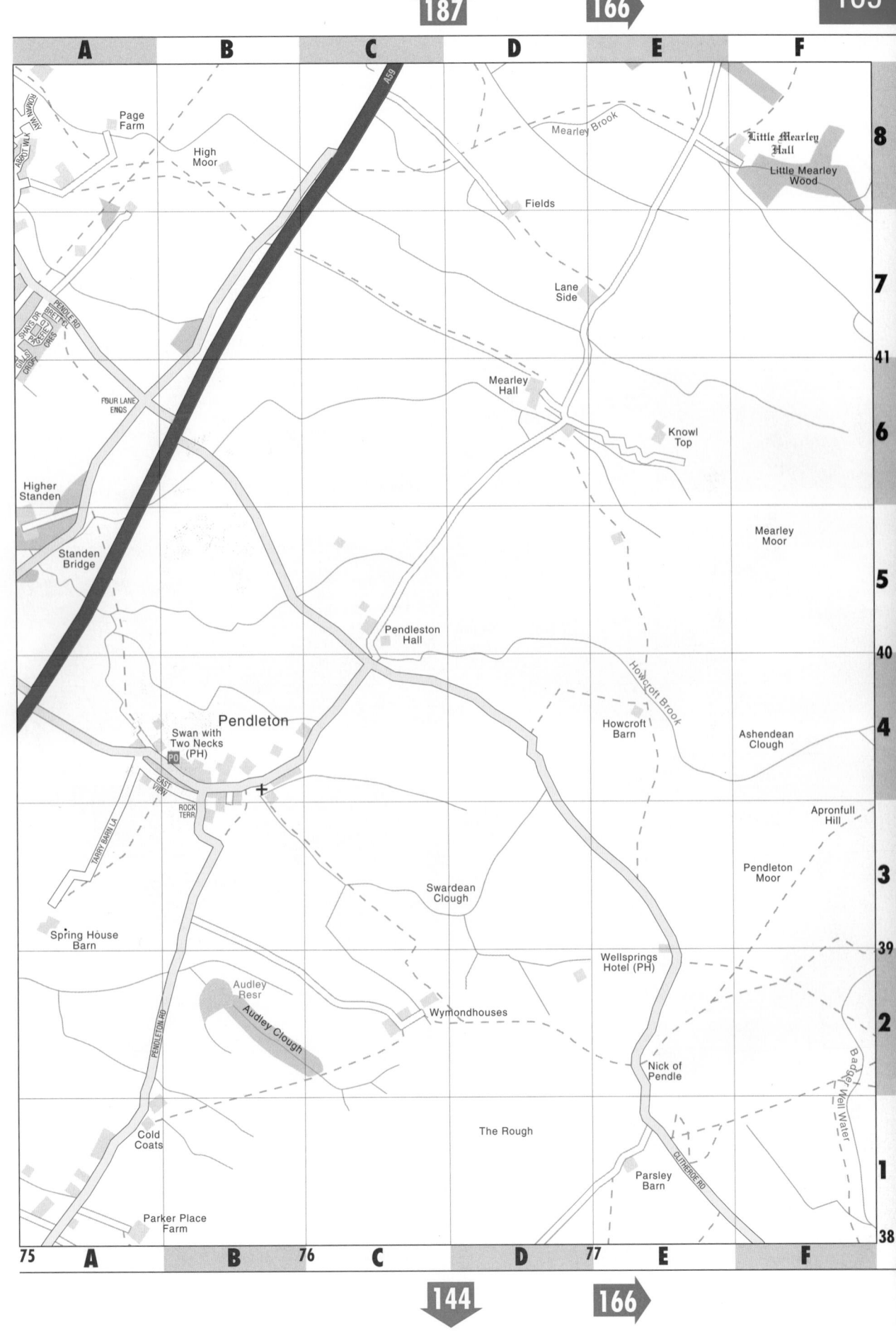

165
188

A **B** **C** **D** **E** **F**

8

Worston Moor

Pendle Hill

Beacon or Big End

Pendle Way

7

Pendle Moor

Pendle House

41

6

Turn Head

Ogden Clough

Under Pendle

5

Mearley Moor

Barley Moor

Ogden Hill

White Slacks

Buttock

Dry Clough

Howcroft Brook

40

Cat Holes

New Fields

4

Black Hill

Ogden Clough

Fox Holes

Pendle Way

Ogden Clough

Badger Wells Hill

Upper Ogden Resr

Spence Moor

3

Deerstones

Cock Dole

Driver Height

Craggs Dole

39

Cock Clough Plantation

2

Bank Hill

Wood House Dale

Lower Dale

Stainscomb Dale

Calf Hill

Churn Clough Resr

Wood House Brook

Sabden Fold

1

Rotten Clough

Stainscomb

Churn Clough

Wood House

Lower Lane

The Old House

38

78 **A** 79 **B** **C** 80 **D** **E** **F**

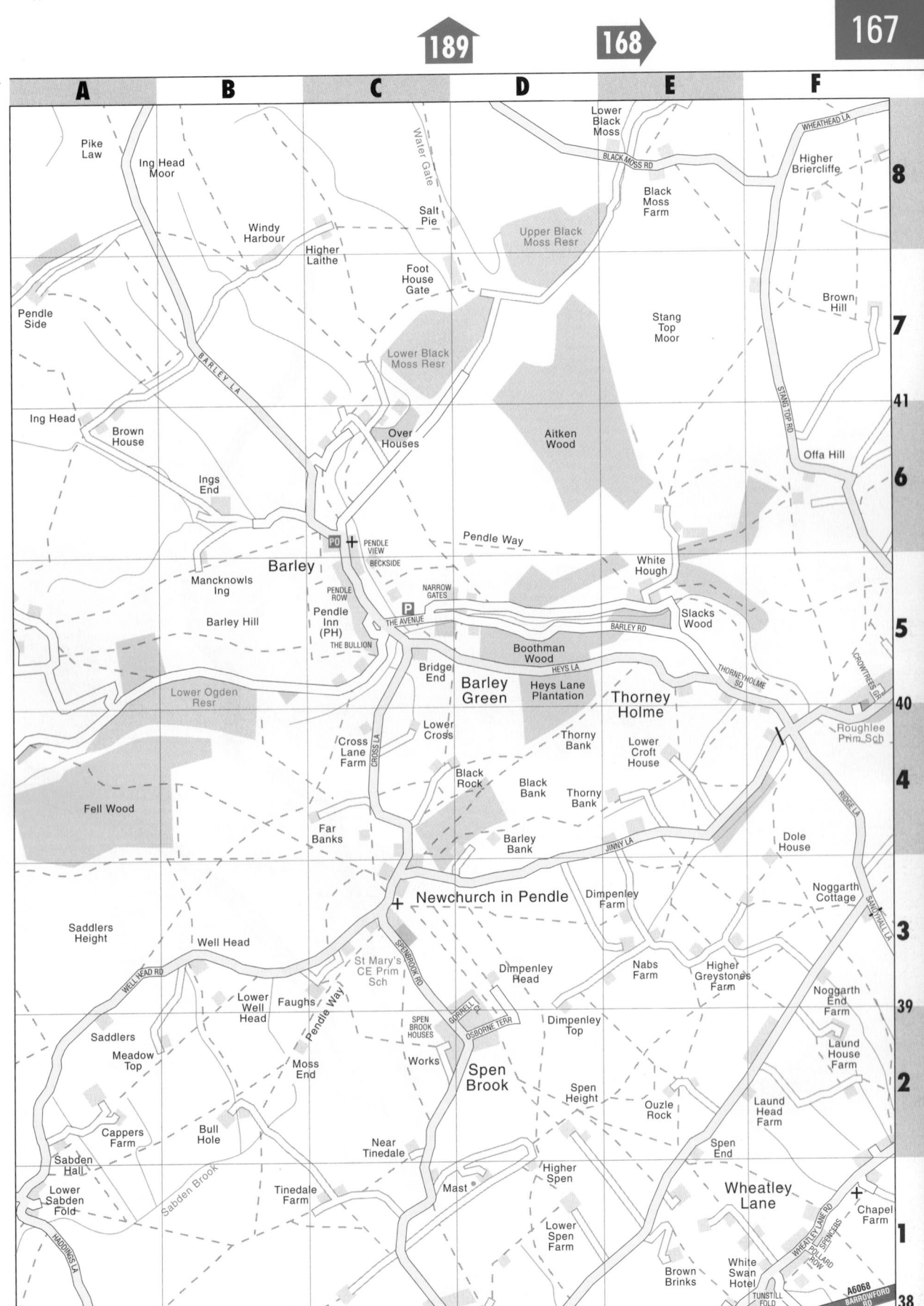

A   B   C   D   E   F

8

7

41

6

5

40

4

3

39

2

1

38

Pike Law

Ing Head Moor

Windy Harbour

Higher Laithe

Salt Pie

Water Gate

Lower Black Moss

Black Moss Rd

Wheathead La

Higher Briercliffe

Black Moss Farm

Upper Black Moss Resr

Foot House Gate

Pendle Side

Brown Hill

Brown House

Ing Head

Barley La

Lower Black Moss Resr

Stang Top Moor

Stang Top Rd

Offa Hill

Ings End

Over Houses

Aitken Wood

Pendle Way

White Hough

Barley

Pendle View

Beckside

PO

Mancknowls Ing

Narrow Gates

Pendle Row

Slacks Wood

Crowtrees Gr

Barley Hill

Pendle Inn (PH)

The Bullion

The Avenue

Barley Rd

P

Boothman Wood

Heys La

Thorneyholme Sq

Bridge End

Barley Green

Heys Lane Plantation

Thorney Holme

Roughlee Prim Sch

Lower Ogden Resr

Cross Lane Farm

Lower Cross

Cross La

Thorny Bank

Lower Croft House

40

Fell Wood

Black Rock

Black Bank

Thorny Bank

Ridge La

Dole House

Far Banks

Barley Bank

Jinny La

Noggarth Cottage

Sandhall La

Newchurch in Pendle

Dimpenley Farm

Saddlers Height

Well Head

Dimpenley Head

Nabs Farm

Higher Greystones Farm

Noggarth End Farm

Well Head Rd

St Mary's CE Prim Sch

Springbrook Rd

Pendle Way

Lower Well Head

Faughs

Dimpenley Top

Laund House Farm

Gurnell La

Osborne Terr

Spen Brook Houses

Saddlers Meadow Top

Moss End

Works

Spen Brook

Spen Height

Ouzle Rock

Laund Head Farm

Cappers Farm

Bull Hole

Near Tinedale

Spen End

Wheatley Lane

Wheatley Lane Rd

Dollard Row

Chapel Farm

Sabden Hall

Sabden Brook

Tinedale Farm

Mast

Higher Spen

Lower Sabden Fold

Haddings La

Lower Spen Farm

Brown Brinks

White Swan Hotel

Tunstill Fold

A6068 Barrowford Rd

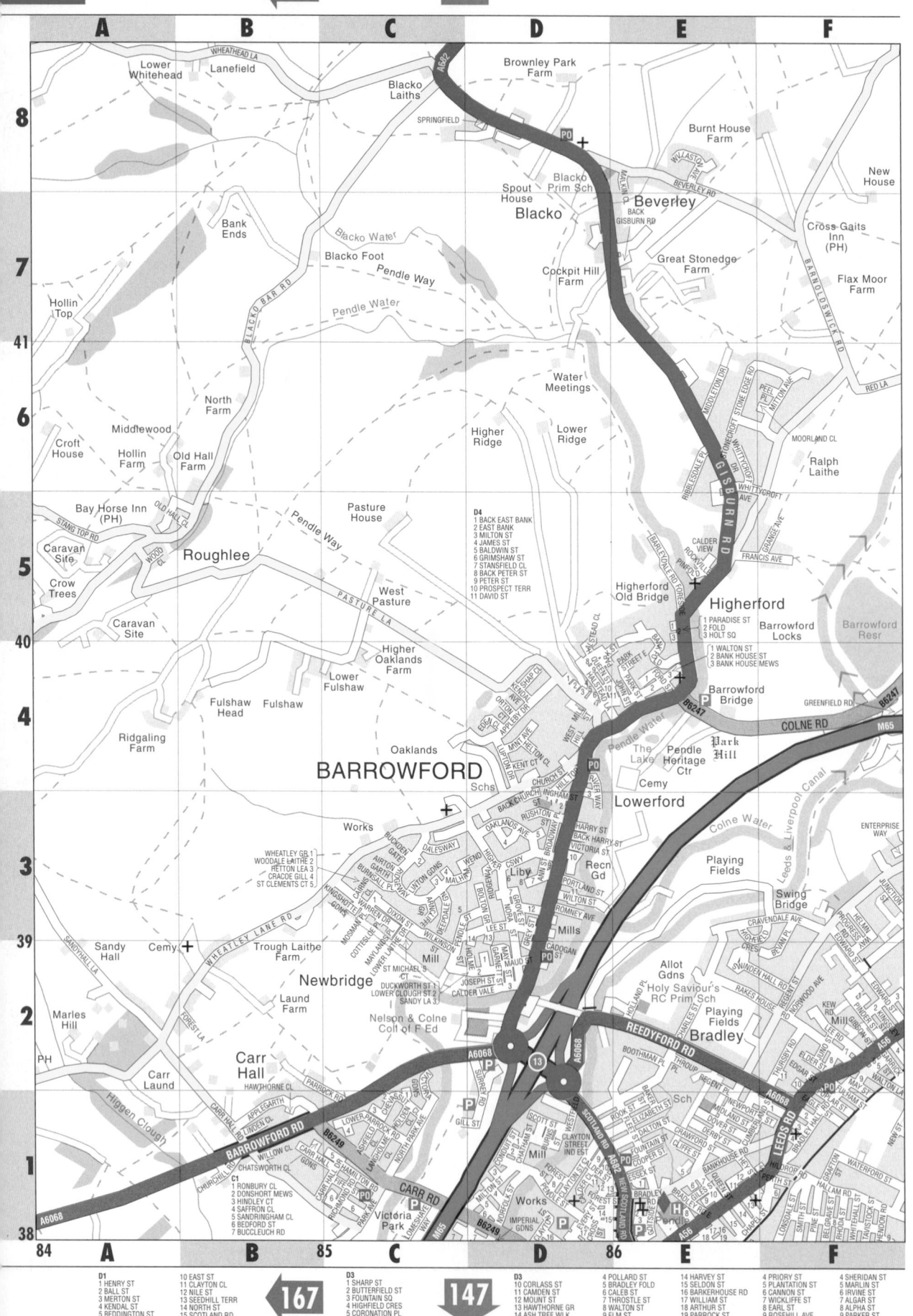

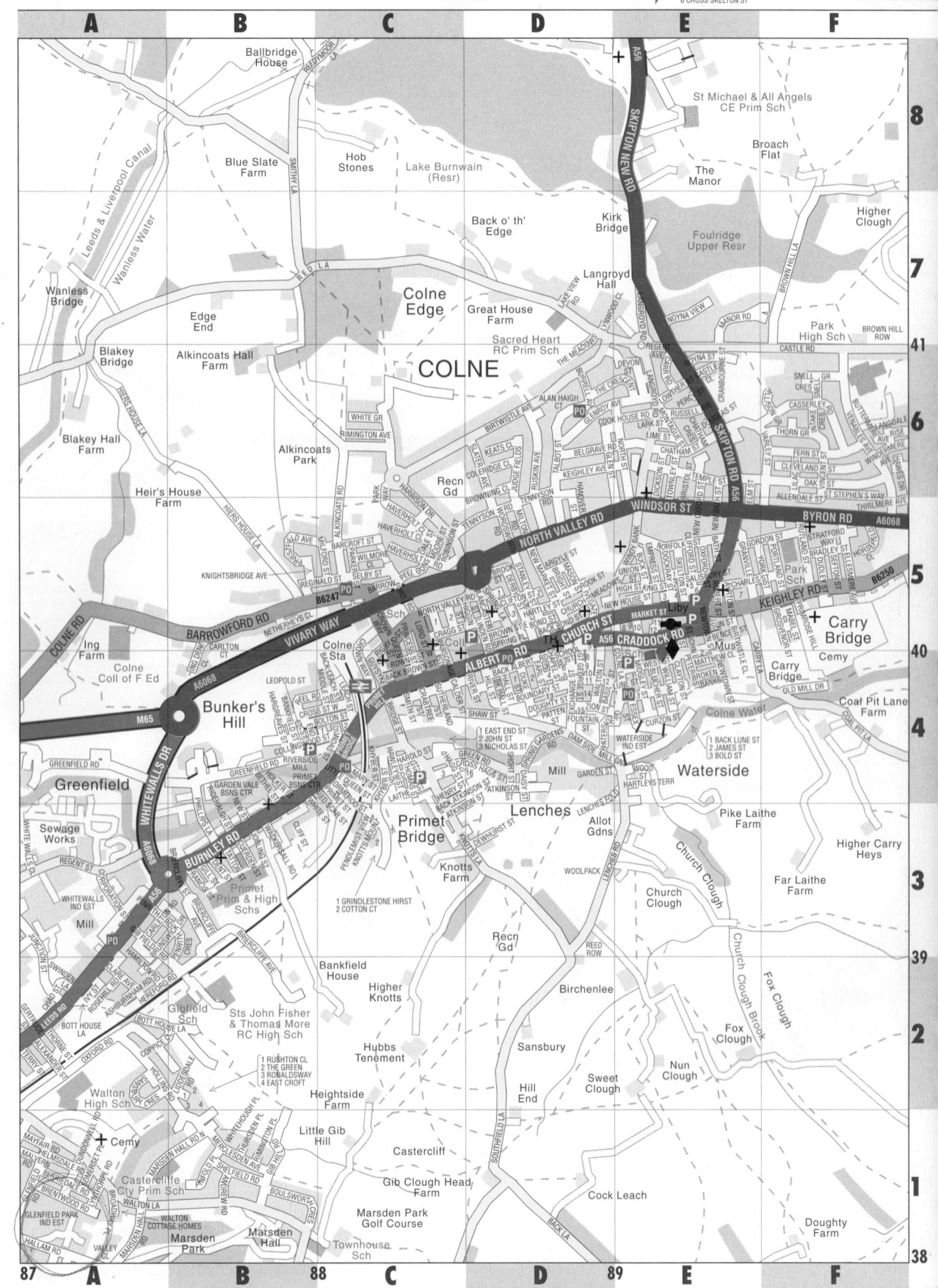

C5
1 FOTHERGILL ST
2 MOORHEAD ST

191

D5
1 BIRTWISTLE HYDE PK
2 MITCHELL ST
3 SPRING YD
4 BACK DERBY ST
5 NELSON ST

170

E5
1 WATER ST
2 DOCKRAY CT
3 ANGEL WAY
4 DOCKRAY YD
5 CUMBERLAND ST
6 CROSS SKELTON ST

7 BIRTWISTLE FOLD
8 POST OFFICE YD
9 ARCADIA
10 MARKET PL
11 PARLIAMENT ST
12 NINEVEH ST

169

148

D4
1 BACK DUKE ST
2 BACK EARL ST
3 KNOWSLEY ST
4 BACK CHAPEL ST
5 CROSS SCHOOL ST
6 LOWER SCHOOL ST
7 WEST EXCHANGE ST
8 RAGLAN ST
9 CAMBRIDGE ST

170

D4
10 BACK CAMBRIDGE ST
11 SELDON ST
12 CHAPEL FOLD
13 BACK BOUNDARY ST
14 BURRANS MEADOW
15 BACK ZION ST
16 CROSS HELLIWELL ST

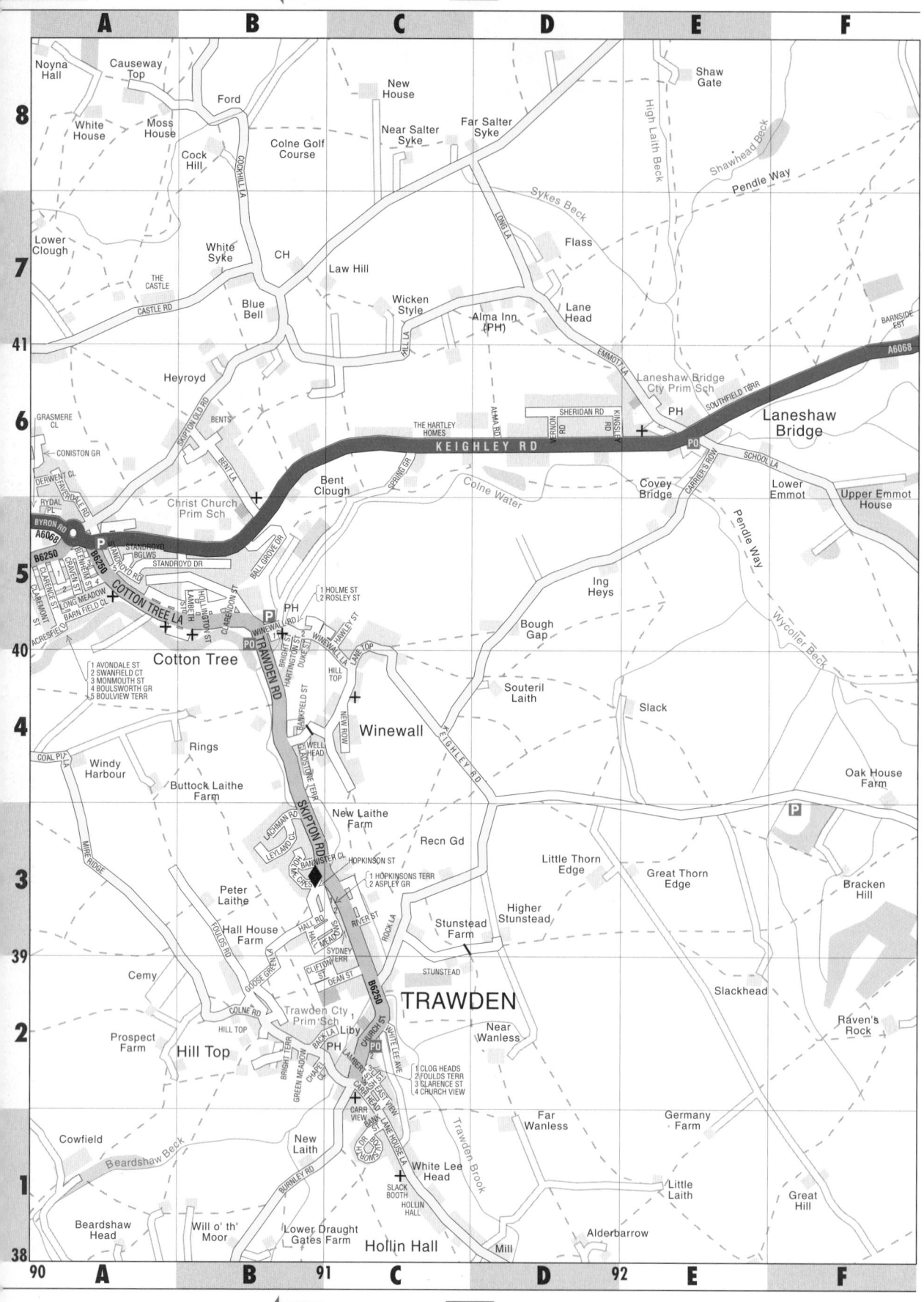

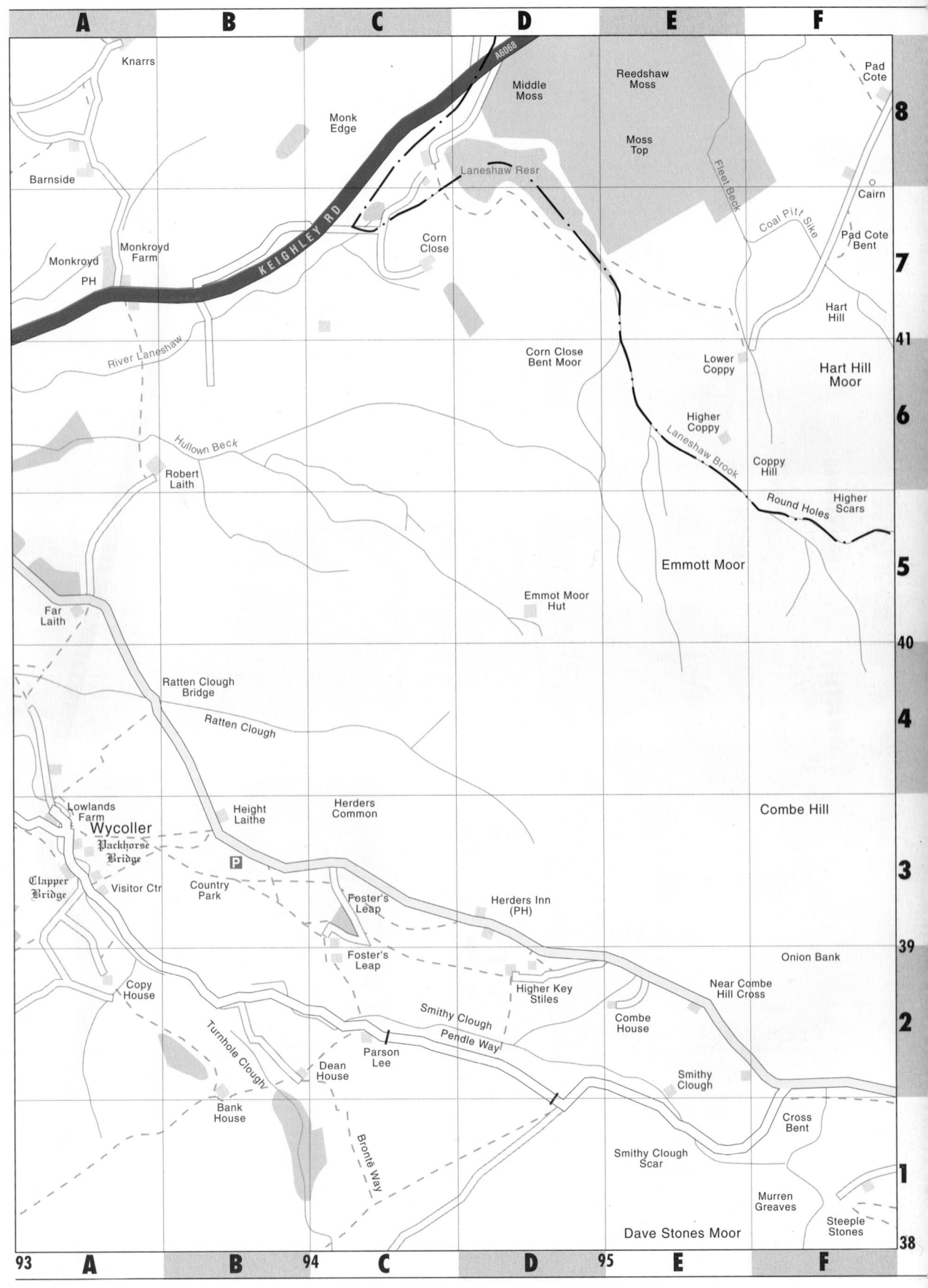

A B C D E F

Knarrs

Middle Moss

A6068

Reedshaw Moss

Pad Cote

Monk Edge

8

Laneshaw Resr

Moss Top

Barnside

Cairn

Corn Close

Monkroyd Farm

Pad Cote Bent

Monkroyd PH

KEIGHLEY RD

Coal Pit Sike

Hart Hill

7

41

River Laneshaw

Corn Close Bent Moor

Lower Coppy

Hart Hill Moor

Hullown Beck

Higher Coppy

Laneshaw Brook

Coppy Hill

6

Robert Laith

Round Holes

Higher Scars

Emmott Moor

Far Laith

Emmot Moor Hut

40

5

Ratten Clough Bridge

Ratten Clough

4

Lowlands Farm

Height Laithe

Herders Common

Combe Hill

Wycoller

Packhorse Bridge

3

Clapper Bridge

Visitor Ctr

Country Park

Foster's Leap

Herders Inn (PH)

Onion Bank

39

Copy House

Foster's Leap

Higher Key Stiles

Near Combe Hill Cross

Turnhole Clough

Smithy Clough

Pendle Way

Combe House

2

Dean House

Parson Lee

Smithy Clough

Bank House

Brontë Way

Cross Bent

Smithy Clough Scar

1

Murren Greaves

Steeple Stones

Dave Stones Moor

38

93 A B 94 C D 95 E F

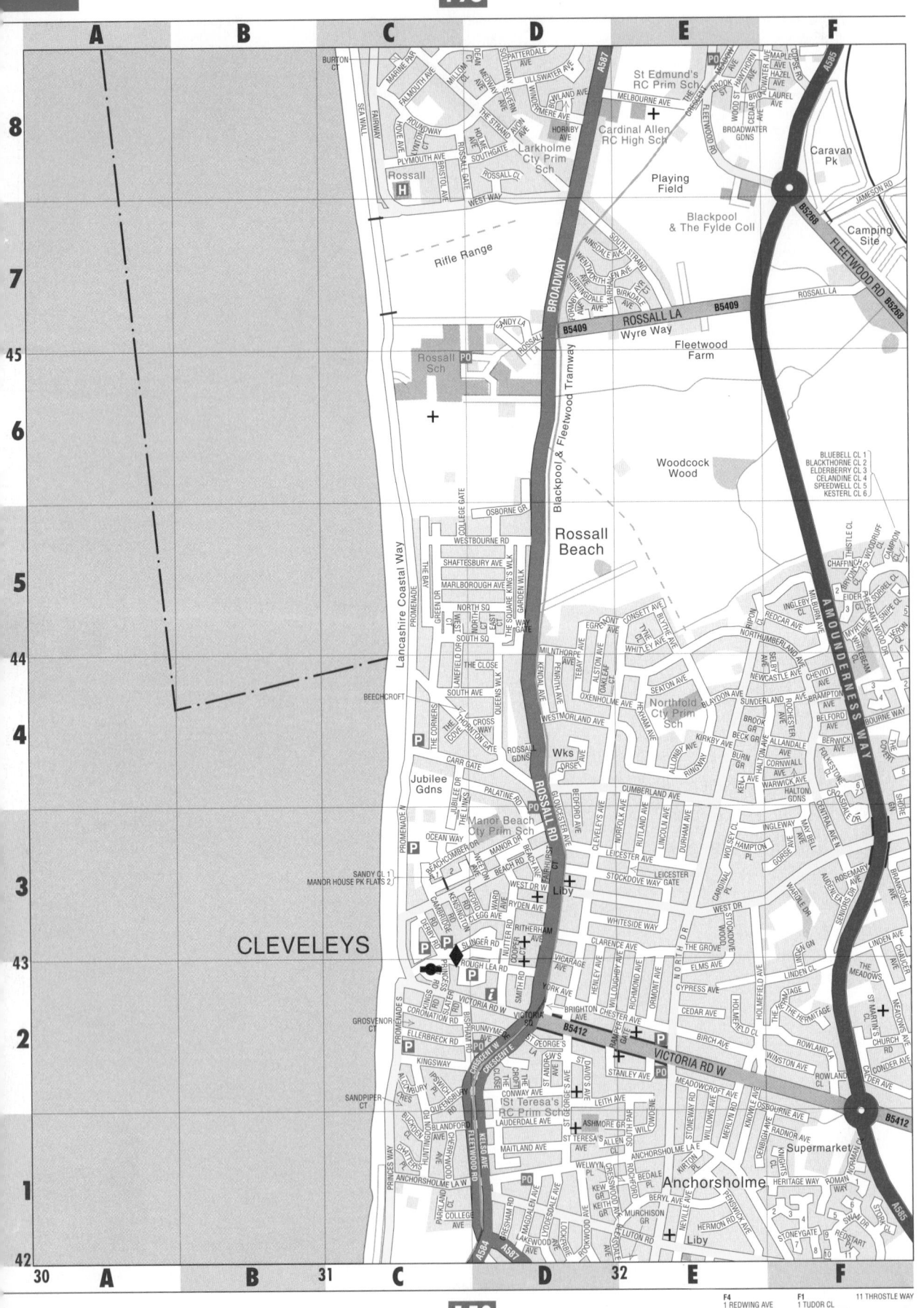

F4
1 REDWING AVE
2 CURLEW CL
3 WHITECREST AVE
4 BARNFIELD CL
5 WIDGEON CL
6 COLCHESTER DR
7 PORTSMOUTH CL

F1
1 TUDOR CL
2 SHERWOOD PL
3 RICHARDS WAY
4 GLADSTONE WAY
5 POCHARD PL
6 DOVE CL
7 INGLENOOK CL
8 HERIOT CL
9 BUNTING PL
10 SANDPIPER PL

11 THROSTLE WAY

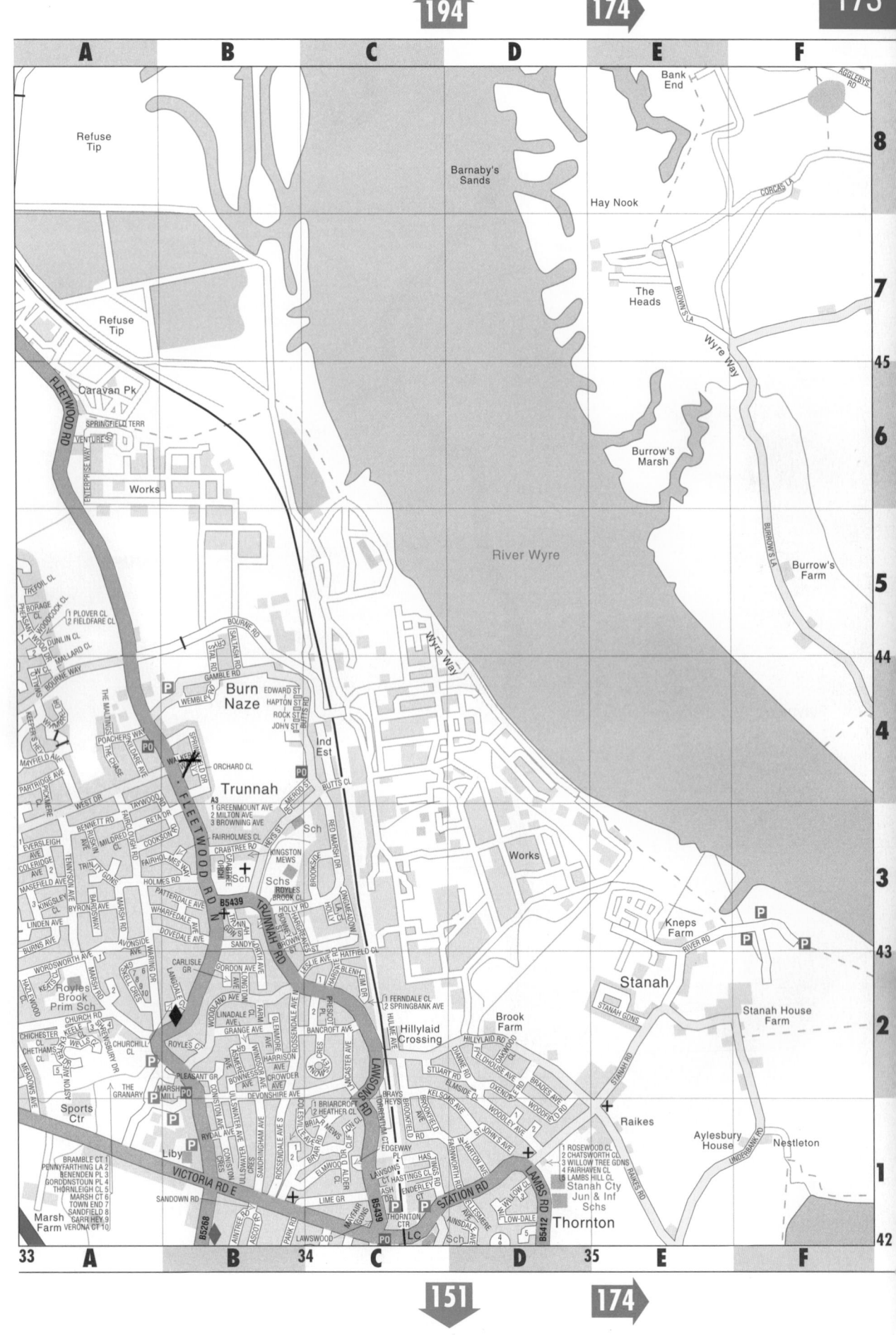

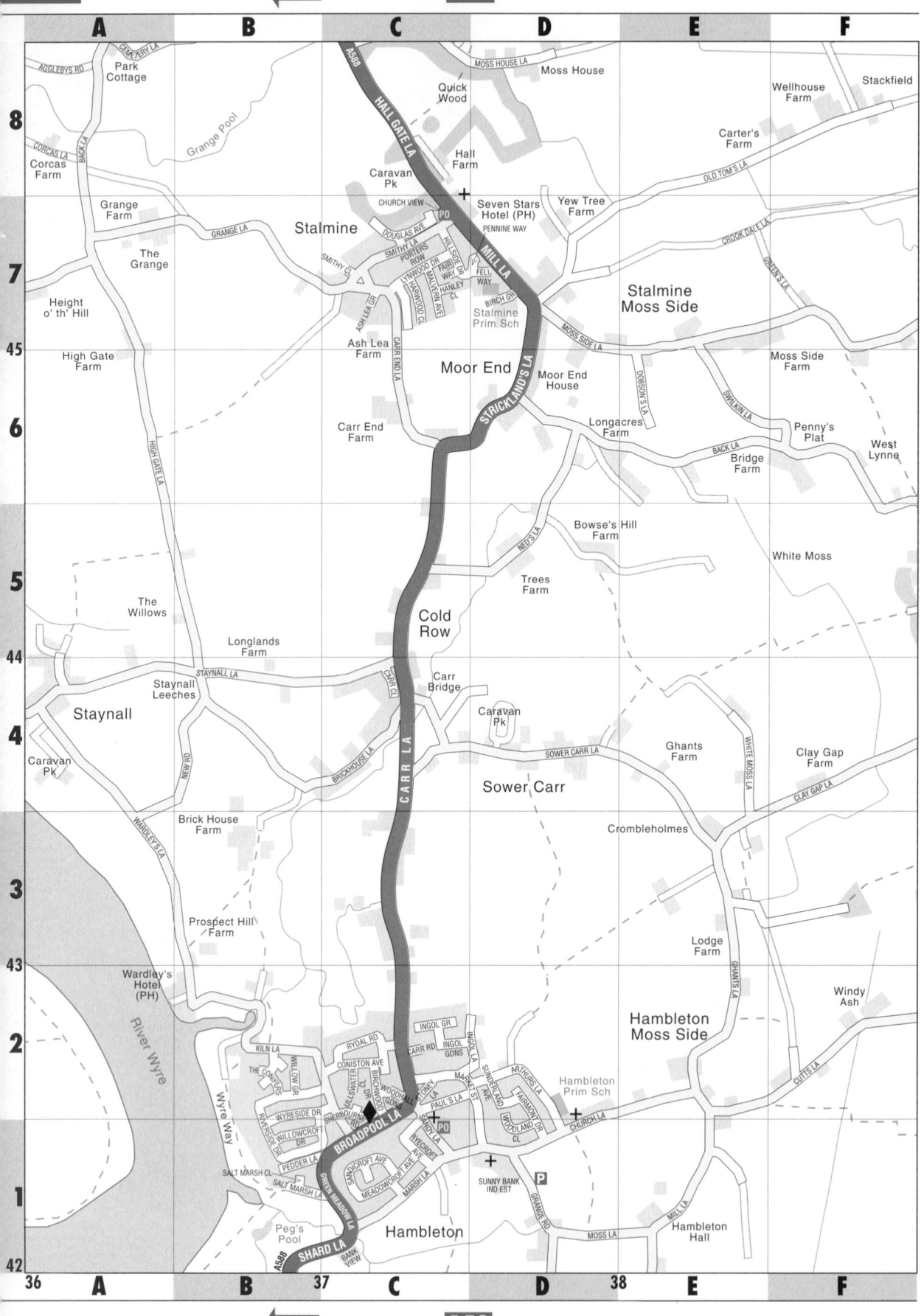

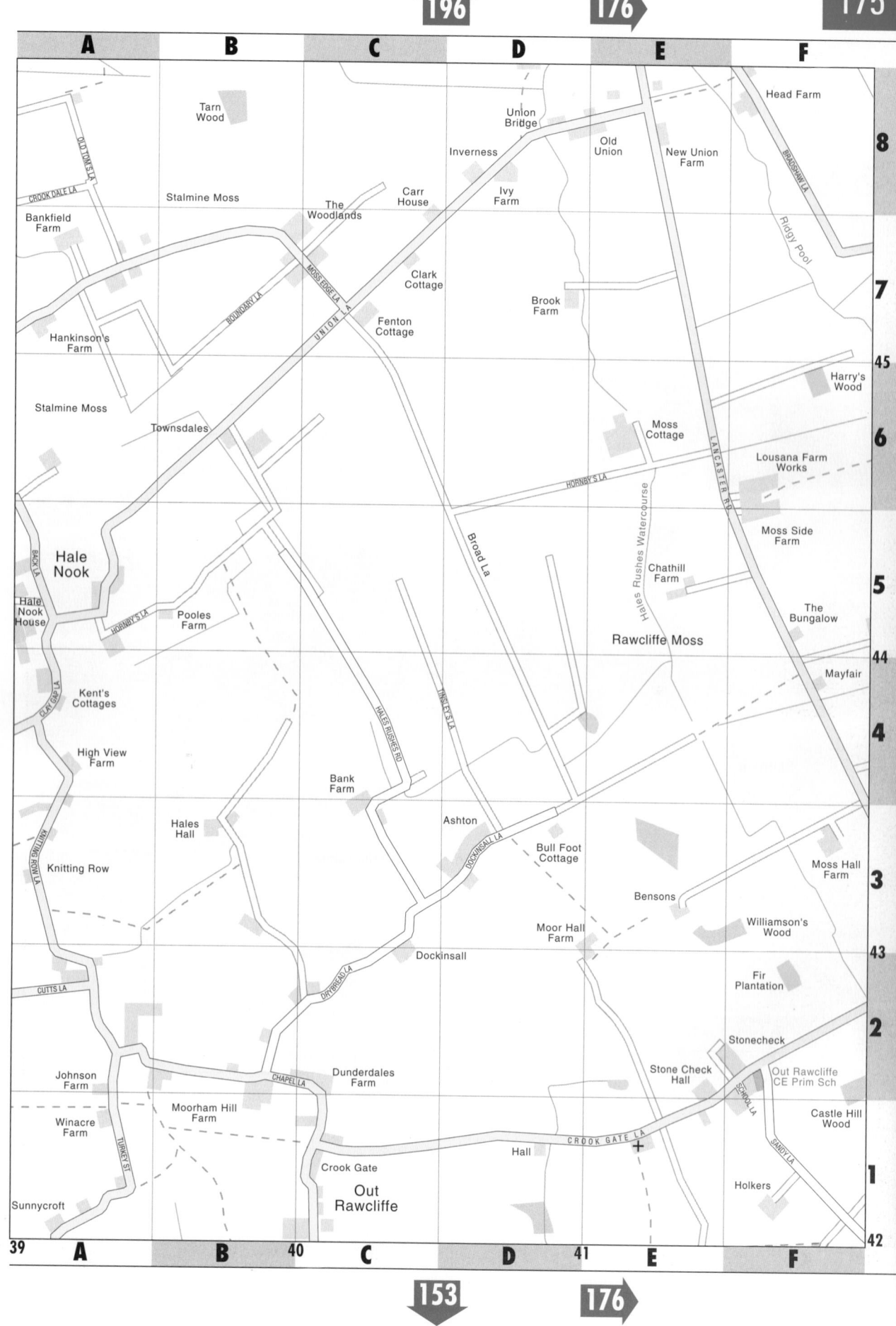

Head Farm

Union
Bridge

Inverness
Old
Union
New Union
Farm

Tarn
Wood

Stalmine Moss

Carr
House
Ivy
Farm

The
Woodlands

Bankfield
Farm

Ridgy Pool

BRADSHAW LA

Clark
Cottage

Brook
Farm

Harry's
Wood

MOSS EDGE LA

Hankinson's
Farm

BOUNDARY LA

Fenton
Cottage

UNION LA

Moss
Cottage

Lousana Farm
Works

Stalmine Moss

Townsdales

HORNBY'S LA

LANCASTER RD

Moss Side
Farm

BACK LA

Hale
Nook

Broad La

Chathill
Farm

Rawcliffe Moss

The
Bungalow

Hale
Nook
House

HORNBY'S LA

Pooles
Farm

Hales Rushes Watercourse

Mayfair

HOPE LA

Kent's
Cottages

HALES RUSHES RD

INSKEY'S LA

High View
Farm

Bank
Farm

Ashton

KNITTING ROW LA

Hales
Hall

Bull Foot
Cottage

Moss Hall
Farm

Knitting Row

DOCKINSALL LA

Bensons

Williamson's
Wood

Moor Hall
Farm

Fir
Plantation

Dockinsall

DRYBREAD LA

Stonecheck

CUTTS LA

Stone Check
Hall

Out Rawcliffe
CE Prim Sch

Johnson
Farm

CHAPEL LA

Dunderdales
Farm

SCHOOL LA

Castle Hill
Wood

Moorham Hill
Farm

Winacre
Farm

TURKEY ST

SANDY LA

CROOK GATE LA

Hall

Crook Gate

Holkers

Sunnycroft

Out
Rawcliffe

CROOK DALE LA

OLD TOM'S LA

175
197

A B C D E F

8

Top Plantation

Black Hill Farm

Northwoods Farm

North Wood's Hill Farm

Eagland Hill

Tarn Farm

Momen Gutter

Momen Farm

NEW LA

7

Upper Birk's Farm

Woodcroft

BRADSHAW LA

South Wood's Hill Farm

45

Birk's Farm

6

Ridgy Pool

Trashy Hill

5

Prospect Farm

Eskham House

44

New Eskham

Rough Holme Farm

Willow Farm

4

Ridgey Pool Farm

SKITHAM LA

Skitham House

Skitham

Grand Agnes Wood

CUCKOO LA

Rawcliffe Moss

3

Moss Edge

Hall

Wilson House Farm

43

CROOK GATE LA

Curlew Farm

2

Valiant's Farm

Equestrian Ctr

LANCASTER RD

CRAB TREE LA

Elswick Ratch Wood

Curlew Wood

1

ALDER LA

Rossall's Wood

Belle Vue Farm

42

42 A B 43 C D 44 E F

175
154

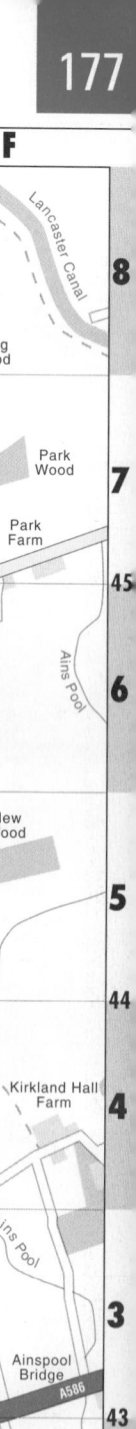

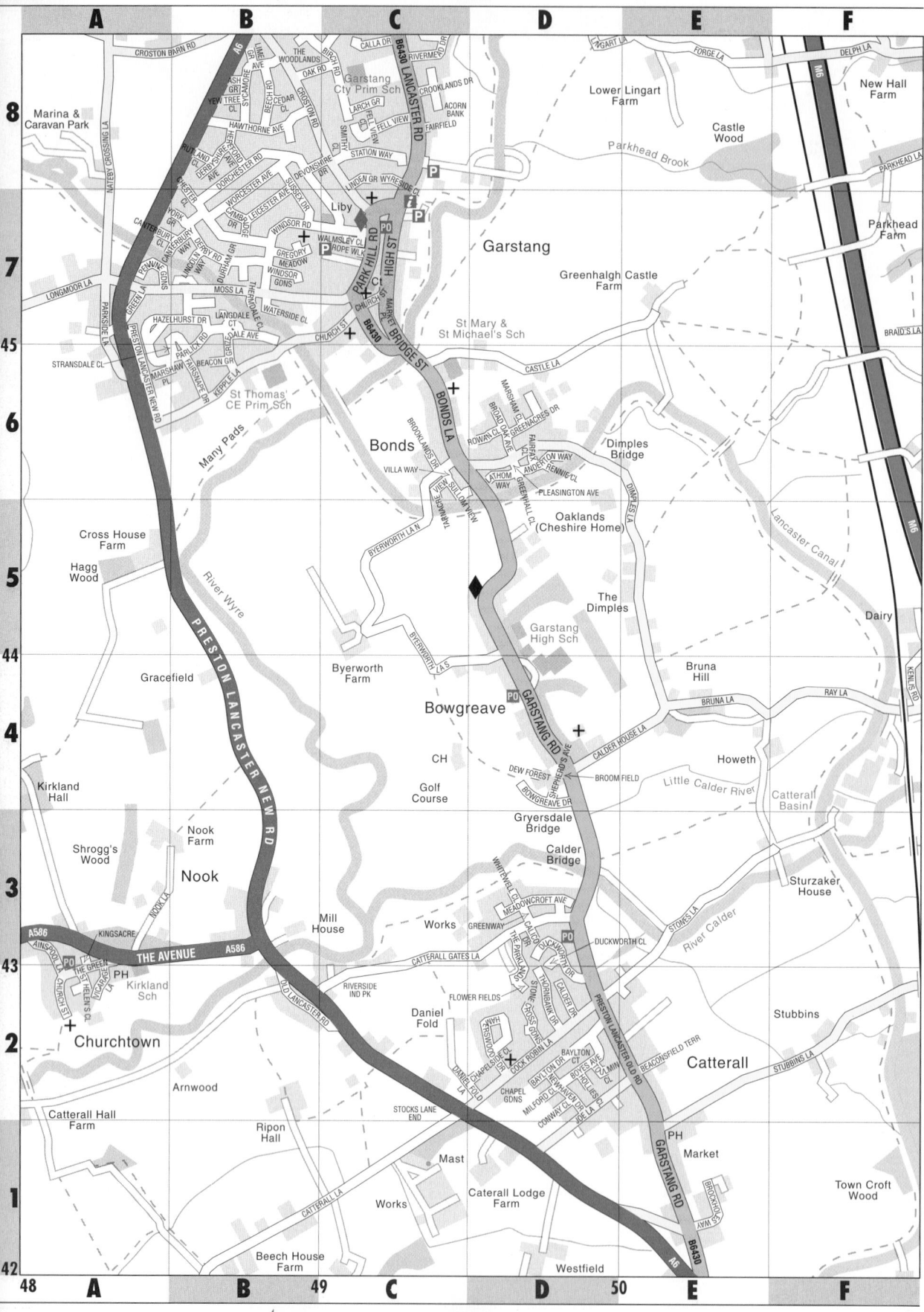

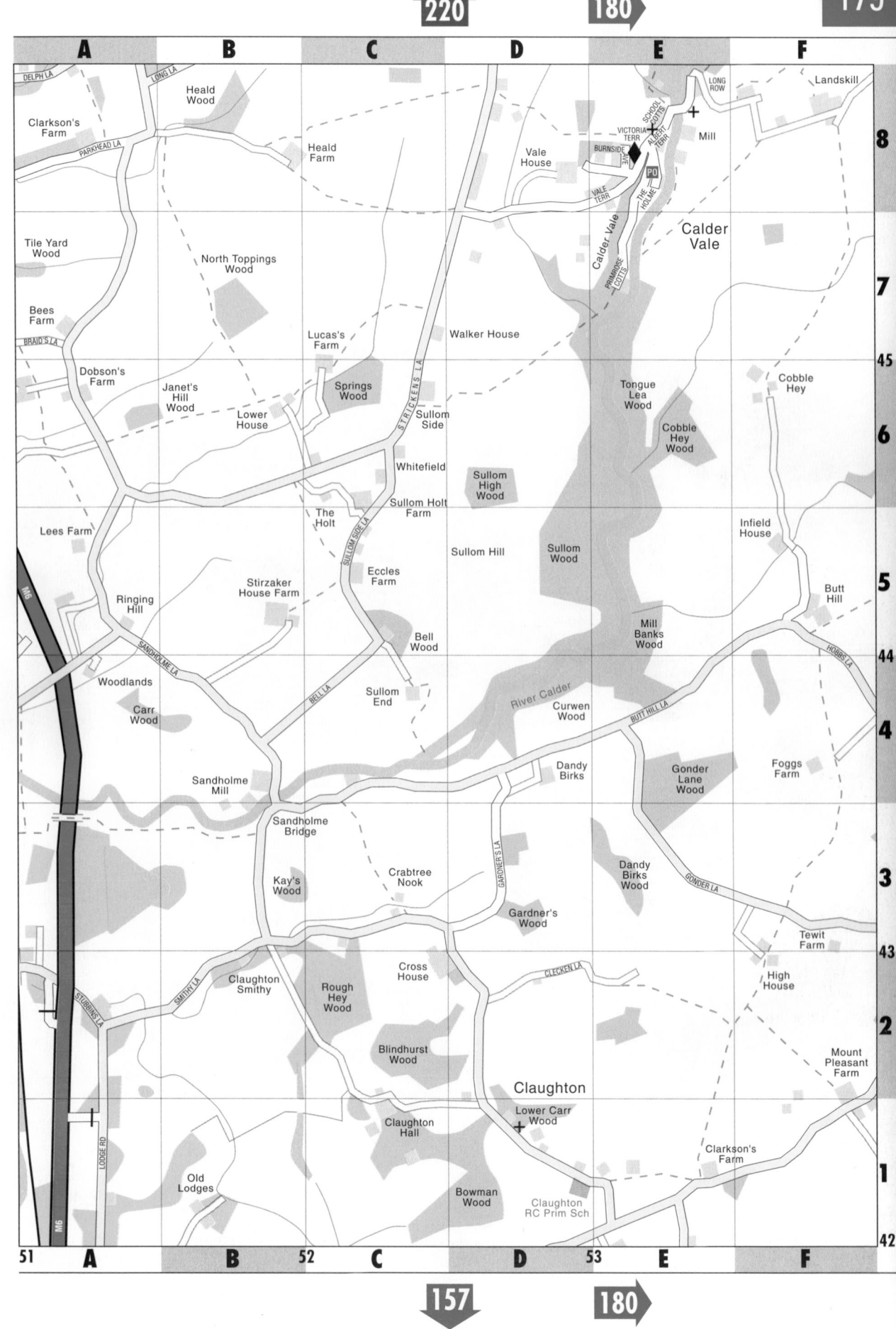

DELPH LA
LONG LA
Heald Wood
Clarkson's Farm
PARKHEAD LA
Heald Farm
Tile Yard Wood
North Toppings Wood
Bees Farm
BRAID'S LA
Lucas's Farm
Walker House
Dobson's Farm
Janet's Hill Wood
Springs Wood
STRICKENS LA
Lower House
Sullom Side
Whitefield
Sullom Holt Farm
Sullom High Wood
Lees Farm
The Holt
SULLOM SIDE LA
Sullom Hill
Sullom Wood
Ringing Hill
Stirzaker House Farm
Eccles Farm
SANDHOLME LA
Woodlands
BELL LA
Bell Wood
Mill Banks Wood
Carr Wood
Sullom End
River Calder
Curwen Wood
BUTT HILL LA
Sandholme Mill
Dandy Birks
Gonder Lane Wood
Foggs Farm
Sandholme Bridge
GARDNER'S LA
Kay's Wood
Crabtree Nook
Dandy Birks Wood
GONDER LA
Tewit Farm
SMITHY LA
Claughton Smithy
Rough Hey Wood
Cross House
Gardner's Wood
CLECKEN LA
High House
STUBBINS LA
Blindhurst Wood
Claughton
LODGE RD
Claughton Hall
Lower Carr Wood
Mount Pleasant Farm
Old Lodges
Bowman Wood
Claughton RC Prim Sch
Clarkson's Farm
M6

Vale House
Calder Vale
VALE TERR
Calder Vale
SCHOOL COTTS
VICTORIA TERR
ALBERT TERR
BURNSIDE AVE
THE HOLME
PRIMROSE COTTS
PO
Mill
LONG ROW
Landskill
Cobble Hey
Tongue Lea Wood
Cobble Hey Wood
Infield House
Butt Hill
HOBBS LA

179
220

A B C D E F

8

7

15

6

5

44

4

3

43

2

1

42

Brooks

Packhorse
Bridge

Delph
Wood

Broadgate
Wood

Broadgate

Broadgate
Meadow
Wood

Lodge
Wood

High
Moor

DELPH LA

Long
Wood

Jack
Anderton
Bridge

Weaver's
Farm

BROCK RAKES

Peacock
Hill

Tootle
Hall

Winshape Brook

New
House

New Bridge
Wood

Huds Brook
Plantation

SNAPE RAKE LA

Moss
Side

Bob's
Wood

Gill Barn
Wood

Huds Brook
Farm

Huds Brook

Brock
Close

Windsnape
Woods

River Brock

Dewhurst
Wood

Black
Wood

Boggy
Wood

Wood
Top

Longfield
Wood

Moor
Wood

SNAPE RAKE LA

Crow
Trees

Longfield
House

Wearden's
Cottage

Higher
Lickhurst

BLEASDALE RD

HOBBS LA

Parker's
Farm

Brock Cott
Farm

Middle
Lickhurst

Tewit
Wood

Brock Mill
Wood

Lickhurst Brook

Lower
Lickhurst

North
Nook

Brock
Mill

Higher Brock
Bridge

Fell
Side

GONDER LA

P

BROCK MILL LA

Nature
Trail

Beacon Fell
Country Park

Lane
Head

Nanny's
Breast

WHITE LEE LA

White Lea
Farm

P

White Lea
Wood

Picnic
Area

Ratcliffe
Brook
Cottage

Salisbury
House

Wood
Fold

Bannister
Hey

Rake Head
Wood

Brock
Bottom

Eccles Moss
Farm

BLEASDALE RD

PO

Crombleholme
Fold

54 A B 55 C D 56 E F

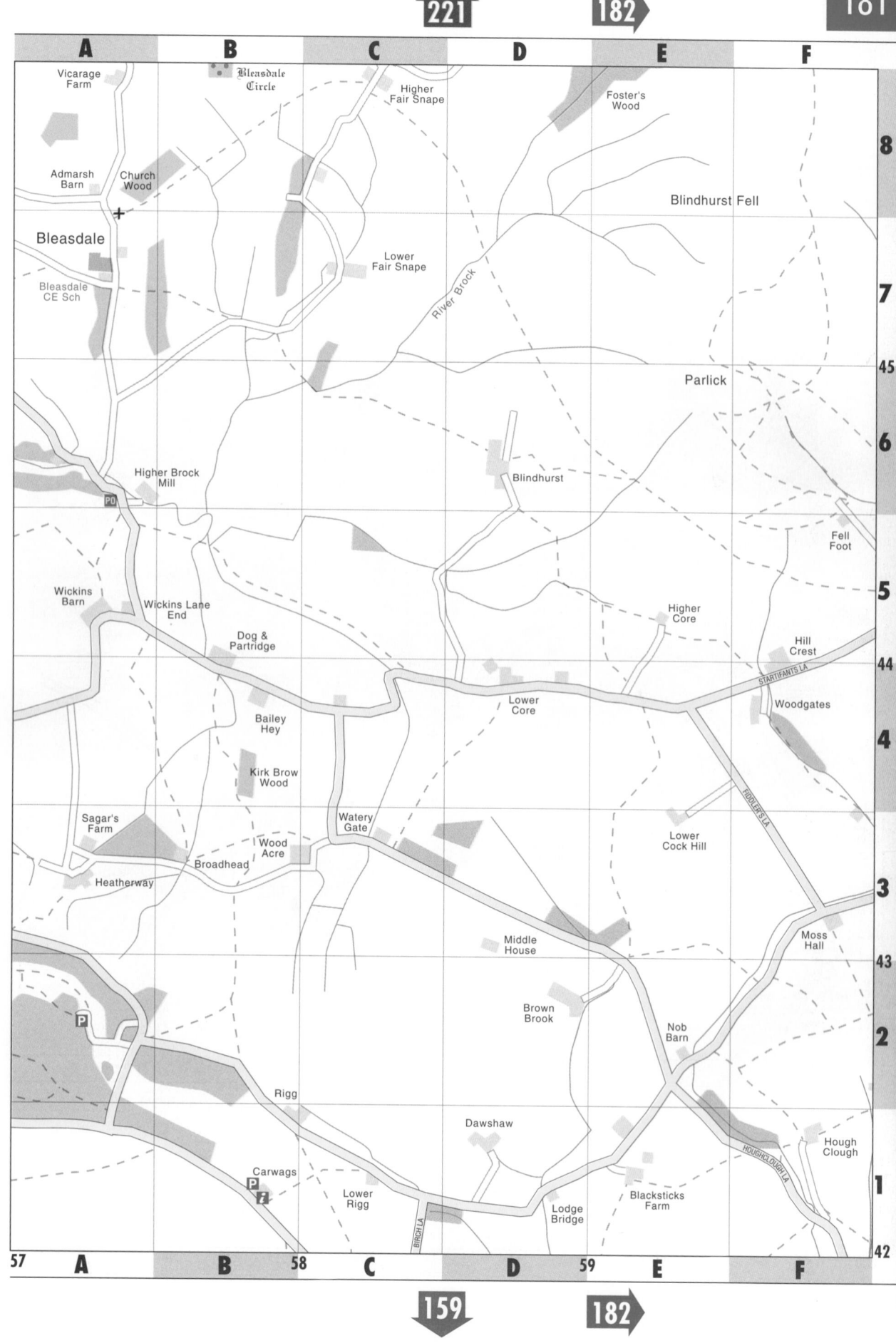

Vicarage Farm

Bleasdale Circle

Higher Fair Snape

Foster's Wood

Admarsh Barn

Church Wood

Blindhurst Fell

Bleasdale

Lower Fair Snape

Bleasdale CE Sch

River Brock

Parlick

Higher Brock Mill

Blindhurst

Fell Foot

Wickins Barn

Wickins Lane End

Higher Core

Hill Crest

Dog & Partridge

STARTIFANTS LA

Woodgates

Bailey Hey

Lower Core

Kirk Brow Wood

Sagar's Farm

Wood Acre

Watery Gate

Lower Cock Hill

FIDDLER'S LA

Broadhead

Heatherway

Moss Hall

Middle House

Brown Brook

Nob Barn

Rigg

Dawshaw

Hough Clough

HOUGHCLOUGH LA

Carwags

Lower Rigg

BIRCH LA

Lodge Bridge

Blacksticks Farm

57 A B 58 C D 59 E F 42

← 181
221 ▲

A B C D E F

8

Ward's End

Stanley

Greenough Clough

Ginney Hey

Park Gate

7

High Barn

Saddle End Farm

Chipping Brook

45

Dobson's Brook

Birchen Lee

6

Wolfen Hall

Bradley

Windy Hill Farm

Laund Farm

Wolfen Hall Plantation

Peacock Hey Farm

Leagram Hall

5

STARTIFANTS LANE END

Windy Harbour

Nan King's Farm

STARTIFANTS LA

44

FISH HOUSE LA

Fish House

4

After Lee

TWEEDY

Works

Out Lane Head

Crag House

Lingey Hill

Clark House

Works

OLD HIVE

MALT KILN BROW

CHURCH RAKE

Springs House

KIRKFIELD

PH

TALBOT ST

WINDY ST

PO

STANLEY CT

GREEN LA

Green Slack

3

Chipping

BROAD MEADOW

CLUB LA

St Mary's Prim Sch

BROOKFIELD CT

BROOKLANDS

Handlesteads Farm

Brabins Endowed Sch

43

Cold Coates

COLLIN'S HILL LA

Ferry Butts

Blackhall

GARSTANG RD

Isaac's Farm

Chipping Brook

2

Cuthbert Hill

Holton Hill

LONGRIDGE RD

Startifants

Richmond Houses

Daub Hall

Abbot Barn

BLACK HOUSE LA

PARSONAGE LA

Radcliffe Hall

New House

Sewage Works

Chipping Dairy

1

Hall Trees Farm

Dairy Farm

MOSS LA

42

60 A B 61 C D 62 E F

183
222

A   B   C   D   E   F

Middle Barn

Radholme Laund

Park Gate

Hagg Clough

Hagg Clough Wood

Roughs

Crow Wood Farm

Cow Ark

South Africa

Cow Ark Bridge

Crow Wood

Browsholme Hall

Crane Wood House

Browsholme Farm

Diamond Jubilee Plantation

Higher Lees

Sugar Hill

Mill Brook Bridge

Bashall Moor Wood

RABBIT LA

Bond Plantation

Cow Ark Brook

Mill Brook

Micklehurst Farm

Lees

Middle Lees

Ayxa Hall

Rough Wood

Ayxa Plantation

Kinder Barn

Lees House

Limes Wood

Sandal Holme

Ox Hey Wood

Broad Meadow Wood

Lees Wood

River Hodder

Plane Barn

Paper Mill Wood

Buck Thorn

Agden Clough

Aigden Farm

Hodder Side Wood

Plantation Farm

Moor Plantation

Armridding

Buck Hill

Agden Wood

Mullineux Wood

Parker's Wood

Lodge Wood

Primrose Wood

Long Plantation

Kenyon Wood

New House Farm

Wallbanks

Chadswell

Knipe Wood

Barracks

New Spring

Crooked Field

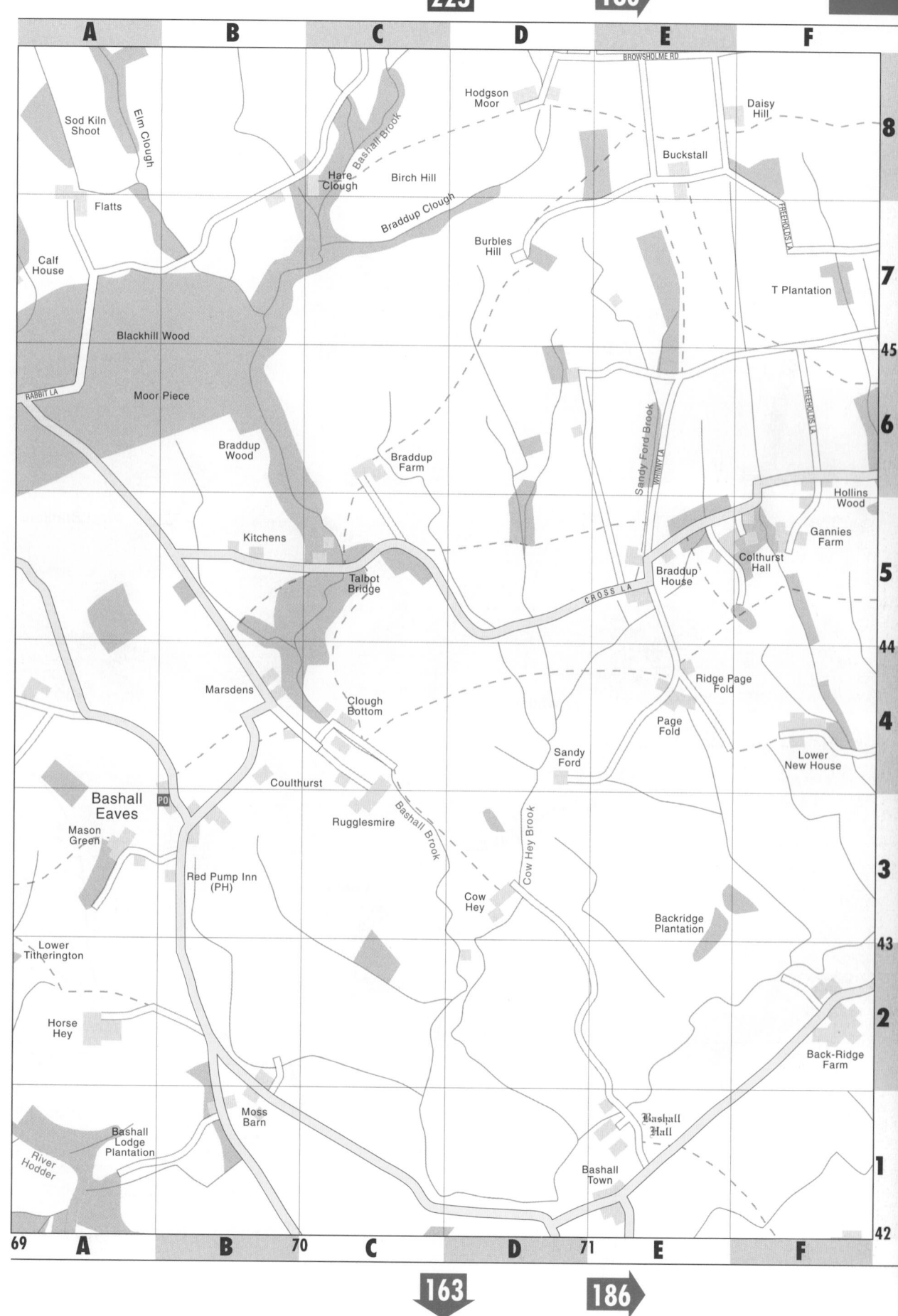

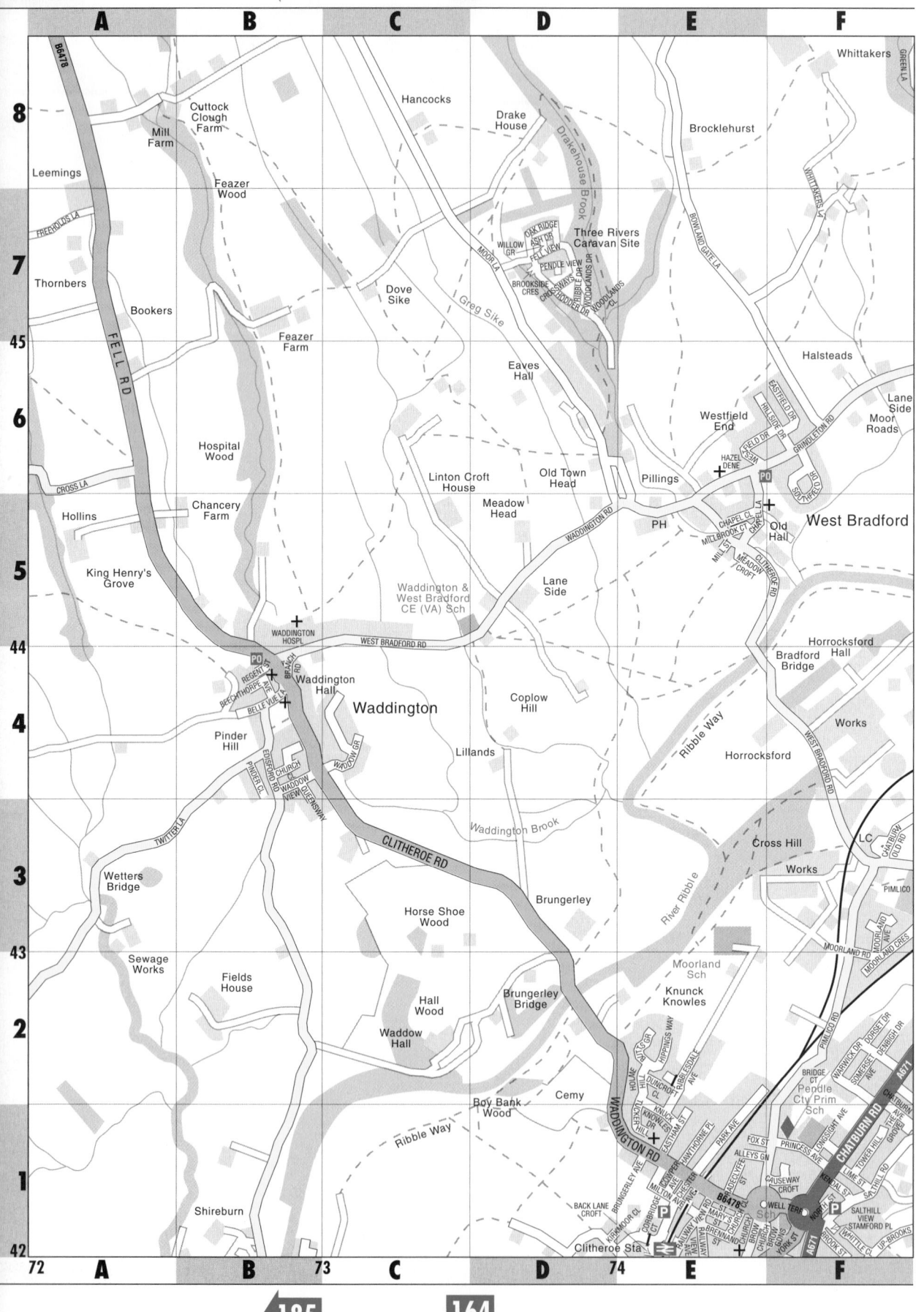

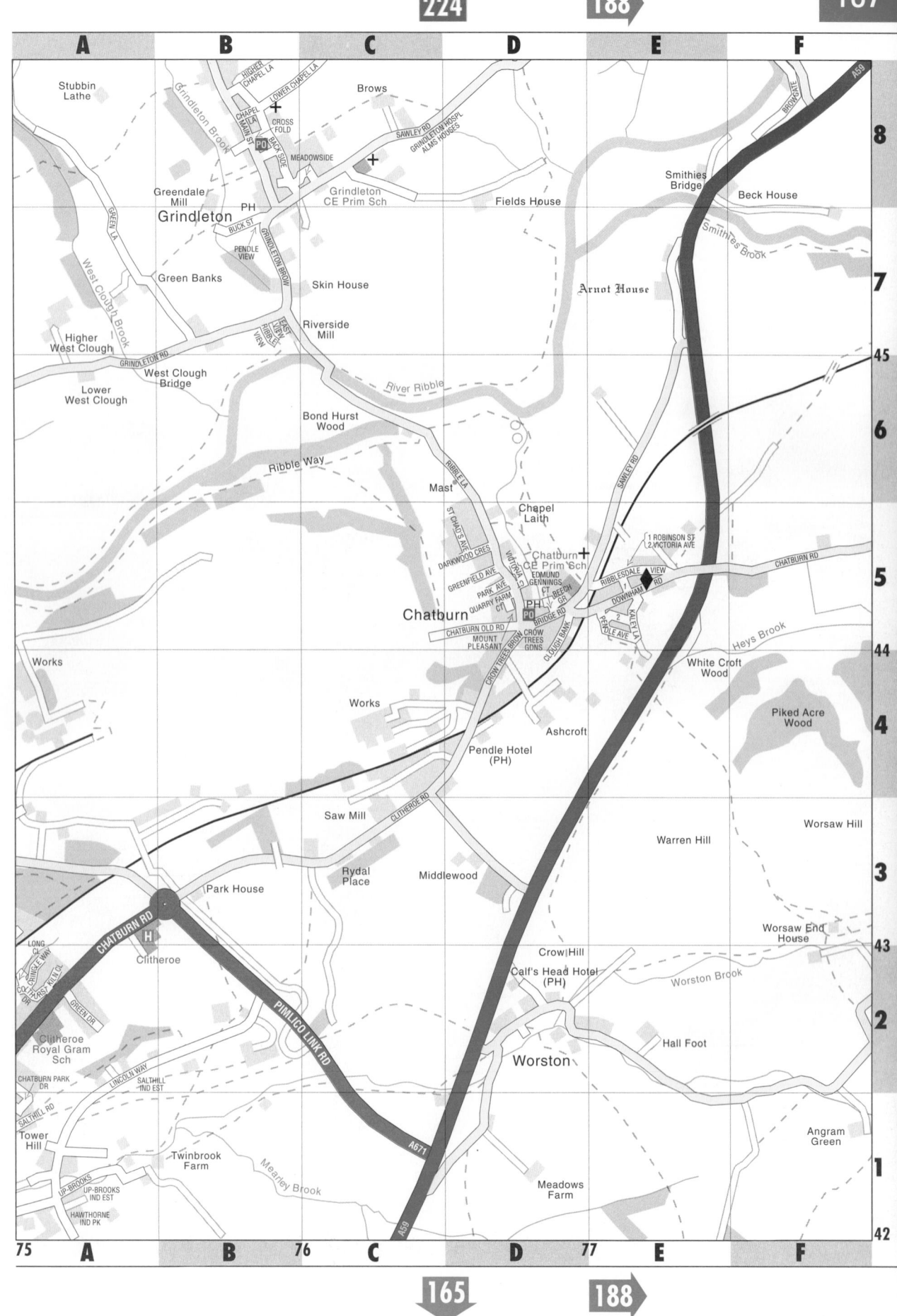

Stubbin Lathe

HIGHER CHAPEL LA
LOWER CHAPEL LA

Brows

Grindleton Brook

CHAPEL MAIN LA
CHAPEL LA

CROSS FOLD

PO

BACK SIDE

MEADOWSIDE

SAWLEY RD

GRINDLETON HOSPL ALMS HOUSES

Fields House

Smithies Bridge

Beck House

Greendale Mill

PH

Grindleton

BUCK ST

PENDLE VIEW

Grindleton CE Prim Sch

Smithies Brook

Green Banks

GRINDLETON BROW

Skin House

Arnot House

8

West Clough Brook

GREEN LA

Higher West Clough

GRINDLETON RD

EAST VIEW

WEST VIEW RIBBLE

Riverside Mill

7

West Clough Bridge

River Ribble

45

Lower West Clough

Bond Hurst Wood

6

Ribble Way

RIBBLE LA

Mast

Chapel Laith

SAWLEY RD

BROAD GATE

A59

Works

ST CHAD'S AVE

DARKWOOD CRES

GREENFIELD AVE

PARK AVE

QUARRY FARM CT

VICTORIA

Chatburn CE Prim Sch

EDMUND GENNINGS

1 ROBINSON ST
2 VICTORIA AVE

RIBBLESDALE VIEW

CHATBURN RD

5

Chatburn

PH PO

BEECH GR

BRIDGE RD

PENDLE AVE

DOWNHAM RD

KALEY LA

CHATBURN OLD RD

MOUNT PLEASANT

CROW TREES GDNS

CLOUGH BANK

White Croft Wood

Heys Brook

44

Works

CROW TREES BROOK

Ashcroft

Piked Acre Wood

4

Pendle Hotel (PH)

CLITHEROE RD

Saw Mill

Warren Hill

Worsaw Hill

Rydal Place

Middlewood

3

Park House

Crow Hill

Worsaw End House

43

Calf's Head Hotel (PH)

Worston Brook

CHATBURN RD

H

Clitheroe

LONG CL

FOREST BRIDGE WAY

CREST KILN CL

GREEN DR

Chatburn Park Dr

LINCOLN WAY

SALTHILL IND EST

Clitheroe Royal Gram Sch

PIMLICO LINK RD

Hall Foot

2

Worston

SALTHILL RD

Meadows Farm

Tower Hill

Twinbrook Farm

Mearley Brook

A671

Angram Green

1

UP-BROOKS

UP-BROOKS IND EST

HAWTHORNE IND PK

A59

42

187
224

Rimington

STOOPS LA

Swanside Beck

Kelriddin

STATION RD

BACK LA

PH

West Croft

Denis Field

Bustards Farm

RIMINGTON LA

Low Laithe

Downham Bridge

Falshaw Wood

The Wood

Stubs Wood

New Field Wood

Mill

Ings Beck

Newfield Barn

Hey House Wood

Torrid Bank Wood

GREEN LA

Downham Green

Hey House Farm

Twiston Beck

Hall RoydsWood

Woolly Hill

Springs

CHATBURN RD

PH
PO

Smithfield Farm

Downham

New Close

TWISTON LA

Twiston Mill

Downham Hall

Downham Beck

P

Cat Gallows Wood

Lane Side

Clay House

Score Clough Beck

Longlands Wood

Hollin's Farm

Hecklin Farm

WEST LA

Gerna Hill

Gerna

Lane Head

PENDLE RD

Ravens Holme

Worsaw End

Ridding Wood

Hookcliffe Plantation

Radbrook

Hook Cliffe

Hook Cliffe

Rad Brook

Barkerfield

Moorside

Downham Moor

Burst Clough

78 A 79 C D 80 E F

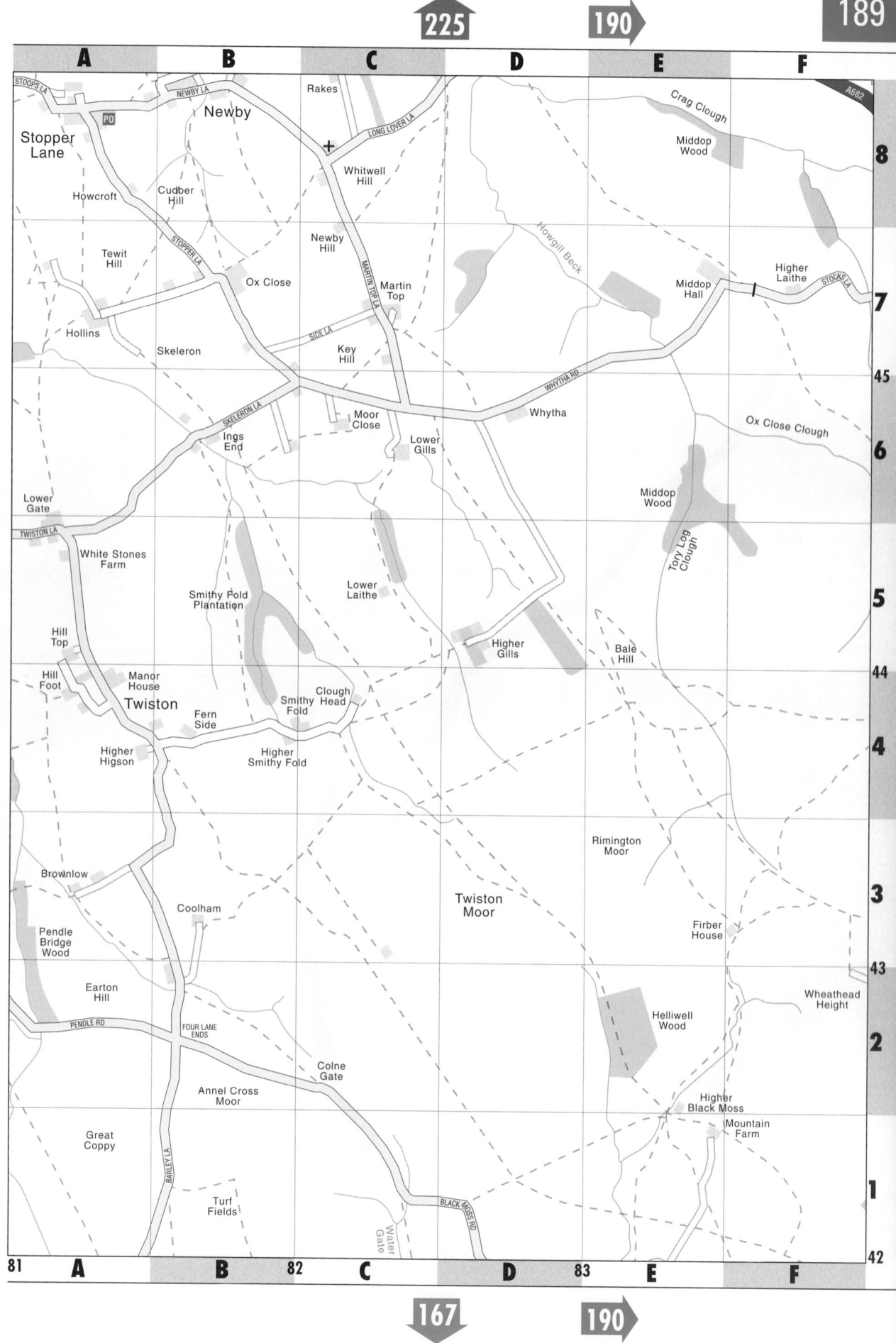

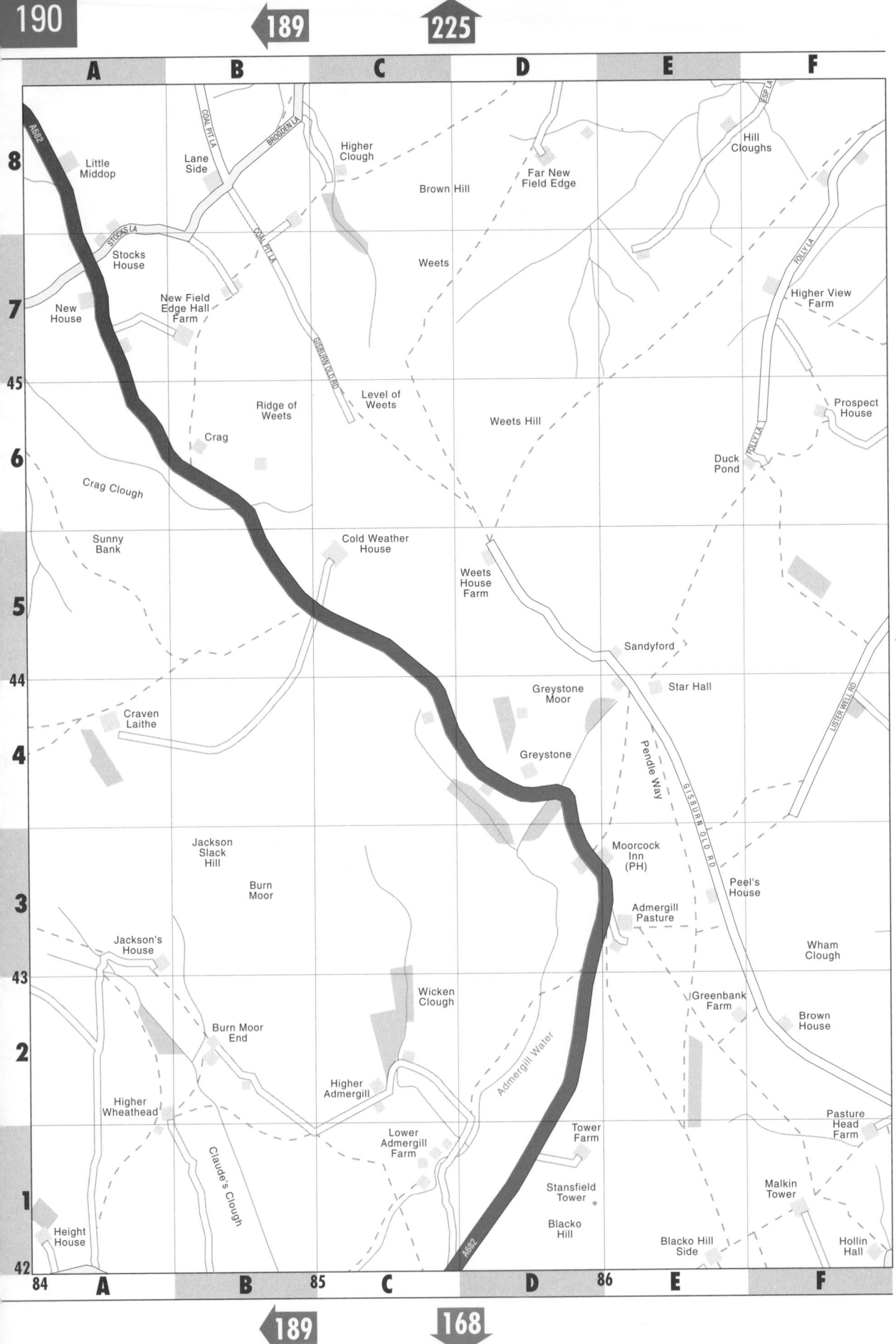

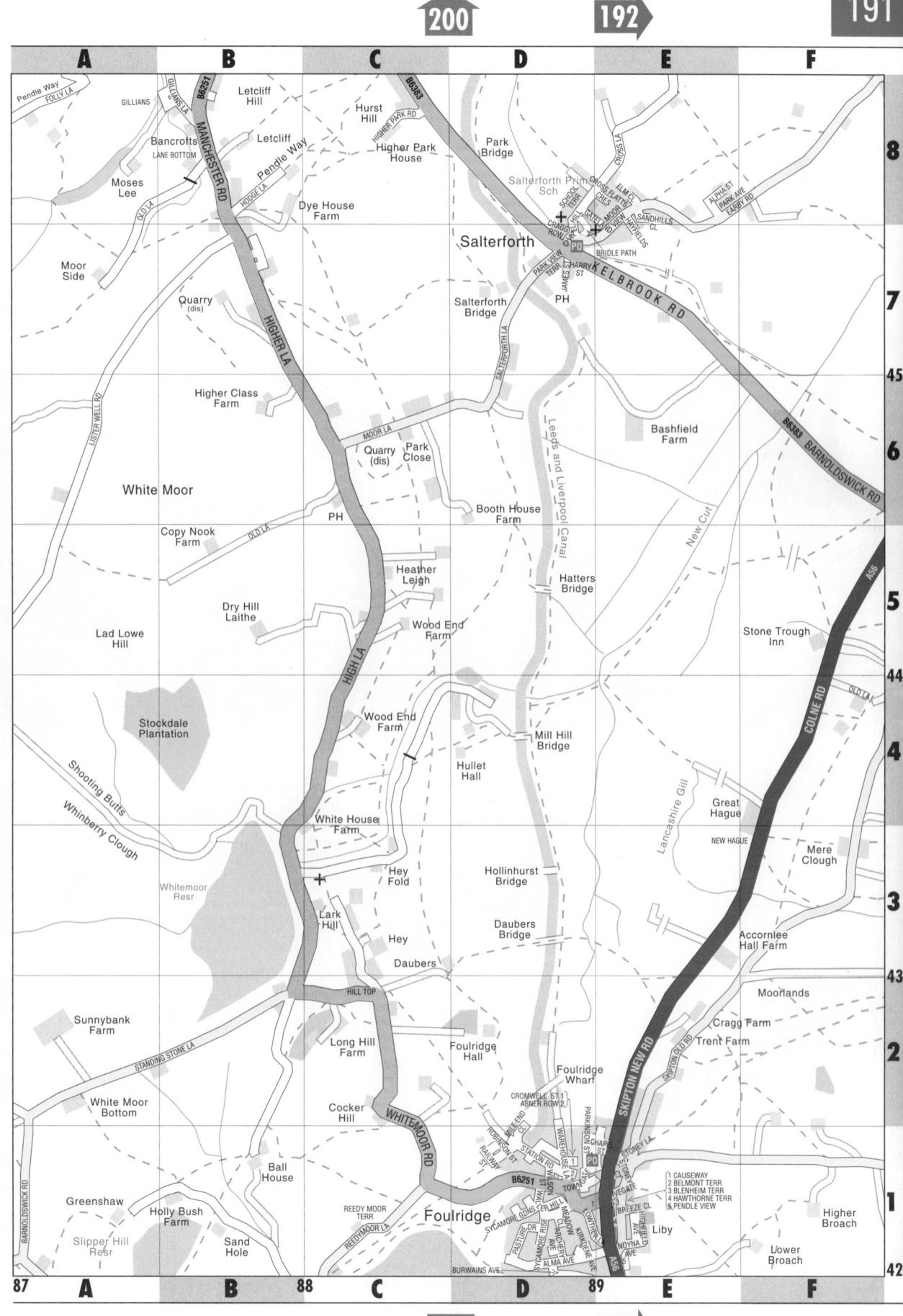

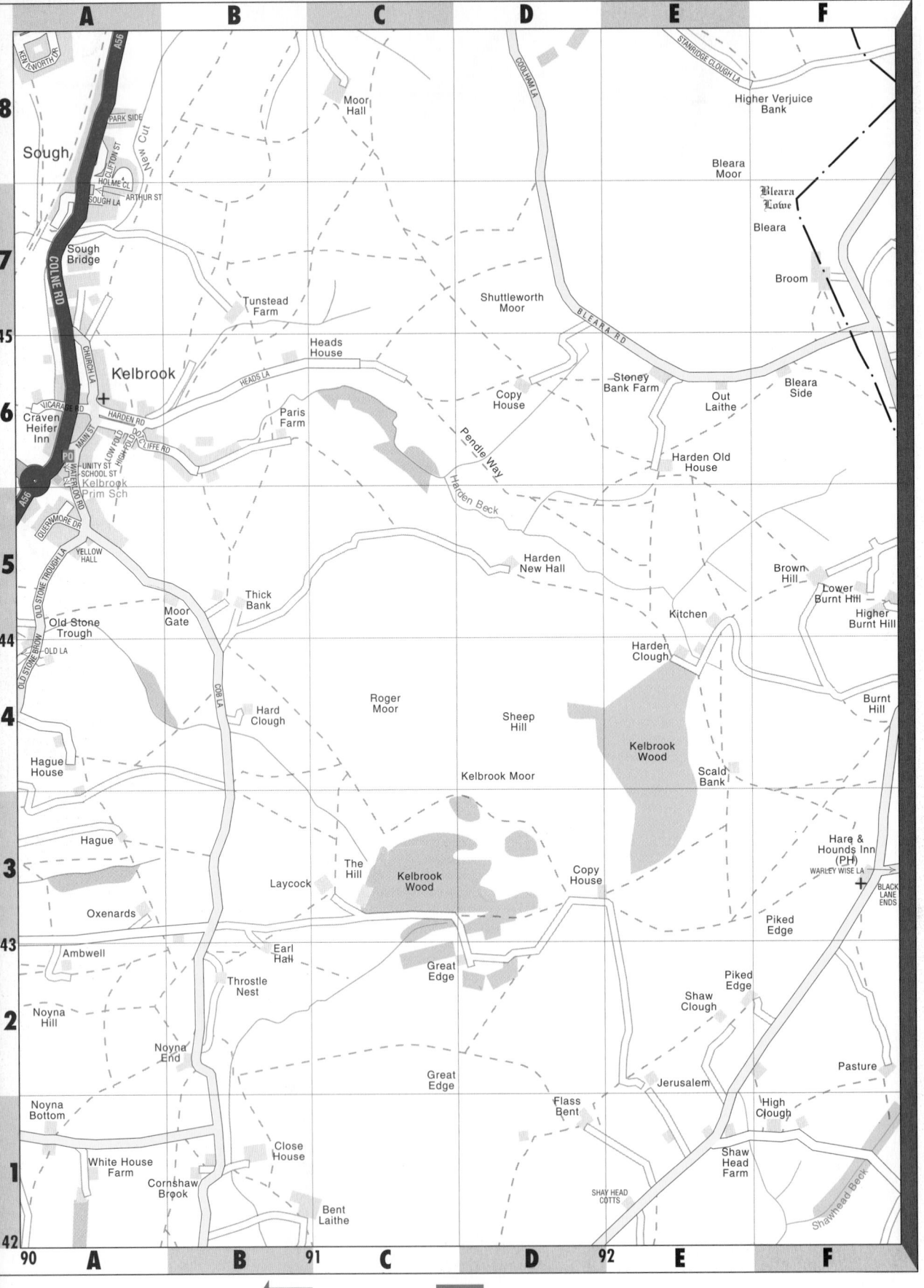

191
201

8

Moor Hall

Higher Verjuice Bank

Sough

Bleara Moor

KENILWORTH

PARK SIDE

CLIFTON ST
HOLME CL
Arthur St
SOUGH LA

Bleara Lowe

Bleara

7

Sough Bridge

COLNE RD

Tunstead Farm

Shuttleworth Moor

BLEARA RD

Broom

45

Heads House

6

Kelbrook

HEADS LA

Copy House

Stoney Bank Farm

Out Laithe

Bleara Side

VICARAGE RD
HARDEN RD
Craven Heifer Inn
MAIN ST
CHURCH LA
LOW FOLD
HIGH FIELD
CLIFFE RD

Paris Farm

Pendle Way

Harden Old House

PO
UNITY ST
SCHOOL ST
WATER LA RD
Kelbrook Prim Sch

Harden Beck

QUENMORE DR

5

YELLOW HALL

Thick Bank

Harden New Hall

Brown Hill

Lower Burnt Hill

OLD STONE BROW
OLD STONE TROUGH LA

Moor Gate

Kitchen

44

Old Stone Trough

OLD LA

Harden Clough

Higher Burnt Hill

4

COB LA

Hard Clough

Roger Moor

Sheep Hill

Kelbrook Wood

Burnt Hill

Hague House

Kelbrook Moor

Scald Bank

Hague

Hare & Hounds Inn (PH)

3

Laycock

The Hill

Kelbrook Wood

Copy House

WARLEY WISE LA

BLACK LANE ENDS

Oxenards

Piked Edge

43

Ambwell

Earl Hall

Great Edge

Piked Edge

Shaw Clough

Noyna Hill

Throstle Nest

2

Noyna End

Great Edge

Jerusalem

Pasture

Noyna Bottom

Flass Bent

High Clough

1

White House Farm

Close House

Shaw Head Farm

Cornshaw Brook

Bent Laithe

SHAY HEAD COTTS

Shawhead Beck

42

90 **A** B 91 **C** D 92 **E** F

A B C D E F

8

7

49

6

5

Outer Prom

Boating Pool

P Marine Gdns

P
Laidley's Wlk
THE ESPLANADE
ELSINORE CL
ABERCROMBIE
GALLOWAY RD
DAPHNE SHIRE

48

Promenade

Cemy

Rossall Point

AVON
MOWBRAY RD
SILVIA WAY
MACBETH
BRUTUS
BIRK
MALDON PL
DUNCAN
ARIEL WAY
HAM PL
DRONSFIELD RD
AGNEY RD
WARREN AVE N
WARREN AVE S
LOWTHER RD

Grasmere Ave
Shakespeare Rd
Shakespeare Prim Sch
BORROWDALE AVE
BRAMLEY AVE
MANOR WOOD
SEYMOUR ST 1
ALBANY RD 2
RIBBLE RD
PERCY
A587

4

West Gate
Lancaster Gate
High Gate
Golf Links
WEST GATE
KNOWSLEY GATE
STANLEY GATE
THE RIDGEWAY
RYDAL AVE
CONISTON AVE
BEACH RD
Liby
POULTON RD
PO
WYREDALE CT
HOLLYWOOD
GR
WELBECK
WARRENHURST
WARRENHURST HOUSE
Meml Gdns

Rossall Grange La
PRINCES WAY
Rossall Ct
ROMNEY AVE
WYRE CT
WESTWOOD AVE
LINCOLN AVE
RUTLAND AVE
DEVON AVE
Schs
CH
SAER CL
LEIGHTON
CRINDRICK
CAMBRIDGE
OXFORD AVE
ADDISON
NELSON
STANLEY RD

Charles Saer Cty Sch
VIOT AVE
LOTHIAN AVE
GRANGE RD
WERLEY AVE
KENILWORTH AVE
LONSDALE AVE
Lincoln Ave
Cambridge
Hatfield Ave
GRENFELL RD
BROMFIELD RD
WYRE ST
GORDON RD

3

Kentmere Cl 1
Honister Cl 2
DOUGLAS AVE
GRETA
KENILWORTH PL
47

EDEN AVE
BRATHAY
St John Ave
DERWENT AVE
Liby
LANGDALE
BROADWAY
Brentwood
WESTFIELD RD
WHINFIELD
HEATHFIELD RD
WINGROVE RD
GREENFIELD
LINDEL RD
DENHAM WAY

MEDLOCK PL
WANSBECK HOUSE
CROFT
THE CROFT
LEYBURN AVE
HENDERSON RD

2

CHATSWORTH AVE
EAMONT PL
TROUTBECK AVE
BIRKBECK PL
TORONTO AVE
Langwood
NORTHFLEET AVE
HAZELDENE RD
LINGFIELD RD
HARBOUR CL
MARITIME ST

ALLEN CL
HODDER AVE
Fleetwood High Sch
Larkholme
BROCK AVE
DUDDON AVE
Flakefleet Cty Sch
WITTON GR
FLEETWOOD RD
HOMESTEAD DR
ORCHARD DR

BURNSIDE AVE
GREENDALE CL
ARNDALE CL
LAUNDRY RD
ALDER CL
YEW CL
TEES LANE
WANSEY
FURNESS AVE
WENSLEY AVE
SOUTHFLEET AVE
Blackpool & Fleetwood Tramway
ROBERTSON CT

1

BRANT CT
TATHAM CT
WRAYWOOD CT
SILVERDALE AVE
POOL
MIDDLETON AVE
MERE AVE
CARLISLE AVE
Larkholme La
KILBANE ST

BENTHAM AVE
THIRLMERE AVE
BOWNESS
NEWBY AVE
SOUTHWAY
KIRKS
PATTERDALE AVE
ULLSWATER AVE
MEADOW AVE
A585

46

30   A   B   31   C   D   32   E   F

F2
1 WESTHEAD WLK
2 HATFIELD MEWS
3 GREGSON DR
4 EDMONDSEN PL
5 ARMISTEAD WAY
6 FORSHAW CL
7 CROOKALL CL
8 ARMISTEAD CT
9 NOBLETT CT

A B C D E F

8

7

49

6

FLEETWOOD

Pier

LB
Sta

Ferry P

FYLDE CT 1
ADDISON CT 2
OCEAN CT 3

P
B5270

SAILSBURY
CT

PH

Lancashire Coastal Way

KINGSTON CL
LEAD RD
DERWENT RD
PENWYTH

ESKDALE
GR

WINDSOR
PL

WINDSOR
RD

Ct
LYNDALE
CT

i

BOLD ST

H

UPPER
LUNE ST

1 WESLEY CT
2 LIGHTHOUSE CL
3 ARTHUR ST N
4 ARTHUR ST
5 LOWER LUNE ST
6 PHAROS CT

Outer Prom

THE ESPLANADE

P

5

P

MOUNT RD

PHAROS
ST

NORTH CHURCH ST

PO

4 3
2 1

6
5

KENT ST

ELIZABETH ST

QUEEN'S TERR

CHERRY TREE
CT

ESPLANADE

3
WORSLEY CL

BOURNE MAY RD

BOURNE RD

P
WAYSIDE

ASHTON AVE

WYRE
VIEW

LUNE VIEW

CLARENCE
THYME GR
BEECH GR

ST BERNARD'S
RD

GRANGE
CL

LANCASTER RD

RYDAL GR

GRASMERE
GR

AMBLESIDE AVE

B5270

THIRLMERE CL

ENNERDALE

BUTTERMERE
DR

WILKINSON
WAY

CH

QUAIL HOLME RD

P

BARTON
AVE

PLANTER
AVE

L Ct

Liby

Knott End-on-Sea

ABBOTTS WLK

Schs

WEST WY

SYKES

JONES

GARFIELD

PHAROS ST

VICTORIA ST

ALBERT ST

ST PETER'S
TERR

Liby

Mkt

Mus

Ferry
Terminal

P

SANTA GDNS

PARKSWAY

HOLMEFIELD
RD

BLEASDALE
RD

INA'S RD

W TRESDALE
RD

48

BURNS RD

DRYDEN RD

BYRON ST

HARRIS ST

BLAKISTON

St Margaret's

LONDON ST

KEMP ST

KINGS RD

PRESTON ST

STREET

HIGH ST

Schs

THE GLEN

HACKENSALL RD

MEADOW LA

5

CARR
RD

TENNYSON
RD

CHAUCER
RD

POULTON
GR

POULTON RD

A587

A587

MILTON RD

WARWICK RD

ALLIANCE

LINDEL RD

WALSON ST

BACK COP LA

COP LA

Knott End & Fleetwood
Golf Links

4

A585

BIRCH ST

OAK ST

ELM ST

WARRENHURST RD

BELMONT
AVE

DEEPDALE
RD

PARK AVE

CLIFTON
RD

NANSON

RADCLIFFE RD

COPSE RD

ASH ST

A587

DOCK ST

BRIDGE RD

River Wyre

Hackensail Brow's

WHINNY LA

Hackensail
Hall

WHINNY LA

Wyre Way

Curwens
Hill

New Heys
Farm

CLOSE CLRK LA

AMOUNDERNESS WAY

LOFTHOUSE STATION RD

SIDING RD

Blackpool & Fleetwood
Tramway

3

ADDISON RD

KEATING
CT

Freeport
Village

Docks

47

A585

DOCK AVE

Works

Cote Walls
Farm

2

Bird
Sanctuary

JAMESON RD

Arm
Hill

MONK'S LA

1

Refuse
Tip

46

33 A B 34 C D 35 E F

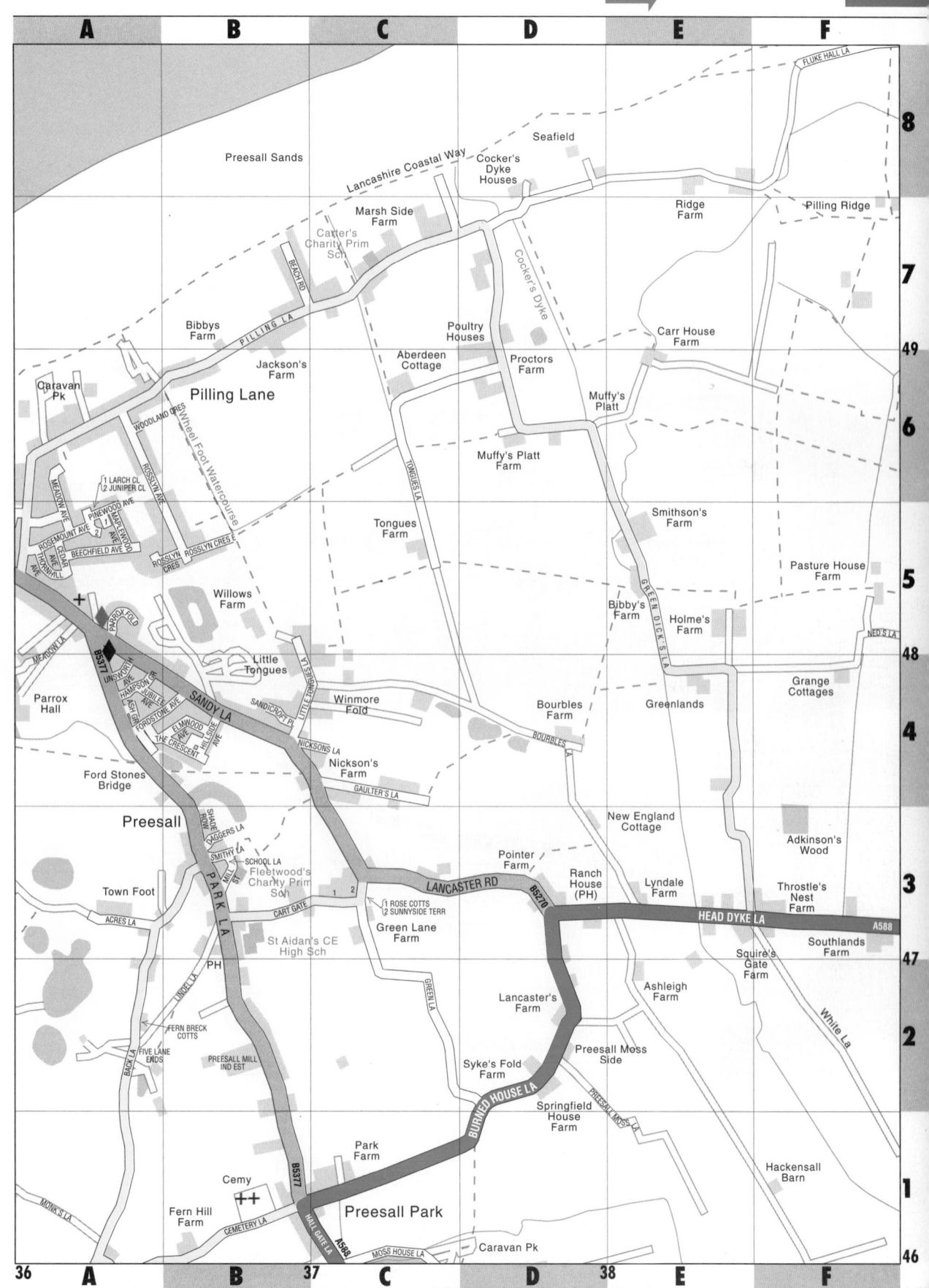

195

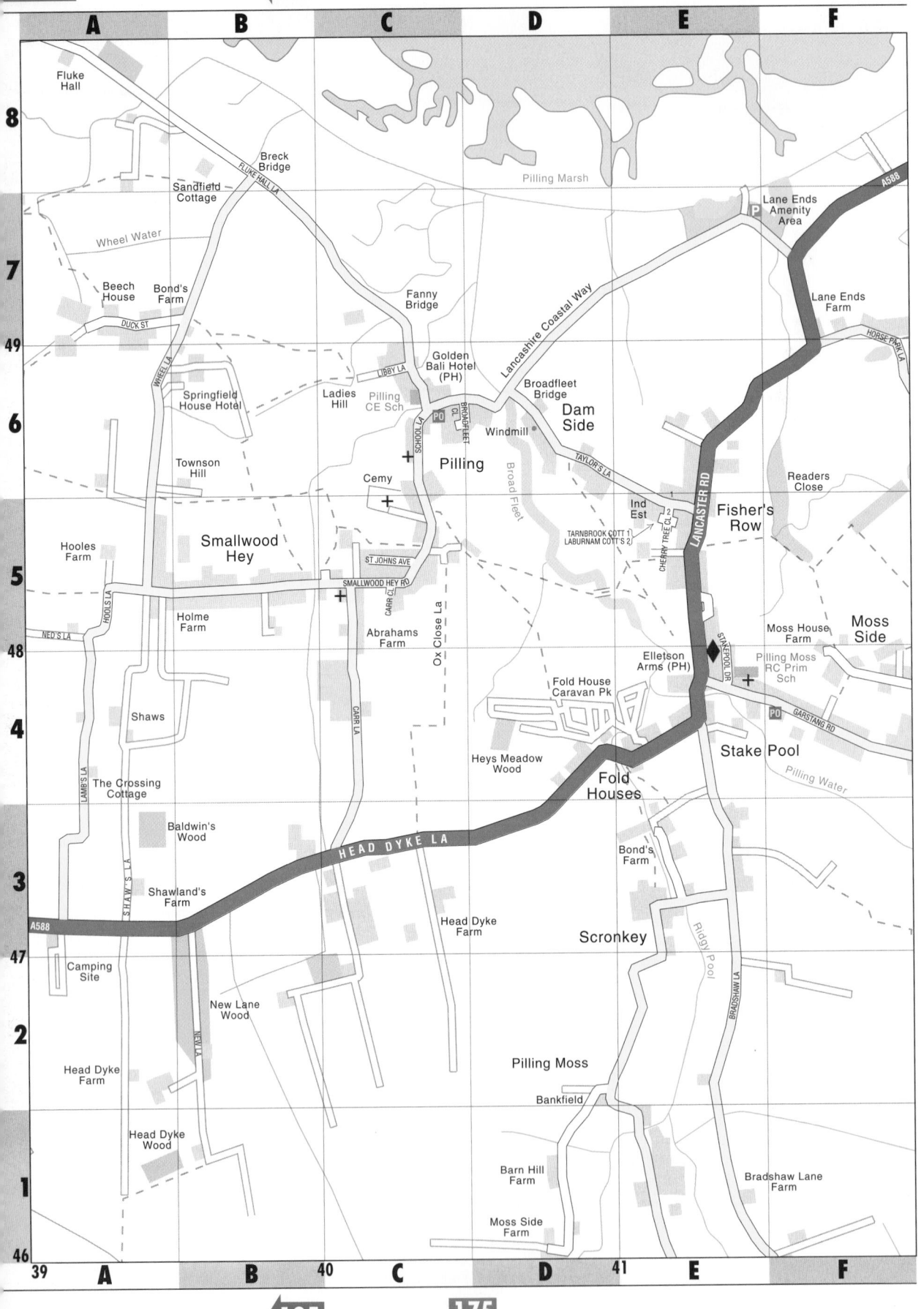

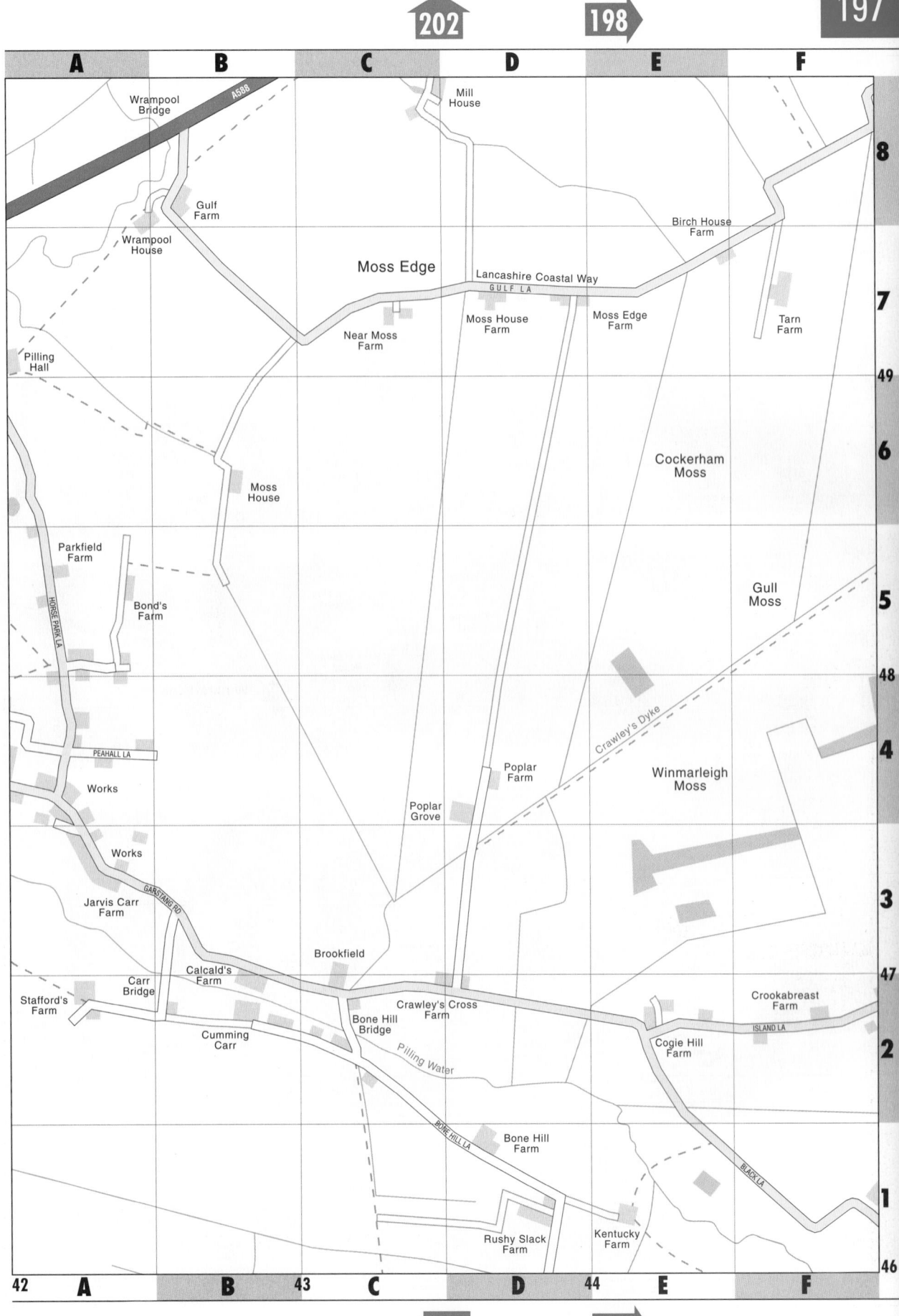

Wrampool
Bridge

A588

Gulf
Farm

Wrampool
House

Mill
House

Moss Edge

Birch House
Farm

Lancashire Coastal Way

GULF LA

Near Moss
Farm

Moss House
Farm

Moss Edge
Farm

Tarn
Farm

Pilling
Hall

Cockerham
Moss

Moss House

Parkfield
Farm

HORSE PARK LA

Bond's
Farm

Gull
Moss

Crawley's Dyke

PEAHALL LA

Works

Poplar
Farm

Winmarleigh
Moss

Poplar
Grove

Works

GARSTANG RD

Jarvis Carr
Farm

Brookfield

Calcald's
Farm

Carr
Bridge

Crawley's Cross
Farm

Crookabreast
Farm

Stafford's
Farm

ISLAND LA

Cumming
Carr

Bone Hill
Bridge

Cogie Hill
Farm

Pilling Water

BONE HILL LA

BLACK LA

Bone Hill
Farm

Rushy Slack
Farm

Kentucky
Farm

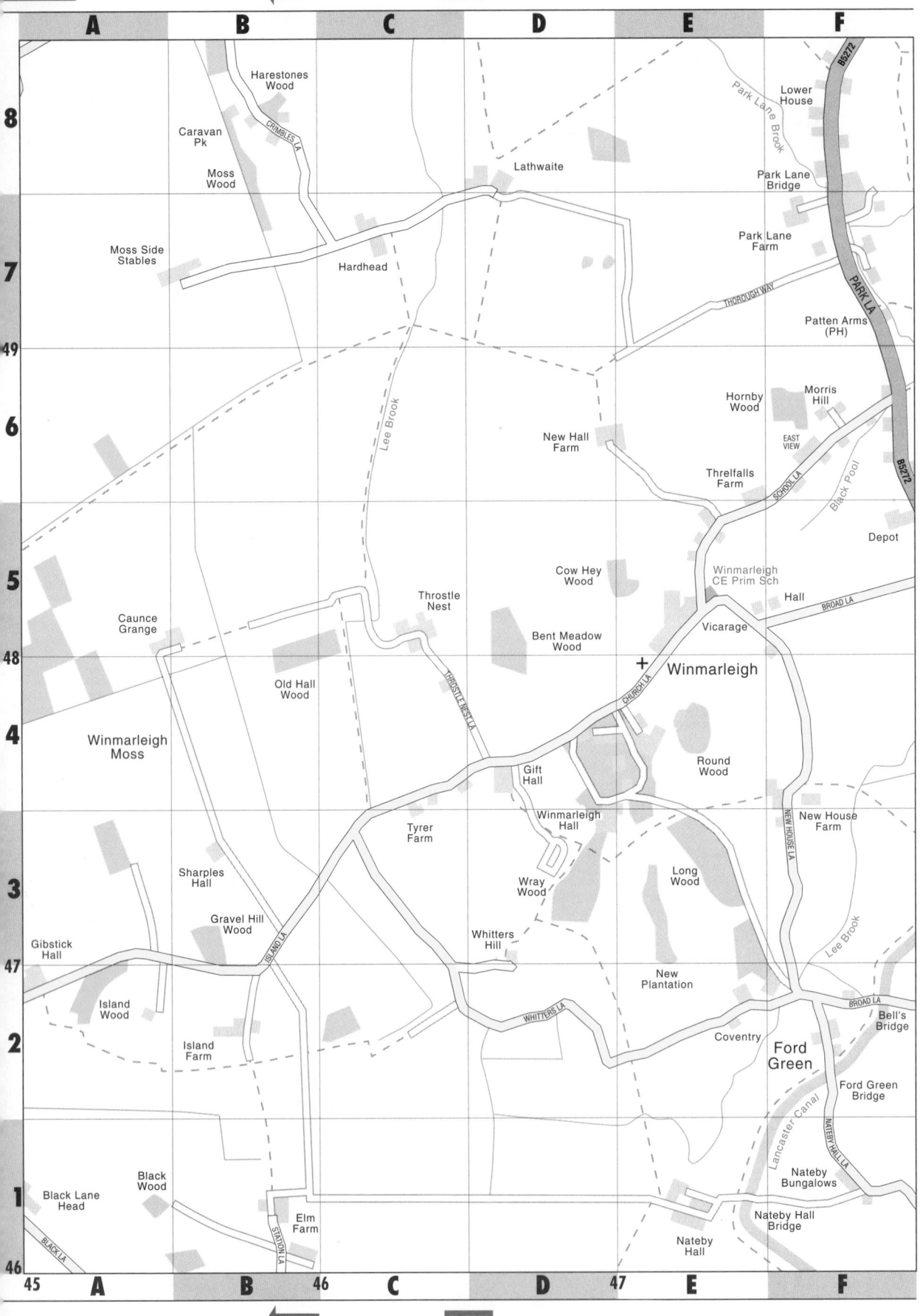

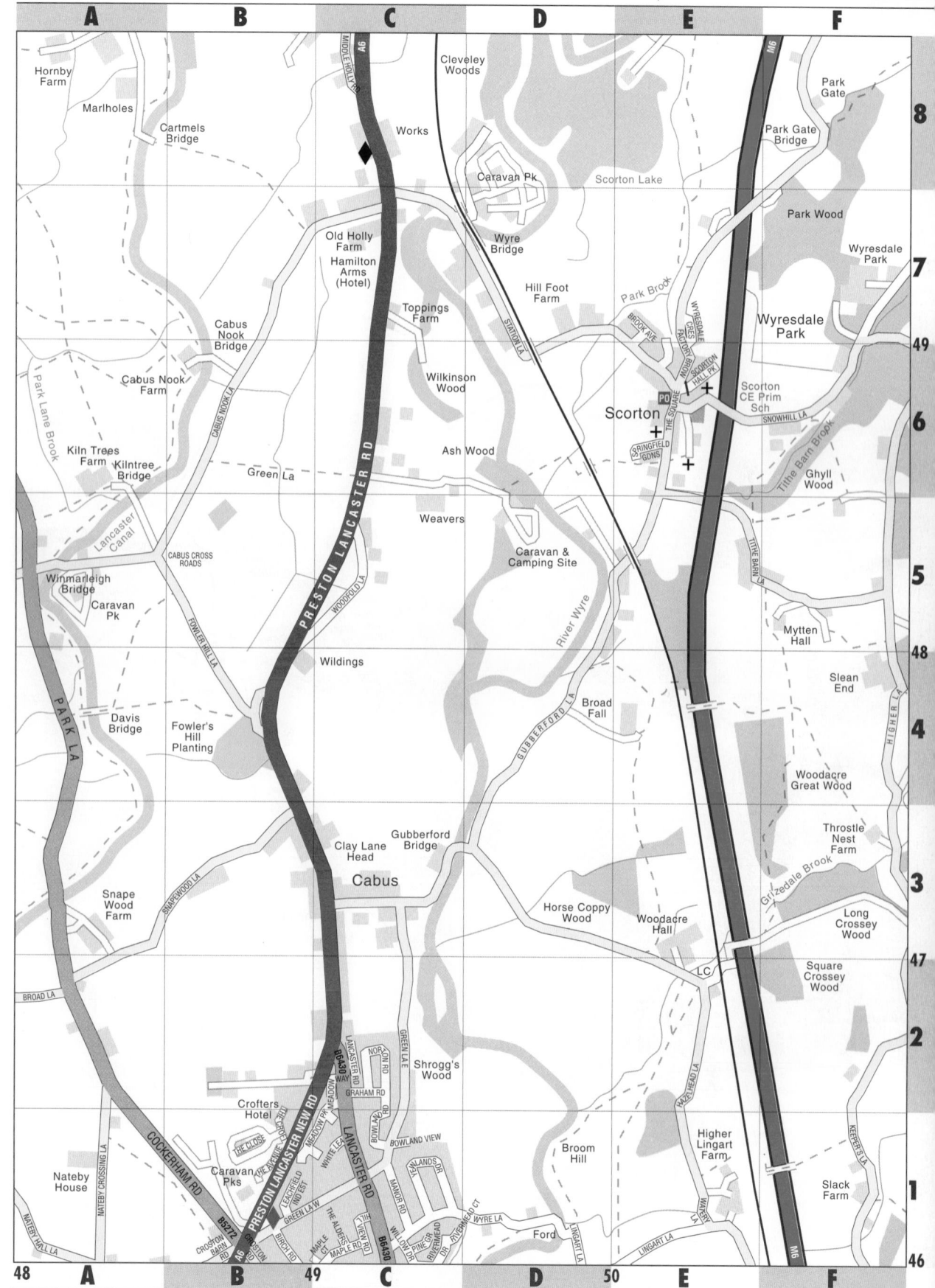

A **B** **C** **D** **E** **F**

8

Hornby Farm

Marlholes

Cartmels Bridge

Park Gate

Park Gate Bridge

Cleveley Woods

Works

MIDDLE HOLLY RD

A6

Caravan Pk

Scorton Lake

Park Wood

Wyresdale Park

7

Old Holly Farm

Hamilton Arms (Hotel)

Wyre Bridge

Hill Foot Farm

Park Brook

Wyresdale Park

Cabus Nook Bridge

Toppings Farm

49

BROOK AVE

WYRESDALE RD

FALCON BROW

SCORTON HALL PK

Park Lane Brook

Cabus Nook Farm

CABUS NOOK LA

PRESTON LANCASTER RD

Wilkinson Wood

STATION LA

PO

Scorton

THE SQUARE

Scorton CE Prim Sch

SNOWHILL LA

6

Kiln Trees Farm

Kilntree Bridge

Green La

Ash Wood

SPRINGFIELD GDNS

Tithe Barn Brook

Ghyll Wood

Lancaster Canal

WOODFOLD LA

Weavers

FOWLER HILL LA

CABUS CROSS ROADS

Winmarleigh Bridge

Caravan Pk

River Wyre

Caravan & Camping Site

TITHE BARN LA

Mytten Hall

5

48

Slean End

Wildings

GUBBERFORD LA

Broad Fall

HIGHER LA

4

PARK LA

Davis Bridge

Fowler's Hill Planting

Woodacre Great Wood

Clay Lane Head

Gubberford Bridge

Throstle Nest Farm

GRIZEDALE BROOK

3

SNAPEWOOD LA

Cabus

Horse Coppy Wood

Woodacre Hall

Long Crossey Wood

Snape Wood Farm

LC

Square Crossey Wood

47

2

BROAD LA

B6430

LANCASTER WAY

NORA RD

GRAHAM RD

GREEN LA

Shrogg's Wood

BOWLAND RD

BOWLAND VIEW

Broom Hill

HAZELHEAD LA

Higher Lingart Farm

KEEPER'S LA

Crofters Hotel

LANCASTER RD

PRESTON LANCASTER NEW RD

WHITE LEA

THE CLOSE

MEADOW PK

MANOR RD

WILLOW RD

Slack Farm

1

NATEBY CROSSING LA

COCKERHAM RD

Caravan Pks

GREEN LAW

THE ALDERS

MAPLE CT

Ford

WYRE LA

LINGART LA

M6

Nateby House

B5272

A6

CROSTON BARN RD

BIRCH RD

MAPLE RD

PINE GR

BUERMEAD DR

RYEMEAD CT

B6430

NATEBY HALL LA

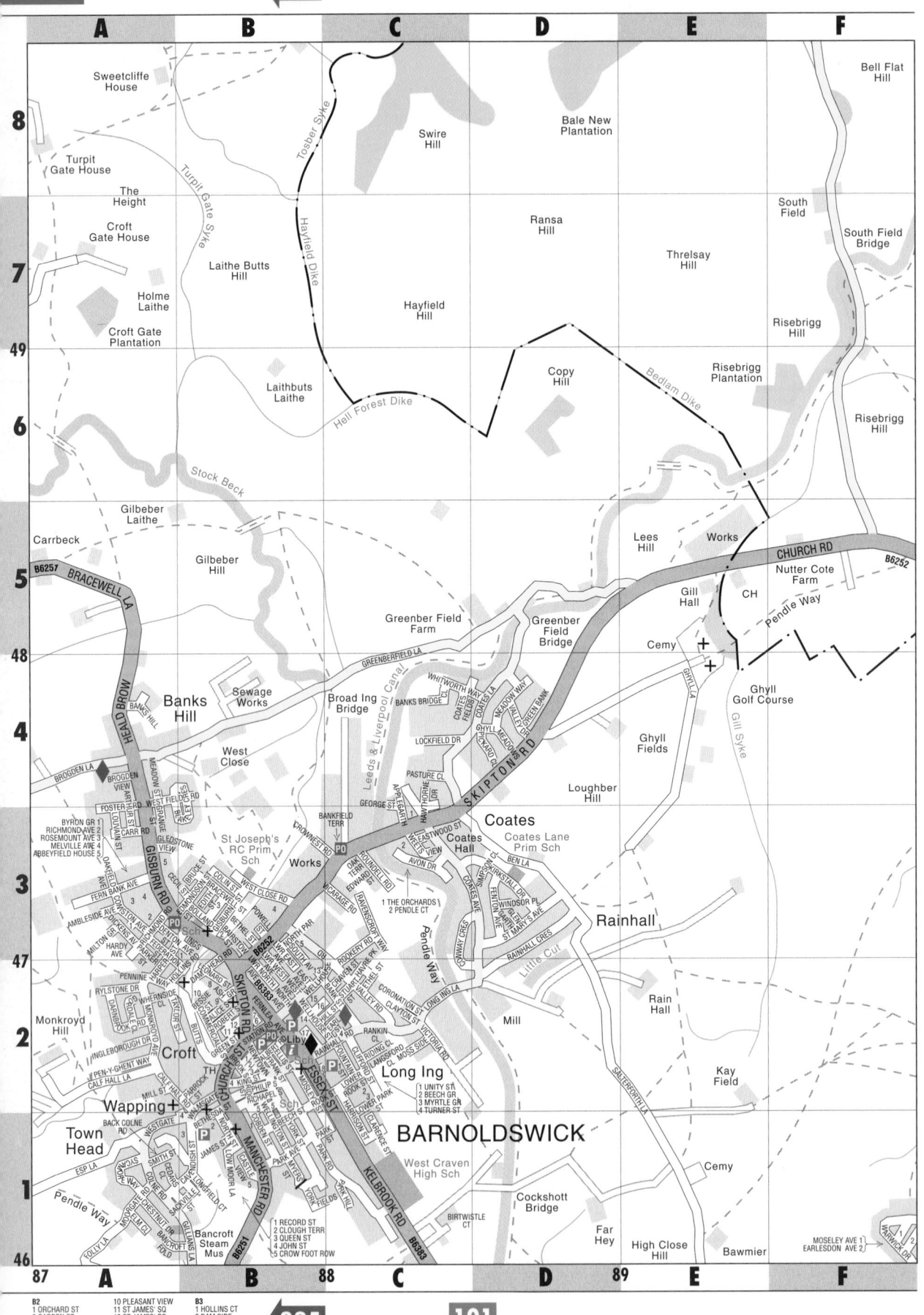

BARNOLDSWICK

B2
1 ORCHARD ST
2 GARDEN ST
3 MARKET ST
4 JEPP HILL
5 BACK CHAPEL ST
6 BACK SKIPTON RD
7 FORESTER'S BLDGS
8 FAR EAST VIEW
9 EAST VIEW

10 PLEASANT VIEW
11 ST JAMES' SQ
12 ST JAMES' RD
13 EAST PAR
14 CO-OPERATIVE ST
15 WELLHOUSE SQ
16 EAST HILLS ST
17 RAILWAY ST
18 SUSSEX ST

B3
1 HOLLINS CT
2 DAM SIDE
3 BROGDEN ST
4 CORNMILL TERR
5 SOUTH PAR

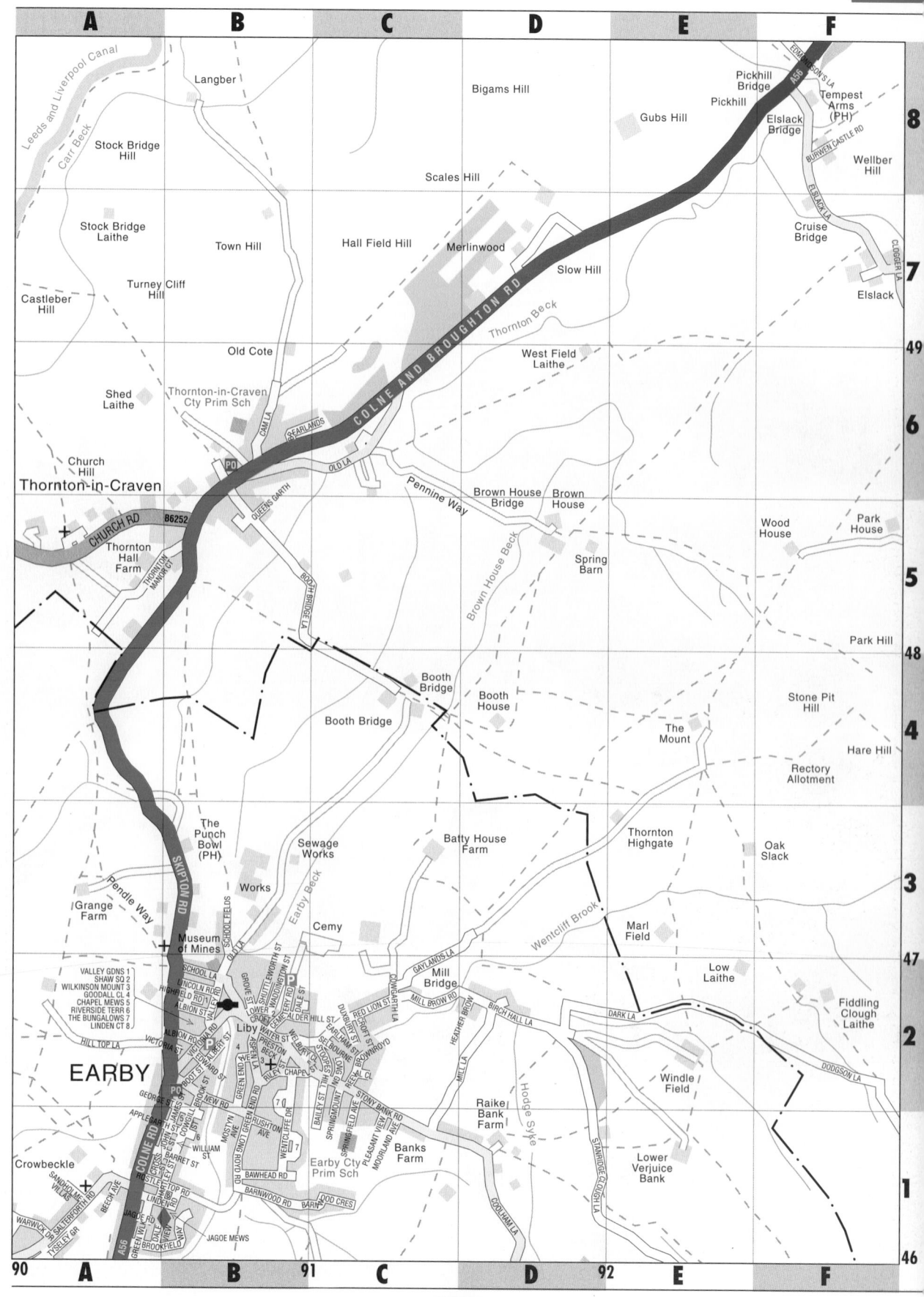

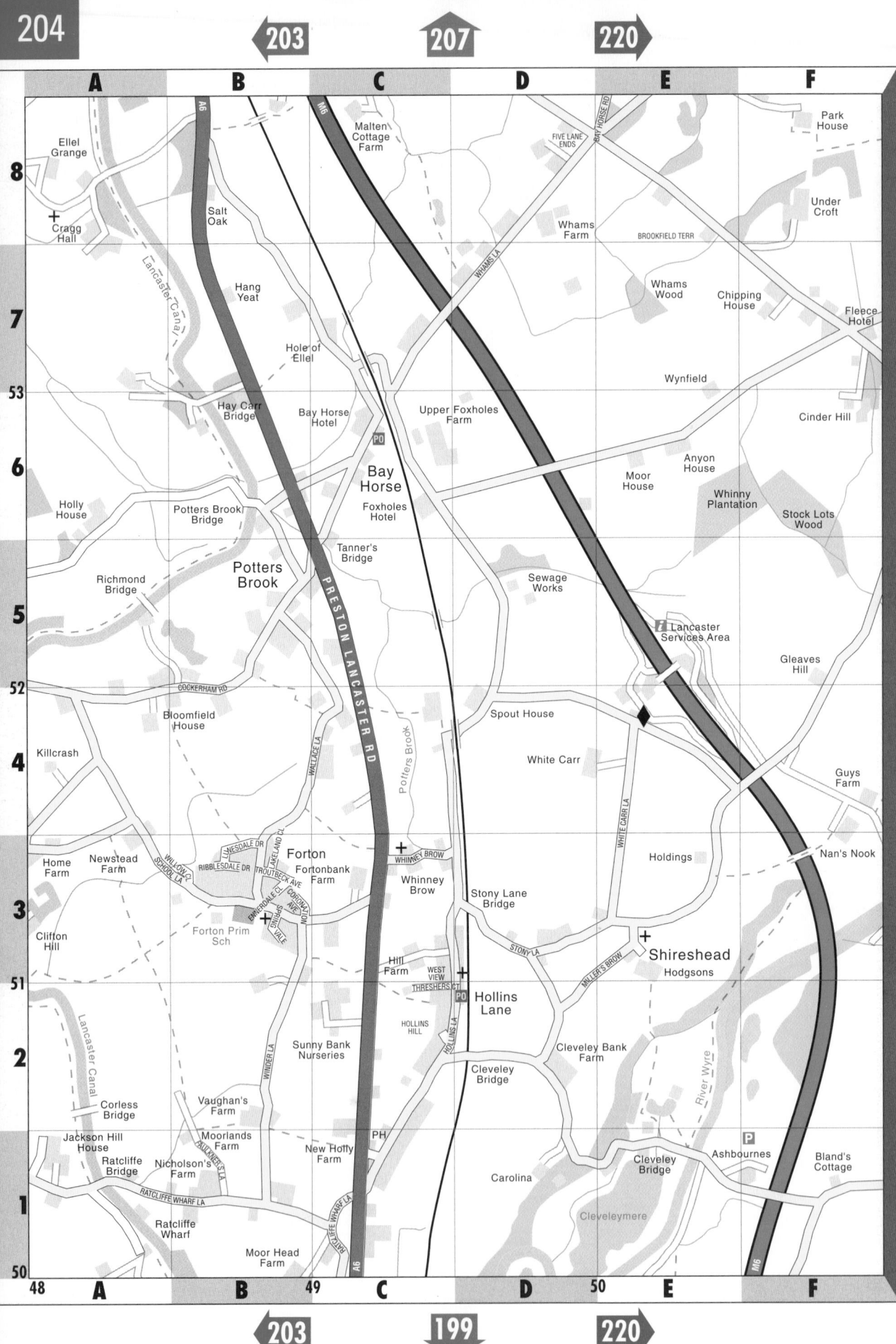

203
207
220

203
199
220

Trumley Farm

Marsh Lea

Trailholme

Lades Bridge

Globe Hotel (PH)

Hall Greave

Overton

STEPHENS GR

CHAPEL CL

MAIN ST

MAIN CL

BACK ST

CHAPEL VIEW

CHAPEL LA

CHURCH PK

ST HELEN'S RD

CHURCH GR

Wandales Point

Dunnal Point

BAZIL GR

BAZIL LA

Lades Marsh

Fiskes Point

Bazil Farm

Bazil

Ferry Cottage

Bazil Point

Wood Bridge

Ford

Chapel Pool

River Lune

Sunderland Brows Farm

Meadow Farm

Ford

Fishnet Point

Works

Dock

RAILWAY PL

RIVER VIEW

VICTORIA TERR

Glasson

PO

B5290

FIRST TERR

THE LANE

PO

TEA ROW

WEST VIEW

TITHEBARN HILL

BOWLAND VIEW

WYRESDALE CRES

LENTHWORTH DR

PENNINE VIEW

P

Marina

Sambo's Grave

Sunderland

SECOND TERR

Glasson Marsh

Old Hall

Christ Church CE Prim Sch

Old Glasson

DOBS LA

Janson Pool

Lancashire Coastal Way

MARSH LA

Sunderland Point

Hall End Skear

Chapel Hill

Crook Farm

Kendal Hill

Moss Grove

Crook Cottage

Tomlinson's Farm

Clarkson's Farm

Thurnham Moss

Abbey Lighthouse Cottage

SLACK LA

Haresnape's Farm

Plover Scar Lighthouse

Gardner's Farm

MOSS LA

42

43

44

8

7

57

6

5

56

4

3

55

2

1

54

A

B

C

D

E

F

205
 210

	A	B	C	D	E	F

8

Ashton Park

Golf Course

Burrow Beck Bridge

Burrow Heights

A6

Lane End

Tarnwater

A588

7

Meldham Wood

CH

Ashton Hall

Crane Wood

Brantbeck Bridge

Brantbeck Farm

Five Ashes

Lower Burrow

River Lune

Waterloo

57

Ashton Park Bridge

6

Seafield Plantation

Long Plantation

Heronswood Farm

Heronswood

Lancaster Canal

Park Coppice

New Park Bridge

Shearset Beck Bridge

5

Conder Green Picnic Area

Conder Green

Old Park Wood

56

B5290

Conder Green Farm

The Stork (PH)

Crow Wood

Parkside

Forerigg Wood

MEADOW PK

4

Brows Farm

Caravan Pk

Conder Bridge

Webster's Farm

Berry's Farm

ELM AVE

ROSE CL

ASH AVE

BEECH AVE

LEACHFIELD RD

OAK AVE

Brick Kiln Bridge

Mill Farm

BIRCH AVE

BANK CL

CONDER GREEN RD

ELLEL HALL GDNS

Ellel Hall Bridge

Ellel Hall

Thurnham Bridge

Lancaster Canal (Glasson Branch)

Thurnham Mill

River Conder

Thurnham Moss

3

Aspley Farm

Bailey Bridge

Bayley Bridge

Sellerly

55

Lower Thurnham

2

Throstle Nest

Forth Lock Bridge

Upper Thurnham

Thurnham Hall

Bamber's Farm

Back Wood

MOSS LA

Brigg's Brow

✝

1

Third Lock Bridge

Second Lock Bridge

A588

54

45	A	B	46	C	D	47	E	F

205
203

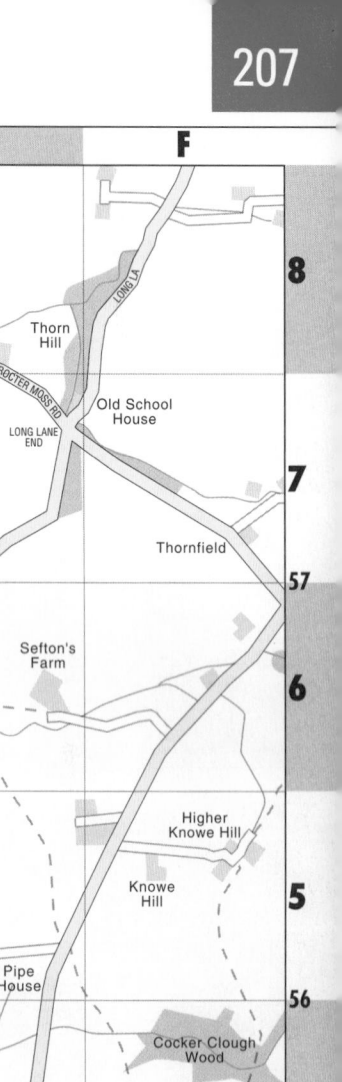

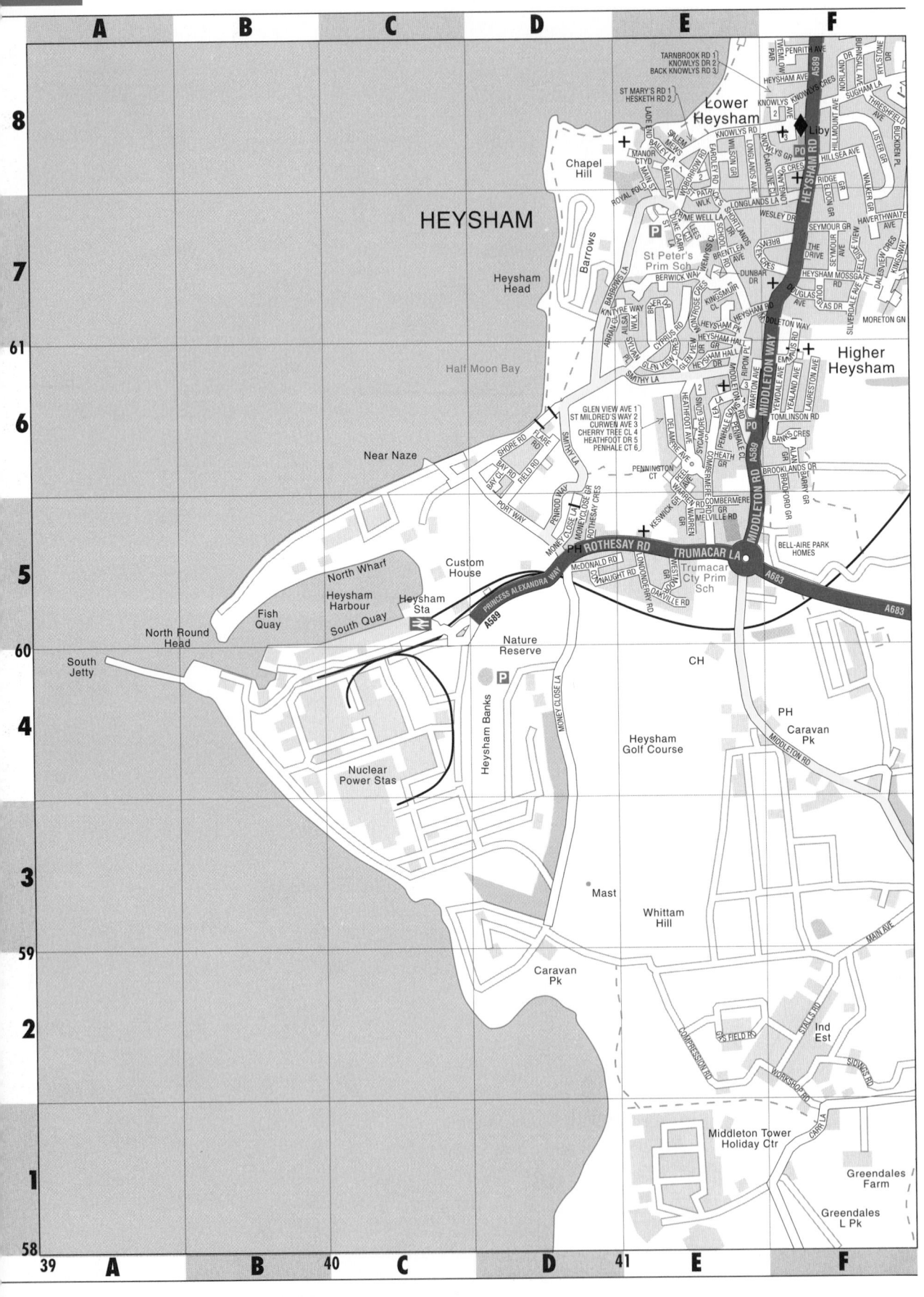

HEYSHAM

Lower Heysham

Chapel Hill

Heysham Head

Half Moon Bay

Higher Heysham

Barrows

St Peter's Prim Sch

Near Naze

North Wharf

Custom House

Heysham Harbour

Heysham Sta

South Quay

Fish Quay

North Round Head

South Jetty

Nature Reserve

Heysham Banks

Nuclear Power Stas

Heysham Golf Course

Trumacar Cty Prim Sch

Bell-Aire Park Homes

Caravan Pk

ROTHESAY RD

TRUMACAR LA

PRINCESS ALEXANDRA WAY

Mast

Whittam Hill

Caravan Pk

Ind Est

Middleton Tower Holiday Ctr

Greendales Farm

Greendales L Pk

GLEN VIEW AVE 1
ST MILDRED'S WAY 2
CURWEN AVE 3
CHERRY TREE CL 4
HEATHFOOT DR 5
PENHALE CT 6

TARNBROOK RD 1
KNOWLYS DR 2
BACK KNOWLYS RD 3

ST MARY'S RD 1
HESKETH RD 2

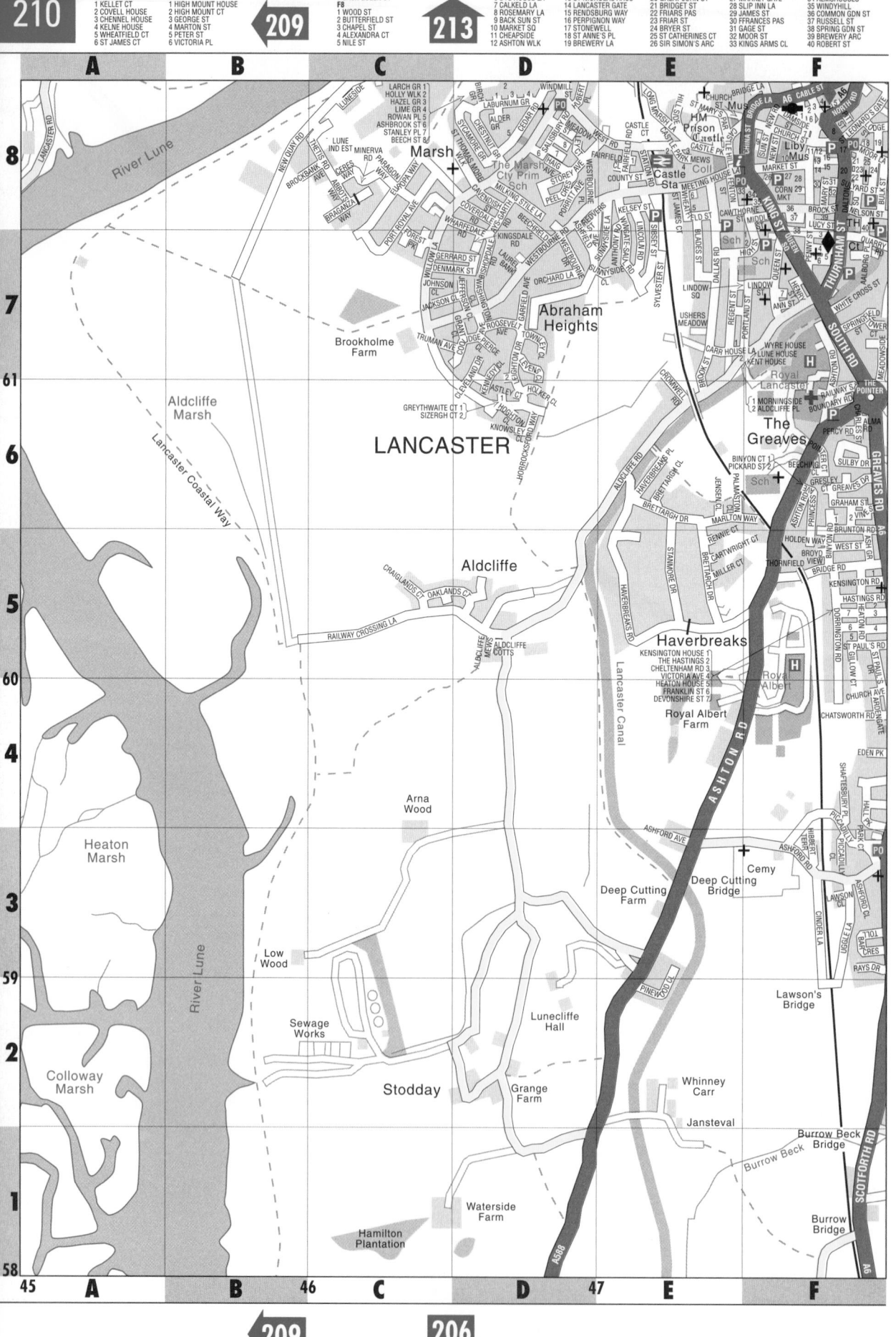

E8
1 KELLET CT
2 COVELL HOUSE
3 CHENNEL HOUSE
4 KELNE HOUSE
5 WHEATFIELD CT
6 ST JAMES CT

F7
1 HIGH MOUNT HOUSE
2 HIGH MOUNT CT
3 GEORGE ST
4 MARTON ST
5 PETER ST
6 VICTORIA PL

7 BACK QUEEN ST
F8
1 WOOD ST
2 BUTTERFIELD ST
3 CHAPEL ST
4 ALEXANDRA CT
5 NILE ST

6 DYE HOUSE LA
7 CALKELD LA
8 ROSEMARY LA
9 BACK SUN ST
10 MARKET SQ
11 CHEAPSIDE
12 ASHTON WLK

13 ST NICHOLAS ARCS
14 LANCASTER GATE
15 RENDSBURG WAY
16 PERPIGNON WAY
17 STONEWELL
18 ST ANNE'S PL
19 BREWERY LA

20 GREAT JOHN ST
21 BRIDGET ST
22 FRIARS PAS
23 FRIAR ST
24 BRYER ST
25 ST CATHERINES CT
26 SIR SIMON'S ARC

27 MARKET GATE
28 SLIP INN LA
29 JAMES ST
30 FRANCES PAS
31 GAGE ST
32 MOOR ST
33 KINGS ARMS CL

34 ALMSHOUSES
35 WINDYHILL
36 COMMON GDN ST
37 RUSSELL ST
38 SPRING GDN ST
39 BREWERY ARC
40 ROBERT ST

← 209

213

214
226
207
226

A8
1 DE VITRE ST
2 SHAW ST
3 GARNET ST
4 SIDNEY TERR
5 SEYMOUR ST
6 PRIORY WLK

7 BATH MILL SQ
8 WHITBARROW SQ
9 HAYLOT SQ
10 CROSSDALE SQ
11 MELBOURNE RD
12 GREENFIELD RD
13 MOOR GATE

14 DAVIDSON ST
15 GLEBE CT
16 CITY HEIGHTS CL
A7
1 SWAN YD
2 GREENFIELD CT
3 ARGYLE ST

4 ELGIN ST
5 DUNKELD ST
6 PRIMROSE CT
7 BRADSHAW ST
8 VINCENT ST

Christ Church CE Prim Sch

Cemy

Lancaster Moor

Freehold

Lancaster Moor

Recess Plantation

Moorlands

Ashton Meml

Williamson Park

The Gables Poultry Farm

Golgotha

Oatlands

Well House

Bowerham

Lancaster L Pk

Filter House

Newlands

West View Farm

Westbourne Heights

Langthwaite House

Langthwaite

Mast

Mast

The Grange

Conderdell

Conder Mill Farm

Recn Gd

Moorside Cty Prim Sch

Middle Langthwaite

Lower Langthwaite

Lee End

Scotforth

Langthwaite Resr

Kirklands Poultry Farm

River Conder

A3
1 SCOTFORTH CT
2 INGLETON HOUSE
3 GRESSINGHAM HOUSE
4 MELLING HOUSE
5 LENTWORTH HOUSE
6 SANDFIELD HOUSE
7 BECK VIEW
8 ABBEYSTEAD HOUSE
9 WINDMILL CT

Scotforth Heights

Mount Vernon

Sunnymede Farm

Conderside Farm

Blea Tarn Resr

Hazelrigg Wood

Blea Tarn Farm

Bailrigg

Bailrigg Farm

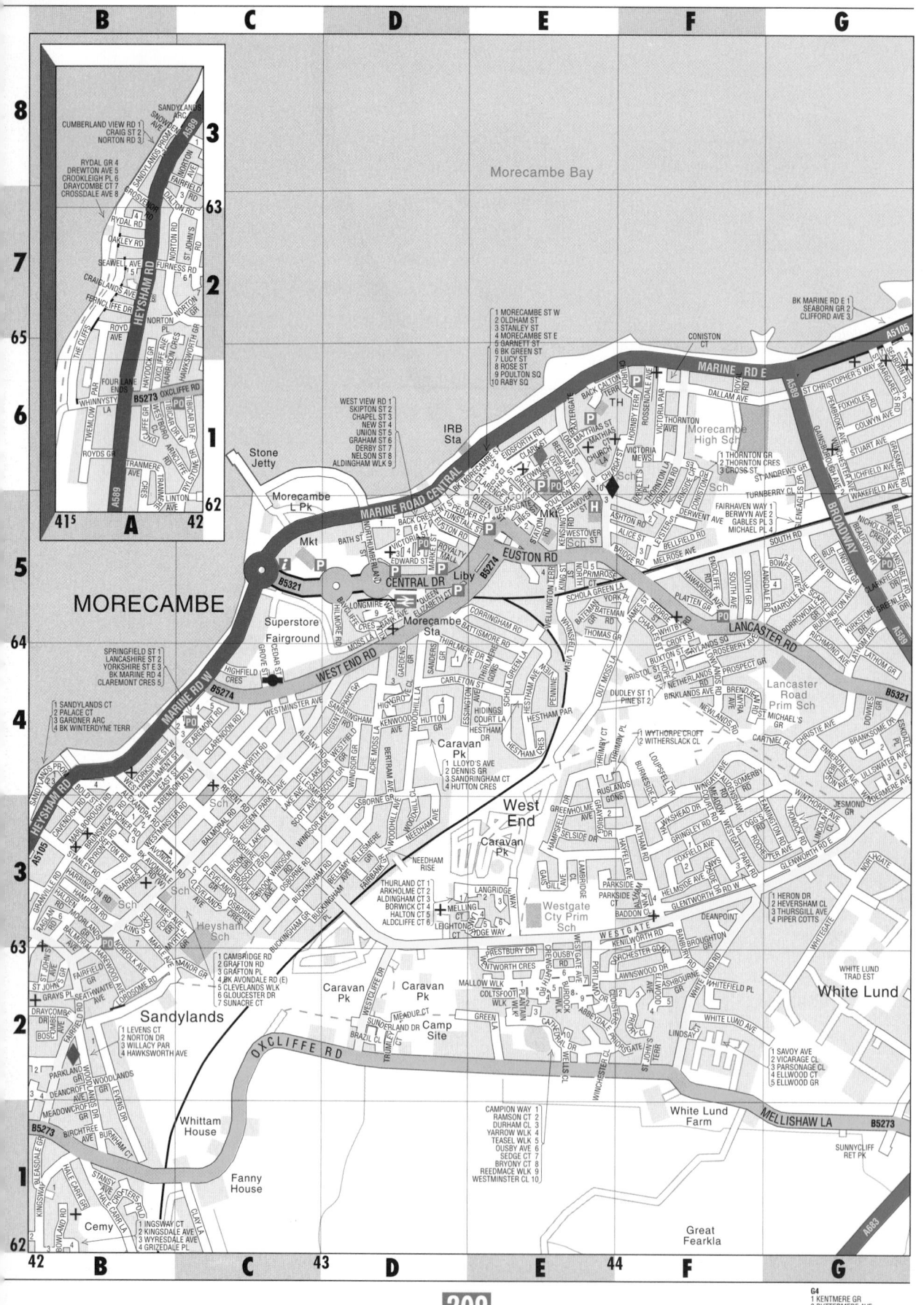

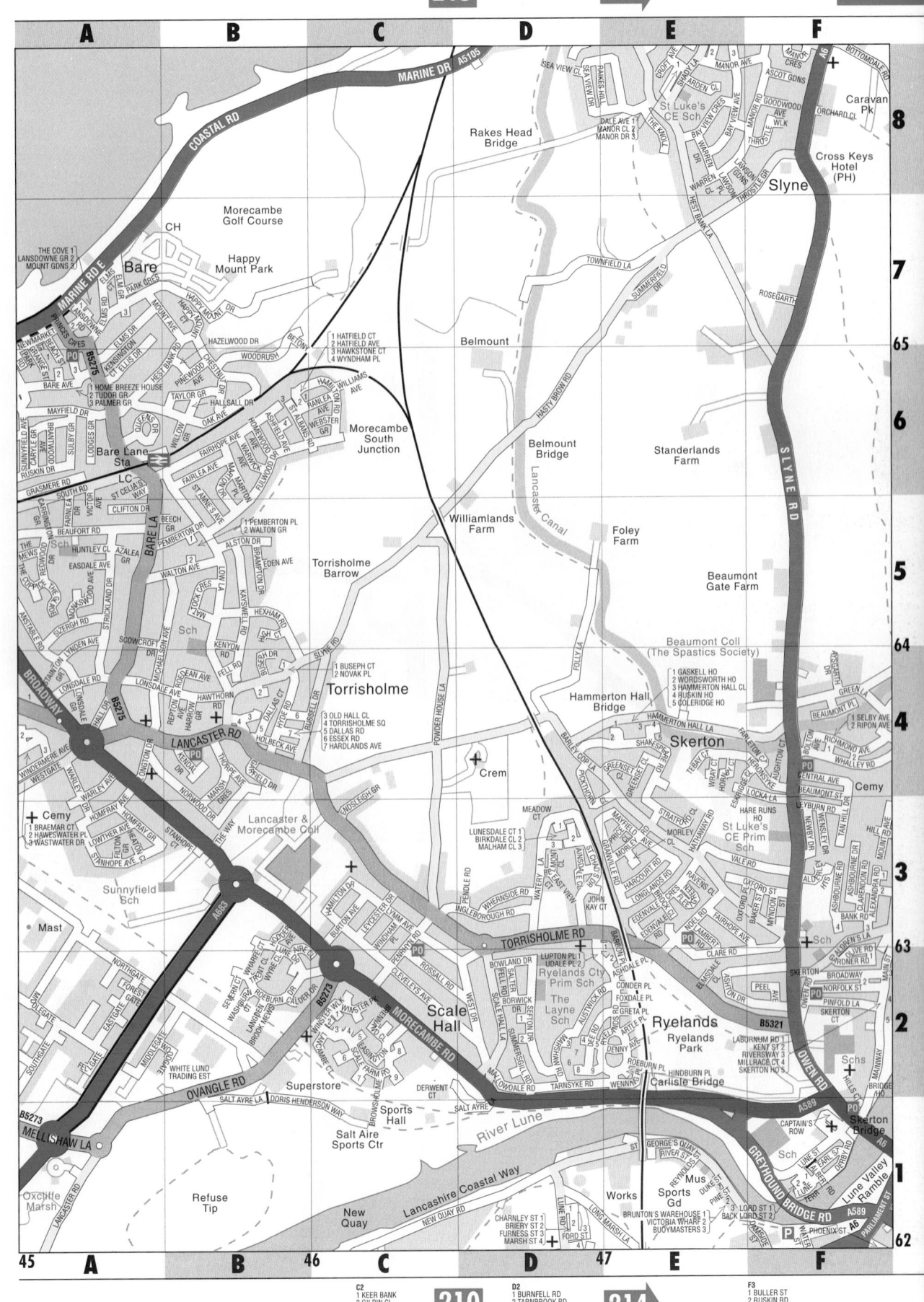

C2
1 KEER BANK
2 GILPIN CL
3 BELA CL
4 CRAKE BANK
5 GREGARETH CL
6 WINDHOLME
7 CROASDALE
8 WHITENDALE
9 BRINDLE CL

D2
1 BURNFELL RD
2 TARNBROOK RD
3 RAYGILL PL
4 AUSTWICK RD
5 RAWTHEY RD
6 MEARBECK PL
7 CROSSHILL PL
8 BROWGILL PL
9 WHITERAY RD

F3
1 BULLER ST
2 RUSKIN RD
3 DAISY ST
4 ASHBOURNE CL

A B C D E F

8

Ancliffe Hall

BOTTOMDALE RD

FOUR LANE
ENDS

Beaumont
Grange

7

Haverbreaks
Farm

FOUNDRY LA

Arrow
Barn

Arrow
Lane Farm

St Wilfrid's CE
Prim Sch

MEADOWFIELD
CL

Halton

65

Cole Beck

Dale
Wood

St
Wilfrid's
Sch

Town End
Mill

6

Carus
Lodge

Carus
House

Halton
Training
Camp

River Lune

Lune Valley Ramble

Church Brow

PH

Bulk
Bridge

Denny
Beck
Farm

Halton
Mills

A683

Halton
Road
Bridge

Hotel

Cottam's
Farm

34

Denny Bank

5

64

RIVERSIDE PARK
IND EST

CH

Lune
Aqueduct

Works

Golf Course

Long Bank
Wood

Moss Syke
Wood

Denny Beck

Old
Parkside
Farm

4

Hill Rd

Lancaster Canal

LANSIL
IND EST

Ridge
Wood

Davies's
Farm

Moor
Side

Old Parkside
Fell

3

63

Lune
Riverside
Park

Newton

TA
Ctr

Trading
Est

Ridge Farm

Ridge

Ridge
Farm

Newton Beck

RIDGE LA

HM Prison

Old Parkside
Fell

2

The
Ridge
Prim
Sch

Central
Lancaster
High Sch

Sports
Ctr

KINGSWAY

CATON RD

A6

Ridge Lea

HM Prison

Stanley
Farm

Stanley Farm
Fell

1

62

Bulk

1 HERLEBECK RISE
2 MONTHALL RISE
3 RIDGE SQ
4 KESWICK CT
5 KESWICK WLK
6 THIRLEMERE CT
7 BUTTERMERE CT

48   A   B   49   C   D   50   E   F

216

A   B   C   D   E   F

8

7

69

6

Priest Skear

Morecambe Bay
Nature Reserve

St MICHEL S LA

Sandside
Caravan
Park

THE SHORE

P

LC

5

Red Bank
Farm

68

PYOAL RD

Morecambe Bay

4

PASTURE LA

A5105

GRANGE VIEW

Bolton
Town End

3

Morecambe
Lodge

Caravan
Pk

COASTAL RD

CHERRY TREE LA

FIR TREE LA

BROMLANDS DR

LILY LEA GR

67

MADISON AVE

ESKDALE CL

TARNBROOK DR

ENDALE DR

GREENWOOD CRES

OAKWOOD GR

GREENWOOD AVE

GREENWOOD AVE

2

Sewage
Works

GREENMOOR RD

ASHWORTH DR

BRYN

HATLEX

PINEWOOD AVE

GREENWOOD
AVE

GREENWOOD DR

LC

COASTAL DR

COASTAL RISE

HATLEX DR

HATLEX HILL

Hest Bank

SLYNE RD A6

MARINE DR

THONS AVE

STATION RD

PO

THE CRESCENT

MOWBRICK LA

HAYFELL GR

PEACOCK CRES

Lancaster
Canal

KIRKLANDS

MANOR RD

A6 MAIN RD

1

SUNNINGDALE CRES

RUSHLEY WAY

RUSHLEY DR

A5105

FELD DR

THE
DRIVE

BANK LA

PEACOCK LA

PROSPECT
AVE

PROSPECT DR

HANGING GREEN LA

SHADY LA

CROFT
AVE

MANOR DR

MANOR
PO

MANOR RD

MANOR
CRES

Manor
House

Slyne
Hall

66

THE
MOORINGS

SUNNINGDALE AVE

45   A   B   46   C   D   47   E   F

215
217
231

A B C D E F

8

7

69

6

5

68

4

3

67

2

1

Black Dike

Crag Bank

GREENGATE LA
CRAG BANK RD
CRAG BANK CRES
LONGFIELD DR
REDRUTH ACRE
ST JUSTELL
CAMBORNE AVE
LONGM CRES CRES
LABURNUM PK

LANCASTER RD

Barker's Bridge

DERTERN LA

Bolton Holmes Farm

Wild Duck Hall

St NICHOLAS LA
WESTFIELD RD
St MARGARET'S RD
ALPINE VIEW
McREFELL RD
MILL LA
HAW THORN AVE
ORCHARD AVE
MEADOW DR
CHEST AVE
LIT
St NICHOLAS RD
WHIN GR
WHIN AVE
THWAITE BROW LA

Mount Pleasant

Crawstone Wood

TORN COTTS

Thwaite House Farm

Whorleys Moss

The Old Mill

SHELLEY CL
SUNNYBANK RD
KEATS AVE
TENNYSON AVE
WORDSWORTH AVE
SONLY TWO
BYRON AVE
RUSKIN GR
BROOKFIELD CL
MAIN RD
Lancaster Canal

Bolton-le-Sands

Hawksheads

BROOKFIELD VIEW
CAVENDISH CT

HILLCREST AVE
MON MONKSWELL AVE
WINDERMERE
St MICHAEL'S CRES
CONISTON RD
RYDAL RD
BYE-PASS RD
MILL DR
PO
PACKET LA
1 CLAYLANDS DR
2 St MICHAEL'S CL
3 St MICHAEL'S GR
3

MOUNT PLEASANT LA

Bolton-le-Sands
CE Prim Sch

Barnes Plantation

Liby
THE NOOK
MAIN RD
CROSS HILL
CT

BOLTON LA

Dale Barns

Lane End Farm

HORNBY BANK

Ash Grove Farm

Nether Kellet

Limeburner's Arms (PH)

BEAR LEA RD
CHURCH HILL
MAIN RD
ASHMEADOW RD
ASHMEADOW GR
LINDETH CL
GRANGE RD
LAITHBUTTS LA

PO
BRIDGE RD
HALLOW
MEADOW CROFT

Nether Kellet
Prim Sch

Lawson's Farm

Channel Head

Hill Top

HILL LA

SLANE LA

BRIDGE RD
CASTLE
Town End
CHURCH

SLYNE RD

CHURCH BROW

CH CH BROW CL

ANCLIFFE LA

Inglebrick

KELLET LA

Cole Wood

Cote Beck

Scargill Farm

Coolbawn

Stub Hall Farm

LONG DALES RD
SCARGILL RD

SLYNE RD
A6

Westfield House

SLYNE HALL HTS

Strellas Bridge

STRELLAS LA

Cote Farm

M6

SCARGILL RD

Leapers Wood

Long Riddings

BACK LA

DUNKIRK AVE
HILLSWAY
LANGDALE RD
CONISTON RD
HIGHFIELD RD
GUMMERS HOWE WLK
GRO KNOTT
RISE

WINDERMERE RD

Ingleborough View

48 A B 49 C D 50 E F

A B C D E F

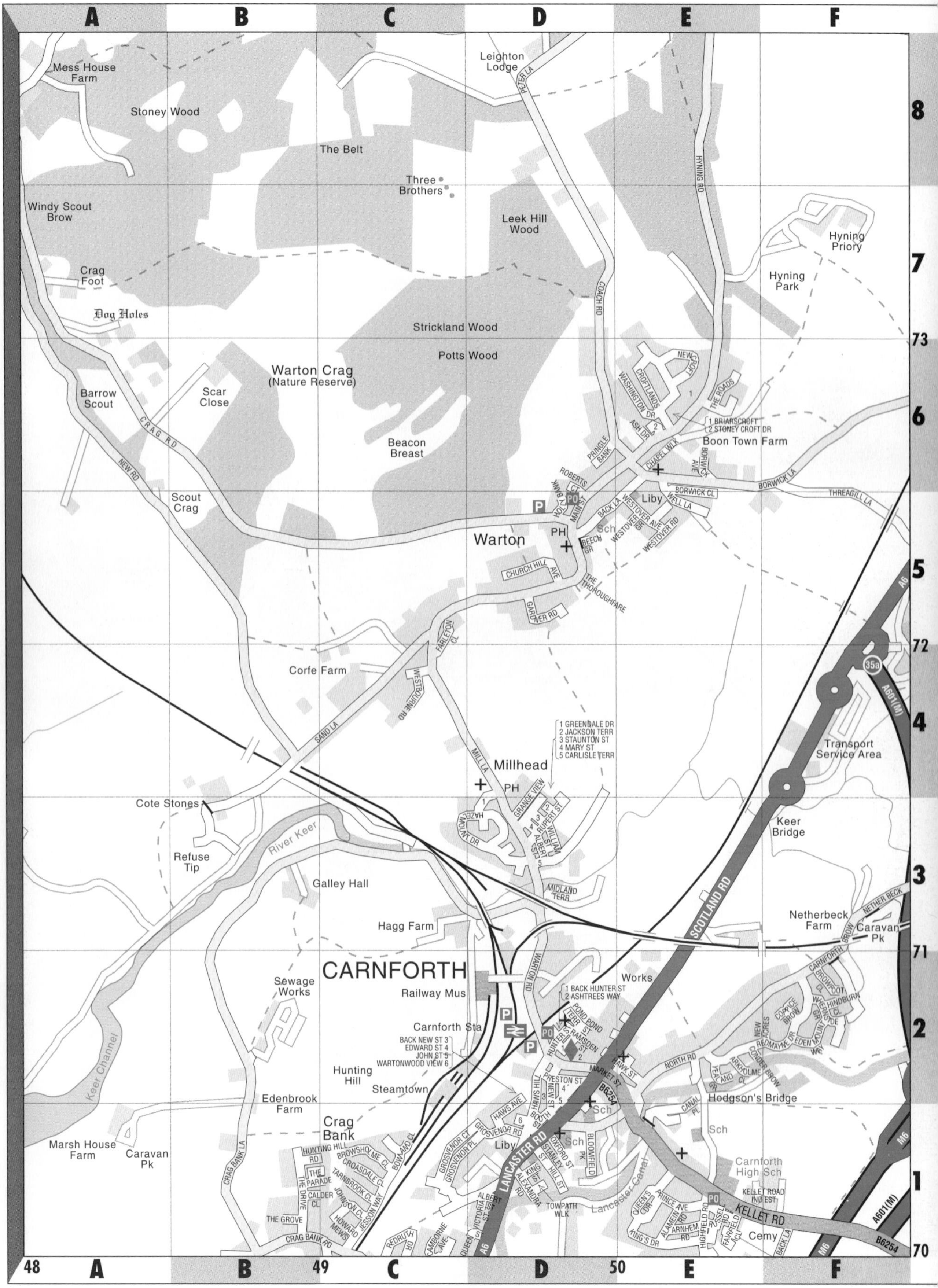

8
7
73
6
5
72
4
71
3
2
1
70

Mess House Farm
Stoney Wood
The Belt
Leighton Lodge
PEEL LA
Three Brothers
Leek Hill Wood
HYNING RD
Hyning Priory
Hyning Park
Windy Scout Brow
Crag Foot
Dog Holes
Strickland Wood
Potts Wood
Barrow Scout
Scar Close
Warton Crag (Nature Reserve)
COACH RD
CRAG RD
NEW CROFT
THE ROADS
1 BRIARSCROFT
2 STONEY CROFT DR
Boon Town Farm
Beacon Breast
Scout Crag
NEW RD
CROFT LANDS
ASH LEA
WASHINGTON DR
PRINGLE BANK
CHAPEL WLK
BORWICK CL
BORWICK LA
THREAGILL LA
ROBERTS
MAIN ST
HILL
Liby
Sch
BACK LA
WESTOVER AVE
WELL LA
WESTOVER DR
WESTOVER RD
Warton
PH
CHURCH HILL
GARNER RD
BEECH GR
THE THOROUGHFARE
Corfe Farm
WESTBOURNE RD
SAND LA
HARTLEY CL
A6
35a
72
Transport Service Area
1 GREENDALE DR
2 JACKSON TERR
3 STAUNTON ST
4 MARY ST
5 CARLISLE TERR
Millhead
PH
MILL LA
GRANGE VIEW
HAZEL
RUPERT ST
WILLIAM
ALBERT ST
A601(M)
Keer Bridge
Cote Stones
River Keer
Refuse Tip
Galley Hall
MIDLAND TERR
SCOTLAND RD
Netherbeck Farm
NETHER BECK
Caravan Pk
Hagg Farm
CARNFORTH
Railway Mus
Carnforth Sta
BACK NEW ST 3
EDWARD ST 4
JOHN ST 5
WARTONWOOD VIEW 6
Sewage Works
Keer Channel
Hunting Hill
Steamtown
Crag Bank
Marsh House Farm
Caravan Pk
Edenbrook Farm
CRAG BANK LA
HUNTING HILL RD
BROWSHQ ME CL
CROASDALE CL
TARNBROOK CL
THE PARADE
CALDER CL
THE DRIVE
JESSOP WAY
JOHNSON CL
HOWARD MEWS
THE GROVE
CRAG BANK RD
REDRUTH CL
CAMBORNE CL WAY
GROSVENOR CT
GROSVENOR PL
GROSVENOR RD
OXFORD ST
HAWS AVE
QUEEN VICTORIA ST
ALBERT ST
A6
LANCASTER RD
THE SWING BRIDGE
NEW ST
PRESTON ST
KING ST
DENNY ST
MILL ST
TOWPATH WLK
1 BACK HUNTER ST
2 ASHTREES WAY
WARTON RD
POND POND
RAMSDEN ST
HUNTER ST
MARKET ST
HAWK ST
B6254
NORTH RD
Works
Sch Pk
BLOOMFIELD
CANAL
Lancaster Canal
Sch
Liby
Hodgson's Bridge
REMDAYNE
COUPE BROW
NEW RD
REDGERS
COUPE BROW
EDEN WAY
AXHOLME
RANDOLF CL
HINDBURN DR
COUPE BROW
Carnforth High Sch
Sch
KELLET ROAD IND EST
PO
KELLET RD
PRINCE AVE
QUEEN'S DR
LANE END
ARNHEM RD
PRIEST HILL
FAIRFIELD RD
ROSSALL RD
King's Dr
Cemy
B6254
M6

237

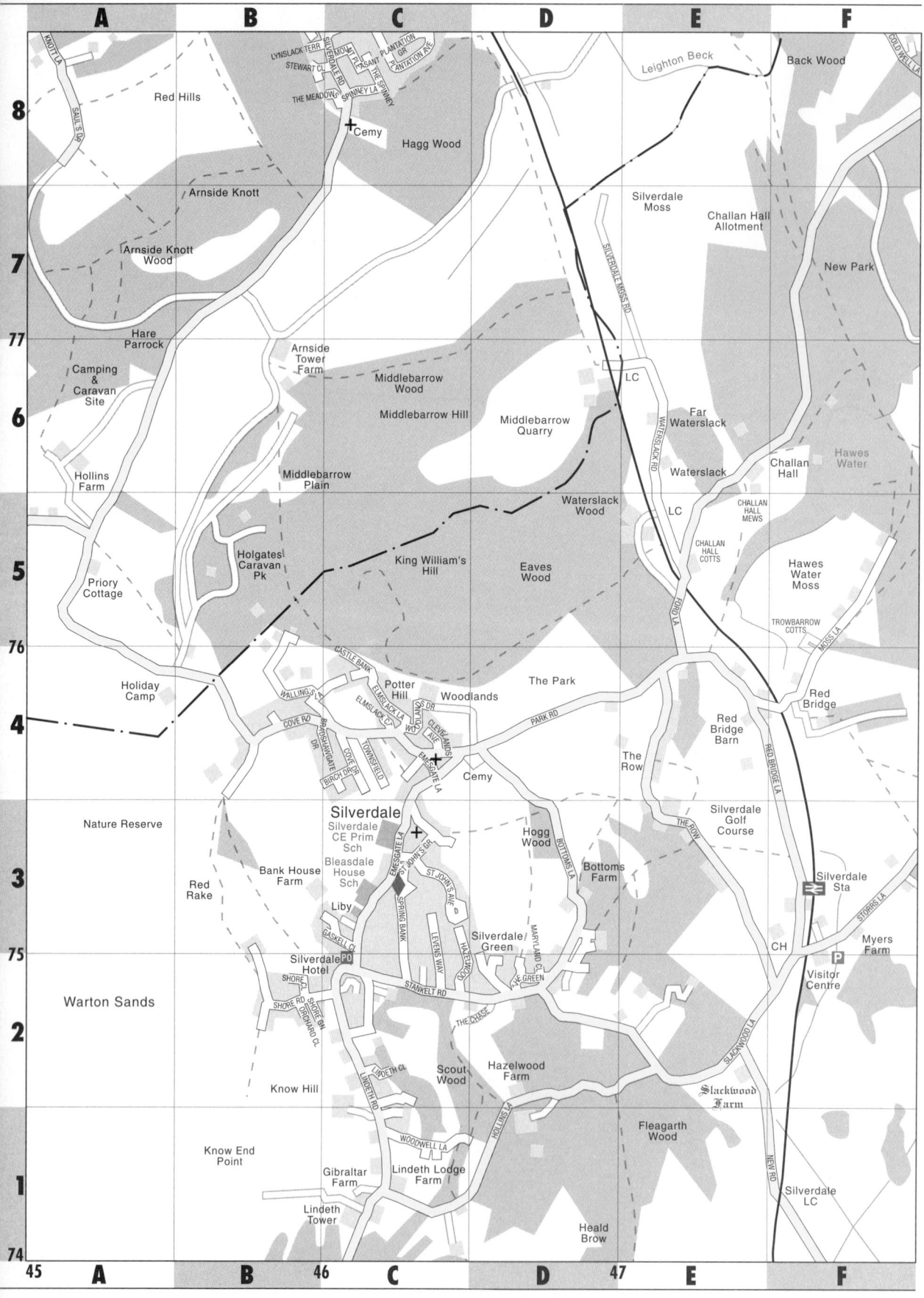

A B C D E F

8 Red Hills
LYNSLACK TERR
STEWART CL
THE MEADOW
SILVERDALE RD
PLEASANT
THE SPINNEY
PLANTATION GR
PLANTATION AVE
SPINNEY LA
Leighton Beck
Back Wood
GOLD WELL LA

Cemy
Hagg Wood
Silverdale
Moss
Challan Hall
Allotment

Arnside Knott

7 Arnside Knott
Wood
New Park

77 Hare
Parrock
Arnside
Tower
Farm
Middlebarrow
Wood
SILVERDALE MOSS RD
LC
Far
Waterslack

6 Camping &
Caravan
Site
Middlebarrow Hill
Middlebarrow
Quarry
WATERSLACK RD
Waterslack
Challan
Hall
Hawes
Water

Hollins
Farm
Middlebarrow
Plain
Waterslack
Wood
LC
CHALLAN HALL
MEWS

5 Priory
Cottage
Holgates
Caravan
Pk
King William's
Hill
Eaves
Wood
FORD LA
CHALLAN
HALL
COTTS
Hawes
Water
Moss
TROWBARROW
COTTS
MOSS LA

76

Holiday
Camp
CASTLE BANK
Potter
Hill
Woodlands
The Park
Red
Bridge
Barn
RED BRIDGE LA
Red
Bridge

4 Nature Reserve
WALLINGS LA
ELMSLACK LA
ELMSLACK CT
ELMSLACK
WAY
CLEVELANDS
AVE
ST ANDREWS DR
EMESGATE LA
Cemy
PARK RD
The
Row
Silverdale
Golf
Course

COVE RD
BRADSHAWGATE
DR
BIRCH DR
COVE DR
TOWNSFIELD
EMESGATE LA
ST JOHN'S GR

3 Red
Rake
Bank House
Farm
Silverdale
Silverdale
CE Prim
Sch
Bleasdale
House
Sch
Hogg
Wood
BOTTOMS LA
Bottoms
Farm
THE ROW
Silverdale
Sta
STORRS LA

Liby
ST JOHN'S AVE
LEVENS WAY
HAZELWOOD
Silverdale
Green
MARYLAND CL
CH
Myers
Farm

75 GASKELL CL
SPRING BANK
Silverdale
Hotel
SHORE CL
VASE GREEN
SLACKWOOD LA
P
Visitor
Centre

SHORE RD
SHORE GN
ORCHARD CL
STANKELT RD
THE CHASE

2 Warton Sands
LINDETH RD
LINDETH CL
Scout
Wood
Hazelwood
Farm
Slackwood
Farm

Know Hill
HOLLINS LA
Fleagarth
Wood
NEW RD

1 Know End
Point
WOODWELL LA
Gibraltar
Farm
Lindeth Lodge
Farm
Heald
Brow
Silverdale
LC

Lindeth
Tower

74

45 A B 46 C D 47 E F

A B C D E F

Leighton House

Leighton Beck Bridge

Beetham Caravan Pk

Silver Ridge Caravan Pk

Fell End Caravan Pk

8

BRACKENTHWAITE RD

Leighton Beck

Hale Moss

Gait Barrows (Nature Reserve)

Brackenthwaite Farm

Hall More Farm

7

East Coppice

Hall More Caravan Pk

Main Drain

77

Thrang End Wood

Thrang End Farm

Hazel Grove

6

West Coppice

Thrang Moss

White Moss

THRANG BROW LA

Thrang Coppice

Birch Cottage

Trough Plantation

Yealand Hall Allotment

Yealand Storrs

5

The Trough

SILVERDALE RD

Yealand Hall

76

Brow Foot Farm

EIGHT ACRE LA

STORRS LA

NINETEEN ACRE LA

4

Storrs Moss

Round Top

Yealand Redmayne

MEADOWS CL

THE MEADOWS

PO

Leighton Moss (Nature Reserve)

Cringlebarrow Wood

WELL LA

Storrs Farm

FOOTBALL LA

Yealand Conyers CE Prim Sch

3

75

FLAT LA

The Pool

Grisedale Farm

Deepdale Wood

Old Hall Farm

ROSE ACRE LA

New Inn (PH)

+

A6

Yealand Manor

Dykes Farm

2

Leighton Hall Home Farm

YEALAND RD

DYKES LA

Dykes House

Grisedale Wood

Leighton Hall

Yealand Conyers

1

Leighton Park

PETER LA

HYNING RD

+

Hermitage Wood

SNAPE LA

74

48 A B 49 C D 50 E F

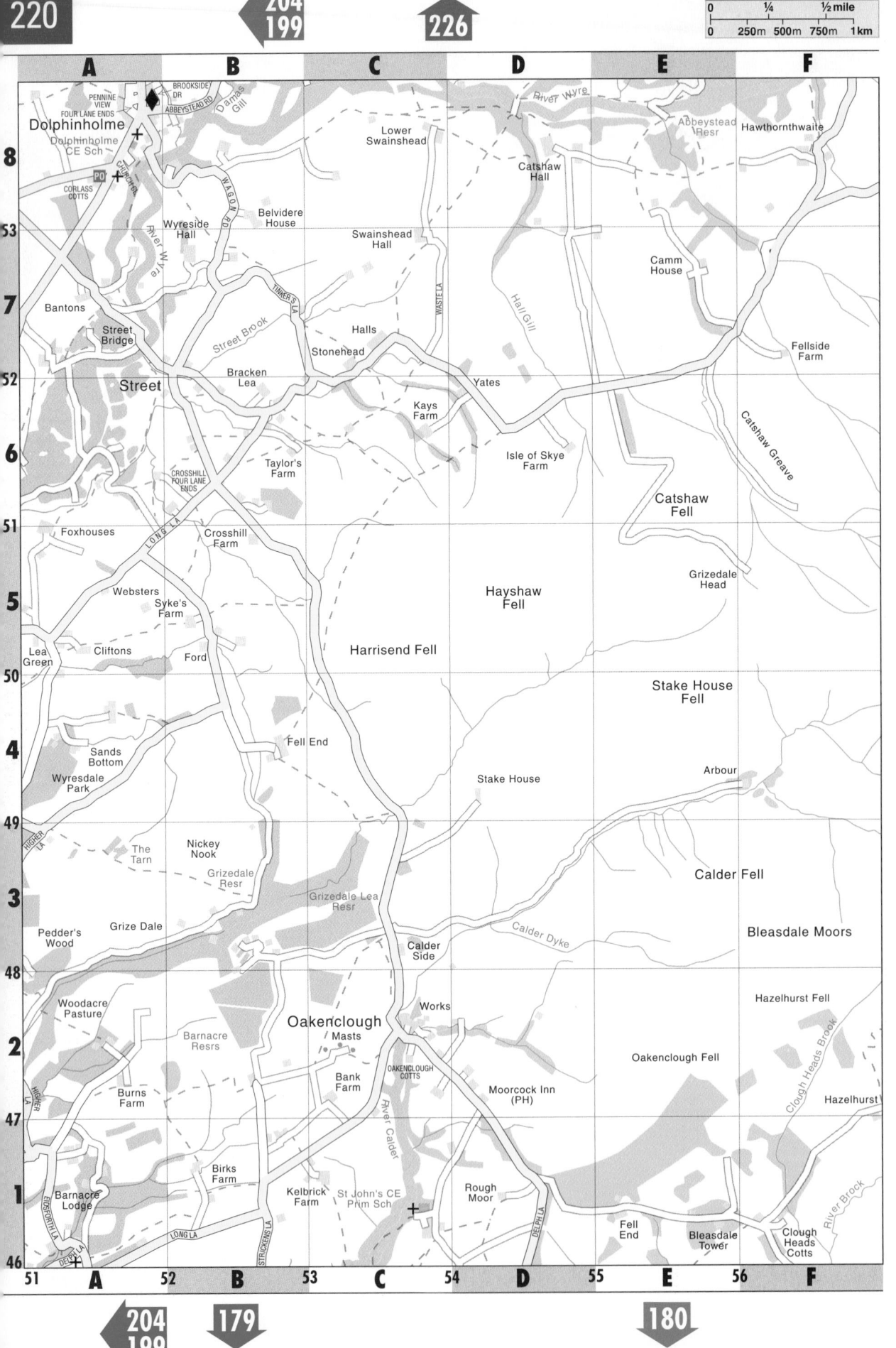

204 199
226

Scale: 1¾ inches to 1 mile
0   ¼   ½ mile
0   250m 500m 750m 1km

A   B   C   D   E   F

PENNINE VIEW
FOUR LANE ENDS
BROOKSIDE DR
ABBEYSTEAD RD
Damas Gill
Dolphinholme
Dolphinholme CE Sch
PO
CORLASS COTTS

8

Lower Swainshead
Catshaw Hall
Abbeystead Resr
Hawthornthwaite

53

Wyreside Hall
Belvidere House
Swainshead Hall
Camm House
WAGON RD
River Wyre

7

Bantons
Street Bridge
Street Brook
TINKER'S LA
Halls
Stonehead
WASTE LA
Hall Gill
Fellside Farm

52

Street
Bracken Lea
Yates
Kays Farm
Catshaw Greave

6

Taylor's Farm
CROSSHILL FOUR LANE ENDS
Isle of Skye Farm
Catshaw Fell

51

Foxhouses
LONG LA
Crosshill Farm
Grizedale Head

5

Websters
Syke's Farm
Hayshaw Fell

50

Lea Green
Cliftons
Ford
Harrisend Fell
Stake House Fell

4

Sands Bottom
Wyresdale Park
Fell End
Stake House
Arbour

49

HIGHER LA
The Tarn
Nickey Nook
Grizedale Resr
Calder Fell

3

Pedder's Wood
Grize Dale
Grizedale Lea Resr
Calder Dyke
Bleasdale Moors

48

Woodacre Pasture
Calder Side
Works
Hazelhurst Fell

2

HIGHER LA
Barnacre Resrs
Oakenclough
Masts
OAKENCLOUGH COTTS
Bank Farm
Moorcock Inn (PH)
Oakenclough Fell
Hazelhurst

47

Burns Farm
River Calder
Clough Heads Brook

1

Barnacre Lodge
EDGEFORTH LA
Birks Farm
Kelbrick Farm
St John's CE Prim Sch
Rough Moor
Fell End
Bleasdale Tower
Clough Heads Cotts
River Brock
DEPTH LA

46

DEPTH LA
LONG LA
STRICKENS LA

51   A   52   B   53   C   54   D   55   E   56   F

204 199
179
180

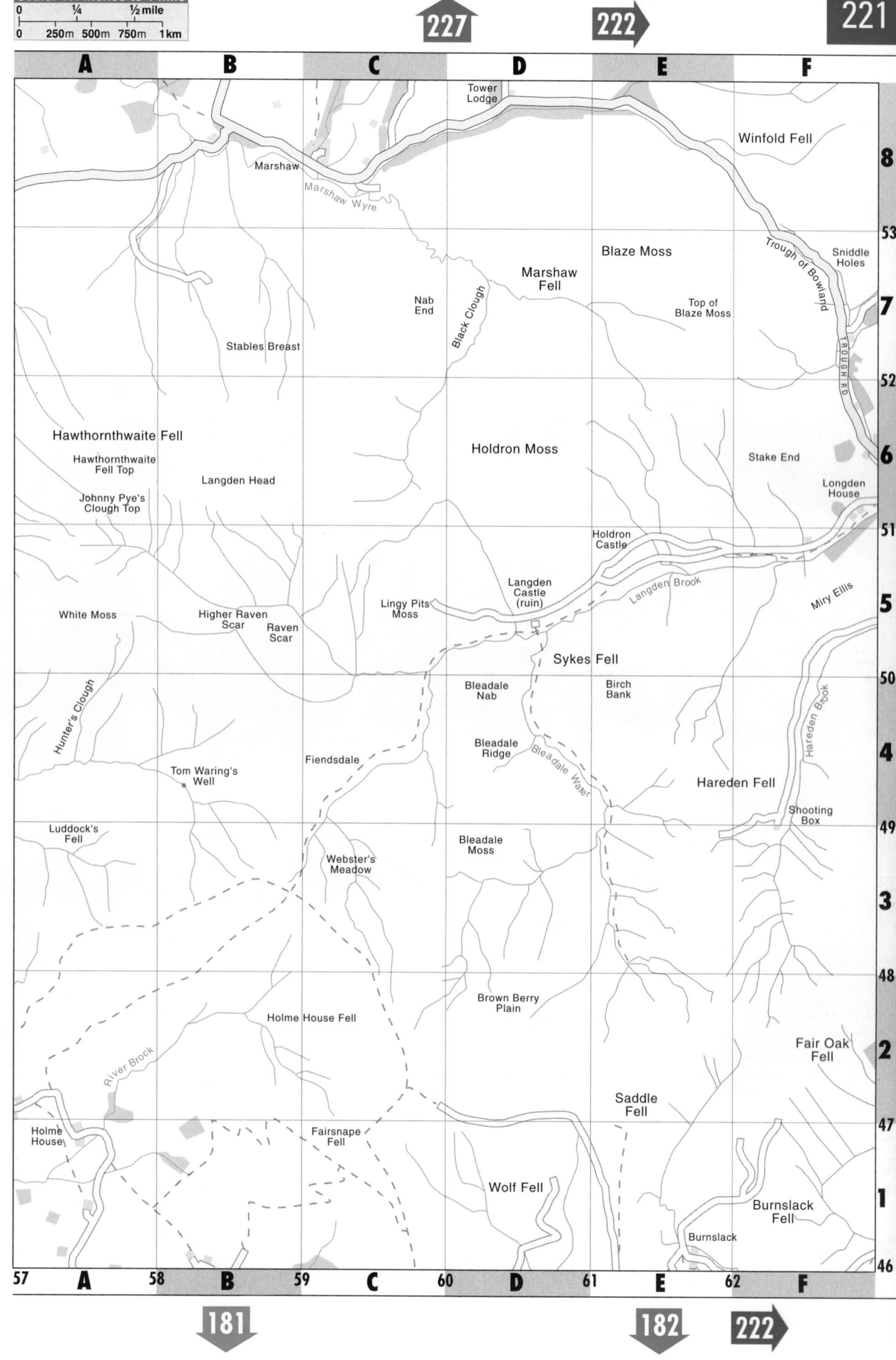

Scale: 1¾ inches to 1 mile

0   ¼   ½ mile
0 250m 500m 750m 1km

227

222

Tower Lodge

Marshaw

Marshaw Wyre

Winfold Fell

Blaze Moss

Trough of Bowland

Sniddle Holes

Nab End

Black Clough

Marshaw Fell

Top of Blaze Moss

TROUGH RD

Stables Breast

Hawthornthwaite Fell

Hawthornthwaite Fell Top

Langden Head

Holdron Moss

Stake End

Longden House

Johnny Pye's Clough Top

Holdron Castle

White Moss

Higher Raven Scar

Raven Scar

Lingy Pits Moss

Langden Castle (ruin)

Langden Brook

Miry Ellis

Hunter's Clough

Sykes Fell

Bleadale Nab

Birch Bank

Tom Waring's Well

Fiendsdale

Bleadale Ridge

Bleadale Water

Hareden Brook

Hareden Fell

Luddock's Fell

Webster's Meadow

Bleadale Moss

Shooting Box

Holme House Fell

Brown Berry Plain

Fair Oak Fell

River Brock

Saddle Fell

Holme House

Fairsnape Fell

Wolf Fell

Burnslack Fell

Burnslack

221
228

Scale: 1¾ inches to 1 mile

0   ¼   ½ mile
0   250m 500m 750m 1km

A B C D E F

Costy Clough

Burn Side

Whins Brow

Whin Fell

Burn Fell

Brennand River

Calder Moor

Rams Clough

Beatrix Fell

Burn House

The Hey

New Biggin

Staple Oak Fell

River Dunsop

Bishops House

Oxenhurst

Brunghill Moor

BACK LA

Sykes Farm

Sykes Nab

Beatrix

Back of Hill Barn

Gamble Hole Farm

Closes Barn

Low Barn

Knot or Sugar Loaf

Moor End

Heaning

Hareden Farm

TROUGH RD

Dunsop Bridge

Boarsden

Hareden Brook

Brown Nab

Bowland Forest RC Sch

THE CRESCENT

PO P

FORESTRY HOUSES

Root

Thorneyholme

Mossthwaite

Fober Farm

Mellor Knoll

Knowlmere Manor

River Hodder

Totridge

New Hay Farm

Langden Bridge

Hodder Bank Fell

Birkett

Burholme

Ing Barn

Hodder Bank Farm

Birkett Fell

Whitmore

Burholme Bridge

Lower Fence Wood

Crag House

Higher Fence Wood

Reed Barn Cottage

Higher Whitewell

Marl Hill

Crimpton

Dinkling Green Farm

New Laund

Whitewell

Marl Hill Moor

The Inn at Whitewell

HALL HILL

New Laund Hill

Spire Farm

Seedalls

Fair Oak

Wilsons

63 A 64 B 65 C 66 D 67 E 68 F

221
183
184

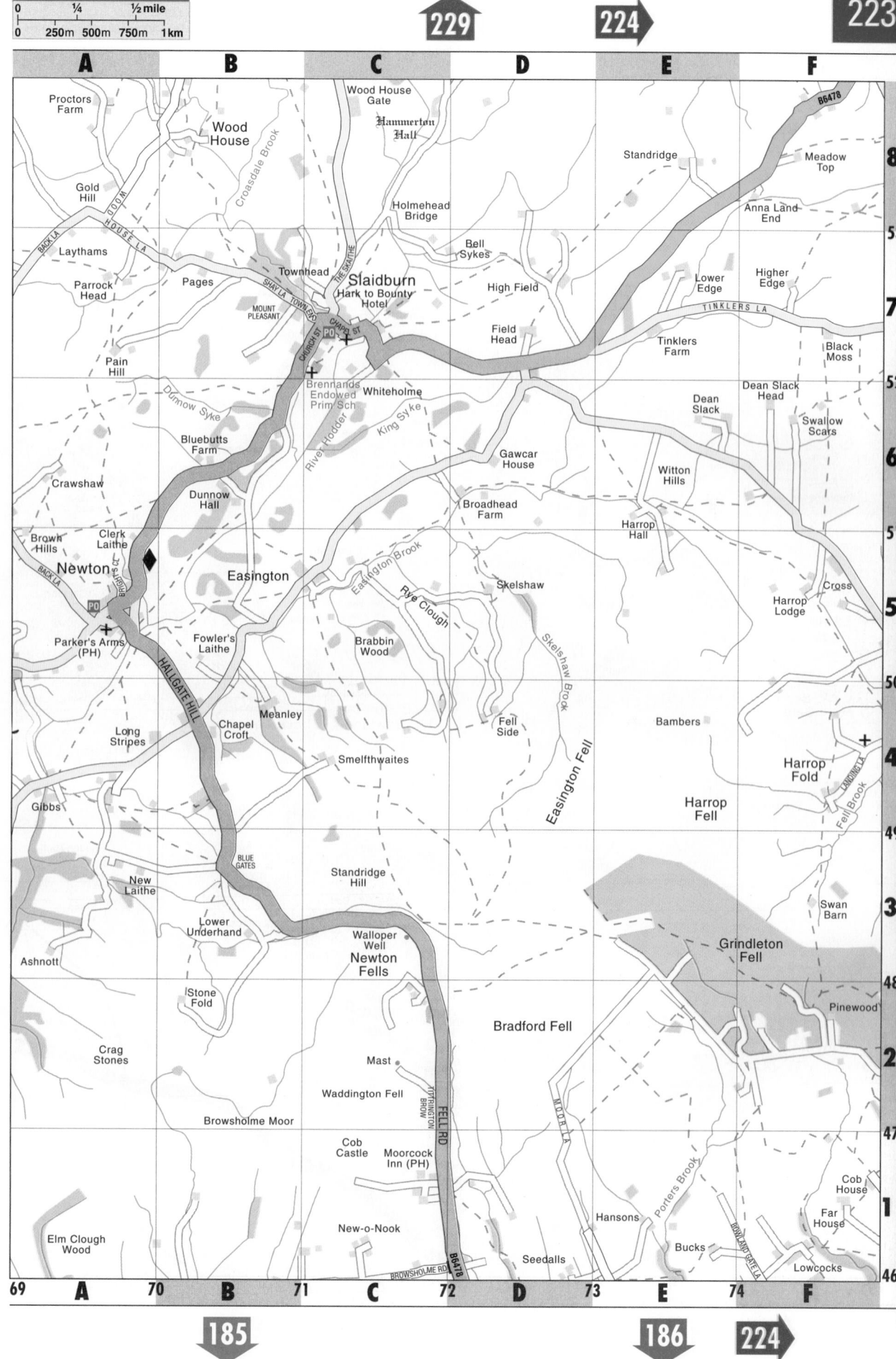

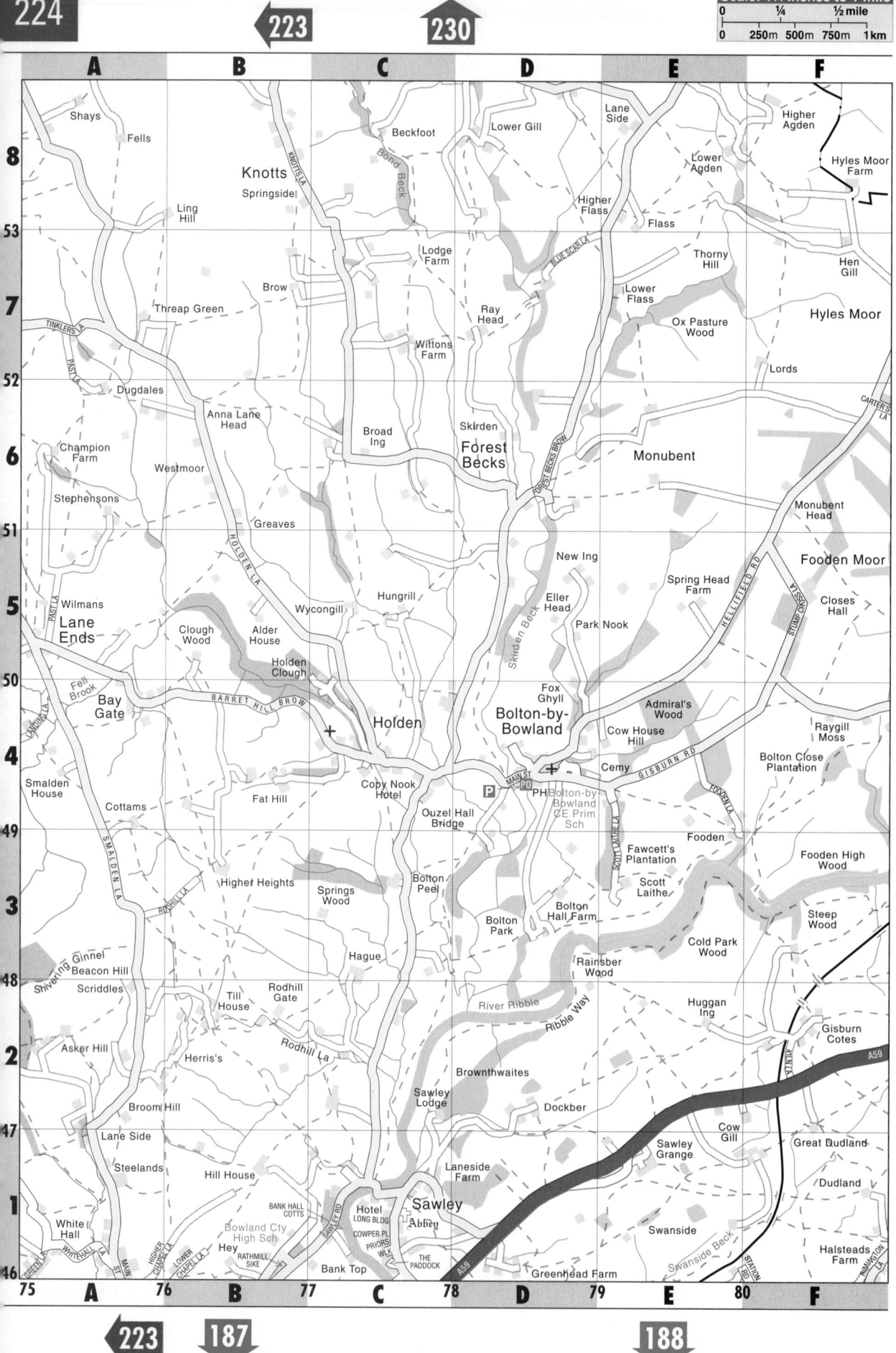

Scale: 1¾ inches to 1 mile

0   ¼   ½ mile
0   250m   500m   750m   1km

A   B   C   D   E   F

8
53
7
52
6
51
5
50
4
49
3
48
2
47
1
46

75   A   76   B   77   C   78   D   79   E   80   F

Shays
Fells
Higher Agden
Hyles Moor Farm
Knotts
Beckfoot
Lower Gill
Lane Side
Lower Agden
Springside
Ling Hill
Higher Flass
Flass
Hen Gill
Brow
Lodge Farm
Hyles Moor
Threap Green
Ray Head
Lower Flass
Thorny Hill
Tinklers La
Dugdales
Wittons Farm
Ox Pasture Wood
Anna Lane Head
Broad Ing
Skirden
Monubent
Lords
Champion Farm
Westmoor
Forest Becks
Stephensons
Greaves
Monubent Head
Holden La
New Ing
Fooden Moor
Wilmans
Wycongill
Hungrill
Spring Head Farm
Closes Hall
Lane Ends
Clough Wood
Alder House
Eller Head
Park Nook
Past La
Holden Clough
Fox Ghyll
Admiral's Wood
Raygill Moss
Fell Brook
Bay Gate
Barret Hill Brow
Holden
Bolton-by-Bowland
Cow House Hill
Bolton Close Plantation
Smalden House
Copy Nook Hotel
Cemy
Gisburn Rd
Cottams
Fat Hill
PH
Bolton-by-Bowland CE Prim Sch
Fooden
Smalden La
Ouzel Hall Bridge
Scott Laithe
Fawcett's Plantation
Fooden High Wood
Higher Heights
Springs Wood
Bolton Peel
Scott Laithe
Steep Wood
Rodhill La
Hague
Bolton Hall Farm
Cold Park Wood
Shivering Ginnel
Beacon Hill
Rodhill Gate
Bolton Park
Rainsber Wood
Scriddles
Till House
River Ribble
Huggan Ing
Asker Hill
Herris's
Rodhill La
Ribble Way
Gisburn Cotes
Broom Hill
Sawley Lodge
Brownthwaites
Dockber
A59
Great Dudland
Lane Side
Sawley Grange
Cow Gill
Steelands
Hill House
Laneside Farm
Swanside
Dudland
Bank Hall Cotts
Hotel
Long Bldg
Sawley
Abbey
White Hall
Bowland Cty High Sch
Rathmill Sike
Cowper Pl
Priors Wlk
The Paddock
Greenhead Farm
Swanside Beck
Halsteads Farm
Green La
Whitehall La
Main St
Higher Chapel La
Lower Chapel La
Sawley Rd
Bank Top
Hey
A59
Station Rd
Carter's La

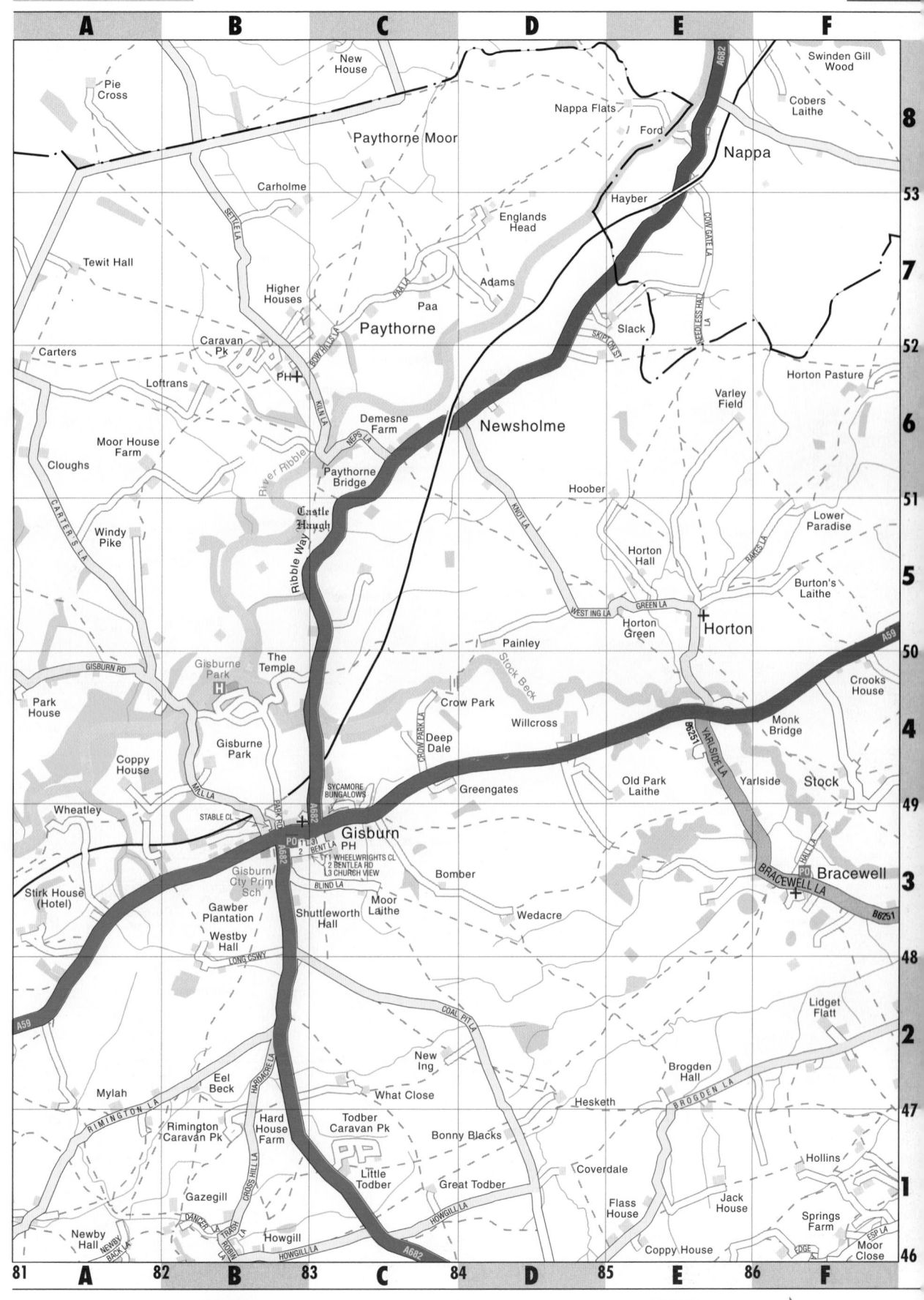

Scale: 1¾ inches to 1 mile

0   ¼   ½ mile
0 250m 500m 750m 1km

A B C D E F

8
Pie Cross
New House
Swinden Gill Wood
Nappa Flats
Cobers Laithe
Paythorne Moor
Ford
Nappa

53
Carholme
Englands Head
Hayber

7
Tewit Hall
Adams
Slack
Higher Houses
Paa
Paythorne
Horton Pasture

52
Carters
Caravan Pk
Varley Field
Loftrans
PH

6
Moor House Farm
Demesne Farm
Newsholme
Cloughs
Hoober
Lower Paradise

51
River Ribble
Paythorne Bridge
Castle Haugh
Ribble Way
Horton Hall
Burton's Laithe

5
Windy Pike
Carter's La
Horton Green
Horton
West Ing La
Green La

50
Gisburn Rd
Gisburne Park
The Temple
Painley
Crooks House
Park House
Crow Park
Stock Beck
Willcross
Monk Bridge

4
Coppy House
Gisburne Park
Deep Dale
Greengates
Old Park Laithe
Yarlside
Stock
Wheatley
Sycamore Bungalows
Stable Cl
Mill La

49
PO
Gisburn
PH
1 Wheelwrights Cl
2 Bentlea Rd
L3 Church View
Bent La
Park Rd
Bomber
Bracewell
Bracewell La

3
Stirk House (Hotel)
Gisburn Cty Prim Sch
Gawber Plantation
Blind La
Moor Laithe
Shuttleworth Hall
Wedacre
Westby Hall
B6251

48
Long Cswy
Coal Pit La

2
A59
Mylah
Eel Beck
New Ing
What Close
Hesketh
Brogden Hall
Brogden La
Lidget Flatt
Rimington La
Hardacre La

47
Rimington Caravan Pk
Hard House Farm
Todber Caravan Pk
Bonny Blacks
Coverdale
Cross Hill La
Hollins

1
Gazegill
Little Todber
Great Todber
Flass House
Jack House
Springs Farm
Newby Hall
Howgill
Howgill La
Coppy House
Moor Close
A682

46

81 A 82 B 83 C 84 D 85 E 86 F

189 190 200

211 207
231

Scale: 1¾ inches to 1 mile

0   ¼   ½ mile
0   250m   500m   750m   1km

A   B   C   D   E   F

Littledale Hall

Foxdale Beck

Corney Hill Farm

Baines Cragg

P

The Cragg

Bellhill Farm

Littledale Hall

8

Friar's Moss Farm

POSTERN GATE RD

FRIAR'S MOSS RD

QUERNMORE RD

LITTLEDALE RD

Cragg Wood

Field Head

Knotts Farm

Askew Hill

61

River Gander

Littledale

Udale Beck

Stock-a-Bank

Greenlot

Windy Clough

Wisp Hill

7

Quernmore CE (VC) Prim Sch

P

RIGG LA

Conder Head

Black Fell

60

Far Lodge

Fell End Farm

Clougha Scar

Clougha

Brownley Hill

6

Narr Lodge

Rowton Brook

Clougha Pike

WYRESDALE RD

Quernmore

PO

Rowton Brook Fell

59

LONG LA

Brow Top Farm

QUERNMORE BROW

Shooters Pile

Grit Fell

Terrace Farm

Gibson's Farm

Middle Brow Top

Hare Appletree Fell

Grizedale Head

5

BAY HORSE RD

Hare Appletree

Burrow Hill

58

Lower Browtop

Damas Gill

Abbeystead Fell

Lee Fell

4

Blackwood End

P

Twr

Rotten Hill

River Grizedale

Longmoor

Westfield House

57

Castle o' Trim

Higher Moor Head

High Moor Cross

Grizedale Barn

3

Yeat House Farm

PROCTER MOSS RD

Lower Moor Head

Damas Gill

Gate House Bridge

Balderstones

56

Lower Castle o' Trim

Tills Farm

Lee

RACEHOUSE BROW

2

Middle Crag

Borwicks

Brook House

Grizedale Bridge

ABBEYSTEAD LA

Summer House Head

River Wyre

55

Hollyhead Farm

Gallows Clough

Chapel House Farm

Abbeystead

LONG LA

PLANTATION LA

Cawthorne Endowed Prim Sch

Lee Bridge

1

Ortner

ABBEYSTEAD RD

THE RAKE

SMITHY BROW

STRAIT LA

Docholme Farm

DOCHOLME RAKE

Starbank

Lower Green Bank

River Wyre

Lentworth Hall

Abbeystead Resr

54

51   A   52   B   53   C   54   D   55   E   56   F

211 207
220

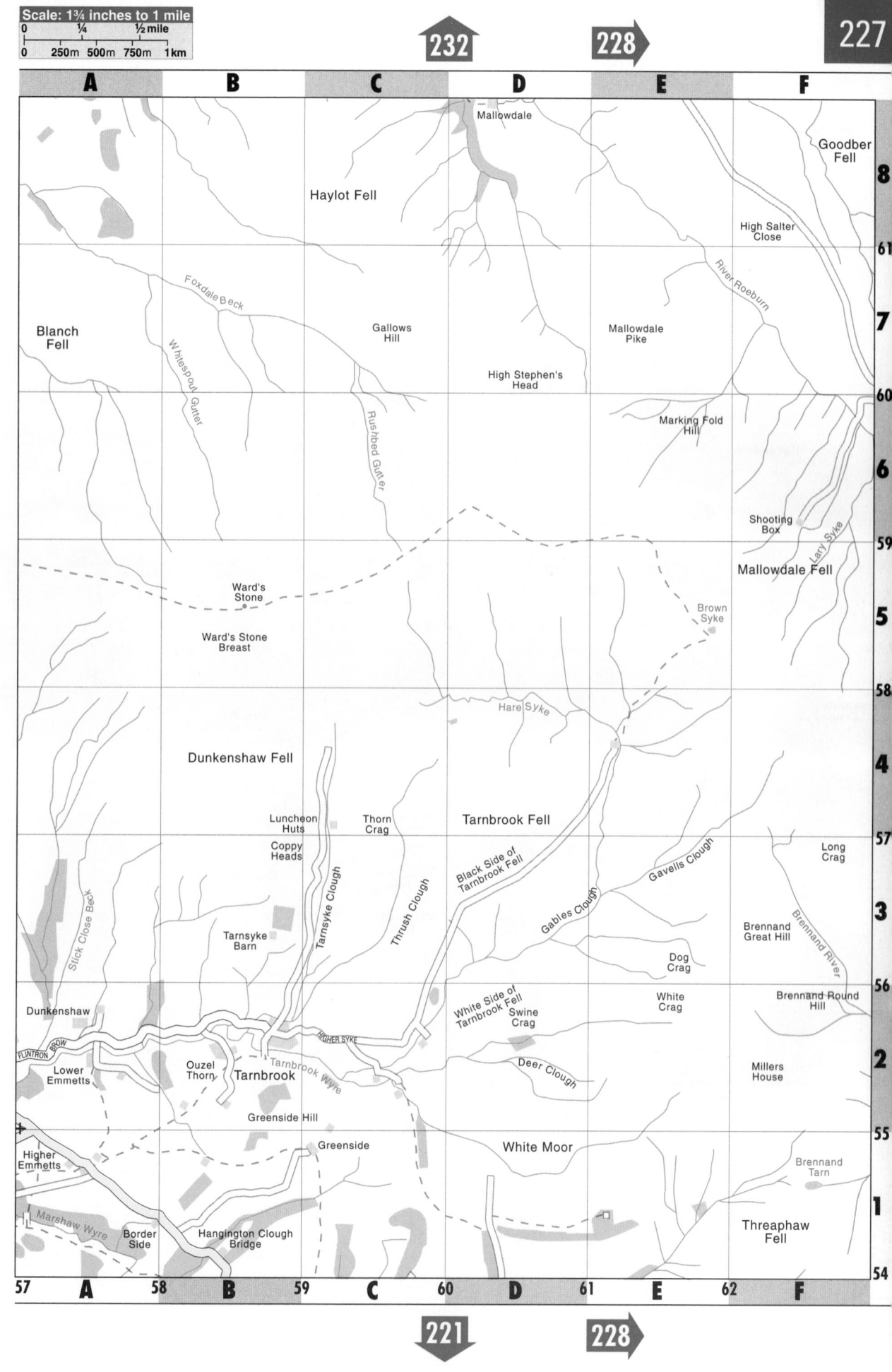

Scale: 1¾ inches to 1 mile

0   ¼   ½ mile

0   250m 500m 750m 1km

232
228

A   B   C   D   E   F

Mallowdale

Goodber
Fell

Haylot Fell

High Salter
Close

Foxdale Beck

61

River Roeburn

7

Blanch
Fell

Gallows
Hill

Mallowdale
Pike

Whitespout Gutter

High Stephen's
Head

60

Marking Fold
Hill

6

Rushbed Gutter

Shooting
Box

Lady Syke

59

Mallowdale Fell

Ward's
Stone

Brown
Syke

5

Ward's Stone
Breast

58

Hare Syke

Dunkenshaw Fell

4

Tarnbrook Fell

Luncheon
Huts

Thorn
Crag

Long
Crag

57

Coppy
Heads

Black Side of
Tarnbrook Fell

Gavells Clough

Tarnsyke Clough

Brennand River

3

Tarnsyke
Barn

Thrush Clough

Gables Clough

Brennand
Great Hill

Slick Close Beck

Dog
Crag

56

Dunkenshaw

White Side of
Tarnbrook Fell

White
Crag

Brennand Round
Hill

FLINTRON BOW

HIGHER SYKE

Swine
Crag

2

Lower
Emmetts

Ouzel
Thorn

Tarnbrook

Tarnbrook Wyre

Deer Clough

Millers
House

Greenside Hill

55

Higher
Emmetts

Greenside

White Moor

Brennand
Tarn

1

Marshaw Wyre

Border
Side

Hangington Clough
Bridge

Threaphaw
Fell

54

57   A   58   B   59   C   60   D   61   E   62   F

221
228

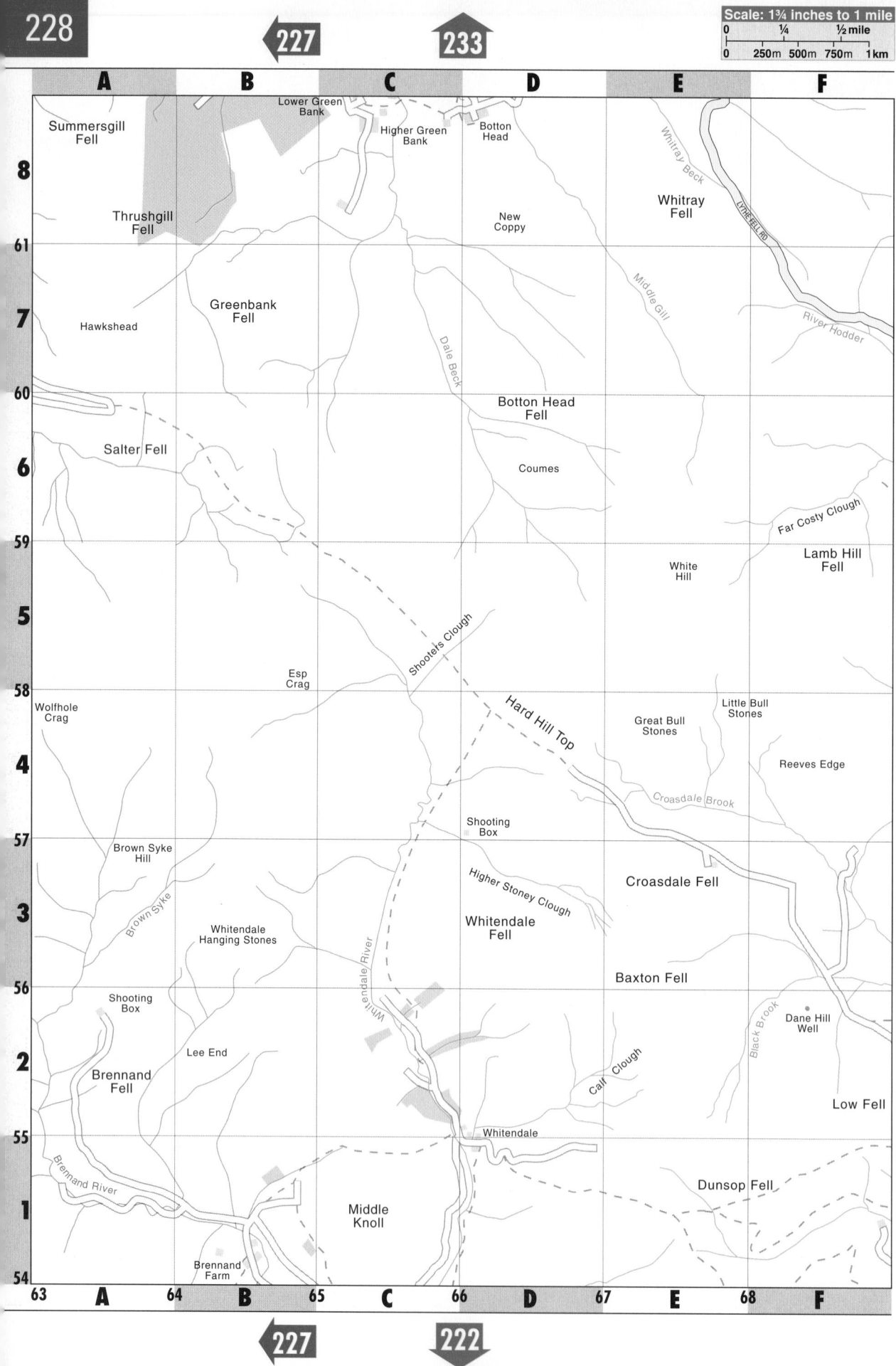

227
233

Scale: 1¾ inches to 1 mile

0	¼	½ mile
0	250m	500m 750m 1km

A   B   C   D   E   F

8

Summersgill Fell

Lower Green Bank

Higher Green Bank

Botton Head

Whitray Beck

Whitray Fell

LYTHE FELL RD

61

Thrushgill Fell

New Coppy

Middle Gill

River Hodder

7

Greenbank Fell

Hawkshead

Dale Beck

60

Botton Head Fell

Salter Fell

6

Coumes

Far Costy Clough

59

White Hill

Lamb Hill Fell

5

Shooters Clough

58

Esp Crag

Hard Hill Top

Wolfhole Crag

Great Bull Stones

Little Bull Stones

4

Reeves Edge

Croasdale Brook

57

Brown Syke Hill

Shooting Box

Higher Stoney Clough

Croasdale Fell

3

Brown Syke

Whitendale Hanging Stones

Whitendale River

Whitendale Fell

Baxton Fell

56

Shooting Box

Black Brook

Dane Hill Well

2

Brennand Fell

Lee End

Calf Clough

Low Fell

55

Whitendale

Brennand River

Dunsop Fell

1

Middle Knoll

Brennand Farm

54

63   A   64   B   65   C   66   D   67   E   68   F

227
222

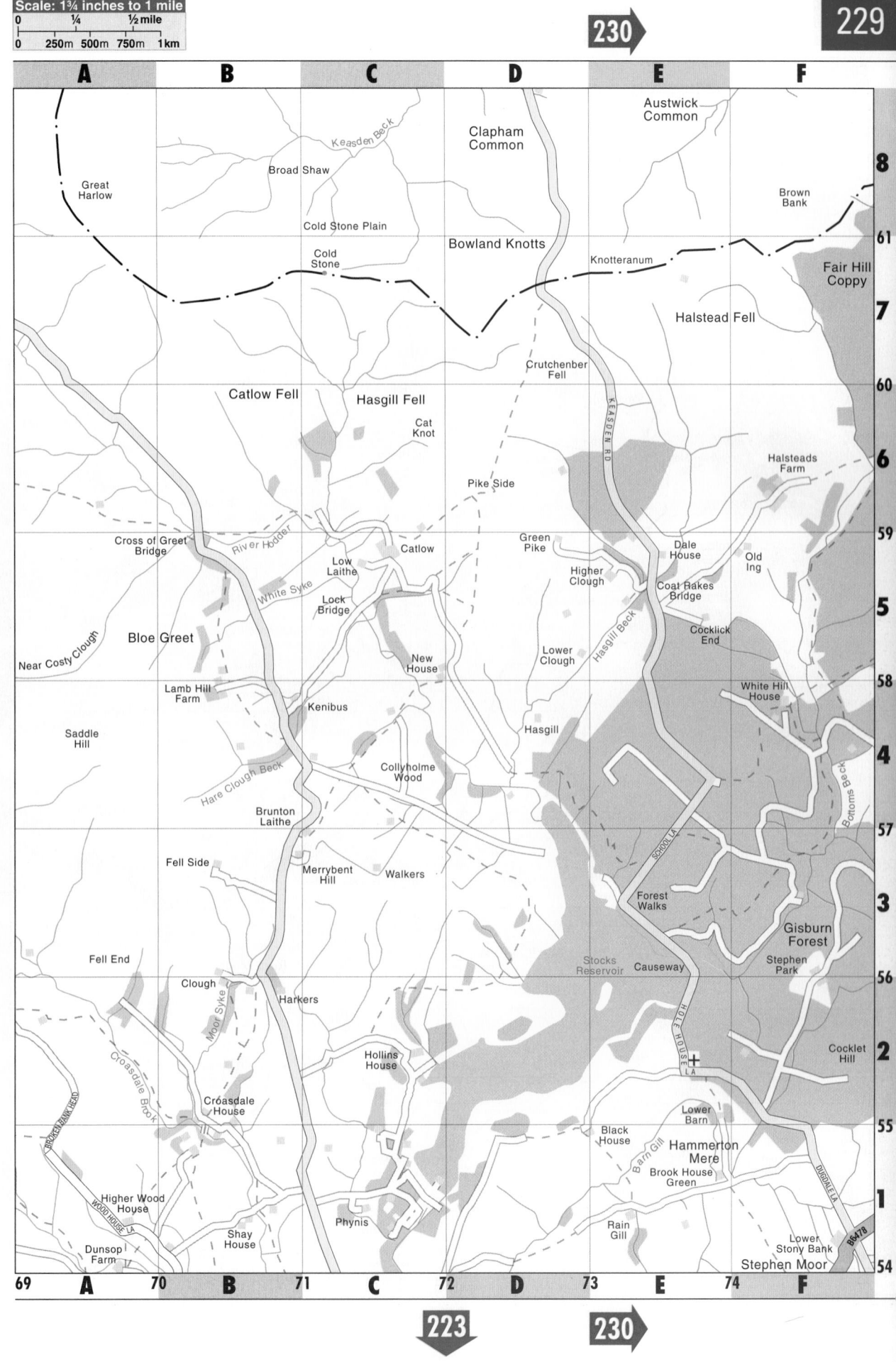

Scale: 1¾ inches to 1 mile

0   ¼   ½ mile
0   250m 500m 750m 1km

A   B   C   D   E   F

8

Austwick
Common

Great
Harlow

Broad Shaw

Clapham
Common

Brown
Bank

Cold Stone Plain

61

Cold
Stone

Bowland Knotts

Knotteranum

Fair Hill
Coppy

7

Halstead Fell

Crutchenber
Fell

60

Catlow Fell

Hasgill Fell

Cat
Knot

6

Pike Side

Halsteads
Farm

KEASDEN RD

Green
Pike

59

Cross of Greet
Bridge

River Hodder

Catlow

Dale
House

Old
Ing

Low
Laithe

White Syke

Higher
Clough

Coat Rakes
Bridge

5

Lock
Bridge

Cocklick
End

Near Costy Clough

Bloe Greet

New
House

Lower
Clough

Hasgill Beck

White Hill
House

58

Lamb Hill
Farm

Kenibus

Hasgill

4

Saddle
Hill

Collyholme
Wood

Hare Clough Beck

Bottoms Beck

Brunton
Laithe

57

Fell Side

Merrybent
Hill

Walkers

SCHOOL LA

Forest
Walks

Gisburn
Forest

3

Fell End

Clough

Moor Syke

Harkers

Stocks
Reservoir

Causeway

Stephen
Park

56

Hollins
House

HOLE HOUSE LA

Cocklet
Hill

2

Croasdale Brook

Croasdale
House

Lower
Barn

Black
House

Barn Gill

Hammerton
Mere

DUGDALE LA

55

SPROKEN PARK HEAD

Brook House
Green

Higher Wood
House

WOOD HOUSE LA

Phynis

Rain
Gill

Lower
Stony Bank

B6478

1

Dunsop
Farm

Shay
House

Stephen Moor

54

69   A   70   B   71   C   72   D   73   E   74   F

Scale: 1¾ inches to 1 mile
0   ¼   ½ mile
0   250m 500m 750m 1km

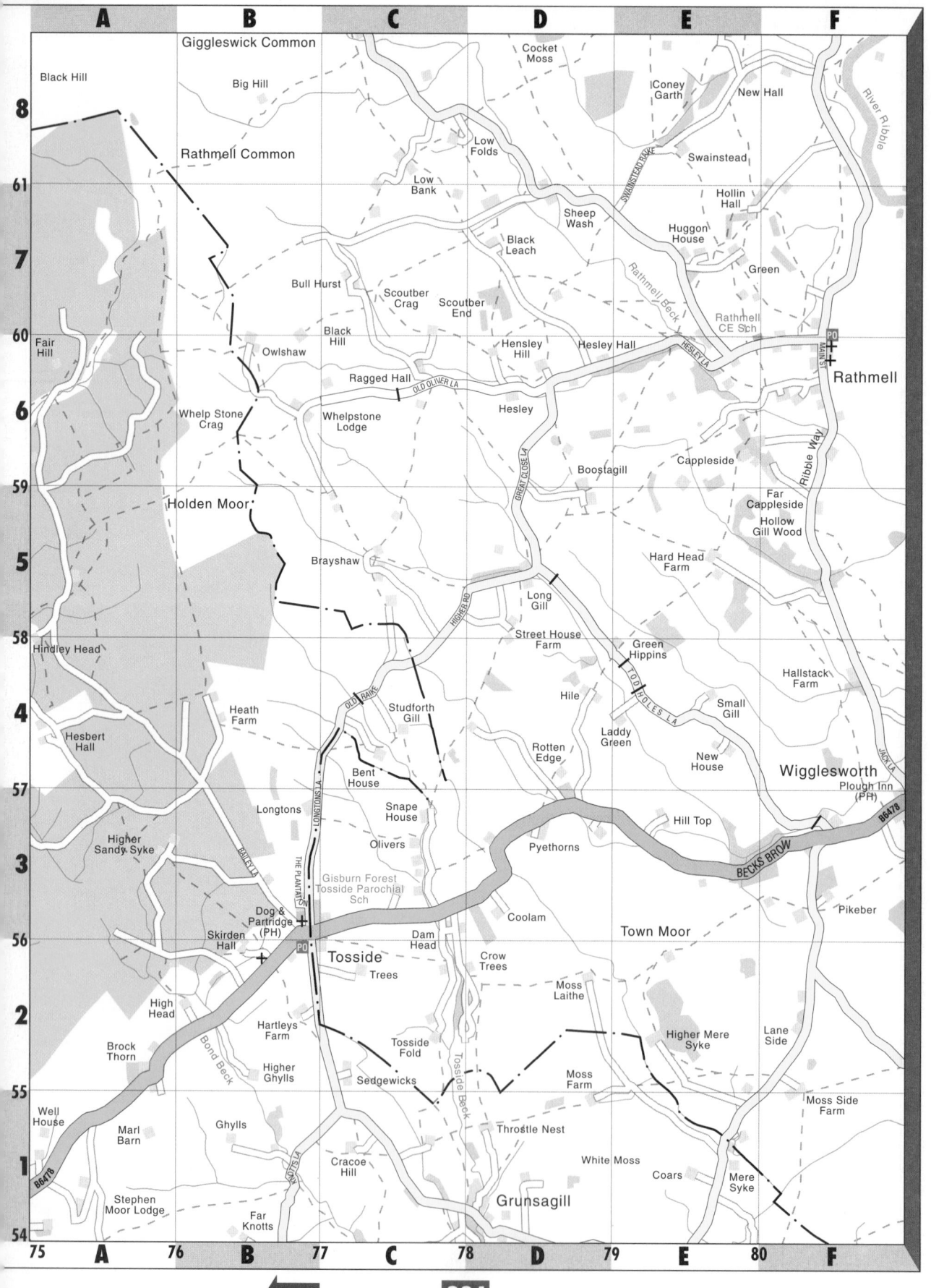

A   **B**   **C**   **D**   **E**   **F**

Giggleswick Common

Black Hill

Big Hill

8

Rathmell Common

Cocket Moss

Coney Garth

New Hall

River Ribble

Low Folds

Swainstead

61

Low Bank

Sheep Wash

Hollin Hall

Huggon House

Green

7

Bull Hurst

Scoutber Crag

Scoutber End

Black Leach

Rathmell CE Sch

Fair Hill

Owlshaw

Black Hill

Hensley Hill

Hesley Hall

60

Ragged Hall

OLD OLIVER LA

Hesley

PO

Rathmell

Whelp Stone Crag

Whelpstone Lodge

Cappleside

Ribble Way

6

Holden Moor

Boostagill

Far Cappleside

Hollow Gill Wood

59

Brayshaw

Hard Head Farm

5

Long Gill

Hindley Head

Street House Farm

Green Hippins

Hallstack Farm

58

Heath Farm

Studforth Gill

Hile

Small Gill

4

Hesbert Hall

Bent House

Rotten Edge

Laddy Green

New House

Wigglesworth

Longtons

OLD RAKE

Snape House

Plough Inn (PH)

57

Higher Sandy Syke

Olivers

Pyethorns

Hill Top

BECKS BROW

B6478

3

THE PLANTATIONS

Gisburn Forest Tosside Parochial Sch

Coolam

Town Moor

Pikeber

Dog & Partridge (PH)

Dam Head

56

Skirden Hall

PO

Tosside

Crow Trees

Trees

Moss Laithe

2

High Head

Hartleys Farm

Tosside Fold

Higher Mere Syke

Lane Side

Brock Thorn

Higher Ghylls

Sedgewicks

Moss Farm

Moss Side Farm

55

Bond Beck

Ghylls

Throstle Nest

Well House

Marl Barn

Tosside Beck

White Moss

Coars

Mere Syke

1

Cracoe Hill

Grunsagill

B6478

Stephen Moor Lodge

Far Knotts

54

A   75   **B**   76   77   **C**   78   **D**   79   **E**   80   **F**

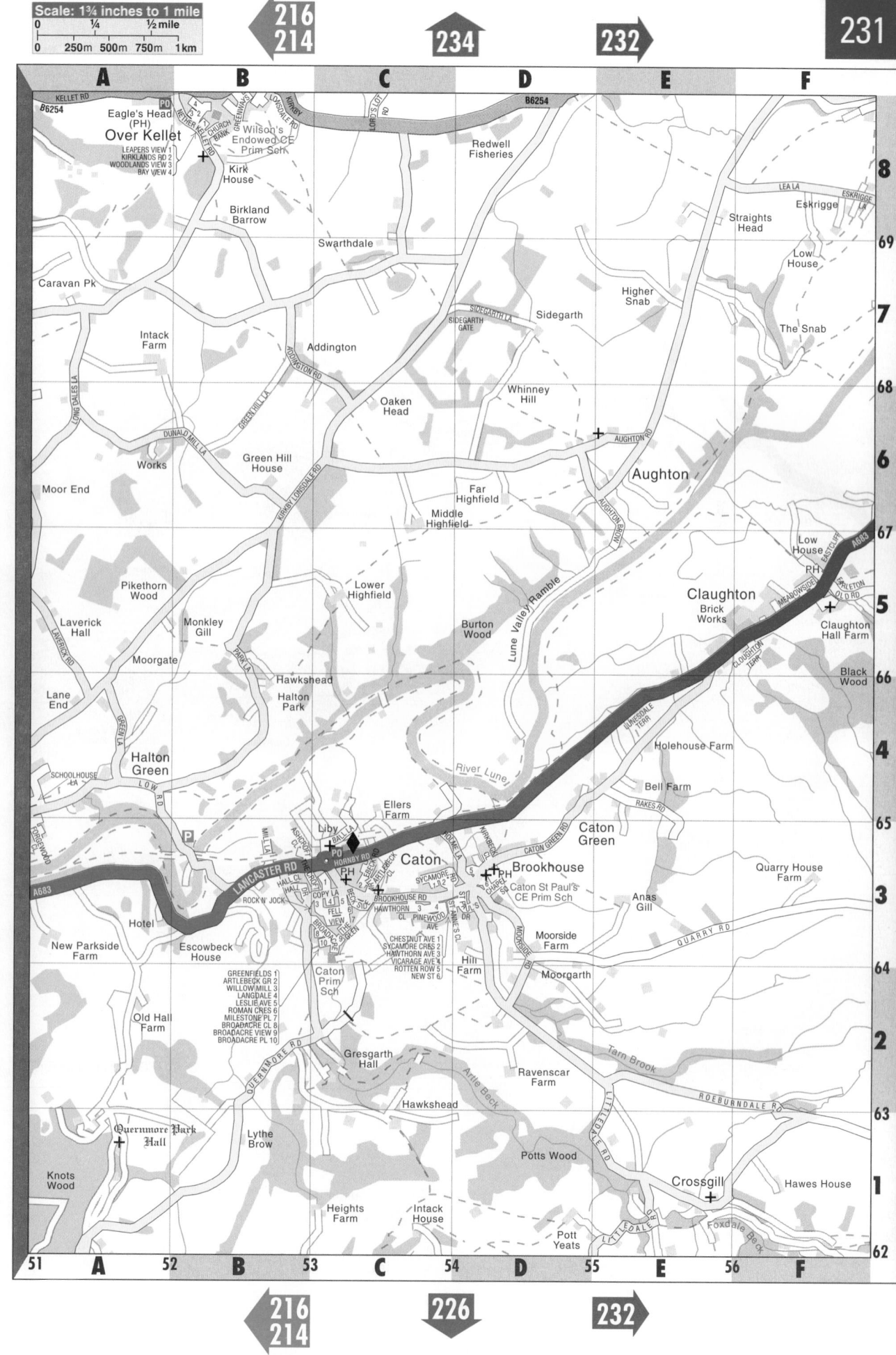

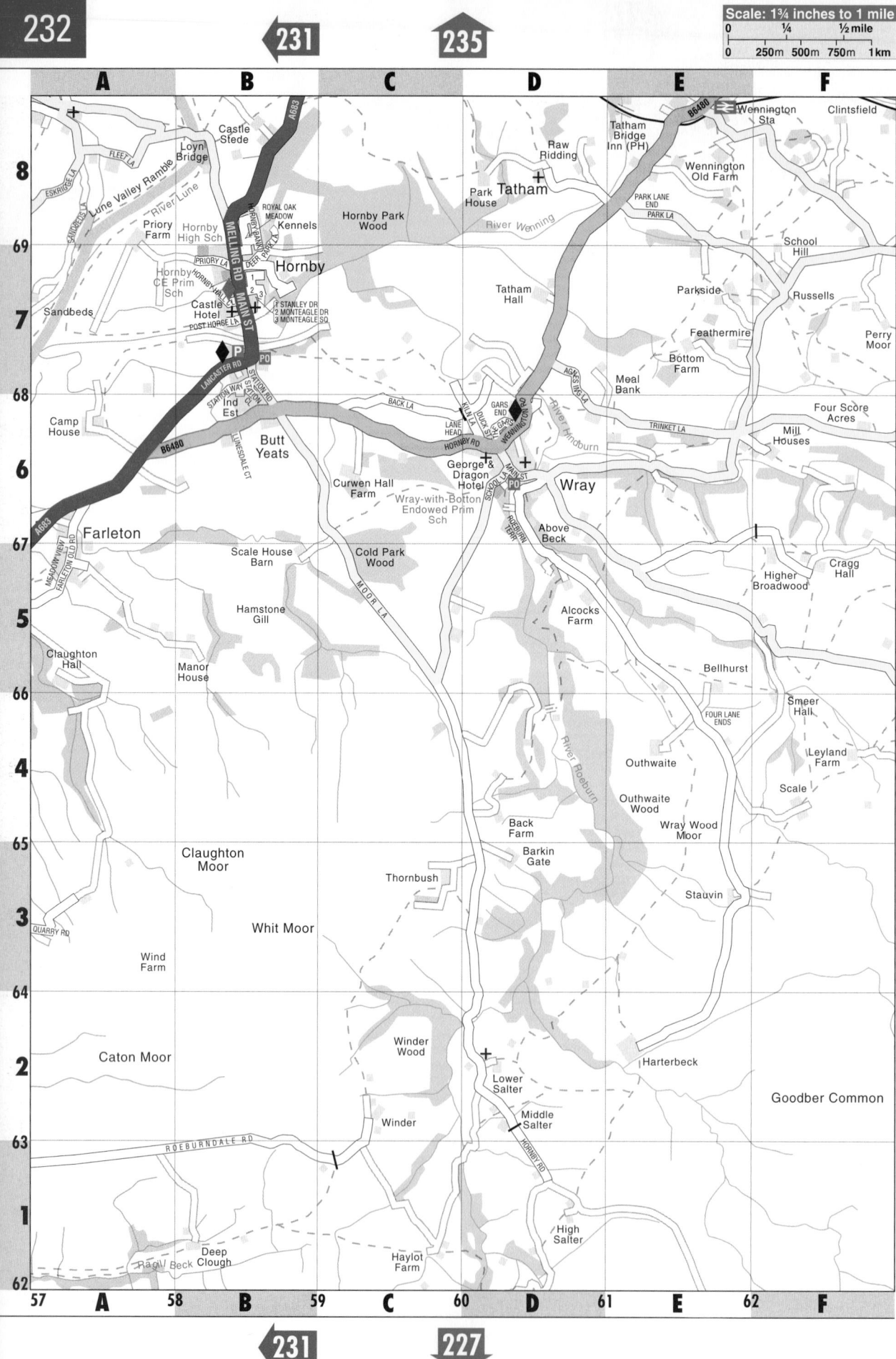

Scale: 1¾ inches to 1 mile

0   ¼   ½ mile
0   250m 500m 750m 1km

A B C D E F

8

69

7

68

6

67

5

66

4

65

3

64

2

63

1

62

Castle
Stede

Loyn
Bridge

FLEET LA

ESKRIGGE LA

SANDBEDS

Lune Valley Ramble

River Lune

Priory
Farm

Hornby
High Sch

Sandbeds

Hornby Hall

Hornby
CE Prim
Sch

PRIORY LA

ROYAL OAK
MEADOW

HORNBY RD

DEER PARK LA

MELLING RD

MAIN ST

A683

Kennels

Hornby Park
Wood

Hornby

1
2
3

1 STANLEY DR
2 MONTEAGLE DR
3 MONTEAGLE SQ

Castle
Hotel

Post Horse La

LANCASTER RD

STATION WAY

STATION RD

STATION CL

P

PO

Ind
Est

Camp
House

B6480

A683

MEADOW VIEW

FARLETON OLD RD

Farleton

Butt
Yeats

LINESDALE CT

BACK LA

Curwen Hall
Farm

Wray-with-Botton
Endowed Prim
Sch

LANE
HEAD

HORNBY RD

DUCK ST

MAIN ST

SCHOOL LA

GARS
END

GARS
RD

WENNINGTON RD

George &
Dragon
Hotel

PO

Wray

HUBRUN TERR

Back Farm

Scale House
Barn

Cold Park
Wood

MOOR LA

Hamstone
Gill

Claughton
Hall

Manor
House

Claughton
Moor

Whit Moor

QUARRY RD

Wind
Farm

Caton Moor

ROEBURNDALE RD

Winder
Wood

Winder

Deep
Clough

Ragill Beck

Haylot
Farm

Lower
Salter

Middle
Salter

HORNBY RD

High
Salter

Thornbush

Barkin
Gate

Stauvin

Harterbeck

Goodber Common

Wray Wood
Moor

Outhwaite
Wood

Outhwaite

Alcocks
Farm

Above
Beck

River Roeburn

FOUR LANE
ENDS

Bellhurst

Higher
Broadwood

Smeer
Hall

Leyland
Farm

Scale

Cragg
Hall

Tatham

Park
House

Raw
Ridding

River Wenning

Tatham
Hall

AGNES HILL LA

River Hindburn

Meal
Bank

TRINKET LA

Bottom
Farm

Feathermire

Parkside

Russells

School
Hill

Perry
Moor

Four Score
Acres

Mill
Houses

Tatham
Bridge
Inn (PH)

B6480

Wennington
Sta

Wennington
Old Farm

PARK LANE
END

PARK LA

Clintsfield

57 58 59 60 61 62

A B C D E F

231
227

D8
1 GOODENBER CRES
2 LAKEBER DR
3 BANKS WAY
4 BANKS RISE
5 LAKEBER CL
6 TWEED ST
7 GRASMERE DR
8 GRASMERE CL
9 LAIRGILL ROW
10 COLLINGWOOD TERR

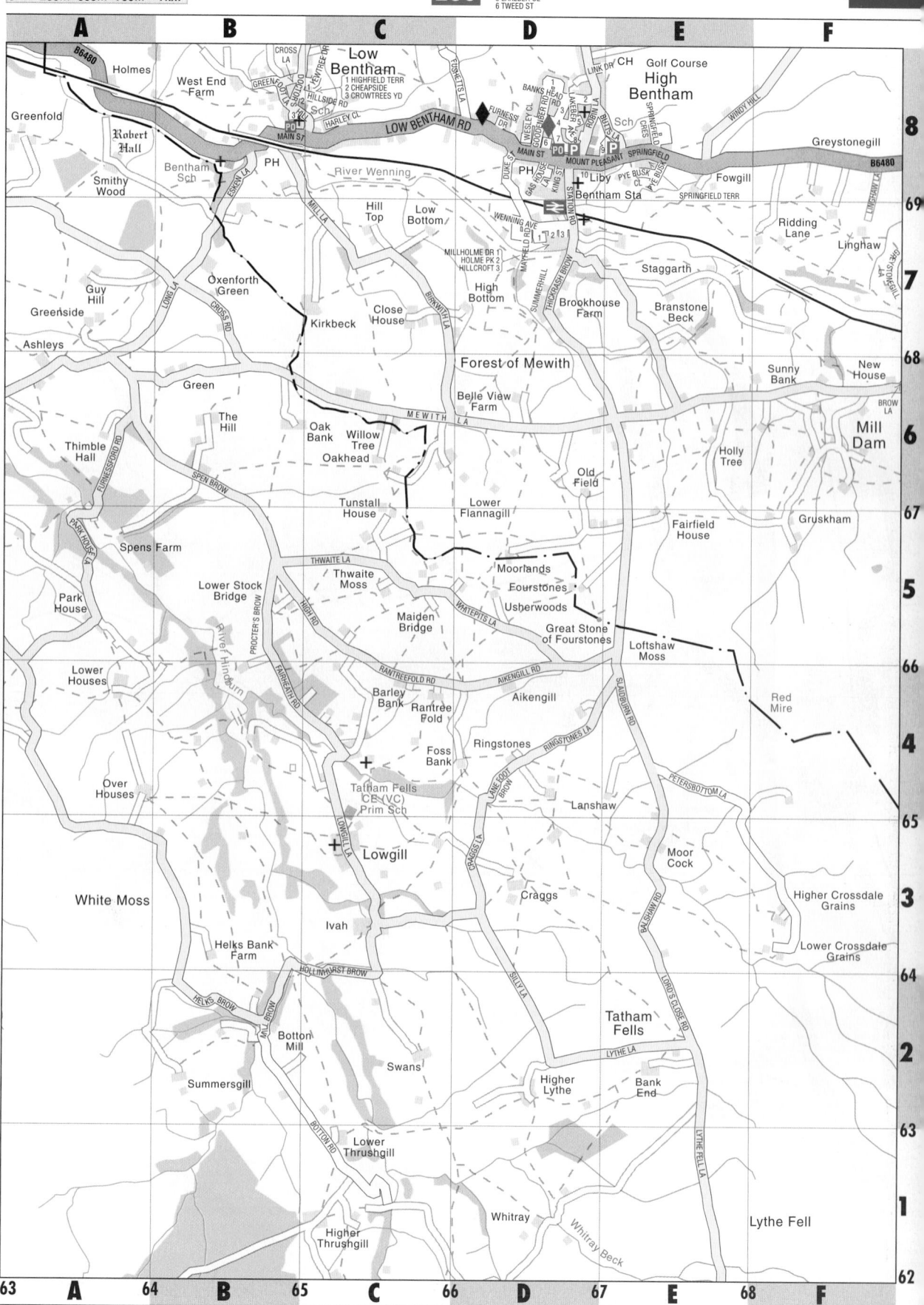

Scale: 1¾ inches to 1 mile

0   ¼   ½ mile
0   250m   500m   750m   1km

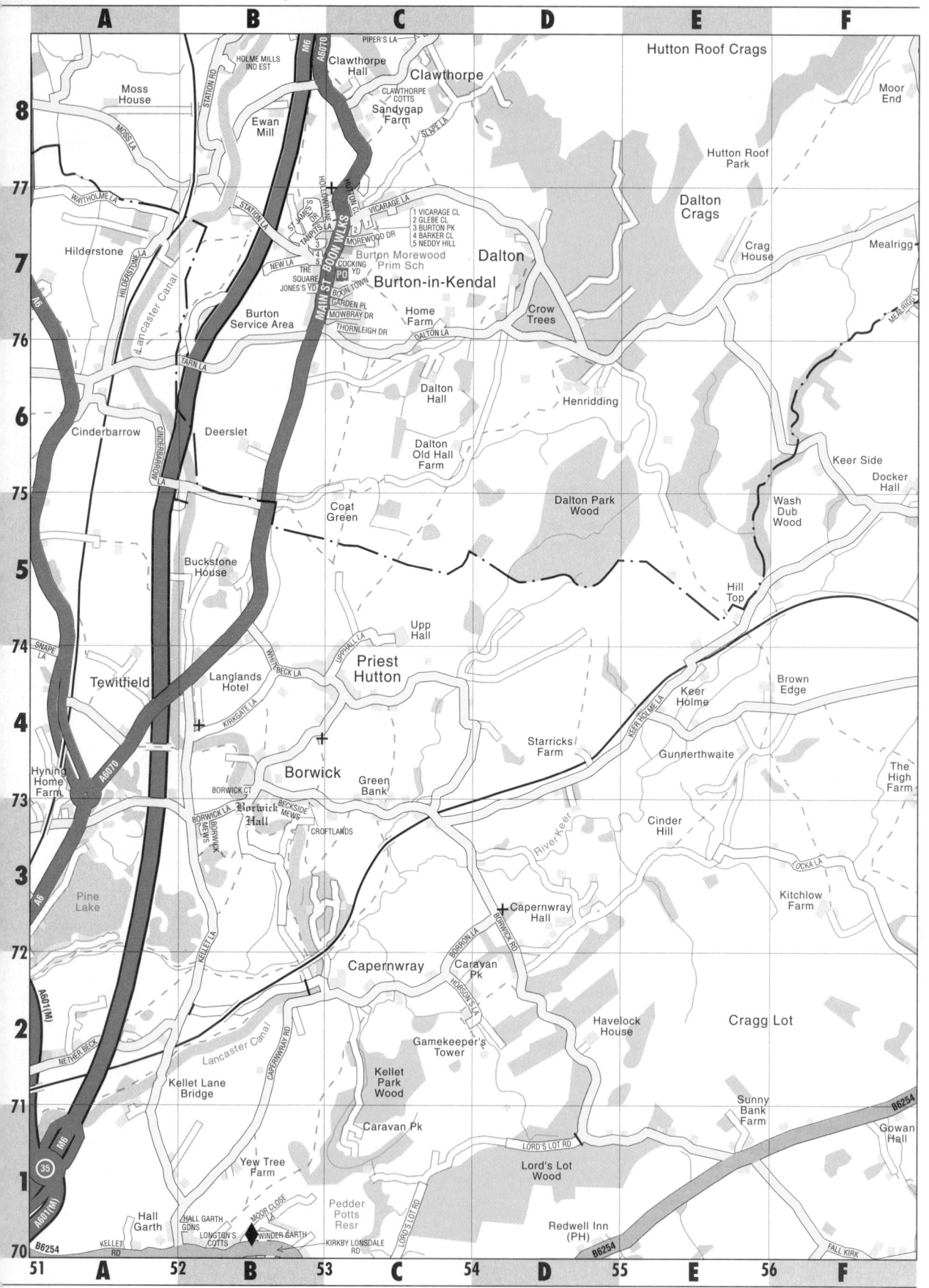

Moss House

Hutton Roof Crags

Moor End

Holme Mills IND EST

Clawthorpe Hall

PIPER'S LA

Clawthorpe

CLAWTHORPE COTTS

Sandygap Farm

STATION RD

Ewan Mill

SLAPE LA

Hutton Roof Park

Dalton Crags

Crag House

Mealrigg

WAITHOLME LA

Hilderstone

HILDERSTONE LA

MOSS LA

1 VICARAGE CL
2 GLEBE CL
3 BURTON PK
4 BARKER CL
5 NEDDY HILL

VICARAGE LA

ST JAMES'S DR

HOLLOWRANE

MOREWOOD DR

Burton Morewood Prim Sch

Dalton

Crow Trees

Keer Side

Docker Hall

Lancaster Canal

STATION RD

Burton Service Area

Burton-in-Kendal

COCKING YD

BCKN TOWN

GARDEN PL

MOWBRAY DR

THORNLEIGH DR

Home Farm

DALTON LA

Wash Dub Wood

A6

Cinderbarrow

TARN LA

Deerslet

Dalton Hall

Henridding

Dalton Old Hall Farm

Dalton Park Wood

CINDERBARROW LA

Buckstone House

SNAPE LA

Coat Green

Hill Top

Upp Hall

Brown Edge

Tewitfield

Langlands Hotel

WHIT BECK LA

UPPHALL LA

Priest Hutton

Keer Holme

KEER HOLME LA

The High Farm

KIRKGATE LA

Hyning Home Farm

A6

A6070

Borwick

Green Bank

Starricks Farm

Gunnerthwaite

BORWICK CT

BORWICK MEWS

Borwick Hall

BECKSIDE MEWS

CROFTLANDS

River Keer

Cinder Hill

OCKA LA

Pine Lake

KELLET LA

Kitchlow Farm

CAPERNWRAY RD

Capernway Hall

BORWICK RD

Lancaster Canal

Capernwray

BORRON LA

Caravan Pk

HOBSON S LA

Havelock House

Cragg Lot

A601(M)

NETHER BECK

Kellet Lane Bridge

Kellet Park Wood

Gamekeeper's Tower

Sunny Bank Farm

B6254

Caravan Pk

LORD'S LOT RD

Gowan Hall

Yew Tree Farm

MOOR CLOSE LA

LORD'S LOT RD

Lord's Lot Wood

M6

35

A601(M)

Hall Garth

HALL GARTH GONS

LONGTON'S COTTS

WINDER GARTH

Pedder Potts Resr

KIRKBY LONSDALE RD

Redwell Inn (PH)

B6254

FALL KIRK

B6254

KELLET RD

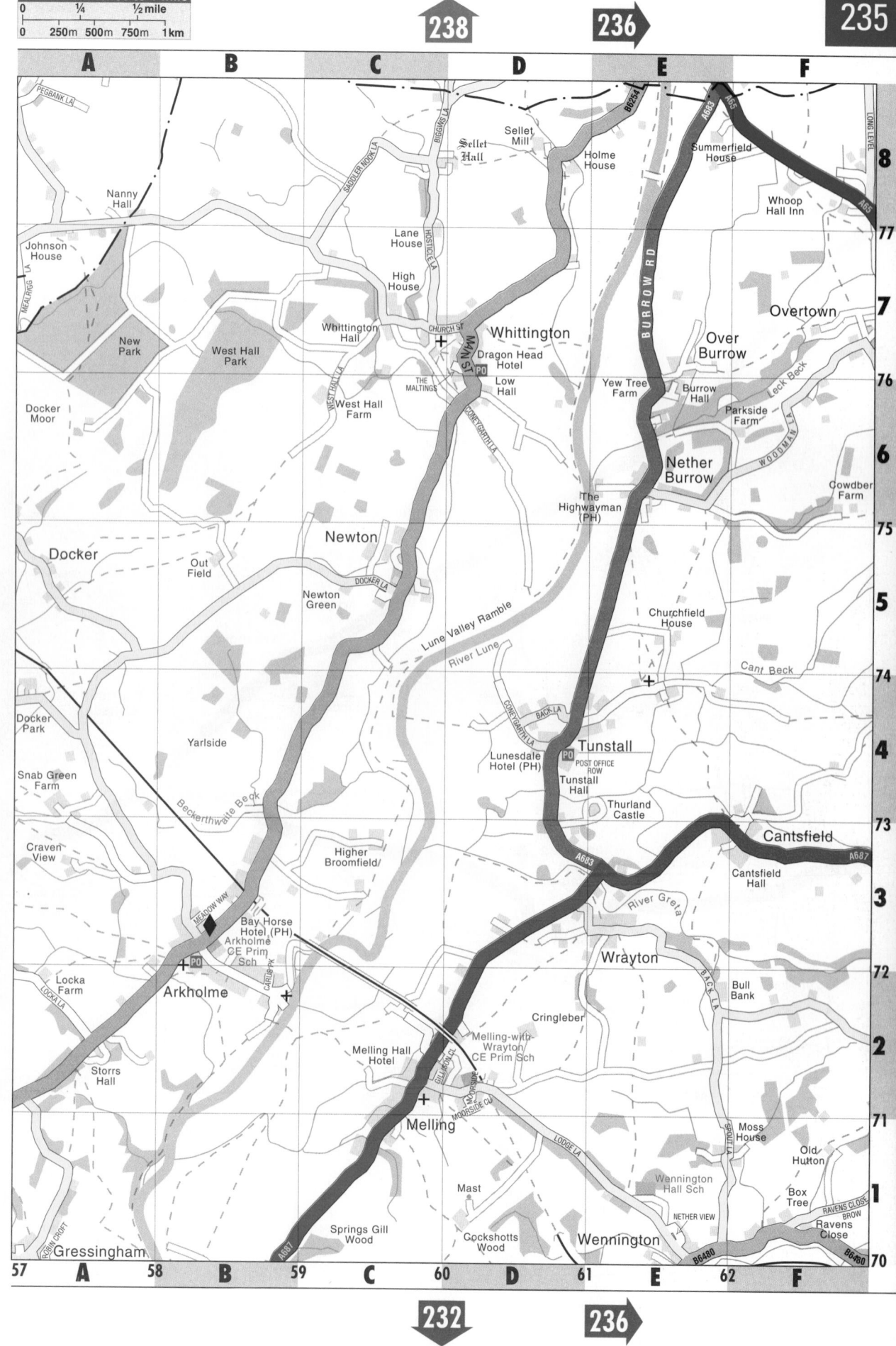

A   B   C   D   E   F

8
77
7
76
6
75
5
74
4
73
3
72
2
71
1
70

PEGBANK LA

Nanny
Hall

Johnson
House

New
Park

MEAL RIGG LA

Docker
Moor

Docker

Docker
Park

Snab Green
Farm

Craven
View

Locka
Farm

LOCKA LA

Storrs
Hall

ROBIN CROFT

Gressingham

West Hall
Park

West Hall
Farm

WEST HALL LA

SADDLER NOOK LA

BIGGINS LA

Whittington
Hall

Lane
House

High
House

CHURCH ST

THE MALTINGS

Newton

Newton
Green

Out
Field

DOCKER LA

Yarlside

Beckerthwaite Beck

MEADOW WAY

CARUS PK

PO

Arkholme

Bay Horse
Hotel (PH)
Arkholme
CE Prim
Sch

Higher
Broomfield

Melling Hall
Hotel

Melling

Springs Gill
Wood

A687

Sellet
Hall

Sellet Mill

Holme
House

HOSTICLE LA

MAIN ST

Whittington

Dragon Head
Hotel

Low
Hall

PO

CONEYGARTH LA

Lune Valley Ramble

River Lune

CONEYGARTH LA

BACK LA

Lunesdale
Hotel (PH)

SILL PONK CK

MOORSIDE CL

Wennington
Hall Sch

Mast

Cockshotts
Wood

LODGE LA

Wennington

NETHER VIEW

B6480

B6254

BURROW RD

A683

A65

Summerfield
House

Over
Burrow

Yew Tree
Farm

Burrow
Hall

Nether
Burrow

The
Highwayman
(PH)

Churchfield
House

Tunstall

PO
POST OFFICE
ROW

Tunstall
Hall

Thurland
Castle

A683

River Greta

Wrayton

Melling-with-
Wrayton
CE Prim Sch

Cringleber

BACK LA

LONG LEVEL

A65

Whoop
Hall Inn

Overtown

Leck Beck

Parkside
Farm

WOODMAN LA

Cowdber
Farm

Cant Beck

Cantsfield

A687

Cantsfield
Hall

Bull
Bank

Moss
House

SELLET LA

Old
Hutton

Box
Tree

RAVENS CLOSE
BROW

Ravens
Close

B6480

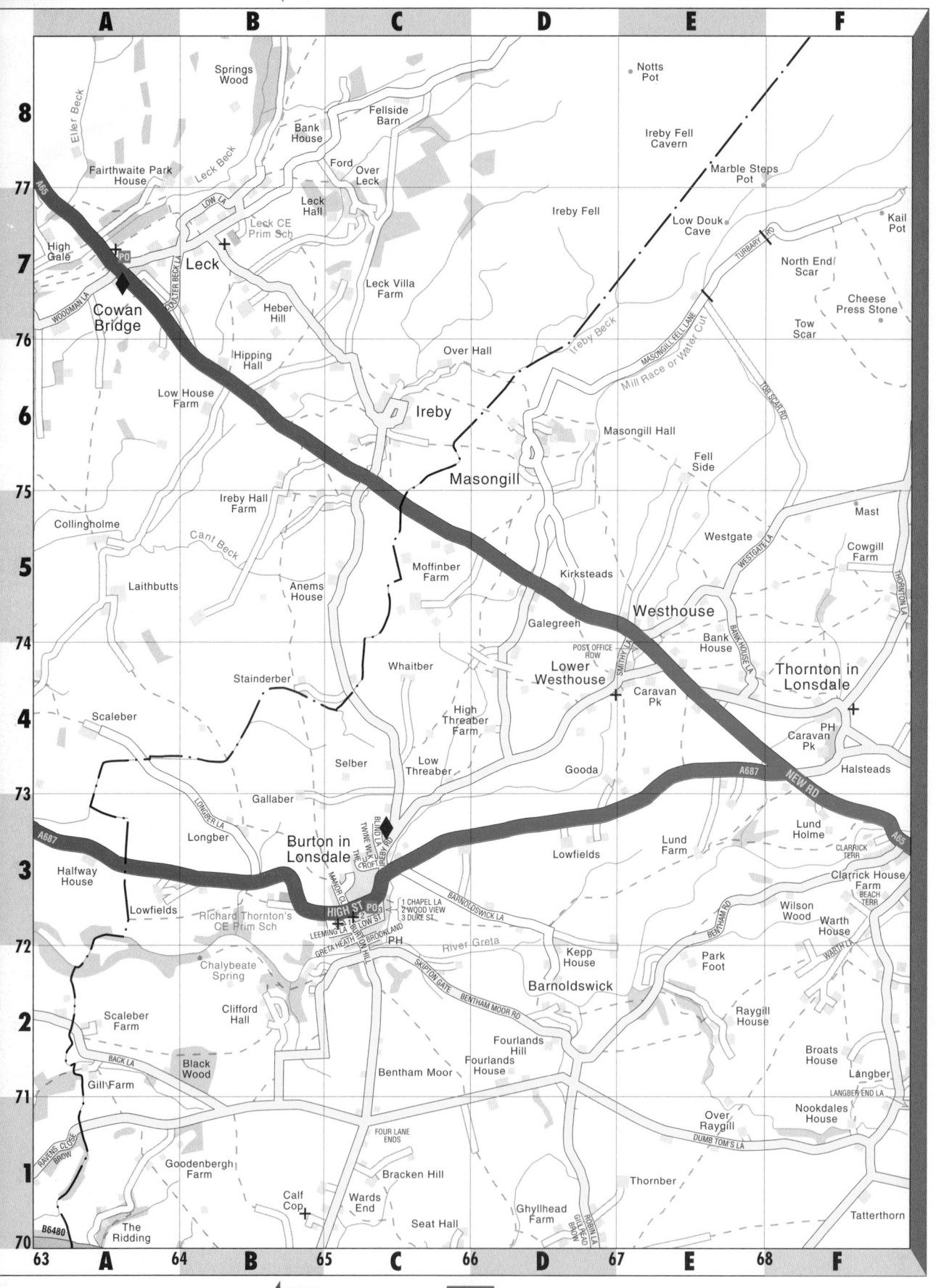

Scale: 1¾ inches to 1 mile

0   ¼   ½ mile

0   250m 500m 750m 1km

A **B** **C** **D** **E** **F**

Notts
Pot

Springs
Wood

Ireby Fell
Cavern

Fellside
Barn

Bank
House

Ford

Over
Leck

Marble Steps
Pot

Fairthwaite Park
House

Leck Beck

Low Douk
Cave

Leck
Hall

Kail
Pot

Low La

Leck CE
Prim Sch

Ireby Fell

North End
Scar

High
Gale

Leck

Cheese
Press Stone

Cowan
Bridge

Heber
Hill

Leck Villa
Farm

Tow
Scar

Woodman La

Baxter Beck La

Hipping
Hall

Over Hall

Mill Race or Water Cut

Low House
Farm

Ireby

Masongill Hall

Collingholme

Ireby Hall
Farm

Masongill

Fell
Side

Cant Beck

Mast

Westgate

Laithbutts

Anems
House

Moffinber
Farm

Kirksteads

Cowgill
Farm

Westhouse

Galegreen

Bank
House

Thornton in
Lonsdale

Stainderber

Whaitber

Lower
Westhouse

POST OFFICE
ROW

Scaleber

High
Threaber
Farm

Caravan
Pk

PH
Caravan
Pk

Selber

Low
Threaber

Gooda

A687

Halsteads

NEW RD

Gallaber

Lund
Farm

Lund
Holme

Longber La

Longber

Burton in
Lonsdale

Lowfields

CLARRICK
TERR

Halfway
House

Clarrick House
Farm

A687

Lowfields

HIGH ST PO

1 CHAPEL LA
2 WOOD VIEW
3 DUKE ST

BARNOLDSWICK LA

BEACH
TERR

Richard Thornton's
CE Prim Sch

Wilson
Wood

Warth
House

Chalybeate
Spring

River Greta

Kepp
House

Park
Foot

WARTH LA

Scaleber
Farm

Clifford
Hall

Black
Wood

SKIPTON GATE

BENTHAM MOOR RD

Barnoldswick

Raygill
House

Broats
House

BACK LA

Gill Farm

Fourlands
Hill

Fourlands
House

Langber

LANGBER END LA

Goodenbergh
Farm

Bentham Moor

Over
Raygill

Nookdales
House

RAVENS CLOSE
BROW

Calf
Cop

Wards
End

DUMB TOM'S LA

Thornber

B6480

The
Ridding

Bracken Hill

Seat Hall

Ghyllhead
Farm

GILLHEAD
BROW

Tatterthorn

A **B** **C** **D** **E** **F**

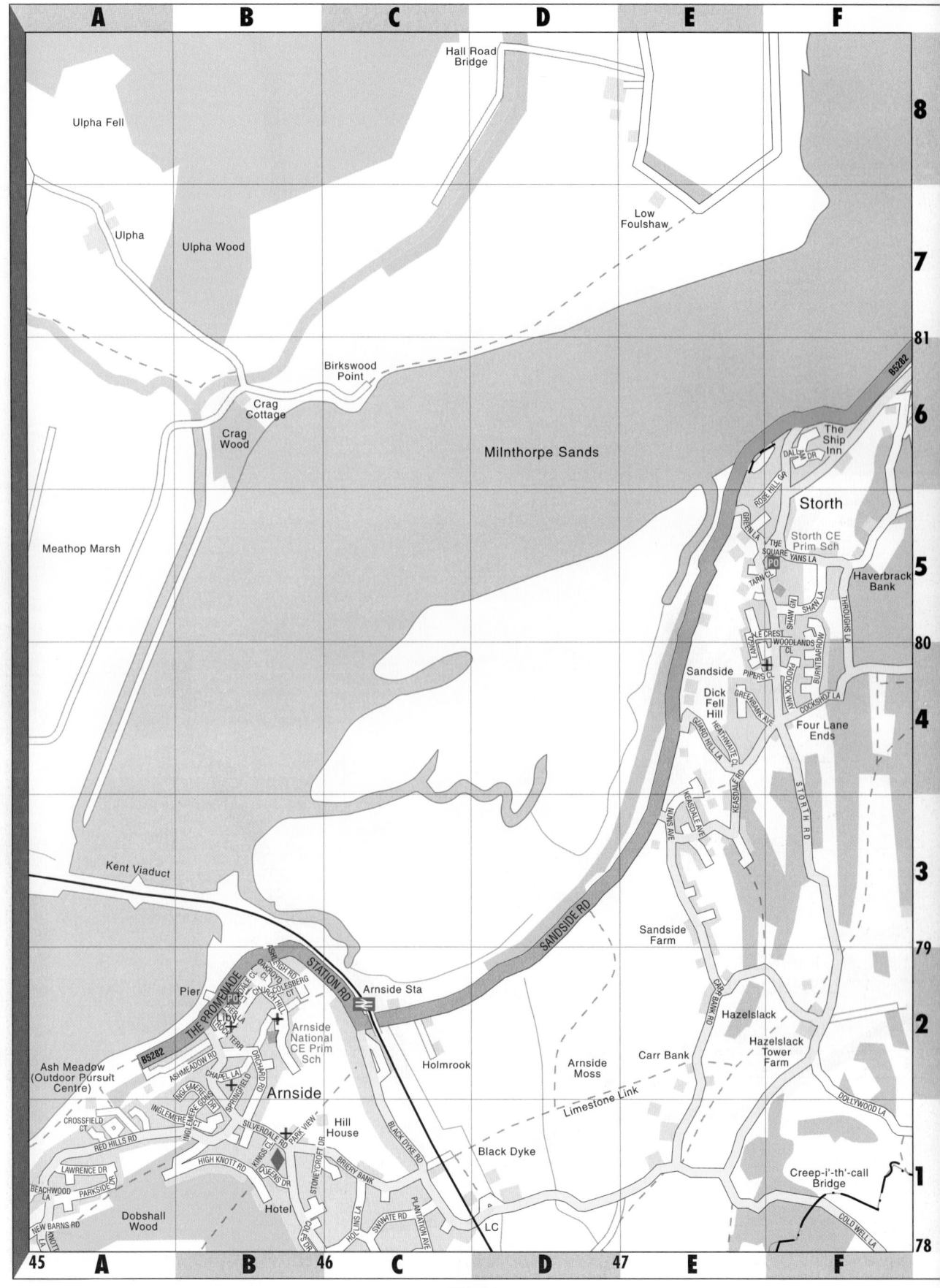

| | A | B | C | D | E | F |

Hall Road Bridge

Ulpha Fell

Low Foulshaw

Ulpha

Ulpha Wood

Birkswood Point

Crag Cottage

Crag Wood

Milnthorpe Sands

The Ship Inn

DALE DR

ROSE HILL DR

Storth

GREEN LA

Storth CE Prim Sch

THE SQUARE

YANS LA

PO

Meathop Marsh

TARN CL

Haverbrack Bank

NUNS LA

SHAW LA

THROUGHS LA

LE CREST CL

PENNY CL

WOODLANDS CL

PIPERS CL

BURNTBARROW

PADDOCK WAY

COCKSHOT LA

Sandside

GREENBANK AVE

Dick Fell Hill

HEATHWAITE CL

SQUAD HILL LA

KEASDALE RD

Four Lane Ends

KEASDALE AVE

STORTH RD

NUNS AVE

Kent Viaduct

Sandside Farm

CARR BANK RD

STATION RD

THE PROMENADE

Pier

OAKROYD

ROSEDALE CL

ROSE HIGH RD

CHV AV COLESBERG CT

SILVERGATE

LIBV LA

Arnside Sta

Hazelslack

Arnside National CE Prim Sch

Ash Meadow (Outdoor Pursuit Centre)

ASHMEADOW RD

ELM TERR

ORCHARD RD

B5282

Holmrook

Arnside Moss

Carr Bank

Hazelslack Tower Farm

CHAPEL LA

Arnside

INGLEMERE DR

SPRINGFIELD

Hill House

Limestone Link

DOLLYWOOD LA

CROSSFIELD CT

INGLEMERE VIADUCT

INGLEMERE GDNS

SILVERDALE RD

KINGS CL

PARK VIEW

RED HILLS RD

HIGH KNOTT RD

KINGSWOOD DR

STONECROFT DR

BRIERY BANK

BLACK DYKE RD

Black Dyke

Creep-i'-th'-call Bridge

LAWRENCE DR

PARKSIDE

Hotel

HOLLINS LA

SWINATE RD

PLANTATION AVE

COLD WELL LA

BEACHWOOD LA

NEW BARNS RD

NEW KNOTT LA

Dobshall Wood

LC

| 45 | A | | B | 46 | C | | D | 47 | E | | F |

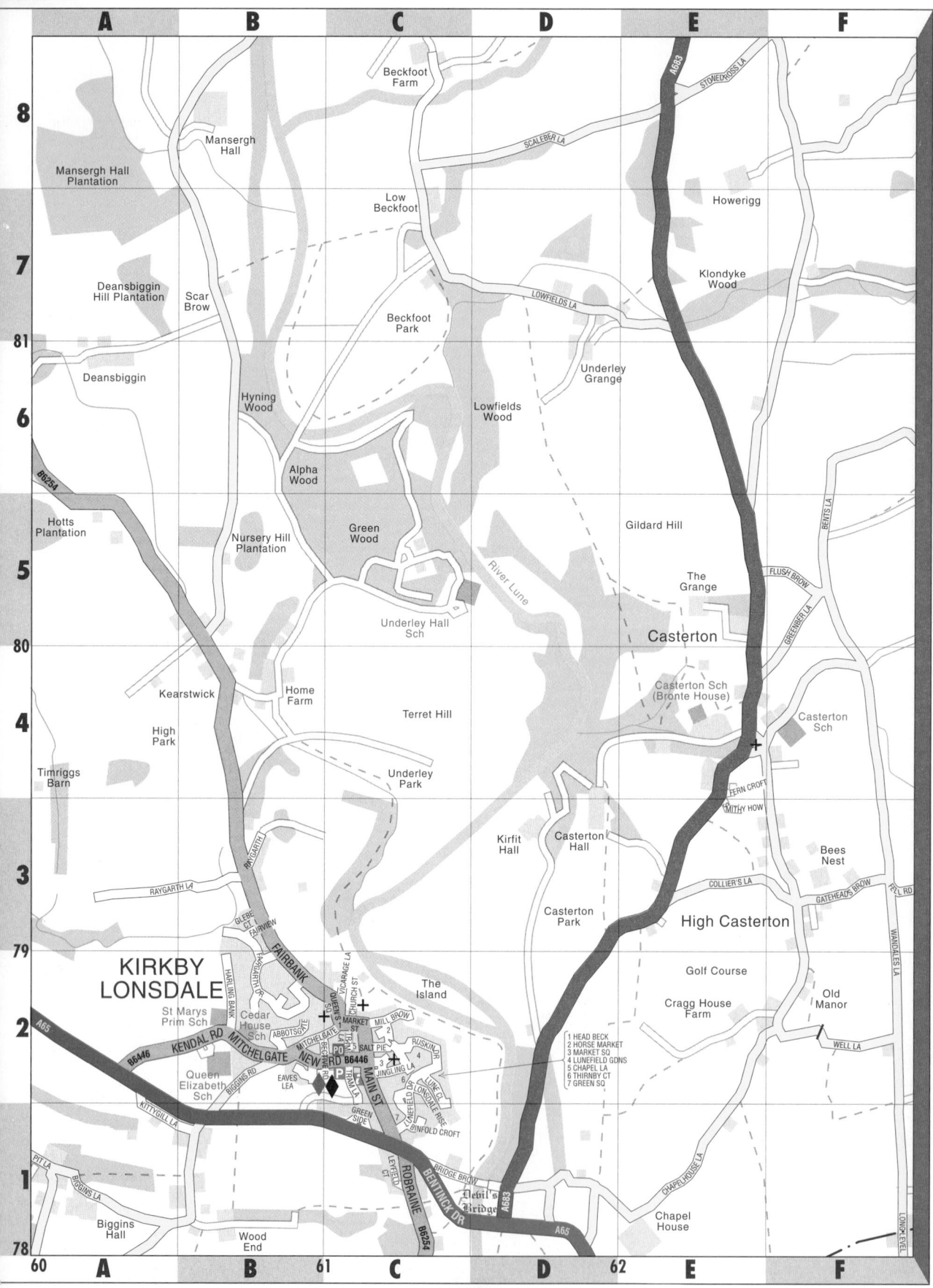

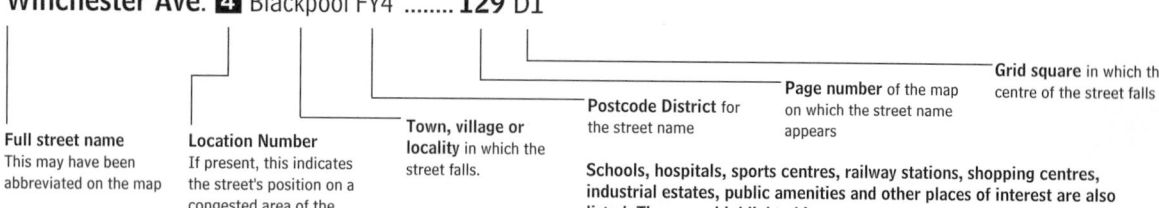

Index

Street names are listed alphabetically and show the locality, the Postcode District, the page number and a reference to the square in which the name falls on the map page

Winchester Ave. **4** Blackpool FY4 .... **129** D1

Full street name
This may have been abbreviated on the map

Location Number
If present, this indicates the street's position on a congested area of the map instead of the name

Town, village or locality in which the street falls.

Postcode District for the street name

Page number of the map on which the street name appears

Grid square in which the centre of the street falls

Schools, hospitals, sports centres, railway stations, shopping centres, industrial estates, public amenities and other places of interest are also listed. These are highlighted in magenta

Abbreviations used in the index

App	Approach	Cl	Close	Espl	Esplanade
Arc	Arcade	Comm	Common	Est	Estate
Ave	Avenue	Cnr	Corner	Gdns	Gardens
Bvd	Boulevard	Cotts	Cottages	Gn	Green
Bldgs	Buildings	Ct	Court	Gr	Grove
Bsns Pk	Business Park	Ctyd	Courtyard	Hts	Heights
Bsns Ctr	Business Centre	Cres	Crescent	Ind Est	Industrial Estate
Bglws	Bungalows	Dr	Drive	Intc	Interchange
Cswy	Causeway	Dro	Drove	Junc	Junction
Ctr	Centre	E	East	La	Lane
Cir	Circus	Emb	Embankment	N	North

Orch	Orchard
Par	Parade
Pk	Park
Pas	Passage
Pl	Place
Prec	Precinct
Prom	Promenade
Ret Pk	Retail Park
Rd	Road
Rdbt	Roundabout
S	South

Sq	Square
Strs	Stairs
Stps	Steps
St	Street, Saint
Terr	Terrace
Trad Est	Trading Estate
Wlk	Walk
W	West
Yd	Yard

A K Bsns Pk. PR9 .... 35 A6
Aalborg Pl. LA1 .... 210 F7
Abbey Cl. Formby L37 .... 12 B2
Abbey Cl. Up Holland WN8 ...... 10 C7
Abbey Cres. BB3 .... 64 C8
Abbey Dale. Appley Bridge WN6 .. 19 D7
Abbey Dale. Burscough L40 ...... 24 F3
Abbey Dr. WN5 .... 10 E6
Abbey Farm. BB7 .... 143 B6
Abbey Fields. BB7 .... 143 C5
Abbey Gdns. PR8 .... 34 A4
Abbey Gr. PR6 .... 30 B7
Abbey La. L40 .... 24 C1
Abbey Rd. Blackpool FY4 .... 109 D5
Abbey Rd. Whalley BB7 .... 143 C5
Abbey St. Accrington BB5 .... 103 C5
Abbey St. Accrington BB5 .... 103 C6
Abbey St. Bacup OL13 .... 86 F4
Abbey St. Preston PR1 .... 95 D8
Abbey Village Cty Prim Sch.
   PR7 .... 79 C1
Abbey Wlk. PR1 .... 95 D3
Abbeydale. LA3 .... 212 E2
Abbeyfield. **5** BB11 .... 127 B4
Abbeyfield Cl. LA1 .... 211 A3
Abbeyfield House.
  Barnoldswick BB8 .... 200 A3
Abbeyfield House.
  Burnley BB11 .... 126 E5
Abbeystead. WN8 .... 9 C7
Abbeystead Dr. LA1 .... 211 A3
Abbeystead House. **8** LA1 ... 211 A3
Abbeystead La. LA2 .... 226 E2
Abbeystead Rd. LA2 .... 226 C1
Abbeyville. FY4 .... 109 C6
Abbeywood. WN8 .... 9 C6
Abbot Meadow. PR1 .... 95 D4
Abbot Wlk. BB7 .... 165 A8
Abbots Cl. Formby L37 .... 12 A1
Abbots Cl. Kirkham PR4 .... 113 C4
Abbots Cl. Rawtenstall BB4 ...... 85 A4
Abbots Croft. BB7 .... 143 C5
Abbots Way. Formby L37 .... 12 B1
Abbots Way. Lancaster LA1 ...... 210 C8
Abbotsford. L39 .... 15 F5
Abbotsford Ave. BB2 .... 100 D1
Abbotsford Rd. FY3 .... 130 A3
Abbotsgate. LA6 .... 238 B2
Abbotsway. PR1 .... 95 C6
Abbott Brow. BB2 .... 120 E3
Abbott Clough Ave. BB1 .... 101 E4
Abbott Clough Cl. BB1 .... 101 E4
Abbott Croft. PR2 .... 116 A7
Abbott St. **14** BL6 .... 31 B4
Abbotts Wlk. FY7 .... 194 A5
Abel St. BB10 .... 127 A8
Abercorn Pl. FY4 .... 109 B5
Abercrombie Rd. FY3 .... 193 F4
Aberdare Cl. BB1 .... 100 E7
Aberdeen Dr. BB1 .... 101 A4
Aberdeen Gdns. OL12 .... 51 D4
Aberdeen Rd. LA1 .... 211 A7
Abernethy St. BL6 .... 31 D2

Abingdon Dr. PR1 & PR2 .... 116 B1
Abingdon Gr. LA3 .... 209 A7
Abingdon Rd. BB12 .... 125 D7
Abingdon St. FY1 .... 129 B5
Abinger St. BB10 .... 147 C1
Abner Row. BB8 .... 191 D1
Abraham St. Accrington BB5 .... 103 B5
Abraham St. Blackburn BB2 ..... 100 E2
Abraham St. **11** Horwich BL6 .... 31 B4
Abrams Fold. PR9 .... 53 F5
Abrams Gn. PR9 .... 53 F5
Acacia Rd. PR2 .... 117 E2
Acacia Wlk. **4** BB1 .... 101 B5
Accrington & District
  Golf Course. BB5 .... 102 B6
Accrington Rd. Blackburn BB1 .. 101 C4
Accrington Rd. Burnley BB11 .... 126 C5
Accrington Rd. Burnley BB11 .... 126 E6
Accrington Rd. Hapton BB11 .... 125 E3
Accrington Rd.
  Whalley BB6 & BB7 .... 143 C4
Accrington & Rossendale Coll.
  Accrington BB5 .... 103 B5
Accrington & Rossendale Coll.
  Accrington BB5 .... 103 D5
Accrington & Rossendale Coll
  Rawtenstall Ctr. BB4 .... 84 F2
Accrington Sta. BB5 .... 103 B6
Accrington Victoria Hospl.
  BB5 .... 103 B7
Ackhurst La. WN5 .... 19 F2
Ackhurst Rd. PR7 .... 41 F8
Ackroyd St. OL14 .... 108 B1
Acorn Ave. BB8 .... 102 F3
Acorn Bank. PR3 .... 178 C8
Acorn Bsns Ctr. L33 .... 1 B1
Acorn Cl. PR5 .... 59 A8
Acorn Cl. Bacup OL13 .... 86 F2
Acorn St. Blackburn BB1 .... 101 B4
Acornfield Rd. L33 .... 1 D2
Acre Ave. OL13 .... 69 D8
Acre Cl. BL0 .... 67 D3
Acre Gate. FY4 .... 109 E7
Acre Gr. PR4 .... 73 F3
Acre Mill Rd. OL13 .... 69 D8
Acre Moss La. LA4 .... 212 D4
Acre St. Brierfield BB10 .... 148 A4
Acre St. Burnley BB10 .... 147 B1
Acre St. Whitworth OL12 .... 70 C1
Acre View. OL13 .... 69 D7
Acrefield. Blackburn BB2 .... 100 A7
Acrefield. Clayton Brook PR5 .... 77 C5
Acrefield. Newburgh WN8 .... 26 A1
Acrefield. Padiham BB12 .... 145 C1
Acregate. WN8 .... 9 C7
Acregate La. PR0 & PR1 .... 117 D1
Acremount. BB12 .... 144 D2
Acres La. Great Altcar L38 .... 3 E8
Acres La. Maghull L31 & L39 .... 4 E7
Acres La. Preesall FY6 .... 195 A3
Acres The. BB6 .... 143 E8
Acresbrook Rd. BB12 .... 145 F6

Acresfield. Adlington PR7 .... 29 F6
Acresfield. Colne BB8 .... 170 A5
Acresfield Cl. Brierfield BB10 .. 147 C5
Acresfield Cl. BL6 .... 30 C3
Acreswood Cl. PR7 .... 28 E8
Active Way. BB11 .... 127 A6
Acton Rd. FY4 .... 129 E1
Ada St. Blackburn BB2 .... 100 C5
Ada St. Burnley BB10 .... 147 B1
Ada St. Nelson BB9 .... 147 E6
Ada St. Ramsbottom BL0 .... 49 B5
Adamson St. Burnley BB12 .... 126 C6
Adamson St. Padiham BB12 .... 145 C1
Addington Rd. LA2 & LA6 ...... 231 B7
Addington St. BB1 .... 101 A4
Addison Cl. BB2 .... 100 C5
Addison Cres. FY3 .... 129 D6
Addison St. FY6 .... 194 C5
Addison Rd. FY7 .... 194 A3
Addison St. BB5 .... 103 C7
Addle St. LA1 .... 211 A4
Adelaide Ave. FY5 .... 151 C8
Adelaide Ct. FY1 .... 129 C5
Adelaide La. BB5 .... 103 C5
Adelaide St. Accrington BB5 .... 103 C5
Adelaide St. Blackpool FY1 ..... 129 B5
Adelaide St. **5** Burnley BB11 .. 126 D6
Adelaide St. Enfield BB5 .... 124 A1
Adelaide St. Fleetwood FY7 .... 194 B5
Adelaide St. Preston PR1 .... 96 B8
Adelaide St. **2** Ramsbottom BL0 49 A4
Adelaide St. Rawtenstall BB4 .... 85 A7
Adelaide St W. FY1 .... 129 B4
Adelaide Terr. BB2 .... 100 C5
Adelphi House. **1** PR1 .... 116 E1
Adelphi Pl. **3** PR1 .... 95 F8
Adelphi St. Blackpool FY1 ...... 129 B5
Adelphi St. Burnley BB11 & BB12127 A7
Adelphi St. Lancaster LA1 ...... 211 A6
Adelphi St. Preston PR1 .... 116 E1
Adelphi St. Standish WN6 .... 28 E2
Adlington Cty Prim Sch. PR7 ... 29 F7
Adlington St. BB11 .... 127 A6
Adlington Sta. PR6 .... 30 A7
Admiral Cl. FY8 .... 109 E1
Admiral St. BB10 .... 127 B5
Admiralty Cl. L40 .... 24 C2
Adrian St. FY1 .... 129 B1
Adstone Ave. FY3 .... 129 F7
Agate St. BB1 .... 121 F1
Agglebys Rd. FY6 .... 173 F8
Agnes La. LA2 .... 232 D7
Agnes St. Blackburn BB2 .... 100 C3
Agnes St. **11** Preston PR1 ..... 96 A8
Agnew Rd. FY7 .... 193 F4
Agnew St. FY8 .... 90 A3
Aiken Ct. PR4 .... 113 A5
Aikengill Rd. LA2 .... 233 D4
Ailsa Ave. FY4 .... 129 F2
Ailsa Cl. PR3 .... 136 B8
Ailsa Rd. BB1 .... 101 D3
Ailsa Wlk. LA3 .... 208 E7
Ainscough Brook House. **1**
  PR2 .... 117 F3

Ainsdale Ave. Blackpool FY2 .. 150 E5
Ainsdale Ave. Brierfield BB10 .. 147 C5
Ainsdale Ave. Edgworth BL7 .... 47 E6
Ainsdale Ave. Fleetwood FY7 .. 172 D7
Ainsdale Ave. Thornton FY5 ... 173 D1
Ainsdale CE Prim Sch. PR8 ..... 20 D4
Ainsdale Cl. LA1 .... 213 D3
Ainsdale Dr. Darwen BB3 .... 64 B5
Ainsdale Dr. Preston PR2 ...... 115 E2
Ainsdale Dr. Whitworth OL12 .... 51 D7
Ainsdale High Sch. PR8 .... 20 C6
Ainsdale Sta. PR8 .... 20 C5
Ainslie Ave. BL6 .... 30 B3
Ainslie Ct. BB6 .... 123 B5
Ainslie Rd. PR2 .... 116 E3
Ainslie St. BB12 .... 126 C6
Ainsworth Ave. BL6 .... 31 E2
Ainsworth St. BB1 .... 100 E5
Aintree Cres. PR8 .... 34 F4
Aintree Rd. Blackpool FY4 ..... 129 D1
Aintree Rd. Thornton FY5 ...... 151 B8
Air Hill Terr. **8** OL12 .... 51 C1
Airdrie Cres. BB11 .... 126 D4
Airdrie Pl. FY2 .... 150 E6
Aire Cl. LA1 .... 213 B3
Airedale Ave. FY3 .... 129 E3
Airedale Ct. FY6 .... 151 C4
Airegate. L31 .... 5 B2
Airey St. BB5 .... 103 D3
Airton Garth. BB9 .... 168 C3
Aitken Cl. BL0 .... 49 B5
Aitken St. Accrington BB5 ...... 103 C7
Aitken St. Irwell Vale BL0 .... 67 C5
Ajax St. **3** BL0 .... 49 B5
Alamein Rd. LA5 .... 217 E1
Alan Gr. LA3 .... 208 F6
Alan Haigh Ct. BB8 .... 169 D6
Alan Ramsbottom Way. BB6 .. 123 E4
Alandale Cl. PR5 .... 59 B7
Alaska St. BB2 .... 100 E2
Albany Ave. FY4 .... 109 B5
Albany Cl. FY6 .... 130 E8
Albany Dr. Bamber Bridge PR5 .. 96 D2
Albany Dr. Copster Green BB1 .. 121 C8
Albany High Sch. PR7 .... 42 E5
Albany Rd. Blackburn BB2 ..... 100 B6
Albany Rd. Fleetwood FY7 .... 193 F4
Albany Rd. Lytham St Anne's FY8 . 89 C5
Albany Rd. Morecambe LA4 ... 212 C4
Albany Rd. Southport PR8 & PR9 . 52 C1
Albatros St. PR1 .... 117 B1
Albemarle House. **1** BB11 .. 126 E5
Albemarle St. BB7 .... 164 D8
Albert Ct. PR9 .... 52 D1
Albert House. BB4 .... 85 D1
Albert Pl. Blackburn BB3 .... 80 F7
Albert Pl. Southport PR8 .... 34 B8
Albert Rd. Barnoldswick BB8 .. 200 B2
Albert Rd. Blackpool FY1 ...... 129 C5
Albert Rd. Colne BB8 .... 169 D4
Albert Rd. Formby L37 .... 2 B8
Albert Rd. Fulwood PR2 .... 116 F3
Albert Rd. Lancaster LA1 ...... 213 F1

Albert Rd. Leyland PR6 .... 59 C8
Albert Rd. Lytham St Anne's FY8 .. 89 A7
Albert Rd. Morecambe LA4 .... 212 C4
Albert Rd. Preston PR1 .... 116 F2
Albert Rd. Rawtenstall BB4 ...... 85 A8
Albert Rd. Rufford L40 .... 38 A3
Albert Rd. Southport PR9 .... 52 D1
Albert Sq. FY7 .... 194 B5
Albert St. Accrington BB5 ...... 103 C5
Albert St. Blackburn BB2 ...... 100 C2
Albert St. Brierfield BB9 .... 147 B5
Albert St. Burnley BB11 .... 127 B6
Albert St. Bury BL9 .... 32 A2
Albert St. Carnforth LA5 .... 217 D1
Albert St. Carnforth LA5 .... 217 D3
Albert St. **1** Chorley PR6 ...... 42 D7
Albert St. **2** Church BB5 ..... 102 E6
Albert St. Clayton-le-M BB5 .. 123 F2
Albert St. Darwen BB3 .... 64 B5
Albert St. Earby BB8 .... 201 B2
Albert St. Egerton BL7 .... 46 D3
Albert St. Fleetwood FY7 ...... 194 B5
Albert St. Great Harwood BB6 .. 123 D4
Albert St. Hoddlesden BB3 ...... 81 F1
Albert St. Horwich BL6 .... 31 B4
Albert St. Kirkham PR4 .... 112 F6
Albert St. Lytham St Anne's FY8 .. 90 C3
Albert St. Nelson BB9 .... 147 D8
Albert St. Oswaldtwistle BB5 .. 102 E4
Albert St. Padiham BB12 .... 125 C8
Albert St. Ramsbottom BL0 ..... 49 B6
Albert St. Rishton BB1 .... 123 B1
Albert St. Wheelton PR6 .... 61 A7
Albert St. Whitewell Bottom BB4 . 85 E5
Albert St. Whitworth OL12 .... 51 C8
Albert Terr. Bacup OL13 .... 86 F3
Albert Terr. **9** Barrowford BB9 168 D3
Albert Terr. Calder Vale PR3 ... 179 E8
Albert Terr. **7** Preston PR1 ... 117 A1
Albert Terr. Rawtenstall BB4 .... 85 B2
Albert Terr. Southport PR8 .... 34 A5
Alberta Cl. BB2 .... 100 B8
Albion Ave. FY3 .... 129 F6
Albion Cl. BB11 .... 126 E4
Albion Mews. LA1 .... 214 A1
Albion Rd. Blackburn BB2 ...... 100 D1
Albion Rd. Earby BB8 .... 201 B2
Albion Rd. Accrington BB5 ..... 103 B6
Albion St. **7** Bacup OL13 ...... 69 C8
Albion St. Blackburn BB2 ...... 100 C1
Albion St. Brierfield BB9 .... 147 B5
Albion St. Burnley BB11 .... 126 E5
Albion St. Chorley PR6 & PR7 .. 42 C7
Albion St. **1** Clitheroe BB7 .. 164 F8
Albion St. Earby BB8 .... 201 B2
Albion St. Lancaster LA1 .... 214 A1
Albion St. **4** Nelson BB9 ..... 147 D8
Albion St. **4** Padiham BB12 .. 125 D7
Albrighton Cl. PR5 .... 76 B7
Albrighton Cres. PR5 .... 76 B7
Albrighton Rd. PR5 .... 76 C7
Albyn Bank Rd. PR1 .... 96 B7

Albyn St E. PR1 96 B7
Alcester Ave. PR1 95 C5
Alconbury Cres. FY5 172 C2
Aldate Gr. PR2 116 A2
Aldcliffe Cotts. LA1 210 D5
Aldcliffe Ct. LA4 212 E3
Aldcliffe Mews. LA1 210 D5
Aldcliffe Pl. LA1 210 E7
Aldcliffe Rd. Lancaster LA1 210 E6
Aldcliffe Rd. Preston PR2 115 E1
Alden Rd. BB4 & BL8 66 F5
Alden Rise. BB4 67 A6
Alder Ave. Bury BL9 32 C3
Alder Ave. Rawtenstall BB4 85 B2
Alder Bank. Blackburn BB2 100 B4
Alder Bank. 20 Rawtenstall BB4 85 A3
Alder Cl. Leyland PR5 58 B8
Alder Cl. Newton-with-S PR4 114 A2
Alder Cl. Thornton FY5 173 C1
Alder Coppice. PR4 115 E3
Alder Ct. FY7 193 C2
Alder Dr. Charnock Richard PR7 41 D3
Alder Dr. Gregson Lane PR5 97 E1
Alder Gr. Blackpool FY3 129 E7
Alder Gr. Coppull PR7 41 F1
Alder Gr. Huncoat BB5 124 E2
Alder Gr. Lancaster LA1 210 D8
Alder Gr. Lytham St Anne's FY8 90 A4
Alder Gr. Poulton-le-F FY6 151 D1
Alder Grange High Sch. BB4 85 A4
Alder Hill St. BB8 201 B2
Alder La. Formby L39 12 E7
Alder La. Moss Edge PR3 176 A1
Alder La. Parbold WN8 26 C1
Alder Meadow Cl. 1 OL12 51 A1
Alder Rd. PR2 118 A4
Alder St. Bacup OL13 86 F3
Alder St. 2 Blackburn BB1 101 A7
Alder St. Burnley BB12 126 C7
Alder St. Rawtenstall BB4 85 B3
Alderbank. BL6 30 F3
Alderbrook Dr. WN8 26 C2
Alderdale Ave. PR8 20 A5
Alderfield. PR1 95 D3
Alderford Cl. BB7 164 C7
Alderley. WN8 9 C6
Alderley Ave. FY4 109 B5
Alderley Hts. LA1 213 F3
Alderman Foley Dr. OL12 51 A2
Alderney Cl. BB2 100 B1
Alders The. PR3 199 C1
Aldersleigh Cres. PR5 97 D1
Alderson Cres. L37 11 F4
Alderway. BL0 67 C1
Alderwood Gr. BL0 67 D4
Aldfield Ave. PR2 115 C1
Aldingham Ct. LA4 212 E3
Aldingham Wlk. LA4 212 D5
Aldon Gr. PR4 94 A1
Aldon Rd. FY6 151 F2
Aldren's La. LA1 213 F3
Aldwych Ave. FY3 129 E3
Aldwych Dr. Bamber Bridge PR5 76 B7
Aldwych Dr. Preston PR2 116 A2
Aldwych Pl. BB1 121 E2
Alert St. PR1 116 C1
Alexander Cl. Accrington BB5 103 E1
Alexander Cl. Burscough L40 24 F3
Alexander Ct. FY6 151 D3
Alexander Dr. L31 5 D3
Alexander Gr. BB12 126 B6
Alexander St. BB9 169 A2
Alexandra Cl. BB5 123 E3
Alexandra Ct. 4 LA1 210 F8
Alexandra House. Blackburn BB1 101 B3
Alexandra House. 10 Preston PR1 117 C1
Alexandra Mews. 1 L39 15 E6
Alexandra Pavilion. 5 PR1 117 A1
Alexandra Pl. BB6 123 D6
Alexandra Rd. Bamber Bridge PR5 96 D3
Alexandra Rd. Blackburn BB2 100 C6
Alexandra Rd. Blackpool FY1 129 B1
Alexandra Rd. Burscough L40 24 D4
Alexandra Rd. Carnforth LA5 217 D1
Alexandra Rd. 8 Darwen BB3 80 F2
Alexandra Rd. Formby L37 11 B1
Alexandra Rd. Kirkham PR4 113 A6
Alexandra Rd. Lancaster LA1 213 F3
Alexandra Rd. Longridge PR3 139 A7
Alexandra Rd. Lytham St Anne's FY8 89 A7
Alexandra Rd. Morecambe LA3 212 B3
Alexandra Rd. Southport PR9 34 D8
Alexandra Rd. Thornton FY5 151 C8
Alexandra St. Clayton-le-M BB5 123 E3
Alexandra St. Preston PR1 96 C7
Alexandra View. 7 BB3 80 F2
Alexandria Dr. FY8 88 F5
Alexandria St. BB4 84 F4
Alford Fold. PR2 116 D7
Alfred St. Blackpool FY1 129 C5
Alfred St. Bury BL9 32 A1
Alfred St. Darwen BB3 64 B6
Alfred St. Egerton BL7 46 D3
Alfred St. Lancaster LA1 211 A8
Alfred St. 10 Ramsbottom BL0 49 B5
Alfred St. Whitworth OL12 70 D2
Algar St. 7 BB9 168 F2
Alice Ave. PR5 76 A1
Alice Sq. 4 PR1 117 A1
Alice St. Accrington BB5 103 D7
Alice St. Barnoldswick BB8 200 B2
Alice St. 7 Darwen BB3 64 A8
Alice St. Morecambe LA4 212 F5
Alice St. Oswaldtwistle BB5 102 E3
Alicia Ct. OL12 51 E1
Alicia Dr. OL12 51 E1
Alisan Rd. FY6 151 B5
Alker La. PR7 60 B3
Alker St. PR7 42 C7
Alkincoats Rd. BB8 169 C5
All Hallows Rd. FY2 150 D5
All Hollows RC High Sch. PR1 95 A3
All Saint's Cl. BB5 102 B4
All Saints CE Prim Sch. Appley Bridge WN6 27 C1
All Saints CE Prim Sch. Chorley PR7 42 B5
All Saints CE Prim Sch. Clayton-le-M BB5 123 F2
All Saints Cl. Padiham BB12 125 F7
All Saints Cl. Rawtenstall BB4 105 A1
All Saints RC High Sch. BB4 84 D1
All Saints Rd. Blackpool FY2 150 E6
All Saints' Rd. Lytham St Anne's FY8 88 E6
Allan St. OL13 86 F1
Allandale. FY4 109 C5
Allandale Ave. FY5 172 F4
Allen Cl. Cleveleys FY5 172 D1
Allen Cl. Fleetwood FY7 193 D2
Allen Ct. BB10 127 A8
Allen St. BB10 127 A8
Allen Way. FY7 193 D2
Allenbury Pl. FY3 130 A2
Allenby Ave. PR2 117 B4
Allenby Rd. FY8 88 E8
Allendale Gr. BB10 127 F4
Allendale St. Burnley BB12 126 B6
Allendale St. Colne BB8 169 F5
Allengate. PR2 116 F4
Allerton Cl. BB3 81 A2
Allerton Dr. BB12 126 D6
Allerton Rd. Bamber Bridge PR5 96 D4
Allerton Rd. Southport PR9 52 E1
Alleys Gn. BB7 186 E1
Alleytroyds. BB5 102 E5
Alliance St. BB5 103 F1
Allison Gr. BB8 169 F6
Allonby Ave. FY5 172 E4
Allsprings Cl. BB6 123 D6
Allsprings Dr. BB6 123 D6
Alma Ave. BB8 191 D1
Alma Cl. WN8 10 C7
Alma Ct. Southport PR8 20 F7
Alma Ct. Up Holland WN8 10 C7
Alma Dr. PR7 41 E4
Alma Hill. WN8 10 C7
Alma Ind Est. 25 OL12 51 F1
Alma Par. WN8 10 C7
Alma Pl. Accrington BB5 83 E8
Alma Pl. Clitheroe BB7 164 D7
Alma Rd. Lancaster LA1 210 F6
Alma Rd. Laneshaw Bridge BB8 170 D6
Alma Rd. Southport PR8 34 A4
Alma Rd. Up Holland WN8 10 C7
Alma Row. PR5 97 E1
Alma St. Bacup OL13 87 A2
Alma St. Blackburn BB2 100 D5
Alma St. 9 Clayton-le-M BB5 123 F3
Alma St. Padiham BB12 125 C8
Alma St. Preston PR1 117 A1
Alma St. 13 Rochdale OL12 51 F1
Alma Terr. BB11 105 C4
Almond Ave. Burscough Bridge L40 24 F6
Almond Ave. 4 Bury BL9 32 C3
Almond Brook Rd. WN6 28 C1
Almond Cl. Abbey Village PR7 79 B2
Almond Cl. Fulwood PR2 117 D6
Almond Cl. Penwortham PR1 95 B3
Almond Cres. BB4 67 F8
Almond St. BB3 64 A8
Almshouses. Aughton L39 6 A7
Almshouses. 34 Lancaster LA1 210 F8
Almshouses. 7 Rawtenstall BB4 84 E2
Alnwick Cl. BB12 126 E7
Alpha St. Darwen BB3 64 B8
Alpha St. 8 Nelson BB9 168 F2
Alpha St. Salterforth BB8 191 E8
Alpic Dr. FY5 150 C7
Alpine Ave. Bamber Bridge PR5 76 B7
Alpine Ave. Blackpool FY4 109 E5
Alpine Cl. Bamber Bridge PR5 76 B7
Alpine Cl. Hoddlesden BB3 81 E1
Alpine Gr. BB2 80 B8
Alpine Rd. PR6 60 E3
Alpine View. LA5 216 A6
Alsop St. PR1 116 F2
Alston Ave. FY5 172 D4
Alston Cl. BB7 144 F8
Alston Dr. LA4 213 B5
Alston La. PR2 & PR3 139 A2
Alston Lane RC Prim Sch. PR3 138 F2
Alston Rd. FY2 150 E2
Alston St. PR1 117 D1
Alt Rd. Formby L37 12 B2
Alt Rd. Hightown L38 3 A4
Altcar La. Formby L37 11 F1
Altcar La. Maghull L31 & L39 5 A4
Altcar La. Runshaw Moor PR5 58 E5
Altcar Rd. L37 12 B2
Altham Bsns Pk. BB5 124 E6
Altham CE Prim Sch. BB5 124 D6
Altham Ind Est. BB5 124 D6
Altham La. BB5 124 F4
Altham Rd. Morecambe LA4 212 F3
Altham Rd. Southport PR8 34 E2
Altham St. 2 Burnley BB10 127 A8
Altham St. 5 Padiham BB12 125 D8
Altham Wlk. LA4 212 F3
Althorp Cl. FY1 129 C7
Althorpe Dr. PR8 34 E3
Altom St. BB1 100 E6
Alton Cl. L38 2 F2
Altys La. L39 15 F3
Alum Scar La. BB2 99 A6
Alvern Ave. PR2 116 D4
Alvern Cres. PR2 116 D4
Alwin St. 12 BB11 126 E5
Alwood Ave. FY3 129 F6
Amber Ave. BB1 121 F2
Amber Gate. PR2 115 F6
Amberbanks Gr. FY1 129 B2
Ambergate. WN8 9 B7
Amberley St. BB2 100 C2
Amberwood. PR4 112 F5
Ambleside Ave. Barnoldswick BB8 200 A3
Ambleside Ave. Euxton PR7 59 D1
Ambleside Ave. Knott End-on-S FY6 194 F6
Ambleside Ave. 2 Rawtenstall BB4 84 E2
Ambleside Cl. Bamber Bridge PR5 96 E2
Ambleside Cl. Blackburn BB1 101 A6
Ambleside Cl. Huncoat BB5 103 E8
Ambleside Dr. BB3 81 C3
Ambleside Rd. Blackpool FY4 130 D1
Ambleside Rd. Fulwood PR2 117 E5
Ambleside Rd. Lancaster LA1 214 B2
Ambleside Rd. Lytham St Anne's FY8 109 E1
Ambleside Rd. Maghull L31 5 D2
Ambleside Wlk. PR2 117 E5
Ambleway. PR5 96 C4
Ambrose. PR5 76 B2
Amelia St. BB1 101 B6
Amersham. WN8 9 C7
Amersham Cl. PR4 74 F8
Amersham Gr. BB10 147 D4
Amethyst St. BB1 121 F2
Amounderness Way. Cleveleys FY5 172 F4
Amounderness Way. Fleetwood FY7 194 A3
Amounderness Way. Thornton FY5 151 C7
Ampleforth Dr. PR5 96 A1
Amy Johnson Way. FY4 109 E4
Amy St. OL11 & OL12 51 B1
Ancenis Ct. PR4 113 B5
Anchor Ave. BB3 80 F4
Anchor Ct. PR1 95 F7
Anchor Dr. PR4 94 D2
Anchor Gr. BB3 80 E5
Anchor Rd. BB3 80 F4
Anchor Ret Pk. 1 BB11 127 A6
Anchor St. PR8 & PR9 34 B7
Anchor Way. FY8 109 E1
Anchorage Ave. PR4 71 F1
Anchorsholme La. FY5 150 F8
Anchorsholme La E. FY5 172 E1
Anchorsholme La W. FY5 172 C1
Anchorsholme Prim Sch. FY5 150 E8
Ancliffe La. LA2 & LA5 216 B2
Andelen Cl. BB11 125 C3
Andersholme La. FY5 151 A8
Anderson Cl. LA1 211 B6
Anderson Rd. BB1 122 A7
Anderson St. FY1 129 C4
Anderton Cl. BB4 68 F7
Anderton La. BL6 30 E4
Anderton Prim Sch. PR6 30 B8
Anderton Rd. Euxton PR7 59 D1
Anderton Rd. Higham BB12 145 F5
Anderton St. Adlington PR6 30 A7
Anderton St. Chorley PR6 & PR7 42 C7
Anderton Way. PR3 178 D6
Andertons Way. PR2 117 D5
Andreas Cl. PR8 34 B4
Andrew Ave. BB4 84 F1
Andrew Cl. Blackburn BB2 80 B8
Andrew Cl. Ramsbottom BL8 48 F1
Andrew Rd. BB9 169 B1
Andrew St. Bury BL9 32 A2
Andrew St. Preston PR1 117 C1
Andrews Cl. L37 11 E1
Andrews La. L37 11 E1
Andrews Yort. L37 11 E1
Anemone Dr. BB4 66 F8
Angel Way. 3 BB8 169 E5
Angela St. BB2 100 B1
Anger's Hill Rd. FY4 129 F1
Angle St. BB10 127 A8
Anglesey Ave. BB12 126 A7
Anglesey St. BB2 80 B8
Anglezarke Rd. PR6 30 A7
Anglian Cl. BB5 102 C5
Angus St. OL13 69 C8
Aniline St. PR6 42 E8
Ann St. Barrowford BB9 168 D3
Ann St. Brierfield BB9 147 B6
Ann St. 4 Clayton-le-M BB5 123 F3
Ann St. Lancaster LA1 210 F7
Ann St. Skelmersdale WN8 8 E8
Anna's Rd. FY4 110 E3
Annan Cres. FY4 130 C1
Annandale Gdns. WN8 10 A7
Annarly Fold. BB10 128 A5
Annaside Cl. FY4 109 E7
Anne Ave. PR8 20 E6
Anne Cl. BB10 127 B5
Anne St. BB11 127 B5
Annesley Ave. FY3 129 E8
Annie St. Accrington BB5 103 C7
Annie St. Ramsbottom BL0 49 A4
Annie St. 5 Rawtenstall BB4 85 A2
Annis St. PR1 96 C8
Ansbro Ave. PR4 92 C6
Ansdell Cty Prim Sch. FY8 89 C5
Ansdell & Fairhaven Sta. FY8 89 D4
Ansdell Gr. Fulwood PR2 116 C3
Ansdell Gr. Southport PR9 53 A4
Ansdell Rd. Blackpool FY1 129 D2
Ansdell Rd. Horwich BL6 31 C4
Ansdell Rd N. FY8 89 D4
Ansdell Rd S. FY8 89 D3
Ansdell St. 3 PR1 117 C1
Ansdell Terr. BB2 100 E1
Anshaw Cl. BL7 45 C5
Anson Cl. FY8 109 D1
Anson Rd. PR4 113 B2
Anstable Rd. LA4 213 A5
Anthony Rd. LA1 210 E7
Antrim Rd. FY2 150 C1
Anvil Cl. WN5 10 D5
Anvil St. OL13 69 E8
Anyon St. BB3 81 B2
Anzio Rd. PR4 131 E5
Apiary The. PR5 57 A6
Appealing La. FY8 109 E2
Apple Cl. BB2 100 C4
Apple Ct. BB2 100 C4
Apple St. BB2 100 C4
Apple Tree Cl. PR3 155 C8
Appleby Cl. Accrington BB5 103 D5
Appleby Cl. Gregson Lane PR5 97 E1
Appleby Dr. BB9 168 D4
Appleby Rd. FY2 150 D1
Appleby St. Blackburn BB1 101 A5
Appleby St. Nelson BB9 147 D8
Appleby St. Preston PR1 116 F1
Applecross Dr. BB10 127 E4
Applefields. PR5 59 B7
Applegarth. Barnoldswick BB8 200 C3
Applegarth. Barrowford BB9 168 B1
Applegarth Rd. LA3 209 A8
Applegarth St. BB8 201 B1
Applesike. PR4 94 A1
Appleton Cl. FY6 151 A2
Appleton Rd. WN8 17 F2
Appletree Cl. Lancaster LA1 211 A3
Appletree Cl. Penwortham PR1 95 C2
Appletree Dr. LA1 211 A3
Applewood Cl. FY8 89 F3
Appley Bridge Sta. WN6 19 C7
Appley Cl. WN6 27 C2
Appley La N. Appley Bridge WN6 19 C8
Appley La N. Appley Bridge WN6 27 C1
Appley La S. WN6 & WN8 19 C6
Approach Way. BB11 126 F2
Apsley Brow. L31 5 B1
Apsley Fold. PR3 139 B6
Aqueduct Rd. Blackburn BB2 100 D1
Aqueduct Rd. Blackburn BB2 100 D2
Aqueduct St. PR1 116 E1
Arago St. BB5 103 C7
Aragon Cl. L31 5 E3
Arbories Ave. BB12 125 B8
Arbory Dr. BB12 125 B8
Arbory The. PR4 111 E7
Arbour La. Kirkby L32 & L33 1 B2
Arbour La. Shevington Moor WN6 28 B1
Arbour Lane End. PR3 160 E7
Arbour St. PR8 34 C6
Arboury St. BB12 125 B8
Arcadia. 9 BB8 169 E5
Arcadia Ave. L31 5 D3
Arch St. Burnley BB11 & BB12 126 F6
Arch St. 4 Darwen BB3 81 A1
Archbishop Hutton's Prim Sch. LA5 217 D5
Archbishop Temple Sch. PR2 116 F5
Archery Ave. BB8 191 D1
Arcon Rd. PR7 41 E1
Ardee Rd. PR1 95 D6
Arden Cl. Ainsdale PR8 20 A5
Arden Cl. Hest Bank LA2 213 E8
Arden Gn. FY7 193 E4
Ardengate. LA1 210 F4
Ardleigh Ave. PR8 34 E3
Ardley Rd. BL6 31 C4
Ardmore Rd. FY2 150 D2
Ardwick St. BB10 127 A8
Argameols Cl. PR8 34 F5
Argarmeols Gr. L37 11 E5
Argarmeols Rd. L37 11 E6
Argosy Ave. FY3 129 F8
Argosy Ct. 1 FY3 130 A8
Argyle Ct. PR9 52 D1
Argyle Rd. 7 Leyland PR5 76 A1
Argyle Rd. Poulton-le-F FY6 151 E3
Argyle Rd. Southport PR9 52 D2
Argyle St. Accrington BB5 103 B6
Argyle St. Colne BB8 169 D5
Argyle St. Darwen BB3 80 F3
Argyle St. Heywood OL10 32 E1
Argyle St. 3 Lancaster LA1 211 A7
Argyll Ct. FY2 150 C1
Argyll Rd. Blackpool FY2 150 C1
Argyll Rd. Preston PR1 117 A1
Ariel Way. FY7 193 E4
Arkholme Ave. FY1 129 D2
Arkholme CE Prim Sch. LA6 235 B3
Arkholme Cl. LA5 217 E2
Arkholme Ct. LA4 212 E3
Arkholme Dr. PR4 93 F1
Arkwright Ct. FY4 110 C7
Arkwright Fold. BB2 80 C8
Arkwright Rd. PR1 116 F2
Arkwright St. Burnley BB12 126 C7
Arkwright St. Horwich BL6 31 C2
Arley Gdns. BB12 126 F7
Arley La. WN1 & WN2 29 D2
Arley Rise. BB2 120 E2
Arley St. PR6 42 D8
Arlington Ave. FY4 109 B7
Arlington Cl. Ainsdale PR8 20 A5
Arlington Cl. Ramsbottom BL9 49 C2
Arlington Rd. BB3 63 F8
Armadale Rd. FY2 150 E1
Armitstead Ct. 8 FY7 193 F2
Armitstead Way. 5 FY7 193 F2
Armstrong St. Horwich BL6 31 C2
Armstrong St. Preston PR1 & PR2 116 B2
Arncliffe Ave. BB5 102 F4
Arncliffe Gr. BB9 168 C3
Arncliffe Rd. Burnley BB10 127 E5
Arncliffe Rd. Morecambe LA3 212 A1
Arndale Cl. FY7 193 C2
Arndale Ctr. 3 BB9 147 E8
Arndale Rd. PR3 139 A7
Arnhem Rd. Carnforth LA5 217 E1
Arnhem Rd. Preston PR1 96 D8
Arnian Ct. L39 6 C7
Arno St. 6 PR1 96 B7
Arnold Ave. FY4 109 C7
Arnold Cl. Burnley BB11 126 E2
Arnold Cl. Fulwood PR2 117 E2
Arnold Jun Sch. FY4 109 C6
Arnold Pl. PR7 42 A5
Arnold Rd. FY8 90 D4
Arnold Sch. FY4 109 C7
Arnold St. 2 BB5 103 C6
Arnott Rd. Blackpool FY4 129 E1
Arnott Rd. Fulwood PR2 116 C2
Arnside Ave. Blackpool FY1 129 D1
Arnside Ave. Lytham St Anne's FY8 89 C7
Arnside Cl. Coupe Green PR5 97 E4
Arnside Cl. Lancaster LA1 211 B3
Arnside Cres. Blackburn BB2 79 E8
Arnside Cres. Morecambe LA4 212 F6
Arnside National CE Prim Sch. LA5 237 B2
Arnside Rd. Broughton PR3 136 D2
Arnside Rd. Preston PR2 115 E2
Arnside Rd. Southport PR9 34 C7
Arnside Sta. LA5 237 C2
Arnside Terr. PR9 34 C7
Arran Ave. BB1 101 D2
Arran Cl. LA3 208 E7
Arran St. BB11 126 D5
Arrow La. LA2 214 F7
Arrowsmith Cl. PR5 97 E2
Arrowsmith Ct. 7 BL6 31 E1
Arrowsmith Dr. PR5 97 E2
Arroyo Way. PR2 117 B4
Arthur St. Bacup OL13 87 B3
Arthur St. Barnoldswick BB8 200 A3
Arthur St. Blackburn BB2 100 C4
Arthur St. Brierfield BB9 147 B6
Arthur St. Burnley BB11 126 E6
Arthur St. Clayton-le-M BB5 123 F3
Arthur St. Fleetwood FY7 194 B5
Arthur St. Great Harwood BB6 123 D6
Arthur St. 18 Nelson BB9 168 E1
Arthur St. Preston PR1 95 E7
Arthur St. Sough BB8 192 A7
Arthur St N. FY7 194 B6
Arthur Way. BB2 100 C4
Arthurs La. FY6 174 D2
Artillery St. BB5 102 F5
Artle Pl. LA1 213 E2
Artlebeck Cl. LA2 231 C3
Artlebeck Gr. LA2 231 C3
Artlebeck Rd. LA2 231 C3
Arundel Ave. FY2 150 B5
Arundel Dr. FY6 151 C5
Arundel Pl. 37 PR1 96 A7
Arundel Rd. Longton PR4 94 A1
Arundel Rd. Lytham St Anne's FY8 89 C4
Arundel Rd. Southport PR8 20 F8
Arundel St. BB1 123 A2
Arundel Way. PR5 & PR6 59 C8
Ascot Cl. Lancaster LA1 211 B4
Ascot Cl. Southport PR8 33 E5
Ascot Gdns. LA2 213 F8
Ascot Rd. Blackpool FY3 129 E6
Ascot Rd. Thornton FY5 151 B8
Ascot Way. BB5 103 D5
Ash Ave. Galgate LA2 206 F4
Ash Ave. Haslingden BB4 84 C3
Ash Ave. Kirkham PR4 113 A4
Ash Bank Cl. PR3 136 B8
Ash Brow. WN8 26 B1
Ash Cl. Appley Bridge WN6 19 D7
Ash Cl. Barrow BB7 164 D1
Ash Cl. Elswick PR4 154 A1
Ash Cl. Ormskirk L39 15 D5
Ash Cl. Rishton BB1 102 B8
Ash Coppice. PR4 115 D2
Ash Ct. PR4 114 D2
Ash Dr. Freckleton PR4 92 A5
Ash Dr. Poulton-le-F FY6 151 E2
Ash Dr. Thornton FY5 173 C1
Ash Dr. Warton PR4 91 D6
Ash Dr. Warton LA5 217 E6
Ash Dr. West Bradford BB7 186 D7
Ash Field. PR6 77 C3
Ash Gr. Bamber Bridge PR5 96 F1
Ash Gr. Barnoldswick BB8 200 B2
Ash Gr. Chorley PR7 42 C5
Ash Gr. Darwen BB3 81 B2
Ash Gr. Formby L37 11 C1
Ash Gr. Garstang PR3 178 B8
Ash Gr. 8 Horwich BL6 31 E1
Ash Gr. Kirkham PR4 113 B7
Ash Gr. Lancaster LA1 210 F5
Ash Gr. Longton PR4 73 F8
Ash Gr. New Longton PR4 74 F6

Ash Gr. Orrell WN5 .... 10 F6
Ash Gr. Preesall FY6 .... 195 A4
Ash Gr. Ramsbottom BL8 .... 48 F3
Ash Gr. 3 Rawtenstall BB4 .... 85 A3
Ash Gr. Skelmersdale WN8 .... 17 D1
Ash Gr. St Michael's on W PR3 .. 155 C7
Ash Gr. Water BB4 .... 86 A8
Ash Gr. Wrea Green PR4 .... 112 C3
Ash La. Clifton PR4 .... 114 E2
Ash Lea Gr. FY6 .... 174 C7
Ash Meadow. PR4 .... 115 E3
Ash Meadow (Outdoor Pursuit Ctr).
LA5 .... 237 A2
Ash Rd. Coppull PR7 .... 28 E8
Ash Rd. Elswick PR4 .... 154 A1
Ash St. Bacup OL13 .... 86 F3
Ash St. Blackburn BB1 .... 101 A4
Ash St. Blackpool FY4 .... 109 C6
Ash St. Burnley BB11 .... 127 B5
Ash St. Bury BL9 .... 32 A2
Ash St. Fleetwood FY7 .... 194 A4
Ash St. Great Harwood BB6 ...... 123 C6
Ash St. Nelson BB9 .... 147 F8
Ash St. Oswaldtwistle BB5 .... 102 D4
Ash St. Southport PR8 .... 34 C5
Ash St. Trawden BB8 .... 170 C2
Ash Tree Gr. LA5 .... 215 F3
Ash Tree Wlk. 14 BB9 .... 168 D3
Ashborne Dr. BL9 .... 49 D2
Ashbourne Cl. 4 LA1 .... 213 E3
Ashbourne Cres. PR2 .... 116 A5
Ashbourne Dr. LA1 .... 213 F3
Ashbourne Gr. LA3 .... 212 F2
Ashbourne Rd. LA1 .... 213 F3
Ashbrook St. LA1 .... 210 D8
Ashburnham Rd. BB8 .... 169 A2
Ashburton Rd. FY1 .... 129 B7
Ashby St. PR7 .... 42 D6
Ashcombe Gate. FY5 .... 151 D7
Ashcroft Ave. L39 .... 15 F6
Ashcroft Cl. LA2 .... 231 B3
Ashcroft Rd. Formby L37 .... 11 F1
Ashcroft Rd. Kirkby L33 .... 1 C3
Ashdale Cl. L37 .... 11 C2
Ashdale Pl. LA1 .... 213 E2
Ashdene. OL12 .... 51 D4
Ashdown Cl. Carleton FY6 .... 151 B5
Ashdown Cl. Southport PR8 ...... 34 E4
Ashdown Mews. PR2 .... 117 E6
Asheldon St. 1 PR1 .... 117 D1
Ashendean View. BB12 .... 145 D1
Ashfield. PR2 .... 116 F8
Ashfield Ave. Lancaster LA1 ... 210 D7
Ashfield Ave. Morecambe LA4 .. 213 B6
Ashfield Cl. BB9 .... 168 C1
Ashfield Ct. Blackpool FY2 ...... 150 E6
Ashfield Ct. Fulwood PR2 .... 115 F6
Ashfield Rd. Adlington PR6 .... 30 B8
Ashfield Rd. Blackpool FY2 ...... 150 E6
Ashfield Rd.
Burnley BB11 & BB12 .... 126 F6
Ashfield Rd. Chorley PR7 .... 42 B7
Ashfield Terr. WN6 .... 19 C8
Ashfields. PR5 .... 75 B1
Ashford Ave. LA2 .... 210 E3
Ashford Cl. LA1 .... 210 F3
Ashford Cres. PR3 .... 136 C3
Ashford Rd.
Lancaster LA1 & LA2 .... 210 F3
Ashford Rd. Preston PR2 .... 115 D8
Ashford St. Heywood OL10 .... 32 F2
Ashford St. Nelson BB9 .... 147 E7
Ashgrove. PR1 .... 117 E1
Ashlands Cl. BL0 .... 67 D2
Ashleigh Ct. PR2 .... 117 A7
Ashleigh Mews. FY3 .... 129 E4
Ashleigh Prim Sch. BB3 .... 64 A6
Ashleigh Rd. LA5 .... 237 B2
Ashleigh St. Darwen BB3 .... 64 B6
Ashleigh St. Preston PR1 .... 96 C7
Ashlet Ct. FY6 .... 151 C3
Ashley Cl. Blackpool FY2 .... 150 D2
Ashley Cl. Thornton FY5 .... 151 B7
Ashley La. PR3 .... 138 C8
Ashley Rd. Lytham St Anne's FY8 109 F1
Ashley Rd. Skelmersdale WN8 .. 18 B3
Ashley Rd. Southport PR9 .... 34 C7
Ashley St. BB12 .... 126 F7
Ashmead Rd. WN8 .... 18 A4
Ashmeadow Gr. LA6 .... 216 F5
Ashmeadow La. PR6 .... 61 F8
Ashmeadow Cl. Arnside LA5 .... 237 B2
Ashmeadow Rd.
Nether Kellet LA6 .... 216 F5
Ashmoor St. PR1 .... 116 E1
Ashmore Gr. FY5 .... 172 D1
Ashmount Dr. OL12 .... 51 F2
Ashness Cl. Fulwood PR2 .... 116 F8
Ashness Cl. Horwich BL6 .... 30 F3
Ashton Ave. FY6 .... 194 D5
Ashton Cl. PR1 .... 95 A8
Ashton Dr. Lancaster LA1 .... 213 E2
Ashton Dr. Nelson BB9 .... 147 E6
Ashton Garden Ct. FY8 .... 88 E7
Ashton House. BB3 .... 64 B8
Ashton La. BB3 .... 64 A8
Ashton & Lea Golf Course.
PR2 & PR4 .... 115 C2
Ashton Meml. LA1 .... 211 B7
Ashton Rd. Blackpool FY1 .... 129 C3
Ashton Rd. Darwen BB3 .... 64 B8
Ashton Rd. Lancaster LA1 & LA2 210 E4
Ashton Rd. Morecambe LA4 .... 212 F5
Ashton Rd. Southport PR8 .... 33 F1
Ashton St. Longridge PR3 .... 139 B6
Ashton St. Lytham St Anne's FY8 . 90 A3
Ashton St. Preston PR1 .... 95 D8

Ash Grlk. 12 LA1 .... 210 F8
Ashton-on-Ribble High Sch.
PR2 .... 115 F2
Ashtongate. PR2 .... 115 F1
Ashtree Ct. PR2 .... 116 A4
Ashtree Gr. PR1 .... 95 B4
Ashtrees. L40 .... 39 C2
Ashtrees Way. LA5 .... 217 D2
Ashurst Cl. L37 .... 11 E2
Ashurst Gdns. WN8 .... 18 B4
Ashurst Rd. Clayton-le-W PR6 .. 76 D1
Ashurst Rd.
Shevington Moor WN6 .... 28 B2
Ashurst Rd. Skelmersdale WN8 .. 18 B4
Ashurst Sch. WN8 .... 17 D1
Ashville Terr. BB2 .... 80 D8
Ashwall St. WN8 .... 8 E8
Ashwell Pl. FY5 .... 150 C7
Ashwood. WN8 .... 18 C3
Ashwood Ave. BL0 .... 49 D7
Ashwood Cl. FY8 .... 89 E4
Ashwood Dr. PR2 .... 116 D7
Ashworth Cl. BB2 .... 100 C5
Ashworth Ct. FY3 .... 129 D7
Ashworth Dr. LA2 & LA5 .... 215 E2
Ashworth Gr. PR1 .... 96 C5
Ashworth Hospl. L31 .... 6 B2
Ashworth La. Newchurch BB4 .... 85 F3
Ashworth La. Preston PR1 .... 96 C6
Ashworth Rd. Blackpool FY4 ... 110 C8
Ashworth Rd. Cheesden OL11 .... 50 E2
Ashworth Rd. Newchurch BB4 ... 85 F2
Ashworth St. Accrington BB5 ... 103 C5
Ashworth St. 3 Bacup OL13 ..... 69 D8
Ashworth St. 15 Bacup OL13 .... 87 A3
Ashworth St. Bamber Bridge PR5 .. 96 F2
Ashworth St. Forest Holme BB4 .. 86 A7
Ashworth St. Newchurch BB4 ... 68 F8
Ashworth St. 7 Preston PR1 .... 96 B7
Ashworth St. Rishton BB1 .... 123 B1
Ashworth St. 7 Bacup OL13 ...... 69 B8
Ashworth Terr. 7 Darwen BB3 .. 81 A1
Askrigg Cl. Accrington BB5 ...... 103 E5
Askrigg Cl. Blackpool FY4 .... 110 A7
Asland Cl. PR5 .... 76 F8
Asland Gdns. PR9 .... 53 C4
Asmall Cl. L39 .... 15 D6
Asmall Cty Prim Sch. L39 .... 15 D6
Asmall La. L39 & L40 .... 15 B7
Aspden St. PR5 .... 96 E1
Aspels Cres. PR1 .... 95 C4
Aspels Nook. PR1 .... 95 C4
Aspels The. PR1 .... 95 C4
Aspen Fold. BB5 .... 102 B5
Aspen Gdns. OL12 .... 51 A1
Aspen Gr. L37 .... 11 C1
Aspen La. Earby BB8 .... 201 B2
Aspen La. Oswaldtwistle BB5 ... 102 C4
Aspendale Cl. PR4 .... 73 F8
Aspinal Cl. PR1 .... 95 D2
Aspinall Cres. L37 .... 12 F1
Aspinall Rd. WN6 .... 28 B1
Aspinall St. BL6 .... 31 C1
Aspley Dr. BB2 .... 170 C3
Asshawes The. PR6 .... 42 F1
Assheton Pl. PR2 .... 117 E4
Assheton Rd. BB2 .... 100 A5
Astland Gdns. PR4 .... 72 F2
Astland St. FY8 .... 88 E6
Astley Cres. PR4 .... 92 C6
Astley Cl. LA1 .... 210 D6
Astley Ctr The. PR7 .... 42 D6
Astley Gate. BB2 .... 100 E5
Astley Hall Dr. BB2 .... 49 C4
Astley Park Sch. PR7 .... 42 B8
Astley Rd. PR7 .... 60 C1
Astley St. Chorley PR6 & PR7 .... 60 C1
Astley St. Darwen BB3 .... 64 A7
Astley St. Longridge PR3 .... 139 A7
Aston Ave. FY5 .... 173 A6
Aston St. PR4 .... 131 E6
Aston Way. PR5 .... 75 C2
Aston Wlk. BB2 .... 81 A8
Athens View. BB10 .... 127 C5
Athelstan Fold. PR2 .... 116 C3
Atherton Rd. PR5 .... 58 D8
Atherton St. Adlington PR7 .... 30 A6
Atherton St. Bacup OL13 .... 69 C8
Atherton Way. OL13 .... 69 B8
Athletic St. BB10 .... 127 C5
Athlone Ave. FY2 .... 150 C2
Athol Gr. PR7 .... 42 E6
Athol St. Nelson BB9 .... 147 F8
Athol St. Ramsbottom BL0 .... 49 C7
Athol St N. BB11 .... 126 D5
Athol St S. BB11 .... 126 D5
Athole Gr. PR9 .... 34 F7
Atholl St. PR1 .... 95 D8
Atkinson Art Gal. PR8 .... 34 B7
Atkinson Liby. PR8 .... 34 B7
Atkinson St. Brierfield BB10 ... 147 F3
Atkinson St. Colne BB8 .... 169 C3
Atkinson St. Colne BB8 .... 169 D4
Atlas Rd. BB3 .... 81 B1
Atlas St. BB5 .... 124 A1
Atrium Ct. BB11 .... 127 B4
Auburn Gr. PR2 .... 116 D4
Auckland St. BB3 .... 64 B7
Audenlea. FY5 .... 172 F3
Audenshaw Rd. L4 .... 15 D6
Audley Cl. Lytham St Anne's FY8 . 89 D5
Audley Cl. Nelson BB9 .... 147 E8
Audley Jun & Inf Sch. BB1 .... 101 A3
Audley La. BB1 .... 101 A4
Audley Range. BB1 .... 101 A5
Audley St. BB1 .... 101 A5
Audlum Ct. 4 BL9 .... 32 A2

Aughton Brow. LA2 .... 231 E6
Aughton Ct. LA1 .... 213 F4
Aughton Hall Cotts. L39 .... 15 C6
Aughton Mews. PR8 .... 34 A5
Aughton Park Dr. L39 .... 15 D2
Aughton Rd. Aughton LA2 ...... 231 E6
Aughton Rd. Southport PR8 ...... 34 A5
Aughton St. Fleetwood FY7 .... 194 B5
Aughton St. Ormskirk L39 .... 15 E4
Aughton St Michael's CE Prim Sch.
L39 .... 15 B1
Aughton Town Green Cty Prim Sch.
L39 .... 6 C8
Aughton Wlk. 2 PR1 .... 116 F1
Augusta Cl. OL12 .... 51 E2
Augusta St. Accrington BB5 .... 103 C4
Augusta St. Rochdale OL12 ...... 51 E1
Auster Cres. PR4 .... 113 B2
Austin Gr. FY1 .... 129 B1
Austin St. 6 Bacup OL13 .... 86 F2
Austin St. Burnley BB11 .... 126 E5
Austin Way. FY4 .... 111 A7
Austin's Cl. PR5 .... 59 A8
Austwick Rd. 4 LA1 .... 213 D2
Austwick Way. BB5 .... 103 E5
Avallon Way. BB3 .... 81 C1
Avalon Dr. PR4 .... 92 C7
Avalwood Ave. PR4 .... 74 B8
Avebury Cl. Blackburn BB2 .... 81 A8
Avebury Cl. Horwich BL6 .... 31 F1
Aveling Dr. PR9 .... 54 A6
Avelon Cl. L31 .... 5 B5
Avenham Colonnade. PR1 .... 96 A6
Avenham Ct. 20 PR1 .... 96 A7
Avenham La. PR1 .... 96 A7
Avenham Pl. Newton-with-S PR4 113 F2
Avenham Pl. Preston PR1 .... 96 A7
Avenham Rd. Chorley PR7 .... 42 C7
Avenham Rd. Preston PR1 .... 96 A7
Avenue Par. BB5 .... 103 D6
Avenue Rd. Hurst Green BB7 .. 162 E1
Avenue Rd. Normoss FY3 .... 130 B7
Avenue The. Adlington PR6 .... 30 A8
Avenue The. Banks PR9 .... 53 F5
Avenue The. Barley BB12 .... 167 C5
Avenue The. Burnley BB11 ..... 127 D3
Avenue The. Carleton FY6 ...... 151 C4
Avenue The. Churchtown PR3 .. 178 B3
Avenue The. Fulwood PR2 ...... 116 A6
Avenue The. Garstang PR3 ..... 199 B1
Avenue The. Leyland PR5 .... 59 A6
Avenue The. Ormskirk L39 .... 15 D6
Avenue The. Ormskirk L39 .... 15 E5
Avenue The. Orrell WN5 .... 10 D3
Avenue The. Penwortham PR1 .. 95 B5
Avenue The. Preston PR1 .... 115 D1
Avenue The. Southport PR8 ...... 35 F5
Avenue Rd. Morecambe LA3 ... 212 B3
Avenue Rd. Nelson BB9 .... 147 D7
Avondale Rd.
Lytham St Anne's FY8 .... 88 C8
Avondale Rd. Morecambe LA3 .. 212 B3
Avondale Rd. Nelson BB9 .... 147 D7
Avondale Rd.
Southport PR8 & PR9 .... 34 B8
Avondale Rd N. Colne BB8 ..... 170 A5
Avondale Rd. Standish WN6 ...... 28 E2
Avondale Ave. Blackburn BB1 .. 101 E5
Avondale Ave. Burnley BB12 ... 126 C7
Avondale Cl. BB3 .... 80 E2
Avondale Cres. FY4 .... 109 F7
Avondale Dr. Bamber Bridge PR5 76 B8
Avondale Dr. Ramsbottom BL0 .. 48 F3
Avondale Dr. Tarleton PR4 .... 56 A8
Avondale Mews. BB3 .... 80 E3
Avondale Prim Sch. BB2 .... 80 E2
Avondale Rd. Chorley PR7 .... 42 C7
Avondale Rd. Darwen BB3 .... 80 E3
Avondale Rd. Lancaster LA1 ... 211 A6
Avonhead Cl. BL6 .... 31 A3
Avonside Ave. FY5 .... 173 A3
Avonwood Cl. BB3 .... 80 E2
Avroe Cres. FY8 .... 109 D4
Aylesbury Ave. FY4 .... 129 D1
Aylesbury Wlk. BB10 .... 147 D3
Ayr Cl. PR8 .... 34 F4
Ayr Gr. BB11 .... 126 C6
Ayr Rd. BB1 .... 101 D3
Ayr St. LA1 .... 211 B7
Ayrefield Gr. WN6 .... 19 D6
Ayrefield La. WN8 .... 19 C4
Ayrton Ave. FY4 .... 109 D7
Ayrton St. BB8 .... 169 E5
Ays-Garth Rd. LA1 .... 210 D8
Aysgarth Ave. PR2 .... 116 F7
Aysgarth Cl. PR4 .... 109 F7
Aysgarth Dr. Accrington BB5 ... 103 D6
Aysgarth Dr. Darwen BB3 .... 80 E2
Aysgarth Dr. Lancaster LA1 ... 213 F4
Azalea Cl. PR2 .... 117 C6
Azalea Rd. LA3 .... 213 A5
Azalea Rd. BB2 .... 100 B6

Babbacombe Ave. FY4 .... 109 B6
Babylon La. PR6 .... 30 B8
Back Albert Rd. BB8 .... 169 D4

Back Albert St. Bury BL9 .... 32 A2
Back Albert St. 3
Padiham BB12 .... 125 C8
Back Alfred St. 11 BL0 .... 49 B5
Back Altham St. 4 BB12 .... 125 D8
Back Andrew St. 13 BL9 .... 32 A2
Back Andrew St N. 12 BL9 .... 32 A2
Back Arthur St. 15 BB5 .... 123 F3
Back Ash St. 7 BL9 .... 32 A2
Back Ashburton Rd. FY1 .... 129 C7
Back Atkinson St. BB8 .... 169 D4
Back Avondale Rd (E). LA3 ..... 212 B3
Back Avondale Rd (W). LA3 .... 212 B3
Back Bath St. PR8 .... 34 B8
Back Beehive Terr. BB4 .... 84 B3
Back Bell La. 8 Bury BL9 .... 32 A3
Back Bell La. Bury BL9 .... 32 A3
Back Benson St. 9 BL9 .... 32 A1
Back Blackburn Rd E. BB7 .... 46 D3
Back Bolton Rd. BB3 .... 64 B7
Back Bond St. BB8 .... 169 D5
Back Bond St W. BL9 .... 32 A2
Back Boundary St. 13 BB8 ...... 169 D4
Back Bourne's Row. PR5 .... 97 E1
Back Bridge St. 2 BL0 .... 49 C6
Back Broading Terr. BB4 .... 105 A3
Back Brook St N. 11 BL9 .... 32 A4
Back Brow. WN8 .... 10 C7
Back Brown St. BB8 .... 169 C4
Back Burnley Rd. BB5 .... 103 C6
Back Calton Terr. LA4 .... 212 E6
Back Cambridge St. 10 BB8 ...... 169 F4
Back Canada St. BL6 .... 31 B3
Back Carr Mill St. BB4 .... 84 B5
Back Cateaton St. BL9 .... 32 A4
Back Cedar St. 3 BL9 .... 32 B3
Back Cedar St N. 1 BL9 .... 32 B3
Back Cemetery Terr. 9 OL13 .... 69 D8
Back Chapel St. 5
Barnoldswick BB8 .... 200 B2
Back Chapel St. 4 Colne BB8 ... 169 D5
Back Chapel St. Horwich BL6 .... 31 C3
Back Chesham Rd N. 6 BL9 ...... 32 A4
Back Chesham Rd S. 7 BL9 .... 32 A4
Back Chester St. BL9 .... 32 A4
Back Church St.
Barrowford BB9 .... 168 D3
Back Church St. Blackpool FY1 . 128 D3
Back Church St. Hapton BB12 . 125 C4
Back Church St. Newchurch BB4 85 E1
Back Clarendon Rd. FY1 .... 129 B2
Back Clayton St. 3 BB9 .... 168 D1
Back Club St. PR5 .... 76 E7
Back Colne Rd. BB8 .... 200 A1
Back Constablelee. BB4 .... 84 F4
Back Cookson St. FY1 .... 129 C5
Back Cop La. FY7 .... 194 B4
Back Cowm La. OL12 .... 70 C2
Back Crescent St. LA4 .... 212 D5
Back Crown St. BL6 .... 31 A4
Back Darwen Rd N. BL7 .... 46 E1
Back Deal St. BL9 .... 32 B2
Back Delamere St N. BL9 .... 32 A5
Back Delamere St S. BL9 .... 32 A5
Back Derby St. 4 BB8 .... 169 D5
Back Drinkhouse La. PR5 .... 57 B1
Back Duckworth St. 4
Bury BL9 .... 32 A4
Back Duckworth St. 12
Darwen BB3 .... 81 A1
Back Duke St. 1 BB8 .... 169 D4
Back Duncan St. BL6 .... 31 C3
Back Earl St. 2 BB8 .... 169 D4
Back East Bank. 1 BB9 .... 168 D4
Back Eaves St. FY1 .... 129 B7
Back Elm St. 10 BL9 .... 32 B2
Back Emmett St. BB3 .... 31 B3
Back Epsom Rd. FY5 .... 150 F8
Back Fazakerley St. 11 PR4 ...... 42 C8
Back Fir St. BL9 .... 32 B2
Back Fletcher St. BL9 .... 32 A2
Back Forest Rd. PR8 .... 34 D6
Back Garston St. BL9 .... 32 A4
Back George St. BL6 .... 31 C3
Back Gisburn Rd. BB9 .... 168 E2
Back Glen Eldon Rd. FY8 .... 88 E7
Back Green St. LA4 .... 212 E6
Back Grimshaw St. 8 PR1 .... 96 A7
Back Hall St. BB8 .... 169 D4
Back Halstead St. 2 BL9 .... 32 A4
Back Hamilton St. 1 BL9 .... 32 A4
Back Harry St. BB9 .... 168 D3
Back Haslam St. BL9 .... 32 A4
Back Headroomgate Rd. FY8 .... 88 F8
Back Heys. BB5 .... 102 E3
Back Heywood St E. 14 BL9 ...... 32 A4
Back Heywood St W. BL9 .... 32 A4
Back High St. Belmont BL7 .... 45 C5
Back High St. Blackpool FY1 ... 129 B6
Back High St. Chapeltown BL7 .. 47 C5
Back Hill St. 13 BB4 .... 85 A7
Back Hilton St. BL9 .... 32 A4
Back Holly St. BL9 .... 32 A2
Back Holly St S. 8 BL9 .... 32 A2
Back Hope St. OL13 .... 86 F4
Back Hunter St. LA5 .... 217 D2
Back Huntley Mount Rd. BL9 .... 32 B3
Back Hurst St. BL9 .... 32 A1
Back Ingham St. BL9 .... 32 A1
Back Ingham St E. BL9 .... 32 A1
Back Kershaw St. 9 BL9 .... 32 A2
Back King St. BB5 .... 103 B6
Back Knowlys Rd. LA3 .... 208 F8
Back La. Accrington BB5 .... 103 C3
Back La. Bolton Green PR7 .... 41 B7
Back La. Bretherton PR5 .... 56 E5
Back La. Burscough Bridge L40 .. 24 E6
Back La. Carnforth LA5 & LA6 .. 216 E7

Back La. Clayton Green PR6 ..... 77 A2
Back La. Clayton Green PR6 ..... 77 B1
Back La. Cumeragh Village PR3 138 C6
Back La. Great Eccleston PR3 .. 154 B5
Back La. Greenhalgh PR4 .... 132 B4
Back La. Hale Nook FY6 & PR3 . 174 A5
Back La. Haskayne L39 .... 13 D3
Back La. Higham BB12 .... 145 E6
Back La. Holt Green L39 .... 5 E6
Back La. Leyland PR5 .... 59 C7
Back La. Longridge PR3 .... 159 B6
Back La. Longton PR4 .... 73 E8
Back La. Mawdesley L40 .... 39 D1
Back La. Newburgh L40 & WN8 . 25 E2
Back La. Newton BB7 .... 222 F6
Back La. Preesall FY6 .... 195 A1
Back La. Rawtenstall BB4 .... 85 B2
Back La. Rimington BB7 .... 188 E8
Back La. Royal Oak L39 .... 7 B2
Back La. Sabden BB12 & BB6 .. 145 C4
Back La. Shevington Moor WN6 .. 27 F1
Back La. Shevington Vale WN6 . 19 E8
Back La. Skelmersdale WN8 .... 9 D6
Back La. Skelmersdale WN8 .... 9 E7
Back La. Trawden BB10 .... 148 F7
Back La. Trawden BB8 .... 170 B2
Back La. Tunstall LA6 .... 235 D4
Back La. Warton LA5 .... 217 D5
Back La. Whitworth OL12 .... 70 C3
Back La. Wiswell BB7 .... 143 F6
Back La. Wray LA2 .... 232 C6
Back La. Wrayton LA6 .... 235 E2
Back La E. L40 .... 39 F1
Back Lane Croft. BB7 .... 186 E1
Back Lane Side. BB4 .... 84 B2
Back Lathom St. 9 BL9 .... 32 A4
Back Laurel St. 2 BL9 .... 32 B2
Back Leach St. BB8 .... 169 C4
Back Lee St. BB4 .... 84 B2
Back Lines St. 2 LA4 .... 212 E5
Back Longworth Rd. BL7 .... 46 D3
Back Lord St. Blackpool FY1 ... 129 B6
Back Lord St. Lancaster LA1 ... 213 F1
Back Lord St. 4
Rawtenstall BB4 .... 85 A7
Back Lune St. BB8 .... 169 E4
Back Manor St. 1 BL9 .... 32 A2
Back Marine Rd. LA4 .... 212 C4
Back Marine Rd E. LA4 .... 212 G6
Back Mason St. 16 BL9 .... 32 A4
Back Morecambe St. LA4 .... 212 E6
Back Moon Ave. FY1 .... 129 B2
Back Moss La. L40 .... 24 F7
Back Mount. 5 PR7 .... 42 C8
Back Myrtle St. N BL9 .... 32 B2
Back Myrtle St S. BL9 .... 32 B2
Back Nelson St. BL6 .... 31 D3
Back New St. LA5 .... 217 D2
Back Nook Terr. OL12 .... 51 F3
Back North Cres. FY8 .... 88 E6
Back o' the Town La. L38 .... 3 E3
Back Oram St. BL9 .... 32 A4
Back Ormrod St. 10 BL9 .... 32 A2
Back Owen's Row. BL6 .... 31 C3
Back Oxford St. BL9 .... 32 A1
Back Parkinson St. BB2 .... 100 B2
Back Parsonage St. 10 BL9 .... 32 A3
Back Patience St. 10 OL12 .... 51 C1
Back Percy St. BL9 .... 32 B3
Back Peter St. 8
Barrowford BB9 .... 168 D4
Back Peter St. 3 Bury BL9 .... 32 A3
Back Pine St. 1 BL9 .... 32 B2
Back Pleasant St. FY1 .... 129 B7
Back Queen St.
Great Harwood BB6 .... 123 C5
Back Queen St. 7
Lancaster LA1 .... 210 F7
Back Queen St. 1
Morecambe LA4 .... 212 E5
Back Railway View. PR6 .... 30 A7
Back Rawlinson St. 16 BL6 .... 31 B4
Back Read's Rd. FY1 .... 129 C4
Back Regent St. 2 BB4 .... 84 B3
Back Rhoden Rd. BB5 .... 102 C3
Back Richard Burch St. 1 BL9 .. 32 A3
Back Rings Row. BB4 .... 105 A1
Back Rochdale Old North Rd. 1
BL9 .... 32 A3
Back Rochdale Old Rd S. BL9 .... 32 B3
Back Rochdale Old South Rd. 3
Bury BL9 .... 32 C3
Back Rochdale Old South Rd.
Bury BL9 .... 32 D3
Back Rochdale Rd. Bury BL9 .... 32 A3
Back Rochdale Rd. Bury BL9 .... 32 B2
Back Rochdale Rd S. 17 BL9 .... 32 A2
Back Rushton St. 5 OL13 .... 69 E8
Back Salford St. BL9 .... 32 A4
Back Sandy Bank Rd. BL7 .... 47 D5
Back School La.
Skelmersdale WN8 .... 17 D2
Back School La. Up Holland WN8 10 C7
Back Scotland Rd. BB1 .... 147 D6
Back Seed St. 9 PR1 .... 95 F8
Back Shannon St. FY1 .... 129 B3
Back Shaw-Street. BL9 .... 32 B3
Back Shepherd St. LA3 .... 208 B8
Back Side. BB7 .... 187 B8
Back Skipton Rd. 6 BB8 .... 200 B2
Back South Cross St E. 15 BL9 . 32 A2
Back Spencer St. BB4 .... 85 A7
Back Springfield Rd N. FY8 .... 88 E6
Back Square St. BL0 .... 49 C6
Back St. LA3 .... 205 D8

Back St Anne's Rd W. FY8 ..... 88 E6
Back St Anne's St. BL9 .... 32 A4
Back St John St. 5 OL13 .... 86 F3
Back Stanley St. BL0 .... 49 B5
Back Starkie St. PR1 .... 95 F6
Back Sun St. 9 LA1 .... 210 F8
Back Teak St. 6 BL9 .... 32 B2
Back Tinline St. 11 BL9 .... 32 A2
Back Union St. BL7 .... 46 D2
Back Virginia St. PR8 .... 34 B6
Back Walmersley Rd E. BL9 .... 32 A3
Back Wash La. BL9 .... 32 B2
Back Wash La S. 6 BL9 .... 32 A2
Back Water St. 11
  Accrington BB5 .... 103 C6
Back Water St. Egerton BL7 ..... 46 D2
Back Waterloo Rd. FY1 .... 129 B1
Back Wellington St. BB5 .... 103 C5
Back West Cres. FY8 .... 88 E6
Back Willow St. BB12 .... 126 E6
Back Winterdyne Terr. LA3 ... 212 B4
Back Wood St. BL6 .... 31 C3
Back Woodfield Rd. FY1 .... 129 B2
Back Wright St. BL6 .... 31 B4
Back York St. Clitheroe BB7 ... 164 F8
Back York St. Rawtenstall BB4 .. 85 A7
Back Zion St. 15 BB8 .... 169 D4
Backhouse St. 1 BB5 .... 102 E4
Backs The. PR3 .... 139 A6
Bacon St. 5 BB9 .... 147 E8
Bacup Golf Course. OL13 .... 86 E2
Bacup Holy Trinity
  Stacksteads CE Sch. OL13 .... 69 C8
Bacup Old Rd. OL13 .... 86 F7
Bacup & Rawtenstall Gram Sch.
  BB4 .... 68 F8
Bacup Rd. Rawtenstall BB4 ..... 85 C2
Bacup Rd. Sharneyford OL14 ... 87 E5
Bacup Rd. Walk Mill BB11 ..... 106 E6
Baddon Cl. LA4 .... 212 F3
Baden Terr. BB2 .... 100 D1
Badge Brow. BB5 .... 102 E5
Badger Cl. BB12 .... 145 D1
Badger Rd. PR5 .... 76 A4
Badger St. BL9 .... 32 A3
Badger Wells Cotts. BB7 .... 145 A8
Badgers Cl. BB5 .... 103 E8
Badgers Croft. PR1 .... 117 F1
Badgers Rake. L37 .... 11 C5
Badgers Way. PR5 .... 96 B3
Badgers Wlk E. FY8 .... 90 C3
Badgers Wlk W. FY8 .... 90 B3
Bagganley La. PR6 .... 60 F2
Bagnold Rd. PR1 .... 117 D1
Bagot St. FY1 .... 129 B1
Baildon Rd. OL11 & OL12 ...... 51 B1
Bailey Bank. BB7 .... 163 A7
Bailey Ct. FY3 .... 129 E6
Bailey La. Heysham LA3 .... 208 E8
Bailey La. Tosside BD23 .... 230 B3
Bailey St. Burnley BB11 .... 126 E5
Bailey St. Earby BB8 .... 201 C2
Bailrigg La. LA1 .... 211 A1
Baines Ave. FY3 .... 150 F1
Baines Endowed CE Prim Sch.
  FY4 .... 129 F1
Baines' Endowed Cty Prim Sch.
  FY5 .... 173 C1
Baines Sch. FY6 .... 151 D1
Bairstow St. Barnoldswick BB8 . 200 B3
Bairstow St. Blackpool FY1 ... 129 B3
Bairstow St. Preston PR1 & PR0 . 95 F7
Baker St. 13 Bacup OL13 ...... 86 F3
Baker St. Blackburn BB1 .... 101 B4
Baker St. Burnley BB11 .... 126 E5
Baker St. Lancaster LA1 .... 213 F3
Baker St. 4 Leyland PR5 .... 76 B2
Baker St. Nelson BB9 .... 168 E1
Baker St. Ramsbottom BL0 ..... 49 B5
Baker's La. PR9 .... 53 A3
Bakers Ct. FY4 .... 109 F7
Bala Cl. BB1 .... 100 E6
Balaclava St. BB1 .... 100 E6
Balcarres Cl. PR5 .... 76 A1
Balcarres Pl. PR5 .... 59 A8
Balcarres Rd. Chorley PR7 ...... 42 B5
Balcarres Rd. Leyland PR5 ...... 59 A8
Balcarres Rd. 5 Leyland PR5 .. 76 B1
Balcarres Rd.
  Preston PR1 & PR2 .... 116 C2
Balderstone CE Prim Sch.
  BB2 .... 120 A5
Balderstone Cl. BB12 .... 147 D2
Balderstone Hall La. BB2 ...... 119 C6
Balderstone La. BB10 .... 147 E2
Balderstone Rd. Freckleton PR4 . 92 B7
Balderstone Rd. Preston PR1 ... 95 D5
Baldwin Gr. FY1 .... 129 D2
Baldwin Hill. BB7 .... 164 D8
Baldwin Rd. BB7 .... 164 D8
Baldwin St. Bacup OL13 .... 69 B8
Baldwin St. 6
  Bamber Bridge PR5 .... 96 E1
Baldwin St. 5 Barrowford BB9 . 168 D4
Baldwin St. Blackburn BB2 .... 100 C3
Baldwin's Bldgs. 14 BB4 .... 85 A3
Balfour Cl. Brierfield BB9 ...... 147 D5
Balfour Cl. Thornton FY5 ...... 151 D7
Balfour House. BB2 .... 100 C4
Balfour Rd. Preston PR2 .... 116 E3
Balfour Rd. Southport PR8 ...... 34 E5
Balfour Rd. 5
  Spotland Fold OL12 .... 51 C1
Balfour St. Blackburn BB2 ..... 100 C4
Balfour St. Great Harwood BB6 . 123 E5
Balfour St. Leyland PR5 .... 76 A1
Balham Ave. FY4 .... 109 E5
Ball Grove Dr. BB8 .... 170 B5
Ball La. LA2 .... 231 C3
Ball St. Blackpool FY1 .... 129 B1
Ball St. 2 Nelson BB9 .... 168 D1
Ball St. Poulton-le-F FY6 ...... 151 D3
Ball's Pl. PR8 .... 34 B7
Balladen Prim Sch. BB4 .... 67 F8
Ballam Rd. Lower Ballam PR4 . 111 C3
Ballam Rd. Lytham St Anne's FY8 . 90 B4
Ballam St. Preston PR2 .... 115 E1
Ballantine St. BB11 .... 127 A4
Ballantrae Rd. BB1 .... 101 D3
Ballater St. BB11 .... 126 D3
Balle St. BB3 .... 64 A8
Ballet Hill Cres. PR3 .... 157 A5
Balliol Cl. BB12 .... 125 D6
Balm St. BL0 .... 49 A4
Balmer Gr. FY1 .... 129 D3
Balmoral. PR7 .... 29 E6
Balmoral Ave. Blackburn BB1 . 122 A4
Balmoral Ave. Clitheroe BB7 . 164 C6
Balmoral Ave. Leyland PR5 .... 59 C8
Balmoral Ave. Morecambe LA3 . 212 B3
Balmoral Cl. Horwich BL6 ...... 31 E2
Balmoral Cl. Ramsbottom BL8 .. 49 A1
Balmoral Cres. BB1 .... 101 F4
Balmoral Dr. Brinscall PR6 ..... 61 E8
Balmoral Dr. Formby L37 .... 11 E1
Balmoral Dr. Southport PR9 .... 53 B3
Balmoral Pl. FY5 .... 151 C8
Balmoral Rd. Accrington BB5 . 103 D7
Balmoral Rd. Bamber Bridge PR5 . 96 D3
Balmoral Rd. Blackpool FY4 .. 109 B8
Balmoral Rd. Chorley PR7 ...... 42 B8
Balmoral Rd. Darwen BB3 ...... 64 B6
Balmoral Rd. Eccleston PR7 .... 40 C7
Balmoral Rd. Haslingden BB4 .. 84 A1
Balmoral Rd. Lancaster LA1 .. 211 A7
Balmoral Rd.
  Lytham St Anne's FY8 .... 89 A5
Balmoral Rd. Maghull L31 .... 5 C1
Balmoral Rd.
  Morecambe LA3 & LA4 .... 212 C3
Balmoral Rd. New Longton PR4 . 95 A1
Balmoral Terr. FY7 .... 194 B5
Balmore Ct. OL10 .... 32 E1
Balniel Cl. PR7 .... 42 A7
Balshaw Ave. PR7 .... 59 D2
Balshaw Cres. PR5 .... 75 F2
Balshaw La. PR7 .... 59 D1
Balshaw Lane Cty Prim Sch.
  PR7 .... 59 E1
Balshaw Rd. Leyland PR5 .... 75 F1
Balshaw Rd. Lowgill LA2 ...... 233 E3
Balshaw St. PR5 .... 96 E2
Balshaw's High Sch. PR5 .... 59 B7
Baltic Rd. BB4 .... 68 E8
Baltimore Rd. FY8 .... 89 B6
Bamber Ave. FY2 .... 150 C4
Bamber Bridge Meth Prim Sch.
  PR5 .... 76 F8
Bamber Bridge Sta. PR5 .... 76 E8
Bamber Gdns. PR9 .... 35 A8
Bamber St. PR7 .... 42 B5
Bamber's Wlk. PR4 .... 112 E7
Bambers La. Blackpool FY4 ... 110 C6
Bambers La. Blackpool FY4 ... 110 C7
Bamburgh Cl. FY4 .... 110 A7
Bamburgh Dr. BB12 .... 126 E7
Bamford Cl. BL9 .... 32 E4
Bamford Cres. BB5 .... 103 D4
Bamford Pl. OL12 .... 51 E1
Bamford Rd. BL0 .... 50 B6
Bamford St. Burnley BB11 .... 127 A6
Bamford St. Nelson BB9 .... 148 A8
Bamfords Fold. PR5 .... 56 F5
Bamton Ave. FY4 .... 109 C7
Banastre. PR7 .... 60 A2
Banastre Rd. PR8 .... 34 B5
Banastre St. BB5 .... 124 A1
Banbury Ave. Blackpool FY2 . 150 D1
Banbury Ave. Oswaldtwistle BB5 . 102 C4
Banbury Cl. 8 Accrington BB5 . 103 A7
Banbury Cl. Blackburn BB2 ..... 79 F3
Banbury Dr. PR2 .... 116 E4
Banbury Rd. Longshaw WN5 ... 10 D2
Banbury Rd.
  Lytham St Anne's FY8 .... 89 A6
Banbury Rd.
  Morecambe LA3 & LA4 ...... 212 F3
Bancroft Ave. FY5 .... 173 C2
Bancroft Fold. BB8 .... 200 A1
Bancroft Rd. BB10 .... 127 C8
Bancroft St. BB11 .... 100 F5
Bancroft Steam Mus. BB8 ..... 200 B1
Band La. PR3 .... 177 D1
Bangor Ave. FY2 .... 150 D4
Bangor St. BB1 .... 100 F7
Bank Ave. WN5 .... 10 D5
Bank Bottom. BB3 .... 81 A1
Bank Bridge. PR4 .... 56 B5
Bank Brow. WN8 .... 19 C5
Bank Cl. Galgate LA2 .... 206 F3
Bank Cl. Longton PR4 .... 74 A8
Bank Cotts. BB7 .... 143 B4
Bank Croft. PR4 .... 74 A8
Bank Fold. BB9 .... 168 E4
Bank Hall Cotts. BB7 .... 224 C1
Bank Head La. PR5 .... 97 D1
Bank Hey Cl. BB1 .... 122 A1
Bank Hey La N. BB1 .... 121 F3
Bank Hey La S. BB1 .... 122 A1
Bank Hey Sq. BB2 .... 80 C7
Bank Hey St. FY1 .... 129 B5
Bank House La. Bacup OL13 .... 86 F2
Bank House La. Westhouse LA6 . 236 E4
Bank House St. BB9 .... 168 E4
Bank La. Blackburn BB1 .... 101 D4
Bank La. Warton PR4 .... 91 D4
Bank Meadow. BL6 .... 31 C4
Bank Mill St. 3 BB4 .... 84 B2
Bank Par. Burnley BB11 .... 127 A6
Bank Par. Preston PR1 .... 96 A6
Bank Pas. PR8 .... 34 A7
Bank Pl. PR1 .... 116 C1
Bank Rd. Lancaster LA1 .... 213 F3
Bank Rd. Shevington Vale WN8 . 19 D4
Bank Sq. PR8 .... 34 B8
Bank St. Accrington BB5 ...... 103 C5
Bank St. Adlington PR6 .... 26 A7
Bank St. 14 Bacup OL13 .... 86 F2
Bank St. Bank Lane BL6 .... 49 E7
Bank St. Barnoldswick BB8 ... 200 C2
Bank St. Brierfield BB9 .... 147 B6
Bank St. Chapeltown BL7 .... 47 C4
Bank St. 9 Church BB5 .... 102 E6
Bank St. Darwen BB3 .... 81 A1
Bank St. Haslingden BB4 .... 84 B3
Bank St. 11 Nelson BB9 .... 168 E1
Bank St. Padiham BB12 .... 145 C1
Bank St. Rawtenstall BB4 .... 85 A2
Bank St. Trawden BB8 .... 170 C1
Bank Terr. Simonstone BB12 .. 124 E8
Bank Terr. Whitworth OL12 .... 51 C8
Bank Top. Baldingstone BL9 .... 49 F1
Bank Top. Blackburn BB2 ...... 100 C4
Bank Top. Burnley BB11 .... 127 A6
Bank View. Hambleton FY6 ... 174 C1
Bank View. Rawtenstall BB11 . 105 C5
Bankcroft Cl. BB12 .... 125 E8
Bankfield. Burnley BB10 .... 127 A6
Bankfield. Skelmersdale WN8 ... 9 C7
Bankfield Cl. FY5 .... 151 B8
Bankfield Gr. FY1 .... 129 E3
Bankfield La. PR9 .... 53 B2
Bankfield St. Bacup OL13 .... 69 D8
Bankfield St. Colne BB8 .... 169 B4
Bankfield St. Colne BB8 .... 170 B4
Bankfield Terr. 1 Bacup OL13 . 69 D8
Bankfield Terr.
  Barnoldswick BB8 .... 200 C3
Bankhouse La. BB9 .... 168 E1
Bankhouse St. Burnley BB11 . 126 F6
Bankhouse St. Burnley BB11 . 127 A6
Banks Bridge Cl. BB8 .... 200 C4
Banks Cres. LA3 .... 208 F6
Banks Head Rd. LA2 .... 233 D8
Banks Hill. BB8 .... 200 A4
Banks Meth Prim Sch. PR9 ...... 54 B7
Banks Rd. Fulwood PR2 .... 116 C3
Banks Rd. Southport PR9 .... 53 D6
Banks Rise. 4 LA2 .... 233 D8
Banks St. Lane Bottom BB10 . 148 B3
Banks Way. 3 LA2 .... 233 D8
Banksbarn. WN8 .... 9 C7
Banksfield Ave. PR2 .... 116 C3
Bankside Pl. PR5 .... 77 A7
Bankside. Blackburn BB2 ...... 100 E2
Bankside. Clayton Green PR6 ... 77 B1
Bankside. Hightown L38 .... 2 F3
Bankside. Penwortham WN8 ... 26 B2
Bankside Cl. OL13 .... 86 E1
Bankside La. OL13 .... 86 F2
Bankwood. WN6 .... 19 E6
Banner Cl. PR7 .... 40 B6
Bannerman Terr. PR4 .... 60 D2
Bannister Brow. L40 & WN8 ... 26 E6
Bannister Cl. Higher Walton PR5 . 97 B4
Bannister Cl. Trawden BB8 ... 170 B3
Bannister Ct. Blackpool FY2 .. 150 B4
Bannister Ct. 12 Nelson BB9 . 147 E8
Bannister Dr. PR5 .... 75 E1
Bannister Gn. PR7 .... 40 C3
Bannister Hall Cres. PR5 .... 97 B4
Bannister Hall Dr. PR5 .... 97 B4
Bannister Hall La. PR5 .... 97 B4
Bannister La. Eccleston PR7 .... 40 C5
Bannister La. Hill Dale L40 & WN8 . 26 E6
Bannister La. Leyland PR5 ...... 75 E4
Bannister St. 10 Chorley PR7 . 42 C7
Bannister St.
  Lytham St Anne's FY8 .... 90 B3
Bannister's Bit. PR1 .... 95 C2
Bannistre Ct. PR4 .... 56 A6
Bar St. BB10 .... 127 B8
Bar Terr. OL12 .... 51 C7
Barbara Castle Way.
  BB1 & BB2 .... 100 E5
Barberry Bank. BL7 .... 46 E2
Barbon Pl. LA1 .... 213 E2
Barbon St. Burnley BB10 ...... 147 C2
Barbon St. 12 Padiham BB12 . 145 C1
Barbrook Cl. WN6 .... 28 B2
Barclay Ave. Blackpool FY4 .. 129 F2
Barclay Ave. Burnley BB11 ... 126 C4
Barclay Rd. PR3 .... 139 A7
Barcroft Gn. BB10 .... 127 E1
Barcroft St. BB8 .... 169 C5
Barden Croft. BB5 .... 123 F4
Barden High Sch. BB10 .... 147 A1
Barden Jun Sch. BB10 .... 147 A1
Barden La. BB10 & BB12 ...... 147 A2
Barden Pl. PR2 .... 117 D1
Barden Rd. BB5 .... 102 F4
Barden St. BB10 .... 147 B1
Barden View. BB10 .... 147 A2
Bardsea Pl. PR2 .... 115 F3
Bardsley Cl. WN8 .... 10 A7
Bardsway. FY5 .... 173 A3
Bardsway Ave. FY3 .... 129 F6
Bare Ave. LA4 .... 213 A6
Bare La. LA4 .... 213 A5
Bare Lane Sta. LA4 .... 213 A6
Barford Cl. Ainsdale PR8 .... 20 A6
Barford Cl. Hall Green WN8 ... 10 A7
Barford Gr. BB12 .... 31 F1
Bargee Cl. BB1 .... 100 F3
Barker Brow. BB1 & PR3 ...... 141 A3
Barker Cl. LA6 .... 234 B7
Barker La. BB1 & BB2 .... 121 C2
Barkerford Cl. BB12 .... 145 F5
Barkerhouse Rd.
  Nelson BB10 & BB9 .... 148 B8
Barkerhouse Rd. 16
  Nelson BB9 .... 168 E1
Barkfield Ave. L37 .... 11 E4
Barkfield La. L37 .... 11 D4
Barley Bank St. BB3 .... 80 F2
Barley Cl. BB2 .... 100 D5
Barley Cop La. LA1 .... 213 D4
Barley Gr. BB10 .... 127 C6
Barley Holme Rd. BB4 .... 85 A8
Barley La.
  Barley BB12 & BB9 & BB7 .. 167 B7
Barley La. Blackburn BB2 ...... 100 D5
Barley Rd. BB12 .... 167 E5
Barley St. BB12 .... 125 C7
Barley Way. BB2 .... 100 D5
Barleydale Rd. BB9 .... 168 E5
Barleyfield. PR5 & PR6 .... 77 C3
Barlow Cres. FY3 .... 129 E4
Barlow Rd. BB3 .... 47 E5
Barlow St. Accrington BB5 .... 103 A6
Barlow St. Bacup OL13 .... 69 B7
Barlow St. Bury BL9 .... 32 A2
Barlow St. Horwich BL6 .... 31 C2
Barlow St. Preston PR1 .... 116 E1
Barlow St. Preston PR1 .... 116 E1
Barlow St. 11 Rawtenstall BB4 . 85 A3
Barlow's La. L39 .... 21 D5
Barlows Bldgs. 4 BB4 .... 84 F1
Barmouth Ave. FY3 .... 130 A3
Barmouth Cres. BB1 .... 121 E1
Barmskin La. PR7 .... 40 B2
Barn Acre. BL6 .... 30 E1
Barn Cl. PR4 .... 55 A2
Barn Croft. Leyland PR5 .... 75 B1
Barn Croft. Penwortham PR1 ... 95 B4
Barn Gill Cl. BB1 .... 100 F3
Barn Hey. PR4 .... 94 A1
Barn Hey Rd. L33 .... 1 A2
Barn Meadow. Clayton Brook PR5 . 77 B6
Barn Meadow. Edgworth BL7 ... 47 D5
Barn Meadow Cres. BB1 ...... 123 C1
Barnacre Cl. Fulwood PR2 .... 117 A8
Barnacre Cl. Lancaster LA1 .. 211 B2
Barnacre Rd. PR3 .... 139 A8
Barnard Cl. BB5 .... 102 C4
Barnbrook St. BL9 .... 32 A3
Barncroft Dr. BL6 .... 31 F3
Barnes Ave. BB4 .... 84 F2
Barnes Cl. BL0 .... 49 A3
Barnes Dr. L31 .... 5 C3
Barnes Rd. Morecambe LA3 .. 212 B3
Barnes Rd. Ormskirk L39 .... 15 E3
Barnes Rd. Skelmersdale WN8 . 17 E1
Barnes Sq. 1 BB5 .... 123 F2
Barnes St. Accrington BB5 .... 103 C6
Barnes St. Burnley BB11 ...... 127 A6
Barnes St. Church BB5 .... 102 E6
Barnes St. Clayton-le-M BB5 . 123 F3
Barnes St. Haslingden BB4 ..... 84 B4
Barnfield. Bamber Bridge PR5 . 76 A8
Barnfield. Kirkham PR4 .... 113 A5
Barnfield. Much Hoole PR4 .... 73 E3
Barnfield Bsns Ctr. BB9 .... 147 F6
Barnfield Cl. Egerton BL7 .... 46 E2
Barnfield Cl. 4 Thornton FY5 . 172 F4
Barnfield Dr. WN8 .... 9 E7
Barnfield Manor. FY6 .... 152 D3
Barnfield St. Accrington BB5 . 103 D5
Barnmeadow La. BB6 .... 123 C5
Barnoldswick CE Prim Sch.
  BB8 .... 200 B2
Barnoldswick La. LA6 .... 236 D3
Barnoldswick Rd.
  Beverley BB8 & BB9 .... 168 F7
Barnoldswick Rd. Kelbrook BB8 . 191 F6
Barns La. PR3 .... 159 C8
Barns The. L37 .... 12 A1
Barnsfold. PR2 .... 116 D6
Barnside. Euxton PR7 .... 59 C3
Barnside. Whitworth OL12 .... 51 B8
Barnside Est. BB8 .... 170 F7
Barnwood Cres. BB8 .... 201 C1
Barnwood Rd. BB8 .... 201 B1
Baron Rd. FY1 .... 129 C1
Baron St. Darwen BB3 .... 80 F2
Baron St. Rawtenstall BB4 ..... 85 D1
Barons Cl. BB3 .... 81 A7
Barons Way. Blackburn BB3 ... 81 A6
Barons Way. Euxton PR7 .... 59 D2
Barracks Rd. BB11 .... 126 D6
Barracks The. L39 .... 22 C2
Barret Hill Brow. BB7 .... 224 B4
Barret St. BB8 .... 201 A1
Barrett Ave. PR8 .... 34 A2
Barrett Rd. 5 BL9 .... 32 A2
Barrett Rd. PR8 .... 34 A2
Barrington Dr. PR8 .... 20 B5
Barrington Gn. L40 .... 23 D2
Barritt Rd. BB4 .... 84 F2
Barronwood Ct. PR4 .... 56 A5
Barrow Nook La. L39 .... 7 E2
Barrow (VC) Prim Sch. BB7 .. 164 D2
Barrow's St. PR3 .... 154 B5
Barrowdale Ave. BB9 .... 147 F2
Barrowdale Rd. Barrowford BB9 . 168 B1
Barrowford Rd. Colne BB8 ... 169 B5
Barrowford Rd.
  Fence BB12 & BB9 .... 146 C7
Barrows La. LA3 .... 208 E7
Barrows La E. PR3 .... 154 B5
Barry Ave. PR2 .... 116 A3
Barry Gr. LA3 .... 208 F6
Barry St. BB12 .... 126 C7
Bartle La. PR4 .... 115 C7
Bartle Pl. PR2 .... 115 E1
Bartle Rd. FY8 .... 89 A8
Bartle St. BB11 .... 126 D5
Barton Ave. Blackpool FY1 ... 129 B2
Barton Ave. Knott End-on-S FY6 . 194 E5
Barton & Broughton Sta. PR3 . 136 B5
Barton Gdns. LA1 .... 211 B5
Barton La. PR3 .... 136 E7
Barton Mansion. FY8 .... 88 C7
Barton Rd. Lancaster LA1 ..... 211 A4
Barton Rd. Lytham St Anne's FY8 . 88 D8
Barton Sq. FY6 .... 194 E5
Barton St. BB2 .... 100 E5
Barton Streety. BB2 .... 100 E5
Bashall Gr. PR5 .... 76 B3
Basil St. Colne BB8 .... 169 D4
Basil St. Preston PR1 .... 117 C2
Basnett St. BB10 .... 147 C1
Bass La. BL9 .... 49 D3
Bassenthwaite Rd. FY3 .... 130 C2
Bassett Way. OL12 .... 51 E2
Bastwell Rd. BB1 .... 100 F7
Bateman Gr. LA4 .... 212 A6
Bateman Rd. LA4 .... 212 E5
Bateman St. BL6 .... 31 D2
Bates St. BB5 .... 123 E3
Bath Mill La. LA1 .... 211 A8
Bath Mill Sq. 7 LA1 .... 211 A8
Bath Rd. FY8 .... 90 B3
Bath Springs. L39 .... 15 F5
Bath St. Accrington BB5 ...... 103 B4
Bath St. Blackburn BB2 .... 100 C4
Bath St. Blackpool FY4 .... 129 B1
Bath St. Colne BB8 .... 169 E5
Bath St. Darwen BB3 .... 81 A1
Bath St. Lytham St Anne's FY8 . 90 B3
Bath St. Morecambe LA4 ...... 212 D5
Bath St. Nelson BB9 .... 147 F8
Bath St. Preston PR1 .... 116 D1
Bath St. Southport PR8 .... 34 B8
Bath St N. PR8 & PR9 .... 34 B8
Bathurst Ave. FY3 .... 130 A7
Bathurst St. BB2 .... 100 D5
Batridge Rd. BL7 .... 47 A7
Battersby St. BL9 .... 32 D3
Battismore Rd. LA4 .... 212 E5
Battle Way. L37 .... 12 B2
Bawdlands. BB7 .... 164 D8
Bawhead Rd. BB8 .... 201 B1
Baxenden CE Prim Sch. BB5 . 103 E1
Baxenden Golf Course. BB5 . 103 F3
Baxter St. WN6 .... 28 F1
Baxtergate. LA4 .... 212 E6
Bay Cl. LA3 .... 208 D6
Bay Horse Dr. LA1 .... 211 B3
Bay Horse La. PR4 .... 134 D4
Bay Horse Rd. LA2 .... 207 E4
Bay Rd. Fulwood PR2 .... 117 E2
Bay Rd. Heysham LA3 .... 208 D6
Bay St. BB1 .... 101 A7
Bay The. FY5 .... 172 C5
Bay View. LA6 .... 231 B8
Bay View Ave. LA2 .... 213 E8
Bay View Cres. LA2 .... 213 E8
Bayard St. BB12 .... 126 A6
Baycliffe Cres. LA4 .... 212 D5
Bayley Fold. BB7 .... 164 E8
Bayley St. BB5 .... 123 E3
Baylton Ct. PR3 .... 178 D2
Baylton Dr. PR3 .... 178 D2
Baynes St. BB3 .... 81 F1
Bayswater. FY2 .... 150 C4
Baytree Cl. Bamber Bridge PR5 . 76 C8
Baytree Cl. Southport PR9 ...... 53 D5
Baytree Gr. BL0 .... 49 B2
Baytree Wlk. OL12 .... 70 C1
Baywood St. BB1 .... 100 F7
Bazil Gr. LA3 .... 205 D7
Bazil La. LA3 .... 205 D7
Bazley Rd. FY8 .... 89 D3
Beach Ave. Cleveleys FY5 .... 172 D3
Beach Ave. Lytham St Anne's FY8 . 89 C3
Beach Priory Gdns. PR8 .... 34 A6
Beach Rd. Cleveleys FY5 ...... 172 D3
Beach Rd. Fleetwood FY7 ..... 193 E3
Beach Rd. Lytham St Anne's FY8 .. 88 D7
Beach Rd. Pilling Lane PR3 ... 195 B7
Beach Rd. Southport PR8 .... 33 F6
Beach St. Lytham St Anne's FY8 . 90 A3
Beach St. Morecambe LA4 .... 213 A4
Beach Terr. LA6 .... 236 F3
Beacham Rd. PR8 .... 34 E7
Beachcomber Dr. FY5 .... 172 C3
Beachley Rd. PR2 .... 116 A4
Beachley Sq. BB12 .... 126 D7
Beachmews. PR8 .... 33 F6
Beachwood La. LA5 .... 237 A1
Beacon Ave. PR2 .... 116 D5
Beacon Crossing. WN8 .... 26 C2
Beacon Cty Pk. WN8 .... 18 E2

Beacon Dr. PR3 137 D6
Beacon Fell Ctry Pk. PR3 180 F2
Beacon Gr. Fulwood PR2 116 D4
Beacon Gr. Garstang PR3 178 B6
Beacon La. L40 & WN8 18 D4
Beacon Rd. Poulton-le-F FY6 152 A3
Beacon Rd. Shevington Moor WN6 28 B2
Beacon St. PR6 & PR7 42 D7
Beacon View. WN6 19 C8
Beacon View Dr. WN8 10 B7
Beacons The. WN6 19 D7
Beaconsfield Ave. PR1 117 E1
Beaconsfield Rd. PR9 34 F6
Beaconsfield St. Accrington BB5 103 D5
Beaconsfield St. Great Harwood BB6 123 C5
Beaconsfield St. 13 Haslingden BB4 84 B3
Beaconsfield Terr. Catterall PR3 178 E2
Beaconsfield Terr. Chorley PR6 60 D2
Beale Rd. BB9 147 B8
Beamont Dr. PR1 & PR2 95 D8
Bean Ave. FY4 109 E8
Bear St. BB12 125 F6
Beardshaw Ave. FY1 129 D2
Beardsworth St. BB1 101 A7
Beardwood. BB2 100 A8
Beardwood Brow. BB2 100 B7
Beardwood Dr. BB2 100 A7
Beardwood Meadow. BB2 100 A7
Beardwood Pk. BB2 100 B7
Bearncroft. WN8 9 D6
Bearswood Croft. PR6 77 B2
Beatie St. BB9 147 B6
Beatrice Ave. BB12 126 C7
Beatrice Mews. 9 BL6 31 B4
Beatrice Pl. BB2 81 A8
Beattock Pl. FY2 150 F6
Beatty Ave. PR7 42 B6
Beatty Cl. FY8 109 D1
Beatty Rd. PR8 34 E5
Beauclerk Rd. FY8 89 B6
Beaufort. L37 12 A2
Beaufort Ave. FY2 150 C5
Beaufort Cl. BB12 144 E2
Beaufort Gr. LA4 212 G5
Beaufort Rd. Morecambe LA4 213 A5
Beaufort Rd. Weir OL13 87 A7
Beaufort St. Nelson BB9 147 E7
Beaufort St. Spotland Fold OL12 51 C1
Beauley Ave. BB12 144 E2
Beaumaris Ave. BB2 100 A1
Beaumaris Cl. 2 BB4 84 B1
Beaumaris Rd. PR5 59 C8
Beaumont Ave. BL6 31 C4
Beaumont Coll (The Spastics Society). LA1 213 F4
Beaumont Cres. L39 15 D2
Beaumont Gdns. FY6 151 A5
Beaumont Pl. LA1 213 F4
Beaumont Rd. BL6 31 C4
Beaumont St. LA1 213 F4
Beaver Cl. BB1 121 F5
Beaver Terr. 13 OL13 87 A3
Beavers La. WN8 9 D6
Bebles Rd. L39 15 C3
Becconsall La. PR4 72 F3
Beck Ct. FY7 193 D1
Beck Gr. FY5 172 E4
Beck Side. LA2 231 C3
Beck View. 7 LA1 213 A3
Beckdean Ave. FY6 151 D2
Beckenham Ct. BB10 147 D3
Beckett Ct. 19 PR1 95 F8
Beckett St. 4 BB3 64 A8
Becks Brow. BD23 230 F3
Beckside. BB12 167 C5
Beckside Mews. LA6 234 B3
Beckway Ave. FY3 129 F7
Bective Rd. LA6 238 C2
Bedale Pl. FY5 172 E1
Beddington St. 5 BB9 168 D1
Bedford Ave. FY5 172 D3
Bedford Cl. BB5 102 C4
Bedford Pl. Lancaster LA1 211 A4
Bedford Pl. Padiham BB12 125 D7
Bedford Rd. Blackpool FY1 129 C8
Bedford Rd. Fulwood PR2 117 A4
Bedford Rd. Lytham St Anne's FY8 90 D4
Bedford Rd. Southport PR8 34 A2
Bedford St. 6 Barrowford BB9 168 C1
Bedford St. Blackburn BB2 100 C2
Bedford St. Darwen BB3 80 F4
Bedford St. Egerton BL7 46 D2
Bedford Terr. Bury BL9 32 A4
Bedford Terr. Haslingden BB4 67 A8
Bedfordshire Ave. BB12 126 B7
Bee La. PR1 & PR5 95 E1
Beech Ave. Adlington PR6 30 B8
Beech Ave. Bilsborrow PR3 157 A5
Beech Ave. Blackpool FY3 129 E5
Beech Ave. Darwen BB3 81 B2
Beech Ave. Earby BB8 201 A1
Beech Ave. Euxton PR7 59 C4
Beech Ave. Galgate LA2 206 F4
Beech Ave. Horwich BL6 31 E1
Beech Ave. Kirkham PR4 113 B4
Beech Ave. Leyland PR5 59 A7
Beech Ave. Parbold WN8 26 C2
Beech Ave. Poulton-le-F FY6 151 D4
Beech Ave. Warton PR4 91 D6
Beech Cl. Bacup OL13 87 A3
Beech Cl. Clitheroe BB7 164 D8
Beech Cl. Oswaldtwistle BB5 102 C2
Beech Cl. Rishton BB1 102 B8
Beech Cl. Rufford L40 38 C4
Beech Cl. Skelmersdale WN8 17 E1
Beech Cl. Whitworth OL12 70 C1
Beech Cl. Wilpshire BB1 121 E6
Beech Cres. BB5 124 A1
Beech Dr. Formby L37 11 D4
Beech Dr. Freckleton PR4 92 A5
Beech Dr. Fulwood PR2 116 D8
Beech Dr. Haslingden BB4 84 C2
Beech Dr. Longridge PR3 139 A7
Beech Dr. Newton-with-S PR4 113 F2
Beech Dr. Poulton-le-F FY6 151 D2
Beech Gdns. PR6 77 B1
Beech Gr. Accrington BB5 103 A4
Beech Gr. Barnoldswick BB8 200 C2
Beech Gr. Brierfield BB10 147 C4
Beech Gr. Chatburn BB7 187 D5
Beech Gr. Darwen BB3 80 D6
Beech Gr. Knott End-on-S FY6 194 E6
Beech Gr. Morecambe LA4 213 A5
Beech Gr. Preston PR1 116 B1
Beech Gr. Ramsbottom BL8 49 A1
Beech Gr. Southport PR9 34 F7
Beech Gr. Warton LA5 217 D5
Beech Grove Cl. BL9 32 B4
Beech Hill Cl. PR5 96 E3
Beech Ind Est. 3 OL13 87 A3
Beech Meadow. L39 16 A4
Beech Mount. BB1 121 F3
Beech Rd. Elswick PR4 153 F1
Beech Rd. Garstang PR3 178 B8
Beech Rd. Halton LA2 214 E7
Beech Rd. Holt Green L39 6 A6
Beech Rd. Leyland PR5 76 A2
Beech St. Accrington BB5 103 C5
Beech St. Bacup OL13 87 A3
Beech St. Barnoldswick BB8 200 B1
Beech St. Blackburn BB1 101 A7
Beech St. Bury BL9 32 B2
Beech St. Clayton-le-M BB5 123 F1
Beech St. Clitheroe BB7 164 D8
Beech St. Edgworth BL7 47 D5
Beech St. Great Harwood BB6 123 C6
Beech St. Lancaster LA1 210 D8
Beech St. 10 Nelson BB9 168 E1
Beech St. Padiham BB12 125 D7
Beech St. Preston PR1 95 D6
Beech St. Ramsbottom BL0 49 C3
Beech St. Rawtenstall BB4 85 A3
Beech St S. PR1 95 E6
Beech Terr. PR1 95 E6
Beech Tree Ave. WN6 19 D8
Beech Tree Cl. BB9 147 E7
Beech Tree Sch. PR5 77 B4
Beechacre. BL0 49 D5
Beecham St. LA4 212 E6
Beechcroft. Cleveleys FY5 172 C4
Beechcroft. Maghull L31 5 D1
Beeches The. Clayton Green PR6 77 C3
Beeches The. Singleton FY6 152 D1
Beeches The. Tarleton PR4 56 A7
Beechfield. Hill Dale WN8 26 C5
Beechfield. Lancaster LA1 210 D7
Beechfield. Maghull L31 5 E1
Beechfield Ave. Blackpool FY3 129 E3
Beechfield Ave. Knott End-on-S FY6 195 A5
Beechfield Ave. Wrea Green PR4 112 C4
Beechfield Ct. PR5 59 B8
Beechfield Gdns. PR8 33 F6
Beechfield Mews. PR9 34 C7
Beechfield Rd. PR5 59 B8
Beechfields. PR7 40 B6
Beeching Cl. LA1 210 F6
Beechthorpe Ave. BB7 186 B4
Beechtrees. WN8 9 D7
Beechway. Fulwood PR2 117 A4
Beechway. Moss Side L31 6 B2
Beechway. Penwortham PR1 95 B3
Beechway Ave. L31 6 B2
Beechwood. WN8 18 C3
Beechwood Ave. Accrington BB5 103 D3
Beechwood Ave. Bamber Bridge PR5 96 D4
Beechwood Ave. Burnley BB11 126 F3
Beechwood Ave. Clitheroe BB7 164 E6
Beechwood Ave. Fulwood PR2 116 C4
Beechwood Ave. Ramsbottom BL0 49 D6
Beechwood Ave. Shevington WN6 19 F5
Beechwood Cres. WN5 10 E6
Beechwood Croft. PR6 77 A3
Beechwood Ct. Maghull L31 5 F1
Beechwood Ct. Skelmersdale WN8 9 D6
Beechwood Dr. Blackburn BB2 79 E8
Beechwood Dr. Formby L37 11 C1
Beechwood Dr. Ormskirk L39 15 D5
Beechwood Dr. Thornton FY5 151 B8
Beechwood Gdns. LA1 211 A2
Beechwood Gr. FY2 150 E4
Beechwood Mews. BB1 81 A8
Beechwood Rd. 9 Blackburn BB1 101 A7
Beechwood Rd. Chorley PR7 42 D6
Beenland St. 3 PR1 117 D1
Beeston Ave. FY6 151 C5
Beetham Ct. BB5 123 E2
Beetham Pl. FY3 129 E6
Begonia St. BB3 81 B1
Beightons Wlk. OL12 51 D4
Bela Cl. 3 LA1 213 C2
Bela Gr. FY1 129 D2
Belfield. WN8 9 D6
Belfield Rd. BB5 103 C4
Belford Ave. FY5 172 F4
Belford St. BB12 126 F7
Belfry Cres. WN6 28 F2
Belfry The. FY8 90 D5
Belgarth Rd. BB5 103 C7
Belgrave Ave. Kirkham PR4 113 A7
Belgrave Ave. Penwortham PR1 95 B3
Belgrave Cl. Blackburn BB2 100 B3
Belgrave Cl. Lytham St Anne's FY8 89 D6
Belgrave Cres. BL6 31 D3
Belgrave Ct. BB12 126 F7
Belgrave Pl. Poulton-le-F FY6 151 B2
Belgrave Pl. Southport PR8 33 F3
Belgrave Rd. Blackpool FY4 129 E1
Belgrave Rd. Colne BB8 169 D6
Belgrave Rd. Darwen BB3 64 A8
Belgrave Rd. 5 Leyland PR5 76 A1
Belgrave Rd. Poulton-le-F FY6 151 B3
Belgrave Rd. Southport PR8 33 F3
Belgrave Sq. 9 BB3 81 A1
Belgrave St. 5 Brierfield BB9 147 A6
Belgrave St. Burnley BB12 126 F7
Belgrave St. Haslingden BB5 84 A8
Belgrave St. Nelson BB9 168 F1
Belgrave St. Spotland Fold OL12 51 D1
Bell La. Bury BL9 32 A3
Bell La. Claughton PR3 179 C4
Bell La. Clayton-le-M BB5 124 B4
Bell St. BB4 84 B3
Bell's Cl. L31 5 C4
Bell's La. L31 5 B3
Bell-Aire Park Homes. LA3 208 F5
Bellamy Ave. LA4 212 D3
Belle Isle Ave. OL12 51 C6
Belle Vue Ave. LA1 211 A5
Belle Vue Dr. LA1 211 A5
Belle Vue La. BB7 186 B4
Belle Vue Pl. BB11 126 E6
Belle Vue St. Blackburn BB2 100 C5
Belle Vue St. Burnley BB11 126 E6
Bellfield Rd. LA4 212 F5
Bellingham Rd. FY8 90 B4
Bellis Ave. PR9 52 F2
Bells La. PR5 97 E3
Belmont Ave. Blackpool FY1 129 C4
Belmont Ave. Fulwood PR2 117 D2
Belmont Ave. Orrell WN5 10 D3
Belmont Ave. Poulton-le-F FY6 151 B3
Belmont Cl. Brinscall PR6 61 E8
Belmont Cl. Burscough L40 24 E3
Belmont Cl. Fulwood PR2 117 D2
Belmont Cl. Lancaster LA1 213 D3
Belmont Cres. PR2 117 D2
Belmont Ct. PR3 139 B7
Belmont Dr. PR6 60 E1
Belmont Gr. BB10 127 D5
Belmont Pl. PR7 28 C6
Belmont Rd. Adlington PR6 30 B7
Belmont Rd. Belmont PR7 & BL7 63 A2
Belmont Rd. Fleetwood FY7 194 A3
Belmont Rd. Fulwood PR2 116 C2
Belmont Rd. Great Harwood BB6 123 B5
Belmont Rd. Horwich BL6 31 C7
Belmont Rd. Leyland PR5 58 D8
Belmont Rd. Lytham St Anne's FY8 89 C5
Belmont Rd. Rivington BL6 44 C3
Belmont Sch. BB4 84 E2
Belmont St. PR8 34 A5
Belmont Terr. 6 Barrowford BB9 168 D3
Belmont Terr. Foulridge BB8 191 E1
Belmont Way. OL12 51 E2
Belper St. BB1 101 A6
Belsfield Dr. PR4 72 E4
Belshaw Ct. BB11 126 A3
Belthorn CE Prim Sch. BB1 81 F6
Belthorn Rd. BB1 81 E6
Belton Hill. PR2 116 D8
Belvedere Ave. Ramsbottom BL8 49 A1
Belvedere Ave. Rawtenstall BB4 86 A1
Belvedere Ct. FY8 89 D4
Belvedere Dr. Chorley PR7 42 B8
Belvedere Dr. Formby L37 11 D1
Belvedere Pk. L39 6 C7
Belvedere Rd. Adlington PR6 30 B8
Belvedere Rd. Ainsdale PR8 20 C5
Belvedere Rd. Blackburn BB1 122 A3
Belvedere Rd. Burnley BB10 & BB11 127 B6
Belvedere Rd. 2 Leyland PR5 76 B2
Belvedere Rd. Thornton FY5 151 C8
Belverdale Gdns. FY4 109 F5
Belvere Ave. FY4 109 D6
Belvoir St. OL12 51 C1
Ben La. Barnoldswick BB8 200 D3
Ben La. Barrow Nook L39 8 A1
Benbow Cl. FY8 109 D2
Bence Rd. PR1 96 B6
Bence St. BB8 169 E5
Bench Carr. OL12 51 E1
Benenden Pl. FY5 173 A2
Bengal St. PR6 60 D1
Bengarth Rd. PR9 34 F8
Benjamin Hargreaves CE Prim Sch. BB5 103 D5
Bennett Ave. FY1 129 C4
Bennett Rd. FY5 173 A3
Bennett St. 2 BB9 168 F2
Bennett's La. FY4 109 F6
Bennington St. BB1 & BB2 100 F3
Benson Ave. LA4 212 G4
Benson House. BB1 101 C8
Benson La. PR4 134 F3
Benson Rd. FY2 150 E1
Benson St. Blackburn BB1 101 B7
Benson St. Bury BL9 32 A1
Benson St. Edgworth BL7 47 E5
Benson's La. PR3 & PR4 156 C1
Bent Est. OL13 87 A7
Bent Gap La. BB2 100 C4
Bent La. Colne BB8 170 B6
Bent La. Gisburn BB7 225 C3
Bent La. Leyland PR5 & PR6 59 C8
Bent St. Blackburn BB2 100 D4
Bent St. Haslingden BB4 67 D8
Bent St. Oswaldtwistle BB5 102 D3
Bentgate Cl. BB4 67 D8
Bentham Ave. Burnley BB10 147 B3
Bentham Ave. Fleetwood FY7 193 A1
Bentham Cl. BB2 100 B1
Bentham Moor Rd. LA6 236 D2
Bentham Pl. WN6 28 F2
Bentham Rd. Barnoldswick LA6 236 E3
Bentham Rd. Blackburn BB2 100 B1
Bentham Rd. Lancaster LA1 211 A2
Bentham Rd. Standish WN6 28 F2
Bentham Sch. LA2 233 B8
Bentham St. Coppull PR7 41 E1
Bentham St. Southport PR8 34 B5
Bentham Sta. LA2 233 D7
Bentham's Way. PR8 34 C2
Bentinck Ave. FY4 109 B5
Bentinck Rd. FY8 88 C8
Bentinck St. 9 OL12 51 C1
Bentlea Rd. BB7 225 C3
Bentley Dr. Kirkham PR4 112 E5
Bentley Dr. Peel Hill FY4 111 A6
Bentley La. Andertons Mill L40 & PR7 40 A1
Bentley La. Baldingstone BL9 50 A1
Bentley La. Bispham Green L40 26 E8
Bentley Park Rd. PR4 73 F7
Bentley St. 8 Bacup OL13 86 F3
Bentley St. Blackburn BB1 101 C5
Bentley St. Darwen BB3 64 C7
Bentley St. Falinge Fold OL12 51 E2
Bentley St. Nelson BB9 147 D7
Bentmeadows. OL12 51 E1
Benton Rd. PR2 117 D4
Bents. BB8 170 B6
Bents La. LA6 238 F5
Bentwood Rd. BB4 84 A3
Beresford Dr. PR9 52 F1
Beresford Gdns. PR9 52 F2
Beresford Rd. BB1 100 D7
Beresford St. Blackpool FY1 129 C7
Beresford St. 6 Burnley BB11 126 D6
Beresford St. Nelson BB9 147 F6
Bergen St. BB11 126 B5
Berkeley Cl. Chorley PR7 42 D5
Berkeley Cl. Nelson BB9 147 E7
Berkeley Cres. BB12 145 C1
Berkeley Dr. Clayton-le-W PR5 76 E4
Berkeley Dr. Simonstone BB12 144 E2
Berkeley St. Brierfield BB9 147 A5
Berkeley St. Nelson BB9 147 E7
Berkeley St. Preston PR1 116 E1
Berkley Cl. PR4 112 E5
Berkshire Ave. BB12 126 B7
Berkshire Cl. BB1 121 F7
Bernard St. OL12 51 E3
Berne Ave. BL6 31 A3
Berridge Ave. BB12 126 A6
Berriedale Rd. BB9 169 A1
Berry Cl. WN8 17 F2
Berry Field. PR1 95 C3
Berry House Rd. L40 37 A4
Berry La. PR3 139 A7
Berry St. Bamber Bridge PR5 76 A8
Berry St. Brierfield BB9 147 B5
Berry St. Burnley BB11 126 F4
Berry St. Preston PR1 96 A7
Berry St. Skelmersdale WN8 17 F2
Berry's La. FY6 151 C4
Berrys La. BB7 143 C1
Bertha St. BB5 103 D6
Bertram Ave. LA4 212 D4
Bertrand Ave. FY3 130 A7
Berwick Ave. Ainsdale PR8 20 D5
Berwick Ave. Cleveleys FY5 172 F4
Berwick Dr. Burnley BB12 126 E7
Berwick Dr. Fulwood PR2 116 D4
Berwick Rd. Blackpool FY4 109 C5
Berwick Rd. Lytham St Anne's FY8 88 F7
Berwick Rd. Preston PR1 96 A6
Berwick St. PR1 117 E1
Berwick Way. LA3 208 E7
Berwyn Ave. LA4 212 G6
Berwyn Cl. BL6 31 C5
Berwyn Ct. PR8 34 D4
Beryl Ave. Blackburn BB1 121 F2
Beryl Ave. Cleveleys FY5 172 E1
Bescar Brow La. L40 22 F7
Bescar La. L40 & PR9 36 B1
Bessie St. BB8 200 B2
Bessie's Well Pl. WN6 28 F1
Best St. PR4 112 F5
Bethel Ave. FY2 150 D4
Bethel Rd. BB1 101 A7
Bethel St. Barnoldswick BB8 200 B3
Bethel St. Colne BB8 169 B4
Bethesda Cl. BB2 100 D3
Bethesda Rd. FY1 129 B3
Bethesda St. Barnoldswick BB8 200 B2
Bethesda St. Burnley BB11 126 F6
Betony. LA4 213 B7
Betony Cl. OL12 51 D3
Bett La. PR6 78 C1
Beulah Ave. LA4 212 G5
Bevan Pl. BB9 168 F2
Beverley Ave. Longshaw WN5 10 E1
Beverley Ave. Poulton-le-F FY6 130 D8
Beverley Cl. Clitheroe BB7 164 E6
Beverley Cl. Preston PR1 95 C8
Beverley Cl. Southport PR9 53 C5
Beverley Cl. Wrea Green PR4 112 A3
Beverley Dr. BB7 164 D6
Beverley Gr. FY4 109 C7
Beverley Rd. BB9 168 E8
Beverley Rd N. FY8 89 A8
Beverley Rd S. FY8 89 A8
Beverley St. Blackburn BB2 100 B1
Beverley St. Burnley BB11 126 E5
Beverly Cl. FY5 151 B8
Bewcastle Dr. L40 16 C3
Bexhill Rd. PR2 116 A4
Bexley Ave. FY3 129 D8
Bexley Pl. FY8 89 E5
Bezza La. BB2 119 C5
Bhailok St. 3 PR1 95 E8
Bibby Dr. FY3 130 E5
Bibby Rd. PR9 53 A1
Bibby's La. FY2 150 E3
Bickerstaffe CE Sch. L39 7 E5
Bickerstaffe St. FY1 129 B3
Bickerton Rd. PR8 33 F4
Bicknell St. BB1 100 E6
Bideford Ave. FY3 130 A6
Bidston St. PR1 96 E8
Big Fold. BL6 30 D2
Bigdale Dr. L33 1 A3
Biggins La. LA6 238 A1
Biggins Rd. LA6 238 B2
Billinge Ave. BB2 100 B5
Billinge Cl. BB2 100 B5
Billinge End. BB2 100 A6
Billinge End Rd. BB2 99 F5
Billinge High Sch. BB2 100 A6
Billinge Side. BB2 99 F5
Billinge St. BB1 101 B4
Billinge View. BB2 99 F2
Billings Hospl. WN5 10 D2
Billington Ave. BB4 85 A5
Billington Gdns. BB6 143 A4
Billington Rd. Burnley BB11 126 A3
Billington Rd. Burnley BB11 126 B4
Billington St. PR4 112 F6
Billington St E. PR4 112 F6
Bilsberry Cotts. BB7 162 F1
Bilsborough Hey. PR1 95 E2
Bilsborough Meadow. PR4 115 E3
Bilsborrow La. Bilsborrow PR3 157 C4
Bilsborrow La. Inglewhite PR3 157 F5
Binbrook Pl. PR7 42 A7
Binfold Croft. LA6 238 C1
Bingley Ave. FY3 129 F6
Binns St. BB4 85 A7
Binyon Ct. LA1 210 F6
Binyon Rd. LA1 210 F5
Birbeck Rd. L33 1 A3
Birbeck Wlk. 8 L33 1 A3
Birch Ave. Burscough L40 24 E4
Birch Ave. Clayton-le-W PR5 76 D3
Birch Ave. Cleveleys FY5 172 E2
Birch Ave. Euxton PR7 59 C4
Birch Ave. Galgate LA2 207 A4
Birch Ave. Haslingden BB4 84 C3
Birch Ave. Newton-with-S PR4 113 F3
Birch Ave. Penwortham PR1 95 A3
Birch Ave. Preston PR2 116 A2
Birch Cl. Huncoat BB5 124 E2
Birch Cl. Maghull L31 5 F1
Birch Cl. Tonacliffe OL12 51 C6
Birch Cres. Gregson Lane PR5 97 E1
Birch Cres. Oswaldtwistle BB5 102 F3
Birch Dr. LA5 218 C4
Birch Field. PR6 77 B3
Birch Gn. L37 11 D4
Birch Gr. Barrow BB7 164 D1
Birch Gr. Lancaster LA1 210 D8
Birch Gr. Ramsbottom BL0 49 A3
Birch Gr. Stalmine FY6 174 D7
Birch Green Rd. WN8 18 C3
Birch Hall Ave. BB3 80 D4
Birch Hall La. BB8 201 D2
Birch La. PR3 181 C1
Birch Rd. Chorley PR6 60 E2
Birch Rd. Coppull PR7 41 E1
Birch Rd. Garstang PR3 178 C8
Birch St. Accrington BB5 103 B6
Birch St. Bacup OL13 86 F3
Birch St. Fleetwood FY7 194 A4
Birch St. Lytham St Anne's FY8 90 C3
Birch St. Skelmersdale WN8 8 E8
Birch St. Southport PR8 34 B4
Birch Terr. BB5 103 D2
Birch Tree Gdns. FY3 130 B2
Birch Tree Way. 4 BL6 31 E1
Birch Way. FY6 151 C4
Birch Wlk. 1 BB1 101 B4
Birchbank Gdns. BB1 101 A7
Birches Rd. BL7 47 D4
Birches The. L37 11 E5
Birchfield. PR4 73 F4
Birchfield Ave. OL10 32 E1
Birchfield Dr. PR3 139 A8
Birchfield Way. L31 5 B5
Birchill Rd. L33 1 C2
Birchin La. PR6 77 D1
Birchover Cl. PR2 116 A5
Birchtree Ave. LA3 212 B1
Birchway Ave. FY3 129 E6
Birchwood. PR5 75 C1
Birchwood Ave. PR4 94 B1
Birchwood Cl. FY8 89 E4
Birchwood Dr. Coppull PR7 41 E2
Birchwood Dr. Fulwood PR2 116 D7
Birchwood Dr. Hambleton FY6 174 C2

Bird i' th' Hand Cotts. **2** L39 ... 15 E6
Bird St. Brierfield BB9 .... 147 B5
Bird St. Preston PR1 .... 95 D6
Birdy Brow. BB7 .... 163 A6
Birk St. PR1 .... 95 E7
Birkacre Brow. PR7 .... 41 F2
Birkacre Rd. PR7 .... 41 F4
Birkbeck Pl. FY7 .... 193 D2
Birkdale Ave. Blackpool FY2 ..... 150 E5
Birkdale Ave. Cleveleys FY7 ..... 172 E7
Birkdale Ave. Longton PR4 .... 73 F8
Birkdale Ave.
  Lytham St Anne's FY8 .... 109 F1
Birkdale Cl. Lancaster LA1 .... 213 D3
Birkdale Cl. Longton PR4 .... 73 F8
Birkdale Cl. Thornton FY5 .... 151 D8
Birkdale Cop. PR8 .... 34 E1
Birkdale Dr. PR2 .... 115 E2
Birkdale High Sch. PR8 .... 20 E7
Birkdale Prim Sch. PR8 .... 34 B3
Birkdale Sch for Hearing
  Impaired. PR8 .... 33 E4
Birkdale Sta. PR8 .... 33 E4
Birkdale Trad Est. PR8 .... 34 A2
Birkett Dr. PR1 & PR2 & PR5 .... 118 A3
Birkett Pl. PR5 .... 118 A3
Birkett Rd. BB5 .... 103 D7
Birkett's Pl. LA4 .... 212 F5
Birkey La. L37 .... 11 F2
Birklands Ave. LA4 .... 212 F4
Birkrig. WN8 .... 9 D6
Birks Brow. PR3 .... 160 D3
Birkside Way. FY4 .... 130 C1
Birkwith La. LA2 .... 233 C7
Birley Bank. PR1 .... 96 C8
Birley Cl. WN6 .... 19 F8
Birley Pl. BB10 .... 127 A8
Birley St. Blackburn BB1 .... 100 F5
Birley St. Blackburn BB1 .... 100 F6
Birley St. Blackpool FY1 .... 129 B5
Birley St. Kirkham PR4 .... 113 B5
Birley St. **30** Preston PR0 & PR1 .. 95 F8
Birley St. **1** Preston PR1 .... 96 A7
Birleywood. WN8 .... 9 D6
Birnam Gn. FY7 .... 193 E4
Birtle Rd. BL9 .... 32 E6
Birtwhistle Cl. BB9 .... 147 B5
Birtwhistle Fold. **7** BB8 .... 169 E5
Birtwistle Ave. BB8 .... 169 D6
Birtwistle Cl. BB8 .... 169 E5
Birtwistle Ct. BB8 .... 200 C1
Birtwistle Hyde Pk. **1** BB8 .... 169 D5
Birtwistle St. Accrington BB5 ... 103 C5
Birtwistle St. Bamber Bridge PR5 76 B7
Birtwistle St.
  Great Harwood BB6 .... 123 B5
Birtwistle Terr. BB6 .... 142 C1
Bisham Cl. BB3 .... 64 C8
Bishop Martin CE Prim Sch.
  WN8 .... 9 D6
Bishop Rawstorne CE High
  Sch The. PR5 .... 57 C2
Bishop St. Accrington BB5 .... 103 C5
Bishop St. Burnley BB10 .... 147 B1
Bishop St. Nelson BB9 .... 147 D8
Bishopdale Cl. BB2 .... 79 D7
Bishopdale Rd. LA1 .... 210 D7
Bishopgate. **14** PR1 .... 96 A8
Bishops David Sheppard CE Sch.
  PR9 .... 35 A7
Bishopsgate. LA1 .... 211 A4
Bishopstone Cl. BB2 .... 81 A8
Bishopsway. PR1 .... 95 D3
Bison Pl. PR5 .... 75 C2
Bispham Ave. PR5 .... 75 C1
Bispham Endowed CE Jun Sch.
  FY2 .... 150 D4
Bispham Hall Bsns Pk. WN5 ..... 10 C2
Bispham Rd. Blackpool FY3 ..... 129 E8
Bispham Rd. Blackpool FY3 ..... 150 D3
Bispham Rd. Blackpool FY2 ..... 150 F6
Bispham Rd.
  Carleton FY5 & FY6 .... 151 A6
Bispham Rd. Cleveleys FY5 ..... 172 C2
Bispham Rd. Nelson BB9 .... 147 E6
Bispham Rd. Southport PR9 ..... 34 F7
Bispham St. **24** PR1 .... 95 F8
Bittern Cl. FY3 .... 130 B6
Bivel St. BB12 .... 126 D6
Black Abbey St. BB5 .... 103 C5
Black Bull La. PR2 .... 116 D5
Black Croft. PR6 .... 77 B3
Black Dyke Rd. LA5 .... 237 C1
Black Horse St. Blackrod BL6 ... 30 C3
Black Horse St. Chorley PR7 .... 42 B6
Black House La. Chipping PR3 .. 182 B1
Black House La.
  Lane Bottom BB10 .... 148 D3
Black La. Nateby PR3 .... 177 A8
Black La. Shuttleworth BL0 .... 50 B7
Black Lane Ends. BB8 .... 192 F3
Black Moor Rd. L40 .... 39 A2
Black Moss La. Ormskirk L39 ..... 15 E3
Black Moss La. Scarisbrick L40 .. 22 D6
Black Moss Rd. BB9 & BB7 ..... 167 E8
Black Moss Sch. WN8 .... 17 D2
Black-a-Moor La. L39 .... 13 F2
Blackacre La. L39 & L40 .... 15 E8
Blackamoor Broadlands & Dame
  Evelyn Fox Special Schs. BB1 81 B8
Blackamoor Rd. BB1 .... 81 C8
Blackberry Hall Cres. LA3 ..... 209 A8
Blackberry Way. PR3 .... 95 B2
Blackburn Brow. PR6 .... 60 E3
Blackburn Coll. BB2 .... 100 D5

Blackburn & East Lancashire
  Royal Infmy. BB2 .... 100 D2
Blackburn Golf Course. BB2 .. 100 C7
Blackburn Old Rd.
  Blackburn BB1 .... 122 D3
Blackburn Old Rd. Egerton BL7 . 46 C4
Blackburn Old Rd.
  Great Harwood BB1 & BB6 .... 122 F5
Blackburn Rd. Accrington BB5 .. 103 A6
Blackburn Rd. Accrington BB5 .. 103 C6
Blackburn Rd. Blackburn BB1 .. 101 E8
Blackburn Rd. Clayton-le-M BB5 123 E1
Blackburn Rd. Darwen BB3 ...... 80 E4
Blackburn Rd. Egerton BL7 & BL1 46 C4
Blackburn Rd. Ewood Bridge BL0 67 D5
Blackburn Rd.
  Great Harwood BB1 & BB6 .... 123 C4
Blackburn Rd. Great Knowley PR6 60 E4
Blackburn Rd.
  Haslingden BB4 & BB5 .... 84 B5
Blackburn Rd. Higher Walton PR5 97 B3
Blackburn Rd.
  Higher Wheelton PR6 .... 78 C1
Blackburn Rd. Longridge PR3 .. 139 D7
Blackburn Rd.
  Oswaldtwistle BB5 & BB1 ...... 102 C5
Blackburn Rd. Padiham BB12 ... 125 A8
Blackburn Rd. Ribchester PR3 .. 140 E3
Blackburn Rd. Rishton BB1 ...... 123 A1
Blackburn Rd. Wheelton PR6 .... 60 F6
Blackburn Rd.
  Whittlestone Head BB3 & BL7 .. 65 B2
Blackburn St. Blackburn BB1 .. 100 E6
Blackburn St. **4** Burnley BB11 .. 126 C6
Blackburn St. Chorley PR6 & PR7 42 E7
Blackburn Sta. BB1 .... 100 F4
Blackcar La. L29 .... 4 B3
Blacker St. BB10 .... 147 A2
Blackfen Pl. FY3 .... 129 D8
Blackfield Rd. PR4 .... 92 B6
Blackgate La. Holmes PR4 .... 55 C3
Blackgate La. Tarleton PR4 ...... 55 E5
Blackhorse Ave. BL6 .... 30 C2
Blackhorse Cl. BL6 .... 30 C3
Blackhurst Rd. L31 .... 5 C5
Blackleach Ave. PR2 .... 138 D1
Blackleach La. PR4 .... 134 F1
Blacko Bar Rd. BB9 .... 168 B7
Blacko Prim Sch. BB9 .... 168 D8
Blackpool Airport. FY8 .... 109 D3
Blackpool & Fleetwood Tramway.
  FY2 .... 150 B2
Blackpool & Fleetwood
  Yacht Club. FY5 .... 151 F7
Blackpool & Fylde Coll.
  Blackpool FY2 .... 150 E6
Blackpool & Fylde Coll.
  Fleetwood FY7 .... 194 A4
Blackpool & Fylde Coll of F Ed.
  FY8 .... 88 E5
Blackpool North Sta. FY1 ...... 129 C6
Blackpool Old Rd.
  Little Eccleston PR3 .... 154 A5
Blackpool Old Rd.
  Poulton-le-F FY3 & FY6 .... 151 B2
Blackpool Rd. Blackpool FY2 .. 150 D4
Blackpool Rd. Blackpool FY1 .. 129 B5
Blackpool Rd. Clifton PR4 .... 93 F8
Blackpool Rd. Longridge PR3 .. 139 A7
Blackpool Rd.
  Lytham St Anne's FY8 .... 89 D5
Blackpool Rd.
  Newton-with-S PR4 .... 114 B2
Blackpool Rd. Preston PR2 ..... 115 E1
Blackpool Rd.
  Preston PR1 & PR2 & PR4 .... 116 C2
Blackpool Rd.
  St Michael's on W PR3 .... 155 B6
Blackpool Rd. Wrea Green PR4 112 C6
Blackpool Rd N. FY8 .... 109 F2
Blackpool Sixth Form Coll The.
  FY3 .... 151 A2
Blackpool South Sta. FY4 ...... 129 B1
Blackpool St. **6** Church BB5 .. 102 E5
Blackpool St. Darwen BB3 .... 64 B6
Blackpool & The Fylde Coll.
  FY1 .... 129 C4
Blackpool & The Fylde Coll.
  FY1 .... 129 D4
Blackpool & The Fylde Coll.
  FY7 .... 172 E7
Blackpool & The Fylde Coll
  Ansdell Campus. FY8 .... 89 C5
Blackrod Brow. BL6 .... 30 B4
Blackrod By-Pass Rd. BL6 .... 30 D2
Blacksnape Rd. BB3 .... 81 D2
Blackstone Rd. FY3 .... 129 E8
Blackthorn Cl. Falinge Fold OL12 51 E2
Blackthorn Cl.
  Newton-with-S PR4 .... 113 F2
Blackthorn Cl. Preston PR2 ..... 115 D1
Blackthorn Cl. Thornton FY5 .. 172 F5
Blackthorn Cres. OL13 .... 86 F3
Blackthorn Croft. PR4 .... 77 A2
Blackthorn Dr. PR1 .... 95 B3
Blackthorn La. OL13 .... 86 F3
Blackwood Pl. LA1 .... 211 B5
Blackwood Rd. OL13 .... 69 B7
Blades St. LA1 .... 210 E7
Blaguegate La. WN8 .... 17 F2
Blainscough Rd. PR7 .... 28 E8
Blair Gr. PR4 .... 34 F7
Blair St. OL12 .... 51 D1
Blairway Ave. FY3 .... 129 F6
Blake Ave. PR5 .... 76 A7
Blake Gdns. BB6 .... 123 B4
Blake St. BB5 .... 103 B6

Blakehall. WN8 .... 9 D7
Blakeley Cres. BB8 .... 200 B3
Blakewater Rd. BB1 .... 101 C7
Blakey Moor. BB2 .... 100 D5
Blakey St. BB11 .... 127 B6
Blakiston St. FY7 .... 194 A4
Blanche St. **6** PR1 .... 116 C1
Blandford Rd. FY5 .... 172 C1
Blandford Cl. PR8 .... 33 F5
Blandford Rise. BL6 .... 31 F1
Blannell St. BB11 .... 126 E6
Blashaw La. PR1 .... 95 A5
Blaydike Moss. PR5 .... 75 B1
Blaydon Pk. PR5 .... 172 E4
Blaydon Pk. WN8 .... 9 D7
Blea Cl. BB12 .... 126 B8
Blea Tarn Pl. **3** LA4 .... 212 G4
Bleachers Dr. PR5 .... 75 E1
Bleak La. L40 .... 25 D5
Bleakholt Rd. BL0 .... 67 F1
Bleara Rd. BB8 .... 192 D7
Bleasdale Ave. Cleveleys FY5 .. 150 E8
Bleasdale Ave. Clitheroe BB7 .. 164 C7
Bleasdale Ave. Kirkham PR4 ... 113 A5
Bleasdale Ave. Poulton-le-F FY6 151 C2
Bleasdale Ave. Staining FY3 ... 130 E5
Bleasdale CE Sch. PR3 .... 181 A7
Bleasdale Cl.
  Bamber Bridge PR5 .... 76 F8
Bleasdale Cl. Leyland PR5 & PR7 59 B7
Bleasdale Cl. Ormskirk L39 .... 6 D7
Bleasdale Ct. PR3 .... 139 B7
Bleasdale Gr. LA3 .... 212 B1
Bleasdale House Sch. LA5 ...... 218 C3
Bleasdale Rd. Bleasdale PR3 ... 180 E4
Bleasdale Rd.
  Cumeragh Village PR3 .... 137 F6
Bleasdale Rd.
  Knott End-on-S FY6 .... 194 D5
Bleasdale Rd.
  Lytham St Anne's FY8 .... 90 C4
Bleasdale Rd. Whitechapel PR3 158 C8
Bleasdale St E. PR1 .... 117 C1
Blelock St. PR1 .... 96 A7
Blenheim Ave. Blackpool FY1 .. 129 D4
Blenheim Ave. Kirkham PR4 ... 113 C1
Blenheim Cl. Bamber Bridge PR5 76 C8
Blenheim Cl. Blackburn BB1 ... 121 E1
Blenheim Dr. Thornton FY5 .... 173 C2
Blenheim Dr. Warton PR4 .... 91 D6
Blenheim Pl. FY8 .... 109 E1
Blenheim Rd. PR8 .... 20 B6
Blenheim St. Colne BB8 .... 170 A5
Blenheim St. **13**
  Spotland Fold OL12 .... 51 C1
Blenheim Terr. BB8 .... 191 E1
Blessed Sacrament RC Prim Sch.
  PR2 .... 117 F3
Blind La. Burton in L LA6 .... 236 C3
Blind La. Gisburn PR3 .... 225 C3
Blind La. Higham BB12 .... 146 A6
Blindman's La. L39 .... 15 C7
Bloom St. **3** BL0 .... 49 A4
Bloomfield Ct. PR1 .... 116 E2
Bloomfield Grange. PR1 .... 95 C2
Bloomfield Pk. LA5 .... 217 D1
Bloomfield Rd. Withnell PR6 .... 79 A1
Bloomfield Road Football Gd
  (Blackpool FC). FY1 .... 129 C2
Blossom Ave. FY4 .... 109 F7
Blossoms The. PR2 .... 117 C6
Blucher St. BB8 .... 169 E4
Blue Bell La. OL14 .... 108 D2
Blue Bell Pl. PR1 .... 96 A7
Blue Gates. BB7 .... 223 B3
Blue Moor. PR4 .... 134 A2
Blue Scar La. BB7 .... 224 D7
Blue Stone La. L40 & PR7 .... 39 C4
Bluebell Ave. BB4 .... 67 A8
Bluebell Ave. Formby L37 .... 11 B4
Bluebell Cl. Lucas Green PR7 ... 60 C5
Bluebell Cl. Thornton FY5 ...... 172 F5
Bluebell Wood. PR5 .... 75 F3
Bluecoat Cres. PR4 .... 114 A2
Bluestone La. L31 .... 5 E1
Blundell Ave. Formby L37 .... 11 B4
Blundell Ave. Hightown L38 .... 2 F3
Blundell Ave. Southport PR8 .... 33 F2
Blundell Cres. PR8 .... 33 F2
Blundell Dr. PR8 .... 33 F2
Blundell Gr. L38 .... 2 F3
Blundell La. Little Scotland BL6 .. 30 A2
Blundell La. Penwortham PR1 ... 95 B6
Blundell La. Southport PR9 ...... 53 C2
Blundell Rd. Fulwood PR2 .... 116 E3
Blundell Rd. Hightown L38 .... 2 F3
Blundell Rd.
  Lytham St Anne's FY8 .... 109 F1
Blundell St. FY1 .... 129 B3
Blythe Ave. FY5 .... 172 E5
Blythe La. L40 .... 24 E1
Blythewood. WN8 .... 9 D7
Board St. BB10 .... 147 A1
Boarded Barn. PR7 .... 59 C3
Boardman Ave. FY1 .... 129 D2
Boardman St. BL6 & PR7 .... 30 D2
Boarsgreave La. BB4 .... 68 F6
Bobbin Cl. BB5 .... 103 A5
Bobbin Mill Cl. OL14 .... 108 B1
Bobbin St. OL14 .... 108 C1
Bobbiners La. PR9 .... 54 A3
Bocholt Way. BB4 .... 85 A2
Bodiam Rd. BL8 .... 48 F2
Bodkin La. PR3 .... 152 F7
Bodmin Ave. PR9 .... 53 B5
Bodmin St. PR1 .... 117 D1
Boegrave Ave. PR5 .... 76 A8
Bog Height Rd. BB3 .... 80 C6

Bogburn La. PR7 .... 28 D6
Boland St. BB1 .... 101 A7
Bold La. L39 .... 6 B7
Bold St. Bacup OL13 .... 86 F1
Bold St. Blackburn BB1 .... 100 E6
Bold St. Bury BL9 .... 32 A3
Bold St. Colne BB8 .... 169 E4
Bold St. Fleetwood FY7 .... 194 B5
Bold St. Morecambe LA3 .... 212 B4
Bold St. Preston PR1 .... 116 D1
Bold St. Southport PR8 & PR9 .. 34 B8
Boleyn Cl. FY3 .... 130 A2
Boleyn The. L31 .... 5 E3
Bolland Prospect. BB7 .... 164 F7
Bolland St. BB8 .... 200 B3
Bolton Ave. Accrington BB5 .... 124 D1
Bolton Ave. Carleton FY5 .... 151 C5
Bolton Ave. Lancaster LA1 ...... 213 F4
Bolton Cl. LA1 .... 12 A2
Bolton Croft. PR5 .... 58 B8
Bolton Gr. BB9 .... 168 D3
Bolton La. LA5 .... 216 C4
Bolton Rd.
  Abbey Village BL6 & PR6 & PR7 ... 79 B3
Bolton Rd. Blackburn BB2 & BB3 80 E7
Bolton Rd. Blackburn BB2 ...... 100 D2
Bolton Rd.
  Grimeford Village BL6 & PR6 .. 30 D6
Bolton Rd. Hawkshaw BL8 .... 48 D2
Bolton Rd. Riley Green BB2 & PR5 78 E6
Bolton Rd. Southport PR8 .... 34 A4
Bolton Rd N. BL0 .... 67 D2
Bolton Rd W. BL0 & BL8 .... 49 A4
Bolton St. Blackpool FY1 .... 129 B2
Bolton St. Chorley PR6 & PR7 .. 42 C7
Bolton St. Colne BB8 .... 169 C4
Bolton St. **4** Newchurch BB4 .. 85 E1
Bolton St. Ramsbottom BL0 ..... 49 B6
Bolton's Cop. PR9 .... 54 D5
Bolton's Ct. **24** BB1 .... 100 E5
Bolton's Meanygate. PR4 .... 55 C7
Bolton-by-Bowland CE Prim Sch.
  BB7 .... 224 D4
Bolton-le-Sands CE Prim Sch.
  LA5 .... 216 B4
Boltons Croft. PR4 .... 114 E7
Boltons Ct. PR1 .... 96 A7
Bombay St. BB2 .... 100 C3
Bonchurch St. BB1 .... 101 C4
Bond Cl. BL6 .... 31 C3
Bond St. Blackpool FY4 .... 109 B7
Bond St. **12** Burnley BB10 ... 127 A8
Bond St. Bury BL9 .... 32 A2
Bond St. Colne BB8 .... 169 D5
Bond St. Darwen BB3 .... 81 A2
Bond St. Edenfield BL0 .... 67 E2
Bond St. Lancaster LA1 .... 211 A8
Bond St. Nelson BB9 .... 147 D7
Bond's La. Adlington PR7 .... 29 F7
Bond's La. Banks PR9 .... 54 A7
Bonds La. Bonds PR3 .... 178 C6
Bonds La. Elswick PR4 .... 154 A2
Bone Croft. PR6 .... 77 B3
Bonfire Hill Cl. BB4 .... 85 B7
Bonfire Hill Rd. BB4 .... 85 A7
Bonney St. FY1 .... 129 B4
Bonny Grass Terr. BB6 .... 143 A4
Bonny St. FY1 .... 129 B4
Bonsall St. BB2 .... 100 B2
Boome St. FY4 .... 109 C6
Boon Town. LA6 .... 234 C7
Boon Wlks. LA6 .... 234 C7
Boot St. BB8 .... 201 B2
Boot Way. BB11 .... 127 A5
Booth Bridge La. BD23 .... 201 B5
Booth Cres. BB4 .... 86 A1
Booth Ct. **4** BB10 .... 127 A8
Booth Rd. OL13 .... 69 B8
Booth St. Accrington BB5 .... 103 C4
Booth St. **10** Bacup OL13 .... 86 F2
Booth St. Carnforth LA5 .... 217 D1
Booth St. Haslingden BB4 .... 84 A4
Booth St. **10** Newchurch BB9 147 B8
Booth St. Newchurch BB4 .... 68 E8
Booth St. Southport PR8 .... 34 B8
Booth's La. L39 .... 14 F4
Boothley Rd. FY1 .... 129 D6
Boothman Pl. BB9 .... 168 E2
Boothman St. BB2 .... 100 D2
Boothroyden. FY1 .... 129 B8
Bootle St. PR1 .... 117 C1
Borage Cl. FY5 .... 173 A5
Bores Hill. WN1 .... 29 C4
Borough Rd. BB3 .... 81 A1
Borron La. LA6 .... 234 C3
Borrowdale Ave. Blackburn BB1 101 C3
Borrowdale Ave. Fleetwood FY7 193 D4
Borrowdale Cl. Accrington BB5 124 D1
Borrowdale Dr. BB10 .... 147 C4
Borrowdale Gr. LA4 .... 212 G5
Borrowdale Rd. Blackpool FY4 130 B1
Borrowdale Rd. Lancaster LA1 211 A8
Borrowdale Rd. Leyland PR5 .... 59 B7
Borwick Ave. LA5 .... 217 E6
Borwick Cl. LA5 .... 217 E6
Borwick Ct. Borwick LA6 .... 234 B4
Borwick Ct. Morecambe LA4 .. 212 E3
Borwick Dr. LA1 .... 213 D2
Borwick La. LA5 & LA6 .... 234 B3
Borwick Mews. LA6 .... 234 B3
Borwick Rd. LA6 .... 234 D3

Bosburn Dr. BB2 .... 120 C2
Boscombe Ave. LA3 .... 212 B2
Boscombe Rd. FY4 .... 109 B6
Bosley Cl. BB3 .... 64 D8
Bostock St. **22** PR1 .... 96 A7
Boston Ave. FY2 .... 150 D6
Boston Rd. Bacup OL13 .... 86 F3
Boston Rd. Lytham St Anne's FY8 89 B6
Boston Way. FY8 .... 147 F6
Bostons. BB6 .... 123 B5
Bostonway. FY4 .... 109 F8
Bosworth Dr. PR8 .... 20 B4
Bosworth Pl. FY4 .... 109 B4
Bosworth St. BL6 .... 31 B4
Botanic Rd. PR9 .... 53 B2
Botany Brow. PR6 .... 60 E2
Bott House La. BB8 & BB9 ..... 169 A2
Bottom o' th' Knotts Brow.
  BL7 .... 47 E3
Bottom o' th' Moor. BL6 .... 31 F3
Bottomdale Rd. LA2 .... 214 A8
Bottomgate. BB1 .... 101 B5
Bottomley Bank La. BB4 .... 85 B8
Bottomley St. BB9 .... 147 E8
Bottoms La. LA5 .... 218 D3
Botton Rd. LA2 .... 233 C1
Boulder St. **8** BB10 .... 85 A7
Bouldsworth Rd. BB10 .... 127 E5
Boulevard. PR1 .... 96 B5
Boulevard The. FY8 .... 89 A4
Boulsworth Cres. BB9 .... 169 B1
Boulsworth Dr. BB8 .... 170 C1
Boulsworth Gr. BB8 .... 170 A5
Boulview Terr. BB8 .... 170 A5
Boundary Cl. Eccleston PR7 ..... 40 B6
Boundary Cl. New Longton PR4 74 F8
Boundary Ct. FY3 .... 151 A1
Boundary La. Becconsall PR4 ... 72 E1
Boundary La. Hale Nook PR3 ... 175 F8
Boundary La. Holmes PR4 & PR9 54 E6
Boundary La. Kirkby L33 .... 1 F2
Boundary La.
  Shevington Moor WN6 .... 28 A3
Boundary Meanygate.
  Becconsall PR4 .... 72 D1
Boundary Meanygate.
  Holmes PR4 .... 54 F7
Boundary Rd. Accrington BB5 .. 103 D7
Boundary Rd. Fulwood PR2 .... 116 D3
Boundary Rd. Lancaster LA1 .. 210 F6
Boundary Rd.
  Lytham St Anne's FY8 .... 90 E5
Boundary Rd. Burnley BB10 ... 147 C2
Boundary Rd. Colne BB8 .... 169 D4
Boundary St. Leyland PR5 .... 76 B2
Boundary St. Southport PR8 .... 34 B4
Bourbles La. BB3 .... 195 D4
Bourne Brow. PR3 .... 157 F5
Bourne May Rd. FY6 .... 194 D5
Bourne Rd. FY5 .... 173 B5
Bourne Way. FY5 .... 173 A4
Bourne's Row. PR5 .... 97 E1
Bournemouth Rd. FY4 .... 109 B6
Bournesfield. PR5 .... 97 E1
Bovington Ave. FY5 .... 150 F8
Bow Brook Rd. PR5 .... 76 C1
Bow Hills La. BB7 .... 225 C6
Bow La. Leyland PR5 .... 76 B1
Bow La. Preston PR1 .... 95 E7
Bow St. PR5 .... 76 B2
Bowden Ave. BB2 .... 99 C1
Bowen St. BB2 .... 100 B3
Bower Cl. BB2 .... 100 B2
Bower St. Blackburn BB2 .... 100 B2
Bower St. Bury BL9 .... 32 C3
Bowerham Cty Prim Sch. LA1 211 A6
Bowerham Rd. LA1 & LA2 ...... 211 A5
Bowerham Rd. LA1 .... 211 A5
Bowers La. PR3 .... 177 E7
Bowes Lyon Pl. FY8 .... 89 C7
Bowfell Ave. LA4 .... 212 G5
Bowfell Cl. FY4 .... 130 D1
Bowfield's La. BB2 .... 119 F4
Bowgreave Cl. FY4 .... 110 A6
Bowgreave Dr. PR3 .... 178 D4
Bowker St. BB4 .... 67 C5
Bowker's Green La. L39 .... 6 E4
Bowland Ave. Burnley BB10 ... 127 E5
Bowland Ave. Chorley PR6 .... 42 D8
Bowland Ave. Fleetwood FY7 .. 172 D8
Bowland Cl. Carnforth LA5 .... 217 C1
Bowland Cl. Longridge PR3 ... 139 B8
Bowland Cres. BB7 .... 130 A8
Bowland Ct. BB7 .... 164 E8
Bowland Cty High Sch. BB7 .. 224 B1
Bowland Dr. LA1 .... 213 D2
Bowland Forest High Division
  Thorneyholme RC Sch. BB7 222 C5
Bowland Gate La. BB7 .... 186 E7
Bowland House. **7** BB1 ...... 100 F6
Bowland Pl. Fulwood PR5 ..... 118 A3
Bowland Pl.
  Lytham St Anne's FY8 .... 89 C6
Bowland Rd.
  Fulwood PR1 & PR5 .... 118 A3
Bowland Rd. Garstang PR3 .... 199 C1
Bowland Rd. Heysham LA3 ..... 209 A8
Bowland View. Brierfield BB9 .. 147 D4
Bowland View. Garstang PR3 .. 199 C1
Bowland View. Glasson LA2 ... 205 B4
Bowlers Cl. PR2 .... 117 C5
Bowlers Wlk. OL12 .... 51 F2
Bowling Green Cl. Darwen BB3 .. 64 B7
Bowling Green Cl.
  Southport PR8 .... 34 F5
Bowlingfield. PR2 .... 116 A4
Bowness Ave. Ainsdale PR8 ... 20 C3
Bowness Ave. Blackpool FY4 .. 130 D1

Bowness Ave.
Lytham St Anne's FY8 .... 109 F2
Bowness Ave. Nelson BB9 .... 147 E6
Bowness Ave. Spotland Fold OL12 51 C1
Bowness Ave. Thornton FY5 ...... 173 B2
Bowness Pl. BB1 .... 101 A6
Bowness Pl. FY7 .... 193 C1
Bowness Rd. Fulwood PR1 .... 118 A1
Bowness Rd. Lancaster LA1 .... 214 A1
Bowness Rd. Padiham BB12 .... 145 C2
Bowood Ct. FY3 .... 130 B7
Bowran St. PR1 .... 95 F8
Box St. BL0 .... 49 D6
Boxer Pl. PR5 .... 75 C2
Boxwood Dr. BB2 .... 79 F8
Boxwood St. BB1 .... 100 F8
Boyd Cl. WN6 .... 28 F1
Boyes Ave. PR3 .... 178 D2
Boyle St. BB1 .... 100 F6
Boys La. PR2 .... 116 C5
Brabiner La. PR2 & PR3 .... 138 B4
Brabins Endowed Sch. PR3 ...... 182 E3
Bracebridge Dr. PR8 .... 34 F2
Bracewell Ave. FY6 .... 152 A3
Bracewell Cl. BB9 .... 147 E8
Bracewell La. BB8 & BD23 .... 225 F3
Bracewell Rd. PR2 .... 117 E5
Bracewell St. Barnoldswick BB8 200 B3
Bracewell St. Burnley BB10 ...... 147 B1
Bracewell St. Nelson BB9 .... 147 F8
Bracken Cl. BB2 .... 79 F8
Bracken Dr. PR4 .... 92 D7
Bracken Gr. BB4 .... 67 A8
Bracken Lea Fold OL12 .... 51 B2
Brackenbury Cl. PR5 .... 76 A7
Brackenbury Rd. PR1 & PR2 .... 116 E3
Brackenbury St. PR1 .... 116 F2
Brackenthaite Rd. LA5 & LA7 ... 219 B7
Brackenway. L37 .... 12 A6
Bradda St. BB2 .... 100 E1
Braddon St. PR0 & PR1 .... 117 D1
Brade St. PR9 .... 53 C4
Brades Ave. FY5 .... 173 D2
Bradford Gr. LA3 .... 208 F6
Bradford St. BB5 .... 103 D6
Bradkirk La. PR5 .... 77 B8
Bradkirk Pl. PR5 .... 77 A7
Bradley Ct. BB7 .... 161 E8
Bradley Cty Prim Sch. BB9 ... 168 E1
Bradley Fold. BB9 .... 168 E1
Bradley Gdns. BB12 .... 126 B5
Bradley Hall Rd. BB9 .... 168 F1
Bradley Hill Trad Est. WN6 ... 29 A2
Bradley La. Eccleston PR7 ..... 40 D6
Bradley La. Standish WN6 ...... 28 F2
Bradley Pl. PR8 .... 34 B7
Bradley Rd. BB9 .... 168 E1
Bradley Rd E. BB9 .... 168 E1
Bradley St. Colne BB8 .... 169 F5
Bradley St. Southport PR9 .... 34 C8
Bradley View. BB9 .... 168 E1
Bradman Rd. L33 .... 1 D3
Bradshaw Brow. L40 .... 39 E2
Bradshaw Cl. Blackburn BB1 .. 100 E8
Bradshaw Cl. Nelson BB9 ...... 147 E7
Bradshaw La. Corner Row PR4 132 D1
Bradshaw La. Eagland Hill PR3 176 A7
Bradshaw La. Mawdesley L40 ... 39 E2
Bradshaw La. Parbold WN8 ...... 26 C1
Bradshaw La. Scronkey PR3 ..... 196 E2
Bradshaw Rd. BL2 .... 47 E1
Bradshaw Row. BB5 .... 102 F6
Bradshaw St. Church BB5 ...... 102 F6
Bradshaw St. Lancaster LA1 ... 211 A7
Bradshaw St. Nelson BB9 .... 147 D7
Bradshaw St E. BB5 .... 103 C6
Bradshaw St W. BB5 .... 102 F6
Bradshaw's La. PR8 .... 20 D6
Bradshawgate Dr. LA5 .... 218 C4
Brady St. BL6 .... 31 A4
Braefield Cres. PR2 .... 117 F2
Braemar Ave. Southport PR9 ... 52 E2
Braemar Ave. Thornton FY5 .... 151 C7
Braemar Ct. LA4 .... 213 A4
Braemar Wlk. FY2 .... 150 F6
Braemore Dr. BL9 .... 32 D2
Braeside. BB2 .... 100 C6
Braewood Cl. BL9 .... 32 D2
Braganza Way. LA1 .... 210 C8
Braid's La. PR3 .... 179 A7
Braidhaven. WN6 .... 19 E7
Braintree Ave. PR1 .... 95 E2
Braith Cl. FY4 .... 109 F8
Braithwaite St. FY1 .... 129 B7
Bramble Cl. PR4 .... 112 E6
Bramble Cl. Penwortham PR1 ... 95 E2
Bramble Cl. Thornton FY5 ..... 173 A2
Bramble Gdns. 151 A2
Bramble St. BB10 .... 147 A1
Bramble Way. WN8 .... 26 C1
Brambles The. Barrow BB9 .... 164 D1
Brambles The. Blackburn BB2 .. 100 A8
Brambles The. Blackpool FY6 .. 109 B4
Brambles The. Coppull PR7 .... 41 F2
Bramblewood. PR5 .... 57 B2
Bramblings The. FY6 .... 151 B2
Bramcote Cl. L33 .... 1 A4
Bramcote Rd. L33 .... 1 A4
Bramhall Rd. WN8 .... 17 C2
Bramley Ave. Burnley BB12 ... 126 C8
Bramley Ave. Fleetwood FY7 .. 193 E4
Bramley View. BB7 .... 143 C8
Brampton Ave. FY5 .... 172 F4
Brampton Dr. LA4 .... 213 B5
Brampton St. PR1 .... 116 C1
Bramwell Rd. PR4 .... 92 B6
Bramworth Ave. BL0 .... 49 B6

Branch Rd. Blackburn BB2 & BB3 80 E7
Branch Rd. Burnley BB11 .... 127 B4
Branch Rd. Clayton-le-M BB5 123 F3
Branch Rd. Mellor Brook BB2 ... 120 C2
Branch Rd. Waddington BB7 .... 186 B4
Branch St. Bacup OL13 .... 106 D8
Branch St. Nelson BB9 .... 147 F8
Brancker St. PR7 .... 42 A5
Brandiforth St. PR5 .... 96 F2
Brandon Cl. WN8 .... 10 A7
Brandon St. WN8 .... 26 C2
Brandreth Delph. WN8 .... 26 C3
Brandreth Dr. WN8 .... 26 C2
Brandreth Hospl. L39 .... 15 E5
Brandreth Pk. WN8 .... 26 D4
Brandreth Rd. WN8 .... 28 F1
Brandwood. BB5 .... 123 E2
Brandwood Fold. BL7 .... 47 E5
Brandwood Gr. BB10 .... 127 C6
Brandwood Pk. OL13 .... 69 B8
Brandwood Rd. OL13 .... 69 B8
Brandwood St. BB3 .... 81 B1
Brandwood Rd.
  Great Harwood BB6 .... 123 D6
Brantwood. BB5 .... 123 E2
Brantwood Ave. Blackburn BB1 101 F5
Brantwood Ave.
  Morecambe LA4 .... 213 A6
Brantwood Dr. Lancaster LA1 211 A2
Brantwood Dr. Leyland PR5 ... 76 E1
Brassey Pl. BB12 .... 126 C7
Brathay Pl. FY7 .... 193 D2
Bray St. PR1 .... 116 C1
Brays Heys. FY5 .... 173 C1
Brays Rd. FY8 .... 111 B1
Brayshaw Pl. PR2 .... 117 E4
Brazil Cl. LA3 .... 212 D2
Brazley Ave. BL6 .... 31 E1
Bread St. BB12 .... 126 D6
Brearlands. BD23 .... 201 B6
Brearley St. OL13 .... 69 D8
Brechin Rd. L33 .... 1 A2
Breck Cl. FY6 .... 151 E5
Breck Cty Prim Sch The. FY6 . 151 F5
Breck Dr. FY6 .... 151 E5
Breck Rd. Blackpool FY3 ..... 129 E4
Breck Rd. Poulton-le-F FY6 .. 151 F6
Breckside Cl. FY6 .... 151 E5
Brecon Ave. BB5 .... 102 C4
Brecon Cl. FY1 .... 129 D3
Brecon Ct. L37 .... 11 E4
Brecon Rd. BB1 .... 101 C5
Bredon Ave. PR7 .... 59 E1
Bredon Cl. FY6 .... 90 D5
Bredon Ct. BB8 .... 191 E1
Breeze Mount. PR5 .... 76 C8
Breeze Rd. PR9 .... 33 E2
Brendan Cres. OL12 .... 70 D1
Brendjean Rd. LA4 .... 212 F4
Brendon Wlk. FY3 .... 129 F8
Brennand Cl. Bamber Bridge PR5 76 B8
Brennand Cl. Lancaster LA1 .. 213 C2
Brennand St. Burnley BB10 ... 147 B1
Brennand St. Clitheroe BB7 ... 186 E1
Brennands Endowed Prim Sch.
  BB7 .... 223 C7
Brent St. BB10 .... 147 C3
Brentlea Ave. LA3 .... 208 E7
Brentlea Cres. LA3 .... 208 E7
Brentwood. FY7 .... 193 E2
Brentwood Ave. Burnley BB11 126 E3
Brentwood Ave. Cleveleys FY5 150 D8
Brentwood Ave.
  Poulton-le-F FY6 .... 151 C3
Brentwood Cl. L38 .... 2 F2
Brentwood Dr. WN8 .... 20 C4
Brentwood Rd. Adlington PR6 30 B8
Brentwood Rd. Nelson BB9 .. 169 A1
Bretherton Cl. PR5 .... 58 C8
Bretherton Cl. L40 .... 24 F3
Bretherton Endowed CE Prim Sch.
  PR5 .... 56 F6
Bretherton Rd. PR5 .... 57 B4
Bretherton Terr. PR5 .... 76 B1
Brett Cl. BB7 .... 165 A7
Brettarch Dr. LA1 .... 210 E6
Brettargh Cl. LA1 .... 210 E6
Brettargh Dr. LA1 .... 210 E6
Bretton Fold. PR8 .... 34 F5
Brewery Arc. LA1 .... 210 F8
Brewery La. Formby L37 .... 11 F6
Brewery La. Lancaster LA1 .. 210 F8
Brewery St. Blackburn BB2 .. 100 D5
Brewery St. Longridge PR3 .. 139 B7
Breworth Fold La. PR6 ...... 78 A3
Briar Ave. PR7 .... 59 C4
Briar Cl. OL12 .... 51 A1
Briar Croft. PR4 .... 74 A7
Briar Field. FY2 .... 150 F6
Briar Gr. PR2 .... 116 A4
Briar Hill Cl. BB1 .... 101 A4
Briar Mews. FY5 .... 173 C1
Briar Rd. Ainsdale PR8 ...... 20 D4
Briar Rd. Blackburn BB1 .... 100 F8
Briar Rd. Thornton FY5 ..... 173 C1
Briar St. OL13 .... 87 A1
Briarcroft. PR5 .... 173 B1
Briarfield. BL7 .... 46 D2

Briarfield Rd. FY6 .... 151 B5
Briars Brook. L40 .... 25 A2
Briars Gn. WN8 .... 18 B4
Briars La. Maghull L31 .... 5 E1
Briars La. Ring o'Bells L40 ... 25 A3
Briars The. Eccleston PR7 .... 40 C6
Briars The. Fulwood PR2 ..... 117 D6
Briars The. Southport PR8 .... 33 F1
Briarscroft. LA5 .... 217 E6
Briarwood Cl. Leyland PR5 ... 58 E8
Briarwood Cl. Weeton PR4 ... 131 F2
Briarwood Ct. FY5 .... 151 B7
Briarwood Dr. FY2 .... 150 E5
Briary Croft. L38 .... 2 F3
Brick Kiln La. L40 .... 38 B3
Brick St. BL9 .... 32 A3
Brickcroft La. PR5 .... 57 B3
Brickhouse La. FY6 .... 174 C4
Bridge Ave. L39 .... 15 E5
Bridge Bank. PR1 .... 96 C6
Bridge Brow. LA6 .... 238 C1
Bridge Cl. PR5 .... 76 A8
Bridge Croft. Bolton-le-S LA5 216 A4
Bridge Croft. Clayton-le-M BB5 123 B4
Bridge Ct. Bamber Bridge PR5 76 A8
Bridge Ct. Clitheroe BB7 ... 186 F2
Bridge Ct. Lytham St Anne's FY8 90 D4
Bridge End. Bamber Bridge PR5 76 C8
Bridge End. Whalley BB7 .... 143 C4
Bridge End Cl. BB4 .... 67 A7
Bridge End St. OL14 .... 108 C1
Bridge Farm Dr. L31 .... 5 F2
Bridge Gr. PR8 .... 34 B6
Bridge Hall Dr. BL9 .... 32 C2
Bridge Hall Fold. BL9 .... 32 C2
Bridge Hall La. BL9 .... 32 D2
Bridge House. LA1 .... 213 F2
Bridge House Rd. FY4 ...... 109 F8
Bridge Houses. Accrington BB5 83 E8
Bridge Houses.
  Whitewell Bottom BB4 ..... 85 F7
Bridge La. LA1 .... 210 F8
Bridge Mill Rd. BB9 .... 147 C8
Bridge Rd. Bamber Bridge PR5 76 C8
Bridge Rd. Chatburn BB7 ... 187 D5
Bridge Rd. Fleetwood FY7 .. 194 B4
Bridge Rd. Lancaster LA1 ... 210 F5
Bridge Rd. Lytham St Anne's FY8 89 F4
Bridge Rd. Morecambe LA4 .. 212 F5
Bridge Rd. Nether Kellet LA6 .. 216 D4
Bridge Rd. Preston PR1 ..... 116 C2
Bridge Row. PR3 .... 155 C7
Bridge St. Accrington BB5 ... 103 C6
Bridge St. Bamber Bridge PR5 76 E7
Bridge St. Blackburn BB1 ... 100 E4
Bridge St. Brierfield BB9 .... 147 B5
Bridge St. Burnley BB11 ..... 127 A6
Bridge St. Bury BL9 .... 32 A3
Bridge St. Church BB5 ...... 102 E6
Bridge St. Colne BB8 .... 169 C4
Bridge St. Darwen BB3 ..... 81 A1
Bridge St. Ewood Bridge BB4 .. 67 C6
Bridge St. Garstang PR3 .... 178 C6
Bridge St.
  Great Harwood BB6 .... 123 C5
Bridge St. Higher Walton PR5 .. 97 B3
Bridge St. Horwich BL6 ..... 31 C4
Bridge St. Newchurch BB4 ... 85 E1
Bridge St. Ormskirk L39 .... 15 E4
Bridge St. Padiham BB12 ... 125 B8
Bridge St. Ramsbottom BL0 .. 49 C6
Bridge St. Rawtenstall BB4 .. 68 E7
Bridge St. Rishton BB1 ..... 123 B2
Bridge St. Southport PR8 ... 34 B6
Bridge St. Wheelton PR6 ... 61 A7
Bridge St. Whitworth OL12 .. 70 C1
Bridge Terr. PR1 .... 96 C6
Bridge Wills La. PR9 .... 53 C5
Bridgefield Dr. BL9 .... 32 D2
Bridgefield St. BB12 .... 125 C4
Bridgehall Dr. WN8 .... 10 B7
Bridgend Dr. PR8 .... 20 C4
Bridget St. LA1 .... 210 F8
Bridgewater Ave. FY5 ...... 150 F7
Bridgeway. PR5 .... 76 C8
Bridle Path. BB8 .... 191 D7
Bridleway. BB4 .... 85 F2
Brief St. BB10 .... 127 A8
Brier Cres. BB9 .... 147 D6
Brier Dr. LA3 .... 208 E7
Briercliffe Ave. Blackpool FY3 129 F7
Briercliffe Ave. Nelson BB8 . 169 B3
Briercliffe Cty Sch. BB10 .. 147 C4
Briercliffe Rd. Brierfield BB10 147 D2
Briercliffe Rd. Burnley BB10 127 B8
Briercliffe Rd. Burnley BB10 147 C1
Briercliffe Rd. Chorley PR6 .. 60 D1
Briercliffe St. BB8 .... 169 B3
Brierfield. New Longton PR4 74 F8
Brierfield. Skelmersdale WN8 .. 9 D6
Brierfield Mansfield High Sch.
  BB9 .... 147 B6
Brierfield Reedley Cty Sch.
  BB10 .... 147 C4
Brierfield St. BB5 .... 147 B5
Brierholme Ave. BL7 ...... 46 E1
Brierley Ave. FY3 .... 129 E7
Brierley La. PR4 .... 135 B8
Brierley Rd. PR5 .... 77 A7
Brierley St. PR1 .... 116 D1
Briers Brow. PR6 .... 61 B7
Briery Bank. LA5 .... 237 C1
Briery Cl. PR2 .... 117 C4
Briery Hey. PR5 .... 77 C6
Briery St. LA1 .... 213 D1
Brieryfield Rd. PR1 ..... 95 D8
Brigg Field. BB5 .... 123 F4

Briggs Fold. BL7 .... 46 E2
Briggs Fold Cl. BL7 .... 46 E2
Briggs Fold Rd. BL7 ...... 46 E2
Briggs Rd. PR2 .... 116 C2
Brighouse Cl. L39 .... 15 D6
Bright St. Blackburn BB1 .. 101 B6
Bright St. Blackpool FY4 .. 109 B8
Bright St. Burnley BB10 ... 147 B1
Bright St. Bury BL9 ...... 32 A3
Bright St. Clitheroe BB7 .. 164 F8
Bright St. Colne BB8 ..... 169 D5
Bright St. Colne BB8 ..... 170 B5
Bright St. Darwen BB3 .... 80 F2
Bright St. Egerton BL7 .... 46 D2
Bright St. Oswaldtwistle BB5 102 D3
Bright St. Padiham BB12 .. 125 D8
Bright St. Rawtenstall BB4 . 85 A3
Bright St. Southport PR9 .. 34 F7
Bright Terr. BB8 .... 170 B2
Bright's Cl. BB7 .... 223 A5
Brighton Ave. Blackpool FY4 109 B8
Brighton Ave. Cleveleys FY5 172 D2
Brighton Ave.
  Lytham St Anne's FY8 .... 88 F7
Brighton Cres. PR2 .... 116 A3
Brighton Rd. Brierfield BB10 147 C3
Brighton Rd. Southport PR8 .. 34 A3
Brighton St. Bury BL9 .... 32 B3
Brighton St. Chorley PR6 .. 42 E8
Brighton St. Cornholme OL14 108 C1
Brighton Terr. Blackburn BB2 100 B6
Brighton Terr. Darwen BB3 .. 80 E2
Brindle Cl. Lancaster LA1 .. 213 C2
Brindle Cl. Longridge PR3 .. 139 B7
Brindle Cl. Walton Summit PR5 .. 77 B8
Brindle Gregson Lane City
  Prim Sch. PR5 .... 97 E1
Brindle Hts. PR6 .... 77 F5
Brindle Rd. Bamber Bridge PR5 96 F2
Brindle Rd.
  Walton Summit PR5 & PR6 .. 77 C7
Brindle St. Blackburn BB2 . 100 C1
Brindle St. Chorley PR6 .... 42 C6
Brindle St. Preston PR1 .... 96 C8
Brindley St. BL6 .... 31 C2
Brink's Row. BL6 .... 31 D5
Brinklow Ct. PR8 .... 20 A5
Brinwell Rd. FY4 .... 130 B1
Brisbane Pl. FY5 .... 150 F7
Brisbane St. BB5 .... 124 A1
Bristol Ave. Blackpool FY2 . 150 E4
Bristol Ave. Fleetwood FY7 172 C8
Bristol Cl. PR5 .... 76 C3
Bristol Ct. BB1 .... 101 A4
Bristol St. Burnley BB11 .. 126 D3
Bristol St. Colne BB8 .... 169 E5
Bristol St. Morecambe LA4 212 F4
Bristow Ave. PR2 .... 116 B2
Britannia Ave. OL13 ..... 87 A2
Britannia Cotts. BB5 .... 102 A1
Britannia Fy1. FY1 ...... 129 B1
Britannia Prim Sch. OL13 .. 70 C8
Britannia St. BB6 .... 123 C5
Britannia Way. BB4 ..... 67 A8
Britannia Wlk. Burnley BB11 127 B4
Britannia Wlk.
  Lytham St Anne's FY8 ... 89 C8
Britten Cl. BB2 .... 101 A2
Britten St. BB3 .... 80 F2
Britwell Cl. BB2 .... 81 A8
Brixey St. PR1 .... 95 D6
Brixham Pl. FY4 .... 109 B6
Brixton Rd. PR1 .... 96 B7
Broad Clough Villas. OL13 86 F5
Broad Croft. PR4 ..... 94 A1
Broad Gate. BB3 ..... 81 B2
Broad Ing. OL12 ..... 51 C1
Broad Ing Cl. BB10 .. 147 A3
Broad La. Downholland Cross L39 14 B2
Broad La. Ford Green PR3 .. 198 F2
Broad La. Great Altcar L37 & L38 . 12 F1
Broad La. Ince Blundell L29 . 4 C2
Broad La. Whalley BB7 ... 143 B5
Broad La. Winmarleigh PR3 198 F5
Broad Meadow.
  Bamber Bridge PR5 ...... 76 A8
Broad Meadow. Chipping PR3 .. 182 D3
Broad Meadow La. PR5 .... 56 F4
Broad Oak Ave. PR3 ...... 178 D6
Broad Oak Cl. PR1 .... 30 A8
Broad Oak Gn. PR1 ...... 95 B3
Broad Oak High Sch. BL9 .. 32 B2
Broad Oak High Sch (Annexe).
  BL9 .... 32 B3
Broad Oak La.
  Penwortham PR1 & PR4 .. 95 B2
Broad Oak La. Penwortham PR1 95 B3
Broad Oak La. Staining FY3 . 130 C5
Broad Oak Rd. BB5 ...... 103 C5
Broad Oak Terr. BL9 .... 32 E3
Broad Sq. PR5 .... 59 A8
Broad St. Leyland PR5 .. 59 A8
Broad St. Nelson BB9 ... 147 D8
Broadacre. Caton LA2 ... 231 C3
Broadacre.
  Shevington Moor WN6 .. 28 B2
Broadacre Cl. LA2 ..... 231 C3
Broadacre Rd. LA2 .... 231 C3
Broadacre View. LA2 .. 231 C3
Broadbent Dr. BL9 .... 32 E4
Broadfield. Accrington BB5 83 B8
Broadfield. Broughton PR3 136 B2
Broadfield. Oswaldtwistle BB5 .. 102 F2
Broadfield Ave. Blackpool FY4 109 F5
Broadfield Ave.
  Poulton-le-F FY6 .... 151 F3
Broadfield Dr. Leyland PR5 .. 75 E1

Broadfield Dr. Penwortham PR1 . 95 D2
Broadfield Jun Sch. PR5 ...... 75 F1
Broadfield Rd. BB5 .... 103 A3
Broadfield Sch. BB5 .... 102 F2
Broadfield St. BB5 .... 102 F3
Broadfields. PR7 .... 60 B2
Broadfleet Cl. PR3 .... 196 C6
Broadfold Ave. BB1 ...... 101 B7
Broadgate. PR1 .... 95 D6
Broadgreen Cl. PR5 ..... 75 F1
Broadhead Rd. BB3 & BB4 & BL7 65 F5
Broadhurst La. WN6 .... 27 F7
Broadhurst Rd. PR5 .... 150 E8
Broadhurst Way. BB10 & BB9 . 147 C4
Broadith La. PR3 ...... 158 L1
Broadlands. PR8 ...... 33 E3
Broadlands Dr. LA5 .. 215 F3
Broadlands Pl. FY8 .. 89 F4
Broadleia Gr. OL12 .. 51 C2
Broadley Fold. OL12 .. 51 B6
Broadley St. BB4 .... 85 A3
Broadmead. WN8 ... 26 B2
Broadness Dr. BB9 .. 147 E6
Broadoak Rd. L31 ... 5 D5
Broadpool La. FY6 .. 174 C1
Broadriding Rd. WN6 . 19 E6
Broadstone Cl. OL12 .. 51 A1
Broadtree Cl. BB2 ... 120 C3
Broadwater Ave. PR7 .. 172 F8
Broadwater Gdns. FY7 172 E8
Broadway. Accrington BB5 103 B6
Broadway. Blackburn BB1 .. 121 E2
Broadway. Blackpool FY4 .. 109 C7
Broadway. Fleetwood FY7 .. 193 E3
Broadway. Fulwood PR2 ... 116 D7
Broadway. Haslingden BB4 . 67 B8
Broadway. Horwich BL6 ... 31 D3
Broadway. Lancaster LA1 .. 213 F2
Broadway. Leyland PR5 ... 59 B8
Broadway. Morecambe LA4 212 G5
Broadway. Nelson BB9 ... 147 D8
Broadway. Preston PR2 .. 115 F2
Broadway Cl. PR8 ..... 20 B5
Broadway Cres. BB4 .. 67 A8
Broadway Cty Prim Sch. LA4 67 C8
Broadway Pl. Barrowford BB9 . 168 D3
Broadway Pl. Nelson BB9 . 169 A1
Broadway St. BB2 ..... 100 B1
Broadwood Cl. PR1 ... 95 B4
Broadwood Dr. PR2 .. 116 F7
Broadwood Way. FY8 . 89 E4
Brock Ave. FY7 ...... 193 D2
Brock Bank. BB4 .... 85 F4
Brock Cl. LA1 .... 213 E3
Brock Clough Rd. BB4 . 85 F4
Brock Mill La. PR3 .. 180 B2
Brock Rakes. PR3 ... 180 F7
Brock Rd. Chorley PR6 . 60 D1
Brock Rd.
  Lane Heads PR3 & PR4 . 154 E3
Brock Side. PR3 ... 157 C6
Brock St. LA1 ..... 210 F8
Brockbank Ave. LA1 210 C8
Brockenhurst St. BB10 127 C5
Brockholes Brow. PR1 118 A1
Brockholes Cres. FY6 . 151 E2
Brockholes View. PR1 96 C7
Brockholes Way. PR3 . 178 E1
Brockholes Wood Cty Prim
  Sch. PR1 .... 118 A1
Brocklebank Rd. PR9 . 52 E2
Brocklehurst Ave. BB5 103 E3
Brocklewood Ave. FY6 . 130 D8
Brockway. FY6 .... 151 D2
Brockway Ave. FY3 . 129 F6
Broderick Ave. FY2 . 150 E4
Brodick Rd. BB1 ... 101 D3
Brogden La. BB8 ... 225 E2
Brogden St. BB8 ... 200 B3
Brogden View. BB8 . 200 A4
Broken Bank Head. BB7 229 A2
Broken Banks. BB8 . 124 A1
Broken Stone Rd. BB2 & BB3 . 80 A6
Bromilow Rd. WN8 . 17 C1
Bromley Cl. FY2 ... 150 E1
Bromley Cross. BL7 . 47 B1
Bromley Ct. FY2 ... 150 E1
Bromley Gn. PR8 .. 60 F4
Bromley House. BB2 100 C5
Bromley Rd. FY8 .. 88 F6
Bromley St. Blackburn BB2 100 C5
Bromley St. Preston PR1 95 D8
Brompton Cl. FY8 . 89 D5
Brompton Rd. Poulton-le-F FY6 130 D8
Brompton Rd. Southport PR8 . 34 E7
Bromsgrove Ave. FY7 . 150 C4
Bromsgrove Rd. BB10 127 B8
Bronte Ave. BB10 .. 127 D6
Bronte Cl. LA2 ... 51 A1
Brood Ford Ct. OL10 . 32 F1
Brooden Dr. BB10 .. 147 C4
Brook Ave. Maghull L31 . 5 E2
Brook Ave. Morecambe LA4 212 C3
Brook Ave. Scorton PR3 . 199 E7
Brook Croft. PR2 .. 116 B4
Brook Gr. Cleveleys FY5 172 E4
Brook Gr. Morecambe LA3 212 C3
Brook Hey. PR4 ... 73 F8
Brook Hey Dr. L33 . 1 A3
Brook Hey Wlk. L33 . 1 A3
Brook House. PR8 .. 34 C5
Brook La. Charnock Richard PR7 41 C4
Brook La. Farington PR4 & PR5 75 D7
Brook La. Much Hoole PR4 . 73 E3

Brook La. Ormskirk L39 .... 15 E4
Brook Meadow. PR2 .... 115 F7
Brook Mill Ind Est. PR4 .... 112 B4
Brook Pl. PR2 .... 115 D2
Brook Rd. Lytham St Anne's FY8 ... 90 C3
Brook Rd. Morecambe LA3 ...... 212 C3
Brook Side. L31 .... 5 E1
Brook St. Adlington PR6 .... 43 A1
Brook St. Barnoldswick BB8 ...... 200 B2
Brook St. Blackburn BB2 .... 100 B2
Brook St. Blackpool FY4 .... 129 E1
Brook St. Bury BL9 .... 32 A3
Brook St. Clitheroe BB7 .... 186 F1
Brook St. Colne BB8 .... 169 D5
Brook St. Earby BB8 .... 201 B2
Brook St. Fleetwood FY7 .... 172 E8
Brook St. Haslingden BB4 .... 84 B5
Brook St. Higher Walton PR5 ..... 97 B3
Brook St. Kirkham PR4 .... 112 F6
Brook St. Lancaster LA1 .... 210 E7
Brook St. Nelson BB9 .... 147 E8
Brook St. Oswaldtwistle BB5 .... 102 E3
Brook St. Padiham BB12 .... 125 D7
Brook St. Preston PR1 & PR2 .... 116 E2
Brook St. Rishton BB1 .... 123 B1
Brook St. Southport PR9 .... 53 D4
Brook St N. PR2 .... 116 D3
Brookdale. Adlington PR6 .... 43 A1
Brookdale. Belmont BL7 .... 45 C5
Brookdale. Lower Healey OL12 ... 51 E3
Brookdale. New Longton PR4 ...... 75 A6
Brookdale Ave. FY5 .... 150 E8
Brookdale Cl. PR5 & PR7 .... 59 B6
Brooke Cl. BB5 .... 103 E2
Brooke St. PR6 & PR7 .... 42 E7
Brookes La. BB7 .... 143 C5
Brookes St. 7 OL13 .... 69 D8
Brookfield. Croston PR5 .... 57 B3
Brookfield. Mawdesley L40 .... 39 C2
Brookfield. Mellor BB2 .... 120 E2
Brookfield. Parbold WN8 .... 26 C2
Brookfield Ave. Blackpool FY4 .. 110 A6
Brookfield Ave. Fulwood PR2 .... 117 C4
Brookfield Ave. Thornton FY5 ... 173 C1
Brookfield Cl. LA5 .... 216 B5
Brookfield Cl. PR3 .... 182 E3
Brookfield Dr. PR2 .... 116 E8
Brookfield La. L35 .... 6 A5
Brookfield Pl. PR5 .... 77 A6
Brookfield Prim Sch. PR2 .... 117 E5
Brookfield Rd.
 Shevington Moor WN6 .... 28 B2
Brookfield Rd. Thornton FY5 .... 173 C1
Brookfield Rd. Up Holland WN8 .. 10 B7
Brookfield St. 2 Blackburn BB1 .. 100 F6
Brookfield St. Cornholme OL14 .. 108 C1
Brookfield St. Preston PR1 ...... 116 F1
Brookfield Terr.
 Hampson Green LA2 .... 204 E8
Brookfield Terr.
 Lytham St Anne's FY8 .... 90 B4
Brookfield View. LA5 .... 216 B5
Brookfield Way. BB8 .... 201 B1
Brookfields Prim Sch. WN8 ...... 17 D2
Brookford Cl. BB12 .... 126 D8
Brookhouse Bsns Ctr. 10 BB1 .. 100 F6
Brookhouse Cl. Blackburn BB1 .. 100 F6
Brookhouse Cl.
 Gregson Lane PR5 .... 97 F2
Brookhouse Dr. PR5 .... 97 F2
Brookhouse Gdns. 12 BB1 ...... 100 F6
Brookhouse La. BB1 .... 100 F6
Brookhouse Prim Sch. BB1 ..... 100 F7
Brookhouse Rd. Caton LA2 ...... 231 C3
Brookhouse Rd. Ormskirk L39 ... 15 D6
Brookhouse St. PR1 .... 116 D1
Brookland. LA6 .... 236 C3
Brookland Cl. BB5 .... 123 F4
Brookland St. BB4 .... 85 D1
Brookland Terr. BB4 .... 68 F7
Brooklands. Chipping PR3 .... 182 E3
Brooklands. Horwich BL6 .... 31 C3
Brooklands. Ormskirk L39 .... 16 A6
Brooklands. Preston PR1 .... 116 A1
Brooklands Ave. Burnley BB11 .. 127 B3
Brooklands Ave. Fulwood PR2 .. 116 E7
Brooklands Ave.
 Haslingden BB4 .... 67 B7
Brooklands Ave. Kirkham PR4 .. 113 A5
Brooklands Dr. Bacup PR3 .... 178 C6
Brooklands Dr. Heysham LA3 ... 208 F6
Brooklands Dr. Orrell WN5 .... 10 D5
Brooklands Gr. L40 .... 24 F3
Brooklands Rd. Burnley BB11 .. 127 B3
Brooklands Rd.
 Lytham St Anne's FY8 .... 89 C6
Brooklands Rd.
 Ramsbottom BL0 .... 49 A2
Brooklands Rd. Up Holland WN8 10 C7
Brooklands Terr. BB1 .... 101 A7
Brooklands The. PR4 .... 112 B4
Brooklyn Ave. FY3 .... 129 E8
Brooklyn Rd. BB1 .... 121 F5
Brooks Rd. L37 .... 11 D2
Brooks Way. L37 .... 11 D2
Brooksbottom Cl. BL0 .... 49 C4
Brookshaw St. BL9 .... 32 A4
Brookside. Brockhall Village BB6 142 C4
Brookside. Coppull PR7 .... 41 F1
Brookside. Euxton PR7 .... 59 C2
Brookside. Kirkham PR4 .... 112 F6
Brookside. Thornton FY5 .... 173 C3
Brookside Cl. Leyland PR5 .... 75 E3
Brookside Cl. Ramsbottom BL0 .. 49 A3
Brookside Cl. Whalley BB7 ...... 143 C5

Brookside Cotts. PR7 .... 61 D3
Brookside Cres. Ramsbottom BL8 48 E1
Brookside Cres.
 West Bradford BB7 .... 186 D7
Brookside Dr. LA2 .... 220 A8
Brookside Ind Est. BB5 .... 103 B5
Brookside La. BB5 .... 102 B3
Brookside Prim Sch. BB7 .... 164 F8
Brookside Rd. Fulwood PR2 .... 116 D7
Brookside Rd. Southport PR8 ... 34 C2
Brookside Rd. Standish WN1 ... 29 B1
Brookside View. BB5 .... 102 B4
Brookvale Ct. PR3 .... 155 E3
Brookview. PR2 .... 117 B5
Brookville. OL12 .... 70 C1
Brookway. Blackburn BB2 .... 80 B8
Brookway. Longton PR4 .... 73 F8
Brookway. Wrea Green PR4 ..... 112 A4
Broom Field. PR3 .... 178 D4
Broome St. PR8 .... 34 B3
Broomfield Mill St. PR1 .... 116 F1
Broomfield Pl. Blackburn BB2 .. 100 B3
Broomfield Pl. Standish WN6 ... 28 E1
Broomfield Rd. Fleetwood FY7 . 193 F2
Broomfield Rd. Standish WN6 ... 28 E2
Broomflat. WN6 .... 19 D7
Broomholme. WN6 .... 19 D7
Brotherod Hall Rd. OL12 .... 51 C2
Brotherton Meadows. 4 BB7 164 F8
Brough Ave. FY2 .... 150 F2
Brougham St. BB12 .... 126 F7
Broughton Ave. Blackpool FY3 . 129 E7
Broughton Ave. Southport PR8 .. 34 D4
Broughton Cl. BB2 .... 101 A1
Broughton Cty High Sch. PR3 136 C2
Broughton Gr. LA3 .... 212 F3
Broughton in Amounderness
 CE Prim Sch. PR3 .... 136 D1
Broughton St. Blackburn BB12 126 D6
Broughton St. 4 Darwen BB3 ... 80 F2
Broughton St.
 Preston PR1 & PR2 .... 116 E2
Broughton Way. FY6 .... 151 C6
Brow Cl. PR3 .... 154 A6
Brow Edge. BB4 .... 85 D1
Brow Hey. PR5 .... 77 B6
Brow La. LA2 .... 233 F4
Brow The. PR4 .... 72 E4
Browfoot Cl. LA5 .... 217 F2
Browgate. BB7 .... 187 F8
Browgill Pl. 8 LA1 .... 213 D2
Browhead Ct. BB10 .... 127 B8
Browhead Rd. BB10 .... 127 B8
Brown Birks Rd. BB5 .... 103 E8
Brown Birks St. OL14 .... 108 B1
Brown Edge Cl. PR8 .... 35 A2
Brown Hill La. BB8 .... 169 F7
Brown Hill Row. BB8 .... 169 F7
Brown La. Bamber Bridge PR5 .. 97 A2
Brown La. Higher Walton PR5 ... 97 A3
Brown St. Accrington BB5 ...... 103 B5
Brown St. Bacup OL13 .... 86 F4
Brown St. Bamber Bridge PR5 ... 76 F8
Brown St. Blackburn BB1 ...... 100 F5
Brown St. Blackrod BL6 .... 30 D2
Brown St. Burnley BB11 .... 126 F6
Brown St. Chorley PR6 .... 42 D8
Brown St. Clitheroe BB7 .... 164 D7
Brown St. 2 Ramsbottom BL0 ... 49 B5
Brown St. Thornton FY5 .... 173 B3
Brown St E. BB8 .... 169 D5
Brown St W. BB8 .... 169 C4
Brown's La. Kirkham PR4 .... 112 D3
Brown's La. Thornton FY6 ...... 173 E7
Browning Ave.
 Lytham St Anne's FY8 .... 90 D4
Browning Ave.
 Oswaldtwistle BB5 .... 102 C5
Browning Ave. 3 Thornton FY5 173 A3
Browning Cl. BB8 .... 169 D6
Browning Cres. PR1 .... 117 D2
Browning Rd. PR1 .... 117 D2
Browning St. BB3 .... 81 F1
Brownley St. Chorley PR7 .... 42 E7
Brownley St. Clayton Green PR6 . 77 B1
Brownlow La. WN5 .... 10 C1
Brownlow Rd. BL6 .... 31 C5
Brownlow St. Blackburn BB1 ... 101 D4
Brownlow St. Clitheroe BB7 .... 164 E7
Brownlow Terr. PR2 .... 99 C1
Brownroyd. BB8 .... 201 C2
Browns Hey. PR7 .... 60 A2
Brownside Mill. BB10 .... 127 F6
Brownside Rd. BB10 .... 127 F5
Brows Cl. L37 .... 11 E3
Brows La. L37 .... 11 E3
Browsholme. LA1 .... 213 C2
Browsholme Ave. Fulwood PR2 117 F3
Browsholme Cl. Carnforth LA5 . 217 C1

Browsholme Cl. Normoss FY3 . 130 B8
Browsholme Hall. BB7 .... 184 F7
Browsholme Rd. BB7 .... 223 C1
Broxfield Ct. FY8 .... 88 D6
Broxton Ave. WN5 .... 10 F7
Broyd View. LA1 .... 210 F5
Bruce St. Barnoldswick BB8 ... 200 B3
Bruce St. Blackburn BB1 .... 101 B6
Bruce St. Burnley BB11 .... 126 D5
Brun Gr. FY1 .... 129 E1
Brun St. BB1 .... 126 F6
Brun Terr. BB10 .... 127 F5
Bruna Dr. PR3 .... 178 E4
Brundhurst Fold. BB2 .... 120 E2
Brunel Dr. BB1 .... 101 A4
Brunel St. Burnley BB12 .... 126 C7
Brunel St. Horwich BL6 .... 31 C2
Brunel Way. FY4 .... 110 C7
Brunel Wlk. BB1 .... 100 F4
Brungerley Ave. BB7 .... 186 E1
Brunshaw Ave. BB10 .... 127 D5
Brunshaw Prim Sch. BB10 ..... 127 D4
Brunshaw Rd. BB10 & BB11 ... 127 D6
Brunswick Ave. BL6 .... 31 E2
Brunswick Dr. BB8 .... 169 A3
Brunswick Pl. 4 PR1 .... 116 C1
Brunswick Rd. LA3 .... 212 B3
Brunswick St. Blackburn BB2 .. 100 D4
Brunswick St. Blackpool FY1 .. 129 B4
Brunswick St. Burnley BB11 .. 127 A4
Brunswick St. Chorley PR6 ...... 42 D8
Brunswick St. Darwen BB3 ...... 64 B8
Brunswick St. Nelson BB9 ...... 147 E7
Brunswick Terr. Accrington BB5 103 B6
Brunswick Terr. Bacup OL13 .... 69 D8
Brunton House. LA1 .... 211 A5
Brunton Rd. LA1 .... 210 F6
Brunton's Warehouse. LA1 .... 213 E1
Brush St. BB11 .... 126 C5
Brussells Rd. BB3 .... 81 C1
Bryan St. FY3 .... 129 D5
Bryan St. BB2 .... 100 B4
Brydeck Ave. PR1 .... 95 E4
Bryer St. 24 PR1 .... 210 F8
Bryer's Croft. BB1 .... 121 F6
Bryn Gr. LA5 .... 215 E2
Bryning Ave. Blackpool FY2 ... 150 C4
Bryning Ave. Wrea Green PR4 .. 112 B3
Bryning Fern La. PR4 .... 112 F4
Bryning Hall La. Moss Side PR4 111 F1
Bryning Hall La. Warton PR4 ... 91 B8
Bryning La. Newton-with-S PR4 . 113 F2
Bryning La. Wrea Green PR4 ... 112 B2
Bryony Cl. Orrell WN5 .... 10 D5
Bryony Cl. Thornton FY5 .... 172 F5
Bryony Ct. LA3 .... 212 E2
Buccleuch Ave. BB7 .... 164 D8
Buccleuch Cl. BB7 .... 164 D8
Buccleuch Rd. 7 BB9 .... 168 C1
Buccleuch St. BB11 .... 126 E5
Buchan St. Blackpool FY1 ...... 129 C6
Buchanan St. Chorley PR6 & PR7 42 D7
Buchanan St. 7
 Ramsbottom BL0 .... 49 B6
Buck St. Burnley BB11 .... 126 E5
Buck St. Colne BB8 .... 169 E5
Buck St. Grindleton BB7 .... 187 B7
Buckden Cl. FY5 .... 172 C1
Buckden Gdns. BB9 .... 168 C3
Buckden Pl. LA3 .... 208 F8
Buckden Rd. 4 BB5 .... 102 F7
Buckfast Dr. LT 12 B2
Buckholes La. PR6 .... 78 C1
Buckhurst Rd. BL9 .... 50 C3
Buckingham Ave. Horwich BL6 .. 31 E2
Buckingham Ave.
 Penwortham PR1 .... 95 E2
Buckingham Cl. BB4 .... 84 A1
Buckingham Dr. BB12 .... 144 D2
Buckingham Gr. Church BB5 ... 102 F7
Buckingham Gr. Formby L37 ... 11 E1
Buckingham Gr.
 Morecambe LA3 .... 212 C3
Buckingham Pl. LA3 & LA4 .... 212 C3
Buckingham Rd.
 Lytham St Anne's FY8 .... 89 D4
Buckingham Rd. Maghull L31 .... 5 C1
Buckingham Rd.
 Morecambe LA3 & LA4 .... 212 C3
Buckingham St. PR7 .... 42 D7
Buckingham Way. FY6 .... 151 C5
Bucklands Ave. PR1 & PR2 .... 116 D2
Buckley Cres. PR5 .... 150 D7
Bucknell Pl. FY5 .... 150 F7
Buckshaw Cty Prim Sch. PR7 ... 60 A2
Buckshaw Hall Cl. PR7 .... 60 B2
Buckshaw Terr. BB12 .... 144 E2
Buff St. 2 BB3 .... 64 A8
Buffalo Rd. PR5 .... 76 A4
Bulcock St. BB10 .... 147 C1
Bulk La. LA1 .... 214 A1
Bulk St. LA1 .... 210 F8
Bull Cop. L37 .... 12 B3
Bull Park La. FY6 .... 152 C8
Bull St. BB11 .... 127 A6
Bullens La. L40 .... 22 E7
Buller Ave. PR1 .... 95 E4
Buller St. 1 Lancaster LA1 .... 213 F3
Buller St. Rawtenstall BB4 ...... 85 A2
Bullfinch Dr. FY5 .... 32 B5
Bullfinch St. 3 PR1 .... 117 B1
Bullion The. BB5 .... 167 E1
Bullough Cl. BB5 .... 103 A5
Bulrush Cl. BB5 .... 103 A5
Buncer La. BB2 .... 100 A4
Bungalows The. Earby BB8 .... 201 B1
Bungalows The.
 Great Eccleston PR3 .... 154 C5

Bunker St. PR4 .... 92 C6
Bunkers Hill Cl. BB2 .... 80 B8
Bunting Pl. 9 FY5 .... 172 F1
Bunyan St. 24 OL12 .... 51 F1
Buoymaster. LA1 .... 213 E1
Burbank St. FY4 .... 109 F5
Burdett St. BB11 .... 126 D5
Burdock Wlk. LA3 .... 212 E2
Burford Cl. Blackpool FY3 ...... 130 A7
Burford Dr. LA3 .... 209 A7
Burgate. FY4 .... 109 D5
Burgess Ave. FY4 .... 109 E5
Burgess Gdns. L31 .... 5 C2
Burgess' La. L37 .... 13 A1
Burgess St. 2 Blackburn BB1 . 101 C5
Burgess St. 5 Haslingden BB4 . 84 B3
Burgh Hall Rd. PR7 .... 42 A3
Burgh La. PR7 .... 42 C4
Burgh La S. PR7 .... 42 B2
Burgh Meadows. PR7 .... 42 C4
Burghley Ct. PR5 .... 76 B1
Burholme Cl. PR1 .... 118 A2
Burholme Pl. PR1 .... 118 A2
Burholme Rd. PR1 .... 118 A2
Burleigh. PR1 .... 95 E7
Burleigh Rd. PR1 .... 95 E7
Burleigh St. BB12 .... 126 F7
Burlington Ave. Formby L37 .... 12 B3
Burlington Ave.
 Morecambe LA4 .... 212 G5
Burlington Ctr The. FY8 .... 88 E6
Burlington Gdns. PR5 .... 59 B8
Burlington Gr. LA4 .... 212 G5
Burlington Rd. Blackpool FY4 .. 109 B6
Burlington Rd. Southport PR8 .. 33 F3
Burlington Rd W. FY4 .... 109 A6
Burlington St. Blackburn BB2 . 100 C5
Burlington St.
 Chorley PR6 & PR7 .... 42 D7
Burlington St. Nelson BB9 ..... 147 C7
Burn Gr. FY5 .... 172 E4
Burn Naze Cty Prim Sch. FY5 173 B3
Burnage Gdns. FY4 .... 109 D7
Burned House La. FY6 .... 195 D2
Burneside Cl. LA4 .... 212 F4
Burnfell Rd. 1 LA1 .... 213 D2
Burnham Cl. BB11 .... 126 E5
Burnham Ct. Blackpool FY3 ... 129 E5
Burnham Ct. Morecambe LA3 .. 212 B1
Burnham Gate. BB11 .... 126 D5
Burnham Trad Pk. 4 BB11 .... 126 E6
Burnley Ave. PR8 .... 20 D5
Burnley Barracks Sta. BB12 ... 126 E6
Burnley Bsns Ctr. 7 BB11 .... 127 A6
Burnley Central Sta. BB12 .... 126 F7
Burnley Coll of Art & Tech.
 BB11 .... 127 A7
Burnley General Hospl. BB10 147 C2
Burnley La. BB11 & BB5 .... 125 A2
Burnley Rd. 9 Accrington BB5 103 C6
Burnley Rd. Accrington BB5 .. 103 D8
Burnley Rd. Ainsdale PR8 ...... 20 C5
Burnley Rd. Baldingstone BL9 .. 49 E1
Burnley Rd. Blackburn BB1 ... 101 C6
Burnley Rd.
 Brierfield BB10 & BB9 .... 147 B5
Burnley Rd. Brierfield BB10 ... 147 F3
Burnley Rd.
 Burnley BB10 & BB11 .... 127 D1
Burnley Rd.
 Clayton-le-M BB12 & BB5 ..... 124 C5
Burnley Rd. Colne BB8 & BB9 .. 169 B3
Burnley Rd. Ewood Bridge BL0 .. 67 D5
Burnley Rd. Hapton BB11 & BB5 125 B1
Burnley Rd. Holme Chapel
 BB10 & OL14 & BB11 & OL13 .. 107 C4
Burnley Rd. Padiham BB12 .... 125 D8
Burnley Rd. Rawtenstall BB4 ... 84 F5
Burnley Rd. Rawtenstall BB4 .. 105 A2
Burnley Rd.
 Trawden BB8 & BB10 .... 170 B1
Burnley Rd. Weir BB11 & BB4 . 106 C3
Burnley Rd. Whalley BB6 ...... 143 F3
Burnley Rd E. Water BB4 .... 106 A2
Burnley Rd E.
 Whitewell Bottom BB4 .... 85 F4
Burnley Wlk. BB11 .... 101 C5
Burnley Wood Prim Sch. BB11 127 A4
Burns Ave. Lytham St Anne's FY8 . 90 D4
Burns Ave. Oswaldtwistle BB5 .. 102 D5
Burns Ave. Thornton FY5 ...... 173 A3
Burns Cl. WN5 .... 10 D1
Burns Dr. BB5 .... 103 E2
Burns Pl. FY4 .... 109 F8
Burns Rd. FY7 .... 194 A5
Burns St. Burnley BB12 .... 126 F7
Burns St. Nelson BB9 .... 168 D1
Burns St. Padiham BB12 .... 125 D7
Burns St. Preston PR1 .... 117 D2
Burns Way. BB6 .... 123 B4
Burns Wlk. BB3 .... 81 B1
Burnsall Ave. Blackpool FY3 .. 151 A1
Burnsall Ave. Heysham LA3 ... 208 F8
Burnsall Cl. BB10 .... 147 E3
Burnsall Pl. Fulwood PR2 ...... 117 E4
Burnsall St. 3 PR1 .... 125 A4
Burnside. Edenfield BL0 .... 67 D2
Burnside. Parbold WN8 .... 26 B2
Burnside Ave. Blackpool FY4 .. 109 E8
Burnside Ave. Calder Vale PR3 . 179 E8
Burnside Ave. Fleetwood FY7 . 193 C2
Burnside Ave. Fulwood PR2 ... 117 C3
Burnside Way. PR1 .... 95 D3

Burnslack Rd. PR2 .... 117 F3
Burntbarrow. LA7 .... 237 F4
Burrans Meadow. 14 BB8 .... 169 D4
Burrell Ave. BB8 .... 169 D6
Burrington Cl. PR2 .... 117 D6
Burrow Rd. Over Burrow LA6 .. 235 E7
Burrow Rd. Preston PR1 .... 117 A1
Burrow's La. FY6 .... 173 F5
Burscough Bridge Meth
 Prim Sch. L40 .... 24 E5
Burscough Bridge Sta. L40 ... 24 E5
Burscough Cty Prim Sch. L40 . 24 F5
Burscough Ind Est. L40 .... 24 E5
Burscough Junc Sta. L40 ...... 24 F4
Burscough RC Prim Sch. L40 . 24 E2
Burscough Rd. L39 .... 15 F7
Burscough St. L39 .... 15 F6
Burton Ave. LA1 .... 213 C3
Burton Cl. FY7 .... 172 C8
Burton Gdns. BB9 .... 147 B5
Burton Hill. LA6 .... 236 C3
Burton Morewood Prim Sch.
 LA6 .... 234 C7
Burton Pk. LA6 .... 234 B7
Burton Rd. FY4 .... 129 F1
Burton St. Burnley BB11 ...... 127 D6
Burton St. Rishton BB1 .... 123 C1
Burwains Ave. BB8 .... 191 D1
Burwell Ave. Coppull PR7 ..... 28 D8
Burwell Ave. Formby L37 .... 11 D1
Burwell Cl. 11 Kirkby L33 .... 1 A3
Burwell Cl. Middle Healey OL12 .. 51 E4
Burwen Castle Rd. BD23 ...... 201 F8
Burwen Cl. BB11 .... 126 D3
Burwood Cl. PR1 .... 95 F2
Burwood Dr. Blackpool FY3 ... 130 A6
Burwood Dr. Fulwood PR2 .... 117 E3
Bury Bsns Ctr. BL9 .... 32 A4
Bury Fold La. BB3 .... 64 A6
Bury La. PR6 & PR7 .... 78 F3
Bury New Rd. Bury BL9 .... 32 C2
Bury New Rd.
 Prettywood BL9 & OL10 .... 32 E2
Bury New Rd. Ramsbottom BL0 .. 49 D6
Bury Old Rd. Edenfield BL0 .... 67 F1
Bury Old Rd.
 Heywood BL9 & OL10 .... 32 E1
Bury Old Rd.
 Nangreaves BL0 & BL9 .... 49 F4
Bury Rd. Edenfield BL0 .... 67 D3
Bury Rd. Haslingden BB4 .... 84 B3
Bury Rd. Rawtenstall BB4 .... 67 E7
Bury Rd. Southport PR8 .... 34 B3
Bury Rd. Turton Bottoms BL7 .. 47 E3
Bury Row. BB7 .... 144 F8
Bury St. Darwen BB3 .... 81 A1
Bury St. Oswaldtwistle BB5 ... 102 D3
Buseph Cl. LA4 .... 213 B4
Buseph Dr. LA4 .... 213 B4
Bush La. Freckleton PR4 .... 92 B5
Bush La. Freckleton PR4 .... 92 B6
Bush St. BB10 .... 147 B1
Bushburn Dr. BB6 .... 142 C1
Bushby's La. L37 .... 11 C2
Bushby's Pk. L37 .... 11 D2
Bushell Pl. PR1 .... 116 F2
Bushell St. PR1 .... 116 F1
Bushell's Hosp. PR3 .... 137 E6
Bushey La. WA11 .... 8 E2
Bussel Rd. PR1 .... 95 E2
Butcher Brow. PR5 .... 96 E5
Butchers La. Maghull L39 .... 5 F5
Butchers La. Moss Side L31 & L39 . 6 B3
Bute Ave. FY1 .... 129 B7
Bute Rd. BB1 .... 101 C3
Bute St. BB11 .... 126 D3
Butler Pl. PR1 .... 116 F2
Butler Rd. FY1 .... 129 B3
Butler St. Blackpool FY1 .... 129 C6
Butler St. Padiham BB12 .... 125 D8
Butler St. Preston PR1 .... 95 F7
Butler St. 7 Burnley BB10 ..... 127 A8
Butler St. Ramsbottom BL0 .... 49 A4
Butler St. Rishton BB1 .... 123 C1
Butlers Meadow. PR4 .... 91 E6
Butt Hill La. PR3 .... 179 E4
Butt's La. PR3 .... 154 B5
Buttercross Cl. BB11 .... 126 D2
Butterfield Gdns. L39 .... 15 D3
Butterfield St. 2
 Barrowford BB9 .... 168 D3
Butterfield St. 2 Lancaster LA1 210 F8
Butterlands. PR1 .... 96 F8
Buttermere Ave. Chorley PR7 .. 42 B6
Buttermere Ave. Colne BB8 ... 169 F6
Buttermere Ave. Fleetwood FY7 193 C2
Buttermere Ave. 2
 Morecambe LA4 .... 212 G4
Buttermere Ave.
 Oswaldtwistle BB5 .... 102 D5
Buttermere Cl.
 Bamber Bridge PR5 .... 96 E2
Buttermere Cl. 5
 Blackburn BB1 .... 100 F6
Buttermere Cl. Formby L37 ..... 11 D3
Buttermere Cl. Fulwood PR2 .. 117 C4
Buttermere Cl. Maghull L31 ..... 5 E1
Buttermere Cres. WA11 .... 8 F2
Buttermere Ct. LA1 .... 214 B1
Buttermere Dr.
 Knott End-on-S FY6 .... 194 F5
Buttermere Dr. Ramsbottom BL0 49 B7
Buttermere Rd. Burnley BB10 . 127 F5
Buttermere Rd. Lancaster LA1 . 214 B1
Buttermere Rd. Longridge PR3 138 F5
Butterworth Brow. Brinscall PR7 62 A7
Butterworth Brow. Chorley PR7 . 42 A4
Buttons Row. BB4 .... 68 F6
Butts. Barnoldswick BB8 .... 200 B2

Butts. Great Harwood BB6 ...... 123 B5
Butts Cl. FY5 ...... 173 C4
Butts Gr. BB7 ...... 186 E2
Butts La. High Bentham LA2 ...... 233 B8
Butts La. Southport PR8 & PR9 .. 34 F5
Butts Mount. BB6 ...... 123 C5
Butts Rd. FY5 ...... 173 C4
Buxton Ave. FY2 ...... 150 D4
Buxton St. Accrington BB5 ...... 103 A5
Buxton St. Morecambe LA4 ...... 212 F4
Buxton St. Whitworth OL12 ...... 70 D3
Bye La. L39 ...... 14 C3
Bye Rd. BL0 ...... 49 E8
Bye-Pass Rd. LA5 ...... 216 A4
Byerworth La N. PR3 ...... 178 C5
Byerworth La S. PR3 ...... 178 C4
Byfield Ave. FY5 ...... 150 E7
Byland Cl. Blackpool FY4 ...... 109 C5
Byland Cl. Formby L37 ...... 12 B2
Byland Cl. Read BB12 ...... 144 D1
Bymbrig Cl. PR5 ...... 76 E8
Byrom Cl. Blackpool BB4 ...... 100 D4
Byrom St. Southport PR9 ...... 34 F7
Byron Ave. Bolton-le-S LA5 ...... 216 A5
Byron Ave. Lytham St Anne's FY8 90 D4
Byron Ave. Thornton FY5 ...... 173 A3
Byron Ave. Warton PR4 ...... 91 E6
Byron Cl. Accrington BB5 ...... 103 E2
Byron Cl. Formby L37 ...... 11 F4
Byron Cl. Orrell WN5 ...... 10 F7
Byron Cl. Oswaldtwistle BB5 ...... 102 C5
Byron Cl. Tarleton PR4 ...... 55 F5
Byron Cres. PR7 ...... 28 E8
Byron Dr. BB8 ...... 200 A3
Byron Rd. Colne BB8 ...... 169 F5
Byron Rd. Maghull L31 ...... 5 D3
Byron Rd. Morecambe LA3 ...... 212 B3
Byron Rd. Ramsbottom BL8 ...... 48 F2
Byron Sq. BB6 ...... 123 B4
Byron St. Blackpool FY4 ...... 129 B1
Byron St. Chorley PR6 ...... 42 D8
Byron St. Fleetwood FY7 ...... 194 A5
Byron St. Padiham BB12 ...... 125 F7
Byron Terr. BB2 ...... 100 B3
Byton Wlk. L33 ...... 1 A4

Cabin End Row. BB1 ...... 101 E4
Cabin Hill. BB2 ...... 99 B2
Cabin La. Banks PR9 ...... 53 F3
Cabin La. Holmeswood PR4 ...... 37 A6
Cabin La. Maghull L31 ...... 4 F4
Cabin La. Shirdley Hill L39 ...... 21 C5
Cable St. Formby L37 ...... 12 A4
Cable St. Lancaster LA1 ...... 210 F8
Cable St. Southport PR8 ...... 34 B7
Cabus Cross Roads. PR3 ...... 199 A5
Cabus Nook La. PR3 ...... 199 B6
Cadby Ave. FY3 ...... 129 F3
Cadley Ave. PR2 ...... 116 B3
Cadley Cswy. PR2 ...... 116 C4
Cadley Dr. PR2 ...... 116 B3
Cadogan Pl. PR1 ...... 96 A6
Cadogan St. BB9 ...... 168 D2
Cadshaw Cl. BB1 ...... 100 E8
Cadwell Rd. L31 ...... 5 B5
Caernarvon Ave. BB12 ...... 126 A7
Caernarvon Cl. BL8 ...... 48 F1
Caernarvon Rd. BB4 ...... 84 A1
Cage La. PR4 ...... 75 B8
Cairn Cl. FY4 ...... 109 C4
Cairndale Dr. PR5 ...... 59 B6
Cairns Cl. BB9 ...... 168 C3
Cairnsmore Ave. PR1 ...... 117 F1
Cairo St. BB12 ...... 126 D6
Caister Cl. WN8 ...... 9 E8
Calcott St. BB11 ...... 126 E2
Caldbeck Cl. BB9 ...... 147 E6
Caldbeck Rd. LA1 ...... 214 B1
Calder Ave. Billington BB7 ...... 143 A4
Calder Ave. Chorley PR7 ...... 42 B5
Calder Ave. Darwen BB3 ...... 80 D4
Calder Ave. Fleetwood FY7 ...... 193 D3
Calder Ave. Freckleton PR4 ...... 92 A5
Calder Ave. Fulwood PR2 ...... 116 F6
Calder Ave. Longridge PR3 ...... 139 A8
Calder Ave. Ormskirk L39 ...... 15 E4
Calder Ave. Thornton FY5 ...... 172 F2
Calder Ave. Whalley BB7 ...... 143 A7
Calder Ave. Withnell PR6 ...... 79 A1
Calder Banks. BB1 ...... 100 F7
Calder Cl. Bury BL9 ...... 32 A8
Calder Cl. Carnforth LA5 ...... 217 B1
Calder Cl. Kirkby L33 ...... 1 A6
Calder Cl. Kirkham PR4 ...... 113 C5
Calder Cl. Lytham St Anne's FY8 109 F2
Calder Cl. Nelson BB9 ...... 168 D1
Calder Cl. BB5 ...... 124 E6
Calder Dr. Catterall PR3 ...... 178 D2
Calder Dr. Lancaster LA1 ...... 213 B2
Calder Dr. Maghull L31 ...... 5 F2
Calder House La. PR3 ...... 178 D4
Calder Pl. Bury BB9 ...... 150 C1
Calder Pl. BB6 ...... 123 E6
Calder Rd. Rawtenstall BB4 ...... 85 A4
Calder St. Blackburn BB1 ...... 100 F7
Calder St. Burnley BB11 ...... 126 F6
Calder St. Colne BB8 ...... 169 C6
Calder St. Nelson BB9 ...... 168 D1
Calder St. Padiham BB12 ...... 125 C8
Calder St. Preston PR1 ...... 116 C1
Calder Terr. BB9 ...... 147 B8
Calder Vale. Barrowford BB9 ...... 168 D2
Calder Vale. Whalley BB7 ...... 143 C4
Calder Vale Rd. BB11 & BB12 .. 126 F6
Calder Vale. BB9 ...... 168 C5
Calderbrook Ave. BB11 ...... 126 E3
Calderbrook Pl. BB11 ...... 126 E3
Caldershaw Ctr The. OL12 ...... 51 B2

Caldershaw La. OL12 ...... 51 A2
Caldershaw Prim Sch. OL12 ...... 51 A1
Caldershaw Rd. OL11 & OL12 ... 51 A1
Calderstones Hospl. BB7 ...... 143 A7
Caldervale Ave. FY6 ...... 151 C3
Calderview Sch. BB12 ...... 126 F8
Caldicott Way. FY6 ...... 151 C6
Caldy Dr. BL8 ...... 49 A3
Caleb St. BB9 ...... 168 E1
Caledonian Ave. FY3 ...... 129 E2
Calendar St. BB1 ...... 100 E5
Calf Croft Pl. FY8 ...... 90 A4
Calf Hall La. BB8 ...... 200 A2
Calf Hall Rd. BB8 ...... 200 A2
Calf Hey. BB5 ...... 123 F4
Calf Hey Rd. BB4 ...... 83 B2
Calfcote La. PR3 ...... 139 B7
Calgary Ave. BB2 ...... 100 B8
Calico Cl. BB5 ...... 102 B4
Calico Dr. BB2 ...... 178 D3
Calico St. BB2 ...... 100 D1
Calico Wood Ave. WN6 ...... 19 F6
Calkeld La. LA1 ...... 210 F8
Calla Dr. PR3 ...... 178 C8
Callander Sq. OL10 ...... 32 F1
Callender St. BL0 ...... 49 B6
Callon St. PR1 ...... 96 E8
Caltha St. BL0 ...... 49 B6
Calva Cl. BB12 ...... 126 B8
Calverley St. PR0 & PR1 ..... 117 D1
Calverley Way. OL12 ...... 51 E4
Calvert Pl. FY3 ...... 130 A7
Cam Cl. PR5 ...... 76 F8
Cam La. Clayton Green PR5 & PR6 77 A4
Cam La. Thornton-in-C BD23 ... 201 B6
Cam St. PR1 ...... 117 C2
Cam Wood Fold. PR5 & PR6 ..... 77 A3
Cambell's Ct. FY8 ...... 88 E7
Camberley Cl. PR8 ...... 33 E5
Camborne Ave. LA5 ...... 216 C8
Camborne Ct. FY3 ...... 130 B2
Camborne Pl. PR4 ...... 92 B6
Cambray Rd. FY1 ...... 150 C1
Cambrian Cl. BB1 ...... 121 F3
Cambrian Way. BB4 ...... 84 B1
Cambridge Arc. PR8 ...... 34 B7
Cambridge Ave. Lancaster LA1 211 B5
Cambridge Ave. Southport PR9 .. 52 F2
Cambridge Cl. Blackburn BB1 ... 100 F4
Cambridge Cl. Padiham BB12 .. 125 D6
Cambridge Cl. Preston PR1 ..... 116 E2
Cambridge Cl. Preston PR1 ..... 116 E2
Cambridge Cl. Southport PR9 ... 52 F2
Cambridge Dr. Blackburn BB1 .. 101 E4
Cambridge Dr. Garstang PR3 ... 178 B7
Cambridge Dr. Padiham BB12 .. 125 D6
Cambridge Gdns. PR9 ...... 52 F2
Cambridge Rd.
  Bamber Bridge PR5 ...... 76 F8
Cambridge Rd. Blackpool FY1 .. 129 D5
Cambridge Rd. Cleveleys FY5 ... 172 C3
Cambridge Rd. Fleetwood FY7 . 193 E3
Cambridge Rd. Formby L37 ..... 11 D1
Cambridge Rd.
  Lytham St Anne's FY8 ...... 89 C3
Cambridge Rd. Morecambe LA3 212 B3
Cambridge Rd. Orrell WN5 ..... 10 F7
Cambridge Rd.
  Skelmersdale WN8 ...... 17 E1
Cambridge Rd. Southport PR9 .. 52 E2
Cambridge St. Accrington BB5 .. 103 D6
Cambridge St. Blackburn BB1 .. 100 F4
Cambridge St. Brierfield BB9 ... 147 B5
Cambridge St. Burnley BB11 ... 126 D5
Cambridge St. Chorley PR6 .... 42 C7
Cambridge St. Colne BB8 ...... 169 D4
Cambridge St. Darwen BB3 ..... 81 C1
Cambridge St.
  Great Harwood BB6 ...... 123 D5
Cambridge St. Haslingden BB4 .. 84 B1
Cambridge St. Nelson BB9 ...... 147 D7
Cambridge St. Preston PR1 ..... 116 E2
Cambridge Wlk. PR1 ...... 116 E2
Cambridge Wlks. PR8 ...... 34 B7
Camden Pl. PR1 ...... 95 F6
Camden Rd. FY3 ...... 129 E6
Camden St. Barrowford BB9 ... 168 D3
Camden St. Nelson BB9 ...... 147 D7
Cameron Ave. FY3 ...... 129 E2
Cameron Ct. BB10 ...... 147 A1
Camforth Hall La. PR3 ...... 138 A7
Camms View. BB4 ...... 67 A8
Camp St. BB10 ...... 147 E3
Campbell Ave. FY3 ...... 129 E2
Campbell St. Blackburn BB1 ... 121 F1
Campbell St. Falinge Fold OL12 .. 51 E2
Campbell St. Padiham BB12 .... 125 F7
Campbell St. Preston PR1 ...... 96 B8
Campbell St. Read BB12 ...... 144 D1
Campion Cl. BB2 ...... 100 A8
Campion Dr. Haslingden BB4 ... 67 A8
Campion Dr. Preston PR2 ...... 115 C1
Campion Way. Lower Fold OL12 .. 51 C3
Campion Way. Morecambe LA3 212 E2
Campions The. PR2 ...... 115 C1
Camwood. PR5 ...... 77 B4
Camwood Dr. PR5 ...... 96 B1
Canada Cres. FY2 ...... 150 E3
Canada St. BL6 ...... 31 B3
Canal Bank. Appley Bridge WN6 . 19 C7
Canal Bank. New Lane L40 ..... 24 B6
Canal Bank. Reeds L40 ...... 25 C2
Canal Bank Cotts. L31 ...... 5 C7
Canal Bank Pygons Hill. L31 .... 5 C7
Canal Mews. BB9 ...... 147 D8
Canal Pl. LA5 ...... 217 E1
Canal Row. WN2 ...... 29 D1

Canal St. Adlington PR7 ...... 30 A6
Canal St. Blackburn BB2 ...... 100 B1
Canal St. Burnley BB11 ...... 126 F6
Canal St. Church BB5 ...... 102 C6
Canal St. Clayton-le-M BB5 ... 123 F2
Canal Wlk. PR6 ...... 42 F8
Canalside. BB1 ...... 100 F3
Canberra Cl. FY5 ...... 150 F7
Canberra Rd. PR5 ...... 59 B8
Canberraway. PR4 ...... 91 E7
Candlemakers Ct. BB7 ...... 164 E8
Candlestick Pk. BL9 ...... 32 D4
Cann Bridge St. PR5 ...... 97 B4
Canning Rd. PR9 ...... 35 A6
Canning St. Burnley BB12 ...... 126 F7
Canning St. Padiham BB12 ..... 125 D7
Cannock Ave. FY3 ...... 129 E8
Cannock Gn. L31 ...... 5 B1
Cannon Hill. PR1 ...... 116 C1
Cannon St. Accrington BB5 ..... 103 B5
Cannon St. Chorley PR7 ..... 42 C8
Cannon St. Nelson BB9 ...... 168 E1
Cannon St. Preston PR1 & PR0 .. 95 F7
Cannon St. Ramsbottom BL0 .. 49 A4
Canon Cl. WN6 ...... 28 F2
Canon St. BL9 ...... 32 A4
Canterbury Ave. Blackpool FY3 129 F3
Canterbury Ave. Lancaster LA1 211 B5
Canterbury Cl. Brinscall PR6 ... 61 E8
Canterbury Cl. Carleton FY6 ... 151 C5
Canterbury Cl. Formby L37 ..... 11 F5
Canterbury Cl. Garstang PR3 .. 178 A7
Canterbury Cl. Southport PR8 .. 33 F4
Canterbury Rd. PR1 ...... 117 D1
Canterbury St. Blackburn BB2 .. 100 E4
Canterbury St. Chorley PR7 .... 42 E6
Canterbury Way. PR3 ...... 178 B7
Cantlow Fold. PR8 ...... 20 A4
Cantsfield Ave. PR2 ...... 116 B4
Canute St. PR1 ...... 117 A1
Cape St. BB4 ...... 85 A2
Capernwray Rd. LA6 ...... 234 B2
Capilano Pk. L39 ...... 6 C8
Capitol Way. PR1 & PR5 ...... 96 C5
Capstan Cl. FY8 ...... 109 E1
Captain Dr. Horwich BL6 ...... 31 B4
Captain St. Weir OL13 ...... 87 A7
Captain's Row. LA1 ...... 213 F1
Carawood Cl. WN6 ...... 19 D7
Carcroft Ave. FY2 ...... 150 D4
Cardale Ave. FY2 ...... 94 D2
Cardiff St. WN7 ...... 17 D1
Cardigan Ave. Burnley BB12 ... 126 A7
Cardigan Ave. Clitheroe BB7 164 E8
Cardigan Ave.
  Oswaldtwistle BB5 ...... 102 C4
Cardigan Cl. Blackburn BB12 .. 164 D8
Cardigan Pl. FY4 ...... 109 A5
Cardigan Pl. PR8 ...... 33 F1
Cardigan St. Lower Healey OL12 . 51 E3
Cardigan St. Preston PR1 ...... 116 D1
Cardinal Allen RC High Sch.
  FY7 ...... 172 E8
Cardinal Newman Coll. PR1 .... 96 B7
Cardinal Pl. FY5 ...... 172 E8
Cardinal St. BB10 ...... 147 B1
Cardwell Cl. PR4 ...... 91 D5
Cardwell Pl. BB2 ...... 100 E5
Cardwell St. BB12 ...... 125 D7
Carfax Fold. OL12 ...... 51 B2
Carfax Rd. L33 ...... 1 A4
Carham Rd. BB1 ...... 100 E8
Carholme Ave. BB10 ...... 127 C6
Carisbrooke Ave. Blackpool FY3 150 F1
Carisbrooke Cl. FY6 ...... 151 C6
Carisbrooke Dr. PR9 ...... 52 F1
Carleton Ave. Blackpool FY3 ... 150 F1
Carleton Ave. Fulwood PR2 .... 117 D4
Carleton Ave. Simonstone BB12 144 E2
Carleton Dr. PR1 ...... 95 A4
Carleton Gate. FY6 ...... 151 C4
Carleton Gdns. FY6 ...... 151 B5
Carleton Green Cty Prim Sch.
  FY6 ...... 151 C6
Carleton Rd. Great Knowley PR6 . 60 F3
Carleton Rd. Nelson BB8 ...... 169 A3
Carleton Sch. FY6 ...... 151 B5
Carleton St. Morecambe LA4 .. 212 D4
Carleton St. Nelson BB9 ...... 147 E7
Carleton Way. FY6 ...... 151 B5
Carley St. BB3 ...... 80 E2
Carlin Gate. FY2 ...... 150 B2
Carlisle Ave. Fleetwood FY7 ... 193 D1
Carlisle Ave. Penwortham PR1 .. 95 A4
Carlisle Gr. FY5 ...... 173 B2
Carlisle House. PR1 ...... 96 A7
Carlisle Pl. PR6 ...... 30 A8
Carlisle Rd. Accrington BB5 .... 103 D7
Carlisle Rd. Southport PR8 .... 34 A2
Carlisle St. Blackburn BB1 ..... 100 F4
Carlisle St. Lower Healey OL12 .. 51 E3
Carlisle Terr. LA5 ...... 217 D3
Carloway Ave. PR2 ...... 117 C5
Carlton Ave. Clayton Green PR6 .. 77 B2
Carlton Ave. Hall Green WN8 ... 10 A7
Carlton Cl. BB6 ...... 30 D2
Carlton Cl. BB5 ...... 169 B5
Carlton Dr. PR1 ...... 96 B5
Carlton Gdns. BB1 ...... 100 E6
Carlton Gr. Blackpool FY2 ..... 150 B4
Carlton Gr. Horwich BL6 ...... 31 D1
Carlton Pl. BB7 ...... 164 E7
Carlton Rd. Ainsdale PR8 ...... 20 C6
Carlton Rd. Blackburn BB1 .... 126 E5
Carlton Rd. Leyland PR5 ...... 58 F8
Carlton Rd. Lytham St Anne's FY8 88 F7
Carlton St. Bacup OL13 ...... 87 A4

Carlton St. Brierfield BB9 ...... 147 B5
Carlton St. Preston PR1 ...... 95 D8
Carluke St. BB1 ...... 101 C5
Carlyle Ave. FY4 ...... 109 B6
Carlyle St. BB10 ...... 147 C3
Carmel Cl. L39 ...... 15 D2
Carnarvon Rd. Blackburn BB2 .. 100 B5
Carnarvon Rd. Preston PR1 .... 95 D7
Carnarvon Rd. Southport PR8 .. 33 F1
Carnfield Pl. PR5 ...... 77 B8
Carnforth Ave. FY7 ...... 150 E5
Carnforth Brow. LA5 ...... 217 F2
Carnforth Cl. BB2 ...... 101 A1
Carnforth Dr. BL8 ...... 49 A2
Carnforth High Sch. LA5 ...... 217 E1
Carnforth Sta. LA5 ...... 217 D2
Carnoustie Cl. PR2 ...... 116 B7
Carnoustie Cl. PR1 ...... 95 A6
Carnoustie Dr. BL0 ...... 49 B5
Caroline Cl. LA3 ...... 208 F8
Caroline Ct. BB11 ...... 126 B4
Caroline St. Blackpool FY1 .... 129 B3
Caroline St. Preston PR1 ...... 96 C8
Carr Bank Ave. BL0 ...... 49 B7
Carr Bank Dr. BL0 ...... 49 B7
Carr Bank Rd. Ramsbottom BL0 .. 49 B7
Carr Bank Rd. Storth LA7 ...... 237 E2
Carr Barn Brow. PR5 ...... 77 C6
Carr Brook Cl. PR6 ...... 60 B8
Carr Cl. Poulton-le-F FY6 ...... 151 E2
Carr Cl. Smallwood Hey PR3 ... 196 C5
Carr Dr. PR4 ...... 112 F2
Carr End La. FY6 ...... 174 C6
Carr Field. PR5 ...... 77 C4
Carr Fold. BL0 ...... 49 B7
Carr Gate. FY5 ...... 172 C4
Carr Hall Dr. BB9 ...... 168 C1
Carr Hall Gdns. BB9 ...... 168 B1
Carr Hall Rd. BB9 ...... 168 B1
Carr Hall St. BB4 ...... 84 A5
Carr Head. BB8 ...... 170 C2
Carr Head La. FY6 ...... 151 E2
Carr Hey. FY5 ...... 173 A2
Carr Hill High Sch. PR4 ...... 113 B4
Carr House La.
  Bretherton PR4 & PR5 ...... 56 D6
Carr House La.
  Heskin Green PR7 &WN6 ...... 40 F1
Carr House La. Ince Blundell L38 .. 3 E4
Carr House La. Lancaster LA1 .. 210 E7
Carr La. Blackburn BB2 ...... 99 F6
Carr La. Chorley PR7 ...... 42 D5
Carr La. Cold Row FY6 ...... 174 C4
Carr La. Croston PR5 & PR7 .... 39 B8
Carr La. Heysham LA3 ...... 208 E7
Carr La. Kirkham PR4 ...... 113 C6
Carr La. Leyland PR5 ...... 76 A3
Carr La. Maghull L31 ...... 4 F5
Carr La. Middleton LA3 ...... 208 F1
Carr La. Much Hoole PR4 ...... 74 A1
Carr La. Newchurch BB4 ...... 68 F7
Carr La. Rawtenstall BB4 ...... 85 A1
Carr La. Ring o'Bells L40 ...... 25 B3
Carr La. Singleton FY6 ...... 152 C1
Carr La. Smallwood Hey PR3 ... 196 C4
Carr La. Southport PR8 ...... 20 F7
Carr La. Tarleton PR4 ...... 55 F7
Carr La. Warton PR4 ...... 91 B6
Carr Meadow. PR5 ...... 77 C6
Carr Mill St. BB4 ...... 84 B5
Carr Moss La. L39 ...... 21 D2
Carr Mount. BB4 ...... 84 F1
Carr Pl. PR5 ...... 77 B7
Carr Rd. Barnoldswick BB8 .... 200 A3
Carr Rd. Blackpool FY5 ...... 150 D6
Carr Rd. Burnley BB11 ...... 126 E3
Carr Rd. Clayton Green PR6 .... 77 B2
Carr Rd. Colne BB8 ...... 169 E6
Carr Rd. Cornholme OL14 ..... 107 F1
Carr Rd. Darwen BB3 ...... 64 B8
Carr Rd. Fleetwood FY7 ...... 194 A4
Carr Rd. Hambleton FY6 ...... 174 C2
Carr Rd. Horwich BL6 ...... 31 B5
Carr Rd. Kirkham PR4 ...... 113 B4
Carr Rd. Nelson BB9 ...... 168 C1
Carr Rd. Rawtenstall BB4 ...... 84 F1
Carr Rd. Water BB4 ...... 86 C7
Carr Royd Est. FY6 ...... 152 A3
Carr Side La. L29 & L38 ...... 4 A3
Carr St. Bamber Bridge PR5 .... 76 E8
Carr St. Blackburn BB1 ...... 100 E6
Carr St. Chorley PR6 ...... 60 E1
Carr St. Preston PR1 ...... 96 B7
Carr St. Ramsbottom BL0 ...... 49 B7
Carr View. BB8 ...... 170 C1
Carr's Cres. L37 ...... 11 E1
Carr's Cres W. L37 ...... 11 D1
Carradice Cl. WN6 ...... 147 D8
Carradon Dr. WN6 ...... 28 E1
Carrier's Row. BB8 ...... 170 E6
Carrington Ave. BB2 ...... 80 C8
Carrington Gr. LA4 ...... 213 A5
Carrington Rd. Adlington PR7 .. 29 F7
Carrington Rd. Chorley PR7 .... 42 C7
Carrol St. PR1 ...... 117 B1
Carroll Cres. L39 ...... 15 F7
Carron La. PR3 ...... 158 A4
Carrs Ind Est. BB4 ...... 84 A4
Carrs Wood. BB2 ...... 99 F6
Carrwood Dr. BB4 ...... 113 A4
Carrwood Gn. BB2 ...... 125 C8
Carrwood Hey. BL0 ...... 49 A4
Carrwood Rd. PR1 & PR5 ...... 96 B3
Carry La. BB9 ...... 169 E4
Carsharlton Rd. FY1 ...... 129 B8
Carsluith Ave. FY3 ...... 129 F3
Carson Rd. FY4 ...... 130 A1

Cart Gate. FY6 ...... 195 B3
Carter Ave. BB11 ...... 125 C4
Carter Fold. PR3 ...... 120 E2
Carter St. Accrington BB5 ...... 103 B4
Carter St. Blackpool FY1 ...... 129 B5
Carter St. Burnley BB12 ...... 126 C7
Carter's Charity Prim Sch.
  PR3 ...... 195 C7
Carter's La. BB7 ...... 225 A5
Carterville Cl. FY4 ...... 110 A7
Cartford Cl. PR3 ...... 154 A6
Cartford La. PR3 ...... 154 A6
Cartmel Ave. Accrington BB5 .. 103 A3
Cartmel Ave. Fleetwood FY7 .. 193 D1
Cartmel Ave. Maghull L31 ...... 5 E2
Cartmel Cl. PR8 ...... 34 F3
Cartmel Dr. Burnley BB12 ..... 126 B8
Cartmel Dr. Coupe Green PR5 .. 97 E4
Cartmel Dr. Formby L37 ...... 12 B2
Cartmel Pl. Morecambe LA4 ... 212 G4
Cartmel Pl. Preston PR2 ...... 115 E2
Cartmel Rd. Blackburn BB2 .... 100 A3
Cartmel Rd. Lancaster LA1 .... 214 B2
Cartmel Rd. Leyland PR5 ...... 58 D8
Cartmell La. Moss Side FY8 .... 90 E4
Cartmell La. Nateby PR3 ...... 177 C7
Cartmell Rd. Blackpool FY4 ... 130 D1
Cartmell Rd.
  Lytham St Anne's FY8 ...... 88 F5
Cartwright Ct. LA1 ...... 210 E8
Carus Ave. BB3 ...... 81 E1
Carus Pk. LA6 ...... 235 B2
Carus St. BB3 ...... 81 F1
Carvers Brow. PR5 ...... 57 B1
Carwood Gr. BL6 ...... 31 D1
Carwood La. Whittle-le-W PR6 .. 60 C8
Carwood La. Whittle-le-W PR6 .. 60 D8
Caryl Rd. FY8 ...... 88 D8
Caryle Gr. LA4 ...... 213 A6
Casserley Rd. BB8 ...... 169 F6
Casson Gate. OL12 ...... 51 E1
Castercliffe Cty Prim Sch.
  BB9 ...... 169 B1
Castercliffe Rd. BB9 ...... 148 B8
Casterton. PR7 ...... 59 C2
Casterton Ave. BB10 ...... 147 C3
Casterton Mews. BB10 ...... 147 C3
Casterton Sch. LA6 ...... 238 F4
Castle Ave. FY6 ...... 151 B6
Castle Bank. LA5 ...... 218 C4
Castle Cl. BB8 ...... 169 E6
Castle Cres. BL6 ...... 31 C5
Castle Cl. LA1 ...... 210 E8
Castle Dr. Formby L37 ...... 11 F1
Castle Fold. PR1 ...... 95 F2
Castle Gate. BB7 ...... 164 E8
Castle Gr. BL0 ...... 49 A2
Castle Hill. LA1 ...... 210 E8
Castle Hill Rd. BL9 ...... 32 D5
Castle House La. PR7 ...... 29 E6
Castle La. Bonds PR3 ...... 178 D6
Castle La. Staining FY3 ...... 130 D5
Castle La. Westhead L40 ...... 16 E5
Castle Mount. PR2 ...... 116 F7
Castle Park Mews. LA1 ...... 210 E8
Castle Pk. LA1 ...... 210 E8
Castle Rd. BB4 ...... 170 A7
Castle St. Brierfield BB9 ...... 147 B6
Castle St. Burnley BB11 ...... 126 F7
Castle St. Clitheroe BB7 ...... 164 E8
Castle St. Hapton BB12 ...... 125 C4
Castle St. Nelson BB9 ...... 147 F8
Castle St. Preston PR1 ...... 116 F1
Castle St. Ramsbottom BL9 .... 49 C2
Castle St. Southport PR9 ...... 34 B8
Castle Sta. LA1 ...... 210 E8
Castle The. BB8 ...... 170 A7
Castle View. Barnoldswick BB8 . 200 B1
Castle View. Clitheroe BB7 .... 164 E8
Castle Wlk. Penwortham PR1 ... 95 C7
Castle Wlk. Southport PR8 ..... 34 A6
Castlecroft Ave. BL6 ...... 30 D2
Castlegate. FY1 ...... 129 B1
Castlehey. WN8 ...... 9 E6
Castlerigg Dr. BB12 ...... 126 B8
Castlerigg Pl. FY4 ...... 130 C1
Castleton Rd. PR1 ...... 117 B1
Castletown Dr. OL13 ...... 87 B1
Cat Tail Rd. PR 35 E1
Catches La. OL11 ...... 51 B1
Catforth Ave. FY4 ...... 130 B1
Catforth Cty Prim Sch. PR4 ... 135 A4
Catforth Rd. Catforth PR4 .... 134 F5
Catforth Rd. Preston PR2 ..... 115 C1
Catharine's La. L39 ...... 15 F1
Cathedral. LA3 ...... 212 E2
Cathedral RC Sch. LA1 ...... 211 A7
Catherine Cl. PR4 ...... 112 F7
Catherine St. Chorley PR7 ..... 42 C6
Catherine St. Kirkham PR4 .... 112 F6
Catherine St. Preston PR1 .. 96 B8
Catherine St E. BL6 ...... 31 B1
Catherine St W. BL6 ...... 31 B5
Cathrow Dr. PR4 ...... 75 A7
Catlow Hall St. BB5 ...... 102 E4
Cato St. BL0 ...... 49 A4
Caton Ave. FY7 ...... 193 D1
Caton Cl. Clayton-le-W PR5 & PR4 76 C2
Caton Cl. Longridge PR3 ...... 139 B8
Caton Cl. Southport PR9 ...... 52 F4
Caton Gr. FY3 ...... 129 F7
Caton Green Rd. LA2 ...... 231 D3
Caton Prim Sch. LA2 ...... 231 C3
Caton Rd. Lancaster LA1 ...... 214 A1

Caton Rd. Lancaster LA1 .... 214 B4
Caton St Paul's CE Prim Sch. LA2 .... 231 D3
Catterall Cl. FY1 .... 129 D7
Catterall Gates La. PR3 .... 178 C3
Catterall La. PR3 .... 178 C1
Catterall St. BB2 .... 80 C8
Catterick Fold. PR8 .... 34 F3
Cattle St. BB6 .... 123 C5
Caunce Ave. PR9 .... 54 A6
Caunce St. FY1 & FY3 .... 129 D6
Caunce's Rd. PR9 .... 36 C5
Causeway. Foulridge BB8 .... 191 D1
Causeway. Great Harwood BB6 . 123 B5
Causeway Ave. PR2 .... 116 C4
Causeway Croft. BB7 .... 186 F1
Causeway Head. BB4 .... 67 A8
Causeway La. Great Altcar L37 .... 13 B1
Causeway La. Rufford L40 .... 38 B2
Causeway St. BB3 .... 64 C7
Causeway The. Chorley PR7 .... 42 E8
Causeway The. Southport PR9 .... 53 C5
Causeway The. Wymott PR5 .... 57 F6
Causey Foot. BB9 .... 147 D7
Cavalry Way. BB11 & BB12 .... 126 D6
Cave St. Blackburn BB2 .... 100 B1
Cave St. Preston PR1 .... 96 D8
Cavendish Cres. PR2 .... 117 F3
Cavendish Ct. Bolton-le-S LA5 ... 216 A5
Cavendish Ct. Southport PR9 .... 34 E8
Cavendish Dr. PR2 .... 117 F3
Cavendish Pl. Bamber Bridge PR5 .... 96 D3
Cavendish Pl. Blackburn BB2 .... 100 B3
Cavendish Rd. Blackpool FY2 .... 150 C4
Cavendish Rd. Lytham St Anne's FY8 .... 88 D8
Cavendish Rd. Morecambe LA3 . 212 B3
Cavendish Rd. 2 Preston PR1 . 117 E1
Cavendish Rd. Southport PR8 .... 33 F3
Cavendish St. Barnoldswick BB8 200 B1
Cavendish St. 1 Chorley PR6 .... 42 E7
Cavendish St. Darwen BB3 .... 80 F3
Cavendish St. Lancaster LA1 .... 210 D8
Cavour St. BB12 .... 126 F7
Cawthorne Endowed Prim Sch. LA2 .... 226 F1
Cawthorne St. LA1 .... 210 E8
Caxton Ave. FY2 .... 150 C5
Caxton Rd. PR2 .... 117 B8
Cecil St. Barnoldswick BB8 .... 200 B3
Cecil St. Blackpool FY1 .... 129 C7
Cecil St. Lytham St Anne's FY8 .... 90 A3
Cecil St. Oswaldtwistle BB5 .... 102 E4
Cecil St. Rishton BB1 .... 123 C2
Cecilia Rd. BB2 .... 100 A2
Cecilia St. PR1 .... 117 D1
Cedar Ave. 1 Bamber Bridge PR5 .... 76 B8
Cedar Ave. Cleveleys FY5 .... 172 E2
Cedar Ave. Euxton PR7 .... 59 C4
Cedar Ave. Fleetwood FY7 .... 172 E8
Cedar Ave. Haslingden BB4 .... 84 C3
Cedar Ave. Horwich BL6 .... 31 E1
Cedar Ave. Knott End-on-S FY6 .. 195 A5
Cedar Ave. Poulton-le-F FY6 .... 130 D8
Cedar Ave. Preston PR2 .... 116 A2
Cedar Ave. Rawtenstall BB4 .... 84 E2
Cedar Ave. Warton PR4 .... 91 D6
Cedar Cl. Garstang PR3 .... 178 B8
Cedar Cl. Grimsargh PR2 .... 138 D1
Cedar Cl. Newton-with-S PR4 .... 114 A3
Cedar Cl. Rishton BB1 .... 102 B8
Cedar Cres. Kirkham PR4 .... 113 A4
Cedar Cres. Ormskirk L39 .... 15 D4
Cedar Cres. Ramsbottom BL0 .... 49 C7
Cedar Dr. L37 .... 11 C1
Cedar Field. PR6 .... 77 C2
Cedar Gr. Longton PR4 .... 94 A1
Cedar Gr. Orrell WN5 .... 10 F6
Cedar Gr. Skelmersdale WN8 .... 17 E1
Cedar House Sch. LA6 .... 238 B2
Cedar Rd. Chorley PR6 .... 60 D2
Cedar Rd. Fulwood PR2 .... 117 E2
Cedar Rd. Lancaster LA1 .... 210 D8
Cedar Sq. FY1 .... 129 B5
Cedar St. Accrington BB5 .... 103 D6
Cedar St. Blackburn BB1 .... 100 F8
Cedar St. Burnley BB11 .... 127 B5
Cedar St. Bury BL9 .... 32 A3
Cedar St. Bury BL9 .... 32 B3
Cedar St. Morecambe LA4 .... 212 C4
Cedar St. Rochdale OL12 .... 51 F1
Cedar St. Southport PR8 .... 34 D4
Cedar Way. PR1 .... 95 B3
Cedar Wlk. PR4 .... 153 F1
Cedars Cl. BB8 .... 200 A1
Cedars Cty Inf Sch The. BB1 .. 100 F8
Cedars The. Chorley PR7 .... 42 B4
Cedars The. Eccleston PR7 .... 40 B7
Cedars The. New Longton PR4 .... 74 F8
Cedarwood Cl. FY8 .... 89 E4
Cedarwood Dr. PR5 .... 58 E8
Cedric Pl. FY2 .... 150 C4
Celandine Cl. FY5 .... 172 F5
Celia St. BB10 .... 127 C5
Cemetery La. Burnley BB11 .... 126 A4
Cemetery La. Preesall Park FY6 195 B1
Cemetery Rd. Earby BB8 .... 201 B2
Cemetery Rd. Padiham BB12 .... 125 C7
Cemetery Rd. Preston PR1 .... 117 C1
Cemetery Rd. Ramsbottom BL0 ... 49 A4
Cemetery Rd. Southport PR8 .... 34 C4
Cemetery View. PR7 .... 30 A6
Centenary Way. BB11 .... 127 A5
Central Ave. Clitheroe BB7 .... 164 D7
Central Ave. Edenfield BL0 .... 67 D2
Central Ave. Gregson Lane PR5 ... 97 E2
Central Ave. Kirkham PR4 .... 112 F6
Central Ave. Lancaster LA1 .... 213 F4
Central Ave. Oswaldtwistle BB5 102 C4
Central Ave. Southport PR8 .... 21 A8
Central Ave N. FY5 .... 172 F3
Central Avnue. PR8 .... 20 F8
Central Beach. FY8 .... 90 B3
Central Dr. Blackpool FY1 .... 129 C3
Central Dr. Lytham St Anne's FY8 89 C5
Central Dr. Morecambe LA4 .... 212 D5
Central Dr. Penwortham PR1 .... 95 A4
Central Lancaster High Sch. LA1 .... 214 B1
Central Sq. 7 Haslingden BB4 .... 84 B3
Central Sq. Maghull L31 .... 5 D2
Central St. BL0 .... 49 C6
Central Terr. PR7 .... 59 D4
Central View. OL13 .... 87 A2
Centre Dr. PR5 & PR6 .... 77 B4
Centurian Way. BB1 .... 81 B6
Centurion Cl. BB1 .... 81 B7
Centurion Ind Est. PR5 .... 76 B3
Centurion Way. PR5 .... 76 A4
Ceres Way. LA1 .... 210 C8
Chad St. BB8 & BB9 .... 169 A2
Chaddock St. 11 Preston PR1 .... 95 F7
Chaddock St. 27 Preston PR1 .... 96 A7
Chadfield Rd. FY1 .... 129 D2
Chadwick St. Blackburn BB2 .... 100 D3
Chadwick St. Blackpool FY1 .... 129 C3
Chadwick St. Bury BL9 .... 32 E4
Chadwick Terr. OL12 .... 51 D4
Chaffinch Cl. FY5 .... 172 F5
Chaffinch Ct. FY3 .... 130 B6
Chaffinch Dr. BL9 .... 32 C4
Chaigley Ct. BB7 .... 163 A8
Chaigley Farm Cotts. BB7 .... 163 A8
Chaigley Rd. PR3 .... 139 B8
Chain Caul Rd. PR2 .... 94 F8
Chain Caul Way. PR2 .... 94 F8
Chain House La. PR4 & PR5 .... 75 D7
Chain La. FY3 .... 130 E4
Chalfont Field. PR2 .... 116 C5
Challan Hall Cotts. LA5 .... 218 E5
Challan Hall Mews. LA5 .... 218 E5
Challenge Way. BB1 .... 101 C7
Chamber St. BB4 .... 86 A8
Chambres Rd. PR8 .... 34 D5
Chambres Rd N. PR8 .... 34 D6
Chancel Pl. BB3 .... 64 C8
Chancel Way. BB3 .... 64 C8
Chancery Rd. PR7 .... 60 B2
Chancery Wlk. 3 BB11 .... 127 A6
Chandler Bsns Pk. PR5 .... 75 E2
Chandler St. 7 PR1 .... 95 F8
Chandlers Croft. PR4 .... 72 E4
Chandley Cl. PR8 .... 20 A5
Change View. OL13 .... 87 B4
Changford Gn. 7 L33 .... 1 A3
Changford Rd. L33 .... 1 A3
Channel Way. PR1 & PR2 .... 95 C8
Channing Rd. FY8 .... 89 C4
Chapel Brow. Leyland PR5 .... 76 B2
Chapel Brow. Longridge PR3 .... 139 B5
Chapel Cl. Kirkham PR4 .... 112 F7
Chapel Cl. Overton LA3 .... 205 C8
Chapel Cl. Trawden BB8 .... 170 B2
Chapel Cl. West Bradford BB7 ... 186 E5
Chapel Cl. Whalley BB7 .... 143 C5
Chapel Ct. BB10 .... 148 A3
Chapel Fields. BL7 .... 47 C4
Chapel Fold. 12 Colne BB8 .... 169 D4
Chapel Fold. Wiswell BB7 .... 143 F7
Chapel Gdns. Catterall PR3 .... 178 D2
Chapel Gdns. Hesketh Bank PR4 . 72 E4
Chapel Grange. BL7 .... 47 C4
Chapel Hill. Longridge PR3 .... 139 A6
Chapel Hill. Salterforth BB8 .... 191 D7
Chapel Hill La. BB4 .... 85 B4
Chapel House. BB1 .... 123 C1
Chapel House Rd. BB9 .... 147 E7
Chapel La. Arnside LA5 .... 237 B2
Chapel La. Banks PR9 .... 54 B7
Chapel La. Burscough L40 .... 24 E2
Chapel La. Burton in L LA6 .... 236 C3
Chapel La. Catforth PR4 .... 134 D4
Chapel La. Coppull PR7 .... 41 F1
Chapel La. Formby L37 .... 11 F3
Chapel La. Grindleton BB7 .... 187 B8
Chapel La. Hoghton PR5 .... 98 D2
Chapel La. Holmeswood PR4 .... 37 B6
Chapel La. Kirkby Lonsdale LA6 . 238 C2
Chapel La. Kirkham PR4 .... 113 B4
Chapel La. Langho BB6 .... 142 B2
Chapel La. Longton PR4 .... 74 C8
Chapel La. New Longton PR4 .... 74 E8
Chapel La. Out Rawcliffe PR3 .... 175 B2
Chapel La. Overton LA3 .... 205 D8
Chapel La. Parbold WN8 .... 26 D1
Chapel La. Ramsbottom BL8 .... 49 A6
Chapel La. West Bradford BB7 ... 186 E5
Chapel La. Wheelton PR6 .... 61 B5
Chapel Meadow. PR4 .... 74 C8
Chapel Meadows. PR4 .... 56 A5
Chapel Mews. Earby BB8 .... 201 B1
Chapel Mews. Ormskirk L39 .... 15 F4
Chapel Park Rd. PR4 .... 74 D8
Chapel Rd. Blackpool FY4 .... 110 B7
Chapel Rd. Fulwood PR2 .... 117 A4
Chapel Rd. Hesketh Bank PR4 .... 72 E4
Chapel Rise. BB7 .... 143 B4
Chapel Sq. LA2 .... 231 D3
Chapel St. 9 Accrington BB5 .... 103 C5
Chapel St. Adlington PR7 .... 29 F6
Chapel St. 14 Bacup OL13 .... 69 C8
Chapel St. Barnoldswick BB8 .... 200 B2
Chapel St. Belmont BL7 .... 45 C5
Chapel St. Belthorn BB1 .... 81 F6
Chapel St. Blackburn BB2 .... 100 D4
Chapel St. Blackpool FY1 .... 129 B4
Chapel St. Blackrod BL6 .... 30 D2
Chapel St. Brierfield BB9 .... 147 B6
Chapel St. Brinscall PR6 .... 61 F8
Chapel St. Burnley BB11 .... 127 A6
Chapel St. Chorley PR6 & PR7 .... 42 C8
Chapel St. Clayton-le-M BB5 .... 123 E3
Chapel St. Colne BB8 .... 169 D4
Chapel St. Coppull PR7 .... 41 E1
Chapel St. Darwen BB3 .... 64 A8
Chapel St. Earby BB8 .... 201 B2
Chapel St. Egerton BL7 .... 46 D3
Chapel St. Foulridge BB8 .... 191 E1
Chapel St. Galgate LA2 .... 207 A3
Chapel St. Great Eccleston PR3 . 154 B5
Chapel St. Haslingden BB4 .... 84 B3
Chapel St. Higham BB12 .... 145 F5
Chapel St. Horwich BL6 .... 31 C3
Chapel St. 3 Lancaster LA1 .... 210 F8
Chapel St. Longridge PR3 .... 139 B7
Chapel St. Lytham St Anne's FY8 . 90 A3
Chapel St. Morecambe LA4 .... 212 D5
Chapel St. Nelson BB9 .... 147 E8
Chapel St. Newchurch BB4 .... 85 E1
Chapel St. Ormskirk L39 .... 15 F4
Chapel St. Oswaldtwistle BB5 .... 102 E4
Chapel St. Poulton-le-F FY6 .... 151 D3
Chapel St. Preston PR1 .... 95 F7
Chapel St. Rawtenstall BB4 .... 85 A8
Chapel St. Rishton BB1 .... 123 C1
Chapel St. Slaidburn BB7 .... 223 C7
Chapel St. Southport PR8 .... 34 B7
Chapel St. Whitworth OL12 .... 51 C8
Chapel St. Worsthorne BB10 .... 128 A5
Chapel Street Ct. 2 FY6 .... 151 D3
Chapel Street Sta. PR8 .... 34 B7
Chapel Veiw. LA3 .... 205 D8
Chapel Way. PR7 .... 28 F8
Chapel Wlk. 2 Padiham BB12 .. 145 C1
Chapel Wlk. Warton LA5 .... 217 E6
Chapel Wlks. Kirkham PR4 .... 113 B4
Chapel Wlks. 4 Preston PR1 .... 95 F7
Chapel Yd. PR5 .... 96 D5
Chapelhouse La. LA6 .... 238 E1
Chapelhouse Wlk. L37 .... 12 A3
Chapels. BB3 .... 81 A3
Chapels Brow. BB3 .... 81 A3
Chapels La. BB3 .... 79 F3
Chapelside Cl. PR3 .... 178 D2
Chapeltown Rd. BL7 .... 47 C2
Chapman Cl. PR3 .... 154 C5
Chapman Rd. Fulwood PR2 .... 117 A3
Chapman Rd. Hoddlesden BB3 .... 81 F1
Chapter Rd. BB3 .... 64 C8
Charlbury Gr. LA3 .... 209 A7
Charles Ave. PR8 .... 20 E6
Charles Cl. PR4 .... 72 E3
Charles Cres. PR5 .... 97 C3
Charles Ct. FY3 .... 129 D7
Charles Gr. PR3 .... 139 A7
Charles La. BB4 .... 84 A2
Charles Saer Cty Sch. FY7 .... 193 D3
Charles St. Blackburn BB2 .... 100 D2
Charles St. Blackpool FY1 .... 129 C6
Charles St. Clayton-le-M BB5 .... 123 E2
Charles St. Colne BB8 .... 169 E5
Charles St. Darwen BB3 .... 81 A2
Charles St. Egerton BL7 .... 46 D2
Charles St. Great Harwood BB6 . 123 C4
Charles St. Lancaster LA1 .... 210 F6
Charles St. Morecambe LA4 .... 212 F5
Charles St. Nelson BB9 .... 168 E2
Charles St. Newchurch BB4 .... 85 F2
Charles St. Oswaldtwistle BB5 ... 102 E3
Charles Way. PR2 .... 115 E1
Charlesbye Ave. L39 & L40 .... 16 B6
Charlesbye Cl. L40 .... 16 B6
Charleston Ct. PR5 .... 96 E2
Charlesway Ct. PR2 .... 115 E1
Charlesworth Cl. L31 .... 5 B5
Charley Wood Rd. L33 .... 1 C1
Charlotte Pl. 33 PR1 .... 96 A7
Charlotte St. Blackburn BB1 .... 100 E6
Charlotte St. Burnley BB11 .... 126 F5
Charlotte St. Chapeltown BL7 .... 47 C4
Charlotte St. Preston PR1 .... 96 A7
Charlotte St. 4 Ramsbottom BL0 49 B5
Charlotte's La. PR4 .... 55 E2
Charnley Cl. PR1 .... 95 C2
Charnley Fold. PR5 .... 96 F3
Charnley Fold La. PR5 .... 96 F3
Charnley Rd. FY1 .... 129 C4
Charnley St. Blackburn BB2 .... 100 C2
Charnley St. Lancaster LA1 .... 213 D1
Charnley St. 1 Preston PR1 .... 95 F7
Charnley's La. PR9 .... 53 E7
Charnock Ave. PR1 .... 95 E2
Charnock Back La. PR6 & PR7 ... 43 C6
Charnock Brow. PR7 .... 41 C7
Charnock Fold. PR1 .... 117 A2
Charnock House. PR6 .... 60 C2
Charnock Richard CE Prim Sch. PR7 .... 41 D4
Charnock St. Chorley PR6 & PR7 . 42 D7
Charnock St. Kirkham PR4 .... 112 F6
Charnock St. 3 Leyland PR5 .... 76 B1
Charnock St. Preston PR1 .... 116 F2
Charnwood Ave. FY3 .... 130 A7
Charnwood Cl. BB2 .... 100 A8
Charter Brook. BB6 .... 123 D5
Charter La. PR7 .... 41 D3
Charter St. BB5 .... 103 A5
Charterhouse Pl. BB2 .... 100 B3
Chartwell Rd. PR8 .... 20 B6
Chartwell Rise. PR5 .... 76 C8
Chasden Cl. PR6 .... 60 C5
Chase Cl. PR8 .... 33 F4
Chase Heys. PR9 .... 53 A1
Chase The. Burnley BB12 .... 126 D8
Chase The. Leyland PR5 .... 76 C2
Chase The. Silverdale LA5 .... 218 D2
Chase The. Thornton FY5 .... 173 A4
Chaseley Rd. OL12 .... 51 E1
Chatburn Ave. Burnley BB10 .... 127 D5
Chatburn Ave. Clitheroe BB7 .... 186 F1
Chatburn CE Prim Sch. BB7 .. 187 D5
Chatburn Cl. Great Harwood BB6 .... 123 E5
Chatburn Cl. Normoss FY3 .... 130 B8
Chatburn Cl. Rawtenstall BB4 .... 85 A4
Chatburn Gdns. OL10 .... 32 F2
Chatburn Old Rd. BB7 .... 187 D5
Chatburn Park Ave. BB9 .... 147 A6
Chatburn Park Dr. Brierfield BB9 .... 147 A6
Chatburn Park Dr. Clitheroe BB7 .... 187 A2
Chatburn Rd. Chatburn BB7 .... 187 F5
Chatburn Rd. Clitheroe BB7 .... 187 A3
Chatburn Rd. Fulwood PR2 .... 117 F4
Chatburn Rd. Longridge PR3 .... 139 A7
Chatburn St. BB2 .... 100 C5
Chatham Ave. FY8 .... 109 E1
Chatham Cres. BB8 .... 169 E6
Chatham Pl. Chorley PR6 .... 42 E8
Chatham Pl. Preston PR1 .... 117 B2
Chatham St. Colne BB8 .... 169 E6
Chatham St. Nelson BB9 .... 168 D1
Chatsworth Ave. Blackpool FY2 150 C6
Chatsworth Ave. Fleetwood FY7 193 D2
Chatsworth Ave. Warton PR4 .... 91 D6
Chatsworth Cl. Barrowford BB9 168 B1
Chatsworth Cl. Chorley PR7 .... 42 B8
Chatsworth Cl. Thornton FY5 .... 173 D1
Chatsworth Ct. PR6 .... 42 F1
Chatsworth Rd. Ainsdale PR8 .... 20 B6
Chatsworth Rd. Bamber Bridge PR5 .... 96 D3
Chatsworth Rd. Lancaster LA1 . 210 F4
Chatsworth Rd. 1 Leyland PR5 . 76 A1
Chatsworth Rd. Lytham St Anne's FY8 .... 88 D7
Chatsworth Rd. Morecambe LA3 & LA4 .... 212 C4
Chatsworth St. Lower Healey OL12 .... 51 E3
Chatsworth St. Preston PR1 .... 96 D8
Chatteris Pl. FY5 .... 172 C1
Chatterton. BL0 .... 67 C2
Chatterton Dr. BB5 .... 103 E2
Chatterton Old La. BL0 .... 67 C2
Chatterton Rd. BL0 .... 67 C1
Chaucer Ave. FY5 .... 172 F2
Chaucer Cl. PR7 .... 40 B6
Chaucer Gdns. BB6 .... 123 B4
Chaucer Prim Sch. FY7 .... 194 A4
Chaucer Rd. FY7 .... 194 A4
Chaucer St. PR1 .... 117 D2
Cheam Ave. PR7 .... 42 D6
Cheapside. Blackpool FY1 .... 129 B5
Cheapside. 5 Chorley PR6 & PR7 42 C7
Cheapside. Formby L37 .... 12 A2
Cheapside. 11 Lancaster LA1 .... 210 F8
Cheapside. Low Bentham LA2 .... 233 B8
Cheapside. 8 Preston PR0 & PR1 95 F7
Cheddar Ave. FY4 .... 109 D6
Cheddar Dr. PR2 .... 117 D6
Chedworth Ave. LA3 .... 209 A7
Cheetham Hill. OL12 .... 70 D3
Cheetham Meadow. PR5 .... 58 B8
Cheetham St. BB2 .... 100 C5
Chelburn Gr. BB10 .... 127 C6
Chelford Ave. FY3 .... 129 E8
Chelford Cl. PR1 .... 95 F2
Chelmsford Cl. LA1 .... 211 B5
Chelmsford Gr. PR7 .... 42 B7
Chelmsford Pl. PR7 .... 42 B7
Chelmsford Wlk. PR5 .... 58 A8
Chelsea Ave. FY2 .... 150 E1
Chelsea Ct. 3 FY2 .... 150 E1
Chelsea Mews. 4 FY2 .... 150 E1
Chelston Dr. BB4 .... 67 A7
Cheltenham Ave. BB5 .... 103 C8
Cheltenham Cres. Lytham St Anne's FY8 .... 90 D5
Cheltenham Cres. Thornton FY5 .... 151 D8
Cheltenham Dr. WN5 .... 10 D2
Cheltenham Rd. Blackburn BB2 100 C5
Cheltenham Rd. Blackpool FY1 . 129 B7
Cheltenham Rd. Lancaster LA1 210 F5
Cheltenham Way. PR8 .... 34 F3
Chennel House. 3 LA1 .... 210 E8
Chepstow Ct. FY3 .... 129 F8
Chepstow Rd. FY3 .... 129 F8
Chequer Cl. WN8 .... 9 F5
Chequer La. WN8 .... 9 F6
Chequers. BB5 .... 123 F2
Chequers Ave. LA1 .... 211 B4
Cheriton Field. PR2 .... 116 C7
Cheriton Gdns. BL6 .... 31 B5
Cherry Ave. BL9 .... 32 C3
Cherry Cl. 2 Blackburn BB1 .... 101 B5
Cherry Cl. Fulwood PR2 .... 117 D6
Cherry Cres. Oswaldtwistle BB5 102 D2
Cherry Cres. Rawtenstall BB4 .... 67 F8
Cherry Gn. L39 .... 15 B1
Cherry Gr. Abbey Village PR7 .... 79 B2
Cherry Gr. Burscough Bridge L40 . 24 E6
Cherry Gr. Longridge PR3 .... 139 A7
Cherry La. PR4 .... 92 B4
Cherry Rd. PR8 .... 20 D2
Cherry St. BB1 .... 101 B5
Cherry Tree Cl. Fisher's Row PR3 .... 196 E5
Cherry Tree Cl. Hest Bank LA5 . 215 F2
Cherry Tree Cl. Heysham LA3 ... 208 E6
Cherry Tree Ct. Blackpool FY4 .. 130 B1
Cherry Tree Ct. Fleetwood FY7 . 194 B5
Cherry Tree Ct. Standish WN6 .... 28 D2
Cherry Tree Gdns. FY4 .... 110 A8
Cherry Tree Gr. PR6 .... 60 C3
Cherry Tree La. Blackburn BB2 ... 79 E8
Cherry Tree La. Ormskirk L39 .... 15 B1
Cherry Tree La. Rawtenstall BB4 67 F8
Cherry Tree Rd. FY4 .... 130 A1
Cherry Tree Rd N. FY4 .... 130 A1
Cherry Tree Sta. BB2 .... 99 F1
Cherry Tree Terr. BB2 .... 99 F1
Cherry Tree Way. Helmshore BB4 .... 67 B7
Cherry Tree Way. 5 Horwich BL6 .... 31 E1
Cherry Trees. PR5 .... 96 C3
Cherry Vale. PR4 .... 72 F2
Cherry Wood. PR1 .... 95 A3
Cherryclough Way. BB2 .... 80 B8
Cherrycroft. WN8 .... 9 E6
Cherrydale. FY2 .... 150 D5
Cherrywood Ave. Cleveleys FY5 172 C1
Cherrywood Ave. Lytham St Anne's FY8 .... 89 E4
Cherrywood Cl. PR5 .... 58 E8
Cheryl Dr. FY5 .... 151 B8
Chesham Cres. BL9 .... 32 A3
Chesham Cty Prim Sch. BL9 .... 32 A5
Chesham Dr. PR4 .... 74 F8
Chesham Fold Rd. BL9 .... 32 B4
Chesham Ind Est. BL9 .... 32 A4
Chesham Rd. BL9 .... 32 A5
Chesham St. PR3 .... 154 B5
Cheshire Ct. BL0 .... 49 D6
Cheshire House Cl. PR5 .... 75 F7
Chesmere Dr. PR1 .... 95 B5
Chessington Gn. BB10 .... 147 D3
Chester Ave. Chorley PR7 .... 42 E4
Chester Ave. Cleveleys FY5 .... 172 E2
Chester Ave. Clitheroe BB7 .... 186 E1
Chester Ave. Poulton-le-F FY6 ... 151 C4
Chester Ave. Southport PR9 .... 34 F8
Chester Cl. Blackburn BB1 .... 101 A3
Chester Cl. Garstang PR3 .... 178 B7
Chester Cres. BB4 .... 67 B8
Chester Dr. BL0 .... 49 A4
Chester Pl. Adlington PR6 .... 30 A8
Chester Pl. Great Eccleston PR3 154 C5
Chester Pl. Lancaster LA1 .... 211 A5
Chester Rd. Blackpool FY3 .... 129 D6
Chester Rd. Preston PR1 .... 117 C1
Chester Rd. Southport PR9 .... 34 F8
Chester St. Accrington BB5 .... 103 A5
Chester St. Blackburn BB1 .... 101 A4
Chester St. Bury BL9 .... 32 A4
Chesterbrook. PR3 .... 140 E4
Chesterfield Cl. PR8 .... 20 C4
Chesterfield Rd. Ainsdale PR8 .... 20 C5
Chesterfield Rd. Blackpool FY1 129 C7
Chestnut Ave. Blackpool FY4 .... 109 F5
Chestnut Ave. Bolton-le-S LA5 ... 216 A5
Chestnut Ave. Bury BL9 .... 32 B2
Chestnut Ave. Caton LA2 .... 231 C3
Chestnut Ave. Chorley PR6 .... 60 E2
Chestnut Ave. Euxton PR7 .... 59 C4
Chestnut Ave. Penwortham PR1 . 95 A4
Chestnut Cl. Bamber Bridge PR5 . 96 E2
Chestnut Cl. Halsall L39 .... 22 C1
Chestnut Cl. Kirkham PR4 .... 113 B5
Chestnut Cres. Barrow BB7 .... 164 D1
Chestnut Cres. Fulwood PR2 .... 117 E2
Chestnut Cres. Longton PR4 .... 73 F8
Chestnut Ct. PR5 .... 59 A7
Chestnut Dr. Barnoldswick BB8 . 200 A1
Chestnut Dr. Fulwood PR2 .... 116 D7
Chestnut Dr. Morecambe LA4 .... 213 B6
Chestnut Dr. Rawtenstall BB4 .... 67 F8
Chestnut Gr. Accrington BB5 .... 103 A4
Chestnut Gr. Clayton-le-M BB5 .. 124 A4
Chestnut Gr. Darwen BB3 .... 64 A5
Chestnut Gr. Lancaster LA1 .... 210 D8
Chestnut Rise. BB11 .... 126 F4
Chestnut St. PR8 .... 34 C5
Chestnut Way. L37 .... 11 C1
Chestnut Wlk. 5 BB1 .... 101 B5
Chestnuts The. PR7 .... 41 F2
Chethams Cl. FY5 .... 173 A2
Chevassut Cl. BB9 .... 168 C1
Cheviot Ave. Burnley BB10 .... 127 E5
Cheviot Ave. Cleveleys FY5 .... 172 F4
Cheviot Cl. Horwich BL6 .... 31 C5
Cheviot Cl. Ramsbottom BL0 .... 49 C4
Cheviot St. PR1 .... 95 C8
Chichester Cl. Burnley BB10 .... 127 B6
Chichester Cl. Thornton FY5 .... 173 A2
Chicken St. BB2 .... 100 C4
Childrey Wlk. BB2 .... 81 A8
Chilgrove Ave. BL6 .... 30 D1
Chiltern Ave. Blackpool FY4 .... 109 D7
Chiltern Ave. Burnley BB10 .... 127 E5
Chiltern Ave. Euxton PR7 .... 59 D1
Chiltern Ave. Poulton-le-F FY6 ... 151 C3
Chiltern Cl. Horwich BL6 .... 31 C5
Chiltern Cl. Lytham St Anne's FY8 90 D5
Chiltern Cl. Ramsbottom BL0 .... 49 C4
Chiltern Meadow. PR6 .... 76 D1
Chiltern Rd. Ainsdale PR8 .... 20 B6
Chiltern Rd. Ramsbottom BL0 .... 49 C4
Chimes The. PR4 .... 113 A4
China St. Accrington BB5 .... 102 F6
China St. Lancaster LA1 .... 210 F8
Chindit Cl. L37 .... 11 D2

Chindits Way. PR2 .... 117 B4
Chines The. PR2 .... 116 E4
Chingford Bank. BB10 .... 147 D3
Chingle Cl. PR2 .... 117 E6
Chipping Ave. PR8 .... 20 A5
Chipping Ct. 4 FY3 .... 130 A8
Chipping Gr. Burnley BB10 ...... 127 C4
Chipping Gr. Normoss FY3 ...... 130 A8
Chipping La. PR3 .... 139 A8
Chipping St. BB12 .... 145 D1
Chisacre Dr. WN6 .... 19 D7
Chisholm Cl. WN6 .... 28 B2
Chisholme Cl. BL8 .... 48 F2
Chislehurst Ave. FY4 .... 129 C1
Chislehurst Gr. BB10 .... 147 D4
Chislehurst Pl. FY8 .... 89 E5
Chislett Cl. L40 .... 24 D4
Chisnall Ave. WN6 .... 27 F6
Chisnall La. Coppull Moor PR7 .. 28 C6
Chisnall La. Heskin Green PR7 .... 40 F2
Chisnall La. Mossy Lea PR7 ...... 28 A5
Chiswell Gr. FY5 .... 151 D8
Chiswick Gr. FY3 .... 130 B2
Chobham Ct. 1 BB4 .... 85 E1
Chorley Bsns & Tech Ctr. PR7 .. 59 E4
Chorley Cl. PR9 .... 53 F5
Chorley & District Hospl. PR7 .. 60 C2
Chorley Golf Course. PR6 ...... 43 A3
Chorley Hall Rd. PR6 & PR7 .... 60 C2
Chorley La. PR7 .... 41 D3
Chorley New Rd. BL6 .... 31 C2
Chorley New Road Prim Sch.
  BL6 .... 31 D2
Chorley North Ind Est. PR6 ...... 60 D3
Chorley Old Rd. PR6 .... 77 C2
Chorley Rd. Adlington BL6 & PR6 . 30 B5
Chorley Rd. Bamber Bridge PR5 .. 96 C3
Chorley Rd. Blackpool FY3 ...... 150 F2
Chorley Rd. Blackrod BL6 ...... 30 C3
Chorley Rd. Hill Dale L40 & WN8 . 26 D6
Chorley Rd.
  Ollerton Fold BB2 & PR6 ...... 78 E4
Chorley Rd. Parbold WN8 ...... 26 C4
Chorley Rd. Standish WN1 ...... 29 C3
Chorley St. PR6 .... 30 B8
Chorley St James CE Prim Sch.
  PR6 .... 42 E7
Chorley Sta. PR6 .... 42 D8
Chorley West Bsns Pk. PR7 .... 41 F8
Chorlton Cl. BB10 .... 147 D2
Chorlton St. BB1 .... 100 F7
Chrisleton Cl. BB10 .... 147 F3
Christ Church CE Prim Sch.
  Carnforth LA5 .... 217 D1
Christ Church CE Prim Sch.
  Glasson LA2 .... 205 E4
Christ Church CE Prim Sch.
  Lancaster LA1 .... 211 B8
Christ Church CE Prim Sch.
  Ormskirk L39 .... 15 C3
Christ Church CE Sch. LA1 ...... 211 A8
Christ Church Prim Sch. BB8 .. 170 B5
Christ Church Sq. 1 BB5 ...... 103 C5
Christ Church St. 2
  Accrington BB5 .... 103 C5
Christ Church St. 6
  Bacup OL13 .... 87 A3
Christ Church St. Preston PR1 .. 95 E7
Christ The King RC High Sch.
  PR1 .... 96 B6
Christ The King RC Prim Sch.
  Blackpool FY3 .... 130 A7
Christ the King RC Prim Sch.
  Burnley BB11 .... 126 E3
Christ The King Sch. PR8 ...... 34 B2
Christian Rd. PR1 .... 95 E7
Christiana Hartley Maternity
  Hospl. PR8 .... 34 D5
Christie Ave. LA4 .... 212 G4
Christines Cres. L40 .... 24 E4
Church Alley. BB5 .... 123 F2
Church Ave. Accrington BB5 .... 103 E2
Church Ave. Lancaster LA1 .... 210 F4
Church Ave. Penwortham PR1 .... 95 C6
Church Ave. Preston PR1 ...... 96 E8
Church Bank. LA6 .... 231 B8
Church Bank St. 19 BB3 ...... 81 A1
Church Brook House. PR1 ...... 95 E4
Church Brow. Bolton-le-S LA5 .. 216 A3
Church Brow. Clitheroe BB7 .... 186 E1
Church Brow. Halton LA2 ...... 214 E6
Church Brow. Walton-le-D PR5 .. 96 E5
Church Brow Cl. LA5 .... 216 A3
Church Brow Gdns. BB7 ...... 186 E1
Church Cl. Clitheroe BB7 ...... 186 E1
Church Cl. Dolphinholme LA2 .. 220 A8
Church Cl. Formby L37 .... 12 A3
Church Cl. Freckleton PR4 ...... 92 A6
Church Cl. Mellor BB2 .... 120 E2
Church Cl. Read BB12 .... 144 D2
Church Cl. Southport PR9 ...... 35 A8
Church Cl. Waddington BB7 .... 186 B4
Church Close Ct. L37 .... 12 A3
Church Ct. Bolton-le-S LA5 .... 216 A3
Church Ct. Edenfield BL0 ...... 67 D4
Church Dr. Lytham St Anne's FY8 . 89 F3
Church Dr. Orrell WN5 .... 10 D5
Church Dr. Whalley BB7 ...... 143 A7
Church Fields. Bescar L40 ...... 22 F7
Church Fields. Ormskirk L39 .... 15 E5
Church Fold.
  Charnock Richard PR7 ...... 41 E4
Church Fold. Coppull PR7 ...... 28 F8
Church Gdns. PR4 .... 91 E6
Church Gn. L37 .... 11 C2
Church Gr. LA3 .... 205 E8
Church Hall. BB5 .... 102 F7

Church Hill. Arnside LA5 ...... 237 B2
Church Hill. Nether Kellet LA6 .. 216 F5
Church Hill. Whittle-le-W PR6 .... 60 C7
Church Hill Ave. LA5 .... 217 D5
Church Hill Rd. Blackburn BB1 . 101 A7
Church Hill Rd. Ormskirk L39 .... 15 D6
Church La. Aughton L39 .... 6 A7
Church La. Aughton L39 .... 6 A7
Church La. Bilsborrow PR3 .... 157 A4
Church La. Broughton PR3 .... 136 D1
Church La. Charnock Richard PR7 . 41 D4
Church La. Edenfield BL0 ...... 67 D4
Church La. Farington PR5 ...... 75 F7
Church La. Galgate LA2 ...... 207 B4
Church La. Goosnargh PR3 .... 137 D6
Church La. Great Harwood BB6 . 123 C6
Church La. Great Mitton BB7 .. 163 E3
Church La. Hambleton FY6 .... 174 D1
Church La. Kelbrook BB8 ...... 192 A6
Church La. Maghull L39 .... 5 A8
Church La. Mellor BB2 .... 120 E2
Church La. Morecambe LA4 .... 212 E6
Church La. Morecambe LA4 .... 212 F6
Church La. Newchurch BB4 ...... 85 E1
Church La. Newton-with-S PR4 .. 114 B3
Church La. 10 Padiham BB12 .. 145 C1
Church La. Whalley BB7 ...... 143 C5
Church La. Whitechapel PR3 .. 158 E7
Church La. Winmarleigh PR3 .. 198 E4
Church La. Wrightington Bar WN6 27 D8
Church Meadows. BB8 ...... 169 D5
Church & Oswaldtwistle Sta.
  BB5 .... 102 E5
Church Pk. Lea Town PR4 ...... 114 F3
Church Pk. Overton LA3 ...... 205 D8
Church Raike. PR3 .... 182 E3
Church Rd. Bamber Bridge PR5 .. 76 E7
Church Rd. Bamber Bridge PR5 .. 76 F6
Church Rd. Banks PR9 .... 54 A6
Church Rd. Bickerstaffe L39 ...... 7 E6
Church Rd. Formby L37 .... 12 A5
Church Rd. Kirkham PR4 ...... 112 F7
Church Rd. Leyland PR5 ...... 59 A8
Church Rd. Lytham FY8 .... 89 F3
Church Rd. Lytham St Anne's FY8 . 89 B6
Church Rd. Rufford L40 .... 38 C4
Church Rd. Shuttleworth BL0 .... 49 E8
Church Rd. Singleton FY6 ...... 152 F1
Church Rd. Skelmersdale WN8 .. 17 F1
Church Rd. Tarleton PR4 ...... 56 A5
Church Rd. Thornton FY5 ...... 173 A2
Church Rd.
  Thornton-in-C BB8 & BD23 .. 201 A5
Church Rd. Warton PR4 .... 91 D6
Church Rd. Weeton PR4 ...... 131 F1
Church Rd. Wharles PR4 ...... 133 F2
Church Row. Preston PR1 ...... 96 A7
Church Row. Wrea Green PR4 .. 112 B4
Church Row Chambers. PR4 .. 74 A8
Church Sq. BB10 .... 128 B5
Church St. Accrington BB5 .... 103 C5
Church St. Adlington PR6 ...... 30 A7
Church St. Bacup OL13 .... 69 C8
Church St. Barnoldswick BB8 .. 200 B2
Church St. Barrowford BB9 .... 168 D4
Church St. Belmont BL7 .... 45 C4
Church St. Blackburn BB1 .... 100 E5
Church St. Blackpool FY1 .... 129 C5
Church St. Blackrod BL6 ...... 30 C2
Church St. Brierfield BB9 .... 147 B5
Church St. Brierfield BB10 .... 147 F2
Church St. Burnley BB11 .... 127 A6
Church St. Bury BL9 .... 32 A3
Church St. Chorley PR6 .... 42 C7
Church St. Church BB5 .... 102 E6
Church St. Churchtown PR3 .. 178 A2
Church St. Clayton-le-M BB5 .. 123 F2
Church St. 1 Clitheroe BB7 .. 164 E8
Church St. Colne BB8 .... 169 D5
Church St. Croston PR5 .... 57 B1
Church St. Darwen BB3 .... 83 A1
Church St. Fleetwood FY7 .... 194 B4
Church St. Garstang PR3 .... 178 C7
Church St.
  Goodshaw Chapel BB4 ...... 105 A1
Church St. Great Harwood BB6 . 123 C5
Church St. Halton LA2 ...... 214 D6
Church St. Haslingden BB4 ...... 84 B4
Church St. Hapton BB12 ...... 125 B1
Church St. Higher Walton PR5 .... 97 B3
Church St. Horwich BL6 .... 31 C3
Church St. Kirkby Lonsdale LA6 . 238 C2
Church St. Kirkham PR4 ...... 113 B5
Church St. Lancaster LA1 .... 210 F8
Church St. Leyland PR5 .... 76 B2
Church St. Longridge PR3 .... 139 B7
Church St. Morecambe LA4 .... 212 E8
Church St. Nelson BB9 .... 147 D6
Church St. Newchurch BB4 ...... 68 E8
Church St. Newchurch BB4 ...... 85 E1
Church St. Ormskirk L39 .... 15 E5
Church St. Orrell WN5 .... 10 E5
Church St. Oswaldtwistle BB5 .. 102 D3
Church St. Padiham BB12 .... 125 C8
Church St. 1 Poulton-le-F FY6 . 151 D3
Church St. Preston PR1 .... 96 A7
Church St. Preston PR1 .... 96 B8
Church St. 5 Ramsbottom BL0 . 49 C6
Church St. Read BB12 .... 144 D2
Church St.
  Ribchester BB1 & PR3 ...... 140 D3
Church St. Rishton BB1 ...... 123 A1
Church St. Slaidburn BB7 ...... 223 C2
Church St. Southport PR9 ...... 34 C7
Church St. Standish WN6 ...... 28 F1
Church St. Trawden BB8 ...... 170 C2
Church St. Up Holland WN8 .... 10 C7
Church St. Whittington LA6 .... 235 C7

Church St. Whitworth OL12 .... 51 C8
Church Terr. 20 BB3 .... 81 A1
Church View. Aughton L39 ...... 6 A7
Church View. Gisburn BB7 .... 225 C3
Church View. Salesbury BB1 .. 121 E6
Church View. Stalmine FY6 .... 174 C7
Church View. Tarleton PR4 ...... 56 A5
Church View. Trawden BB8 .... 170 C2
Church View Ct. L39 .... 15 E5
Church Way. L37 .... 11 C2
Church Wlk. Blackburn BB1 .... 121 F3
Church Wlk. Euxton PR7 .... 59 C2
Church Wlk. Kirkham PR4 .... 112 F7
Church Wlk. Tarleton PR4 ...... 56 A6
Church Wlks. L39 .... 15 E5
Churchfield. PR2 .... 116 F6
Churchfields. PR8 .... 33 F3
Churchgate. Goosnargh PR3 .. 137 D6
Churchgate. Southport PR9 .... 52 F1
Churchgate Mews. PR9 ...... 53 A1
Churchill Ave. Rishton BB1 .. 102 A8
Churchill Ave. Southport PR9 .. 52 F2
Churchill Cl. FY5 .... 173 B2
Churchill Ct. FY3 .... 129 D6
Churchill Dr. PR2 .... 117 D4
Churchill Rd. Barrowford BB9 . 168 B1
Churchill Rd. Brinscall PR7 ...... 62 A8
Churchill Rd. Fulwood PR2 .... 117 C4
Churchill St. OL11 & OL12 .... 51 C1
Churchill Way. Leyland PR5 .... 76 A2
Churchill Way. Nelson BB9 .... 147 B7
Churchlands La. WN6 .... 28 F1
Churchside. PR4 .... 74 F8
Churchtown Cres. OL13 ...... 87 B1
Churchtown Ct. PR9 .... 53 A2
Churchtown Prim Sch. PR9 .. 53 B2
Churchward Sq. BL6 .... 31 C2
Churton Gr. WN6 .... 28 B2
Cicely La. BB1 .... 100 F5
Cicely St. BB1 .... 100 F4
Cinder La. Lancaster LA1 & LA2 . 210 F3
Cinder La. Lewth PR4 .... 135 A6
Cinder La. Mere Brow PR4 ...... 55 C5
Cinderbarrow La. LA5 & LA6 .. 234 A6
Cinnamon Brow. WN8 .... 10 C6
Cinnamon Ct. PR1 .... 95 C2
Cinnamon Hill Dr N. PR5 ...... 96 D3
Cinnamon Hill Dr S. PR5 ...... 96 D3
Cintra Ave. PR2 .... 116 D3
Cintra Terr. PR2 .... 116 D3
Circus The. 10 BB3 .... 81 A1
City Heights Cl. 16 LA1 ...... 211 A8
Clairane Ave. PR2 .... 116 E6
Clairville. PR8 .... 33 F5
Clancut La. PR7 .... 41 F2
Clanfield. PR2 .... 116 E7
Clara St. Preston PR1 .... 96 C7
Clara St. Whitworth OL12 ...... 70 D1
Clare Ave. BB8 .... 169 A2
Clare Rd. LA1 .... 213 E2
Clare St. Blackpool FY1 .... 129 B1
Clare St. Burnley BB11 ...... 126 E6
Claremont Ave. Chorley PR7 .... 42 B7
Claremont Ave. Clitheroe BB7 .. 164 F7
Claremont Cres. LA4 .... 212 C4
Claremont Ct. FY1 .... 129 C7
Claremont Dr. Clitheroe BB7 .... 164 F7
Claremont Dr. Ormskirk L39 .... 15 D3
Claremont Gdns. PR8 .... 34 A4
Claremont Pl. FY8 .... 88 E8
Claremont Prep Sch. BB1 .... 100 D6
Claremont Rd. Accrington BB5 . 103 B8
Claremont Rd. Blackpool FY1 .. 129 C8
Claremont Rd. Chorley PR7 .... 42 B7
Claremont Rd. Morecambe LA4 212 C4
Claremont Rd. Southport PR8 .. 34 A4
Claremont St. Brierfield BB9 .. 147 A6
Claremont St. Burnley BB12 .. 126 D6
Claremont St. Colne BB8 .... 170 A5
Claremont Terr. BB9 .... 147 D7
Claremount Ave. PR5 .... 59 B8
Clarence Ave. Cleveleys FY5 .. 172 D3
Clarence Ave. 4
  Haslingden BB4 .... 84 A1
Clarence Ave.
  Knott End-on-S FY6 .... 194 E5
Clarence Ct. FY4 .... 129 B1
Clarence Pk. BB2 .... 100 B7
Clarence Rd. Accrington BB5 .. 103 A4
Clarence Rd. Southport PR9 .... 34 A4
Clarence St. Barnoldswick BB8 . 200 C1
Clarence St. Blackburn BB1 .. 100 D6
Clarence St. Burnley BB11 .. 127 B4
Clarence St. Chorley PR6 ...... 42 D7
Clarence St. Colne BB8 .... 170 A5
Clarence St. Darwen BB3 .... 80 F3
Clarence St. Lancaster LA1 .... 211 A7
Clarence St. Leyland PR5 ...... 76 B2
Clarence St. Lower Fold OL12 ... 51 D2
Clarence St. Morecambe LA4 .. 212 E6
Clarence St. Rawtenstall BB4 ... 85 A7
Clarence St. Trawden BB8 .... 170 C2
Clarendon Gr. L31 .... 5 C5
Clarendon Rd. Blackburn BB1 .. 100 D6
Clarendon Rd. Blackpool FY1 .. 129 B2
Clarendon Rd. Lancaster LA1 .. 213 C4
Clarendon Rd.
  Lytham St Anne's FY8 ...... 89 A8
Clarendon Rd E. Blackburn BB1 101 A8
Clarendon Rd E.
  Morecambe LA4 .... 212 C4
Clarendon Rd N. FY8 .... 88 F8
Clarendon Rd W. LA3 & LA4 .... 212 B4
Clarendon St. Accrington BB5 .. 103 D6
Clarendon St. Bury BL9 .... 32 A4
Clarendon St. Chorley PR7 .... 42 E7

Clarendon St. Colne BB8 ...... 170 B5
Clarendon St. Preston PR1 ...... 96 A6
Claret St. BB5 .... 103 A3
Clark St. LA4 .... 212 E6
Clarke Holme St. BB4 .... 85 C7
Clarke St. Poulton-le-F FY6 .... 151 F3
Clarke St. 5 Rishton BB1 .... 123 B1
Clarke Wood Cl. BB7 .... 143 F8
Clarke's Cotts. L40 .... 26 A8
Clarkes Croft. BL9 .... 32 C3
Clarkfield Dr. LA4 .... 212 G5
Clarksfield Rd. LA5 .... 216 A4
Clarrick Terr. LA4 .... 236 F3
Claughton Ave. PR6 .... 76 C1
Claughton Dr. LA1 .... 211 A3
Claughton RC Prim Sch. PR3 179 D1
Claughton St. BB10 .... 147 B1
Clawthorpe Cotts. LA6 ...... 234 C8
Clay Brow Rd. WN8 .... 9 E6
Clay Gap La. FY6 & PR3 ...... 174 F4
Clay Hill La. PR3 .... 140 B8
Clay La. LA3 .... 209 B8
Clay St. BB11 .... 126 C5
Claybank. BB12 .... 145 C1
Clayburn Cl. PR6 .... 60 E2
Claylands Dr. LA5 .... 216 A4
Claypool Prim Sch. BL6 ...... 31 F1
Claypool Rd. BL6 .... 31 E1
Clayton Ave. Leyland PR5 ...... 58 D7
Clayton Ave. Rawtenstall BB4 ... 67 E8
Clayton Brook Cty Prim Sch.
  PR5 .... 77 B5
Clayton Brook Rd. PR5 ...... 77 C6
Clayton Cl. 11 BB9 .... 168 C1
Clayton Cres. FY4 .... 109 E6
Clayton Ct. PR3 .... 139 B7
Clayton Gdns. L40 .... 24 E4
Clayton Gr. BB1 .... 121 D6
Clayton Green RC Prim Sch
  (St Bede's). PR5 .... 77 C4
Clayton Hall Dr. BB5 .... 123 F4
Clayton Mews. WN8 .... 17 D1
Clayton Row. BB6 .... 142 D1
Clayton St. 5
  Bamber Bridge PR5 .... 96 E1
Clayton St. Barnoldswick BB8 .. 200 C2
Clayton St. Blackburn BB2 .... 100 E4
Clayton St. Colne BB8 .... 169 E4
Clayton St. Enfield BB5 ...... 124 A1
Clayton St. Great Harwood BB6 . 123 C5
Clayton St. Nelson BB9 ...... 168 D1
Clayton St. 7
  Oswaldtwistle BB5 .... 102 E5
Clayton St. Skelmersdale WN8 . 17 D1
Clayton Street Ind Est. BB9 .. 168 D1
Clayton's Gate. 12 PR1 ...... 95 F8
Clayton-le-Moors Ind Est.
  BB5 .... 123 E2
Clayton-le-Woods CE Prim Sch.
  PR6 .... 77 A2
Claytongate. PR7 .... 41 F2
Claytonhalgh. PR3 .... 140 E3
Cleator Ave. FY2 .... 150 C1
Cleaver St. Blackburn BB1 .... 100 F5
Cleaver St. Burnley BB10 .... 127 B8
Clecken La. PR3 .... 179 D2
Clegg Ave. FY5 .... 172 D3
Clegg St. 6 Bacup OL13 ...... 69 C8
Clegg St. Brierfield BB9 ...... 147 B5
Clegg St. Burnley BB10 ...... 127 A8
Clegg St. Haslingden BB4 ...... 84 B3
Clegg St. Nelson BB9 .... 147 E6
Clegg St. Skelmersdale WN8 .. 17 D1
Clegg St. Worsthorne BB10 .... 128 A5
Clegg St E. BB10 .... 127 A8
Clegg's Ct. OL12 .... 70 C2
Clematis St. BB2 .... 100 B6
Clement St. Accrington BB5 .. 103 C5
Clement St. 3 Darwen BB3 .... 64 A8
Clement View. 14 BB9 ...... 147 D8
Clementina St. OL12 .... 51 F1
Clements Dr. BB10 .... 147 C4
Clengers Brow. PR9 .... 53 A3
Clent Ave. L31 .... 5 C3
Clent Gdns. L31 .... 5 C3
Clent Rd. L31 .... 5 C3
Clerkhill St. BB1 .... 101 B5
Cleve Way. L37 .... 12 B2
Clevedon Rd. Blackpool FY1 .. 129 B7
Clevedon Rd. Fulwood PR2 .... 116 A4
Cleveland Ave. PR2 .... 117 C4
Cleveland Cl. BL0 .... 49 C3
Cleveland Dr. LA4 .... 210 D7
Cleveland Rd. Leyland PR5 .... 75 F7
Cleveland Rd.
  Lytham St Anne's FY8 ...... 90 B3
Cleveland St. Chorley PR6 .... 42 C8
Cleveland St. Colne BB8 ...... 169 F6
Cleveland St. Coppull PR7 .... 41 E1
Cleveland St. Cornholme OL14 . 108 B1
Clevelands Ave.
  Morecambe LA3 .... 212 C3
Clevelands Ave. Silverdale LA5 . 218 C4
Clevelands Gr. Burnley BB11 .. 126 E4
Clevelands Gr. Morecambe LA3 212 C3
Clevelands Rd. BB11 .... 126 F4
Clevelands Wlk. LA3 .... 212 C3
Cleveleys Ave. Cleveleys FY5 .. 172 D3
Cleveleys Ave. Fulwood PR2 .. 116 C4
Cleveleys Ave. Lancaster LA1 .. 213 C2
Cleveleys Ave. Southport PR9 .. 53 A4
Cleveleys Rd. Accrington BB5 .. 103 B8
Cleveleys Rd. Blackburn BB2 .. 100 F1
Cleveleys Rd. Coupe Green PR5 . 97 E3

Cleveleys Rd. Southport PR9 .. 53 A3
Cleves Ct. FY3 .... 130 A2
Cleves The. L31 .... 5 E3
Clieves Hills La. L39 .... 14 E3
Clieves Rd. L32 .... 1 A1
Clifden Ct. L37 .... 11 F3
Cliff Ave. BL9 .... 49 C2
Cliff Mount. BL0 .... 49 B7
Cliff Pl. FY2 .... 150 B4
Cliff Rd. PR9 .... 52 D1
Cliff St. Colne BB8 .... 169 B3
Cliff St. Padiham BB12 ...... 145 D1
Cliff St. Preston PR1 .... 95 E6
Cliff St. Rishton BB1 .... 123 B2
Cliffe Cl. PR1 .... 96 D8
Cliffe Dr. PR6 .... 60 B8
Cliffe La. BB6 .... 123 C6
Cliffe St. BB9 .... 168 E1
Clifford Ave. Longton PR4 ...... 94 A1
Clifford Ave. Morecambe LA4 .. 212 G6
Clifford Rd. Blackpool FY1 .... 129 C7
Clifford St. Barnoldswick BB8 .. 200 C2
Clifford St. Chorley PR6 ...... 42 D8
Clifford St. Colne BB8 .... 169 E5
Cliffs The. LA3 .... 212 A2
Clifton Ave. Accrington BB5 .... 103 C7
Clifton Ave. Blackpool FY4 .... 130 C1
Clifton Ave. Leyland PR5 ...... 59 B8
Clifton Ave. Preston PR2 ...... 116 A2
Clifton Ave. Warton PR4 ...... 91 E6
Clifton Cl. FY5 .... 173 C1
Clifton Cres. Blackpool FY3 .. 130 A2
Clifton Cres. Fulwood PR2 .... 117 C2
Clifton Ct. Blackpool FY4 .... 109 B6
Clifton Dr. Blackpool FY4 .... 109 B5
Clifton Dr. Blackrod BL6 ...... 30 C3
Clifton Dr. Great Harwood BB6 . 123 C5
Clifton Dr. Lytham St Anne's FY8 . 89 D3
Clifton Dr. Morecambe LA4 .... 213 A5
Clifton Dr. Penwortham PR1 .... 95 C5
Clifton Dr N. FY8 .... 109 B2
Clifton Dr S. FY8 .... 88 E5
Clifton Gdns. FY8 .... 89 C6
Clifton Gn. PR4 .... 114 C2
Clifton Gr. Chorley PR7 ...... 42 B7
Clifton Gr. Fulwood PR1 ...... 117 C3
Clifton Gr. Wilpshire BB1 .... 121 F4
Clifton Hospl. FY8 .... 89 B5
Clifton La. PR4 .... 114 D2
Clifton Lodge. FY8 .... 88 E7
Clifton Pl. PR4 .... 92 B6
Clifton Rd. Blackpool FY4 .... 110 C8
Clifton Rd. Brierfield BB9 .... 147 A5
Clifton Rd. Burnley BB12 .... 126 C7
Clifton Rd. Fleetwood FY7 .... 194 A3
Clifton Rd. Formby L37 ...... 12 A5
Clifton Rd. Southport PR8 .... 34 F6
Clifton Sq. FY8 .... 90 B3
Clifton St. Accrington BB5 .... 103 A4
Clifton St. Blackpool FY1 .... 129 B5
Clifton St. Burnley BB11 & BB12 126 F6
Clifton St. Colne BB8 .... 169 D5
Clifton St. Darwen BB3 ...... 80 F4
Clifton St. Lytham St Anne's FY8 . 90 B3
Clifton St. Preston PR1 ...... 95 D6
Clifton St. Rishton BB1 ...... 123 B1
Clifton St. Sough BB8 ...... 192 A5
Clifton St. Trawden BB8 ...... 170 C2
Clifton Terr. BB3 .... 81 E2
Clifton Wlk. PR3 .... 90 B3
Clinkham Rd. BB6 .... 123 A5
Clinning Rd. PR8 .... 34 A2
Clinton Ave. FY1 .... 129 C4
Clinton St. BB1 .... 101 A6
Clippers Quay. BB1 .... 100 F4
Clitheroe Castle. BB8 ...... 164 E8
Clitheroe Hospl. BB7 .... 187 A3
Clitheroe Pl. FY4 .... 110 A8
Clitheroe Rd. Brierfield BB9 .. 147 A5
Clitheroe Rd. Chatburn BB7 .. 187 C3
Clitheroe Rd.
  Lytham St Anne's FY8 ...... 89 C6
Clitheroe Rd. Sabden BB7 .... 165 E1
Clitheroe Rd. Waddington BB7 .. 186 C3
Clitheroe Rd.
  West Bradford BB7 .... 186 F5
Clitheroe Rd. Whalley BB7 .... 143 C7
Clitheroe Royal Gram Sch.
  Clitheroe BB7 .... 186 F1
Clitheroe Royal Gram Sch.
  Clitheroe BB7 .... 187 A2
Clitheroe St. 8 Padiham BB12 . 125 C8
Clitheroe St. Preston PR1 ...... 96 C7
Clitheroe Sta. BB7 .... 186 E1
Clitheroes La. PR4 .... 92 B6
Clive Ave. FY8 .... 109 C1
Clive Lodge. PR8 .... 33 F2
Clive Rd. Penwortham PR1 .... 95 B6
Clive Rd. Southport PR8 ...... 33 F2
Clive St. BB12 .... 126 F8
Clockhouse Ave. BB10 ...... 147 D3
Clockhouse Ct. BB10 .... 147 D3
Clockhouse Gr. BB10 .... 147 D3
Clod La. BB4 .... 67 C8
Clods Carr La. FY6 .... 194 F3
Clog Heads. BB8 .... 170 C2
Clogger La. BD23 .... 201 F7
Cloister Dr. BB3 .... 81 C1
Cloister Gn. L37 .... 12 B2
Cloisters. LA3 .... 212 F2
Cloisters The. Blackpool FY3 . 129 E5
Cloisters The. Formby L37 .... 11 F3

Cloisters The. Leyland PR5 .... 76 C2
Cloisters The. Preston PR1 .... 95 D8
Cloisters The. Tarleton PR4 .... 56 A6
Cloisters The. Whalley BB7 .... 143 D5
Clorain Cl. L33 .... 1 A3
Clorain Rd. L33 .... 1 A3
Close The. Banks PR9 .... 54 A5
Close The. Clayton-le-M BB5 ...... 123 F4
Close The. Cleveleys FY5 .... 172 D2
Close The. Cleveleys FY5 .... 172 D4
Close The. Fulwood PR2 .... 117 E6
Close The. Garstang PR3 .... 199 B1
Close The. Haslingden BB4 .... 84 A8
Close The. Ince Blundell L38 ...... 3 E3
Close The. Kirkham PR4 .... 113 B4
Close The. New Longton PR4 ...... 75 A7
Close The. Weeton PR4 .... 131 E2
Close The. Withnell Fold PR6 ...... 78 C3
Clough Acre. PR7 .... 60 A2
Clough Ave. PR1 .... 96 B3
Clough Bank. BB7 .... 187 D5
Clough End Rd. BB4 .... 84 B5
Clough Fold Prim Sch. WN8 ...... 18 C2
Clough La. Hesketh Lane PR3 ...... 161 A7
Clough La. Simonstone BB12 ...... 144 F1
Clough Rd. Bacup OL13 .... 87 A3
Clough Rd. Nelson BB9 .... 148 A8
Clough St. 8 Bacup OL13 .... 69 D8
Clough St. Burnley BB11 .... 126 D5
Clough St. Darwen BB3 .... 64 C6
Clough St. 5 Newchurch BB4 ...... 85 F1
Clough Terr. BB8 .... 200 B1
Clough The. Clayton Green PR6 .. 77 A3
Clough The. Darwen BB3 .... 64 C6
Clougha Ave. Halton LA2 .... 214 F7
Clougha Ave. Lancaster LA1 ...... 211 B6
Cloughfold Cty Prim Sch. BB4 .. 85 C2
Cloughton Terr. LA2 .... 231 F5
Cloughwood Cres. WN6 .... 19 C6
Clovelly Ave. Blackpool FY5 ...... 150 D6
Clovelly Ave. Fulwood PR2 .... 116 D3
Clovelly Dr. Newburgh WN8 ...... 26 A1
Clovelly Dr. Penwortham PR1 ...... 95 A5
Clovelly Dr. Southport PR8 .... 20 E8
Clover Ave. FY8 .... 110 A1
Clover Crescent. BB12 .... 126 D8
Clover Ct. FY2 .... 150 F6
Clover Dr. PR4 .... 92 D7
Clover Field. PR6 .... 77 B2
Clover Hill Rd. BB9 .... 147 F7
Clover Mews. FY3 .... 129 E6
Clover Rd. PR7 .... 42 A5
Clover St. OL13 .... 87 A3
Cloverfield. PR1 .... 95 B4
Cloverfields. BB1 .... 101 A6
Cloverhill House. BB9 .... 147 F7
Club La. PR3 .... 182 E3
Club St. Bamber Bridge PR5 ...... 76 F7
Club St. Cornholme OL14 .... 108 B1
Clucas Gdns. L39 .... 15 E6
Clyde St. Blackburn BB2 .... 100 B3
Clyde St. Blackpool FY1 .... 129 B7
Clyde St. Preston PR1 .... 95 C8
Clydesdale Pl. PR5 .... 75 C2
Clyffes Farm Cl. L40 .... 23 A7
Co-operation St. Bacup OL13 .... 87 A2
Co-operation St.
  Newchurch BB4 .... 85 F2
Co-operation St. 8
  Rake Foot BB4 .... 85 A7
Co-operation St.
  Rawtenstall BB4 .... 85 B2
Co-operative Bldgs. BB10 .... 106 F8
Co-operative St. 1
  Bamber Bridge PR5 .... 76 E8
Co-operative St. 14
  Barnoldswick BB8 .... 200 B2
Co-operative St.
  Haslingden BB4 .... 66 F7
Coach Rd. Barrow Nook L39 ...... 8 A1
Coach Rd. Church BB5 .... 102 E5
Coach Rd. Warton LA5 .... 217 D7
Coal Clough Jun & Inf Sch.
  BB11 .... 126 D5
Coal Clough La. BB11 .... 126 E4
Coal Clough Rd. OL14 .... 108 B2
Coal Hey St. 10 BB4 .... 84 B3
Coal Pit La. Accrington BB5 ...... 102 F4
Coal Pit La. Bacup OL13 .... 87 B3
Coal Pit La.
  Barnoldswick BB7 & BB8 .... 190 B7
Coal Pit La. Colne BB8 .... 169 F4
Coal Pit La. Darwen BB3 .... 80 B3
Coal Pit La. Gisburn BB7 .... 225 D2
Coal Pit La.
  Rainford Junction L39 & WN8 .. 8 D4
Coal Pit La. Rawtenstall BB4 ...... 86 A4
Coal Rd. BL0 & OL12 .... 50 C8
Coal St. 11 BB11 .... 126 F6
Coastal Dr. LA2 .... 215 E2
Coastal Rd. Ainsdale PR8 .... 20 A4
Coastal Rd. Hest Bank LA2 & LA5 215 F2
Coastal Rd.
  Morecambe LA2 & LA4 .... 213 B8
Coastal Rd. Southport PR8 .... 33 C3
Coastal Rise. LA2 .... 215 E2
Coates Ave. BB8 .... 200 D3
Coates Fields. BB8 .... 200 C4
Coates La. BB8 .... 200 D3
Coates Lane Prim Sch. BB8 ...... 200 D3
Cob Castle Rd. BB4 .... 83 E3
Cob La. BB8 .... 192 B4
Cob Moor Ave. WN5 .... 10 D1
Cob Moor Rd. WN5 .... 10 D1
Cobb's Brow La. Newburgh WN8 18 B6

Cobb's Brow La.
  Skelmersdale L40 .... 17 F5
Cobb's Clough Rd. L40 .... 17 F5
Cobbs Brow Cty Prim Sch.
  WN8 .... 18 A3
Cobbs St. BB8 .... 82 E8
Cobden Ct. 3 BB1 .... 100 E5
Cobden House. BB4 .... 85 D1
Cobden Rd. PR9 .... 35 A6
Cobden Rd. Bacup OL13 .... 70 B8
Cobden St. Barnoldswick BB8 .. 200 B1
Cobden St. Brierfield BB10 ...... 147 F3
Cobden St. Burnley BB10 .... 127 B8
Cobden St. 4 Bury BL9 .... 32 A3
Cobden St. Chorley PR6 .... 60 E1
Cobden St. 9 Darwen BB3 ...... 64 A8
Cobden St. Egerton BL7 .... 46 D2
Cobden St. Hapton BB12 .... 125 C4
Cobden St. Nelson BB9 .... 147 D7
Cobden St. Padiham BB12 .... 145 D1
Cobham Rd. BB5 .... 103 D5
Cobourg Cl. BB2 .... 100 F2
Cochran St. 24 BB3 .... 81 A1
Cock Hall La. OL12 .... 70 B1
Cock Robin. PR5 .... 57 C2
Cock Robin La. PR3 .... 178 D2
Cocker Ave. FY6 .... 152 A2
Cocker Bar Rd. PR5 .... 57 D8
Cocker La. PR5 .... 75 C1
Cocker Rd. PR5 .... 77 B7
Cocker Sq. FY1 .... 129 B6
Cocker St. Blackpool FY1 .... 129 B6
Cocker St. Darwen BB3 .... 64 C7
Cockerham Parochial CE
  Prim Sch. LA2 .... 203 D4
Cockerham Rd. Garstang PR3 .. 199 B1
Cockerham Rd.
  Potters Brook LA2 & PR3 ...... 204 B4
Cockerham Wlk. FY3 .... 130 A8
Cockerill St. BB4 .... 84 B4
Cockerill Terr. BB7 .... 164 D1
Cockermouth Cl. BB3 .... 80 F7
Cockersand Ave. PR4 .... 94 C1
Cockersand Dr. LA1 .... 211 A3
Cockhall La. OL12 .... 70 C1
Cockhill La. BB8 .... 170 B8
Cocking Yd. LA6 .... 234 C7
Cockle Dick's La. PR9 .... 52 E2
Cockle Lane Ends. LA2 .... 160 A2
Cockridge Cl. BB2 .... 80 B7
Cockshot La. LA7 .... 237 F4
Codale Ave. FY2 .... 150 D5
Coddington St. BB1 .... 101 B5
Coe La. PR4 .... 56 A5
Cog La. Burnley BB11 .... 126 C5
Cog La. Burnley BB11 .... 126 D4
Cog St. BB11 .... 126 D5
Colbran St. Burnley BB10 .... 127 B8
Colbran St. 10 Nelson BB9 ...... 168 F2
Colburne Cl. L40 .... 24 F5
Colchester Ave. LA1 .... 211 B5
Colchester Dr. 6 FY5 .... 172 F2
Colchester Rd. Blackpool FY3 .. 129 F3
Colchester Rd. Southport PR8 .. 34 F3
Cold Bath St. 4 PR1 .... 95 A8
Cold Well La. LA7 .... 237 F1
Coldstream Pl. BB2 .... 100 E2
Coldweather Ave. BB9 .... 147 F5
Coldwell Inn Activity Ctr.
  BB10 .... 149 A5
Cole Cres. L39 .... 6 C8
Colebatch. PR2 .... 116 E5
Coleman St. 4 BB9 .... 147 F8
Colenso Rd. Blackburn BB1 ...... 100 D7
Colenso Rd. Fulwood PR2 .... 116 C2
Coleridge Ave. FY5 .... 173 A3
Coleridge Cl. BB8 .... 169 D6
Coleridge Dr. BB5 .... 103 E2
Coleridge Pl. BB6 .... 123 B4
Coleridge Rd. Blackpool FY1 .... 129 D6
Coleridge Rd. Longshaw WN5 .. 10 D1
Coleridge Rd. Ramsbottom BL8 .. 48 F2
Coleridge St. BB2 .... 100 C3
Coles Dr. LA5 .... 237 B3
Colesberg Ct. LA5 .... 237 B2
Coleshill Ave. BB10 .... 127 D5
Colesville Ave. FY5 .... 173 B1
Colin St. Barnoldswick BB8 ...... 200 B3
Colin St. Burnley BB11 .... 126 D5
Colinmander Gdns. L39 .... 15 C3
Colinton. WN8 .... 9 E7
Colldale Terr. BB4 .... 84 B2
College Ave. Cleveleys FY5 ...... 172 C1
College Ave. Formby L37 .... 11 E4
College Cl. Formby L37 .... 11 D4
College Cl. Longridge PR3 .... 139 A5
College Cl. Padiham BB12 .... 125 D6
College Cl. Southport PR8 .... 34 A3
College Ct. PR1 .... 116 F2
College Gate. FY5 .... 172 C5
College Path. L37 .... 11 D5
College Rd. WN8 .... 19 B1
College Rd. Accrington BB5 ...... 103 A6
College Rd. Cornholme OL14 .... 108 C1
Collegiate High Sch. FY3 .... 151 A1
Collier St. BB5 .... 103 E2
Collier's La. LA6 .... 238 E3
Collier's Row. BB1 .... 101 F1
Collins St. BB5 .... 102 E5
Collin's Hill La. PR3 .... 182 A3
Colling St. 9 BL0 .... 49 B5
Colline Fold La. BB4 .... 84 F4
Collinge St. Padiham BB12 ...... 125 C2
Collinge St. Rawtenstall BB4 .... 84 F4
Collingham Pk. LA1 .... 211 A2
Collingwood Ave.
  Blackpool FY3 .... 129 E6

Collingwood Ave.
  Lytham St Anne's FY8 .... 109 E1
Collingwood Pl. FY3 .... 129 E6
Collingwood Rd. PR7 .... 42 B7
Collingwood St. Colne BB8 ...... 169 C4
Collingwood Terr. 10 LA2 .... 233 D8
Collins Ave. FY2 .... 150 E3
Collins Dr. BB5 .... 103 E2
Collins Rd. PR5 .... 96 F1
Collins Rd N. PR5 .... 96 F2
Collinson St. PR1 .... 117 C1
Collisdene Rd. WN5 .... 10 E6
Collison Ave. PR7 .... 42 C8
Collyhurst Ave. FY4 .... 109 E6
Colman Ct. PR1 .... 95 D6
Colnbrook. WN6 .... 28 B1
Colne and Broughton Rd.
  BB8 & BB23 .... 201 C6
Colne Coll of F Ed. BB8 .... 169 A5
Colne Golf Course. BB8 .... 170 B8
Colne La. BB8 .... 169 E4
Colne Rd. Barnoldswick BB8 .... 200 A1
Colne Rd. Barrowford BB8 & BB9 168 F4
Colne Rd. Brierfield BB9 .... 147 B6
Colne Rd. Burnley BB10 & BB11 . 127 A8
Colne Rd. Burnley BB10 .... 147 B3
Colne Rd. Sough BB8 .... 192 A1
Colne Rd. Trawden BB8 .... 170 B2
Colne Sta. BB8 .... 169 C4
Colt House Cl. PR5 .... 59 A7
Colthurst Dr. BB7 .... 187 A2
Coltsfoot Dr. PR6 .... 60 D2
Coltsfoot Wlk. LA3 .... 212 E2
Columbia Way. BB2 .... 100 B8
Columbine Cl. OL12 .... 51 C3
Colville Ave. 1 FY4 .... 109 C5
Colville Rd. BB3 .... 80 E4
Colville St. BB10 .... 127 A8
Colwall Cl. L33 .... 1 A2
Colwall Rd. L33 .... 1 A2
Colwall Wlk. L33 .... 1 A2
Colwyn Ave. Blackpool FY4 .... 129 E1
Colwyn Ave. Morecambe LA4 .. 212 G6
Colwyn Pl. PR2 .... 116 A3
Colyton Cl. PR6 .... 42 E8
Colyton Rd. PR6 .... 42 E8
Colyton Rd E. 2 PR6 .... 42 E8
Combermere Gr. LA3 .... 208 E5
Combermere Rd. LA3 .... 208 E6
Comer Gdns. L31 .... 5 C3
Comet Rd. PR5 .... 75 C2
Comet St. OL13 .... 87 A7
Commerce St. Bacup OL13 ...... 86 F2
Commerce St. Haslingden BB4 .. 84 A4
Commercial Rd. Chorley PR6 .... 60 C1
Commercial Rd.
  Great Harwood BB6 .... 123 C5
Commercial Rd. Nelson BB9 .... 147 E8
Commercial St. Bacup OL13 .... 69 D8
Commercial St.
  Barnoldswick BB8 .... 200 B2
Commercial St. Blackpool FY1 .. 129 B1
Commercial St. Brierfield BB9 .. 147 B6
Commercial St. 7 Church BB5 102 E6
Commercial St. 10
  Great Harwood BB6 .... 123 C5
Commercial St.
  Oswaldtwistle BB5 .... 102 D3
Commercial St.
  Rawtenstall BB4 .... 105 A3
Commercial St. Rishton BB1 .... 123 B1
Common Bank Employment
  Area. PR7 .... 41 F8
Common Bank La. PR7 .... 41 F8
Common Edge Rd. FY4 .... 109 F6
Common End. PR7 .... 29 E5
Common Gdn St. 3B LA1 .... 210 F8
Common La. PR9 .... 54 C1
Common The. Adlington PR7 .... 29 E5
Common The. Parbold WN8 .... 26 C3
Commons La. BB2 .... 120 B5
Commonside. PR7 .... 89 D4
Commonwealth Cl. FY8 .... 89 C8
Como Ave. FY4 .... 126 C4
Company St. 6 BB1 .... 123 B1
Compley Ave. FY6 .... 151 C2
Compley Gn. FY6 .... 151 C2
Compression Rd. LA3 .... 208 E2
Compston Ave. BB4 .... 105 A1
Compton Cl. FY6 .... 151 C5
Compton Gn. PR2 .... 116 D7
Compton Rd. PR8 .... 34 B3
Comrie Cres. BB11 .... 126 D3
Concourse Sh Ctr. WN8 .... 18 B1
Conder Ave. FY3 .... 172 F2
Conder Brow. LA5 .... 217 E2
Conder Green Rd. LA2 .... 206 F3
Conder Pl. LA1 .... 213 E2
Conder Rd. PR2 .... 115 E1
Condor Gr. Blackpool FY1 ...... 129 D3
Condor Gr. Lytham St Anne's FY8 88 E8
Conduit St. BB9 .... 168 D1
Coneygarth La. Tunstall LA6 .... 235 D4
Coneygarth La. Whittington LA6 235 F6
Congress St. PR6 .... 60 C1
Conifer Ct. L37 .... 12 A2
Conifers The. Barton PR3 .... 136 B8
Conifers The. Hambleton FY6 .. 174 B2
Conifers The. Kirkham PR4 ...... 113 B5
Conifers The. Maghull L31 .... 5 C3
Conisber Cl. BL7 .... 46 E1
Coniston Ave. Accrington BB5 .. 102 F4
Coniston Ave. Adlington PR6 .... 30 B8
Coniston Ave.
  Barnoldswick BB8 .... 200 A3
Coniston Ave. Carleton FY6 .... 151 B4
Coniston Ave. Euxton PR7 ...... 59 D1

Coniston Ave. Fleetwood FY7 .. 193 E4
Coniston Ave. Fulwood PR2 .... 116 D2
Coniston Ave. Hambleton FY6 .. 174 C2
Coniston Ave.
  Knott End-on-S FY6 .... 194 E6
Coniston Ave.
  Lytham St Anne's FY8 .... 109 F2
Coniston Ave. Orrell WN5 ...... 10 F7
Coniston Ave. Padiham BB12 .. 145 C2
Coniston Ave. Thornton FY5 .... 173 B1
Coniston Cl. Longridge PR3 .... 139 A5
Coniston Cl. Ramsbottom BL0 .. 49 C7
Coniston Cres. PR5 .... 173 B1
Coniston Ct. Ainsdale PR8 ...... 20 C3
Coniston Ct. Morecambe LA4 .. 212 F6
Coniston Dr. Bamber Bridge PR5 96 E2
Coniston Dr. Darwen BB3 .... 81 C2
Coniston Gr. BB8 .... 170 A6
Coniston Rd. Blackburn BB1 .... 101 A8
Coniston Rd. Blackpool FY4 .... 109 C2
Coniston Rd. Blackrod BL6 ...... 30 D3
Coniston Rd. Bolton-le-S LA5 .. 216 A4
Coniston Rd. Carnforth LA5 .... 216 E8
Coniston Rd. Chorley PR7 ...... 42 B6
Coniston Rd. Formby L37 .... 11 D2
Coniston Rd. Fulwood PR2 ...... 117 C4
Coniston Rd. Lancaster LA1 .... 214 A2
Coniston Rd. Maghull L31 .... 5 E2
Coniston Rd. Morecambe LA4 .. 212 F6
Coniston St. BB12 .... 126 C6
Coniston Way. Croston PR5 .... 57 B3
Coniston Way.
  Rainford Junction WA11 .... 8 F2
Coniston Way. Rishton BB1 .... 122 F1
Connaught Rd. Heysham LA3 .. 208 D5
Connaught Rd. Lancaster LA1 .. 214 A2
Connaught Rd. Preston PR1 .... 95 E5
Consett Ave. FY5 .... 172 E5
Constable Ave.
  Bamber Bridge PR5 .... 76 A7
Constable Ave. Burnley BB11 .. 126 F3
Constable Lee Cres. BB4 .... 85 A4
Constable Lee St Paul's CE Sch.
  BB4 .... 85 A4
Constable St. 7 PR1 .... 96 A8
Convent Cl. Bamber Bridge PR5 96 D1
Convent Cl. Leyland PR5 .... 76 C2
Convent Cl. Ormskirk L39 ...... 15 E2
Convent Cres. FY3 .... 130 A8
Conway Ave. Bamber Bridge PR5 96 A1
Conway Ave. Blackburn BB1 .... 100 E7
Conway Ave. Cleveleys FY5 .... 172 D2
Conway Ave. Clitheroe BB7 .... 164 C6
Conway Ave. Leyland PR5 ...... 59 C8
Conway Ave. Normoss FY3 .... 130 B7
Conway Cl. Catterall PR3 .... 178 D2
Conway Cl. Euxton PR7 .... 59 D1
Conway Cl. Haslingden BB4 .... 84 B1
Conway Cl. Ramsbottom BL0 .. 49 B6
Conway Cres. Barnoldswick BB8 200 C3
Conway Cres. Ramsbottom BL8 . 48 F2
Conway Dr. Bury BL9 .... 32 D2
Conway Dr. Fulwood PR2 ...... 116 C6
Conway Dr. Oswaldtwistle BB5 .. 102 B4
Conway Gr. BB10 .... 147 C3
Conway House. 4 PR1 .... 96 D8
Conway Rd. Eccleston PR7 .... 40 C7
Conway Rd. Rawtenstall BB4 .. 85 C2
Conyers Ave. PR8 .... 33 F3
Cook Gdns. BB1 .... 101 B4
Cook Green La. PR3 .... 140 C7
Cook House Rd. BB8 .... 169 E6
Cook St. BL9 .... 32 A2
Cooke St. PR4 .... 92 B6
Cookson Cl. FY5 .... 173 B3
Cookson St. FY1 .... 129 C5
Coolham La. BB8 .... 201 D1
Coolidge Ave. LA1 .... 210 D7
Coombes The. PR2 .... 116 F5
Coop St. FY1 .... 129 B3
Cooper Ct. PR5 .... 172 D3
Cooper Hill Cl. PR5 .... 96 D5
Cooper Hill Dr. PR5 .... 96 D5
Cooper Rd. PR1 .... 95 D8
Cooper St. Bacup OL13 .... 86 F4
Cooper St. Burnley BB11 .... 127 A5
Cooper St. Horwich BL6 .... 31 B4
Cooper St. Nelson BB9 .... 168 E1
Cooper's La. PR7 .... 27 B8
Cooper's Way. FY1 .... 129 D7
Coopers Cl. BB5 .... 102 D3
Coote La. PR5 .... 75 F7
Cop La. Fleetwood FY7 .... 194 D3
Cop La. Penwortham PR1 .... 95 C4
Cop Lane CE Prim Sch. PR1 .... 95 C3
Cop Royd Terr. BB10 .... 127 F1
Copeland Dr. WN6 .... 28 F1
Copeland Pl. FY8 .... 90 C4
Copp CE Prim Sch. PR3 .... 154 A3
Copp La. PR3 & PR4 .... 154 A2
Copper Beech Cl. PR4 .... 73 E3
Copperas La. BL6 .... 30 B1
Copperfield Cl. BB10 .... 127 F6
Copperfield St. BB1 .... 100 F3
Copperwood Way. PR7 .... 41 F7
Coppice Ave. BB5 .... 103 D7
Coppice Brow. LA5 .... 217 E2
Coppice Cl. Chorley PR6 .... 60 E1
Coppice Dr. Longshaw WN5 .. 10 D2
Coppice Dr. Whitworth OL12 .. 51 D7
Coppice Dr. PR6 & PR7 .... 61 C3
Coppice Leys. L37 .... 11 E3
Coppice St. BL9 .... 32 C3
Coppice The. Blackburn BB2 .. 100 A7
Coppice The. Clayton-le-M BB5 123 F4

Coppice The. Fulwood PR2 ...... 116 B4
Coppice The. Kirkham PR4 ...... 113 A6
Coppice The. Longton PR4 ...... 74 A7
Coppice The. Morecambe LA4 . 213 A5
Coppice The. Ramsbottom BL0 49 A4
Coppice Vale. BL0 .... 49 C3
Coppingford Cl. OL12 .... 51 A2
Coppins Gn. FY6 .... 151 E1
Coppull & District Cty Prim Sch.
  PR7 .... 41 E1
Coppull Hall La. PR7 .... 42 A1
Coppull Moor La. PR7 .... 28 E6
Coppull Parish CE Prim Sch.
  PR7 .... 28 F8
Coppull Parish Church Prim Sch.
  PR7 .... 41 F1
Coppull Rd. Chorley PR7 .... 42 A4
Coppull Rd. Maghull L31 .... 5 C4
Copse The. PR7 .... 193 F2
Copse The. Accrington BB5 .... 102 F5
Copse The. Chapeltown BL7 .... 47 C2
Copse The. Chorley PR7 .... 42 B4
Copster Dr. PR3 .... 139 B7
Copthurst Ave. BB12 .... 145 F6
Copthurst La. PR6 .... 60 F7
Copthurst St. 14 BB12 .... 145 C1
Copy La. LA2 .... 231 C3
Copy Nook. BB1 .... 101 A5
Coral Cl. FY4 .... 130 A1
Coral Leach Cotts. PR5 .... 56 F6
Corbridge Cl. Blackpool FY4 .. 110 A7
Corbridge Cl. Carleton FY6 .... 151 C5
Corbridge Cl. BB7 .... 186 E1
Corcas La. FY6 .... 173 F8
Cork Rd. LA1 .... 211 B5
Cork St. BL9 .... 32 A2
Corka La. FY8 .... 111 F1
Corlass St. 10 BB9 .... 168 D3
Corless Cotts. LA2 .... 220 A8
Corn Mill Lodge. L31 .... 5 C2
Corn Mill Yd. BB5 .... 123 F2
Cornbrook. WN8 .... 9 F7
Corncroft. PR1 .... 95 C3
Corneghie Ct. PR8 .... 33 F4
Cornel Gr. BB11 .... 126 C4
Cornelian St. BB1 .... 121 F2
Corner Bank Cl. PR4 .... 111 F7
Corners The. FY5 .... 172 C4
Cornfield. PR4 .... 115 E6
Cornfield Gr. BB12 .... 126 A8
Cornfield St. BB3 .... 81 B2
Cornflower Cl. PR6 .... 60 D2
Cornford Rd. FY4 .... 110 B8
Cornhill. 8 BB5 .... 103 C6
Cornhill Arc. BB5 .... 103 B6
Cornholme. BB10 .... 147 E2
Cornholme Jun & Infs Sch.
  OL14 .... 108 A1
Cornholme Terr. OL14 .... 108 B1
Cornmill Terr. 4 BB8 .... 200 B3
Cornthwaite Rd. PR2 .... 116 E3
Cornwall Ave. Blackburn BB1 .. 101 E4
Cornwall Ave. Blackpool FY2 .. 150 C2
Cornwall Ave. Cleveleys FY5 .. 172 F4
Cornwall Cres. WN1 .... 29 B1
Cornwall Pl. Blackpool FY3 .... 130 B2
Cornwall Pl. Church BB5 .... 102 F7
Cornwall Rd. BB1 .... 123 A1
Cornwall Way. PR8 .... 20 C2
Corona Ave. 3 FY5 .... 5 C5
Coronation Ave. Blackburn BB2 . 79 C7
Coronation Ave. Formby L37 .... 12 A2
Coronation Ave. Forton PR3 .... 204 B3
Coronation Ave. Padiham BB12 125 C7
Coronation Cres. PR1 .... 96 B7
Coronation Gr. BB4 .... 85 E1
Coronation Pl. 5 BB9 .... 168 D3
Coronation Rd. Brierfield BB9 . 147 C5
Coronation Rd. Cleveleys FY5 . 172 C2
Coronation Rd. Kirkham PR4 .. 113 A5
Coronation Rd.
  Lytham St Anne's FY8 .... 89 C4
Coronation Rd. Maghull L31 .... 5 D3
Coronation St.
  Barnoldswick BB8 .... 200 C2
Coronation St. Blackpool FY1 .. 129 B4
Coronation St.
  Great Harwood BB6 .... 123 D6
Coronation Terr. BB6 .... 142 C1
Coronation Way. LA1 .... 214 A4
Coronation Wlk. PR8 .... 34 A7
Corporation St. Accrington BB5 103 A5
Corporation St. 10
  Blackburn BB2 .... 100 E5
Corporation St. Blackpool FY1 .. 129 B5
Corporation St. Chorley PR6 .. 60 D1
Corporation St. Clitheroe BB7 . 164 D8
Corporation St. Nelson BB8 .... 169 A8
Corporation St. Preston PR1 .... 95 F7
Corporation St. Preston PR1 .... 95 F8
Corporation St. Southport PR8 .. 34 B7
Corpus Christi RC High Sch.
  PR2 .... 116 E5
Corrib Rd. FY2 .... 150 D2
Corrick Mews. FY3 .... 130 B2
Corringham Rd. LA4 .... 212 E5
Corston Gr. BL6 .... 30 D1
Corwen Cl. BB1 .... 100 E7
Cosford St. PR4 .... 131 E6
Cotswold Ave. PR7 .... 59 D1
Cotswold Cl. Eccleston PR7 .... 40 D6
Cotswold Cl. Ramsbottom BL0 .. 49 C4
Cotswold Dr. BL6 .... 31 C5
Cotswold Rd. Blackpool FY2 .... 150 D1
Cotswold Rd. Chorley PR7 ...... 42 C6
Cotswold Rd.
  Lytham St Anne's FY8 .... 90 D5

Cottage Cl. L39 .... 15 D4
Cottage Fields. PR7 .... 42 B5
Cottage La. Bamber Bridge PR5 .... 96 F3
Cottage La. Ormskirk L39 .... 15 D5
Cottage Mews. L39 .... 15 D5
Cottage St. PR1 .... 96 A8
Cottage Wlk. OL12 .... 51 C4
Cottam Ave. PR2 .... 116 A4
Cottam Cl. Lytham St Anne's FY8 109 F2
Cottam Cl. Whalley BB5 .... 143 C5
Cottam Gn. PR4 .... 115 F6
Cottam Hall La. PR2 & PR4 ...... 115 F5
Cottam La. PR2 .... 116 A2
Cottam Pl. FY6 .... 151 C2
Cottam St. PR7 .... 42 C6
Cottam Way. PR2 & PR4 ...... 115 D4
Cottesloe Pl. BB9 .... 168 C3
Cottesmore Pl. FY3 .... 130 A6
Cottom Croft. BB5 .... 123 F4
Cotton Ct. Colne BB8 .... 169 C3
Cotton Ct. Preston PR1 .... 96 A8
Cotton Dr. L39 .... 15 D6
Cotton Gn. L39 .... 12 B3
Cotton Hall St. BB3 .... 81 A2
Cotton St. Accrington BB5 ...... 103 B5
Cotton St. Burnley BB12 .... 126 D7
Cotton St. Padiham BB12 .... 125 C7
Cotton Tree La. BB8 .... 170 A5
Cottys Brow. PR9 .... 52 F3
Coudray Rd. PR9 .... 52 E1
Coulston Ave. FY2 .... 150 B3
Coulston Rd. LA1 .... 211 B6
Coultate St. BB12 .... 126 C6
Coulter Beck La. LA6 .... 236 A7
Coulthard St. 1 BL0 .... 49 B6
Coulthurst St. 1 BL0 .... 49 B6
Countess Cl. PR4 .... 113 A7
Countess Cres. FY2 .... 150 C3
Countess Rd. BB3 .... 81 A7
Countess St. BB5 .... 103 A6
Countess Way. PR7 .... 59 D2
Countessway. 2 PR5 .... 96 E1
County Cl. PR5 .... 76 A4
County Rd. Kirkby L32 .... 1 A1
County Rd. Ormskirk L39 .... 15 E6
County St. LA1 .... 210 E8
Coupe Gn. PR5 .... 97 E4
Coupe Green Cty Prim Sch.
  PR5 .... 97 E4
Coupland St. OL12 .... 51 C8
Courage Low La. WN6 .... 27 D5
Course La. L40 & WN8 .... 25 D1
Court Hey. L31 .... 5 E1
Court Rd. PR9 .... 34 C8
Court The. PR2 .... 116 C7
Courtfield. L39 .... 15 D7
Courtfield Ave. FY3 .... 129 D8
Courtgreen. L39 .... 15 D7
Courtyard The. 8 OL13 .... 87 A3
Courtyard Works. L33 .... 1 C2
Cousin's La. L40 .... 38 A3
Cove Dr. LA5 .... 218 C4
Cove Rd. LA5 .... 218 B4
Cove The. Cleveleys FY5 .... 172 C4
Cove The. Morecambe LA4 ...... 213 A4
Covell House. 2 LA1 .... 210 E8
Coventry St. PR7 .... 42 C6
Coverdale Dr. BB2 .... 79 D7
Coverdale Rd. LA1 .... 210 D8
Coverdale Way. BB12 .... 126 D7
Covert The. FY5 .... 172 F4
Coveway Ave. FY3 .... 129 E6
Cow Gate La. BD23 .... 225 E7
Cow Well La. PR6 .... 60 B8
Cowan Brae. BB1 .... 100 D6
Cowell Way. BB2 .... 100 D5
Cowes Ave. BB4 .... 84 C2
Cowgarth La. BB8 .... 201 C2
Cowgill St. 16 Bacup OL13 .... 87 A3
Cowgill St. Earby BB18 .... 201 B1
Cowhill La. BB1 .... 101 F7
Cowley Cres. BB12 .... 125 E7
Cowley Rd. Blackpool FY4 ...... 109 F8
Cowley Rd. Fulwood PR2 ...... 117 E4
Cowling Brow. PR7 .... 42 E7
Cowling Brow Ind Est. PR7 .... 42 F6
Cowling La. PR5 .... 75 D1
Cowling Rd. PR7 .... 42 F6
Cowm Park Way N. OL12 ...... 70 D2
Cowm Park Way S. OL12 ...... 70 C1
Cowm St. OL12 .... 70 E5
Cowpe Rd. BB4 .... 68 F7
Cowper Ave. BB6 .... 186 E1
Cowper Pl. BB7 .... 224 C1
Cowper St. Blackburn BB1 ...... 100 F7
Cowper St. Burnley BB11 ...... 126 C5
Cowslip Way. PR6 .... 60 D2
Cowtoot La. OL13 .... 87 A4
Cox Green Cl. BL7 .... 46 D3
Cox Green Rd. BL7 .... 46 E2
Coxfield. WN6 .... 19 D7
Coyford Dr. PR9 .... 53 A4
Crab Tree La. PR3 .... 176 C2
Crabtree Ave. Bacup OL13 .... 87 A1
Crabtree Ave. Newchurch BB4 .. 85 F2
Crabtree Ave. Penwortham PR1 .. 95 A3
Crabtree Bldgs. BB4 .... 85 F4
Crabtree Cl. L40 .... 24 D4
Crabtree La. L40 .... 24 D6
Crabtree Orch. FY5 .... 173 B3
Crabtree Rd. FY5 .... 173 B3
Crabtree St. Blackburn BB1 .... 101 B5
Crabtree St. Brierfield BB9 .... 147 B8
Crabtree St. Bury BL9 .... 32 B3
Crabtree St. Colne BB8 .... 169 C4
Crabtree St.
  Whitewell Bottom BB4 .... 85 F4
Cracoe Gill. BB9 .... 168 C3

Craddock Rd. BB8 .... 169 E5
Crag Ave. BL9 .... 49 D2
Crag Bank Cres. LA5 .... 216 C8
Crag Bank La. LA5 .... 217 B1
Crag La. BL9 .... 49 D2
Crag Rd. Lancaster LA1 .... 214 B1
Crag Rd. Warton LA5 .... 217 A6
Cragg Row. BB8 .... 191 D7
Cragg St. Blackpool FY1 ...... 129 B3
Cragg St. Colne BB8 .... 169 C5
Cragg's Row. 17 PR1 .... 95 F8
Craggs La. LA3 .... 233 D3
Craig St. LA3 .... 212 A3
Craigflower Ct. PR5 .... 77 C7
Craiglands Ave. LA3 .... 212 A2
Craiglands Ct. LA1 .... 210 C5
Crail Pl. OL10 .... 32 F1
Crake Ave. FY7 .... 193 C2
Crake Bank. 4 LA1 .... 213 C2
Cranberry Cl. BB3 .... 64 D6
Cranberry La. BB3 .... 64 D6
Cranborne Cl. Horwich BL6 .... 31 F1
Cranborne Cl. Standish WN6 .. 28 D1
Cranborne St. 5
  Bamber Bridge PR5 .... 76 E8
Cranborne St. 10 Preston PR1 .. 96 C8
Cranborne Terr. BB2 .... 100 C6
Cranbourne Dr. Chorley PR7 .. 42 E7
Cranbourne Dr. Church BB5 .. 103 A8
Cranbourne Gr. FY5 .... 151 E7
Cranbourne St. Chorley PR7 .. 42 D7
Cranbourne St. Colne BB8 .... 169 E6
Cranbrook Ave. Blackpool FY4 .. 150 E5
Cranbrook Ave.
  Oswaldtwistle BB5 .... 102 C4
Cranbrook St. BB2 .... 100 D2
Crane St. PR7 .... 28 D6
Cranes La. L40 .... 16 E7
Cranfield View. BB3 .... 64 C6
Crank Rd. WN5 .... 10 D1
Crankshaw St. 9 BB4 .... 85 A3
Cranleigh Ave. FY2 .... 150 C3
Cranleigh Cl. BL6 .... 30 D1
Cranmer St. 5 BB11 .... 126 E6
Cranshaw Dr. BB11 .... 100 F8
Cranston Rd. L33 .... 1 C2
Cranwell Ave. LA1 .... 211 B5
Cranwell Cl. 2 BB1 .... 101 A4
Cranwell Ct. PR4 .... 112 F5
Craven Cl. PR2 .... 116 F7
Craven Ct. BL6 .... 31 D2
Craven St. Accrington BB5 .... 103 A5
Craven St. Barnoldswick BB8 .. 200 C2
Craven St. Brierfield BB9 ...... 147 B5
Craven St. Burnley BB11 ...... 127 A5
Craven St. Bury BL9 .... 32 C3
Craven St. Clitheroe BB7 ...... 164 E7
Craven St. Colne BB8 .... 170 A5
Craven St. Nelson BB9 .... 147 C8
Craven St. Rawtenstall BB4 .... 84 F2
Craven St E. BB4 .... 31 D2
Craven's Ave. BB2 .... 80 D6
Craven's Brow. BB2 .... 80 E7
Cravendale Ave. BB9 .... 168 F3
Crawford Ave. Adlington PR7 .. 29 E5
Crawford Ave. Blackpool FY2 .. 150 D5
Crawford Ave. Chorley PR7 .... 42 B7
Crawford Ave. Leyland PR5 .... 59 B8
Crawford Ave. Maghull L31 .... 5 B3
Crawford Ave. Preston PR1 .... 117 F1
Crawford Rd. WA11 & WN8 .... 9 D2
Crawford St. BB3 .... 168 E1
Crawford Village Prim Sch.
  WN8 .... 9 E3
Crawshaw Dr. BB4 .... 85 A6
Crawshaw La. BB10 .... 148 D6
Crawshaw St. BB5 .... 103 B6
Crawshaw's Bldgs. BB4 ...... 85 A1
Crawshawbooth Cty Prim Sch.
  BB4 .... 85 A8
Crediton Ave. PR9 .... 53 B5
Crediton Cl. BB2 .... 80 C8
Crescent Ave. L37 .... 11 E1
Crescent Ct. FY4 .... 109 A5
Crescent E. FY5 .... 172 D2
Crescent Gn. L39 .... 15 B1
Crescent Rd. Poulton-le-F FY6 .. 151 E4
Crescent Rd. Southport PR8 .. 33 F3
Crescent St. PR1 .... 117 C1
Crescent The. Lostock Hall PR5 .. 76 C8
Crescent The.
  Bamber Bridge PR5 .... 96 F2
Crescent The. Blackburn BB2 .. 99 E1
Crescent The. Blackpool FY4 .. 109 B7
Crescent The. Brierfield BB10 .. 147 B4
Crescent The. Bury BL9 .... 32 A3
Crescent The. Carleton FY6 .. 151 C4
Crescent The.
  Chorley PR6 & PR7 .... 60 C2
Crescent The. Clitheroe BB7 .. 164 D7
Crescent The. Colne BB8 ...... 169 E6
Crescent The.
  Dunsop Bridge BB7 .... 222 D1
Crescent The. Fleetwood FY7 .. 172 E8
Crescent The. Freckleton PR4 .. 92 C5
Crescent The. Hest Bank LA2 .. 215 D1
Crescent The. Horwich BL6 .... 31 E1
Crescent The. Preesall FY6 .... 195 B4
Crescent The. Preston PR2 .... 115 D1
Crescent The. Preston PR2 .... 116 B2
Crescent The. Southport PR9 .. 53 C3
Crescent The. Warton PR4 .... 91 C4
Crescent The. Whalley BB7 .... 164 D8
Crescent The. Whitworth OL12 .. 51 C8
Crescent The. Worsthorne BB10 128 A5
Crescent W. PR2 .... 172 D2
Cressell Pk. WN6 .... 28 B1
Cressingham Wlk. LA1 .... 211 B3

Cresswood Ave. FY5 .... 172 D1
Crestway. Blackpool FY3 ...... 129 F6
Crestway. Tarleton PR4 .... 56 A8
Creswell Ave. PR2 .... 115 F3
Creswick Ave. BB11 .... 126 F3
Creswick Cl. BB11 .... 126 F3
Crewdson St. BB3 .... 80 F2
Crewgarth Rd. LA3 & LA4 .... 212 D4
Cribden End La. BB4 .... 84 D4
Cribden House Sch. BB4 ...... 84 E1
Cribden La. BB4 .... 84 E5
Cribden St. BB4 .... 84 F4
Criccieth Cl. 3 BB4 .... 84 B1
Crichton Pl. FY4 .... 109 B5
Cricket Path. Formby L37 .... 11 F5
Cricket Path. Southport PR8 .. 33 F3
Cricketers Gn. PR7 .... 40 B6
Crimbles La. LA2 .... 203 B2
Crime Well La. LA3 .... 208 E7
Crimea St. OL13 .... 87 A2
Crinan Sq. OL10 .... 32 F1
Cringle Way. BB7 .... 187 A2
Cripple Gate. WN6 .... 28 A2
Cripple Gate La. PR5 .... 98 C4
Croasdale. 7 LA1 .... 213 C2
Croasdale Ave. Brierfield BB10 .. 147 E2
Croasdale Ave. Fulwood PR2 .. 117 E4
Croasdale Cl. LA5 .... 217 C1
Croasdale Dr. Cleveleys FY5 .. 172 F4
Croasdale Dr. Clitheroe BB7 .. 164 F7
Croasdale Dr. Parbold WN8 .. 26 C3
Croasdale Sq. BB1 .... 101 A3
Croasdale Wlk. FY3 .... 130 B8
Crockleford Ave. PR8 .... 34 E3
Crocus Cl. BB4 .... 66 F8
Crocus Field. PR5 .... 59 A7
Croft Acres. BL0 .... 67 D2
Croft Ave. Burscough L40 .... 24 F3
Croft Ave. Hest Bank LA2 .... 213 E8
Croft Ave. Orrell WN5 .... 10 D5
Croft Bank. PR1 .... 95 C3
Croft Butts La. PR4 .... 92 C6
Croft Cl. BB4 .... 85 A5
Croft Ct. FY7 .... 193 E2
Croft Field. L31 .... 5 E1
Croft Head Rd. BB1 .... 122 B1
Croft Hey. L40 .... 38 B4
Croft Heys. L39 .... 15 B1
Croft La. BB12 .... 145 F6
Croft Manor. PR4 .... 92 C6
Croft Meadow. PR5 .... 77 C6
Croft Rd. PR7 .... 42 E7
Croft St. Bacup OL13 .... 86 F3
Croft St. Burnley BB11 .... 127 A5
Croft St. Bury BL9 .... 32 A2
Croft St. Clitheroe BB7 .... 164 E7
Croft St. 17 Darwen BB3 .... 81 A1
Croft St. Earby BB18 .... 201 C2
Croft St. Great Harwood BB6 .. 123 C4
Croft St. Morecambe LA4 .... 212 F5
Croft St. Preston PR1 .... 95 D8
Croft St. Preston PR1 .... 95 E8
Croft The. Blackburn BB1 .... 100 D7
Croft The. Burton in L LA6 .. 236 C3
Croft The. Caton LA2 .... 231 C3
Croft The. Cleveleys FY5 ...... 172 D2
Croft The. Eccleston PR7 .... 40 C7
Croft The. Euxton PR7 .... 59 B3
Croft The. Fleetwood FY7 .... 193 E2
Croft The. Garstang PR3 ...... 199 B1
Croft The. Goosnargh PR3 .... 137 D6
Croft The. Great Plumpton PR4 .. 111 E7
Croft The. Hoghton PR5 ...... 98 B2
Croft The. Lytham St Anne's FY8 110 B1
Croft The. Maghull L31 .... 5 B5
Croft The. Orrell WN5 .... 10 D3
Croft The. Poulton-le-F FY6 .. 151 D2
Croft Way. FY5 .... 151 C8
Crofters Fold. LA3 .... 212 B1
Crofters Gn. Euxton PR7 .... 59 C3
Crofters Gn. Preston PR6 .... 116 E2
Crofters Mews. FY1 .... 129 C7
Crofters Wlk. PR1 .... 95 D2
Croftgate. PR2 .... 116 F5
Croftlands. Borwick LA6 ...... 234 B3
Croftlands. Orrell WN5 .... 10 D4
Croftlands. Ramsbottom BL0 .. 49 A3
Croftlands. Warton LA5 .... 217 C6
Crofton Ave. FY2 .... 150 D5
Crofts Cl. PR4 .... 113 C5
Crofts The. PR4 .... 94 A1
Croftson Ave. L39 .... 15 F7
Croichley Fold. BL8 .... 48 D2
Cromarty Sq. OL10 .... 32 F1
Cromblehome Rd. PR1 .... 117 E1
Cromer Ave. BB10 .... 147 C1
Cromer Gr. BB10 .... 147 C1
Cromer Pl. Blackburn BB1 .... 100 E7
Cromer Pl. Fulwood PR2 ...... 116 A4
Cromer Rd. Blackpool FY2 .... 150 E4
Cromer Rd.
  Lytham St Anne's FY8 ...... 110 A1
Cromer Rd. Southport PR8 .. 33 E2
Cromer St. OL12 .... 51 E1
Cromfield. L39 .... 15 C2
Cromford Wlk. 9 PR1 .... 96 D8
Crompton Ave. FY4 .... 109 E7
Crompton Pl. BB2 .... 100 C5
Crompton St. PR1 .... 117 C1
Cromwell Ave. PR1 .... 95 C3
Cromwell Cl. L39 .... 15 C2
Cromwell Rd. Blackpool FY1 .. 129 C7
Cromwell Rd. Fulwood PR2 .. 117 D3
Cromwell Rd. Lancaster LA1 .. 216 E6
Cromwell Rd. Penwortham PR1 .. 95 C3
Cromwell St. Accrington BB5 .. 103 B8
Cromwell St. 20 Blackburn BB1 101 A4
Cromwell St. Burnley BB12 .. 126 F8

Cromwell St. Foulridge BB8 .. 191 D1
Cromwell St. 3 Preston PR1 .. 117 A1
Cronkeyshaw Rd. OL12 .... 51 F1
Cronkshaw St. BB10 .... 127 A7
Cronshaw Dr. BB6 .... 142 C1
Crook Dale La. FY6 & PR3 .... 174 E7
Crook Gate La. PR3 .... 175 E1
Crook Nook. LA3 .... 209 B2
Crook St. Adlington PR7 ...... 29 F7
Crook St. Chorley PR7 .... 42 B5
Crook St. Preston PR1 .... 96 B8
Crookall Cl. 7 FY7 .... 193 F2
Crooked La. PR1 .... 96 A8
Crooked Shore. OL13 .... 86 F3
Crookfield Rd. PR7 .... 63 B3
Crookhalgh Ave. BB10 .... 127 F6
Crookings La. PR1 .... 95 A6
Crooklands Dr. PR3 .... 178 C8
Crookleigh Pl. LA3 .... 212 A2
Croos St. BB5 .... 103 C5
Cropper Gdns. PR4 .... 72 D3
Cropper Rd. FY4 .... 110 C6
Cropper's La. L39 .... 16 A1
Cropton Rd. L37 .... 11 F3
Crosby Cl. BB3 .... 64 B6
Crosby Gr. FY3 .... 129 F3
Crosby Pl. PR2 .... 116 A4
Crosby Rd. Blackburn BB2 .... 100 E1
Crosby Rd. Lytham St Anne's FY8 109 F1
Crosby Rd. Southport PR8 .... 34 A3
Crosby St. OL12 .... 51 F2
Crosfield Ave. BL9 .... 49 C2
Crosier Wlk. PR4 .... 115 E5
Crosland Rd. L32 .... 1 A1
Crosland Rd N. FY8 .... 89 A8
Crosland Rd S. FY8 .... 89 A8
Crosley Cl. BB5 .... 103 B3
Cross Bank. FY8 .... 125 D8
Cross Barn Gr. BB3 .... 64 B8
Cross Barn La. L38 .... 3 E3
Cross Barn Wlk. BB3 .... 64 B8
Cross Brow. PR7 .... 41 C8
Cross Edge. BB5 .... 103 A1
Cross Field. PR4 .... 94 C1
Cross Flatts Cres. BB8 .... 191 E8
Cross Fold. BB7 .... 187 B8
Cross Gn. LA3 .... 12 A2
Cross Green Cl. L37 .... 12 A2
Cross Green Rd. PR2 .... 116 E6
Cross Hagg St. BB8 .... 169 C4
Cross Halls. PR1 .... 95 C3
Cross Helliwell St. 16 BB8 .. 169 D4
Cross Hill Ct. LA5 .... 216 A4
Cross Hill Four Lane Ends.
  PR3 .... 220 B6
Cross Hill La. BB7 .... 225 B1
Cross La. Barley Green BB12 .. 167 C4
Cross La. Halsall L39 .... 22 C1
Cross La. Low Bentham LA2 .. 233 B8
Cross La. Moor Side PR4 ...... 133 D1
Cross La. Orrell WN5 .... 10 D3
Cross La. Ramsbottom BL8 .... 49 A6
Cross La. Salterforth BB18 .... 191 E8
Cross La. Waddington BB7 .... 185 E5
Cross Meanygate. L40 & PR4 .. 37 C5
Cross Rd. LA2 .... 233 B7
Cross School St. 5 BB8 ...... 169 D4
Cross Skelton St. 6 BB8 .... 169 C5
Cross St. 4 Bacup OL13 .... 87 A3
Cross St. Blackburn BB3 ...... 80 F7
Cross St. Blackpool FY1 ...... 129 B4
Cross St. Brierfield BB9 ...... 147 B5
Cross St. Brierfield BB10 ...... 147 F3
Cross St. Chorley PR6 .... 60 C1
Cross St. Clayton-le-M BB5 .. 123 C3
Cross St. Clitheroe BB7 ...... 164 D8
Cross St. Darwen BB3 .... 64 B7
Cross St. Earby BB8 .... 201 A1
Cross St. Fleetwood FY7 ...... 194 B5
Cross St. Great Harwood BB6 .. 123 C5
Cross St. Higham BB12 ...... 145 F6
Cross St. 3 Leyland PR5 .... 76 B2
Cross St. Longridge PR3 ...... 139 A6
Cross St. Lytham St Anne's FY8 .. 88 D8
Cross St. Morecambe LA4 .... 212 F5
Cross St. Nelson BB9 .... 147 D8
Cross St. Oswaldtwistle BB5 .. 102 D4
Cross St. Preston PR0 & PR1 .. 95 F7
Cross St. Ramsbottom BL0 .... 49 C6
Cross St. 14 Rawtenstall BB4 .. 85 A7
Cross St. Southport PR8 ...... 34 B6
Cross St. Standish WN6 ...... 28 E1
Cross St. Worsthorne BB10 .. 128 B6
Cross St N. BB4 .... 84 B5
Cross St S. BB4 .... 84 B4
Cross St W. BB8 .... 169 B4
Cross Swords Cl. PR7 .... 42 A5
Cross Way. FY5 .... 172 D4
Crossdale Ave. LA3 .... 212 A2
Crossdale Sq. 10 LA1 .... 211 A8
Crosse Hall La. PR6 & PR7 .. 42 F7
Crosse Hall St. PR6 & PR7 .. 42 F7
Crossens CE Prim Sch. PR9 .. 53 C6
Crossens Way. PR9 .... 53 C6
Crossfield Ct. LA5 .... 237 A1
Crossfield St. BB1 & BB2 .... 100 F3
Crosshall Brow. WN6 .... 16 C4
Crosshall High Sch. L40 ...... 16 B5
Crosshill Pl. 7 LA2 .... 213 C1
Crosshill Rd. BB2 .... 100 B5
Crosshill Sch. BB1 .... 101 C2
Crosshills. 5 BB4 .... 145 C1
Crossing The. PR5 .... 98 B2
Crossland Rd. FY4 .... 129 E1
Crossland St. BB5 .... 103 A5
Crossley Fold. BB11 .... 126 D4
Crossways. BB7 .... 186 D7

Cuncliffe House. BB4 .... 85 D1
Cunliffe Ave. BL0 .... 49 A4
Cunliffe Cl. BB1 .... 122 B1
Cunliffe La. BB7 .... 143 F8
Cunliffe Rd. Blackburn BB1 ..... 122 C1
Cunliffe Rd. Blackpool FY1 ...... 129 D2
Cunliffe Rd. Chorley PR6 .... 42 D7
Cunliffe St. 10 Preston PR1 ...... 96 A8
Cunliffe St. Ramsbottom BL0 .... 49 C7
Cunnery Meadow. PR6 .... 76 E1
Cunningham Ave. PR7 .... 42 A6
Cunningham Gr. BB12 .... 126 B6
Cunscough La. L31 & L39 .... 6 D3
Curate St. Chorley PR6 .... 60 E1
Curate St. Great Harwood BB6 .. 123 C5
Curlew Cl. Blackburn BB1 .... 100 E8
Curlew Cl. Leyland PR5 .... 58 C7
Curlew Cl. Oswaldtwistle BB5 ... 102 D3
Curlew Cl. 2 Thornton FY5 ...... 172 F4
Curlew Gdns. BB11 .... 126 C5
Curlew La. L40 .... 37 E2
Curteis St. BL6 .... 31 B4
Curtis. 8 BB4 .... 85 A3
Curve St. OL13 .... 86 F1
Curven Edge. BB4 .... 67 A7
Curwen Ave. LA3 .... 208 E6
Curwen La. PR3 .... 158 C2
Curwen St. 7 PR1 .... 117 C1
Curzon Pl. BB2 .... 100 C3
Curzon Rd. Lytham St Anne's FY8 89 A7
Curzon Rd. Poulton-le-F FY6 .... 151 E3
Curzon Rd. Southport PR8 .... 34 C5
Curzon St. Burnley BB11 .... 126 F6
Curzon St. Clitheroe BB7 .... 164 D8
Curzon St. Colne BB8 .... 169 E4
Cusson Rd. L33 .... 1 B1
Custom House La. FY7 .... 194 C5
Cut La. 5 Caldershaw OL12 ...... 51 A1
Cut La. Ormskirk L39 & L40 ...... 14 F6
Cut La. Rishton BB1 .... 122 F1
Cutgate Rd. OL12 .... 51 B1
Cutler Cl. BB2 .... 100 C5
Cutler Cres. OL13 .... 69 D7
Cutler La. Bacup OL13 .... 69 D7
Cutler La. Hesketh Lane PR3 ... 160 C8
Cutt Cl. PR5 .... 57 F6
Cutts La. FY6 & PR3 .... 174 F2
Cygnet Cl. L39 .... 15 C2
Cygnet Cl. L33 .... 1 A2
Cypress Ave. FY5 .... 172 E2
Cypress Cl. PR2 .... 118 A4
Cypress Gr. Bamber Bridge PR5 76 B8
Cypress Gr. Blackpool FY3 ...... 129 D7
Cypress Rd. PR8 & PR9 .... 34 F6
Cypress Ridge. BB2 .... 79 F8
Cyprus Ave. FY8 .... 89 B4
Cyprus Rd. LA3 .... 208 E7
Cyprus St. BB3 .... 64 B6

D'urton La. PR2 & PR3 .... 136 F1
Daffodil Cl. Haslingden BB4 ...... 67 A8
Daffodil Cl. Lower Healey OL12 .. 51 E3
Dagger Rd. PR4 .... 114 C8
Daggers Hall La. FY4 .... 109 E8
Daggers La. FY6 .... 195 B3
Dahlia Cl. BB2 .... 51 D3
Dailton Rd. WN8 .... 10 A7
Daisy Bank. 12 Bacup OL13 ...... 86 F3
Daisy Bank. Lancaster LA1 ...... 211 D7
Daisy Bank Cl. PR5 .... 75 D1
Daisy Bank Cres. BB10 .... 127 E5
Daisy Bank St. OL14 .... 108 B1
Daisy Croft. PR2 .... 94 D8
Daisy Hill. BB4 .... 85 A3
Daisy Hill Dr. PR5 .... 30 A8
Daisy La. Blackburn BB1 .... 100 F6
Daisy La. Fulwood PR1 .... 117 C3
Daisy La. Ring o'Bells L40 .... 25 B4
Daisy Meadow. PR5 .... 77 B5
Daisy St. Blackburn BB1 .... 101 A6
Daisy St. Colne BB8 .... 169 D4
Daisy St. 3 Lancaster LA1 .... 213 F3
Daisyfield Prim Sch. BB1 .... 101 A6
Daisyfield St. BB3 .... 80 E5
Daisyfields. PR2 .... 115 F7
Dalby Cl. Cleveleys FY5 .... 150 F7
Dalby Cl. Fulwood PR1 .... 117 D3
Dalby Cres. BB2 .... 100 A1
Dalby Lea. BB2 .... 100 A1
Dale Ave. Euxton PR7 .... 59 D1
Dale Ave. Hest Bank LA2 ...... 213 E8
Dale Ave. Longton PR4 .... 73 E8
Dale Cl. Burnley BB12 .... 126 D6
Dale Cl. Maghull L31 .... 5 C2
Dale Cl. Parbold WN8 .... 26 B2
Dale Cres. BB2 .... 79 E7
Dale La. L33 .... 1 B4
Dale St. Accrington BB5 .... 103 A6
Dale St. Bacup OL13 .... 69 C8
Dale St. Blackburn BB2 .... 100 D4
Dale St. Blackpool FY1 .... 129 B3
Dale St. Brierfield BB9 .... 147 A5
Dale St. Burnley BB12 .... 126 D6
Dale St. Colne BB8 .... 169 C5
Dale St. Earby BB8 .... 201 B2
Dale St. Haslingden BB4 .... 84 B3
Dale St. Lancaster LA1 .... 211 A7
Dale St. Nelson BB9 .... 147 C8
Dale St. 4 Oswaldtwistle BB5 .. 102 E4
Dale St. Preston PR1 .... 96 B8
Dale St. Ramsbottom BL0 .... 67 C1
Dale St E. BL6 .... 31 D2
Dale St W. BL6 .... 31 D2
Dale Street Mews. FY1 .... 129 B3
Dale View. Chorley PR7 .... 42 C4
Dale View. Darwen BB2 & BB3 .. 80 E6
Dale View. Earby BB8 .... 201 A1
Dale View. 5 Rawtenstall BB4 .. 84 F1
Dalecrest. WN5 .... 10 D1
Daleford Cl. FY5 .... 151 C8
Dalegarth Cl. FY4 .... 130 C1
Dalegarth Rd. PR5 & PR7 .... 59 B7
Dales Ct. FY4 .... 109 D6
Dales The. BB6 .... 122 A8
Dalesford. BB4 .... 84 B1
Dalesview Cres. LA3 .... 208 F7
Dalesway. BB9 .... 168 C3
Dalewood Ave. FY4 .... 129 E1
Dalkeith Ave. FY3 .... 130 A2
Dalkeith Rd. BB9 .... 147 C8
Dall St. BB11 .... 127 A4
Dallam Ave. LA4 .... 212 F6
Dallam Dr. LA7 .... 237 F6
Dallas Ct. LA4 .... 213 B4
Dallas Rd. Lancaster LA1 .... 210 E7
Dallas Rd. Morecambe LA4 ..... 213 B4
Dallas Road Sch. LA1 .... 210 E7
Dallas St. PR1 & PR2 .... 116 E2
Dalmore Rd. PR2 .... 116 A3
Dalton Ave. FY4 .... 109 D5
Dalton Cl. BL0 .... 49 A4
Dalton La. LA6 .... 234 C7
Dalton Rd. Lancaster LA1 ...... 211 A8
Dalton Rd. Morecambe LA3 .... 212 A3
Dalton Sq. LA1 .... 210 F8
Dalton St. Burnley BB11 .... 126 D3
Dalton St. Lytham St Anne's FY8 88 D8
Dalton St. Nelson BB9 .... 168 E1
Dalton St Michael's CE
  Prim Sch. PR9 .... 18 D5
Dalweb Ind Pk. PR9 .... 54 C3
Dam Head Rd. BB8 .... 200 B2
Dam La. L40 .... 23 C6
Dam Side. 2 Barnoldswick BB8 200 B3
Dam Side. Colne BB8 .... 169 D4
Dam Top. BB4 .... 85 B2
Dam Wood La. L40 .... 23 C5
Dame Fold. Higham BB12 ...... 145 F6
Dame Fold. 2 Padiham BB12 .. 125 C8
Damfield La. L31 .... 5 C1
Damside Cotts. LA2 .... 207 B5
Damside St. LA1 .... 210 F8
Danbers. WN8 .... 9 F6
Dancer La. BB7 .... 225 B1
Dandy Wlk. BB1 .... 100 E4
Dane Hall La. PR7 .... 58 D2
Dane St. BB10 .... 127 A7
Danes Cl. PR4 .... 113 C5
Danes Dr. PR5 .... 59 A4
Danes House Rd. BB10 & BB12 127 A8
Danesbury Pl. FY1 .... 129 C5
Danesmoor Dr. BL9 .... 32 B4
Danesway. Bamber Bridge PR5 .. 96 D1
Danesway. Penwortham PR1 .... 95 A4
Daneswood Ave. OL12 .... 51 C8
Daneswood Cl. OL12 .... 51 C8
Daneway. PR8 .... 20 B6
Danewerke St. 8 PR1 .... 96 A8
Daniel Fold. PR3 .... 51 B2
Daniel Fold La. PR3 .... 178 D2
Daniel St. 10 Clayton-le-M BB5 123 F3
Daniel St. Whitworth OL12 ...... 70 D2
Daniell St. BB1 .... 123 A2
Daniels La. WN8 .... 9 C7
Danson Gdns. FY3 .... 129 D8
Danvers St. BB1 .... 123 B2
Darbishire Rd. FY7 .... 193 F4
Daresbury Ave. PR8 .... 20 A5
Darfield. WN8 .... 9 F7
Dark Rd. Blackrod BL6 .... 30 B3
Dark La. Earby BB8 .... 201 E2
Dark La. Johnson's Hillock PR6 .. 60 E6
Dark La. Maghull L31 .... 5 E1
Dark La. Mawdesley L40 .... 39 E3
Dark La. Newchurch BB4 .... 85 E1
Dark La. Ormskirk L40 .... 16 C3
Dark Wood La. PR5 .... 98 B6
Darkinson La. Lea Town PR4 .. 114 F1
Darkinson La. Preston PR4 .... 115 B2
Darkwood Cres. BB7 .... 187 D5
Darley Ave. FY4 .... 109 E7
Darley St. BL6 .... 31 B5
Darlington St. PR7 .... 41 E1
Darmond Rd. L33 .... 1 A3
Darnbrook Rd. BB8 .... 200 A2
Darnhill Cty Prim Sch. OL10 ... 32 F1
Darnley St. BB10 .... 127 C5
Dart St. PR1 .... 95 C8
Dartford Cl. 1 BB1 .... 101 A4
Dartmouth Cl. PR4 .... 112 F5
Darul-uloom Islamic Coll. BL8 .. 80 F4
Darwen Cl. PR3 .... 139 B7
Darwen Ent Ctr. BB3 .... 81 A2
Darwen Golf Course. BB3 ...... 80 C3
Darwen Moorland High Sch.
  BB3 .... 81 B3
Darwen Rd. BL7 .... 46 E1
Darwen Rd. Blackburn BB1 & BB2 100 E4
Darwen Rd. Padiham BB12 .... 125 C8
Darwen St. Preston PR1 .... 96 C7
Darwen Sta. BB3 .... 81 A1
Darwen Vale High Sch. BB3 .... 80 E5
Darwen View. PR5 .... 96 E5
Darwin St. BB10 .... 147 A2
Daub Hall La. PR5 .... 97 E3
Daub La. L40 .... 39 A1
Dauntesey Ave. FY3 .... 130 A6
Davenham Rd. Darwen BB3 ..... 80 E3
Davenham Rd. Formby L37 ...... 11 F3
Davenport Ave. FY2 .... 150 C5
Daventry Ave. FY2 .... 150 B4
David St. Bacup OL13 .... 69 D8
David St. 11 Barrowford BB9 .. 168 D4
David St. Burnley BB11 .... 126 F4
David St. 16 Rochdale OL12 ..... 51 F1
David St N. 15 OL12 .... 51 F1
Davidson St. 14 LA1 .... 211 A8
Davies Rd. BB1 .... 101 D6
Davis St. PR3 .... 139 A8
Davitt Cl. 4 BB4 .... 84 B3
Davy Field Rd. BB1 & BB3 .... 81 B6
Dawber's La. PR7 .... 58 E2
Dawlish Ave. FY3 .... 129 F8
Dawlish Cl. BB2 .... 80 C8
Dawlish Dr. PR9 .... 53 A5
Dawlish Lodge. FY8 .... 88 D7
Dawlish Pl. PR2 .... 116 A3
Dawnay Rd. PR2 .... 117 E3
Dawson Ave. Simonstone BB12 144 E2
Dawson Ave. Southport PR9 .... 53 C5
Dawson Gdns. L31 .... 5 C2
Dawson La. PR5 & PR7 .... 59 E7
Dawson Pl. PR1 .... 77 A7
Dawson Rd.
  Lytham St Anne's FY8 .... 109 F1
Dawson Rd. Ormskirk L39 .... 15 F7
Dawson Sq. BB11 .... 127 A7
Dawson St. BL9 .... 32 A4
Dawson Wlk. PR1 .... 116 F1
Day St. BB11 .... 147 E2
Daybrook. WN8 .... 9 F7
Dayfield. WN8 .... 10 B7
Dayton Pl. FY4 .... 109 C6
De Lacy House. BB2 .... 100 C5
De Lacy Rd. Clitheroe BB7 ...... 164 D8
De Lacy St. Preston PR1 & PR2 . 116 D2
De Vitre St. 4 LA1 .... 214 A1
Deakin's Terr. BL7 .... 45 C5
Deakins Bsns Pk. BL7 .... 46 D2
Deal Pl. FY8 .... 109 F1
Deal St. Blackburn BB1 .... 100 F7
Deal St. 9 Bury BL9 .... 32 B2
Dean Brow. PR3 .... 140 F8
Dean Cl. Edenfield BL0 .... 67 D3
Dean Cl. Up Holland WN8 .... 10 C7
Dean Ct. Clayton-le-M BB5 .... 123 F3
Dean Ct. Fleetwood FY7 .... 172 D8
Dean Fold. BB4 .... 86 A8
Dean Head La. PR7 .... 44 A4
Dean La. Billington BB6 & BB7 . 143 C1
Dean La. Darwen BB3 .... 80 B1
Dean La. Salmesbury PR5 ...... 118 F3
Dean La. Water BB4 .... 86 B8
Dean Meadow. BB7 .... 164 D7
Dean Rd. BB4 .... 84 B1
Dean St. Bamber Bridge PR5 ... 96 E1
Dean St. Blackpool FY4 .... 109 B8
Dean St. Burnley BB11 .... 126 E6
Dean St. Darwen BB3 .... 80 E5
Dean St. Padiham BB12 .... 145 D1
Dean St. Trawden BB8 .... 170 C2
Dean Wood Ave. WN5 .... 10 E8
Dean Wood Golf Course. WN8 . 10 D8
Deancroft Ave. LA3 .... 212 B2
Deanpoint. LA3 .... 212 F3
Deans Ct. L37 .... 11 F5
Deans La. L40 & WN8 .... 25 E3
Deansgate. Blackpool FY1 ..... 129 B5
Deansgate. Morecambe LA4 ... 212 E5
Deansgate La. L37 .... 12 B5
Deansgate La N. L37 .... 12 A6
Deansgrave. BB4 .... 84 B1
Deansgrave Rd. OL13 .... 70 B7
Dearden Clough. BL0 .... 67 E2
Dearden Fold. BL0 .... 67 E2
Dearden Nook. BB4 .... 85 A1
Deardengate. BB4 .... 84 B3
Deben Cl. WN6 .... 28 D1
Deborah Ave. PR2 .... 117 A7
Dee Rd. LA1 .... 213 D2
Dee St. FY8 .... 88 E6
Deepdale Ave. FY6 .... 151 B5
Deepdale Cty Inf Sch. PR1 ..... 117 B2
Deepdale Cty Jun Sch. PR1 .... 117 B2
Deepdale Dr. BB10 .... 147 C4
Deepdale Gn. BB9 .... 168 C3
Deepdale La. BB8 .... 201 A6
Deepdale Mill St. PR1 .... 117 B1
Deepdale Rd. Blackpool FY4 .. 130 C1
Deepdale Rd. Fleetwood FY7 . 194 A3
Deepdale Rd.
  Preston PR0 & PR1 .... 117 B2
Deepdale St. 8 PR1 .... 96 B8
Deeply Vale La. BL9 .... 50 C2
Deer Chace. BB12 .... 146 D8
Deer Park La. LA2 .... 232 B7
Deer Park Rd. BB10 & BB11 ... 127 E4
Deer Pk. BB5 .... 103 E8
Deerfield. PR7 .... 60 B2
Deerhurst Rd. FY5 .... 150 E7
Deerplay Cl. BB10 .... 147 E2
Deerstone Ave. BB10 .... 127 C6
Deerstone Rd. BB9 .... 148 B8
Deeside. FY4 .... 109 C5
Deganwy Ave. BB1 .... 100 E7
Deighton Ave. 7 PR5 .... 59 A8
Deighton Rd. PR7 .... 42 B6
Delamere Ave. LA3 .... 208 E6
Delamere Cl. BB2 .... 100 B2
Delamere Pl. PR5 .... 42 D8
Delamere Rd. Ainsdale PR8 .... 20 C5
Delamere Rd. Brierfield BB10 . 147 F3
Delamere Rd. Skelmersdale WN8 17 F2
Delamere St. BB5 .... 32 A5
Delamere Way. WN8 .... 17 A7
Delany Dr. PR4 .... 92 A6
Delaware St. PR0 & PR1 .... 117 D1
Delf La. Cornholme OL14 ...... 108 D3
Delf La. Haskayne L39 .... 14 A5
Delfby Cres. L32 .... 1 A1
Dell Gdns. OL12 .... 51 B2
Dell Meadow. OL12 .... 51 C5
Dell Rd. OL12 .... 51 B3
Dell Side Way. OL12 .... 51 C2
Dell The. Appley Bridge WN6 ... 19 D7
Dell The. Fulwood PR2 .... 116 D7
Dell The. Up Holland WN8 ...... 10 B7
Dell The. Wrea Green PR4 ..... 112 B3
Dellar St. OL12 .... 51 C1
Dellfield La. L31 .... 5 E1
Dellway The. PR4 .... 94 D2
Delma Rd. BB10 .... 127 E5
Delph App. BB1 .... 101 C4
Delph Ave. BL7 .... 46 D3
Delph Brook Way. BL7 .... 46 D2
Delph Cl. BB1 .... 101 C4
Delph Common Rd. L39 .... 15 C1
Delph Ct. 2 BB6 .... 123 C5
Delph La. Blackburn BB1 .... 101 C3
Delph La. Blackburn BB1 .... 101 C4
Delph La. Charnock Green PR7 . 41 D6
Delph La. Coppull PR7 .... 41 L5
Delph La. Formby L37 .... 11 C3
Delph La. Garstang PR3 .... 178 F8
Delph La. Oakenclough PR3 .. 180 B7
Delph La. Ormskirk L39 .... 15 C1
Delph Lane Est. BB1 .... 101 C4
Delph Mount.
  Great Harwood BB6 .... 123 B6
Delph Mount. Nelson BB9 ..... 147 D6
Delph Park Ave. L39 .... 15 B1
Delph Rd. BB6 .... 123 C5
Delph St. Haslingden BB4 ...... 84 B4
Delph St. The. WN8 .... 26 C3
Delph Top. L39 .... 16 A6
Delphene Ave. Blackpool FY5 . 150 D6
Delphene Ave. Blackpool FY5 . 150 D6
Delphside Cl. WN5 .... 10 D5
Delphside Prim Sch. WN5 .... 9 C8
Delta La. FY7 .... 194 A4
Delta Park Ave. PR4 .... 72 E4
Delta Park Dr. PR4 .... 72 E4
Delves La. BB10 .... 148 E7
Demming Cl. PR2 .... 94 C8
Denbigh Ave. Cleveleys FY5 .. 150 D7
Denbigh Ave. Southport PR9 ... 52 F3
Denbigh Cl. PR5 .... 76 B1
Denbigh Dr. BB7 .... 186 F2
Denbigh Gr. BB12 .... 126 A7
Denbigh Way. 34 PR1 .... 96 A7
Denby Cl. PR5 .... 96 C3
Dene Bank Rd. BB5 .... 102 E3
Dene The. Blackburn BB2 ...... 100 B7
Dene The. Hurst Green BB6 ... 141 E8
Denebank. PR2 .... 150 D5
Deneway Ave. FY3 .... 129 F6
Denford Ave. Leyland PR5 ...... 59 B8
Denford Ave.
  Lytham St Anne's FY8 .... 89 A4
Denham La. PR6 .... 77 E2
Denham Way. FY7 .... 193 F2
Denholme. Hall Green WN8 ..... 10 A7
Denholme. Skelmersdale WN8 .. 9 F7
Denholme Gr. FY2 .... 150 E5
Denis St. LA1 .... 211 A8
Denmark Rd.
  Lytham St Anne's FY8 .... 89 D4
Denmark Rd. Southport PR9 .... 53 A2
Denmark St. LA1 .... 210 D7
Dennis Gr. LA4 .... 212 D4
Denny Ave. LA1 .... 213 E2
Denny Bank. LA2 .... 214 E5
Denny Beck La. LA2 .... 214 E5
Denshaw. WN8 .... 9 F7
Denstone Ave. FY2 .... 150 D4
Dent Row. BB11 .... 126 F5
Dent St. BB8 .... 169 B3
Denton St. Barnoldswick BB8 .. 200 A3
Denton St. 7 Rochdale OL12 ... 51 F1
Denville Ave. FY5 .... 150 F8
Denville Rd. Blackburn BB2 ... 100 C5
Denville Rd. Preston PR1 ...... 117 C1
Denville St. BB2 .... 100 C5
Depot Rd. Blackpool FY2 ...... 150 E1
Depot Rd. Kirkby L33 .... 1 D4
Derbe Rd. FY8 .... 88 E5
Derby Cl. BB3 .... 64 B5
Derby Cres. PR4 .... 134 C8
Derby Hill Cres. L39 .... 16 A5
Derby Hill Rd. L39 .... 16 A5
Derby Pl. PR6 .... 30 A8
Derby Rd. Blackpool FY1 ...... 129 B7
Derby Rd. Cleveleys FY5 ...... 172 C3
Derby Rd. Formby L37 .... 11 E5
Derby Rd. Fulwood PR2 .... 116 D3
Derby Rd. Garstang PR3 .... 178 B7
Derby Rd. Kirkham PR4 .... 113 A6
Derby Rd. Lancaster LA1 ...... 213 F1
Derby Rd. Longridge PR3 ...... 139 A7
Derby Rd. Lytham St Anne's FY8 89 C7
Derby Rd. Poulton-le-F FY6 ... 151 D4
Derby Rd. Skelmersdale WN8 ... 8 C8
Derby Rd. Southport PR8 & PR9 . 34 C7
Derby Sq. PR1 .... 96 B8
Derby St. Accrington BB5 ...... 103 C6
Derby St. Blackburn BB1 .... 101 A6
Derby St. Brinscall PR7 .... 62 A8
Derby St. Burnley BB11 .... 126 E5
Derby St. Clitheroe BB7 .... 164 D8
Derby St. Colne BB8 .... 169 D5
Derby St. Horwich BL6 .... 31 C1
Derby St. Leyland PR5 .... 76 B2
Derby St. Morecambe LA4 .... 212 D5
Derby St. Nelson BB9 .... 168 A1
Derby St. Ormskirk L39 .... 15 F5
Derby St. 10 Preston PR1 ...... 96 A8
Derby St. Ramsbottom BL0 ..... 49 D6
Derby St. Rishton BB1 .... 123 C1
Derby St W. L39 .... 15 C5
Derbyshire Ave. PR3 .... 178 B8
Derek Rd. PR6 .... 77 C1
Derham St. BB2 .... 100 E3
Derry Rd. PR2 .... 117 E3
Dertern La. LA5 .... 216 A7
Derwent Ave. Burnley BB10 .. 147 A2
Derwent Ave. Fleetwood FY7 . 193 D2
Derwent Ave. Formby L37 ...... 11 D2
Derwent Ave. Morecambe LA4 212 F1
Derwent Ave. Padiham BB12 .. 145 C2
Derwent Ave. Southport PR9 ... 52 F1
Derwent Cl. Colne BB8 .... 170 A6
Derwent Cl. Freckleton PR4 .... 92 A6
Derwent Cl. Horwich BL6 .... 31 C2
Derwent Cl. Knott End-on-S FY6 194 F6
Derwent Cl. Maghull L31 .... 5 F2
Derwent Cl. Rishton BB1 ...... 122 F1
Derwent Cres. BB7 .... 164 C7
Derwent Ct. LA2 .... 213 C2
Derwent Dr. Freckleton PR4 .... 92 A6
Derwent Dr. Longridge PR3 ... 138 F5
Derwent Hall. 3 PR1 .... 116 E1
Derwent House. 6 PR1 .... 96 D8
Derwent Pl. Cleveleys FY5 .... 150 D8
Derwent Pl. Poulton-le-F FY6 . 151 D1
Derwent Rd. Chorley PR7 .... 42 B5
Derwent Rd. Lancaster LA1 .. 211 B8
Derwent Rd.
  Lytham St Anne's FY8 .... 110 A1
Derwent Rd. Orrell WN5 .... 10 F8
Derwent St. 6 Darwen BB3 ..... 80 F2
Derwent St. 11 Rochdale OL12 . 51 F1
Derwentwater Pl. PR1 .... 116 F2
Dever Ave. PR5 .... 75 D1
Devereux Prep Sch. BB9 ...... 147 D8
Devon Ave. Fleetwood FY7 .... 193 E3
Devon Ave. Oswaldtwistle BB5 102 B6
Devon Cl. PR5 .... 96 D3
Devon Cres. BB4 .... 67 B8
Devon Dr. WN1 .... 29 B1
Devon Farm Way. L37 .... 12 B3
Devon Gr. BB12 .... 126 A7
Devon Pl. 2 Church BB5 .... 102 E5
Devon Pl. Lancaster LA1 ...... 211 A4
Devon Rd. BB1 .... 101 C5
Devon St. Blackpool FY4 ...... 129 D1
Devon St. Colne BB8 .... 169 E6
Devon St. Darwen BB3 .... 64 B6
Devona Ave. FY4 .... 130 B1
Devonport Rd. BB2 .... 100 C5
Devonport Way. PR6 .... 42 E8
Devonshire Ave. FY5 .... 173 B2
Devonshire Cl. 8 PR7 .... 42 C8
Devonshire Dr.
  Clayton-le-M BB5 .... 124 A3
Devonshire Dr. Garstang PR3 . 178 B8
Devonshire House. FY3 .... 129 D6
Devonshire Jun Sch. FY3 ...... 129 D6
Devonshire Pl. PR1 .... 117 E1
Devonshire Rd. Blackpool FY2 150 D2
Devonshire Rd. Burnley BB10 . 127 A8
Devonshire Rd. Chorley PR7 ... 42 C7
Devonshire Rd. Fulwood PR2 . 117 A4
Devonshire Rd.
  Lytham St Anne's FY8 .... 88 D7
Devonshire Rd. Morecambe LA3 212 C3
Devonshire Rd. Rishton BB1 .. 123 A1
Devonshire Rd. Southport PR9 . 35 A8
Devonshire Sq. FY3 .... 129 D5
Devonshire Square Mews.
  FY3 .... 129 C5
Devonshire St. Accrington BB5 103 B7
Devonshire St. Lancaster LA1 . 210 F5
Dew Forest. PR3 .... 178 D4
Dew Meadow Cl. OL12 .... 51 E2
Dewhirst Rd. OL12 .... 51 F4
Dewhirst Way. OL12 .... 51 F4
Dewhurst Ave. FY4 .... 109 E8
Dewhurst Cl. BB3 .... 64 C6
Dewhurst Clough Rd. BL7 .... 46 D2
Dewhurst Rd. BL7 .... 46 D3
Dewhurst Rd. BB6 .... 141 F4
Dewhurst Row. PR5 .... 76 D7
Dewhurst St. Blackburn BB1 .. 101 A3
Dewhurst St. Blackburn BB1 .. 101 A4
Dewhurst St. Colne BB8 .... 169 D3
Dewhurst St. Darwen BB3 ...... 64 B6
Dewhurst St. Preston PR1 .... 116 D1
Deycroft Ave. L33 .... 1 A4
Deycroft Wlk. L33 .... 1 A4
Deyes End. L31 .... 5 E1
Deyes High Sch. L31 .... 5 D1
Deyes La. Maghull L31 .... 5 D1
Deyes La. Maghull L31 .... 5 F1
Diamond Jubilee Rd. L40 .... 38 C6
Dianne Rd. FY5 .... 173 D2
Dib Rd. PR4 .... 72 B5
Dicconson Terr. FY8 .... 90 B3
Dicconson Way. L39 .... 16 A5
Dicconson's La. L39 .... 14 D4
Dick La. PR6 .... 61 E7
Dick's La. L40 .... 16 F4
Dickens Ave. BB8 .... 200 A3
Dickens Rd. PR7 .... 28 E8
Dickens St. BB1 .... 101 A3
Dickensons Field. PR1 .... 95 E2
Dicket's La. WN8 & L40 .... 17 A2
Dickie's La. FY4 .... 110 B7
Dickie's La S. FY4 .... 110 C6
Dickinson Cl. Blackburn BB2 .. 100 C3
Dickinson Cl. Formby L37 ...... 11 F2
Dickinson Ct. 1 BL6 .... 31 B4
Dickinson Rd. L37 .... 11 F2

Dickinson St. BB2 .... 100 D3
Dickinson St W. BL6 .... 31 B4
Dickson Ave. PR1 .... 117 D2
Dickson Hey. PR4 .... 74 F8
Dickson Rd. FY1 .... 129 B7
Dickson St. Burnley BB12 .... 126 C6
Dickson St. Colne BB8 .... 169 E6
Dickson St. **5** Preston PR1 .... 96 B7
Dickson St W. BL6 .... 31 A4
Didsbury St. BB1 .... 101 C5
Digham Ave. FY5 .... 150 D6
Digmoor Dr. WN8 .... 9 C7
Digmoor Rd. WN8 .... 9 D6
Dill Hall La. BB5 .... 102 F7
Dilworth La. PR3 .... 139 C7
Dimmock St. BB2 .... 100 C2
Dimple Pk. BL7 .... 46 D3
Dimples La. PR3 .... 178 E5
Dinckley Gr. FY1 .... 129 D3
Dinckley Sq. BB2 .... 100 B6
Dinely St. BB5 .... 102 F6
Dingle Ave. Blackpool FY3 .... 129 F8
Dingle Ave. Shevington Vale WN6 .. 19 E8
Dingle Ave. Up Holland WN8 .... 10 C8
Dingle Cl. L39 .... 15 C1
Dingle Rd. WN8 .... 10 B7
Dingle The. PR2 .... 116 D7
Dinmore Ave. FY3 .... 130 A8
Dinmore Pl. FY3 .... 130 A7
Dinorwic Rd. PR8 .... 34 A2
Dirty Leech. OL12 .... 51 F6
Disraeli St. BB10 .... 147 A2
District General Hospl. PR8 ... 34 E4
Ditchfield. L37 .... 12 A2
Division La. FY4 .... 110 C3
Dixey St. BL6 .... 31 A3
Dixon Rd. PR3 .... 139 B7
Dixon St. Barrowford BB9 ... 168 C3
Dixon St. Blackburn BB2 .... 100 C4
Dixon St. Horwich BL6 .... 31 B3
Dixon's Farm Mews. PR4 ... 114 D1
Dob Brow. PR7 .... 41 F4
Dob La. PR4 .... 74 A4
Dobbin Cl. BB4 .... 85 C2
Dobbin La. BB4 .... 85 C2
Dobbs Dr. L37 .... 12 A4
Dobs La. LA2 .... 205 E3
Dobson Ave. FY8 .... 88 E8
Dobson Cl. WN6 .... 27 E2
Dobson St. **2** BB3 .... 80 F2
Dobson's La. FY6 .... 174 E6
Dock Ave. FY7 .... 194 A2
Dock Rd. FY8 .... 90 D4
Dock St. Blackburn BB1 .... 101 A5
Dock St. Fleetwood FY7 .... 194 B4
Docker La. LA6 .... 235 C5
Dockinsall La. PR3 .... 175 D3
Dockray Ct. **2** BB8 .... 169 E5
Dockray St. BB8 .... 169 E5
Dockray Yd. **4** BB8 .... 169 E5
Docky Pool La. FY4 .... 110 A6
Doctor's Hill. BB2 .... 233 B8
Doctor's La. Eccleston PR7 ... 40 B6
Doctor's La. Great Altcar L37 ... 12 E2
Doctor's La. Sollom PR4 .... 55 F3
Doctors Row. PR3 .... 139 A6
Dodd Way. PR5 .... 77 A6
Dodd's La. L31 .... 5 D2
Dodgeons Cl. FY6 .... 151 C2
Dodgson La. BB8 .... 201 F2
Dodgson Pl. PR1 .... 117 C1
Dodgson Rd. PR1 .... 117 C1
Dodney Dr. PR2 .... 115 C1
Dodson Rd. FY3 .... 130 B7
Dodworth Ave. PR8 .... 34 E5
Doe Meadow. MK 26 A1
Doeholme Rake. LA2 .... 226 F1
Dog Pits La. OL13 .... 87 A6
Dole La. Abbey Village PR7 ... 79 C1
Dole La. Chorley PR7 .... 42 C8
Doles La. PR4 & PR5 .... 57 A7
Dolly's La. PR9 .... 53 E1
Dollywood La. LA7 .... 237 F1
Dolphin House. BB11 .... 126 E5
Dolphinholme CE Sch. LA2 ... 220 A8
Dombey St. Blackburn BB1 ... 101 A3
Dombey St. Blackburn BB1 ... 101 A4
Dominion Rd. BB2 .... 100 C8
Don St. FY8 .... 88 E7
Doncaster Rd. FY3 .... 130 A3
Donnington Lodge. PR8 ... 33 F6
Donnington Rd. Carleton FY6 ... 151 C6
Donnington Rd.
  Lytham St Anne's FY8 .... 88 F7
Donshort Mews. **2** BB9 ... 168 C1
Doodson Ave. PR5 .... 96 B1
Doodstone Cl. PR5 .... 96 B1
Doodstone Dr. PR5 .... 96 B1
Doodstone Nook. PR5 .... 96 B1
Dora St. BL0 .... 49 A4
Dorchester Ave. BB5 .... 102 C4
Dorchester Cl. Blackburn BB1 ... 101 B3
Dorchester Cl. Thornton FY5 ... 151 C8
Dorchester Gdns. LA3 .... 212 F2
Dorchester Rd. Blackpool FY1 ... 129 B8
Dorchester Rd. Garstang PR3 ... 178 B8
Dorchester Rd. Hall Green WN8 .. 10 A7
Doric Gn. WN5 .... 10 D3
Doris Henderson Way. LA3 ... 213 A1
Doris St. Burnley BB11 .... 127 B7
Doris St. Chorley PR6 .... 60 D1
Dorking Rd. PR6 .... 60 F4
Dorman Rd. PR2 .... 117 E3
Dorothy Ave. PR5 .... 76 A1
Dorothy St. Blackburn BB2 ... 80 C8
Dorothy St. **13** Ramsbottom BL0 .. 49 B5
Dorrington Rd. LA1 .... 210 F5
Dorritt Rd. FY4 .... 109 E6

Dorritt St. **19** BB1 .... 101 A4
Dorset Ave. Ainsdale PR8 .... 20 C2
Dorset Ave. Bamber Bridge PR5 .. 96 D3
Dorset Ave. Cleveleys FY5 .... 172 D4
Dorset Ave. Darwen BB3 .... 80 F3
Dorset Ave. Padiham BB12 .... 125 D7
Dorset Dr. Blackburn BB1 .... 101 E4
Dorset Dr. Clitheroe BB7 .... 186 F2
Dorset Dr. Haslingden BB4 .... 67 A8
Dorset Pl. BB5 .... 102 F7
Dorset Rd. Lytham St Anne's FY8 .. 88 F8
Dorset Rd. Preston PR1 .... 117 A1
Dorset Rd. Rishton BB1 .... 123 A1
Dorset Rd. Standish WN1 .... 29 B1
Dorset St. **8** Blackpool FY4 .... 129 D1
Dorset St. Burnley BB12 .... 126 A6
Dotcliffe Rd. BB8 .... 192 A6
Double Row. BB12 .... 125 C8
Doughty St. BB8 .... 169 D4
Douglas Ave. Becconsall PR4 ... 72 F1
Douglas Ave. Blackpool FY3 .... 129 D7
Douglas Ave. Heysham LA3 .... 208 F7
Douglas Ave. Horwich BL6 .... 31 C5
Douglas Ave. Stalmine FY6 .... 174 C7
Douglas Ave. Up Holland WN8 ... 10 B7
Douglas Cl. Bamber Bridge PR5 ... 76 F7
Douglas Cl. Horwich BL6 .... 31 C5
Douglas Cl. Rufford L40 .... 38 C3
Douglas Ct. Freckleton PR4 .... 92 B6
Douglas Dr. Heysham LA3 .... 208 F7
Douglas Dr. Maghull L31 .... 5 F2
Douglas Dr. Ormskirk L39 .... 15 D7
Douglas Dr. Orrell WN5 .... 10 F5
Douglas Dr. Shevington WN6 ... 19 F5
Douglas Gr. BB3 .... 80 D4
Douglas Leatham House. **3**
  FY1 .... 129 D1
Douglas Pl. Blackburn BB1 .... 121 F1
Douglas Pl. Fleetwood FY7 .... 193 D3
Douglas Rd. Bacup OL13 .... 87 A1
Douglas Rd. Brierfield BB10 ... 148 A3
Douglas Rd. Fulwood PR2 .... 116 D3
Douglas Rd.
  Shevington Moor WN6 .... 28 B2
Douglas Rd N. Southport PR9 ... 53 C4
Douglas Rd N. PR2 .... 116 D3
Douglas Sq. **8** OL10 .... 32 F1
Douglas St. Colne BB8 .... 169 E6
Douglas St. Lytham St Anne's FY8 88 D6
Douglas St. Preston PR1 .... 95 C8
Douglas St. Ramsbottom BL0 ... 49 B6
Douglas Street Back. **4** BL0 .... 49 B6
Douglas Way. BB10 .... 148 A3
Doultons The. PR5 .... 96 C3
Dove Ave. PR1 .... 95 E4
Dove Cl. **6** FY5 .... 172 F1
Dove Dr. BL9 .... 32 B4
Dove La. BB3 .... 80 F2
Dove St. Lytham St Anne's FY8 ... 88 D6
Dove St. Preston PR1 .... 117 B1
Dove Tree Ct. FY4 .... 130 B1
Dovecote. PR5 & PR6 .... 77 A3
Dovedale Ave. Blackpool FY3 ... 130 C2
Dovedale Ave. Fulwood PR2 .... 116 A5
Dovedale Ave. Maghull L31 .... 5 C2
Dovedale Ave. Thornton FY5 .... 173 B3
Dovedale Cl. Brierfield BB10 ... 147 C4
Dovedale Cl. Burnley BB12 .... 126 C8
Dovedale Cl. Fulwood PR2 .... 116 A4
Dovedale Cl. Leyland PR5 .... 59 A6
Dovedale Dr. WN6 .... 28 E2
Dover Cl. Blackburn BB1 .... 101 C4
Dover Cl. Ramsbottom BL8 .... 49 A1
Dover Ct. FY1 .... 129 D2
Dover Gdns. FY6 .... 151 B5
Dover La. PR5 .... 78 C8
Dover Rd. Blackpool FY1 .... 129 E2
Dover Rd. Lytham St Anne's FY8 ... 88 F8
Dover Rd. Southport PR8 .... 33 F2
Dover St. Accrington BB5 .... 103 A4
Dover St. Blackburn BB3 .... 80 F7
Dover St. Nelson BB9 .... 168 E1
Dovetree Cl. PR1 .... 96 A3
Dowbridge. PR4 .... 113 C4
Dowbridge Way. PR4 .... 113 C5
Downes Gr. LA4 .... 212 G4
Downeyfield Rd. LA3 .... 209 C3
Downfield Cl. BL0 .... 49 B6
Downham Ave.
  Great Harwood BB6 .... 123 F6
Downham Ave. Rawtenstall BB4 . 85 A4
Downham Dr. BB5 .... 103 A3
Downham Gr. BB10 .... 127 D5
Downham Pl. Blackpool FY4 .... 109 B4
Downham Pl.
  Lytham St Anne's FY8 .... 89 C6
Downham Pl. Preston PR2 .... 115 E2
Downham Rd. Chatburn BB7 .... 187 E5
Downham Rd. Leyland PR5 .... 75 D1
Downham St. BB2 .... 100 C4
Downham Wlk. WN5 .... 10 F6
Downholland Haskayne CE Sch.
  L39 .... 13 E3
Downing Ct. PR3 .... 136 C3
Downing St. PR1 .... 96 E8
Downley Cl. OL10 .... 51 B2
Downs The. FY6 .... 151 D4
Dowry St. BB5 .... 103 C6
Dragon St. **5** BB12 .... 125 C8
Drake Cl. Lytham St Anne's FY8 . 109 E1
Drake Cl. Ormskirk L39 .... 15 C2
Drakelowe Ave. FY4 .... 109 F6
Drakes Hollow. PR5 .... 96 A4
Drammen Ave. BB11 .... 126 B5
Draperfield. PR7 .... 42 A4
Drapers Ave. PR7 .... 40 C6
Draw Well Rd. L33 .... 1 D2

Draycombe Ct. LA3 .... 212 A2
Draycombe Dr. LA3 .... 212 B2
Draycot Ave. FY3 .... 129 F8
Drayton Rd. LA3 .... 209 A7
Drew St. BB11 .... 126 B5
Drewitt Cres. PR9 .... 53 D4
Drewton Ave. LA3 .... 212 A2
Drinkhouse La. PR5 .... 57 A1
Drinkhouse Rd. PR5 .... 57 B1
Driscoll St. **1** PR1 .... 96 B8
Drive The. Bacup OL13 .... 86 F2
Drive The. Carnforth LA5 .... 217 B1
Drive The. Edenfield BL0 .... 67 D3
Drive The. Fulwood PR2 .... 117 B4
Drive The. Hest Bank LA2 .... 215 E1
Drive The. Heysham LA3 .... 208 F7
Drive The. Longton PR4 .... 74 A3
Drive The. Walton-le-D PR5 .... 96 F5
Driver St. **12** BB7 .... 85 A7
Driving Gate. 105 A1
Dronsfield Rd. FY7 .... 193 F4
Druids Cl. BL7 .... 46 D3
Drumacre La. PR4 .... 74 D6
Drumacre La W. PR4 .... 74 A6
Drummersdale La. L40 .... 23 D7
Drummond Ave. FY3 .... 129 E7
Drybread La. PR8 .... 175 C2
Dryburgh Ave. FY3 .... 129 F3
Dryden Gr. BB6 .... 123 C4
Dryden Rd. FY7 .... 194 A4
Dryden St. **6** Clayton-le-M BB5 123 F3
Dryden St. Padiham BB12 .... 125 E7
Dryfield La. BB1 .... 31 A5
Duchess Ct. FY2 .... 150 B3
Duchess Dr. FY2 .... 150 B3
Duchess St. BB3 .... 80 F7
Duchy Ave. PR2 .... 117 B4
Ducie Pl. PR1 .... 117 F1
Duck St. **2** Clitheroe BB7 .... 164 F8
Duck St. Smallwood Hey PR3 ... 196 A7
Duck St. Wray LA2 .... 232 D6
Duckett St. **3** BB11 .... 126 E6
Duckshaw Rd. BB3 .... 63 F6
Duckworth Cl. PR3 .... 178 D3
Duckworth Dr. PR3 .... 178 D3
Duckworth Hall Brow. BB5 ... 102 A1
Duckworth Hill La. BB1 & BB5 . 102 B1
Duckworth La. Rawtenstall BB4 . 67 E8
Duckworth La. Tarleton PR4 .... 55 F8
Duckworth St. Barrowford BB9 ... 168 D2
Duckworth St. Blackburn BB2 ... 100 D3
Duckworth St. **3** Bury BL9 .... 32 A4
Duckworth St. Church BB5 .... 102 E6
Duckworth St. Darwen BB3 .... 80 F2
Duddle La. PR5 .... 96 D2
Duddon Ave. Darwen BB3 .... 80 E3
Duddon Ave. Fleetwood FY7 .... 193 D2
Duddon Ave. Maghull L31 .... 5 F2
Dudley Ave. Blackpool FY2 .... 150 A4
Dudley Ave. Oswaldtwistle BB5 .. 102 C4
Dudley Cl. PR2 .... 94 A1
Dudley St. Brierfield BB9 .... 147 C5
Dudley St. Colne BB8 .... 169 F5
Dudley St. Morecambe LA4 .... 212 F4
Duerden St. BB9 .... 147 D2
Duffins Cl. OL12 .... 51 D3
Dugdale Ct. FY4 .... 109 F5
Dugdale Rd. BB12 .... 126 C7
Dugdale St. BB11 .... 127 A5
Dugie St. BL0 .... 49 B7
Duke Ave. PR8 .... 34 C4
Duke of Sussex St. BB2 .... 80 B8
Duke St. Bamber Bridge PR5 .... 76 E7
Duke St. Blackburn BB2 .... 100 D5
Duke St. Blackpool FY1 .... 129 B1
Duke St. Brierfield BB10 .... 147 B4
Duke St. Burnley BB11 .... 127 B4
Duke St. Burton in L LA6 .... 236 C3
Duke St. Chorley PR7 .... 42 C6
Duke St. Clayton-le-M BB5 .... 124 A2
Duke St. Colne BB8 .... 169 D4
Duke St. Formby L37 .... 11 F2
Duke St. Great Harwood BB6 .... 123 B5
Duke St. Heysham LA3 .... 208 E7
Duke St. High Bentham LA2 .... 233 D8
Duke St. Lancaster LA1 .... 213 C1
Duke St. Newchurch BB4 .... 68 E8
Duke St. Oswaldtwistle BB5 .... 102 D3
Duke St. Preston PR1 .... 96 B7
Duke St. Ramsbottom BL0 .... 49 A4
Duke St. Rochdale OL12 .... 51 F1
Duke St. Southport PR8 .... 34 B5
Duke St. Trawden BB8 .... 170 B5
Duke St Cty Prim Sch. PR7 ... 42 C6
Duke's Wood La. WN8 .... 9 D3
Dukes Brow. BB2 .... 100 C6
Dukes Ct. BB2 .... 100 B6
Dukes Dr. BB3 .... 81 F1
Dukes Meadow. PR2 .... 116 A5
Dukes Way. L37 .... 11 F2
Dulas La. L32 .... 1 A1
Dulas Rd. L32 .... 1 A1
Dumb Tom's La. L6 .... 236 E1
Dumbarton Rd. LA1 .... 211 A7
Dumfries Cl. FY2 .... 150 F5
Dunald Mill La. LA2 & LA6 ... 231 B6
Dunbar Cl. FY4 .... 110 A6
Dunbar Cres. PR8 .... 20 F8
Dunbar Rd. Fulwood PR2 .... 116 D4
Dunbar Rd. Heysham LA3 .... 208 E2
Dunbar Rd. Fulwood PR2 .... 115 F3
Dunbar Rd. Southport PR8 .... 33 F1
Duncan Ave. PR2 .... 150 C6
Duncan Cl. Brownside BB10 ... 127 F5
Duncan Cl.
  Lytham St Anne's FY8 .... 109 D1
Duncan Pl. FY7 .... 193 E4

Duncan St. Burnley BB12 .... 126 A5
Duncan St. Horwich BL6 .... 31 C3
Duncroft St. PR2 .... 186 E2
Dundas St. BB8 .... 169 C4
Dundee Cl. OL10 .... 32 F1
Dundee Dr. BB1 .... 101 A4
Dundee La. BL0 .... 49 B6
Dundee St. LA1 .... 211 A7
Dunderdale Ave. BB9 .... 147 C7
Dunderdale St. PR3 .... 139 B7
Dundonald St. PR1 .... 96 D8
Dundonnell Rd. BB9 .... 169 A1
Dunedin Rd. BB8 .... 48 F2
Dunelt Rd. FY1 .... 129 D2
Dunes Ave. FY4 .... 109 B5
Dunes Dr. L37 .... 11 C4
Dungeon La. WN8 .... 18 C7
Dunkeld St. **5** LA1 .... 211 A7
Dunkenhalgh Way. Church BB5 102 E7
Dunkenhalgh Way.
  Clayton-le-M BB5 .... 123 E1
Dunkenshaw Cres. LA1 .... 211 B2
Dunkirk Ave. Carnforth LA5 .... 216 E8
Dunkirk Ave. Fulwood PR2 .... 116 C3
Dunkirk La. BB5 .... 75 A1
Dunkirk Rd. PR8 .... 33 F2
Dunlin Cl. FY5 .... 173 A5
Dunlop Ave. PR8 .... 20 C2
Dunmail Ave. FY3 .... 129 F2
Dunmore St. PR1 .... 96 B8
Dunny Shop Ave. BB5 .... 103 A4
Dunoon Cl. PR2 .... 115 F4
Dunoon Dr. BB1 .... 101 D3
Dunoon St. BB1 .... 126 D5
Dunrobin Dr. PR7 .... 59 D1
Dunscar Dr. PR6 .... 60 E1
Dunscar Golf Course. BL7 ... 46 C1
Dunsop Cl.
  Bamber Bridge PR5 .... 76 F8
Dunsop Cl. **1** Blackpool FY1 ... 129 D1
Dunsop Cl. **2** FY1 .... 129 D1
Dunsop Rd. PR2 .... 117 D4
Dunsop St. BB1 .... 100 F7
Dunster Ave. BB5 .... 102 C5
Dunster Gr. BB7 .... 164 C6
Dunster Rd. PR8 .... 20 E8
Dunvegan Cl. FY4 .... 110 A6
Dunvegan Ct. **2** OL10 .... 32 F1
Durban Gr. BB11 .... 126 E4
Durham Ave. Burnley BB12 .... 126 D5
Durham Ave. Cleveleys FY5 .... 172 E3
Durham Ave. Lancaster LA1 .... 211 A4
Durham Ave.
  Lytham St Anne's FY8 .... 88 E7
Durham Cl. Blackburn BB1 .... 100 F4
Durham Cl. Leyland PR5 .... 58 E6
Durham Cl. Morecambe LA3 ... 212 E2
Durham Dr. Oswaldtwistle BB5 .. 102 F3
Durham Dr. Ramsbottom BL0 ... 49 B3
Durham Dr. Wilpshire BB1 .... 121 F6
Durham Gr. PR3 .... 178 B7
Durham House. PR1 .... 96 A6
Durham Rd. Blackpool FY1 .... 129 D5
Durham Rd. Darwen BB3 .... 80 F2
Durham Rd. Wilpshire BB1 .... 121 F6
Durham St. Accrington BB5 .... 103 D7
Durham St. Skelmersdale WN8 ... 17 D2
Durley Rd. FY1 .... 129 D2
Durn St. OL14 .... 108 A1
Dutch Barn Cl. PR7 .... 60 B2
Dutton Ct. FY3 .... 129 D5
Dutton Rd. FY3 .... 129 D5
Dutton St. **16** BB5 .... 103 C6
Duxbury Cl. L31 .... 5 E3
Duxbury Dr. BL9 .... 32 C2
Duxbury Hall Rd. PR7 .... 42 E3
Duxbury Jubilee Pk. PR7 .... 42 D3
Duxbury St. Darwen BB3 .... 64 B6
Duxbury St. Earby BB8 .... 201 C2
Dye House La. **6** LA1 .... 210 F8
Dyer St. PR4 .... 112 F5
Dyers La. L39 .... 15 E4
Dyke Nook. BB7 .... 164 F6
Dykes La. LA5 .... 219 F2
Dymock Rd. PR1 .... 117 D1
Dymock Rd N. PR1 .... 117 D1
Dyneley Ave. BB10 .... 127 F4
Dyneley Rd. BB1 .... 101 C7
Dyson St. BB2 .... 100 E2

Eachill Gdns. BB1 .... 102 B8
Eachill Rd. **2** BB1 .... 123 B1
Eager La. L31 .... 5 B8
Eagle St. Accrington BB5 .... 103 B5
Eagle St. Blackburn BB1 .... 101 C4
Eagle St. Nelson BB9 .... 168 F1
Eagle St. Oswaldtwistle BB5 .... 102 C2
Eagles The. FY5 .... 151 E5
Eagley Bank. OL12 .... 70 E6
Eagley Rd. BB10 .... 147 C4
Ealing Gr. PR6 .... 60 F3
Eamont Ave. PR9 .... 53 B5
Eamont Pl. FY7 .... 193 D2
Eanam. BB1 .... 100 F5
Eanam Old Rd. BB1 .... 100 F5
Earby Cty Prim Sch. BB8 .... 201 C1
Earby Rd. BB8 .... 191 F8
Eardley Rd. LA3 .... 208 F3
Earl Rd. BL0 .... 49 B6
Earl St. Barnoldswick BB8 .... 200 C2
Earl St. Blackburn BB1 .... 100 E6
Earl St. Burnley BB10 .... 127 B8
Earl St. Clayton-le-M BB5 .... 123 F2
Earl St. Colne BB8 .... 169 D4
Earl St. Great Harwood BB6 .... 123 C5
Earl St. Lancaster LA1 .... 213 F1
Earl St. **8** Nelson BB9 .... 168 F1
Earl St. Preston PR0 & PR1 ... 95 F8

Earl St. Ramsbottom BL0 .... 49 D6
Earlesdon Ave. BB8 .... 200 F1
Earlham St. BB8 .... 201 C2
Earls Ave. PR5 .... 76 E8
Earls Dr. BB3 .... 81 E1
Earls Way. PR7 .... 59 D2
Earlsway. FY3 .... 130 D5
Earlswood. WN8 .... 18 E1
Earnsdale Ave. BB3 .... 80 D2
Earnsdale Cl. BB3 .... 80 E2
Earnsdale Rd. BB3 .... 80 E3
Earnshaw Ave. OL12 .... 51 E3
Earnshaw Bridge Cty Infs Sch.
  PR5 .... 75 E2
Earnshaw Dr. PR5 .... 75 D1
Earnshaw Rd. OL13 .... 86 F3
Earnshaw Ave. **19** OL13 .... 86 F3
Easby Cl. L37 .... 12 A2
Easdale Ave. LA4 .... 213 A5
Easedale Cl. Burnley BB12 .... 126 B8
Easedale Cl. Hest Bank LA5 .... 215 F2
Easedale Dr. PR8 .... 20 B4
Easington. LA1 .... 213 C2
Easington Cres. FY3 .... 130 B8
Easington Wlk. **4** BB1 .... 100 F3
East Ave. BB8 .... 200 B2
East Bank. **2** Barrowford BB9 . 168 D4
East Bank. Water BB4 .... 106 A1
East Bank Ave. BB4 .... 84 B2
East Bank Rd. FY8 .... 88 E5
East Beach. FY8 .... 90 C3
East Boothroyden. FY1 .... 129 B8
East Cecil St. FY8 .... 90 A3
East Cliff. PR1 .... 95 F6
East Cliff Rd. PR1 .... 95 F6
East Cliffe. FY8 .... 90 C3
East Cres. BB5 .... 103 B8
East Croft. BB9 .... 169 B2
East Ct. FY5 .... 172 D5
East Dene. WN8 .... 26 B2
East End St. BB8 .... 169 C4
East Gate. BB4 .... 84 B3
East Hills St. **16** BB8 .... 200 B2
East Holme. FY8 .... 90 C4
East La. L29 & L38 .... 4 B2
East Lancashire Rd. BB1 .... 121 F3
East Lancashire Rly. BL0 .... 49 C5
East Leigh. WN8 .... 18 D1
East Lodge Pl. BB10 .... 127 E1
East Mead. Blackpool FY3 .... 129 F3
East Mead. Ormskirk L39 .... 15 B2
East Meade. L31 .... 5 C2
East Mount. WN5 .... 10 F6
East Par. **13** Barnoldswick BB8 .. 200 B2
East Par. **17** Rawtenstall BB4 .... 85 A3
East Park Ave. Blackburn BB1 .. 100 C8
East Park Ave. Darwen BB3 .... 63 F8
East Park Dr. FY3 .... 130 A5
East Park Rd. BB1 & BB2 .... 100 D6
East Rd. Fulwood PR2 .... 117 A3
East Rd. Lancaster LA1 .... 211 A8
East Rd. Maghull L31 .... 5 F1
East Sq. PR4 .... 94 A1
East St. Bamber Bridge PR5 .... 76 E7
East St. Blackburn BB2 .... 79 D8
East St. Blackburn BB2 .... 100 C3
East St. Brierfield BB9 .... 147 C5
East St. Chorley PR6 .... 42 D8
East St. Edenfield BL0 .... 67 D4
East St. Hapton BB12 .... 125 C4
East St. Helmshore BB4 .... 67 A7
East St. Leyland PR5 .... 76 B1
East St. Leyland PR5 .... 76 B2
East St. Morecambe LA3 & LA4 .. 212 B4
East St. **10** Nelson BB9 .... 168 D1
East St. Padiham BB12 .... 145 C1
East St. **12** Preston PR1 .... 96 A8
East St. Rawtenstall BB4 .... 84 F5
East St. Southport PR9 .... 34 D7
East Terr. PR7 .... 59 D4
East Topping St. FY1 .... 129 C5
East View. Bacup OL13 .... 86 F2
East View. **9** Barnoldswick BB8 200 B2
East View. Grindleton BB7 .... 187 B7
East View. Haslingden BB5 .... 84 A8
East View. Pendleton BB7 .... 165 B4
East View. Preston PR1 .... 96 A8
East View. Preston PR1 .... 96 C6
East View. Ramsbottom BL0 ... 49 C3
East View. Read BB12 .... 144 D2
East View. Stubbins BL0 .... 67 C1
East View. Trawden BB8 .... 170 C2
East View. Winmarleigh PR3 ... 198 F6
East View. LA1 .... 213 D3
East View Terr. PR6 .... 79 B3
East Ward Cty Prim Sch. BL9 .. 32 B2
East Ward Cty Prim Sch
  (Annexe). BL9 .... 32 B3
East Wlk. BL7 .... 46 D2
Eastbank Ave. FY4 .... 110 A7
Eastbank St. PR8 .... 34 B6
Eastbourne Cl. PR2 .... 115 C4
Eastbourne Rd. Blackpool FY4 . 109 B6
Eastbourne Rd. Southport PR8 . 34 A3
Eastcliff. LA2 .... 231 F5
Eastcott Cl. BB2 .... 81 A8
Eastern Ave. BB10 .... 147 C1
Eastfield Dr. West Bradford BB7 186 F6
Eastgate. Accrington BB5 .... 103 C6
Eastgate. Fulwood PR2 .... 116 C4
Eastgate. Morecambe LA3 .... 213 A4
Eastgate. Rochester PR3 .... 140 E4
Eastgate. Wallbank OL12 .... 51 C7
Eastham Pl. BB11 .... 127 B6

Eastham St. Burnley BB11 .... 127 B5
Eastham St. Clitheroe BB7 .... 186 E1
Eastham St. Lancaster LA1 .... 211 A7
Eastham St. Preston PR1 .... 116 E1
Eastlands. Heysham LA3 .... 209 A7
Eastlands. Leyland PR5 .... 58 C7
Eastmoor Dr. BB7 .... 164 F7
Easton Cl. PR2 .... 117 D6
Eastpines Dr. FY5 .... 150 F8
Eastside. FY4 .... 109 F8
Eastway. Freckleton PR4 .... 92 A6
Eastway. Fulwood PR2 & PR3 .... 117 B6
Eastway. Maghull L31 .... 5 E1
Eastway Bsns Village. PR2 .... 117 B8
Eastwood Ave. Blackpool FY3 .... 129 E8
Eastwood Ave. Fleetwood FY7 .... 193 F3
Eastwood Cl. ⑥ BL9 .... 32 B2
Eastwood Cres. BB4 .... 85 C2
Eastwood Rd. PR5 .... 75 F1
Eastwood St. Barnoldswick BB8 .... 200 C3
Eastwood St. Blackburn BB1 .... 101 A6
Eastwood St. Rawtenstall BB4 .... 85 C2
Eaton Ave. FY1 .... 129 C1
Eaton Ct. FY8 .... 88 F6
Eaton Pl. PR4 .... 112 F5
Eaton Way. FY6 .... 130 E8
Eaves Ave. BB11 .... 126 D2
Eaves Cl. BB5 .... 124 F1
Eaves Green La. PR3 .... 137 F8
Eaves Green Rd. PR7 .... 42 B5
Eaves La. Chorley PR6 & PR7 .... 42 E7
Eaves La. Cuddy Hill PR4 .... 135 D7
Eaves La. Fulwood PR2 .... 116 E3
Eaves Lane Hospl. PR6 .... 42 E8
Eaves Lea. 238 B2
Eaves Rd. FY8 .... 110 A1
Eaves St. FY1 .... 129 B7
Eavesdale. WN8 .... 9 E8
Eaveswood Cl. PR5 .... 96 E1
Ebony St. ⑥ BB1 .... 101 A7
Ebor St. BB10 .... 147 B2
Eccles Rd. L37 .... 11 D1
Eccles St. Accrington BB5 .... 103 B7
Eccles St. Blackburn BB2 .... 100 E3
Eccles St. Preston PR1 .... 117 C1
Eccles St. Ramsbottom BL0 .... 49 B6
Eccles's La. L40 & WN8 .... 26 B7
Ecclesgate Rd. FY4 .... 110 A5
Eccleshill Gdns. BB3 .... 81 C4
Eccleshill St. ⑦ BB12 .... 125 C8
Eccleston Cty Prim Sch. PR7 .... 40 B6
Eccleston Rd. FY1 .... 129 D1
Eclipse Rd. BB2 .... 79 D8
Ecroyd Rd. PR1 & PR2 .... 116 C2
Ecroyd St. Leyland PR5 .... 76 A1
Ecroyd St. Nelson BB9 .... 147 C8
Edale Ave. BB4 .... 84 C2
Edale Cl. PR5 .... 59 A7
Edale Cl. PR1 .... 116 F1
Edale Dr. WN6 .... 28 E2
Eddington Rd. FY8 .... 89 B4
Eddleston Cl. FY3 .... 130 D5
Edelston Rd. FY1 .... 129 C6
Eden Ave. Edenfield BL0 .... 67 D3
Eden Ave. Fleetwood FY7 .... 193 D2
Eden Ave. Lytham St Anne's FY8 .... 89 E3
Eden Ave. Morecambe LA4 .... 213 B5
Eden Ave. Southport PR9 .... 52 F2
Eden Cl. BB0 .... 67 D2
Eden Cl. BL0 .... 67 D2
Eden Gdns. PR3 .... 139 B8
Eden Hall. PR1 .... 116 E1
Eden Mount Way. LA5 .... 217 F2
Eden Pk. LA1 .... 210 F4
Eden St. Accrington BB5 .... 103 A5
Eden St. Blackburn BB1 .... 101 A5
Eden St. Blackpool FY1 .... 129 C6
Eden St. Leyland PR5 .... 59 A8
Eden St. Ramsbottom BL0 .... 67 D1
Edenfield Ave. FY6 .... 151 F2
Edenfield CE Prim Sch. BL0 .... 67 D4
Edenfield Cl. PR8 .... 34 E3
Edenfield Rd.
Cheesden OL11 &OL12 .... 50 E4
Edenfield Rd.
Passmonds OL11 & OL12 .... 51 B1
Edenfield St. OL11 & OL12 .... 51 C1
Edenhurst Cl. L37 .... 11 C2
Edenhurst Dr. L37 .... 11 C2
Edensor Terr. BB3 .... 80 F2
Edenvale Ave. FY2 .... 150 B4
Edenvale Cres. LA1 .... 213 E3
Edenvale Rd. LA1 .... 213 E3
Edenway. PR2 .... 116 D7
Edgar St. Accrington BB5 .... 103 B6
Edgar St. Huncoat BB5 .... 124 E2
Edgar St. Nelson BB9 .... 168 F2
Edgar St. Ramsbottom BL0 .... 49 B5
Edgar St W. ⑰ BL0 .... 49 B5
Edge End. BB6 .... 123 B5
Edge End Ave. BB9 .... 147 D6
Edge End High Sch. BB9 .... 147 D6
Edge End La. Brierfield BB9 .... 147 D6
Edge End La.
Great Harwood BB6 .... 123 B6
Edge End Rd. BB6 .... 123 B5
Edge End Terr. BB3 .... 79 B3
Edge Gate La. PR7 .... 62 A6
Edge Hall Rd. WN5 .... 10 E5
Edge Hill Coll. ....
Edge Hill Coll of HE. L39 .... 16 A3
Edge La. Bacup OL13 .... 69 F8
Edge La. Barnoldswick BB8 .... 225 F1
Edge La. Entwistle BB3 & BL7 .... 47 A8
Edge La. Rawtenstall BB4 .... 85 D3
Edge Yate La. BB4 .... 85 B5
Edgecott Cl. LA3 .... 209 A7
Edgefield. PR7 .... 60 B2
Edgefield Cl. FY3 .... 130 B8
Edgehill Cl. PR2 .... 116 D4
Edgehill Cres. PR5 .... 75 E2
Edgehill Dr. PR2 .... 116 D4
Edgemoor Cl. OL12 .... 70 E5
Edgeside. BB6 .... 123 B5
Edgeside La. BB4 .... 85 F2
Edgeware Rd. BB2 .... 100 C6
Edgeway Pl. FY5 .... 173 C1
Edgeway Rd. FY4 .... 109 E5
Edgeworth CE/Meth Prim Sch.
BL7 .... 47 D5
Edgley Dr. L39 .... 16 A5
Edinburgh Cl. PR5 .... 76 C1
Edinburgh Dr. BB5 .... 102 F3
Edinburgh Rd. Formby L37 .... 11 E1
Edinburgh Rd. Haslingden BB4 .... 83 F1
Edisford Cty Prim Sch. BB7 .... 164 C7
Edisford Rd. Clitheroe BB7 .... 164 C8
Edisford Rd. Waddington BB7 .... 186 B4
Edison St. BB3 .... 80 F1
Edith St. Barnoldswick BB8 .... 200 B3
Edith St. Blackburn BB1 .... 101 A4
Edith St. Nelson BB9 .... 147 F8
Edith St. Shuttleworth BL0 .... 49 E8
Edleston St. BB5 .... 102 F4
Edmondsen Pl. ④ FY7 .... 193 F2
Edmondson St. BB8 .... 200 B3
Edmondson's La. BD23 .... 201 F8
Edmonton Pl. FY2 .... 150 F3
Edmund Gennings Ct. BB7 .... 187 D5
Edmund St. Accrington BB5 .... 103 C5
Edmund St. Blackburn BB2 .... 80 D7
Edmund St. Burnley BB10 .... 147 B1
Edmund St. Darwen BB3 .... 81 B1
Edmund St. ③ Preston PR1 .... 96 B8
Edmundson St. Blackburn BB2 .... 100 C5
Edmundson St. ③ Church BB5 .... 102 E4
Edward Cl. BB5 .... 102 E6
Edward Sq. ⑧ PR1 .... 117 A1
Edward St. Accrington BB5 .... 103 E1
Edward St. ⑫ Bacup OL13 .... 87 A3
Edward St. Bamber Bridge PR5 .... 76 E8
Edward St. Barnoldswick BB8 .... 200 C3
Edward St. Blackpool FY1 .... 129 B5
Edward St. Burnley BB11 .... 127 A6
Edward St. Carnforth LA5 .... 217 D2
Edward St. Chorley PR6 .... 42 D7
Edward St. Darwen BB3 .... 81 A2
Edward St. ⑧ Church BB5 .... 102 E6
Edward St. Darwen BB3 .... 81 A2
Edward St. Earby BB8 .... 201 B2
Edward St. ⑤
Great Harwood BB6 .... 123 C5
Edward St. Haslingden BB4 .... 84 B6
Edward St. Horwich BL6 .... 31 A3
Edward St. Lancaster LA1 .... 211 A8
Edward St. ③ Leyland PR5 .... 59 A8
Edward St. Lytham St Anne's FY8 .... 88 F7
Edward St. Morecambe LA4 .... 212 D5
Edward St. Nelson BB9 .... 168 F2
Edward St. Preston PR1 .... 95 B4
Edward St. Rawtenstall BB4 .... 85 A8
Edward St. ③ Rishton BB1 .... 123 B1
Edward St. Thornton FY5 .... 173 B4
Edward St. Walton-le-D PR4 .... 96 C5
Edward St. Whitworth OL12 .... 70 D2
Edward VII Quay. PR2 .... 95 B8
Edwell Ave. FY4 .... 109 D8
Edwin Waugh Gdns. OL12 .... 51 D3
Edwinstowe Rd. FY8 .... 89 D6
Egan St. PR1 .... 96 A8
Egbert St. PR1 .... 117 A1
Egerton Gr. PR7 .... 42 B6
Egerton Prim Sch. BL7 .... 46 D3
Egerton Rd. Belmont BL7 .... 45 E4
Egerton Rd. Blackpool FY1 .... 129 B7
Egerton Rd. Leyland PR5 .... 75 C2
Egerton Rd. Preston PR1 .... 116 B1
Egremont Ave. FY5 .... 172 D5
Egypt Mount. BB4 .... 84 D2
Egypt Terr. ③ BB4 .... 84 E2
Eider Cl. FY5 .... 172 F5
Eidsforth La. PR3 .... 220 A1
Eidsforth Rd. LA4 .... 212 E6
Eight Acre Ave. BB2 .... 144 F8
Eight Acre La.
Yealand Redmayne LA5 .... 219 E4
Eildon Dr. FY6 .... 151 D1
Elaine Ave. FY4 .... 129 F1
Elbow La. L37 .... 11 F3
Elbow St. PR7 .... 42 C7
Elbut La. BL9 .... 32 F5
Elcho St. PR1 .... 117 A2
Elder Cl. Clayton Green PR6 .... 77 C2
Elder Cl. Fulwood PR2 .... 117 D6
Elder Cl. Warton PR4 .... 91 E6
Elder Cl. BB5 .... 103 E8
Elder St. BB9 .... 168 F2
Elderberry Cl. FY5 .... 172 F5
Elderwood Ave. FY5 .... 151 B7
Eldon Cl. FY8 .... 88 F7
Eldon Cty Prim Sch. PR1 .... 116 E2
Eldon Gr. LA3 .... 208 F7
Eldon Rd. BB1 .... 100 D7
Eldon St. Chorley PR7 .... 42 D7
Eldon St. Preston PR1 .... 116 D2
Eldons Croft. PR8 .... 20 D5
Eldwick St. BB10 .... 147 C1
Eleanor St. Blackburn BB1 .... 100 F5
Eleanor St. ③ Nelson BB9 .... 168 E1
Electricity St. BB5 .... 103 B6
Elgar Cl. BB2 .... 101 A2
Elgin Cres. BB11 .... 126 D4
Elgin Pl. BB2 .... 130 A7
Elgin St. ④ Lancaster LA1 .... 211 A7
Elgin St. Preston PR1 .... 117 A2
Elijah St. PR1 .... 96 D8
Elim Ct. FY8 .... 90 C3
Elim Gdns. BB2 .... 100 C1
Eliza St. Burnley BB10 & BB11 .... 127 B5
Eliza St. Ramsbottom BL0 .... 49 D6
Elizabeth Ave. PR8 .... 20 E6
Elizabeth Cl. FY3 .... 130 D5
Elizabeth Cl. Blackpool FY3 .... 129 D6
Elizabeth Ct. Poulton-le-F FY6 .... 151 D3
Elizabeth Dr. 67 A8
Elizabeth House.
Blackburn BB1 .... 101 A3
Elizabeth House. Darwen BB3 .... 81 B1
Elizabeth Sq. ⑥ PR1 .... 117 A1
Elizabeth St. Accrington BB5 .... 102 F5
Elizabeth St. Blackburn BB1 .... 100 F5
Elizabeth St. Blackpool FY1 .... 129 C6
Elizabeth St. Burnley BB11 .... 127 A5
Elizabeth St. Edenfield BL0 .... 67 D3
Elizabeth St. Fleetwood FY7 .... 194 B5
Elizabeth St. Nelson BB9 .... 168 E1
Elizabeth St. Padiham BB12 .... 125 C7
Elizabeth St. Preston PR1 .... 95 F8
Elizabeth St.
Whitewell Bottom BB4 .... 85 F4
Elker Cotts. BB6 .... 142 F4
Elker La. BB7 .... 142 F5
Elker Mews. BB6 .... 142 F3
Elkin Rd. LA4 .... 212 G5
Elland Pl. FY1 .... 129 C6
Elland Rd. BB9 .... 147 C6
Ellel Hall Gdns. LA2 .... 206 F3
Ellen Cl. PR1 .... 116 F2
Ellen St. Bamber Bridge PR5 .... 96 E1
Ellen St. Darwen BB3 .... 64 A7
Ellen St. ⑪ Nelson BB9 .... 147 D8
Ellen St. Preston PR1 .... 116 E1
Ellen St. Preston PR1 .... 116 F2
Ellenrod Dr. OL12 .... 51 A2
Ellenrod La. OL12 .... 51 A2
Ellenshaw Cl. BB3 .... 81 B1
Eller Brook Cl. PR6 .... 42 F1
Ellerbeck Ave. PR2 .... 117 E5
Ellerbeck Cl. BB10 .... 147 E3
Ellerbeck Rd. BB5 .... 103 B7
Ellerbreck Rd. FY5 .... 172 C2
Ellerbrook Dr. L40 .... 24 F3
Ellerbrook Rd. BB3 .... 81 B1
Ellerbrook Way. L39 .... 15 E6
Ellerslie Rd. PR1 .... 116 B1
Ellesmere Ave. Colne BB8 .... 169 F5
Ellesmere Ave. Thornton FY5 .... 173 D1
Ellesmere Gr. LA4 .... 212 D3
Ellesmere Rd. Blackpool FY4 .... 129 E1
Ellesmere Rd. Darwen BB3 .... 80 E3
Ellesmere Rd. Morecambe LA4 .... 212 C4
Elletson St. FY6 .... 151 D4
Elliott Ave. BB3 .... 64 B6
Elliott Cl. PR1 .... 116 E2
Elliott St. Burnley BB10 .... 127 C5
Elliott St. Preston PR1 .... 116 E1
Elliott St. Preston PR1 .... 116 E2
Elliott Wlk. PR1 .... 116 F2
Ellis Dr. LA4 .... 213 A6
Ellis St. Barnoldswick BB8 .... 200 B2
Ellis St. Burnley BB11 .... 126 E5
Ellis St. ⑪ Ramsbottom BL0 .... 49 B5
Ellisland. FY4 .... 130 C1
Ellison Fold. BB5 .... 123 E3
Ellison Fold La. BB3 .... 81 C1
Ellison Fold Terr. BB3 .... 81 B1
Ellison St. Accrington BB5 .... 103 B6
Ellison St. Darwen BB3 .... 81 A2
Ellwood Ave. Lancaster LA1 .... 214 A4
Ellwood Ave. Morecambe LA3 .... 212 F2
Ellwood Cl. LA3 .... 212 G2
Ellwood Gr. LA3 .... 212 F2
Elm Ave. Blackpool FY3 .... 129 E5
Elm Ave. Poulton-le-F FY6 .... 151 D3
Elm Ave. Preston PR2 .... 116 A2
Elm Ave. Warton PR4 .... 91 D6
Elm Brow. PR3 .... 160 C4
Elm Cl. Barnoldswick BB8 .... 200 A1
Elm Cl. Haslingden BB4 .... 84 B3
Elm Cl. Rishton BB1 .... 102 B8
Elm Cl. Salterforth BB8 .... 191 E8
Elm Cl. FY5 .... 151 D3
Elm Dr. ③ Bamber Bridge PR5 .... 96 F1
Elm Cl. Formby L37 .... 11 D1
Elm Gr. Chorley PR6 .... 60 E2
Elm Gr. Clayton-le-W PR5 .... 76 D3
Elm Gr. Darwen BB3 .... 81 B3
Elm Gr. Fulwood PR2 .... 117 E2
Elm Gr. ⑥ Horwich BL6 .... 31 E1
Elm Gr. Kirkham PR4 .... 113 B7
Elm Gr. Morecambe LA4 .... 213 A7
Elm Gr. Skelmersdale WN8 .... 17 E1
Elm Mill. BB10 .... 127 A8
Elm Pl. L39 .... 15 E4
Elm Rd. Burscough L40 .... 24 E3
Elm Rd. Southport PR9 .... 34 B4
Elm St. ⑦ Bacup OL13 .... 87 A3
Elm St. Blackburn BB1 .... 101 A7
Elm St. Burnley BB10 .... 147 A8
Elm St. Bury BL9 .... 32 B2
Elm St. Colne BB8 .... 169 E6
Elm St. Edenfield BL0 .... 67 D3
Elm St. Fleetwood FY7 .... 194 A4
Elm St. Great Harwood BB6 .... 123 C4
Elm St. Haslingden BB4 .... 84 B3
Elm St. ⑨ Nelson BB9 .... 168 E1
Elm St. Ramsbottom BL0 .... 49 D6
Elm St. Rawtenstall BB4 .... 85 A3
Elm St. Rochdale OL12 .... 51 F1
Elm St. Whitworth OL12 .... 70 D2
Elmbank Ave. FY5 .... 150 C7
Elmcroft La. L38 .... 3 A3
Elmdale Cl. L37 .... 11 D2
Elmhurst Rd. FY8 .... 89 B8
Elmpark Gate. OL12 .... 51 B3
Elmpark Gr. OL12 .... 51 B3
Elmpark Vale. OL12 .... 51 B3
Elmpark View. OL12 .... 51 B3
Elmpark Way. OL12 .... 51 B3
Elmridge. WN8 .... 9 D8
Elmridge Cres. FY2 .... 150 F3
Elms Ave. Cleveleys FY5 .... 172 G2
Elms Ave. Lytham St Anne's FY8 .... 89 E3
Elms Ct. LA4 .... 213 A7
Elms Dr. Morecambe LA4 .... 213 A7
Elms Dr. Wrea Green PR4 .... 112 B4
Elms Rd. LA4 .... 213 A7
Elms Sch. PR1 .... 117 A3
Elms The. Clayton Green PR6 .... 77 C1
Elms The. Maghull L31 .... 5 D3
Elms The. Southport PR8 .... 33 F6
Elms The. Southport PR8 .... 34 C5
Elmsdale Cl. LA1 .... 213 E2
Elmsfield Pk. L39 .... 6 A6
Elmside Cl. FY5 .... 173 D2
Elmslack Cl. LA5 .... 218 C4
Elmslack La. LA5 .... 218 C4
Elmsley St. PR1 & PR2 .... 116 E2
Elmslie Girls Sch. FY3 .... 129 E3
Elmstead. WN8 .... 9 D8
Elmswood Cl. FY8 .... 89 F4
Elmwood. Chorley PR7 .... 60 B1
Elmwood. Skelmersdale WN8 .... 18 C3
Elmwood Ave. Leyland PR5 .... 75 E1
Elmwood Ave. Preesall FY6 .... 195 B4
Elmwood Cl. BB5 .... 103 D6
Elmwood Dr. PR4 .... 131 F2
Elmwood Dr. Penwortham PR1 .... 95 B4
Elmwood Dr. Thornton FY5 .... 173 C1
Elmwood Gdns. LA1 .... 211 A2
Elmwood St. BB11 .... 126 D5
Elsby Ave. FY5 .... 151 C8
Elsie St. ⑩ Church BB5 .... 49 A4
Elsinore Cl. FY7 .... 193 F5
Elslack La. BD23 .... 201 F7
Elson Rd. L37 .... 11 D1
Elston Ave. FY3 .... 130 A8
Elston Gn. PR2 .... 138 E1
Elston La. PR2 .... 118 F7
Elswick. WN8 .... 9 C8
Elswick Gdns. BB2 .... 120 D3
Elswick Gn. PR9 .... 53 A5
Elswick Lodge. BB2 .... 120 E3
Elswick Pl. Blackpool FY4 .... 109 E8
Elswick Pl. Lytham St Anne's FY8 .... 89 B8
Elswick Rd. Leyland PR5 .... 58 D8
Elswick Rd. Preston PR2 .... 115 E1
Elswick Rd. Southport PR9 .... 52 F4
Elswick St. BB3 .... 81 B1
Elterwater. FY6 .... 194 E5
Elterwater Pl. Blackpool FY3 .... 130 A2
Elterwater Pl. Lancaster LA1 .... 214 A1
Eltham Ct. FY6 .... 151 B1
Elton Rd. BB1 & BB5 .... 82 B5
Elton St. ③ PR1 .... 116 C1
Elvaston Way. FY6 .... 151 C6
Elvington Rd. L38 .... 3 A2
Ely Cl. Darwen BB3 .... 81 C1
Ely Cl. Wilpshire BB1 .... 121 F6
Emerald Ave. BB1 .... 121 F2
Emerald Cotts. BL8 .... 48 F3
Emerald St. BB1 .... 121 F2
Emerson Ave. FY4 .... 109 D7
Emerson Cl. L38 .... 3 A4
Emerson Rd. PR1 .... 117 D2
Emerson St. LA1 .... 211 A4
Emesgate La. LA5 .... 218 C3
Emily St. Bamber Bridge PR5 .... 76 A8
Emily St. Blackburn BB1 .... 101 A6
Emily St. Burnley BB11 .... 127 A4
Emily St. BB5 .... 102 F6
Emmanuel Holcombe CE
Prim Sch. BL8 .... 49 A6
Emmanuel Rd. PR9 .... 52 F2
Emmanuel St. PR1 & PR2 .... 116 E2
Emmaus Rd. LA3 .... 208 F6
Emmerdale Cl. BB5 .... 102 D5
Emmett St. Horwich BL6 .... 31 B3
Emmett St. Preston PR1 .... 116 F1
Emmott La. BB8 .... 170 D6
Emnie La. PR5 .... 58 C7
Empire Gr. FY3 .... 129 D7
Empire St. BB6 .... 123 D6
Empress Ave. PR2 .... 116 E4
Empress Cl. L31 .... 6 A7
Empress Dr. FY2 .... 150 B1
Empress St. Accrington BB5 .... 102 F6
Empress St. Blackburn BB5 .... 80 F7
Empress St. Colne BB8 .... 169 C5
Empress Way. PR7 .... 59 E2
End St. BB8 .... 169 B4
Endcliffe Rd. LA4 .... 212 F5
Enderley Ct. FY5 .... 173 C1
Ending Rake. OL12 .... 51 C4
Endsleigh Gdns. FY4 .... 109 E6
Endsleigh Gr. LA1 .... 213 C3
Enfield Cl. Eccleston PR7 .... 40 C5
Enfield Cl. Huncoat BB5 .... 124 E2
Enfield Rd. Accrington BB5 .... 103 C2
Enfield Rd. Blackpool FY1 .... 129 C7
Engine La. L37 .... 3 E8
England Ave. FY2 .... 150 C4
English Martyrs' Pl. PR1 .... 116 F2
English Martyrs' RC Prim Sch.
PR1 .... 116 E1
Ennerdale. WN8 .... 9 D8
Ennerdale Ave. Blackburn BB1 .... 101 C3
Ennerdale Ave. Fleetwood FY7 .... 193 C6
Ennerdale Ave. Maghull L31 .... 5 E2
Ennerdale Ave. Morecambe LA4 .... 212 G4
Ennerdale Cl. Clitheroe BB7 .... 164 C7
Ennerdale Cl. Formby L37 .... 11 D3
Ennerdale Cl. Forton PR3 .... 204 B3
Ennerdale Cl.
Knott End-on-S FY6 .... 194 F6
Ennerdale Cl. Lancaster LA1 .... 214 B2
Ennerdale Cl. Leyland PR5 .... 59 A7
Ennerdale Dr. Ormskirk L39 .... 15 E2
Ennerdale Dr. Walton-le-D PR5 .... 96 E5
Ennerdale Rd. Blackpool FY4 .... 130 C1
Ennerdale Rd. Burnley BB10 .... 127 E5
Ennerdale Rd. Chorley PR7 .... 42 A6
Ennerdale Rd. Clitheroe BB7 .... 164 C7
Ennerdale Rd. Formby L37 .... 11 E3
Ennerdale Rd. Longridge PR3 .... 138 F5
Ennismore St. BB10 .... 147 C1
Enstone. WN8 .... 18 D1
Enterprise Dr. PR5 .... 76 A4
Enterprise Way.
Nelson BB8 & BB9 .... 168 F3
Enterprise Way. Thornton FY5 .... 173 A6
Enterprise Workshops. PR9 .... 35 A6
Entwisle Rd. BB5 .... 103 B8
Entwistle Hall La. BL7 .... 47 B8
Entwistle St. BB3 .... 81 A1
Entwistle Sta. BL7 .... 47 B8
Ephraim St. PR1 .... 96 C7
Epping Cl. FY2 .... 150 E5
Epping Pl. PR6 .... 42 D8
Epsom Cl. PR6 .... 60 F4
Epsom Croft. PR6 .... 30 B7
Epsom Rd. FY5 .... 150 F8
Epsom Way. BB5 .... 103 D5
Epworth St. BB3 .... 64 B6
Equity St. BB3 .... 64 A8
Erdington Rd. FY1 .... 129 C3
Erith Gr. FY2 .... 150 C5
Ermine Cl. BB2 .... 81 A8
Ernest St. Bacup OL13 .... 70 C8
Ernest St. ⑥ Church BB5 .... 102 E6
Ernest St. Clayton-le-M BB5 .... 123 F1
Ernest St. Cornholme OL14 .... 108 C1
Ernlouen Cl. BB2 .... 80 A8
Erskine Rd. PR6 .... 60 E1
Escar St. BB11 .... 126 F5
Escott Gdns. ⑩ BB10 .... 127 A8
Esher Pond. PR2 .... 116 C6
Eshton Terr. BB7 .... 164 C7
Esk Ave. Edenfield BL0 .... 67 D5
Esk Ave. Fleetwood FY7 .... 193 D2
Eskbank. WN8 .... 9 C8
Eskbrook. WN8 .... 18 C1
Eskdale. WN8 .... 9 B8
Eskdale Ave. Fleetwood FY7 .... 193 D1
Eskdale Ave. Ormskirk L39 .... 15 C2
Eskdale Cl. Blackpool FY4 .... 129 F1
Eskdale Cl. Brierfield BB10 .... 147 C4
Eskdale Cl. Formby L37 .... 11 D2
Eskdale Cl. Fulwood PR2 .... 116 F6
Eskdale Cres. BB2 .... 79 E8
Eskdale Dr. Formby L37 .... 11 D2
Eskdale Dr. Kirkham PR4 .... 113 A7
Eskdale Dr. Maghull L31 .... 5 E2
Eskdale Gdns. BB12 .... 145 C2
Eskdale Gr. FY6 .... 194 F6
Eskdale Pl. LA4 .... 212 G4
Eskdale Rd. Leyland PR5 .... 59 C7
Eskdale Rd. Longridge PR3 .... 138 F6
Eskew La. LA2 .... 233 B8
Eskham Cl. PR4 .... 112 E6
Eskrigge Cl. LA1 .... 213 F4
Eskrigge La. LA2 .... 232 A8
Esp La. BB8 .... 225 F1
Esplanade. Knott End-on-S FY6 .... 194 D6
Esplanade. Preston PR1 .... 96 B5
Esplanade. Southport PR8 .... 33 F7
Esplanade The. Fleetwood FY7 .... 194 A5
Esplanade The. Rishton BB1 .... 102 A8
Essex Ave. Burnley BB12 .... 126 B7
Essex Ave. Heywood OL10 .... 32 E1
Essex Cl. BB2 .... 100 D3
Essex Pl. FY2 .... 150 F2
Essex Rd. Morecambe LA4 .... 213 B4
Essex Rd. ④ Rishton BB1 .... 123 A1
Essex Rd. Southport PR8 .... 21 A5
Essex Rd. Standish WN1 .... 29 B1
Essex St. Accrington BB5 .... 103 D6
Essex St. Barnoldswick BB8 .... 200 B2
Essex St. Colne BB8 .... 169 A4
Essex St. Darwen BB3 .... 81 C1
Essex St. Horwich BL6 .... 31 D1
Essex St. Nelson BB9 .... 168 A5
Essex St. Preston PR1 .... 117 A1
Essington Ave. LA4 .... 212 D4
Est Bank Rd. BL0 .... 49 A3
Esther St. BB1 .... 101 C5
Ethel St. Barnoldswick BB8 .... 200 C2
Ethel St. Whitworth OL12 .... 70 D2
Ethersall Rd. BB9 .... 147 E6
Eton Ave. BB5 .... 103 C2
Eton Cl. BB12 .... 125 E6
Eton Pk. PR2 .... 117 C5

Eton Way. WN5 10 F8
Ettington Dr. PR8 20 A5
Ettrick Ave. FY7 193 D3
Euro Trad Est. BB1 100 F7
Europa Way. LA1 210 C8
Euston Rd. LA4 212 E5
Euston St. PR1 95 E7
Euxton CE Sch. PR7 59 C2
Euxton Hall Ct. PR7 59 C2
Euxton Hall Gdns. PR7 59 C1
Euxton Hall Hospl. PR7 59 C1
Euxton Hall Mews. PR7 59 C2
Euxton La. Chorley PR7 60 B3
Euxton La. Euxton PR7 59 E4
Evans St. Burnley BB11 126 F4
Evans St. Horwich BL6 31 D4
Evans St. Preston PR1 116 D1
Evelyn Rd. BB3 80 E5
Evelyn St. BB10 147 A1
Evenwood. WN8 18 D1
Evenwood Ct. WN8 18 C1
Everard Cl. L40 22 F7
Everard Rd. PR8 34 D4
Everest Cl. FY8 110 A1
Everest Ct. PR4 112 F6
Everest Dr. FY2 150 C5
Everest Rd. FY8 110 A2
Evergreen Ave. PR5 59 A7
Evergreens The. Blackburn BB2 79 F8
Evergreens The. Fulwood PR4 115 E4
Eversholt Cl. BB12 146 D7
Eversleigh Ave. FY5 173 A3
Eversleigh St. PR1 116 E1
Eversley. WN8 18 D1
Everton. BB2 101 A1
Everton Rd. Blackpool FY4 109 C6
Everton Rd. Southport PR8 34 A4
Everton St. BB3 80 F1
Every St. Brierfield BB9 147 B6
Every St. Burnley BB11 126 E5
Every St. Nelson BB9 147 C8
Every St. Nelson BB9 147 D8
Every St. Ramsbottom BL0 49 D6
Evesham Ave. PR1 95 E2
Evesham Cl. 5 Accrington BB5 103 A7
Evesham Cl. Blackpool FY5 150 E7
Evesham Cl. Hutton PR4 94 C1
Evesham Rd. Lytham St Anne's FY8 89 A5
Evesham Rd. Normoss FY3 130 B7
Evington. WN8 18 D1
Ewell Cl. PR6 60 F4
Ewood. BB2 100 D1
Ewood Bridge & Edenfield Sta. BB4 67 D6
Ewood Ct. BB2 100 C2
Ewood La. BB4 67 C7
Ewood Park (Blackburn Rovers FC). BB2 80 D8
Exchange St. Accrington BB5 102 F5
Exchange St. 18 Blackburn BB1 100 E5
Exchange St. Blackpool FY1 129 B6
Exchange St. Colne BB8 169 D4
Exchange St. Darwen BB3 81 A2
Exchange St. Edenfield BL0 67 D3
Exe St. PR1 117 B2
Exeter Ave. LA1 211 B6
Exeter Dr. FY5 173 A2
Exeter Pl. PR2 115 E2
Exeter St. Blackburn BB2 100 D2
Exeter St. Blackpool FY4 129 C1
Exmoor Cl. PR9 53 B6
Exmouth St. BB11 127 A5
Exton St. BB9 147 A5
Extwistle Rd. BB10 128 B7
Extwistle Sq. BB10 127 E5
Extwistle St. Burnley BB10 127 B8
Extwistle St. Nelson BB9 147 D7
Eyes La. Bretherton L40 & PR5 56 E3
Eyes La. Newburgh WN8 26 A3

Factory Brow. Blackrod BL6 30 D3
Factory Brow. Scorton PR3 199 E6
Factory Hill. Horwich BL6 31 D4
Factory Hill. 2 Lancaster LA1 214 A1
Factory La. Adlington PR6 30 B8
Factory La. 15 Padiham BB12 145 C1
Factory La. Penwortham PR1 95 F3
Factory St. BL0 49 C7
Fair Hill. BB4 67 A7
Fair Oak Cl. PR2 117 F3
Fair View. OL13 70 C8
Fair View Cres. OL13 87 B3
Fair View Rd. BB11 127 B5
Fair Way. FY6 174 C7
Fairacres. WN6 28 B1
Fairbairn Ave. BB12 126 C8
Fairbairn St. BL6 31 B3
Fairbank. LA6 238 B2
Fairbank Gr. LA4 212 D3
Fairburn. WN8 18 B3
Fairclough Rd. Accrington BB5 103 A3
Fairclough Rd. Thornton FY5 173 A3
Fairfax Ave. FY2 150 E5
Fairfax Cl. PR3 178 D6
Fairfax Pl. PR5 96 D2
Fairfax Rd. PR2 117 E4
Fairfield. PR3 178 C8
Fairfield Ave. Newchurch BB4 85 F2
Fairfield Ave. Normoss FY3 130 B7
Fairfield Ave. Poulton-le-F FY6 151 D3
Fairfield Cl. Carnforth LA5 217 E1
Fairfield Cl. Clitheroe BB7 164 C7
Fairfield Cl. Lancaster LA1 210 E8
Fairfield Cl. 2 Ormskirk L39 15 E7
Fairfield Ct. FY7 193 F2
Fairfield Dr. Brierfield BB10 147 C3
Fairfield Dr. Bury BL9 32 D3
Fairfield Dr. Clitheroe BB7 164 C7
Fairfield Dr. 1 Ormskirk L39 15 E7
Fairfield Dr. Preston PR2 116 B2
Fairfield General Hospl. BL9 32 E4
Fairfield Gr. LA3 212 A5
Fairfield Prim Sch. BL9 32 D3
Fairfield Rd. Ainsdale PR8 20 C5
Fairfield Rd. Blackpool FY1 129 C8
Fairfield Rd. Fulwood PR2 117 A4
Fairfield Rd. Lancaster LA1 210 E8
Fairfield Rd. Leyland PR5 58 F8
Fairfield Rd. Morecambe LA3 212 B2
Fairfield Rd. Nelson BB9 148 B8
Fairfield Rd. Poulton-le-F FY6 130 F7
Fairfield St. Accrington BB5 102 F4
Fairfield St. Bamber Bridge PR5 76 B7
Fairfields Dr. BB3 80 F6
Fairgarth Dr. LA6 238 B2
Fairham Ave. PR1 95 D2
Fairhaven. WN8 18 C3
Fairhaven Ave. FY7 172 D7
Fairhaven Cl. FY5 173 D1
Fairhaven Golf Course. FY8 89 E6
Fairhaven La. FY8 88 E5
Fairhaven Rd. Blackburn BB2 100 F1
Fairhaven Rd. Leyland PR5 75 D1
Fairhaven Rd. Lytham St Anne's FY8 88 F5
Fairhaven Rd. Penwortham PR1 95 E5
Fairhaven Rd. Southport PR9 53 B4
Fairhaven Way. LA4 212 G5
Fairheath Rd. LA2 233 B4
Fairhill Terr. BB4 67 A7
Fairholme Rd. BB11 127 B3
Fairholmes Cl. FY5 173 B3
Fairholmes Way. FY5 173 B3
Fairhope Ave. Lancaster LA1 213 E3
Fairhope Ave. Morecambe LA4 213 B6
Fairhope Ct. BB2 100 C6
Fairhurst Ave. WN6 28 D3
Fairhurst Ct. FY5 172 D3
Fairhurst St. FY1 129 C6
Fairhurst's Dr. WN8 26 B2
Fairlawn Rd. FY8 89 F3
Fairlea Ave. LA4 213 B6
Fairlie. WN8 18 C3
Fairlie Cty Prim Sch. WN8 18 C3
Fairmont Dr. FY6 174 D2
Fairsnape Ave. PR3 139 B7
Fairsnape Dr. PR3 178 B6
Fairsnape Rd. FY8 90 D4
Fairstead. WN8 18 C3
Fairthorn Wlk. 9 L33 1 A3
Fairview. Kirkby Lonsdale LA6 238 B3
Fairview. Rawtenstall BB4 84 F5
Fairview Ave. FY8 89 A7
Fairview Cl. PR4 73 F5
Fairway. Chorley PR7 60 C2
Fairway. Fleetwood FY7 193 C1
Fairway. Penwortham PR1 95 B6
Fairway. Poulton-le-F FY6 151 A2
Fairway. Southport PR9 52 C2
Fairway. Wallbank OL12 51 C7
Fairway Gdns. FY6 194 D5
Fairway Rd. FY4 109 E8
Fairways. Fulwood PR2 117 A6
Fairways. Horwich BL6 31 C3
Fairways. Lytham St Anne's FY8 89 A6
Fairways Ave. PR3 136 C3
Fairways Ct. Formby L37 11 C5
Fairways Ct. Wilpshire BB1 121 F5
Fairways Dr. BB11 126 E2
Fairways The. WN8 18 D3
Fairweather Ct. BB12 145 D1
Fairwinds Ave. PR4 72 D4
Falcon Ave. BB3 80 E3
Falcon Cl. Blackburn BB1 100 D8
Falcon Cl. Bury BL9 32 B4
Falcon Ct. BB5 123 F2
Falcon Dr. FY6 151 B2
Falcon St. PR1 117 B2
Falinge Fold. OL12 51 D1
Falinge Park High Sch. OL12 51 D1
Falinge Rd. OL12 51 E1
Falkirk Ave. FY2 150 C6
Falkland. WN8 18 C3
Falkland Ave. FY4 129 F2
Falkland Rd. PR8 34 D5
Falkland St. PR1 95 F7
Fall Barn Rd. BB4 85 B2
Fall Birch Hospl. BL6 31 F1
Fall Kirk. LA2 234 F1
Fallbarn Cres. BB4 85 A1
Fallbarn Rd. BB4 85 B2
Fallowfield Cl. PR4 112 E6
Fallowfield Dr. Burnley BB12 126 D8
Fallowfield Dr. Falinge Fold OL12 51 D2
Fallowfield Rd. FY8 89 C6
Falmouth Ave. Fleetwood FY7 172 C8
Falmouth Ave. Haslingden BB4 84 C2
Falmouth Rd. FY1 129 C2
Falshaw Dr. BL9 49 E1
Falstone Ave. BL0 49 C4
Falstone Rd. L33 1 A4
Far Croft. PR5 96 A1
Far East View. 8 BB8 200 B2
Far Field. PR1 95 D3
Far Moor La. LA1 211 C8
Far Nook. PR6 60 B7
Faraday Ave. BB7 164 D8
Faraday Dr. PR2 117 C7
Faraday St. BB12 126 D7
Farholme La. OL13 69 D8
Faringdon Ave. FY4 109 E5
Farington Ave. PR5 58 D7
Farington Cty Prim Sch. PR5 76 B3
Farington Rd. PR5 76 A6
Farington St Paul's CE Prim Sch. PR5 75 F7
Farleton Cl. LA5 217 C5
Farleton Ct. LA1 213 F4
Farleton Old Rd. LA2 232 A5
Farley La. WN8 19 A3
Farm Ave. Adlington PR6 30 A8
Farm Ave. Bacup OL13 86 F4
Farm Cl. Southport PR9 35 A8
Farm Cl. Thornton FY5 173 B2
Farm House Cl. BB1 101 C4
Farm Meadow Rd. WN5 10 E5
Farmdale Dr. L31 5 E1
Farmdale Rd. LA1 211 B5
Farmend Cl. PR4 74 B8
Farmer's Row. BB2 80 B7
Farnborough Rd. PR8 20 F8
Farnborough Road Inf & Jun Sch. PR8 21 A8
Farnell Pl. FY4 109 D6
Farnham Way. FY6 151 C5
Farnlea Dr. LA4 213 A5
Farnworth Rd. FY5 173 D1
Farrer St. BB9 147 C7
Farrier Rd. L33 1 A2
Farringdon Cl. PR1 117 F1
Farringdon Cres. PR1 117 F1
Farringdon La. PR2 117 F3
Farringdon Pl. PR1 117 F1
Farrington Cl. BB11 126 C3
Farrington Ct. BB11 126 C3
Farrington Dr. L39 15 E6
Farrington Pl. BB11 126 C3
Farrington Rd. BB11 126 B3
Farrington St. PR7 42 C8
Farthings The. PR7 59 F1
Faulkner Cl. PR8 20 C6
Faulkner Gdns. PR8 20 C6
Faulkner's La. PR3 204 B1
Faverdale Rd. BB8 170 A5
Fawcett. WN8 18 B3
Fawcett Cl. BB2 100 D3
Fawcett Rd. L31 5 D3
Fayles Gr. FY4 130 A1
Fazackerley St. PR1 116 C1
Fazakerley St. 10 PR6 & PR7 42 C8
Fearnhead Ave. BL6 31 B5
Fearns Cty High Sch. OL13 86 A1
Fearns Moss. BB4 & OL13 86 A1
Fecit La. BL0 & OL12 50 C8
Fecitt Brow. BB1 101 D4
Fecitt Rd. BB2 100 B6
Federation St. BB8 200 A3
Feilden Pl. BB2 79 D8
Feilden St. BB2 100 D5
Felgate Brow. FY3 129 E5
Felix St. BB11 127 B7
Fell Brow. PR3 139 B7
Fell Cl. 2 PR5 76 F8
Fell Rd. High Casterton LA6 238 F3
Fell Rd. Morecambe LA4 213 B4
Fell Rd. Waddington BB7 186 A6
Fell View. Brierfield BB10 147 D3
Fell View. Caton LA2 231 C3
Fell View. Chorley PR7 42 E6
Fell View. Garstang PR3 178 C8
Fell View. Grimsargh PR2 138 C2
Fell View. West Bradford BB7 186 D7
Fell View Cl. PR3 178 C8
Fell Way. FY6 174 D7
Fellborough Lodge. FY8 89 A8
Fellery St. PR6 42 D8
Fellgate. LA3 213 A2
Fellside Cl. BL8 48 F1
Fellside View. LA3 208 F7
Fellstone Vale. PR6 79 A1
Fellstone View. PR6 79 A1
Fellview. PR9 53 D6
Fellway Cl. 4 PR5 76 C8
Felstead. WN8 18 B2
Felstead St. PR1 96 D8
Felton Way. PR4 73 F3
Feltons. WN8 18 B2
Fenber Ave. FY4 109 C7
Fengrove. PR4 74 A8
Feniscliffe Dr. BB2 100 A2
Feniscowles Prim Sch. BB2 79 D8
Fenney Ct. WN8 18 C1
Fennyfold Terr. BB12 125 C6
Fensway. PR4 94 D2
Fenton Ave. BB8 200 D3
Fenton Rd. Blackpool FY1 129 C6
Fenton Rd. Fulwood PR2 117 C4
Fenton St. LA1 210 E8
Fenwick St. BB11 126 D3
Ferguson Rd. FY1 129 E2
Ferguson St. BB2 80 D7
Fermor Rd. Becconsall PR4 72 E1
Fermor Rd. Preston PR1 117 E1
Fern Ave. BB5 102 F3
Fern Bank. Chorley PR6 60 D3
Fern Bank. Lancaster LA1 211 A5
Fern Bank. Maghull L31 5 E1
Fern Bank Ave. BB8 200 A3
Fern Breck Cotts. FY6 195 A2
Fern Cl. Bamber Bridge PR5 76 B8
Fern Cl. Skelmersdale WN8 17 E1
Fern Croft. LA6 238 E4
Fern Ct. FY7 193 C1
Fern Dene. OL12 51 B2
Fern Gore Ave. BB5 103 A3
Fern Gr. FY1 129 C3
Fern Hill La. OL12 51 A3
Fern Isle Cl. OL12 51 B6
Fern Lea St. BB4 68 D8
Fern Meadow. PR6 77 C2
Fern Rd. BB11 126 E4
Fern St. Bacup OL13 86 F3
Fern St. Colne BB8 169 F6
Fern St. Newchurch BB4 85 F1
Fern St. Ramsbottom BL0 49 D7
Fern Terr. BB4 84 A3
Fernbank Ct. BB9 147 E7
Ferncliffe Dr. LA3 212 A2
Ferndale. Blackburn BB1 101 A6
Ferndale. Skelmersdale WN8 18 C2
Ferndale Ave. FY4 109 D7
Ferndale Cl. Freckleton PR4 92 D7
Ferndale Cl. Leyland PR5 59 B7
Ferndale Cl. Thornton FY5 173 C2
Ferndale St. BB10 127 C8
Ferngrove. BL9 32 B5
Fernhill Ave. OL13 69 E8
Fernhill Cl. OL13 69 E8
Fernhill Cres. OL13 86 E1
Fernhill Dr. OL13 69 E8
Fernhill Gr. 1 OL13 69 E8
Fernhill Pk. OL13 69 E8
Fernhill Way. 3 OL13 69 E8
Fernhills. BL7 46 E2
Fernhurst Ave. FY4 129 D1
Fernhurst Gate. L39 15 B1
Fernhurst St. BB2 80 D8
Fernlea Ave. Barnoldswick BB8 200 B2
Fernlea Ave. Oswaldtwistle BB5 103 A3
Fernlea Cl. Blackburn BB2 80 B8
Fernlea Cl. Caldershaw OL12 51 B2
Fernlea Dr. BB5 123 F4
Fernleigh. PR5 58 A8
Fernleigh Cl. FY2 150 D4
Fernley Rd. PR8 34 A5
Ferns The. Bacup OL13 87 A1
Ferns The. Bamber Bridge PR5 96 C3
Ferns The. Preston PR1 116 C2
Fernside Way. OL12 51 A1
Fernview Dr. BL0 49 B1
Fernville Terr. 6 OL13 69 D8
Fernwood Ave. FY5 151 B8
Fernwood Cl. FY8 89 E4
Ferny Knoll Rd. WA11 8 F4
Fernyhalgh Ct. PR2 117 D6
Fernyhalgh Gdns. PR2 117 D6
Fernyhalgh La. PR2 117 D7
Fernyhalgh Pl. PR2 117 D6
Ferrier Bank. PR4 91 D5
Ferrier Cl. 1 BB1 101 C5
Ferry Side La. PR9 53 C5
Ffrances Pas. 30 LA1 210 F8
Fiddler's La. Chipping PR3 181 F4
Fiddler's La. Clayton Green PR6 77 B2
Fidler La. PR5 75 F5
Field Rd. LA3 208 D6
Field St. Blackburn BB2 100 B2
Field St. Blackpool FY1 129 C2
Field St. Padiham BB12 125 C7
Field St. Skelmersdale WN8 17 D2
Field Top. OL13 87 A7
Fielden St. Burnley BB11 126 D5
Fielden St. Chorley PR6 42 E8
Fielden St. Leyland PR5 75 D1
Fieldfare Cl. FY5 173 A5
Fieldhouse Ave. FY5 173 D2
Fieldhouse Ind Est. OL12 51 F2
Fieldhouse Rd. OL12 51 F2
Fielding Cres. BB2 100 A1
Fielding La. Great Harwood BB6 123 B5
Fielding La. Oswaldtwistle BB5 102 E3
Fielding Pl. PR6 30 B8
Fielding Rd. FY1 129 D8
Fielding St. BB1 123 C1
Fields End. BB6 122 C8
Fields Rd. BB4 84 C1
Fields The. PR7 40 B7
Fieldsend. LA3 209 A7
Fieldside Ave. PR7 59 C1
Fieldside Cl. PR5 96 C3
Fieldway. FY8 109 E2
Fife Cl. PR7 42 E6
Fife St. Accrington BB5 103 A4
Fife St. Barrowford BB9 168 C1
Fifth Ave. Blackpool FY4 109 C7
Fifth Ave. Burnley BB10 147 B3
Fifth Ave. Bury BL9 32 D4
Filberts Cl. PR2 116 C3
Filberts The. PR2 116 C3
File St. PR7 42 C7
Filey Pl. Blackpool FY1 129 B6
Filey Pl. Fulwood PR2 116 A4
Filey Rd. FY8 110 A1
Filton Gr. LA3 213 A3
Finch Cl. BB1 100 E6
Finch La. WN6 27 B1
Finch Mill Ave. WN6 19 D7
Finch St. 5 BB3 80 F2
Finches The. FY6 151 B2
Finchley Rd. FY1 129 B8
Fine Jane's Way. PR9 35 B8
Finnington La. BB2 79 A6
Finsbury Ave. Blackpool FY1 129 D2
Finsbury Ave. Lytham St Anne's FY8 89 B4
Finsbury Pl. BB2 80 D8
Finsley Gate. BB11 127 A5
Finsley St. BB10 147 E3
Fir Cl. FY7 193 C2
Fir Cotes. L31 5 E1
Fir Ct. BB5 103 E8
Fir Gr. Blackpool FY1 129 E2
Fir Gr. Warton PR4 91 D6
Fir Grove Rd. BB11 127 B4
Fir St. Blackburn BB1 100 F7
Fir St. Burnley BB10 127 B5
Fir St. Bury BL9 32 A2
Fir St. Haslingden BB4 84 B3
Fir St. Nelson BB9 147 F8
Fir St. Ramsbottom BL0 49 D7
Fir St. Southport PR8 34 F6
Fir Tree Ave. PR2 116 B4
Fir Tree Cl. Hest Bank LA5 215 F2
Fir Tree Cl. Much Hoole PR4 73 E3
Fir Tree Cl. Skelmersdale WN8 9 D7
Fir Tree La. L39 14 F3
Fir Tree Pl. FY5 150 F8
Fir Tree Way. 3 BL6 31 E1
Fir Trees Ave. Bamber Bridge PR5 76 A8
Fir Trees Ave. Fulwood PR2 118 A4
Fir Trees Cres. 1 PR5 76 A8
Fir Trees Gr. BB12 145 E5
Fir Trees La. BB12 145 E5
Fir Trees Pl. PR2 117 F4
Fir Trees Rd. PR5 96 A1
Firbank. PR7 59 C2
Firbank Ave. PR4 56 A7
Firbank Rd. LA1 214 A1
Firbeck. WN8 18 C1
Fircroft. WN6 28 A2
Firfield Cl. PR4 112 E5
Firs Cl. L37 11 D5
Firs Cres. L37 11 D5
Firs La. L39 14 E3
Firs Link. L37 11 D4
Firshill Cl. FY5 151 B8
First Ave. Blackpool FY4 109 C7
First Ave. Church BB5 103 A8
First Ave. Clifton PR4 114 C1
First Ave. Poulton-le-F FY6 151 E3
First Ave. Preston PR2 116 A2
First Ave. Wrea Green PR4 112 B4
First Terr. LA3 205 B5
Firswood Cl. FY8 89 E4
Firswood Rd. L40 & WN8 17 C3
Firtree Cl. Blackburn BB2 79 F8
Firtree Cl. Chorley PR7 42 C3
Firwood. WN8 18 D3
Firwood La. PR5 98 B5
Fish House La. PR3 182 B5
Fish La. L40 37 B2
Fish Rake La. BL0 67 E6
Fisher Dr. Orrell WN5 10 E7
Fisher Dr. Southport PR9 34 F7
Fisher St. FY1 129 C6
Fisher's La. FY4 110 A5
Fishergate. PR0 & PR1 95 F7
Fishergate Ctr. PR1 95 F7
Fishergate Hill. PR1 95 E6
Fishergate Wlk. 7 PR4 95 F7
Fishermans Cl. L37 11 E6
Fishmoor Dr. BB2 & BB3 80 F8
Fishwick Cty Prim Sch. PR1 117 E1
Fishwick Hall Golf Course. PR1 96 F8
Fishwick La. PR6 78 B1
Fishwick Par. PR1 96 D8
Fishwick Rd. PR1 96 C8
Fishwick View. PR1 96 D8
Fitchfield. PR1 95 F2
Fitzgerald St. PR1 117 C1
Fitzroy Rd. FY2 150 D3
Fitzroy St. PR1 95 E7
Five Acres. PR5 75 E4
Five Lane Ends. Hampson Green LA2 204 D8
Five Lane Ends. Preesall FY6 195 A2
Five Lane Ends. Singleton FY6 152 D4
Flag La. Bamber Bridge PR5 95 F1
Flag La. Bretherton PR5 57 A5
Flag La. Limbrick PR7 42 F5
Flag La. Runshaw Moor PR5 & PR7 58 D4
Flag St. OL13 69 E8
Flakefleet Ave. FY7 193 E1
Flakefleet Cty Sch. FY7 193 E2
Flamstead. WN8 18 C1
Flare Rd. LA3 208 D6
Flash La. L40 38 B4
Flat La. LA5 219 E3
Flatfield Way. L31 5 E1
Flatman's La. L39 13 E1
Flats Ret Pk The. PR1 & PR5 96 C5
Flats The. PR4 113 B4
Flax Cl. BB4 67 A8
Flax La. L40 24 F2
Flax Moss Cl. BB4 67 A8
Flax St. 8 BL0 49 A4
Flaxfield Rd. L37 12 A3
Flaxfield Way. PR4 113 A5
Flaxton. WN8 18 C1
Fleet La. LA2 232 A8
Fleet St. Blackpool FY1 129 C4
Fleet St. Chorley PR7 42 C7
Fleet St. Horwich BL6 31 D3
Fleet St. Longridge PR3 139 A7
Fleet St. Lytham St Anne's FY8 88 D8
Fleet St. Nelson BB9 168 E1
Fleet St. 3 Preston PR1 95 F7
Fleet Street La. PR3 140 A6
Fleet Wlk. 5 BB11 127 A6
Fleetgreen. LA1 213 E3
Fleetwood Cl. Blackburn BB2 100 F1
Fleetwood Cl. Southport PR9 52 F3
Fleetwood Cres. PR9 54 A6
Fleetwood Dr. PR9 54 A6
Fleetwood High Sch. FY7 193 D2
Fleetwood High Sch Beach Rd Site. FY7 193 E3
Fleetwood Hospl. FY7 194 B5
Fleetwood Old Rd. PR4 132 E3
Fleetwood Rd. Blackpool FY5 150 D7
Fleetwood Rd. Burnley BB10 147 C2
Fleetwood Rd. Carleton FY6 151 B5
Fleetwood Rd. Esprick PR4 132 D5
Fleetwood Rd. Fleetwood FY7 193 E1

Fleetwood Rd. Kirkham PR4 ..... 112 F7
Fleetwood Rd. Padiham BB12 .. 125 D8
Fleetwood Rd. Southport PR9 ..... 52 E3
Fleetwood Rd. Thornton FY7 ..... 173 A6
Fleetwood Rd N. FY5 .... 173 E3
Fleetwood Rd S. FY5 .... 151 B7
Fleetwood St. 6 Leyland PR5 ... 76 B2
Fleetwood St. Preston PR1 ...... 116 D1
Fleetwood's Charity Prim Sch. FY6 .... 195 B3
Fleming Sq. BB2 .... 100 E4
Flemming Sq. PR3 .... 139 B7
Flensburg Way. Farington PR5 ... 75 E6
Flensburg Way. Leyland PR5 ...... 75 D4
Fletcher Ave. PR4 .... 56 A6
Fletcher Rd. Preston PR0 & PR1 117 C1
Fletcher Rd. Rishton BB1 .... 102 A8
Fletcher St. Blackburn BB2 .... 100 D3
Fletcher St. Bury BL9 .... 32 A2
Fletcher St. Nelson BB9 .... 147 F7
Fletcher's Dr. L40 .... 24 E4
Flett St. PR1 .... 116 C1
Flimby. WN8 .... 18 D1
Flimby Cl. BB2 .... 80 F8
Flintron Brow. LA2 .... 227 A2
Flip Rd. BB4 .... 84 A2
Flockton Ct. 7 BL6 .... 31 B4
Flordon. WN8 .... 18 D2
Florence Ave. Burnley BB11 ...... 126 C4
Florence Ave. Warton PR4 .... 91 D5
Florence Pl. BB1 .... 101 A6
Florence St. Blackburn BB1 ...... 101 A6
Florence St. Blackpool FY4 .... 110 A6
Florence St. Burnley BB11 .... 126 C5
Florence St. 1 Church BB5 .... 102 E6
Flower Fields. PR3 .... 178 D2
Flower Scar Rd. OL14 .... 87 E6
Flowerfield. PR4 .... 115 E6
Floyd Rd. PR2 .... 117 E3
Floyer St. PR1 .... 96 B7
Fluke Hall La. PR3 .... 196 B8
Flush Brow. LA6 .... 238 F5
Fold. BB9 .... 168 E5
Fold Gdns. OL12 .... 51 B4
Fold House Caravan Pk. PR3 196 D4
Fold View. BL7 .... 46 E1
Folds. BL6 .... 30 C3
Folds St. BB12 .... 126 F8
Foldside. PR4 .... 92 C7
Folkestone Cl. FY5 .... 172 F4
Folkestone Rd. Lytham St Anne's FY8 .... 88 F8
Folkestone Rd. Southport PR8 .... 34 F3
Folly La. Barnoldswick BB8 .... 190 F7
Folly La. Lancaster LA1 & LA2 .... 213 D4
Folly Terr. BB4 .... 85 B8
Folly Wlk. 20 OL12 .... 51 F1
Fontwell Cl. WN6 .... 28 F1
Fooden La. BB7 .... 224 E4
Foot Mill Cres. OL12 .... 51 D2
Foot Wood Cres. OL12 .... 51 D2
Footeran La. LA5 .... 219 E3
Forbes Ct. BB11 .... 126 A3
Ford La. Goosnargh PR3 .... 158 F2
Ford La. Silverdale LA5 .... 218 E5
Ford St. Barrowford BB9 .... 168 E4
Ford St. Burnley BB10 .... 147 B1
Ford St. Lancaster LA1 .... 213 D1
Fordham Cl. PR8 .... 34 E3
Fordside Ave. BB5 .... 123 E4
Fordstone Ave. FY6 .... 195 A4
Fordway Ave. FY3 .... 129 F6
Fore St. BB3 .... 80 F7
Foregate. PR2 .... 116 E4
Foreside. BB9 .... 168 E5
Forest Bank. BB4 .... 85 A7
Forest Bank Rd. BB4 .... 85 A7
Forest Becks Brow. BB7 .... 224 D6
Forest Cl. PR5 .... 96 C3
Forest Dr. Lytham St Anne's FY8 .. 89 F4
Forest Dr. Shevington Moor WN6 28 A2
Forest Dr. Skelmersdale WN8 ...... 18 C3
Forest Gate. Blackpool FY3 .... 129 E5
Forest Gate. Morecambe LA3 ..... 213 A2
Forest Gr. PR3 .... 136 B8
Forest Holme Cl. BB4 .... 86 A7
Forest La. BB9 .... 168 B2
Forest Pk. LA1 .... 210 C7
Forest Rd. PR8 .... 34 D6
Forest St. Burnley BB11 .... 127 B6
Forest St. Forest Holme BB4 .... 86 A7
Forest St. Nelson BB9 .... 168 D1
Forest View. Brierfield BB9 .... 147 A5
Forest View. Falinge Fold OL12 ... 51 D2
Forest Way. PR2 .... 116 F6
Forester's Bldgs. 7 BB8 .... 200 B2
Foresters Hall. 13 PR4 .... 95 F8
Forestry Houses. BB7 .... 222 C5
Forestway. PR5 .... 58 F8
Forfar Gr. BB11 .... 126 D3
Forfar St. BB11 .... 126 D3
Forge Cl. L40 .... 16 E4
Forge La. PR3 .... 178 E8
Forge St. 3 OL13 .... 86 F2
Forgewood Cl. LA2 .... 231 A3
Forgewood Dr. LA2 .... 214 F6
Formby Ave. FY7 .... 172 D7
Formby Bridge. L37 .... 11 E2
Formby Bsns Pk. L37 .... 12 B3
Formby By-Pass. L37 .... 12 B5
Formby Cl. BB2 .... 80 F8
Formby Cres. PR4 .... 73 F8
Formby Fields. L37 .... 12 A2
Formby Gdns. L37 .... 11 F4
Formby High Sch. L37 .... 11 E4
Formby La. Formby L37 .... 12 B2
Formby La. Ormskirk L39 .... 14 E2
Formby Pl. PR2 .... 115 E2
Formby Point Caravan Pk. L37 11 B1
Formby Rd. FY8 .... 109 F1
Formby St. L37 .... 11 E2
Formby Sta. L37 .... 11 E2
Forrest Ct. FY3 .... 129 E8
Forrest St. BB1 .... 101 A5
Forrester Cl. PR5 .... 75 E1
Forrester Dr. BB12 .... 146 D8
Forshaw Ave. Blackpool FY3 ...... 129 F8
Forshaw Ave. Lytham St Anne's FY8 .... 88 D8
Forshaw Cl. 6 FY7 .... 193 F2
Forshaw Rd. PR1 .... 95 D2
Fort Ave. PR3 .... 140 D3
Fort St. Accrington BB5 .... 103 B6
Fort St. Blackburn BB1 .... 101 A5
Fort St. 11 Clayton-le-M BB5 ...... 123 F3
Fort St. Clitheroe BB7 .... 164 D7
Fort St. Read BB12 .... 144 D2
Forton Primary Sch. PR3 .... 204 B3
Forton Rd. PR2 .... 115 E1
Forty Acre La. PR3 .... 161 B5
Foscote Rd. L33 .... 1 A4
Fossdale Moss. PR5 .... 75 C1
Fosse Cl. BB1 & BB2 .... 81 A8
Foster Croft. PR1 .... 95 C6
Foster Ct. Bury BL9 .... 32 D4
Foster Ct. Chorley PR6 .... 60 E1
Foster Rd. Barnoldswick BB8 ..... 200 A3
Foster Rd. Formby L37 .... 11 D2
Foster St. Accrington BB5 .... 103 C7
Foster St. Chorley PR6 .... 60 E1
Fosterfield Pl. PR6 .... 60 E1
Fosters Cl. PR9 .... 35 B8
Fosters Green Rd. WN8 .... 18 D3
Fothergill St. 1 BB8 .... 169 C5
Foul La. PR8 & PR9 .... 35 A5
Fouldrey Ave. FY6 .... 151 F5
Foulds Rd. BB8 .... 170 B3
Foulds Terr. BB8 .... 170 C2
Foulridge Wharf. BB8 .... 191 D2
Foundry La. Halton LA2 .... 214 C7
Foundry La. Halton LA2 .... 214 D6
Foundry St. 1 Bacup OL13 .... 86 F2
Foundry St. Blackburn BB2 .... 100 D4
Foundry St. Burnley BB11 .... 126 F6
Foundry St. Chorley PR7 .... 42 C8
Foundry St. 22 Darwen BB3 .... 81 A1
Foundry St. Rawtenstall BB4 .... 84 F1
Fountain Sq. 3 BB9 .... 168 D3
Fountain St. Accrington BB5 ...... 103 A5
Fountain St. Barnoldswick BB8 . 200 C2
Fountain St. Bury BL9 .... 32 A2
Fountain St. Colne BB8 .... 169 D4
Fountain St. Darwen BB3 .... 64 A8
Fountain St. Nelson BB9 .... 168 E1
Fountain St N. 12 BL9 .... 32 A3
Fountains Ave. Blackburn BB1 ... 101 B8
Fountains Ave. Read BB12 .... 144 D1
Fountains Cl. PR7 .... 42 D5
Fountains The. L39 .... 15 E6
Fountains Way. Formby L37 .... 12 B2
Fountains Way. Oswaldtwistle BB5 .... 102 B5
Four Acre La. PR3 .... 160 E5
Four Lane Ends. Barley BB7 ..... 189 B2
Four Lane Ends. Burton in L LA6 .... 236 C1
Four Lane Ends. Carleton FY6 .. 151 B5
Four Lane Ends. Charnock Richard PR7 .... 41 C4
Four Lane Ends. Clitheroe BB7 . 165 A6
Four Lane Ends. Dolphinholme LA2 .... 220 A8
Four Lane Ends. Gregson Lane PR5 .... 97 D2
Four Lane Ends. Halsall L39 .... 22 D3
Four Lane Ends. Halton LA2 ..... 214 B7
Four Lane Ends. Knowley PR6 .... 61 C4
Four Lane Ends. Morecambe LA3 .... 212 A1
Four Lane Ends. Sabden BB12 . 144 F4
Four Lane Ends. Wray LA2 .... 232 E4
Four Lanes End Rd. OL13 .... 69 B8
Four Oaks Rd. Walton Summit PR5 .... 77 A6
Four Oaks Rd. Walton Summit PR5 .... 77 B7
Fouracre. BB2 .... 120 E2
Fourfields. PR5 .... 96 E2
Fourth Ave. Blackpool FY4 .... 109 C7
Fourth Ave. Bury BL9 .... 32 D4
Fowler Ave. PR5 .... 76 B6
Fowler Cl. PR5 .... 98 C2
Fowler Height Cl. BB2 .... 80 B7
Fowler Hill La. PR3 .... 199 B5
Fowler Ind Pk. BL6 .... 31 C2
Fowler La. Farington PR5 .... 75 F6
Fowler La. Leyland PR5 .... 76 B5
Fowler St. PR2 .... 116 D3
Fox Gr. LA3 .... 212 B3
Fox Ind Est. 2 FY2 .... 150 E1
Fox La. Coupe Green PR5 .... 97 E3
Fox La. Leyland PR5 .... 58 E7
Fox Lane Ends. PR4 .... 112 A5
Fox St. Accrington BB5 .... 103 B6
Fox St. Burnley BB12 .... 125 F6
Fox St. Clitheroe BB7 .... 186 E1
Fox St. Horwich BL6 .... 31 C2
Fox St. Preston PR1 .... 95 F7
Foxcote. PR7 .... 60 C2
Foxcroft. BB12 .... 126 D8
Foxdale Ave. FY3 .... 129 D7
Foxdale Cl. Bacup OL13 .... 87 A1
Foxdale Cl. Edgworth BL7 .... 47 E7
Foxdale Cl. Southport PR8 .... 34 E3
Foxdale Gr. PR1 & PR2 .... 117 D3
Foxdale Pl. LA1 .... 213 E2
Foxen Dole La. BB12 .... 146 A5
Foxes Terr. PR3 .... 155 C7
Foxfield Ave. LA4 .... 212 F3
Foxfold. WN8 .... 18 D3
Foxglove Cl. WN6 .... 28 D2
Foxglove Ct. OL12 .... 51 D3
Foxglove Dr. Bury BL9 .... 32 D3
Foxglove Dr. Lucas Green PR6 & PR7 .... 60 C5
Foxglove Way. PR4 .... 92 D7
Foxhall Rd. FY1 .... 129 B3
Foxhall Sq. FY1 .... 129 B3
Foxhill Bank Brow. BB5 .... 102 E5
Foxhill Cl. L37 .... 11 C3
Foxhill Dr. BB4 .... 85 F4
Foxhole Rd. Chorley PR7 .... 41 F8
Foxhole Rd. Chorley PR7 .... 59 F1
Foxholes Rd. Horwich BL6 .... 31 D4
Foxholes Rd. Morecambe LA4 .. 212 G6
Foxhouse La. L31 .... 5 F1
Foxhouse St. BB2 .... 100 C5
Foxleigh. PR5 .... 58 D7
Foxstones Cres. BB2 .... 80 A8
Foxstones La. BB10 .... 128 B2
Foxwell Cl. BB4 .... 84 C2
Foxwood Chase. BB5 .... 103 E8
Foxwood Dr. PR4 .... 112 E5
Foxwood The. PR7 .... 41 C1
Frailey Cl. PR8 .... 20 C4
France St. Blackburn BB2 .... 100 D4
France St. Church BB5 .... 102 E6
Frances St. 3 BB3 .... 80 F2
Francis Ave. BB9 .... 168 F5
Francis St. Blackburn BB2 .... 100 B1
Francis St. Blackpool FY1 .... 129 B6
Francis St. Burnley BB10 .... 147 A1
Francis St. 3 Clayton-le-M BB5 123 F3
Francis St. Colne BB8 .... 169 B3
Francis St. Preston PR1 .... 116 C1
Frank St. Barnoldswick BB8 .... 200 B2
Frank St. Enfield BB5 .... 124 A1
Frank St. Preston PR1 .... 116 F1
Frankland Science Schs (Royal Gram Sch Annexe). LA1 .... 211 B7
Franklands. PR4 .... 94 A1
Franklands Dr. PR2 .... 118 A5
Franklands Fold. PR4 .... 74 A8
Franklin Rd. BB2 .... 100 B3
Franklin St. Burnley BB12 .... 126 C6
Franklin St. Clitheroe BB7 .... 164 D7
Franklin St. 26 Darwen BB3 .... 81 A1
Franklin St. Lancaster LA1 .... 210 F5
Fraser Ave. PR1 .... 95 E5
Fraser St. Accrington BB5 .... 103 A4
Fraser St. Burnley BB10 .... 147 B1
Frazer Gr. FY4 .... 129 B1
Freckleton CE Prim Sch. PR4 .. 92 C7
Freckleton Rd. Kirkham PR4 ...... 113 B3
Freckleton Rd. Southport PR9 ..... 52 F4
Freckleton St. Blackburn BB2 .... 100 E4
Freckleton St. Blackpool FY1 .... 129 C3
Freckleton St. Kirkham PR4 .... 113 B4
Freckleton St. Lytham St Anne's FY8 .... 90 C3
Frederick Row. BB1 .... 101 B5
Frederick St. Accrington BB5 .... 103 A6
Frederick St. 6 Blackburn BB2 100 E3
Frederick St. Blackpool FY4 .... 109 D8
Frederick St. Chorley PR7 .... 42 E7
Frederick St. Darwen BB3 .... 81 A2
Frederick St. Oswaldtwistle BB5 102 E4
Frederick St. 12 Ramsbottom BL0 .... 49 B5
Fredora Ave. FY3 .... 130 A2
Free La. BB4 .... 67 A6
Free Trade St. 7 BB11 .... 126 F6
Freeholds La. Waddington BB7 . 185 F6
Freeholds La. Waddington BB7 . 185 F7
Freeholds Rd. OL12 .... 70 E6
Freeholds Terr. OL12 .... 70 E6
Freeman's La. PR7 .... 41 E3
Freemantle Ave. FY4 .... 109 B4
French Cl. BB2 .... 100 B4
French Rd. BB2 .... 100 B4
Frenchwood Ave. Lytham St Anne's FY8 .... 89 F3
Frenchwood Ave. Preston PR1 .. 96 B6
Frenchwood Cty Prim Sch. PR1 96 B6
Frenchwood Knoll. PR1 .... 96 B6
Frenchwood St. PR1 .... 96 A6
Freshfield Ave. BB5 .... 123 E3
Freshfield Caravan Pk. L37 .... 11 B6
Freshfield Ct. L37 .... 11 E4
Freshfield Prim Sch. L37 .... 12 A4
Freshfield Rd. L37 .... 11 E4
Freshfield Sta. L37 .... 11 E5
Freshfields. PR4 .... 115 D3
Friar St. 23 LA1 .... 210 F8
Friar's Moss Rd. LA2 .... 226 A8
Friar's Pas. 22 LA1 .... 210 F8
Friargate. Preston PR1 .... 95 F7
Friargate. Preston PR1 .... 95 F8
Friargate Wlk. 6 PR4 .... 95 F7
Friars The. PR2 .... 116 E4
Friars Wlk. L37 .... 12 B2
Friary Cl. PR4 .... 113 C4
Friday St. PR6 .... 42 D8
Frieldhurst Rd. OL14 .... 108 C1
Frinton Gr. FY2 .... 150 E6
Friths Ave. PR5 .... 97 E1
Frobisher Dr. FY8 .... 109 D1
Frog La. L40 .... 25 D3
Frome St. PR1 .... 117 D1
Froom St. PR6 .... 42 F8
Fry St. BB9 .... 147 F8
Fryent Cl. BL6 .... 30 D2
Fryer Cl. PR1 .... 95 D2
Fulford Ave. PR2 .... 115 C1
Fulham St. BB9 .... 168 F2
Full View. BB2 .... 80 B8
Fullers Terr. OL13 .... 86 F1
Fulmars The. FY6 .... 151 B2
Fulshaw Rd. PR2 .... 116 B2
Fulwood Ave. Becconsall PR4 ..... 72 F1
Fulwood Ave. Blackpool FY3 ..... 129 F8
Fulwood Ave. Southport PR8 ...... 34 D4
Fulwood & Cadley Prim Sch. PR2 .... 116 D4
Fulwood Dr. LA2 & LA4 .... 213 B6
Fulwood Hall Hospl. PR2 .... 117 C5
Fulwood Hall La. PR2 .... 117 B4
Fulwood High Sch. PR2 .... 116 D6
Fulwood Hts. PR2 .... 117 C5
Fulwood Row. PR2 .... 117 E6
Funchal Ave. L37 .... 11 D1
Furlong Cres. FY3 .... 151 A1
Furlong La. FY6 .... 151 D5
Furness Ave. Blackburn BB1 ...... 101 B8
Furness Ave. Fleetwood FY7 ...... 193 D1
Furness Ave. Formby L37 .... 11 F3
Furness Ave. Normoss FY3 .... 130 A8
Furness Ave. Ormskirk L39 .... 15 E4
Furness Ave. Read BB12 .... 144 D1
Furness Cl. Ainsdale PR8 .... 20 B3
Furness Cl. Chorley PR7 .... 42 D5
Furness Ct. 3 Normoss FY3 .... 130 A8
Furness Dr. High Bentham LA2 . 233 D8
Furness Dr. Poulton-le-F FY6 ..... 152 A3
Furness Rd. LA3 .... 212 A2
Furness St. 8 Burnley BB10 ...... 147 B1
Furness St. Lancaster LA1 .... 213 D1
Furnessford Rd. LA2 .... 233 A6
Furnival Dr. L40 .... 24 D4
Further Ends Rd. PR4 .... 92 B6
Further Heights Rd. 1 OL12 .... 51 F1
Further La. BB2 & PR5 .... 99 A8
Further Wilworth. BB1 .... 121 E2
Furthergate. BB1 .... 101 B5
Fushetts La. LA2 .... 233 D8
Fylde Ave. PR5 .... 75 E4
Fylde Coast Hospl. FY3 .... 129 F7
Fylde Ct. FY6 .... 194 C5
Fylde Rd. Lytham St Anne's FY8 ... 89 D5
Fylde Rd. Poulton-le-F FY6 .... 151 E4
Fylde Rd. Preston PR1 .... 116 D1
Fylde Rd. Southport PR9 .... 53 B4
Fylde Sch. FY3 .... 130 C8
Fylde St. Kirkham PR4 .... 113 A4
Fylde St. Preston PR1 .... 95 E8
Fylde View Cl. FY6 .... 151 D2
Gabbot St. PR6 .... 30 A7
Gable Mews. L37 .... 12 A1
Gables Pl. LA4 .... 212 G5
Gables The. PR4 .... 115 E4
Gadfield St. BB3 .... 64 B8
Gadsby St. FY1 .... 129 B2
Gage St. 31 LA1 .... 210 F8
Gaghills Rd. BB4 .... 85 F1
Gaghills Terr. 3 BB4 .... 85 F1
Gainsborough Ave. Bamber Bridge PR5 .... 76 A7
Gainsborough Ave. Blackburn BB2 .... 100 C6
Gainsborough Ave. Burnley BB11 .... 126 F3
Gainsborough Ave. Morecambe LA4 .... 212 G6
Gainsborough Rd. Blackpool FY1 .... 129 D4
Gainsborough Rd. Ramsbottom BL0 .... 49 B1
Gainsborough Rd. Southport PR8 .... 33 E3
Gaisgill Ave. LA4 .... 212 E3
Gait Barrows (Nature Reserve). LA5 .... 219 A7
Gale St. OL12 .... 51 F3
Gales La. L40 .... 39 A3
Galgate Silk Mills Ind Est. LA2 .... 207 B4
Gall La. OL14 .... 108 C3
Gallery The. L37 .... 11 F3
Galligreaves St. BB2 .... 100 D3
Galligreaves Way. BB2 .... 100 D3
Galloway Cl. 4 OL10 .... 32 F1
Galloway Cres. FY2 .... 150 F5
Galloway Rd. FY7 .... 193 F5
Gallows La. PR3 .... 141 A6
Galway Ave. FY2 .... 150 D3
Gamble Rd. FY5 .... 173 B4
Gambleside Cl. BB4 .... 105 A1
Game St. BB6 .... 123 C5
Gamull La. PR2 .... 117 F5
Gandy La. OL12 .... 51 D4
Gannow La. BB12 .... 126 C6
Gantley Ave. WN5 .... 10 D3
Gantley Cres. WN5 .... 10 D3
Gantley Rd. WN5 .... 10 D4
Ganton Cl. PR8 .... 34 E3
Ganton Ct. PR1 .... 95 A6
Garbett St. BB5 .... 103 A4
Garden Ave. PR4 .... 112 B4
Garden City. BL0 .... 49 A2
Garden Pl. LA6 .... 234 C7
Garden Row. OL12 .... 51 D2
Garden St. Abbey Village BB2 & PR7 .... 79 C2
Garden St. Accrington BB5 .... 103 B7
Garden St. Bamber Bridge PR5 .... 76 B7
Garden St. 2 Barnoldswick BB8 200 B2
Garden St. Blackburn BB2 .... 100 C4
Garden St. Brierfield BB9 .... 147 B5
Garden St. Brookbottoms BL0 ...... 49 C3
Garden St. Colne BB8 .... 169 D4
Garden St. Great Harwood BB6 . 123 C4
Garden St. Higham BB12 .... 145 F5
Garden St. Kirkham PR4 .... 113 A4
Garden St. Lytham St Anne's FY8 . 88 E6
Garden St. Nelson BB9 .... 147 E8
Garden St. Oswaldtwistle BB5 .. 102 D4
Garden St. Padiham BB12 .... 145 C1
Garden St. Preston PR1 .... 95 F7
Garden St. Ramsbottom BL0 .... 49 C6
Garden Terr. Blackpool FY4 .... 129 B1
Garden Terr. Chorley PR6 .... 60 C1
Garden Terr. Middleton LA3 ...... 209 A2
Garden Vale Bsns Ctr. BB8 .... 169 B4
Garden Wlk. Cleveleys FY5 .... 172 D5
Garden Wlk. Preston PR1 .... 116 B1
Gardeners Mews. FY1 .... 129 C7
Gardeners Row. BB7 .... 144 F7
Gardens Gr. LA4 .... 212 D4
Gardiners Pl. WN8 .... 8 E8
Gardner Arc. LA3 .... 212 B4
Gardner Rd. Formby L37 .... 12 B4
Gardner Rd. Lancaster LA1 .... 213 F2
Gardner Rd. Morecambe LA3 ..... 212 B3
Gardner Rd. Warton LA5 .... 217 D5
Gardner St. 21 PR0 & PR1 .... 95 F8
Gardner's La. PR3 .... 179 D3
Garfield Ave. LA1 .... 210 D7
Garfield Dr. LA4 .... 213 B4
Garfield St. Accrington BB5 .... 103 D5
Garfield St. Cornholme OL14 ..... 108 C1
Garfield St. Fleetwood FY7 .... 194 B5
Garfield Terr. PR6 .... 60 D2
Garnall's Bldgs. 6 BB4 .... 84 E2
Garnet St. 3 LA1 .... 211 A8
Garnett Gn. L39 .... 15 D4
Garnett Pl. WN8 .... 9 A7
Garnett Rd. BB7 .... 164 C7
Garnett St. Barrowford BB9 .... 168 D2
Garnett St. Darwen BB3 .... 81 B1
Garnett St. Morecambe LA4 .... 212 E6
Garnett St. Ramsbottom BL0 .... 49 B5
Garrick Gr. FY3 .... 129 E7
Garrick Par. PR8 .... 34 A6
Garrick St. BB9 .... 168 F2
Garrison Rd. PR2 .... 117 B3
Gars End. LA2 .... 232 D6
Gars The. LA2 .... 232 D6
Garsdale Ave. BB10 .... 147 B4
Garsdale Cl. PR5 .... 96 E5
Garsdale Rd. PR2 .... 117 E4
Garsden Ave. BB1 .... 101 E3
Garstang Cl. FY6 .... 151 C3
Garstang Cty Prim Sch. PR3 .. 178 C8
Garstang High Sch. PR3 .... 178 D4
Garstang New Rd. FY6 .... 152 E3
Garstang Rd. Bilsborrow PR3 ..... 157 A4
Garstang Rd. Bowgreave PR3 .... 178 D4
Garstang Rd. Catterall PR3 .... 178 E1
Garstang Rd. Chipping PR3 .... 182 C2
Garstang Rd. Cockerham LA2 & PR3 .... 203 E2
Garstang Rd. Fulwood PR1 & PR2 & PR3 .... 116 E5
Garstang Rd. Kirkham PR4 .... 112 F6
Garstang Rd. Little Eccleston PR3 & FY6 .... 153 D5
Garstang Rd. Newsham PR3 ...... 136 B4
Garstang Rd. Singleton FY6 .... 152 C3
Garstang Rd. Southport PR9 .... 53 A5
Garstang Rd. St Michael's on W PR3 .... 155 C7
Garstang Rd. Stake Pool PR3 ..... 197 B3
Garstang Rd E. FY6 .... 151 E3
Garstang Rd N. PR4 .... 112 F7
Garstang Rd S. PR4 .... 112 F6
Garstang Rd W. FY6 .... 151 B2
Garstang St. BB3 .... 81 A2
Garston St. BL9 .... 32 A4
Garstone Croft. PR2 .... 116 D6
Garswood Cl. Brierfield BB12 .... 146 F2
Garswood Cl. Maghull L31 .... 5 E3
Garton Ave. FY4 .... 109 D6
Gas Field Rd. LA3 .... 208 E2
Gas House La. LA2 .... 233 D8
Gas St. Adlington PR7 .... 30 A6
Gas St. Bacup OL13 .... 86 F2
Gas St. Burnley BB11 .... 126 F6
Gas St. Haslingden BB4 .... 83 F1
Gas St. Longridge PR3 .... 139 A8
Gas Terr. PR5 .... 76 B2
Gaskell Cl. LA5 .... 218 C3
Gaskell Cres. FY5 .... 173 A2
Gaskell House. LA1 .... 213 E4
Gaskell Rd. PR1 .... 95 E5
Gaskell St. PR6 .... 42 E8
Gate St. BB1 .... 101 A5
Gategill Gr. WN5 .... 10 D3
Gateheads Brow. LA6 .... 238 F3
Gateland. BB8 .... 191 D8
Gates La. L29 .... 4 C1
Gatesgarth Ave. PR2 .... 116 F7
Gateside Ct. 2 FY3 .... 130 A8
Gateside Dr. FY3 .... 129 F8
Gateway Cl. FY5 .... 151 D7
Gathurst Golf Course. WN6 .... 19 F5
Gathurst La. WN6 .... 19 F5
Gathurst Rd. Fulwood PR2 .... 116 C2
Gathurst Rd. Gathurst WN5 .... 19 F2
Gathurst Rd. Orrell WN5 .... 10 E8
Gaulter's La. FY6 .... 195 C4
Gaw Hill La. L39 .... 15 B3
Gaw Hill View. L39 .... 15 B3
Gawthorpe Edge Pk. BB12 .... 125 F8
Gawthorpe High Sch. BB12 .... 125 E8
Gawthorpe Rd. BB12 .... 126 D7
Gawthorpe St. 11 BB12 .... 145 C1

Gawthorpe View. BB12 .... 145 F5
Gaydon Way. FY5 .... 150 E7
Gaylands La. BB8 .... 201 C2
Gayle Way. **1** BB5 .... 102 F4
Gaythorne Ave. PR1 .... 96 F8
Geddes St. BB2 .... 99 F2
Geldof Dr. FY1 .... 129 C8
General St. FY1 .... 129 B6
Geneva St. PR2 .... 117 C4
Genoa St. BB11 .... 126 C4
Geoffrey St. Bury BL9 .... 32 A4
Geoffrey St. Chorley PR6 .... 60 E1
Geoffrey St. Preston PR1 .... 96 C8
Geoffrey St. Ramsbottom BL0 .... 49 A4
George Ave. FY4 .... 129 F1
George Dr. PR8 .... 20 E5
George La. BB12 .... 144 C2
George Rd. BL0 .... 49 B5
George St. Accrington BB5 .... 102 F4
George St. **4** Bacup OL13 .... 69 C8
George St. Barnoldswick BB8 .... 200 C4
George St. Blackburn BB1 & BB2 .. 100 E4
George St. Blackpool FY1 .... 129 C5
George St. Blackpool FY1 .... 129 C6
George St. Burnley BB11 .... 126 F5
George St. Chorley PR6 .... 42 C7
George St. **13** Clayton-le-M BB5 .. 123 F3
George St. Clitheroe BB7 .... 164 D6
George St. Darwen BB3 .... 81 A2
George St. Earby BB8 .... 201 B1
George St. Great Harwood BB6 . 123 C5
George St. Haslingden BB4 .... 84 B3
George St. Horwich BL6 .... 31 C3
George St. **3** Lancaster LA1 .... 210 F7
George St. Leyland PR5 .... 76 B2
George St. Longridge PR3 .... 139 A8
George St. Lytham St Anne's FY8 .. 90 B3
George St. Morecambe LA4 .... 212 F5
George St. **8** Nelson BB9 .... 168 D1
George St. Oswaldtwistle BB5 .. 102 E5
George St. Preston PR1 .... 96 B7
George St. Rishton BB1 .... 123 B1
George St. Whalley BB7 .... 143 C5
George St. Whitworth OL12 .... 51 C8
George St W. BB2 .... 100 D4
George's La. Banks PR9 .... 54 A7
George's La. Horwich BL6 .... 31 E5
George's Rd. PR1 .... 95 F7
George's Row. **2** BB4 .... 68 F8
George's Terr. WN5 .... 10 D5
Georgian Pl. L37 .... 11 E1
Gerald Ct. **6** BB11 .... 127 B4
German La. PR7 .... 41 D7
Gerrard Pl. WN8 .... 8 F7
Gerrard St. Lancaster LA1 .... 210 D7
Gerrard St. Preston PR1 .... 95 E7
Gerrard's Fold. PR7 .... 79 B2
Gerrard's Terr. FY6 .... 151 C4
Gertrude St. Nelson BB9 .... 169 A2
Gertrude St. Shawforth OL12 .... 70 E6
Ghants La. FY6 .... 174 E2
Ghyll Golf Course. BB8 .... 200 E4
Ghyll La. BB8 .... 200 E4
Ghyll Meadows. BB8 .... 200 D4
Gib Field Rd. BB8 .... 169 A3
Gib Hey La. PR3 .... 159 F7
Gib Hill La. BB4 .... 105 B2
Gib Hill Rd. BB9 .... 169 B1
Gib La. Blackburn BB2 .... 80 A7
Gib La. Hoghton PR5 .... 98 C3
Gibfield Rd. BB8 .... 169 B2
Gibraltar Rd. PR4 .... 131 E5
Gibraltar St. BB2 .... 100 B6
Gibson St. BB9 .... 168 F2
Giddygate La. L31 .... 6 B1
Gidlow Ave. PR6 .... 30 A7
Gilbert St. Brierfield BB10 .... 147 E2
Gilbert St. Chorley PR7 .... 42 C6
Gilbert St. Ramsbottom BL0 .... 67 C1
Gilbert St. Rawtenstall BB4 .... 85 D1
Gilbertson Rd. PR6 .... 42 E2
Gildabrook Rd. FY4 .... 109 D5
Gilderdale Ct. FY8 .... 90 C4
Gildow St. **1** PR1 .... 95 E8
Giles St. Clitheroe BB7 .... 164 E7
Giles St. Nelson BB9 .... 168 E1
Gilhouse Ave. PR2 .... 115 C1
Gill Ct. FY4 .... 109 B5
Gill La. PR4 .... 74 C5
Gill Nook. PR4 .... 74 A5
Gill St. Burnley BB12 .... 126 E6
Gill St. Colne BB8 .... 169 C8
Gill St. Nelson BB9 .... 168 D1
Gillcroft. PR7 .... 40 B7
Giller Cl. PR1 .... 95 F2
Giller Dr. PR1 .... 95 F2
Giller Fold. PR1 .... 95 F2
Gillett St. **6** PR1 .... 117 C1
Gillhead Brow. LA6 .... 236 D1
Gillians. BB8 .... 191 B8
Gillians La. BB8 .... 191 B8
Gillibrand Cty Prim Sch. PR7 .. 42 B6
Gillibrand House. PR6 .... 60 C2
Gillibrand St. Chorley PR7 .... 42 C7
Gillibrand St. Darwen BB3 .... 80 F3
Gillibrand St.
  Walton-le-D PR1 & PR5 .... 96 D5
Gillibrand Wlks. PR7 .... 42 C7
Gillibrands Rd. WN8 .... 9 A7
Gillies St. Accrington BB5 .... 103 C6
Gillies St. Blackburn BB2 .... 100 F3
Gillison Cl. LA6 .... 235 C2
Gillow Cl. LA1 .... 210 F5
Gillow Pk. PR3 .... 153 F6
Gillow Rd. PR4 .... 112 F5
Gills Croft. BB7 .... 165 A7
Gilpin Ave. L31 .... 5 E2
Gilpin Cl. **2** LA1 .... 213 C2

Gilsecroft Ave. L33 .... 1 A4
Gilstead Ave. LA3 .... 209 A8
Gin Bow. PR7 .... 42 D6
Gin Croft La. BL0 .... 67 E4
Gingham Brow. BL6 .... 31 E4
Girvan Gr. BB11 .... 126 D5
Girvan Wlk. **3** OL10 .... 32 F1
Gisburn Ave. FY8 .... 89 C6
Gisburn Cty Prim Sch. BB7 .. 225 C3
Gisburn Forest Tosside
  Parochial Sch. BD23 .... 230 B3
Gisburn Gr. Blackpool FY3 .... 129 E7
Gisburn Gr. Blackburn BB10 .. 127 D5
Gisburn Old Rd.
  Barnoldswick BB7 & BB9 .... 190 C7
Gisburn Old Rd. Foulridge BB9 . 190 E4
Gisburn Rd. Barnoldswick BB8 .. 200 A3
Gisburn Rd. Barrowford BB9 .. 168 E5
Gisburn Rd. Bolton-by-B BB7 .. 224 E4
Gisburn Rd. Fulwood PR2 .... 117 E4
Gisburn Road Prim Sch. BB8 . 200 B3
Gisburn St. Barnoldswick BB8 .. 200 B3
Gisburn St. Blackburn BB2 .... 100 C4
Gisburne Park Hospl. BB7 .... 225 B4
Gladden Pl. WN8 .... 8 E8
Glade The. LA4 .... 213 A5
Glades The. FY8 .... 90 C4
Gladeway. FY5 .... 151 D7
Gladstone Cres. OL13 .... 87 A2
Gladstone Rd. PR9 .... 34 F6
Gladstone St. Bacup OL13 .... 87 A2
Gladstone St. Blackburn BB1 .. 101 B6
Gladstone St. Blackpool FY4 .. 129 C1
Gladstone St. Bury BL9 .... 32 B3
Gladstone St. Cornholme OL14 .. 108 B1
Gladstone St.
  Great Harwood BB6 .... 123 C5
Gladstone Terr.
  Abbey Village PR7 .... 79 C1
Gladstone Terr. Blackburn BB2 .. 99 F1
Gladstone Terr. Colne BB8 .. 170 B4
Gladstone Terr. **1**
  Lancaster LA1 .... 214 A1
Gladstone Way. **4** FY5 .... 172 F1
Glaisdale Dr. PR8 .... 34 F3
Glamis Dr. Chorley PR7 .... 42 B8
Glamis Dr. Southport PR9 .... 53 B3
Glamis Rd. PR5 & PR6 .... 59 C8
Glamorgan Gr. BB12 .... 126 A7
Glasson Cl. BB2 .... 100 F1
Glastonbury Ave. FY1 .... 129 E2
Glebe Cl. Accrington BB5 .... 103 B5
Glebe Cl. Burton-in-K LA6 .... 234 C7
Glebe Cl. Fulwood PR2 .... 116 F4
Glebe Cl. Maghull L31 .... 5 B1
Glebe Cl. Standish WN6 .... 28 F1
Glebe Cotts. BB4 .... 85 A2
Glebe Ct. Kirkby Lonsdale LA6 .. 238 B3
Glebe Ct. **15** Lancaster LA1 .. 211 A8
Glebe La. Banks PR9 .... 54 A7
Glebe La. Kirkham PR4 .... 113 C4
Glebe Pl. PR8 .... 34 B7
Glebe Rd. Skelmersdale WN8 .. 9 A8
Glebe Rd. Standish WN6 .... 28 F1
Glebe St. Burnley BB11 .... 127 B4
Glebe St. Great Harwood BB6 .. 123 C5
Gledhill Way. BL7 .... 47 A1
Gledstone View. BB8 .... 200 A3
Glegside Rd. L33 .... 1 A2
Glen Cres. OL13 .... 69 A8
Glen Dr. WN6 .... 19 E8
Glen Eldon Rd. FY8 .... 88 E7
Glen Garth. BB8 .... 200 D3
Glen Gdns. OL12 .... 51 F2
Glen Gr. PR2 .... 117 F5
Glen Park Dr. PR4 .... 72 D4
Glen Rd. BB4 .... 68 F8
Glen Royd. **1** OL12 .... 51 C1
Glen Sq. BB11 .... 126 F2
Glen St. Bacup OL13 .... 69 E8
Glen St. Blackpool FY3 .... 129 E4
Glen St. Burnley BB11 .... 126 E6
Glen St. Colne BB8 .... 169 D6
Glen St. Ramsbottom BL0 .... 49 B7
Glen The. Caton LA2 .... 231 C3
Glen The. Fulwood PR1 .... 117 F2
Glen The. Knott End-on-S FY6 .. 194 E4
Glen View Ave. LA3 .... 208 E6
Glen View Cres. LA3 .... 208 E6
Glen View Dr. LA3 .... 208 E6
Glen View Rd. BB11 .... 126 E2
Glen View St. OL14 .... 108 B1
Glen Way. BB9 .... 147 B6
Glenarden Ave. FY5 .... 150 F8
Glenavon Dr. OL12 .... 51 D3
Glenborough Ave. OL13 .... 69 C8
Glenbrook Cl. L33 .... 1 A2
Glenburn High Sch. WN8 .... 9 B8
Glenburn Rd. WN8 .... 18 A1
Glencarron Cl. BB3 .... 64 F8
Glencoe Ave. Blackpool FY6 .. 151 A2
Glencoe Ave. Hoddlesden BB3 .. 81 E1
Glencoe Cl. OL10 .... 32 F1
Glencourse Dr. PR2 .... 117 D5
Glencoyne Dr. PR9 .... 53 B3
Glencroft. PR7 .... 59 C3
Glencross Pl. FY4 .... 109 E7
Glendale Ave. PR5 .... 96 C1
Glendale Cl. Blackpool FY2 .. 150 F5
Glendale Cl. Burnley BB11 .. 127 A3
Glendale Cl. Leyland PR5 .... 59 B7
Glendale Cl. Poulton-le-F FY6 .. 151 C3
Glendale Cres. PR5 .... 96 C1
Glendale Dr. BB2 .... 120 E2
Glendale Gr. PR1 & PR2 .... 117 D2
Glendale Way. L37 .... 11 F2
Glenden Foot. OL12 .... 51 D2
Glendor Rd. BB10 .... 127 E5

Gleneagles Ave. BB3 .... 81 E1
Gleneagles Ct. PR4 .... 113 B4
Gleneagles Dr. Ainsdale PR8 .. 20 C3
Gleneagles Dr. Fulwood PR2 .. 116 B7
Gleneagles Dr. Morecambe LA4 212 G6
Gleneagles Dr. Penwortham PR1 95 A6
Gleneagles Way. **1** BL0 .... 49 B5
Glenfield Ave. PR2 .... 150 E6
Glenfield Park Ind Est.
  Blackburn BB1 .... 101 B7
Glenfield Park Ind Est.
  Nelson BB9 .... 169 A1
Glenfield Rd. BB9 .... 169 A1
Glengarry. FY8 .... 90 C3
Glengreave Ave. BB3 .... 121 E3
Glenholme Gdns. FY6 .... 151 C2
Glenluce Cres. BB1 .... 101 D3
Glenluce Dr. PR1 .... 96 F8
Glenmarsh Way. L37 .... 12 B3
Glenmere Cres. FY5 .... 150 C7
Glenmore Ave. FY5 .... 173 B2
Glenmore Cl. BB5 .... 103 E2
Glenmore Rd. BL8 .... 48 F2
Glenpark Dr. PR9 .... 53 B4
Glenrose Ave. BB8 .... 169 D6
Glenrose Terr. PR8 .... 34 A5
Glenroyd Cl. FY3 .... 129 E3
Glenroyd Dr. L40 .... 22 E4
Glenshiels Ave. BB3 .... 64 E8
Glenside. WN6 .... 27 B2
Glentworth Rd W. LA4 .... 212 F3
Glenview Cl. PR2 .... 118 A3
Glenview Cl. PR2 .... 118 A3
Glenway. PR1 .... 95 C4
Glossop Cl. FY2 .... 150 C6
Gloucester Ave. Accrington BB5 103 A7
Gloucester Ave. **8**
  Clayton-le-M BB5 .... 123 F3
Gloucester Ave. Cleveleys FY5 172 D3
Gloucester Ave. Horwich BL6 .. 31 D2
Gloucester Ave. Lancaster LA1 . 211 A4
Gloucester Ave. Leyland PR5 .. 76 C3
Gloucester Ct. Blackpool FY3 .. 129 D4
Gloucester Ct. Horwich BL6 .. 31 D2
Gloucester Dr. LA3 .... 212 B3
Gloucester Rd. Blackburn BB1 . 101 D5
Gloucester Rd. Chorley PR7 .. 42 C6
Gloucester Rd.
  Lytham St Anne's FY8 .... 89 D4
Gloucester Rd. Rishton BB1 .. 102 A8
Gloucester Rd. Southport PR8 .. 33 F5
Glover St. PR5 .... 57 F6
Glover St. Horwich BL6 .... 31 B4
Glover St. Preston PR1 .... 96 A7
Glover's Ct. **24** PR1 .... 96 A7
Glynn St. BB5 .... 102 F7
Godiva St. BB10 .... 147 A1
Godley St. BB11 .... 127 B6
Godwin Ave. FY3 .... 129 E3
Goe La. PR4 .... 92 B6
Goit St. Blackburn BB2 .... 100 C2
Goit St. Newchurch BB4 .... 85 F1
Goitside. BB9 .... 168 E1
Golbourne St. PR1 .... 117 B1
Goldacre La. BB6 .... 123 A7
Goldburn Cl. PR2 .... 115 F6
Golden Hill. **9** PR5 .... 76 B2
Golden Hill La. PR5 .... 75 F2
Goldfield Ave. BB10 .... 127 F6
Goldfinch Dr. BL9 .... 32 C4
Goldfinch Gn. BB11 .... 126 C4
Goldfinch St. PR1 .... 117 B1
Goldhey St. **10** BB1 .... 101 A7
Goldsboro Ave. FY3 .... 129 F3
Golf Rd. L37 .... 11 E5
Golf View. PR2 .... 116 A6
Golgotha Rd. LA1 .... 211 A6
Gonder La. PR2 .... 179 E3
Gooch St. BL6 .... 31 C2
Good St. PR1 .... 95 E7
Goodall Cl. BB8 .... 201 B2
Goodenber Cres. **1** LA2 .. 233 D8
Goodenber Rd. LA2 .... 233 D8
Goodshaw Ave.
  Rawtenstall BB4 .... 105 A1
Goodshaw Ave N. BB4 .... 105 A2
Goodshaw Cl. BB1 .... 100 B8
Goodshaw Fold Rd. BB4 .... 104 F2
Goodshaw La. Accrington BB5 . 104 C1
Goodshaw La. Rawtenstall BB4 105 B2
Goodwood Ave. Blackpool FY2 150 D1
Goodwood Ave. Fulwood PR2 .. 116 F7
Goodwood Ave. Hest Bank LA2 213 F8
Goodwood Cl. LA1 .... 211 B4
Goodwood Rd. LA1 .... 211 B4
Goose Cote Hill. BL7 .... 46 E1
Goose Foot Cl. PR5 .... 98 D7
Goose Foot La. PR5 .... 98 C6
Goose Green Ave. PR7 .... 41 F1
Goose Green La. BB8 .... 170 B2
Goose Hill St. **14** OL13 .... 86 F3
Goose House Rd. BB3 .... 81 A3
Goosebutts La. BB7 .... 164 F7
Gooseleach La. BB12 .... 144 E1
Goosnargh La. PR3 .... 137 B7
Gordale Cl. Barnoldswick BB8 .. 200 A2
Gordale Cl. Blackpool FY4 .. 110 A8
Gorden St. **11** OL13 .... 69 C8
Gordon Ave. Accrington BB5 .. 103 A4
Gordon Ave. Maghull L31 .... 5 C3
Gordon Ave. Southport PR9 .. 52 C1
Gordon Ave. Thornton FY5 .. 173 B2

Gordon Rd. Fleetwood FY7 .. 193 F3
Gordon Rd.
  Lytham St Anne's FY8 .... 89 D4
Gordon Rd. **7** Nelson BB9 .. 168 D1
Gordon St. Bacup OL13 .... 86 F4
Gordon St. Blackpool FY4 .. 129 B1
Gordon St. Burnley BB12 .. 126 F7
Gordon St. Chorley PR6 .... 42 D7
Gordon St. Church BB5 .... 102 E5
Gordon St. Clayton-le-M BB5 .. 124 A2
Gordon St. Colne BB8 .... 169 F5
Gordon St. Darwen BB3 .... 81 A3
Gordon St. Preston PR1 .... 116 E1
Gordon St. Rawtenstall BB4 .. 84 F2
Gordon St. Southport PR9 .. 34 C8
Gordon St. Worsthorne BB10 .. 128 B6
Gordon Way. OL10 .... 32 F1
Gordonstoun Cres. WN5 .... 10 F7
Gordonstoun Pl. FY5 .... 173 A2
Gore Dr. BL9 .... 15 E3
Gore La. BB12 .... 11 F5
Gores La. L37 .... 11 F5
Gores Rd. L33 .... 1 C1
Goring St. PR6 & PR7 .... 42 D7
Gorple Gn. BB10 .... 128 B5
Gorple Rd. BB10 .... 128 D5
Gorple St. BB10 .... 147 E3
Gorrell Cl. BB12 .... 167 D3
Gorse Ave. FY5 .... 172 F3
Gorse Bank. BL9 .... 32 C3
Gorse Cl. Great Knowley PR6 .. 60 E5
Gorse Cl. Tarleton PR4 .... 56 A6
Gorse Gr. Fulwood PR2 .... 117 E3
Gorse Gr. Haslingden BB4 .... 67 A8
Gorse Gr. Longton PR4 .... 94 A1
Gorse La. PR4 .... 55 D5
Gorse Rd. Blackburn BB2 .... 100 B5
Gorse Rd. Blackpool FY3 .... 129 E4
Gorse St. BB1 .... 101 B6
Gorse Way. L37 .... 11 C4
Gorsefield. L37 .... 12 A6
Gorsewood. PR5 .... 75 E1
Gorsey La. Banks PR9 .... 54 C7
Gorsey La. Barton L39 .... 13 B7
Gorsey La. Hambleton L38 .... 2 B7
Gorsey La. Mawdesley L40 .. 39 C1
Gorsey Pl. WN8 .... 9 B7
Gorst La. L40 & PR9 .... 24 A6
Gorsuch La. L39 & L40 .... 22 D4
Gorton Fold. BL6 .... 31 C3
Gorton St. FY1 .... 129 C6
Gosforth Rd. Blackpool FY2 .. 150 C1
Gosforth Rd. Southport PR9 .. 34 F8
Gough La. Clayton Brook PR5 .. 77 C5
Gough La. Walton Summit PR5 .. 77 B6
Goulding Ave. PR5 .... 76 B1
Goulding St. PR7 .... 42 D6
Gowans La. PR4 .... 78 A8
Gower Ct. PR5 .... 75 D3
Gower Gdns. L40 .... 24 F3
Gower Gr. PR4 .... 74 A5
Goyt St. FY8 .... 88 F7
Grab La. LA1 .... 211 C7
Graburn Rd. L37 .... 11 F4
Gracamy Ave. PR4 .... 91 D5
Grace St. BL6 .... 31 B3
Gradwell St. **2** PR1 .... 95 E8
Grafton Ave. Accrington BB5 .. 103 E2
Grafton Ave. Brierfield BB10 .. 147 B5
Grafton Ct. Chorley PR7 .... 42 B5
Grafton Ct. Darwen BB3 .... 80 F2
Grafton Dr. PR8 .... 20 A5
Grafton Pl. LA3 .... 212 B3
Grafton Rd. Fulwood PR2 .... 117 F4
Grafton Rd. Morecambe LA3 .. 212 B3
Grafton St. Adlington PR7 .... 29 F6
Grafton St. Blackburn BB2 .. 100 D2
Grafton St. Blackpool FY1 .. 129 C7
Grafton St. Clitheroe BB7 .. 164 F7
Grafton St. Nelson BB9 .... 168 F1
Grafton St. Preston PR1 .... 95 E6
Grafton Villas. OL13 .... 86 F1
Graham Ave. Appley Bridge WN6 27 C2
Graham Ave. Bamber Bridge PR5 76 C8
Graham Rd. PR3 .... 199 C2
Graham St. Hoddlesden BB3 .. 81 F1
Graham St. Lancaster LA1 .. 210 F6
Graham St. Morecambe LA4 .. 212 D5
Graham St. **1** Padiham BB12 .. 125 D7
Graham St. **4** Preston PR1 .. 117 B1
Granary The. FY5 .... 173 A2
Granby Ave. FY3 .... 129 E8
Granby Gr. PR9 .... 52 F3
Granby St. BB12 .... 126 D7
Grane Pk. BB4 .... 84 A2
Grane Rd. BB4 & BB1 & BB5 .. 83 C7
Grane St. BB4 .... 84 B2
Grange Ave. Barrowford BB9 .. 168 F5
Grange Ave. Fulwood PR2 .... 117 F4
Grange Ave. Fulwood PR2 .... 118 A4
Grange Ave. Great Harwood BB6 123 C6
Grange Ave. Rawtenstall BB4 .. 85 B3
Grange Ave. Southport PR9 .. 34 E8
Grange Ave. Thornton FY5 .. 173 B2
Grange Cl. Great Harwood BB6 . 123 C6
Grange Cl. Knott End-on-S FY6 .. 194 F6
Grange Cl. Oswaldtwistle BB5 .. 103 A3
Grange Cl. Rawtenstall BB4 .. 85 B2
Grange Cres. BB4 .... 85 A2
Grange Ct. FY1 .... 129 C8
Grange Dr. Coupe Green PR5 .. 97 E4
Grange Dr. Euxton PR7 .... 59 C4
Grange Farm Cotts. PR4 .... 92 E5
Grange Gdns. FY6 .... 151 D2
Grange La. Accrington BB5 .. 85 D1
Grange La. Formby L37 .... 11 E5
Grange La. Longton PR4 .... 93 D3
Grange La. Newton-with-S PR4 .. 113 F2

Grange La. Stalmine FY6 .... 174 B7
Grange Park Cl. PR1 .... 95 A6
Grange Park Cty Prim Sch.
  FY3 .... 130 A7
Grange Pl. PR2 .... 117 F4
Grange Prim Sch. PR2 .... 118 A4
Grange Rd. Blackburn BB2 .. 100 B2
Grange Rd. Blackpool FY3 .. 129 F7
Grange Rd. Egerton BL7 .... 47 C1
Grange Rd. Elswick PR4 .... 153 F1
Grange Rd. Fleetwood FY7 .. 193 D3
Grange Rd. Fulwood PR2 .... 116 C3
Grange Rd. Hambleton FY6 .. 174 C1
Grange Rd. Hightown L38 .... 2 E6
Grange Rd. Leyland PR5 .... 75 D2
Grange Rd. Lytham St Anne's FY8 88 E7
Grange Rd. Over Town BB10 .. 107 A7
Grange Rd. Rawtenstall BB4 .. 85 B2
Grange Rd. Singleton FY6 .. 153 A3
Grange Rd. Southport PR9 .. 34 E7
Grange Rd. Whitworth OL12 .. 70 D3
Grange Rd. Accrington BB5 .. 103 C5
Grange Rd. Barnoldswick BB8 .. 200 A3
Grange Rd. Burnley BB11 .... 126 E5
Grange Rd. Clayton-le-M BB5 .. 123 E3
Grange Rd. Morecambe LA4 .. 213 A6
Grange St. **2** Rawtenstall BB4 .. 85 A2
Grange Terr. **19** BB4 .... 85 A3
Grange View. Carnforth LA5 .. 217 D3
Grange View. Hest Bank LA5 .. 215 F3
Grange View Rd. LA6 .... 216 F6
Grangefield. PR4 .... 93 F1
Granings The. PR4 .... 115 D6
Granny's Bay. FY8 .... 89 C3
Grant Cl. LA1 .... 210 D7
Grant Dr. PR4 .... 74 A5
Grant Rd. BB2 .... 100 B3
Grant St. Accrington BB5 .. 103 A6
Grant St. Burnley BB11 .... 126 E5
Grantham Cl. PR8 .... 34 A1
Grantham Rd. Blackpool FY1 .. 129 C7
Grantham Rd. Southport PR8 .. 34 A1
Grantham St. BB2 .... 100 B2
Granton Cl. L37 .... 11 E3
Granton Wlk. PR2 .... 116 A4
Grants La. BL0 .... 49 C6
Grants Mews. BL0 .... 49 B7
Granville Ave. Becconsall PR4 .. 72 E2
Granville Ave. Maghull L31 .... 5 C2
Granville Cl. L39 .... 6 B8
Granville Cl. Chorley PR6 .... 60 E1
Granville Ct. Southport PR9 .. 52 E1
Granville Gdns. BB5 .... 103 D3
Granville Pk. L39 .... 6 C8
Granville Rd. Accrington BB5 .. 103 D3
Granville Rd. Blackburn BB2 .. 100 B5
Granville Rd.
  Blackpool FY1 & FY3 .... 129 D5
Granville Rd. Brierfield BB9 .. 147 C6
Granville Rd. Chorley PR6 .... 60 E1
Granville Rd. Darwen BB3 .... 63 F8
Granville Rd.
  Great Harwood BB6 .... 123 C6
Granville Rd. Lancaster LA1 .. 213 D3
Granville Rd. Morecambe LA3 .. 212 B3
Granville Rd. Southport PR8 .. 33 D4
Granville St. Adlington PR6 .. 30 A7
Granville St. Brierfield BB10 .. 147 F2
Granville St. **13** Burnley BB10 .. 127 A8
Granville St. Colne BB8 .... 169 E5
Granville St. Helmshore BB4 .. 67 A4
Grape La. PR5 .... 57 C1
Grasmere Ave. Blackburn BB1 .. 121 C5
Grasmere Ave. Fleetwood FY7 .. 193 E3
Grasmere Ave. Leyland PR5 .. 76 A3
Grasmere Ave. Orrell WN5 .. 10 F5
Grasmere Ave. Padiham BB12 .. 145 C1
Grasmere Ave. Thornton FY5 .. 173 B2
Grasmere Ave. Up Holland WN8 .. 10 B7
Grasmere Cl. Accrington BB5 .. 103 D8
Grasmere Cl. Bamber Bridge PR5 96 C3
Grasmere Cl. Colne BB8 .... 170 A5
Grasmere Cl. Euxton PR7 .... 59 E1
Grasmere Cl. Fulwood PR2 .. 117 C4
Grasmere Cl. **8**
  High Bentham LA2 .... 233 D8
Grasmere Dr. **7**
  High Bentham LA2 .... 233 D8
Grasmere Dr. Rishton BB1 .. 123 A1
Grasmere Gr. Longridge PR3 .. 138 F5
Grasmere Gr. Whittle-le-W PR6 .. 60 F7
Grasmere Rd. Blackpool FY1 .. 129 D5
Grasmere Rd. Formby L37 .... 11 D3
Grasmere Rd. Haslingden BB4 .. 67 C8
Grasmere Rd.
  Knott End-on-S FY6 .... 194 F6
Grasmere Rd. Lancaster LA1 .. 211 A8
Grasmere Rd.
  Lytham St Anne's FY8 .... 109 E1
Grasmere Rd. Maghull L31 .... 5 D2
Grasmere Rd. Morecambe LA3 .. 213 A6
Grasmere St. Burnley BB10 .. 147 A2
Grasmere St. **10** Rochdale OL12 . 51 F1
Grasmere Terr. Bacup OL13 .. 86 F4
Grasmere Terr. Chorley PR7 .. 42 B8
Grassington Dr. Brierfield BB10 147 D3
Grassington Dr. Bury OL10 .. 32 D1
Grassington Pl. FY5 .... 150 D2
Grassington Rd. FY8 .... 89 C7
Gratton Pl. WN8 .... 9 A8
Grave-Yard La. L39 .... 7 A6
Gravel La. Banks PR9 .... 53 F5
Gravel La. Banks PR9 .... 54 A5
Gravel La. Banks PR9 .... 54 B3
Gravel The. PR4 .... 54 F2

Graver Weir Terr. BB4 ...... **106** A1
Graving Dock Rd. FY8 ...... **90** D4
Grayrigg Dr. LA4 ...... **212** E3
Grays Pl. LA3 ...... **212** B2
Great Arley Sch. FY5 ...... 173 B3
Great Avenham St. PR1 ...... **96** A6
Great Bolton St. BB2 ...... **100** E3
Great Close La. BD23 ...... **230** D6
Great Eaves Rd. BL0 ...... **49** C7
Great Flatt. OL12 ...... **51** B1
Great George St. Colne BB8 ...... **169** D5
Great George St. Preston PR1 ...... **117** A1
Great Gill. PR4 ...... **74** A5
Great Greens La. PR5 ...... **77** C5
Great Hanover St. PR1 ...... **117** A1
Great Harwood Cty Prim Sch.
  BB6 ...... 123 C5
Great Harwood Golf Course.
  BB6 ...... 123 F7
Great Hey. PR4 ...... **73** D3
Great John St. 20 LA1 ...... **210** F8
Great Lee. OL12 ...... **51** D3
Great Lee Wlk. OL12 ...... **51** D2
Great Meadow.
  Bamber Bridge PR5 ...... **76** A8
Great Meadow. Chorley PR7 ...... **60** A2
Great Shaw St. PR1 ...... **95** F8
Great Stone of Fourstones.
  LA2 ...... 233 D5
Great Stones Cl. BL7 ...... **46** F2
Great Townley St. PR1 ...... **96** D8
Great Tunstead. PR4 ...... **74** A7
Great Wood Cty Prim Sch.
  LA4 ...... 213 A5
Greave. BB4 ...... **85** A4
Greave Clough Cl. 9 OL13 ...... **87** A3
Greave Clough Dr. OL13 ...... **87** B3
Greave Cres. 10 OL13 ...... **87** A3
Greave Rd. OL13 ...... **87** B3
Greave Terr. OL13 ...... **87** B3
Greaves Cl. WN6 ...... **19** F8
Greaves Dr. LA1 ...... **210** F6
Greaves Hall Hosp. PR9 ...... 54 B5
Greaves Meadow. PR1 ...... **95** E2
Greaves Rd. LA1 ...... **210** F6
Greaves St. Haslingden BB4 ...... **83** F2
Greaves St. 9 Preston PR1 ...... **96** A7
Greaves-Town La. PR2 ...... **115** E1
Grebe Cl. FY3 ...... **130** B7
Green Acre. PR3 ...... **137** D6
Green Acres. PR4 ...... **92** C7
Green Ave. FY4 ...... **109** C6
Green Bank. Bacup OL13 ...... **69** D8
Green Bank. Barnoldswick BB8 ...... **200** D4
Green Bank Ind Est. BB1 ...... 101 C7
Green Bridge N. BB4 ...... **68** E7
Green Bridge S. BB4 ...... **68** E7
Green Brook Cl. BL9 ...... **32** A4
Green Cl. BB11 ...... **126** E2
Green Close Pk. BB2 ...... **100** C2
Green Dick's La. PR3 ...... **195** E5
Green Dr. Bamber Bridge PR5 ...... **96** C1
Green Dr. Barton PR3 ...... **136** B8
Green Dr. Cleveleys FY5 ...... **172** C5
Green Dr. Clitheroe BB7 ...... **187** A2
Green Dr. Fulwood PR2 ...... **116** A3
Green Dr. Lytham St Anne's FY8 ...... **89** F5
Green Dr. Penwortham PR1 ...... **95** B5
Green Dr. Poulton-le-F FY6 ...... **130** E8
Green Dr. Saltcotes FY8 ...... **90** C5
Green Drive Golf Course. FY8 . 90 B5
Green End. BB2 ...... **98** E7
Green End Ave. BB8 ...... **201** B2
Green End Cl. 11 OL13 ...... **87** A3
Green End Rd. BB8 ...... **201** B1
Green Gate. Fulwood PR2 ...... **116** C3
Green Gate. Hutton PR4 ...... **94** C1
Green Haworth CE Prim Sch.
  BB5 ...... 103 B1
Green Haworth Golf Course.
  BB5 ...... 103 B1
Green Hey. Lytham St Anne's FY8 **90** D4
Green Hey. Much Hoole PR4 ...... **73** E3
Green Heys Dr. L31 ...... **5** F1
Green Hill. OL13 ...... **87** A1
Green Hill La. LA2 & LA6 ...... **231** B6
Green Hill Rd. OL13 ...... **87** A1
Green Howarth View. BB5 ...... **103** A3
Green La. Banks PR9 ...... **54** C4
Green La. Bilsborrow PR3 ...... **157** B2
Green La. Bispham Green L40 ...... **26** B7
Green La. Blackburn BB2 ...... **100** A1
Green La. Bretherton PR4 & PR5 ...... **57** C7
Green La. Chipping PR3 ...... **182** F3
Green La. Coppull PR7 ...... **29** A8
Green La. Downham BB7 ...... **188** B6
Green La. Ellel LA1 & LA2 ...... **207** B6
Green La. Farington PR5 ...... **75** E7
Green La. Formby L37 ...... **11** F5
Green La. Freckleton PR4 ...... **92** C6
Green La. Garstang PR3 ...... **178** A7
Green La. Grindleton BB7 ...... **187** A7
Green La. Halton Green LA2 ...... **231** A4
Green La. Holmes PR4 ...... **55** C4
Green La. Horwich BD23 ...... **225** D5
Green La. Lancaster LA1 & LA2 ...... **214** A6
Green La. Longridge PR3 ...... **139** B8
Green La. Maghull L31 ...... **5** A2
Green La. Maghull L31 ...... **5** C1
Green La. Morecambe LA3 ...... **212** E2
Green La. New Gate PR4 ...... **95** C1
Green La. Ormskirk L39 ...... **15** E6
Green La. Orrell WN5 ...... **10** D3

Green La. Padiham BB12 ...... **125** C8
Green La. Preesall FY6 ...... **195** C2
Green La. Riley Green PR5 ...... **78** E8
Green La.
  Samlesbury Bottoms PR5 ...... **98** B7
Green La. Skelmersdale L40 ...... **18** A6
Green La. Sollom PR4 ...... **55** D1
Green La. Standish WN6 ...... **28** D1
Green La. Storth LA7 ...... **237** E5
Green La. Woodsfold PR4 ...... **134** E6
Green La E. PR3 ...... **199** C2
Green La W. Freckleton PR4 ...... **92** B5
Green La W. Garstang PR3 ...... **199** B1
Green Link. L31 ...... **5** B2
Green Meadow. BB8 ...... **170** B2
Green Meadow La. FY6 ...... **174** C1
Green Moor La. PR3 ...... **140** B7
Green Mount. BB6 ...... **143** D8
Green Nook La. PR3 ...... **138** F6
Green Oak Pl. FY5 ...... **151** A8
Green Park Dr. L31 ...... **5** B1
Green Park Prim Sch. L31 ...... 5 B2
Green Pk. BB7 ...... **143** C5
Green Pl. PR5 ...... **77** A6
Green Rd. BB8 ...... **169** D4
Green Row. BB3 ...... **80** B6
Green Side. LA6 ...... **238** C1
Green Sq. LA6 ...... **238** C1
Green St. Adlington PR6 ...... **30** B8
Green St. Barnoldswick BB8 ...... **200** B2
Green St. Burnley BB10 ...... **147** B1
Green St. Chorley PR7 ...... **42** A5
Green St. Darwen BB3 ...... **81** A1
Green St. Edenfield BL0 ...... **67** E3
Green St. Great Harwood BB6 ...... **123** B5
Green St. Lancaster LA1 ...... **214** A1
Green St. Lytham St Anne's FY8 ...... **90** A3
Green St. Morecambe LA4 ...... **212** E6
Green St. Oswaldtwistle BB5 ...... **102** C2
Green St. Padiham BB12 ...... **125** C7
Green St. Rawtenstall BB4 ...... **85** A3
Green St. 16 BB8 ...... **81** A1
Green The. Adlington PR6 ...... **42** F2
Green The. Bispham Green L40 ...... **26** B8
Green The. Churchtown PR3 ...... **178** A2
Green The. 5 Darwen BB3 ...... **81** A1
Green The. Eccleston PR7 ...... **40** C6
Green The. Fulwood PR1 & PR2 ...... **117** F2
Green The. Hesketh Bank PR4 ...... **72** E3
Green The. Nelson BB9 ...... **169** B2
Green The. Parbold WN8 ...... **26** D2
Green The. Ramsbottom BL8 ...... **48** F1
Green The. Silverdale LA5 ...... **218** D2
Green The. Weeton PR4 ...... **131** F2
Green Way. FY4 ...... **109** F7
Green Wlk. Ainsdale PR8 ...... **20** D5
Green Wlk. Earby BB8 ...... **201** A1
Green's La.
  Downholland Cross L31 & L39 ...... **14** C1
Green's La. Stalmine FY6 ...... **174** F7
Greenacre. Blackburn BB3 ...... **80** F6
Greenacre. Westhead L40 ...... **16** E4
Greenacre Cl. BL0 ...... **49** E7
Greenacre Ct. LA1 & LA2 ...... **211** B3
Greenacre Pk. LA5 ...... **215** E2
Greenacre Rd. LA2 & LA5 ...... **215** E2
Greenacre St. BB7 ...... **164** E7
Greenacres. Edgworth BL7 ...... **47** E6
Greenacres. Fulwood PR2 ...... **116** B7
Greenacres. Read BB12 ...... **144** D2
Greenacres Ave. PR4 ...... **113** A4
Greenacres Dr. PR3 ...... **178** D6
Greenacres The. PR4 ...... **94** D2
Greenbank. Broadley OL12 ...... **51** C5
Greenbank. Poulton-le-F FY6 ...... **151** E3
Greenbank Ave. Maghull L31 ...... **5** C3
Greenbank Ave. Orrell WN5 ...... **10** D3
Greenbank Ave. Preston PR1 ...... **116** E3
Greenbank Ave. Storth LA7 ...... **237** E4
Greenbank Dr. Fence BB12 ...... **146** E8
Greenbank Dr. Southport PR8 ...... **33** E2
Greenbank High Sch. PR8 ...... 33 E1
Greenbank Pk. BB4 ...... **85** B2
Greenbank Pl. PR1 ...... **116** E1
Greenbank Rd. Blackburn BB1 ... **101** B6
Greenbank Rd. Penwortham PR1 **95** E4
Greenbank Rd. Rochdale OL12 ... **51** F2
Greenbank Sch. OL12 ...... 51 F1
Greenbank St. Preston PR1 ...... **116** D2
Greenbank St. Preston PR1 ...... **116** E1
Greenbank St. Rawtenstall BB4 ... **85** B2
Greenbank Terr. BB3 ...... **80** F6
Greenbanks. FY2 ...... **150** F3
Greenbarn Way. BL6 ...... **30** D1
Greenber La. LA6 ...... **238** D5
Greenberfield La. BB8 ...... **200** C4
Greenbrook Cl. BB12 ...... **125** F6
Greenbrook Rd. BB12 ...... **125** F6
Greenbrook St. 6 BL9 ...... **32** A4
Greencliffe La. BB10 ...... **128** A1
Greencroft. PR1 ...... **95** D3
Greendale Ave. BB4 ...... **85** E2
Greendale Cl. Fleetwood FY7 ... **193** C2
Greendale Cl. Over Town BB10 . **107** A7
Greendale Dr. LA5 ...... **217** D3
Greendale Mews. PR2 ...... **115** E2
Greenfield. PR4 ...... **72** D4
Greenfield Ave. Chatburn BB7 . **187** D5
Greenfield Ave. Clitheroe BB7 .. **164** C8
Greenfield Cl. Parbold WN8 ...... **26** B2
Greenfield Cl. Fleetwood FY7 ... **193** F2
Greenfield Cl. Southport PR9 .... **53** A3
Greenfield Ct. 2 LA1 ...... **211** A7
Greenfield Dr. PR5 ...... **76** A8
Greenfield Gdns. 1 BB4 ...... **84** B2
Greenfield Rd. Adlington PR6 ... **30** A8

Greenfield Rd. Burnley BB10 ...... **127** D4
Greenfield Rd. Chorley PR6 ...... **42** E8
Greenfield Rd. Cleveleys FY5 ...... **150** E8
Greenfield Rd. Colne BB8 ...... **169** D4
Greenfield Rd. Darwen BB3 ...... **64** C6
Greenfield Rd. Fleetwood FY7 ...... **193** F2
Greenfield Rd. Nelson BB8 ...... **169** A4
Greenfield St. Haslingden BB4 ...... **84** B3
Greenfield St. 12
  Lancaster LA1 ...... **211** A8
Greenfield St. Rawtenstall BB4 ... **85** A3
Greenfield Terr.
  Cornholme OL14 ...... **108** A1
Greenfield Terr.
  Oswaldtwistle BB5 ...... **102** A1
Greenfield View. BB3 ...... **81** A7
Greenfield Way. PR2 ...... **116** B5
Greenfields. LA2 ...... **231** C3
Greenfields Cres. PR4 ...... **112** E6
Greenfinch Ct. FY3 ...... **130** B6
Greenfold Dr. BB4 ...... **105** A2
Greenfoot La. LA2 ...... **233** B8
Greenford Cl. WN5 ...... **10** D6
Greenford Rd. PR8 ...... **20** C4
Greengate Cl. BB12 ...... **126** D7
Greengate La. LA5 ...... **216** C8
Greenhalgh La. Adlington PR6 ... **30** B8
Greenhalgh La.
  Greenhalgh PR4 ...... **132** D4
Greenhall Cl. PR3 ...... **178** D6
Greenhaven. WN8 ...... **10** B7
Greenhead Ave. BB1 ...... **101** B7
Greenhead La. BB12 ...... **146** D5
Greenhey Pl. WN8 ...... **8** F8
Greenheys Ave. FY6 ...... **151** B4
Greenheys Cres. BL8 ...... **48** F1
Greenhill. BB6 ...... **123** B5
Greenhill Ave. PR4 ...... **113** A6
Greenhill Pl. FY1 ...... **129** C6
Greenholme Ave. LA4 ...... **212** E3
Greenhurst Cl. BB2 ...... **100** D4
Greenings La. PR9 ...... **36** C3
Greenland Ave. WN6 ...... **28** E1
Greenland La. PR4 ...... **26** D5
Greenlands Cres. PR4 ...... **117** E3
Greenlands Cty Prim Sch.
  PR2 ...... 117 E3
Greenlands High Sch. FY2 ...... 150 E2
Greenlea Cl. WN5 ...... **10** D5
Greenlea Dr. LA4 ...... **212** G5
Greenloon's Dr. L37 ...... **11** C3
Greenloon's Wlk. L37 ...... **11** C2
Greenmead Cl. PR4 ...... **115** E5
Greenmount Ave. Kirkham PR4 **113** A5
Greenmount Ave. 1
  Thornton FY5 ...... 173 A3
Greenmount Cl. BL8 ...... **48** F2
Greenmount Dr. BL8 ...... **48** F2
Greenmount Golf Course. BL8 .. 48 E1
Greenmount Prim Sch. BL8 ...... 48 E2
Greenock Cl. BB11 ...... **126** D4
Greenock Dr. OL10 ...... **32** F1
Greenock St. BB11 ...... **126** D4
Greenpark Cl. BB8 ...... **48** F1
Greens Arms Rd. BL7 ...... **46** E7
Greens La. Bacup OL13 ...... **69** D7
Greens La. Bacup OL13 ...... **87** A3
Greens La. Haslingden BB4 ...... **67** C7
Greens The. OL12 ...... **70** C1
Greenset Cl. LA1 ...... **213** E4
Greenside. Euxton PR7 ...... **59** C3
Greenside. Fulwood PR4 ...... **115** D4
Greenside. Ribchester PR3 ...... **140** E3
Greenside Ave. Blackburn BB2 ... **80** A8
Greenside Ave. Preston PR2 ...... **115** C1
Greenside Cl. BL8 ...... **48** B3
Greenside Dr. BL8 ...... **48** F1
Greenside Gdns. PR5 ...... **58** B7
Greenslate Ave. WN6 ...... **19** E8
Greenslate Ct. WN5 ...... **10** E3
Greenslate Rd. WN5 ...... **10** E3
Greensnook La. OL13 ...... **87** A3
Greensnook Mews. 5 OL13 ...... **87** A3
Greensnook Terr. 1 OL13 ...... **87** A3
Greenstone Ave. BL6 ...... **31** B3
Greensward Cl. WN6 ...... **28** B1
Greensway. PR3 ...... **136** C3
Greenthorn Cres. PR1 ...... **118** A2
Greenthorne Cl. BL7 ...... **47** E7
Greenvale. WN6 ...... **19** F4
Greenville Dr. L31 ...... **5** C1
Greenway. Catterall PR3 ...... **178** D3
Greenway. Eccleston PR7 ...... **40** B7
Greenway. Fulwood PR2 ...... **116** D7
Greenway. Horwich BL6 ...... **31** F3
Greenway. Penwortham PR1 ...... **95** B4
Greenway Ave. WN8 ...... **9** B8
Greenway Cl. WN8 ...... **17** E2
Greenway Mews. BL0 ...... **49** C4
Greenway St. BB3 ...... **80** F3
Greenways. Becconsall PR4 ...... **72** F1
Greenways. Lytham St Anne's FY8 **89** B6
Greenways. Orrell WN5 ...... **10** D3
Greenways. Over Kellet LA6 ...... **231** B8
Greenwich Dr. FY8 ...... **89** D5
Greenwood. PR5 ...... **77** B4
Greenwood Ave. Blackpool FY1 **129** C2
Greenwood Ave. Hest Bank LA5 **215** F2
Greenwood Ave. Horwich BL6 ... **31** D1
Greenwood Cl.
  Lytham St Anne's FY8 ...... **89** E4
Greenwood Cl. Ormskirk L39 ...... **15** C1
Greenwood Dr. LA5 ...... **215** F2
Greenwood Rd. LA4 ...... **216** B1
Greenwood Rd. WN6 ...... **28** E2
Greenwood St.
  Bamber Bridge PR5 ...... **96** E1

Greenwood St. Preston PR1 ...... **96** B7
Greetby Hill. L39 & L40 ...... **16** A6
Gregareth Cl. 5 LA1 ...... **213** C2
Gregory Ave. PR2 ...... **150** C5
Gregory Fold. BB4 ...... **67** A7
Gregory La. L39 ...... **22** B3
Gregory Meadow. PR3 ...... **178** B7
Gregory Pl. PR1 ...... **90** A3
Gregory's Ct. LA1 ...... **211** A4
Gregson Cl. FY4 ...... **109** F7
Gregson Dr. 3 FY7 ...... **193** F2
Gregson La. Blackburn BB2 ...... **100** D5
Gregson La. Gregson Lane PR5 ... **97** E1
Gregson La. Higher Walton PR5 ... **97** C2
Gregson Rd. LA1 ...... **211** A7
Gregson St. Darwen BB3 ...... **64** A8
Gregson St.
  Lytham St Anne's FY8 ...... **90** A3
Gregson Way. PR2 ...... **117** B5
Gregson's Ave. L37 ...... **11** E5
Grenfell Ave. FY3 ...... **129** E7
Grenville Ave.
  Bamber Bridge PR5 ...... **96** D2
Grenville Ave.
  Lytham St Anne's FY8 ...... **109** E1
Gresham House. 4 BB11 ...... **126** E5
Gresham Rd. FY5 ...... **172** D1
Gresham St. BB4 ...... **85** F1
Gresley Cl. LA1 ...... **210** F6
Gresley Pl. FY2 ...... **150** E2
Gressingham Dr. LA2 ...... **211** A4
Gressingham House. 3 LA1 ...... **211** A3
Greta Heath. LA6 ...... **236** C3
Greta Pl. Fleetwood FY7 ...... **193** D3
Greta Pl. Lancaster LA1 ...... **213** E2
Gretdale Ave. FY8 ...... **88** E8
Gretna Cres. FY5 ...... **150** D8
Gretna Rd. BB1 ...... **101** C2
Grey Heights View. PR6 ...... **42** E8
Grey St. Barrowford BB9 ...... **168** D3
Grey St. Burnley BB10 ...... **127** A8
Greyfriars Ave. PR2 ...... **116** D5
Greyfriars Cres. PR2 ...... **116** D5
Greyfriars Dr. PR1 ...... **95** C5
Greyfriars Rd. PR8 ...... **20** B6
Greyhound Bridge Rd. LA1 ...... **213** F1
Greymont Rd. BL9 ...... **32** A6
Greystock Ave. PR2 ...... **116** E6
Greystock Cl. PR5 ...... **77** B8
Greystoke Ave. BB2 ...... **79** E8
Greystoke Pl. FY4 ...... **109** B5
Greystokes. L39 ...... **15** D2
Greystone Ct. FY4 ...... **109** B5
Greystone Dr. BB12 ...... **146** E8
Greystonegill La. LA2 ...... **233** F7
Greystones. PR5 ...... **75** B1
Greythwaite Ct. LA1 ...... **210** D6
Greywood Ave. BL9 ...... **32** B2
Griffin Cl. Accrington BB5 ...... **124** F1
Griffin Cl. Burnley BB11 ...... **126** B5
Griffin Cl. Bury BL9 ...... **32** A4
Griffin Ct. BB2 ...... **100** C2
Griffin Park Prim Sch. BB2 .. 100 B3
Griffin Rd. BB2 ...... **100** B3
Griffiths Dr. PR9 ...... **34** F8
Griffon House. PR9 ...... **52** F2
Grime Row. BB5 ...... **124** F2
Grime St. Chorley PR7 ...... **42** D6
Grime St. Darwen BB3 ...... **80** F2
Grime St. 7 Ramsbottom BL0 ... **49** A4
Grimeford La. BL6 & PR6 ...... **30** C5
Grimeshaw La. LA2 ...... **214** D3
Grimrod Pl. WN8 ...... **9** A7
Grimsargh St. PR1 ...... **117** D1
Grimsargh St Michaels CE Sch.
  PR2 ...... 138 C1
Grimshaw Green La. WN8 ...... **26** C6
Grimshaw La. L39 ...... **15** E7
Grimshaw Pk. BB2 ...... **100** F3
Grimshaw Rd. WN8 ...... **9** D8
Grimshaw St. Accrington BB5 ... **103** A5
Grimshaw St. 6
  Barrowford BB9 ...... **168** D4
Grimshaw St. Burnley BB10 ...... **147** B1
Grimshaw St. 5 Church BB5 ... **102** E6
Grimshaw St. 2
  Clayton-le-M BB5 ...... **123** F2
Grimshaw St. Darwen BB3 ...... **64** B7
Grimshaw St.
  Great Harwood BB6 ...... **123** C5
Grimshaw St. Preston PR1 ...... **96** A7
Grindlestone Ct. PR3 ...... **137** E6
Grindlestone Hirst. BB8 ...... **169** C3
Grindleton Brow. BB7 ...... **187** B7
Grindleton CE Prim Sch. BB7 187 C8
Grindleton Cl. FY3 ...... **130** B8
Grindleton Gr. BB10 ...... **127** D5
Grindleton Hospl Alms Houses.
  BB7 ...... 187 C8
Grindleton Rd. Blackburn BB2 . **100** D6
Grindleton Rd. Grindleton BB7 . **187** A6
Gringley Rd. LA4 ...... **212** F3
Grinstead Cl. PR8 ...... **33** F1
Grisedale Ave. BB1 ...... **101** C2
Grisedale Cl. LA1 ...... **11** E3
Grisedale Dr. BB12 ...... **126** E8
Grisedale Pl. PR7 ...... **42** B5
Grizedale Ave. Garstang PR3 ... **178** B7
Grizedale Ave. Poulton-le-F FY6 **151** C3
Grizedale Ave. Clayton-le-M BB5 . **123** C2
Grizedale Cl. Fulwood PR2 ...... **117** F2
Grizedale Cres.
  PR1 & PR2 & PR5 ...... **118** A2
Grizedale Pl. Fulwood PR2 ...... **117** F2
Grizedale Pl. Morecambe LA3 ... **212** B1
Grizedale Rd. Blackpool FY4 ... **130** C1

Grizedale Rd. Lancaster LA1 ...... **214** B1
Grosvenor Cl. PR8 ...... **33** E3
Grosvenor Ct. Carnforth LA5 ...... **217** C1
Grosvenor Ct. Cleveleys FY5 ...... **172** C2
Grosvenor Ct.
  Lytham St Anne's FY8 ...... **89** A8
Grosvenor Gdns. PR8 ...... **33** F3
Grosvenor Lodge. BB1 ...... **121** F6
Grosvenor Pl. Carnforth LA5 ...... **217** C1
Grosvenor Pl.
  Preston PR1 & PR2 ...... **116** B2
Grosvenor Pl. Southport PR8 ...... **33** F3
Grosvenor Rd. Carnforth LA5 ...... **217** D1
Grosvenor Rd. Chorley PR7 ...... **42** B6
Grosvenor Rd. Morecambe LA3 **212** A3
Grosvenor Rd. Southport PR8 ...... **33** E4
Grosvenor St. Blackpool FY1 ...... **129** C5
Grosvenor St. Burnley BB12 ...... **126** F7
Grosvenor St. Colne BB8 ...... **169** F5
Grosvenor St.
  Lytham St Anne's FY8 ...... **90** C3
Grosvenor St. Preston PR1 ...... **96** B7
Grosvenor Way. 4
  Blackburn BB1 ...... **100** C5
Grosvenor Way. Horwich BL6 ...... **31** C3
Grouse St. OL12 ...... **51** F1
Grove Ave. Adlington PR6 ...... **30** A7
Grove Ave. Longton PR4 ...... **73** F8
Grove Cres. PR6 ...... **30** A7
Grove Ct. BB5 ...... **102** C3
Grove La. BB12 ...... **145** E1
Grove Mead. L31 ...... **5** F1
Grove Mill Development Ctr.
  PR7 ...... 40 C5
Grove Pk. Ormskirk L39 ...... **15** F7
Grove Pk. Southport PR9 ...... **34** F8
Grove Rd. Preston PR1 ...... **96** C6
Grove Rd. Up Holland WN8 ...... **10** C8
Grove St. Accrington BB5 ...... **103** A6
Grove St. Bacup OL13 ...... **87** A3
Grove St. 12 Bamber Bridge PR5 . **76** F8
Grove St. Barrowford BB9 ...... **168** D3
Grove St. Blackburn BB2 ...... **100** E2
Grove St. 3 Burnley BB11 ...... **126** D5
Grove St. Bury BL9 ...... **32** C3
Grove St. Earby BB8 ...... **201** B2
Grove St. Leyland PR5 ...... **58** D8
Grove St. Lytham St Anne's FY8 ... **88** F7
Grove St. Morecambe LA4 ...... **212** C4
Grove St. Nelson BB9 ...... **147** E8
Grove St. Oswaldtwistle BB5 ...... **102** D3
Grove St. Southport PR8 ...... **34** A4
Grove Terr. PR8 ...... **34** A5
Grove The. Appley Bridge WN6 ... **27** C2
Grove The. Bilsborrow PR3 ...... **157** A5
Grove The. Burnley BB12 ...... **126** B6
Grove The. Carnforth LA5 ...... **217** B1
Grove The. Chorley PR6 & PR7 ... **60** C2
Grove The. Cleveleys FY5 ...... **172** E3
Grove The. Clitheroe BB7 ...... **186** F1
Grove The. Lancaster LA1 ...... **211** A7
Grove The. Ormskirk L39 ...... **6** C7
Grove The. Penwortham PR1 ...... **95** B4
Grove The. Preston PR1 ...... **116** B1
Grove The. Rufford L40 ...... **38** A3
Grove The. Whalley BB7 ...... **143** C5
Grovewood. PR8 ...... **33** E5
Grovewood Dr. WN6 ...... **19** E8
Grundy Cl. PR8 ...... **34** E5
Grundy Homes. PR8 ...... **34** E5
Grundy Mews. FY4 ...... **109** C2
Grundy St. 7 PR5 ...... **76** B2
Grundy's La. PR6 & PR7 ...... **42** D1
Guard Hill La. LA7 ...... **237** E4
Gubberford La. PR3 ...... **199** D4
Guide. BB12 ...... **146** A7
Guide Rd. PR4 ...... **72** E6
Guide Sq. BB1 ...... **81** B8
Guild Hall Arc. 5 PR1 ...... **96** A7
Guild Row. 7 PR1 ...... **96** A7
Guild Way. PR1 ...... **95** D7
Guildford Ave. Blackpool FY2 ... **150** D6
Guildford Ave.
  Great Knowley PR6 ...... **60** E4
Guildford Rd. 30 Preston PR1 ... **96** A7
Guildford Rd. Southport PR8 ...... **34** B2
Guildford Way. FY6 ...... **151** C6
Guildhall St. PR1 ...... **95** F7
Guilford St. BB9 ...... **147** B5
Guinea Hall La. PR9 ...... **54** A5
Gulf La. LA2 & PR3 ...... **197** D7
Gummers Howe Wlk. LA5 ...... **216** E8
Gunsmith Pl. 8 BB11 ...... **127** A6
Gurney St. BB2 ...... **100** B3
Gutter La. BL0 ...... **49** B7
Guy St. BB12 ...... **145** C1
Guysyke. BB8 ...... **169** C4
Gynn Ave. FY1 ...... **129** B8
Gynn Sq. FY1 ...... **129** B8

Habergham Dr. BB12 ...... **125** F8
Habergham High Sch. BB12 .. 126 A7
Habergham High Sch &
  Sixth Form Ctr. BB12 ...... 125 F7
Habergham St. 16 BB12 ...... **145** C1
Hackensall Rd. FY6 ...... **194** E5
Hacking Cl. BB6 ...... **142** C1
Hacking Dr. BB9 ...... **138** F5
Hacking St. Bury BL9 ...... **32** A2
Hacking St. Darwen BB3 ...... **80** F1
Hacking St. 3 Nelson BB9 ...... **168** F2
Hacklands Ave. PR2 ...... **115** C1
Haddon Pl. PR2 ...... **116** D3
Haddon Rd. FY2 ...... **150** C5
Hadleigh Rd. FY6 ...... **151** C6
Hadstock Ave. L37 ...... **11** D1
Hagg La. PR3 ...... **154** C8

Hagg St. BB8 ... 169 C4
Haig Ave. Lancaster LA1 ... 210 D8
Haig Ave. Leyland PR5 ... 75 F1
Haig Ave. Preston PR1 ... 116 D2
Haig Ave. Southport PR8 ... 34 E5
Haig Ave. Tarleton PR4 ... 56 A7
Haig Rd. FY1 ... 129 B1
Haigh Cl. PR7 ... 42 A7
Haigh Cres. Chorley PR7 ... 42 B7
Haigh Cres. Maghull L31 ... 5 C4
Haigh Ct. PR8 ... 34 F6
Haigh Hall Cl. BL0 ... 49 B4
Haighton Ct. PR2 ... 117 A7
Haighton Dr. PR2 ... 117 E6
Haighton Green La. PR2 ... 137 E2
Hail St. BL0 ... 49 A4
Hala Cres. LA1 ... 211 A3
Hala Gr. LA1 ... 211 A3
Hala Hill. LA1 & LA2 ... 211 B3
Hala Rd. LA1 ... 211 A3
Hala Sq. LA1 ... 211 A3
Haldane Rd. BB3 ... 80 E4
Haldane St. BB10 ... 147 B2
Halden Rd. LA3 ... 212 B3
Hale Carr Gr. LA3 ... 212 B1
Hale Carr La. LA3 ... 212 B1
Hale St. BB11 ... 127 A4
Hales Rushes Rd. PR3 ... 175 C4
Half Acre. PR5 ... 76 A8
Half Acre La. BL6 ... 30 C2
Halford Pl. FY5 ... 150 E7
Halfpenny La. Andertons Mill PR7 40 B3
Halfpenny La. Longridge PR3 ... 138 F8
Halifax Rd. Ainsdale PR8 ... 20 C5
Halifax Rd. Brierfield BB9 ... 147 C5
Halifax Rd. Lane Bottom BB10 .. 148 D3
Halifax Rd. Nelson BB10 & BB9 .. 147 E5
Halifax Rd. Widdop BB10 ... 149 B1
Halifax St. FY3 ... 129 F3
Hall Ave. FY4 ... 129 C1
Hall Brow Cl. L39 & L40 ... 16 B4
Hall Carr La. PR4 ... 73 D6
Hall Carr Mill Cotts. BB4 ... 85 B2
Hall Carr Rd. BB4 ... 85 A1
Hall Cl. Caton LA2 ... 231 B3
Hall Cl. Rawtenstall BB4 ... 85 A6
Hall Coppice The. BL7 ... 46 E1
Hall Croft. PR4 ... 94 D2
Hall Dr. Caton LA2 ... 231 B3
Hall Dr. Middleton LA3 ... 209 A2
Hall Dr. Morecambe LA4 ... 213 A4
Hall Fold. OL12 ... 51 C8
Hall Garth Gdns. LA6 ... 234 B1
Hall Gate. PR7 ... 60 A2
Hall Gate La. FY6 ... 174 C8
Hall Gdns. OL12 ... 51 C2
Hall Gn. WN8 ... 10 B7
Hall Gr. LA3 ... 209 A2
Hall Green Cl. WN8 ... 10 B7
Hall Green La. PR7 ... 40 A3
Hall Hill. BB7 ... 222 D1
Hall Hill St. 4 BB12 ... 145 C1
Hall La. Appley Bridge WN6 ... 27 D2
Hall La. Bickerstaffe L39 ... 7 E4
Hall La.
Bispham Green L40 & WN8 ... 26 A6
Hall La. Bracewell BD23 ... 225 F3
Hall La. Great Eccleston PR3 ... 154 C4
Hall La. Ince Blundell L38 ... 3 F3
Hall La. Kirkby L33 & L39 ... 1 A8
Hall La. Lathom L40 ... 17 A6
Hall La. Leyland PR5 ... 75 F2
Hall La. Longton PR4 ... 73 E7
Hall La. Maghull L31 ... 5 B7
Hall La. Mawdesley L40 ... 39 D3
Hall La. Orrell WN3 & WN5 ... 10 F4
Hall La. Rivington BL6 ... 44 A2
Hall La. St Michael's on W PR3 ... 155 E6
Hall Meadows. BB8 ... 170 C3
Hall Park Ave. BB10 ... 127 F4
Hall Park Ctr. FY8 ... 89 F4
Hall Park Dr. FY8 ... 89 E6
Hall Park Prim Sch. FY8 ... 89 F3
Hall Pk. LA1 ... 210 F4
Hall Rd. Bescar L40 ... 23 B6
Hall Rd. Fulwood PR2 ... 116 E5
Hall Rd. Penwortham PR1 ... 95 E3
Hall Rd. Trawden BB8 ... 170 B3
Hall St. Bacup OL13 ... 86 F3
Hall St. Blackburn BB2 ... 100 E2
Hall St. Burnley BB11 ... 127 A6
Hall St. Clitheroe BB7 ... 164 E7
Hall St. Colne BB8 ... 169 D4
Hall St. Haslingden BB4 ... 84 B2
Hall St. Morecambe LA4 ... 212 E6
Hall St. Preston PR1 ... 116 C1
Hall St. Ramsbottom BL0 ... 49 C2
Hall St. 12 Rawtenstall BB4 ... 85 A3
Hall St. Southport PR9 ... 34 C7
Hall St. Whitworth OL12 ... 51 B8
Hall St. Whitworth OL12 ... 51 C8
Hall St. Worsthorne BB10 ... 128 A5
Hallam Cres. BB9 ... 148 A8
Hallam La. LA3 ... 209 A2
Hallam Rd. BB9 ... 148 A8
Hallam St. BB5 ... 124 A1
Hallbridge Gdns. WN8 ... 10 B8
Hallcroft. WN8 ... 18 C2
Halley Rd. BB3 ... 80 E3
Hallfield Rd. BB6 ... 123 D6
Hallgate Hill. BB7 ... 223 B4
Halliwell Cl. 6 PR6 ... 42 C7
Halliwell La. PR6 ... 60 C4
Halliwell Pl. 7 PR6 ... 42 C7
Halliwell St. Accrington BB5 ... 103 E2
Halliwell St. Chorley PR6 & PR7 .. 42 C7
Hallmoor Cl. L39 ... 15 E2
Hallows Cl. PR3 ... 155 C6
Hallows Farm Ave. OL12 ... 51 D2
Hallows St. BB10 ... 147 A2
Hallsall Dr. LA4 ... 213 B6
Hallsalls Sq. PR3 ... 154 B5
Hallwell St. BB10 ... 127 A8
Hallwood Cl. BB10 ... 147 B4
Hallwood Rd. PR7 ... 42 A5
Halmot Ct. 2 BB4 ... 85 E1
Halmote Ave. BB12 ... 145 F5
Halsall Ct. L39 ... 15 D6
Halsall Hall Dr. L39 ... 22 B1
Halsall La. Formby L37 ... 11 F3
Halsall La. Halsall L39 ... 14 D6
Halsall La. Ormskirk L39 ... 15 D6
Halsall Rd. Halsall L39 ... 22 C2
Halsall Rd. Southport PR8 ... 21 A8
Halsbury St. PR1 ... 96 B6
Halstead Cl. BB9 ... 168 D4
Halstead La. BB9 ... 168 D4
Halstead Rd. PR2 ... 117 E5
Halstead St. Burnley BB11 ... 126 F5
Halstead St. Bury BL9 ... 32 A4
Halstead St. Worsthorne BB10 .. 128 A6
Halstead Wlk. BL9 ... 32 A5
Halton Ave. Clayton-le-W PR5 ... 76 D1
Halton Ave. Cleveleys FY5 ... 172 E4
Halton Chase. L40 ... 16 E4
Halton Ct. LA4 ... 212 E3
Halton Gdns. Blackpool FY4 ... 109 F8
Halton Gdns. Cleveleys FY5 ... 172 F4
Halton Pl. Fulwood PR2 ... 117 F4
Halton Pl. Longridge PR3 ... 139 B8
Halton Rd. Lancaster LA1 ... 214 A4
Halton Rd. Maghull L31 ... 5 D3
Halton Rd. Nether Kellet LA6 ... 216 E5
Halton St. PR4 ... 131 E6
Hambledon Dr. PR1 ... 95 E2
Hambledon St. BB12 ... 125 D8
Hambledon Terr. Higham BB12 145 F6
Hambledon Terr.
Padiham BB12 ... 125 F7
Hambledon View.
Padiham BB12 ... 125 F7
Hambledon View. Read BB12 . 144 D1
Hambleton Cl. PR4 ... 93 F1
Hambleton Prim Sch. FY6 ... 174 D2
Hameldon App. BB11 ... 126 D5
Hameldon Ave. BB5 ... 103 E2
Hameldon Cl. BB11 ... 125 C2
Hameldon Rd. Hapton BB11 ... 125 D2
Hameldon Rd. Rawtenstall BB4 105 A2
Hameldon View. BB6 ... 123 D5
Hamer Ave. Blackburn BB1 ... 101 D5
Hamer Ave. Rawtenstall BB4 ... 105 A1
Hamer Rd. PR2 ... 116 D3
Hamer St. Darwen BB3 ... 64 A8
Hamer St. Ramsbottom BL0 ... 49 B2
Hamer St. Rawtenstall BB4 ... 85 A2
Hamerswood Dr. PR3 ... 178 D2
Hamilton Dr. LA1 ... 213 C3
Hamilton Gr. PR2 ... 117 E3
Hamilton House. 6 BB11 ... 126 E5
Hamilton Rd. Barrowford BB9 ... 168 C1
Hamilton Rd. Chorley PR7 ... 42 C7
Hamilton Rd. Fulwood PR2 ... 117 D4
Hamilton Rd.
Morecambe LA2 & LA4 ... 213 C6
Hamilton Rd. Nelson BB8 ... 169 A2
Hamilton St. BB2 ... 100 D2
Hamilton Way. OL10 ... 32 E1
Hamlet Cl. BB2 ... 100 C3
Hamlet Rd. FY7 ... 193 F4
Hamlet The. FY8 ... 109 F2
Hammer Terr. BL0 ... 49 C3
Hammerton Gn. 18 OL13 ... 86 F3
Hammerton Hall Cl. LA1 ... 213 E4
Hammerton Hall La. LA1 ... 213 E4
Hammerton Pl. FY3 ... 130 A8
Hammerton St. Bacup OL13 ... 86 F4
Hammerton St. Burnley BB11 ... 126 F5
Hammond Ave. OL13 ... 69 D8
Hammond Ct. PR1 ... 116 E1
Hammond Dr. BB12 ... 144 C2
Hammond Rd. L33 ... 1 C3
Hammond St. Nelson BB9 ... 147 F7
Hammond St. Preston PR1 ... 116 E1
Hammond St. Preston PR1 ... 116 E2
Hammond St. Preston PR1 ... 116 F2
Hammond's Row. 17 PR1 ... 96 A8
Hampden Ave. BB3 ... 64 B7
Hampden Rd. PR5 ... 76 A2
Hampden St. 7 Burnley BB11 .. 127 B4
Hampden St. Hapton BB12 ... 125 C4
Hampsfell Dr. LA4 ... 212 E3
Hampshire Cl. BB1 ... 122 A7
Hampshire Pl. FY4 ... 109 F6
Hampshire Rd.
Bamber Bridge PR5 ... 96 D3
Hampshire Rd. Rishton BB1 ... 123 A1
Hampson Ave. PR6 ... 76 D1
Hampson Cotts. LA2 ... 207 B1
Hampson Gr. FY6 ... 195 A4
Hampson La. LA2 ... 207 C1
Hampson St. BL6 ... 31 B4
Hampstead Cl. FY8 ... 89 E6
Hampstead Mews. FY1 ... 129 C7
Hampstead Rd.
Fulwood PR1 & PR2 ... 117 D2
Hampstead Rd. Standish WN6 ... 28 D1
Hampton Cl. PR7 ... 42 B8
Hampton Ct. FY8 ... 89 C8
Hampton Pl. FY5 ... 172 E3
Hampton Rd. Blackpool FY4 ... 109 C8
Hampton Rd. Formby L37 ... 11 E1
Hampton Rd. Morecambe LA3 ... 212 B3
Hampton Rd. Southport PR8 ... 34 C5
Hampton St. PR1 ... 116 C2
Hanbury St. PR1 ... 116 C1
Hancock St. BB2 ... 100 C3
Hand La. PR7 ... 39 F5
Handbridge The. PR2 ... 116 E5
Handley Rd. FY1 ... 129 C6
Handsworth Ct. FY1 ... 129 C7
Handsworth Rd. FY1 ... 129 C7
Handsworth Wlk. PR8 ... 34 F3
Hane Row. BB11 ... 106 D7
Hanging Green La. LA2 ... 215 E1
Hanley Cl. FY6 ... 174 C7
Hannah St. Accrington BB5 ... 103 B5
Hannah St. 14 Bacup OL13 ... 87 A3
Hannah St. Darwen BB3 ... 64 B8
Hanover Cres. FY2 ... 150 C5
Hanover St. Colne BB8 ... 169 D5
Hanover St. Morecambe LA4 ... 212 E5
Hanover St. 4 Preston PR1 ... 116 F1
Hanson St. Great Harwood BB6 . 123 C4
Hanson St. Rishton BB1 ... 123 C1
Hants La. L39 ... 15 E6
Happy Mount Ct. LA4 ... 213 B7
Happy Mount Dr. LA2 & LA4 ... 213 B7
Hapton CE Meth Prim Sch.
BB11 ... 125 C4
Hapton Rd. BB12 ... 125 C7
Hapton St. Padiham BB12 ... 125 D8
Hapton St. Thornton FY5 ... 173 B4
Hapton Sta. BB11 ... 125 C4
Hapton Way. BB4 ... 105 A2
Harbour Ave. PR4 ... 91 E6
Harbour Cl. FY7 ... 193 F2
Harbour La. Brinscall PR6 ... 61 D7
Harbour La. Edgworth BL7 ... 47 D5
Harbour La. Warton PR4 ... 91 E6
Harbury Ave. PR8 ... 20 A4
Harcles Dr. BL0 ... 49 B2
Harcourt Mews. 10 BL6 ... 31 B4
Harcourt Rd. Accrington BB5 ... 103 D3
Harcourt Rd. Blackburn BB2 ... 100 C6
Harcourt Rd. Blackpool FY4 ... 109 D8
Harcourt Rd. Lancaster LA1 ... 213 E3
Harcourt St. 15 Bacup OL13 ... 86 F3
Harcourt St. 1 Burnley BB11 .. 126 D5
Harcourt St. Preston PR1 ... 116 E1
Hard Knott Rise. LA5 ... 216 E8
Hardacre La.
Lucas Green PR6 & PR7 ... 60 C5
Hardacre La. Rimington BB7 ... 225 B2
Hardacre St. L39 ... 15 F6
Hardcastle Rd. PR2 ... 116 E3
Harden Rd. BB8 ... 192 A6
Hardhorn Ct. FY6 ... 151 D3
Hardhorn Rd. FY6 ... 151 D2
Hardhorn Way. FY6 ... 151 D2
Harding Rd. L40 ... 24 D4
Harding St. PR6 ... 30 B8
Hardlands Ave. LA4 ... 213 B4
Hardman Ave. BB4 ... 85 A1
Hardman Cl. Blackburn BB1 ... 101 F4
Hardman Cl. Newchurch BB4 ... 68 F7
Hardman Dr. BB4 ... 68 F7
Hardman St. FY1 ... 129 C6
Hardman Terr. OL13 ... 69 D8
Hardman Way. 23 BB3 ... 81 A1
Hardsough La. BL0 ... 67 D5
Hardwicke St. 4 PR1 ... 96 A8
Hardy Ave. Barnoldswick BB8 ... 200 A3
Hardy Ave. Brierfield BB9 ... 147 B6
Hardy Ct. 10 BB9 ... 147 E8
Hardy Dr. PR7 ... 42 A7
Hardy St. Blackburn BB1 ... 121 F1
Hardy St. Brierfield BB9 ... 147 B6
Hare Clough Cl. BB2 ... 100 F3
Hare Runs House. LA1 ... 213 F3
Harebell Cl. Blackburn BB2 ... 79 D8
Harebell Cl. Formby L37 ... 11 F1
Harebell Cl. Lower Fold OL12 ... 51 D3
Hareden Brook Cl. BB1 ... 100 F3
Hareden Cl. PR5 ... 76 F8
Hareden Rd. PR1 ... 117 F2
Harefield Rise. BB12 ... 126 D7
Hareholme La. BB4 ... 85 D2
Hares La. PR8 ... 35 D1
Harestone Ave. PR7 ... 42 A5
Harewood Ave. Ainsdale PR8 ... 20 C6
Harewood Ave. Blackpool FY3 ... 151 A1
Harewood Ave. Lancaster LA1 .. 211 A3
Harewood Ave. Morecambe LA3 212 B2
Harewood Ave.
Simonstone BB12 ... 144 E2
Harewood Cl. FY6 ... 151 C5
Harewood Rd. PR1 ... 117 C2
Hargate Ave. OL12 ... 51 A2
Hargate Cl. BL9 ... 49 C2
Hargate Rd. FY5 ... 173 C2
Hargher Clough Jun Sch.
BB11 ... 126 D5
Hargher St. BB11 ... 126 D5
Hargreaves Ave. PR5 ... 59 B8
Hargreaves Ct. Clitheroe BB7 ... 164 C7
Hargreaves Ct. Fulwood PR2 ... 115 F4
Hargreaves Ct.
Whitewell Bottom BB4 ... 85 F6
Hargreaves Dr. BB4 ... 84 F2
Hargreaves Fold La. BB4 ... 86 A7
Hargreaves La. 2 BB2 ... 100 E3
Hargreaves Rd. BB5 ... 102 C4
Hargreaves St. 8
Accrington BB5 ... 103 C5
Hargreaves St. Brierfield BB10 . 147 F3
Hargreaves St. 10
Burnley BB11 ... 126 F6
Hargreaves St. Colne BB8 ... 169 B4
Hargreaves St. Haslingden BB4 .. 84 B3
Hargreaves St. Hoddlesden BB3 . 81 F1
Hargreaves St. Nelson BB9 ... 147 C7
Hargreaves St. Southport PR8 ... 34 C6
Hargreaves St. Thornton FY5 ... 173 B3
Hargreaves St.
Whitewell Bottom BB4 ... 85 E5
Hargrove Ave. Burnley BB12 ... 126 D7
Hargrove Ave. Padiham BB12 ... 145 C1
Hargrove Rd. BB12 ... 126 D8
Harington Cl. L37 ... 11 D3
Harington Gn. L37 ... 11 D3
Harington Rd. L37 ... 11 D4
Harland St. PR2 ... 116 D3
Harland Way. OL12 ... 51 B2
Harlech Ave. FY1 ... 129 D1
Harlech Cl. BB4 ... 84 B1
Harlech Dr. Leyland PR5 ... 76 C1
Harlech Dr. Oswaldtwistle BB5 .. 102 C4
Harleston Rd. L33 ... 1 A3
Harleston Wlk. 10 L33 ... 1 A3
Harley Cl. LA2 ... 233 C8
Harley Rd. FY3 ... 129 E4
Harley St. BB12 ... 126 C6
Harling Bank. LA6 ... 238 B2
Harling Rd. PR1 ... 117 D1
Harling St. BB12 ... 126 B6
Harold Ave. Blackpool FY4 ... 110 A6
Harold Ave. Burnley BB11 ... 126 C4
Harold St. Burnley BB11 ... 126 D5
Harold St. Colne BB8 ... 169 C4
Harold Terr. PR5 ... 76 A8
Harper St. BB8 ... 200 A3
Harper's La. PR6 ... 60 D1
Harperley. PR7 ... 60 B2
Harpers La. BB12 ... 146 D8
Harridge Ave. OL12 ... 51 C3
Harridge La. L40 ... 23 A1
Harridge St. OL12 ... 51 C3
Harridge The. OL12 ... 51 C3
Harrier Dr. BB1 ... 100 D8
Harriet St. BB11 ... 126 E5
Harrington Ave. FY4 ... 109 B5
Harrington Rd. Chorley PR7 ... 42 B8
Harrington Rd. Morecambe LA3 212 B3
Harrington St. Accrington BB5 .. 124 A1
Harrington St. Preston PR1 ... 116 F1
Harris Ave. FY1 ... 129 D1
Harris Cl. OL10 ... 32 E1
Harris Ct. 2 BB7 ... 164 E8
Harris Ctr. PR2 ... 116 E5
Harris Cty Prim Sch. PR2 ... 116 B7
Harris Rd. WN6 ... 28 B3
Harris St. Fleetwood FY7 ... 194 A4
Harris St. 2 Preston PR1 ... 96 A7
Harrison Ave. FY5 ... 173 B2
Harrison Cres. Blackrod BL6 ... 30 C3
Harrison Cres. Morecambe LA3 212 A1
Harrison Dr. BB8 ... 169 C6
Harrison La. PR4 ... 95 B2
Harrison Rd. Adlington PR7 ... 30 A6
Harrison Rd. Chorley PR7 ... 42 C6
Harrison Rd. Fulwood PR2 ... 116 E6
Harrison St. Bacup OL13 ... 70 A8
Harrison St. Barnoldswick BB8 .. 200 C1
Harrison St. Blackburn BB2 ... 100 D4
Harrison St. Blackpool FY1 ... 129 C3
Harrison St. Brierfield BB10 ... 147 F2
Harrison St. Cornholme OL14 ... 108 B1
Harrison St. Horwich BL6 ... 31 B4
Harrison St. Ramsbottom BL0 ... 49 C7
Harrock La. L40 & WN6 & WN8 ... 26 F6
Harrock Rd. PR6 ... 76 D1
Harrod Dr. PR8 ... 33 E3
Harrogate Cres. BB10 ... 147 D2
Harrogate Rd. FY8 ... 89 C7
Harrogate Way. PR9 ... 53 C6
Harrop Pl. PR2 ... 117 E4
Harrow Ave. Accrington BB5 ... 103 C7
Harrow Ave. Fleetwood FY7 ... 193 F3
Harrow Cl. Orrell WN5 ... 10 F8
Harrow Cl. Padiham BB12 ... 125 E6
Harrow Dr. BB1 ... 101 B3
Harrow Gr. LA4 ... 213 B4
Harrow Pl. Blackpool FY4 ... 109 A5
Harrow Pl. Lytham St Anne's FY8 . 89 E5
Harrow St. BB5 ... 102 E4
Harrow Stiles La. OL13 ... 106 E1
Harrowdale Pk. LA2 ... 214 F7
Harrowside. FY4 ... 109 B6
Harrowside W. FY4 ... 109 A5
Harry St. Barrowford BB9 ... 168 D3
Harry St. Salterforth BB8 ... 191 D7
Harsnips. WN8 ... 18 C2
Hart St. Blackburn BB1 ... 100 F4
Hart St. Burnley BB11 ... 127 A6
Hart St. Southport PR8 & PR9 ... 34 E6
Hart's Houses. BL6 ... 31 D5
Hart's La. WN8 ... 9 F8
Hartford Ave. FY1 ... 129 D2
Hartington Rd. Brinscall PR7 ... 62 A8
Hartington Rd. Darwen BB3 ... 80 E4
Hartington Rd. Preston PR1 ... 95 D7
Hartington St. Brierfield BB9 ... 147 B5
Hartington St. Colne BB8 ... 170 B5
Hartington St. Lancaster LA1 ... 211 B8
Hartington St. Rishton BB1 ... 123 A1
Hartland. WN8 ... 18 C2
Hartland Ave. PR9 ... 53 B5
Hartlands Cl. BB10 ... 147 D3
Hartlet St. BB6 ... 123 D5
Hartley Ave. BB5 ... 103 A3
Hartley Cres. PR8 ... 33 F2
Hartley Homes The. BB8 ... 170 C6
Hartley Rd. PR8 ... 33 F2
Hartley St. 3 Blackburn BB1 ... 100 E6
Hartley St. Burnley BB11 ... 126 C5
Hartley St. Colne BB8 ... 169 D5
Hartley St. Earby BB8 ... 201 B1
Hartley St. 1 Haslingden BB4 ... 84 B3
Hartley St. Horwich BL6 ... 31 B3
Hartley St. Nelson BB9 ... 147 E7
Hartley St. 2 Oswaldtwistle BB5 102 E4
Hartley St. Passmonds OL12 ... 51 B1
Hartleys Terr. BB8 ... 169 E4
Hartmann St. BB5 ... 103 A6
Hartshead. WN8 ... 18 C2
Hartwood Gn. PR6 ... 60 C3
Hartwood Rd. PR9 ... 34 D7
Harvey St. 14 Nelson BB9 ... 168 E1
Harvey St. Oswaldtwistle BB5 ... 102 D4
Harvington Dr. PR8 ... 20 B5
Harwich Rd. FY8 ... 110 A1
Harwin Cl. OL12 ... 51 D3
Harwood Ave. FY8 ... 88 E8
Harwood Cl. FY6 ... 174 C7
Harwood Gate. BB1 ... 101 B6
Harwood La. BB6 ... 123 E6
Harwood New Rd. BB6 ... 123 E6
Harwood Rd. Rishton BB1 ... 123 A2
Harwood Rd. Wilpshire BB1 ... 122 D4
Harwood St. 12 Blackburn BB1 . 101 A7
Harwood St. Blackburn BB1 ... 101 B6
Harwood St. Darwen BB3 ... 80 E2
Harwood's La. BB3 ... 81 E1
Haskoll St. BL6 ... 31 D1
Haslam Dr. L39 ... 15 D7
Haslam St. BL9 ... 32 A4
Haslemere Ave. FY3 ... 129 E3
Haslemere Ind Est. PR5 ... 75 F3
Haslingden Cty High Sch. BB4 67 B8
Haslingden Old Rd. BB4 ... 84 E2
Haslingden Prim Sch. BB4 ... 84 B2
Haslingden Rd.
Blackburn BB1 & BB2 ... 101 B2
Haslingden Rd.
Blackburn BB1 & BB5 ... 101 E3
Haslingden Rd.
Oswaldtwistle BB5 ... 82 D7
Haslingden Rd. Rawtenstall BB4 84 E2
Haslingden St James CE
Prim Sch. BB4 ... 84 B3
Haslow Pl. FY3 ... 129 F7
Hassall Dr. PR4 ... 154 A1
Hassett Cl. PR1 ... 95 E6
Hastings Ave. Blackpool FY2 ... 150 E5
Hastings Ave. Warton PR4 ... 91 E7
Hastings Cl. Blackburn BB1 ... 101 C4
Hastings Cl. Thornton FY5 ... 173 C1
Hastings Pl. FY8 ... 90 A3
Hastings Rd. Kirkham PR4 ... 113 B2
Hastings Rd. Lancaster LA1 ... 210 F5
Hastings Rd. Leyland PR5 ... 76 B2
Hastings Rd. Preston PR1 ... 116 B1
Hastings Rd. Southport PR8 ... 33 E1
Hastings Rd. Thornton FY5 ... 173 C1
Hastings The. LA1 ... 210 F5
Haston Lee Ave. BB1 ... 121 F3
Hasty Brow Rd. LA2 ... 213 D6
Hatfield Ave. Fleetwood FY7 ... 193 F3
Hatfield Ave. Morecambe LA4 ... 213 B6
Hatfield Cl. FY5 ... 173 C2
Hatfield Ct. LA4 ... 213 B6
Hatfield Gdns. FY7 ... 193 E2
Hatfield Mews. 2 FY7 ... 193 F2
Hatfield Rd. Accrington BB5 ... 103 D7
Hatfield Rd. Ainsdale PR8 ... 20 C6
Hatfield Rd. Fulwood PR2 ... 117 E3
Hatfield Wlk. FY7 ... 193 E2
Hathaway. FY4 ... 109 E8
Hathaway Fold. 2 BB12 ... 125 D7
Hathaway Rd. Fleetwood FY7 ... 193 E4
Hathaway Rd. Lancaster LA1 ... 213 E3
Hatlex Dr. LA2 ... 215 E2
Hatlex Hill. LA2 ... 215 E2
Hatlex La. LA2 ... 215 E2
Hattersley St. BB11 ... 126 E6
Hatton St. PR7 ... 29 F6
Haugh Ave. BB12 ... 144 E2
Haunders La. PR4 ... 73 B1
Havelock Cl. BB2 ... 100 D3
Havelock Rd. Bamber Bridge PR5 76 E7
Havelock Rd. Penwortham PR1 ... 95 E5
Havelock St. Blackburn BB2 ... 100 C2
Havelock St. Blackpool FY1 ... 129 B4
Havelock St. Burnley BB12 ... 126 B6
Havelock St. Lancaster LA1 ... 211 A6
Havelock St. Oswaldtwistle BB5 102 D3
Havelock St. 9 Padiham BB12 . 145 C1
Havelock St. Preston PR1 ... 116 D2
Havelock St. Preston PR1 ... 116 E2
Havelock St. Preston PR1 ... 116 F2
Haven Brow. L39 ... 6 C8
Haven Rd. FY8 ... 90 C3
Haven St. BB10 ... 127 C5
Haven Wlk. L31 ... 5 C4
Havenbrook Gr. BL0 ... 49 A3
Haverbreaks Pl. LA1 ... 210 E6
Haverbreaks Rd. LA1 ... 210 E5
Haverholt Cl. BB8 ... 169 C5
Haverholt Rd. BB8 ... 169 C5
Haverthwaite Ave. LA3 ... 208 F7
Havre Pk. BB8 ... 200 C2
Hawarden Ave. LA4 ... 212 F5
Hawarden Rd. 1 PR1 ... 117 E1
Hawarden St. BB9 ... 147 E7
Hawes Dr. BB8 ... 169 F6
Hawes Side La. FY4 ... 109 E8
Hawes Side Prim Sch. FY4 ... 109 E7
Hawes Terr. BB10 ... 147 B2
Hawesside St. PR8 & PR9 ... 34 C7
Haweswater Ave. PR7 ... 42 B6
Haweswater Gr. L31 ... 5 F2
Haweswater Pl. LA4 ... 213 A4
Haweswater Rd. BB5 ... 124 D1
Hawick Gr. OL10 ... 32 E1
Hawk Cl. BL9 ... 32 B4
Hawk St. Burnley BB11 ... 127 A6

Hawk St. Carnforth LA5 .... 217 E2
Hawkeshead Cl. BB2 .... 100 B4
Hawkhurst Ave. PR2 .... 116 D6
Hawkhurst Cres. PR2 .... 116 D6
Hawkhurst Rd. Penwortham PR1 . 95 E5
Hawkhurst Rd. Preston PR1 .... 117 B1
Hawkins Cl. PR1 .... 116 E1
Hawkins St. Blackburn BB2 .... 100 B2
Hawkins St. Preston PR1 .... 116 E1
Hawks Gr. BB4 .... 85 A1
Hawksbury Dr. PR1 .... 95 D2
Hawksclough. WN8 .... 18 D2
Hawkshaw Ave. BB3 .... 80 E3
Hawkshaw Bank Rd. BB1 .... 100 D8
Hawkshaw La. BL8 .... 48 B5
Hawkshaw St. BL6 .... 31 B3
Hawkshead. PR1 .... 95 E3
Hawkshead Ave. PR7 .... 59 D1
Hawkshead Cl. L31 .... 5 E2
Hawkshead Dr. LA4 .... 212 F3
Hawkshead Rd. Fulwood PR2 ... 117 E5
Hawkshead Rd.
Knott End-on-S FY6 .... 194 F6
Hawkshead St. Blackburn BB2 .. 100 B4
Hawkshead St.
Southport PR8 & PR9 .... 34 D7
Hawkshead Terr. FY4 .... 110 D8
Hawksheath Cl. BL7 .... 46 E1
Hawksley St. BL6 .... 31 D2
Hawkstone Cl. Accrington BB5 .. 124 F1
Hawkstone Cl. Thornton FY5 .... 151 D8
Hawkstone Ct. LA4 .... 213 B6
Hawkswood. PR7 .... 40 B6
Hawkswood Gdns. BB9 .... 147 A4
Hawksworth Ave. LA3 .... 212 B2
Hawksworth Cl. L37 .... 12 A6
Hawksworth Dr. L37 .... 12 A6
Hawksworth Gr. LA3 .... 212 A2
Hawksworth Rd. BB5 .... 103 B8
Hawley Gn. OL12 .... 51 D2
Hawley St. Colne BB8 .... 169 C4
Hawley St. Winewall BB8 .... 170 C5
Haworth Ave. Accrington BB5 .. 103 D3
Haworth Ave. Ramsbottom BL0 . 49 A2
Haworth Ave. Rawtenstall BB4 ... 84 F2
Haworth Dr. OL13 .... 69 C8
Haworth St. Accrington BB5 ..... 124 B1
Haworth St. Edgworth BL7 .... 47 D5
Haworth St. Oswaldtwistle BB5 . 102 E4
Haworth St. Rishton BB1 .... 123 B1
Haws Ave. LA5 .... 217 D1
Haws Hill. LA5 .... 217 D1
Hawthorn Ave. Caton LA2 .... 231 C3
Hawthorn Ave. Darwen BB3 .... 81 C2
Hawthorn Ave. Edenfield BL0 ..... 67 D2
Hawthorn Ave. Fleetwood FY7 . 172 E8
Hawthorn Ave. Orrell WN5 .... 10 F6
Hawthorn Ave.
Oswaldtwistle BB5 .... 102 F3
Hawthorn Ave. Ramsbottom BL0 . 49 A2
Hawthorn Bank. BB5 .... 124 A3
Hawthorn Cl. Caton LA2 .... 231 C3
Hawthorn Cl. Kirkham PR4 .... 112 E6
Hawthorn Cl. Langho BB6 .... 122 D8
Hawthorn Cl. Leyland PR5 .... 75 D2
Hawthorn Cl. New Longton PR4 .. 75 A7
Hawthorn Cres. Preston PR2 .... 115 D1
Hawthorn Cres.
Skelmersdale WN8 .... 17 E1
Hawthorn Dr. BB1 .... 102 B8
Hawthorn Rd. Bacup OL13 .... 87 A2
Hawthorn Rd. Blackpool FY1 .... 129 C7
Hawthorn Rd. Bolton-le-S LA5 .. 216 A6
Hawthorn Rd. Fulwood PR2 ...... 117 E2
Hawthorn Rd. Morecambe LA4 . 213 B4
Hawthorne Ave. Brierfield BB10 147 C5
Hawthorne Ave. Garstang PR3 . 178 B8
Hawthorne Ave.
Higher Walton PR5 .... 97 C3
Hawthorne Ave. Horwich BL6 ..... 31 E1
Hawthorne Ave.
Newton-with-S PR4 .... 113 F3
Hawthorne Cl. Barrowford BB9 . 168 B1
Hawthorne Cl.
Clayton Green PR6 .... 77 B3
Hawthorne Cl. Nelson BB9 .... 148 B8
Hawthorne Cres. 12 A2
Hawthorne Dr. BB8 .... 200 C4
Hawthorne Gr. **13**
Barrowford BB9 .... 168 D3
Hawthorne Gr. Carleton FY6 .... 151 B5
Hawthorne Gr. Southport PR9 .... 34 F7
Hawthorne Ind Pk. BB7 .... 187 A1
Hawthorne Lea. FY5 .... 151 C8
Hawthorne Meadows. BB4 .... 105 A1
Hawthorne Pl. BB7 .... 186 E1
Hawthorne Rd. Burnley BB11 ... 126 F4
Hawthorne Rd. Thornton FY5 ... 151 C8
Hawthorne St. BB1 .... 100 F8
Hawthorne Terr. BB8 .... 191 E1
Hawthornes Cty Jun Sch. BB1 100 F8
Hawthorns The. L40 .... 38 B3
Hawthorns The. Eccleston PR7 .. 40 B7
Hawthorns The. Fulwood PR2 .. 116 F6
Hawthorns The. Newburgh WN8 . 26 A1
Hawthorns The.
Newchurch BB4 .... 85 F1
Hawthorns The. Wilpshire BB1 121 F6
Haydock Ave. PR5 .... 59 A8
Haydock Gr. BB3 .... 212 A1
Haydock La. Egerton BL7 .... 47 A1
Haydock La. Egerton BL7 .... 47 A1
Haydock Rd. LA1 .... 211 B3
Haydock Sq. **1** BB6 .... 123 C5
Haydock St. Bamber Bridge PR5 . 96 E2

Haydock St. Blackburn BB1 ...... 121 E1
Haydock St. Burnley BB10 .... 147 C1
Haydocks La. PR4 .... 115 D5
Haydon Ave. PR5 .... 76 A7
Hayfell Ave. LA4 .... 212 F3
Hayfell Cres. LA4 .... 215 D1
Hayfell Gr. LA2 .... 215 D1
Hayfield. BB2 .... 100 A7
Hayfield Ave. Blackpool FY2 .... 150 E2
Hayfield Ave. Gregson Lane PR5 . 97 E1
Hayfield Ave. Poulton-le-F FY6 . 151 E3
Hayfield Cl. Gregson Lane PR5 .. 97 E1
Hayfield Cl. Ramsbottom BL8 ..... 48 F1
Hayfield Rd. L39 .... 15 E7
Hayhurst Cl. BB7 .... 191 E8
Hayhurst Cl. BB7 .... 143 C6
Hayhurst Rd. BB7 .... 143 C6
Hayhurst St. BB7 .... 164 F7
Hayling Pl. PR2 .... 116 A4
Haylot Dr. LA2 .... 214 F7
Haylot Sq. **9** LA1 .... 211 A8
Haymans Gn. L31 .... 5 E1
Haymarket. FY8 .... 89 B6
Haysworth St. PR1 .... 116 F2
Haywood Cl. BB5 .... 103 B8
Haywood Rd. BB5 .... 103 B8
Hazebank Gdns. L37 .... 11 E5
Hazel Ave. Bamber Bridge PR5 .. 97 A1
Hazel Ave. Bury BL9 .... 32 B3
Hazel Ave. Clayton-le-M BB5 ... 123 F2
Hazel Ave. Darwen BB3 .... 81 B2
Hazel Ave. Fleetwood FY7 .... 172 F8
Hazel Ave. Ramsbottom BL0 .... 49 B1
Hazel Cl. Bamber Bridge PR5 ..... 96 F1
Hazel Cl. Blackburn BB2 .... 100 C4
Hazel Cl. Penwortham PR1 .... 95 B3
Hazel Coppice. PR2 & PR4 .... 115 E3
Hazel Dene. BB7 .... 186 E6
Hazel Gr. Bacup OL13 .... 87 B3
Hazel Gr. Bamber Bridge PR5 ..... 97 A1
Hazel Gr. Blackburn BB1 .... 101 F5
Hazel Gr. Blackpool FY3 .... 129 E5
Hazel Gr. Chorley PR6 .... 60 C3
Hazel Gr. Clayton-le-M BB5 ..... 124 A2
Hazel Gr. Fulwood PR2 .... 118 A4
Hazel Gr. Lancaster LA1 .... 210 D8
Hazel Gr. Rawtenstall BB4 .... 84 F2
Hazel Gr. Southport PR8 & PR9 .. 34 E7
Hazel Gr. Tarleton PR4 .... 55 F8
Hazel Hall La. BL0 .... 49 B1
Hazel La. WN8 .... 18 B4
Hazel Mount. BL7 .... 46 E2
Hazel St. Haslingden BB5 .... 84 A8
Hazel St. Ramsbottom BL0 .... 49 A4
Hazeldene Ave. **2** BB4 .... 84 B2
Hazeldene Rd. FY7 .... 193 F2
Hazelhead La. PR3 .... 199 E2
Hazelhurst Cl. BL0 .... 49 B4
Hazelhurst Cty Prim Sch. BL0 .. 49 A4
Hazelhurst Rd. PR1 .... 118 A2
Hazelmere Cty F HQ. PR3 .... 116 D8
Hazelmere Rd. Fulwood PR2 .... 116 B8
Hazelmere Rd. Preston PR1 ...... 116 A1
Hazelmoor. BB1 .... 121 E6
Hazelmount Dr. LA5 .... 217 C3
Hazels The. Coppull PR7 .... 41 E4
Hazels The. Wilpshire BB1 .... 121 E6
Hazelwood. L31 .... 218 C2
Hazelwood Ave. L40 .... 24 A4
Hazelwood Cl. Blackburn BB1 .. 122 A1
Hazelwood Cl. Leyland PR5 .... 75 C1
Hazelwood Dr.
Hesketh Bank PR4 .... 72 E4
Hazelwood Dr. Morecambe LA4 213 B6
Hazelwood Gdns. LA1 .... 211 A2
Hazelwood Rd. BB9 .... 148 A8
Hazlehurst Cl. L37 .... 11 C2
Hazlewood Cl. FY5 .... 173 A2
Head Beck. LA6 .... 238 C2
Head Cl. OL12 .... 51 E4
Head Dyke La. FY6 & PR3 .... 196 C3
Headbolt La. Ainsdale PR8 .... 21 A4
Headbolt La. Kirkby L33 .... 1 A5
Headfort Cl. FY2 .... 150 D2
Headingley Cl. BB5 .... 124 F1
Headlands St. L21 .... 51 E1
Headley Rd. PR5 .... 75 E1
Headroomgate Rd. FY8 .... 88 F8
Heads La. BB8 .... 192 B6
Heald Brow. BB8 .... 200 A4
Heald Cl. OL12 .... 51 C3
Heald Dr. OL12 .... 51 C3
Heald House Rd. PR5 & PR7 .... 59 C7
Heald La. OL13 .... 87 A8
Heald Rd. BB10 & BB12 .... 147 A2
Heald St. Blackpool FY3 .... 129 D6
Heald St. **4** Chorley PR6 .... 42 E8
Healdwood Cl. BB12 .... 146 F3
Healdwood Dr. BB12 .... 146 F3
Healey Ave. OL12 .... 51 D4
Healey Ct. BB11 .... 126 F5
Healey Dell Cotts. OL12 .... 51 B4
Healey Dell Nature Reserve.
OL12 .... 51 A6
Healey Gr. OL12 .... 51 C5
Healey Hall Farm. OL12 .... 51 C4
Healey Hall Mews. OL12 .... 51 C4
Healey La. OL12 .... 51 B3
Healey Mount. BB11 .... 126 F4
Healey Prim Sch. OL12 .... 51 B3
Healey Road Inf Sch. BB11 ...... 126 F4
Healey Row. BB11 .... 126 F5
Healey St. FY3 .... 129 D7
Healey Stones. OL12 .... 51 B4
Healey Wood Rd. BB11 .... 126 F4
Heaning Ave. Accrington BB5 ... 103 D8

Heaning Ave. Blackburn BB1 .... 101 D4
Heanor Dr. PR8 .... 34 F3
Heap Bridge Prim Sch. BL9 .... 32 D1
Heap Brow. BL9 .... 32 D1
Heap Clough. BB4 .... 83 C3
Heap St. Brierfield BB9 .... 147 A5
Heap St. Burnley BB10 .... 147 B1
Heap St. Bury BL9 & OL10 .... 32 D1
Heap St. Rawtenstall BB4 .... 85 A8
Heap St. Worsthorne BB10 .... 128 B6
Heapey Fold La. PR6 & PR7 .... 43 C7
Heapey Rd. PR6 .... 60 F7
Heaplands. BL8 .... 48 F1
Heapworth Ave. BL0 .... 49 B6
Heartwood Cl. BB2 .... 100 A8
Heasandford Cty Prim Sch.
BB10 .... 127 B8
Heasandford Ind Est.
Burnley BB10 .... 127 D8
Heasandford Ind Est.
Burnley BB10 .... 147 D2
Heath Ave. BB1 .... 49 B1
Heath Gr. LA3 .... 208 E6
Heath Hill Dr. OL13 .... 69 C8
Heath St. BB10 .... 127 B8
Heathbourne Rd. OL13 .... 69 C8
Heather Bank. Burnley BB11 .... 126 C4
Heather Bank. Rawtenstall BB4 .. 67 F8
Heather Brow. BB8 .... 201 D2
Heather Cl. Ainsdale PR8 .... 20 D2
Heather Cl. Brierfield BB9 .... 147 D4
Heather Cl. Burscough L40 .... 24 E4
Heather Cl. Formby L37 .... 12 E5
Heather Cl. Haslingden BB4 .... 67 A8
Heather Cl. Horwich BL6 .... 31 B4
Heather Cl. Thornton FY5 .... 173 B1
Heather Gr. PR2 .... 117 E3
Heather Lea Dr. PR6 .... 61 F8
Heatherfield. BL7 .... 47 E6
Heatherlands. OL12 .... 70 D4
Heatherlea Cl. WN8 .... 10 C7
Heatherlea Rd. BB12 .... 146 D7
Heathers The. PR5 .... 77 C4
Heatherside Rd. BB4 .... 49 C7
Heatherway. PR2 .... 117 E6
Heatherways. L37 .... 12 A6
Heathey La. L39 & PR8 .... 22 A7
Heathfield. PR6 .... 42 F1
Heathfield Ave. OL13 .... 69 C8
Heathfield Cl. L37 .... 12 A6
Heathfield Dr. PR7 .... 117 E4
Heathfield Pk. BB2 .... 99 F6
Heathfield Rd. Bacup OL13 .... 69 C8
Heathfield Rd. Fleetwood FY7 .. 193 E2
Heathfield Rd. Southport PR8 ..... 20 F6
Heathfoot Ave. LA3 .... 208 E6
Heathfoot Dr. LA3 .... 208 E6
Heathgate. Fence BB12 .... 146 D8
Heathgate. Skelmersdale WN8 ... 18 C2
Heathrow Pl. PR7 .... 42 A7
Heathwaite Cl. LA7 .... 237 E4
Heathway. PR2 .... 116 F5
Heathway Ave. FY3 .... 129 E6
Heatley La. L39 & PR8 .... 13 B8
Heatley Cl. BB2 .... 100 D3
Heatley St. PR1 .... 95 F8
Heaton Bottom Rd. LA3 .... 209 E5
Heaton Cl. Bamber Bridge PR5 ... 96 D4
Heaton Cl. Burscough L40 .... 24 D4
Heaton Cl. Carleton FY6 .... 151 C5
Heaton Cl. Hall Green WN6 .... 10 A7
Heaton Cl. Morecambe LA3 ...... 213 A3
Heaton Cl. Thornton FY5 .... 151 C8
Heaton House. LA1 .... 210 F5
Heaton Mount Ave. PR2 .... 116 F7
Heaton Pl. PR1 .... 117 E1
Heaton Rd. Lancaster LA1 .... 210 F5
Heaton Rd. Lytham St Anne's FY8 89 A8
Heaton St. Blackburn BB2 .... 100 E4
Heaton St. Leyland PR5 .... 75 E2
Heaton St. Standish WN6 .... 28 E1
Heatons Bridge Rd. L40 .... 23 D3
Heaviley Gr. BL6 .... 31 A5
Hebden Ave. FY1 .... 129 D1
Heber St. BB11 .... 105 B4
Hebrew Rd. BB10 .... 127 A8
Hebrew Sq. **11** BB10 .... 127 A8
Heckenhurst Ave. BB10 .... 128 A6
Hector Rd. BB3 .... 80 E5
Hedge Row. PR4 .... 112 B3
Hedge Rows. OL12 .... 70 C1
Hedgerow The. BB2 .... 100 A8
Hedgerows. PR5 .... 58 A8
Heeley Rd. FY8 .... 88 E8
Height Barn La. OL13 .... 70 A8
Height Croft. BB9 .... 147 E5
Height La. PR3 .... 159 F7
Height Side La. BB4 .... 85 B7
Heights Ave. OL12 .... 51 E2
Heights Cl. OL12 .... 51 E2
Heights Cotts. BB5 .... 103 F4
Heights La. OL12 .... 51 E1
Heights Rd. BB9 .... 147 D6
Heights The. BL6 .... 31 D1
Heightside Ave. BB4 .... 85 E2
Heightside Mews. BB4 .... 85 E2
Helen's Cl. FY4 .... 109 E6
Helena St. BB10 & BB11 .... 127 B5
Helks Brow. LA2 .... 233 B2
Hellifield. PR2 .... 116 F7
Hellifield Rd. BB7 .... 224 F5
Helm Cl. BB11 .... 126 D2
Helmcroft. **3** BB4 .... 84 A1
Helmcroft. **1** BB4 .... 84 B1
Helmn Way. BB9 .... 168 F3
Helmsdale. WN8 .... 18 C2
Helmsdale Cl. BL0 .... 49 A4
Helmsdale Rd. Blackpool FY4 ... 109 F7

Helmsdale Rd. Nelson BB9 .... 169 A1
Helmshore Prim Sch. BB4 .... 67 A7
Helmshore Rd. Haslingden BB4 .. 67 A7
Helmshore Rd. Ramsbottom BL0 67 A3
Helmside Ave. LA4 .... 212 F3
Helmsley Gn. **2** PR5 .... 76 B1
Helston Cl. Burnley BB11 .... 126 B4
Helston Cl. Southport PR9 .... 53 B5
Helton Cl. BB9 .... 168 D4
Helvellyn Dr. BB12 .... 126 C8
Hemingway. FY4 .... 109 D8
Hemp St. OL13 .... 87 A1
Hempshaw Ave. BB4 .... 105 A2
Henderson Rd. Fleetwood FY7 . 193 F2
Henderson Rd.
Weeton Camp PR4 .... 131 E6
Henderson St. PR1 & PR2 .... 116 E2
Hendon Pl. PR2 .... 115 E2
Hendon Rd. BB9 .... 147 F8
Hendriff Pl. **4** OL12 .... 51 F1
Henley Ave. FY5 .... 172 D2
Henley Ct. **7** Blackpool FY2 .. 150 E1
Henley Ct. Southport PR9 .... 52 E1
Henley Dr. PR9 .... 52 F1
Henley St. **9** OL12 .... 51 F1
Hennel House. PR5 .... 96 C3
Hennel La. Bamber Bridge PR5 .. 96 C3
Hennel La. Bamber Bridge PR5 .. 96 C4
Henrietta St. Bacup OL13 .... 86 F2
Henrietta St. Blackburn BB2 .... 100 C5
Henrietta St. Preston PR1 .... 96 B8
Henrietta Street Ind Est. **2**
OL13 .... 86 F2
Henry St. Accrington BB5 .... 103 D3
Henry St. Bank Lane BL0 .... 49 D7
Henry St. Blackpool FY1 .... 129 C2
Henry St. Church BB5 .... 102 F6
Henry St. Colne BB8 .... 169 C4
Henry St. Enfield BB5 .... 124 A2
Henry St. Lancaster LA1 .... 210 F7
Henry St. Lytham St Anne's FY8 . 90 A3
Henry St. **1** Nelson BB9 .... 168 D1
Henry St. Rawtenstall BB4 .... 84 F2
Henry St. Rishton BB1 .... 123 B1
Henry Whalley St. BB2 .... 100 A2
Henson Ave. FY4 .... 109 E6
Henthorn Cl. BB7 .... 164 D7
Henthorn Rd. BB7 .... 164 C6
Henthorne St. FY1 .... 129 C6
Henwick Hall Ave. BL0 .... 49 B4
Herbert St. Bacup OL13 .... 69 D8
Herbert St. Blackburn BB2 .... 100 D2
Herbert St. Burnley BB11 .... 126 E5
Herbert St. Horwich BL6 .... 31 B4
Herbert St. Leyland PR5 .... 76 A1
Herbert St. Padiham BB12 .... 125 D7
Herbert St. Preston PR1 .... 117 B1
Hereford Ave. Blackpool FY3 ... 129 E3
Hereford Ave. Burnley BB12 .... 126 B7
Hereford Ave. Garstang PR3 .... 178 B8
Hereford Cl. BB5 .... 103 B7
Hereford Dr. BB7 .... 164 F7
Hereford Rd. Blackburn BB1 .... 101 C5
Hereford Rd. Nelson BB8 & BB9 169 A4
Hereford Rd. Southport PR9 ...... 34 F7
Herevale Hall Dr. BL0 .... 49 B4
Heriot Cl. **8** FY5 .... 172 F1
Heritage Way. FY5 .... 172 F1
Herkomer Ave. BB11 .... 126 E2
Herlbeck Rise. LA1 .... 214 B2
Hermitage Cl. WN6 .... 19 E7
Hermitage St. BB1 & BB5 .... 123 C1
Hermitage The. FY5 .... 172 F2
Hermon Rd. FY5 .... 172 F1
Hermon St. **2** Preston PR1 .... 117 C1
Hermon St. Preston PR1 .... 117 D1
Hern Ave. PR5 .... 76 A8
Heron Cl. Blackburn BB1 .... 100 D8
Heron Cl. Thornton FY5 .... 172 F5
Heron Cl. BB11 .... 126 C5
Heron Dr. LA4 .... 212 F3
Heron Way. Blackpool FY3 .... 130 B6
Heron Way. Kirkham PR4 .... 112 B3
Heron Way. Oswaldtwistle BB5 . 102 E3
Herons Ct. L31 .... 5 B4
Heronsyke. LA1 .... 213 F4
Herschel Ave. BB12 .... 126 C8
Herschell St. Blackburn BB2 .... 100 C5
Herschell St. Preston PR1 .... 96 B6
Hertford St. BB2 .... 100 C2
Hesketh Ave. Banks PR9 .... 54 A6
Hesketh Ave. Blackpool FY2 .... 150 B4
Hesketh Cl. BB3 .... 64 C6
Hesketh Cl. FY2 .... 150 B4
Hesketh Dr. Maghull L31 .... 5 F1
Hesketh Dr. Rufford L40 .... 38 A3
Hesketh Dr.
Shevington Moor WN6 .... 28 A2
Hesketh Dr. Southport PR9 .... 52 F1
Hesketh La. BB9 .... 48 B4
Hesketh La. Becconsall PR4 .... 72 E4
Hesketh La. Hesketh Lane PR3 . 160 D7
Hesketh La. Tarleton PR4 .... 56 A7
Hesketh Pl. FY7 .... 194 B5
Hesketh Rd. Burscough L40 .... 24 D4
Hesketh Rd. Fulwood PR1 & PR2 117 E7
Hesketh Rd. Heysham LA3 .... 208 E8
Hesketh Rd. Longridge PR3 ...... 139 A8
Hesketh Rd.
Lytham St Anne's FY8 .... 110 A1
Hesketh Rd. Southport PR9 .... 52 D2
Hesketh St. Great Harwood BB6 123 C5
Hesketh St. Preston PR1 .... 116 C1
Hesketh-with-Becconsall
All Saints CE Sch. PR4 .... 72 E4

Heskin Cl. L31 .... 5 D4
Heskin Hall Ct. L39 .... 15 D8
Heskin La. L39 .... 15 D8
Hesley La. BD23 .... 230 E6
Hesse St. **1** BB3 .... 64 A8
Hest Bank La. LA2 .... 213 C4
Hest Bank Rd. LA4 .... 213 A6
Hester Cl. L38 .... 2 F4
Hestham Ave. LA4 .... 212 E4
Hestham Cres. LA4 .... 212 E4
Hestham Dr. LA4 .... 212 E4
Hestham Par. LA4 .... 212 E4
Hetherington Pl. FY2 .... 150 E2
Hetton Lea. BB9 .... 168 C3
Heversham Ave. WN8 .... 18 C2
Heversham Ave. PR2 .... 116 F7
Heversham Cl. Lancaster LA1 ... 211 B3
Heversham Cl. Morecambe LA4 212 F3
Hewart Dr. BL9 .... 32 C3
Hewitt St. **8** PR5 .... 76 B2
Hewlett St. PR7 .... 41 D1
Hexham Ave. FY5 .... 172 E4
Hexham Rd. LA4 .... 213 B5
Hey Bottom La. OL12 .... 51 F6
Hey End. PR4 .... 74 F8
Hey Head Ave. BB4 .... 69 A8
Hey House Mews. BL8 .... 48 F4
Hey St. BB9 .... 168 E1
Heycrofts View. BL0 .... 67 E3
Heydon Cl. L37 .... 11 D1
Heyes Rd. WN5 .... 10 E6
Heyes St. WN6 .... 19 C7
Heyes The. PR6 .... 77 B2
Heyescroft. L39 .... 7 D6
Heyfold Gdns. BB3 .... 80 E3
Heyhead St. BB9 .... 147 C5
Heyhouses Ct. FY8 .... 89 B8
Heyhouses Endowed CE Inf Sch.
FY8 .... 89 F7
Heyhouses Endowed CE Jun Sch.
FY8 .... 88 F8
Heyhouses La. FY8 .... 89 C7
Heyhurst Rd. BB2 .... 100 D5
Heymoor Ave. BB6 .... 123 D6
Heys Cl. Blackburn BB2 .... 80 C7
Heys Cl. Rawtenstall BB4 .... 85 C1
Heys Ct. BB8 .... 80 C8
Heys La. Barley Green BB12 ..... 167 D5
Heys La. Blackburn BB2 & BB3 .. 80 C7
Heys La. Darwen BB3 .... 80 F2
Heys La. Oswaldtwistle BB5 ..... 102 E3
Heys St. Bacup OL13 .... 86 F1
Heys St. Great Harwood BB6 .... 123 C5
Heys St. Haslingden BB4 .... 84 A3
Heys St. Rawtenstall BB4 .... 85 C1
Heys St. Thornton FY5 .... 173 B3
Heys The. Coppull PR7 .... 41 F2
Heys The. Parbold WN8 .... 26 C3
Heys The. Southport PR8 .... 33 D4
Heysham Ave. LA3 .... 208 F8
Heysham Cres. BB2 .... 100 F1
Heysham City High Sch. LA3 ... 212 C3
Heysham Hall Dr. LA3 .... 208 E6
Heysham Hall Gr. LA3 .... 208 E7
Heysham Mossgate Rd. LA3 .... 208 E7
Heysham Pk. LA3 .... 208 E7
Heysham Rd. Heysham LA3 ...... 208 E7
Heysham Rd. Morecambe LA3 . 212 A2
Heysham Rd. Southport PR9 ...... 34 F7
Heysham St. **2** PR1 .... 116 E1
Heysham Sta. LA3 .... 208 C5
Heywood. L37 .... 11 E3
Heywood Comm High Sch.
OL10 .... 32 E1
Heywood Rd. PR2 .... 115 E2
Heywood Rd. Bury BL9 .... 32 A1
Heywood St.
Great Harwood BB6 .... 123 C4
Heyworth Ave. BB2 .... 80 C7
Hibbert Terr. LA1 .... 210 F3
Hibson Rd. Nelson BB9 .... 147 D7
Hibson Rd. Nelson BB9 .... 147 D8
Hic Bibi La. PR7 .... 28 E6
Hick's Terr. **4** BB1 .... 123 B1
Hickory St. BB1 .... 100 F7
Hickson Ave. L31 .... 5 C3
Hidings Court La. LA4 .... 212 E4
Hiers House La. BB8 .... 169 B5
Higgin St. Burnley BB10 .... 127 B5
Higgin St. Colne BB8 .... 169 D5
Higgin St. Worsthorne BB10 .... 128 B5
Higgin's La. L40 .... 24 C4
High Banks. L31 .... 5 C3
High Barn La. OL12 .... 70 C3
High Bentham Prim Sch. LA2 233 D8
High Cop. PR6 .... 77 F4
High Ct. LA4 .... 213 B5
High Fold. BB8 .... 192 A6
High Gate. FY7 .... 193 D3
High Gate La. FY6 .... 174 A6
High Gn. PR5 .... 75 F1
High Knott Rd. LA5 .... 237 B1
High La. Ormskirk L40 .... 24 B1
High La. Salterforth BB8 .... 191 C5
High La. Stanley Gate L39 .... 7 C8
High Moor La. WN6 .... 27 B4
High Moss. L39 .... 15 E3
High Mount Ct. **2** LA1 .... 210 F7
High Mount House. **1** LA1 .. 210 F7
High Park Pl. PR9 .... 35 A8
High Park Rd. PR9 .... 35 A8
High Peak Rd. OL12 .... 51 C6
High Rd. Halton LA2 .... 214 E2
High Rd. Lowgill LA2 .... 233 C5
High St. Belmont BL7 .... 45 C4
High St. Blackburn BB1 .... 100 E5
High St. Blackpool FY1 .... 129 B6
High St. Brierfield BB9 .... 147 B5

High St. Chapeltown BL7 47 C4
High St. Chorley PR6 & PR7 42 C8
High St. Clitheroe BB7 164 B8
High St. Colne BB8 169 E5
High St. Darwen BB3 81 A1
High St. Elswick PR4 153 F1
High St. Fleetwood FY7 194 B4
High St. Garstang PR3 178 C7
High St. Great Eccleston PR3 154 B5
High St. Haslingden BB4 84 B4
High St. Horwich BL6 31 B4
High St. Lancaster LA1 210 F7
High St. Mawdesley L40 39 B1
High St. Nelson BB9 147 D7
High St. Oswaldtwistle BB5 102 F3
High St. Padiham BB12 145 D1
High St. 13 Preston PR1 96 A8
High St. Rishton BB1 123 B1
High St. Skelmersdale WN8 8 E8
High St. Standish WN6 28 E1
Higham CE Prim Sch. BB12 146 A6
Higham Gr. FY3 129 F2
Higham Hall Rd. BB12 145 F5
Higham Rd. BB12 145 C3
Higham Side Rd. PR4 134 C6
Higham St. BB12 145 D1
Highbank. BB1 121 F1
Highbank Ave. FY4 110 A8
Highbury Ave. Blackpool FY3 129 E8
Highbury Ave. Fleetwood FY7 193 F3
Highbury Pl. BB1 100 E6
Highbury Rd. FY8 109 E1
Highbury Rd E. FY8 109 E1
Highbury Rd W. FY8 109 D1
Highcroft Ave. FY2 150 E5
Highcroft Way. OL12 51 F4
Highcross Ave. FY6 130 D8
Highcross Hill. FY6 130 D8
Highcross Rd. FY6 151 D1
Higher Antley St. BB5 103 B5
Higher Audley St. BB1 100 F4
Higher Bank Rd. PR2 116 F3
Higher Bank St. Blackburn BB2 100 B6
Higher Bank St. Withnell PR6 79 A1
Higher Barn. BL6 31 F3
Higher Barn St. 2 BB1 101 A5
Higher Blackthorn. OL13 86 F4
Higher Booths La. BB4 105 A1
Higher Change Villas. OL13 87 B4
Higher Chapel La. BB7 224 A1
Higher Church St. BB3 81 B1
Higher Cockcroft. 13 BB1 100 E5
Higher Commons La. BB2 120 C4
Higher Croft. PR1 95 C2
Higher Croft Rd. BB2 & BB3 80 F8
Higher Cross Row. 9 OL13 86 F3
Higher Cswy. BB9 168 D3
Higher Dunscar. BL7 46 E1
Higher Eanam. BB1 101 A5
Higher Feniscowles La. BB2 79 B8
Higher Field. BB6 122 C8
Higher Fold La. BL0 49 E7
Higher Furlong. PR4 73 F6
Higher Gate. BB5 124 F1
Higher Gate Rd. BB5 124 F1
Higher Gn. FY6 151 E3
Higher Greenfield. PR2 116 B5
Higher Heys. BB5 102 E3
Higher Hill Mus. BB4 66 F8
Higher House Cl. BB2 80 A7
Higher House La. PR6 & PR7 61 B2
Higher La. Barnoldswick BB8 191 B7
Higher La. Dalton WN8 18 C7
Higher La. Haslingden BB4 84 B4
Higher La. Holmes PR4 55 C3
Higher La. Scorton PR3 199 F4
Higher La. Up Holland WN8 10 C7
Higher Lawrence St. 12 BB3 80 F2
Higher London Terr. BB3 81 B2
Higher Meadow. Chorley PR6 59 E8
Higher Meadow.
Clayton-le-W PR6 76 E1
Higher Mill St. BB4 85 A3
Higher Moor Cotts. FY2 150 F2
Higher Moor Rd. FY3 151 A2
Higher Moss La. L37 13 A2
Higher Moulding. BL9 32 E5
Higher Park Rd. BB8 191 C8
Higher Peel St. BB5 102 D3
Higher Perry St. BB3 81 B2
Higher Ramsgreave Rd.
BB1 & BB2 121 C3
Higher Rd. Longridge PR3 139 C8
Higher Rd. Tosside BD23 230 C5
Higher Reedley Rd.
BB10 & BB9 147 D5
Higher Row. BL9 32 B3
Higher Saxifield. BB10 147 E3
Higher South St. BB3 81 A1
Higher Summerseat. BL0 49 B2
Higher Syke. LA2 227 C2
Higher Tentre. BB11 127 B5
Higher Walton CE Prim Sch.
PR5 97 B3
Higher Walton Rd. PR5 96 E4
Higher Witton Rd. BB2 100 B4
Highergate Cl. BB5 124 F2
Highfield. Bacup OL13 86 F2
Highfield. Brinscall PR6 61 F8
Highfield. Great Harwood BB6 123 B5
Highfield. Rawtenstall BB4 85 A7
Highfield Ave.
Bamber Bridge PR5 96 C1
Highfield Ave. Brierfield BB10 147 B3
Highfield Ave. Foulridge BB8 191 E1
Highfield Ave. Fulwood PR2 117 C4
Highfield Ave. Inskip PR4 134 C8
Highfield Ave. Leyland PR5 76 C3
Highfield Cl. Adlington PR6 30 A7
Highfield Cl. Clifton PR4 114 C1
Highfield Cl. Oswaldtwistle BB5 102 F3
Highfield Cres. 4
Barrowford BB9 168 D3
Highfield Cres. Morecambe LA4 212 C4
Highfield Cres. Nelson BB9 168 E3
Highfield Dr. Fulwood PR2 116 E8
Highfield Dr. Hest Bank LA2 215 D1
Highfield Dr. Longridge PR3 139 B6
Highfield Dr. Longton PR4 73 F6
Highfield Dr. Penwortham PR1 95 D2
Highfield Gdns. BB2 100 E2
Highfield Gr. PR5 96 C2
Highfield High Sch. FY4 109 E6
Highfield Ind Est. PR6 60 D2
Highfield La. L40 23 D7
Highfield Mews. BB3 64 B8
Highfield Pk. L31 5 F1
Highfield Prim Sch. Chorley PR6 42 E8
Highfield Prim Sch.
Fulwood PR2 117 F5
Highfield Rd. Adlington PR6 30 A7
Highfield Rd. Blackburn BB2 100 E3
Highfield Rd. Blackpool FY4 109 E6
Highfield Rd. Blackrod BL6 30 E1
Highfield Rd. Carnforth LA5 216 E8
Highfield Rd. Clitheroe BB7 164 F7
Highfield Rd. Croston PR5 57 D2
Highfield Rd. Darwen BB3 81 B1
Highfield Rd. Earby BB8 201 B2
Highfield Rd. Edenfield BL0 67 D3
Highfield Rd. Ormskirk L39 15 E7
Highfield Rd. Rawtenstall BB4 85 D1
Highfield Rd. 5 Rishton BB1 123 A1
Highfield Rd. Southport PR9 53 B3
Highfield Rd N. Adlington PR6 30 A8
Highfield Rd N. Chorley PR7 60 C2
Highfield Rd S. PR7 60 C1
Highfield St. Darwen BB3 64 B8
Highfield St. Haslingden BB4 84 A2
Highfield Terr. LA2 233 C8
Highfurlong Sch. FY3 151 A2
Highgale Gdns. PR5 76 C7
Highgate. Blackpool FY4 109 D5
Highgate. Goosnargh PR3 137 D6
Highgate. Nelson BB9 147 D7
Highgate. Penwortham PR1 95 B5
Highgate Ave. PR2 116 E4
Highgate Cl. Fulwood PR2 116 F4
Highgate Cl. Newton-with-S PR4 113 F3
Highgate Cres. WN6 19 E7
Highgate La. Broadley OL12 51 C5
Highgate La. Warton PR4 91 E6
Highgate Pl. FY8 89 D6
Highgate Rd. Hall Green WN8 10 B7
Highgate Rd. Maghull L31 5 D3
Highgrove Ave. PR7 40 F3
Highgrove Cl. LA4 212 D4
Highgrove Ct. PR5 57 F8
Highland Ave. PR1 95 B4
Highland Brow. LA2 207 A4
Highland Rd. BL6 31 E1
Highmoor. BB5 147 F6
Highmoor Pk. BB7 164 F8
Highrigg Dr. PR3 136 F1
Highsands Ave. L40 38 A3
Hightown. BB4 85 E4
Hightown Rd. BB4 85 F4
Hightown Sta. L38 3 A4
Highways Ave. PR7 59 D1
Higson St. BB2 100 D5
Hilary Ave. FY2 150 C5
Hilary St. BB10 147 A1
Hilbre Cl. PR9 52 F1
Hilbre Dr. PR9 52 F1
Hilderstone La. LA5 & LA6 234 A7
Hildrop Rd. BB9 168 F1
Hill Cl. WN6 19 E8
Hill Cres. PR4 114 A2
Hill Crest. OL13 86 D1
Hill Crest Ave. Burnley BB10 127 F4
Hill Crest Ave. Fulwood PR2 116 E8
Hill Crest Ave. Longridge PR3 139 A7
Hill End La. BB4 85 C1
Hill House Fold La. WN6 27 C5
Hill House La.
Jack Green PR5 & PR6 78 A7
Hill House La. Robin Hood WN6 27 C5
Hill La. Blackrod BL6 30 C2
Hill La. Colne BB8 170 C7
Hill La. Nether Kellet LA6 216 F4
Hill Pl. BB9 147 D6
Hill Rd. Lancaster LA1 213 F3
Hill Rd. Leyland PR5 & PR6 76 C1
Hill Rd. Penwortham PR1 95 D4
Hill Rd S. PR1 95 D3
Hill Rise. Haslingden BB4 84 C1
Hill Rise. 1 Ramsbottom BL0 49 A4
Hill Side. LA1 210 E8
Hill St. Accrington BB5 103 C5
Hill St. Barnoldswick BB8 200 C2
Hill St. Blackburn BB1 101 B5
Hill St. Blackpool FY4 129 B1
Hill St. Brierfield BB12 & BB9 146 F6
Hill St. Brierfield BB9 147 B5
Hill St. Carnforth LA5 217 D1
Hill St. Colne BB8 169 D4
Hill St. Enfield BB5 124 A1
Hill St. Oswaldtwistle BB5 102 D5
Hill St. Padiham BB12 125 C8
Hill St. Preston PR1 95 F8
Hill St. Ramsbottom BL9 49 C3
Hill St. Rawtenstall BB4 85 A7
Hill St. Southport PR9 34 B7
Hill Top. Barrowford BB9 168 D4
Hill Top. Colne BB8 170 C4
Hill Top. Foulridge BB8 191 C2
Hill Top. New Longton PR4 75 A6
Hill Top. Trawden BB8 170 B2
Hill Top Cl. PR4 92 D7
Hill Top La. Earby BB8 201 A2
Hill Top La. Whittle-le-W PR6 60 D8
Hill View. Blackburn BB1 121 E1
Hill View. 2 Rawtenstall BB4 84 F1
Hill View Dr. PR7 28 D8
Hill View Rd. PR3 199 C1
Hill Wlk. PR5 76 A2
Hillam La. LA2 203 B7
Hillary Cres. L31 5 D1
Hillbrook Rd. PR5 75 F2
Hillcrest. Maghull L31 5 F1
Hillcrest. Skelmersdale WN8 9 B8
Hillcrest Ave. Bolton-le-S LA5 216 A5
Hillcrest Ave. Fulwood PR2 116 A4
Hillcrest Cl. PR4 56 A8
Hillcrest Dr. Bescar L40 22 F7
Hillcrest Dr. Longridge PR3 139 A7
Hillcrest Dr. Tarleton PR4 56 A8
Hillcrest Rd. Blackburn BB2 99 F2
Hillcrest Rd. Blackpool FY4 109 B4
Hillcrest Rd. Langho BB6 122 C8
Hillcrest Rd. Ormskirk L39 15 E6
Hillcroft. Fulwood PR2 116 C7
Hillcroft. High Bentham LA2 233 D7
Hilldean. WN8 10 C8
Hillingdon Rd. BB10 147 D3
Hillingdon Rd N. BB10 147 D3
Hillmount Ave. LA3 208 F8
Hillock Cl. L40 23 A7
Hillock La. Bescar L40 23 A7
Hillock La. Dalton WN8 18 D7
Hillock La. Warton PR4 91 E7
Hillocks The. PR5 57 B1
Hillpark Ave. Fulwood PR2 116 D4
Hillpark Ave. Gregson Lane PR5 97 D1
Hills Ct. LA1 213 F1
Hillsborough Ave. BB9 147 D5
Hillsea Ave. LA3 208 F8
Hillside. BB11 126 D3
Hillside Autistic Ctr. PR3 139 D7
Hillside Ave. Blackburn BB1 101 C4
Hillside Ave. Blackrod BL6 30 E1
Hillside Ave. Brierfield BB10 147 C5
Hillside Ave. 11 Darwen BB3 64 A8
Hillside Ave. Egerton BL7 47 B1
Hillside Ave. Farington PR5 75 F7
Hillside Ave. Fulwood PR2 116 D4
Hillside Ave. Hill Dale WN8 26 D5
Hillside Ave. Horwich BL6 31 C4
Hillside Ave. Kirkham PR4 113 C5
Hillside Ave. Ormskirk L39 15 D3
Hillside Ave. Preesall FY6 195 B4
Hillside Cl. Blackburn BB1 101 C4
Hillside Cl. Blackpool FY3 129 E6
Hillside Cl. Brierfield BB9 147 C5
Hillside Cl. Burnley BB11 126 D2
Hillside Cl. Clitheroe BB7 164 E6
Hillside Cl. Euxton PR7 59 C1
Hillside Cl. Great Harwood BB6 123 C6
Hillside Cl. Thornton FY5 151 D8
Hillside Cres. Horwich BL6 31 C4
Hillside Cres. Weir OL13 86 F7
Hillside Cres. Whittle-le-W PR6 60 C8
Hillside Cty Prim Sch. WN8 9 D8
Hillside Dr. Newchurch BB4 85 E2
Hillside Dr. Stalmine FY6 174 C7
Hillside Dr. West Bradford BB7 186 F6
Hillside Golf Links. PR8 20 C8
Hillside Rd. Haslingden BB4 84 C3
Hillside Rd. Low Bentham LA2 233 C8
Hillside Rd. Preston PR1 96 C6
Hillside Rd. Ramsbottom BL0 49 A5
Hillside Rd. Southport PR8 33 E1
Hillside Sta. PR8 33 E1
Hillside View. BB9 147 C5
Hillside Way. OL12 70 C1
Hillside Wlk. Blackburn BB1 101 C4
Hillside Wlk. Middle Healey OL12 51 D4
Hillstone Ave. OL12 51 D4
Hillstone Cl. BL8 48 F2
Hillsview Rd. PR8 20 C4
Hilltop. OL12 51 C5
Hilltop Dr. BB4 67 C7
Hilltop Wlk. L39 15 C3
Hillview Rd. PR4 113 A6
Hillylaid Rd. FY5 173 D2
Hilmont Terr. BB1 100 F7
Hilmore Rd. LA4 212 D5
Hilstone La. FY2 150 D1
Hilton Ave. Blackpool FY1 129 B1
Hilton Ave. Horwich BL6 31 A3
Hilton Ave. Lytham St Anne's FY8 89 C6
Hilton Ct. FY8 88 E5
Hilton Rd. BB3 64 B8
Hilton St. Bury BL9 32 A4
Hilton St. Darwen BB3 64 A8
Hilton's Brow. PR6 78 B4
Hinchley Gn. L31 5 B1
Hind St. Burnley BB10 147 B2
Hind St. Preston PR1 95 E6
Hind's Head Ave. WN6 27 F6
Hindburn Ave. L31 5 F2
Hindburn Cl. LA5 217 F2
Hindburn Pl. LA1 213 E2
Hinde St. LA1 214 A1
Hindle Fold La. BB6 123 C6
Hindle St. Accrington BB5 103 B6
Hindle St. Bacup OL13 69 D8
Hindle St. Darwen BB3 80 F2
Hindle St. Haslingden BB4 84 B3
Hindley Beech. L31 5 C2
Hindley Ct. 3 BB9 168 C1
Hindley St. PR7 42 C6
Hinton St. BB10 127 B5
Hippings Meth Prim Sch. BB5 102 E3
Hippings Vale. BB5 102 D4
Hippings Way. BB7 186 E2
Hirst St. Burnley BB11 127 B4
Hirst St. Cornholme OL14 108 B1
Hirst St. Padiham BB12 145 C1
Hoarstones Ave. BB12 146 D7
Hob Gn. BB2 120 F2
Hob La. BL7 47 C7
Hobart Pl. FY5 150 F8
Hobart St. BB10 & BB11 127 B6
Hobbs La. PR3 180 A4
Hobcross La. L40 25 A2
Hobson St. BB4 84 F4
Hobson's La. LA6 234 C2
Hockley Pl. FY3 129 F7
Hodder Ave. Blackpool FY1 129 D1
Hodder Ave. Chorley PR7 42 B5
Hodder Ave. Fleetwood FY7 193 D2
Hodder Ave. Maghull L31 5 F2
Hodder Ave. Morecambe LA1 213 B3
Hodder Brook. PR2 118 A3
Hodder Cl. 3
Bamber Bridge PR5 76 F8
Hodder Cl. Fleetwood FY7 193 C2
Hodder Ct. BB7 163 C4
Hodder Dr. BB7 186 D7
Hodder Gr. Clitheroe BB7 164 C7
Hodder Gr. Darwen BB3 80 E4
Hodder Pl. Blackburn BB1 100 F6
Hodder Pl. Lancaster LA1 211 B5
Hodder Pl. Lytham St Anne's FY8 89 C7
Hodder St. Accrington BB5 103 D6
Hodder St. 1 Blackburn BB1 100 E6
Hodder St. Brierfield BB10 147 C3
Hodder Way. FY6 151 D2
Hoddlesden Fold. BB3 81 F1
Hoddlesden Rd. BB3 81 E1
Hodge Brow. PR7 43 F4
Hodge La. BB8 191 B8
Hodge St. PR8 34 B7
Hodgson Ave. PR4 92 A5
Hodgson High Sch. FY6 151 F3
Hodgson Pl. FY6 151 D2
Hodgson Rd. FY1 129 C8
Hodgson St. Darwen BB3 81 B1
Hodgson St. 3
Oswaldtwistle BB5 102 E4
Hodson St. Bamber Bridge PR5 96 E1
Hodson St. Southport PR8 34 C6
Hogarth Ave. BB11 126 F3
Hogarth Cres. PR4 133 F4
Hogg's La. PR7 42 F5
Hoggs Hill La. L37 11 F1
Hoghton Ave. OL13 70 A8
Hoghton Cl. Lancaster LA1 210 D6
Hoghton Cl.
Lytham St Anne's FY8 109 F2
Hoghton Gr. PR9 34 C8
Hoghton La. PR5 97 D3
Hoghton Pl. PR9 34 B7
Hoghton Rd. Leyland PR5 75 D1
Hoghton Rd. Longridge PR3 139 C7
Hoghton St. 6
Bamber Bridge PR5 76 A8
Hoghton St. Southport PR8 & PR9 34 C7
Hoghton Tower. PR5 98 E1
Hoghton View. PR1 96 C6
Holbeck Ave. Blackpool FY4 109 E6
Holbeck Ave. Middle Healey OL12 51 D4
Holbeck Ave. Morecambe LA4 213 B4
Holbeck St. BB10 147 A1
Holborn Dr. L39 15 C3
Holborn Hill. L39 15 C4
Holcombe Brook Prim Sch.
BL0 49 A2
Holcombe Ct. BL0 48 F2
Holcombe Dr. BB10 127 B6
Holcombe Gr. PR6 60 E1
Holcombe Lee. BL0 49 A4
Holcombe Mews. BL8 48 F3
Holcombe Old Rd. BL8 & BL0 49 A4
Holcombe Rd. Blackpool FY2 150 E1
Holcombe Rd. Haslingden BB4 66 F8
Holcombe Rd. Ramsbottom BL8 48 F2
Holcombe Village. BL8 49 A6
Holcroft Pl. FY8 89 F4
Holden Ave. Bury BL9 32 E4
Holden Ave. Ramsbottom BL0 49 A5
Holden Cl. BB9 168 C1
Holden Fold. BB3 81 B3
Holden La. BB7 224 B5
Holden Rd. Brierfield BB9 147 A5
Holden Rd. Brierfield BB10 147 B3
Holden St. Accrington BB5 103 B5
Holden St. Adlington PR7 29 F7
Holden St. Belthorn BB1 81 F6
Holden St. Blackburn BB2 100 C4
Holden St. Burnley BB11 126 F5
Holden St. Clitheroe BB7 164 F8
Holden Way. LA1 210 F5
Hole House La. BB7 229 E2
Hole House St. BB1 101 C5
Holgate. FY4 109 F6
Holgate Dr. WN5 10 E6
Holgate St. Brierfield BB10 147 F3
Holgate St. Great Harwood BB6 123 C5
Holhouse La. BL8 48 F2
Holker Cl. Coupe Green PR5 97 E3
Holker Cl. Lancaster LA1 210 D6
Holker La. PR5 58 B4
Holker St. Colne BB8 169 B4
Holker St. Darwen BB3 64 B8
Holland Ave. Bamber Bridge PR5 96 E2
Holland Ave. Rawtenstall BB4 84 F3
Holland Lodge. 4 PR2 117 F4
Holland Moor Prim Sch. WN8 9 E7
Holland Moss. WA11 & WN8 9 A5
Holland Pl. BB9 168 E2
Holland Rd. PR1 116 C1
Holland St. Accrington BB5 102 F6
Holland St. Blackburn BB1 100 D6
Holland St. Padiham BB12 125 B8
Holland's La. WN8 17 A1
Holliers Cl. L31 5 E1
Hollies Cl. Blackburn BB2 79 F8
Hollies Cl. Catterall PR3 178 D2
Hollies Rd. BB1 122 A7
Hollies The. PR8 33 F6
Hollin Bridge St. BB2 100 D2
Hollin Hall. BB8 170 C1
Hollin Hill. BB11 127 B3
Hollin La. Knowley PR7 61 C2
Hollin La. Rawtenstall BB4 85 A4
Hollin Mill St. BB9 147 B6
Hollin St. BB2 100 C2
Hollin Way. Rawtenstall BB4 85 A4
Hollin Way. Rawtenstall BB4 85 A6
Hollingreave Rd. BB11 127 A4
Hollings. PR4 74 F7
Hollington St. BB8 170 B5
Hollinhead Cres. PR2 116 B4
Hollinhurst Ave. PR1 95 C6
Hollinhurst Brow. LA2 233 C2
Hollins Ave. BB10 127 F4
Hollins Cl. Accrington BB5 103 C4
Hollins Cl. Hoghton PR5 98 C3
Hollins Ct. 1 BB8 200 B3
Hollins Gr. PR2 116 B3
Hollins Grove St. BB3 80 F3
Hollins High Sch The. BB5 103 D2
Hollins Hill. PR3 204 C2
Hollins La. Accrington BB5 103 D3
Hollins La. Arnside LA5 237 C1
Hollins La. Edenfield BL0 67 E2
Hollins La. Hollins Lane PR3 204 C2
Hollins La. Runshaw Moor PR5 58 C4
Hollins Rd. Barnoldswick BB8 200 A2
Hollins Rd. Darwen BB3 80 F4
Hollins Rd. Nelson BB9 169 A2
Hollins Rd. Preston PR1 117 B2
Hollinshead St. PR6 42 C8
Hollinshead St Sch. PR6 42 C8
Hollinshead Terr. BB3 63 B7
Hollowell La. BL6 31 D1
Hollowford La. L40 25 D2
Hollowforth La. PR4 135 E5
Hollowhead Ave. BB1 121 F5
Hollowhead Cl. BB1 121 F5
Hollowhead La. BB1 122 A5
Hollowrane. LA6 234 C7
Holly Ave. BB4 84 C1
Holly Bank. Accrington BB5 103 C4
Holly Bank. Entwistle BL7 47 B7
Holly Bank. Fulwood PR2 116 C5
Holly Bank. Warton LA5 217 D5
Holly Cl. Clayton Green PR6 77 B2
Holly Cl. Skelmersdale WN8 17 E1
Holly Cl. Thornton FY5 173 C3
Holly Cl. Westhead L40 16 E4
Holly Cres. PR7 41 E2
Holly Fold La. WA11 8 E3
Holly Gr. Longridge PR3 139 A8
Holly Gr. Tarleton PR4 56 A7
Holly La. Ormskirk L39 15 B4
Holly La.
Rainford Junction WA11 & WN8 8 E4
Holly La. Rufford L40 38 C3
Holly Mews. FY8 109 F2
Holly Mount. BB4 67 A7
Holly Mount RC Prim Sch. BL8 48 D1
Holly Pl. PR5 77 B6
Holly Rd. Blackpool FY1 150 C1
Holly Rd. Thornton FY5 173 B3
Holly St. Blackburn BB1 100 F7
Holly St. Burnley BB10 127 B5
Holly St. Bury BL9 32 A2
Holly St. Nelson BB9 147 F8
Holly St. Oswaldtwistle BB5 102 D4
Holly St. Ramsbottom BL0 49 C3
Holly Terr. BB1 100 F8
Holly Tree Cl. BB3 64 A6
Holly Tree Way. BB2 79 F8
Holly Wlk. LA1 210 D8
Hollybank Cl. PR2 115 F5
Hollybrook Rd. PR8 34 A5
Hollywood Ave. Blackpool FY3 129 E5
Hollywood Ave.
Penwortham PR1 95 C3
Hollywood Gr. FY7 193 F4
Holman St. 5 PR1 117 C1
Holmbrook Cl. BB2 80 F8
Holmby St. BB10 147 B2
Holmdale Ave. PR9 53 C4
Holme Ave. FY7 172 D8
Holme Bank. BB4 84 F1
Holme CE Prim Sch. BB10 107 B6
Holme Cl. BB8 192 A7
Holme Cres. BB8 170 B3
Holme End. BB12 146 F4
Holme Hill. BB7 186 E2
Holme House Rd. OL14 108 C1
Holme La. Caton LA2 231 C3
Holme La. Haslingden BB4 67 D8
Holme La. Rawtenstall BB4 67 E8
Holme Lea. BB5 123 F4
Holme Mills Ind Est. LA6 234 B8
Holme Pk. LA2 233 D7
Holme Rd. Bamber Bridge PR5 76 E8
Holme Rd. Burnley BB12 126 E7
Holme Rd. Clayton-le-M BB5 123 E4
Holme Rd.
Penwortham PR1 & PR4 95 B7
Holme Slack La. PR1 & PR2 117 C3

Holme Slack Prim Sch. PR1 ... 117 C3
Holme St. Accrington BB5 .... 103 C6
Holme St. Bacup OL13 .... 69 D8
Holme St. Barrowford BB9 .... 168 D2
Holme St. Colne BB8 .... 170 B5
Holme St. Darwen BB3 .... 64 A8
Holme St. Nelson BB9 .... 147 E8
Holme Terr. Haslingden BB4 ...... 67 D8
Holme Terr. Nelson BB9 .... 147 C8
Holme The. PR3 .... 179 E7
Holme Vale. BB4 .... 67 A6
Holmefield Ave. FY5 .... 172 E2
Holmefield Cl. FY5 .... 172 E2
Holmefield Ct. BB9 .... 168 D3
Holmefield Gr. L31 .... 5 C1
Holmefield Rd.
  Knott End-on-S FY6 .... 194 E5
Holmefield Rd.
  Lytham St Anne's FY8 .... 89 A7
Holmes Ct. PR1 .... 116 E3
Holmes Dr. OL13 .... 86 F4
Holmes La. OL13 .... 86 F3
Holmes Meadow. PR5 .... 75 B1
Holmes Rd. FY5 .... 173 B3
Holmes Sq. BB10 .... 127 B5
Holmes St. Burnley BB11 .... 127 B5
Holmes St. Forest Holme BB4 ..... 86 A7
Holmes St. Padiham BB12 .... 125 D8
Holmes St. Rawtenstall BB4 .... 85 B3
Holmes Terr. BB4 .... 84 F5
Holmes The. BB4 .... 84 F5
Holmestrand Ave. BB11 .... 126 B4
Holmeswood. PR4 .... 113 A5
Holmeswood Cres. PR3 .... 136 B3
Holmeswood Four Lane Ends.
  PR4 .... 37 C6
Holmeswood Meth Sch. PR4 ...... 37 C6
Holmeswood Pk. BB4 .... 67 E8
Holmeswood Rd. L40 & PR4 .... 37 D6
Holmfield Cres. PR2 .... 115 D1
Holmfield Rd. Blackpool FY2 ..... 150 B2
Holmfield Rd. Fulwood PR2 ...... 117 A4
Holmrook Rd. PR1 .... 117 B1
Holmsley St. BB10 .... 127 B5
Holmwood Cl. L37 .... 11 D3
Holmwood Dr. L37 .... 11 D4
Holsands Cl. PR2 .... 117 E6
Holstein Ave. OL12 .... 51 D4
Holstein St. PR1 .... 96 A8
Holt Ave. PR7 .... 41 F2
Holt Brow. PR5 .... 59 A6
Holt Coppice. L39 .... 6 A7
Holt La. PR6 .... 77 E3
Holt Mill Rd. BB4 .... 68 D8
Holt Sq. BB9 .... 168 E5
Holt St. Newchurch BB4 .... 68 E8
Holt St. Orrell WN5 .... 10 D5
Holt St. Ramsbottom BL0 .... 49 D6
Holt St. Rishton BB1 .... 123 C1
Holt St. Whitworth OL12 .... 70 C1
Holt St W. BL0 .... 49 B5
Holt's Terr. OL12 .... 51 E2
Holts La. FY6 .... 151 F2
Holwood Gdns. L37 .... 11 D4
Holy Cross RC High Sch. PR7 ...... 42 C4
Holy Family RC Jun Sch. FY1 .. 129 C6
Holy Family RC Prim Sch.
  Fulwood PR2 .... 115 F4
Holy Family RC Prim Sch.
  Southport PR9 .... 34 E7
Holy Family RC Prim Sch.
  Warton PR4 .... 91 E6
Holy Saviour's RC Prim Sch.
  BB9 .... 168 E4
Holy Souls RC Prim Sch. BB1 ... 121 E1
Holy Trinity CE Prim Sch.
  Burnley BB11 .... 126 E5
Holy Trinity CE Prim Sch.
  Darwen BB3 .... 81 A1
Holy Trinity CE Prim Sch.
  Formby L37 .... 11 F3
Holy Trinity CE Prim Sch.
  Southport PR9 .... 34 E7
Holy Trinity RC Prim Sch. BB9 .. 147 B5
Holyoake Ave. FY2 .... 150 E4
Holyoake St. Burnley BB12 .... 126 A6
Holyoake St. Cornholme OL14 ... 108 A1
Home Breeze House. LA4 .... 213 A6
Homecare Ave. BB7 .... 144 F8
Homechase Hse. PR8 .... 33 F4
Homer Ave. PR4 .... 55 F7
Homer St. BB11 .... 126 C5
Homesands House. PR9 .... 34 D8
Homestead. PR5 .... 77 B4
Homestead Cl. PR5 .... 75 D1
Homestead Dr. FY7 .... 193 E1
Homestead The. FY8 .... 90 A3
Homestead Way. FY7 .... 193 E1
Homewood Ave. LA4 .... 213 B6
Homfray Ave. LA3 & LA4 .... 213 A3
Homfray Gr. LA3 .... 213 A3
Hondel St. OL12 .... 51 B8
Honey Hole. BB2 .... 100 E2
Honey Holme La. BB10 .... 106 F7
Honeypot La. FY6 .... 152 D4
Honeysuckle Pl. FY2 .... 150 F6
Honeysuckle Row. PR2 .... 117 E2
Honeysuckle Way. OL12 .... 51 D6
Honeywood Cl. BL0 .... 49 A3
Honister Ave. FY3 .... 129 F2
Honister Cl. FY7 .... 193 D3
Honister Rd. Brierfield BB10 ..... 147 B3
Honister Rd. Lancaster LA1 ...... 214 B2
Honister Sq. FY8 .... 109 F2
Honiton Ave. BB2 .... 80 C8

Hoo Hill Ind Est. FY3 .... 129 E8
Hood House St. BB11 .... 126 E4
Hood St. 4 BB5 .... 103 C6
Hoole CE Prim Sch. PR4 .... 73 C1
Hoole La. Banks PR9 .... 54 A6
Hoole La. Nateby PR3 .... 177 B5
Hools La. PR3 .... 196 A5
Hope La. PR3 .... 160 E5
Hope Sq. PR9 .... 34 D7
Hope St. Accrington BB5 .... 103 B5
Hope St. Adlington PR6 .... 30 B8
Hope St. Bacup OL13 .... 86 F4
Hope St. Blackburn BB2 .... 100 D5
Hope St. Brierfield BB9 .... 147 B5
Hope St. Chorley PR6 .... 60 C1
Hope St. Darwen BB3 .... 80 F1
Hope St. Great Harwood BB6 .... 123 C4
Hope St. Haslingden BB4 .... 84 B2
Hope St. Horwich BL6 .... 31 B4
Hope St. Lancaster LA1 .... 211 A7
Hope St. Lytham St Anne's FY8 ... 89 A7
Hope St. Morecambe LA4 .... 212 F4
Hope St. Nelson BB9 .... 147 D8
Hope St. 8 Padiham BB12 .... 125 D8
Hope St. 5 Preston PR1 .... 95 F8
Hope St. Ramsbottom BL0 .... 49 B5
Hope St. Rawtenstall BB4 .... 85 C1
Hope St. Southport PR9 .... 34 C7
Hope St. Worsthorne BB10 .... 128 B6
Hope St N. BB5 .... 31 B5
Hope Terr. 4
  Bamber Bridge PR5 .... 76 A8
Hope Terr. Blackburn BB2 .... 100 C6
Hope Terr. Nelson BB9 .... 147 D8
Hopkinson St. BB8 .... 170 B3
Hopkinsons Terr. BB8 .... 170 C3
Hopton Rd. FY1 .... 129 B2
Hopwood Ave. BL6 .... 31 C4
Hopwood St. Accrington BB5 ..... 103 B4
Hopwood St. 4
  Bamber Bridge PR5 .... 76 E8
Hopwood St. Bamber Bridge PR5 76 F7
Hopwood St. Blackburn BB2 ..... 100 E3
Hopwood St. 7 Burnley BB11 .... 126 B6
Hopwood St. Preston PR1 .... 96 A8
Horace St. 4 BB12 .... 126 D6
Horatio House. 3 BB11 .... 126 E5
Horden Rake. BB2 .... 79 E7
Horden View. BB2 .... 79 E7
Hordley St. BB12 .... 126 A6
Hornbeam Cl. PR1 .... 95 B3
Hornby Ave. Fleetwood FY7 ...... 172 D8
Hornby Ave. Fulwood PR2 .... 117 E4
Hornby Bank. Hornby LA2 .... 232 B8
Hornby Bank. Nether Kellet LA6 216 F5
Hornby CE Prim Sch. LA2 .... 232 B7
Hornby Croft. PR5 .... 58 B3
Hornby Ct. Kirkham PR4 .... 113 B4
Hornby Ct. Lancaster LA1 .... 213 E4
Hornby Dr. Lancaster LA1 .... 211 A4
Hornby Dr. Newton-with-S PR4 .. 113 F2
Hornby Hall Cl. LA2 .... 232 B7
Hornby High Sch. LA2 .... 232 B7
Hornby La. PR3 & PR4 .... 154 F2
Hornby Park Ct. FY3 .... 129 D4
Hornby Rd. Blackpool FY1 .... 129 C4
Hornby Rd. Caton LA2 .... 231 C3
Hornby Rd. Chorley PR7 .... 42 E6
Hornby Rd. Longridge PR3 .... 139 B8
Hornby Rd. Lytham St Anne's FY8 88 E5
Hornby Rd. Southport PR9 .... 53 A4
Hornby Rd. Wray LA2 .... 232 D1
Hornby Rd. Wray LA2 .... 232 D6
Hornby St. Burnley BB11 .... 126 C8
Hornby St. Oswaldtwistle BB5 ... 102 E3
Hornby Terr. LA4 .... 212 F6
Hornby's La. Hale Nook PR3 ..... 175 A5
Hornby's La. Moss Edge PR3 ..... 175 D6
Hornbyx Ct. BB2 .... 100 C4
Hornchurch Dr. PR7 .... 42 A7
Horncliffe Cl. BB4 .... 67 E8
Horncliffe Rd. FY4 .... 109 B6
Horncliffe View. BB4 .... 67 B8
Horne St. BB5 .... 103 C7
Horning Cres. BB10 .... 147 D2
Horns La. PR3 .... 159 B3
Hornsea Cl. PR2 .... 116 A4
Hornsey Ave. FY8 .... 109 B4
Horridge Fold. BL7 .... 46 E3
Horrobin Fold. BL7 .... 47 C2
Horrobin La. Chapeltown BL7 ..... 47 C2
Horrobin La.
  Rivington BL6 & PR6 & PR7 ..... 43 E1
Horrocks Rd. BL7 .... 47 D6
Horrocksford Way. LA1 .... 210 D6
Horse Market. LA6 .... 238 C2
Horse Park La. PR3 .... 197 A5
Horsebridge Rd. FY3 .... 130 B8
Horsefield Ave. OL12 .... 51 C6
Horsefield Cl. BB8 .... 169 F5
Horsfall Ave. FY8 .... 90 A3
Horsfall Cl. BB5 .... 103 B7
Horton Ave. BB10 .... 147 B3
Horwich Coll of F Ed. BL6 .... 31 D2
Horwich L Ctr. BL6 .... 31 C3
Horwich Parish CE Prim Sch.
  BL6 .... 31 C4
Hoscar Moss Rd. L40 .... 25 D3
Hospital Cotts. PR3 .... 139 F6
Hosticle La. LA6 .... 235 C7
Hothersall La. PR3 .... 139 D4
Hough La. PR5 .... 76 A1
Houghclough La. PR3 .... 181 F1
Houghton Ave. FY4 .... 109 D8
Houghton Cl. PR1 .... 95 C3
Houghton Ct. LA2 .... 214 E7
Houghton La. WN6 .... 19 F6
Houghton Rd. PR1 .... 95 C3
Houghton St. PR6 .... 42 D8

Houghton's La. WN8 .... 18 C1
Houghtons Rd. WN8 .... 18 B3
Houldsworth Rd. PR2 .... 116 E3
Hounds Hill. FY1 .... 129 B4
Hounds Hill Ctr. FY1 .... 129 B5
Houseman Pl. FY4 .... 109 E7
Houses Hill. BB3 .... 64 A8
Hove Ave. FY7 .... 172 C8
Hove Cl. BL8 .... 48 F1
Hove Rd. FY8 .... 88 F6
Howard Cl. Accrington BB5 ...... 102 F5
Howard Cl.
  Lytham St Anne's FY8 .... 109 E1
Howard Cl. Maghull L31 .... 5 E1
Howard Ct. PR9 .... 52 D1
Howard Dr. PR4 .... 55 F7
Howard Mews. LA5 .... 217 C1
Howard Rd. PR7 .... 42 C5
Howard St. Blackpool FY1 .... 129 C6
Howard St. Burnley BB11 .... 126 D5
Howard St. Nelson BB9 .... 147 C8
Howard St. Rishton BB1 .... 123 A1
Howard St. Rochdale OL12 .... 51 F1
Howards La. WN5 .... 10 F7
Howarth Ave. BB5 .... 102 F7
Howarth Cl. BB11 .... 127 A3
Howarth Cres. FY6 .... 151 E3
Howarth Rd. PR2 .... 116 D3
Howarth's St. BB4 .... 86 A8
Howe Ave. FY4 .... 109 E8
Howe Croft. BB7 .... 164 F8
Howe Dr. BL0 .... 49 B2
Howe Gr. PR7 .... 42 A7
Howe Wlk. 4 BB11 .... 127 A6
Howells Cl. L31 .... 5 D2
Howgill Ave. LA1 .... 214 A4
Howgill Cl. BB9 .... 147 F6
Howgill La. BB7 .... 225 C1
Howgills The. PR2 .... 117 A7
Howick CE Prim Sch. PR1 .... 94 F3
Howick Cross La. PR1 .... 94 E5
Howick Moor La. PR1 .... 95 A3
Howick Park Ave. PR1 .... 94 F4
Howick Park Cl. PR1 .... 94 F4
Howick Park Dr. PR1 .... 94 F4
Howick Row. PR1 .... 94 D5
Howorth Rd. BB11 .... 127 A3
Howsin St. BB10 .... 147 A1
Hoylake Cl. PR2 .... 116 B6
Hoyle Ave. FY8 .... 109 F2
Hoyle St. Bacup OL13 .... 69 E8
Hoyle St. Haslingden BB5 .... 84 A8
Hoyle St. Whitworth OL12 .... 70 D3
Hoyles La. PR4 .... 115 D6
Hozier St. BB1 .... 101 C5
Hubert Pl. LA1 .... 210 D8
Hubie St. BB12 .... 126 F7
Huck La. FY8 .... 90 E7
Hud Hey Ind Est. BB4 .... 84 B5
Hud Hey Rd. BB4 .... 84 B5
Hudcar La. BL9 .... 32 A4
Hudson Cl. BB2 .... 100 B8
Hudson Ct. PR5 .... 77 C8
Hudson Rd. FY1 .... 129 D2
Hudson St. Accrington BB5 ...... 103 C4
Hudson St. Brierfield BB9 .... 147 B5
Hudson St. Burnley BB11 .... 126 D5
Hudson St. Cornholme OL14 .... 108 C1
Hudson St. Preston PR1 .... 96 A7
Hufling Ct. 9 BB11 .... 127 B4
Hufling La. BB11 .... 127 B4
Hugh Barn La. PR4 .... 74 F7
Hugh La. PR5 .... 75 D3
Hugh Rake. BB4 .... 84 F6
Hughes Ave. BL6 .... 31 A4
Hughes Cl. 11 BL9 .... 32 A3
Hughes Gr. FY2 .... 150 E1
Hughes St. BB11 .... 127 A5
Hull Rd. FY1 .... 129 B4
Hull St. Burnley BB11 .... 127 B5
Hull St. Preston PR1 .... 95 C8
Hullet Cl. WN6 .... 19 E8
Hulme Ave. FY5 .... 173 C2
Hulme St. PR8 .... 34 A7
Hulton Dr. BB9 .... 147 E6
Humber Ave. FY3 .... 129 E8
Humber Sq. BB10 .... 147 C2
Humber St. PR3 .... 139 A7
Humblescough La. PR3 .... 177 D5
Humphrey St. BB9 .... 147 B6
Huncoat Cty Prim Sch. BB5 .... 124 F2
Huncoat Ind Est. BB5 .... 103 D8
Huncoat Stn. BB5 .... 124 E2
Hundred End La. PR4 .... 71 F1
Hungerford Rd. FY8 .... 88 F5
Hunslet St. Burnley BB11 .... 127 B6
Hunslet St. Nelson BB9 .... 147 F7
Hunt Fold Dr. BL8 .... 48 F1
Hunt Rd. L31 .... 5 D1
Hunt St. PR1 .... 95 D7
Hunter Ave. PR4 .... 56 A6
Hunter Rd. BB4 .... 113 B2
Hunter St. Brierfield BB10 & BB9 147 B5
Hunter St. Carnforth LA5 .... 217 D2
Hunter's La. PR4 .... 55 B3
Hunters Dr. BB12 .... 126 D8
Hunters Fold. PR4 .... 74 A5
Hunters Gn. BL8 .... 48 F3
Hunters Lodge. BB2 .... 99 F1
Hunters Rd. PR6 .... 76 D1
Hunting Hill Rd. LA5 .... 217 B1
Huntingdon Cl. L31 .... 5 C4
Huntingdon Hall Rd. PR3 .... 162 A2
Huntingdon Rd. FY5 .... 172 C1
Huntington Dr. BB3 .... 64 A7
Huntley Ave. FY3 .... 129 E7
Huntley Cl. LA4 .... 213 A5

Huntley La. PR5 .... 119 E1
Huntley Mount Rd. BL9 .... 32 B3
Huntly Rd. BL9 .... 32 B3
Huntly Way. OL10 .... 32 E1
Huntroyde Ave. BB12 .... 125 B8
Huntroyde Cl. BB12 .... 126 D7
Hunts Field. PR6 .... 77 C2
Huntsmans Chase. PR4 .... 113 F6
Hurlston Dr. L39 .... 15 E7
Hurlston La. L40 .... 23 C1
Hurn Gr. PR7 .... 42 A7
Hurst Brook. PR7 .... 41 F1
Hurst Cres. BB4 .... 85 B3
Hurst Gn. L40 .... 39 C2
Hurst La. BB4 .... 85 B3
Hurst Pk. PR1 .... 95 C4
Hurst St. BL9 .... 32 C2
Hurst's La. L39 .... 7 B2
Hurstead St. BB5 .... 103 E1
Hurstleigh Dr. LA3 .... 209 A7
Hurstmere Ave. FY4 .... 109 E8
Hurstway. PR2 .... 116 D7
Hurstway Cl. PR2 .... 116 D7
Hurstwood Ave. Blackburn BB2 100 A1
Hurstwood Ave. Burnley BB10 .. 127 D5
Hurstwood Ent Pk. BB4 .... 84 A2
Hurstwood Gdns. BB9 .... 147 D4
Hurstwood La. BB10 .... 128 B4
Hurtley St. BB10 .... 127 A8
Hut La. PR6 .... 43 B3
Hutch Bank Rd. BB4 .... 83 F2
Hutchinson Ct. BB3 .... 81 A2
Hutchinson St. 4 BB2 .... 100 E3
Huttock End La. OL13 .... 69 D8
Hutton Cl. LA6 .... 234 C7
Hutton Cres. LA4 .... 212 D4
Hutton Ct. WN8 .... 17 D1
Hutton Dr. BB12 .... 126 F7
Hutton Gr. LA4 .... 212 D4
Hutton Gram Sch. PR4 .... 94 D2
Hutton Hall Ave. PR4 .... 94 F1
Hutton Rd. WN8 .... 17 D1
Hutton St. Blackburn BB1 .... 100 E6
Hutton St. Standish WN1 .... 29 A3
Hutton Way. L39 .... 7 C8
Huyton Rd. PR6 .... 30 A6
Huyton Terr. PR6 .... 30 B6
Hyacinth Cl. BB4 .... 66 F8
Hyatt Cres. WN6 .... 28 C3
Hyde Rd. Blackpool FY1 .... 129 B2
Hyde Rd. Morecambe LA4 .... 213 B4
Hygiene. BB5 .... 123 E2
Hynd Brook House. BB5 .... 103 A5
Hyndburn Bridge. BB5 .... 123 F5
Hyndburn Park Cty Prim Sch.
  BB5 .... 103 A6
Hyndburn Rd. Accrington BB5 .. 103 A6
Hyndburn Rd. Church BB5 .... 102 F6
Hyndburn Rd.
  Great Harwood BB6 .... 123 F5
Hyning Rd. LA5 .... 217 E8
Hynings The. BB6 .... 123 B6
Hythe Cl. Blackburn BB1 .... 101 C4
Hythe Cl. Southport PR8 .... 34 E3

Ibbison Ct. FY1 .... 129 C3
Icconhurst Cl. BB5 .... 103 E2
Ice St. BB1 .... 100 E7
Iddesleigh Rd. 3 PR1 .... 117 E1
Iddon Ct. FY1 .... 129 C6
Idlewood Pl. FY5 .... 150 F8
Idstone Cl. BB2 .... 81 A8
Ighten Rd. BB12 .... 126 C7
Ightenhill Jun Sch. BB12 .... 126 C6
Ightenhill Park La.
  Burnley BB12 .... 126 C8
Ightenhill Park La.
  Padiham BB12 .... 126 C6
Ightenhill Prim Inf Sch. BB12 .. 126 C6
Ightenhill St. BB12 .... 145 C1
Ilford Rd. FY4 .... 129 C1
Ilkley Ave. Lytham St Anne's FY8 .. 89 C6
Ilkley Ave. Southport PR9 .... 53 D4
Ilkley Gr. FY5 .... 150 E8
Illingworth Rd. PR1 .... 117 E1
Ilway. PR7 .... 96 E3
Imperial Gdns. BB9 .... 168 D1
Imperial St. FY1 .... 129 B7
Ince Cres. L37 .... 11 D3
Ince La. PR7 .... 40 C6
Inch Field. BB10 .... 128 B6
Inchfield. WN8 .... 18 B2
India St. Accrington BB5 .... 102 F6
India St. Ramsbottom BL0 .... 49 C3
Industrial Cotts. 9 BB4 .... 68 F8
Industrial Pl. 4 OL13 .... 86 F2
Industrial St. Bacup OL13 .... 87 A2
Industrial St. Ramsbottom BL0 ... 67 C1
Industrial Terr. BB6 .... 143 A4
Industry Rd. 6 OL12 .... 51 F1
Industry St. Darwen BB3 .... 81 B2
Industry St. Whitworth OL12 ...... 70 D2
Infant St. 12 BB5 .... 103 C6
Infirmary Rd. BB2 .... 100 E3
Infirmary Cl. BB2 .... 100 E3
Infirmary St. BB2 .... 100 E2
Ing Dene Cl. BB8 .... 169 B4
Ingersol Rd. BL6 .... 31 E1
Ingham Brow. BL6 .... 31 F4
Ingham St. Barrowford BB9 ...... 168 D3
Ingham St. Bury LA2 .... 32 A1
Ingham St. Padiham BB12 .... 125 D8
Ingle Head. PR2 .... 116 D6
Ingle Mews. PR6 .... 60 D1
Ingle Nook. BB10 .... 127 F4

Ingleborough Dr. BB8 .... 200 A2
Ingleborough Rd. LA1 .... 213 D3
Ingleborough View. LA5 .... 216 E8
Ingleborough Way. PR5 .... 76 C2
Ingleby Cl. Cleveleys FY5 .... 172 F5
Ingleby Cl. Standish WN6 .... 28 D2
Inglehurst Rd. BB11 .... 126 B5
Inglemere Ct. LA5 .... 237 B1
Inglemere Dr. LA5 .... 237 B2
Inglemere Gdns. LA5 .... 237 B1
Inglenook Cl. 7 FY5 .... 172 F1
Ingleton Ave. FY2 .... 150 F4
Ingleton Cl. BB5 .... 103 C5
Ingleton Dr. LA1 .... 211 A4
Ingleton House. 2 LA1 .... 211 A3
Ingleton Rd. Fulwood PR2 .... 117 E4
Ingleton Rd. Southport PR8 .... 34 E3
Ingleway. FY5 .... 172 F3
Ingleway Ave. FY3 .... 129 F6
Inglewhite. WN8 .... 18 A2
Inglewhite Rd. PR3 .... 159 C3
Inglewood Cl. Fleetwood FY7 ... 193 C1
Inglewood Cl. Warton PR4 .... 91 D6
Inglewood Gr. FY2 .... 150 E5
Ingol Gdns. FY6 .... 174 C2
Ingol Gr. FY6 .... 174 C2
Ingol La. FY6 .... 174 D2
Ingol Prim Sch. PR2 .... 115 F4
Ingot St. PR1 .... 95 D8
Ingram. WN8 .... 18 B1
Ings Ave. Barnoldswick BB8 .... 200 B3
Ings Ave. Caldershaw OL12 .... 51 B2
Ings La. OL12 .... 51 C2
Ingthorpe Ave. FY3 .... 150 D5
Inkerman Rd. PR4 .... 131 F6
Inkerman St. Bacup OL13 .... 87 A2
Inkerman St. Blackburn BB1 .... 100 E6
Inkerman St. 4 Padiham BB12 .. 125 C8
Inkerman St. Preston PR1 & PR2 116 D2
Inkerman St. 12 Rochdale OL12 .. 51 F1
Inner Prom. FY8 .... 89 B3
Innes St. OL12 .... 51 C1
Inskip. WN8 .... 18 A2
Inskip Pl. Blackpool FY4 .... 109 E5
Inskip Pl. Lytham St Anne's FY8 .. 89 A8
Inskip Rd. Leyland PR5 .... 75 D2
Inskip Rd. Preston PR2 .... 115 E1
Inskip Rd. Southport PR9 .... 53 A4
Inskip Rd. Wharles PR4 .... 134 A5
Inskip St. BB12 .... 125 C8
Institute St. BB12 .... 125 D8
Intack La. BB2 .... 120 B2
Intack Prim Sch. BB1 .... 101 D5
Intack Rd. PR4 .... 74 B8
Intake Cres. BB12 .... 169 F6
Intake La.
  Barrow Nook L39 & WA11 .... 8 B2
Intake La. Bickerstaffe L39 .... 7 F4
Intake La. Maghull L39 .... 4 E8
Inver Rd. FY2 .... 150 D3
Inverness Rd. BB3 .... 63 F8
Ipswich Pl. FY5 .... 172 C2
Ipswich Rd. PR2 .... 117 D2
Ireby Rd. LA6 .... 236 C3
Irene Pl. BB2 .... 100 B5
Irene St. BB10 .... 127 C5
Iris St. BL0 .... 49 B6
Iron St. Blackburn BB2 .... 100 E3
Iron St. Horwich BL6 .... 31 C2
Irongate. PR5 .... 76 C8
Ironside Cl. PR2 .... 117 B4
Irton Rd. PR9 .... 34 E8
Irvin Ave. PR9 .... 53 C5
Irvine Cl. FY2 .... 150 F5
Irvine Ct. LA2 .... 232 B1
Irvine St. 6 BB9 .... 168 F2
Irving Pl. BB2 .... 100 B5
Irving St. PR8 .... 52 B1
Irwell. WN8 .... 18 A3
Irwell Rd. WN5 .... 10 F7
Irwell St. 7 Bacup OL13 .... 86 F2
Irwell St. Burnley BB12 .... 126 A6
Irwell St. Longridge PR3 .... 139 B7
Irwell St. Longridge PR3 .... 139 B8
Irwell St. Ramsbottom BL0 .... 49 C6
Irwell Terr. 12 OL13 .... 86 F2
Irwell Vale Rd. BB4 .... 67 C6
Isa St. 5 BL0 .... 49 A4
Isabella St. Longridge PR3 .... 139 A8
Isabella St. Lower Healey OL12 ... 51 F2
Isherwood Fold. BL7 .... 47 D7
Isherwood St. Blackburn BB2 ... 100 D1
Isherwood St. 1 Preston PR1 ... 117 B1
Isherwood St. Preston PR1 .... 117 C1
Island Cotts. BL9 .... 49 C2
Island La. PR3 .... 198 B3
Islay Rd. FY8 .... 89 E6
Isle of Man. BB1 .... 121 E4
Isle of Man St. BB4 .... 86 A7
Isleworth Dr. PR7 .... 42 B7
Islington. BB2 .... 100 E3
Islington Cl. BB10 .... 147 D3
Islington St. PR9 .... 53 D2
Ivan St. BB10 .... 147 B2
Ivegate. Colne BB8 .... 169 D5
Ivegate. Foulridge BB8 .... 191 E1
Ivinson Rd. BB3 .... 81 B3
Ivory St. BB12 .... 126 C6
Ivy Ave. Blackpool FY4 .... 109 C5
Ivy Ave. Haslingden BB4 .... 84 C3
Ivy Bank. PR2 .... 117 D6
Ivy Bank High Sch. BB12 .... 125 F7
Ivy Cotts. BB4 .... 68 F8
Ivy Gr. 2 BB4 .... 85 A3
Ivy St. Blackburn BB2 .... 100 E2
Ivy St. Burnley BB10 .... 147 B1
Ivy St. Nelson BB8 & BB9 .... 169 A2
Ivy St. 1 Newchurch BB4 .... 68 F8
Ivy St. Southport PR8 .... 34 D6

Entry	Ref
Ivy Terr. BB3	64 B6
Ivybridge. WN8	18 B2
Ivydale. WN8	18 B2
Jack La. BD23	230 F4
Jackdaw Rd. BL8	48 F2
Jacks Key Dr. BB3	64 C5
Jacksmere La. L40 & PR8	22 B8
Jackson Cl. Haskayne L39	13 F5
Jackson Cl. Lancaster LA1	210 C7
Jackson Heights Rd. BB1	82 B4
Jackson Rd. Chorley PR7	42 A5
Jackson Rd. Leyland PR5	75 D1
Jackson St. 7 Bamber Bridge PR5	76 F8
Jackson St. Blackpool FY3	129 E7
Jackson St. Burnley BB10	127 A8
Jackson St. Chorley PR7	42 D6
Jackson St. 1 Church BB5	102 E5
Jackson St. 5 Clayton-le-M BB5	123 F3
Jackson Terr. LA1	217 D3
Jackson's Banks Rd. BB2	119 E6
Jackson's Common La. L40	23 B1
Jackson's La. L40	26 E7
Jacob St. BB5	103 C5
Jacob's La. PR4	114 A7
Jacson St. 3 PR1	96 A7
Jade Cl. 6 L33	1 A3
Jagoe Mews. BB8	201 B1
Jagoe Rd. BB8	201 A1
James Ave. Blackpool FY4	129 F1
James Ave. Great Harwood BB6	123 B5
James Pl. Coppull PR7	28 E8
James Pl. Standish WN6	28 D2
James Sq. WN6	28 D2
James St. Bacup OL13	69 B7
James St. Bamber Bridge PR5	96 E1
James St. Barnoldswick BB8	200 B1
James St. 4 Barrowford BB9	168 D4
James St. Belthorn BB1	81 F6
James St. Blackburn BB1	100 E5
James St. Burnley BB10	147 A1
James St. Bury BL9	32 A1
James St. 12 Clayton-le-M BB5	123 F3
James St. Colne BB8	169 E4
James St. 1 Darwen BB3	81 A1
James St. Earby BB8	201 B1
James St. Egerton BL7	46 D3
James St. Great Harwood BB6	123 B5
James St. Haslingden BB4	84 A2
James St. Horwich BL6	30 F3
James St. Huncoat BB5	124 E2
James St. 20 Lancaster LA1	210 F8
James St. Morecambe LA4	212 F5
James St. Oswaldtwistle BB5	102 D3
James St. Preston PR1	96 B7
James St. Rawtenstall BB4	85 A2
James St. Rishton BB1	123 C1
James St. Salterforth BB8	191 D7
James St. Whitworth OL12	70 D2
James St W. 6 BB3	81 A1
Jameson Rd. FY7	194 A1
Jameson St. FY1	129 C3
Jane La. Catforth PR4	134 E5
Jane La. Leyland PR5	75 A3
Jane St. OL12	70 E6
Jane's Brook Rd. PR8	34 E4
Janice Dr. PR2	116 D7
Jannat Cl. BB5	103 B5
Jarrett Rd. L33	1 A4
Jarrett Wlk. L33	1 A4
Jarvis Cl. L33	51 F1
Jasmine Rd. PR1	96 A3
Jasper St. BB1	121 F1
Jefferson Cl. LA1	210 D7
Jefferson Way. OL12	51 F3
Jeffrey Ave. PR3	139 B7
Jeffrey Sq. FY1	129 D3
Jellicoe Cl. FY8	109 E1
Jem Gate. FY5	150 D8
Jemmett St. PR1	116 E2
Jenny La. Blackpool FY4	110 C7
Jenny La. Higher Wheelton PR6	78 C1
Jenny St. BB9	147 D6
Jensen Cl. LA1	210 E6
Jensen Dr. FY4	111 A6
Jepheys Pl. 17 OL12	51 F1
Jepheys St. OL12	51 F1
Jepp Hill. 4 BB8	200 B2
Jepps Ave. PR3	136 B7
Jepps La. PR3	136 B8
Jepson St. 8 BB3	64 A8
Jepson Way. FY4	109 F4
Jericho Rd. BL9	32 E4
Jersey Ave. FY2	150 E2
Jersey St. BB2	100 B1
Jervis Cl. FY8	109 D1
Jesmond Ave. FY4	109 B7
Jesmond Gr. LA4	212 G3
Jessel St. BB2	100 B2
Jesson Way. LA5	217 C1
Jevington Way. LA3	209 A7
Jib Hill Cotts. BB10	147 D2
Jingling La. LA6	238 C2
Jinny La. BB12	167 E4
Jobling St. BB8	169 B3
Jockey St. BB4	126 C5
Joe Connolly Way. BB4	68 E8
Joe La. PR3	178 D2
John Cross CE Prim Sch. PR3	157 A4
John Henry St. OL12	70 D4
John Hill St. FY4	129 F2
John Kay Ct. LA1	213 D3
John o' Gaunt St. 13 BB12	145 C1
John St. 1 Bamber Bridge PR5	96 E1
John St. Barnoldswick BB8	200 B1
John St. Barrowford BB9	168 E4
John St. Blackpool FY1	129 B2
John St. Brierfield BB9	147 B6
John St. Carnforth LA5	217 D2
John St. Church BB5	102 E7
John St. Clayton-le-M BB5	123 F3
John St. Colne BB8	169 C4
John St. Coppull PR7	41 E1
John St. Darwen BB3	80 F2
John St. Earby BB8	201 B1
John St. Galgate LA2	207 A3
John St. Haslingden BB4	84 B3
John St. Leyland PR5	76 A1
John St. Newchurch BB4	85 F1
John St. Oswaldtwistle BB5	102 D3
John St. Thornton FY5	173 B4
John St. Whitworth OL12	70 D2
John Wall St. BB7	164 D8
John William St. 7 PR1	96 C8
Johnny Barn Cl. BB4	85 D2
Johnny Barn Cotts. BB4	85 D2
Johnson Cl. Carnforth LA5	217 C1
Johnson Cl. Lancaster LA1	210 C7
Johnson New Rd. BB3	81 E2
Johnson Rd. Blackpool FY4	129 F2
Johnson St. Waterside BB3	81 D4
Johnson St. PR8 & PR9	34 B8
Johnson's Meanygate. PR4	55 D7
Johnspool. PR2	116 C6
Johnston Cl. BB2	100 C5
Johnston St. BB2	100 C5
Johnsville Ave. FY4	109 E7
Joiner's Row. BB1 & BB2	100 E3
Joiners Alley. 8 BB6	123 C5
Jolly Tar La. PR7	29 B7
Jonathan Cl. BB4	67 A8
Jones' Gr. FY7	194 B5
Jones St. BL6	31 B4
Jones's Yd. LA6	234 B7
Joseph St. Barrowford BB9	168 D2
Joseph St. Darwen BB3	81 B1
Joseph St. Falinge Fold OL12	51 D2
Joy Pl. OL12	51 F2
Joy St. Lower Healey OL12	51 F2
Joy St. Ramsbottom BL0	49 B6
Joyce Ave. FY4	129 F2
Jubilee Ave. Ormskirk L39	15 F6
Jubilee Ave. Orrell WN5	10 D4
Jubilee Ave. Preesall FY6	195 A4
Jubilee Cl. BB4	84 A1
Jubilee Cl. 1 BB4	84 A1
Jubilee Cts. PR5	58 E8
Jubilee Dr. Cleveleys FY5	172 C4
Jubilee Dr. Skelmersdale WN8	8 F8
Jubilee La. Blackpool FY4	110 B5
Jubilee La. Blackpool FY4	110 B6
Jubilee Rd. 5 Bamber Bridge PR5	76 A8
Jubilee Rd. Church BB5	102 F7
Jubilee Rd. Formby L37	11 D1
Jubilee Rd. Haslingden BB4	84 A1
Jubilee Rd. Blackburn BB1 & BB2	100 E4
Jubilee Rd. Brierfield BB10	147 F3
Jubilee St. Darwen BB3	81 A1
Jubilee St. Enfield BB5	124 A1
Jubilee St. Oswaldtwistle BB5	102 E4
Jubilee St. Read BB12	144 D2
Jubilee Terr. PR4	92 C7
Jubilee Trad Est. PR1	116 E1
Jubilee Way. FY8	89 C8
Judd Holmes La. PR3	160 D7
Jude St. BB9	147 D8
Judeland. PR7	60 A2
Judge Fields. BB8	169 D6
Judith St. OL12	51 C3
Julia Mews. 4 BL6	31 B4
Julia St. BL6	31 B4
July St. 16 BB1	101 A4
Jumbles Ctry Pk. BL7	47 D2
Jumps La. OL14	108 E1
Junction La. L40	24 E3
Junction Rd. Preston PR1 & PR2	95 D7
Junction Rd. Rainford Junction WA11	8 F1
Junction St. Brierfield BB9	147 B6
Junction St. Burnley BB11 & BB12	126 E6
Junction St. Burnley BB12	126 E7
Junction St. Darwen BB3	64 B7
Junction St. Nelson BB8 & BB9	169 A3
June Ave. FY4	130 A1
June St. 16 BB1	101 A4
June's Wlk. PR4	74 A5
Juniper Cl. FY6	195 A5
Juniper Croft. PR6	77 A1
Juniper Cts. BB5	103 E8
Juniper St. 4 BB1	101 A7
Juno St. BB9	168 F2
Jutland St. PR1	96 A8
Kairnryan Cl. FY2	150 F5
Kaley La. BB7	187 C5
Kane St. PR1	116 C1
Kate St. 3 BL0	49 B6
Kateholm. OL13	87 A7
Kay Brow. BL0	49 C6
Kay Gdns. BB11	127 B5
Kay St. Blackburn BB2	100 E3
Kay St. Blackpool FY1	129 B4
Kay St. Brierfield BB9	147 B5
Kay St. Bury BL9	32 A3
Kay St. Chapeltown BL7	47 C4
Kay St. Clitheroe BB7	164 D6
Kay St. Darwen BB3	81 B1
Kay St. Oswaldtwistle BB5	102 D3
Kay St. Padiham BB12	145 D1
Kay St. Preston PR1	95 E7
Kay St. Ramsbottom BL0 & BL9	49 C3
Kay St. Rawtenstall BB4	85 A2
Kaymar Ind Est. PR1	96 C7
Kayswell Rd. LA4	213 B5
Kearsley Ave. PR4	56 A6
Keasdale Ave. LA7	237 E3
Keasdale Rd. LA7	237 E3
Keasden Ave. FY4	109 D7
Keasden Rd. BB7	229 E6
Keating Ct. FY7	194 A3
Keats Ave. Bolton-le-S LA5	216 A5
Keats Ave. Caldershaw OL12	51 A1
Keats Ave. Longshaw WN5	10 D1
Keats Ave. Warton PR4	91 E6
Keats Cl. Accrington BB5	103 E2
Keats Cl. Colne BB8	169 D6
Keats Cl. Eccleston PR7	40 D5
Keats Cl. Thornton FY5	173 A2
Keats Rd. BB8	48 F2
Kebs Rd. OL14	108 E3
Keeper's Hey. FY5	173 A4
Keeper's La. PR3	199 F1
Keer Bank. 1 LA1	213 C2
Keer Holme La. LA6	234 E4
Keighley Ave. BB8	169 D6
Keighley Cl. BB8	169 F5
Keighley Rd. Laneshaw Bridge BB8 & BB22	170 D6
Keighley Rd. Trawden BB8	170 C4
Keirby Wlk. BB11	127 A6
Keith Gr. FY5	172 D1
Keith St. BB12	126 C6
Kelbrook Dr. BB11	126 E3
Kelbrook Prim Sch. BB8	192 A6
Kelbrook Rd. BB8	191 D7
Kelbeck Cl. L31	5 F2
Kellet Acre. PR5	76 A7
Kellet Ave. PR6	76 D1
Kellet Ct. 1 LA1	210 E8
Kellet La. Bolton-le-S LA5 & LA2	216 C3
Kellet La. Borwick LA6	234 B3
Kellet La. Walton Summit PR5	77 B7
Kellet Rd. Carnforth LA5 & LA6	217 C1
Kellet Rd. Over Kellet LA6	234 A1
Kellett St. 7 PR6	42 C8
Kelmarsh Cl. FY3	130 B2
Kelne House. 4 LA1	210 E8
Kelsall Ave. BB1	101 B8
Kelsey St. LA1	210 E8
Kelso Ave. FY5	172 D1
Kelsons Ave. FY5	173 C2
Kelswick Dr. BB9	147 E6
Kelverdale Rd. FY5	150 F8
Kelvin Rd. FY5	150 D6
Kelvin St. BB1	80 F1
Kelwood Ave. BL9	32 D5
Kem Mill La. PR6	60 B8
Kemble Cl. BL6	31 B5
Kemp Ct. BB1	121 F3
Kemp St. FY7	194 B4
Kemple View. BB7	164 D6
Kempton Ave. FY3	129 E3
Kempton Park Fold. PR8	34 F3
Kempton Rd. LA1	211 B4
Kempton Rise. BB1	100 F3
Kenbury Cl. L33	1 A4
Kenbury Rd. L33	1 A4
Kendal Ave. Barrowford BB9	168 D4
Kendal Ave. Blackpool FY3	151 A1
Kendal Ave. Cleveleys FY5	172 D4
Kendal Dr. Maghull L31	5 E2
Kendal Dr. Morecambe LA4	213 B4
Kendal Dr. Rainford Junction WA11	8 F2
Kendal Rd. Lytham St Anne's FY8	109 D1
Kendal Rd. Ramsbottom BL0	49 A2
Kendal Rd W. BL0	48 F2
Kendal Row. BB1	81 F6
Kendal St. Blackburn BB1	100 E6
Kendal St. Clitheroe BB7	186 F1
Kendal St. 4 Nelson BB8	168 D1
Kendal St. Preston PR1	95 E8
Kendal Way. PR8	20 B3
Kenilworth Ave. FY7	193 E3
Kenilworth Cl. BB12	125 E8
Kenilworth Ct. FY8	88 F6
Kenilworth Dr. Clitheroe BB7	164 C6
Kenilworth Dr. Earby BB8	192 A8
Kenilworth Gdns. FY4	109 B7
Kenilworth Pl. Fleetwood FY7	193 E3
Kenilworth Pl. Lancaster LA1	211 A5
Kenilworth Rd. Ainsdale PR8	20 B4
Kenilworth Rd. Lytham St Anne's FY8	88 F6
Kenilworth Rd. Morecambe LA3	212 F3
Kenlis Rd. PR3	178 F4
Kenmay Way. 12 L33	1 A3
Kenmure Pl. PR1	116 F2
Kennedy Cl. Lancaster LA1	210 D6
Kennedy Cl. Standish WN6	28 F1
Kennelwood Ave. 4 L33	1 A3
Kennet Dr. PR2	116 F8
Kennington Cty Prim Sch. PR2	117 A4
Kennington Ave. PR1	95 B6
Kennington Rd. PR2	117 A4
Kensington Ave. PR1	95 B6
Kensington Cl. BL8	49 A1
Kensington Dr. BL6	31 D3
Kensington Ind Pk. PR9	34 C6
Kensington Pl. BB11	126 D4
Kensington Rd. Blackpool FY3	129 E4
Kensington Rd. Chorley PR7	42 B7
Kensington Rd. Cleveleys FY5	172 C3
Kensington Rd. Formby L37	11 E1
Kensington Rd. Lancaster LA1	210 F5
Kensington Rd. Lytham St Anne's FY8	89 D4
Kensington Rd. Morecambe LA4	212 C4
Kensington Rd. Southport PR9	34 C6
Kensington St. BB9	147 C5
Kent Ave. Bamber Bridge PR5	96 E3
Kent Ave. Cleveleys FY5	172 E4
Kent Ave. Formby L37	12 A1
Kent Ct. BB9	168 D4
Kent Dr. Blackburn BB1	101 E4
Kent Dr. Clayton-le-W PR5 & PR6	76 D1
Kent House. LA1	210 F7
Kent Rd. Blackpool FY1	129 C3
Kent Rd. Formby L37	12 A1
Kent Rd. Southport PR8	34 A4
Kent St. Blackburn BB1	100 F4
Kent St. Burnley BB12	126 F7
Kent St. Fleetwood FY7	194 B5
Kent St. Lancaster LA1	213 F2
Kent St. Preston PR1	116 F2
Kent Wlk. LA1	67 A8
Kent's Cl. PR4	112 E7
Kentmere Ave. Bamber Bridge PR5	96 E1
Kentmere Ave. Leyland PR5	76 A3
Kentmere Cl. Burnley BB12	126 B8
Kentmere Cl. Fleetwood FY7	193 D3
Kentmere Dr. Blackburn BB2	79 E8
Kentmere Dr. Blackpool FY4	130 C1
Kentmere Dr. Longton PR4	74 B8
Kentmere Gr. 1 LA4	212 G4
Kentmere Rd. LA1	214 A1
Kenton Cl. L37	11 F6
Kenwood Ave. LA4	212 D4
Kenworthy St. BB1	100 F6
Kenworthys Flats. PR8	34 B8
Kenwyn Ave. FY3	129 E3
Kenyon La. PR6	60 F7
Kenyon La. Morecambe LA4	213 B5
Kenyon Rd. Nelson BB9	147 B7
Kenyon Rd. Standish WN6	28 D2
Kenyon St. 6 Accrington BB5	103 C6
Kenyon St. Bacup OL13	70 B8
Kenyon St. Bury BL9	32 A1
Kenyon St. Ramsbottom BL0	49 B6
Kenyon St. Rawtenstall BB4	85 A3
Kenyon's La. L37	12 A3
Kenyons La. L31	5 E3
Keppel Pl. BB11	126 E6
Kepple La. PR3	178 B6
Kerenhappuch St. 5 BL0	49 B5
Kerfoot's La. WN8	8 C8
Kerr Pl. PR1	95 D8
Kershaw Ave. BB5	85 A7
Kershaw St. 8 Bacup OL13	86 F2
Kershaw St. Bury BL9	32 A2
Kershaw St. Chorley PR6	60 E1
Kershaw St. Church BB5	102 E7
Kerslake Way. L38	3 A4
Kerslea Ave. FY3	130 D8
Keston Gr. FY4	109 C5
Kestor Gr. PR3	139 A7
Kestrel Cl. Blackburn BB1	100 D8
Kestrel Cl. Cleveleys FY5	172 F4
Kestrel Cl. Knowley PR6	61 A3
Kestrel Cl. PR9	34 D7
Kestrel Dr. BL9	32 B4
Kestrel Mews. WN8	18 C4
Kestrel Pk. WN8	18 C4
Keswick Cl. Accrington BB5	124 D1
Keswick Cl. Ainsdale PR8	20 C3
Keswick Cl. Maghull L31	5 E2
Keswick Cl. LA1	214 B1
Keswick Dr. BB2	79 E8
Keswick Gr. Heysham LA3	208 E5
Keswick Gr. Knott End-on-S FY6	194 F5
Keswick Rd. Blackpool FY1	129 C3
Keswick Rd. Burnley BB10	147 B2
Keswick Rd. Lancaster LA1	214 B1
Keswick Rd. Lytham St Anne's FY8	88 E8
Keswick Way. WA11	8 F2
Keswick Wlk. LA1	214 B1
Kettering Rd. PR8	20 B5
Kevin Ave. FY6	151 F5
Kevin Gr. LA3	209 D1
Kew Gdns. Leyland PR5	76 B3
Kew Gdns. Penwortham PR1	95 B5
Kew Gr. FY5	172 D1
Kew Rd. Formby L37	11 D1
Kew Rd. Nelson BB9	168 F2
Kew Rd. Southport PR8	34 B3
Kew Woods Cty Prim Sch. PR8	34 F3
Key View. BB5	64 C5
Keynsham Gr. BB12	126 D7
Khyber St. BB8	169 C4
Kibble Cres. BB10	147 C3
Kibble Gr. BB9	147 D4
Kibboth Crew. BL0	49 B7
Kidder St. BB2	80 D8
Kiddlington Cl. PR5	76 D8
Kiddrow La. BB12	126 A7
Kidsgrove. PR2	115 F5
Kielder Ct. FY5	90 C4
Kielder Dr. BB12	126 E7
Kilbane St. FY7	193 F1
Kilburn Rd. WN5 & WN8	10 C5
Kilcrash La. PR3	177 D7
Kildale Cl. L31	5 C2
Kildare Ave. FY5	173 A4
Kildare Rd. FY2	150 D3
Kilgrimol Gdns. FY8	109 C1
Killer St. 1 BL0	49 C6
Killiard La. BB2	99 E5
Killingbeck Cl. L40	24 C4
Killington St. BB10	147 C2
Killingworth Mews. BL6	31 D1
Killon St. BL9	32 A1
Kilmory Pl. FY2	150 F5
Kilmuir Cl. PR2	117 C5
Kiln Bank. OL12	70 C2
Kiln Bank La. OL12	70 C2
Kiln Cl. BB7	187 A2
Kiln Croft. PR6	77 B3
Kiln Hill. BB12	145 F6
Kiln House Way. BB5	103 A3
Kiln La. Hambleton FY6	174 B2
Kiln La. Paythorne BB7	225 C6
Kiln La. Rimington BB7	224 F2
Kiln La. Skelmersdale WN8	17 E1
Kiln La. Wray LA2	232 D6
Kiln St. Nelson BB9	147 B8
Kiln St. 5 Ramsbottom BL0	49 B5
Kiln Terr. 5 OL13	69 B2
Kilnbank Ave. LA4	212 D5
Kilngate. PR5	96 C3
Kilnhouse La. FY8	110 A1
Kilns The. BB1	127 B3
Kilruddery Rd. PR1	95 C5
Kilworth Height. PR2	116 C5
Kimberley Ave. FY4	109 D5
Kimberley Cl. BB10	147 F3
Kimberley Rd. PR1	116 C2
Kimberley St. Bacup OL13	69 A7
Kimberley St. Brierfield BB10	147 F3
Kimberley St. Coppull PR7	41 E1
Kimberly Cl. PR4	92 B6
Kimble Cl. BL8	48 F2
Kime St. BB12	126 C6
Kincraig Pl. FY2	150 F6
Kincraig Rd. FY2	150 F5
King Edward Ave. Blackpool FY2	150 B1
King Edward Ave. Lytham St Anne's FY8	89 A4
King Edward St. BB5	102 C3
King Edward VII & Queen Mary Jun Sch. FY8	89 A4
King Edward VII Sch. FY8	89 B4
King George Ave. FY2	150 B1
King George V Coll. PR8	34 E5
King St. BB7	164 B8
King St. Accrington BB5	103 B6
King St. 5 Bacup OL13	86 F2
King St. Bamber Bridge PR5	76 B7
King St. Barnoldswick BB8	200 B2
King St. Blackburn BB2	100 A4
King St. Brierfield BB9	147 A5
King St. Brierfield BB10	147 F3
King St. Carnforth LA5	217 D1
King St. Chorley PR7	42 D1
King St. 4 Clayton-le-M BB5	123 F2
King St. Clitheroe BB7	164 E8
King St. Colne BB8	169 E5
King St. Fleetwood FY7	194 A4
King St. 12 Great Harwood BB6	123 C5
King St. Haslingden BB4	84 B4
King St. High Bentham LA2	233 D8
King St. Horwich BL6	31 A4
King St. Lancaster LA1	210 F8
King St. Leyland PR5	76 A1
King St. Longridge PR3	139 B7
King St. Morecambe LA4	212 E5
King St. Newchurch BB4	68 B8
King St. Padiham BB12	125 C8
King St. Ramsbottom BL0	49 C6
King St. Southport PR8	34 A6
King St. Whalley BB7	143 C5
King St. Whitworth OL12	70 D3
King Street Terr. PR3	147 A5
King William St. BB1 & BB2	100 E5
King's Bridge Cl. BB2	100 B1
King's Bridge St. BB2	100 B1
King's Bridge Wharfe. BB2	100 B1
King's Cl. FY5	151 E3
King's Cres. LA3	212 B3
King's Croft. PR5	96 D5
King's Croft Mews. PR5	96 D5
King's Cswy. BB9	147 E5
King's Dr. LA5	217 C1
King's Highway. Accrington BB5 & BB4	104 B2
King's Highway. Huncoat BB5	103 F8
King's Rd. Accrington BB5	103 B7
King's Rd. Blackburn BB2	100 B1
King's Rd. Lytham St Anne's FY8	88 E5
King's Sq. FY1	129 C5
King's Wlk. FY5	172 D5
Kingfisher Bank. BB11	126 C4
Kingfisher Cl. BB1	100 E8
Kingfisher Ct. Oswaldtwistle BB5	102 E3
Kingfisher Ct. Southport PR9	34 D8
Kingfisher Dr. Bury BL9	32 B4
Kingfisher Dr. Poulton-le-F FY6	151 B2
Kingfisher Mews. FY6	151 B2
Kingfisher Pk. WN8	18 C4
Kingfisher St. PR1	117 B1
Kings Arms Cl. 13 LA1	210 F8
Kings Ave. BB4	85 A1
Kings Cl. Arnside LA5	237 B1
Kings Cl. Formby L37	11 E2
Kings Cres. PR5	76 A1
Kings Ct. PR5	76 A1
Kings Dr. Fulwood PR2	116 D5
Kings Dr. Hoddlesden BB3	81 F1
Kings Dr. Padiham BB12	125 E6

Kings Hey Dr. PR9 .... 52 F1
Kings Rd. Cleveleys FY5 .... 172 C2
Kings Rd. Formby L37 .... 11 E2
Kingsacre. PR3 .... 178 A3
Kingsbridge Cl. PR1 .... 95 E2
Kingsbury Cl. PR8 .... 20 B4
Kingsbury Ct. WN8 .... 18 C4
Kingsbury Pl. BB10 .... 147 D3
Kingscote Dr. FY3 .... 129 E7
Kingsdale Ave. Brierfield BB10 .. 147 C3
Kingsdale Ave. Fulwood PR2 ..... 117 D5
Kingsdale Ave. Morecambe LA3 212 B1
Kingsdale Cl. Leyland PR5 .... 59 B6
Kingsdale Cl. Walton-le-D PR5 .... 96 F5
Kingsdale Rd. LA1 .... 210 D7
Kingsfold Christian Sch. PR4 .... 72 F2
Kingsfold Dr. PR1 .... 95 D2
Kingsfold Prim Sch. PR1 .... 95 D2
Kingshaven Dr. PR1 .... 95 E2
Kingshotte Gdns. BB9 .... 168 C3
Kingsland Gr. FY1 .... 129 D3
Kingsland Rd. BB11 .... 127 B4
Kingslea. PR7 .... 29 F8
Kingsley Ave. BB12 .... 125 E7
Kingsley Cl. Church BB5 .... 102 F7
Kingsley Cl. Maghull L31 .... 5 C5
Kingsley Cl. Thornton FY5 .... 173 A3
Kingsley Dr. PR7 .... 42 A5
Kingsley Rd. Blackpool FY3 ..... 130 B2
Kingsley St. BB9 .... 168 F2
Kingsmead. Blackburn BB1 ...... 101 D4
Kingsmead. Chorley PR7 .... 42 C5
Kingsmede. FY4 .... 109 E6
Kingsmere Ave. FY8 .... 109 F1
Kingsmill Ave. BB7 .... 143 A8
Kingsmuir Ave. PR2 .... 117 D4
Kingsmuir Cl. LA3 .... 208 E2
Kingston Ave. Accrington BB5 ... 103 A4
Kingston Ave. Blackpool FY4 .... 109 C5
Kingston Cl. FY4 .... 194 F6
Kingston Cres. Haslingden BB4 ... 67 A7
Kingston Cres. Southport PR9 .... 53 C5
Kingston Dr. FY8 .... 89 D6
Kingston Mews. FY5 .... 173 B3
Kingston Pl. BB3 .... 80 F7
Kingsway. Accrington BB5 ...... 103 A8
Kingsway. Bamber Bridge PR5 .... 76 E8
Kingsway. Blackburn BB3 .... 81 A7
Kingsway. Blackpool FY4 .... 109 C7
Kingsway. Burnley BB11 .... 127 A6
Kingsway. Cleveleys FY5 .... 172 C2
Kingsway. Euxton PR7 .... 59 E2
Kingsway. Great Harwood BB6 .. 123 F6
Kingsway. Hapton BB11 .... 125 C3
Kingsway. Heysham LA3 .... 209 A8
Kingsway. Huncoat BB5 .... 124 F1
Kingsway. Lancaster LA1 .... 214 A1
Kingsway. Leyland PR5 .... 58 E2
Kingsway. Lytham St Anne's FY8 . 89 C4
Kingsway. Penwortham PR1 ...... 95 B6
Kingsway. Preston PR2 .... 115 F2
Kingsway. Southport PR8 .... 34 A2
Kingsway Ave. PR3 .... 136 C3
Kingsway Ct. Broughton PR3 ..... 136 C3
Kingsway Ct. Morecambe LA3 .. 212 B1
Kingsway Sports Ctr. LA1 ...... 214 A1
Kingsway W. PR1 .... 95 B6
Kingswood Cl. FY8 .... 89 E4
Kingswood Rd. PR5 .... 76 A2
Kingswood Schs. PR8 .... 33 F5
Kingswood St. PR1 .... 95 E7
Kinloch Way. L39 .... 15 D6
Kinnerton Pl. FY5 .... 150 F8
Kinross Cl. BB1 .... 101 A4
Kinross Cres. FY4 .... 130 A1
Kinross St. BB11 .... 126 D4
Kinross Wlk. 7 BB1 .... 101 A4
Kintbury Rd. FY8 .... 88 F4
Kintour Rd. FY8 .... 89 E6
Kintyre Cl. FY4 .... 109 F7
Kintyre Way. LA3 .... 208 E2
Kipling Dr. FY3 .... 130 B2
Kipling Pl. BB6 .... 123 B4
Kirby Dr. PR4 .... 92 B6
Kirby Rd. Blackburn BB2 .... 100 D1
Kirby Rd. Blackpool FY1 .... 129 B2
Kirby Rd. Nelson BB9 .... 147 B8
Kirk Ave. BB7 .... 164 C8
Kirk Head. PR4 .... 73 E2
Kirk Hill Rd. BB4 .... 84 C3
Kirk House. BB5 .... 102 E6
Kirk Rd. BB5 .... 102 E7
Kirk View. BB4 .... 86 A1
Kirkbeck Cl. LA2 .... 231 D3
Kirkby Ave. Clayton-le-W PR6 .. 76 E1
Kirkby Ave. Cleveleys FY5 ..... 172 E4
Kirkby Bank Rd. L33 .... 1 C2
Kirkby Londsdale Rd. LA2 ..... 214 F7
Kirkby Lonsdale Rd.
    Over Kellet LA2 & LA6 ...... 231 B6
Kirkby Lonsdale Rd.
    Over Kellet LA6 .... 234 B1
Kirkdale Ave.
    Lytham St Anne's FY8 .... 88 F7
Kirkdale Ave. Newchurch BB4 ... 85 E1
Kirkdale Cl. BB3 .... 64 C6
Kirkdale Gdns. WN8 .... 10 A7
Kirkdale Rd. BB6 .... 122 C8
Kirkdene Ave. BB8 .... 191 D4
Kirkes Rd. LA1 .... 211 A2
Kirkfell Dr. BB12 .... 126 C8
Kirkfield. PR3 .... 182 D3
Kirkgate. Burnley BB11 .... 127 B4
Kirkgate. Kirkham PR4 .... 113 B4
Kirkgate La. LA6 .... 234 B4

Kirkham Ave. FY1 .... 129 E2
Kirkham By-Pass. PR4 .... 113 B4
Kirkham Cl. PR5 .... 75 D1
Kirkham Gram Jun Sch. PR4 .. 112 F4
Kirkham Gram Sch. PR4 .... 112 F5
Kirkham Rd. Freckleton PR4 .... 92 B8
Kirkham Rd. Kirkham PR4 ..... 113 A4
Kirkham Rd. Kirkham PR4 ..... 113 E6
Kirkham Rd. Southport PR9 ..... 53 A4
Kirkham Rd. Weeton PR4 ...... 131 F2
Kirkham St. PR1 .... 95 E8
Kirkham Trad Pk. PR4 .... 113 B4
Kirkham & Wesham Cty
    Prim Sch. PR4 .... 112 F5
Kirkham & Wesham Sta. PR4 .. 112 F6
Kirklake Bank. L37 .... 11 C2
Kirklake Rd. L37 .... 11 D2
Kirkland Pl. PR2 .... 94 E8
Kirkland Sch. PR3 .... 178 A2
Kirklands. Chipping PR3 .... 182 E3
Kirklands. Hest Bank LA2 ...... 215 E1
Kirklees Rd. PR8 .... 33 F1
Kirkmoor Cl. BB7 .... 186 D1
Kirkstall Ave. Blackpool FY1 .. 129 E2
Kirkstall Ave. Read BB12 ...... 144 D1
Kirkstall Cl. PR7 .... 42 D5
Kirkstall Dr. Barnoldswick BB8 . 200 D3
Kirkstall Dr. Chorley PR7 ...... 42 D5
Kirkstall Dr. Chorley PR7 ...... 42 D5
Kirkstall Rd. Southport PR7 .... 33 F2
Kirkstone Ave. Blackburn BB2 .. 79 E8
Kirkstone Ave. Fleetwood FY7 . 193 E2
Kirkstone Dr. Blackpool FY5 ... 150 C7
Kirkstone Dr. Morecambe LA4 . 212 G6
Kirkstone Rd. FY8 .... 109 D1
Kirton Cres. FY8 .... 89 C6
Kirton Pl. FY5 .... 172 E1
Kit Brow La. LA2 .... 207 D6
Kittiwake Rd. PR6 .... 61 A3
Kittlingborne Brow. PR5 .... 97 A3
Kitty La. FY4 .... 110 B4
Kittygill La. LA6 .... 238 A1
Knacks La. OL12 .... 51 A5
Knaresboro Ave. FY3 .... 129 F3
Knaresborough Cl. PR4 .... 151 D5
Knighton Ave. BB1 & BB2 ...... 100 C8
Knights Cl. FY5 .... 172 F1
Knightsbrdige Cl. PR4 .... 112 E6
Knightsbridge Ave.
    Blackpool FY4 .... 109 D6
Knightsbridge Ave. Colne BB8 . 169 B5
Knightsbridge Cl. Kirkham PR4 112 E6
Knightsbridge Cl.
    Lytham St Anne's FY8 .... 89 D6
Knightscliffe Cres. WN6 .... 19 D6
Knitting Row La. PR3 .... 175 A3
Knob Hall La. PR9 .... 52 F3
Knoll La. PR4 .... 74 A4
Knoll The. LA2 .... 213 E8
Knot Acre. PR4 .... 75 A8
Knot La.
    Newsholme BB7 & BD23 ..... 225 D5
Knot La. Walton-le-D PR5 ...... 96 F5
Knott End & Fleetwood
    Golf Links. FY6 .... 194 D4
Knott Hill St. OL12 .... 70 E6
Knott La. LA5 .... 218 A8
Knott St. BB3 .... 81 A1
Knotts Brow. BL7 .... 47 F4
Knotts La. Colne BB8 .... 169 D3
Knotts La. Knotts BB7 & BD23 .. 224 B8
Knotts La. Padiham BB12 ...... 125 E6
Knotts Mount. BB8 .... 169 C3
Knowe Hill Cres. LA1 .... 211 B3
Knowl Cl. BL0 .... 49 C4
Knowl Gap Ave. BB4 .... 84 A1
Knowl Meadow. BB4 .... 67 A6
Knowle Ave. Ainsdale PR8 ...... 20 C6
Knowle Ave. Blackpool FY2 .... 150 C1
Knowle Ave. Cleveleys FY5 .... 172 E2
Knowle Green Rd. PR3 .... 140 A8
Knowle The. FY2 .... 150 C2
Knowles Brow. BB7 .... 163 B3
Knowles Rd. FY8 .... 88 E7
Knowles St. Chorley PR7 .... 42 C6
Knowles St. Preston PR1 .... 96 D8
Knowles St. Rishton BB1 ...... 123 B1
Knowlesly Meadows. BB3 .... 64 C6
Knowlesly Rd. BB3 .... 64 B6
Knowley Brow. PR6 .... 60 E2
Knowlmere St. BB5 .... 103 B7
Knowlys Ave. LA3 .... 208 F8
Knowlys Cres. LA3 .... 208 F8
Knowlys Dr. LA3 .... 208 F8
Knowlys Gr. LA3 .... 208 F8
Knowlys Rd. LA3 .... 208 E8
Knowsley Ave. Blackpool FY3 .. 129 E3
Knowsley Ave. Leyland PR5 .... 76 C4
Knowsley Cl. Gregson Lane PR5 . 97 F2
Knowsley Cl. Shawforth OL12 .. 70 E6
Knowsley Cres. Thornton FY5 . 173 C1
Knowsley Cres. Weeton PR4 .. 131 E2
Knowsley Dr. PR5 .... 97 F2
Knowsley Gate. FY7 .... 193 D4
Knowsley Gr. BL6 .... 31 D1
Knowsley Ind Est. L33 .... 1 C2
Knowsley La.
    Edgworth BL7 .... 65 C4
Knowsley La.
    Rivington PR6 & PR7 .... 43 E4
Knowsley Park Way. BB4 .... 67 B8
Knowsley Rd. Haslingden BB4 ... 67 B8
Knowsley Rd. Leyland PR6 ...... 59 C8
Knowsley Rd. Ormskirk L39 .... 15 F5

Knowsley Rd.
    Southport PR8 & PR9 .... 52 C1
Knowsley Rd. Wilpshire BB1 ... 121 F5
Knowsley Rd Ind Est. BB4 ..... 67 B8
Knowsley Rd W. BB1 .... 121 F5
Knowsley Road Ind Est. BB4 ... 84 B1
Knowsley St. 3 Colne BB8 .... 169 D4
Knowsley St. 32 Preston PR1 ... 96 A7
Knox Gr. FY1 .... 129 D3
Knuck Knowles Dr. BB7 .... 186 L1
Knutsford Rd. FY3 .... 130 B2
Knutsford Wlk. L31 .... 5 D4
Korea Rd. PR2 .... 117 B4
Kumara Cres. FY4 .... 130 B1
Kyan St. BB10 .... 147 B2
Kylemore Ave. FY2 .... 150 D3
Kyston Cl. FY1 .... 129 D7

Laburnam Cotts. PR3 .... 196 E5
Laburnum Ave.
    Bamber Bridge PR5 .... 76 B8
Laburnum Ave.
    Lytham St Anne's FY8 .... 90 B5
Laburnum Cl. Burnley BB11 ... 126 D3
Laburnum Cl. Fulwood PR2 .... 117 C3
Laburnum Dr. Fulwood PR2 ... 116 D8
Laburnum Dr.
    Oswaldtwistle BB5 .... 102 F3
Laburnum Gr.
    Burscough Bridge L40 .... 24 E6
Laburnum Gr. Horwich BL6 .... 31 E1
Laburnum Gr. Lancaster LA1 .. 210 D8
Laburnum Gr. Maghull L31 ...... 5 F1
Laburnum Gr.
    Southport PR8 & PR9 .... 34 F7
Laburnum Pk. LA5 .... 216 C8
Laburnum Rd. Blackburn BB1 .. 101 A8
Laburnum Rd. Chorley PR6 ..... 60 D3
Laburnum Rd. Helmshore BB4 .. 67 A7
Laburnum Rd. Lancaster LA1 .. 213 F2
Laburnum St. Blackpool FY3 .. 129 D7
Laburnum St. Haslingden BB4 .. 84 A3
Lacey St. 16 BB4 .... 84 B3
Lachman Rd. BB8 .... 170 B3
Lacy Ave. PR1 .... 95 C2
Ladbrooke Gr. BB11 .... 126 E2
Ladbury Ave. FY8 .... 89 B5
Lade End. LA3 .... 208 E8
Ladies Row. PR4 .... 133 F4
Ladies Wlk. LA1 .... 214 A2
Lady Alice's Dr. L40 .... 16 E8
Lady Anne Cl. L40 .... 23 B7
Lady Crosse Dr. PR6 .... 60 C7
Lady Green Cl. L38 .... 3 E3
Lady Green La. L38 .... 3 D4
Lady Hey Cres. PR2 .... 115 C1
Lady Pl. PR5 .... 96 E4
Lady St. PR1 .... 95 F8
Lady's Wlk. L40 .... 16 C6
Ladyman St. PR1 .... 95 E7
Ladysmith Ave. BL9 .... 32 A5
Ladysmith Rd. PR1 .... 116 C2
Ladywell St. PR1 .... 95 E8
Lafford La. WN8 .... 19 C2
Laidley's Wlk. FY7 .... 193 E5
Lairgill Row. 9 LA2 .... 233 D8
Laithbutts La. LA6 .... 216 F5
Laithe St. Burnley BB11 ...... 126 F4
Laithe St. Colne BB8 .... 169 C4
Lake Ave. LA4 .... 212 C4
Lake Gr. LA4 .... 212 C4
Lake Point. FY8 .... 89 D3
Lake Rd. Blackpool FY3 ...... 130 A3
Lake Rd. Morecambe LA3 & LA4 212 C3
Lake Rd N. FY8 .... 89 C4
Lake Side Cotts. WN1 .... 29 C1
Lake View. BL7 .... 45 C5
Lake View Rd. BB8 .... 169 D7
Lakeber Ave. LA2 .... 233 D8
Lakeber Cl. 5 LA2 .... 233 D8
Lakeber Dr. 2 LA2 .... 233 D8
Lakeland Cl. Billington BB6 ... 143 A3
Lakeland Cl. Forton PR3 ...... 204 B3
Lakeland Gdns. PR7 .... 42 A5
Lakeland Way. BB12 .... 126 B8
Lakes Dr. WN5 .... 10 E6
Lakeside Ave. WN5 .... 10 E3
Lakeway. FY3 .... 129 F6
Lakewood Ave. FY5 .... 172 D1
Lamaleach Dr. PR4 .... 92 A6
Lamb Row. BB7 .... 144 E7
Lamb's La. PR3 .... 196 A4
Lambert Cl. PR2 .... 117 E3
Lambert Rd. Fulwood PR2 .... 117 E3
Lambert Rd. Lancaster LA1 ... 213 E3
Lambert St. BB8 .... 170 C2
Lambeth Cl. Blackburn BB1 ... 101 A4
Lambeth Cl. Horwich BL6 ...... 31 D3
Lambeth St. Blackburn BB1 .. 101 A4
Lambeth St. Blackburn BB1 .. 101 B4
Lambeth St. Colne BB8 .... 170 B5
Lambing Clough La. BB6 ...... 141 E7
Lambourne. WN8 .... 18 B4
Lambridge Cl. LA4 .... 212 E3
Lambs Hill Cl. FY5 .... 173 D1
Lambshear La. L31 .... 5 C4
Lambton Gates. BB4 .... 85 C2
Lamlash Rd. BB1 .... 101 D4
Lammack Prim Sch. BB2 ..... 121 C1
Lammack Rd. Blackburn BB1 .. 100 C8
Lammack Rd. Blackburn BB1 .. 100 D8
Lanark Ave. FY2 .... 150 C6
Lanark Cl. OL10 .... 32 F1
Lanark St. BB11 .... 126 D4
Lancambe Ct. LA1 .... 213 C2
Lancashire Coll. PR7 .... 42 A8

Lancashire Constabulary HQ.
    PR4 .... 94 E1
Lancashire Rd. PR5 .... 76 A4
Lancashire St. LA4 .... 212 B4
Lancaster Ave. Accrington BB5 . 103 B7
Lancaster Ave. Clayton-le-W PR6 76 E1
Lancaster Ave.
    Great Eccleston PR3 .... 154 C5
Lancaster Ave. Haslingden BB4 . 67 B8
Lancaster Ave. Horwich BL6 .... 31 D2
Lancaster Ave.
    Lytham St Anne's FY8 .... 88 F4
Lancaster Ave. Ramsbottom BL0 49 A4
Lancaster Ave. Thornton FY5 . 173 C2
Lancaster Cl. Adlington PR6 .... 30 B7
Lancaster Cl.
    Great Eccleston PR3 .... 154 C5
Lancaster Cl. Knott End-on-S FY6 194 F5
Lancaster Cl. Maghull L31 .... 5 F1
Lancaster Cl. Southport PR8 .... 33 E4
Lancaster Cres. WN8 .... 17 C1
Lancaster Ct. PR6 .... 60 C2
Lancaster Dr. Banks PR9 .... 53 F5
Lancaster Dr. Brinscall PR6 .... 61 E8
Lancaster Dr. Clayton-le-M BB5 124 A3
Lancaster Dr. Clitheroe BB7 ... 164 C7
Lancaster Dr. Padiham BB12 .. 125 D6
Lancaster Gate. Banks PR9 .... 53 F5
Lancaster Gate. Fleetwood FY7 193 D4
Lancaster Gate. 14
Lancaster Gate.
    Lancaster LA1 .... 210 F8
Lancaster Gate. Nelson BB9 ... 147 F8
Lancaster Gdns. PR8 .... 33 E4
Lancaster Girls' Gram Sch.
    LA1 .... 210 E7
Lancaster House. 29 PR1 ...... 96 A7
Lancaster L Pk. LA1 .... 211 B6
Lancaster La.
    Clayton-le-W PR5 & PR6 ..... 76 E2
Lancaster La. Parbold WN8 .... 26 C3
Lancaster & Lakeland
    Nuffield Hospl The. LA1 .... 211 A7
Lancaster Lane Prim Sch.
    PR6 .... 76 D1
Lancaster Moor Hospl. LA1 ... 211 C8
Lancaster & Morecambe Coll.
    LA1 .... 213 B3
Lancaster & Morecambe Coll
    (Annexe). LA4 .... 212 E5
Lancaster Pl. Adlington PR6 .... 30 A8
Lancaster Pl. Blackburn BB2 .. 100 B5
Lancaster Rd. Blackpool FY3 .. 130 A3
Lancaster Rd. Carnforth LA5 .. 216 B7
Lancaster Rd. Caton LA2 ...... 231 B3
Lancaster Rd. Cockerham LA2 . 203 C6
Lancaster Rd. Fisher's Row PR3 196 C5
Lancaster Rd. Formby L37 ...... 11 E1
Lancaster Rd. Garstang PR3 .. 199 C1
Lancaster Rd. Hornby LA2 .... 232 B7
Lancaster Rd.
    Knott End-on-S FY6 .... 194 F5
Lancaster Rd. Morecambe LA4 . 212 F5
Lancaster Rd.
    Moss Edge PR3 .... 175 E6
Lancaster Rd. Overton LA3 ... 209 D3
Lancaster Rd. Preesall PR6 ... 195 C3
Lancaster Rd. Preston PR1 ..... 95 F8
Lancaster Rd. Preston PR1 ..... 96 A8
Lancaster Rd. Ratten Row PR3 . 154 A3
Lancaster Rd. Southport PR8 .. 33 E4
Lancaster Rd N. PR1 .... 116 F1
Lancaster Road Prim Sch.
    LA4 .... 212 G4
Lancaster St. Blackburn BB2 .. 100 C4
Lancaster St. Colne BB8 ...... 169 D5
Lancaster St. Coppull PR7 ..... 41 F1
Lancaster St. Oswaldtwistle BB5 102 C3
Lancaster Way. 15 PR1 .... 96 A8
Lancastergate. PR5 .... 58 F8
Lancia Cres. FY4 .... 111 A6
Lancing Pl. BB2 .... 100 C3
Land End. L31 .... 6 C1
Land Gate. OL12 .... 70 F5
Land La. New Longton PR4 ...... 74 D5
Land La. Southport PR9 .... 53 D4
Land Foot Brow. LA2 .... 233 D4
Land Head. LA2 .... 232 D6
Land Head La. OL13 .... 86 F3
Land House Cl. BB2 .... 80 B8
Land House La. BB8 .... 170 C1
Land Side. OL13 .... 87 A4
Lane The. LA3 .... 205 A5
Lane Top. BB8 .... 170 C5
Lanedale. PR4 .... 74 A8
Lanefield Dr. FY5 .... 172 C4
Laneshaw Bridge Cty
    Prim Sch. BB8 .... 170 E6
Laneside. Altham BB5 .... 124 D6
Laneside. Great Harwood BB6 . 123 F6
Laneside Ave. Accrington BB5 . 103 B8
Laneside Ave. Higham BB12 .. 145 F6
Laneside Rd. BB4 .... 84 C1
Lang St. Accrington BB5 ...... 103 A6
Lang St. Blackpool FY1 ...... 129 C6

Langber End La. LA6 .... 236 F1
Langcliffe Rd. PR2 .... 117 E4
Langdale. LA2 .... 231 C3
Langdale Ave. Clitheroe BB7 .. 164 C7
Langdale Ave. Croston PR5 .... 57 B3
Langdale Ave. Formby L37 ...... 11 D2
Langdale Ave. Hesketh Bank PR4 72 D4
Langdale Ave. Rawtenstall BB4 . 84 E2
Langdale Cl. Accrington BB5 .. 124 D1
Langdale Cl. Blackburn BB2 .... 79 E8
Langdale Cl. Formby L37 .... 11 D2
Langdale Cl. Freckleton PR4 ... 92 A6
Langdale Cl. Thornton FY5 ... 173 B3
Langdale Cres. PR2 .... 117 E3
Langdale Crest. LA7 .... 237 E5
Langdale Ct. Fleetwood FY7 .. 193 E2
Langdale Ct. Garstang PR3 ... 178 B7
Langdale Ct. Penwortham PR1 .. 95 C4
Langdale Dr. Burscough L40 .... 24 E4
Langdale Dr. Maghull L31 .... 5 E2
Langdale Gdns. PR8 .... 33 F1
Langdale Gr. PR6 .... 60 B7
Langdale Pl. 1 Blackpool FY4 . 130 C1
Langdale Pl. Lancaster LA1 ... 214 A2
Langdale Rd. Blackburn BB2 ... 79 E8
Langdale Rd. Blackpool FY4 .. 130 C1
Langdale Rd. Carnforth LA5 .. 216 E8
Langdale Rd. Fulwood PR2 .... 117 E3
Langdale Rd. Lancaster LA1 .. 214 A2
Langdale Rd. Leyland PR5 & PR7 59 B6
Langdale Rd. Longridge PR3 .. 138 F5
Langdale Rd.
    Lytham St Anne's FY8 ...... 109 D1
Langdale Rd. Morecambe LA4 . 212 G5
Langdale Rd. Padiham BB12 .. 145 C2
Langdale Rise. BB8 .... 169 F6
Langden Brook Mews. LA1 ... 213 B2
Langden Brook Sq. BB1 ...... 101 A3
Langden Cres. PR5 .... 76 F8
Langden Dr. PR2 .... 118 A3
Langden Fold. PR2 .... 138 C1
Langdon Way. FY2 .... 150 E2
Langfield. BB10 .... 128 B6
Langfield Ave. FY4 .... 109 C5
Langfield Cl. PR2 .... 116 F8
Langford St. BB5 .... 103 E1
Langham Ave. BB5 .... 103 B8
Langham Rd. Blackburn BB1 .. 100 D7
Langham Rd. Standish WN6 .... 28 D1
Langham St. BB12 .... 126 B6
Langho St. BB2 .... 100 C1
Langho Sta. BB6 .... 142 C1
Langholm Cl. PR5 .... 75 D1
Langholm Rd. LA3 .... 168 C1
Langholme Rd. PR1 .... 95 B4
Langholme St. BB9 .... 147 E6
Langley Cl. Hightown L38 .... 2 F2
Langley Cl. Standish WN6 ...... 28 E2
Langley Ct. L40 .... 24 B5
Langley La. Goosnargh PR3 .. 136 F6
Langley La. Inglewhite PR3 .. 158 B2
Langley Pl. L40 .... 24 B4
Langley Rd. Burscough L40 .... 24 B4
Langley Rd. Lancaster LA1 ... 211 A7
Langport Cl. PR2 .... 116 F8
Langridge Way. LA4 .... 212 E3
Langroyd Rd. BB8 .... 169 E6
Langsford Cl. BB8 .... 200 C2
Langshaw Dr. BB7 .... 164 F6
Langshaw La. LA2 .... 207 D5
Langstone Cl. BL6 .... 31 B3
Langthwaite Rd. LA1 & LA2 .. 211 E5
Langton Ave. WN6 .... 28 E1
Langton Brow. Eccleston PR7 .. 40 D5
Langton Brow. Longridge PR3 . 139 B7
Langton Cl. Lancaster LA1 ... 214 A4
Langton Cl. Leyland PR5 ...... 58 C8
Langton Pl. WN6 .... 28 E1
Langton Rd. PR4 .... 113 A5
Langton St. PR1 .... 95 D7
Langtree. WN8 .... 18 B3
Langtree La. Elswick PR4 .... 153 F2
Langtree La. Standish WN6 .... 28 D3
Langwood. FY7 .... 193 G2
Langwood La. WA11 .... 9 C1
Langwyth Rd. BB10 .... 127 E5
Lansborough Cl. PR5 .... 58 B8
Lansbury Pl. 1 BB9 .... 168 F2
Lansdown Hill. PR2 .... 116 C7
Lansdown Rd. PR4 .... 113 A7
Lansdowne Cl. BB11 .... 126 F4
Lansdowne Gr. LA4 .... 213 A7
Lansdowne Pl. FY1 .... 129 B6
Lansdowne Rd. Burnley BB11 . 126 F4
Lansdowne Rd.
    Lytham St Anne's FY8 .... 89 D5
Lansdowne Rd. Morecambe LA4 213 A7
Lansdowne Rd. Southport PR8 . 34 E6
Lansdowne St. BB2 .... 100 B3
Lansil Ind Est. LA1 .... 214 A3
Lansil Way. LA1 .... 214 A3
Lanterns The. FY6 .... 151 D4
Lapford Cres. L33 .... 1 A4
Lapford Wlk. L33 .... 1 A4
Lappet Gr. PR4 .... 115 E5
Lapwings The. FY6 .... 151 B2
Larbreck Ave. PR4 .... 154 A1
Larbreck Rd. FY3 .... 129 E7
Larch Ave. Chorley PR6 .... 60 E2
Larch Ave. Oswaldtwistle BB5 . 102 F3
Larch Cl. Blackburn BB2 ...... 79 E8
Larch Cl. Freckleton PR4 ..... 92 A5
Larch Cl. Knott End-on-S FY6 . 195 A5
Larch Cl. Rawtenstall BB4 ..... 67 F8
Larch Cl. Skelmersdale WN8 ... 17 E1
Larch Dr. PR6 .... 61 F7
Larch Gate. PR5 .... 97 E2

Larch Gr. Bamber Bridge PR5 ...... 96 F1
Larch Gr. Garstang PR3 ...... 178 C8
Larch Gr. Lancaster LA1 ...... 210 D8
Larch St. Blackburn BB1 ...... 101 A7
Larch St. Burnley BB12 ...... 126 C7
Larch St. Bury BL9 ...... 32 B2
Larch St. Nelson BB9 ...... 147 F8
Larch St. Southport PR8 ...... 34 E6
Larch Way. L37 ...... 11 D4
Larches Ave. PR2 ...... 115 F1
Larches La. PR2 ...... 115 E1
Larchgate. PR2 ...... 117 C7
Larchwood. Lancaster LA1 ...... 211 B4
Larchwood. Penwortham PR1 ...... 95 B4
Larchwood. Preston PR2 ...... 115 E1
Larchwood Cl. FY8 ...... 89 F4
Larchwood Cres. PR5 ...... 75 C1
Largs BB1 ...... 101 C3
Lark Ave. PR1 ...... 95 E4
Lark Ct. FY7 ...... 193 D1
Lark Hill. Blackburn BB1 ...... 100 F6
Lark Hill. Higher Walton PR5 ...... 97 B3
Lark Hill. Rawtenstall BB4 ...... 85 A3
Lark St. Burnley BB12 ...... 126 C7
Lark St. Colne BB8 ...... 169 E6
Lark St. Darwen BB3 ...... 64 B5
Larkfield. PR7 ...... 40 B6
Larkfield Cl. BL8 ...... 48 F1
Larkfield Ct. PR9 ...... 53 A3
Larkfield La. PR9 ...... 53 A3
Larkfield Prim Sch. PR9 ...... 53 A3
Larkhill. Brockhall Village BB6 ...... 142 C5
Larkhill. Skelmersdale WN8 ...... 18 B4
Larkhill Ave. Brierfield BB10 ...... 147 C5
Larkhill Ave. Standish WN6 ...... 28 F1
Larkhill Gr. L38 ...... 2 F3
Larkhill La. L37 ...... 11 C4
Larkhill Rd. PR1 ...... 96 B7
Larkhill St. Blackpool FY1 ...... 129 C6
Larkhill St. Preston PR1 ...... 96 B7
Larkholme Ave. FY7 ...... 193 E1
Larkholme Cty Prim Sch. FY7 172 D8
Larkholme La. FY7 ...... 193 E1
Larkholme Par. FY7 ...... 193 D1
Larkspur Cl. BB2 ...... 79 D8
Last Drop Village. BL7 ...... 47 A1
Latham Ave. Blackpool FY3 ...... 129 E3
Latham Ave. Ormskirk L39 ...... 16 A5
Latham Cres. PR4 ...... 56 A6
Latham Rd. BL6 ...... 30 C3
Latham St. Burnley BB10 ...... 147 B1
Latham St. Bury BL9 ...... 32 A4
Latham St. Preston PR1 ...... 96 A6
Lathom Ave. Morecambe LA4 ...... 212 G4
Lathom Ave. Parbold WN8 ...... 26 B3
Lathom Cl. L40 ...... 24 E4
Lathom Dr. L31 ...... 5 E3
Lathom Gr. LA4 ...... 212 G4
Lathom High Sch. WN8 ...... 17 F3
Lathom La. L40 ...... 16 C7
Lathom Park CE Prim Sch. L40 17 A8
Lathom Rd. Southport PR8 & PR9 52 C1
Lathom Rd. Stanley Gate L39 ...... 7 F8
Lathom St James CE Prim Sch.
L39 ...... 16 E4
Lathom Way. PR3 ...... 178 D6
Latimer Cl. WN5 ...... 10 F7
Latimer Dr. PR7 ...... 74 F7
Lauderdale Ave. FY5 ...... 172 D1
Lauderdale Cres. PR2 ...... 117 F4
Lauderdale Rd. PR2 ...... 117 F4
Lauderdale St. PR1 ...... 95 E6
Laund Gate. BB12 ...... 146 D8
Laund Gr. BB5 ...... 103 D3
Laund Hey View. BB4 ...... 84 B1
Laund La. Haslingden BB4 ...... 84 C3
Laund La. Ollerton Fold PR6 ...... 78 E4
Laund Rd. BB5 ...... 103 D3
Laund St. BB4 ...... 84 F4
Laund The. PR5 ...... 75 A1
Laundry Rd. FY4 ...... 110 A5
Laura St. BL0 ...... 49 C2
Laurel Ave. Blackpool FY1 ...... 129 E2
Laurel Ave. Burscough Bridge L40 24 E6
Laurel Ave. Darwen BB3 ...... 81 B2
Laurel Ave. Euxton PR7 ...... 59 B3
Laurel Ave. Fleetwood FY7 ...... 172 F8
Laurel Ave. Lytham St Anne's FY8 90 B5
Laurel Bank. LA1 ...... 210 D7
Laurel Bank Ave. PR2 ...... 116 C3
Laurel Dr. Skelmersdale WN8 ...... 17 E2
Laurel Dr. Thornton FY5 ...... 151 B8
Laurel Gr. PR8 & PR9 ...... 34 E7
Laurel St. Bacup OL13 ...... 86 F3
Laurel St. Burnley BB11 ...... 127 B4
Laurel St. Bury BL9 ...... 32 B2
Laurel St. Preston PR1 ...... 96 A7
Laurels The. PR7 ...... 41 F3
Laureston Ave. LA3 ...... 208 F6
Laurie Pl. OL12 ...... 51 F1
Laurier Ave. FY4 ...... 109 C6
Laurier Rd. BB10 ...... 147 B2
Lauriston Cl. FY4 ...... 110 A6
Laverton Rd. FY4 ...... 89 A4
Lavender Cl. PR7 ...... 42 C5
Lavender Gr. PR7 ...... 42 C5
Lavender Hill. BB4 ...... 67 F8
Laverick Rd. LA2 ...... 231 A5
Lawn Ct. FY3 ...... 129 D4
Lawn St. BB10 ...... 127 A8
Lawley Rd. BB1 ...... 100 A5
Lawn Tennis Ct. FY4 ...... 109 D5
Lawns Ave. WN5 & WN8 ...... 10 C5
Lawns The. PR9 ...... 52 F2
Lawnswood Ave. Lancaster LA1 211 A3

Lawnswood Ave.
Poulton-le-F FY6 ...... 151 C2
Lawnswood Cres. FY3 ...... 130 C2
Lawnswood Dr. LA3 ...... 212 F2
Lawnswood Ave. PR7 ...... 42 A5
Lawrence Ave.
Bamber Bridge PR5 ...... 96 D2
Lawrence Ave. Burnley BB11 ...... 126 C4
Lawrence Ave. Burnley BB11 ...... 126 C5
Lawrence Ave.
Lytham St Anne's FY8 ...... 89 A4
Lawrence Ave. Preston PR1 ...... 96 B5
Lawrence Ave.
Simonstone BB12 ...... 144 B3
Lawrence Cl. 2 OL12 ...... 51 A1
Lawrence Dr. LA5 ...... 237 A1
Lawrence La. PR7 ...... 40 C7
Lawrence Rd. Chorley PR7 ...... 42 E7
Lawrence Rd. Penwortham PR1 ... 95 B5
Lawrence St. Blackburn BB2 ...... 100 C4
Lawrence St. Blackpool FY4 ...... 129 B1
Lawrence St. Fulwood PR2 ...... 116 D3
Lawrence St. Padiham BB12 ...... 145 D1
Lawrence St.
Whitewell Bottom BB4 ...... 85 F4
Lawrie Ave. BL0 ...... 49 B5
Lawson Cl. LA1 ...... 210 F3
Lawson Gdns. LA2 ...... 213 E8
Lawson Pl. LA2 ...... 213 E8
Lawson Rd. Blackpool FY3 ...... 130 A3
Lawson Rd. Horwich BL6 ...... 31 C4
Lawson Rd.
Lytham St Anne's FY8 ...... 110 A2
Lawson St. 3 Chorley PR6 ...... 42 E7
Lawson St. Preston PR1 ...... 95 F8
Lawson St. Rawtenstall BB4 ...... 85 A8
Lawson St. Southport PR9 ...... 35 A7
Lawsons Ct. FY5 ...... 173 C2
Lawsons Rd. FY5 ...... 173 C2
Lawswood. FY5 ...... 173 C1
Lawton Cl. PR6 ...... 78 B1
Laxey Gr. PR2 ...... 117 D3
Laxey Rd. BB2 ...... 100 E1
Laycock Gate. FY3 ...... 129 D6
Layne Sch The. LA1 ...... 213 D2
Layton Cty Prim Sch. FY3 ...... 129 E8
Layton Rd. Blackpool FY3 ...... 129 E6
Layton Rd. Preston PR1 ...... 115 E1
Layton Sta. FY3 ...... 150 E1
Lazenby Ave. FY7 ...... 193 C2
Lea Bank. BB4 ...... 85 D2
Lea Cres. L39 ...... 15 F7
Lea Cty Prim Sch. PR2 ...... 115 D1
Lea Endowed CE Prim Sch.
PR4 ...... 115 C4
Lea La. Claughton LA2 ...... 231 F8
Lea La. Heysham LA3 ...... 208 E6
Lea La. Lea Town PR4 ...... 115 B5
Lea Mount Dr. BL9 ...... 32 D4
Lea Rd. Lucas Green PR6 & PR7 .... 60 C5
Lea Rd. Preston PR2 & PR4 ...... 115 D3
Lea Way Cl. FY5 ...... 151 D7
Leach Cres. FY5 ...... 109 F2
Leach La. FY8 ...... 109 E1
Leach Pl. PR5 ...... 77 B8
Leach St. Blackburn BB2 ...... 100 E2
Leach St. Colne BB8 ...... 169 C4
Leaches Rd. BL0 ...... 49 C8
Leachfield Cl. LA2 ...... 207 A4
Leachfield Ind Est. PR3 ...... 199 B1
Leachfield Rd. LA2 ...... 206 F4
Leacroft. BB3 ...... 81 A6
Leadale. PR2 ...... 115 D2
Leadale Cl. WN6 ...... 28 D1
Leadale Gn. PR5 ...... 75 E1
Leadale Rd. PR5 ...... 75 E1
Leaford Ave. FY3 ...... 129 E8
Leafy Cl. PR5 ...... 59 B7
Leagram Cres. PR2 ...... 118 A3
Leamington Ave. Ainsdale PR8 ... 20 D5
Leamington Ave.
Baldingstone BL9 ...... 49 E1
Leamington Ave. Burnley BB10 147 C1
Leamington Rd. Ainsdale PR8 ...... 20 D5
Leamington Rd. Blackburn BB2 100 B6
Leamington Rd. Blackpool FY1 129 D5
Leamington Rd.
Lytham St Anne's FY8 ...... 88 F4
Leamington Rd.
Morecambe LA4 ...... 212 G3
Leamington St. BB9 ...... 147 E7
Leander Ave. FY6 ...... 151 D2
Leapers View. LA6 ...... 231 B8
Leaside Cl. OL12 ...... 51 D2
Leathwood. L31 ...... 5 E1
Leavengreave Ct. OL12 ...... 70 D4
Leaver St. BB12 ...... 126 A5
Leaverholme Cl. BB10 ...... 107 A7
Leavesley Rd. FY1 ...... 129 D8
Lebanon St. BB10 ...... 127 C5
Leck CE Prim Sch. LA6 ...... 236 B7
Leckhampton Rd. FY1 ...... 129 B8
Leconby St. PR3 ...... 154 B5
Ledburn. WN8 ...... 18 B3
Ledbury Rd. FY3 ...... 130 B7
Ledson Gr. L39 ...... 6 B7
Lee Brook Cl. BB4 ...... 85 A4
Lee Gr. BB10 ...... 127 F4
Lee Green St. 3 BB10 ...... 127 A8
Lee La. Bispham Green L40 ...... 26 C7
Lee La. Great Harwood BB1 ...... 123 B3
Lee La. Whittlestone Head BL7 .... 65 B2
Lee Rd. Bacup OL13 ...... 69 E8
Lee Rd. Nelson BB9 ...... 168 F2
Lee St. Accrington BB5 ...... 103 C6

Lee St. Bacup OL13 ...... 86 F2
Lee St. Barrowford BB9 ...... 168 D3
Lee St. Longridge PR3 ...... 139 A7
Lee St. Rawtenstall BB4 ...... 85 A4
Lee's St. OL13 ...... 70 C8
Leebrook Rd. BB4 ...... 84 F4
Leeds Cl. 15 BB1 ...... 101 A4
Leeds Rd. Blackpool FY1 ...... 129 D5
Leeds Rd. Nelson BB9 ...... 168 F1
Leehouse Dr. FY6 ...... 130 D8
Leek St. PR1 ...... 96 E8
Leeming La. LA6 ...... 236 C3
Lees Cotts. BL7 ...... 47 C2
Lees La. LA3 ...... 208 E7
Lees La. WN8 ...... 18 E7
Lees Rd. Adlington PR6 ...... 30 B8
Lees Rd. Kirkby L33 & L32 ...... 1 B2
Lees The. BB10 ...... 107 A7
Leesands Cl. PR2 ...... 117 E5
Leeson Ave. PR7 ...... 41 D4
Leeswood. WN8 ...... 18 B3
Leet Rd. BB12 ...... 145 F5
Legh La. PR4 ...... 55 B4
Leicester Ave. Cleveleys FY5 ...... 172 E3
Leicester Ave. Garstang PR3 ...... 178 B7
Leicester Ave. Horwich BL6 ...... 31 A3
Leicester Gate. FY5 ...... 172 E3
Leicester Lodge. 3 PR2 ...... 117 F4
Leicester Rd. Blackburn BB1 ...... 101 C5
Leicester Rd. Blackpool FY1 ...... 129 D5
Leicester Rd. Preston PR1 ...... 117 A1
Leicester St. PR8 & PR9 ...... 34 B8
Leigh Brow. PR1 ...... 96 B2
Leigh Row. PR7 ...... 42 C7
Leigh St. PR7 ...... 42 C7
Leighton Ave. Fleetwood FY7 ...... 193 D3
Leighton Ave. Maghull L31 ...... 5 D2
Leighton Ct. LA4 ...... 212 D3
Leighton Dr. LA1 ...... 210 D7
Leighton Hall. LA5 ...... 219 C1
Leighton Moss
(Nature Reserve). LA5 ...... 219 A3
Leinster Rd. LA1 ...... 211 A5
Leith Ave. FY5 ...... 172 D2
Lemon Tree Ct. FY8 ...... 109 B4
Lemonious St. BB5 ...... 103 C4
Lench Rd. BB4 ...... 68 D8
Lench St. BB4 ...... 68 F8
Lenches Fold. BB8 ...... 169 D4
Lenches Rd. BB8 ...... 169 D3
Lendel Cl. L37 ...... 11 E3
Lennon St. 2 PR7 ...... 42 C7
Lennox Ct. PR7 ...... 109 D6
Lennox Gate. FY4 ...... 109 D7
Lennox Rd. OL14 ...... 108 A1
Lennox St. 19 Preston PR1 ...... 96 A7
Lennox St. Worsthorne BB10 ...... 128 A6
Lennox Wlk. OL10 ...... 32 F1
Lenton Ave. L37 ...... 11 D4
Lentworth Ave. FY2 ...... 150 D5
Lentworth Dr. LA1 ...... 211 A4
Lentworth House. 5 LA1 ...... 211 A3
Leonard Ave. Barnoldswick BB8 .... 200 B3
Leonard St. Nelson BB9 ...... 147 E7
Leonard Terr. BB3 ...... 81 E3
Leopold Gr. FY1 ...... 129 B5
Leopold Rd. BB2 ...... 100 B6
Leopold St. BB8 ...... 169 B4
Leopold Way. BB8 ...... 81 A8
Lesley Rd. PR8 & PR9 ...... 34 E7
Leslie Ave. Caton LA2 ...... 231 C3
Leslie Ave. Thornton FY5 ...... 173 C2
Letchworth Dr. PR7 ...... 42 B6
Letchworth Pl. 2 PR7 ...... 42 B6
Lethbridge Rd. PR8 ...... 34 D5
Letitia St. BL6 ...... 31 A3
Levant St. BB12 ...... 125 C7
Leven Ave. FY7 ...... 193 D3
Leven Gr. BB3 ...... 80 E4
Leven St. BB11 ...... 127 B4
Levens Cl. Blackburn BB2 ...... 80 B8
Levens Cl. Poulton-le-F FY6 ...... 130 E8
Levens Ct. LA3 ...... 212 B2
Levens Dr.
Clayton-le-W PR5 & PR6 ...... 76 D2
Levens Dr. Morecambe LA3 ...... 212 B2
Levens Dr. Poulton-le-F FY6 ...... 151 D1
Levens Gr. FY1 ...... 129 D3
Levens St. 12 PR1 ...... 117 D1
Levens Way. LA5 ...... 218 C2
Levensgarth Ave. PR2 ...... 116 F8
Lever House La. PR5 ...... 76 C2
Lever Park Ave. BL6 ...... 31 B5
Lever St. Blackpool FY3 ...... 129 E4
Lever St. Ramsbottom BL0 ...... 49 C6
Lever St. Rawtenstall BB4 ...... 85 B4
Leverhouse Prim Sch. PR5 ...... 76 C3
Levine Ave. FY4 ...... 130 A1
Lewis Cl. PR7 ...... 29 E6
Lewis Dr. OL10 ...... 32 F1
Lewis St. BB6 ...... 123 D5
Lewtas St. FY1 ...... 129 B6
Lewth La. PR4 ...... 135 B5
Lex St. PR1 ...... 96 C8
Lexton Dr. PR9 ...... 53 B3
Ley Ct. LA1 ...... 210 D8
Ley St. BB5 ...... 103 E2
Leybourne Ave. PR8 ...... 20 F7
Leyburn Ave. Blackpool FY2 ...... 150 C5
Leyburn Ave. Fleetwood FY7 ...... 193 E2
Leyburn Ave. Accrington BB5 ...... 103 E5
Leyburn Cl. Fulwood PR2 ...... 117 E5
Leyburn Rd. Blackburn BB2 ...... 100 E7
Leyburn Rd. Lancaster LA1 ...... 213 F3
Leycester Dr. LA1 ...... 213 C3

Leyfield. PR1 ...... 95 E2
Leyfield Ct. LA6 ...... 238 C1
Leyfield Rd. PR5 ...... 58 F8
Leyland Cl. Banks PR9 ...... 53 E5
Leyland Cl. Trawden BB8 ...... 170 B3
Leyland Golf Course. PR6 ...... 59 D8
Leyland La. Leyland PR5 ...... 58 D7
Leyland La. Leyland PR5 ...... 75 D2
Leyland La.
Runshaw Moor PR5 & PR7 ...... 58 D4
Leyland Meth Inf Sch. PR5 ...... 76 B1
Leyland Meth Jun Sch. PR5 ...... 76 B1
Leyland Rd. Burnley BB11 ...... 127 B6
Leyland Rd. Penwortham PR1 ...... 95 D6
Leyland Rd.
Penwortham PR1 & PR5 ...... 95 E3
Leyland Rd. Southport PR8 & PR9 52 C1
Leyland St. BB5 ...... 102 F5
Leyland Sta. PR5 ...... 76 B2
Leyland Warden High Sch. PR5 75 E1
Leyland Way. Leyland PR5 ...... 76 C1
Leyland Way. Ormskirk L39 ...... 15 F5
Leylands The. FY5 ...... 89 F2
Leys Cl. Elswick PR4 ...... 154 A1
Leys Cl. Wiswell BB7 ...... 143 F8
Leys Rd. FY7 ...... 150 D1
Leyster St. LA4 ...... 212 F5
Leyton Ave. PR5 ...... 58 D7
Leyton St. OL12 ...... 51 F2
Libby La. PR5 ...... 196 C6
Library Mews. FY4 ...... 109 E7
Library Rd. PR5 & PR6 ...... 77 B4
Library St. Chorley PR7 ...... 42 C7
Library St. Church BB5 ...... 102 E6
Library St. 16 Preston PR1 ...... 96 A7
Lichen Cl. PR7 ...... 41 D4
Lichfield Ave. LA4 ...... 212 G6
Lichfield Rd. Blackpool FY1 ...... 129 C8
Lichfield Rd. Chorley PR7 ...... 42 C6
Lichfield Rd. Preston PR2 ...... 115 F2
Liddesdale Rd. BB2 ...... 169 B2
Liddington Cl. BB2 ...... 81 A8
Liddington Hall Dr. BL0 ...... 49 B4
Lidget Ave. PR2 ...... 115 C1
Lidum Park Ind Est. FY8 ...... 90 E5
Liege Rd. 5 PR5 ...... 59 A8
Lifeboat St. LA3 ...... 11 B1
Lifton Rd. L33 ...... 1 A2
Lightbown Ave. FY3 ...... 129 E3
Lightbown St. BB3 ...... 81 A3
Lightburne Ave. FY1 ...... 88 F5
Lightfoot Cl. PR2 ...... 116 D8
Lightfoot Green La. PR2 & PR4 116 B8
Lightfoot La.
Fulwood PR2 & PR4 ...... 116 A7
Lightfoot La.
Fulwood PR2 & PR4 ...... 116 B7
Lightfoot La. Fulwood PR2 ...... 116 D8
Lighthorne Dr. PR8 ...... 20 A4
Lighthouse Cl. FY7 ...... 194 B5
Lighthurst Ave. PR7 ...... 42 C6
Lighthurst La. PR7 ...... 42 D5
Lightwood Ave. Blackpool FY1 ... 129 C1
Lightwood Ave.
Lytham St Anne's FY8 ...... 89 D3
Lilac Ave.
Abbey Village BB2 & PR7 ...... 79 C2
Lilac Ave. Ainsdale PR8 ...... 20 D2
Lilac Ave. Blackpool FY1 ...... 129 D2
Lilac Ave. Haslingden BB4 ...... 84 B3
Lilac Ave. Lytham St Anne's FY8 ... 90 B5
Lilac Ave. Penwortham PR5 ...... 95 C2
Lilac Cres. PR4 ...... 133 F4
Lilac Gr. Clitheroe BB7 ...... 164 C7
Lilac Gr. Darwen BB3 ...... 81 B3
Lilac Gr. Fulwood PR2 ...... 117 C3
Lilac Gr. Skelmersdale WN8 ...... 17 E1
Lilac Rd. BB1 ...... 101 A8
Lilac St. BB8 ...... 169 F6
Lilac Terr. 2 OL13 ...... 69 D8
Lilburn Cl. BL0 ...... 49 C4
Lilford Rd. BB1 ...... 100 D6
Lily Gr. Fulwood PR1 ...... 117 C3
Lily Gr. Lancaster LA1 ...... 211 A5
Lily St. 16 Bacup OL13 ...... 86 F2
Lily St. Blackpool FY1 ...... 129 C5
Lily St. Darwen BB3 ...... 81 B1
Lily St. Nelson BB9 ...... 147 F6
Lima Rd. FY8 ...... 89 B6
Lima St. BL9 ...... 32 B3
Limbrick. 21
Blackburn BB1 & BB2 ...... 100 C5
Limbrick. Blackburn BB1 ...... 100 E6
Limbrick Rd. PR7 ...... 42 E7
Lime Ave. Galgate LA2 ...... 207 A4
Lime Ave. Kirkham PR4 ...... 113 B4
Lime Ave. Oswaldtwistle BB5 ...... 102 D2
Lime Chase. PR2 ...... 116 C8
Lime Cl. PR1 ...... 95 B4
Lime Ct. WN8 ...... 17 E1
Lime Gr. Blackpool FY2 ...... 150 E2
Lime Gr. Chorley PR7 ...... 42 C5
Lime Gr. Garstang PR3 ...... 178 B8
Lime Gr. Lancaster LA1 ...... 210 D8
Lime Gr. Longridge PR3 ...... 139 A8
Lime Gr. Lytham St Anne's FY8 .... 88 D8
Lime Gr. Poulton-le-F FY6 ...... 151 C2
Lime Gr. Preston PR2 ...... 115 C2
Lime Gr. Ramsbottom BL0 ...... 49 D7
Lime Gr. Skelmersdale WN8 ...... 17 E1
Lime Gr. Thornton FY5 ...... 173 C1
Lime Rd. Accrington BB5 ...... 103 C4
Lime Rd. Haslingden BB4 ...... 84 C3
Lime St. Blackburn BB1 ...... 100 E6
Lime St. Clitheroe BB7 ...... 186 F1
Lime St. Colne BB8 ...... 169 E6
Lime St. Great Harwood BB6 ...... 123 C4
Lime St. Nelson BB9 ...... 147 D8

Lime St. Southport PR8 ...... 34 E6
Lime Tree Gr. BB4 ...... 85 A4
Lime Tree Way. L37 ...... 11 C2
Limebrest Ave. FY5 ...... 151 B8
Limefield Ave. Brierfield BB9 .... 147 C6
Limefield Ave. Whalley BB7 ...... 143 C6
Limefield Ct. BB2 ...... 100 B5
Limefield Dr. WN8 ...... 9 E7
Limefield St. BB5 ...... 103 D5
Limerick Rd. FY2 ...... 150 D3
Limers Gate. Sharneyford OL14 ... 87 E4
Limers Gate. Syke OL12 ...... 51 F5
Limes Ave. Darwen BB3 ...... 64 A8
Limes Ave. Euxton PR7 ...... 59 C4
Limes Ave. Morecambe LA3 ...... 212 B3
Limewood Cl. BB5 ...... 103 D6
Limey La. BB11 & BB4 ...... 105 E6
Limont Rd. PR8 ...... 20 D5
Lina St. BB5 ...... 102 F6
Linacre La. L37 & L38 ...... 4 B7
Linadale Ave. FY5 ...... 173 B2
Linaker Dr. L39 ...... 14 B8
Linaker Prim Sch. PR8 ...... 34 B5
Linaker St. PR8 ...... 34 B5
Linby St. BB10 ...... 127 B5
Lincoln Ave. Cleveleys FY5 ...... 172 E3
Lincoln Ave. Fleetwood FY7 ...... 193 E3
Lincoln Chase. PR2 ...... 115 C1
Lincoln Cl. Blackburn BB1 ...... 101 B4
Lincoln Cl. Morecambe LA4 ...... 212 G3
Lincoln Cl. Blackpool FY1 ...... 129 C4
Lincoln Ct. 1 Church BB5 ...... 103 A7
Lincoln House. 4 PR1 ...... 96 B7
Lincoln Pl. BB4 ...... 84 A3
Lincoln Rd. Blackburn BB1 ...... 101 B4
Lincoln Rd. Blackpool FY1 ...... 129 C5
Lincoln Rd. Earby BB8 ...... 201 B2
Lincoln Rd. Lancaster LA1 ...... 210 E7
Lincoln Rd. Southport PR8 ...... 34 A1
Lincoln St. Burnley BB11 ...... 127 A4
Lincoln St. Cornholme OL14 ...... 108 B1
Lincoln St. 2 Haslingden BB4 .... 84 A3
Lincoln St. Preston PR1 ...... 117 B1
Lincoln Way. Clitheroe BB7 ...... 187 A2
Lincoln Way. Garstang PR3 ...... 178 B7
Lindadale Ave. BB5 ...... 103 A3
Lindale Ave. PR2 ...... 138 E1
Lindale Cl. LA5 ...... 237 B2
Lindale Cres. BB10 ...... 147 A2
Lindale Gdns. FY4 ...... 109 E6
Lindale Rd. Fulwood PR2 ...... 117 A4
Lindale Rd. Longridge PR3 ...... 138 F5
Lindbeck Ct. FY4 ...... 110 C8
Lindbeck Rd. FY4 ...... 130 C1
Lindel La. FY6 ...... 195 B2
Lindel Rd. FY7 ...... 193 E2
Linden Ave. Blackburn BB1 ...... 100 D6
Linden Ave. Orrell WN5 ...... 10 E6
Linden Ave. Ramsbottom BL0 ...... 49 D6
Linden Ave. Thornton FY5 ...... 172 F3
Linden Cl. Bamber Bridge PR5 .... 96 B1
Linden Cl. Barrowford BB9 ...... 168 B1
Linden Cl. Cleveleys FY5 ...... 172 E2
Linden Cl. Edenfield BL0 ...... 67 D2
Linden Cres. BB3 ...... 81 C2
Linden Ct. Earby BB8 ...... 201 B1
Linden Ct. Orrell WN5 ...... 10 E6
Linden Dr. Bamber Bridge PR5 .... 96 B1
Linden Dr. Clitheroe BB7 ...... 164 F7
Linden Gn. FY5 ...... 172 F2
Linden Gr. Chorley PR6 ...... 60 D3
Linden Gr. Fulwood PR2 ...... 117 E3
Linden Gr. Garstang PR3 ...... 178 C8
Linden Gr. Orrell WN5 ...... 10 E6
Linden Lea. Blackburn BB2 ...... 79 F8
Linden Lea. Rawtenstall BB4 ...... 67 F8
Linden Mews. FY7 ...... 109 F2
Linden Pl. FY2 ...... 150 E3
Linden Rd. Colne BB8 ...... 169 D5
Linden Rd. Earby BB8 ...... 201 B1
Linden St. BB10 ...... 127 B5
Linden Wlk. WN5 ...... 10 E6
Lindeth Cl. Nether Kellet LA6 ... 216 F6
Lindeth Cl. Silverdale LA5 ...... 218 C2
Lindeth Rd. LA5 ...... 218 C2
Lindholme. WN8 ...... 18 C3
Lindisfarne Cl. BB12 ...... 126 E7
Lindle Ave. PR4 ...... 94 E2
Lindle Cl. PR4 ...... 94 E2
Lindle Cres. PR4 ...... 94 E2
Lindle La. PR1 & PR4 ...... 95 A2
Lindley Ave. WN5 ...... 10 C5
Lindley Dr. WN8 ...... 26 C3
Lindley St. Bamber Bridge PR5 .... 76 B8
Lindley St. Blackburn BB2 ...... 100 B2
Lindon Pk. BB4 ...... 67 C7
Lindow Sq. LA1 ...... 210 E7
Lindow St. LA1 ...... 210 F7
Lindred Rd. BB9 ...... 147 B7
Lindsay Ave. Blackpool FY3 ...... 129 E3
Lindsay Ave. Leyland PR5 ...... 76 B1
Lindsay Ave.
Lytham St Anne's FY8 ...... 89 B6
Lindsay Ave. Poulton-le-F FY6 .. 151 D2
Lindsay Cl. Blackpool FY8 ...... 109 A4
Lindsay Ct. Morecambe LA3 ...... 212 F2
Lindsay Ct. PR7 ...... 42 A7
Lindsay Pk. BB10 ...... 127 F5
Lindsay St. BL6 ...... 31 D1
Lindsay House. 2 BB5 ...... 103 A4
Linedred La. BB9 ...... 147 B7
Lines St. LA4 ...... 212 E5

Linfield Terr. FY4 .... 109 E6
Lingart La. PR3 .... 199 D1
Lingdales. L37 .... 12 B5
Lingfield Ave. BB7 .... 164 E6
Lingfield Cl. LA1 .... 211 B3
Lingfield Ct. BB2 .... 79 C8
Lingfield Rd. FY7 .... 193 E2
Lingfield Way. BB2 .... 79 D8
Linghaw La. LA2 .... 233 F8
Lingmoor Dr. BB12 .... 126 A8
Lingmoor Rd. LA1 .... 214 B1
Lingwell Cl. PR6 .... 60 C5
Link Dr. LA2 .... 233 D8
Links Ave. PR9 .... 52 F3
Links Field. PR2 .... 116 C3
Links Gate. Fulwood PR2 .... 116 C3
Links Gate. Lytham St Anne's FY8 89 A6
Links Gate. Thornton FY5 .... 151 D7
Links Rd. Blackburn BB2 .... 79 C8
Links Rd. Blackpool FY1 ...... 129 C8
Links Rd. Kirkby L32 .... 1 A1
Links Rd. Knott End-on-S FY6 194 D5
Links Rd. Lytham St Anne's FY8 .. 88 E5
Links Rd. Penwortham PR1 .... 95 B6
Links The. FY5 .... 172 C4
Links View. FY8 .... 89 C5
Linkside Ave. BB9 .... 148 B8
Linley Gr. BL0 .... 49 A2
Linnet Cl. FY3 .... 130 B6
Linnet Dr. BL9 .... 32 B4
Linnet St. PR1 .... 117 B2
Linsdale Cres. L33 .... 1 A4
Linton Ave. LA3 .... 212 A1
Linton Dr. BB11 .... 126 D3
Linton Gdns. BB9 .... 168 C3
Linton Gr. PR1 .... 95 B5
Linton St. PR2 .... 116 D3
Lion Ct. 10 BB5 .... 102 E6
Lion La. BL6 .... 30 C2
Lion St. BB5 .... 102 E6
Lionel St. BB12 .... 126 C6
Liptrott Rd. PR7 .... 42 A5
Lisbon Dr. BB3 .... 81 C1
Lisbon St. 17 OL12 .... 51 C1
Lisieux Hall Hospl. PR6 .... 60 A7
Lister Gr. LA3 .... 208 F8
Lister St. Accrington BB5 .... 103 A6
Lister St. 3 Blackburn BB2 .. 100 E3
Lister Well Rd. BB8 & BB9 .. 191 A6
Little Acre. Longton PR4 .... 74 A8
Little Acre. Thornton FY5 .... 151 D8
Little Banks Cl. PR5 .... 77 B6
Little Brewery La. L37 .... 11 F6
Little Carr La. PR7 .... 42 D5
Little Cl. PR1 .... 95 C3
Little Digmoor Cty Sch. WN8 .... 9 B6
Little Fell La. LA2 .... 211 E3
Little Fell Rd. LA2 .... 211 F6
Little Flatt. OL12 .... 51 B1
Little Hey La. L37 .... 18 B7
Little Hoole Cty Prim Sch. PR4 74 A5
Little La. Banks PR9 .... 54 B7
Little La. Longridge PR3 ...... 139 A7
Little La. Southport PR9 .... 53 B1
Little Meadow La. L40 .... 38 D4
Little Moor. BB7 .... 164 E6
Little Moor Clough. BL7 .... 46 E2
Little Moor View. BB7 .... 164 E6
Little Peel St. BB4 .... 100 D5
Little Poulton La. FY6 .... 151 F4
Little Queen St. BB8 .... 169 C4
Little Scotland. BL6 & WN2 .... 30 B2
Little St. BB5 .... 103 A6
Little Stones Rd. BL7 .... 46 E2
Little Toms La. BB10 .... 147 D3
Little Tongues La. FY6 & PR3 .. 195 B4
Little Twining. PR4 .... 74 A7
Little Wood. FY7 .... 193 E3
Littledale Ave. LA3 .... 209 A8
Littledale Mews. LA2 .... 214 B6
Littledale Rd. Crossgill LA2 231 E1
Littledale Rd. Littledale LA .. 226 C8
Littlemoor Cl. BB7 .... 145 A8
Littlemoor Rd. BB7 .... 164 E7
Littleton Gr. WN6 .... 28 E2
Littondale Garden. BB2 .... 79 D7
Liverpool Ave. PR8 .... 20 D5
Liverpool New Rd. PR4 .... 73 F5
Liverpool Old Rd.
  Ainsdale PR8 . 20 C1
Liverpool Old Rd.
  Much Hoole PR4 ...... 73 C1
Liverpool Old Rd.
  Much Hoole PR4 ...... 73 B4
Liverpool Old Rd. Sollom PR4 .... 56 B2
Liverpool Old Rd.
  Walmer Bridge PR4 .... 73 F5
Liverpool Rd. Ainsdale PR8 .... 20 C3
Liverpool Rd. Ainsdale PR8 .... 20 D5
Liverpool Rd. Ainsdale PR8 .... 20 E6
Liverpool Rd. Blackpool FY1 .. 129 D5
Liverpool Rd. Burnley BB12 .. 126 A6
Liverpool Rd. Formby L37 .... 12 A1
Liverpool Rd. Hutton PR4 .... 94 C2
Liverpool Rd. Hutton PR1 & PR4 . 94 F1
Liverpool Rd. Longton PR4 .... 73 F7
Liverpool Rd. Maghull L31 ...... 5 D4
Liverpool Rd. Much Hoole PR4 .. 73 D2
Liverpool Rd. Ormskirk L39 .... 15 B2
Liverpool Rd. Penwortham PR1 .. 95 B5
Liverpool Rd. Preston PR1 .... 95 D6
Liverpool Rd. Royal Oak L39 .... 6 F4
Liverpool Rd. Rufford L40 .... 38 C5
Liverpool Rd. Skelmersdale WN8 .. 8 E7
Liverpool Rd. Sollom PR4 ...... 56 A3
Liverpool Rd. Southport PR8 .. 34 A3

Liverpool Rd. Stanley Gate L39 .... 7 C5
Liverpool Rd N.
  Burscough Bridge L40 .... 24 E5
Liverpool Rd N. Maghull L31 .... 5 C2
Liverpool Rd S. Burscough L40 24 D2
Liverpool Rd S. Maghull L31 .... 5 C1
Livesey Branch Rd. BB2 .... 80 D8
Livesey Ct. BB2 .... 100 C2
Livesey Fold. PR6 .... 79 A1
Livesey Hall Cl. BB2 .... 99 E1
Livesey St. Lytham St Anne's FY8 .. 90 A3
Livesey St. Padiham PR6 ...... 125 C8
Livesey St. Preston PR1 .... 96 B7
Livesey St. Rishton BB1 .... 123 B2
Livesley's La. L37 .... 12 F2
Livet Ave. BB12 .... 126 E8
Livingstone Rd. Accrington BB5 103 B8
Livingstone Rd. Blackburn BB2 100 B4
Livingstone Rd. Blackpool FY1 129 C4
Livingstone St. BB9 .... 147 B5
Livingstone Wlk. BB9 .... 147 B6
Lloyd Cl. 5 BB9 .... 147 E8
Lloyd St. Darwen BB3 .... 80 F3
Lloyd St. Whitworth OL12 .... 70 C1
Lloyd Wlk. 6 BB9 .... 147 E8
Lloyd's Ave. LA4 .... 212 D4
Lobden Cres. OL12 .... 51 D8
Lobden Golf Course. OL12 .... 51 E6
Lochinch Cl. FY4 .... 110 A6
Lock Gate. BB4 .... 84 C1
Lock La. L40 & PR4 .... 56 B2
Lock St. 10 BB5 .... 102 E4
Locka La. Arkholme LA2 ...... 234 F3
Locka La. Lancaster LA1 ...... 213 F4
Locke Ind Est. BL6 .... 31 B3
Lockerbie Ave. FY5 .... 150 D8
Lockfield Dr. BB8 .... 200 C4
Lockhart Ave. FY5 .... 150 F8
Lockhurst Ave. FY5 .... 150 F8
Lockside. BB2 .... 100 D2
Lockside Rd. PR2 .... 94 F8
Lockwood Ave. FY6 .... 151 D4
Lockyer Ave. BB12 .... 126 B7
Locomotion Ind Est. BL6 .... 31 B2
Lodge Bank. PR6 & PR7 .... 61 F7
Lodge Cl. 2 Bamber Bridge PR5 .. 96 F1
Lodge Cl. Blackpool FY5 ...... 150 C7
Lodge Cl. Freckleton PR4 .... 92 B7
Lodge Cl. Blackpool FY5 ...... 150 C7
Lodge Cl. Inskip PR4 .... 155 B1
Lodge Cl. Staining FY3 .... 130 D5
Lodge La. Bacup OL13 .... 86 F1
Lodge La. Clifton PR4 .... 114 D1
Lodge La. Elswick PR4 .... 154 B1
Lodge La. Farington PR5 .... 75 E6
Lodge La. Melling LA2 .... 235 D1
Lodge La.
  Rainford Junction WA11 .... 8 D1
Lodge La. Singleton FY6 ...... 152 D2
Lodge La. Warton PR4 .... 90 F5
Lodge Mill La. BL0 .... 68 A1
Lodge Rd. Catterall PR3 ...... 179 A1
Lodge Rd. Orrell WN5 .... 10 E4
Lodge St. Accrington BB5 .... 103 C7
Lodge St. Lancaster LA1 ...... 210 F8
Lodge St. Preston PR1 .... 95 E8
Lodge St. Ramsbottom BL0 .... 49 C6
Lodge St. Shuttleworth BL0 .... 49 E8
Lodge Terr. BB9 .... 102 E5
Lodge View. PR3 .... 139 A6
Lodges Gr. LA4 .... 213 A6
Lodgeside. BB5 .... 123 F3
Lodgings The. PR2 .... 117 C5
Lodore Rd. FY4 .... 109 C6
Lofthouse Way. FY7 .... 194 A4
Loftos Ave. FY4 .... 109 D8
Logwood St. BB1 .... 100 F7
Lois Pl. BB2 .... 100 C5
Lomas La. BB4 .... 84 F1
Lomax St. 7 Bury BL9 .... 32 A3
Lomax St. Great Harwood BB6 .. 123 C5
Lomax St. Rochdale OL12 .... 51 F1
Lomeshaye Bsns Village. BB9 147 C8
Lomeshaye Cty Jun Sch. BB9 147 B8
Lomeshaye Ind Est. BB9 ...... 147 B7
Lomeshaye Pl. BB9 .... 147 C8
Lomeshaye Rd. Nelson BB9 147 C8
Lomeshaye Rd. Nelson BB9 147 D7
Lomeshaye Way. BB9 .... 147 C8
Lomond Ave.
  Lytham St Anne's FY8 .... 89 B5
London La. PR8 .... 21 D8
London Rd. Blackburn BB1 .. 100 E6
London Rd. Blackpool FY3 .. 129 D6
London Rd. Preston PR1 .... 96 C6
London Sq. PR8 .... 34 B7
London St. Fleetwood FY7 .. 194 B4
London St. Southport PR8 & PR9 . 34 B7
London Terr. BB3 .... 81 B2
London Way. PR1 & PR5 .... 96 C3
London Wlk. BB1 .... 100 E6
Londonderry Rd. LA3 .... 208 E5
Long Acre. PR5 .... 77 C5
Long Acre. LA5 .... 216 C8
Long Acre Pl. FY8 .... 90 A4
Long Acres Dr. OL12 .... 70 D2
Long Barn Brow. PR5 .... 98 E2
Long Bldg. BB7 .... 224 A1
Long Butts. PR1 .... 95 D2
Long Cl. Clitheroe BB7 .... 187 A2
Long Cl. Leyland PR5 .... 58 A8
Long Copse. PR7 .... 59 F1
Long Croft. Barton PR3 .... 136 B8
Long Croft. Longton PR4 .... 94 A1
Long Croft Meadow. PR7 .... 60 B2
Long Cswy. PR7 .... 225 B2
Long Cswy The. BB10 .... 107 E3

Long Dales La. LA6 .... 231 A6
Long Gn. BB8 .... 201 C2
Long Hey La. BB1 & BB3 .... 82 A2
Long Heys or Back La. WN8 .. 18 F5
Long Ing La. BB8 .... 200 C2
Long La. Abbeystead LA2 .... 226 F1
Long La. Banks PR9 .... 54 B6
Long La. Darwen BB3 .... 80 A3
Long La. Ince Blundell L29 ...... 4 B1
Long La. Laneshaw Bridge BB8 . 170 D7
Long La. Low Bentham LA2 .. 233 B7
Long La. Oakenclough PR3 .. 220 B1
Long La. Ormskirk L39 .... 15 D2
Long La. Pleasington BB2 .... 99 A2
Long La. Quernmore LA2 ...... 226 A5
Long La. Skelmersdale WN8 .... 9 E3
Long La. Stanley Gate L39 .... 7 B7
Long La. Street PR3 .... 220 B5
Long Lane End. LA2 .... 207 E7
Long Level. LA6 .... 235 F8
Long Lover La. BB7 .... 189 C8
Long Marsh La. LA1 .... 213 D1
Long Meadow. Chorley PR7 .. 42 A5
Long Meadow. Colne BB8 .... 170 A5
Long Meadow. Kirkham PR4 112 E5
Long Meadow.
  Mellor Brook BB2 .... 120 B2
Long Meadow. Much Hoole PR4 . 73 F4
Long Meanygate. PR9 .... 36 C7
Long Moss. PR5 .... 58 A8
Long Moss La. PR4 .... 75 A6
Long Row. Blackburn BB2 .... 121 B2
Long Row. Calder Vale PR3 .. 179 E8
Long Royd Rd. BB8 .... 201 B1
Long Wham La. PR4 .... 74 D1
Longacre. Longton PR4 .... 73 F8
Longacre. Southport PR9 .... 52 F3
Longacres La. OL12 .... 70 D2
Longber La. LA6 .... 236 B3
Longbrook Ave. PR5 .... 96 E1
Longcliffe Dr. PR8 .... 20 C4
Longcroft Cotts. BL9 .... 49 F1
Longfield. Formby L37 .... 12 B5
Longfield. Fulwood PR2 .... 116 F8
Longfield Ave. Penwortham PR1 .. 95 B4
Longfield Ave. Coppull PR7 .. 41 E2
Longfield Ave. Poulton-le-F FY6 151 D4
Longfield Dr. LA5 .... 216 C8
Longfield Pl. FY6 .... 151 D4
Longfield Terr. BB10 .... 106 E8
Longfold. Maghull L31 .... 5 E1
Longfold. Mere Brow PR4 .... 54 F2
Longford Ave. FY2 .... 150 E5
Longford Rd. PR8 .... 34 A2
Longholme Rd. 6 BB4 .... 85 A2
Longhouse La. FY6 .... 130 D8
Longlands Ave. LA3 .... 208 E8
Longlands Cres. LA3 .... 208 F8
Longlands La. LA3 .... 208 E7
Longlands Rd. LA1 .... 213 E3
Longley Cl. PR2 .... 116 F8
Longmeadow La. FY5 .... 173 C3
Longmeadow Ave. LA3 .... 208 F8
Longmeanygate. Leyland PR5 .. 75 A2
Longmeanygate. Leyland PR5 .. 75 C3
Longmeanygate. Leyland PR5 .. 75 D2
Longmire Way. LA4 .... 212 D5
Longmoor La. PR3 .... 177 E6
Longridge Ave. FY4 .... 109 E5
Longridge CE Cty High Sch. PR3 .. 139 A7
Longridge Cty High Sch. PR3 139 A4
Longridge Cty Prim Sch. PR3 138 F8
Longridge Dr. OL10 .... 32 F2
Longridge Golf Course. PR3 .. 160 F3
Longridge Heath. BB10 & BB9 147 D4
Longridge Rd. Fulwood PR2 .. 118 B6
Longridge Rd.
  Hurst Green BB6 & PR3 ...... 141 D8
Longridge Rd. Longridge PR3 160 C4
Longsands Cty Prim Sch. PR2 117 D5
Longsands La. PR2 .... 117 C6
Longshaw Ave. WN5 .... 10 E1
Longshaw Cl. WN5 .... 10 E1
Longshaw Inf Sch. BB2 .... 80 E8
Longshaw Jun Sch. BB2 ...... 100 E1
Longshaw La. BB2 .... 100 D2
Longshaw Old Rd. WN5 .... 10 E1
Longshaw St. BB2 .... 100 D1
Longsight Ave. Clitheroe BB7 186 F1
Longsight Ave. Huncoat BB5 103 E8
Longsight Rd.
  Langho BB6 & BB1 .... 142 B2
Longsight Rd. Langho BB6 .. 142 D2
Longsight Rd.
  Osbaldeston BB2 & BB1 .... 120 E4
Longsight Rd. Ramsbottom BL0 .. 49 A2
Longton Ave. FY5 .... 173 B2
Longton By-Pass. PR4 .... 74 C6
Longton Cl. BB1 .... 101 C5
Longton Cty Prim Sch. PR4 .. 74 A8
Longton Dr. Formby L37 .... 12 A6
Longton Dr. Morecambe LA4 213 A4
Longton Rd. Blackpool FY1 .. 129 C5
Longton Rd. Burnley BB12 .. 126 E8
Longton St. Blackburn BB1 .. 101 C5
Longton St. Chorley PR7 .... 42 E8
Longton's Cotts. LA6 .... 234 B1
Longway. FY4 .... 109 F8
Longwood Cl. FY6 .... 151 D1
Longworth Ave. Blackrod BL6 .. 30 C3
Longworth Ave. Burnley BB10 127 D6
Longworth Ave. Coppull PR7 41 F2
Longworth La. BL7 & BL1 .... 46 C2

Longworth Rd. Billington BB7 143 B4
Longworth Rd. Egerton BL7 .. 46 B3
Longworth Rd. Horwich BL6 .. 31 C4
Longworth Rd N. BL7 .... 45 D5
Longworth St.
  Bamber Bridge PR5 .... 96 E2
Longworth St. Chorley PR7 .... 42 E8
Longworth St. Preston PR1 .. 117 C1
Lonsdale Ave. Fleetwood FY7 193 E3
Lonsdale Ave. Morecambe LA4 213 A4
Lonsdale Ave. Ormskirk L39 .... 15 F7
Lonsdale Cl. PR5 .... 59 A6
Lonsdale Cres. FY7 .... 193 E3
Lonsdale Dr. PR5 .... 57 B3
Lonsdale Gr. LA4 .... 213 A4
Lonsdale Pl. LA1 .... 211 A5
Lonsdale Rd. Blackpool FY1 129 B2
Lonsdale Rd. Formby L37 ...... 11 F3
Lonsdale Rd. Hest Bank LA2 215 D1
Lonsdale Rd. Morecambe LA4 213 A4
Lonsdale Rd. Preston PR1 .... 117 C1
Lonsdale Rd. Southport PR8 .. 34 D4
Lonsdale Rise. LA4 .... 238 C2
Lonsdale St. Accrington BB5 102 F5
Lonsdale St. Burnley BB12 .. 126 C7
Lonsdale St. Nelson BB9 ...... 168 F1
Lord Ave. OL13 .... 86 C1
Lord Sefton Way. L37 .... 12 E2
Lord Sq. BB1 .... 100 E5
Lord St. Accrington BB5 ...... 103 B6
Lord St. Blackburn BB2 .... 100 E5
Lord St. Blackpool FY1 .... 129 B6
Lord St. Brierfield BB9 .... 147 B5
Lord St. Burscough Bridge L40 24 F1
Lord St. Bury BL9 .... 32 C1
Lord St. Chorley PR6 .... 42 D7
Lord St. Clayton Green PR6 .. 77 C1
Lord St. Colne BB8 .... 169 C5
Lord St. Darwen BB3 .... 81 A2
Lord St. Eccleston PR7 .... 40 C5
Lord St. Fleetwood FY7 .... 194 B4
Lord St. Great Harwood BB6 123 C4
Lord St. Horwich BL6 .... 31 B4
Lord St. Lancaster LA1 .... 213 F1
Lord St. Lytham St Anne's FY8 .. 88 E7
Lord St. Morecambe LA4 ...... 212 E6
Lord St. Oswaldtwistle BB5 .. 102 E4
Lord St. Preston PR1 .... 96 A8
Lord St. Rawtenstall BB4 .... 85 A2
Lord St. Rawtenstall BB4 .... 85 A7
Lord St. Rishton BB1 .... 123 B1
Lord St. Southport PR8 & PR9 .. 34 B7
Lord St W. 11 Blackburn BB2 .. 100 E5
Lord St W. Southport PR8 ...... 34 A6
Lord Street Cty Prim Sch.
  BB8 .... 169 C5
Lord Street Mall. 9 BB1 ...... 100 E5
Lord Street Prim Sch. BL6 .... 31 B4
Lord's Ave. PR7 .... 76 B7
Lord's Close Rd. LA2 .... 233 E2
Lord's La. Bamber Bridge PR5 95 E1
Lord's La. Longridge PR3 .... 160 B2
Lord's Lot Rd. Over Kellet LA6 234 D1
Lord's Lot Rd. Over Kellet LA6 234 D1
Lord's Wlk. PR1 .... 96 A8
Lords Croft. PR5 .... 77 A2
Lordsgate Dr. L40 .... 24 E3
Lordsgate La. L40 .... 24 C2
Lordsgate Township CE
  Prim Sch. L40 .... 24 E3
Lordsome Rd. LA3 .... 212 B2
Lorne Rd. FY2 .... 150 D2
Lorne St. Chorley PR7 .... 42 C7
Lorne St. Darwen BB3 .... 80 F2
Lorne St. Lytham St Anne's FY8 90 D4
Lorne Way. OL10 .... 32 F1
Lorraine Ave. PR2 .... 116 E3
Lorton Cl. Burnley BB12 ...... 126 B8
Lorton Cl. Fulwood PR2 .... 116 F6
Lostock Gdns. FY4 .... 109 F8
Lostock Hall Cty Prim Sch. PR5 96 B1
Lostock Hall High Sch. PR5 .... 96 C1
Lostock Hall Sta. PR5 .... 76 B8
Lostock La. PR5 .... 76 D7
Lostock Meadow. PR6 .... 77 A1
Lostock Rd. PR5 .... 57 C3
Lostock Sq. PR5 .... 76 B7
Lostock View. PR5 .... 76 B7
Lothersdale Cl. BB10 .... 147 D3
Lothian Ave. FY7 .... 193 D3
Lothian Pl. FY2 .... 150 E5
Lottice La. BB5 & BB1 .... 102 A1
Lotus Dr. FY4 .... 111 A6
Loughrigg Cl. BB12 .... 126 B7
Loughrigg Terr. FY4 .... 130 C1
Louis St. BL0 .... 67 D5
Louis William St. BB1 .... 81 D8
Louise St. FY1 .... 129 B3
Loupsfell Dr. LA4 .... 212 F4
Lourdes Ave. PR5 .... 96 A1
Louvain St. BB8 .... 200 A3
Lovat Rd. PR1 .... 116 F2
Love Clough Rd. BB4 .... 104 F2
Love La. BL0 .... 67 E1
Lovely Hall La. BB1 .... 121 D7
Low Bank. BB7 .... 192 A6
Low Bentham Prim Sch. LA2 233 B8
Low Bentham Rd. LA2 .... 233 C8
Low Croft. PR3 .... 136 B2
Low Fold. BB8 .... 192 A6
Low Gn. PR5 .... 75 F1
Low Hill. BB3 .... 64 A6
Low La. Leck LA6 .... 236 B7
Low La. Morecambe LA4 ...... 213 B5
Low Moor Rd. FY2 .... 150 E3
Low Rd. Halton Green LA2 .. 231 A4

Low Rd. Middleton LA3 .... 209 A2
Low St. LA6 .... 236 C3
Lowcroft. WN8 .... 18 C3
Lowcross Rd. FY6 .... 151 E2
Low View. BB4 .... 86 A1
Lowe Alt Rd. L38 .... 2 F4
Lowe Antley St. BB5 .... 102 F5
Lowe Ashworth Cl. BB2 ...... 100 C4
Lower Audley St. BB1 & BB2 100 F4
Lower Bank Rd. PR2 .... 116 F3
Lower Bank St. PR7 .... 79 A1
Lower Barn St. BB3 .... 64 C7
Lower Barnes St. BB5 .... 123 E4
Lower Burgh Way. PR7 .... 42 B4
Lower Carr La. L38 .... 4 B7
Lower Chapel La. BB7 .... 187 B8
Lower Clough St. BB9 .... 168 D2
Lower Clowes. BB4 .... 67 E8
Lower Clowes Rd. BB4 .... 67 E8
Lower Cockcroft. 12 BB2 .... 100 E5
Lower Copthurst La. PR6 .... 60 E7
Lower Cribden Ave. BB4 .... 84 D2
Lower Croft. PR1 .... 95 D2
Lower Croft. BB8 .... 201 B2
Lower Cross St. 23 BB1 .... 81 A1
Lower Darwen Prim Sch. BB3 . 81 A6
Lower East Ave. BB8 .... 200 B3
Lower Eccleshill Rd. BB3 ...... 81 A5
Lower Field. PR5 .... 75 F6
Lower Gate Rd. BB5 .... 124 F2
Lower Gn. Poulton-le-F FY6 151 E3
Lower Gn. 3 Spotland Fold OL12 51 C1
Lower Greenfield. PR2 .... 116 B5
Lower Hazel Cl. BB2 .... 100 C4
Lower Hey. PR4 .... 94 A1
Lower Hill Dr. PR6 .... 42 F1
Lower Hollin Bank St. BB2 .. 100 D2
Lower House Gn. BB4 .... 86 A8
Lower House Rd. PR5 .... 58 E8
Lower La. Freckleton PR4 ...... 92 D7
Lower La. Haslingden BB4 ...... 84 B4
Lower La. Kirkham PR4 .... 113 C1
Lower La. Longridge PR3 .... 139 B7
Lower Laithe Dr. BB9 .... 168 C3
Lower Lune St. PR7 .... 194 B5
Lower Makinson Fold. BL6 .... 31 D1
Lower Manor La. BB12 .... 146 F2
Lower Mead. PR7 .... 46 F1
Lower Mead Dr. BB12 .... 146 F2
Lower Meadow. BL7 .... 47 D6
Lower Park St. BB8 .... 200 C4
Lower Parrock Rd. BB9 .... 168 C1
Lower Philips Rd. BB1 .... 101 C8
Lower Prom. Southport PR8 .. 34 A7
Lower Prom. Southport PR8 .. 34 B8
Lower Rd. BL0 .... 49 E8
Lower Ridge Cl. BB10 .... 127 B6
Lower Rook St. BB8 .... 200 C2
Lower Rosegrove La. BB12 .. 126 A5
Lower School St. 6 BB8 ...... 169 D4
Lower Tentre. BB11 .... 127 B5
Lower Timber Hill La. BB11 .. 127 A2
Lower Waterside Farm Cotts.
  BB3 .... 81 E3
Lower West Ave. BB8 .... 200 B2
Lower Wilworth. BB1 .... 121 E1
Lower Wlk. FY2 .... 150 C7
Lowerfield. BB6 .... 122 C8
Lowerfields. BB12 .... 125 F6
Lowerfields. BB6 .... 123 C6
Lowerfold Cl. OL12 .... 51 C4
Lowerfold Cres. OL12 .... 51 C4
Lowerfold Dr. OL12 .... 51 C4
Lowerfold Rd. BB6 .... 123 C6
Lowerfold Way. OL12 .... 51 C4
Lowergate. BB7 .... 164 E8
Lowerhouse Cres. BB12 ...... 126 A6
Lowerhouse Cty Jun Sch.
  BB12 .... 126 A6
Lowerhouse Fold. BB12 ...... 126 A6
Lowerhouse La. Burnley BB12 125 F6
Lowerhouse La. Burnley BB12 126 B6
Lowes Ct. FY1 .... 129 B1
Lowes Gn. L37 .... 12 B3
Lowes Park Golf Course. BL9 32 A7
Lowes Rd. BL9 .... 32 A6
Loweswater Cres. BB12 ...... 126 B8
Loweswater Dr. 5 LA4 .... 212 G4
Lowesway. FY4 .... 109 F8
Lowfield Cl. PR4 .... 113 F2
Lowfield Rd. FY4 .... 109 F2
Lowfields La. LA6 .... 238 D2
Lowgill La. LA2 .... 233 C3
Lowick Cl. PR5 .... 97 E4
Lowick Dr. FY6 .... 151 D1
Lowland Way. FY2 .... 150 F6
Lowlands Rd. Bolton-le-S LA5 216 A5
Lowlands Rd. Morecambe LA4 212 F4
Lowndes St. PR1 & PR2 .... 116 E2
Lowood Gr. PR2 .... 115 D1
Lowood Lodge. FY8 .... 90 A3
Lowood Pl. BB2 .... 100 A6
Lowrey Terr. FY1 .... 129 B2
Lowry Cl. PR5 .... 76 A7
Lowry Hill La. L40 .... 25 E2
Lowstead Pl. FY4 .... 109 E6
Lowstern Cl. BL7 .... 46 E1
Lowswood. L37 .... 11 E5
Lowther Ave. Blackpool FY2 150 E4
Lowther Ave. Maghull L31 ...... 5 F2
Lowther Ave. Morecambe LA3 213 A3
Lowther Cres. PR5 .... 75 D2
Lowther Dr. PR7 .... 152 B2
Lowther Dr. PR5 .... 75 D3
Lowther La. BB8 .... 191 C1
Lowther Pl. BB1 .... 101 A8
Lowther Rd. Fleetwood FY7 193 F4

Lowther Rd. Lancaster LA1 214 B1
Lowther St. Colne BB8 169 E6
Lowther St. Nelson BB9 147 C8
Lowther St. Preston PR1 116 C1
Lowther Terr. Appley Bridge WN6 19 C8
Lowther Terr. Lytham St Anne's FY8 90 A3
Lowthian St. 28 PR1 95 F8
Lowthorpe Cres. PR1 117 B2
Lowthorpe Pl. PR1 117 B2
Lowthorpe Rd. PR1 117 B2
Lowthwaite Dr. BB9 147 E6
Lowton Rd. FY8 89 A8
Loxham Gdns. FY4 109 D6
Loxley Pl. FY5 150 E7
Loxley Pl E. FY5 150 F7
Loxley Rd. PR8 34 D4
Loynd St. 9 Great Harwood BB6 123 C5
Loynd St. Ramsbottom BL0 49 D6
Lubbock St. BB12 126 C6
Lucas Ave. PR7 41 D8
Lucas La. PR6 60 C6
Lucas St. BL9 32 A3
Lucerne Cl. PR2 117 C4
Lucerne Rd. PR2 117 C4
Lucy St. 7 Barrowford BB9 168 D3
Lucy St. Lancaster LA1 210 F8
Lucy St. Morecambe LA4 212 E6
Ludlow. WN8 18 C4
Ludlow Dr. L39 15 D7
Ludlow Gr. FY2 150 F2
Ludlow St. WN6 28 D3
Luke St. 17 OL13 69 C8
Lulworth. WN8 18 C4
Lulworth Ave. Blackpool FY3 130 A3
Lulworth Ave. Preston PR1 & PR2 116 D2
Lulworth Pl. PR5 96 D2
Lulworth Rd. Fulwood PR2 117 A4
Lulworth Rd. Southport PR8 33 F5
Lumb Carr Ave. BL0 & BL8 49 A4
Lumb Carr Rd. BL0 & BL8 49 A4
Lumb Cotts. BL0 67 A4
Lumb Flats. BL0 67 A4
Lumb Holes La. BB4 68 E7
Lumb La. BB4 85 F4
Lumb Scar. 9 OL13 86 F2
Lund St. Blackburn BB2 100 C4
Lund St. 2 Preston PR1 96 A8
Lunds La. PR4 73 D1
Lune Ave. L31 5 E2
Lune Cl. Kirkby Lonsdale LA6 238 C2
Lune Cl. Kirkham PR4 113 C5
Lune Dr. Clayton-le-W PR5 & PR6 76 E2
Lune Dr. Morecambe LA1 213 B3
Lune Gr. FY1 129 C3
Lune House. LA1 210 F7
Lune Ind Est. LA1 210 C8
Lune Rd. Fleetwood FY7 193 F4
Lune Rd. Lancaster LA1 213 D1
Lune St. Colne BB8 169 E4
Lune St. Lancaster LA1 213 F1
Lune St. Longridge PR3 139 B8
Lune St. Padiham BB12 125 D8
Lune St. Preston PR1 95 F7
Lune Terr. LA1 213 F1
Lune View. FY6 194 E6
Lunedale Ave. FY1 129 C1
Lunefield Dr. LA6 238 C1
Lunefield Gdns. LA6 238 C2
Lunesdale Cl. FY8 89 C7
Lunesdale Ct. Butt Yeats LA2 232 B6
Lunesdale Ct. Lancaster LA1 213 D3
Lunesdale Ct. Lancaster LA1 214 B1
Lunesdale Dr. PR3 204 B3
Lunesdale Rd. PR4 113 A5
Lunesdale Terr. LA2 231 E4
Lunesdale View. LA2 214 F7
Luneside. LA1 210 C8
Lunt Rd. L29 4 C1
Lupin Cl. Accrington BB5 103 A7
Lupin Cl. Lucas Green PR7 60 B5
Lupin Rd. BB5 103 B7
Lupton Dr. BB9 168 D4
Lupton Pl. LA1 213 D3
Lupton St. PR7 42 C6
Lutner St. BB11 127 A5
Luton Rd. Cleveleys FY5 172 E1
Luton Rd. Preston PR2 115 F2
Lutwidge Ave. PR1 117 C1
Lyceum Ave. FY3 129 D4
Lychfield. PR5 76 E7
Lychgate. 19 PR1 96 A8
Lydd Gr. PR7 42 A7
Lyddesdale Ave. FY5 150 D8
Lydgate. Brierfield BB10 147 E2
Lydgate. Chorley PR7 42 A5
Lydia St. BB5 103 B4
Lydiate Cty Prim Sch. L31 5 C4
Lydiate La. Bilsborrow PR3 157 C6
Lydiate La. Leyland PR5 76 C4
Lydiate La. Newton PR7 58 B1
Lydiate Lane End. PR7 58 B2
Lydiate Station Rd. L31 4 E5
Lydric Ave. PR5 97 E2
Lyelake La. L40 & L39 16 F2
Lymbridge Dr. BL6 30 D1
Lyme Gr. FY6 194 E5
Lymm Ave. LA1 213 C3
Lyncroft Cres. FY3 129 E7
Lyndale. WN8 18 B4
Lyndale Ave. Bamber Bridge PR5 96 E4
Lyndale Ave. Haslingden BB4 84 B2
Lyndale Ave. Wilpshire BB1 122 A7
Lyndale Cl. Leyland PR5 59 B6
Lyndale Cl. Rawtenstall BB4 85 A7
Lyndale Cl. Wilpshire BB1 122 A7
Lyndale Ct. FY7 194 B5
Lyndale Gr. PR5 96 C2
Lyndale Rd. BB11 125 C3
Lynden Ave. LA4 213 A5
Lyndhurst. Maghull L31 5 D1
Lyndhurst. Skelmersdale WN8 18 A4
Lyndhurst Ave. Blackburn BB1 101 E5
Lyndhurst Ave. Blackpool FY4 129 D1
Lyndhurst Dr. PR2 115 E2
Lyndhurst Gr. BB6 123 E6
Lyndhurst Rd. Blackburn BB2 100 E2
Lyndhurst Rd. Burnley BB10 & BB11 127 C5
Lyndhurst Rd. Darwen BB3 80 E3
Lyndhurst Rd. Darwen BB3 80 F3
Lyndhurst Rd. Southport PR8 34 B2
Lyndon Ave. BB6 123 E6
Lyndon Ct. BB6 123 E6
Lynfield Rd. BB6 123 E6
Lynn Gr. FY1 129 B7
Lynn Pl. PR1 117 D2
Lynslack Terr. LA5 218 B8
Lynthorpe Rd. Blackburn BB2 100 E2
Lynthorpe Rd. Nelson BB9 169 A1
Lynton Ave. Blackpool FY4 109 D8
Lynton Ave. Leyland PR5 59 C8
Lynton Ct. FY7 172 C8
Lynton Dr. PR8 33 E1
Lynton Rd. Accrington BB5 102 F4
Lynton Rd. Southport PR8 33 E1
Lynwood Ave. Blackpool FY3 129 E8
Lynwood Ave. Clayton-le-M BB5 123 F4
Lynwood Ave. Darwen BB3 80 E4
Lynwood Ave. Grimsargh PR2 138 C2
Lynwood Ave. Ormskirk L39 15 C3
Lynwood Cl. Clayton-le-M BB5 123 F4
Lynwood Cl. Colne BB8 169 D7
Lynwood Cl. Darwen BB3 80 E3
Lynwood Cl. Skelmersdale WN8 9 D7
Lynwood Dr. FY6 174 C7
Lynwood End. L39 15 C3
Lynwood Rd. Blackburn BB2 100 B6
Lynwood Rd. Huncoat BB5 124 E2
Lyons La. PR6 42 D7
Lyons Rd. PR8 34 A5
Lyth Rd. LA1 214 B2
Lythall Ave. FY8 90 D4
Lytham CE Prim Sch. FY8 90 B4
Lytham Cl. PR2 116 D3
Lytham Rd. Blackburn BB2 100 F1
Lytham Rd. Blackpool FY4 109 C6
Lytham Rd. Blackpool FY1 129 B3
Lytham Rd. Brierfield BB10 147 C2
Lytham Rd. Freckleton PR4 92 B6
Lytham Rd. Fulwood PR2 116 D3
Lytham Rd. Moss Side FY8 111 E1
Lytham Rd. Southport PR9 53 A4
Lytham Rd. Warton PR4 91 D5
Lytham St. Chorley PR7 42 E7
Lytham St. Lower Healey OL12 51 E3
Lytham St Anne's High Sch. FY8 89 C5
Lytham Sta. FY8 90 A3
Lytham Windmill (Mus). FY8 90 C3
Lythcoe Ave. PR2 116 C4
Lythe Fell Ave. LA2 214 F7
Lythe Fell Rd. LA2 228 F8
Lythe La. LA2 233 E2
Lytles Cl. L37 12 A2
Lytton St. BB12 125 F7

Mabel St. Colne BB8 169 F5
Mabel St. Falinge Fold OL12 51 D2
Maberry Cl. WN6 19 D7
Macaulay St. BB11 126 C5
Macauley Ave. FY4 109 F8
Macbeth Rd. FY7 193 E4
Maclaren Cl. FY3 130 D5
Macleod St. BB9 147 D8
Maddy St. PR1 95 D8
Madeley Gdns. OL12 51 C1
Maden Rd. OL13 86 F2
Maden St. BB5 102 E6
Maden Way. OL13 86 F2
Madison Ave. Blackpool FY2 150 B5
Madison Ave. Hest Bank LA5 215 E2
Madryn Ave. L33 1 A2
Mafeking Ave. BL9 32 A5
Mafeking Rd. PR1 116 C2
Magdalen Ave. FY5 172 D1
Maggots Nook Rd. WA11 9 A1
Maghull La. L31 6 B1
Maghull Smallholdings Est. L31 5 F3
Magnolia Cl. PR2 117 C6
Magnolia Rd. PR1 95 B3
Magpie Cl. BB11 126 C5
Maharishi Sch of the Age of Enlightenment. L40 18 A5
Maida Vale. FY5 150 D8
Maiden St. BB4 84 B6
Main Ave. LA3 208 F3
Main Cl. LA3 205 D8
Main Dr. FY6 151 E2
Main Rd. Bolton-le-S LA5 216 A4
Main Rd. Bolton-le-S LA5 216 B5
Main Rd. Galgate LA2 207 A3
Main Rd. Hest Bank LA2 215 F1
Main Rd. Nether Kellet LA6 216 F5
Main Sprit Weind. PR1 96 A7
Main St. Bolton-by-B BB7 224 D4
Main St. Burton-in-K LA6 234 B7
Main St. Cockerham LA2 203 D4
Main St. Grindleton BB7 187 B8
Main St. Heysham LA3 208 E8
Main St. High Bentham LA2 233 D8
Main St. Hornby LA2 232 B7
Main St. Kelbrook BB8 192 A6
Main St. Kirkby Lonsdale LA6 238 C2
Main St. Lancaster LA1 213 F2
Main St. Low Bentham LA2 233 B8
Main St. Overton LA3 205 D8
Main St. Rathmell BD23 230 F6
Main St. Warton LA5 217 D5
Main St. Whittington LA6 235 D7
Main St. Wray LA2 232 D6
Mains La. Bispham Green L40 26 A6
Mains La. Poulton-le-F FY6 152 B4
Mainway. LA1 213 F2
Mairscough La. L39 14 B1
Maitland Ave. FY5 172 D1
Maitland Cl. 5 PR1 96 C8
Maitland Pl. BB4 85 A1
Maitland St. 18 Bacup OL13 86 F2
Maitland St. 4 Preston PR1 96 C8
Maitland St. 1 Preston PR5 96 D8
Majestic The. FY8 88 D6
Major St. Accrington BB5 103 B4
Major St. Ramsbottom BL0 49 B6
Major St. Rawtenstall BB4 85 A7
Makinson Ave. BL6 31 E1
Makinson La. BL6 31 F4
Makinsons Row. LA2 207 A4
Malcolm Pl. FY7 193 E4
Malcolm St. PR1 117 D1
Malden St. PR5 76 A1
Maldern Ave. FY6 151 C5
Maldon Pl. PR2 117 D2
Malham Ave. Accrington BB5 102 F4
Malham Ave. Blackpool FY4 109 D8
Malham Cl. Lancaster LA1 213 D3
Malham Cl. Southport PR8 34 E3
Malham Pl. PR2 117 E4
Malham Rd. BB10 147 D3
Malham Wend. BB9 168 C3
Maliff Rd. BB10 149 B2
Malkin Cl. BB9 168 E8
Malkin La. BB7 163 F6
Mall The. Burnley BB11 127 A6
Mall The. Fulwood PR2 117 E2
Mall The. Lytham St Anne's FY8 89 C7
Mallard Cl. Leyland PR5 58 D8
Mallard Cl. Ormskirk L39 15 C2
Mallard Cl. Thornton FY5 173 A4
Mallard Ct. FY3 130 B6
Mallard Dr. BL6 31 A3
Mallard House. L31 5 B4
Mallard Pl. BB5 102 D3
Mallards Wlk. PR5 77 A5
Mallee Ave. PR9 53 A3
Mallee Cres. PR9 53 A3
Malley La. PR4 & PR3 135 C8
Mallom Ave. PR7 59 E1
Mallory Ave. L31 5 B4
Mallow Wlk. LA3 212 E2
Mallowdale Ave. LA3 209 A8
Mallowdale Rd. LA1 213 D2
Malt Kiln Brow. PR3 182 E4
Malt Kiln Gr. PR3 154 A5
Malt St. BB5 103 B7
Maltby Pl. FY4 129 F2
Malthouse Ct. PR1 116 D1
Malthouse The. PR1 116 D1
Malthouse Way. PR1 95 D3
Maltings The. Longton PR4 73 F8
Maltings The. Thornton FY5 173 A4
Maltings The. Whittington LA6 235 D7
Maltkiln La. Bispham Green L40 & WN8 26 C7
Maltkiln La. Ormskirk L39 6 E8
Malton Dr. PR5 76 A7
Malvern Ave. Blackburn BB2 100 D1
Malvern Ave. Blackpool FY1 129 D2
Malvern Ave. Lancaster LA1 211 A6
Malvern Ave. Oswaldtwistle BB5 102 E3
Malvern Ave. Padiham BB12 125 D6
Malvern Ave. Preston PR1 96 B6
Malvern Ave. Stalmine FY6 174 C7
Malvern Cl. 6 Accrington BB5 103 A7
Malvern Cl. Bamber Bridge PR5 76 C8
Malvern Cl. Horwich BL6 31 C5
Malvern Rd. Lytham St Anne's FY8 89 D5
Malvern Rd. Nelson BB9 169 A1
Malvern Rd. Preston PR1 96 B6
Malvern St. Preston PR1 96 B5
Malvern St. Standish WN6 28 D3
Malvern Way. BB4 67 A7
Manby Cl. PR5 97 E3
Manchester Rd. Accrington BB5 103 D3
Manchester Rd. Barnoldswick BB8 200 B1
Manchester Rd. Blackpool FY3 129 D6
Manchester Rd. Blackrod BL6 30 E1
Manchester Rd. Burnley BB11 126 E4
Manchester Rd. Burnley BB11 126 F5
Manchester Rd. Clow Bridge BB11 & BB4 105 D6
Manchester Rd. Hapton BB11 & BB12 125 C4
Manchester Rd. Haslingden BB4 67 D7
Manchester Rd. Haslingden BB4 84 B2
Manchester Rd. Nelson BB9 147 D7
Manchester Rd. Preston PR1 96 B7
Manchester Rd. Ramsbottom BL0 & BL9 49 E4
Manchester Rd. Southport PR9 34 C7
Manchester Road Sta. BB11 126 F5
Mancknols St. BB9 147 F7
Mandella Ct. BB1 100 E6
Mandeville Rd. PR8 20 B5
Mandeville Terr. BL8 48 B2
Manfield. WN8 18 A3
Manghales. BB4 84 B7
Manion Ave. L31 5 B5
Manion Cl. L31 5 B5
Manitoba Cl. BB2 100 B8
Manley Cl. BL9 49 C2
Manner Sutton St. BB1 100 F5
Manning Rd. 4 Preston PR1 117 E1
Manning Rd. Southport PR8 34 E6
Manor Ave. Burscough L40 24 D2
Manor Ave. Fulwood PR2 117 B4
Manor Ave. Hest Bank LA2 213 E8
Manor Ave. Penwortham PR1 95 B4
Manor Ave. Ribchester PR3 140 D3
Manor Beach Cty Prim Sch. FY5 172 D3
Manor Brook. 1 BB5 103 C6
Manor Cl. Burton in L LA6 236 C3
Manor Cl. Coupe Green PR5 97 F3
Manor Cl. Hest Bank LA2 213 E8
Manor Cres. Burscough L40 24 D2
Manor Cres. Hest Bank LA2 213 F8
Manor Ct. Blackpool FY4 129 E1
Manor Ct. Fulwood PR2 116 B7
Manor Ctyd. LA3 208 E8
Manor Dr. Burscough L40 24 D2
Manor Dr. Cleveleys FY5 172 D3
Manor Dr. Hest Bank LA2 213 E8
Manor Dr. Kirkham PR4 113 C4
Manor Fields. BB7 143 C5
Manor Gdns. L40 24 D2
Manor Gr. Morecambe LA3 212 C2
Manor Gr. Penwortham PR1 95 A4
Manor Gr. Skelmersdale WN8 17 F1
Manor House Cl. Leyland PR5 58 B8
Manor House Cl. Maghull L31 5 C1
Manor House Cres. PR1 117 B3
Manor House Dr. WN8 9 E3
Manor House La. PR1 & PR2 117 C3
Manor House Park Flats. FY5 172 C3
Manor La. Hest Bank LA2 215 F1
Manor La. Penwortham PR1 95 B4
Manor Lodge. L37 11 E4
Manor Pk. PR2 117 C4
Manor Pl. BB5 102 F7
Manor Rd. Blackburn BB2 100 B5
Manor Rd. Blackpool FY1 129 D4
Manor Rd. Burnley BB12 126 B7
Manor Rd. Burscough L40 24 D2
Manor Rd. Clayton Green PR6 77 B3
Manor Rd. Clitheroe BB7 164 D7
Manor Rd. Colne BB8 169 E7
Manor Rd. Darwen BB3 63 F8
Manor Rd. Fleetwood FY7 193 E4
Manor Rd. Garstang PR3 199 C1
Manor Rd. Hest Bank LA2 213 F8
Manor Rd. Horwich BL6 31 D4
Manor Rd. Inskip PR4 134 C8
Manor Rd. Shevington WN6 19 F6
Manor Rd. Southport PR9 53 A2
Manor Rd. Whalley BB7 143 C5
Manor Rd. Wrea Green PR4 112 B4
Manor Road Cty Prim Sch. PR6 77 B2
Manor St. Accrington BB5 103 D7
Manor St. Bacup OL13 86 F1
Manor St. Bury BL9 32 A2
Manor St. Nelson BB9 147 F8
Manor St. Ramsbottom BL0 49 B7
Manor Steet. BB9 147 F8
Manor Way. PR4 112 B3
Manor Wood. Fleetwood FY7 193 E4
Manor Wood. Kirkham PR4 113 B7
Manorcroft. PR4 73 F8
Manse Ave. WN6 27 F5
Mansergh St. BB10 147 C2
Mansfield Ave. BL0 49 B2
Mansfield Cres. BB9 147 C6
Mansfield Dr. PR5 97 E3
Mansfield Gr. BB9 147 C6
Mansfield Rd. FY3 129 D8
Mansion House Bldgs. 2 BB4 85 A7
Mansion St S. BB5 103 D6
Manston Gr. PR7 42 A7
Manx Jane's La. PR9 53 A4
Manxman Rd. BB2 100 F1
Maple Ave. Blackpool FY3 129 D5
Maple Ave. Brinscall PR6 61 F7
Maple Ave. Burscough L40 24 E4
Maple Ave. 7 Bury BL9 32 B2
Maple Ave. Fleetwood FY7 172 F8
Maple Ave. Haslingden BB4 84 C3
Maple Ave. Horwich BL6 31 E1
Maple Ave. Morecambe LA3 212 B2
Maple Ave. Thornton FY5 151 C8
Maple Cl. Formby L37 11 C1
Maple Cl. Newton-with-S PR4 113 F2
Maple Cl. Whalley BB7 143 D6
Maple Cl. Wilpshire BB1 121 E6
Maple Cres. BB1 102 B8
Maple Ct. PR3 199 C1
Maple Dr. Bamber Bridge PR5 96 F1
Maple Dr. Oswaldtwistle BB5 102 F3
Maple Dr. Poulton-le-F FY6 151 E2
Maple Gr. Chorley PR6 60 D3
Maple Gr. Fulwood PR2 118 A4
Maple Gr. Grimsargh PR2 138 D1
Maple Gr. Penwortham PR1 95 B4
Maple Gr. Ramsbottom BL0 49 D6
Maple Gr. Warton PR4 91 D6
Maple Rd. PR3 199 C1
Maple St. Blackburn BB1 101 A7
Maple St. Clayton-le-M BB5 123 F1
Maple St. Great Harwood BB6 123 D6
Maple St. 1 Rishton BB1 123 B1
Maple St. Southport PR8 34 E6
Maplebank. PR2 115 C1
Maples The. PR5 57 F6
Maplewood. Skelmersdale WN8 18 A4
Maplewood. Southport PR9 52 F2
Maplewood Ave. FY6 195 A5
Maplewood Cl. Leyland PR5 58 E8
Maplewood Cl. Lytham St Anne's FY8 89 F4
Maplewood Dr. FY5 150 C8
Maplewood Gdns. LA1 211 A2
Mapsden Dr. BB9 147 D6
Marabou Dr. BB3 80 E3
Marathon Pl. PR5 75 C3
Marble Pl. PR8 34 B7
Marble St. BB5 102 E4
March St. BB12 126 F8
Marchbank Rd. WN8 17 D1
Marchwood Rd. FY3 130 B8
Marcroft Ave. FY4 109 E7
Mardale Ave. Blackpool FY4 130 C1
Mardale Ave. Morecambe LA4 212 G5
Mardale Cl. PR8 20 B4
Mardale Cres. PR5 59 B7
Mardale Rd. Fulwood PR1 118 A1
Mardale Rd. Lancaster LA1 214 A1
Mardale Rd. Longridge PR3 138 F5
Maresfield Rd. PR1 95 E5
Marewood. PR7 60 B2
Margaret Rd. PR1 95 E4
Margaret St. Blackburn BB1 101 D4
Margaret St. Burnley BB10 127 A8
Margaret St. Oswaldtwistle BB5 102 C2
Margaret St. 1 Preston PR1 96 A8
Margaret St. Rawtenstall BB4 84 F4
Margate Ave. FY4 109 E6
Margate Rd. Fulwood PR2 116 A4
Margate Rd. Lytham St Anne's FY8 88 F8
Maria Ct. 10 BB11 127 B4
Maria Sq. BL7 45 D4
Maria St. BB3 64 B6
Marians Dr. L39 15 E7
Maricourt Ave. BB1 101 D5
Marilyn Ave. 2 PR5 76 B8
Marina Ave. Blackpool FY1 129 D2
Marina Ave. Poulton-le-F FY3 130 D8
Marina Cl. PR5 96 A1
Marina Dr. Bamber Bridge PR5 96 A1
Marina Dr. Fulwood PR2 116 E7
Marina Gr. PR5 96 A1
Marina Rd. L37 11 F1
Marine Ave. BB11 126 C4
Marine Dr. Hest Bank LA2 215 D1
Marine Dr. Lytham St Anne's FY8 89 D3
Marine Dr. Southport PR8 & PR9 52 D4
Marine Ind Ctr. FY8 90 D4
Marine Par. Fleetwood FY7 193 C1
Marine Par. Southport PR8 34 A8
Marine Rd E. LA4 212 F6
Marine Rd W. LA3 & LA4 212 C4
Marine Road Central. LA4 212 D5
Mariners Cl. FY7 193 E1
Mariners Way. PR1 & PR2 95 B8
Marino Cl. FY5 151 D8
Maritime St. FY7 193 F2
Mark Cl. PR5 95 F1
Mark Rd. L38 2 F4
Mark Sq. PR4 56 A6
Mark St. Bacup OL13 69 C8
Mark St. Burnley BB10 147 B1
Mark's Ave. PR5 75 E5
Market Ave. 2 BB1 100 E5
Market Cross. L39 15 E5
Market Gate. 27 LA1 210 F8
Market Pl. Adlington PR6 30 A7
Market Pl. 12 Chorley PR7 42 C8
Market Pl. 8 Clitheroe BB7 164 E8
Market Pl. 10 Colne BB8 169 E5
Market Pl. Edenfield BL0 67 D3
Market Pl. Garstang PR3 178 C7
Market Pl. 1 Leyland PR5 59 A8
Market Pl. Longridge PR3 139 B7
Market Pl. 3 Poulton-le-F FY6 151 D3
Market Pl. Ramsbottom BL0 49 C7
Market Pl. Standish WN6 28 E1
Market Sq. Burnley BB11 127 A6
Market Sq. Kirkby Lonsdale LA6 238 C2
Market Sq. Kirkham PR4 113 B5
Market Sq. 10 Lancaster LA1 210 F8
Market Sq. Lytham St Anne's FY8 90 A3
Market Sq. Nelson BB9 147 D8
Market St. Adlington PR6 30 A6
Market St. Bacup OL13 86 F2
Market St. 8 Barnoldswick BB8 200 B2
Market St. Blackpool FY1 129 B5
Market St. Carnforth LA5 217 D2
Market St. Chorley PR6 & PR7 42 C7
Market St. Church BB5 102 E5
Market St. Colne BB8 169 E5
Market St. Darwen BB3 81 A1
Market St. Edenfield BL0 67 D4
Market St. Hambleton FY6 174 C2
Market St. Kirkby Lonsdale LA6 238 C2
Market St. Kirkham PR4 112 F6
Market St. Lancaster LA1 210 F8
Market St. Morecambe LA4 212 D5
Market St. 9 Nelson BB9 147 D8
Market St. 5 Newchurch BB4 68 F8
Market St. Preston PR1 95 F8
Market St. Southport PR8 34 B7
Market St. Standish WN6 28 E1
Market St. Whitworth OL12 & OL13 70 D4
Market St W. PR1 95 F8
Market Street La. BB2 100 E4
Market Way. 7 Blackburn BB1 100 E5
Market Way. Ormskirk L39 15 E5
Market Wlk. PR6 42 C8
Markham Dr. PR8 34 E2
Markham Rd. BB2 100 B3
Markham St. PR1 116 C1

Markland St. Preston PR1 .... 95 E7
Markland St. 6 Ramsbottom BL0 49 C6
Marklands Rd. BL6 .... 31 E5
Markross St. BB4 .... 85 A2
Marl Ave. PR1 .... 95 B4
Marl Cop. PR5 .... 57 A6
Marl Croft. PR1 .... 95 D2
Marl Gr. WN5 .... 10 D4
Marl Hill Cres. PR1 & PR5 .... 118 A2
Marl Pits. BB4 .... 85 B3
Marl Pits Sports Complex. BB4 85 C3
Marl Rd. L33 .... 1 C3
Marland. WN8 .... 18 A4
Marlboro Rd. FY3 .... 129 E4
Marlborough. WN8 .... 18 A4
Marlborough Ave.
 Cleveleys FY5 .... 172 D5
Marlborough Ave. Maghull L31 ...... 5 D3
Marlborough Ave. Warton PR4 .. 91 D6
Marlborough Cl.
 Ramsbottom BL0 .... 49 C3
Marlborough Cl. Whitworth OL12 51 C7
Marlborough Dr.
 Bamber Bridge PR5 .... 96 D3
Marlborough Dr. Fulwood PR2 116 C7
Marlborough Rd.
 Accrington BB5 .... 103 C7
Marlborough Rd.
 Lytham St Anne's FY8 .... 109 E1
Marlborough Rd.
 Morecambe LA3 .... 212 B3
Marlborough Rd. Southport PR9 34 C7
Marlborough St. Burnley BB11 .. 127 A4
Marlborough St. Chorley PR6 ...... 60 C1
Marlborough St. 14
 Spotland Fold OL12 .... 51 C1
Marled Hey. BL7 .... 47 D5
Marles Ct. BB10 .... 127 B8
Marlfield. PR4 .... 73 F4
Marlfield Cl. PR2 .... 115 F5
Marlhill Rd. FY3 .... 130 B8
Marlin St. 6 BB9 .... 168 F2
Marlowe Ave. Accrington BB5 .. 103 E2
Marlowe Ave. Padiham BB12 .... 125 F7
Marlowe Cres. BB6 .... 123 B4
Marlton Rd. BB2 .... 100 D1
Marlton Way. LA1 .... 210 E6
Marple Cl. WN6 .... 28 B2
Marquis Cl. BB3 .... 80 F7
Marquis Dr. PR4 .... 92 C7
Marquis PR4 .... 112 F5
Marron Cl. PR7 .... 58 E8
Mars St. BL7 .... 47 E6
Marsden Cl. PR7 .... 40 B7
Marsden Cres. BB9 .... 148 A8
Marsden Ct. BB10 .... 147 C3
Marsden Gr. BB9 .... 147 C5
Marsden Hall Rd. BB9 .... 148 A8
Marsden Hall Rd N. BB9 .... 169 B1
Marsden Hall Road S. BB9 .... 148 A8
Marsden Height Cl. BB9 .... 147 F5
Marsden Mall. 2 BB9 .... 147 E8
Marsden Park Golf Course.
 BB9 .... 148 C8
Marsden Prim Sch. BB9 .... 147 D7
Marsden Rd. Blackpool FY4 ..... 109 D8
Marsden Rd. Brierfield BB10 .... 147 C3
Marsden Rd. Southport PR9 ...... 34 E7
Marsden Sq. BB4 .... 84 A4
Marsden St. Accrington BB5 ..... 103 B4
Marsden St. Blackburn BB2 ..... 100 B2
Marsden St. 5 Haslingden BB4 .. 84 A3
Marsden St. Kirkham PR4 .... 113 B5
Marsett Cl. OL12 .... 51 A1
Marsett Pl. PR2 .... 117 E5
Marsh Brows. L37 .... 11 E2
Marsh Cl. LA2 .... 203 B4
Marsh Cres. LA4 .... 213 B4
Marsh Ct. FY5 .... 173 A2
Marsh Cty Prim Sch The. LA1 210 D8
Marsh Dr. PR4 .... 92 D7
Marsh Gates. PR4 .... 92 D7
Marsh House La. BB3 .... 81 C1
Marsh Houses. LA2 .... 203 B4
Marsh La. Brindle PR6 .... 78 B5
Marsh La. Cockerham LA2 .... 203 B4
Marsh La. Glasson LA2 .... 205 D3
Marsh La. Hambleton FY6 .... 174 C1
Marsh La. Lady Green L38 .... 3 E6
Marsh La. Longton PR4 .... 73 D8
Marsh La. Ormskirk L40 .... 23 D1
Marsh La. Preston PR1 .... 95 E1
Marsh La. Preston PR1 .... 95 E8
Marsh La. 6 Preston PR1 .... 95 F8
Marsh Mill. FY5 .... 173 B2
Marsh Moss La. L40 .... 24 C7
Marsh Rd. Banks PR4 & PR9 ..... 71 D1
Marsh Rd. Hesketh Bank PR4 .... 72 F4
Marsh Rd. Thornton FY5 .... 173 A2
Marsh Rd. Thornton FY5 .... 173 A3
Marsh St. Blackburn BB1 .... 100 E6
Marsh St. Horwich BL6 .... 31 A4
Marsh St. Lancaster LA1 .... 213 D1
Marsh Terr. BB3 .... 81 A2
Marsh View. PR4 .... 113 F2
Marsh Way. PR1 .... 95 C2
Marshall Ave. BB5 .... 124 F2
Marshall Gr. PR2 .... 116 A4
Marshall's Brow. PR1 .... 95 E3
Marshall's Cl. Maghull L31 .... 5 C4
Marshall's Cl. Penwortham PR1 .. 95 E4
Marshallsay. L37 .... 12 A2
Marsham Cl. PR3 .... 178 D6
Marsham Gr. BB3 .... 81 C1
Marshaw Pl. PR3 .... 178 A6

Marshaw Rd. LA1 .... 213 D2
Marshdale Rd. FY4 .... 109 F7
Marshes La The. PR4 .... 37 A8
Marshside Rd. PR9 .... 52 F4
Marshside Prim Sch. PR9 .... 53 A5
Marston Cl. PR2 .... 116 C7
Marston Cres. L38 .... 3 C1
Marston Moor. PR2 .... 116 C7
Mart La. L40 .... 24 E5
Martholme La. BB6 .... 123 F8
Martin Ave. FY8 .... 109 C4
Martin Croft Rd. BB4 .... 84 A5
Martin La. Drummersdale L40 .... 23 E6
Martin La. Passmonds OL12 ...... 51 B1
Martin Mere
 (The Wildfowl Trust). L40 ...... 37 B1
Martin St. Burnley BB10 .... 147 B1
Martin St. Bury BL9 .... 32 B3
Martin St. Turton Bottoms BL7 .... 47 D4
Martin Top La. BB7 .... 189 C7
Martindale Cl. BB1 .... 101 C2
Martinfield. PR2 .... 116 F8
Martinfields. BB10 .... 147 C4
Martins Ave. PR6 .... 42 E2
Martins La. WN8 .... 9 D7
Martland Ave. WN6 .... 19 F5
Marton Dr. Blackpool FY4 .... 109 D8
Marton Dr. Burnley BB11 .... 126 E3
Marton Dr. Morecambe LA4 .... 213 B6
Marton Pl. LA4 .... 213 B6
Marton Rd. PR2 .... 94 F8
Marton St. 4 LA1 .... 210 F7
Marwick Cl. WN6 .... 28 D2
Mary Ave. PR8 .... 20 E6
Mary St. Blackburn BB1 .... 101 A4
Mary St. Burnley BB10 .... 127 B5
Mary St. Carnforth LA5 .... 217 D3
Mary St. Colne BB8 .... 169 C4
Mary St. Lancaster LA1 .... 210 F8
Mary St. Ramsbottom BL0 .... 49 B5
Mary St. Rishton BB1 .... 123 B1
Mary St E. BL6 .... 31 B4
Mary St W. Horwich BL6 .... 31 A4
Mary St W. Longridge PR3 .... 139 A8
Marybank Cl. PR2 .... 117 C5
Maryport Cl. BB2 & BB3 .... 80 F8
Maryland Cl. LA5 .... 218 D2
Masefield Ave. Padiham BB12 .. 125 E7
Masefield Ave. Thornton FY5 ... 173 A3
Masefield Cl. BB6 .... 123 B4
Masefield Pl. PR5 .... 96 D2
Mason Cl. PR4 .... 92 C6
Mason Hill View. PR2 .... 117 A4
Mason House Cres. PR2 .... 116 A5
Mason St. 7 Accrington BB5 ... 103 C6
Mason St. Bury BL9 .... 32 A2
Mason St. Chorley PR6 .... 60 C2
Mason St. Colne BB8 .... 169 D5
Mason St. Egerton BL7 .... 46 E1
Mason St. Horwich BL6 .... 31 D3
Mason St. Oswaldtwistle BB5 ... 102 D3
Masonfield. PR5 .... 77 B5
Masongill Fell Lane. LA6 .... 236 E7
Masonwood. PR2 .... 117 A6
Massam's La. L37 .... 11 F6
Massey Croft. OL12 .... 51 C8
Massey St. BB9 .... 147 A5
Massey St. Brierfield BB9 .... 147 A4
Massey St. Burnley BB11 .... 127 A6
Massey St. Bury BL9 .... 32 B3
Masterson Ave. BB12 .... 144 D2
Mather Ave. BB5 .... 103 B8
Mather St. FY3 .... 129 D7
Mathias Ct. LA4 .... 212 E6
Matlock Ave. PR8 .... 34 B4
Matlock Cl. PR8 .... 34 B4
Matlock Cres. PR8 .... 34 B4
Matlock Gr. BB10 .... 147 C2
Matlock Pl. PR2 .... 116 A5
Matlock Rd. PR8 .... 34 B4
Matlock St. 11 BB3 .... 80 F2
Matterdale Rd. PR5 .... 59 B7
Matthew Cl. BB8 .... 169 E4
Matthew St. BB2 .... 100 B2
Matthews Ct. FY4 .... 109 D7
Matthias St. LA4 .... 212 E6
Mattock Cres. LA4 .... 213 B5
Maud St. Barrowford BB9 .... 168 D2
Maud St. Chorley PR7 .... 42 B6
Maudland Bank. PR1 .... 95 E8
Maudland Rd. Blackpool FY1 .. 129 C2
Maudland Rd. Preston PR1 .... 95 E8
Maudsley St. Accrington BB5 .. 103 C6
Maudsley St. Blackburn BB1 .. 100 F5
Maureen Ave. 3 PR5 .... 76 B8
Maurice Gr. FY2 .... 150 E1
Maurice St. BB9 .... 147 D8
Mavis Dr. PR7 .... 41 E2
Mavis Rd. BB2 .... 100 A5
Mawdesley CE Prim Sch. L40 .. 39 C3
Mawdesley RC Prim Sch. L40 .. 39 F2
Mawdsley Cl. L37 .... 12 B3
Mawdsley Terr. L39 .... 15 F7
Maxwell Gr. FY2 .... 150 E2
Maxwell St. BL9 .... 32 B3
May Bell Ave. FY5 .... 172 F3
May St. Barrowford BB9 .... 168 D2
May St. Blackburn BB1 .... 101 A4
May St. Burnley BB11 .... 127 B4
May St. Edgworth BL7 .... 47 E6
May St. Nelson BB9 .... 168 F2
May Terr. BB7 .... 143 A4
Maybank Cl. PR9 .... 53 A1
Maybury Cl. BB12 .... 126 B7

Maycroft Ave. FY6 .... 151 B5
Mayfair. BL6 .... 31 D3
Mayfair Cl. Haslingden BB4 ..... 67 A7
Mayfair Cl. Hightown L38 .... 2 F2
Mayfair Cl. Lytham St Anne's FY8 89 D6
Mayfair Cotts. WN1 .... 29 C1
Mayfair Cres. BB1 .... 121 F5
Mayfair Dr. FY5 .... 151 C8
Mayfair Gdns. FY5 .... 173 C1
Mayfair Rd. Blackpool FY1 ..... 129 E2
Mayfair Rd. Nelson BB9 .... 169 A1
Mayfayre Ave. L31 .... 5 B5
Mayfield. BB3 .... 64 B7
Mayfield Ave. Adlington PR6 .... 30 A7
Mayfield Ave.
 Bamber Bridge PR5 .... 76 C8
Mayfield Ave. Blackpool FY4 .. 109 C5
Mayfield Ave. Clitheroe BB7 ... 164 F7
Mayfield Ave. Formby L37 .... 11 C1
Mayfield Ave. Fulwood PR2 ... 116 A5
Mayfield Ave. Fulwood PR2 ... 116 B4
Mayfield Ave. Haslingden BB4 .. 84 A1
Mayfield Ave. Kirkham PR4 .... 113 A5
Mayfield Ave. Lancaster LA1 .. 213 E3
Mayfield Ave.
 Oswaldtwistle BB5 .... 102 F4
Mayfield Ave. Thornton FY5 ... 173 A4
Mayfield Cl. BL0 .... 49 A2
Mayfield Cl. L37 .... 11 F5
Mayfield Dr. LA4 .... 213 A6
Mayfield Dr. Burnley BB11 .... 126 E3
Mayfield Dr. Formby L37 .... 11 F2
Mayfield Rd.
 Lytham St Anne's FY8 .... 88 E8
Mayfield Prim Sch. FY8 .... 88 E8
Mayfield Rd. Blackburn BB1 ... 121 E3
Mayfield Rd. Chorley PR6 .... 60 D1
Mayfield Rd. High Bentham LA2 233 D7
Mayfield Rd. Leyland PR5 .... 59 A7
Mayfield Rd. Preston PR1 .... 116 B1
Mayfield Rd. Ramsbottom BL0 .. 49 A2
Mayfield Sch. PR7 .... 42 C6
Mayfield St. BB2 .... 100 E3
Mayflower Ave. PR1 .... 95 A3
Mayflower Ind Est. L37 .... 12 A1
Mayflower Rd. BB9 .... 168 C3
Maylands Pl. BB9 .... 168 C3
Maylands Sq. LA4 .... 212 F4
Maynard St. PR1 .... 116 D2
Mayo Dr. PR4 .... 56 A6
Mayor Ave. FY1 .... 129 C2
Maypark. PR5 .... 77 A5
Mayson St. BB1 .... 100 E4
Maytree Wlk. WN8 .... 18 B4
Mayville Rd. BB9 .... 147 B6
McCall Cl. PR8 .... 112 A3
McDonald Rd. LA3 .... 208 D5
McKenzie St. 8 PR5 .... 76 F8
Mead Ave. PR5 .... 59 B8
Meadow Ave. Fleetwood FY7 .. 193 E1
Meadow Ave.
 Knott End-on-S FY6 .... 195 A6
Meadow Ave. Southport PR8 .... 34 C4
Meadow Bank. Maghull L31 ...... 5 B2
Meadow Bank. Ormskirk L39 .... 15 F5
Meadow Bank Ave. BB10 .... 147 B6
Meadow Bank Rd. 15 BB9 ...... 147 D8
Meadow Bolton. PR5 .... 58 A8
Meadow Brow. PR9 .... 53 D5
Meadow Cl. Accrington BB5 ... 124 F1
Meadow Cl. Billington BB6 ..... 143 A3
Meadow Cl. Brierfield BB10 ... 147 C4
Meadow Cl. Clifton PR4 .... 114 D2
Meadow Cl. Foulridge BB8 ..... 169 D7
Meadow Cl. Skelmersdale WN8 .. 9 D7
Meadow Cl. Westhead L40 .... 16 E4
Meadow Cl. Wrea Green PR4 .. 112 B3
Meadow Clough. WN8 .... 18 B4
Meadow Cotts. OL12 .... 70 D3
Meadow Court Rd. LA4 .... 212 F3
Meadow Cr. PR4 .... 112 F6
Meadow Cres. FY6 .... 151 A3
Meadow Croft.
 Nether Kellet LA6 .... 216 F4
Meadow Croft.
 West Bradford BB7 .... 186 E5
Meadow Ct. Lancaster LA1 .... 213 D3
Meadow Ct. 11
 Oswaldtwistle BB5 .... 102 E4
Meadow Ct. Preston PR1 .... 95 E6
Meadow Dr. Bolton-le-S LA5 .. 216 A5
Meadow Dr. Ormskirk L39 ...... 15 C2
Meadow Dr. Warton PR4 .... 91 C5
Meadow Field. PR1 .... 95 E2
Meadow Gate. BB3 .... 81 B2
Meadow Head Ave. OL12 .... 51 D6
Meadow Head Cl. BB2 .... 100 A1
Meadow Head La. Darwen BB3 .. 80 B4
Meadow Head La. Longton PR4 . 73 F7
Meadow La. Ainsdale PR8 .... 20 D3
Meadow La. Clayton Brook PR5 .. 77 B4
Meadow La. Croston L40 & PR5 .. 56 E1
Meadow La. Hesketh Bank PR4 .. 72 F4
Meadow La. Hoscar L40 .... 25 C6
Meadow La. Knott End-on-S FY6 194 F4
Meadow La.
 Lytham St Anne's FY8 .... 90 E4
Meadow St. Maghull L31 .... 5 F1
Meadow La. Rufford L40 .... 38 D3
Meadow Pk. Galgate LA2 .... 206 F4
Meadow Pk. Garstang PR3 ..... 199 C1
Meadow Pk. Irwell Vale BL0 ..... 67 C4
Meadow Pk. Staining FY3 ...... 130 D5
Meadow Rise. BB2 .... 80 A8
Meadow St. Accrington BB5 ... 103 C6

Meadow St. Adlington PR6 .... 30 A6
Meadow St. Barnoldswick BB8 200 A4
Meadow St. 6 Burnley BB11 .. 126 F6
Meadow St. Darwen BB3 .... 64 B6
Meadow St. Great Harwood BB6 123 C4
Meadow St. Lancaster LA1 ..... 210 B8
Meadow St. Leyland PR5 .... 76 A1
Meadow St. Padiham BB12 .... 145 C1
Meadow St. Preston PR1 .... 96 A8
Meadow St. Wheelton PR6 .... 61 A7
Meadow View. Clitheroe BB7 .. 164 C8
Meadow View. Farleton LA2 ... 232 A6
Meadow View.
 Great Plumpton PR4 .... 111 F7
Meadow View. Passmonds OL12 51 A1
Meadow View. Southport PR8 ... 34 D4
Meadow Way. Arkholme LA6 ... 235 B3
Meadow Way. Bacup OL13 ...... 86 F2
Meadow Way.
 Barnoldswick BB8 .... 200 D4
Meadow Way. Blackrod BL6 .... 30 C1
Meadow Way. Coppull PR7 ...... 28 D8
Meadow Way. Edgworth BL7 .... 47 E6
Meadow Way. Garstang PR3 .. 199 C2
Meadow Way. Formby L37 .... 11 F2
Meadow Way. Ramsbottom BL9 .. 49 C2
Meadow Way.
 Lytham St Anne's FY8 .... 110 A1
Meadowcroft.
 Skelmersdale WN8 .... 18 B4
Meadowcroft. Blackburn BB3 ... 81 A6
Meadowcroft. Euxton PR7 .... 59 B3
Meadowcroft. Formby L37 .... 11 F2
Meadow Way. Edgworth BL7 .... 47 E6
Meadowcroft.
 Lytham St Anne's FY8 .... 110 A1
Meadowcroft Gr. LA3 .... 212 B1
Meadowcroft Rd. PR5 .... 58 D7
Meadowfield. Fulwood PR2 ... 116 F8
Meadowfield. Halton LA2 .... 214 E7
Meadowfield. LA2 .... 214 E7
Meadowfield Ave.
 Catterall PR3 .... 178 D3
Meadowfield Ave.
 Cleveleys FY5 .... 172 E2
Meadowfield Ave.
 Hambleton FY6 .... 174 C1
Meadowlands. PR7 .... 41 D4
Meadows Ave. Bacup OL13 ...... 86 F4
Meadows Ave. Haslingden BB4 .. 84 C2
Meadows Ave. Thornton FY5 ... 172 F2
Meadows Cl. LA5 .... 219 E4
Meadows The. Arnside LA5 ..... 218 C8
Meadows The. Billington BB6 .. 143 A4
Meadows The. Colne BB8 .... 169 D7
Meadows The. Darwen BB3 ..... 80 E5
Meadows The. Elswick PR4 .... 153 F1
Meadows The. Heskin Green PR7 40 E2
Meadows The. Leyland PR5 ..... 75 B1
Meadows The.
 Oswaldtwistle BB5 .... 102 F3
Meadows The. Thornton FY5 .. 172 F2
Meadows The. Whitworth OL12 .. 70 C1
Meadows The.
 Yealand Redmayne LA5 ...... 219 E3
Meadowside. Claughton LA2 .. 231 F5
Meadowside. Croston PR5 .... 57 A2
Meadowside. Grindleton BB7 .. 187 C8
Meadowside. Lancaster LA1 .. 210 F7
Meadowside. Walmer Bridge PR4 74 A5
Meadowside Ave. BB5 .... 123 E3
Meadowside Dr. PR5 .... 97 E1
Meadway. Becconsall PR4 .... 72 F2
Meadway. Clayton Green PR6 .. 77 B3
Meadway. Clayton Green PR6 .. 77 B3
Meadway. Penwortham PR1 .... 95 A5
Meadway. Ramsbottom BL0 ..... 67 C1
Meadway Cl. BL6 .... 31 D3
Meagles La. PR3 & PR4 .... 153 E3
Mealhouse La. 6 PR7 .... 42 C8
Mealrigg La. LA6 .... 235 A7
Meanwood Ave. FY4 .... 109 F7
Meanwood Brow. 16 OL12 ..... 51 C1
Meanwood Prim Sch. OL12 ..... 51 C1
Meanygate. PR5 .... 96 E1
Mearbeck Pl. LA2 .... 213 D2
Mearley Brook Fold. BB2 .... 164 F7
Mearley Rd. PR2 .... 117 E4
Mearley St. BB7 .... 164 F7
Mearley Syke. BB7 .... 164 F8
Meath Rd. PR1 .... 95 D6
Mede The. PR4 .... 113 B3
Medina Cl. BB5 .... 103 B5
Medlar Cl. PR4 .... 112 E6
Medlar Rd. PR4 .... 113 A6
Medlar Gate. PR4 .... 113 A6
Medlar La. PR4 .... 132 E4
Medley St. OL12 .... 51 F1
Medlock Ave. FY7 .... 193 D2
Medlock Pl. FY7 .... 193 D2
Medway. PR2 .... 116 F6
Medway Ave. FY7 .... 172 D8
Medway Cl. PR5 .... 96 B1
Medway Dr. BL6 .... 31 D3
Medway House. 3 PR1 .... 96 D8
Meeting House La. LA1 .... 210 E8
Meins Croft. BB2 .... 100 A6
Meins Rd. BB2 .... 99 F6
Melba Rd. PR2 .... 117 E3
Melbert Ave. PR2 .... 116 C3
Melbourne Ave. Cleveleys FY5 . 150 F7
Melbourne Ave. Fleetwood FY7 172 E8
Melbourne Cl. BL6 .... 31 C3
Melbourne Ct. FY5 .... 150 E8

Melbourne Gr. BL6 .... 31 C3
Melbourne Rd. 11 LA1 .... 211 A8
Melbourne St. Darwen BB3 ...... 64 B6
Melbourne St. Enfield BB5 ..... 124 A1
Melbourne St. 2
 Newchurch BB4 .... 85 F1
Melbourne St.
 Oswaldtwistle BB5 .... 102 D3
Melbourne St. Padiham BB12 . 125 D7
Melbreck. WN8 .... 18 A4
Melbury Dr. BL6 .... 31 F1
Meldon Grange. LA3 .... 209 A8
Meldon Rd. LA3 .... 209 A8
Meldreth Cl. L37 .... 11 C1
Melford Dr. WN5 .... 10 D3
Melia Cl. BB4 .... 84 F2
Melita St. BB3 .... 64 B8
Melling Ct. LA4 .... 212 D3
Melling House. 4 LA1 .... 211 A3
Melling La. Hornby LA2 .... 232 B7
Melling Rd. Southport PR9 ...... 34 E7
Melling St. 20 PR1 .... 95 F8
Melling's La. FY8 .... 110 A1
Melling-with-Wrayton
 CE Prim Sch. LA6 .... 235 D2
Mellings. PR1 .... 96 C6
Mellings Ave. WN5 .... 10 E1
Mellings Fold. PR1 .... 96 C6
Mellings Wood. FY8 .... 110 A1
Mellishaw La. LA3 .... 212 G1
Mellor Brow. BB2 .... 120 D2
Mellor Cl. BB11 .... 126 D3
Mellor Ct. PR3 .... 139 B7
Mellor La. BB2 .... 120 F3
Mellor Pl. PR1 .... 96 B7
Mellor Rd. Kirkham PR4 .... 113 A5
Mellor Rd. Leyland PR5 .... 75 D2
Mellowfield Dr. PR9 .... 34 C7
Mellwood Ave. FY3 .... 150 F1
Melrose Ave. Blackpool FY3 .. 129 E8
Melrose Ave. Burnley BB11 ... 126 D4
Melrose Ave. Fulwood PR2 ... 117 C5
Melrose Ave. Morecambe LA4 . 212 F5
Melrose Ave. Oswaldtwistle BB5 102 F3
Melrose Ave. Southport PR9 ... 53 B5
Melrose St. 10 Darwen BB3 .... 80 F2
Melrose St. Lancaster LA1 ..... 211 A7
Melrose St. Ramsbottom BL0 .. 49 B2
Melrose Terr. OL13 .... 87 A7
Melrose Way. PR7 .... 42 D5
Melton Gr. FY8 .... 89 E3
Melton Pl. Cleveleys FY5 .... 150 C8
Melton Pl. Leyland PR5 .... 76 B1
Melville Ave. BB8 .... 200 A3
Melville Dr. BB2 .... 100 D5
Melville Gdns. BB3 .... 64 A8
Melville Rd. Blackpool FY2 ... 150 C4
Melville Rd. Heysham LA3 .... 208 E5
Melville St. Burnley BB10 ..... 147 C1
Melville St. Darwen BB3 .... 64 A8
Memory Cl. PR4 .... 92 B7
Menai Dr. PR2 .... 116 D7
Mendip Cl. BL6 .... 31 C5
Mendip Rd. Clayton-le-W PR6 .. 76 D1
Mendip Rd. Leyland PR6 .... 59 D8
Menivale Cl. PR9 .... 53 B5
Meols Cl. L37 .... 11 E2
Meols Cop Ctr The. PR9 .... 35 A4
Meols Cop High Sch. PR8 .... 34 F5
Meols Cop Sta. PR9 .... 34 F7
Meols Ct. PR9 .... 54 A6
Meolsgate Ave. PR4 .... 56 A7
Mercer Cres. BB4 .... 67 A8
Mercer Ct. PR6 .... 42 F1
Mercer Rd. PR5 .... 96 A1
Mercer St. Burnley BB12 .... 125 F7
Mercer St. 16 Clayton-le-M BB5 123 F3
Mercer St. Great Harwood BB6 . 123 D5
Mercer St. Preston PR1 .... 96 C3
Mercer's La. L39 .... 7 B4
Merchants Landing. BB1 .... 100 F3
Merchants Quay. 1 BB1 .... 100 F3
Merclesden Ave. PR9 .... 169 B1
Mere Ave. Burscough Bridge L40 . 24 D1
Mere Ave. Fleetwood FY7 ...... 193 D1
Mere Brook. FY3 .... 130 E5
Mere Brow La. PR4 .... 55 A2
Mere Cl. Broughton PR3 .... 136 C3
Mere Cl. Skelmersdale WN8 ..... 17 F2
Mere Ct. Burnley BB11 .... 126 B4
Mere Ct. Burscough Bridge L40 . 24 E1
Mere Fold. PR7 .... 41 D3
Mere La. Banks PR9 .... 54 A2
Mere La. Holmeswood PR4 ...... 37 A7
Mere La. Rufford L40 .... 37 E3
Mere Park Ct. PR3 .... 130 A2
Mere Rd. Blackpool FY3 .... 129 D5
Mere Rd. Formby L37 .... 11 D2
Mere Sands Wood
 Nature Reserve. L40 .... 37 F4
Meredith St. BB9 .... 147 E7
Merefell Rd. LA5 .... 216 A6
Merefield. PR7 .... 60 A1
Merefield Sch. Ainsdale PR8 ... 20 B4
Merefield Sch. Southport PR9 .. 53 B3
Merefold. BL6 .... 30 F3
Mereland Cl. WN5 .... 10 E6
Mereland Rd. PR3 .... 130 A2
Merepark Dr. PR9 .... 53 B4
Mereside Cl. PR4 .... 73 F7
Mereside Inf Sch. FY4 .... 130 B1
Merewood. WN8 .... 18 A4
Meriden Cl. PR8 .... 20 B5
Merlecrest Dr. PR4 .... 56 A8
Merlewood. BL0 .... 67 C3
Merlewood Ave. PR9 .... 53 B3
Merlin Cl. PR6 .... 61 A3

Merlin Dr. BB5 .... 102 D3
Merlin Gr. PR5 .... 58 C8
Merlin Rd. BB2 .... 100 B6
Merlyn Rd. FY5 .... 172 E1
Merrick Ave. PR1 .... 96 F8
Merrilox La. L31 .... 5 D3
Merry Trees La. PR2 & PR4 .. 115 E5
Merryburn Cl. PR2 .... 117 A4
Merscar La. L40 .... 23 D6
Mersey Ave. Darwen BB3 .. 80 D3
Mersey Ave. Formby L37 .. 11 E6
Mersey Ave. Maghull L31 .. 5 F2
Mersey Rd. Blackpool FY4 .. 109 B8
Mersey Rd. Fleetwood FY7 .. 193 F4
Mersey Rd. Orrell WN5 .. 10 F7
Mersey St. Bacup OL13 .. 87 A1
Mersey St. Burnley BB12 .. 126 A6
Mersey St. Longridge PR3 .. 139 B8
Mersey St. Preston PR1 .. 95 C8
Merton Ave. PR2 .... 116 F6
Merton Gr. PR6 .... 60 F3
Merton St. Burnley BB12 .. 126 F7
Merton St. 3 Nelson BB9 .. 168 D1
Messenger St. BB9 .... 148 A7
Meta St. BB2 .... 100 E2
Metcalf Dr. BB5 .... 124 D6
Metcalfe St. BB12 .... 126 B5
Mete St. PR1 .... 96 D8
Methuen Ave. Coupe Green PR5 . 97 E3
Methuen Ave. Fulwood PR2 .. 116 E6
Methuen Cl. PR5 .... 97 F3
Methuen Dr. PR5 .... 97 F3
Metropolitan Bsns Pk. FY3 .. 130 B2
Metropolitan Dr. FY3 .... 130 B2
Mettle Cote. OL13 .... 87 A1
Mewith La. LA2 .... 233 C6
Mews The. Morecambe LA3 .. 213 A5
Mews The. 1 Padiham BB12 .. 145 C1
Mexford Ave. FY3 .... 129 D8
Meyler Ave. FY3 .... 129 E8
Michael Pl. LA4 .... 212 G5
Michael Wife La. Edenfield BL0 .. 67 F2
Michael Wife La. Edenfield BL0 .. 67 F3
Michael's La. L39 .... 21 C3
Michaels Cl. L37 .... 11 E3
Michaelson Ave. LA4 .... 213 A4
Mickering La. L39 .... 6 C5
Mickleden Ave. PR2 .... 116 F7
Mickleden Rd. FY4 .... 130 C1
Micklegate. FY5 .... 150 C7
Micklehurst Cres. BB11 .. 126 D2
Middle Hey. PR4 .... 73 E3
Middle Hill. OL12 .... 51 F4
Middle Holly Rd. PR3 .... 199 C8
Middle Meanygate. PR4 .. 55 C7
Middle St. Blackpool FY1 .. 129 B3
Middle St. Colne BB8 .. 169 C4
Middle St. Lancaster LA1 .. 210 F8
Middle St. Whitworth OL12 .. 70 D1
Middle Withins La. L37 & L38 ... 4 A7
Middlefield. PR5 .... 58 A8
Middleforth CE Prim Sch. PR1 95 D3
Middleforth Gn. PR1 .... 95 E4
Middlegate. LA3 .... 213 A3
Middlegate Gn. BB4 .... 105 A1
Middlesex Ave. BB12 .... 126 B7
Middleton Ave. FY7 .... 193 D1
Middleton Dr. BB9 .... 168 E6
Middleton Rd. Heysham LA3 . 208 E5
Middleton Rd. Middleton LA3 . 209 B2
Middleton Tower Holiday Ctr.
LA3 .... 208 E1
Middleton Way. Heysham LA3 . 208 F6
Middleton Way. Heysham LA3 . 208 F7
Middlewood. WN8 .... 18 A4
Middlewood Cl. Eccleston PR7 .. 40 C6
Middlewood Cl. Ormskirk L39 .. 6 C7
Middlewood Dr. PR7 .... 6 C7
Middlewood Rd. L39 .... 6 C7
Midfield. BB6 .... 122 C8
Midge Hall La.
Drummersdale L40 & PR9 .. 36 C3
Midge Hall La.
Leyland PR4 & PR5 .... 74 F4
Midgeland Rd. FY4 .... 110 B5
Midgery La. Fulwood PR2 & PR3 117 A8
Midgery La. Fulwood PR2 .. 117 B7
Midgery La. Fulwood PR2 .. 117 C6
Midgley St. BB8 .... 169 E4
Midhurst Dr. PR8 .... 20 B4
Midland St. 11 Accrington BB5 .. 103 C5
Midland St. Nelson BB9 .. 168 E1
Midland Terr. LA5 .... 217 D3
Midsummer St. BB2 .... 100 C5
Midville Pl. 14 BB3 .... 81 A1
Milbanke Ave. PR4 .... 113 A5
Milbeck Cl. PR3 .... 138 F5
Milbourne Rd. BL9 .... 32 A6
Milbourne St. FY1 .... 129 C5
Milbrook Cl. BB11 .... 126 B5
Milburn Ave. FY5 .... 172 F5
Mildred Cl. PR5 .... 173 A3
Mile End Cl. BB8 .... 191 D1
Mile End Row. BB2 .... 100 B6
Mile Rd. FY6 .... 153 A1
Miles Ave. OL13 .... 69 D8
Miles La. WN6 .... 19 E6
Miles St. PR1 .... 116 F2
Miles Wlk. PR1 .... 116 E2
Milestone Pl. LA2 .... 231 C3
Miletas Pl. FY8 .... 89 C4
Milford Ave. FY8 .... 150 D1
Milford Cl. Catterall PR3 .. 178 D2
Milford Cl. Formby L37 .. 11 C1
Milford Cl. Colne BB8 .. 169 C1
Milford St. 6 Rochdale OL12 .. 51 F1

Milk St. BL0 .... 49 B5
Milking La. BB3 .... 81 A6
Milking Stile La. LA1 .. 210 D8
Mill Bank. WN6 .... 19 D7
Mill Brow. Kirkby Lonsdale LA6 . 238 C2
Mill Brow. Lowgill LA2 .. 233 B2
Mill Brow Rd. BB8 .... 201 C2
Mill Cl. PR4 .... 134 C8
Mill Cotts. BB3 .... 81 F3
Mill Ct. PR3 .... 139 B8
Mill Dam Cl. L40 .... 24 C2
Mill Dam La. L40 .... 24 D1
Mill Entrance. BB5 .... 123 F2
Mill Field. Clayton-le-M BB5 . 123 F4
Mill Field. Parbold WN8 .. 26 C1
Mill Gap St. BB3 .... 64 A8
Mill Gate. Fulwood PR2 .. 116 D3
Mill Gate. 15 Rawtenstall BB4 .. 85 A3
Mill Gn. BB8 .... 169 D4
Mill Haven. PR2 .... 116 D3
Mill Hey Ave. FY6 .... 151 E1
Mill Hey La. L40 .... 38 C3
Mill Hill. Oswaldtwistle BB5 .. 102 E4
Mill Hill. Preston PR1 .. 95 E8
Mill Hill Bridge St. BB2 .. 100 B2
Mill Hill Gr. LA3 .... 209 A2
Mill Hill La. BB11 .... 125 B3
Mill Hill St. BB2 .... 100 B2
Mill Hill Sta. BB2 .... 100 B2
Mill House La. PR3 .... 140 A8
Mill Laithe. BB1 .... 100 E6
Mill Lane View. WN8 .. 10 C7
Mill La. Appley Bridge WN6 .. 19 D7
Mill La. Becconsall PR4 .. 72 F2
Mill La. Blackburn BB2 .. 100 E4
Mill La. Bolton Green PR7 .. 41 A8
Mill La. Bolton Green PR7 .. 59 A1
Mill La. Bolton-le-S LA5 .. 216 A6
Mill La. Burscough L40 .. 24 E4
Mill La. Carnforth LA5 .. 217 D4
Mill La. Caton LA2 .... 231 B3
Mill La. Clayton Green PR6 .. 77 C1
Mill La. Coppull PR7 .... 41 E2
Mill La. Darwen PR7 .. 63 A5
Mill La. Earby BB8 .... 201 D2
Mill La. Eccleston PR7 .. 40 C5
Mill La. Elswick PR4 .... 154 B1
Mill La. Fleetwood FY7 .. 194 B4
Mill La. Fulwood PR2 .. 116 C4
Mill La. Gisburn BB7 .... 225 B4
Mill La. Goosnargh PR3 .. 137 E6
Mill La.
Great Harwood BB5 & BB6 .. 124 A6
Mill La. Hall Green WN8 .. 10 A8
Mill La. Halton LA2 .... 214 F6
Mill La. Hambleton FY6 .. 174 E1
Mill La. Hesketh Lane PR3 .. 160 C8
Mill La. Heskin Green PR7 .. 41 A2
Mill La. Horwich BL6 .... 31 D4
Mill La. Leyland PR5 .. 58 D8
Mill La. Leyland PR5 .... 75 E3
Mill La. Low Bentham LA2 .. 233 C7
Mill La. Ormskirk L39 .. 14 F1
Mill La. Parbold WN8 .. 26 C1
Mill La. Skelmersdale WN8 .. 17 F2
Mill La. Southport PR9 .. 53 A1
Mill La. Staining FY3 .. 130 D5
Mill La. Stalmine FY6 .. 174 D7
Mill La. Walton-le-D PR5 .. 96 D5
Mill La. Warton PR4 .... 91 F6
Mill La. Wrea Green PR4 .. 112 A3
Mill Lane Cres. PR9 .. 53 A1
Mill Leat Cl. WN8 .... 26 C2
Mill Leat Mews. WN8 .. 26 C2
Mill Rd. Ainsdale PR8 .. 20 D5
Mill Rd. Orrell WN5 .. 10 D5
Mill Row. BB4 .... 84 F5
Mill St. Accrington BB5 .. 103 F1
Mill St. Adlington PR6 .. 30 B8
Mill St. Bacup OL13 .... 86 F3
Mill St. Barnoldswick BB8 .. 200 A2
Mill St. Barrowford BB9 .. 168 D4
Mill St. Church BB5 .... 102 F6
Mill St. Clayton-le-M BB5 .. 123 F2
Mill St. Coppull PR7 .... 41 E1
Mill St. Great Harwood BB6 .. 123 C5
Mill St. Haslingden BB4 .. 84 B5
Mill St. Kirkham PR4 .... 113 A5
Mill St. Lancaster LA1 .. 211 A8
Mill St. Leyland PR5 .. 58 D8
Mill St. Leyland PR5 .... 76 B3
Mill St. Ormskirk L39 .. 15 F5
Mill St. Oswaldtwistle BB5 .. 102 D3
Mill St. Padiham BB12 .. 125 C8
Mill St. Preesall FY6 .. 195 B3
Mill St. Preston PR1 .. 95 D8
Mill St. Ramsbottom BL0 .. 49 A4
Mill St. Southport PR9 .. 34 C6
Mill St. West Bradford BB7 .. 186 E5
Mill View. PR4 .... 92 B7
Mill View Ct. L39 .... 7 E6
Mill Wood Cl. PR7 .... 78 C3
Mill Yd. BL9 .... 32 A3
Millar Barn La. BB4 .. 68 F8
Millar's Pace. PR9 .. 53 B5
Millbank. Fulwood PR2 .. 116 C3
Millbank. 4 Preston PR1 .. 96 B8
Millbank Brow. L40 .... 24 F3
Millbank La. L31 & L39 .. 5 F3
Millbrook. BB12 .... 146 E8
Millbrook Cl. Skelmersdale WN8 17 C2
Millbrook Cl. Wheelton PR6 .. 61 A7
Millbrook Ct. BB7 .. 186 E5
Millbrook Mews. FY8 .. 90 C3
Millbrook Row. PR6 .. 43 B1
Millbrook St. BB3 .... 80 F7
Millbrook Way. PR1 .. 95 C3
Millcroft. Chorley PR7 .. 60 A2
Millcroft. Fulwood PR2 .. 116 D4

Millcroft Ave. WN5 .. 10 D5
Milldyke Cl. FY4 .... 109 F6
Miller Ave. PR7 .... 79 B2
Miller Cl. BB5 .... 102 C5
Miller Cres. FY6 .... 152 E1
Miller Ct. LA1 .... 210 E5
Miller Field. PR2 & PR4 .. 115 E3
Miller Fold Ave. BB5 .. 103 B3
Miller House. 4 PR1 .. 96 A7
Miller La. Catforth PR4 .. 134 E4
Miller La. Fulwood PR4 .. 115 E5
Miller Rd. PR1 & PR2 .... 117 E2
Miller St. Blackpool FY1 .. 129 B1
Miller St. 11 Preston PR1 .. 96 C8
Miller St. Ramsbottom BL9 .. 49 C2
Miller's Brow. PR3 .... 204 E3
Millers Ct. L39 .... 15 F5
Millersdale Cl. FY5 .. 151 E7
Millersgate. PR4 .... 115 E4
Millett St. BL0 .... 49 D7
Millfield Cl. PR4 .... 91 F6
Millfield High Sch. FY5 .. 151 C8
Millfield Rd. Blackpool FY4 .. 109 F6
Millfield Rd. Chorley PR7 .. 60 C1
Millfold. OL12 .... 70 D2
Millgate. BL7 .... 46 D2
Millgate Rd. 18 BB4 .. 85 A3
Millgate St. BB1 .... 101 A5
Millgate Terr. OL12 .. 70 E5
Millholme Dr. LA2 .... 233 D7
Millhouse Lodge. PR8 .. 20 C5
Millhouse St. BL0 .... 49 E8
Millington Ave. FY4 .. 109 E8
Millom Ave. FY2 .... 150 D4
Millom Cl. FY7 .... 172 C8
Millrose Cl. WN8 .... 17 F2
Mills St. OL12 .... 70 D1
Millstone Cl. PR7 .... 41 F1
Millthorne Ave. BB7 .. 164 D7
Millwood Glade. PR7 .. 60 B1
Millwood Rd. PR1 & PR5 .. 96 B3
Milman Cl. L39 .... 15 D3
Milne St. BB4 .... 67 C5
Milner Rd. Darwen BB3 .. 80 E4
Milner Rd. Lytham St Anne's FY8 . 89 E4
Milner St. Burnley BB10 .. 127 A8
Milner St. Preston PR1 .. 117 A2
Milner St. Whitworth OL12 .. 51 C8
Milner St. Whitworth OL12 .. 70 C1
Milnshaw Gdns. BB5 .. 103 B7
Milnshaw La. BB5 .... 103 B6
Milnthorpe Ave. FY5 .. 172 D5
Milton Ave. Blackpool FY3 .. 129 F5
Milton Ave. Clitheroe BB7 .. 186 E1
Milton Ave. 2 Thornton FY5 . 173 A3
Milton Cl. Bamber Bridge PR5 .. 96 D2
Milton Cl. Darwen BB3 .. 81 C1
Milton Cl. Great Harwood BB6 .. 123 B4
Milton Cres. Kirkham PR4 .. 113 A5
Milton Cres. Poulton-le-F FY6 . 130 D8
Milton Ct. PR7 .... 41 E1
Milton Gr. Barnoldswick BB8 .. 200 A3
Milton Gr. Orrell WN5 .. 10 F6
Milton Rd. Colne BB8 .. 169 D5
Milton Rd. Coppull PR7 .. 41 E1
Milton St. 3 Barrowford BB9 .. 168 D4
Milton St. 1 Blackburn BB1 .. 101 A5
Milton St. Brierfield BB10 .. 147 F3
Milton St. Clayton-le-M BB5 .. 123 F3
Milton St. Fleetwood FY7 .. 194 A4
Milton St. Nelson BB9 .. 168 D1
Milton St. Oswaldtwistle BB5 .. 102 E4
Milton St. Padiham BB12 .. 125 E7
Milton St. Ramsbottom BL0 .. 49 B6
Milton St. Southport PR9 .. 35 A7
Milton Terr. PR6 .... 60 D2
Milton Way. L31 .... 5 B1
Mimosa Rd. PR2 .... 117 E2
Mincing La. BB2 .... 100 E4
Minden Rd. PR4 .... 131 E5
Minehead Ave. BB10 .. 147 D2
Minerva Rd. LA1 .... 210 C8
Minnie St. OL12 .... 70 D2
Minnie Terr. BB2 .... 100 C6
Minor St. 11 BB4 .... 85 A7
Minstead Ave. L33 .... 1 A2
Minster Cres. BB3 .... 64 C8
Minster Pk. PR4 .... 115 E5
Minstrel Wlk. FY6 .. 151 D4
Mint Ave. BB9 .... 168 D4
Mint St. BL0 .... 67 C2
Mintholme Ave. PR5 .. 97 E2
Mintor Rd. L33 .... 1 A2
Mire Ash Brow. BB2 .. 120 D1
Mire Ridge. BB8 .... 170 A3
Mirfield Gr. 9 FY4 .. 129 D1
Miry La. WN8 .... 26 D2
Mission Cotts. L40 .... 25 B8
Mitcham Rd. FY4 .... 110 B8
Mitchelgate. LA6 .... 238 D2
Mitchell St. Burnley BB12 .. 126 C6
Mitchell St. Clitheroe BB7 .. 164 D7
Mitchell St. 2 Colne BB8 .. 169 D5
Mitella St. BB10 .... 127 C5
Mitre St. BB11 .... 126 E6
Mitten's La. L37 .... 12 B3
Mitton Ave. Barrowford BB9 .. 168 F6
Mitton Ave. Rawtenstall BB4 .. 85 A4
Mitton Cl. OL10 .... 32 F2
Mitton Dr. PR2 .... 118 A3
Mitton Rd. Great Mitton BB7 .. 163 F2
Mitton Rd. Whalley BB7 .. 143 B7

Mitton St. BB1 .... 100 F8
Mizpah St. BB10 .... 127 C5
Mizzy Rd. OL12 .... 51 F1
Moels Cop Rd. PR8 .. 34 F4
Moira Cres. PR2 .... 117 F4
Moleside Cl. BB5 .... 103 D6
Mollington Rd. BB2 .. 100 B7
Molly Wood La. BB12 .. 125 F5
Molyneux St. 18 PR1 .. 96 A8
Molyneux Dr. FY4 .. 109 D7
Molyneux Pl. FY8 .. 90 A4
Molyneux Rd. L39 .. 6 C7
Mona Pl. PR1 .... 95 E8
Mona Rd. BB2 .... 100 E1
Monarch Cres. FY8 .. 89 B8
Monarch House. 7 BB11 .. 126 E5
Monarch St. BB5 .... 102 E4
Money Close La. BB2 .. 100 D4
Money Close La. Heysham LA3 208 D4
Moneyclose Gr. LA3 .. 208 D5
Monk Hall St. BB10 .. 127 A7
Monk St. Accrington BB5 .. 103 A6
Monk St. Clitheroe BB7 .. 164 D7
Monk's La. PR5 .... 195 A1
Monkroyd Ave. BB8 .. 200 A2
Monks Carr La. L38 .. 4 A6
Monks Cl. L37 .... 12 A1
Monks Dr. Formby L37 .. 12 A1
Monks Dr. Longridge PR3 .. 139 A6
Monks Dr. Withnell PR6 .. 79 A1
Monks Wlk. PR1 .... 95 C6
Monkswell Ave. LA5 .. 216 A5
Monkswell Dr. LA5 .. 216 A5
Monkswood Ave. LA4 .. 213 A5
Monmouth Rd. BB1 .. 101 C5
Monmouth St. 2 Burnley BB12 126 D6
Monmouth St. Colne BB8 .. 170 A5
Montagu Rd. L37 .. 11 E5
Montague Cl. BB2 .. 100 D4
Montague Rd. BB11 .. 126 E5
Montague St. Blackburn BB2 .. 100 D5
Montague St. Blackpool FY4 .. 109 B8
Montague St. Brierfield BB9 .. 147 B5
Montague St. Clitheroe BB7 .. 164 D8
Montague St. Colne BB8 .. 169 E6
Montcliffe Rd. PR6 .. 60 E1
Monteagle Dr. LA2 .. 232 B7
Monteagle Sq. LA2 .. 232 B7
Montford Rd. BB12 & BB9 .. 146 F6
Montgomery Ave. PR9 .. 35 B6
Montgomery Ct. BB5 .. 103 E2
Montgomery Gr. BB12 .. 126 C7
Montgomery High Sch. FY2 . 150 D5
Montgomery St. 6 PR5 .. 76 B3
Monthall Rise. LA1 .. 214 B1
Montjoly St. PR1 .... 96 C7
Monton Rd. BB3 .... 80 E4
Montpelier Ave. FY2 .. 150 C5
Montreal Ave. FY1 .. 129 D4
Montreal Rd. BB2 .. 100 D5
Montrose Ave. Blackpool FY1 . 129 C3
Montrose Ave. Ramsbottom BL0 . 49 A2
Montrose Cl. PR7 .... 42 E6
Montrose Cres. LA3 .. 208 E2
Montrose Dr. PR9 .... 52 F1
Montrose St. Blackburn BB2 .. 100 C3
Montrose St. Brierfield BB9 .. 147 B6
Montrose St. Burnley BB11 .. 126 F4
Moody La. L40 .... 39 E1
Moody St. WN6 .... 28 E1
Moon Ave. FY1 .... 129 B2
Moon St. PR5 .... 76 E8
Moor St. Penwortham PR1 .. 95 A4
Moor Ave. Shevington Vale WN6 .. 19 E8
Moor Cl. Ainsdale PR8 .. 20 D2
Moor Cl. Darwen BB3 .. 64 D8
Moor Cl. Lancaster LA1 .. 211 A8
Moor Close La. LA6 .. 234 B1
Moor Dr. WN8 .... 9 D7
Moor Edge. BB7 .... 143 B6
Moor Field. New Longton PR4 . 75 A7
Moor Field. Whalley BB7 .. 143 B6
Moor Gate. 13 LA1 .. 211 A8
Moor Hall La. PR4 .. 113 A4
Moor Hall St. PR1 .. 116 E2
Moor Hey Cotts. PR5 .. 57 A6
Moor Hey Sch. PR5 .. 96 A1
Moor La. Ainsdale PR8 .. 20 C2
Moor La. Billington BB6 & BB7 .. 143 B2
Moor La. Clitheroe BB7 .. 164 E8
Moor La. Darwen BB3 .. 81 B3
Moor La. Haslingden BB4 .. 83 F6
Moor La. Hutton PR4 .. 94 D1
Moor La. Ince Blundell L38 .. 3 E2
Moor La. Ince Blundell L29 .. 4 D1
Moor La. Lancaster LA1 .. 211 A8
Moor La. Langho BB6 .. 122 B8
Moor La. Padiham BB12 .. 145 C1
Moor La. Preston PR1 .. 116 F1
Moor La. Salterforth BB18 .. 191 C6
Moor La. Waddington BB7 .. 223 D2
Moor La. West Bradford BB7 .. 186 D7
Moor La. Whalley BB7 .. 143 B6
Moor La. Wiswell BB7 .. 143 F7
Moor Nook Cty Prim Sch.
PR2 .... 118 A3
Moor Park Ave. Blackpool FY2 . 150 D4
Moor Park Ave. Preston PR1 .. 117 A2
Moor Park High Sch. PR1 .. 117 A2
Moor Park Inf & Jun Sch. FY2 150 D4
Moor Platt Cl. BL6 .... 31 F3
Moor Rd. Barber's Moor PR5 .. 57 D3
Moor Rd. Chorley PR7 .. 42 B5
Moor Rd. Helmshore BB4 .. 66 F5
Moor Rd. Orrell WN5 .. 10 E6
Moor Rd. Ramsbottom BL8 .. 49 A6

Moor Rd. Rivington PR7 .. 43 E7
Moor Side La. Shuttleworth BL0 . 50 A7
Moor Side La. Wiswell BB7 .. 143 F7
Moor St. Clayton-le-M BB5 .. 123 F3
Moor St. Kirkham PR4 .. 113 A5
Moor St. 32 Lancaster LA1 .. 210 F8
Moor St. Ormskirk L39 .. 15 F5
Moor View. Bacup OL13 .. 87 A4
Moor View. Newchurch BB4 .. 68 F6
Moor View. Newchurch OL13 .. 69 B7
Moor View. Salterforth BB18 .. 191 E8
Moor Way. BL8 .... 48 C3
Moorbottom Rd. BL8 .. 48 E3
Moorbrook Sch. PR2 .. 116 E3
Moorbrook St. PR1 .. 116 E1
Moorcroft. Blackburn BB3 .. 81 A6
Moorcroft. Broughton PR3 .. 136 B2
Moorcroft. Edenfield BL0 .. 67 D2
Moorcroft Cres. PR2 .. 117 D3
Moore Dr. BB12 .... 145 F5
Moore St. Blackpool FY4 .. 129 B1
Moore St. Colne BB8 .. 169 C5
Moore St. Nelson BB9 .. 147 F7
Moore St. Padiham BB12 .. 125 F7
Moore St. Preston PR1 .. 96 C7
Moore Tree Dr. FY4 .. 110 A8
Moorend. BB7 .... 164 F7
Moores La. WN6 .... 28 D2
Moorfield. Edgworth BL7 .. 47 D6
Moorfield. Kirkby L33 .. 1 A1
Moorfield Ave. Blackburn BB1 . 121 E3
Moorfield Ave. Blackpool FY3 . 129 E6
Moorfield Ave. Carleton FY6 .. 151 B4
Moorfield Ave. Huncoat BB5 .. 103 F8
Moorfield Cl. Clayton-le-M BB5 . 124 B3
Moorfield Cl. Fulwood PR2 .. 116 E8
Moorfield Dr. Clayton-le-M BB5 124 B3
Moorfield Dr. Fulwood PR2 .. 117 E3
Moorfield Dr.
Lytham St Anne's FY8 .. 90 A4
Moorfield Ind Est. BB5 .. 124 B3
Moorfield La. L40 .... 23 C3
Moorfield Pl. 3 OL12 .. 51 F1
Moorfield Rd. Clayton-le-M BB5 124 B3
Moorfield Rd. Leyland PR5 .. 58 C8
Moorfield Sch. PR1 .. 117 A3
Moorfield Way. BB5 .. 124 B3
Moorfields. Blackpool FY2 .. 150 F4
Moorfields Ave. PR2 .. 116 E8
Moorgate. Accrington BB5 .. 103 B2
Moorgate. Blackpool FY4 .. 109 F6
Moorgate. Bury BL9 .. 32 A3
Moorgate. Fulwood PR2 .. 116 F5
Moorgate. Ormskirk L39 .. 15 E4
Moorgate Rd. BB8 .. 200 A1
Moorgate St. BB2 .. 100 C1
Moorhead High Sch. BB5 .. 103 A7
Moorhead St. 2 BB8 .. 169 C5
Moorhey Cres. Penwortham PR1 95 B5
Moorhey Cres.
Walton Summit PR5 .. 77 A8
Moorhey Dr. PR1 .. 95 B5
Moorhouse Ave. BB5 .. 103 A4
Moorhouse Cl. BB5 .. 103 A4
Moorhouse St. Accrington BB5 . 103 A4
Moorhouse St. Blackpool FY1 .. 129 B7
Moorhouse St. Burnley BB11 .. 126 C5
Moorhouses. L38 .... 2 F3
Moorings The. Burnley BB12 .. 126 E7
Moorings The. Hest Bank LA2 .. 215 D1
Moorings The. Maghull L31 .. 5 B4
Moorland Ave. Blackburn BB2 .. 79 D7
Moorland Ave. Broadley OL12 .. 51 C7
Moorland Ave. Clitheroe BB7 .. 186 F3
Moorland Ave. Darwen BB3 .. 80 D2
Moorland Ave. Earby BB8 .. 201 C1
Moorland Ave. Fulwood PR2 .. 117 D4
Moorland Ave. Poulton-le-F FY6 151 E4
Moorland Cl. BB9 .... 168 F6
Moorland Cres. Broadley OL12 . 51 C7
Moorland Cres. Clitheroe BB7 .. 186 F2
Moorland Cres. Fulwood PR2 .. 117 D4
Moorland Dr. Brierfield BB9 .. 147 D4
Moorland Dr. Horwich BL6 .. 31 F3
Moorland Dr. Nelson BB9 .. 147 E6
Moorland Gate. PR7 .. 42 F6
Moorland Gdns. FY6 .. 151 E4
Moorland Rd. Blackburn BB2 .. 80 C7
Moorland Rd. Burnley BB11 .. 126 F3
Moorland Rd. Clitheroe BB7 .. 186 F2
Moorland Rd. Langho BB6 .. 142 C1
Moorland Rd.
Lytham St Anne's FY8 .. 89 A7
Moorland Rd. Poulton-le-F FY6 . 151 F4
Moorland Rise. BB4 .. 84 C2
Moorland Sch. BB7 .. 186 E2
Moorland St. OL12 .. 51 E1
Moorland Terr. OL12 .. 51 A1
Moorlands. PR1 .... 116 E3
Moorlands Gr. LA3 .. 212 B3
Moorlands Terr. OL13 .. 87 A1
Moorlands The. OL13 .. 87 A8
Moorlands View. BL0 .. 67 D5
Moorside. Melling LA6 .. 235 D2
Moorside. Moor Side PR4 .. 133 D3
Moorside Ave. Blackburn BB1 .. 101 D4
Moorside Ave. Brierfield BB9 .. 147 D4
Moorside Ave. Fulwood PR2 .. 117 F3
Moorside Ave. Horwich BL6 .. 31 F4
Moorside Cl. LA6 .... 235 D2
Moorside Cres. OL13 .. 87 A4
Moorside Cty Prim Sch. LA1 . 211 B4
Moorside La. PR4 .... 135 C4
Moorside Prim Sch. WN8 .. 9 E7

Moorside Rd. Caton LA2 .... **231** D3
Moorside Rd. Edgworth BL7 ...... **65** E1
Moorsview. BL0 .... **49** B6
Moorthorpe CI. BB3 .... **64** A6
Moorview CI. BB10 .... **147** E2
Moorview Ct. FY4 .... **109** F7
Moorway. FY6 .... **151** F4
Moray CI. BL0 .... **49** A4
Morecambe Bay
  Nature Reserve. LA5 ...... **215** D5
Morecambe Bay Prim Sch.
  LA4 .... **212** E5
Morecambe Golf Course. LA4 .. **213** B7
Morecambe High Sch. LA4 ...... **212** F6
Morecambe L Pk. LA4 .... **212** D7
Morecambe Rd. Blackburn BB2 . **100** F1
Morecambe Rd.
  Lancaster LA1 & LA3 & LA4 .... **213** C2
Morecambe Sta E. LA4 .... **212** E6
Morecambe St W. LA4 .... **212** E6
Morecambe Sta. LA4 .... **212** D5
Moresby Ave. FY3 .... **130** B7
Moreton Dr. Poulton-le-F FY6 .. **151** D2
Moreton Dr. Staining FY3 .... **130** D5
Moreton Gn. LA3 .... **208** F7
Moreton St. BB5 .... **103** B6
Morewood Dr. LA6 .... **234** C7
Morland Ave. Bamber Bridge PR5 **76** A7
Morland Ave. Kirkham PR4 ...... **112** F7
Morley Ave. BB2 .... **100** A1
Morley CI. LA1 .... **213** E3
Morley Rd. Blackpool FY4 .... **129** E1
Morley Rd. Lancaster LA1 .... **213** E3
Morley Rd. Southport PR9 .... **34** E8
Morley St. **2** Burnley BB11 ...... **127** B4
Morley St. Padiham BB12 .... **125** C8
Morningside. LA1 .... **210** E7
Mornington Rd. Adlington PR6 .. **30** B8
Mornington Rd.
  Lytham St Anne's FY8 .... **90** E4
Mornington Rd.
  Penwortham PR1 .... **95** B5
Mornington Rd. Preston PR1 .... **117** F1
Mornington Rd. Southport PR9 . **34** C7
Morris Cres. PR1 & PR2 .... **117** D2
Morris Ct. PR1 .... **117** D2
Morris Hey. L39 .... **22** D3
Morris La. L39 & L40 .... **22** E3
Morris Rd. Chorley PR6 .... **60** E1
Morris Rd. Fulwood PR1 & PR2 . **117** D2
Morris Rd. Hall Green WN8 ...... **10** A7
Morrison St. PR6 .... **60** D2
Morse St. BB10 .... **127** D5
Morston Ave. FY2 .... **150** E1
Mort St. BL6 .... **31** B4
Mortimer Gr. LA3 .... **209** A8
Morton Cty Prim Sch. FY4 ...... **109** F7
Morton St. **22** BB1 .... **100** E5
Morton Wlk. BB3 .... **64** B6
Morven Gr. PR8 & PR9 .... **34** C7
Moscow Mill St. BB5 .... **102** E5
Mosedale Dr. BB12 .... **126** B8
Moseley Ave. BB8 .... **200** F1
Moseley Rd. BB11 .... **127** A3
Mosley Ave. BL0 .... **49** B2
Mosley St. Barnoldswick BB8 .. **200** B2
Mosley St. Blackburn BB2 .... **100** E2
Mosley St. **4** Leyland PR5 ...... **76** A1
Mosley St. Nelson BB9 .... **147** D8
Mosley St. Preston PR1 .... **96** C8
Mosley St. Southport PR8 .... **34** B4
Mosman Pl. BB9 .... **168** C3
Moss Acre Rd. PR1 .... **95** E2
Moss Ave. Orrell WN5 .... **10** D3
Moss Ave. Preston PR2 .... **116** A2
Moss Bank. Coppull PR7 .... **41** E1
Moss Bank. Ormskirk L39 .... **15** D2
Moss Bank Ct. L39 .... **15** D2
Moss Bank Pl. FY4 .... **109** F8
Moss Bridge. L40 .... **25** C3
Moss Bridge La. L40 .... **25** C2
Moss Bridge Pk. PR5 .... **76** C8
Moss CI. Chorley PR6 .... **42** E8
Moss CI. Haslingden BB4 .... **67** A8
Moss Delph La. L39 .... **15** C1
Moss Dr. BL6 .... **31** F3
Moss Edge La. Blackpool FY4 . **110** A4
Moss Edge La. Hale Nook PR3 . **175** C3
Moss Edge La.
  Lytham St Anne's FY8 .... **110** B2
Moss End Way. L33 .... **1** D3
Moss Fold Rd. BB3 .... **80** E5
Moss Gate. BB1 .... **101** B6
Moss Gn. L37 .... **12** B4
Moss Hall La. FY8 .... **89** E7
Moss Hall Rd. BB5 .... **103** C8
Moss Hey Hey. PR4 .... **55** A3
Moss House La.
  Great Plumpton PR4 .... **111** C7
Moss House La.
  Much Hoole PR4 .... **74** B2
Moss House Rd. Blackpool FY4 **110** A6
Moss House Rd. Broughton PR3 **136** B2
Moss La. Bamber Bridge PR5 ... **76** B8
Moss La. Banks PR9 .... **54** D6
Moss La. Barrow Nook L39 .... **7** F2
Moss La. Becconsall PR4 .... **72** C1
Moss La. Blackburn BB1 & BB5 **101** F3
Moss La. Bretherton PR4 & PR5 . **72** E5
Moss La. Burscough L40 .... **25** A7
Moss La. Burton-in-K LA5 & LA6 . **234** A8
Moss La. Catforth PR4 .... **134** D5
Moss La. Chipping PR3 .... **183** A1
Moss La. Clayton-le-W PR5 ...... **76** D2

Moss La. Coppull PR7 .... **41** E1
Moss La. Croston PR5 & PR7 .... **39** A8
Moss La. Duncombe PR3 .... **156** D2
Moss La. Farington PR5 .... **75** D5
Moss La.
  Formby L37 & L39 & L38 & L23 . **12** D5
Moss La. Garstang PR3 .... **178** B7
Moss La. Glasson LA2 .... **205** D3
Moss La. Hambleton FY6 .... **174** D1
Moss La. Hesketh Lane PR3 .... **160** F8
Moss La. Hightown L38 .... **3** C2
Moss La. Horwich BL6 .... **30** F7
Moss La. Inskip PR4 .... **155** B3
Moss La. Kirkby L33 .... **1** B3
Moss La. Leyland PR5 .... **76** C2
Moss La. Lucas Green PR6 .... **60** D5
Moss La. Lydiate L31 .... **5** D5
Moss La. Maghull L31 .... **5** E2
Moss La. Morecambe LA4 .... **212** D5
Moss La. New Longton PR4 ...... **74** E7
Moss La. Robin Hood WN6 .... **27** E3
Moss La. Silverdale LA5 .... **218** F5
Moss La. Southport PR9 .... **35** B8
Moss La. Skelmersdale WN8 ..... **8** F4
Moss La. St Michael's on W PR3 . **155** B8
Moss La. Walmer Bridge PR4 .... **74** C4
Moss La. Wymott PR5 .... **57** F5
Moss La E. PR4 .... **114** A8
Moss Lane W. PR4 .... **113** F7
Moss Lane View. WN8 .... **8** F6
Moss Nook. Burscough Bridge L40 **24** E6
Moss Nook. Ormskirk L39 .... **15** C2
Moss Pl. LA1 .... **214** A4
Moss Rd. Heaton LA3 .... **209** D7
Moss Rd. Orrell WN5 .... **10** D3
Moss Rd. Southport PR8 .... **34** C2
Moss Side. Barnoldswick BB8 .. **200** C2
Moss Side. Formby L37 .... **12** B4
Moss Side Cty Prim Sch. PR5 .. **75** B1
Moss Side La. Lane Heads PR3 . **154** E5
Moss Side La. Mere Brow PR4 ... **54** F4
Moss Side La. Stalmine FY6 .... **174** D7
Moss Side La. Wrea Green PR4 **112** A3
Moss Side Sta. FY8 .... **111** D1
Moss Side Way. PR5 .... **58** C8
Moss St. Bamber Bridge PR5 .... **76** B8
Moss St. Blackburn BB1 .... **101** A6
Moss St. Clitheroe BB7 .... **164** D8
Moss St. Great Harwood BB6 .. **123** C4
Moss St. Preston PR1 .... **95** E8
Moss St. Ramsbottom BL9 .... **49** D2
Moss View. Ainsdale PR8 .... **20** E5
Moss View. Maghull L31 .... **5** F1
Moss Way. FY4 .... **109** F7
Mossbank. BB1 .... **101** A6
Mossbourne Rd. FY6 .... **151** C2
Mossbrook Dr. PR4 .... **115** F5
Mosscroft. L33 .... **1** A5
Mossdale. BB1 .... **101** A6
Mossdale Ave. PR2 .... **117** D4
Mossfield CI. Bamber Bridge PR5 **76** B8
Mossfield CI. Bury BL9 .... **32** B4
Mossfield Rd. PR6 .... **42** E8
Mossgiel Ave. PR8 .... **20** B5
Mosshill CI. L31 .... **5** C3
Mosslands. PR5 .... **75** D1
Mosslawn Rd. L32 .... **1** A1
Mosslea Dr. PR3 .... **136** B8
Mossock Hall Golf Course.
  L39 .... **6** D3
Mossom La. FY5 .... **150** D7
Mossway. PR4 .... **74** F7
Mossy Lea Cty Prim Sch. WN6 **27** F6
Mossy Lea Fold. WN6 .... **28** A3
Mossy Lea Rd. WN6 .... **27** F5
Mostyn St. BB3 .... **80** E4
Motherwell Cres. PR8 .... **34** F3
Motive Power Mus. FY8 .... **90** E4
Mottram Mews. **6** BL6 .... **31** B4
Mottram St. BL6 .... **31** B4
Moulden Brow. BB2 .... **79** B7
Moulding CI. BB2 .... **100** B4
Mounsey Rd. PR5 .... **76** F8
Mount Ave. Lancaster LA1 ...... **213** F3
Mount Ave. Morecambe LA4 .... **212** F4
Mount Ave. Newchurch BB4 ..... **68** F8
Mount Carmel Prep Sch. L39 ... **15** D2
Mount Carmel RC High Sch.
  BB5 .... **103** A4
Mount Cres. Orrell WN5 .... **10** F6
Mount Cres. Over Town BB10 . **107** A8
Mount Gdns. LA4 .... **213** A4
Mount House CI. L37 .... **12** B5
Mount House Rd. L37 .... **12** B5
Mount La. Burnley BB10 .... **127** F1
Mount La. Cornholme OL14 .... **108** C3
Mount Pleasant. Adlington PR6 . **30** A8
Mount Pleasant. Arnside LA5 .. **218** C8
Mount Pleasant. **16** Bacup OL13 **69** C8
Mount Pleasant. Blackburn BB1 **100** F5
Mount Pleasant. Brinscall PR7 .. **62** A8
Mount Pleasant. Chatburn BB7 **187** D5
Mount Pleasant. Edgworth BL7 . **47** D5
Mount Pleasant.
  High Bentham LA2 .... **233** D8
Mount Pleasant.
  Nangreaves BL9 .... **49** F3
Mount Pleasant. **8** Preston PR1 **95** F8
Mount Pleasant.
  Rawtenstall BB4 .... **84** E2
Mount Pleasant. Sabden BB7 .. **145** A7
Mount Pleasant. Slaidburn BB7 **223** B7
Mount Pleasant.
  Whittle-le-W PR6 .... **60** C8
Mount Pleasant La. LA5 .... **216** B5
Mount Pleasant Prim Sch.
  BB5 .... **123** F2

Mount Pleasant St.
  Burnley BB11 .... **126** F5
Mount Pleasant St.
  Cornholme OL14 .... **108** A1
Mount Pleasant St.
  Horwich BL6 .... **31** D1
Mount Pleasant St. **6**
  Oswaldtwistle BB5 .... **102** E4
Mount Rd. Burnley BB11 .... **126** F4
Mount Rd. Fleetwood FY7 .... **194** A5
Mount St. Accrington BB5 .... **103** B4
Mount St. **12** Barrowford BB9 .. **168** D3
Mount St. Blackpool FY1 .... **129** B6
Mount St. Brierfield BB9 .... **147** B5
Mount St. Clayton-le-M BB5 ... **124** A2
Mount St. Fleetwood FY7 .... **194** A4
Mount St. Great Harwood BB6 . **123** C6
Mount St. Horwich BL6 .... **31** D2
Mount St. Preston PR1 .... **95** F7
Mount St. Ramsbottom BL0 ...... **49** B6
Mount St. Rawtenstall BB4 .... **84** E2
Mount St. Southport PR9 .... **34** D7
Mount St James. BB1 .... **101** F4
Mount Terr. BB4 .... **85** A2
Mount The. Blackburn BB2 ...... **100** C6
Mount The. Skelmersdale WN8 . **9** B8
Mountain Ash. OL12 .... **51** B3
Mountain Ash CI. OL12 .... **51** B3
Mountain La. BB5 .... **103** C4
Mountain Rd. PR7 .... **28** E8
Mountainside CI. OL12 .... **51** F2
Mountbatten Rd. PR7 .... **42** B6
Mountfield Ct. WN5 .... **10** F7
Mountwood. WN8 .... **18** A4
Mountwood Lodge. PR8 .... **20** C5
Mowbray Ave. BB2 .... **100** A8
Mowbray Dr. Blackpool FY3 ... **150** F1
Mowbray Dr. Burton-in-K LA6 . **234** C7
Mowbray Rd. FY7 .... **193** E4
Mowbreck Ct. PR4 .... **113** A6
Mowbreck La. PR4 .... **113** B7
Mowbrick La. LA2 .... **215** D1
Mowgrain View. **2** OL13 .... **86** F3
Muirfield. PR1 .... **95** A6
Muirfield CI. PR2 .... **116** B6
Muirfield Dr. PR8 .... **20** C4
Mulberry Ave. PR1 .... **95** A3
Mulberry Mews. FY2 .... **150** F6
Mulberry St. BB1 .... **101** B5
Mulberry Wlk. **3** BB1 .... **101** B5
Mulgrave Ave. PR1 .... **116** A1
Mullion CI. PR9 .... **53** B5
Muncaster Rd. PR2 .... **116** F2
Munro Ave. WN5 .... **10** E6
Munro Cres. PR2 .... **117** E3
Munster Ave. FY2 .... **150** D3
Murchison Gr. FY5 .... **172** E1
Murdock Ave. PR1 & PR2 ...... **116** D2
Murdock St. BB2 .... **100** B4
Murray Ave. PR5 .... **75** C5
Murray St. Burnley BB10 .... **147** B1
Murray St. Leyland PR5 .... **76** B1
Murray St. Preston PR1 .... **116** E1
Musbury Cres. BB4 .... **85** A1
Musbury Rd. BB4 .... **66** F7
Musbury View. BB4 .... **83** F1
Musden Ave. FY4 .... **67** A7
Museum of Mines. BB8 .... **201** B3
Museum St. **15** BB1 .... **100** E5
Myers St. Barnoldswick BB8 .. **200** B1
Myers St. Burnley BB10 .... **127** A8
Myerscough Ave. Blackpool FY4 **109** F5
Myerscough Ave.
  Lytham St Anne's FY8 .... **88** D8
Myerscough Coll. PR3 .... **156** D3
Myerscough Coll - Hutton Ctr.
  PR4 .... **94** F1
Myerscough Hall Dr. PR3 ...... **156** E5
Myerscough Planks. PR3 .... **156** E5
Myerscough Smithy Rd. BB2 .. **119** E4
Myndon St. LA1 .... **213** F3
Myra Ave. LA4 .... **212** F4
Myra Rd. FY8 .... **89** B4
Myrescough Smithy Rd. BB2 .. **120** C3
Myrtle Ave. Blackpool FY3 .... **129** D5
Myrtle Ave. Burnley BB10 ...... **126** D4
Myrtle Ave. Poulton-le-F FY6 .. **151** E5
Myrtle Ave. Thornton FY5 ...... **172** F5
Myrtle Bank Inf Sch. BB11 .... **126** D4
Myrtle Bank Rd. **10** Bacup OL13 **86** F3
Myrtle Bank Rd. Blackburn BB2 .. **80** C8
Myrtle Dr. PR4 .... **113** C4
Myrtle Gdns. BL9 .... **32** B2
Myrtle Gr. Barnoldswick BB8 .. **200** C2
Myrtle Gr. Burnley BB7 .... **127** F4
Myrtle Gr. Haslingden BB4 ...... **84** A1
Myrtle Gr. Morecambe LA4 .... **212** C3
Myrtle Gr. Southport PR9 .... **34** C7
Myrtle St N. BL9 .... **32** B2
Myrtle St S. BL9 .... **32** B2
Mythop Ave. FY8 .... **90** C4
Mythop CI. FY8 .... **90** C4
Mythop Pl. FY8 .... **115** F1
Mythop Rd.
  Lytham St Anne's FY8 .... **90** C4
Mythop Rd. Weeton PR4 .... **131** C2
Mythop Village. FY4 .... **130** F2
Mytton St. BB12 .... **125** D8
Mytton View. BB7 .... **164** D7

Nab La. Blackburn BB2 .... **100** D5
Nab La. Oswaldtwistle BB5 .... **102** B4
Nab Rd. PR6 .... **60** L1
Nab's Head La. BB2 & PR5 ...... **98** E8
Nabbs Fold. BL8 .... **48** F3
Nabbs Way. BL8 .... **49** A1
Nairn CI. Blackpool FY4 .... **110** A7
Nairn CI. Standish WN6 .... **28** C1

Nairne St. BB11 .... **126** D5
Nancy St. BB3 .... **81** B1
Nansen Rd. Blackburn BB2 .... **100** B3
Nansen Rd. Fleetwood FY7 ... **194** A3
Nantwich Ave. OL12 .... **51** F3
Napier Ave. Blackpool FY4 .... **109** B6
Napier Ave. Tarleton PR4 .... **55** F8
Napier CI. FY8 .... **109** E1
Napier St. **5** Accrington BB5 .. **103** C5
Napier St. Nelson BB9 .... **147** E2
Napier Terr. PR8 .... **34** A5
Naples Ave. BB11 .... **126** D4
Naples Rd. BB3 .... **81** C1
Naptha La. PR4 & PR5 .... **75** C6
Narcissus Ave. BB4 .... **67** A8
Nares Rd. BB2 .... **100** B3
Nares St. PR1 .... **116** C1
Narrow Croft Rd. L39 .... **15** B1
Narrow Gates. BB12 .... **167** C5
Narrow La. Leyland PR5 .... **74** F2
Narrow La. Ormskirk L39 .... **15** B1
Narrow Lane (Clieves Hills).
  L39 .... **14** E6
Narrow Moss La. L40 .... **23** D1
Nasmyth St. BL6 .... **31** C3
Nateby Ave. FY4 .... **109** E5
Nateby CI. Longridge PR3 ...... **138** F8
Nateby CI. Lytham St Anne's FY8 **89** B7
Nateby Crossing La. PR3 ...... **178** A8
Nateby Cty Prim Sch. PR3 .... **177** C6
Nateby Hall La. PR3 .... **198** F1
Nateby Pl. PR2 .... **115** F1
Nave CI. BB3 .... **81** C1
Navena Ave. FY7 .... **193** E2
Navigation Bsns Village. PR2 .. **95** A8
Navigation Way. Blackburn BB1 **100** F3
Navigation Way. Preston PR2 ... **95** A7
Naylor's Terr. BL7 .... **45** C5
Naylorfarm Ave. WN6 .... **19** F5
Naze CI. **3** BB4 .... **85** E1
Naze La. BB3 .... **81** C1
Naze La E. PR4 .... **92** C5
Naze La Ind Est. PR4 .... **92** C4
Naze Rd. PR4 .... **85** E1
Naze View Ave. BB4 .... **85** E2
Neargates. PR7 .... **41** D3
Neath CI. BB1 .... **100** E7
Ned's La. Cold Row FY6 .... **174** D5
Ned's La. Smallwood Hey PR3 **196** A5
Neddy Hill. LA6 .... **234** B7
Neddy La. BB7 .... **143** A4
Nedens Gr. L31 .... **5** C3
Nedens La. L31 .... **5** C3
Needham Ave. LA4 .... **212** D3
Needham Rise. LA4 .... **212** D3
Needless Hall La. BD23 .... **225** E7
Nell Carrs. BL0 .... **49** E8
Nell La. PR5 .... **76** E4
Nell's La. L39 .... **24** E3
Nelson Ave. PR5 .... **76** B1
Nelson & Colne Coll of F Ed.
  BB9 .... **168** D2
Nelson & Colne FE Coll. BB8 **169** D5
Nelson Cres. PR2 .... **115** D2
Nelson Ct. FY7 .... **193** F3
Nelson Dr. PR2 .... **115** D2
Nelson Gdns. PR4 .... **134** C8
Nelson Golf Course. BB9 ...... **147** E4
Nelson Rd. Blackpool FY1 ..... **129** B2
Nelson Rd. Brierfield BB10 ... **148** A4
Nelson Rd. Chorley PR7 .... **42** C7
Nelson Rd. Fleetwood FY7 .... **193** F3
Nelson Sq. BB11 .... **126** F5
Nelson St. Accrington BB5 .... **103** C5
Nelson St. Bacup OL13 .... **70** C8
Nelson St. **3** Bamber Bridge PR5 **76** B8
Nelson St. Clitheroe BB7 ...... **164** B8
Nelson St. Colne BB8 .... **169** D5
Nelson St. **1** Darwen BB3 .... **80** F2
Nelson St. Great Harwood BB6 . **123** D6
Nelson St. Horwich BL6 .... **31** D3
Nelson St. Kirkham PR4 .... **112** F5
Nelson St. Lancaster LA1 ...... **210** F8
Nelson St. Lytham St Anne's FY8 **90** D3
Nelson St. Morecambe LA4 ... **212** D5
Nelson St. Southport PR8 .... **34** A6
Nelson Sta. BB9 .... **147** E8
Nelson Terr. PR1 .... **95** D8
Nelson Way. PR2 .... **94** E8
Nene CI. PR5 .... **59** B7
Neps La. BB7 .... **225** C6
Neptune House. **2** BB11 .... **126** E5
Neptune St. BB11 .... **126** F6
Nesswood Ave. FY4 .... **109** E6
Neston St. PR1 .... **96** E8
Nether Beck. LA5 & LA6 .... **234** A2
Nether Kellet Prim Sch. LA6 .. **216** E4
Nether Kellet Rd. LA6 .... **231** B8
Nether View. LA2 .... **235** E1
Netherby St. BB11 .... **126** E4
Netherfield CI. BB2 .... **126** D7
Netherfield Gdns. **6** BB9 ...... **147** E8
Netherfield Rd. BB9 .... **147** E8
Netherheys CI. BB8 .... **169** B5
Netherlands Rd. LA4 .... **212** F4
Nethertown CI. BB7 .... **143** B6
Netherwood Rd. BB10 .... **127** D7
Netherwood St. BB10 .... **147** E2
Nethway Ave. FY3 .... **129** F6
Netley Ave. OL12 .... **51** F3
Neverstitch CI. WN8 .... **17** F2
Neverstitch Rd. WN8 .... **17** D2
Nevett St. PR1 .... **96** D8
Neville Ave. FY5 .... **172** E1
Neville Dr. FY5 .... **151** B8

Neville St. PR3 .... **139** A7
Nevy Fold Ave. BL6 .... **31** F3
New Acres. Carnforth LA5 ...... **217** F2
New Acres. Newburgh WN8 ..... **26** A1
New Bank Rd. BB2 .... **100** B6
New Barn. BB4 .... **67** B6
New Barn La. BB4 .... **68** A8
New Barns Rd. LA5 .... **237** A1
New Bath St. BB8 .... **169** E6
New Bonny St. FY1 .... **129** B4
New Briggs Fold. BL7 .... **46** E2
New Brown St. **17** BB9 .... **168** D1
New Brunswick St. BL6 .... **31** B3
New Bury CI. BB5 .... **102** C3
New Chapel La. BL6 .... **31** F2
New Chapel St. BB2 .... **100** B2
New Church CI. **14** BB5 .... **123** F3
New Church Mews. **5** BB10 .. **147** B1
New Cock Yd. **28** PR1 .... **96** A7
New Court Dr. BL7 .... **46** E3
New Court Way. L39 .... **15** F5
New Cswy. L37 & L38 .... **3** B7
New Cut CI. PR8 .... **21** A8
New Cut La. L39 & PR8 .... **21** D6
New Fold. WN5 .... **10** C4
New Foul La. PR8 .... **35** A4
New Garden Fields. BB4 .... **86** A7
New Garden St. **1** BB12 .... **100** E3
New Ground Ct. BB12 .... **147** C3
New Hague. BB8 .... **191** F3
New Hall Ave. Blackpool FY4 . **110** B5
New Hall Ave. Blackpool FY4 . **110** B5
New Hall Hey Bsns Pk. BB4 .... **84** F1
New Hall Hey Rd. BB4 .... **84** F1
New Hall La. PR1 .... **96** C8
New Hall Rd. BL9 .... **32** E4
New Hall St. BB10 & BB12 .... **147** A1
New Hey La. PR4 .... **113** E5
New House La. PR3 .... **198** F4
New House St. BB8 .... **169** E5
New La. Banks PR9 .... **53** E3
New La. Bilsborrow PR3 .... **157** A8
New La. Burton-in-K LA6 ...... **234** B7
New La. Eagland Hill PR3 ..... **176** D7
New La. Great Mitton BB7 ..... **163** E6
New La. Haskayne L39 .... **13** E3
New La. New Lane L40 .... **24** B6
New La. Newton PR5 & PR7 .... **58** A1
New La. Ormskirk L39 .... **15** E2
New La. Oswaldtwistle BB5 ... **102** C2
New La. Penwortham PR1 .... **95** E3
New La. Smallwood Hey PR3 . **196** B2
New La. Tarleton PR4 .... **55** D6
New Lane Head. PR5 .... **58** A2
New Lane Pace. PR9 .... **54** B8
New Line. L40 .... **24** B7
New Line. OL13 .... **70** B8
New Links Ave. PR2 .... **116** A6
New Longton CE Prim Sch.
  PR4 .... **74** F7
New Market St. **15**
  Blackburn BB1 .... **100** E5
New Market St. Chorley PR6 ... **42** C8
New Market St. Clitheroe BB7 . **164** E8
New Market St. Colne BB8 .... **169** D5
New Meadow La. L37 & L38 ..... **3** F8
New Miles La. WN6 .... **19** F5
New Mill St. Blackburn BB1 ... **100** F6
New Mill St. Eccleston PR7 ..... **40** C6
New Moss La. PR5 .... **60** C5
New Oxford St. BB8 .... **169** E6
New Park Ormskirk Golf Course.
  L40 .... **16** E6
New Park St. BB2 .... **100** D5
New Pastures. **6** PR5 .... **76** C8
New Quay Rd. LA1 .... **210** B8
New Rd. Adlington PR6 .... **43** C1
New Rd. Bamber Bridge PR5 ... **96** B1
New Rd. Blackpool FY8 .... **109** B4
New Rd. Burnley BB11 .... **127** B2
New Rd. Coppull PR7 .... **41** F3
New Rd. Cornholme OL14 ..... **108** C4
New Rd. Croston PR5 & PR7 .... **39** B7
New Rd. Earby BB8 .... **201** B2
New Rd. Formby L37 .... **12** A5
New Rd. Grimeford Village PR6 . **30** D8
New Rd. Kirkby Lonsdale LA6 . **238** C2
New Rd. Lancaster LA1 .... **210** F8
New Rd. Newchurch BB4 .... **85** C7
New Rd. Rufford L40 .... **38** B3
New Rd. Silverdale LA5 .... **218** F1
New Rd. Staynall FY6 .... **174** B4
New Rd. Thornton FY5 .... **151** C7
New Rd. Thornton in L LA6 .... **236** F4
New Rd. Warton LA5 .... **217** A6
New Rd. Whitworth OL12 .... **70** B1
New Rough Hey. PR2 .... **115** F6
New Row. Altham BB5 .... **124** E6
New Row. Colne BB8 .... **170** C4
New Row. Knowle Green PR3 . **161** D1
New Scotland Rd. BB9 .... **168** E1
New St. Blackrod BL6 .... **30** D2
New St. Brinscall PR6 & PR7 ... **61** F8
New St. Carnforth LA5 .... **217** D2
New St. Caton LA2 .... **231** D3
New St. Colne BB8 .... **169** B3
New St. Eccleston PR7 .... **40** C6
New St. Falinge Fold OL12 ...... **51** E2
New St. Halsall L39 .... **14** B8
New St. Halton LA2 .... **214** D6
New St. **11** Haslingden BB4 .... **84** B3
New St. Lancaster LA1 .... **210** F8
New St. Mawdesley L40 .... **39** C2
New St. Morecambe LA4 .... **212** D5
New St. Nelson BB9 .... **168** F1
New St. Padiham BB12 .... **125** B8
New Taylor Fold. BB10 .... **147** F3
New Way. Barrow Nook L39 ...... **7** C2

New Way. Whitworth OL12 .... 70 C1
New Wellington Cl. BB2 .... 100 C1
New Wellington Gdns. BB2 .... 100 C1
New Wellington St. BB2 .... 100 C1
Newark Pl. Fulwood PR2 .... 116 D8
Newark Pl. Preston PR2 .... 115 E2
Newark Rd. OL12 .... 51 F3
Newark Sq. OL12 .... 51 F3
Newark St. BB5 .... 102 F5
Newarth La. PR4 .... 72 E3
Newbigging Ave. BB4 .... 85 F2
Newburgh CE Prim Sch. WN8 . 26 A1
Newbury Ave. FY4 .... 109 D8
Newbury Cl. PR2 .... 116 C8
Newbury Gn. PR2 .... 116 C8
Newbury Rd. FY8 .... 89 A4
Newby Ave. Fleetwood FY7 .... 193 D1
Newby Ave. Poulton-le-F FY6 .... 151 D1
Newby Back La. BB7 .... 225 A1
Newby Cl. Ainsdale PR8 .... 20 B3
Newby Cl. Burnley BB11 .... 126 E2
Newby Dr.
Clayton-le-W PR5 & PR6 .... 76 E2
Newby Dr. Lancaster LA1 .... 213 F3
Newby La. BB7 .... 189 B8
Newby Pl. Blackpool FY4 .... 130 B1
Newby Pl. Fulwood PR2 .... 117 D4
Newcastle Ave. Blackpool FY3 . 129 D4
Newcastle Ave. Cleveleys FY5 .. 172 F4
Newcastle St. BB2 .... 100 C3
Newchurch CE Prim Sch. BB4 . 85 E1
Newchurch Cl. BB2 .... 100 F2
Newchurch Old Rd. OL13 .... 86 E1
Newchurch Rd. Bacup OL13 .... 69 C8
Newchurch Rd. Rawtenstall BB4 85 C2
Newcombe Rd. BL0 .... 49 B2
Newcroft. LA5 .... 217 E6
Newfield Dr.
Blackburn BB1 & BB2 .... 81 A8
Newfield Dr. Nelson BB9 .... 147 E8
Newfield Rd. PR5 .... 77 A7
Newgate. PR2 .... 116 E4
Newgate Ave. WN6 .... 19 E8
Newgate La. PR4 .... 75 C8
Newgate Rd. WN8 .... 9 F7
Newhaven Dr. PR3 .... 178 D2
Newhouse Rd. Accrington BB5 . 124 D1
Newhouse Rd. Blackpool FY4 .... 129 F2
Newington Ave. BB1 .... 121 F3
Newlands. PR7 .... 40 C6
Newlands Ave. Blackpool FY3 .. 129 F2
Newlands Ave. Burscough L40 .... 24 F4
Newlands Ave. Clitheroe BB7 .... 164 C7
Newlands Ave. Lancaster LA1 ... 211 B5
Newlands Ave.
Lower Healey OL12 .... 51 F3
Newlands Ave. Penwortham PR1 95 B5
Newlands Cl. Blackburn BB2 .... 79 E8
Newlands Cl. Lower Healey OL12 51 F3
Newlands Rd. Lancaster LA1 .... 211 C5
Newlands Rd.
Lancaster LA1 & LA2 .... 211 E6
Newlands Rd.
Lytham St Anne's FY8 .... 89 C5
Newlands Rd. Morecambe LA4 .. 212 F4
Newlands Way. FY6 .... 151 C1
Newlyn Ave. Blackpool FY4 .... 109 E5
Newlyn Ave. Maghull L31 .... 5 E1
Newlyn Ct. FY4 .... 109 E5
Newlyn Dr. WN8 .... 9 D7
Newlyn Pl. PR2 .... 115 F5
Newman Rd. FY1 .... 129 D8
Newman St. BB10 .... 147 B1
Newmarket Ave. LA1 .... 211 B3
Newmarket St. LA4 .... 213 A7
Newport St. BB9 .... 168 E1
News La. WA11 .... 8 F2
Newsham Hall La. PR4 & PR3 .. 135 F3
Newsham Pl. LA1 .... 211 A5
Newsham Rd. LA1 .... 211 A5
Newsham St. PR1 .... 116 D1
Newsham St Mary's &
St Andrews RC Sch. PR4 .... 136 A5
Newsome St. PR5 .... 76 A1
Newstet Rd. L33 .... 1 C2
Newthorn. BB5 .... 103 A1
Newton Ave. Poulton-le-F FY6 ... 151 C2
Newton Ave. Preston PR1 .... 97 A8
Newton Bluecoat CE Prim Sch.
PR4 .... 114 A2
Newton Cl. Freckleton PR4 .... 92 C7
Newton Cl. Leyland PR5 .... 58 B8
Newton Dr. Accrington BB5 .... 103 D3
Newton Dr. Blackpool FY3 .... 129 E5
Newton Dr. Over Town BB10 .... 107 A7
Newton Dr. Ramsbottom BL8 .... 49 A1
Newton Dr E. FY3 .... 130 B7
Newton Gr. FY5 .... 151 D7
Newton Pl. FY3 .... 130 A7
Newton Rd.
Lytham St Anne's FY8 .... 89 A7
Newton Rd. Preston PR1 & PR2 . 116 B2
Newton St. Blackburn BB1 .... 101 B5
Newton St. Burnley BB12 .... 126 C7
Newton St. Clitheroe BB7 .... 164 D7
Newton St. Darwen BB3 .... 81 B2
Newton St. Oswaldtwistle BB5 ... 102 C5
Newton St. 2 Preston PR1 .... 96 B8
Newton St. Southport PR9 .... 35 A7
Newton Terr. LA1 .... 214 A3
Newtown. BB8 .... 200 B2
Newtown St. BB8 .... 169 E5
Nib La. PR5 .... 75 E8
Nichol St. PR6 & PR7 .... 60 C1
Nicholas St. Brierfield BB10 .... 147 E3
Nicholas St. Burnley BB11 .... 127 A5
Nicholas St. Colne BB8 .... 169 C4
Nicholas St. Darwen BB3 .... 80 F1
Nicholl St. 1 BB10 .... 127 A8
Nicholson Cres. LA4 .... 212 G5
Nick Hilton's La. PR6 .... 43 D3
Nickey La. BB2 .... 120 F2
Nickleton Brow. PR6 .... 43 C2
Nicksons La. FY6 .... 195 B4
Nightfield La. BB2 .... 119 F6
Nightingale Cres. BB11 .... 126 C4
Nightingale Dr. FY6 .... 151 B2
Nightingale Rd. BL6 .... 30 C3
Nightingale St. PR6 .... 30 A8
Nile St. 5 Lancaster LA1 .... 210 F8
Nile St. 12 Nelson BB9 .... 168 D1
Nile St. Preston PR1 .... 96 A7
Nimes St. PR1 .... 96 D8
Nine Elms. PR2 .... 116 C6
Nineteen Acre La. LA5 .... 219 F4
Nineveh St. 12 BB8 .... 169 E5
Nipe La. WA11 & WN8 .... 9 B5
Nithside. FY4 .... 130 C1
Niton Cl. BB4 .... 84 C1
Nixon La. PR5 .... 58 A8
Nixon's La. PR8 .... 20 E7
Nixons Ct. PR5 .... 57 F8
Nixons La. WN8 .... 9 D7
Noble St. Darwen BB3 .... 64 A8
Noble St. Great Harwood BB6 .... 123 C4
Noble St. Rishton BB1 .... 123 B1
Noblett Ct. 9 FY7 .... 193 F2
Noblett St. BB1 .... 100 F5
Noel Gate. L39 .... 15 B1
Noel Jones Ct. FY8 .... 88 E7
Noel Rd. LA1 .... 213 E3
Noel Sq. PR2 .... 117 E1
Nolan St. PR8 .... 34 C5
Nook Cres. PR2 .... 138 C1
Nook Farm Ave. OL12 .... 51 F3
Nook Field. PR3 .... 137 D6
Nook Glade. PR2 .... 138 C1
Nook La. Bamber Bridge PR5 .... 76 D6
Nook La. Blackburn BB2 .... 99 F1
Nook La. Churchtown PR3 .... 178 A3
Nook La. Mawdesley PR7 .... 39 E5
Nook La. Oswaldtwistle BB5 .... 102 B2
Nook Terr. Blackburn BB2 .... 100 A1
Nook Terr. Lower Healey OL12 .... 51 F3
Nook The. Bolton-le-S LA5 .... 216 A4
Nook The. Shevington Vale WN6 .. 19 E7
Nook The. Staining FY3 .... 130 D5
Nookfield. PR5 .... 75 A1
Nookfield Cl. FY8 .... 90 A4
Nooklands. PR2 .... 116 E4
Noon Sun St. OL12 .... 51 F1
Noor St. PR1 .... 117 A1
Nora St. BB9 .... 168 D3
Norbeck Cl. BB2 .... 80 F8
Norbreck Dr. PR2 .... 115 E1
Norbreck Rd. FY5 .... 150 C7
Norbreck Sch (Prim). FY5 .... 150 D8
Norburn Cres. L37 .... 11 F2
Norbury Cl. PR9 .... 53 C5
Norcliffe Rd. FY2 .... 150 C5
Norcross Brow. PR7 .... 62 B8
Norcross La. FY5 .... 151 A7
Norcross Pl. PR2 .... 115 F1
Norden Cty High Sch. BB1 .... 123 A2
Norfield. L39 .... 15 F5
Norfolk Ave. Blackpool FY2 .... 150 B3
Norfolk Ave. Burnley BB12 .... 126 B7
Norfolk Ave. Cleveleys FY5 .... 172 E3
Norfolk Ave. Morecambe LA3 .... 212 B2
Norfolk Ave. Padiham BB12 .... 125 D6
Norfolk Cl. 7 Clayton-le-M BB5 123 F3
Norfolk Cl. Leyland PR5 .... 58 E7
Norfolk Gr. Church BB5 .... 103 A7
Norfolk Gr. Southport PR8 .... 33 F1
Norfolk Rd. Bamber Bridge PR5 .. 96 D4
Norfolk Rd. Blackpool FY3 .... 130 A2
Norfolk Rd. Longshaw WN5 .... 10 E1
Norfolk Rd. Lytham St Anne's FY8 90 C5
Norfolk Rd. Preston PR1 .... 117 A1
Norfolk Rd. Southport PR8 .... 33 F1
Norfolk St. Accrington BB5 .... 103 D7
Norfolk St. Blackburn BB2 .... 100 C2
Norfolk St. Colne BB8 .... 169 E5
Norfolk St. Darwen BB3 .... 81 B1
Norfolk St. Lancaster LA1 .... 213 F2
Norfolk St. Nelson BB9 .... 168 D1
Norfolk St. Rishton BB1 .... 123 A1
Norkeed Rd. FY5 .... 150 C7
Norland Dr. LA3 .... 208 F8
Norman Cl. FY5 .... 172 F1
Norman Rd. BB5 .... 102 C5
Norman St. Blackburn BB2 .... 100 C3
Norman St. Burnley BB10 .... 127 A7
Norman St. Bury BL9 .... 32 B4
Normandie Ave. FY2 .... 150 D3
Normandy Rd. PR3 .... 136 B3
Normanhurst. L39 .... 16 A4
Normington Cl. L31 .... 5 C4
Normoss Ave. FY3 .... 130 A7
Normoss Rd. FY3 .... 130 C7
Norris House Dr. L39 .... 6 C8
Norris St. Chorley PR7 .... 42 C6
Norris St. Darwen BB3 .... 81 B1
Norris St. Fulwood PR2 .... 116 D3
Norris St. Preston PR1 & PR2 .... 116 E2
Norris Way. L37 .... 12 B3
North Albert St. FY7 .... 194 B5
North Albion St. FY7 .... 194 A4
North Arthur St. FY7 .... 194 B5
North Ave. Barnoldswick BB8 .... 200 B2
North Ave. Blackpool FY3 .... 129 D7
North Ave. Ramsbottom BL8 .... 48 F1
North Bank Ave. BB1 .... 121 E1
North Church St. FY7 .... 194 B5
North Cliff St. PR1 .... 95 E6
North Cliffe Sch. BB6 .... 123 B6
North Clifton St. FY8 .... 90 B3
North Cres. FY8 .... 88 E6
North Ct. FY5 .... 172 D5
North Dr. Appley Bridge WN6 .... 27 C2
North Dr. Blackpool FY5 .... 150 D6
North Dr. Cleveleys FY5 .... 172 E2
North Dr. Inskip PR4 .... 155 C1
North Dr. Kirkham PR4 .... 112 F6
North Dr. Whalley BB7 .... 143 B7
North End Football Gd (Preston
North End FC). PR1 .... 117 B2
North End La. L38 .... 3 A6
North Gr. 1 PR5 .... 76 C8
North Highfield. PR2 .... 117 E6
North Houses La. FY8 .... 110 D1
North Leach Dr. PR8 .... 20 A5
North Meade. L31 .... 5 C2
North Meadowside. PR4 .... 74 A6
North Mersey Bsns Ctr. L33 .... 1 D4
North Moor La. L39 .... 22 E2
North Moss La. L37 & L39 .... 12 D7
North Par. BB8 .... 200 B3
North Park Ave. BB9 .... 168 C1
North Park Dr. FY3 .... 129 F5
North Perimeter Rd. L33 .... 1 D4
North Prom. FY8 .... 88 D7
North Rd. Blackburn BB1 .... 101 C3
North Rd. Bretherton PR5 & PR4 .. 57 B7
North Rd. Carnforth LA5 .... 217 E2
North Rd. Lancaster LA1 .... 210 F8
North Rd. Preston PR0 & PR1 .... 116 F1
North Rd. Rawtenstall BB4 .... 85 C2
North Rd. Southport PR9 .... 53 C4
North Ribble St. PR1 .... 96 C6
North Road Sch. LA5 .... 217 D1
North Shore Golf Course. FY2 150 C3
North Sq. Blackpool FY3 .... 129 D6
North Sq. Cleveleys FY5 .... 172 D5
North St. Barnoldswick BB8 .... 200 B1
North St. Brierfield BB10 .... 147 F3
North St. Burnley BB10 .... 147 A1
North St. Chorley PR6 .... 60 D2
North St. Clitheroe BB7 .... 186 F1
North St. Colne BB8 .... 169 E6
North St. Fleetwood FY7 .... 194 B5
North St. Hapton BB12 .... 125 C5
North St. Haslingden BB4 .... 84 C1
North St. Morecambe LA4 .... 212 E5
North St. 14 Nelson BB9 .... 168 D1
North St. Newchurch BB4 .... 85 E1
North St. Padiham BB12 .... 145 C1
North St. Preston PR1 .... 95 F8
North St. Ramsbottom BL0 .... 67 C2
North St. Rawtenstall BB4 .... 85 A2
North St. Southport PR9 .... 34 C8
North St. Water BB4 .... 86 A8
North St. Whitworth OL12 .... 70 C1
North Syke Ave. PR2 .... 115 C1
North Terr. PR7 .... 59 D4
North Vale. PR6 .... 42 F1
North Valley Rd. Colne BB8 .... 169 C5
North Valley Rd. Colne BB8 .... 169 D5
North View. Kirkham PR4 .... 112 F5
North View. Leyland PR5 .... 58 F8
North View. Ramsbottom BL0 .... 49 B2
North View. Rawtenstall BB4 .... 85 A8
North View. Strongstry BL0 .... 67 C2
North View Cl. PR3 .... 154 C5
North Warton St. FY8 .... 90 C3
Northall. PR4 .... 73 E2
Northam Cl. PR9 .... 53 A5
Northbrook Gdns. PR5 .... 75 E1
Northbrook Rd. PR5 .... 75 F1
Northcliffe. BB6 .... 123 B6
Northcote Rd. Langho BB6 .... 142 C3
Northcote Rd. Preston PR1 .... 95 D7
Northcote St. Darwen BB3 .... 64 B6
Northcote St. 4 Haslingden BB4 84 B2
Northcote St. 8 Leyland PR5 .... 76 A1
Northdene. WN8 .... 26 B2
Northdunes. L38 .... 2 F4
Northenden Rd. PR7 .... 41 E1
Northern Ave. PR4 .... 73 E2
Northern Cty Prim Sch. OL13 ... 86 F6
Northfield. WN8 .... 18 B4
Northfield Ave. FY1 .... 129 B8
Northfield Rd. Blackburn BB1 .... 100 E7
Northfield Rd. Haslingden BB5 .... 84 A8
Northfleet Ave. FY7 .... 193 E2
Northfold Cty Prim Sch. FY5 .. 172 E4
Northgate. 14 Blackburn BB2 .... 100 E5
Northgate. Blackpool FY2 .... 150 C4
Northgate. Goosnargh PR3 .... 137 D6
Northgate. Leyland PR5 .... 76 B2
Northgate. Lytham St Anne's FY8 . 88 D6
Northgate.
Morecambe LA1 & LA3 & LA4 ..... 213 A2
Northgate. Wallbank OL12 .... 51 C7
Northgate Dr. PR6 .... 60 E2
Northlands. Fulwood PR2 .... 116 E6
Northlands. Leyland PR5 .... 58 C7
Northleach Ave. PR1 .... 95 F2
Northside. PR7 .... 59 C3
Northumberland Ave.
Blackpool FY2 .... 150 B1
Northumberland Ave.
Cleveleys FY5 .... 172 F5
Northumberland House. 14
PR4 .... 95 F8
Northumberland St. 2
Chorley PR6 .... 42 D7
Northumberland St.
Morecambe LA4 .... 212 D5
Northway. Broughton PR3 .... 136 C3
Northway. Fleetwood FY7 .... 193 D1
Northway. Fulwood PR2 .... 116 D7
Northway. Maghull L31 & L39 .... 5 E4
Northway. Ormskirk L39 .... 15 A1
Northway. Skelmersdale WN8 .... 18 B2
Northway Prim Sch. L31 .... 5 E3
Northways. WN6 .... 28 D2
Northwood Cl. Burnley BB12 ... 126 D7
Northwood Cl.
Lytham St Anne's FY8 .... 89 E4
Northwood Way. FY6 .... 151 D2
Norton Ave. LA3 .... 212 A3
Norton Dr. LA3 .... 212 B2
Norton Gr. LA3 .... 212 A2
Norton Pl. LA3 .... 212 A2
Norton Rd. LA3 .... 212 A2
Norton Rd. Garstang PR3 .... 199 C2
Norton Rd. Lower Healey OL12 .... 51 F3
Norton St. BB12 .... 125 C4
Norwich Pl. Blackpool FY2 .... 150 D5
Norwich Pl. 35 Preston PR1 .... 96 A7
Norwich St. BB1 .... 100 F7
Norwood Ave. Becconsall PR4 .... 72 F2
Norwood Ave. Blackburn BB2 .... 100 E2
Norwood Ave. Blackpool FY3 .... 129 E8
Norwood Ave. Nelson BB9 .... 168 F2
Norwood Ave. Southport PR9 .... 34 E7
Norwood Cl. PR6 .... 30 A8
Norwood Cres. PR9 .... 34 E7
Norwood Dr. LA4 .... 213 B3
Norwood Gdns. PR9 .... 34 F7
Norwood Prim Sch. PR9 .... 34 E7
Norwood Rd.
Lytham St Anne's FY8 .... 88 C8
Norwood Rd.
Southport PR8 & PR9 .... 34 F6
Notre Dame Gdns. BB1 .... 101 A6
Nottingham Rd. PR1 .... 117 A1
Nottingham St. BB1 .... 101 A4
Novak Pl. LA4 .... 213 B4
Nowell Gr. BB12 .... 144 D2
Nowell St. 13 BB6 .... 123 C5
Noyna Ave. BB8 .... 191 E1
Noyna St. BB8 .... 169 E6
Noyna View. BB8 .... 169 E7
Nun's St. LA1 .... 211 A8
Nuns Ave. LA7 .... 237 E3
Nurseries The. L37 .... 12 A2
Nursery Ave. L39 .... 16 A6
Nursery Cl. Coppull PR7 .... 41 E4
Nursery Cl. Leyland PR5 .... 58 F8
Nursery Dr. Becconsall PR4 .... 72 F1
Nursery Dr. Formby L37 .... 11 F2
Nursery La. PR4 .... 74 E8
Nursery Nook. BB3 .... 81 D5
Nursery Rd. L31 .... 5 C4
Nuthall Rd. PR8 .... 34 F3
Nuttall Ave. Great Harwood BB6 123 C4
Nuttall Ave. Horwich BL6 .... 31 A3
Nuttall Cl. BL0 .... 49 C5
Nuttall Hall Cotts. BL0 .... 49 D5
Nuttall Hall Rd. BL0 .... 49 D5
Nuttall La. BL0 .... 49 C4
Nuttall Rd. Blackpool FY1 .... 129 D2
Nuttall Rd. Ramsbottom BL0 .... 49 D4
Nuttall St. Accrington BB5 .... 103 C5
Nuttall St. Bacup OL13 .... 87 B3
Nuttall St. Blackburn BB2 .... 80 D8
Nuttall St. Blackburn BB2 .... 100 D1
Nuttall St. 8 Burnley BB11 .... 127 B4
Nuttall St. Bury BL9 .... 32 A1
Nuttall St. Rawtenstall BB4 .... 85 B3
Nuttall St Mews. 3 BB5 .... 103 C5
Nutter Cres. BB12 .... 145 F5
Nutter Rd. Accrington BB5 .... 103 C7
Nutter Rd. Cleveleys FY5 .... 172 D3
Nutter Rd. Preston PR1 .... 95 E7

O'Hagan Ct. BB9 .... 147 B6
Oak Ave. Blackpool FY4 .... 109 D8
Oak Ave. Euxton PR7 .... 59 D3
Oak Ave. Galgate LA2 .... 206 F4
Oak Ave. Haslingden BB5 .... 84 A8
Oak Ave. 9 Horwich BL6 .... 31 E1
Oak Ave. Kirkham PR4 .... 113 B4
Oak Ave. Longridge PR3 .... 139 A7
Oak Ave. Morecambe LA4 .... 213 B6
Oak Ave. Ormskirk L39 .... 15 D4
Oak Ave. Penwortham PR1 .... 95 B3
Oak Ave. Ramsbottom BL0 .... 49 A2
Oak Ave. Thornton FY5 .... 151 C8
Oak Bank. Accrington BB5 .... 124 D2
Oak Bank. Gregson Lane PR5 .... 97 E1
Oak Cl. Barrow BB7 .... 164 D1
Oak Cl. Rishton BB1 .... 102 B8
Oak Cl. Whitworth OL12 .... 70 D4
Oak Cres. WN8 .... 17 D1
Oak Croft. PR6 .... 77 B2
Oak Dr. Chorley PR6 .... 60 C3
Oak Dr. Freckleton PR4 .... 92 A5
Oak Dr. Halton LA2 .... 214 F7
Oak Gates. BL7 .... 46 E1
Oak Gn. L39 .... 15 F5
Oak Gr. Darwen BB3 .... 81 B2
Oak Gr. New Longton PR4 .... 75 A6
Oak Hill Cl. BB5 .... 103 C4
Oak La. Accrington BB5 .... 103 D5
Oak La. Newton-with-S PR4 .... 113 F2
Oak Rd. PR3 .... 178 B8
Oak Ridge. BB7 .... 186 D7
Oak St. Accrington BB5 .... 103 C5
Oak St. Blackburn BB1 .... 100 F7
Oak St. Brierfield BB9 .... 147 B6
Oak St. Burnley BB12 .... 126 C6
Oak St. Clayton-le-M BB5 .... 123 F1
Oak St. Colne BB8 .... 169 F6
Oak St. Fleetwood FY7 .... 194 A4
Oak St. Great Harwood BB6 .... 123 C6
Oak St. 2 Nelson BB9 .... 168 E1
Oak St. Oswaldtwistle BB5 .... 102 D3
Oak St. Preston PR1 .... 96 A7
Oak St. Ramsbottom BL0 .... 49 B5
Oak St. Rawtenstall BB11 .... 105 B4
Oak St. Southport PR8 .... 34 E6
Oak St. Whitworth OL12 .... 70 D5
Oak Terr. BB8 .... 200 C3
Oak Tree Ct. WN8 .... 18 D3
Oak View. Leyland PR5 .... 75 E2
Oak View. Whitworth OL12 .... 70 D4
Oakdene Ave. BB5 .... 124 E1
Oaken Bank. BB10 .... 147 E3
Oaken Cl. OL13 .... 87 B3
Oakenclough Cotts. PR3 .... 220 C2
Oakenclough Rd. OL13 .... 87 B3
Oakeneaves Ave. BB11 .... 126 D2
Oakengate. PR2 .... 117 C7
Oakengates. WN6 .... 28 F1
Oakenhead St. PR1 .... 117 E1
Oakenhead Wood Old Rd. BB4 84 E3
Oakenhurst Rd. BB2 .... 100 D4
Oakenshaw Ave. OL12 .... 51 C6
Oakenshaw View. OL12 .... 51 C6
Oakfield. Fulwood PR2 .... 116 F7
Oakfield. Preston PR1 .... 116 B1
Oakfield Ave. Accrington BB5 .... 124 E1
Oakfield Ave. Barnoldswick BB8 200 A3
Oakfield Ave. Clayton-le-M BB5 . 123 E3
Oakfield Cl. BL6 .... 31 F2
Oakfield Cres. BB5 .... 102 F4
Oakfield Dr. Formby L37 .... 11 D4
Oakfield Dr. Leyland PR5 .... 58 B8
Oakfield Rd. Blackburn BB2 .... 80 D7
Oakfield Rd. Hightown L38 .... 2 F2
Oakgate Cl. PR4 .... 55 F5
Oakgrove. FY4 .... 109 D6
Oakham Ct. 13 PR1 .... 96 A7
Oakhill Cl. L31 .... 5 D2
Oakhill Coll. BB7 .... 143 D6
Oakhill Cottage La. L31 .... 5 D4
Oakhill Dr. L31 .... 5 D4
Oakhill Rd. L31 .... 5 D3
Oakhurst Ave. BB5 .... 124 E1
Oakland Ave. FY5 .... 150 D6
Oakland Glen. PR1 .... 96 A3
Oakland St. 3
Bamber Bridge PR5 .... 96 E1
Oakland St. Nelson BB9 .... 147 E8
Oaklands Ave. Barrowford BB9 168 D3
Oaklands Ave. Tarleton PR4 .... 56 A7
Oaklands Ct. LA1 .... 210 C5
Oaklands Dr. Penwortham PR1 ... 95 A4
Oaklands Dr. Rawtenstall BB4 .... 84 E2
Oaklands Gr. PR2 .... 115 F1
Oaklands Rd. BL0 .... 67 D2
Oaklea. WN6 .... 28 A2
Oakleaf Cl. PR3 .... 137 C6
Oakleaf Ct. FY5 .... 172 D4
Oakleaf Way. FY4 .... 130 D1
Oaklee Gr. L33 .... 1 A4
Oakleigh. WN8 .... 9 D2
Oakleigh Terr. OL14 .... 108 B1
Oakley Rd. Morecambe LA3 .... 212 A2
Oakley Rd. Rawtenstall BB4 .... 84 F2
Oakley St. BB4 .... 84 E2
Oakmere. PR6 .... 77 C3
Oakmere Ave. PR6 .... 78 D2
Oakmoor Ave. FY2 .... 150 E4
Oakridge Cl. PR2 .... 116 F7
Oakroyd Cl. LA5 .... 237 B2
Oaks Bar. BB1 .... 121 C8
Oaks Brow. BB1 .... 121 C7
Oaks The. Bamber Bridge PR1 .... 96 B3
Oaks The. Chorley PR7 .... 42 B4
Oaks The. Leyland PR5 .... 58 A7
Oaks The. Poulton-le-F FY6 .... 151 D4
Oaks The.
St Michael's on W PR3 .... 155 C7
Oaksfield. BB3 .... 80 E5
Oakshaw Dr. OL12 .... 51 A1
Oakshott Pl. PR5 .... 77 B7
Oaktree Ave. Clayton-le-W PR5 ... 76 D4
Oaktree Ave. Fulwood PR2 .... 116 A4
Oaktree Cl. PR2 .... 116 A4
Oakville Rd. LA3 .... 208 E5
Oakwood. WN8 .... 18 D3
Oakwood Ave. Ainsdale PR8 .... 20 D6
Oakwood Ave.
Bamber Bridge PR5 .... 96 C4
Oakwood Ave. Blackburn BB1 ... 122 B1
Oakwood Ave.
Lytham St Anne's FY8 .... 89 E4
Oakwood Ave. Shevington WN6 .. 19 F5
Oakwood Cl. Blackpool FY4 .... 109 F4
Oakwood Cl. Brierfield BB10 .... 147 D3
Oakwood Cl. Thornton FY5 .... 173 D2
Oakwood Dr. Ainsdale PR8 .... 20 E5
Oakwood Dr. Fulwood PR2 .... 116 D8
Oakwood Gdns. LA1 .... 211 A2
Oakwood Gr. LA5 .... 215 F2
Oakwood Rd. Accrington BB5 .... 103 D3
Oakwood Rd. Chorley PR7 .... 42 B6
Oakwood Rd. Coppull PR7 .... 41 F2
Oakwood View. PR7 .... 42 B4
Oakworth Ave. PR2 .... 117 F5
Oasis Cl. L40 .... 38 B3
Oat St. BB12 .... 125 D7
Oban Cres. PR2 .... 117 D3
Oban Ct. PR2 .... 138 D1
Oban Dr. BB1 .... 101 C3
Oban Pl. FY2 .... 150 E6
Oban St. BB10 .... 127 C8
Observatory Rd. BB2 .... 101 A2
Ocean Bvd. FY4 .... 109 A7
Ocean Ct. FY6 .... 194 C5
Ocean Way. FY5 .... 172 C3
Oddfellows Terr. BB4 .... 85 F3
Off Botanic Rd. PR9 .... 53 A1

Off Mount Pleasant St. 7
BB5 .... 102 E4
Offerton St. BL6 .... 31 A3
Old Acre. L38 .... 2 F3
Old Back La. BB7 .... 143 F7
Old Bank La. Blackburn BB2 .. 101 A2
Old Bank La.
Blackburn BB1 & BB2 .... 101 B2
Old Bank St. BB2 .... 100 E4
Old Boundary Way. L39 ...... 15 F6
Old Bridge La. FY6 .... 152 B7
Old Bridge Way. PR6 .... 60 D1
Old Buckley La. PR3 .... 140 D7
Old Clitheroe Rd. PR3 ...... 161 C3
Old Cock Yd. PR1 .... 96 A7
Old Croft. PR2 .... 116 D8
Old Dawber's La. PR7 .... 59 B1
Old Engine La. Ramsbottom BL0 . 49 D6
Old Engine La.
Skelmersdale WN8 .... 17 C2
Old Gates Dr. BB2 .... 79 F8
Old Green. BL8 .... 48 F1
Old Greenwood La. BL6 .... 31 D1
Old Ground St. 8 BL0 .... 49 C6
Old Hall Cl. Bamber Bridge PR5 ... 76 E8
Old Hall Cl. Morecambe LA4 ... 213 B4
Old Hall Cl. Roughlee BB9 .. 168 B5
Old Hall Dr. Accrington BB5 . 124 F1
Old Hall Dr. Bamber Bridge PR5 .. 76 E8
Old Hall La. Charnock Green PR7 . 41 B6
Old Hall La. Pleasington BB2 .. 99 C2
Old Hall Sq. BB10 .... 128 A5
Old Hall St. BB10 .... 127 A8
Old Hey Croft. PR1 .... 95 D2
Old Hive. PR3 .... 182 D4
Old House La. FY4 .... 110 D7
Old Kiln. OL13 .... 69 D8
Old La. Barnoldswick BB8 ..... 191 A8
Old La. Bispham Green L40 ..... 26 D8
Old La. Earby BB8 .... 201 B2
Old La. Formby L37 .... 11 F6
Old La. Haskayne L39 .... 13 E3
Old La. Horwich BL6 .... 31 F2
Old La. Kelbrook BB8 .... 191 F4
Old La. Maghull L31 .... 5 E4
Old La. Salterforth BB8 ..... 191 B5
Old La. Shawforth OL12 & OL13 .. 70 E6
Old La. Thornton-in-C BD23 ... 201 C6
Old Lancaster La. PR1 ...... 116 D1
Old Lancaster Rd. PR3 ...... 178 B2
Old Langho Rd. BB6 & BB7 .. 142 C5
Old Laund St. BB12 .... 146 E8
Old Links Cl. PR9 .... 35 B8
Old Lord's Cres. BL6 .... 31 B5
Old Lostock La. PR5 .... 76 E7
Old Mains La. FY6 .... 151 F6
Old Meadow Ct. FY3 .... 129 E3
Old Meadow La. FY3 .... 129 E3
Old Meadows Rd. OL13 .... 87 A5
Old Mill Ct. PR4 .... 73 F5
Old Mill Dr. BB8 .... 169 F4
Old Mill Hill. L39 .... 15 D3
Old Mill La. Formby L37 .... 11 F4
Old Mill La. Hill Dale L40 ... 26 F6
Old Mill St. BB1 .... 100 F6
Old Mill Terr. PR6 .... 60 E1
Old Mill The. PR5 .... 96 F2
Old Millstones. PR1 .... 95 D7
Old Moss La. L39 .... 13 B5
Old Nab Rd. BB6 .... 122 E8
Old Oak Gdns. PR1 .... 96 A2
Old Oliver La. BD23 .... 230 C6
Old Park La. PR9 .... 35 A8
Old Parsonage La. BB12 ..... 125 B8
Old Pepper La. WN6 .... 28 B2
Old Prescot Cl. L31 .... 6 C2
Old Quarry La. BL7 .... 46 F1
Old Raike. BD23 .... 230 C4
Old Rake. BL6 .... 31 E5
Old Rectory Gn. L39 .... 6 A7
Old Roman Rd. BB12 & BB7 . 144 A3
Old Rough La. L33 .... 1 A2
Old Row. Barrow BB7 .... 164 D2
Old Row. Kirkham PR4 .... 113 B4
Old Row. 4 Rawtenstall BB4 ... 84 E2
Old School Cl. PR5 .... 58 A8
Old School La. Adlington PR7 .. 29 E5
Old School La.
Bamber Bridge PR5 .... 76 C6
Old School La. Euxton PR7 ... 59 D3
Old School La. Tockholes BB3 .. 79 F2
Old School Mews. 12 OL13 .... 69 C8
Old School Row. BB12 .... 126 B6
Old St. BB4 .... 85 F1
Old Station Cl. PR2 .... 138 D1
Old Station Ct. Clitheroe BB7 . 164 E8
Old Station Ct. 4
Clitheroe BB7 .... 164 E8
Old Stone Brow. BB8 .... 192 A4
Old Stone Trough La. BB8 .. 192 A5
Old Swan Cl. BL7 .... 46 E2
Old Swan Cotts. BL7 .... 46 E2
Old Tom's La. FY6 & PR 174 E8
Old Town La. L37 .... 11 E4
Old Tram Rd. Bamber Bridge PR5 76 F4
Old Tram Rd. Preston PR1 .... 96 A4
Old Vicarage. PR1 .... 96 A8
Old Vicarage Rd. BL6 .... 31 F3
Old Will's La. BL6 .... 31 B6
Oldbury Pl. FY5 .... 150 F8
Oldfield. Much Hoole PR4 ..... 73 F4
Oldfield. Penwortham PR1 ..... 95 D2
Oldfield Ave. Blackpool FY2 . 150 C4
Oldfield Ave. Darwen BB3 ..... 80 E3
Oldfield Carr La. FY6 .... 151 E1

Oldfield Cl. FY6 .... 151 E1
Oldfield Cres. FY6 .... 151 E3
Oldfield Rd. PR5 .... 77 A7
Oldham St. Burnley BB11 ..... 126 F4
Oldham St. Morecambe LA4 . 212 E6
Olivant St. BB12 .... 126 C7
Olive Cl. PR6 .... 60 C5
Olive Gr. Blackpool FY3 ...... 129 E5
Olive Gr. Skelmersdale WN8 .. 17 E1
Olive Gr. Southport PR8 & PR9 . 34 E7
Olive Gr. Warton PR4 .... 91 D6
Olive La. BB3 .... 81 B2
Olive Rd. LA1 .... 213 F2
Olive St. OL13 .... 69 E8
Olive Terr. BB4 .... 84 F5
Oliver St. 10 OL13 .... 69 C8
Oliver's Pl. PR2 .... 117 B8
Olivers Pl. PR2 .... 117 A8
Oliverson's Ce Prim Sch. PR3 137 D6
Ollerton La. PR6 .... 78 E4
Ollerton Rd. FY8 .... 89 D5
Ollerton St. PR6 .... 43 A1
Ollerton Terr. PR6 .... 78 E3
Olympia St. BB10 .... 127 C5
Onchan Dr. OL13 .... 87 B1
Onchan Rd. BB2 .... 100 E1
One Ash Cl. OL12 .... 51 F2
Onslow Cres. PR8 .... 34 A2
Onslow Rd. FY3 .... 129 F7
Ontario Cl. BB2 .... 100 A8
Oozebooth Terr. BB1 .... 100 E7
Oozehead La. BB2 .... 100 B5
Opal Cl. BB1 .... 121 F2
Openshaw Dr. BB1 .... 100 E8
Openshaw St. BL9 .... 32 A1
Oram Rd. PR5 .... 77 F8
Oram St. BL9 .... 32 A4
Orange St. BB5 .... 103 B8
Orchard Ave. Blackpool FY4 .. 109 C8
Orchard Ave. Bolton-le-S LA5 . 216 A6
Orchard Ave. New Longton PR4 .. 75 A7
Orchard Ave. Poulton-le-F FY6 . 151 E1
Orchard Bridge. 3 BB11 .... 126 F6
Orchard Cl. Becconsall PR4 ... 72 F3
Orchard Cl. Freckleton PR4 ... 92 A6
Orchard Cl. Fulwood PR2 .... 116 A5
Orchard Cl. Hest Bank LA2 ... 213 F8
Orchard Cl. Silverdale LA5 ... 218 B2
Orchard Cl. Thornton FY5 ... 173 B4
Orchard Cl. Wrea Green PR4 .. 112 B3
Orchard Croft. 2 PR5 .... 76 A8
Orchard Ct. L31 .... 5 F1
Orchard Dr. Fleetwood FY7 .. 193 E1
Orchard Dr. Lucas Green PR6 .. 60 C5
Orchard End. PR3 .... 154 C5
Orchard La. Ainsdale PR8 ..... 20 D4
Orchard La. Lancaster LA1 ... 210 D7
Orchard La. Longton PR4 ...... 73 F8
Orchard Lodge. L39 .... 15 F6
Orchard Rd. Arnside LA5 ..... 237 B2
Orchard Rd.
Lytham St Anne's FY8 ..... 88 G6
Orchard St. 1
Barnoldswick BB8 .... 200 B2
Orchard St. Great Harwood BB6 123 C4
Orchard St. 1 Leyland PR5 ... 76 B1
Orchard St. 29 Preston PR1 ... 95 F8
Orchard The. Burnley BB11 .. 126 C4
Orchard The. Croston PR5 ..... 57 C3
Orchard The. Ormskirk L39 ... 15 D5
Orchard The. Warton PR4 ..... 91 E6
Orchard The.
Woodplumpton PR4 .... 135 E1
Orchard View. L39 .... 15 D1
Orchards The.
Barnoldswick BB8 .... 200 C3
Orchards The. Carleton FY6 .. 151 B5
Orchid Way. OL12 .... 51 D3
Ord Ave. FY4 .... 129 F1
Ord Rd. PR2 .... 116 C2
Orders La. PR4 .... 113 A4
Ordnance St. BB1 .... 101 A5
Oregon Ave. FY3 .... 129 E8
Oriole Cl. 9 BB5 .... 100 F6
Orkney Cl. BB1 .... 101 D3
Orkney Rd. FY1 .... 129 C2
Orme St. FY1 .... 129 C3
Ormerod Rd. BB10 & BB11 ... 127 B7
Ormerod St. Accrington BB5 . 103 B5
Ormerod St. Burnley BB11 ... 127 A5
Ormerod St. Colne BB8 ...... 169 C4
Ormerod St.
Haslingden BB4 & BB5 ..... 84 B7
Ormerod St. 5 Nelson BB9 .. 147 F8
Ormerod St. Rawtenstall BB4 .. 85 B2
Ormerod St. Thornton FY5 ... 173 B4
Ormerod St. Worsthorne BB10 .. 128 A5
Ormerod Terr. BB8 .... 143 D8
Ormond Ave. Blackpool FY1 . 129 B8
Ormond Ave. Westhead L40 . 16 E4
Ormond St. BL9 .... 32 A3
Ormonde Cres. L33 .... 1 A2
Ormont Ave. FY5 .... 172 E2
Ormrod St. BL9 .... 32 A2
Ormrods The. BL9 .... 32 F5
Orms Way. L37 .... 11 E3
Ormsby Cl. WN6 .... 28 E2
Ormskirk Bsns Pk. L39 .... 15 F6
Ormskirk CE Prim Sch. L39 .. 16 A6
Ormskirk & District
General Hospl. L39 .... 16 A4
Ormskirk Gram Sch. L39 ...... 15 F4
Ormskirk Old Rd. L39 .... 7 F7
Ormskirk Rd. Hall Green WN8 . 10 A7
Ormskirk Rd. Preston PR1 ..... 96 A8
Ormskirk Rd.
Rainford Junction WA11 ..... 8 D1
Ormskirk Rd. Skelmersdale WN8 . 9 D7

Ormskirk Rd. Skelmersdale WN8 .. 9 F7
Ormskirk Rd. Skelmersdale WN8 17 C1
Ormskirk Rd. Stanley Gate L39 .. 7 E7
Ormskirk Sta. L39 .... 15 F5
Ormskirk West End
Cty Prim Sch. L39 .... 15 E7
Ormston Ave. BL6 .... 31 C5
Orpen Ave. BB11 .... 126 F3
Orpington Sq. BB10 .... 147 D3
Orrell Cl. PR5 .... 75 D1
Orrell Gdns. WN5 .... 10 F6
Orrell Hill La. L38 .... 3 C4
Orrell Holgate Prim Sch. WN5 10 E5
Orrell La. L40 .... 24 D5
Orrell Rd. WN5 .... 10 E7
Orrell St James' Road
Cty Jun & Inf Sch. WN5 ... 10 D4
Orrell Sta. WN5 .... 10 E4
Orrell Water Pk. WN5 .... 10 E4
Orrest Rd. PR9 .... 118 A1
Orton Ct. BB9 .... 168 D4
Orwell Cl. L37 .... 11 D1
Osbaldeston La. BB2 .... 120 D5
Osbert Croft. PR4 .... 94 A1
Osborne Cres. LA3 .... 212 C3
Osborne Gr. Cleveleys FY5 .. 172 D5
Osborne Gr. Morecambe LA4 . 212 D3
Osborne Rd. Ainsdale PR8 ..... 20 B6
Osborne Rd. Bamber Bridge PR5 . 96 D3
Osborne Rd. Blackburn BB2 . 100 B6
Osborne Rd. Cleveleys FY5 .. 172 D5
Osborne Rd. Formby L37 ...... 11 E1
Osborne Rd.
Lytham St Anne's FY8 ..... 88 F5
Osborne Rd.
Morecambe LA3 & LA4 ... 212 C3
Osborne Terr. Bacup OL13 ... 86 D1
Osborne Terr. Darwen BB3 .... 80 E2
Osborne Terr. 1
Rawtenstall BB4 .... 84 E2
Osborne Terr. Spen Brook BB12 167 D2
Osborne Terr.
Whitewell Bottom BB4 ..... 85 F4
Osborne Way. BB4 .... 84 A1
Osbourne Ave. FY5 .... 172 F1
Osbourne Rd. FY4 .... 109 B8
Oscar St. FY4 .... 129 F2
Oslo Rd. BB11 .... 126 B5
Osprey Cl. BB1 .... 100 D8
Oswald Rd.
Lytham St Anne's FY8 ..... 90 D4
Oswald Rd. Preston PR1 ...... 116 C1
Oswald St. Accrington BB5 .. 103 D6
Oswald St. Blackburn BB1 .. 100 E6
Oswald St. Burnley BB12 ... 126 F8
Oswald St. Oswaldtwistle BB5 . 102 D3
Oswald St. Rishton BB1 ..... 123 C2
Otley Rd. FY8 .... 89 B7
Ottawa Cl. BB2 .... 100 A8
Otterburn Cl. FY6 .... 151 B1
Otterburn Gr. BB10 .... 127 D6
Otterburn Rd. BB2 .... 80 C7
Otters Cl. PR1 .... 117 F2
Ottershaw Gdns. BB1 .... 100 E8
Ottery Cl. PR9 .... 53 A5
Otway St. PR1 .... 116 E2
Oulton Cl. L31 .... 5 B4
Our Lady of Compassion Hospl.
BB2 .... 100 A6
Our Lady Of Compassion
RC Prim Sch. L37 .... 12 A3
Our Lady of Lourdes RC
Prim Sch. Carnforth LA5 ... 217 E1
Our Lady of Lourdes RC
Prim Sch. Southport PR8 ... 34 A1
Our Lady of Perpetual
Succour RC Prim Sch. BB2 .. 80 E8
Our Lady of the Assumption
RC Prim Sch. FY4 .... 109 F5
Our Lady Queen of Peace RC
High Sch. WN8 .... 17 F4
Our Lady & St Edward's RC
Prim Sch. PR2 .... 116 D8
Our Lady & St Gerard's RC
Prim Sch. PR5 .... 76 A3
Our Lady & St John RC
High Sch. BB1 .... 101 C3
Our Lady & St Paul's RC
Prim Sch. OL10 .... 32 F1
Our Lady Star of the Sea RC
Prim Sch. FY8 .... 88 F6
Our Lady's RC High Sch.
Fulwood PR2 .... 116 C4
Our Lady's RC High Sch.
Lancaster LA1 .... 213 F1
Ousby Ave. LA3 .... 212 E2
Ousby Rd. LA3 .... 212 E2
Ouseburn Rd. BB2 .... 80 C8
Out La. PR5 .... 57 C2
Out Moss La. LA4 .... 212 E4
Out Rawcliffe CE Prim Sch.
PR3 .... 175 F2
Outer Prom. FY7 .... 193 E5
Outlet La. L31 & L39 .... 6 F1
Outram La. BB1 .... 121 E1
Outram Way. PR5 .... 76 E8
Outterside St. PR7 .... 30 A6
Outwood Rd. BB11 .... 127 B4
Oval The. WN6 .... 19 F5
Ovangle Rd. LA1 & LA3 ...... 213 B2
Over Houses. BB7 .... 47 B6
Overdale Gr. FY3 .... 130 A8
Overdell Dr. OL12 .... 51 C4
Overfield Way. OL12 .... 51 F2
Overshores Rd. BL7 .... 47 B8
Overton Rd. PR2 .... 94 E8
Ovington Dr. PR8 .... 34 E3

Owen Ave. L39 .... 15 F6
Owen Rd. LA1 .... 213 F2
Owen St. Accrington BB5 .... 103 C7
Owen St. Burnley BB12 ...... 126 A5
Owen St. Darwen BB3 .... 81 A3
Owen St. Preston PR1 .... 96 B8
Owen's La. L39 .... 13 E2
Owen's Row. BL6 .... 31 C3
Owens St. PR7 .... 42 E7
Owlet Hall Rd. BB3 .... 80 E2
Ox Hey. BB5 .... 123 F4
Ox Hey Ave. PR2 .... 115 C1
Ox St. 15 BL0 .... 49 B5
Oxcliffe Ave. LA3 .... 212 A2
Oxcliffe Gr. LA3 .... 212 A1
Oxcliffe Rd. LA3 .... 212 C2
Oxendale Rd. FY5 .... 173 D2
Oxenholme Ave. FY5 .... 172 D4
Oxenhurst Rd. FY3 .... 130 A8
Oxford Ave. BB5 .... 124 A3
Oxford Cl. Blackburn BB1 ... 100 F4
Oxford Cl. Padiham BB12 ... 125 D6
Oxford Ct. Lytham St Anne's FY8 . 89 D4
Oxford Ct. Blackburn BB1 ... 101 E4
Oxford Dr. Kirkham PR4 ...... 113 C4
Oxford Gdns. PR8 .... 33 E4
Oxford Pl. Burnley BB10 ..... 127 B5
Oxford Pl. Lancaster LA1 ... 213 E3
Oxford Rd. Bamber Bridge PR5 .. 76 F8
Oxford Rd. Blackpool FY1 .. 129 D5
Oxford Rd. Burnley BB10 ... 127 B5
Oxford Rd. Cleveleys FY5 .. 172 D3
Oxford Rd. Fleetwood FY7 .. 193 E3
Oxford Rd. Fulwood PR2 .... 116 D4
Oxford Rd. Lytham St Anne's FY8 . 88 E8
Oxford Rd. Lytham St Anne's FY8 . 89 D4
Oxford Rd. Nelson BB9 ...... 169 A2
Oxford Rd. Orrell WN5 .... 10 F8
Oxford Rd. Southport PR8 .... 33 E4
Oxford St. Accrington BB5 .. 103 B6
Oxford St. Adlington PR7 ..... 30 A6
Oxford St. Brierfield BB9 ... 147 B5
Oxford St. 8 Chorley PR6 .... 42 C7
Oxford St. Carnforth LA5 ... 217 D1
Oxford St. Colne BB8 .... 169 E5
Oxford St. Darwen BB3 .... 80 F4
Oxford St. Lancaster LA1 ... 213 F3
Oxford St. Morecambe LA4 . 212 E6
Oxford St. Preston PR1 ...... 96 A6
Oxhey Cl. BB10 .... 127 F6
Oxheys Ind Est. PR1 .... 116 D2
Oxheys St. PR1 .... 116 D2
Oxhill Pl. FY5 .... 150 F7
Oxhouse Rd. WN5 .... 10 D4
Oxley Pl. PR1 .... 117 D1
Oxley Rd N. PR1 .... 117 D1

Paa St. BB7 .... 225 C2
Packet La. LA5 .... 216 A4
Paddington Ave. PR3 .... 155 C7
Paddock Dr. FY3 .... 130 C2
Paddock Rd. WN8 .... 9 C5
Paddock St. 9 BB5 .... 102 E4
Paddock The. Ainsdale PR8 ... 20 C4
Paddock The. Blackburn BB2 . 100 A8
Paddock The. Carleton FY6 .. 151 C5
Paddock The. Formby L37 ..... 12 A1
Paddock The. Fulwood PR2 .. 117 A6
Paddock The. Ormskirk L39 .. 15 C3
Paddock The. Penwortham PR1 . 95 E2
Paddock The. Ramsbottom BL0 . 49 B7
Paddock The. Rufford L40 ... 38 C4
Paddock The. Thornton FY5 .. 151 B8
Paddock Way. LA7 .... 237 D4
Padgate Pl. BB11 .... 126 B4
Padiham Cty Prim Sch. BB12 . 125 D8
Padiham Green CE Sch. BB12 125 C8
Padiham Rd. Burnley BB12 .. 126 C7
Padiham Rd.
Burnley BB11 & BB12 ..... 126 E6
Padiham Rd. Padiham BB12 . 125 F7
Padiham Rd.
Sabden BB12 & BB7 ...... 145 A7
Padstow Cl. PR9 .... 53 A5
Padway. PR1 .... 95 D2
Page Ct. L37 .... 11 F3
Pagefield Cres. BB7 .... 165 A7
Pages Ct. PR5 .... 76 B7
Paignton Rd. BB1 .... 100 D7
Painley Cl. FY8 .... 90 A4
Paisley Cl. FY8 .... 126 D5
Palace Cl. LA3 .... 212 B4
Palace Gdns. BB12 .... 126 B7
Palace Rd. PR8 .... 33 E5
Palace St. Burnley BB12 .... 126 C7
Palace St. Bury BL9 .... 32 A2
Palais Bldgs. LA4 .... 24 E5
Palatine Ave. LA1 .... 211 A5
Palatine Cl. FY3 .... 130 C6
Palatine High Sch. FY4 ..... 109 C8
Palatine Rd. Blackburn BB2 . 100 C4
Palatine Rd. Blackpool FY1 . 129 C4
Palatine Rd. Cleveleys FY5 . 172 D4
Palatine Rd. Southport PR8 . 33 E5
Palatine Sq. BB11 .... 126 C5
Palatine St. 10 BL0 .... 49 C6
Paley Rd. PR1 .... 95 D7
Pall Mall. Blackburn BB1 .... 100 C4
Pall Mall. Chorley PR7 .... 42 C6
Palm Ct. WN8 .... 17 E2
Palm Gr. PR8 & PR9 .... 34 E6
Palm St. Blackburn BB1 ...... 101 A7
Palm St. 4 Burnley BB11 .... 126 D5

Palma St. OL14 .... 108 B1
Palmaston Cl. LA1 .... 210 E6
Palmer Ave. FY1 .... 129 C2
Palmer Gr. LA4 .... 213 A6
Palmer St. BB1 .... 100 D6
Palmerston Cl. BL0 .... 49 C4
Palmerston Rd. PR9 .... 34 F6
Palmerston St. BB12 .... 125 D7
Pansy St N. BB5 .... 103 B7
Pansy St S. BB5 .... 103 B7
Panton St. BL6 .... 31 D1
Parade The. LA5 .... 217 B1
Paradise La. Blackburn BB2 . 100 E4
Paradise La. Formby L37 ..... 12 A6
Paradise La. Leyland PR5 ..... 75 B1
Paradise St. Accrington BB5 . 103 B5
Paradise St. Barrowford BB9 168 E5
Paradise St. Blackburn BB2 . 100 D4
Paradise St. 9 Burnley BB11 . 126 F6
Paradise St. Little Knowley PR6 . 60 F3
Paradise St. Newchurch BB4 . 85 F2
Paradise St. Ramsbottom BL0 . 49 C7
Paragon Way. LA1 .... 210 C8
Parbold Cl. L40 .... 24 E3
Parbold Douglas CE Prim Sch.
WN8 .... 26 D3
Parbold Hill. WN8 .... 26 E2
Parbold Our Lady & All Saints
RC Prim Sch. WN8 .... 26 C2
Parbold St. WN8 .... 26 C2
Pardoe Cl. PR4 .... 72 E3
Pardoe Cl. L40 .... 24 F3
Paris. BB1 .... 121 E4
Parish St. 1 BB12 .... 125 C8
Park Ave. Barnoldswick BB8 . 200 B1
Park Ave. Barrowford BB9 ... 168 C1
Park Ave. Blackburn BB1 .... 100 D6
Park Ave. Burnley BB11 ..... 126 E4
Park Ave. Chatburn BB7 .... 187 D5
Park Ave. Clitheroe BB7 .... 186 C1
Park Ave. Euxton PR7 .... 59 D2
Park Ave. Fleetwood FY7 ... 193 F3
Park Ave. Formby L37 .... 11 F1
Park Ave. Great Harwood BB6 . 123 D6
Park Ave. Haslingden BB4 .... 84 B1
Park Ave. Lancaster LA1 .... 211 B7
Park Ave. Longshaw WN5 .... 10 E1
Park Ave. Lytham St Anne's FY8 . 89 E3
Park Ave. Maghull L31 .... 5 D3
Park Ave. Much Hoole PR4 ... 73 E2
Park Ave. New Longton PR4 . 74 F8
Park Ave. Ormskirk L39 .... 15 E5
Park Ave. Preston PR1 ...... 117 B2
Park Ave. Ramsbottom BL0 .. 49 D6
Park Ave. Salterforth BB8 .. 191 E8
Park Ave. Southport PR9 ..... 34 E8
Park Bridge Rd. BB10 & BB11 . 127 D3
Park Brow Dr. L32 .... 1 A1
Park Cl. Formby L37 .... 2 E8
Park Cl. Parbold WN8 .... 26 D3
Park Cl. Penwortham PR1 ..... 95 D4
Park Cotts. BB8 .... 149 D7
Park Cres. Accrington BB5 .. 103 A4
Park Cres. Bacup OL13 .... 69 E8
Park Cres. Blackburn BB2 ... 100 C6
Park Cres. Haskayne L39 ..... 13 F4
Park Cres. Haslingden BB4 ... 84 C1
Park Cres. Morecambe LA4 . 213 A7
Park Cres. Southport PR9 .... 52 D1
Park Ct. LA1 .... 210 F3
Park Cty Prim Sch. BB8 ..... 169 F5
Park Dr. Brierfield BB9 ...... 147 C5
Park Dr. Nelson BB9 .... 147 F7
Park Dr. Preston PR1 .... 115 D1
Park Farm Rd. BB2 .... 79 D8
Park Gate Rd. BB1 .... 141 D1
Park Hall L Ctr. PR7 .... 41 A4
Park Hall Rd. PR7 .... 40 F3
Park Hey Dr. WN6 .... 19 E7
Park High Sch. BB8 .... 169 F6
Park Hill. Barnoldswick BB8 . 200 C1
Park Hill. 21 Rochdale OL12 .. 51 F1
Park Hill Convent Prep Sch.
BB12 .... 126 A8
Park Hill Rd. PR3 .... 178 C7
Park House La. LA2 .... 233 A5
Park La. Brierfield BB10 & BB9 . 147 C5
Park La. Caton LA2 .... 231 B5
Park La. Garstang PR3 .... 199 A4
Park La. Great Harwood BB6 . 123 D6
Park La. Holmes PR4 .... 55 B2
Park La. Horwich BL6 .... 31 D3
Park La. Kirkham PR4 .... 113 A7
Park La. Maghull L31 .... 5 F3
Park La. Moss Side L31 .... 6 A2
Park La. Oswaldtwistle BB5 . 102 E3
Park La. Penwortham PR1 .... 95 E3
Park La. Preesall FY6 .... 195 B3
Park La. Wennington LA2 ... 232 E8
Park Lane Dr. L31 .... 6 B2
Park Lane End. LA2 .... 232 E8
Park Lee Hospl. BB2 .... 100 E2
Park Lee Rd. BB2 .... 100 E2
Park Link. L39 .... 15 B1
Park Mill Pl. PR1 .... 117 A1
Park Pl. Blackburn BB2 .... 79 D7
Park Pl. Blackburn BB2 ..... 100 B3
Park Pl. 25 Preston PR1 ...... 96 A7
Park Pl. Walton-le-D PR5 .... 96 E4
Park Prim Sch. WN8 .... 17 E1
Park Rd. Accrington BB5 .... 103 A6
Park Rd. Adlington PR7 .... 29 C6
Park Rd. Bacup OL13 .... 86 F1
Park Rd. Barnoldswick BB8 . 200 B1
Park Rd. Blackburn BB1 & BB2 . 100 E3
Park Rd. Blackpool FY1 ..... 129 D3
Park Rd. Burnley BB10 ...... 127 C1
Park Rd. Chorley PR6 & PR7 . 42 C8

Park Rd. Coppull PR7 .... 41 E1
Park Rd. Darwen BL3 .... 64 B6
Park Rd. Edgworth BL7 .... 47 E5
Park Rd. Formby L37 .... 11 E1
Park Rd. Fulwood PR2 .... 117 A4
Park Rd. Gisburn BB7 .... 225 B3
Park Rd. Great Harwood BB6 ... 123 D5
Park Rd. Haslingden BB4 .... 66 F7
Park Rd. Kirkham PR4 .... 112 F4
Park Rd. Lancaster LA1 .... 211 A8
Park Rd. Leyland PR5 .... 59 A7
Park Rd. Longshaw WN5 .... 10 F1
Park Rd. Lytham St Anne's FY8 ... 88 E6
Park Rd. Mellor Brook BB2 .... 120 A1
Park Rd. Morecambe LA4 .... 213 A6
Park Rd. Newchurch BB4 .... 85 F1
Park Rd. Ormskirk L39 .... 15 E5
Park Rd. Padiham BB12 .... 125 C8
Park Rd. Penwortham PR1 .... 95 D4
Park Rd. Poulton-le-F FY6 .... 151 E4
Park Rd. Ramsbottom BL8 .... 48 F3
Park Rd. Rishton BB1 .... 123 C1
Park Rd. Silverdale LA5 .... 218 D4
Park Rd. Southport PR9 .... 34 D8
Park Rd. Thornton FY5 .... 173 B1
Park Rd W. PR9 .... 52 C1
Park Sch. FY3 .... 129 E4
Park Side. BB8 .... 192 A8
Park Sq. LA1 .... 211 A8
Park Sreet E. PR7 .... 168 E4
Park St. Accrington BB5 .... 103 C6
Park St. Barnoldswick BB8 .... 200 B1
Park St. Barrowford BB9 .... 168 D4
Park St. Chorley PR6 & PR7 .... 60 C1
Park St. Clitheroe BB7 .... 164 E7
Park St. Eccleston PR7 .... 40 C6
Park St. Great Harwood BB6 ... 123 D5
Park St. Haslingden BB4 .... 66 F7
Park St. Haslingden BB4 .... 84 B3
Park St. Lytham St Anne's FY8 ... 90 B3
Park Terr. BB1 .... 100 D7
Park View. Arnside LA5 .... 237 B1
Park View. Newchurch BB4 .... 85 F1
Park View. Padiham BB12 ... 125 C8
Park View. Penwortham PR1 .... 95 D4
Park View Ave. PR2 .... 116 B2
Park View Cl. BB9 .... 147 B7
Park View Rd. FY8 .... 90 B4
Park View Terr.
  Abbey Village PR7 .... 79 C1
Park View Terr. Salterforth BB8 191 D7
Park Wall Rd. L29 & L38 .... 4 B2
Park Way. Colne BB8 .... 169 C6
Park Way. Formby L37 .... 11 F1
Park Way. Penwortham PR1 .... 95 D4
Park Wlk. PR7 .... 117 A4
Park Wood Dr. BB4 .... 84 E2
Parkbourn. L31 .... 6 A2
Parkbourn Dr. L31 .... 6 A2
Parkbourn N. L31 .... 6 A2
Parkbourn Sq. L31 .... 6 A2
Parke Mews. PR6 .... 78 C3
Parke Rd. PR6 .... 61 E8
Parker Ave. BB7 .... 164 E6
Parker Cres. L39 .... 15 F7
Parker La. Burnley BB11 .... 127 A5
Parker La.
  New Longton PR4 & PR5 .... 75 C6
Parker St. Accrington BB5 .... 103 E2
Parker St. Accrington BB5 .... 103 E8
Parker St. Barnoldswick BB8 .... 200 A3
Parker St. Blackpool FY1 .... 129 C5
Parker St. Brierfield BB10 .... 147 F3
Parker St. Burnley BB11 .... 127 A6
Parker St. Bury BL9 .... 32 A2
Parker St. Chorley PR6 .... 60 C1
Parker St. Colne BB8 .... 169 C5
Parker St. Lancaster LA1 .... 211 A8
Parker St. 9 Nelson BB9 .... 168 F2
Parker St. Preston PR1 & PR2 ... 116 D2
Parker St. Rishton BB1 .... 123 C2
Parkfield Ave. PR2 .... 116 B2
Parkfield Cl. Leyland PR5 .... 58 C8
Parkfield Cl. Preston PR2 .... 115 C1
Parkfield Cres. PR2 .... 115 C1
Parkfield Dr. Lancaster LA1 .... 211 A6
Parkfield Dr. Preston PR2 .... 94 C8
Parkfield Gr. L31 .... 6 A2
Parkfield View. PR2 .... 94 C8
Parkgate. PR3 .... 137 D5
Parkgate Dr. PR5 .... 58 F7
Parkhead La. PR3 .... 179 A8
Parkinson La. PR3 .... 160 B8
Parkinson St. Blackburn BB2 .... 100 C2
Parkinson St. Burnley BB11 .... 127 A4
Parkinson St. Foulridge BB8 ... 191 D1
Parkinson St. Haslingden BB4 .... 84 A3
Parkinson Way. FY4 .... 129 C1
Parkland Cl. FY5 .... 172 C1
Parkland Gr. LA2 .... 212 B2
Parkland View. BB11 .... 126 E2
Parklands. Skelmersdale WN8 ... 18 D2
Parklands. Southport PR9 .... 34 E8
Parklands Ave. PR1 .... 95 A4
Parklands Cl. PR1 .... 95 A4
Parklands Dr. PR2 .... 116 E8
Parklands Gr. PR2 .... 116 E8
Parklands High Sch.
  Chorley PR7 .... 42 A8
Parklands High Sch.
  Preston PR1 .... 116 F2
Parklands The. PR3 .... 178 D3
Parklands Way. BB2 .... 80 B8
Parkside. Fulwood PR2 .... 117 B3
Parkside. Morecambe LA4 .... 212 F3
Parkside. Preston PR2 .... 115 D2
Parkside Ave. PR7 .... 42 C8
Parkside Cl. OL14 .... 108 B1

Parkside Cres. WN5 .... 10 F6
Parkside Ct. LA4 .... 212 F3
Parkside Dr. Arnside LA5 .... 237 A1
Parkside Dr. Lucas Green PR7 ... 60 B6
Parkside Dr S. PR6 & PR7 .... 60 B6
Parkside La. PR3 .... 178 A7
Parkside Rd.
  Lytham St Anne's FY8 .... 89 A7
Parkside Rd. Nelson BB9 .... 148 B8
Parkside Sch. L39 .... 15 E5
Parkstone Ave. Carleton FY6 ... 151 B5
Parkstone Ave. Thornton FY5 ... 151 D8
Parksway. FY6 .... 194 D5
Parkthorn Rd. PR2 .... 94 C8
Parkway. Blackpool FY3 .... 130 A6
Parkway. Shevington Moor WN6 ... 28 A2
Parkwood. BL7 .... 46 D2
Parkwood Ave. BB12 .... 126 D7
Parkwood Rd. BB1 .... 101 B4
Parliament St. Burnley BB11 .... 127 B5
Parliament St. 11 Colne BB8 .... 169 E5
Parliament St. 18 Darwen BB3 ... 81 A1
Parliament St. Lancaster LA1 ... 213 F1
Parliament St.
  Morecambe LA3 & LA4 .... 212 B4
Parliament St. Up Holland WN8 ... 10 C7
Parlick Ave. PR2 .... 139 B7
Parlick Rd. Fulwood PR1 .... 118 A3
Parlick Rd. Garstang PR3 .... 178 B6
Parr Cottage Cl. PR7 .... 40 C7
Parr La. PR7 .... 40 C7
Parr's La. L39 .... 15 D1
Parramatta St. 8 BB4 .... 85 A2
Parrock Cl. PR1 .... 95 E3
Parrock Rd. BB9 .... 168 C2
Parrock St. Barnoldswick BB8 .... 200 B2
Parrock St. 19 Nelson BB9 .... 168 E1
Parrock St. 7 Rawtenstall BB4 ... 85 A7
Parrox Fold. PR6 .... 195 A5
Parson La. BB7 .... 164 E8
Parson's Brow. 3 PR7 .... 42 C7
Parson's Bullough Rd. PR7 .... 43 E5
Parsonage Ave. PR3 .... 140 D3
Parsonage Brow. WN8 .... 10 A8
Parsonage Cl. Bury BL9 .... 32 A2
Parsonage Cl. Morecambe LA3 .. 212 F2
Parsonage Dr. BB10 & BB9 .... 147 C5
Parsonage La. PR3 .... 182 C1
Parsonage Rd. BB1 .... 122 A4
Parsonage Rd. Bury BL9 .... 32 A3
Parsonage St. 3 Church BB5 .... 102 E5
Parsonage St. Colne BB8 .... 169 C4
Part St. PR8 .... 34 B6
Parth St. OL10 .... 32 D1
Partridge Ave. FY5 .... 173 A4
Partridge Dr. BB5 .... 103 F1
Partridge Hill. BB12 .... 145 D1
Partridge Hill St. BB12 .... 145 D1
Partridge Wlk. BB11 .... 126 C4
Passmonds Cres. OL11 & OL12 ... 51 D1
Past La. Lane Ends BB7 .... 224 A5
Past La. Lane Ends BB7 .... 224 A7
Pasture Cl. Barnoldswick BB8 ... 200 C4
Pasture Cl. Burnley BB11 .... 126 E3
Pasture Dr. BB8 .... 191 D1
Pasture Field Cl. PR5 .... 75 C1
Pasture La. Barrowford BB9 ... 168 C5
Pasture La. Hest Bank LA5 ... 215 E4
Pasturegate. BB11 .... 126 E4
Pasturegate Ave. BB11 .... 126 E4
Pasturelands Dr. BB6 .... 143 A3
Pastures The. Blackburn BB2 .... 100 A8
Pastures The. Grimsargh PR2 ... 138 D1
Pastures The. Southport PR9 .... 53 D5
Paterson St. BB2 .... 100 E3
Patience St. 11 OL12 .... 51 C1
Patmos St. BL0 .... 49 D6
Paton St. OL12 .... 51 D3
Patrick Ave. BB12 .... 144 D2
Patrick Cres. BB4 .... 85 C2
Patten St. Blackburn BB1 .... 101 C5
Patten St. Colne BB8 .... 169 D4
Patten St. Preston PR1 .... 95 F8
Patterdale Ave. Blackburn BB1 .. 101 C3
Patterdale Ave. Blackpool FY3 .. 129 F2
Patterdale Ave. Fleetwood FY7 .. 193 D1
Patterdale Ave.
  Oswaldtwistle BB5 .... 102 D5
Patterdale Ave. Thornton FY5 ... 173 B3
Patterdale Cl. Ainsdale PR8 .... 20 B3
Patterdale Cl. Brierfield BB10 ... 147 C4
Patterdale Cres. L31 .... 5 E2
Patterdale Rd. LA1 .... 214 B1
Pattison St. OL12 .... 51 D3
Paul's La. Hambleton FY6 .... 174 C2
Paul's La. Southport PR9 .... 52 F3
Paulhan St. BB10 .... 147 B2
Pavey Cl. FY4 .... 109 F8
Pavilion St. OL12 .... 51 F2
Pavilion View. PR5 .... 57 B2
Pavilions The. PR5 .... 95 C7
Paxton St. WN8 .... 9 C4
Paythorne Ave. BB10 .... 127 D5
Paythorne Cl. FY6 .... 151 B1
Peabody St. BB3 .... 81 A2
Peace St. BB1 .... 126 D5
Peacehaven. WN8 .... 17 E1
Peachtree Cl. PR2 .... 117 D6
Peacock Cres. LA2 .... 215 D1
Peacock Hall Rd. PR5 .... 58 D7
Peahall La. PR3 .... 197 A4
Peace St. BL9 .... 32 C3
Pear Pl. OL14 .... 108 B1
Pear St. OL14 .... 108 B1

Pear Tree Ave. PR7 .... 41 F3
Pear Tree Cl. PR5 .... 96 E2
Pear Tree Cres. PR5 .... 96 E2
Pear Tree Croft. PR4 .... 74 A8
Pear Tree La. PR7 .... 59 E3
Pear Tree Rd. PR6 .... 77 B3
Pear Tree Sch. PR4 .... 113 A5
Pear Tree St. PR5 .... 96 E2
Pearfield. PR5 .... 76 A2
Pearl Ave. 6 FY2 .... 150 E1
Pearl Brook Ind Est. BL6 .... 31 B3
Pearl St. Accrington BB5 .... 102 F5
Pearl St. Blackburn BB1 .... 121 F1
Pearson St. Blackburn BB2 .... 100 D4
Pearson St. Bury BL9 .... 32 B3
Peartree Rd. PR5 .... 57 B3
Pechell St. 5 PR1 .... 116 C1
Pedder Ave. LA3 .... 209 C1
Pedder Dr. LA3 .... 209 D1
Pedder Gr. LA3 .... 209 D1
Pedder La. FY6 .... 174 B1
Pedder St. Morecambe LA4 .... 212 D5
Pedder St. Preston PR1 .... 95 E8
Pedder's La. Blackpool FY4 .... 109 D7
Pedder's La. Preston PR1 & PR2 116 A1
Pedders Gr. PR2 .... 95 A8
Pedders La. PR1 & PR2 .... 95 A8
Pedders Way. PR1 & PR2 .... 95 A8
Peebles Gr. BB11 .... 126 D3
Peel Ave. Blackpool FY3 .... 129 D7
Peel Ave. Heysham LA3 .... 208 E6
Peel Ave. Lancaster LA1 .... 213 F2
Peel Ave. Ramsbottom BL0 .... 49 A5
Peel Bank Rd. BB5 .... 102 B4
Peel Brow. BL0 .... 49 A4
Peel Brow Prim Sch. BL0 .... 49 D6
Peel Cres. LA1 .... 210 D8
Peel Dr. OL13 .... 87 B1
Peel Gdns. BB8 .... 169 C5
Peel Hall Rd. BL0 .... 49 B2
Peel Hall St. PR1 .... 117 B1
Peel Hill. FY4 .... 110 E7
Peel Mount. Blackburn BB1 .... 101 F4
Peel Mount. Ramsbottom BL0 ... 49 A4
Peel Mount Cl. BB1 .... 101 F4
Peel Park Ave. Accrington BB5 .. 103 D7
Peel Park Ave. Clitheroe BB7 ... 164 F7
Peel Park Cl. Accrington BB5 ... 103 D7
Peel Park Cl. Clitheroe BB7 ... 164 F7
Peel Park Cty Prim Sch. BB5 .. 103 D7
Peel Pl. BB5 .... 168 F6
Peel Rd. Colne BB8 .... 169 B4
Peel Rd. Fleetwood FY7 .... 193 F3
Peel Rd. Peel FY4 .... 110 F4
Peel Rd. Skelmersdale WN8 .... 9 F5
Peel St. Accrington BB5 .... 103 C6
Peel St. Adlington PR6 .... 30 B8
Peel St. Blackburn BB2 .... 100 C2
Peel St. Chorley PR7 .... 42 C7
Peel St. Clitheroe BB7 .... 164 E8
Peel St. Haslingden BB4 .... 84 A3
Peel St. Oswaldtwistle BB5 .... 102 D3
Peel St. Padiham BB12 .... 125 D8
Peel St. Preston PR1 .... 95 E8
Peel St. Rawtenstall BB4 .... 85 C2
Peel St. Southport PR8 & PR9 .. 34 F6
Peel Wlk. L31 .... 5 B2
Peers Clough Rd. BB4 .... 85 F7
Peet Ave. L39 .... 15 D4
Peet's La. PR9 .... 53 A1
Peg's La. PR6 .... 90 B8
Pegbank La. LA6 .... 235 A8
Pelham Ave. FY3 .... 129 E8
Pelham St. BB1 .... 101 A6
Pemberton Dr. LA4 .... 213 B5
Pemberton Pl. LA4 .... 213 B5
Pemberton St. BB1 .... 121 E1
Pemberton's CE Sch. PR7 .... 40 E2
Pembroke Ave. Blackpool FY2 .. 150 B3
Pembroke Ave.
  Morecambe LA4 .... 212 G6
Pembroke Cl. BL6 .... 31 A4
Pembroke Ct. Blackpool FY2 ... 150 B3
Pembroke Ct. 14 Rochdale OL12 51 F1
Pembroke Pl. Chorley PR7 .... 42 B2
Pembroke Pl. 11 Preston PR1 ... 96 A7
Pembroke Rd. FY8 .... 89 D4
Pembroke St. Accrington BB5 ... 103 D6
Pembroke St. Bacup OL13 .... 86 F1
Pembroke St. Blackburn BB2 .... 100 E3
Pembroke St. 12 Burnley BB10 147 B1
Pembury Ave. PR1 .... 95 F3
Pen-Y-Ghent Way. BB8 .... 200 A2
Pendle Ave. Bacup OL13 .... 87 A3
Pendle Ave. Chatburn BB7 .... 187 E5
Pendle Ave. Clayton-le-M BB5 ... 123 F4
Pendle Bridge. BB12 .... 146 F3
Pendle Cl. Bacup OL13 .... 87 A2
Pendle Cl. Blackpool FY3 .... 150 F1
Pendle Comm Hospl. BB9 .... 168 E1
Pendle Ct. Barnoldswick BB8 ... 200 C3
Pendle Ct. Kirkham PR4 .... 113 A6
Pendle Ct. Longridge PR3 .... 139 A7
Pendle Cty Prim Sch. BB7 .... 186 F1
Pendle Dr. Blackburn BB2 .... 100 F2
Pendle Dr. Horwich BL6 .... 31 C5
Pendle Dr. Ormskirk L39 .... 16 A6
Pendle Dr. Whalley BB7 .... 143 A7
Pendle Fields. BB12 .... 146 D7
Pendle Heritage Ctr. BB9 .... 168 E4
Pendle House. BB1 .... 100 F5
Pendle Ind Est. BB9 .... 147 F7
Pendle Mount. BB7 .... 164 F8
Pendle Pl. Lytham St Anne's FY8 . 90 C4

Pendle Pl. Skelmersdale WN8 ... 9 D4
Pendle Rd. Brierfield BB9 .... 147 A5
Pendle Rd.
  Clayton-le-W PR5 & PR6 .... 76 D1
Pendle Rd. Clitheroe BB7 .... 165 A7
Pendle Rd. Downham BB7 .... 188 D3
Pendle Rd. Great Harwood BB6 . 123 F6
Pendle Rd. Lancaster LA1 .... 213 D3
Pendle Row. BB12 .... 167 C5
Pendle St. Accrington BB5 .... 103 A5
Pendle St. Barrowford BB9 .... 168 C3
Pendle St. Blackburn BB1 .... 101 A5
Pendle St. Nelson BB9 .... 168 D1
Pendle St. Padiham BB12 .... 125 D8
Pendle St E. BB7 .... 144 F7
Pendle St W. BB7 .... 144 F7
Pendle View. Barley BB12 .... 167 C6
Pendle View. Clayton-le-M BB5 . 124 A3
Pendle View. Foulridge BB8 ... 191 E1
Pendle View. Grindleton BB7 ... 187 B7
Pendle View. Higham BB12 .... 145 F6
Pendle View.
  West Bradford BB7 .... 186 D7
Pendle Way. Burnley BB12 .... 126 E6
Pendle Way. 4 Nelson BB9 .... 147 E8
Pendlehurst St. BB11 .... 126 E4
Pendlemist View. BB8 .... 169 C3
Pendleside CE Sch. BB7 .... 144 F7
Pendleton Ave. Accrington BB5 . 102 F4
Pendleton Ave. Rawtenstall BB4 . 85 A4
Pendleton Rd. Pendleton BB7 ... 165 A2
Pendleton Rd. Wiswell BB7 .... 143 F8
Penfold. L31 .... 5 E1
Pengarth Rd. BL6 .... 31 C4
Penguin St. PR1 .... 117 B2
Penhale Cl. LA3 .... 208 E6
Penhale Cl. LA3 .... 208 E6
Penhale Gdns. LA3 .... 208 E6
Penhill Cl. FY3 .... 129 D8
Penistone St. 3 BB12 .... 126 D6
Penketh Pl. WN8 .... 9 C5
Penn St. BL6 .... 31 C3
Pennine Ave. PR7 .... 59 D1
Pennine Cl. BL6 .... 31 C5
Pennine Cres. BB9 .... 147 C5
Pennine Gdns. PR3 .... 178 A7
Pennine Gr. Padiham BB12 .... 145 C2
Pennine Gr. Padiham BB12 .... 145 C3
Pennine Pl. WN8 .... 9 B6
Pennine Rd. Bacup OL13 .... 87 A2
Pennine Rd. Chorley PR6 .... 42 E8
Pennine Rd. Horwich BL6 .... 31 C5
Pennine View.
  Dolphinholme LA2 .... 220 A8
Pennine View. Glasson LA2 .... 205 E4
Pennine View.
  Great Eccleston PR3 .... 154 C5
Pennine View. Kirkham PR4 .... 113 C5
Pennine View. Morecambe LA4 . 212 F4
Pennine Way.
  Barnoldswick BB8 .... 200 A4
Pennine Way. Brierfield BB9 ... 147 C5
Pennine Way.
  Great Eccleston PR3 .... 154 C5
Pennines The. PR2 .... 117 A4
Pennington Ave. L39 .... 15 E6
Pennington Ct. LA3 .... 208 E6
Pennington La. WN2 .... 29 E1
Penny House La. BB5 .... 103 C7
Penny St. Blackburn BB1 .... 100 F5
Penny St. Lancaster LA1 .... 210 F7
Penny St. 3 Preston PR1 .... 96 A8
Penny Stone Rd. LA2 .... 214 E2
Pennyfarthing La. FY5 .... 173 A4
Pennystone Rd. FY2 .... 150 B4
Penrhos Ave. FY7 .... 193 E1
Penrhyn Rd. LA1 .... 213 C2
Penrith Ave. Ainsdale PR8 .... 20 C3
Penrith Ave. Cleveleys FY5 .... 172 D4
Penrith Ave. Heysham LA3 .... 208 F8
Penrith Cres. Maghull L31 .... 5 E2
Penrith Cres. Nelson BB8 .... 169 B3
Penrith Rd. BB8 .... 169 A3
Penrod Way. LA3 .... 208 D5
Penrose Ave. FY4 .... 129 F1
Penrose Pl. WN8 .... 9 E4
Penshaw Cl. BB1 .... 121 E1
Penswick Ave. FY5 .... 172 C1
Pentland Cl. L33 .... 1 A4
Penwortham Broad Oak
  Cty Prim Sch. PR1 .... 95 C2
Penwortham Ct. PR1 .... 95 D6
Penwortham Girls High Sch.
  PR1 .... 95 C5
Penwortham Golf Course. PR1 95 B7
Penwortham Holme Rec Sch.
  PR1 .... 95 A5
Penwortham Priory High Sch.
  PR1 .... 95 A5
Penwortham Way.
  Farington PR4 & PR5 .... 75 D7
Penwortham Way.
  Penwortham PR1 & PR4 .... 95 C3
Penzance St. BB2 .... 100 B2
Peplow Rd. LA3 .... 209 B8
Pepper La. WN6 .... 28 B3
Perch Pool La. PR9 & L40 .... 35 F4
Percival Ct. PR8 .... 34 A6
Percival St. Accrington BB5 .... 102 F5
Percival St. Blackburn BB1 .... 100 F7
Percival St. Darwen BB3 .... 80 F7
Percy Rd. LA1 .... 210 F6
Percy St. Accrington BB5 .... 103 D6
Percy St. Blackburn BB2 .... 100 B2
Percy St. Blackpool FY1 .... 129 C2
Percy St. Bury BL9 .... 32 B3
Percy St. 4 Chorley PR6 & PR7 . 42 D7

Percy St. Colne BB8 .... 169 E6
Percy St. Fleetwood FY7 .... 193 F4
Percy St. Nelson BB9 .... 147 E7
Percy St. Oswaldtwistle BB5 .... 102 B5
Percy St. Preston PR1 .... 96 A8
Percy St. Ramsbottom BL0 .... 49 B5
Percy St. Shawforth OL12 .... 70 E6
Peregrine Dr. BB3 .... 80 D3
Peregrine Pl. PR5 .... 75 D2
Peridot Cl. BB1 .... 121 F2
Perimeter Rd. L33 .... 1 E2
Peronne Cres. BB1 .... 101 D5
Perpignon Way. 16 LA1 .... 210 F8
Perry St. BB2 .... 81 B2
Perryn Pl. WN6 .... 28 F1
Pershore Gdns. FY3 .... 130 B8
Pershore Gr. PR8 .... 20 A4
Pershore Rd. FY8 .... 89 B5
Persia St. BB5 .... 102 F6
Perth Cl. FY5 .... 150 F7
Perth St. Accrington BB5 .... 103 A5
Perth St. Blackburn BB2 .... 100 C3
Perth St. Burnley BB11 .... 126 D5
Perth St. Lancaster LA1 .... 211 A7
Perth St. Nelson BB9 .... 168 F1
Peter La. LA5 .... 219 E1
Peter Martin St. 2 LA6 .... 31 B4
Peter St. Accrington BB5 .... 103 A5
Peter St. 9 Barrowford BB9 ... 168 D4
Peter St. Blackburn BB1 .... 101 A6
Peter St. Blackpool FY1 .... 129 D5
Peter St. Bury BL9 .... 32 A3
Peter St. Chorley PR7 .... 42 C8
Peter St. Colne BB8 .... 169 E4
Peter St. 5 Lancaster LA1 .... 210 F7
Peter St. Rawtenstall BB4 .... 85 A2
Peterfield Rd. PR1 .... 95 E2
Peters Ave. L40 .... 24 E4
Petersbottom La. LA2 .... 233 E4
Petre Cres. BB1 .... 102 B8
Petre Rd. BB5 .... 123 F2
Petrel Cl. BB1 .... 100 D8
Petworth Rd. PR8 .... 20 B6
Pharos Ct. FY7 .... 194 B5
Pharos Gr. FY7 .... 194 B5
Pharos Pl. FY7 .... 194 B5
Pharos St. FY7 .... 194 B5
Pheasant Wood Dr. FY5 .... 172 F5
Pheasantford Gn. BB10 .... 127 B8
Pheasantford St. BB10 .... 127 B8
Philip Ave. PR4 .... 113 B4
Philip Dr. PR8 .... 20 F6
Philip St. Barnoldswick BB8 .... 200 B2
Philip St. Darwen BB3 .... 81 B1
Philips Rd. Blackburn BB1 .... 101 B8
Philips Rd. Weir OL13 .... 87 A7
Phillip St. FY4 .... 129 E5
Phillip's Cl. L37 .... 11 F2
Phillip's La. L37 .... 11 F2
Phillips La. BB8 .... 169 B3
Phillipstown. BB4 .... 85 E4
Phoenix St. Lancaster LA1 .... 213 F1
Phoenix St. Spotland Fold OL12 . 51 C1
Phoenix Way. BB11 .... 126 C5
Phyllis St. OL11 & OL12 .... 51 B1
Piccadilly. LA1 .... 210 F3
Piccadilly Cl. LA1 .... 210 F3
Piccadilly Rd. BB11 .... 126 E5
Piccadilly Sq. 9 BB11 .... 126 E5
Piccadilly St. BB8 .... 84 B3
Pickard Cl. BB8 .... 200 D4
Pickard St. LA1 .... 210 F6
Pickering Cl. FY8 .... 89 B7
Pickering Fold. BB1 .... 81 B7
Pickering St. BB9 .... 147 B5
Pickerings The. 2 PR5 .... 76 C8
Pickles Dr. L40 .... 24 D4
Pickles St. BB12 .... 126 D7
Pickmere Ave. FY4 .... 109 E8
Pickmere Cl. FY5 .... 173 A4
Pickthorn Cl. LA1 .... 213 D4
Pickup Fold. BB3 .... 64 C7
Pickup Fold Rd. BB3 .... 64 C7
Pickup Rd. BB1 .... 102 A8
Pickup St. Accrington BB5 .... 102 F5
Pickup St. 11 Bacup OL13 .... 86 F2
Pickup St. Blackburn BB1 .... 101 A6
Pickup St. Clayton-le-M BB5 ... 123 F3
Picton St. BB2 .... 80 B8
Pier La. LA5 .... 237 B2
Pier St. FY1 .... 129 B3
Pierce Cl. Lancaster LA1 .... 210 D7
Pierce St. Padiham BB12 .... 145 C1
Piercefield Rd. L37 .... 11 F5
Piercy Meadow. BB4 .... 85 F3
Piercy Mount. BB4 .... 85 F3
Piercy Rd. BB4 .... 85 F3
Piercy Terr. BB4 .... 85 F3
Pierston Ave. FY2 .... 150 C1
Pike Cl. FY7 .... 193 C2
Pike View. BL6 .... 31 D4
Pikelaw Pl. WN8 .... 9 C5
Pilgrim St. BB9 .... 147 F6
Pilgrims Rd. PR8 .... 34 D5
Pilkington St. Blackburn BB1 .. 100 E4
Pilkington St. 14
  Ramsbottom BL0 .... 49 B5
Pilling Ave. Accrington BB5 .... 103 E2
Pilling Ave.
  Lytham St Anne's FY8 .... 89 C7
Pilling CE Sch. PR3 .... 196 C6
Pilling Cl. Chorley PR6 .... 42 D6
Pilling Cl. Southport PR9 .... 53 F5
Pilling Cres. FY3 .... 130 A8
Pilling Field. BL7 .... 46 E1

Pilling La. Chorley PR7 .... 42 D6
Pilling La. Maghull L31 .... 5 A5
Pilling La.
  Pilling Lane FY6 & PR3 ...... 195 B7
Pilling Moss RC Prim Sch.
  PR3 .... 196 E4
Pilling Pl. WN8 .... 9 C5
Pilling St. Haslingden BB4 .... 84 B6
Pilling St. 3 Newchurch BB4 ..... 68 F8
Pilmuir Rd. BB2 .... 100 E1
Pilot St. BB5 .... 103 B7
Pimbo La. WN5 & WN8 .... 9 F3
Pimbo Rd. WN8 .... 9 C5
Pimhole Rd. BL9 .... 32 B2
Pimlico. BB7 .... 186 F3
Pimlico Link Rd. BB7 .... 187 C2
Pimlico Rd. BB7 .... 186 F2
Pinch Clough Rd. BB4 .... 85 F5
Pincock Brow. PR7 .... 41 C8
Pincock St. PR7 .... 41 C8
Pinder Cl. BB7 .... 186 B4
Pinder St. BB9 .... 168 F2
Pine Ave. Blackpool FY1 .... 129 E2
Pine Ave. Much Hoole PR4 .... 73 D4
Pine Ave. Ormskirk L39 .... 15 F7
Pine Cl. Fulwood PR2 .... 117 F4
Pine Cl. Halton LA2 .... 214 E6
Pine Cl. Newburgh WN8 .... 26 A1
Pine Cl. Rishton BB1 .... 102 B8
Pine Cl. Skelmersdale WN8 .... 17 F1
Pine Cres. Oswaldtwistle BB5 ... 102 F3
Pine Cres. Poulton-le-F FY6 ..... 151 E2
Pine Crest. L39 .... 15 B2
Pine Dr. L39 .... 15 F6
Pine Gr. Chorley PR6 .... 60 D3
Pine Gr. Garstang PR3 .... 199 C1
Pine Gr. Ormskirk L39 .... 15 F7
Pine Gr. Southport PR9 .... 34 D7
Pine St. Bacup OL13 .... 87 A1
Pine St. Blackburn BB1 .... 101 A7
Pine St. Burnley BB11 .... 127 B5
Pine St. Bury BL9 .... 32 B3
Pine St. Darwen BB3 .... 64 B8
Pine St. Haslingden BB4 .... 84 C3
Pine St. Lancaster LA1 .... 213 E1
Pine St. Morecambe LA4 .... 212 F4
Pine St. Nelson BB9 .... 147 F8
Pine St. BL9 .... 32 B2
Pine Walks. PR2 .... 115 C1
Pine Way. PR4 .... 113 B7
Pines Cl. PR5 .... 77 C4
Pines The. PR5 .... 58 A8
Pineway. PR2 .... 116 C4
Pinewood. Blackburn BB2 .... 79 F8
Pinewood. Skelmersdale WN8 ... 18 D3
Pinewood Ave. Blackpool FY2 .. 150 E4
Pinewood Ave. Broughton PR3 . 136 C3
Pinewood Ave. Caton LA2 .... 231 C3
Pinewood Ave. Formby L37 ...... 11 D1
Pinewood Ave. Hest Bank LA5 .. 215 F2
Pinewood Ave.
  Knott End-on-S FY6 .... 195 A5
Pinewood Ave. Morecambe LA4 213 B6
Pinewood Ave. Thornton FY5 ... 151 B7
Pinewood Cl. Formby L37 .... 11 D2
Pinewood Cl. Lancaster LA2 .... 210 E2
Pinewood Cres. Leyland PR5 ..... 58 E8
Pinewood Cres.
  Lytham St Anne's FY8 .... 89 D4
Pinewood Cres. Orrell WN5 ...... 10 E6
Pinewood Cres.
  Ramsbottom BL0 .... 49 B2
Pinewood Dr. BB5 .... 103 E6
Pinfold. Barrowford BB9 .... 168 E5
Pinfold. Longton PR4 .... 74 A8
Pinfold Cl. PR8 .... 20 B3
Pinfold La. Ainsdale PR8 .... 20 B3
Pinfold La. Inskip PR4 .... 155 C2
Pinfold La. Lancaster LA1 .... 213 F2
Pinfold La. Longridge PR3 ...... 139 B4
Pinfold La. Pinfold L40 .... 22 F3
Pinfold Pl. Nelson BB9 .... 169 B1
Pinfold Pl. Skelmersdale WN8 ... 9 D4
Pinfold St. PR1 .... 96 E8
Pingle Croft. PR6 .... 77 A2
Pingwood La. L33 .... 1 A5
Pink Pl. BB2 .... 100 B3
Pink St. BB12 .... 126 C6
Pinnacle Dr. BL7 .... 46 E2
Pinner La. BB4 .... 84 F7
Pioneer St. BL6 .... 31 C4
Piper Cotts. LA4 .... 212 F3
Piper Lea. BB4 .... 86 A1
Piper's La. LA6 .... 234 C8
Pipers Cl. LA7 .... 237 E4
Pippin St. Ormskirk L40 .... 24 A2
Pippin St. Thorpe Green PR6 .... 77 E5
Pit Hey Pl. WN8 .... 9 C5
Pitt St. Lancaster LA1 .... 210 F8
Pitt St. 9 Padiham BB12 .... 125 D8
Pitt St. Preston PR1 .... 95 E7
Pitt St. Southport PR9 .... 34 F6
Pittman Ct. PR2 .... 117 B8
Pittman Way. PR2 & PR3 .... 117 C7
Pitts House La. PR9 .... 35 B8
Pittsdale Ave. FY3 .... 130 A2
Pitville St. BB3 .... 80 F3
Place-de-Criel. 12 BB9 .... 147 D8
Plain Pl. LA2 .... 100 B3
Plane St. Bacup OL13 .... 86 F4
Plane St. Blackburn BB1 .... 101 A4
Plane Tree Cl. BB11 .... 126 D3
Plane Tree Rd. BB12 .... 101 A7
Plant St. Oswaldtwistle BB5 ... 102 D3
Plant St. Preston PR1 .... 116 C1

Plantain Wlk. LA3 .... 212 E2
Plantation Ave. Arnside LA5 ... 218 C8
Plantation Ave.
  Knott End-on-S FY6 .... 194 E5
Plantation Gr. LA5 .... 218 C8
Plantation La. LA2 .... 218 D7
Plantation Rd. Accrington BB5 . 103 E6
Plantation Rd. Blackburn BB2 .. 100 B1
Plantation Rd. Burscough L40 ... 24 B4
Plantation Rd. Edgworth BL7 ... 47 F7
Plantation Sq. BB5 .... 103 D6
Plantation St. Accrington BB5 . 103 D6
Plantation St. Bacup OL13 ...... 69 C8
Plantation St. Burnley BB10 ... 127 A7
Plantation St. 5 Nelson BB9 ... 168 F1
Plantation St. Rawtenstall BB4 . 85 B2
Plantation The. BD23 .... 230 B3
Plantation View. Bacup OL13 ... 86 F6
Plantation View.
  Ramsbottom BL0 .... 49 C3
Plantation View.
  Barnoldswick BB8 .... 200 B2
Plantation View. Coppull PR7 ... 41 F2
Plantation View. Earby BB8 .... 201 C1
Plantation View. Hoddlesden BB3 . 81 F1
Plantation View. Leyland PR5 .. 75 C3
Plantation View. Newchurch BB4 . 85 F1
Plantation View. Withnell PR6 .. 79 A1
Pleasington Ave. PR3 .... 178 D6
Pleasington Cl. Blackburn BB2 . 100 B4
Pleasington Cl. Blackpool FY4 . 110 A8
Pleasington Gr. BB10 .... 127 D5
Pleasington Golf Course. BB2 .. 99 A1
Pleasington Rd. Pleasington BB2 99 B5
Pleasington Rd. Pleasington BB2 99 C1
Pleasington St. BB2 .... 100 B4
Pleasington Sta. BB2 .... 99 C1
Pleasure Beach. FY4 .... 109 B7
Pleasure Beach Sta. FY4 .... 109 B6
Pleasureland. PR8 .... 33 F7
Pleck Farm Ave. BB1 .... 100 E8
Pleck Rd. BB5 .... 103 C6
Pleckgate Fold. BB1 .... 121 E1
Pleckgate High Sch. BB1 .... 121 D1
Pleckgate Rd. BB1 .... 121 E1
Plevna Rd. PR1 .... 96 C8
Plex La. L39 .... 14 C5
Plex Moss La. L39 & PR8 .... 13 D8
Plock Gn. PR7 .... 42 C5
Plough La. L40 & WN8 .... 17 A4
Plough Yd. BB6 .... 123 D5
Plover Cl. FY5 .... 173 A5
Plover Dr. BL9 .... 32 B4
Plover St. Burnley BB12 .... 126 D6
Plover St. Preston PR1 .... 117 B1
Plover View. 1 BB12 .... 126 D6
Plox Brow. PR4 .... 56 A6
Plumbe St. BB11 .... 127 A5
Plumpton Ave. FY4 .... 109 F5
Plumpton Field. PR4 .... 135 E2
Plumpton La.
  Great Plumpton PR4 .... 111 E7
Plumpton La. Halsall L39 .... 21 E2
Plumpton Rd. PR1 & PR2 .... 116 C2
Plumtree Cl. PR2 .... 117 C6
Plunge Rd. BL0 .... 67 E3
Plungington Rd. PR1 & PR2 ... 116 E2
Plymouth Ave. FY7 .... 172 C8
Plymouth Gr. PR6 .... 42 E8
Plymouth Rd. FY2 .... 150 E1
Poachers Way. FY5 .... 173 A4
Pochard Pl. 5 FY5 .... 172 F1
Pocklington St. BB5 .... 103 D2
Podiham Cty Prim Sch. BB12 . 125 E8
Poets' Rd. BB12 .... 125 F7
Pointer Cl. LA1 .... 210 F6
Pointer Gr. LA2 .... 214 F7
Pointer The. LA1 .... 210 F6
Poland St. BB5 .... 102 F6
Pole La. BB3 .... 64 C8
Pole St. Preston PR1 .... 96 A8
Pole St. Standish WN6 .... 28 E1
Polefield. PR2 .... 116 E7
Police St. BB3 .... 81 A1
Pollard Pl. LA1 .... 214 A4
Pollard Row. BB12 .... 167 F1
Pollard St. Accrington BB5 ..... 103 C7
Pollard St. 4 Nelson BB9 .... 168 E1
Pollard St. 6 Preston PR1 ...... 95 E8
Pollards La. BL9 .... 49 C2
Pollux Gate. FY8 .... 89 C4
Polly Gn. OL12 .... 51 B3
Polperro Dr. PR4 .... 92 A6
Pomfret St. Blackburn BB2 .... 100 D3
Pomfret St. Burnley BB11 ...... 126 E6
Pompian Brow. PR5 .... 56 E6
Pond St. LA5 .... 217 D2
Pond Terr. LA5 .... 217 D2
Pont St. BB9 .... 147 D7
Pontville Sch. L39 .... 15 D3
Pool Ct. FY7 .... 193 D1
Pool Foot La. FY6 .... 152 E4
Pool Hey La. PR8 & PR9 .... 35 B3
Pool House Cty Prim Sch.
  PR2 .... 116 A6

Pool House La. PR2 .... 116 A5
Pool La. PR4 .... 92 A4
Pool St. PR9 .... 53 D5
Poole Rd. BB1 .... 101 C5
Poolhill Cl. FY5 .... 150 E7
Poolside Wlk. PR9 .... 53 C4
Poot Hall. OL12 .... 51 F3
Pope La. Fulwood PR2 & PR5 .. 118 A3
Pope La. Penwortham PR1 & PR4 . 95 C2
Pope Wlk. PR1 .... 95 D3
Poplar Ave. Bamber Bridge PR5 .. 96 F1
Poplar Ave. Blackpool FY3 ...... 129 D5
Poplar Ave. Bury BL9 .... 32 B3
Poplar Ave. Euxton PR7 .... 59 C4
Poplar Ave. Great Harwood BB6 123 D6
Poplar Ave. Horwich BL6 .... 31 E1
Poplar Ave. Kirkham PR4 .... 113 A4
Poplar Ave. Longton PR4 .... 74 B8
Poplar Ave. Poulton-le-F FY6 .. 151 E2
Poplar Ave. 4
  Spotland Fold OL12 .... 51 C1
Poplar Ave. Warton PR4 .... 91 D6
Poplar Bank. PR9 .... 52 D1
Poplar Cl. Bamber Bridge PR5 .. 96 F1
Poplar Cl. Oswaldtwistle BB5 .. 102 F3
Poplar Cl. Rishton BB1 .... 102 B8
Poplar Dr. Freckleton PR4 .... 92 A5
Poplar Dr. Longridge PR3 ...... 139 A8
Poplar Dr. Penwortham PR1 ..... 95 C5
Poplar Dr. Skelmersdale WN8 .. 17 F1
Poplar Gr. Bamber Bridge PR5 .. 96 F1
Poplar Gr. Fulwood PR2 .... 118 A4
Poplar Gr. Ramsbottom BL0 ..... 49 D7
Poplar St. Blackburn BB1 ...... 100 F7
Poplar St. Chorley PR7 .... 42 D6
Poplar St. Haslingden BB4 ...... 84 B3
Poplar St. Nelson BB9 .... 168 F1
Poplar St. Southport PR8 .... 34 E6
Poplar Terr. BB4 .... 84 F6
Poplars The. PR7 .... 29 F6
Poppy La. L39 .... 16 B1
Porritt Ave. LA1 .... 210 B8
Porritt St. Bury BL9 .... 32 A4
Porritt St. Bury BL9 .... 32 B4
Porritt Way. BL0 .... 49 C7
Port Royal Ave. LA1 .... 210 C8
Port Way. Heysham LA3 .... 208 D5
Port Way. Preston PR1 & PR2 .. 95 C7
Portal Gr. BB12 .... 126 B6
Porter Pl. PR1 .... 96 A6
Porter St. Accrington BB5 ..... 102 F5
Porter St. Preston PR1 .... 117 B1
Porter St E. PR4 .... 112 F6
Porters Row. FY6 .... 174 C7
Portfield La. BB6 .... 143 F3
Portfield Rd. BB7 .... 143 E4
Portland Cotts. BB5 .... 61 D8
Portland Dr. LA3 & LA4 .... 212 E2
Portland Ind Est. 10 BL9 .... 32 A4
Portland Rd. Blackpool FY1 ... 129 D4
Portland Rd. Langho BB6 .... 122 C8
Portland St. Accrington BB5 ... 103 A6
Portland St. Barrowford BB9 .. 168 D3
Portland St. Blackburn BB2 ... 100 C3
Portland St. Bury BL9 .... 32 A4
Portland St. Chorley PR6 .... 42 D8
Portland St. Colne BB8 .... 169 F5
Portland St. Darwen BB3 .... 64 B6
Portland St. Lancaster LA1 .... 210 F7
Portland St. Nelson BB9 .... 147 D8
Portland St. Preston PR1 .... 95 D7
Portland St. Southport PR8 ..... 34 B5
Portman St. PR1 .... 117 B1
Portree Cl. PR2 .... 117 C5
Portree Cres. BB1 .... 101 D3
Portree Rd. FY2 .... 150 E5
Portsmouth Ave. BB10 .... 147 E2
Portsmouth Cl. 7 FY5 .... 172 F4
Portsmouth Dr. PR6 .... 42 E8
Portway. FY2 .... 150 E6
Post Horse La. LA2 .... 232 B7
Post Office Ave. PR9 .... 53 D5
Post Office Row. Tunstall LA6 . 235 D4
Post Office Row.
  Westhouse LA6 .... 236 E4
Post Office Yd. 8 BB8 .... 169 E5
Postern Gate Rd. LA2 .... 226 A8
Pot Gn. BB12 .... 49 A3
Pot House La. Darwen BB3 ...... 81 C3
Pot House La.
  Oswaldtwistle BB5 .... 102 F2
Potter La. Coupe Green PR5 .... 97 D5
Potter La. Samlesbury PR5 .... 118 C2
Potter Pl. WN8 .... 9 D5
Potter St. 5 BL9 .... 32 A3
Poulton Ave. Accrington BB5 .. 103 A8
Poulton Ave.
  Lytham St Anne's FY8 .... 89 B8
Poulton Cres. PR5 .... 97 D3
Poulton Gr. FY7 .... 194 A4
Poulton Old Rd. FY3 .... 150 F1
Poulton RC St John's
  Prim Sch. FY6 .... 151 E4
Poulton Rd. Blackpool FY3 .... 129 E8
Poulton Rd. Carleton FY6 ...... 151 C5
Poulton Rd. Fleetwood FY7 ... 193 F4
Poulton Rd. Morecambe LA4 .. 212 E5
Poulton Rd. Southport PR9 ..... 34 F7
Poulton Sq. LA4 .... 212 E6
Poulton St. Fleetwood FY7 .... 194 A4
Poulton St. Kirkham PR4 .... 113 B6
Poulton St. Preston PR1 .... 116 C1
Poulton-le-Fylde CE
  Prim Sch. FY6 .... 151 D3
Poulton-le-Fylde Sta. FY6 ..... 151 D4
Poulton-le-Sands CE
  Prim Sch. LA4 .... 212 E6

Powder House La. LA1 & LA2 .. 213 C4
Powderworks La. L31 .... 6 C3
Powell Ave. FY4 .... 109 D8
Powell St. Barnoldswick BB8 . 200 B3
Powell St. Burnley BB11 .... 126 E4
Powell St. Darwen BB3 .... 81 A2
Powis Dr. PR4 .... 56 A8
Powis Rd. PR1 .... 95 B8
Powys Cl. BB4 .... 84 B1
Poynter St. 4 PR1 .... 117 C1
Poynton St. BL9 .... 32 A1
Prairie Cres. BB10 .... 147 B2
Pratt St. BB10 .... 147 B1
Precinct The. BL8 .... 48 F3
Preece Gdns. PR4 .... 154 A1
Preesall Cl. Lytham St Anne's FY8 89 B7
Preesall Cl. Preston PR2 .... 115 C1
Preesall Cl. Southport PR9 ...... 52 F4
Preesall Mill Ind Est. FY6 ..... 195 B2
Preesall Moss La. FY6 .... 195 D2
Preesall Rd. PR2 .... 115 C1
Prescot Cl. BL9 .... 32 A1
Prescot Gn. L39 .... 15 D3
Prescot Pl. Blackpool FY3 ..... 130 A2
Prescot Pl. Thornton FY5 ...... 173 C2
Prescot Rd. L31 & L39 .... 6 D6
Prescott Rd. WN8 .... 9 F4
Prescott St. BB10 .... 127 C5
Press Rd. FY4 .... 88 D8
Pressfield Sch. PR9 .... 53 A3
Prestbury Ave. Ainsdale PR8 .. 20 B5
Prestbury Ave. Blackpool FY4 . 109 C5
Prestbury Cl. BL9 .... 32 A1
Prestbury Dr. LA3 .... 212 E3
Preston Beck. BB8 .... 201 B2
Preston Coll. PR2 .... 116 F5
Preston Coll Trinity Building.
  PR1 .... 95 F8
Preston Coll Winkley Building.
  PR1 .... 95 F7
Preston Enterprise Ctr. 1
  PR1 .... 116 F1
Preston Golf Course. PR2 ..... 117 A6
Preston Lancaster New Rd.
  PR3 .... 178 B4
Preston Lancaster Old Rd.
  PR3 .... 178 D2
Preston Lancaster Rd.
  Bilsborrow PR3 .... 157 A6
Preston Lancaster Rd.
  Cabus PR3 .... 199 B4
Preston Lancaster Rd.
  Galgate LA2 .... 207 A5
Preston Lancaster Rd.
  Potters Brook LA2 & PR3 .... 204 C5
Preston New Rd.
  Blackburn BB2 .... 100 B5
Preston New Rd.
  Blackpool FY1 & FY3 .... 130 C2
Preston New Rd. Clifton PR4 ... 93 C7
Preston New Rd.
  Freckleton PR4 .... 92 D7
Preston New Rd.
  Little Plumpton PR4 .... 111 C6
Preston New Rd.
  Mellor Brook BB2 & PR5 ..... 119 D1
Preston New Rd. Peel Hill FY4 110 E7
Preston New Rd.
  Samlesbury PR1 & PR5 .... 118 E1
Preston New Rd. Southport PR9 53 B4
Preston Nook. PR7 .... 40 C5
Preston Old Rd. Blackburn BB2 . 79 D8
Preston Old Rd. Blackpool FY3 130 A2
Preston Old Rd. Clifton PR4 ... 114 C1
Preston Old Rd. Freckleton PR4 . 92 C6
Preston Rd.
  Charnock Richard PR7 .... 41 C4
Preston Rd. Chorley PR6 & PR7 . 60 C2
Preston Rd.
  Clayton Brook PR5 & PR6 & PR7 . 77 B4
Preston Rd. Coppull Moor WN6 . 28 D5
Preston Rd. Grimsargh PR2 ... 138 C1
Preston Rd.
  Grimsargh PR2 & PR3 .... 138 E2
Preston Rd. Inskip PR4 .... 134 D7
Preston Rd. Leyland PR5 .... 76 B2
Preston Rd. Longridge PR3 ... 139 A3
Preston Rd. Longridge PR3 ... 139 E6
Preston Rd. Lucas Green PR6 .. 60 C4
Preston Rd.
  Lytham St Anne's FY8 .... 90 D4
Preston Rd. Ribchester PR3 ... 140 B5
Preston Rd. Southport PR9 ..... 34 E8
Preston St. Carnforth LA5 .... 217 D2
Preston St. 9 Chorley PR6 ...... 60 C1
Preston St. Darwen BB3 .... 80 F3
Preston St. Fleetwood FY7 .... 194 B4
Preston St. Kirkham PR4 .... 113 B5
Preston St. 16
  Spotland Fold OL12 .... 51 C1
Preston Sta. PR1 .... 95 E7
Prestwich St. BB11 .... 126 E5
Prestwood Pl. WN8 .... 9 F4
Pretoria St. 2 OL12 .... 51 C1
Price Cl. LA1 .... 213 E3
Price St. Blackpool FY1 .... 129 B1
Price St. Bury BL9 .... 32 A1
Prickshaw. OL12 .... 51 B6
Prickshaw La. OL12 .... 51 B6
Priestfield Ave. BB8 .... 169 B5
Priesthouse Cl. L37 .... 12 A3
Priesthouse La. L37 .... 12 A3
Priestley Nook. 4 BB5 .... 103 C5
Primet Bridge. BB8 .... 169 C4
Primet Bsns Ctr. BB8 .... 169 B4
Primet High Sch. BB8 .... 169 B3
Primet Hill. BB8 .... 169 C4

Primet Prim Sch. BB8 .... 169 B3
Primet St. BB8 .... 169 C4
Primrose Ave. FY4 .... 109 D6
Primrose Bank. 1 Bacup OL13 . 69 C8
Primrose Bank. Blackburn BB1 . 100 F6
Primrose Bank. Blackpool FY2 . 150 F6
Primrose Cl. Blackburn BB2 ... 100 B2
Primrose Cl. Formby L37 .... 12 B5
Primrose Cl. Southport PR9 ... 53 C6
Primrose Cotts. PR3 .... 179 E7
Primrose Ct. 3 Blackburn BB2 . 100 B2
Primrose Ct. 6 Lancaster LA1 211 A7
Primrose Ct. Morecambe LA4 212 E5
Primrose Dr. Bury BL9 .... 32 D4
Primrose Dr. PR1 .... 117 C3
Primrose Hill. Colne BB8 ...... 169 F5
Primrose Hill. Mellor BB1 & BB2 121 A3
Primrose Hill. Preston PR1 ...... 96 B7
Primrose Hill Prim Sch. PR7 .. 59 B4
Primrose Hill Rd. PR4 .... 59 B4
Primrose Hill Sch. BB10 .... 147 D2
Primrose La. Fulwood PR2 .... 117 C3
Primrose La. Standish WN6 .... 28 D2
Primrose Rd. Clitheroe BB7 ... 164 D6
Primrose Rd. Fulwood PR1 .... 117 C3
Primrose St. Accrington BB5 . 103 A4
Primrose St. 9 Bacup OL13 .... 69 C8
Primrose St. Brierfield BB9 ... 147 B5
Primrose St. Burnley BB10 ... 147 C1
Primrose St. Chorley PR6 ...... 42 D8
Primrose St. Clitheroe BB7 ... 164 D7
Primrose St. Darwen BB3 .... 64 B8
Primrose St. Lancaster LA1 .. 211 A7
Primrose St. 5 Morecambe LA4 212 E5
Primrose Terr. Blackburn BB2 . 100 B2
Primrose Terr. Langho BB6 .... 142 C1
Primrose Way. BB5 .... 102 E7
Prince Ave. LA5 .... 217 E1
Prince Charles Gdns. PR8 ..... 33 F4
Prince Lee Meadows. BB3 ...... 64 B8
Prince St. Bacup OL13 .... 70 D7
Prince St. Burnley BB11 .... 126 E5
Prince St. Darwen BB3 .... 80 F1
Prince St. Ramsbottom BL0 .... 49 C6
Prince's Pk. WN6 .... 19 F4
Prince's St. PR5 .... 96 E5
Prince's St. BB2 .... 100 D4
Princes Cres. LA4 .... 213 A7
Princes Ct. PR1 .... 95 B6
Princes Dr. PR2 .... 116 E6
Princes Rd.
  Lytham St Anne's FY8 .... 89 D4
Princes Rd. Penwortham PR1 .. 95 B4
Princes Reach. PR2 .... 95 A7
Princes St. Rishton BB1 .... 123 B1
Princes St. Southport PR8 ...... 34 A6
Princes Way. Cleveleys FY5 .. 172 C1
Princes Way. Fleetwood FY7 .. 193 D3
Princess Alexandra Way. LA3 208 D5
Princess Ave. Clitheroe BB7 .. 186 F1
Princess Ave. Kirkham PR4 ... 112 F6
Princess Ave. Lancaster LA1 . 210 F6
Princess Ave. Poulton-le-F FY6 . 151 D3
Princess Cl. FY1 .... 129 B3
Princess Gdns. BB2 .... 79 C7
Princess Par. PR1 .... 129 B6
Princess Rd. Adlington PR6 .... 30 B8
Princess Rd. Cleveleys FY5 ... 172 C2
Princess St. Accrington BB5 .. 102 F6
Princess St. 17 Bacup OL13 ... 86 F2
Princess St. Bamber Bridge PR5 . 76 B7
Princess St. 10
  Bamber Bridge PR5 .... 76 B8
Princess St. Blackburn BB2 .. 100 C2
Princess St. Blackpool FY1 ... 129 B3
Princess St. Chorley PR7 .... 42 D6
Princess St. Colne BB8 .... 169 C4
Princess St. Great Harwood BB6 123 D5
Princess St. Haslingden BB4 .. 84 B2
Princess St. Leyland PR5 .... 76 B1
Princess St. Nelson BB9 .... 147 D7
Princess St. Padiham BB12 ... 125 B8
Princess St. Preston PR1 .... 96 B7
Princess St. Rochdale OL12 .... 51 F1
Princess St. Whalley BB7 ...... 143 C5
Princess St. Whitworth OL12 .. 51 C8
Princess Way. Burnley BB12 . 126 F7
Princess Way. Euxton PR7 ..... 59 E2
Princeway. FY4 .... 109 C7
Pringle Bank. LA5 .... 217 D6
Pringle St. BB1 .... 101 A3
Pringle Wood. PR3 .... 136 C2
Prinny Hill Rd. BB4 .... 84 A3
Printers Fold. BB12 .... 125 E6
Prior's Cl. BB2 .... 100 A6
Priors Wlk. BB7 .... 224 C1
Priorsgate. LA3 .... 212 F2
Priorswood Pl. WN8 .... 9 F4
Priory Cl. Formby L37 .... 12 B2
Priory Cl. Leyland PR5 .... 76 C2
Priory Cl. Morecambe LA3 .... 212 F2
Priory Cl. Newchurch BB4 ...... 85 E2
Priory Cl. Penwortham PR1 .... 95 C6
Priory Cl. Tarleton PR4 .... 56 A6
Priory Cres. PR1 .... 95 C6
Priory Ct. Blackpool FY1 ...... 129 C5
Priory Ct. Burnley BB11 .... 127 B2
Priory Ct. Pleasington BB2 ..... 99 C2
Priory Dr. BB3 .... 64 C8
Priory Gate. FY4 .... 109 C5
Priory Gdns. PR8 .... 33 F4
Priory Gr. L39 .... 15 C4
Priory Grange. Darwen BB3 .... 64 C8
Priory Grange. Southport PR8 . 34 E4
Priory High Sch. L40 .... 24 E5
Priory La. Hornby LA2 .... 232 B7

Priory La. Penwortham PR1 .... 95 C6
Priory Mews. PR8 .... 33 F6
Priory Nook. WN8 .... 10 C7
Priory Pl. BB3 .... 64 C8
Priory St. 4 Nelson BB9 .... 168 F1
Priory St. Preston PR1 .... 95 D8
Priory Wlk. 6 LA1 .... 211 A8
Pritchard St. Blackburn BB2 .... 100 E2
Pritchard St. Burnley BB11 .... 126 E5
Private La. BB4 .... 67 C8
Procter Moss Rd.
  Lancaster LA2 .... 211 D1
Procter Moss Rd.
  Lower Green Bank LA2 .... 226 B3
Procter St. BB2 .... 100 F3
Procter's Brow. LA2 .... 233 B5
Proctor Cl. BB9 .... 147 F5
Proctor Rd. L37 .... 11 C4
Progress Ave. BB11 .... 101 A7
Progress Bsns Pk. PR4 .... 113 A4
Progress Ct. FY3 .... 130 B8
Progress Rd. BB9 .... 168 F3
Progress St. Chorley PR6 .... 42 E8
Progress St. Darwen BB3 .... 81 B1
Progress Way. FY4 .... 110 B6
Promenade. Blackpool FY4 .... 109 A6
Promenade. Blackpool FY1 .... 129 B5
Promenade. Blackpool FY2 .... 150 B6
Promenade. Cleveleys FY5 .... 172 C5
Promenade. Southport PR8 .... 34 B8
Promenade Hospl. PR8 .... 34 B8
Promenade N. FY5 .... 172 C3
Promenade Rd. FY7 .... 194 A5
Promenade S. FY5 .... 172 C2
Promenade The. LA5 .... 237 B2
Prospect Ave.
  Bamber Bridge PR5 .... 76 B8
Prospect Ave. Darwen BB3 .... 80 E2
Prospect Ave. Hest Bank LA2 ...... 215 E1
Prospect Ct. PR3 .... 139 B6
Prospect Dr. LA2 .... 215 E1
Prospect Gr. LA2 .... 212 F4
Prospect Hill. Haslingden BB4 ...... 84 A2
Prospect Hill. 4
  Rawtenstall BB4 .... 85 A3
Prospect Pl. Penwortham PR1 .... 95 E4
Prospect Pl. Preston PR1 .... 116 B1
Prospect Pl. Skelmersdale WN8 ...... 9 F5
Prospect Rd. BB4 .... 85 A3
Prospect St.
  Great Harwood BB6 .... 123 D5
Prospect St. Lancaster LA1 .... 211 A7
Prospect St. Newchurch BB4 .... 85 F1
Prospect Terr. Bacup OL13 .... 69 E7
Prospect Terr. 10
  Barrowford BB9 .... 168 D4
Prospect Terr. Belthorn BB1 .... 81 F6
Prospect Terr. Brinscall PR7 .... 62 A8
Prospect Terr. Huncoat BB5 .... 124 E2
Prospect Terr.
  Rawtenstall BB11 .... 105 B4
Providence St. BB1 .... 101 A8
Prudy Hill. FY6 .... 151 D4
Pudding La. OL14 .... 108 C2
Pudding Pie Nook La. PR3 .... 136 F4
Puddle House La. FY6 .... 130 F8
Pudsey Rd. OL14 .... 108 B2
Pump House La. PR5 .... 57 F6
Pump St. Blackburn BB2 .... 100 D4
Pump St. Burnley BB11 .... 126 E4
Pump St. Clitheroe BB7 .... 164 D8
Pump St. Preston PR1 .... 96 A8
Punnell's La. L31 .... 4 F5
Punstock Rd. BB3 .... 80 F1
Purbeck Dr. BL6 .... 31 F1
Pye Busk. LA2 .... 233 E8
Pye Busk Cl. LA2 .... 233 E8
Pye's Cotts. L39 .... 5 E7
Pygon's Hill La. L31 .... 5 D6

Quail Holme Rd. FY6 .... 194 E5
Quaile Holme Rd. FY6 .... 194 D5
Quaker Brook La. PR5 .... 98 A3
Quaker La. BB3 .... 81 A2
Quakerfields. BB3 .... 81 A2
Quakers' Pl. WN6 .... 28 E1
Quakers Terr. WN6 .... 28 D3
Quarlton Dr. BL8 .... 48 B3
Quarry Bank. BB4 .... 83 F1
Quarry Bank St. BB12 .... 126 C7
Quarry Dr. L39 .... 15 C1
Quarry Farm Ct. BB7 .... 187 D5
Quarry Hill. OL12 .... 51 E3
Quarry Hill Nature Reserve.
  BB9 .... 147 F6
Quarry Mount Mews. LA1 .... 211 A7
Quarry Rd. Brinscall PR7 .... 61 F7
Quarry Rd. Caton Green LA2 ...... 231 E3
Quarry Rd. Chorley PR7 .... 42 E6
Quarry Rd. Lancaster LA1 .... 211 A7
Quarry St. 12 Accrington BB5 ..... 103 C5
Quarry St. Bacup OL13 .... 87 A2
Quarry St. Blackburn BB1 .... 100 F5
Quarry St. Hapton BB11 .... 125 C2
Quarry St. Padiham BB12 .... 145 D1
Quarry St. Ramsbottom BL0 .... 49 D6
Quarry St. Rochdale OL12 .... 51 E1
Quarry St. Shawforth OL12 .... 70 C6
Quarrybank. FY5 .... 150 F8
Quarryside Dr. L33 .... 1 A3
Quay West. FY8 .... 88 E5
Quayle Ave. FY4 .... 109 E8
Quebec Ave. FY2 .... 150 E3
Quebec Rd. BB2 .... 100 B8
Queen Anne St. 3
  Haslingden BB4 .... 84 A3
Queen Anne St. Southport PR8 ..... 34 B7

Queen Elizabeth Cres. BB5 .... 103 D5
Queen Elizabeth Ct. LA4 .... 212 D5
Queen Elizabeth Sch. LA6 .... 238 B2
Queen Elizabeth's Gram Sch.
  BB2 .... 100 C6
Queen Elizabeth's Gram Sch
  (Annexe). BB2 .... 100 D6
Queen House. BB4 .... 85 D1
Queen Mary Ave. FY8 .... 89 A5
Queen Mary Rd. FY8 .... 89 A4
Queen Sq. Blackpool FY1 .... 129 B6
Queen Sq. Lancaster LA1 .... 210 F7
Queen St. 13 Accrington BB5 ..... 103 C6
Queen St. 5 Bacup OL13 .... 69 C8
Queen St. Bacup OL13 .... 86 F2
Queen St. Bamber Bridge PR5 ...... 76 B7
Queen St. Barnoldswick BB8 ...... 200 B1
Queen St. Barrowford BB9 .... 168 D4
Queen St. Blackpool FY1 .... 129 B6
Queen St. Brierfield BB10 .... 147 F2
Queen St. Burnley BB11 .... 126 F5
Queen St. Bury BL9 .... 32 A2
Queen St. Carnforth LA5 .... 217 D1
Queen St. Clayton-le-M BB5 .... 123 F3
Queen St. Clitheroe BB7 .... 164 C8
Queen St. Colne BB8 .... 169 C4
Queen St. Darwen BB3 .... 80 F2
Queen St. Fleetwood FY7 .... 194 A4
Queen St. Great Harwood BB6 ... 123 D5
Queen St. Hoddlesden BB3 .... 81 F1
Queen St. Horwich BL6 .... 31 B3
Queen St. Lancaster LA1 .... 210 F7
Queen St. Lytham St Anne's FY8 ... 90 A3
Queen St. Morecambe LA4 .... 212 E5
Queen St. Nelson BB9 .... 168 E1
Queen St. Ormskirk L39 .... 15 E4
Queen St. Oswaldtwistle BB5 ..... 102 E4
Queen St. Padiham BB12 .... 125 C8
Queen St. Preston PR1 .... 96 B7
Queen St. Ramsbottom BL0 .... 49 B6
Queen St. Rawtenstall BB4 .... 85 A2
Queen St. Whalley BB7 .... 143 C5
Queen St E. PR7 .... 42 D6
Queen Vera Rd. FY1 .... 129 B5
Queen Victoria Hospl. LA4 .... 212 E5
Queen Victoria Rd.
  Blackpool FY1 .... 129 C2
Queen Victoria Rd.
  Burnley BB10 .... 127 B8
Queen Victoria Rd.
  Burnley BB10 .... 147 B1
Queen Victoria St. BB2 .... 100 B2
Queen's Cl. Clitheroe BB7 .... 164 E7
Queen's Cl. Poulton-le-F FY6 ...... 151 E3
Queen's Cres. PR4 .... 113 B4
Queen's Ct. FY2 .... 150 B2
Queen's Dr. Carnforth LA5 .... 217 E1
Queen's Dr. Oswaldtwistle BB5 .. 102 F3
Queen's Gr. PR7 .... 42 C8
Queen's Lancashire Way.
  BB11 .... 126 F6
Queen's Park High Sch. BB1 ..... 101 C2
Queen's Park Hospl. BB2 .... 101 A2
Queen's Park Rd.
  Blackburn BB1 .... 101 A3
Queen's Park Rd. Burnley BB10 .. 127 C7
Queen's Prom. FY2 .... 150 B5
Queen's Rd. Accrington BB5 .... 103 C7
Queen's Rd. Blackburn BB1 .... 101 B3
Queen's Rd. Burnley BB10 .... 147 B2
Queen's Rd. Chorley PR7 .... 42 C8
Queen's Rd. Darwen BB3 .... 64 B6
Queen's Rd. Formby L37 .... 11 D2
Queen's Rd. Fulwood PR2 .... 116 E3
Queen's Rd.
  Lytham St Anne's FY8 .... 88 F5
Queen's Rd. Walton-le-D PR5 ...... 96 E4
Queen's Sq. Hoddlesden BB3 .... 81 F1
Queen's Sq.
  Kirkby Lonsdale LA6 .... 238 C2
Queen's Sq. Poulton-le-F FY6 .... 151 D3
Queen's Sq. 7 Rawtenstall BB4 .... 85 A2
Queen's Terr. 2 Bacup OL13 .... 69 E8
Queen's Terr. Blackburn BB2 ...... 100 B1
Queen's Terr. Fleetwood FY7 ...... 194 C5
Queens Ave. L37 .... 11 E5
Queens Croft. L37 .... 11 D2
Queens Ct. PR2 .... 116 E3
Queens Dr. Arnside LA5 .... 237 B1
Queens Dr. Fulwood PR2 .... 116 D6
Queens Dr. Longridge PR3 .... 139 A7
Queens Dr. Morecambe LA4 .... 213 A6
Queens Dr. Staining FY3 .... 130 E5
Queens Drive Prim Sch. PR2 ..... 116 D5
Queens Garth. BD23 .... 201 B5
Queens Gn. L39 .... 13 F5
Queens Pl. Kirkham PR4 .... 112 F7
Queens Pl. Ramsbottom BL9 .... 49 C2
Queens Rd. Clitheroe BB7 .... 164 E7
Queens Rd. Orrell WN5 .... 10 C5
Queens Rd. Southport PR9 .... 34 C8
Queens Rd W. BB5 .... 103 A4
Queens Ret Pk. PR1 .... 96 B7
Queens Wlk. FY5 .... 172 A4
Queensberry Rd. BB11 .... 126 E5
Queensborough Rd. BB5 .... 103 B7
Queensbury Rd. FY5 .... 172 C2
Queenscourt Ave. PR1 .... 95 E2
Queensdale Cl. PR5 .... 96 E4
Queensgate. Chorley PR7 .... 42 B7
Queensgate. Nelson BB9 .... 147 D7
Queensway.
  Bamber Bridge PR5 .... 96 E1
Queensway. Blackburn BB2 .... 80 A8
Queensway. Blackpool FY4 .... 109 C7
Queensway. Brinscall PR6 .... 61 F7
Queensway. Church BB5 .... 102 F7
Queensway. Clitheroe BB7 .... 164 E7
Queensway. Euxton PR7 .... 59 E2

Queensway. Leyland PR5 .... 58 E7
Queensway.
  Lytham St Anne's FY4 & FY8 .... 110 B2
Queensway. Newchurch BB4 .... 85 E1
Queensway. Penwortham PR1 ...... 95 B6
Queensway. Poulton-le-F FY6 .... 151 D3
Queensway. Preston PR2 .... 115 F2
Queensway. Shevington WN6 .... 19 F4
Queensway. Waddington BB7 ..... 186 B4
Queensway. Warton PR4 .... 91 E7
Queensway Cl. PR1 .... 95 B6
Queensway Cl. FY8 .... 110 A1
Queensway Ind Est. FY8 .... 110 A2
Quernmore Ave. FY3 .... 130 A3
Quernmore Brow. LA2 .... 226 B5
Quernmore CE (VC) Prim Sch.
  LA2 .... 226 A7
Quernmore Dr. Glasson LA2 ...... 205 E4
Quernmore Dr. Kelbrook BB8 .... 192 A5
Quernmore Ind Est. PR4 .... 92 C6
Quernmore Rd. Caton LA2 .... 231 B2
Quernmore Rd. Kirkby L33 .... 1 A3
Quernmore Rd.
  Lancaster LA1 & LA2 .... 211 D7
Quernmore Wlk. 6 L33 .... 1 A3
Quin St. PR5 .... 76 A1
Quinton Cl. PR8 .... 20 A4

Rabbit La. Burscough L40 .... 23 F3
Rabbit La. Cow Ark BB7 .... 184 F6
Raby Sq. LA4 .... 212 E6
Raby St. 3 Morecambe LA4 .... 212 E5
Raby St. 1 Rawtenstall BB4 .... 85 A2
Radburn Brow. PR6 .... 77 B3
Radburn Cl. PR6 .... 77 B3
Radcliffe Rd. P7 .... 193 F2
Radclyffe St. BB7 .... 186 E1
Radfield Ave. 10 BB3 .... 64 A8
Radfield Rd. BB3 .... 63 F8
Radford Gdns. BB3 .... 64 A7
Radford St. BB3 .... 64 A8
Radley Ave. FY3 .... 129 E8
Radnor Ave. Burnley BB12 .... 126 A7
Radnor Ave. Cleveleys FY5 .... 172 F1
Radnor Cl. BB5 .... 102 C4
Radnor Dr. PR9 .... 52 F3
Radnor St. Accrington BB5 .... 103 B7
Radnor St. 6 Preston PR1 .... 95 C8
Radway Cl. FY5 .... 150 F7
Radworth Cres. FY4 .... 130 B1
Raeburn Ave. BB11 .... 126 E3
Raedale Ave. BB10 .... 147 B4
Raglan Ave. Burnley BB11 .... 126 E5
Raglan Rd. Morecambe LA3 ...... 212 B3
Raglan St. 8 Colne BB8 .... 169 D4
Raglan St. 5 Nelson BB9 .... 147 D8
Raglan Terr. Preston PR1 .... 116 D2
Raikes Hill. FY1 .... 129 C5
Raikes Hill Dr. LA2 .... 213 E8
Raikes Par. FY1 .... 129 C5
Raikes Rd. Great Eccleston PR3 . 154 C5
Raikes Rd. Preston PR1 .... 117 C1
Raikes Rd. Thornton FY5 .... 151 E8
Railgate. OL13 .... 70 C8
Railton Ave. BB2 .... 80 A8
Railway App. L39 .... 15 F5
Railway Ave. PR9 .... 53 F5
Railway Cotts. Coppull PR7 .... 41 F1
Railway Cotts. Preston PR4 .... 115 C3
Railway Cotts. Salwick PR4 .... 114 C4
Railway Crossing La. LA1 .... 210 C5
Railway Gr. 3 BB1 .... 101 A7
Railway Path. L39 .... 15 E4
Railway Pl. LA2 .... 205 F5
Railway Rd. Adlington PR6 .... 30 A7
Railway Rd. Blackburn BB1 .... 100 E5
Railway Rd. Brinscall PR7 .... 62 A8
Railway Rd. Chorley PR6 .... 60 D1
Railway Rd. Darwen BB3 .... 81 A1
Railway Rd. Haslingden BB4 .... 84 B4
Railway Rd. Ormskirk L39 .... 15 F5
Railway Rd. Skelmersdale WN8 ..... 8 E8
Railway St. Bacup OL13 .... 69 B8
Railway St. 17
  Barnoldswick BB8 .... 200 B2
Railway St. Brierfield BB9 .... 147 B5
Railway St.
  Burnley BB11 & BB12 .... 126 F7
Railway St. Chorley PR6 .... 42 D7
Railway St. Foulridge BB8 .... 191 D1
Railway St. Lancaster LA1 .... 210 F6
Railway St. Leyland PR5 .... 76 B2
Railway St. Nelson BB9 .... 147 E7
Railway St.
  Ramsbottom BL0 & BL9 .... 49 C2
Railway St. Ramsbottom BL0 .... 49 C6
Railway St. Southport PR8 .... 34 B5
Railway Terr. Brierfield BB9 .... 147 B5
Railway Terr. Entwistle BL7 .... 47 B8
Railway Terr.
  Great Harwood BB6 .... 123 C4
Railway Terr. Kirkham PR4 .... 112 F6
Railway Terr. Rawtenstall BB4 ..... 84 F1
Railway Terr. Simonstone BB12 .. 124 E8
Railway Terr. Southport PR8 .... 34 A5
Railway View. 5
  Accrington BB5 .... 103 C6
Railway View. Billington BB7 ..... 143 B4
Railway View. Blackburn BB2 ... 100 B2
Railway View. Brierfield BB9 ..... 147 B6
Railway View. Croston PR5 .... 57 A2
Railway View Ave. BB7 .... 186 E1
Railway View Rd. BB7 .... 186 E1
Rainford By-pass. WA11 .... 8 D1
Rainford Junction Sta. WA11 .... 8 F2
Rainford Rd.
  L39 & WA11 & WN8 .... 8 C4

Rainhall Cres. BB8 .... 200 D3
Rainhall Prim Sch. BB8 .... 200 B2
Rainhall Rd. BB8 .... 200 B2
Rake Fold. BL0 .... 49 A6
Rake Foot. BB4 .... 84 B3
Rake La. PR4 .... 91 D5
Rake The. LA2 .... 226 E1
Rake Top Ave. BB12 .... 145 F6
Rakehead La. OL13 .... 69 B8
Rakehouse Brow. LA 226 F2
Rakes Bridge. BB3 .... 81 A7
Rakes House Rd. BB9 .... 168 F2
Rakes La. BD23 .... 225 F5
Rakes Rd. LA2 .... 231 E4
Raleigh Ave. FY4 .... 109 B5
Raleigh Cl. FY8 .... 109 D1
Raleigh Rd. PR2 .... 116 E6
Raleigh St. BB12 .... 125 E7
Ralph St. BB5 .... 103 C8
Ralph's Wife's La. PR9 .... 53 E6
Ramparts The. LA1 .... 214 A2
Ramper Gate. FY5 .... 172 D2
Rams Clough La. BB5 .... 83 A8
Ramsbottom Cottage Hospl.
  BL0 .... 49 C5
Ramsbottom La. BL0 .... 49 C7
Ramsbottom Rd.
  Hawkshaw BL8 & BL7 .... 48 A3
Ramsbottom Rd. Horwich BL6 ..... 31 C3
Ramsbottom St.
  Accrington BB5 .... 103 B7
Ramsbottom St.
  Newchurch BB4 .... 85 E1
Ramsbottom Sta. BL0 .... 49 C6
Ramsden St. LA5 .... 217 D2
Ramsey Ave. Bacup OL13 .... 87 A1
Ramsey Ave. Blackpool FY3 ...... 129 D5
Ramsey Ave. Fulwood PR2 .... 117 D3
Ramsey Cl. FY8 .... 109 D1
Ramsey Gr. BB12 .... 147 C2
Ramsey Rd. BB2 .... 100 D1
Ramsgate Rd. FY8 .... 89 A8
Ramsgreave Cl. BB1 .... 121 D2
Ramsgreave Dr. BB1 .... 121 D1
Ramsgreave & Wilpshire Sta.
  BB1 .... 121 F4
Ramshill Ave. FY6 .... 151 B5
Ramson Ct. LA3 .... 212 E2
Ranaldsway. PR5 .... 58 D8
Randal St. BB1 .... 100 E6
Randall St. 11 BB1 .... 147 B1
Randolph St. 21 BB1 .... 101 A4
Ranelagh Dr. PR8 .... 20 F7
Ranger St. BB5 .... 103 B5
Rangeway Ave. FY4 .... 109 C7
Ranglet Rd. PR5 .... 77 B7
Rangletts Ave. PR7 .... 42 C6
Ranglit Ave. PR2 .... 115 C1
Rankin Cl. BB8 .... 200 C2
Rankin Dr. BB3 .... 81 E1
Ranlea Ave. LA2 & LA4 .... 213 C6
Ranleigh Dr. WN8 .... 26 A1
Rantreefold Rd. LA2 .... 233 C4
Rapley La. PR4 & PR3 .... 135 A8
Ratcliffe Fold. 6 BB4 .... 84 B3
Ratcliffe St. Darwen BB3 .... 64 B8
Ratcliffe St. 9 Haslingden BB4 ... 84 B3
Ratcliffe Wharf La. PR3 .... 204 A1
Rathbone Rd. L38 .... 2 F4
Rathlyn Ave. FY3 .... 129 E7
Rathmell CE Sch. BD23 .... 230 E7
Rathmill Sike. BB7 .... 224 B1
Rathmore Cres. PR9 .... 53 B3
Ratten La. PR4 .... 94 D3
Raven Ave. BB4 .... 67 A7
Raven Croft. BB4 .... 67 B8
Raven Meols La. L37 .... 11 F2
Raven Oak La. BB10 .... 128 B5
Raven Pk. BB4 .... 67 B8
Raven Rd. BB2 .... 100 A5
Raven St. 2 Nelson BB9 .... 168 F1
Raven St. Preston PR1 .... 117 C2
Raven's Cl. FY3 .... 130 B7
Ravendale Cl. OL12 .... 51 A1
Ravenglass Ave. L31 .... 5 D2
Ravenglass Cl. Blackburn BB2 ... 101 A1
Ravenglass Cl. Blackpool FY4 ... 109 E7
Ravenglass Cl. Kirkham PR4 ..... 113 A7
Ravenhead Dr. WN8 .... 10 A7
Ravenhead Way. WN8 .... 9 F6
Ravenhill Dr. PR7 .... 60 C1
Ravens Cl. LA1 .... 213 E3
Ravens Close Brow. LA2 .... 235 F1
Ravens Gr. BB10 .... 147 C4
Ravens Wood. BB2 .... 100 B5
Ravenscroft. L37 .... 11 F2
Ravenscroft Ave. L39 .... 15 E4
Ravenscroft Cl. BB1 .... 122 A1
Ravenscroft Way. BB8 .... 200 C3
Ravensthorpe. PR7 .... 60 A1
Ravenswing Ave. BB3 .... 81 B7
Ravenswood. Fulwood PR2 .... 117 E2
Ravenswood.
  Great Harwood BB6 .... 123 B6
Ravenswood Ave. FY3 .... 130 B7
Ravenswood Ave. FY4 .... 109 D5
Rawcliffe Dr. PR2 .... 94 E8
Rawcliffe Rd. 11 Chorley PR7 ...... 42 C7
Rawcliffe Rd. Ratten Row PR3 ... 154 C7
Rawcliffe St. Blackpool FY4 .... 108 F8
Rawcliffe St. Burnley BB11 .... 127 A6
Rawlinson Ct. PR9 .... 34 D8
Rawlinson Gr. PR9 .... 52 E1
Rawlinson La. PR6 .... 42 E1
Rawlinson Rd. PR9 .... 52 E1
Rawlinson St. Darwen BB3 .... 64 B6

Rawlinson St. 13 Horwich BL6 ..... 31 B4
Rawlinson St. Kirkham PR4 .... 112 F6
Raws St. BB11 .... 127 A6
Rawson Ave. BB5 .... 103 A4
Rawson St. BB11 .... 147 B1
Rawsons Rake. BL0 & BL8 .... 49 A6
Rawsthorne Ave. Edenfield BL0 .. 67 D2
Rawsthorne Ave.
  Haslingden BB4 .... 84 B2
Rawsthorne Cl. PR4 .... 92 A6
Rawstorne Rd. PR1 .... 95 B5
Rawstorne St. BB2 .... 100 C4
Rawstron St. OL12 .... 70 C1
Rawtenstall Rd. BB4 .... 84 C1
Rawtenstall St Mary's CE
  Prim Sch. BB4 .... 84 F3
Rawtenstall Sta. BB4 .... 84 F1
Rawthey Rd. 5 LA1 .... 213 D2
Ray La. PR3 .... 178 F4
Raybourne Ave. FY6 .... 151 C3
Raygarth. LA6 .... 238 B3
Raygarth La. LA6 .... 238 A3
Raygill Ave. BB1 .... 126 D3
Raygill Pl. 3 LA11 .... 213 D2
Raymond Ave. FY3 .... 129 D8
Raynor St. BB2 .... 100 D5
Rays Dr. LA1 .... 210 F3
Read CE Sch. BB12 .... 144 D2
Read St. BB5 .... 124 A1
Read's Ave. FY1 .... 129 C4
Reading Cl. 14 BB1 .... 101 A4
Reads Ct. FY1 .... 129 C4
Reaney Ave. FY4 .... 109 E7
Record St. BB8 .... 200 B1
Rectory Cl. Chorley PR7 .... 42 C8
Rectory Cl. Croston PR5 .... 57 C2
Rectory Cl. Darwen BB3 .... 64 C8
Rectory Cl. Newchurch BB4 .... 85 E1
Rectory Gdns. LA2 .... 203 C5
Rectory La. Bury BL9 .... 32 D4
Rectory La.
  Standish WN1 & WN6 .... 29 A1
Rectory Paddock. LA2 .... 214 E6
Rectory Rd. Blackpool FY4 .... 129 E1
Rectory Rd. Burnley BB12 .... 126 F7
Rectory Rd. Southport PR9 .... 53 A1
Red Bank Rd. FY2 .... 150 C4
Red Barnes. L37 .... 11 F5
Red Bridge La. LA5 .... 218 F4
Red Cat La. L40 .... 24 E7
Red Cross St. PR1 .... 95 E7
Red Delph La. WA11 .... 8 E1
Red Fold. L39 .... 15 C2
Red Hills Rd. LA5 .... 237 A1
Red House La. PR7 .... 40 B6
Red La. Colne BB8 & BB9 .... 169 B7
Red La. Eccleston PR7 .... 40 E6
Red Lees Ave. BB10 .... 127 F4
Red Lees Rd. BB10 .... 128 A2
Red Lion Cl. L31 .... 5 C1
Red Lion St. Burnley BB11 .... 127 A5
Red Lion St. Earby BB8 .... 201 C2
Red Marsh Dr. FY5 .... 173 C3
Red Marsh Sch. FY5 .... 173 B3
Red Rake. BB1 .... 100 C7
Red Sands. L39 .... 15 D3
Red Scar Ind Est. PR2 .... 118 B5
Red Scar St. BB8 .... 169 C4
Red Shell La. BB1 & BB5 .... 82 B7
Red Spar Rd. BB10 .... 147 D3
Redcar Ave. Cleveleys FY5 .... 172 F5
Redcar Ave. Fulwood PR2 .... 116 A4
Redcar Cl. PR8 .... 34 F3
Redcar Rd. Blackpool FY1 .... 129 B8
Redcar Rd. Lancaster LA1 .... 211 B3
Redcliffe Gdns. L39 .... 15 E3
Redcross St. L31 .... 51 F1
Redcross St N. OL12 .... 51 F1
Rede Ave. FY7 .... 193 C2
Redearth Rd. BB3 .... 64 A8
Redearth St. BB3 .... 64 A8
Redeswood Ave. FY5 .... 150 E8
Redfearn Wood. OL12 .... 51 B2
Redgate. Formby L37 .... 12 A2
Redgate. Ormskirk L39 .... 15 D5
Redgate Cl. BB11 .... 127 B3
Redgate Dr. L37 .... 12 B2
Redgate Prim Sch. L37 .... 12 A2
Redhill. PR4 .... 94 C1
Redhill Gn. PR6 .... 60 E3
Redhills Dr. PR8 .... 34 F3
Redisher Cl. BL8 .... 48 E3
Redisher La. BL8 .... 48 E3
Redlam. BB2 .... 100 B3
Redlam Brow. BB2 .... 100 C3
Redman Rd. BB10 .... 147 B4
Redmayne Dr. LA5 .... 217 F2
Redmayne St. 2 PR1 .... 96 D8
Redness Cl. BB9 .... 147 E6
Redruth St. LA5 .... 217 C1
Redruth St. BB12 .... 126 D6
Redsands Dr. PR2 .... 117 D5
Redstart Pl. FY5 .... 172 F1
Redvers Rd. BB3 .... 80 E5
Redvers St. Burnley BB10 .... 147 B1
Redvers St. Lancaster LA1 .... 210 F4
Redvers Terr. FY1 .... 129 B8
Redwing Ave. 1 FY5 .... 172 F4
Redwing Rd. BL8 .... 48 F2
Redwood Ave. Leyland PR5 .... 58 B9
Redwood Ave. Maghull L31 .... 5 C3
Redwood Cl. OL12 .... 51 B3
Redwood Dr. Morecambe LA4 ... 213 A5
Redwood Dr. Ormskirk L39 .... 15 D4
Redwood Dr. Rawtenstall BB4 ..... 67 F8

Reed Row. BB8 169 C3
Reed St. Bacup OL13 87 A3
Reed St. Burnley BB11 127 A4
Reedfield. Brierfield BB10 147 C4
Reedfield. Clayton Brook PR5 77 C4
Reedfield Pl. PR5 77 A6
Reedley Ave. BB9 147 F7
Reedley Dr. Brierfield BB10 147 B4
Reedley Dr. Brierfield BB10 147 C4
Reedley Gr. BB10 147 B3
Reedley Rd. BB10 & BB9 147 C5
Reedmace Wlk. LA3 212 E2
Reeds Brow. WA11 9 C1
Reeds Cl. BB4 85 A6
Reeds La. BB4 85 A6
Reeds The. L39 15 D6
Reedsholme Cl. BB4 85 A6
Reedy Acre Pl. FY8 89 F4
Reedyford Rd. BB9 168 E2
Reedymoor La. BB8 191 C1
Reeford Gr. BB7 164 D7
Rees Pk. L40 24 F4
Reeth Way. 3 BB5 102 F4
Reeval Cl. BB8 201 C2
Reeveswood. PR7 40 B6
Reform St. OL12 51 F1
Regal Ave. FY4 109 E6
Regency Ave. PR5 76 D8
Regency Cl. PR4 112 E5
Regent Ave. Colne BB8 169 E6
Regent Ave.
Lytham St Anne's FY8 89 D6
Regent Cl. Padiham BB12 125 C7
Regent Cl. Southport PR8 33 F4
Regent Ct. Blackpool FY1 129 B6
Regent Ct. Fulwood PR2 116 E5
Regent Ct. Lytham St Anne's FY8 88 D8
Regent Ct. Southport PR9 34 C8
Regent Dr. PR2 116 D4
Regent Gr. PR2 116 E5
Regent Park Ave. LA3 & LA4 212 C3
Regent Park Gr. LA4 212 D4
Regent Pk. PR2 116 E5
Regent Pl. BB9 168 E2
Regent Rd. Bamber Bridge PR5 96 D4
Regent Rd. Blackpool FY1 129 C5
Regent Rd. Chorley PR7 42 C7
Regent Rd. Church BB5 102 F7
Regent Rd. 6 Leyland PR5 76 A1
Regent Rd. Morecambe LA4 212 C3
Regent Rd. Southport PR8 33 F4
Regent Rd E. FY1 129 C5
Regent St. Bacup OL13 87 A2
Regent St. Blackburn BB1 100 E5
Regent St. Brierfield BB9 147 B5
Regent St. Coppull PR7 41 E1
Regent St. Haslingden BB4 84 B3
Regent St. Lancaster LA1 210 E7
Regent St. Longridge PR3 139 A7
Regent St. Nelson BB8 & BB9 168 F2
Regent St. Preston PR1 95 F6
Regent St. Ramsbottom BL0 49 A4
Regent St. Rochdale OL12 51 F1
Regent St. Waddington BB7 186 B4
Regents Cl. BB2 99 C2
Regents Terr. FY6 151 E3
Regents Way. PR7 59 D2
Regentsway. 6 PR5 76 E8
Reginald St. BB8 169 C5
Reigate. PR6 60 F3
Reiver Rd. PR5 75 C3
Renacres Hall. L39 22 B5
Renacres La. L39 22 B5
Rendel St. BB12 126 C7
Rendsburg Way. 15 LA1 210 F8
Renfrey Cl. L39 15 E8
Rennie Cl. PR3 178 D6
Rennie Ct. LA1 210 E5
Rennie St. BB10 127 C5
Renshaw Dr. Bamber Bridge PR5 96 E2
Renshaw Dr. Bury BL9 32 C3
Renshaw St. 9 BB10 147 B1
Renwick Ave. FY4 109 D8
Repton Ave. Blackpool FY1 129 C8
Repton Ave. Morecambe LA4 213 B4
Reservoir St. Burnley BB11 126 F4
Reservoir St. Darwen BB3 80 F1
Reta Dr. FY5 173 A3
Retford Rd. L33 1 A2
Revidge Rd. BB1 & BB2 100 C7
Revoe Sch (Jun & Inf). FY1 129 C3
Rewe Cl. BB2 80 C8
Rexington Units. BB11 126 C4
Reynolds St. Burnley BB11 126 E3
Reynolds St. Lancaster LA1 213 E1
Rhoda St. BB9 168 F1
Rhoden Rd. Leyland PR5 75 C1
Rhoden Rd. Oswaldtwistle BB5 102 D2
Rhodes Ave. Blackburn BB1 100 D8
Rhodes Ave. Haslingden BB4 67 A7
Rhodesway. PR5 97 E2
Rhuddlan Cl. BB4 84 B1
Rhyddings Cty High Sch. BB5 102 E4
Rhyddings St. BB5 102 E4
Rhyl Ave. BB1 100 E7
Rhyl St. FY7 194 B5
Ribble Ave. Brierfield BB10 147 C2
Ribble Ave. Darwen BB3 80 E4
Ribble Ave. Freckleton PR4 92 A6
Ribble Ave. Great Harwood BB6 123 E6
Ribble Ave. Maghull L31 5 E2
Ribble Ave. Southport PR9 53 C4
Ribble Ave. Whalley BB7 143 A7
Ribble Bank. PR1 95 B6
Ribble Bank St. PR1 95 E7
Ribble Brook House. PR1 116 F1
Ribble Cl. Freckleton PR4 92 A6
Ribble Cl. Penwortham PR1 95 E4
Ribble Cl. Withnell PR6 79 A1
Ribble Cres. Kirkham PR4 113 B5
Ribble Cres. Preston PR1 96 C6
Ribble Dr. Baldingstone BL9 49 F1
Ribble Dr. Hesketh Bank PR4 72 E4
Ribble Dr. West Bradford BB7 186 D7
Ribble Hall. PR1 116 F1
Ribble House. Blackburn BB1 100 F5
Ribble House. 8 Preston PR1 96 D8
Ribble La. BB7 187 D6
Ribble Lodge. FY8 90 A3
Ribble Rd. Blackpool FY1 129 C4
Ribble Rd. Fleetwood FY7 193 F4
Ribble Rd. Leyland PR5 58 D8
Ribble Rd. Shevington Moor WN6 28 B2
Ribble St. Bacup OL13 70 A8
Ribble St. Blackburn BB1 100 E6
Ribble St. Lytham St Anne's FY8 88 D6
Ribble St. Padiham BB12 125 D8
Ribble St. Preston PR1 95 E7
Ribble View. BB7 187 B7
Ribble View Cl. PR4 91 F6
Ribble Way. BB7 164 C8
Ribblesdale Ave.
Accrington BB5 103 B8
Ribblesdale Ave. Clitheroe BB7 186 E2
Ribblesdale Ave. Wilpshire BB1 122 A7
Ribblesdale Cl. Blackpool FY4 110 A8
Ribblesdale Cl. Kirkham PR4 113 A5
Ribblesdale Ct. 4 LA4 212 E5
Ribblesdale Cty High Sch.
BB7 164 E7
Ribblesdale Dr. Forton PR3 204 B3
Ribblesdale Dr. Grimsargh PR2 138 C1
Ribblesdale Pl.
Barrowford BB9 168 E6
Ribblesdale Pl. Blackburn BB2 100 C5
Ribblesdale Pl. Chorley PR7 42 B7
Ribblesdale Pl. Preston PR1 95 F6
Ribblesdale Rd. PR3 140 E3
Ribblesdale St. BB10 127 B8
Ribblesdale View. BB7 187 E5
Ribbleton Ave.
Fulwood PR1 & PR2 117 E2
Ribbleton Ave. Fulwood PR2 117 E3
Ribbleton Avenue Cty Inf Sch.
PR1 117 D2
Ribbleton Avenue Meth
Jun Sch. PR1 117 D2
Ribbleton Dr. BB5 103 C8
Ribbleton Hall Cres. 2 PR2 117 F3
Ribbleton Hall Dr. PR2 117 F3
Ribbleton Hall High Sch. PR2 117 F3
Ribbleton Hospl. PR2 117 F2
Ribbleton La. PR0 & PR1 117 C1
Ribbleton Pl. 6 PR1 96 B8
Ribbleton St. PR1 96 B8
Ribby Ave. Kirkham PR4 112 F5
Ribby Ave. Wrea Green PR4 112 C4
Ribby Pl. Blackpool FY4 130 B1
Ribby Pl. Preston PR2 115 F1
Ribby Rd. Kirkham PR4 112 F4
Ribby Rd. Wrea Green PR4 112 C4
Ribby-with-Wrea Endowed
CE Prim Sch. PR4 112 B4
Ribchester Ave. Blackpool FY4 130 B1
Ribchester Ave. Burnley BB10 127 D5
Ribchester CE Prim Sch. PR3 140 E3
Ribchester Hospl. PR3 139 F6
Ribchester Rd.
Copster Green BB1 141 A1
Ribchester Rd.
Lytham St Anne's FY8 90 D4
Ribchester Rd.
Ribchester BB6 & PR3 141 C4
Ribchester Rd. Wilpshire BB1 121 E6
Ribchester Way. BB9 147 C4
Rice Gr. FY1 129 D8
Richard Burch St. 2 BL9 32 A3
Richard Durning's Endowed
Prim Sch. L40 26 D7
Richard St. Blackburn BB2 100 D4
Richard St. Brierfield BB9 147 B5
Richard St. Burnley BB11 127 B5
Richard St. Shuttleworth BL0 49 E7
Richard St. Weir OL13 87 A7
Richard Thornton's CE
Prim Sch. LA6 236 B3
Richard's St. PR4 112 F6
Richard's Way. FY8 109 E2
Richards Rd. WN6 29 E3
Richards Way. 3 FY5 172 F1
Richardson Cl. PR4 92 C6
Richardson St. FY1 129 B4
Richmond Ave.
Barnoldswick BB8 200 A3
Richmond Ave. Burnley BB10 127 F4
Richmond Ave. Burscough L40 24 E3
Richmond Ave. Cleveleys FY5 172 E2
Richmond Ave. Haslingden BB4 84 C2
Richmond Ave. Lancaster LA1 213 F4
Richmond Ave.
Morecambe LA4 212 G4
Richmond Ave.
Wrea Green PR4 112 B3
Richmond Cl. Brinscall PR6 61 E8
Richmond Cl. Hightown L38 2 F2
Richmond Cres. BB1 101 E5
Richmond Ct. Burscough L40 24 E3
Richmond Ct. Chorley PR7 42 C6
Richmond Ct. Leyland PR5 75 B1
Richmond Gr. L31 5 E3
Richmond Hill. 23 BB1 100 E5
Richmond Hill St. BB5 103 B5
Richmond House. 12 PR1 96 A7
Richmond Ind Est. BB5 103 B5
Richmond Mews. L40 24 E3
Richmond Pk. BB3 81 A2
Richmond Rd. Accrington BB5 103 A4
Richmond Rd.
Barnoldswick BB8 200 A3
Richmond Rd. Barrowford BB9 168 C1
Richmond Rd. Blackpool FY1 129 B7
Richmond Rd. Chorley PR7 42 E6
Richmond Rd. Eccleston PR7 40 C7
Richmond Rd.
Lytham St Anne's FY8 88 E6
Richmond Rd. Southport PR8 33 F2
Richmond St. Accrington BB5 103 A5
Richmond St. Accrington BB5 103 B5
Richmond St. Burnley BB11 126 E5
Richmond St. Horwich BL6 31 B3
Richmond St. 2 Preston PR1 96 B7
Richmond Terr. 17
Blackburn BB1 & BB2 100 E5
Richmond Terr. Clitheroe BB7 164 D7
Richmond Terr. Darwen BB3 81 A2
Rickard Rd. BB9 147 E6
Ridding La. BB7 143 B5
Riddings Ave. BB10 127 F6
Riddings La. BB7 143 C6
Ridehalgh La. BB10 148 F2
Ridehalgh St. BB8 169 B3
Ridge Ave. BB10 127 D6
Ridge Cl. PR9 53 C5
Ridge Ct. Burnley BB10 127 C7
Ridge Ct. Longridge PR3 139 C8
Ridge Gr. LA3 208 F8
Ridge La. Lancaster LA1 214 A1
Ridge La. Lancaster LA1 & LA2 214 C2
Ridge La. Roughlee BB12 167 F4
Ridge Prim Sch The. LA1 214 B1
Ridge Rd. Burnley BB11 127 B6
Ridge Rd. Chorley PR7 42 E7
Ridge Row. BB10 127 D6
Ridge Sq. LA1 214 B1
Ridge St. Barnoldswick BB8 200 B2
Ridge St. Lancaster LA1 214 A1
Ridge Way. PR1 95 E4
Ridgeford Gdns. PR2 116 D5
Ridgemont. PR2 116 C6
Ridgemont Cl. BL6 31 F3
Ridgeway. Barrowford BB9 168 C3
Ridgeway. Barrowford BB9 168 D3
Ridgeway. Great Harwood BB6 123 B6
Ridgeway Ave. BB2 81 A8
Ridgeway Dr. Maghull L31 5 E3
Ridgeway Dr. Thornton FY5 151 D8
Ridgeway The. Fleetwood FY7 193 D3
Ridgeway The. Nelson BB9 147 D7
Ridgeways. BB4 84 C2
Ridgmont Dr. BL6 31 F3
Ridgway. BL6 31 F3
Ridgway Ct. FY8 89 A7
Ridgwood Ave. FY3 129 E5
Riding Barn St. BB5 102 F7
Riding Cl. BB8 200 C2
Riding Head La. BL0 49 F8
Riding La. L39 13 E4
Riding St. Burnley BB11 126 E5
Riding St. Preston PR1 116 F1
Riding St. Southport PR8 34 B6
Ridings The. Burnley BB12 126 D8
Ridings The. Lucas Green PR6 60 C6
Ridings The. Southport PR9 53 A3
Ridley La. Barber's Moor PR5 57 D5
Ridley La. Maghull L31 5 D1
Ridley La. Mawdesley L40 & PR7 39 F2
Ridley Rd. PR1 & PR2 116 C2
Ridley St. FY3 129 D5
Rifle St. BB9 84 B2
Rigby Ave. BL6 30 C2
Rigby Cl. PR4 92 C6
Rigby Rd. Blackpool FY1 129 B3
Rigby Rd. Maghull L31 5 B3
Rigby St. Colne BB8 169 C5
Rigby St. Nelson BB9 147 D8
Rigby St. Preston PR1 96 C8
Rigg La. LA2 226 B7
Rigg St. BB9 147 E8
Riley Ave. FY8 88 F5
Riley Ct. FY8 88 F4
Riley Green Switch Rd.
BB2 & PR5 78 F7
Riley St. Accrington BB5 103 B4
Riley St. Bacup OL13 86 F5
Riley St. Brierfield BB9 147 B5
Riley St. Burnley BB11 127 B4
Riley St. Earby BB8 201 B2
Rimington Ave. Accrington BB5 103 A3
Rimington Ave. Burnley BB10 127 D5
Rimington Ave. Colne BB8 169 C6
Rimington Cl. BB2 100 F2
Rimington La. BB7 188 D7
Rimington Pl.
Lytham St Anne's FY8 89 B6
Rimington Pl. Nelson BB9 169 B1
Rimmer Gn. PR8 35 D1
Rimmer's Ave. Formby L37 11 E6
Rimmer's Ave. Southport PR8 34 B6
Ring Dyke Way. FY8 90 A4
Ring Lows La. OL12 51 F4
Ring O'Bells La. L40 25 B2
Ring Way. PR0 & PR1 95 F7
Rings St. BB4 105 A2
Ringstone Cres. BB9 148 B8
Ringstones La. LA2 233 D4
Ringtail Ct. L40 24 B4
Ringtail Pl. L40 24 B4
Ringtail Rd. L40 24 B4
Rington Ave. FY6 151 B6
Ringway. Chorley PR7 42 A7
Ringway. Cleveleys FY5 172 E4
Ringwood Ave. BL0 49 A4
Ringwood Cl. FY8 89 F3
Ringwood Rd. PR1 117 C2
Ripley Cl. L31 5 E1
Ripley Dr. FY8 89 B6
Ripley St Thomas' CE
Sec Sch. LA1 210 F6
Ripon Ave. LA1 213 F4
Ripon Cl. Cleveleys FY5 172 E5
Ripon Cl. Great Eccleston PR3 154 C5
Ripon Cl. Southport PR8 34 F3
Ripon Hall Ave. BL0 49 B4
Ripon Pl. LA3 208 E6
Ripon Rd. Blackpool FY1 129 D4
Ripon Rd. Lytham St Anne's FY8 89 D5
Ripon Rd. Oswaldtwistle BB5 102 C5
Ripon St. Blackburn BB1 101 B4
Ripon St. Nelson BB9 147 D7
Ripon St. Preston PR1 116 E2
Ripon Terr. PR1 117 F1
Rise The. LA5 216 B6
Risedale Dr. PR3 139 B7
Risedale Gr. BB2 80 A7
Rishton Golf Course. BB1 102 B7
Rishton Meth Sch. BB1 123 B1
Rishton Rd. Clayton-le-M BB5 123 E3
Rishton Rd. Wilpshire BB1 122 C5
Rishton St. FY1 129 C4
Rishton Sta. BB1 102 A8
Rising Bridge Rd. BB4 & BB5 84 A7
Ritherham Ave. FY5 172 D3
River Bank Terr. BB5 124 E6
River Cl. L37 12 B1
River Dr. BB12 125 D8
River Hts. PR5 76 C8
River Par. PR1 95 D6
River Rd. FY5 173 E3
River St. Bacup OL13 86 F1
River St. Blackburn BB1 100 F4
River St. Colne BB8 169 D4
River St. Darwen BB3 80 F2
River St. Lancaster LA1 213 E1
River St. Preston PR1 95 E7
River St. Ramsbottom BL0 49 C6
River St. Trawden BB8 170 C3
River View. Glasson LA2 205 E5
River View. Tarleton PR4 56 A8
River Way. BB9 168 D4
Rivermead Ct. PR3 199 C1
Rivermead Dr. PR3 178 C8
Rivermeade. PR8 34 D4
Rivers St. WN5 10 E6
Riversedge Rd. PR5 58 C8
Riversgate. FY7 193 F4
Riverside. Bamber Bridge PR5 76 E7
Riverside. Clitheroe BB7 164 B8
Riverside. Hightown L38 2 F4
Riverside. Penwortham PR1 95 E5
Riverside. Preston PR1 95 E5
Riverside Ave. PR5 75 E4
Riverside Cl. Halton LA2 214 E6
Riverside Cl. Leyland PR5 75 E4
Riverside Cres. PR5 57 A2
Riverside Ct. OL12 70 D4
Riverside Dr. Hambleton FY6 174 B1
Riverside Dr. Ramsbottom BL0 49 B2
Riverside Ind Pk. PR3 178 C2
Riverside Mill. BB8 169 B4
Riverside Park Ind Est. LA1 214 B4
Riverside Rd. PR1 95 E5
Riverside Terr. BB8 201 B1
Riversleigh Ave. Blackpool FY1 150 C1
Riversleigh Ave.
Lytham St Anne's FY8 89 E3
Riversway. Blackpool FY3 129 F6
Riversway. Lancaster LA1 213 F2
Riversway. Poulton-le-F FY6 151 F5
Riversway. Preston PR2 & PR4 94 D8
Riversway Bsns Village. PR2 95 A8
Riversway Enterprise
Workshops. PR2 94 E8
Riversway Managed
Workshops. PR2 94 F8
Riverway Cl. PR5 76 D8
Rivington Ave. Adlington PR6 30 B7
Rivington Ave. Blackpool FY2 150 D5
Rivington & Blackrod
High Sch. BL6 31 B6
Rivington & Blackrod
High Sch (Annexe). BL6 31 B4
Rivington Cl. Poulton-le-F FY6 151 D3
Rivington Cl. Southport PR8 34 A3
Rivington Cl. Tarleton PR4 55 F8
Rivington Dr. Burscough L40 24 E3
Rivington Dr. Up Holland WN8 10 C7
Rivington Hall Cl. BL0 49 C4
Rivington La.
Grimeford Village PR6 30 D6
Rivington La. Horwich BL6 31 A7
Rivington La. Rivington BL6 43 F1
Rivington Pl. PR7 28 D6
Rivington Rd. Belmont BL6 & BL7 45 B4
Rivington Rd. Chorley PR6 60 E1
Rivington Service Area. PR6 30 E4
Rivington St. Blackburn BB1 101 B4
Rivington St. Blackrod BL6 30 D2
Rivington St. Rochdale OL12 51 F1
Roach Bridge Cotts. PR5 97 E6
Roach Rd. PR5 98 B4
Roach St. BL9 32 C2
Road La. OL12 51 D4
Roads The. LA5 217 E6
Robbin's Bridge. L31 5 E5
Robert St. Accrington BB5 103 C7
Robert St. Barnoldswick BB8 200 B2
Robert St. Blackburn BB2 100 E3
Robert St. Colne BB8 169 E5
Robert St. 13 Darwen BB3 80 F2
Robert St. Great Harwood BB6 123 D5
Robert St. 40 Lancaster LA1 210 F8
Robert St. Newchurch BB4 85 F2
Robert St. Oswaldtwistle BB5 102 D3
Robert St. Ramsbottom BL0 67 C1
Roberts Ct. LA5 217 D6
Roberts St. 1 Chorley PR7 42 C7
Roberts St. Nelson BB9 147 F8
Roberts St. 7 Rawtenstall BB4 85 A3
Robertson Ct. FY7 193 E2
Robin Bank Rd. BB3 81 A2
Robin Cl. PR7 41 D3
Robin Croft. LA2 235 A1
Robin Hey. PR5 75 B1
Robin Hill Dr. WN6 28 B2
Robin Hill La. WN6 28 C3
Robin Hood La. WN6 27 B3
Robin House La. BB10 148 C4
Robin La. High Bentham LA2 233 D8
Robin La. Hill Dale WN8 26 C5
Robin La. Rimington BB7 225 B1
Robin Rd. BL0 49 B2
Robin St. PR1 & PR2 117 D1
Robins Cl. FY6 151 A4
Robins La. Blackpool FY6 151 A4
Robins La. Carleton FY2 151 A6
Robinson La.
BB10 & BB12 & BB9 147 A4
Robinson St. Blackburn BB1 101 B7
Robinson St. Burnley BB10 127 A8
Robinson St. Chatburn BB7 187 E5
Robinson St. Colne BB8 169 C5
Robinson St. Foulridge BB8 191 D1
Robinson St. Fulwood PR2 116 D3
Robinson St. 15 Horwich BL6 31 B4
Robraine. LA6 238 C1
Robson St. BB9 147 B6
Robson Way. FY3 151 A2
Roby Mill. WN8 19 B3
Roby Mill CE Prim Sch. WN8 19 B3
Rochdale Infmy. OL12 51 F1
Rochdale Old Rd. BL9 32 D4
Rochdale Rd. Bacup OL13 87 A1
Rochdale Rd. Bury BL9 32 B2
Rochdale Rd. Edenfield BL0 67 F2
Rochdale Rd.
Shuttleworth BL0 & BL9 50 B7
Rochester Ave. Cleveleys FY5 172 F4
Rochester Ave.
Morecambe LA4 212 G3
Rochester Cl. OL13 87 A7
Rochford Ave. FY5 172 E1
Rock Bridge Fold. BB4 85 E5
Rock Brow. PR3 161 B7
Rock Fold. BL7 46 F1
Rock Hall Rd. BB4 84 B3
Rock La. Burnley BB11 127 B3
Rock La. Darwen BB3 80 A3
Rock La. Trawden BB8 170 C3
Rock n' Jock. LA2 231 B3
Rock St. Accrington BB5 103 E2
Rock St. Clitheroe BB7 164 E8
Rock St. 15 Haslingden BB4 84 B3
Rock St. Horwich BL6 31 B3
Rock St. Shuttleworth BL0 49 E7
Rock St. Thornton FY5 173 B4
Rock Terr. Arnside LA5 237 B2
Rock Terr. Egerton BL7 46 F1
Rock Terr. Pendleton BB7 165 B4
Rock Terr. 9 Rawtenstall BB4 85 A7
Rock Villa Rd. PR6 60 C8
Rock Water (Bird
Conservation Centre). BB10 128 C2
Rockburgh Cres. PR4 74 A5
Rockcliffe Ave. OL13 86 E1
Rockcliffe Dr. OL13 86 E1
Rockcliffe Rd. OL13 86 F1
Rockcliffe St. BB2 100 E2
Rockcliffe Villas. OL13 69 E8
Rockfield Gdns. L31 5 C2
Rockfield St. BB2 100 E3
Rockhaven Ave. BL6 31 C4
Rockingham Rd. FY2 150 D3
Rockliffe La. OL13 87 A1
Rockliffe Rd. OL13 86 F1
Rockliffe St. 5 BB4 85 A3
Rockville. BB9 168 E5
Rockville Ave. FY5 150 F8
Rockwood Cl. BB10 147 E3
Roddlesworth La. PR7 62 E8
Rodhill La. BB7 224 B3
Rodney Ave. FY8 109 E1
Rodney St. Blackburn BB2 100 C3
Rodney St. 4 Preston PR1 95 F8
Rodwell Wlk. FY3 129 F8
Roe Greave Rd. BB5 102 D3
Roe Hey Dr. PR7 41 F2
Roe La. PR9 34 E8
Roe Lee Park Prim Sch. BB1 121 F2
Roe Lee Pk. BB1 121 F2
Roe St. OL12 51 C1
Roebuck Cl. BB2 100 D3
Roebuck Cty Prim Sch. PR1 116 D2
Roebuck St. PR1 116 C2
Roeburn Dr. LA1 213 B2
Roeburn Pl. LA1 213 E2
Roeburn Terr. LA2 232 D6
Roeburndale Cres. LA3 209 A8
Roedean Ave. LA4 213 B4
Roedean Cl. L31 5 D2
Roefield L Ctr. BB7 164 B8
Rogerley Cl. FY8 90 A4
Rogersfield. Langho BB6 122 B8
Rogersfield. Langho BB6 122 C8
Rolleston Rd. BB2 100 B4
Roman Cres. LA2 231 C3
Roman Rd. Blackburn BB1 & BB2 81 B8
Roman Rd. Preston PR1 96 B7

Roman Rd.
Whittlestone Head BB3 .... 65 A4
Roman Road Prim Sch. BB2 .... 80 F8
Roman Way. Cleveleys FY5 .... 172 F1
Roman Way. Clitheroe BB7 .... 165 A8
Roman Way. Kirkham PR4 .... 113 C4
Roman Way. Red Scar PR2 .... 118 C6
Roman Way Ind Est. PR2 .... 118 C5
Rome Ave. BB11 .... 126 C4
Romford Rd. PR1 .... 117 C2
Romford St. BB12 .... 126 C7
Romiley Dr. WN8 .... 17 F2
Romney Ave. Barrowford BB9 .... 168 D3
Romney Ave. Blackpool FY4 ...... 129 D1
Romney Ave. Burnley BB11 .... 126 E3
Romney Ave. Fleetwood FY7 ..... 193 E3
Romney St. BB9 .... 147 D7
Romney Wlk. BB1 .... 101 C4
Romsey Ave. L37 .... 12 B2
Ronald St. Blackburn BB1 .... 101 C5
Ronald St. Burnley BB12 .... 126 A5
Ronaldsway.
Fulwood PR1 & PR2 .... 117 D3
Ronaldsway. Nelson BB9 .... 169 B2
Ronaldsway Cl. OL13 .... 87 B1
Ronbury Cl. [1] BB9 .... 168 C1
Roney St. BB2 .... 100 C5
Ronwood Cl. PR4 .... 153 F1
Ronwood Ct. FY6 .... 95 B8
Roocroft Sq. BL6 .... 30 C2
Rook Hill Rd. [2] OL13 .... 69 B8
Rook St. Barnoldswick BB8 ...... 200 B2
Rook St. Colne BB8 .... 169 D5
Rook St. Nelson BB9 .... 168 E1
Rook St. Preston PR1 .... 117 B1
Rook St. [3] Ramsbottom BL0 .... 49 C6
Rookery Ave. WN6 .... 19 E8
Rookery Cl. Chorley PR7 .... 42 A6
Rookery Cl. Penwortham PR1 .... 95 F2
Rookery Dr. PR1 .... 95 F2
Rookery Rd. Barnoldswick BB8 .. 200 C3
Rookery Rd. Southport PR9 ...... 52 F1
Rookwood. PR7 .... 40 B6
Rookwood Ave. Chorley PR7 .... 60 C2
Rookwood Ave. Cleveleys FY5 . 172 D1
Rooley Moor Rd.
Bacup OL12 & OL13 .... 69 C4
Rooley Moor Rd.
Caldershaw OL12 .... 51 A3
Rooley Moor Rd.
Spotland Fold OL12 .... 51 C1
Rooley St. OL11 & OL12 .... 51 C1
Rooley View. OL13 .... 86 E1
Roosevelt Ave. LA1 .... 210 D7
Roots La. PR4 .... 134 E2
Rope Wlk. PR3 .... 178 C7
Rosary Ave. FY4 .... 129 E1
Roscoe Lowe Brow. PR6 .... 30 D7
Rose Acre La. LA5 .... 219 F2
Rose Ave. Blackpool FY1 .... 129 D2
Rose Ave. Burnley BB11 .... 126 E4
Rose Ave. Fulwood PR2 .... 116 C3
Rose Bank. Lancaster LA1 .... 211 A5
Rose Bank. Rawtenstall BB4 .... 85 A3
Rose Bank St. OL13 .... 86 F3
Rose Cotts. FY6 .... 195 C3
Rose Cres. Ainsdale PR8 .... 20 C2
Rose Cres. Skelmersdale WN8 .. 17 E1
Rose Fold. PR1 .... 95 D4
Rose Gdns. PR4 .... 72 E4
Rose Gr. LA2 .... 206 F4
Rose Grove Sta. BB11 .... 126 B5
Rose Hill. Ramsbottom BL0 ...... 49 B6
Rose Hill. Southport PR8 & PR9 .. 34 D6
Rose Hill Ave. BB1 .... 101 A4
Rose Hill Gr. LA7 .... 237 F6
Rose Hill Rd. BB2 .... 99 C1
Rose Hill St. Bacup OL13 .... 86 F2
Rose Hill St. Darwen BB3 .... 64 B8
Rose Hill St. Rawtenstall BB4 ... 105 A1
Rose Hill Terr. BB3 .... 64 B8
Rose La. PR1 .... 117 C3
Rose Lea. PR2 .... 117 D6
Rose Pl. L39 .... 15 D2
Rose St. Accrington BB5 .... 103 B4
Rose St. Bacup OL13 .... 86 F2
Rose St. [7] Blackburn BB2 ...... 100 E3
Rose St. Darwen BB3 .... 81 B1
Rose St. Leyland PR5 .... 75 B3
Rose St. Morecambe LA4 .... 212 E6
Rose St. Newchurch BB4 .... 85 E2
Rose St. [15] Preston PR1 .... 96 A7
Rose Terr. PR1 .... 116 B2
Rose Vale St. BB4 .... 85 B2
Roseacre. FY4 .... 109 C5
Roseacre Dr. PR4 .... 154 A1
Roseacre Pl.
Lytham St Anne's FY8 .... 89 B8
Roseacre Pl. Preston PR2 .... 115 E1
Roseacre Rd. PR4 .... 133 D6
Rosebank. PR2 .... 115 C1
Rosebank Ave. [3] FY4 .... 109 C5
Rosebay Ave. BB2 .... 79 D8
Rosebay Cl. L37 .... 12 A3
Roseberry Ave. PR4 .... 115 E5
Roseberry Cl. BL0 .... 49 C3
Roseberry Ave. OL14 .... 108 B1
Rosebery Ave. Blackpool FY4 ... 109 B6
Rosebery Ave. Lancaster LA1 ... 211 A5
Rosebery Ave.
Lytham St Anne's FY8 .... 89 B4
Rosebery Ave. Morecambe LA4 . 212 F4
Rosebery St. Burnley BB10 ..... 147 B2
Rosebery St. Southport PR9 .... 35 A6
Rosecroft. L39 .... 15 E6
Rosedale Ave. Blackpool FY4 .. 130 A2
Rosedale Ave. Heysham LA3 ... 209 A8
Rosedale St. BB4 .... 84 F5

Rosegarth. LA2 .... 213 F7
Rosegrove La. BB12 .... 126 B5
Rosegrove Prim Sch. BB12 ..... 126 A6
Rosehill Ave. Burnley BB11 ..... 126 E4
Rosehill Ave. [9] Nelson BB9 ... 168 F1
Rosehill Dr. L39 .... 15 C2
Rosehill Inf Sch. BB11 .... 126 F3
Rosehill Jun Sch. BB11 .... 126 E3
Rosehill Rd. Burnley BB11 ...... 126 F3
Rosehill Rd. Nelson BB8 .... 169 A2
Roseland Ave. BB9 .... 147 C6
Roseland Cl. L31 .... 5 B4
Roselea Dr. PR9 .... 53 C4
Roselyn Ave. FY4 .... 109 C5
Rosemary Ave. Blackpool FY4 .. 109 C5
Rosemary Ave. Cleveleys FY5 . 172 F3
Rosemary Ct. PR1 & PR4 .... 95 C2
Rosemary La. Formby L37 ...... 11 F3
Rosemary La. Haskayne L39 .... 14 B4
Rosemary La. [8] Lancaster LA1 210 F8
Rosemary La. Swillbrook PR4 .. 135 A1
Rosemeade Ave. PR5 .... 76 B8
Rosemere Ave. FY4 .... 129 F2
Rosemount. OL13 .... 87 A4
Rosemount Ave.
Barnoldswick BB8 .... 200 A3
Rosemount Ave. Burnley BB11 . 126 E4
Rosemount Ave.
Knott End-on-S FY6 .... 195 A5
Rosendale Cl. OL13 .... 87 B3
Rosendale Cres. OL13 .... 87 B3
Roseway. Blackpool FY4 .... 109 C5
Roseway. Lytham St Anne's FY8 .. 89 B6
Roseway. Nelson BB9 .... 147 A4
Roseway. Poulton-le-F FY6 .... 151 C3
Roseway. Preston PR1 .... 116 B4
Rosewood Ave. Blackburn BB1 . 100 F8
Rosewood Ave. Burnley BB12 .. 126 F1
Rosewood Ave. Haslingden BB4 . 84 C3
Rosewood Ave.
Higher Walton PR5 .... 97 C3
Rosewood Cl.
Lytham St Anne's FY8 .... 89 E4
Rosewood Cl. Thornton FY5 .... 173 D1
Rosewood Dr. PR5 .... 97 B3
Roshaw. PR2 .... 138 C1
Rosklyn Rd. PR7 .... 42 E7
Rosley St. BB8 .... 170 B5
Ross St. Brierfield BB9 .... 147 B5
Ross St. Darwen BB3 .... 64 A6
Rossall Cl. Coupe Green PR5 ... 97 E3
Rossall Cl. Fleetwood FY7 ...... 172 B8
Rossall Cl. Padiham BB12 .... 125 D6
Rossall Ct. FY7 .... 193 E3
Rossall Dr. PR2 .... 116 C4
Rossall Gate. FY7 .... 172 C8
Rossall Gdns. FY5 .... 172 D4
Rossall Grange La. FY7 .... 193 D3
Rossall Hospl. FY7 .... 172 C8
Rossall La. FY7 .... 172 E7
Rossall Rd. Blackpool FY3 ...... 129 D7
Rossall Rd. Chorley PR6 .... 60 E1
Rossall Rd. Cleveleys FY5 ...... 172 D3
Rossall Rd. Fulwood PR2 .... 116 C4
Rossall Rd. Lancaster LA1 ...... 213 C2
Rossall Rd.
Lytham St Anne's FY8 .... 89 D4
Rossall Sch. FY7 .... 172 C6
Rossall St. PR1 .... 116 C1
Rossall Terr. BB2 .... 100 E1
Rossendale Ave. Burnley BB11 . 126 E1
Rossendale Ave.
Morecambe LA4 .... 212 F6
Rossendale Ave N. FY5 .... 173 B2
Rossendale Ave S. FY5 .... 173 B1
Rossendale General Hospl.
BB4 .... 84 D2
Rossendale Golf Course. BB4 .. 67 B7
Rossendale Rd. Burnley BB11 .. 126 C3
Rossendale Rd.
Lytham St Anne's FY8 .... 89 A7
Rossendale Sch. BL0 .... 50 A7
Rosser Ct. [13] BB9 .... 147 E8
Rossett Ave. FY4 .... 130 C1
Rossetti Ave. BB1 .... 126 F3
Rossington Ave. FY2 .... 150 E5
Rosslyn Ave. FY6 .... 195 A6
Rosslyn Cres. FY6 .... 195 B5
Rosslyn Cres E. FY6 .... 195 B5
Rossmoyne Rd. LA1 .... 211 A4
Rostle Top Rd. BB8 .... 201 B1
Rostrevor Cl. PR5 .... 75 B1
Rostron Cl. L37 .... 11 E1
Rostron Rd. BL0 .... 49 B6
Rostron's Bldgs. BB4 .... 85 D1
Rothay Ave. FY7 .... 193 D2
Rothbury Pl. FY7 .... 90 C4
Rotherwick Ave. PR7 .... 42 B7
Rothesay Cres. LA3 .... 208 D5
Rothesay Rd. Blackburn BB1 ... 101 D3
Rothesay Rd. Brierfield BB9 .... 147 C6
Rothesay Rd. Heysham LA3 .... 208 D5
Rothley Ave. PR8 .... 20 A4
Rothsay Rd. LA3 .... 208 E5
Rothwell Ave. BB5 .... 103 C4
Rothwell Cl. L39 .... 15 D5
Rothwell Cres. PR2 .... 117 F4
Rothwell Ct. PR5 .... 76 A2
Rothwell Dr. Ainsdale PR8 ...... 20 A4
Rothwell Dr. Ormskirk L39 ...... 15 B2
Rothwell Lodge. [5] PR2 .... 117 F4
Rothwell Rd. PR6 .... 30 B7
Rothwell St. BL0 .... 49 B6
Rotten Row. Caton LA2 .... 231 D3
Rotten Row. Southport PR8 .... 33 F6
Rough Hey Pl. PR2 .... 118 B7
Rough Hey Rd. PR2 .... 118 B7
Rough Heys La. BB5 .... 103 A2

Rough Heys La. FY4 .... 109 E7
Rough Hill La. BL9 .... 32 E4
Rough Lea Rd. FY5 .... 172 D2
Rough Lee Rd. BB5 .... 103 C4
Roughlee Gr. BB10 .... 127 D5
Roughlee Prim Sch. BB12 ...... 167 F4
Roughlee Terr. BB11 .... 105 B4
Roughwood Dr. L33 .... 1 A4
Round Acre. Bamber Bridge PR5 . 96 A1
Round Acre.
Nab's Head BB2 & PR5 .... 98 E7
Round Barn. BL7 .... 65 B3
Round Hill Pl. BB10 .... 127 E1
Round Meade The. L31 .... 5 C2
Round Meadow. PR5 .... 75 C1
Round Wood. PR1 .... 95 C7
Roundel St. BB10 .... 147 B2
Roundell Rd. BB8 .... 200 C3
Roundhay. FY4 .... 109 F8
Roundhill La. BB4 .... 84 A7
Roundhill Rd. BB4 & BB5 .... 83 E6
Roundhill View. BB5 .... 84 A6
Roundway. FY7 .... 172 C8
Roundway Down. PR2 .... 116 C7
Roundway The. L38 .... 2 F3
Roundwood Ave. BB10 .... 147 A4
Row The. Knowley PR7 .... 61 D3
Row The. Silverdale LA5 .... 218 E3
Rowan Ave. Fulwood PR2 .... 118 A4
Rowan Ave. [2] Horwich BL6 .... 31 E1
Rowan Ave. Oswaldtwistle BB5 102 D2
Rowan Cl. Blackburn BB1 .... 122 B1
Rowan Cl. Bonds PR3 .... 178 D6
Rowan Cl. Caldershaw OL12 ... 51 B3
Rowan Cl. Penwortham PR1 .... 95 B3
Rowan Croft. PR6 .... 77 B1
Rowan Gr. PR6 .... 60 C3
Rowan La. WN8 .... 18 B4
Rowan Tree Cl. BB5 .... 103 D7
Rowangate. PR2 .... 117 C2
Rowans The. Aughton L39 ...... 6 A7
Rowans The. Poulton-le-F FY6 . 151 A2
Rowberrow Cl. PR2 .... 117 D6
Rowen Pk. BB2 .... 100 B8
Rowland Ave. BB9 .... 148 A8
Rowland Cl. FY5 .... 172 F2
Rowland La. PR5 .... 172 F2
Rowland St. BB5 .... 103 A5
Rowlands Rd. BL9 .... 49 D2
Rowntree Ave. FY7 .... 193 F3
Rowsley Rd. FY8 .... 88 D7
Rowton Heath. PR2 .... 116 C7
Roxburgh Rd. FY4 .... 110 A6
Roxton Cl. BL6 .... 31 B5
Roy St. OL14 .... 108 A1
Royal Albert Hospl. LA1 .... 210 F5
Royal Ave. Blackpool FY3 ...... 129 F3
Royal Ave. Fulwood PR2 .... 116 E6
Royal Ave. Kirkham PR4 .... 113 B4
Royal Ave. Leyland PR5 .... 58 E7
Royal Bank Rd. FY3 .... 129 E3
Royal Beach Ct. FY8 .... 88 D7
Royal Birkdale Golf Links. PR8 33 D3
Royal Cl. BB10 .... 12 A1
Royal Cres. L37 .... 12 A1
Royal Cross Prim Sch. PR2 .... 115 E1
Royal Cross Sch for the Deaf.
PR1 .... 118 A1
Royal Ct. BB10 .... 147 F3
Royal Fold. LA2 .... 208 E8
Royal Gram Sch. LA1 .... 211 A8
Royal Lancaster Infmy. LA1 ... 210 F7
Royal Lytham St Anne's
Golf Course. FY8 .... 89 B5
Royal Oak Ave. BB1 .... 121 E1
Royal Oak Meadow. LA2 .... 232 B8
Royal Pl. FY8 .... 89 C8
Royal Preston Hospl The. PR2 116 F7
Royal Rd. LA4 .... 212 F6
Royal Terr. PR8 .... 34 A7
Royal Troon Ct. PR4 .... 113 A4
Royalty Ave. PR4 .... 95 A1
Royalty Gdns. PR4 .... 75 A8
Royalty La. PR4 .... 75 A8
Royalty Mall. LA4 .... 212 D5
Royds Ave. Accrington BB5 .... 103 C3
Royds Ave. Morecambe LA3 ... 212 A2
Royds Gr. LA3 .... 212 A1
Royds Rd. OL13 .... 69 A7
Royds St. Accrington BB5 ...... 103 C4
Royds St. Bury BL9 .... 32 D4
Royds St. Lytham St Anne's FY8 .. 88 E5
Royle Rd. Burnley BB11 & BB12 . 126 F6
Royle Rd. Burnley BB12 .... 126 F7
Royle Rd. Chorley PR7 .... 42 C8
Royle St. FY1 .... 129 B1
Roylen Ave. FY6 .... 151 B5
Royles Brook Cl. FY5 .... 173 B3
Royles Brook Prim Sch. FY5 .. 173 A2
Royles Ct. FY5 .... 173 B2
Roynton Rd. BL6 .... 31 B7
Royshaw Ave. BB1 .... 100 E8
Royshaw Cl. BB1 .... 100 E8
Royston Cl. BL8 .... 48 F1
Royston Rd. FY6 .... 151 F5
Ruby St. Blackburn BB1 .... 121 F2
Ruby St. Ramsbottom BL0 & BL9 ... 49 B7
Rudd St. BB4 .... 84 A3
Ruddington Rd. PR8 .... 34 E2
Rudman St. OL12 .... 51 E2
Rudyard Ave. WN6 .... 28 E2
Rudyard Dr. BB3 .... 64 D8
Rudyard Pl. Blackpool FY3 ..... 129 F7
Rudyard Pl.
Lytham St Anne's FY8 .... 88 B7
Ruff La. L39 & L40 .... 16 B4
Rufford Ave. L31 .... 5 E3

Rufford CE Prim Sch. L40 ..... 38 B4
Rufford Dr. PR9 .... 53 F5
Rufford Hospl. L40 .... 38 B5
Rufford Rd. Bispham Green L40 . 38 B1
Rufford Rd. Lytham St Anne's FY8 89 D5
Rufford Rd. Southport PR9 ..... 53 C4
Rufford Sta. L40 .... 38 D4
Rufus St. PR1 .... 117 C2
Rugby Ave. BB5 .... 103 C7
Rugby Dr. WN5 .... 10 F8
Rugby St. [7] FY4 .... 129 D1
Rumley Rd. BB1 .... 127 A4
Runcorn Ave. FY2 .... 150 F2
Rundle Rd. PR2 .... 116 D3
Runnel The. L39 .... 22 B1
Runnymede Ave. FY5 .... 172 D2
Runshaw Ave. WN6 .... 19 E8
Runshaw Coll. PR5 .... 59 B6
Runshaw La.
Euxton PR7 .... 59 B3
Runshaw La.
Runshaw Moor PR7 & PR5 .. 58 E3
Rupert St. Carnforth LA5 .... 217 D3
Rupert St. Nelson BB9 .... 147 C7
Rupert St. Spotland Fold OL12 . 51 C1
Rush Hey Bank. BB11 .... 106 D8
Rushbed Cotts. BB4 .... 85 A6
Rushbed Dr. BB4 .... 85 A6
Rushden Rd. L32 .... 1 A1
Rushes Farm Cl. BB5 .... 102 C4
Rushley Dr. LA2 .... 215 D1
Rushley Way. LA2 .... 215 D1
Rushton Ave. BB8 .... 201 B1
Rushton Cl. BB9 .... 169 B2
Rushton St. [4] Bacup OL13 ... 69 E8
Rushton St. Barrowford BB9 ... 168 D3
Rushton St. Great Harwood BB6 123 B4
Rushworth Bldgs. 69 C8
Rushworth St. E. [6] BB10 ..... 147 B1
Rushworth St W. [7] BB10 ..... 147 B1
Rushy Field. BB5 .... 123 F5
Rushy Hey. PR5 .... 76 A7
Rushy Hill View. OL12 .... 51 C1
Ruskin Ave. Blackpool FY1 .... 129 B2
Ruskin Ave. Colne BB8 .... 169 D6
Ruskin Ave. Leyland PR5 .... 76 A1
Ruskin Ave. Oswaldtwistle BB5 . 102 C5
Ruskin Ave. Padiham BB12 .... 125 E7
Ruskin Ave. Thornton FY5 ..... 173 A3
Ruskin Cl. PR4 .... 55 F6
Ruskin Dr. Kirkby Lonsdale LA6 . 238 C2
Ruskin Dr. Morecambe LA4 .... 213 A6
Ruskin Gr. Bolton-le-S LA5 .... 216 A5
Ruskin Gr. Hapton BB12 .... 125 C4
Ruskin House. LA1 .... 213 E4
Ruskin Rd. Freckleton PR4 ..... 92 B6
Ruskin Rd. [2] Lancaster LA1 .. 213 F3
Ruskin St. Burnley BB10 .... 147 A2
Ruskin St. Preston PR1 .... 96 B6
Rusland Ave. FY4 .... 130 D1
Rusland Dr. PR5 .... 97 E4
Ruslands Gdns. LA4 .... 212 F4
Russel St. OL13 .... 86 F4
Russell Ave. Cleveleys FY5 .... 150 D8
Russell Ave. Colne BB8 .... 169 D6
Russell Ave. Leyland PR5 & PR6 . 59 C8
Russell Ave. Preston PR1 ...... 95 A7
Russell Ave. Southport PR9 .... 35 A7
Russell Ct. Burnley BB11 ...... 127 A5
Russell Ct. Lytham St Anne's FY8 . 88 F6
Russell Ct. Southport PR9 ..... 53 B4
Russell Pl. BB6 .... 123 B5
Russell Rd. Carnforth LA5 ..... 217 E1
Russell Rd. Southport PR9 ..... 35 A6
Russell Sq. PR6 .... 60 D1
Russell Sq W. PR6 .... 60 D1
Russell St. Accrington BB5 .... 103 C5
Russell St. Blackburn BB1 & BB2 100 E3
Russell St. [37] Lancaster LA1 .. 210 F8
Russell St. [6] Nelson BB9 ..... 147 D8
Russell Terr. BB12 .... 125 D7
Russia St. BB5 .... 102 F6
Ruth St. Bury BL9 .... 32 A4
Ruth St. Edenfield BL0 .... 67 D2
Ruth St. Whitworth OL12 .... 70 D1
Rutherford Pl. FY8 .... 109 B4
Ruthin Cl. BB1 .... 100 E7
Rutland Ave. Bamber Bridge PR5 96 D3
Rutland Ave. Blackburn BB1 ... 101 E4
Rutland Ave. Burnley BB12 .... 126 A6
Rutland Ave. Cleveleys FY5 ... 172 E3
Rutland Ave. Fleetwood FY7 ... 193 F3
Rutland Ave. Freckleton PR4 ... 92 C7
Rutland Ave. Lancaster LA1 ... 211 A5
Rutland Ave. Poulton-le-F FY6 . 151 C3
Rutland Cl. Clayton-le-M BB5 .. 123 F3
Rutland Cl. Garstang PR3 ...... 178 B8
Rutland Cres. L39 .... 15 E7
Rutland Ct. FY8 .... 89 D5
Rutland Pl. [5] BB12 .... 125 D7
Rutland St.
Lytham St Anne's FY8 .... 89 D5
Rutland St. Southport PR8 ..... 34 D5
Rutland St. Accrington BB5 .... 102 F5
Rutland St. Blackburn BB2 .... 100 B3
Rutland St. Colne BB8 .... 169 F5
Rutland St. [1] Nelson BB9 ..... 168 F1
Rutland St. Preston PR1 .... 96 C8
Rutland Wlk. BB4 .... 67 A8
Ryburn Ave. Blackburn BB2 ... 100 B6
Ryburn Ave. Blackpool FY4 ... 129 E1
Ryburn Rd. L39 .... 15 E4
Rycliffe St. BB12 .... 145 C1
Rydal Ave. Bamber Bridge PR5 .. 96 D2
Rydal Ave. Blackpool FY1 ...... 129 C3
Rydal Ave. Darwen BB3 .... 64 A8
Rydal Ave. Fleetwood FY7 ..... 193 E4

Rydal Ave. Formby L37 .... 11 D3
Rydal Ave. Freckleton PR4 ..... 92 A5
Rydal Ave. Freckleton PR4 ..... 92 A6
Rydal Ave. Orrell WN5 .... 10 C7
Rydal Ave. Penwortham PR1 ... 95 C3
Rydal Ave. Poulton-le-F FY6 ... 151 D3
Rydal Ave. Thornton FY5 .... 173 B1
Rydal Cl. Accrington BB5 .... 124 D1
Rydal Cl. Blackrod BL6 .... 30 C3
Rydal Cl. Fulwood PR2 .... 117 C4
Rydal Cl. Padiham BB12 .... 145 C1
Rydal Gr. Knott End-on-S FY6 . 194 F6
Rydal Gr. Morecambe LA3 ..... 212 A2
Rydal Mount. BB1 .... 81 F6
Rydal Pl. Chorley PR7 .... 42 C6
Rydal Pl. Colne BB8 .... 170 A5
Rydal Rd. Blackburn BB1 .... 101 A7
Rydal Rd. Hambleton FY6 ...... 174 C2
Rydal Rd. Haslingden BB4 ...... 67 C8
Rydal Rd. West Bank LA5 ...... 215 F4
Rydal Rd. Lancaster LA1 .... 211 A8
Rydal Rd. Lytham St Anne's FY8 . 88 E8
Rydal Rd. Morecambe LA3 ..... 212 A2
Rydal Rd. Preston PR1 .... 117 D2
Rydal St. BB10 .... 147 A2
Ryddingwood. PR1 .... 95 B6
Ryde Cl. BB4 .... 84 C1
Ryden Ave. Cleveleys FY5 ..... 172 D3
Ryden Ave. Leyland PR5 & PR6 . 76 C1
Ryden Rd. BB1 .... 121 D6
Ryder Cl. L39 .... 15 C2
Ryder Cres. Ormskirk L39 ...... 15 C1
Ryder Cres. Southport PR8 ..... 20 E7
Ryding's La. PR9 .... 54 D8
Rydinge The. L37 .... 12 A6
Rydings The. BB6 .... 142 A1
Rye Moss La. L37 & L38 .... 4 B8
Rye St. PR1 .... 117 A1
Ryecroft. PR6 .... 61 A7
Ryecroft Ave. FY6 .... 174 C1
Ryecroft La. BL7 .... 45 C5
Ryefield. PR6 .... 61 A7
Ryefield Ave. Haslingden BB4 .. 84 B2
Ryefield Ave. Penwortham PR1 . 95 D2
Ryefield Ave W. BB4 .... 84 B2
Ryefield Pl. BB4 .... 84 B2
Ryeground La. L37 .... 12 A5
Ryeheys Rd. FY8 .... 88 E8
Ryelands Cres. PR2 .... 94 E8
Ryelands Cty Prim Sch. LA1 .. 213 D2
Ryelands Rd. LA1 .... 213 E2
Ryland Ave. FY6 .... 151 C3
Rylands Rd. PR7 .... 42 B7
Rylands St. BB10 .... 147 B1
Ryldon Pl. FY4 .... 130 A2
Rylstone Dr. Barnoldswick BB8 . 200 A2
Rylstone Dr. Morecambe LA3 .. 212 A1
Rymers Gn. L37 .... 11 E4
Ryson Ave. FY4 .... 129 F1

Sabden Cty Prim Sch. BB7 .... 144 F8
Sabden Pl. FY8 .... 89 C7
Sabden Rd. Higham BB12 ...... 145 F6
Sabden Rd. Sabden BB12 ...... 145 B4
Sabden Rd. Whalley BB7 .... 144 A4
Sabden Wlk. BB8 .... 100 F2
Saccary La. BB1 .... 121 A4
Sackville Gdns. BB9 .... 147 A5
Sackville St. Barnoldswick BB8 . 200 B3
Sackville St. Blackpool FY4 .... 109 C6
Sackville St. Brierfield BB9 .... 147 B5
Sackville St. Burnley BB11 .... 126 F5
Sackville St. [6] Bury BL9 ...... 32 A3
Sackville St. Chorley PR7 ...... 42 E7
Sackville St. Nelson BB9 .... 147 F7
Sacred Heart RC Prim Sch.
Blackburn BB2 .... 100 B6
Sacred Heart RC Prim Sch.
Chorley PR6 & PR7 .... 42 E7
Sacred Heart RC Prim Sch.
Church BB5 .... 102 F6
Sacred Heart RC Prim Sch.
Colne BB8 .... 169 D7
Sacred Heart RC Prim Sch.
Preston PR1 .... 116 C1
Sacred Heart RC Prim Sch.
Thornton FY5 .... 173 B3
Saddler Nook La. LA6 .... 235 C8
Sadler St. [4] BB5 .... 102 F5
Saer Cl. FY7 .... 193 D2
Saffron Cl. [4] BB9 .... 168 C1
Sagar Dr. PR4 .... 92 A2
Sagar Fold. L39 .... 6 D8
Sagar Holme Terr. BB4 .... 85 E5
Sagar La. OL14 .... 108 D3
Sagar St. Eccleston PR7 .... 40 C6
Sagar St. Nelson BB9 .... 147 E8
Sage Ct. PR1 .... 95 C2
Sage La. PR1 .... 117 B3
Sahara Fold. [1] BB1 .... 101 A7
Sailsbury Cl. FY6 .... 194 F5
St Aidan's Ave. Blackburn BB2 . 100 D2
St Aidan's Ave. Darwen BB3 ... 64 B8
St Aidan's CE High Sch. FY6 .. 195 B3
St Aidan's CE Prim Sch.
Bamber Bridge PR5 .... 96 F1
St Aidan's CE Prim Sch.
Blackburn BB2 .... 100 C2
St Aidan's Cl. BB2 .... 100 C1
St Aidan's Rd. PR5 .... 96 E2
St Alban's Ct. [2] BB1 .... 100 F6
St Alban's RC Prim Sch. BB1 . 100 F6
St Alban's Rd. Blackpool FY1 .. 129 D4
St Alban's Rd. Darwen BB3 .... 80 E4

St Alban's Rd.
Lytham St Anne's FY8 .... 88 F7
St Albans Rd. Morecambe LA4 ...... 213 B6
St Albans Rd. Rishton BB1 .... 102 A8
St Ambrose Terr. 5 PR5 .... 76 B2
St Andrew's Ave. Cleveleys FY5 172 D2
St Andrew's Ave. Preston PR2 .. 116 B2
St Andrew's CE Prim Sch.
Blackburn BB2 .... 80 B8
St Andrew's CE Prim Sch.
Leyland PR5 .... 58 F8
St Andrew's CE Prim Sch.
Oswaldtwistle BB5 .... 102 D4
St Andrew's CE Prim Sch.
Preston PR1 .... 116 B1
St Andrew's CE Prim Sch.
Ramsbottom BL0 .... 49 B5
St Andrew's Cl. Leyland PR5 ...... 59 A7
St Andrew's Cl.
Oswaldtwistle BB5 .... 102 D4
St Andrew's Cl.
Ramsbottom BL0 .... 49 C4
St Andrew's Cl. BB5 .... 102 D3
St Andrew's Pl. Blackburn BB1 100 D6
St Andrew's Pl. Southport PR8 .. 34 B6
St Andrew's Rd. RB1 .... 117 A2
St Andrew's Rd N. FY8 .... 88 E7
St Andrew's Rd S. FY8 .... 88 F6
St Andrew's St. Blackburn BB1 100 D6
St Andrew's St. 4
Burnley BB10 .... 147 B1
St Andrews Gr. LA4 .... 212 G6
St Andrews Maghull CE
Prim Sch. L31 .... 5 D1
St Andrews Way. PR5 .... 59 A8
St Ann's Sq. BB7 .... 164 C8
St Ann's St. 5 BB2 .... 100 E3
St Anne Edgeside CE
Church & Day Sch. BB4 .... 85 F3
St Anne's Ave. LA4 .... 213 B5
St Anne's CE Prim Sch. PR4 .... 135 D2
St Anne's Cl. Caton LA2 .... 231 C3
St Anne's Cl. Formby L37 .... 11 F6
St Anne's Coll Jun Sch. FY8 .... 88 E5
St Anne's Cres. BB4 .... 85 F3
St Anne's Ct. WN6 .... 19 F5
St Anne's Dr. BB12 .... 146 D7
St Anne's Old Links
Golf Course. FY8 .... 109 D2
St Anne's Path. L37 .... 11 F6
St Anne's Pl. 18 LA1 .... 210 F8
St Anne's RC Inf Sch. BB5 ...... 103 D5
St Anne's RC Prim Sch.
Blackburn BB2 .... 100 D4
St Anne's RC Prim Sch.
Leyland PR5 .... 58 D8
St Anne's RC Prim Sch.
Ormskirk L39 .... 15 E4
St Anne's Rd. Formby L37 .... 11 F6
St Anne's Rd. Leyland PR5 .... 76 C3
St Anne's Rd. Ormskirk L39 ...... 15 D4
St Anne's Rd E. FY8 .... 88 F7
St Anne's Rd W. FY8 .... 88 E6
St Anne's St. Padiham BB12 .... 125 C7
St Anne's St. Preston PR1 .... 117 A2
St Anne's Sta. FY8 .... 88 E7
St Anne's War Meml Hospl.
FY8 .... 89 A8
St Anne's Way. BB12 .... 146 D7
St Annes Cl. 3 Blackpool FY4 .. 109 D7
St Annes Cl. 5 Church BB5 .... 102 E5
St Annes Ct. FY4 .... 129 C1
St Annes Rd. Blackpool FY4 .... 109 D7
St Annes Rd. 4
Chorley PR6 & PR7 .... 42 E7
St Annes Rd.
Great Eccleston PR3 .... 154 C5
St Annes Rd. Horwich BL6 .... 31 C4
St Annes Rd. Southport PR9 .... 52 F4
St Anselm's RC Prim Sch.
OL12 .... 70 D2
St Anthony's Cl. PR2 .... 116 C4
St Anthony's Cres. PR2 .... 116 C4
St Anthony's Dr. PR2 .... 116 C4
St Anthony's Pl. FY1 .... 129 C7
St Anthony's RC Prim Sch.
PR2 .... 116 C4
St Anthony's Rd. PR1 .... 117 A2
St Anthonys Pl. PR4 .... 113 A4
St Antony's RC Sch. BB1 ...... 101 C3
St Augustine's RC High Sch.
BB6 .... 143 A4
St Augustine's RC Prim Sch.
Burnley BB12 .... 126 B6
St Augustine's RC Prim Sch.
Preston PR1 .... 96 A7
St Austell Dr. BL8 .... 48 F2
St Austell Pl. LA5 .... 216 C8
St Austin's Pl. PR1 .... 96 A7
St Austin's Rd. PR1 .... 96 A7
St Barnabas CE Prim Sch. BB3 64 C6
St Barnabas' Pl. PR1 .... 116 A4
St Barnabas St. Blackburn BB2 100 C5
St Barnabas St. Darwen BB3 .. 64 B6
St Barnabas' & St Paul's CE
Prim Sch. BB2 .... 100 D5
St Bartholomew Parish
CE Sch. BB6 .... 123 C6
St Bartholomew's CE
Prim Sch. Blackburn BB2 .... 80 D8
St Bartholomew's CE
Prim Sch. Whitworth OL12 ...... 51 C8
St Bede's Ave. FY1 .... 129 B1
St Bede's RC High Sch.
Blackburn BB2 .... 80 A8

St Bede's RC High Sch.
Lytham St Anne's FY8 .... 90 C4
St Bede's RC High Sch.
Ormskirk L39 .... 15 D4
St Bedes Cl. L39 .... 15 D3
St Bee's Cl. BB2 .... 100 F1
St Bernadette's RC Prim Sch.
FY2 .... 150 D5
St Bernadettes Sch. LA1 .... 211 B4
St Bernard Ave. FY3 .... 129 F7
St Bernard's RC Prim Sch.
PR2 .... 115 C1
St Bernard's Rd. FY6 .... 194 E6
St Brides Cl. BL6 .... 31 A4
St Catherine's CE Prim Sch.
BL6 .... 31 B3
St Catherine's Dr. PR2 .... 116 C4
St Catherine's RC Prim Sch.
PR5 .... 76 C2
St Catherines Cl. PR5 .... 76 C2
St Catherines Ct. 25 LA1 ...... 210 F8
St Cecilia St. BB6 .... 123 D5
St Cecilio's RC High Sch. PR3 139 A6
St Celia's Way. LA4 .... 213 A6
St Chad's Ave. BB7 .... 187 D5
St Chad's Dr. LA1 .... 213 D3
St Chad's RC Prim Sch. PR6 .... 60 F6
St Chad's Rd. Blackpool FY1 .. 129 B2
St Chad's Rd. Preston PR1 ...... 117 C1
St Chads Cl. FY6 .... 151 D2
St Charles' RC Prim Sch. BB1 123 B1
St Charles' Rd. BB1 .... 123 B1
St Christines Ave. PR5 .... 76 C4
St Christopher's CE High Sch.
BB5 .... 103 A7
St Christopher's Rd. PR1 ...... 117 A2
St Christopher's Way. LA4 .... 212 G6
St Clair Dr. PR9 .... 53 A1
St Clair Rd. BL8 .... 48 F3
St Clare's RC Prim Sch. PR2 .. 116 F7
St Clares Ave. PR2 .... 117 A6
St Clement St. Blackburn BB1 . 101 B4
St Clement St. Blackburn BB1 . 101 B5
St Clement's Ave. FY3 .... 129 E5
St Clements Ave. PR5 .... 76 C3
St Clements Cl. 3 BB1 .... 101 B4
St Clements Cl. BB9 .... 168 C3
St Crispin Way. BB4 .... 84 A2
St Cuthbert St. BB10 .... 147 C2
St Cuthbert's CE (Aided)
Prim Sch. L39 .... 22 B1
St Cuthbert's CE
Prim Sch. BB3 .... 80 E3
St Cuthbert's Cl. Fulwood PR2 116 D3
St Cuthbert's CE Prim Sch.
Lytham St Anne's FY8 .... 90 A3
St Cuthbert's Cl. Southport PR9 . 53 A2
St Cuthbert's RC Prim Sch.
FY4 .... 109 C8
St Cuthbert's Rd.
Bamber Bridge PR5 .... 96 A1
St Cuthbert's Rd. Preston PR1 117 A2
St Cuthbert's Rd. Southport PR9 53 A2
St Cuthberts Cl. BB3 .... 80 E3
St David's Ave. Blackburn BB2 . 79 E7
St David's Ave. Cleveleys FY5 .. 172 D2
St David's Gr. FY8 .... 88 D8
St David's Rd. Leyland PR5 ...... 76 C2
St David's Rd. Preston PR1 .... 117 A2
St David's Rd N. FY8 .... 88 D8
St David's Rd S. FY8 .... 88 F6
St Edmund Hall Cl. BL0 .... 49 C4
St Edmund's RC Prim Sch.
Fleetwood FY7 .... 172 E8
St Edmund's RC Prim Sch.
Skelmersdale WN8 .... 17 F1
St Edmund's Rd. FY4 .... 129 C1
St Edmund's St. BB6 .... 123 D5
St Edward's RC Prim Sch. BB3 80 E4
St Frances Cl. 2 BB1 .... 100 F3
St Francis CE Prim Sch. BB2 .. 99 F1
St Francis Ct. PR2 .... 117 A7
St Francis' Rd. BB2 .... 100 A2
St Francis's RC Prim Sch.
PR3 .... 159 A2
St Gabriel Cl. WN8 .... 19 C3
St Gabriel's Ave. BB1 .... 121 F3
St Gabriel's CE Prim Sch.
BB1 .... 121 E2
St George Ct. FY1 .... 129 D6
St George's Ave. Blackburn BB2 100 B1
St George's Ave. Cleveleys FY5 172 D2
St George's Ave.
Lytham St Anne's FY8 .... 88 E7
St George's CE Prim Sch. PR7 42 E5
St George's High Sch. FY4 .... 110 A8
St George's La. Cleveleys FY5 . 172 D2
St George's La.
Lytham St Anne's FY8 .... 88 E6
St George's Pl. PR8 & PR9 .... 34 B7
St George's Quay. LA1 .... 213 E1
St George's Rd. Blackpool FY4 . 109 C6
St George's Rd. Formby L37 .. 11 E4
St George's Rd. Hightown L38 ...... 2 C1
St George's Rd.
Lytham St Anne's FY8 .... 88 E6
St George's Rd. Preston PR1 .. 117 A2
St George's Sh Ctr. 6 PR4 .... 95 F7
St George's Sq. FY8 .... 88 D7
St George's St. PR6 & PR7 .... 42 C7
St George's Terr. BB4 .... 69 A6
St Georges Rd. BB9 .... 147 F7
St Georges Terr. BB3 .... 80 F1
St Gerrard's Rd. PR5 .... 96 A1
St Giles St. 6 BB2 .... 145 C1
St Gregory Rd. PR1 .... 117 B2
St Gregory's Pl. PR7 .... 42 C5
St Gregory's RC Inf Sch. L31 ...... 5 C4

St Gregory's RC Jun Sch. L31 ...... 5 C4
St Gregory's RC Prim Sch.
Chorley PR7 .... 42 C5
St Gregory's RC Prim Sch.
Fulwood PR1 .... 117 B3
St Helen's CE Sch. LA3 .... 209 D1
St Helen's Cl. PR3 .... 178 A2
St Helen's Rd.
Clayton Green PR6 .... 77 C1
St Helen's Rd. Overton LA3 .. 205 E8
St Helens Rd. BB5 .... 102 F3
St Helens Rd. Ormskirk L39 .... 15 F4
St Helens Rd. Scarth Hill L39 .. 16 A2
St Helier Cl. BB2 .... 80 C8
St Helier's Pl. PR3 .... 136 A7
St Heliers Rd. FY1 .... 129 C1
St Hilda's Cl. PR7 .... 42 C4
St Hilda's RC Girls' Sch.
BB11 .... 126 C3
St Hilda's Rd. FY8 .... 88 D8
St Hubert's Rd. BB6 .... 123 C4
St Hubert's St. BB6 .... 123 D5
St Ignatius' Pl. 6 PR1 .... 96 A8
St Ignatius's RC Prim Sch. PR1 . 96 A8
St Ignatius' Sq. 5 PR1 .... 96 A8
St Ives Ave. Blackpool FY1 .. 129 E3
St Ives Ave. Freckleton PR4 .... 92 A6
St Ives Cres. PR2 .... 116 A4
St Ives Rd. BB12 .... 101 D4
St Jame's CE Prim Sch. BB3 .... 81 B2
St Jame's Terr. PR5 .... 98 E7
St James CE Prim Sch.
Blackburn BB3 .... 81 A7
St James CE Prim Sch.
Brindle PR6 .... 77 F5
St James CE Prim Sch.
Leyland PR5 .... 58 B8
St James Cl. Bamber Bridge PR5 76 B8
St James Cl. Church BB5 ...... 102 E7
St James Cl. 3 Haslingden BB4 . 84 B3
St James Cl. Scarth Hill L40 .. 16 C3
St James' Cres. BB3 .... 81 B2
St James Ct. 6 Lancaster LA1 . 210 E8
St James Ct. 4 BB11 .... 127 A6
St James Mews. BB5 .... 102 E7
St James Pl. 3 BB12 .... 125 D8
St James' RC Prim Sch.
Orrell WN5 .... 10 D4
St James' RC Prim Sch.
Skelmersdale WN8 .... 18 B4
St James' Rd. 12
Barnoldswick BB8 .... 200 B2
St James Rd. Blackpool FY4 .. 109 C6
St James Rd. Church BB5 .... 102 E7
St James' Rd. Orrell WN5 ...... 10 D4
St James Row. BB4 .... 85 A3
St James Sq. 16 Bacup OL13 .. 86 F3
St James' Sq. 11
Barnoldswick BB8 .... 200 B2
St James' St. Accrington BB5 . 103 B5
St James St. Bacup OL13 ...... 86 F2
St James St. Blackburn BB2 .. 100 C1
St James St. 1 Rawtenstall BB4 85 A3
St James St. Southport PR8 .... 34 B6
St James St. Waterfoot BB4 .... 68 E8
St James's CE Sch. BB7 ...... 164 E7
St James's Dr. LA6 .... 234 B7
St James's Gdns. PR5 .... 58 B8
St James's Pl. Blackburn BB1 . 100 E7
St James's Pl. 6 Chorley PR7 .. 42 E7
St James's Rd. Blackburn BB1 . 100 E7
St James's Rd. Preston PR1 .. 116 F2
St James's Row. 12 BB11 .... 126 F6
St James's St. Brierfield BB9 .. 147 B5
St James's St. 7 Chorley PR7 .. 42 E7
St James's St. Clitheroe BB7 .. 164 E7
St James-the-Less RC
Prim Sch. BB4 .... 85 A3
St Jerome's RC Prim Sch. L37 11 C3
St John Ave. FY7 .... 193 D2
St John Bosco RC
Prim Sch. L30 .... 5 B2
St John RC Jun Sch. BB10 .... 147 C3
St John Rigby RC Coll. WN5 .... 19 F2
St John Southworth RC
Prim Sch. BB9 .... 147 D7
St John St. Bacup OL13 .... 86 F3
St John St. Colne BB8 .... 169 E5
St John St. Horwich BL6 .... 31 B3
St John Stone RC Prim Sch.
PR8 .... 20 D2
St John the Baptist RC Sch.
BB12 .... 125 C7
St John Vianney RC Sch. FY1 129 E2
St John with St Michael CE
Prim Sch. OL12 .... 70 E5
St John's Ave. Darwen BB3 .... 64 B8
St John's Ave. Morecambe LA3 . 212 B2
St John's Ave. Poulton-le-F FY6 151 E5
St John's Ave. Silverdale LA5 .. 218 C3
St John's Ave. Thornton FY5 .. 173 D1
St John's CE Meth Prim Sch.
PR6 .... 61 E7
St John's CE Prim Sch.
Accrington BB5 .... 103 C4
St John's CE Prim Sch.
Burscough Bridge L40 .... 24 F5
St John's CE Prim Sch.
Coppull Moor PR7 .... 28 D6
St John's CE Prim Sch.
Galgate LA2 .... 207 A3
St John's CE Prim Sch.
Oakenclough PR3 .... 220 C1

St John's Cl. Accrington BB5 .. 103 E2
St John's Cl. 5 Rawtenstall BB4 85 A7
St John's Cl. Read BB12 .... 144 D2
St John's Cl. 6 Bacup OL13 .... 86 F3
St John's Cl. Burnley BB12 .. 126 C6
St John's Ct.
Lytham St Anne's FY8 .... 90 C3
St John's Gn. PR5 .... 75 E1
St John's Gr. Morecambe LA3 . 212 B2
St John's Gr. Silverdale LA5 .. 218 C3
St John's Mkt. FY1 .... 129 C5
St John's Pl. Nelson BB9 ...... 148 A8
St John's Pl. 17 Preston PR1 .... 96 A7
St John's Prim Sch.
Blackburn FY1 .... 129 C5
St John's Prim Sch.
Great Harwood BB6 .... 123 C4
St John's RC Inf Sch. BB10 .. 147 B1
St John's Rd. Burnley BB12 .. 126 C6
St John's Rd. Morecambe LA3 . 212 A2
St John's Rd. Padiham BB12 .. 125 C7
St John's Rd. Southport PR8 .... 33 F1
St John's Rd. Walton-le-D PR5 . 96 D5
St John's Rd. St Darwen BB3 .. 64 B8
St John's St.
Great Harwood BB6 .... 123 C4
St John's St.
Lytham St Anne's FY8 .... 90 C3
St John's St. Newchurch BB4 .. 68 F8
St John's Terr. LA3 .... 212 F2
St Johns Ave. Kirkham PR4 .. 112 F4
St Johns Ave.
Smallwood Hey PR3 .... 196 C5
St Johns' CE Prim Sch. BB1 .. 100 E7
St Johns Cl. PR6 .... 60 B7
St Johns RC Prim Sch. WN8 .. 18 C1
St Johns Wood. FY8 .... 89 E3
St Joseph's Con Ctr. WN8 .... 19 B2
St Joseph's Inf Sch. PR6 ...... 60 D1
St Joseph's RC Prim Sch.
Adlington PR6 .... 30 D8
St Joseph's RC Prim Sch.
Bacup OL13 .... 86 D1
St Joseph's RC Prim Sch.
Barnoldswick BB8 .... 200 B3
St Joseph's RC Prim Sch.
Chorley PR6 .... 60 D2
St Joseph's RC Prim Sch.
Darwen BB3 .... 64 A8
St Joseph's RC Prim Sch.
Gregson Lane PR5 .... 97 E1
St Joseph's RC Prim Sch.
Hurst Green BB7 .... 162 F1
St Joseph's RC Prim Sch.
Kirkham PR4 .... 112 F7
St Joseph's RC Prim Sch.
Lancaster LA1 .... 213 F3
St Joseph's RC Prim Sch.
Preston PR1 .... 117 C1
St Joseph's RC Prim Sch.
Ramsbottom BL0 .... 49 B6
St Joseph's RC Prim Sch.
Shevington Moor WN6 .... 28 A3
St Joseph's RC Prim Sch.
Withnell PR6 .... 79 A1
St Joseph's RC Sch. BL6 .... 31 E1
St Joseph's & St Bede's RC
Prim Sch. BL9 .... 32 B4
St Joseph's Terr. 1 PR1 ...... 117 C1
St Josephs Cl. FY3 .... 129 E5
St Jude's RC Prim Sch. PR5 .. 96 D1
St Judes Ave. PR5 .... 76 C4
St Katherines Dr. BL6 .... 30 C3
St Kentigern's Sch. FY3 .... 129 D5
St Lames Lodge. FY8 .... 89 A5
St Laurence's CE Prim Sch.
PR7 .... 60 C1
St Lawrence Ave. BB2 .... 100 B8
St Lawrence CE Prim Sch.
PR3 .... 136 B7
St Lawrence St. BB6 .... 123 C5
St Lawrence's Ave. PR3 .... 136 B8
St Leger Ct. 10 BB5 .... 103 C5
St Leonard Ct. 3 LA1 .... 214 A1
St Leonard's Ave. BB6 .... 31 F1
St Leonard's CE Cty Prim Sch.
BB12 .... 145 C1
St Leonard's CE Prim Sch.
PR5 .... 96 C4
St Leonard's CE Sch. BB6 .... 142 E2
St Leonard's Cl. PR2 .... 116 A3
St Leonard's Ct. FY8 .... 88 D8
St Leonard's Gate. LA1 .... 210 F8
St Leonard's Rd. FY3 .... 130 A3
St Leonard's Rd E. FY8 .... 88 E8
St Leonard's Rd W. FY8 .... 88 D8
St Leonard's St. 7 BB12 ...... 145 C1
St Louis Ave. FY3 .... 129 F7
St Luke & St Philip's CE
Prim Sch. BB2 .... 100 D3
St Luke's CE Prim Sch.
Formby L37 .... 11 D1
St Luke's CE Prim Sch.
Lancaster LA1 .... 213 F3
St Luke's CE Sch. LA2 .... 231 E8
St Luke's Church Rd. L37 & L38 ... 2 C8
St Luke's Dr. Formby L37 .... 11 C2
St Luke's Dr. Orrell WN5 .... 10 E4
St Luke's Gr. PR9 .... 34 E7
St Luke's Pl. 9 PR1 .... 96 A7
St Luke's RC Prim Sch. WN8 .... 9 E6
St Luke's Rd. Blackpool FY4 .. 109 C6
St Luke's Rd. Southport PR9 .. 34 D7
St Margaret's Ct. 1
Blackburn BB1 .... 101 B5
St Margaret's Ct.
Fleetwood FY7 .... 194 A4
St Margaret's Gdns. BB11 .... 125 C4

St Margaret's Rd.
Bolton-le-S LA5 .... 216 B6
St Margaret's Rd. Leyland PR5 .. 76 C2
St Margaret's Rd.
Morecambe LA4 .... 212 G6
St Margarets Cl. PR2 .... 116 A4
St Margarets Way. BB1 .... 101 B5
St Maria Goretti RC Prim Sch.
PR2 .... 117 F5
St Marie's RC Jun Mix Inf Sch.
L33 .... 1 A3
St Marie's RC Prim Sch.
Southport PR8 .... 34 B8
St Marie's RC Prim Sch.
Standish WN6 .... 28 E2
St Mark's CE Prim Sch.
Bury BL9 .... 32 A4
St Mark's CE Prim Sch.
Scarisbrick L40 .... 22 D7
St Mark's Pl. Blackburn BB2 .. 100 B4
St Mark's Pl. Blackpool FY3 .. 129 E8
St Mark's Pl E. PR1 .... 95 D8
St Mark's Pl W. PR1 .... 95 D8
St Mark's Rd. Blackburn BB2 .. 100 B4
St Mark's Rd. Preston PR1 .... 95 D8
St Marks RC Prim Sch. WN8 ...... 9 E8
St Marlow Ave. PR5 .... 76 C3
St Martin's Cl. FY5 .... 172 F2
St Martin's Coll. LA1 .... 211 B6
St Martin's Dr. BB2 .... 79 D8
St Martin's Rd. Blackpool FY4 . 109 C6
St Martin's Rd. Lancaster LA1 . 211 A7
St Martin's Rd. Preston PR1 .. 117 A2
St Martins Cl. FY6 .... 151 B5
St Mary Magdalen RC
Prim Sch. PR1 .... 95 E4
St Mary Magdalen's CE
Prim Sch. BB5 .... 103 B7
St Mary Magdalene's RC
Prim Sch. BB12 .... 126 D8
St Mary's Ave.
Bamber Bridge PR5 .... 96 D1
St Mary's Ave.
Barnoldswick BB8 .... 200 D3
St Mary's CE Prim Sch.
Eccleston PR7 .... 40 C6
St Mary's CE Prim Sch.
Hawkshaw BL8 .... 48 C2
St Mary's CE Prim Sch.
Mellor BB2 .... 120 D2
St Mary's CE Prim Sch.
Spen Brook BB12 .... 167 C3
St Mary's Cl. PR5 .... 96 D1
St Mary's Ct. Clayton-le-M BB5 .. 123 F2
St Mary's Ct. Preston PR1 ...... 96 B8
St Mary's Dr. BB6 .... 142 D1
St Mary's Gate. Burnley BB11 . 127 B5
St Mary's Gate. Euxton PR7 .... 59 C3
St Mary's Gdns. Mellor BB2 .. 120 E2
St Mary's Gdns. Southport PR8 .. 20 F7
St Mary's Par. LA1 .... 210 E8
St Mary's Pl. BB4 .... 84 F2
St Mary's RC High Sch. FY3 .. 129 F7
St Mary's RC Prim Sch.
Accrington BB5 .... 102 F4
St Mary's RC Prim Sch.
Bacup OL13 .... 87 B2
St Mary's RC Prim Sch.
Burnley BB10 .... 127 B6
St Mary's RC Prim Sch.
Chipping PR3 .... 182 E3
St Mary's RC Prim Sch.
Chorley PR7 .... 42 A7
St Mary's RC Prim Sch.
Clayton-le-M BB5 .... 123 F3
St Mary's RC Prim Sch.
Euxton PR7 .... 59 C3
St Mary's RC Prim Sch.
Great Eccleston PR3 .... 154 B5
St Mary's RC Prim Sch.
Haslingden BB4 .... 84 C2
St Mary's RC Prim Sch.
Horwich BL6 .... 31 B4
St Mary's RC Prim Sch.
Horwich BL6 .... 31 D2
St Mary's RC Prim Sch.
Leyland PR5 .... 75 F1
St Mary's RC Prim Sch.
Morecambe LA4 .... 212 F6
St Mary's RC Prim Sch.
Osbaldeston BB2 .... 120 D4
St Mary's RC Primary Sch.
PR4 .... 114 F2
St Mary's RC Sch.
Fleetwood FY7 .... 194 A5
St Mary's RC Sch. Langho BB6 . 142 C1
St Mary's RC Sch. Langho BB6 142 D2
St Mary's RC Sch. Leyland PR5 . 58 F7
St Mary's RC Sch. Sabden BB7 144 F7
St Mary's Rd. Bamber Bridge PR5 96 E1
St Mary's Rd.
Great Eccleston PR3 .... 154 B5
St Mary's Rd. Heysham LA3 .. 208 E8
St Mary's Sixth Form Coll.
BB1 .... 100 E2
St Mary's St. Clitheroe BB7 .. 186 E1
St Mary's St. Nelson BB9 .... 147 C8
St Mary's St. Preston PR1 ...... 96 B8
St Mary's & St Benedicts RC
Prim Sch. PR5 .... 96 E1
St Mary's & St Joseph's RC
Prim Sch. BB1 .... 100 F3
St Mary's St N. 7 PR1 .... 96 B8
St Mary's Terr. 6 BB4 .... 85 A2
St Mary's Way. BB4 .... 85 A2
St Marys Cl. Blackburn BB1 .. 101 B5
St Marys Cl. Longridge PR3 .. 139 A8
St Marys Cl. 8 Preston PR1 .... 96 C8

St Marys Prim Sch. LA6 — 238 B2
St Marys Wharfe. BB1 — 100 F3
St Matthew's RC Prim Sch. WN8 — 9 D7
St Matthew St. BB11 — 126 E5
St Matthew's CE Prim Sch. BB1 — 100 F4
St Matthew's CE Sch. PR1 — 96 D8
St Michael & All Angels CE Prim Sch. BB8 — 169 E8
St Michael Rd. L39 — 5 F7
St Michael & St John's RC Prim Sch. BB7 — 164 E8
St Michael with St John CE Prim Sch. BB1 — 100 E6
St Michael's CE High Sch. PR7 — 60 C1
St Michael's CE Prim Sch. Croston PR5 — 57 B1
St Michael's CE Prim Sch. Croston PR5 — 57 C2
St Michael's CE Prim Sch. Kirkham PR4 — 113 B5
St Michael's Cl. Blackburn BB2 — 79 E7
St Michael's Cl. Bolton-le-S LA5 — 216 A4
St Michael's Cl. Chorley PR7 — 60 B1
St Michael's Cl. Southport PR9 — 52 F3
St Michael's Cres. LA5 — 216 A4
St Michael's Ct. Barrowford BB9 — 168 C2
St Michael's Ct. [1] Blackburn BB1 — 100 F6
St Michael's Gr. Bolton-le-S LA5 — 216 A4
St Michael's Gr. Morecambe LA4 — 212 F4
St Michael's La. LA5 — 216 A4
St Michael's on Wyre CE Prim Sch. PR3 — 155 C6
St Michael's Pl. Bolton-le-S LA5 — 216 A4
St Michael's Pl. Newsham PR3 — 136 B5
St Michael's Rd. Duncombe PR3 — 156 D4
St Michael's Rd. Leyland PR5 — 76 C3
St Michael's Rd. Preston PR1 — 117 A2
St Michael's St. BB1 — 100 F7
St Michaels Pk. L39 — 6 A7
St Michaels Rd. Blackpool FY2 — 150 D3
St Michaels Rd. Kirkham PR4 — 113 C5
St Mildred's Way. LA3 — 208 E6
St Monica's Way. FY4 — 130 D1
St Nicholas Arcs. [13] LA1 — 210 F8
St Nicholas' Ave. LA1 — 144 F8
St Nicholas' CE Prim Sch. Blackpool FY4 — 110 A4
St Nicholas' CE Prim Sch. Church BB5 — 102 F7
St Nicholas Cres. LA5 — 216 B6
St Nicholas Gr. PR4 — 112 B4
St Nicholas La. LA5 — 216 A6
St Nicholas Rd. Blackpool FY4 — 110 B5
St Nicholas Rd. Church BB5 — 102 F7
St Ogg's Rd. LA4 — 212 F3
St Oswald St. LA1 — 211 A6
St Oswald's CE Prim Sch. BB1 — 101 E4
St Oswald's Cl. Blackburn BB1 — 101 E4
St Oswald's Cl. Preston PR1 — 117 C2
St Oswald's RC Prim Sch. Accrington BB5 — 103 A3
St Oswald's RC Prim Sch. Coppull PR7 — 28 D8
St Oswald's RC Prim Sch. Longton PR4 — 74 B2
St Oswald's Rd. BB1 — 101 E4
St Patrick's RC Prim Sch. Heysham LA3 — 209 A8
St Patrick's RC Prim Sch. Rochdale OL12 — 51 F1
St Patrick's RC Prim Sch. Southport PR9 — 53 A2
St Patrick's RC Prim Sch. Walton-le-D PR5 — 96 E4
St Patrick's Rd N. FY8 — 88 E7
St Patrick's Rd S. FY8 — 88 F6
St Patrick's Wlk. LA3 — 208 E7
St Paul's Ave. Blackburn BB2 — 100 D5
St Paul's Ave. Lytham St Anne's FY8 — 89 B4
St Paul's Ave. Preston PR1 — 117 A1
St Paul's CE Prim Sch. Adlington PR6 — 30 A7
St Paul's CE Prim Sch. Bury BL9 — 32 B4
St Paul's CE Prim Sch. Hoddlesden BB3 — 81 F1
St Paul's CE Prim Sch. Nelson BB9 — 147 D6
St Paul's CE Prim Sch. Oswaldtwistle BB5 — 102 E4
St Paul's CE Prim Sch. Ramsbottom BL0 — 49 C6
St Paul's CE Prim Sch. Warton PR4 — 91 D6
St Paul's Cl. Adlington PR6 — 30 A8
St Paul's Cl. Clitheroe BB7 — 164 C8
St Paul's Ct. [3] Burnley BB11 — 126 F5
St Paul's Ct. [12] Oswaldtwistle BB5 — 102 E4
St Paul's Ct. [9] Preston PR1 — 96 A8
St Paul's Dr. Caton LA2 — 231 D3
St Paul's Dr. Lancaster LA1 — 210 F5
St Paul's Pas. PR8 — 34 A6
St Paul's RC Prim Sch. BB2 — 79 D8
St Paul's Rd. Fleetwood FY7 — 129 B8
St Paul's Rd. Lancaster LA1 — 210 F5
St Paul's Rd. Nelson BB9 — 147 E6
St Paul's Rd. Preston PR0 & PR1 — 117 A1
St Paul's Rd. [1] Rishton BB1 — 123 A1

St Paul's Sq. Preston PR1 — 96 A8
St Paul's Sq. Southport PR8 — 34 A6
St Paul's St. Blackburn BB2 — 100 D5
St Paul's St. Bury BL9 — 32 A3
St Paul's St. Clitheroe BB7 — 164 C8
St Paul's St. Oswaldtwistle BB5 — 102 E4
St Paul's St. [4] Ramsbottom BL0 — 49 C6
St Paul's St. Southport PR8 — 34 A6
St Paul's Terr. Clitheroe BB7 — 164 C8
St Paul's Terr. Hoddlesden BB3 — 81 E2
St Paul's Villas. BL9 — 32 A3
St Pauls Cl. PR5 — 75 F7
St Peter St. Blackburn BB2 — 100 E4
St Peter St. [2] Rishton BB1 — 123 A1
St Peter's Ave. Formby L37 — 11 D4
St Peter's Ave. Haslingden BB4 — 84 B2
St Peter's CE Prim Sch. Accrington BB5 — 103 A2
St Peter's CE Prim Sch. Burnley BB11 — 127 A6
St Peter's CE Prim Sch. Chorley PR6 — 60 E2
St Peter's CE Prim Sch. Darwen BB3 — 64 B8
St Peter's CE Prim Sch. Formby L37 — 12 A5
St Peter's CE Prim Sch. Fulwood PR2 — 116 F7
St Peter's Cl. Darwen BB3 — 64 B8
St Peter's Cl. Formby L37 — 11 D4
St Peter's Cl. [1] Preston PR4 — 95 F8
St Peter's Cl. Salesbury BB1 — 121 D6
St Peter's Pl. Fleetwood FY7 — 194 B4
St Peter's Pl. [6] Haslingden BB4 — 84 B2
St Peter's Prim Sch. LA3 — 208 E7
St Peter's RC Cath. LA1 — 211 A8
St Peter's RC High Sch. WN5 — 10 F7
St Peter's RC Inf Sch. BB2 — 100 B2
St Peter's RC Jun Sch. BB2 — 100 B2
St Peter's RC Prim Sch. Lytham St Anne's FY8 — 90 C5
St Peter's RC Prim Sch. Newchurch BB4 — 85 E2
St Peter's Rd. Lancaster LA1 — 211 A8
St Peter's Rd. Newchurch BB4 — 85 E2
St Peter's Rd. Southport PR8 — 34 A3
St Peter's Sq. [8] PR1 — 95 E8
St Peter's St. Chorley PR6 — 60 E1
St Peter's St. [2] Preston PR1 — 95 F8
St Peter's St Paul's CE Prim Sch. BB1 — 123 A2
St Philip St. BB10 — 147 A1
St Philip's CE Prim Sch. BB9 — 147 E8
St Philip's Prim Sch. PR8 — 34 C5
St Philip's Rd. PR1 — 117 A2
St Philip's St. Blackburn BB2 — 100 B3
St Philip's St. [13] Nelson BB9 — 168 E1
St Pius X Prep Sch. PR2 — 116 E4
St Richards RC Prim Sch. WN8 — 17 D1
St Saviour's CE Prim Sch. PR5 — 76 F7
St Saviour's Cl. PR5 — 76 F7
St Saviour's Cty Prim Sch. OL13 — 69 F8
St Saviours Cl. OL13 — 86 F1
St Silas's CE Jun Sch. BB2 — 100 B6
St Silas's Rd. BB2 — 100 B6
St Stephen's Ave. [11] Blackburn BB1 — 101 A7
St Stephen's Ave. Blackpool FY2 — 150 B2
St Stephen's CE Inf Sch. BB1 — 101 B7
St Stephen's CE Jun Sch. BB1 — 101 B7
St Stephen's CE Prim Sch. PR1 — 95 E6
St Stephen's Prim Sch. BB11 — 127 B4
St Stephen's Rd. [8] Blackburn BB1 — 101 A7
St Stephen's Rd. Hightown L38 — 2 F4
St Stephen's Rd. Preston PR1 — 117 A2
St Stephen's Rd. Preston PR1 — 117 B2
St Stephen's Rd. Standish WN6 — 28 C1
St Stephen's St. [4] BB11 — 127 B4
St Stephen's Way. BB8 — 169 F6
St Stephens' CE Prim Sch. PR9 — 54 A6
St Stephens Rd. PR4 — 112 F4
St Teresa's Ave. FY5 — 172 D1
St Teresa's RC Inf Sch. PR8 — 34 A4
St Teresa's RC Prim Sch. Cleveleys FY5 — 172 D1
St Teresa's RC Prim Sch. Penwortham PR1 — 95 A5
St Teresa's RC Prim Sch. Preston PR1 — 117 E1
St Teresa's RC Prim Sch. Up Holland WN8 — 19 B1
St Theodore's RC High Sch. BB10 — 127 B7
St Theresa's Dr. PR2 — 116 C4
St Thomas' CE Prim Sch. BB1 — 101 B5
St Thomas' CE Prim Sch. Bury BL9 — 32 B1
St Thomas' CE Prim Sch. Garstang PR3 — 178 B6
St Thomas' CE Prim Sch. Lytham St Anne's FY8 — 88 F6
St Thomas CE Prim Sch. Maghull L31 — 5 D4
St Thomas Cl. BB4 — 67 A7
St Thomas Cl. [3] BL9 — 32 A2
St Thomas More Wlk. LA1 — 210 D8
St Thomas' Pl. PR1 — 116 F1
St Thomas Rd. Kirkham PR4 — 113 A4
St Thomas' Rd. Lytham St Anne's FY8 — 88 F6
St Thomas' Rd. Preston PR1 — 117 A2
St Thomas' St. Blackburn BB1 — 100 B4

St Thomas' St. Preston PR1 — 116 F1
St Thomas the Martyr CE Prim Sch. WN8 — 10 B7
St Thomas's Ct. WN8 — 10 C7
St Thomas's Rd. Chorley PR7 — 42 C8
St Thomas's Rd. Rawtenstall BB4 — 85 A7
St Thomas's Sq. [4] PR7 — 42 C8
St Veronica's RC Prim Sch. BB7 — 67 B7
St Vincent Ave. FY3 — 129 E3
St Vincent RC Prim Sch. OL12 — 51 A1
St Vincent's Way. BB8 — 34 A4
St Vincents Rd. FY2 — 116 F5
St Walburga's Rd. FY3 — 129 F7
St Walburge Ave. PR1 — 95 E8
St Walburges Gdns. PR1 — 95 E8
St Wifrid's CE Inf & Jun Sch. FY4 — 130 C1
St Wilfred's CE Jun & Inf Schs. WN6 — 28 F1
St Wilfred's Dr. OL12 — 51 D4
St Wilfred's RC Sch. PR1 — 95 F7
St Wilfrid St. [7] PR3 — 139 A7
St Wilfrid's CE (Lower) Sch. BB2 — 100 D4
St Wilfrid's CE Prim Sch. LA2 — 214 E7
St Wilfrid's CE (Upper) Sch. BB2 — 100 D3
St Wilfrid's Pk. LA2 — 214 E7
St Wilfrid's RC Prim Sch. PR3 — 139 A8
St Wilfrid's Rd. WN6 — 28 E1
St Wilfrid's Sch. LA2 — 214 E6
St Wilfrid's Terr. PR3 — 139 A7
St Wilfrid's Way. WN6 — 28 E1
St Wulstan's RC Sch. FY7 — 193 E3
St Wulston's Prim Sch. BB6 — 123 C5
Salcombe Ave. FY2 — 150 F2
Salcombe Dr. PR9 — 53 A5
Salcombe Rd. FY8 — 109 C1
Salem Ct. PR9 — 34 E8
Salem St. PR3 — 84 B3
Salerno St. BB11 — 126 C4
Sales's La. BL9 — 50 B3
Salesbury CE Prim Sch. BB1 — 121 D7
Salford. BB1 — 100 E5
Salford Rd. Ainsdale PR8 — 20 C5
Salford Rd. Galgate LA2 — 207 A3
Salford St. BL9 — 32 A4
Salisbury Ave. FY6 — 194 E5
Salisbury Rd. Blackpool FY1 — 129 D4
Salisbury Rd. Brinscall PR6 & PR7 — 61 F8
Salisbury Rd. Darwen BB3 — 80 E3
Salisbury Rd. Horwich BL6 — 31 F1
Salisbury Rd. Lancaster LA1 — 210 D8
Salisbury Rd. Preston PR1 — 95 D7
Salisbury St. [3] Chorley PR6 — 42 D7
Salisbury St. Colne BB8 — 169 E5
Salisbury St. Great Harwood BB6 — 123 E6
Salisbury St. [12] Haslingden BB4 — 84 B3
Salisbury St. [5] Preston PR0 & PR1 — 117 D1
Salisbury St. Southport PR9 — 35 A6
Sallowfields. WN5 — 10 D5
Sally's La. PR9 — 53 B2
Salmesbury Ave. FY2 — 150 C2
Salmon St. PR1 — 96 C1
Salmsbury Hall Cl. BL0 — 49 C4
Salop Ave. FY2 — 150 C4
Salt Aire Sports Ctr. LA1 — 213 C1
Salt Ayre La. Lancaster LA1 — 213 B2
Salt Ayre La. Lancaster LA1 — 213 D1
Salt Marsh Cl. FY6 — 174 B1
Salt Marsh La. FY6 — 174 B1
Salt Pie La. LA6 — 238 C2
Salt Pit La. L40 & PR7 — 39 F3
Saltash Rd. FY7 — 173 B5
Saltburn St. BB12 — 126 B6
Saltcotes Pl. FY8 — 90 D4
Saltcotes Rd. Lytham St Anne's FY8 — 90 D4
Saltcotes Rd. Lytham St Anne's FY8 — 90 D7
Salter Fell Rd. LA1 — 213 D2
Salter St. PR1 — 116 F1
Salterford La. BB10 — 128 A4
Salterforth La. Barnoldswick BB8 — 200 E2
Salterforth La. Salterforth BB8 — 191 D7
Salterforth Prim Sch. BB8 — 191 D8
Salterforth Rd. BB8 — 201 A1
Salthill Ind Est. BB7 — 187 A2
Salthill Rd. BB7 — 186 F1
Salthill View. BB7 — 186 F1
Salthouse Ave. FY1 — 129 C3
Saltpit La. L31 — 5 E1
Salus St. BB10 — 147 C1
Salwick Ave. FY2 — 150 D5
Salwick Cl. PR9 — 52 F5
Salwick Pl. Lytham St Anne's FY8 — 89 A8
Salwick Pl. Preston PR2 — 115 E1
Salwick Rd. PR4 — 134 B3
Salwick Sta. PR4 — 114 C5
Sambourn Fold. PR8 — 20 A5
Samlesbury Aerodrome. BB2 — 119 F3
Samlesbury Prim Sch. PR5 — 118 D1
Samuel St. Bury BL9 — 32 A3
Samuel St. Preston PR1 — 96 D8
Sand Beds La. BL0 & OL12 — 68 B5
Sand Castle. FY4 — 109 A8
Sand La. LA5 — 217 C4
Sandbank Gdns. OL12 — 70 C2
Sandbeds La. LA2 — 232 A8
Sandbrook Gdns. WN5 — 10 D5
Sandbrook Rd. Ainsdale PR8 — 20 D4

Sandbrook Rd. Orrell WN5 — 10 C5
Sandbrook Way. PR8 — 20 C3
Sanderling Cl. FY5 — 150 F8
Sanderling Rd. L33 — 1 A3
Sanders Gr. LA4 — 212 D4
Sanderson La. PR7 — 27 A8
Sanderson St. [9] BL9 — 32 A3
Sandersons Way. FY4 — 109 F8
Sandfield. FY5 — 173 A2
Sandfield House. [6] LA1 — 211 A3
Sandfield St. L31 — 87 A1
Sandfield St. [7] PR5 — 76 B1
Sandford Rd. WN5 — 10 C5
Sandgate. Blackpool FY4 — 109 D5
Sandgate. Chorley PR7 — 42 D5
Sandgate. Lytham St Anne's FY8 — 88 C7
Sandham St. BB3 — 64 B5
Sandheys Dr. PR9 — 52 F1
Sandhills. L38 — 2 F3
Sandhills Ave. FY4 — 109 B5
Sandhills Cl. BB8 — 191 E8
Sandholme La. PR3 — 179 A4
Sandholme Villas. BB8 — 201 A1
Sandhurst Ave. Lytham St Anne's FY8 — 88 E7
Sandhurst Cl. Formby L37 — 11 C1
Sandhurst Cl. Kirkham PR4 — 112 F5
Sandhurst Cl. FY8 — 88 D6
Sandhurst Grange. FY8 — 88 E7
Sandhurst St. BB11 — 127 B6
Sandhurst Way. L31 — 5 B5
Sandicroft Ave. FY6 — 174 C1
Sandicroft Pl. FY6 — 195 B4
Sandicroft Rd. FY1 — 150 C1
Sandilands Gr. L38 — 2 F3
Sandiway Dr. BB10 — 147 F3
Sandiway. Cl. PR9 — 34 E8
Sandiways Cl. FY5 — 151 C8
Sandon Pl. FY4 — 109 C4
Sandon Rd. PR8 — 33 F1
Sandon St. Blackburn BB2 — 100 C3
Sandon St. Darwen BB3 — 81 B2
Sandon Terr. BB2 — 100 C3
Sandown Cl. PR4 — 115 D1
Sandown Ct. [31] Preston PR1 — 96 A7
Sandown Ct. Southport PR9 — 34 C8
Sandown Rd. Haslingden BB4 — 84 C2
Sandown Rd. Lancaster LA1 — 211 B3
Sandown Rd. Thornton FY5 — 151 C8
Sandpiper Cl. BB1 — 100 F6
Sandpiper Cl. FY5 — 172 C2
Sandpiper Sq. BB11 — 126 C5
Sandpipre Pl. [10] FY5 — 172 F1
Sandridge Ave. PR7 — 42 B7
Sandridge Pl. FY4 — 109 B4
Sandringham Ave. Leyland PR5 & PR6 — 76 C1
Sandringham Ave. Thornton FY5 — 173 B1
Sandringham Cl. Adlington PR7 — 29 E6
Sandringham Cl. [5] Barrowford BB9 — 168 C1
Sandringham Ct. Lytham St Anne's FY8 — 89 D4
Sandringham Ct. Morecambe LA4 — 212 D4
Sandringham Ct. Southport PR8 — 34 B8
Sandringham Dr. Brinscall PR6 — 61 F8
Sandringham Dr. Ramsbottom BL8 — 49 A1
Sandringham Gr. [2] BB4 — 84 A1
Sandringham Park Dr. PR4 — 75 A8
Sandringham Rd. Ainsdale PR8 — 20 C5
Sandringham Rd. Bamber Bridge PR5 — 96 D3
Sandringham Rd. Chorley PR7 — 42 B8
Sandringham Rd. Darwen BB3 — 80 E4
Sandringham Rd. Eccleston PR7 — 40 C7
Sandringham Rd. Formby L37 — 11 E1
Sandringham Rd. Horwich BL6 — 31 E2
Sandringham Rd. Lytham St Anne's FY8 — 89 A5
Sandringham Rd. Morecambe LA4 — 212 D4
Sandringham Rd. Southport PR8 — 33 E3
Sands Cl. BB1 — 123 B2
Sands Rd. BB5 — 123 B2
Sands The. BB7 — 143 C5
Sandsdale Ave. PR2 — 117 C5
Sandside Dr. LA4 — 212 F3
Sandside Rd. LA5 & LA7 — 237 D3
Sandwich Cl. BB1 — 101 C4
Sandwick Cl. PR2 — 116 E7
Sandy Bank Rd. BL7 — 47 D5
Sandy Cl. FY5 — 172 C3
Sandy La. Accrington BB5 — 103 E5
Sandy La. Adlington PR7 — 29 F6
Sandy La. Barrowford BB9 — 168 D2
Sandy La. Bispham Green L40 — 38 F2
Sandy La. Blackpool FY4 — 110 A4
Sandy La. Brindle PR5 & PR6 — 78 C6
Sandy La. Brinscall PR6 — 61 E8
Sandy La. Clayton Green PR6 — 77 C3
Sandy La. Darwen BB3 — 80 E6
Sandy La. Fleetwood FY7 — 172 D6
Sandy La. Hambleton FY6 — 174 C1
Sandy La. Hightown L38 — 3 A3
Sandy La. Holmeswood L40 & PR4 — 37 E5
Sandy La. Holmeswood L40 — 37 E5
Sandy La. Holt Green L39 — 6 B6
Sandy La. Leyland PR5 — 59 A8
Sandy La. Lower Bartle PR4 — 115 D7

Sandy La. Maghull L31 — 5 C5
Sandy La. Mawdesley L40 — 39 A1
Sandy La. Newburgh WN8 — 25 F1
Sandy La. Ormskirk L40 — 16 D7
Sandy La. Orrell WN5 — 10 D4
Sandy La. Out Rawcliffe PR3 — 175 F1
Sandy La. Pleasington BB2 — 99 C2
Sandy La. Preesall FY6 — 195 B4
Sandy La. Skelmersdale WN8 — 17 D1
Sandy La. Sollom L40 — 38 A8
Sandy La. Thorpe Green PR6 — 77 E4
Sandy La Ctr. [9] — 17 D1
Sandy Pl. [8] PR5 — 59 A8
Sandy Way. L40 — 37 D4
Sandybeds Cl. BB5 — 103 D2
Sandybrook Cl. PR2 — 117 E5
Sandycroft. PR2 — 117 F2
Sandyforth Ave. FY5 — 173 B3
Sandyforth La. PR4 — 116 A8
Sandygate. BB11 — 126 F6
Sandygate La. PR3 — 136 B2
Sandyhall La. BB9 & BB12 — 168 A2
Sandylands Arc. LA3 — 212 A3
Sandylands Ct. LA3 — 212 B4
Sandylands Prim Sch. LA3 — 212 B3
Sandylands Prom. LA3 — 212 A3
Sanfield Cl. L39 — 15 E6
Sangara Dr. BB3 — 80 F7
Sangness Dr. PR8 — 34 E3
Sansbury Cres. BB9 — 169 A2
Santon Cl. PR4 — 113 A7
Sanvino Ave. PR8 — 20 D5
Sapphire St. BB1 — 121 F5
Sarah La. PR5 — 56 F5
Sarah St. Bacup OL13 — 70 C8
Sarah St. Darwen BB3 — 81 B1
Sarah St. Edenfield BL0 — 67 E3
Sarscow La. PR5 — 57 E2
Saswick Ct. PR4 — 133 B7
Saul St. PR1 — 95 F8
Saul's Dr. LA5 — 218 A8
Saunder Bank. BB11 — 127 A5
Saunder Height La. BB4 — 85 E3
Saunders Cl. BB4 — 85 A7
Saunders' La. Hutton PR4 — 94 D2
Saunders' La. Hutton PR4 — 94 E1
Saunders Mews. PR7 — 42 C3
Saunders Rd. BB2 — 100 C5
Saunders St. PR8 & PR9 — 52 C1
Savick Ave. PR2 — 115 D1
Savick Cl. PR5 — 76 F8
Savick Cty Prim Sch. PR2 — 115 E2
Savick Rd. PR2 — 116 D4
Savick Way. PR2 — 115 E3
Saville Ave. FY6 — 151 B6
Saville Rd. Blackpool FY1 — 129 C1
Saville Rd. Maghull L31 — 5 C3
Saville St. PR7 — 42 C5
Savon Hook. L37 — 12 B1
Savoy Ave. LA3 — 212 F3
Savoy St. Accrington BB5 — 102 F5
Savoy St. Preston PR1 — 95 E7
Sawdon Ave. PR8 — 34 E3
Sawley Ave. Accrington BB5 — 103 D7
Sawley Ave. Blackpool FY4 — 109 D5
Sawley Ave. Lytham St Anne's FY8 — 89 C6
Sawley Ave. Read BB12 — 144 F3
Sawley Cl. BB3 — 64 C8
Sawley Cres. PR7 — 117 F2
Sawley Dr. BB6 — 123 F5
Sawley Rd. Chatburn BB7 — 187 E6
Sawley Rd. Sawley BB7 — 224 C1
Sawrey St. BB5 — 123 E2
Sawyer St. [5] OL12 — 51 F1
Saxby Gr. FY4 — 129 F1
Saxenholme. PR8 — 33 F5
Saxifield St. BB10 — 147 E3
Saxon Cl. Oswaldtwistle BB5 — 102 C5
Saxon Cl. Thornton FY5 — 151 C8
Saxon Hey. PR2 — 116 C3
Saxon Rd. PR8 — 33 F5
Saxon St. BB10 — 127 A7
Scafell Ave. LA4 — 212 G5
Scafell Cl. BB12 — 126 C8
Scafell Rd. Lancaster LA1 — 214 A2
Scafell Rd. Lytham St Anne's FY8 — 110 A2
Scaffold La. L38 — 3 D4
Scaitcliffe St. BB5 — 103 B5
Scale Farm Rd. LA1 — 213 C2
Scale Hall La. Newton-with-S PR4 — 114 A2
Scaleber La. LA6 — 238 D8
Scar St. BB2 — 100 B3
Scarborough Rd. Blackburn BB2 — 101 A1
Scarborough Rd. Lytham St Anne's FY8 — 110 A1
Scargill Rd. LA2 & LA6 — 216 F1
Scarisbrick Ave. Parbold WN8 — 26 C2
Scarisbrick Ave. Southport PR8 — 34 A4
Scarisbrick Cl. L31 — 5 E3
Scarisbrick Cl. PR8 — 34 C6
Scarisbrick Cty Prim Sch. L40 — 23 A3
Scarisbrick New Rd. PR8 — 34 D5
Scarisbrick St. Ormskirk L39 — 15 E6
Scarisbrick St. Southport PR9 — 34 B7
Scarlet St. PR7 — 42 E7
Scarlett St. BB11 — 126 E5
Scarr Dr. OL12 — 51 F3
Scarr La. BB2 — 100 A6
Scarsdale Ave. FY4 — 109 C5
Scarth Hill La. L39 & L40 — 16 B2

Scarth La. BB12 ... 125 B5
Scawfell Rd. PR7 ... 42 B5
Schleswig St. PR1 ... 96 A8
Schleswig Way. PR5 ... 75 C1
Schofield Ave. FY3 ... 130 B7
Schofield Rd. BB4 ... 84 F2
Schofield St. Darwen BB4 ... 67 A6
Schofield St. Helmshore BB4 ... 67 A6
Schofield St. Newchurch BB4 ... 68 E8
Schola Green La.
 Morecambe LA4 ... 212 E4
Schola Green La.
 Morecambe LA4 ... 212 E5
Scholars Gn. PR2 ... 115 C1
Scholefield Ave. BB9 ... 147 E5
Scholefield La. BB9 ... 147 F5
Scholes Bank. BL6 ... 31 A5
Scholes St. BB3 ... 80 F2
Scholey Head La. BB10 ... 107 A8
School Ave. L37 ... 11 F3
School Brow. PR6 ... 60 B7
School Cl. L39 ... 15 C1
School Cotts. PR3 ... 179 E8
School Ct. Edenfield BL0 ... 67 D2
School Ct. Egerton BL7 ... 46 E2
School Field. PR5 ... 77 B5
School Fields. BB8 ... 201 B3
School House Gn. L39 ... 15 F5
School House La. BB5 ... 103 B1
School La. Bamber Bridge PR5 ... 96 F2
School La. Blackburn BB1 ... 81 D8
School La. Brinscall PR6 & PR7 ... 61 E8
School La. Burnley BB11 ... 127 A7
School La. Burscough Bridge L40 ... 24 F5
School La. Catforth PR4 ... 135 A4
School La. Earby BB8 ... 201 B2
School La. Edgworth BL7 ... 47 D8
School La. Euxton PR7 ... 59 D3
School La. Farington PR5 ... 76 F7
School La. Formby L37 ... 11 F3
School La. Forton LA2 & PR3 ... 204 B3
School La. Freckleton PR4 ... 92 C7
School La.
 Hammerton Mere BB7 ... 229 E3
School La. Haskayne L39 ... 13 F4
School La. Inskip PR3 ... 155 D1
School La. Kirkham PR4 ... 113 B5
School La.
 Laneshaw Bridge BB8 ... 170 E6
School La. Leyland PR5 ... 58 A8
School La. Leyland PR5 ... 76 A1
School La. Longton PR4 ... 74 A8
School La. Lytham St Anne's FY8 ... 90 A3
School La. Mawdesley L40 ... 39 C1
School La. Mereclough BB10 ... 128 A1
School La. Moss Side L31 ... 6 A1
School La. Newton-with-S PR4 ... 114 A2
School La. Overton Fold PR6 ... 78 F4
School La. Out Rawcliffe PR3 ... 175 F2
School La. Pilling PR3 ... 196 C6
School La. Preesall FY6 ... 195 B3
School La. Roby Mill WN8 ... 19 B3
School La. Simonstone BB12 ... 144 F1
School La. Skelmersdale WN8 ... 17 E1
School La. Standish WN6 ... 28 D1
School La.
 Up Holland WN5 & WN8 ... 10 C7
School La. Westhead L40 ... 16 E3
School La. Winmarleigh PR3 ... 198 F6
School La. Wray LA2 ... 232 D6
School Rd. Blackpool FY4 ... 110 B5
School Rd. Heysham LA3 ... 208 E7
School Rd. Hightown L38 ... 2 F4
School Rd. Thornton FY5 ... 151 C8
School St. Accrington BB5 ... 103 B6
School St. Bacup OL13 ... 69 B8
School St. Bamber Bridge PR5 ... 96 F2
School St. Bury BL9 ... 32 B1
School St. Colne BB8 ... 169 D4
School St. Darwen BB3 ... 81 A1
School St. Great Harwood BB6 ... 123 C4
School St. Horwich BL6 ... 31 C3
School St. Kelbrook BB8 ... 192 A6
School St. Leyland PR5 ... 76 B2
School St. Nelson BB9 ... 147 C8
School St. Preston PR1 ... 96 F8
School St. Ramsbottom BL0 ... 49 B5
School St. Rawtenstall BB4 ... 85 A8
School St. Rishton BB1 ... 123 B1
School St. Walmer Bridge PR4 ... 73 F5
School St. Whitewell Bottom BB4 ... 85 F4
School Terr. Salterforth BB8 ... 191 D8
School Terr. Whitworth OL12 ... 70 D1
School View. BL7 ... 47 D8
School Villas. LA2 ... 207 B5
Schoolfold. PR4 ... 72 E4
Schoolhouse La. LA2 ... 214 F7
Schwartzman Dr. PR9 ... 54 A6
Scorton Ave. FY3 ... 129 F7
Scorton Hall Pk. PR3 ... 199 E6
Scotch Green La. PR3 ... 158 A6
Scotforth CE Prim Sch. LA1 ... 211 A4
Scotforth Ct. [1] LA1 ... 211 A3
Scotforth Rd.
 Lancaster LA1 & LA2 ... 211 A4
Scotforth Rd. Preston PR1 ... 96 C8
Scotland Bank Terr. BB2 ... 80 C8
Scotland La. BL9 ... 32 D8
Scotland Pl. [1] BL0 ... 49 C6
Scotland Rd. Carnforth LA5 ... 217 E3
Scotland Rd. [5] Nelson BB9 ... 147 D8
Scotshaw Brook Ind Est. BB2 ... 80 E7
Scotsword Ave. FY4 ... 109 D6
Scott Ave. Accrington BB5 ... 103 E2
Scott Ave. Morecambe LA4 ... 212 C3

Scott Ave. Simonstone BB12 ... 144 E2
Scott Cl. Blackpool FY4 ... 109 F8
Scott Cl. Maghull L31 ... 5 D1
Scott Cl. Oswaldtwistle BB5 ... 102 D5
Scott Dr. L39 ... 15 F7
Scott Gr. LA4 ... 212 D4
Scott Laithe La. BB7 ... 224 E3
Scott Mews. FY4 ... 109 F8
Scott Park Rd. BB11 ... 126 E4
Scott Rd. LA3 & LA4 ... 212 C3
Scott St. Clayton-le-M BB5 ... 123 F3
Scott St. Nelson BB9 ... 168 D1
Scott St. Padiham BB12 ... 125 F7
Scott St. Southport PR9 ... 35 A7
Scott's Terr. BB11 ... 126 D6
Scott's Wood. PR2 ... 116 D7
Scout End Rd. BL0 ... 68 A2
Scout Rd. Egerton BL1 ... 46 B1
Scout Rd. Newchurch BB4 ... 85 F3
Scow Croft La. PR6 & PR7 ... 61 D4
Scowcroft Dr. LA4 ... 213 A5
Scriffen La. LA2 ... 207 D3
Scudamore Cres. FY4 ... 129 D1
Sea View. Lancaster LA1 ... 211 A5
Sea View. Longridge PR3 ... 159 D2
Sea View. Walmer Bridge PR4 ... 73 F5
Sea View Cl. LA2 ... 213 D8
Sea View Dr. LA2 ... 213 D8
Sea Wall. FY7 ... 193 C3
Seabank Rd. Fleetwood FY7 ... 194 A3
Seabank Rd.
 Southport PR8 & PR9 ... 34 B8
Seaborn Gr. LA4 ... 212 G6
Seaborn Rd. LA4 ... 212 G6
Seabourne Ave. FY4 ... 109 B7
Seabrook Dr. FY5 ... 150 E8
Seacrest Ave. FY1 ... 129 C8
Seacroft Cres. PR9 ... 53 B5
Seafield. L37 ... 12 A2
Seafield Rd. Ainsdale PR8 ... 20 C6
Seafield Rd. Blackpool FY1 ... 129 B8
Seafield Rd.
 Lytham St Anne's FY8 ... 89 F3
Seafore Cl. L31 ... 5 B4
Sealand Ave. L37 ... 11 E2
Sealand Cl. L37 ... 11 D2
Seascale Cl. BB2 ... 101 A1
Seathwaite Ave. Blackpool FY4 ... 130 C1
Seathwaite Ave.
 Morecambe LA3 ... 212 B2
Seaton Ave. FY5 ... 172 E4
Seaton Pl. WN8 ... 17 E3
Seaton Way. PR9 ... 53 A5
Seattle Ave. FY2 ... 150 E2
Seawell Ave. LA3 ... 212 A2
Second Ave. Blackpool FY4 ... 109 C7
Second Ave. Bury BL9 ... 32 D4
Second Ave. Church BB5 ... 103 A8
Second Terr. LA3 ... 205 B4
Sedberg St. PR2 ... 116 D3
Sedbergh Ave. FY4 ... 129 F1
Sedbergh Cl. BB5 ... 103 D5
Sedburgh St. BB10 ... 147 C2
Seddon Pl. WN8 ... 17 E3
Sedge Ct. LA3 ... 212 E2
Sedgefield. PR4 ... 73 E8
Sedgfield Cl. FY4 ... 109 F6
Sedgley Ave. PR4 ... 92 A6
Sedgwick St. PR1 ... 117 A1
Sedwell Cl. FY8 ... 89 F4
Seed St. Blackpool FY1 ... 129 C6
Seed St. Preston PR1 ... 95 F8
Seedall Ave. BB7 ... 164 D7
Seedhill Terr. [3] BB9 ... 168 D1
Seedlee Rd. PR5 ... 77 A6
Sefton Ave. Burnley BB11 ... 126 E5
Sefton Ave. Orrell WN5 ... 10 D5
Sefton Ave. Poulton-le-F FY6 ... 151 D1
Sefton Cl. Darwen BB3 ... 64 C6
Sefton Cl. Orrell WN5 ... 10 D5
Sefton Ct. FY8 ... 88 D7
Sefton Dr. Bury BL9 ... 32 A6
Sefton Dr. Lancaster LA1 ... 213 D2
Sefton Gdns. L39 ... 6 D7
Sefton La. BL6 ... 31 D1
Sefton Rd. Bamber Bridge PR5 ... 96 D3
Sefton Rd. Formby L37 ... 11 E2
Sefton Rd. Lytham St Anne's FY8 ... 88 F7
Sefton Rd. Morecambe LA3 ... 212 B3
Sefton Rd. Orrell WN5 ... 10 D5
Sefton St. Brierfield BB9 ... 147 B5
Sefton St. Colne BB8 ... 169 F5
Sefton St. Southport PR8 ... 34 C5
Sefton Terr. [10] BB11 ... 126 E5
Segar St. [15]
 Great Harwood BB6 ... 123 C5
Segar St. Kirkham PR4 ... 112 F6
Segar's La. PR8 & L39 ... 20 E4
Selborne Mews. BB2 ... 100 B3
Selborne St. Blackburn BB2 ... 100 B3
Selborne St. Preston PR1 ... 96 B6
Selbourne. BB8 ... 201 C2
Selbourne Rd. FY1 ... 129 D6
Selby Ave. Blackpool FY4 ... 109 D5
Selby Ave. Cleveleys FY5 ... 172 F4
Selby Ave. Lancaster LA1 ... 213 F4
Selby Cl. BB5 ... 103 E3
Selby Dr. L37 ... 12 B2
Selby Pl. WN8 ... 17 D2
Selby Rd. PR4 ... 112 F5
Selby St. Colne BB8 ... 169 C5
Selby St. Nelson BB9 ... 147 E7
Selby St. Preston PR1 ... 116 D1
Seldon St. [11] Colne BB8 ... 169 D4
Seldon St. [16] Nelson BB9 ... 168 E1
Selkirk St. [6] BB1 ... 101 A4

Selkirk Dr. PR5 ... 96 D2
Selkirk St. BB11 ... 126 D4
Sellers St. PR1 ... 117 C1
Selous Rd. BB2 ... 100 B3
Selside Dr. LA4 ... 212 E3
Selworthy Rd. Southport PR8 ... 33 D3
Selworthy Rd. Southport PR8 ... 33 E3
Senior Ave. FY5 ... 129 F1
Seniors Dr. FY5 ... 172 F3
Sephton Dr. L39 ... 15 F7
Sephton St. [7] PR5 ... 76 A8
Sergeant St. [11] PR5 ... 76 F8
Serpentine Rd. BB11 ... 126 F4
Serpentine The.
 Lytham St Anne's FY8 ... 90 A3
Serpentine The. Ormskirk L39 ... 6 D8
Sett End Rd. BB1 ... 101 C1
Settle La. BB7 & BD23 ... 225 B7
Settle Pl. FY8 ... 89 C7
Settle Terr. BB10 ... 147 C2
Seven Acres. PR5 ... 77 C5
Seven Houses. BB1 ... 101 D4
Seven Sands. PR4 ... 90 B2
Seven Stars Prim Sch. PR5 ... 58 D7
Seven Stars Rd. PR5 ... 58 D7
Seven Trees Ave. BB1 ... 101 A8
Sevenoaks. PR7 ... 42 C4
Sevenoaks Ave. PR8 ... 20 B5
Sevenoaks Dr. FY5 ... 150 F8
Seventh Ave. FY4 ... 109 C6
Severn Ave. FY7 ... 172 D8
Severn Ct. LA1 ... 213 B2
Severn Dr. PR5 ... 96 C2
Severn Gdns. BB10 ... 147 C2
Severn Hill. PR2 ... 116 C8
Severn House. [7] PR1 ... 96 D8
Severn Rd. FY4 ... 109 B7
Severn St. PR3 ... 139 A7
Seville Ct. FY8 ... 89 D3
Seymour Ave. LA3 ... 208 F7
Seymour Pl. PR1 ... 116 D2
Seymour Rd. L31 ... 5 E3
Seymour Gr. LA3 ... 208 F7
Seymour Rd. Blackpool FY1 ... 129 C2
Seymour Rd. Fulwood PR2 ... 116 C3
Seymour Rd.
 Lytham St Anne's FY8 ... 89 D4
Seymour Rd. Chorley PR6 ... 42 E8
Seymour Rd. Fleetwood FY7 ... 193 F4
Seymour St. [5] Lancaster LA1 ... 211 A8
Shacklady Rd. L33 ... 1 A4
Shackleton Rd. PR4 ... 113 B2
Shackleton St. Burnley BB10 ... 127 B8
Shackleton St. Cornholme OL14 ... 108 C1
Shade Row. FY6 ... 195 B3
Shadsworth Cl. BB1 ... 101 C4
Shadsworth Cty Inf Sch. BB1 ... 101 D4
Shadsworth Cty Jun Sch. BB1 ... 101 C4
Shadsworth L Ctr. BB1 ... 101 C4
Shadsworth Rd. BB1 ... 101 C3
Shady La.
 Clayton-le-W PR5 & PR6 ... 76 E3
Shady La. Hest Bank LA2 ... 213 E8
Shaftesbury Ave. Blackpool FY2 ... 150 C2
Shaftesbury Ave. Burnley BB11 ... 126 F3
Shaftesbury Ave. Cleveleys FY5 ... 172 D5
Shaftesbury Ave. Darwen BB3 ... 80 E3
Shaftesbury Ave.
 Great Harwood BB6 ... 123 E6
Shaftesbury Ave.
 New Longton PR4 ... 74 F8
Shaftesbury Ave. Normoss FY3 ... 130 B6
Shaftesbury Ave.
 Penwortham PR1 ... 95 B6
Shaftesbury Ave. Southport PR8 ... 21 A8
Shaftesbury Gr. PR8 ... 34 A1
Shaftesbury Pl. Lancaster LA1 ... 210 F4
Shaftesbury Pl. Preston PR1 ... 34 A1
Shakeshaft St. [11] BB1 ... 101 A4
Shakespear Prim Sch. FY7 ... 193 E4
Shakespeare Ave. BB6 ... 123 B4
Shakespeare Rd.
 Fleetwood FY7 ... 193 E4
Shakespeare Rd.
 Lancaster LA1 ... 213 E4
Shakespeare Rd. Preston PR1 ... 117 D1
Shakespeare St. Padiham BB12 ... 125 D7
Shakespeare St. Southport PR8 ... 34 B5
Shakespeare Terr. PR6 ... 60 D2
Shakespeare Way. BB2 ... 100 C3
Shalbourn Rd. FY8 ... 89 A4
Shale St. BB12 ... 126 D6
Shalgrove Field. PR2 ... 116 C7
Shannon Sq. BB10 ... 147 C2
Shannon St. FY1 ... 129 B3
Shap Cl. Accrington BB5 ... 103 E3
Shap Cl. Barrowford BB9 ... 168 D4
Shap Ct. FY7 ... 193 D1
Shap Gr. BB10 ... 147 A3
Shard La. FY6 ... 152 B8
Shard Rd. FY6 ... 152 B6
Sharley Fold. PR3 ... 139 B7
Sharman Rd. FY8 ... 109 F1
Sharneyford Cty Prim Sch.
 OL13 ... 87 C5
Sharoe Bay Ct. PR2 ... 116 F6
Sharoe Green Hospl. PR2 ... 116 F4
Sharoe Green La. PR2 ... 116 F7
Sharoe Green Pk. PR2 ... 117 A5
Sharoe Mount Ave. PR2 ... 116 F7
Sharon Gr. FY1 ... 129 C8
Sharp St. [1] Barrowford BB9 ... 168 D3
Sharp St. Burnley BB10 ... 147 B1
Sharpe's Ave. LA1 ... 211 A5
Sharples Gn. BL7 ... 47 D6
Sharples Meadow. BL7 ... 47 D6
Sharples St. Accrington BB5 ... 102 F5

Sharples St. Blackburn BB2 ... 100 D3
Sharrats Path. PR7 ... 41 F4
Sharrock St. PR8 ... 34 B7
Shaw Bridge St. [3] BB7 ... 164 F8
Shaw Brook Cl. BB1 ... 102 A8
Shaw Brook Rd. PR5 ... 58 E6
Shaw Brow. PR6 ... 60 B7
Shaw Cl. Blackburn BB2 ... 100 D5
Shaw Cl. Shirdley Hill L39 ... 22 A6
Shaw Clough Rd. BB4 ... 85 F3
Shaw Clough St. BB4 ... 85 F3
Shaw Cres. L37 ... 12 B3
Shaw Gn. LA7 ... 237 F5
Shaw Hill. PR6 & PR7 ... 60 B7
Shaw Hill Dr. PR6 & PR7 ... 60 B6
Shaw Hill Golf Course. PR7 ... 60 B6
Shaw Hill St. PR7 ... 42 C7
Shaw La. Barton L39 ... 13 E6
Shaw La. Cornholme OL14 ... 108 C3
Shaw La. Nether Kellet LA6 ... 216 F4
Shaw La. Storth LA7 ... 237 F5
Shaw Rd. Blackpool FY1 ... 129 B1
Shaw Rd. Horwich BL6 ... 31 B5
Shaw Sq. BB8 ... 201 B2
Shaw St. Blackburn BB2 ... 100 D5
Shaw St. Bury BL9 ... 32 B3
Shaw St. Colne BB8 ... 169 D4
Shaw St. Haslingden BB4 ... 84 B6
Shaw St. [2] Lancaster LA1 ... 211 A8
Shaw St. [1] Preston PR0 & PR1 ... 117 A1
Shaw's Ave. PR8 ... 34 A1
Shaw's La. PR3 ... 196 A3
Shaw's Rd. PR8 ... 34 A1
Shawbridge Ct. BB7 ... 164 F8
Shawbrook Cl. PR7 ... 59 C5
Shawbury Cl. BL6 ... 30 D1
Shawcliffe La. BB6 & BB7 ... 143 B2
Shawclough Cl. OL12 ... 51 D3
Shawclough Cty Prim Sch.
 OL12 ... 51 E3
Shawclough Dr. OL12 ... 51 D3
Shawclough Rd. OL12 ... 51 C3
Shawclough Way. OL12 ... 51 D3
Shawes Dr. PR6 ... 30 C7
Shawfield. [3] BB4 ... 84 F1
Shawfield La. OL12 ... 51 A2
Shaws Garth. L39 ... 22 A6
Shay Head Cotts. BB8 ... 192 E1
Shay La. Longridge PR3 ... 138 F6
Shay La. Slaidburn BB7 ... 223 B7
Shays Dr. BB7 ... 165 A7
Shear Bank Cl. BB1 ... 100 D6
Shear Bank Gdns. BB1 ... 100 D6
Shear Bank Rd. BB1 & BB2 ... 100 D6
Shear Brow. BB1 ... 100 D7
Shearing Ave. OL12 ... 51 A2
Shearwater Dr. BB1 ... 100 F6
Shed St. Colne BB8 ... 169 C4
Shed St. Oswaldtwistle BB5 ... 102 D3
Shed St. Whitworth OL12 ... 70 D1
Sheddon Gr. BB10 ... 127 E5
Sheep Gap. OL12 ... 51 B1
Sheep Gn. BB4 ... 84 B3
Sheep Hill Brow. PR6 ... 77 A3
Sheep Hill La. Clayton Green PR6 ... 77 A3
Sheep Hill La. Clayton-le-W PR6 ... 76 F2
Sheep House La. BL6 & PR7 ... 44 A3
Sheephill La. PR4 ... 75 A7
Sheffield Dr. PR2 ... 115 D1
Sheldon Ave. WN6 ... 28 E2
Shelfield La. BB10 ... 148 F7
Shelfield Rd. BB9 ... 169 B1
Shelley Cl. Bolton-le-S LA5 ... 216 A5
Shelley Cl. Coppull PR7 ... 28 F8
Shelley Dr. Accrington BB5 ... 103 E2
Shelley Dr. Ormskirk L39 ... 15 D6
Shelley Gdns. BB6 ... 123 B4
Shelley Gr. Cleveleys FY5 ... 150 D8
Shelley Gr. Darwen BB3 ... 81 C1
Shelley Gr. Southport PR8 & PR9 ... 34 F6
Shelley Rd. PR1 & PR2 ... 116 C2
Shellfield Rd. PR9 ... 53 A4
Shellingford Cl. WN6 ... 19 D7
Shelly Dr. PR7 ... 40 D5
Shelton Dr. PR8 ... 20 A4
Shenley Way. PR9 ... 53 D5
Shenstone Rd. FY3 ... 129 F7
Shepherd Rd. FY8 ... 89 A7
Shepherd Rd N. FY8 ... 89 A8
Shepherd St. Bacup OL13 ... 86 F3
Shepherd St. Bury BL9 ... 32 A1
Shepherd St. Darwen BB3 ... 64 A7
Shepherd St.
 Lytham St Anne's FY8 ... 90 B3
Shepherd St. Preston PR1 ... 96 A7
Shepherd's Ave. PR3 ... 178 D4
Shepherd's La. L39 ... 14 E5
Shepherds Cl. Blackrod BL6 ... 30 C3
Shepherds Cl. Ramsbottom BL8 ... 48 F1
Shepherds Way. PR6 ... 42 D8
Sheppard St. FY1 ... 129 B4
Sheraton Pk. PR2 ... 116 A6
Sherborne Lodge. [6] PR2 ... 117 F4
Sherborne Rd. BB5 ... 103 E3
Sherbourne Cl. FY6 ... 151 C5
Sherbourne Cres. PR1 ... 117 B3
Sherbourne Cl. FY6 ... 151 C5
Sherbourne Rd. Blackpool FY1 ... 129 C7
Sherbourne Rd. Hambleton FY6 ... 174 C2
Sherbourne Rd. Preston PR6 ... 42 D7
Sherburn Rd. PR1 ... 95 E3
Sherburn Sch. PR1 ... 117 A3
Sherburne Ave. PR4 ... 112 F5
Sherdley Rd. PR5 ... 76 B7
Sherfin Nook. BB5 ... 84 B7
Sherfin Side. BB5 ... 84 B7
Sheridan Rd. BB8 ... 170 D4

Sheridan St. [4] BB9 ... 168 F2
Sheriff St. OL12 ... 51 E1
Sheringham Ave. FY5 ... 150 D7
Sheringham Way. FY6 ... 151 D7
Sherrat St. WN8 ... 17 D1
Sherwood Ave. Blackpool FY3 ... 129 E6
Sherwood Ave. Ormskirk L39 ... 15 C2
Sherwood Cl. BB10 ... 127 C5
Sherwood Cty Prim Sch. PR2 ... 117 A7
Sherwood Dr. WN8 ... 18 D3
Sherwood House. ... 20 C5
Sherwood Pl. Chorley PR6 ... 42 D8
Sherwood Pl. [2] Blackburn BB1 ... 101 B3
Sherwood Rd.
 Lytham St Anne's FY8 ... 89 C6
Sherwood Way. PR2 ... 117 A7
Shetland Cl. Blackburn BB1 ... 101 C3
Shetland Cl. Wilpshire BB1 ... 121 F7
Shetland Rd. FY1 ... 129 C2
Shevington Cswy. PR5 ... 57 B2
Shevington La. WN6 ... 28 B1
Shevington Moor. WN6 ... 28 A2
Shevington Prim Sch. WN6 ... 19 F6
Shevington Vale Prim Sch.
 WN6 ... 19 E8
Shevington's La. L33 ... 1 A6
Shilton St. L40 ... 49 B5
Shipley Cl. FY6 ... 151 B1
Shipley Rd. FY8 ... 89 B7
Shipper Bottom La. BL0 ... 49 D5
Shirdley Cres. PR8 ... 20 C3
Shire Bank Cres. PR2 ... 116 E5
Shire La. BB6 ... 141 D8
Shireburn Ave. BB7 ... 164 C5
Shireburn Cotts. BB7 ... 162 E1
Shireburn Rd. L37 ... 11 D5
Shireshead Cres. LA1 ... 211 A2
Shirley Cres. FY2 ... 150 D6
Shirley Gdns. BB3 ... 79 F2
Shirley Hts. FY6 ... 151 D4
Shirley La. PR4 ... 94 A1
Shop La. Accrington BB5 ... 103 D5
Shop La. Higher Walton PR5 ... 97 B4
Shop La. Maghull L31 ... 5 C1
Shore Cl. LA5 ... 218 B2
Shore Gn. Cornholme OL14 ... 108 C2
Shore Gn. Silverdale LA5 ... 218 B2
Shore Rd. Ainsdale PR8 ... 20 B6
Shore Rd. Cleveleys FY5 ... 150 C8
Shore Rd. Hesketh Bank PR4 ... 72 C4
Shore Rd. Heysham LA3 ... 208 D6
Shore Rd. Silverdale LA5 ... 218 B2
Shore The. LA5 ... 215 F5
Shorefield Mount. BL7 ... 46 E1
Shoreside Cty Prim Sch. PR8 ... 20 B4
Shorey Bank. BB11 ... 127 A6
Shorrock La. BB2 ... 100 B1
Shorrock St. BB3 ... 64 A8
Shorrocks Ave. PR3 ... 155 C8
Short Clough Cl. BB4 ... 85 A6
Short Clough La. BB4 ... 85 A6
Short Croft La. L37 ... 12 D1
Short St. Bacup OL13 ... 69 B8
Short St. Colne BB8 ... 169 D4
Shorten Brook Dr. BB5 ... 124 E6
Shorten Brook Way. BB5 ... 124 E6
Shortlands Dr. LA3 ... 208 E7
Shortridge Rd. FY4 ... 109 F8
Showfield. BB10 ... 128 B6
Showley Ct. BB1 ... 121 E6
Showley Rd. BB1 ... 121 A6
Shrewsbury Ct. PR4 ... 113 C5
Shrewsbury Dr. Lancaster LA1 ... 211 B5
Shrewsbury Dr. Thornton FY5 ... 173 A2
Shropshire Dr. BB1 ... 121 F6
Shuttle Cl. BB5 ... 103 A6
Shuttleworth Rd. PR1 ... 116 F2
Shuttleworth St. Burnley BB10 ... 147 B2
Shuttleworth St. Earby BB8 ... 201 B2
Shuttleworth St. [6]
 Padiham BB12 ... 125 C8
Shuttleworth St. Rishton BB1 ... 123 B2
Shuttling Fields La. PR5 ... 97 B2
Sibbering Brow Preston Rd.
 PR7 ... 41 C7
Sibsey St. LA1 ... 210 E7
Siddow's Ave. BB7 ... 164 D7
Side La. BB7 ... 189 C2
Sidebeet La. BB1 ... 101 E7
Sidegarth Gate. LA2 ... 231 C7
Sidegarth La. LA2 ... 231 C7
Sidgreaves La. PR4 ... 115 B4
Siding La. Kirkby L33 ... 1 C7
Siding La.
 Rainford Junction WA11 ... 8 C1
Siding St. OL13 ... 69 C8
Sidings Rd. LA3 ... 208 F2
Sidings The. Bacup OL13 ... 70 A8
Sidings The. Whalley BB7 ... 143 C6
Sidmouth Ave. BB4 ... 84 C2
Sidmouth Rd. FY8 ... 109 C1
Sidney Ave. Becconsall PR4 ... 72 F3
Sidney Ave. Blackpool FY2 ... 150 E2
Sidney Rd. PR9 ... 34 F8
Sidney Terr. [4] LA1 ... 211 A8
Siemens St. BL6 ... 31 C2
Silbury Cl. BB2 ... 81 A8
Silk Mill La. PR3 ... 158 B3
Silloth Cl. BB2 ... 100 F1
Silly La. LA2 ... 233 D2
Silsden Ave. PR2 ... 117 C5
Silsden Cl. FY6 ... 151 B1

Silver Birch Way. L31 .... 5 B5
Silver St. Clifton PR4 .... 114 D1
Silver St. Ramsbottom BL0 .... 49 C6
Silverburn. FY8 .... 89 A8
Silverdale. Becconsall PR4 .... 72 F3
Silverdale. Blackpool FY2 .... 150 E6
Silverdale. Southport PR8 .... 33 E4
Silverdale Ave. Fleetwood FY7 .. 193 D1
Silverdale Ave. Heysham LA3 .... 208 F7
Silverdale CE Prim Sch. LA5 .. 218 C3
Silverdale Cl. Blackburn BB2 .... 80 F8
Silverdale Cl. Brierfield BB10 .... 147 B3
Silverdale Cl. Clayton-le-M BB5 .. 123 E2
Silverdale Cl. Coupe Green PR5 .. 97 E4
Silverdale Cl. Leyland PR5 .... 59 B6
Silverdale Dr. PR2 .... 117 E5
Silverdale Golf Course. LA5 .... 218 E3
Silverdale Moss Rd. LA5 .... 218 D7
Silverdale Rd. Arnside LA5 .... 237 B1
Silverdale Rd. Chorley PR7 .... 42 E7
Silverdale Rd.
  Lytham St Anne's FY8 .... 89 C7
Silverdale Rd.
  Yealand Redmayne LA5 .... 219 E4
Silverdale Sta. LA5 .... 218 F3
Silverstone Gr. L31 .... 5 B4
Silverthorne Dr. PR9 .... 52 F1
Silverwell St. BL6 .... 31 B4
Silverwood Ave. FY4 .... 109 D8
Silverwood Cl. FY4 .... 89 E4
Silvester Rd. PR7 .... 42 C6
Silvester St. BL6 .... 30 D2
Silvia Way. FY7 .... 193 E4
Simmons Way. BB9 .... 147 B7
Simmons Ave. PR1 .... 96 B3
Simmons' St. BB2 .... 100 D5
Simonstone CE Prim Sch.
  BB12 .... 144 F1
Simonstone La. BB12 .... 124 E8
Simonstone Rd. BB12 & BB7 .... 144 F6
Simonswood Ind Pk. L33 .... 1 B6
Simonswood La. Kirkby L32 & L33 .. 1 A2
Simonswood La. Royal Oak L39 .. 7 A2
Simonswood Prim Sch. L33 .... 1 A2
Simonswood Wlk. L33 .... 1 A1
Simpson Cl. BB8 .... 200 D3
Simpson St. Blackpool FY4 ...... 109 B8
Simpson St. Hapton BB12 .... 125 C4
Simpson St. Oswaldtwistle BB5 .. 102 D3
Simpson St. Preston PR1 .... 95 F8
Sinclair Ct. FY8 .... 89 B7
Sineacre La. L33 & L39 .... 1 E8
Singleton. PR2 .... 116 F7
Singleton Ave. Horwich BL6 .... 31 C5
Singleton Ave.
  Lytham St Anne's FY8 .... 89 B8
Singleton Ave. Read BB12 .... 144 D2
Singleton CE Prim Sch. FY6 .. 152 E1
Singleton Cl. PR2 .... 116 F7
Singleton Rd. Weeton PR4 .... 131 F4
Singleton Rd.
  Weeton Camp PR4 .... 131 E6
Singleton Row. [18] PR1 .... 95 F8
Singleton St. FY1 .... 129 B3
Sion Cl. PR2 .... 117 F4
Sion Hill. PR2 .... 117 F4
Sir Simon's Arc. [22] LA1 .... 210 F8
Six Acre La. PR4 .... 74 C6
Sixpenny La. PR8 .... 20 D1
Sixth Ave. Blackpool FY4 .... 109 C7
Sixth Ave. Bury BL9 .... 32 D4
Size House Village. [5] BB4 .... 84 B2
Size St. OL12 .... 70 D1
Sizehouse St. [22] PR1 .... 95 F8
Sizer St. PR1 .... 116 F1
Sizergh Cl. LA1 .... 210 D7
Sizergh Rd. LA4 .... 213 A5
Skaithe The. BB7 .... 223 C7
Skeffington Rd. PR0 & PR1 ...... 117 C1
Skeleron La. BB7 .... 189 B6
Skelmersdale Coll.
  Skelmersdale WN8 .... 18 B1
Skelmersdale Coll.
  Skelmersdale WN8 .... 18 B4
Skelmersdale Coll.
  (Westbrook Ctr). WN8 .... 9 B8
Skelmersdale Rd. L39 & WN8 ...... 8 B7
Skelmersdale Sports Ctr. WN8 .. 9 C7
Skelshaw Cl. BB1 .... 101 A3
Skelton. BB8 .... 169 E5
Skelwith Rd. FY3 .... 130 B2
Skerton. LA1 .... 213 F2
Skerton Ct. LA1 .... 213 F2
Skerton High Sch. LA1 .... 213 F2
Skerton House. LA1 .... 213 F2
Skerton Prim Sch. LA1 .... 213 F2
Skiddaw Cl. BB12 .... 146 C1
Skiddaw Rd. Blackpool FY4 ..... 109 F8
Skiddaw Rd. Lancaster LA1 ...... 214 A2
Skiddaw St. BB1 .... 101 A5
Skip La. PR4 .... 94 B3
Skippool Ave. FY6 .... 151 E5
Skippool Rd. FY6 .... 151 E7
Skipton Ave. Carleton FY6 .... 151 C5
Skipton Ave. Southport PR9 .... 53 C6
Skipton Cl. FY1 .... 129 F1
Skipton Cres. PR2 .... 117 E5
Skipton Gate. LA6 .... 236 C2
Skipton New Rd. BB8 .... 191 E2
Skipton Old Rd. Colne BB8 ...... 170 B6
Skipton Old Rd. Foulridge BB8 .. 191 E2
Skipton Rd. Barnoldswick BB8 .. 200 B2
Skipton Rd. Barnoldswick BB8 .. 200 D4
Skipton Rd. Colne BB8 .... 169 E6
Skipton Rd. Earby BB8 .... 201 B3
Skipton Rd.
  Lytham St Anne's FY8 .... 89 B6
Skipton Rd. Trawden BB8 .... 170 B3

Skipton St. Morecambe LA4 ...... 212 D5
Skipton St. Nappa BB7 .... 225 E7
Skitham La. PR3 .... 176 D4
Skull House La. WN6 .... 19 D8
Skye Cl. OL10 .... 32 F1
Skye Cres. BB1 .... 101 C3
Slack. BB12 .... 145 F6
Slack Booth. BB5 .... 170 C1
Slack Gate. OL12 .... 51 F8
Slack House Cotts. L39 .... 16 A3
Slack La. LA2 .... 205 C1
Slack's La. PR6 .... 43 B2
Slackwood La. LA5 .... 218 E2
Slade La. Padiham BB12 .... 145 C1
Slade La. Padiham BB12 .... 145 C2
Slade St. PR1 .... 95 E7
Sladen St. OL12 .... 51 F1
Slaidburn Ave. Burnley BB10 ... 127 D5
Slaidburn Ave. Rawtenstall BB4 .. 85 A4
Slaidburn Cres. PR9 .... 53 B5
Slaidburn Dr. Accrington BB5 .... 103 A4
Slaidburn Dr. Lancaster LA1 ..... 211 A3
Slaidburn Pl. PR2 .... 118 A2
Slaidburn Rd. Fulwood PR2 ...... 118 A2
Slaidburn Rd. Lowgill LA2 .... 233 E4
Slaidburn Wlk. [5] FY3 .... 130 A8
Slape La. LA6 .... 234 C8
Slate La. WN8 .... 17 C2
Slater Ave. Colne BB8 .... 169 D6
Slater Ave. Horwich BL6 .... 31 C4
Slater La. Leyland PR5 .... 58 C8
Slater La. Leyland PR5 .... 58 D8
Slater Rd. FY5 .... 172 C2
Slater St. BB2 .... 100 C1
Slinger Rd. FY5 .... 172 C3
Slip Inn La. [22] LA1 .... 210 F8
Sliven Clod Rd. BB4 .... 104 E2
Sluice La. LA40 .... 38 B3
Slyne Hall Hts. LA2 .... 216 A1
Slyne Rd. Bolton-le-S LA2 & LA5 . 216 A2
Slyne Rd. Lancaster LA1 & LA2 .. 213 F6
Slyne Rd. Morecambe LA2 & LA4 213 C4
Smalden La. BB7 .... 224 A3
Small La. Clieves Hills L39 .... 15 A3
Small La. Drummersdale L40 ..... 23 E8
Small La. Ormskirk L39 .... 15 F4
Small La N. L39 .... 22 E2
Small La S. L39 .... 14 D6
Smalley Croft. PR1 .... 95 F3
Smalley St. Burnley BB11 .... 127 B4
Smalley St. Standish WN6 .... 28 E1
Smalley Thorn Brow. BB6 .... 122 F6
Smalley Way. BB2 .... 100 E2
Smallshaw Ind Est. BB11 .... 126 C4
Smallshaw La. Burnley BB11 .... 126 B5
Smallshaw La. Burnley BB12 .... 126 B6
Smallshaw Rd. OL12 .... 51 A4
Smallwood Hey Rd. PR3 .... 196 C5
Smeaton St. BL6 .... 31 C2
Smethurst Hall Pk. WN5 .... 10 C2
Smethurst Hall Rd. BL9 .... 32 F4
Smethurst Rd. WN5 .... 10 C2
Smirthwaite St. BB11 .... 126 D5
Smith Ave. PR4 .... 72 F1
Smith Brow. BL6 .... 30 C3
Smith Croft. PR5 .... 58 B8
Smith La. BL7 .... 46 F1
Smith Rd. FY5 .... 172 D2
Smith St. Adlington PR7 .... 29 F6
Smith St. [13] Bamber Bridge PR5 76 F8
Smith St. Barnoldswick BB8 .... 200 A1
Smith St. Burnley BB12 .... 126 E6
Smith St. Bury BL9 .... 32 A3
Smith St. Chorley PR7 .... 42 D6
Smith St. Colne BB8 .... 169 C4
Smith St. Kirkham PR4 .... 112 F5
Smith St. Nelson BB9 .... 147 F8
Smith St. Ramsbottom BL0 .... 49 B5
Smith St. Skelmersdale WN8 ..... 17 D1
Smith St. Whittle-le-W PR6 .... 60 C8
Smith St. Worsthorne BB10 ...... 128 B5
Smith's La. PR4 .... 56 A1
Smithills Cl. PR6 .... 60 E1
Smithills Hall Cl. BL6 .... 49 C5
Smithy Bridge St. BB5 .... 102 D3
Smithy Brow. Abbeystead LA2 .. 226 F1
Smithy Brow. Haslingden BB4 .... 84 B4
Smithy Brow. Newburgh WN8 .... 26 A1
Smithy Brow.
  Wrightington Bar WN6 .... 27 C8
Smithy Cl. Brindle PR6 .... 77 F5
Smithy Cl. Formby L37 .... 12 B4
Smithy Cl. Garstang PR3 .... 178 C8
Smithy Cl. Stalmine FY6 .... 174 C7
Smithy Croft. FY8 .... 89 C6
Smithy Fold. Spotland Fold OL12 51 C1
Smithy Fold. Wrea Green PR4 ... 112 B4
Smithy Gn. L37 .... 12 B4
Smithy How. LA4 .... 238 E3
Smithy La. Barton L39 .... 14 A6
Smithy La. Brindle PR6 .... 77 F5
Smithy La. Claughton PR3 .... 179 B2
Smithy La. Colne BB8 .... 169 B8
Smithy La. Heysham LA3 .... 208 E6
Smithy La. Holmeswood PR4 ..... 37 C6
Smithy La. Holt Green L39 .... 6 A6
Smithy La. Hurlston Green L40 .. 23 B3
Smithy La. Lytham St Anne's FY8 . 89 C6
Smithy La. Mawdesley L40 .... 39 C2
Smithy La. Much Hoole PR4 .... 73 E2
Smithy La. Preesall FY6 .... 195 B3
Smithy La. Staining FY3 .... 130 E6
Smithy La. Stalmine FY6 .... 174 C7
Smithy La. Westhouse LA6 .... 236 E4
Smithy Lane Ends. L40 .... 23 D6
Smithy Mews. FY1 .... 129 C7
Smithy Row. BB7 .... 162 E1
Smithy St. [2] Bamber Bridge PR5 76 E8

Smithy St. [8] Haslingden BB4 .... 84 B3
Smithy St. [7] Ramsbottom BL0 .. 49 C6
Smithy Wlk. L40 .... 24 E5
Smithyfield Ave. BB10 .... 127 F6
Snaefell Rd. BB2 .... 100 C1
Snape Gn. PR8 .... 22 D8
Snape La. LA5 .... 219 F1
Snape Rake La. PR3 .... 180 D4
Snape St. BB3 .... 80 F3
Snapewood La. PR3 .... 199 B3
Snell Cres. BB8 .... 169 F6
Snell Gr. BB8 .... 169 F6
Sniddle Hill La. BB3 .... 63 E8
Snipe Cl. Blackpool FY3 .... 130 B6
Snipe Cl. Thornton FY5 .... 172 F5
Snipewood. PR7 .... 40 B6
Snodworth Rd. BB6 .... 122 D7
Snow Hill. PR1 .... 95 F8
Snow St. BB1 .... 100 F6
Snowden Ave. Blackburn BB1 ... 100 E7
Snowden Ave. Morecambe LA3 . 212 A3
Snowden St. BB12 .... 126 B6
Snowdon Cl. FY1 .... 129 D3
Snowdon Dr. BL6 .... 31 C5
Snowdon Rd. FY8 .... 110 A2
Snowdrop Cl. BB4 .... 66 F8
Snowhill La. PR3 .... 199 F6
Snowshill Cres. FY5 .... 150 F7
Sod Hall La. PR4 & PR5 .... 75 A5
Sollam's Cl. PR5 .... 96 F2
Sollom La. PR5 .... 56 B2
Solway Cl. Blackpool FY2 .... 150 C6
Solway Cl. Penwortham PR1 .... 95 E3
Somerby Rd. LA4 .... 212 F4
Somerford Cl. BB12 .... 126 D7
Somerset Ave. Blackpool FY1 ... 129 D3
Somerset Ave. Chorley PR7 .... 60 C1
Somerset Ave. Clitheroe BB7 ... 186 F2
Somerset Ave. Darwen BB3 .... 80 F3
Somerset Ave. Lancaster LA1 ... 211 A6
Somerset Ave. Wilpshire BB1 ... 121 F6
Somerset Cl. BB5 .... 102 F3
Somerset Ct. FY1 .... 129 D3
Somerset Dr. PR8 .... 20 C3
Somerset Gr. Church BB5 .... 102 F7
Somerset Gr. [6]
  Passmonds OL12 .... 51 A1
Somerset Pl. PR7 .... 116 B7
Somerset Pl. BB9 .... 169 A1
Somerset Rd. Leyland PR5 .... 76 B2
Somerset Rd. Preston PR1 .... 117 A1
Somerset Rd. Rishton BB1 .... 123 A1
Somerset Wlk. BB8 .... 67 B8
Sorrel Cl. FY5 .... 172 F5
Sorrel Ct. PR1 .... 95 C2
Soudan St. BB10 .... 147 B2
Sough La. Belthorn BB1 .... 82 A7
Sough La. Blackburn BB1 & BB5 101 F2
Sough La. Sough BB8 .... 192 A7
Sough Rd. BB3 .... 64 B7
South Ave. Barnoldswick BB8 ... 200 B3
South Ave. Chorley PR7 .... 42 D6
South Ave. Cleveleys FY5 .... 172 C4
South Ave. Morecambe LA4 ..... 212 F5
South Ave. New Longton PR4 .... 74 F8
South Cliff St. FY8 .... 95 E6
South Clifton St. FY8 .... 90 B3
South Cross St. BL9 .... 32 A1
South Dr. Appley Bridge WN6 .... 27 C2
South Dr. Fulwood PR2 .... 116 E7
South Dr. Inskip PR4 .... 134 C8
South Dr. Padiham BB12 .... 125 E8
South End. PR1 .... 95 E5
South Gr. Barton PR3 .... 136 B8
South Gr. Fulwood PR2 .... 116 E8
South Gr. Morecambe LA4 .... 212 F5
South Hey. BB5 .... 89 C6
South Holme. FY8 .... 90 B4
South King St. FY1 .... 129 C5
South Lawn. FY1 .... 129 E2
South Meade. L31 .... 5 B1
South Meadow La. PR1 .... 95 E6
South Meadow St. PR1 .... 96 A8
South Moss Rd. FY8 .... 89 C7
South Par. [5] Barnoldswick BB8 200 B3
South Par. Cleveleys FY5 .... 172 E1
South Park Dr. FY3 .... 129 F2
South Pier. [4]
  Blackpool FY4 .... 109 A8
South Pine St. BL9 .... 32 B2
South Pk. FY8 .... 90 A4
South Prom. FY8 .... 88 E5
South Rd. Bretherton PR5 .... 56 F5
South Rd. Coppull PR7 .... 41 E1
South Rd. Lancaster LA1 .... 210 F7
South Rd. Morecambe LA4 ...... 212 G5
South Shore St. Church BB5 .... 102 E5
South Shore St. Haslingden BB4 84 A3
South Sq. Blackpool FY3 .... 129 D6
South Sq. Cleveleys FY5 .... 172 D5
South St. Accrington BB5 .... 103 C5
South St. Accrington BB5 .... 103 E8
South St. Bacup OL13 .... 87 A2
South St. Burnley BB11 .... 127 A6
South St. [15] Darwen BB3 .... 81 A1
South St. Great Eccleston PR3 .. 154 B5
South St. Haslingden BB4 .... 84 C1
South St. Lytham St Anne's FY8 . 90 D4
South St. Newchurch BB4 .... 85 E1
South St. [16] Rawtenstall BB4 .. 85 A3
South Strand. FY7 .... 172 E7
South Terr. Euxton PR7 .... 59 D4
South Terr. Morecambe LA3 ...... 15 E4
South Terr. Ramsbottom BL0 ..... 67 C2
South View. Bamber Bridge PR5 . 76 B7
South View. Belmont BL7 .... 45 C5

South View. [3]
  Great Harwood BB6 .... 123 C5
South View. [17] Haslingden BB4 .. 84 B3
South View. Kirkham PR4 .... 113 A4
South View. Moss Side FY8 ...... 111 D1
South View. Nelson BB9 .... 147 D7
South View. Simonstone BB12 .. 144 E3
South View. St OL14 .... 108 C1
South View Terr. [2] PR5 .... 59 A8
South Warton St. FY8 .... 90 C3
South Westby St. FY8 .... 90 B3
Southbank Ave. FY4 .... 110 A7
Southbank Rd. PR8 .... 34 C5
Southbourne Ave. FY6 .... 151 C2
Southbourne Rd. PR3 .... 130 A2
Southbrook Rd. PR5 .... 75 F1
Southcliffe. BB6 .... 123 B6
Southcliffe Ave. BB12 .... 126 C7
Southdene. WN8 .... 26 B2
Southdown Dr. FY5 .... 151 D8
Southdowns Rd. PR7 .... 42 C6
Southern Ave. Burnley BB12 .... 126 C7
Southern Ave. Preston PR1 .... 96 C6
Southern Cl. PR3 .... 139 A6
Southern Par. PR1 .... 96 B6
Southern Rd. PR8 .... 34 A6
Southey Cl. PR2 .... 116 F7
Southey St. [2] BB11 .... 126 E6
Southfield. PR4 .... 73 E3
Southfield Dr. New Longton PR4 . 74 F7
Southfield Dr. Poulton-le-F FY3 . 130 C8
Southfield Dr.
  West Bradford BB7 .... 186 F5
Southfield Gdns. PR4 .... 73 E3
Southfield La. BB10 & BB8 ...... 148 C7
Southfield Rd. BL0 .... 49 A2
Southfield Sq. BB9 .... 147 F8
Southfield Terr. BB8 .... 170 E6
Southfleet Ave. FY7 .... 193 E1
Southfleet Pl. FY7 .... 193 E1
Southfold Pl. FY8 .... 90 A4
Southgate. Fleetwood FY7 .... 172 D8
Southgate. Fulwood PR2 .... 116 D5
Southgate. Morecambe LA3 ..... 213 A2
Southgate. Preston PR1 .... 116 F1
Southgate. Wallbank OL12 .... 51 C7
Southgates. PR7 .... 41 D3
Southlands. PR4 .... 113 A4
Southlands Ave. PR5 .... 96 C1
Southlands Dr. PR5 .... 58 C8
Southlands High Sch. PR7 .... 42 A5
Southport & Ainsdale
  Golf Links. PR8 .... 20 C7
Southport Coll. PR9 .... 34 C7
Southport General Hospl. PR8 34 D5
Southport New Rd.
  Banks PR4 & PR9 .... 54 D3
Southport New Rd. Holmes PR4 55 D3
Southport Old Links
  (Golf Course). PR9 .... 35 B8
Southport Old Rd. L37 & PR8 .... 12 B7
Southport Rd. Barton L39 .... 14 A6
Southport Rd. Brown Edge PR8 .. 35 B2
Southport Rd. Chorley PR7 .... 42 A8
Southport Rd. Formby L37 .... 12 A5
Southport Rd. Hurlston L40 .... 23 A2
Southport Rd. Maghull L31 & L39 . 5 B5
Southport Rd.
  Newton PR5 & PR7 .... 58 B2
Southport Rd.
  Scarisbrick L40 & PR8 .... 22 E7
Southport Terr. PR6 & PR7 .... 42 E7
Southport Zoo. PR9 .... 33 F7
Southside. PR7 .... 59 C3
Southway. Fleetwood FY7 .... 193 D1
Southway. Skelmersdale WN8 ... 18 B1
Southwood Ave. FY7 .... 193 F3
Southwood Cl. FY8 .... 89 E4
Southwood Dr. BB5 .... 103 E3
Southworth Ave. FY4 .... 109 E7
Southworth St. BB2 .... 100 D2
Sow Clough Rd. OL13 .... 86 D1
Sower Carr La. FY6 .... 174 D4
Sowerby Ave. FY4 .... 109 D8
Sowerby Rd. PR3 .... 155 E3
Sowerby St. BB12 .... 125 C8
Spa Garth. BB2 .... 164 F8
Spa La. L40 & WN8 .... 17 C4
Spa Rd. PR1 .... 95 D7
Spa St. Burnley BB12 .... 126 E7
Spa St. Padiham BB12 .... 125 D8
Spa St. Preston PR1 .... 95 D8
Spark La. L40 .... 38 B6
Sparrow Hill. WN6 & WN8 .... 10 A7
Sparth Ave. BB5 .... 123 F3
Sparth Rd. BB5 .... 123 F3
Speakmans Dr. WN6 .... 19 C6
Speedwell Cl. FY5 .... 172 F5
Speedwell St. BB2 .... 100 B2
Speke St. BB2 .... 100 B2
Spen Brook Houses. BB12 ...... 167 C2
Spen Brow. LA2 .... 233 B6
Spen Cnr. FY4 .... 129 D1
Spen Farm. FY4 .... 110 D8
Spen La. PR4 .... 113 E6
Spen Pl. PR4 .... 109 F8
Spenbrook Rd. BB12 .... 167 C3
Spencer Ct. FY1 .... 129 C7
Spencer St. Accrington BB5 .... 103 D6
Spencer St. Burnley BB10 .... 147 A1
Spencer St. Ramsbottom BL0 .... 49 B5
Spencer St. [10] Rawtenstall BB4 85 A7
Spencer's La. Ainsdale L39 ...... 21 B3
Spencer's La. Orrell WN5 .... 10 D7
Spencers. BB12 .... 167 F1

Spencers Dr. PR4 .... 56 A8
Spencers La. WN8 .... 9 B7
Spendmore La. PR7 .... 41 E1
Spenleach La. BL8 .... 48 D3
Spenser Cl. BB10 .... 128 C4
Spenser St. BB12 .... 125 D7
Spey Cl. Leyland PR5 .... 58 E8
Spey Cl. Standish WN6 .... 28 D1
Speyside. FY4 .... 109 D7
Spinners Gn. OL12 .... 51 F2
Spinners Sq. PR5 .... 76 F2
Spinney Brow. PR2 .... 117 D4
Spinney Cl. Lucas Green PR7 .... 60 B6
Spinney Cl. New Longton PR4 ... 74 F8
Spinney Cl. Ormskirk L39 .... 15 D3
Spinney La. LA5 .... 218 C8
Spinney The. Arnside LA5 .... 218 C8
Spinney The. Blackburn BB2 ... 100 A8
Spinney The. Chapeltown BL7 .. 47 C2
Spinney The. Chorley PR6 & PR7 60 C3
Spinney The. Cleveleys FY5 .... 150 F7
Spinney The. Formby L37 .... 12 A5
Spinney The. Lancaster LA1 ... 211 B5
Spinney The. Penwortham PR1 .. 94 F3
Spinney The. Poulton-le-F FY3 . 151 E4
Spinney The. Tarleton PR4 .... 56 A7
Spinnings The. BL0 .... 49 C3
Spiredale Dr. WN6 .... 28 F2
Spires Gr. PR4 .... 115 E5
Spod Rd. OL12 .... 51 D1
Spodden Cotts. OL12 .... 70 D2
Spodden Fold. OL12 .... 51 C8
Spotland Tops. OL12 .... 51 B1
Spout La. LA2 .... 235 F1
Spouthouse La. BB5 .... 124 F1
Spread Eagle St. BB5 .... 102 C5
Spring Ave. BB6 .... 123 C6
Spring Bank. Appley Bridge WN6 19 C5
Spring Bank. Middle Healey OL12 51 D4
Spring Bank. Preston PR1 .... 95 E7
Spring Bank. Silverdale LA5 .... 218 C3
Spring Bank Terr. BB2 .... 100 C2
Spring Brook House. BB5 .... 123 F2
Spring Cl. Ramsbottom BL0 ...... 49 B6
Spring Cl. Southport PR8 .... 34 A5
Spring Cres. PR6 .... 60 E5
Spring Field. WA11 .... 8 E2
Spring Gardens Rd. BB8 .... 169 D4
Spring Gardens St. [4] BB4 ...... 68 F8
Spring Gardens Terr. [3] BB12 145 C1
Spring Gdn St. [38] LA1 .... 210 F8
Spring Gdns. [7] Accrington BB5 103 C5
Spring Gdns. [2] Bacup OL13 .... 87 A3
Spring Gdns. Darwen BB3 .... 64 A8
Spring Gdns. Freckleton PR4 ..... 92 B8
Spring Gdns. [12] Horwich BL6 .. 31 B4
Spring Gdns. Leyland PR5 .... 58 F8
Spring Gdns.
  Lytham St Anne's FY8 .... 109 F1
Spring Gdns. Newchurch BB4 .... 68 F6
Spring Gdns. Penwortham PR1 .. 95 F2
Spring Gr. BB8 .... 170 C6
Spring Hall. BB5 .... 123 F5
Spring Hill. [5] Blackburn BB1 .. 100 E5
Spring Hill. Freckleton PR4 .... 92 B7
Spring Hill Cty Prim Sch. BB5 103 B5
Spring Hill Rd. Accrington BB5 .. 102 F4
Spring Hill Rd. Burnley BB11 ... 126 F4
Spring La. Blackburn BB2 .... 100 B3
Spring La. Colne BB8 .... 169 D5
Spring La. Haslingden BB4 .... 84 B4
Spring La. Nab's Head BB2 & PR5 98 C8
Spring Meadow. PR6 .... 76 B3
Spring Meadows. BB3 .... 64 D7
Spring Mews. PR6 .... 60 E6
Spring Pl. Colne BB8 .... 169 D5
Spring Pl. Whitworth OL12 .... 70 D3
Spring Rd. Gathurst WN5 .... 19 F1
Spring Rd. Orrell WN5 .... 10 F8
Spring Side. Newchurch BB4 ..... 68 F6
Spring Side. Whitworth OL12 ..... 70 D4
Spring Side Cotts. BL7 .... 46 A2
Spring St. Accrington BB5 .... 102 F4
Spring St. Bacup OL13 .... 86 F1
Spring St. Bank Lane BL0 .... 49 D7
Spring St. Cornholme OL14 ..... 108 C1
Spring St. Horwich BL6 .... 31 B4
Spring St. Leyland PR5 .... 76 B1
Spring St. Nelson BB9 .... 147 C7
Spring St. [5] Oswaldtwistle BB5 102 E4
Spring St. Ramsbottom BL0 ...... 49 B6
Spring St. Rawtenstall BB4 .... 85 A8
Spring St. Rishton BB1 .... 123 B2
Spring Terr. [4] Bacup OL13 ...... 69 D8
Spring Terr. Langho BB6 .... 142 D1
Spring Terr. Oswaldtwistle BB5 102 D4
Spring Terr. Passmonds OL12 .... 51 A1
Spring Terr S. [5] BB4 .... 84 E2
Spring Vale. PR3 .... 204 D3
Spring Vale Garden Village.
  BB3 .... 64 C6
Spring View. BB3 .... 64 B7
Spring View. BB2 .... 100 C5
Spring Villas. OL14 .... 108 B1
Spring Wood St. BL0 .... 49 B7
Spring Yd. [3] BB8 .... 169 D5
Springbank Ave. FY5 .... 173 C2
Springbrook Ave. FY5 .... 150 F8
Springcroft. PR5 .... 76 C3
Springdale Rd. BB6 .... 122 C8
Springfield. Arnside LA5 .... 237 B2
Springfield. Blacko BB9 .... 168 D8
Springfield. High Bentham LA2 . 233 E8
Springfield Ave. Accrington BB5 102 F4

Springfield Ave. Bacup OL13 ...... 87 A3
Springfield Ave. Blackburn BB2 .... 99 E1
Springfield Ave. Earby BB8 .... 201 C1
Springfield Ave. Kirkham PR4 ...... 112 E5
Springfield Bank. BB11 .... 127 B5
Springfield Cl. Burscough L40 ...... 24 D2
Springfield Cl. Formby L37 .... 11 C2
Springfield Cl. Whalley BB7 .... 143 D6
Springfield Cres. LA2 .... 233 E8
Springfield Ct. FY3 .... 129 E3
Springfield Dr. Newchurch BB4 .... 85 E1
Springfield Dr. Thornton FY5 .... 173 B4
Springfield Flats. **6** BB3 .... 64 A8
Springfield Gdns. BB23 .... 199 E6
Springfield Rd. Adlington PR6 ...... 30 A8
Springfield Rd. Blackpool FY1 ...... 129 B6
Springfield Rd. Burnley BB11 ...... 127 A4
Springfield Rd. Burnley BB11 ...... 127 B5
Springfield Rd. **1** Chorley PR7 .. 42 C8
Springfield Rd. Coppull PR7 .... 28 E8
Springfield Rd.
    Great Harwood BB6 .... 123 B4
Springfield Rd. Holt Green L39 ..... 5 F6
Springfield Rd. Horwich BL6 .... 31 D1
Springfield Rd. Leyland PR5 .... 58 D7
Springfield Rd.
    Lytham St Anne's FY8 .... 88 E6
Springfield Rd. Nelson BB9 .... 198 E6
Springfield Rd. Ramsbottom BL0 .. 49 A2
Springfield Rd. Rawtenstall BB4 ... 85 B3
Springfield Rd N. PR7 .... 41 E1
Springfield St. Blackburn BB2 ...... 100 B3
Springfield St. Darwen BB3 .... 64 A8
Springfield St. Lancaster LA1 ...... 210 F7
Springfield St. Morecambe LA4 .... 212 C4
Springfield St.
    Oswaldtwistle BB5 .... 102 D4
Springfield St. Preston PR1 .... 116 E1
Springfield Terr.
    Blackburn BB2 .... 100 A1
Springfield Terr.
    High Bentham LA2 .... 233 E8
Springfield Terr. Thornton FY5 .... 173 A6
Springfield View. BB11 .... 105 C5
Springhill Ave. OL13 .... 69 D8
Springhill Prim Sch. BB5 .... 103 A4
Springhill Villas. OL13 .... 69 D8
Springmount. BB8 .... 201 C2
Springmount Dr. WN8 .... 26 C5
Springs Brow. PR7 .... 28 D5
Springs Rd. Chorley PR6 .... 60 D2
Springs Rd. Longridge PR3 .... 139 B8
Springsands Cl. PR2 .... 117 E5
Springthorpe St. BB3 .... 64 B6
Springvale. BB5 .... 102 F4
Springvale Bsns Pk. BB3 .... 64 B6
Springwater Ave. BL0 .... 49 A3
Springwood Cl. PR1 .... 96 A3
Springwood Dr. PR7 .... 42 E5
Springwood Rd. BB10 .... 127 E5
Sprodley Dr. WN8 .... 27 B2
Spruce Ave. BL9 .... 32 B2
Spruce Cl. BB5 .... 103 E8
Spruce St. BL0 .... 49 B5
Spruce Way. L37 .... 11 C3
Sprucewood Cl. BB5 .... 103 D6
Spurrier St. PR5 .... 76 A4
Spymers Croft. L37 .... 12 A6
Square House La. PR9 .... 54 C6
Square La. Burscough L40 .... 24 E3
Square La. Catforth PR4 .... 134 F4
Square St. BL0 .... 49 C6
Square The. Blackpool FY3 .... 130 A2
Square The. Brinscall PR6 .... 61 F7
Square The. Burton-in-K LA6 ...... 234 B7
Square The. Cleveleys FY5 .... 172 D5
Square The.
    Cumeragh Village PR3 .... 137 F5
Square The.
    Great Eccleston PR3 .... 154 B5
Square The. **1** Leyland PR5 ..... 76 B2
Square The. Scorton PR3 .... 199 E6
Square The. Storth LA7 .... 237 F5
Squire Rd. BB9 .... 147 F8
Squire's Gate Rd. PR2 .... 116 C3
Squires Cl. PR5 .... 97 E2
Squires Gate La. FY4 .... 109 D5
Squires Gate Link Rd. FY4 .... 110 C7
Squires Rd. PR1 .... 95 C6
Squires Wood. PR2 .... 117 D6
Squirrel Fold. PR1 .... 117 F2
Squirrel Gn. L37 .... 11 C5
Squirrel La. BL6 .... 31 A4
Squirrel's Chase. PR5 .... 76 A7
Squirrels Cl. BB5 .... 103 E8
Stable Cl. Gisburn BB7 .... 225 B3
Stable Cl. Kirkham PR4 .... 113 A6
Stable La. PR6 .... 61 A7
Stables Cl. BB4 .... 85 A6
Stack Croft. PR4 .... 77 A2
Stack La. OL13 .... 70 B8
Stackhouses The. **2** BB11 ...... 127 A6
Stadium Ave. FY4 .... 109 E5
Staffa Cres. BB1 .... 101 D4
Stafford Ave. FY6 .... 151 D1
Stafford Moreton Way. L31 .... 5 D1
Stafford Rd. **9** Preston PR1 .... 96 B8
Stafford Rd. Southport PR8 .... 34 A1
Stafford St. Burnley BB10 .... 127 A7
Stafford St. Darwen BB3 .... 80 F4
Stafford St. Nelson BB9 .... 148 A8
Stafford St. Skelmersdale WN8 ... 17 E2
Staghills Rd. BB4 .... 85 D1
Stainburn Cl. WN6 .... 19 E6
Stainforth Ave. FY2 .... 150 E5

Staining Ave. PR2 .... 94 F8
Staining CE Sch. FY3 .... 130 D5
Staining Old Rd. FY3 .... 130 D7
Staining Rd. FY3 .... 130 C6
Staining Rise. FY3 .... 130 E5
Stainton Dr. BB12 .... 126 E8
Stainton Gr. LA4 .... 213 A4
Stakepool Dr. PR3 .... 196 E4
Stakes Hall Pl. BB2 .... 100 C2
Stalls Rd. LA3 .... 208 F2
Stalmine Prim Sch. FY6 .... 174 D7
Stamford Ave. FY4 .... 109 D7
Stamford Ct. FY8 .... 88 D8
Stamford Dr. PR6 .... 60 C5
Stamford Pl. BB7 .... 186 F1
Stamford Rd. Skelmersdale WN8 . 17 D2
Stamford Rd. Southport PR8 ...... 34 B2
Stanagate. PR4 .... 114 C1
Stanah Cty Jun Sch. FY5 .... 173 D1
Stanah Cty Jun Sch. FY5 .... 173 D1
Stanah Gdns. FY5 .... 173 E2
Stanah Rd. FY5 .... 173 E2
Stanbury Cl. OL10 .... 32 D1
Stanbury Dr. BB10 .... 147 E2
Stancliffe St. BB2 .... 100 C3
Standen Hall Cl. BB10 .... 147 E3
Standen Hall Dr. BB10 .... 147 D3
Standen Rd. BB7 .... 164 F7
Standen Road Bglws. BB7 .... 164 F7
Standhouse La. L39 .... 15 C2
Standing Stone La. BB8 & BB9 .. 191 B2
Standish Comm High Sch.
    WN6 .... 28 C2
Standish St. Burnley BB11 .... 127 A6
Standish St. Chorley PR6 & PR7 .. 42 D7
Standroyd Bglws. BB8 .... 170 A5
Standroyd Dr. BB8 .... 170 A5
Standroyd Rd. BB8 .... 170 A5
Stanedge Cl. BL0 .... 49 C4
Stanford Gdns. BB2 .... 101 A1
Stanford Hall Cres. BL0 .... 49 B4
Stang Top Rd. BB9 .... 167 F7
Stangate. L31 .... 5 B2
Stanhill Ave. BB5 .... 102 C4
Stanhill Rd. BB1 & BB5 .... 101 F4
Stanhope Ave. LA3 .... 213 A3
Stanhope Ct. LA3 .... 213 B3
Stanhope Rd. FY1 .... 129 C7
Stanhope St. Burnley BB12 ...... 126 F7
Stanhope St. Darwen BB3 .... 81 A2
Stanhope St. Preston PR1 .... 116 E2
Stanier Pl. BL6 .... 31 C2
Stanifield Cl. PR5 .... 76 B3
Stanifield La. PR5 .... 76 C5
Stankelt Rd. LA5 .... 218 C2
Stanlawe Rd. L37 .... 11 E6
Stanley Ave. Cleveleys FY5 ...... 172 E2
Stanley Ave. Hutton PR4 .... 94 D2
Stanley Ave. Leyland PR5 .... 76 C4
Stanley Ave. Poulton-le-F FY6 .. 151 D3
Stanley Ave. Southport PR8 ...... 33 F3
Stanley Cl. PR3 .... 139 B7
Stanley Croft. PR5 .... 136 B3
Stanley Ct. Burscough Bridge L40 24 E5
Stanley Ct. Chipping PR3 .... 182 E3
Stanley Ct. Kirkham PR4 .... 113 B4
Stanley Dr. Darwen BB3 .... 64 B5
Stanley Dr. Hornby LA2 .... 232 B7
Stanley Fold. PR5 .... 75 F8
Stanley Gate. Fleetwood FY7 .... 193 D3
Stanley Gate. Mellor BB2 .... 120 E2
Stanley Gr. Horwich BL6 .... 31 D1
Stanley Gr. Penwortham PR1 .... 95 A5
Stanley High St. PR9 .... 52 F4
Stanley Mount. **7** OL13 .... 86 F3
Stanley Park FY3 .... 129 F3
Stanley Park Golf Course.
    FY3 .... 130 B6
Stanley Pl. Chorley PR6 .... 42 C8
Stanley Pl. Lancaster LA1 .... 210 D8
Stanley Pl. Preston PR1 .... 95 E7
Stanley Prim & Inf Sch. FY3 ..... 130 B2
Stanley Range. BB2 .... 100 B1
Stanley Rd. Blackpool FY1 .... 129 C4
Stanley Rd. Fleetwood FY7 ...... 193 F3
Stanley Rd. Formby L37 .... 11 E6
Stanley Rd. Hall Green WN8 ..... 10 B7
Stanley Rd. Kirkham PR4 .... 112 F7
Stanley Rd. Leyland PR5 .... 76 C4
Stanley Rd.
    Lytham St Anne's FY8 .... 89 D3
Stanley Rd. Morecambe LA3 ..... 212 B3
Stanley Rd. Accrington BB5 ...... 103 D6
Stanley Rd. Bacup OL13 .... 86 F4
Stanley Rd. Blackburn BB1 .... 101 B6
Stanley Rd. Brierfield BB9 .... 147 B6
Stanley Rd. Burnley BB11 .... 126 F5
Stanley Rd. Carnforth LA5 .... 217 D1
Stanley Rd. Colne BB8 .... 169 D5
Stanley Rd. Kirkham PR4 .... 113 B4
Stanley Rd. **6** Leyland PR5 .... 76 B1
Stanley Rd. Longridge PR3 .... 139 A8
Stanley Rd. Morecambe LA4 ..... 212 B6
Stanley Rd. Nelson BB9 .... 147 D8
Stanley Rd. Ormskirk L39 .... 15 F5
Stanley Rd. Oswaldtwistle BB5 .. 102 D3
Stanley Rd. Preston PR1 .... 96 B8
Stanley Rd. Ramsbottom BL0 .... 49 B5
Stanley Rd. Rochdale OL12 ...... 51 E1
Stanley Rd. Southport PR8 & PR9 . 34 B8
Stanley Terr. PR1 .... 95 E7
Stanley Way. WN8 .... 17 E3
Stanleyfield Cl. PR1 .... 117 A1
Stanleyfield Rd. PR1 .... 117 A1
Stanmore Ave. FY4 .... 109 F6
Stanmore Dr. LA1 .... 210 E5
Stannanought Rd. WN8 .... 18 E2

Stanning St. PR5 .... 59 A8
Stanridge Clough La. BB8 .... 201 D1
Stanrose Cl. BL7 .... 46 E1
Stansfeld St. BB2 .... 100 C3
Stansfield Ave. L31 .... 5 F1
Stansfield Cl. **7** BB9 .... 168 D4
Stansfield Rd. BB4 .... 68 E8
Stansfield St. **2** Bacup OL13 .. 69 C8
Stansfield St. Blackpool FY1 ..... 129 C1
Stansfield St. Burnley BB11 ...... 126 B5
Stansfield St. **5** Darwen BB3 .. 64 A8
Stansfield St. Nelson BB9 .... 147 E8
Stansfield Terr. OL14 .... 108 B1
Stansford Ct. PR1 .... 95 D4
Stansted Rd. PR7 .... 42 A7
Stansy Ave. LA3 .... 212 B1
Stanworth Rd. BB9 .... 147 D8
Stanworth St. Burnley BB10 ..... 127 A8
Stanworth St. Worsthorne BB10 128 B5
Stanworth Terr. PR6 .... 79 B4
Stapleton Rd. L37 .... 11 D1
Star La. BL6 .... 30 F3
Star La. **1** Accrington BB5 ...... 102 F5
Star St. Darwen BB3 .... 81 B1
Starbeck Ave. FY4 .... 129 D1
Starfield Cl. FY8 .... 90 A4
Starkie St. Blackburn BB1 .... 100 F5
Starkie St. Burnley BB11 .... 126 E5
Starkie St. Darwen BB3 .... 64 B8
Starkie St. **8** Leyland PR5 ...... 76 B1
Starkie St. Preston PR1 .... 95 F6
Starr Gate. FY4 .... 109 B4
Starrgate Dr. PR2 .... 115 E1
Startifants La. PR3 .... 181 F4
Startifants Lane End. PR3 .... 182 A5
Startley Nook. PR4 .... 75 B6
States Rd. FY8 .... 89 B6
Statham Rd. WN8 .... 17 E3
Statham Way. L39 .... 15 E4
Station App.
    Burscough Bridge L40 .... 24 E5
Station App. Ormskirk L39 .... 15 F5
Station Ave. WN5 .... 10 D5
Station Brow. PR5 .... 76 B2
Station Cl. Hornby LA2 .... 232 B7
Station Cl. Rishton BB1 .... 102 A8
Station Cl. Wilpshire BB1 .... 121 F4
Station La. Burton-in-K LA6 ...... 234 B7
Station La. Nateby PR3 .... 198 B1
Station La.
    Newsham PR3 & PR4 .... 136 A5
Station La. Scorton PR3 .... 199 D7
Station Par. OL14 .... 107 F1
Station Rd. Adlington PR7 .... 30 A6
Station Rd. Ainsdale PR8 .... 20 C5
Station Rd. Arnside LA5 .... 237 C2
Station Rd. Bamber Bridge PR5 .. 76 E8
Station Rd. Banks PR9 .... 53 F5
Station Rd. Barnoldswick BB8 .... 200 B2
Station Rd. Barton L39 .... 13 E7
Station Rd. Blackpool FY4 .... 109 B8
Station Rd. Blackrod BL6 .... 30 E1
Station Rd. Broadley OL12 .... 51 C5
Station Rd. Burton-in-K LA6 ...... 234 B8
Station Rd. Chapeltown BL7 ...... 47 C4
Station Rd. Clitheroe BB7 .... 164 E8
Station Rd. Coppull PR7 .... 41 F1
Station Rd. Cornholme OL14 ..... 108 C1
Station Rd. Croston PR5 .... 57 B3
Station Rd. Fleetwood FY7 .... 194 A4
Station Rd. Foulridge BB8 .... 191 D1
Station Rd. Great Harwood BB6 .. 123 D5
Station Rd. Haslingden BB4 ...... 84 B4
Station Rd. Helmshore BB4 ...... 67 A7
Station Rd. Hesketh Bank PR4 ... 72 F3
Station Rd. Hest Bank LA2 .... 215 D1
Station Rd. High Bentham LA2 ... 233 D7
Station Rd. Hoghton PR5 .... 98 B2
Station Rd. Hornby LA2 .... 232 B7
Station Rd. Huncoat BB5 .... 124 E2
Station Rd. Kirkham PR4 .... 112 F6
Station Rd. Lancaster LA1 .... 210 E8
Station Rd. Leyland PR5 .... 75 A3
Station Rd. Lytham St Anne's FY8 90 B3
Station Rd. Maghull L31 .... 5 A6
Station Rd. Morecambe LA4 ..... 212 E5
Station Rd. New Longton PR4 .... 74 F8
Station Rd. Ormskirk L39 .... 15 F6
Station Rd. Padiham BB12 .... 125 C8
Station Rd. Parbold WN8 .... 26 C2
Station Rd. Poulton-le-F FY6 .... 151 E4
Station Rd. Ramsbottom BL8 .... 48 F1
Station Rd. Rimington BB7 .... 188 E8
Station Rd. Rishton BB1 .... 123 A1
Station Rd. Rufford L40 .... 38 D4
Station Rd. Salwick PR4 .... 114 C4
Station Rd. Singleton FY6 .... 152 E1
Station Rd. Thornton FY5 .... 173 D1
Station Rd. Walmer Bridge PR4 .. 73 D4
Station Rd. Whalley BB7 .... 143 C5
Station Rd. Whitworth OL12 ..... 70 D3
Station Rd. Wrea Green PR4 ..... 112 B4
Station Sq. FY8 .... 90 A3
Station Terr. Abbey Village BB2 .. 79 C2
Station Terr. Blackpool FY4 ...... 108 B8
Station Way. Garstang PR3 ...... 178 C8
Station Way. Hornby LA2 .... 232 B7
Staunton St. LA5 .... 217 D3
Staveley Pl. PR2 .... 115 E2
Staveley Rd. Ainsdale PR8 .... 20 C4
Staveley Rd. Skelmersdale WN8 . 17 E3
Staynall La. FY6 .... 174 B4
Steamtown (Carnforth). LA5 .... 217 C2
Steeley La. PR6 .... 42 D7
Steeple View. Preston PR1 .... 95 D8

Steeple View. Preston PR1 .... 116 D1
Steer St. BB10 .... 147 B1
Steeton Rd. FY6 .... 151 B1
Stefano Rd. **1** PR1 .... 96 C8
Steiner St. BB5 .... 103 A6
Steiner's La. BB5 .... 102 E7
Step Row. OL13 .... 86 F5
Stephen St. Blackburn BB2 ...... 100 B2
Stephen St.
    Lytham St Anne's FY8 .... 88 E7
Stephendale Ave. PR5 .... 77 B8
Stephens Gr. LA3 .... 205 D8
Stephenson Dr. BB12 .... 126 C7
Stephenson St. **2** Chorley PR6 . 42 E7
Stephenson St. Horwich BL6 .... 31 B2
Stephenson Way. L37 .... 12 C3
Sterling Pl. **5** OL10 .... 32 F1
Sterndale Ave. WN6 .... 28 E2
Stevenson Ave. PR5 .... 76 C3
Stevenson St E. BB5 .... 103 A5
Stevenson St W. BB5 .... 102 F5
Steward Ave. LA1 .... 211 B5
Stewart Cl. LA5 .... 218 B8
Stewart St. Blackburn BB2 .... 80 D8
Stewart St. Burnley BB11 .... 127 B4
Stewart St. Preston PR1 .... 95 D8
Stiles Ave. PR4 .... 94 C1
Stiles The. L39 .... 15 E5
Stirling Cl. Chorley PR7 .... 42 E7
Stirling Cl. Clitheroe BB7 .... 164 C6
Stirling Cl. **1** Leyland PR5 ..... 76 C1
Stirling Ct. Lane Bottom BB10 .. 148 B4
Stirling Ct. Southport PR9 .... 53 A2
Stirling Dr. BB1 .... 100 F4
Stirling Rd. Blackpool FY3 .... 129 D7
Stirling Rd. Lancaster LA1 .... 211 A7
Stirling St. BB2 .... 100 B1
Stock's Park Sch. BL6 .... 31 C3
Stockbridge Cotts. BB7 .... 162 E3
Stockbridge Dr. BB12 .... 125 E8
Stockbridge Rd. BB12 .... 125 D7
Stockclough La. BB2 .... 79 D6
Stockdale Cres. PR5 .... 76 F8
Stockdove Way. FY5 .... 172 E3
Stockdove Wood. FY5 .... 172 E3
Stockholm St. BB11 .... 126 B5
Stockley Cres. L39 .... 7 E6
Stockley Dr. WN6 .... 19 E8
Stockpit Rd. L33 .... 1 D2
Stocks Ct. **4** FY6 .... 151 D3
Stocks La.
    Barnoldswick BB7 & BB8 & BB9 . 190 A7
Stocks La. Blackpool FY6 .... 151 A3
Stocks La. Heskin Green PR7 .... 40 E3
Stocks Lane End. PR3 .... 178 C2
Stocks Park Dr. BL6 .... 31 C3
Stocks Rd. PR1 & PR2 .... 116 C2
Stocks St. PR1 .... 95 E8
Stockwood Cl. BB2 .... 100 A8
Stockydale Rd. FY4 .... 110 A6
Stoke Ave. FY1 .... 129 C2
Stokes Hall Ave. PR5 .... 59 A8
Stone Bridge La. BB5 .... 102 E3
Stone Cl. BL0 .... 49 A4
Stone Croft. PR1 .... 95 D2
Stone Cross Gdns. PR3 .... 178 C2
Stone Edge Rd. BB9 .... 168 E6
Stone Hall La. WN8 .... 19 A5
Stone Hill Dr. BB1 .... 122 A1
Stone Hill La. OL12 .... 51 A2
Stone Holme Terr. BB4 .... 85 A8
Stone House Fold. BB10 .... 106 E6
Stone Moor Bottom. BB12 ...... 125 C6
Stone Park Rd. PR3 .... 136 C3
Stone Pits. BL0 .... 67 B3
Stone Row Head. LA1 .... 211 C8
Stone St. Haslingden BB4 .... 83 F2
Stone St. Newchurch BB4 .... 68 F8
Stonebarn Dr. L31 .... 5 C3
Stonebridge Cl. **5** PR5 .... 76 C8
Stonebridge Terr. PR3 .... 139 A7
Stonechat Cl. FY3 .... 130 B6
Stonecroft. BB9 .... 168 E6
Stonecroft Rd. PR5 .... 58 D7
Stonedross La. LA6 .... 238 C6
Stonefield. Longton PR4 .... 73 F8
Stonefield. Penwortham PR1 .... 95 E4
Stonefold Ave. PR1 .... 96 B8
Stonefold CE Prim Sch. BB4 .... 84 A7
Stonegate Fold. PR6 .... 43 B1
Stonehill Cres. OL12 .... 51 A3
Stonehill Dr. OL12 .... 51 B3
Stonehill Rd. OL12 .... 51 B3
Stoneholme Ind Est. BB4 .... 85 A8
Stoneholme Rd. BB4 .... 85 A8
Stonehouse Gn. PR6 .... 77 B3
Stoneleigh Cl. PR8 .... 20 C4
Stoner Rd. PR7 .... 29 F7
Stones Bank Rd. BL7 .... 46 B5
Stones La. BB3 .... 178 E3
Stoneway Rd. FY5 .... 172 E1
Stonewell. **17** LA1 .... 210 F8
Stoney Brow. WN8 .... 19 B1
Stoney Butts. PR2 .... 94 D8
Stoney Croft Dr. LA5 .... 217 E6
Stoney Ct. BB8 .... 191 E1
Stoney Holt. PR6 .... 76 E1
Stoney La. Adlington PR7 .... 29 E4
Stoney La. Bamber Bridge PR5 .. 76 E6
Stoney La. Foulridge BB8 .... 191 E1
Stoney La. Freckleton PR4 ...... 92 B5
Stoney La. Galgate PR3 .... 207 B3
Stoney La. Hambleton FY6 ...... 174 C2
Stoney La. **7** BB11 .... 127 B4
Stoneybutts. **8** BB1 .... 100 E5
Stoneycroft. BB10 .... 128 A6
Stoneycroft Ave. BL6 .... 31 D4

Stoneycroft Cl. BL6 .... 31 D5
Stoneycroft Dr. LA5 .... 237 B1
Stoneygate. Cleveleys FY5 ...... 172 F1
Stoneygate. **18** Preston PR1 .. 96 A7
Stoneygate La. WN6 .... 27 B2
Stoneyholme Prim Sch. BB12 ... 126 F8
Stoneyhurst Ave. FY5 .... 151 D8
Stoneyhurst Height. BB9 .... 147 D4
Stoneyroyd. OL12 .... 70 D1
Stony Bank. PR6 .... 78 A6
Stony Bank Rd. BB8 .... 201 C2
Stony Croft Pl. **2** FY4 .... 109 C5
Stony Hill Ave. FY4 .... 109 C5
Stony La. Cockerham PR3 .... 203 F2
Stony La. Cornholme OL14 ...... 108 E2
Stony La. Hollins Lane PR3 ...... 204 D3
Stony La. Parbold WN6 & WN8 .. 26 E4
Stonycroft Ave. FY4 .... 109 C5
Stonygate La. PR3 .... 140 D6
Stonyhurst. PR7 .... 42 C4
Stonyhurst Ave. BB10 .... 127 D5
Stonyhurst Cl. Blackburn BB2 .. 100 D4
Stonyhurst Cl. Padiham BB12 ... 125 E6
Stonyhurst Coll. BB7 .... 163 A3
Stonyhurst Rd. BB2 .... 100 D4
Stoop St. BB11 .... 126 C5
Stoopes Hill. BB8 .... 201 C2
Stoops Fold. BB2 .... 120 E2
Stoops La. BB7 .... 188 F8
Stopes Brow. BB1 & BB3 .... 81 A7
Stopford Ave. FY2 .... 150 E2
Stopford Ct. **1** BB5 .... 123 F3
Stopgate La. L33 .... 1 C7
Stopper La. BB7 .... 189 B7
Store St. Blackburn BB3 .... 81 A7
Store St. **14** Haslingden BB4 .. 84 B3
Store St. Horwich BL6 .... 31 C4
Store Yard. PR4 .... 114 E7
Storey Ave. LA1 .... 210 D8
Storey Institute (Coll of F Ed).
    LA1 .... 210 E8
Stork Cl. FY5 .... 172 F1
Storrs La. LA5 .... 219 B4
Storth CE Prim Sch. LA7 .... 237 F5
Storth Rd. LA7 .... 237 F3
Stott St. **2** Nelson BB9 .... 147 D8
Stott St. Rochdale OL12 .... 51 F1
Stour Lodge. PR2 .... 116 C6
Stourton Rd. PR8 .... 20 C4
Stourton St. BB1 .... 123 A2
Stout St. BB2 .... 100 D4
Straight Up La. PR9 .... 35 D8
Strait La. LA2 .... 226 F1
Straits. BB5 .... 102 E4
Straits La. BB12 .... 144 D2
Strand Rd. PR1 .... 95 D3
Strand St W. PR1 .... 95 C8
Strand The. Blackpool FY1 ...... 129 B6
Strand The. Fleetwood FY7 ..... 172 D8
Strand The. Horwich BL6 .... 31 D3
Strang St. **9** BL0 .... 49 C6
Strange St. BB11 .... 127 B4
Stransdale Cl. PR3 .... 178 A6
Stratford Cl. Ainsdale PR8 ...... 20 A6
Stratford Cl. Lancaster LA1 ..... 213 E3
Stratford Dr. PR2 .... 116 D4
Stratford Pl. Blackpool FY1 ..... 129 D2
Stratford Pl. Fleetwood FY7 .... 193 E4
Stratford Rd. Chorley PR6 ...... 42 D8
Stratford Rd.
    Lytham St Anne's FY8 .... 89 B7
Stratford Way. **7**
    Accrington BB5 .... 103 A7
Stratford Way. Colne BB8 .... 169 F5
Strathaven Pl. **7** OL10 .... 32 F1
Strathclyde Rd. BB1 .... 101 A4
Strathdale. FY4 .... 109 F7
Strathmore Cl. BL0 .... 49 C4
Strathmore Gr. PR7 .... 42 B7
Strathmore Rd. PR2 .... 116 E3
Strathyre Cl. FY2 .... 150 F5
Stratton Gr. BL0 .... 31 B5
Strawberry Bank. BB1 & BB2 ... 100 D5
Streatly Wlk. BB2 .... 81 A8
Street The. PR7 .... 43 E3
Strellas La. LA5 .... 216 C1
Stretton Ave. FY4 .... 109 E8
Stretton Dr. PR9 .... 34 F8
Stretton Rd. BL0 .... 49 A2
Strickens La. PR3 .... 179 C6
Strickland Dr. LA4 .... 213 A5
Strickland's La. FY5 .... 174 D6
Stricklands La. PR1 .... 95 E4
Strike La. PR4 .... 92 B8
Strike Lane Cty Prim Sch. PR4 .. 92 B8
Strine The. L40 & PR4 .... 56 A1
Stromness Gr. **6** OL10 .... 32 F1
Strongstry Rd. BL0 .... 67 C2
Stronsay Pl. FY2 .... 150 F6
Stroyan St. BB10 .... 127 C5
Strutt St. **2** PR1 .... 117 B1
Stryands. PR4 .... 94 C1
Sts John Fisher & Thomas
    More RC High Sch. BB8 ...... 169 B2
Stuart Ave. Bacup OL13 .... 69 D8
Stuart Ave. Morecambe LA4 .... 212 G6
Stuart Cl. **13** Darwen BB3 ..... 81 A1
Stuart Cl. Fulwood PR2 .... 117 E3
Stuart Rd. Fulwood PR2 .... 117 D3
Stuart Rd. Thornton FY5 .... 173 C2
Stuart St. Accrington BB5 .... 103 B7
Stuart St. Barnoldswick BB8 .... 200 C2
Stub La. PR4 .... 24 A2
Stubbins Cty Prim Sch. BL0 ..... 67 D1
Stubbins La. Catterall PR3 ...... 178 F2
Stubbins La. Ramsbottom BL0 .. 49 C8
Stubbins La. Sabden BB6 .... 145 A2
Stubbins St. BL0 .... 67 C1

Stubbins Vale Rd. BL0 .... 67 C1
Stubbins Vale Terr. BL0 .... 67 B1
Stubbylee La. OL13 .... 69 F8
Stubley Holme. OL14 .... 108 A1
Stubley La. OL14 .... 108 B1
Studfold. PR7 .... 60 B2
Studholme Ave. PR1 .... 95 E2
Studholme Cl. PR1 .... 95 E2
Studholme Cres. PR1 .... 95 E2
Stump Cross La. BB7 .... 224 F5
Stump La. PR6 .... 42 D8
Stunstead. BB8 .... 170 C2
Sturgess Cl. L39 .... 15 F7
Sturminster Cl. PR1 .... 95 E2
Styan St. FY7 .... 194 A4
Stydd La. PR3 .... 140 E4
Sudell Ave. L31 .... 5 F2
Sudell Cl. BB3 .... 81 C1
Sudell Cross. 20 BB1 .... 100 E5
Sudell La. L31 & L37 .... 5 E6
Sudell Prim Sch. BB3 .... 81 B1
Sudell Rd. BB3 .... 81 B1
Sudellside St. BB3 .... 81 B1
Suffolk Ave. BB12 .... 126 A6
Suffolk Cl. PR5 .... 58 E6
Suffolk Rd. Blackpool FY3 .. 130 A2
Suffolk Rd. Preston PR1 ...... 117 A1
Suffolk Rd. Southport PR8 ... 21 A8
Suffolk St. BB2 .... 100 C2
Sugar Stubbs La. PR9 .... 54 C4
Sugham La. LA3 .... 208 F8
Sulby Cl. PR8 .... 33 F3
Sulby Dr. Fulwood PR2 .... 117 F5
Sulby Dr. Lancaster LA1 ...... 210 F6
Sulby Gr. Fulwood PR2 .... 118 A5
Sulby Gr. Morecambe LA4 ... 213 A6
Sulby Rd. BB2 .... 100 E1
Sullivan Dr. BB2 .... 101 A1
Sullom Side La. PR3 .... 179 C5
Sullom View. PR3 .... 178 C6
Sultan St. BB5 .... 103 D7
Sulyard St. LA1 .... 210 F8
Summer St. Horwich BL6 ...... 31 B4
Summer St. Nelson BB9 .... 147 C4
Summer St. Skelmersdale WN8 ... 18 A4
Summer Trees Ave. PR4 .... 115 D3
Summerdale Dr. BL0 .... 49 B2
Summerer Rd. PR4 .... 131 F6
Summerfield. PR5 .... 75 F3
Summerfield Dr. LA2 .... 213 E7
Summerfields. FY8 .... 88 C8
Summerhill. LA2 .... 233 D7
Summerseat La. BL0 .... 49 A2
Summerseat Meth Prim Sch.
  BL9 .... 49 D2
Summerseat Special Sch. BL0 . 49 B2
Summerseat Sta. BL9 .... 49 C2
Summersgill Rd. LA1 .... 213 D2
Summerton Wlk. BB3 .... 81 A2
Summerville. FY4 .... 109 C6
Summerville Ave. FY3 .... 130 E5
Summerville Wlk. BB2 .... 100 D5
Summerwood Cl. FY2 .... 150 D1
Summerwood La. L39 .... 22 C1
Summit Cl. BL9 .... 32 F4
Summit Dr. PR4 .... 92 C6
Summit St. OL10 .... 32 F3
Summit Works. BB11 .... 126 E2
Sumner Ave. L39 .... 13 F4
Sumner Rd. L37 .... 11 F3
Sumner St. Blackburn BB2 .. 100 E3
Sumner St. Leyland PR5 .... 76 A1
Sumner's La. PR7 .... 39 A7
Sumpter Croft. PR1 .... 95 E2
Sumpter Ct. PR1 .... 95 F2
Sun St. Clitheroe BB7 .... 164 E7
Sun St. Colne BB8 .... 169 E5
Sun St. Lancaster LA1 .... 210 F8
Sun St. Nelson BB9 .... 147 C8
Sun St. Ramsbottom BL0 ...... 49 B7
Sun Terr. LA1 .... 108 B1
Sunacre Ct. LA3 .... 212 B3
Sunbank Cl. OL12 .... 51 D2
Sunbury Ave. PR1 .... 95 D3
Sunbury Dr. PR8 .... 20 B4
Suncliffe Rd. BB9 .... 147 D4
Sunderland Ave. Cleveleys FY5 ... 172 F4
Sunderland Ave.
  Hambleton FY6 .... 174 D2
Sunderland Dr. LA3 .... 212 D2
Sunderland St. BB12 .... 126 B6
Sunfield Cl. FY4 .... 110 A7
Sunnindale Ave. BB4 .... 86 A1
Sunningdale. PR3 .... 136 B3
Sunningdale Ave.
  Blackpool FY2 .... 130 A2
Sunningdale Ave.
  Fleetwood FY7 .... 172 D7
Sunningdale Ave.
  Hest Bank LA2 .... 215 D1
Sunningdale Cl. PR4 .... 113 A4
Sunningdale Cres. LA2 .... 215 D1
Sunningdale Dr. FY5 .... 151 D8
Sunningdale Gdns. BB10 .... 147 D3
Sunningdale Pl. PR4 .... 134 C8
Sunny Bank. PR4 .... 135 F4
Sunny Bank Ave. Blackpool FY2 150 C4
Sunny Bank Ave.
  Newton-with-S PR4 .... 114 A2
Sunny Bank Cl. BB4 .... 67 A6
Sunny Bank Cotts. BB4 .... 66 F5
Sunny Bank Mill. PR4 .... 112 F5
Sunny Bank Rd. Blackburn BB2 100 E1
Sunny Bank Rd. Helmshore BB4 ... 66 F6
Sunny Bank Terr. OL14 .... 108 B1
Sunny Bower Cl. BB1 .... 122 B1
Sunny Bower Rd. BB1 .... 122 B1
Sunny Brow. PR7 .... 42 A2

Sunny Dr. WN5 .... 10 F6
Sunny Lea St. BB4 .... 84 F5
Sunny Rd. PR9 .... 53 A2
Sunny View. BB2 .... 79 C2
Sunnybank Dr. BB5 .... 102 C2
Sunnybank Rd. LA5 .... 216 A5
Sunnybank St. Darwen BB3 ... 81 A1
Sunnybank St. 6
  Haslingden BB4 .... 84 A3
Sunnycliff Ret Pk. LA3 .... 212 G1
Sunnyfield Ave.
  Morecambe LA4 .... 213 A6
Sunnyfield Ave.
  Over Town BB10 .... 107 A8
Sunnyfield Cl. BB3 .... 65 A8
Sunnyfield Sch. LA3 .... 213 B3
Sunnyfields. BB3 .... 16 A5
Sunnyhill Cl. BB3 .... 80 D2
Sunnyhurst Ave. FY4 .... 109 D6
Sunnyhurst Cl. BB3 .... 80 D2
Sunnyhurst La. BB3 .... 80 D2
Sunnyhurst Rd. Blackburn BB2 100 D5
Sunnyhurst Rd. Blackburn BB2 100 D4
Sunnymede Dr. L31 .... 5 D3
Sunnymede Sch. PR8 .... 33 F6
Sunnymede Vale. BL0 .... 49 A3
Sunnymere Dr. BB3 .... 80 E2
Sunnyside. Ormskirk L39 .... 6 C7
Sunnyside. Southport BB8 .... 33 F3
Sunnyside Ave. Billington BB7 143 B4
Sunnyside Ave. Blackburn BB2 79 E8
Sunnyside Ave. Ribchester PR3 140 D3
Sunnyside Ave. Warton BB1 ... 91 E6
Sunnyside Ave. Wilpshire BB1 122 A7
Sunnyside Cl. Freckleton PR4 ... 92 B7
Sunnyside Cl. Lancaster LA1 ... 210 E7
Sunnyside Cl. Rawtenstall BB4 ... 85 A6
Sunnyside La. LA1 .... 210 E7
Sunnyside Terr. FY6 .... 195 C3
Suoth Ribble St. PR1 .... 96 C6
Super St. BB5 .... 123 E4
Surgeon's Ct. PR1 .... 95 F7
Surrey Ave. Burnley BB12 .... 126 B7
Surrey Ave. Darwen BB3 .... 80 F3
Surrey Cl. PR9 .... 53 C5
Surrey Rd. Barrowford BB9 .. 168 D2
Surrey Rd. Blackburn BB1 ... 101 D5
Surrey St. Accrington BB5 .... 103 D6
Surrey St. Preston PR1 .... 96 C8
Sussex Ave. OL10 .... 32 E1
Sussex Cl. Church BB5 .... 102 F7
Sussex Cl. Standish WN1 .... 29 B1
Sussex Dr. Garstang PR3 ..... 178 B7
Sussex Dr. Haslingden BB4 .... 67 B8
Sussex Rd. Blackpool FY3 ... 129 E6
Sussex Rd. Rishton BB1 ...... 101 E6
Sussex Rd. Southport PR8 & PR9 . 34 D6
Sussex St. 18 Barnoldswick BB8 200 B2
Sussex St. Burnley BB10 ...... 127 B4
Sussex St. 1 Nelson BB9 ...... 168 E1
Sussex St. Preston PR1 .... 117 A1
Sussex Wlk. 10 BB1 .... 101 A4
Sutch La. L40 .... 25 B5
Sutcliffe St. Bacup OL13 .... 70 C8
Sutcliffe St. Brierfield BB10 147 F3
Sutcliffe St. Burnley BB11 ... 126 F6
Sutcliffe St. Chorley PR6 .... 42 D7
Sutcliffe Terr. BB1 .... 81 F6
Sutherland Cl. BB1 .... 122 A7
Sutherland Rd. Blackpool FY1 129 C8
Sutherland Rd. Heywood OL10 . 32 F1
Sutherland St. BB8 .... 169 C4
Sutherland View. FY1 .... 129 C7
Sutton Ave. Brierfield BB10 147 D2
Sutton Ave. Tarleton PR4 ...... 56 A8
Sutton Cres. BB5 .... 124 F1
Sutton Dr. PR2 .... 94 D8
Sutton Gr. PR6 .... 60 F4
Sutton La. Adlington PR6 ...... 43 A1
Sutton La. Tarleton PR4 .... 55 F5
Sutton Pl. FY1 .... 129 C4
Sutton Rd. L37 .... 11 E1
Sutton St. Blackburn BB2 ...... 79 D8
Sutton St. Weeton Camp PR4 . 111 B1
Sutton's La. L37 .... 12 E3
Sutton's Yd. FY6 .... 151 E4
Swain St. OL12 .... 51 E1
Swainbank St. BB11 .... 127 B5
Swaine St. BB9 .... 147 C8
Swainson St. Blackpool FY1 129 C6
Swainson St.
  Lytham St Anne's FY8 .... 89 F3
Swainstead Raike. BD23 ..... 230 E8
Swaledale Ave. BB10 .... 147 B4
Swalegate. L31 .... 5 C2
Swallow Ave. PR1 .... 95 E4
Swallow Cl. FY5 .... 173 A4
Swallow Cl. PR6 .... 77 C1
Swallow Dr. Blackburn BB1 . 100 E6
Swallow Dr. Bury BL9 .... 32 B4
Swallow Field. PR4 .... 73 E3
Swallow Pk. BB11 .... 126 C5
Swallowfields. BB1 .... 100 E8
Swan Alley. L39 .... 15 E5
Swan Delph. L39 .... 15 C2
Swan Dr. FY5 .... 172 F1
Swan Farm Cl. BB3 .... 80 F7
Swan La. L39 .... 5 F6
Swan Rd. BL8 .... 48 F2
Swan St. Blackburn BB2 ...... 100 E3
Swan St. Darwen BB3 .... 64 B6
Swan St. Preston PR1 .... 96 C8
Swan Yd. 1 LA1 .... 211 A7
Swanage Ave. FY4 .... 109 B6
Swanage Rd. BB10 .... 147 C1
Swanfield Ct. BB8 .... 170 A5
Swanpool La. L39 .... 15 C2

Swansea St. PR1 .... 95 C8
Swansey La. PR6 .... 77 C1
Swarbrick Cl. FY1 .... 129 D7
Swarbrick Ct. PR3 .... 139 B7
Swarbrick St. PR4 .... 113 A4
Sweet Briar Cl. OL12 .... 51 E2
Sweet Briar La. OL12 .... 51 E2
Swift Cl. BB1 .... 100 F5
Swilkin La. FY8 .... 174 E6
Swill Brook La. PR1 .... 96 C6
Swinate Rd. LA5 .... 237 C1
Swinburn Gr. WN5 .... 10 D1
Swinburne St. BB9 .... 103 E2
Swinden Hall Rd. BB9 .... 168 E2
Swinden La. BB8 .... 169 A2
Swindon Ave. FY4 .... 109 D8
Swindon St. BB11 .... 126 D5
Swinless St. BB10 .... 127 B8
Swinshaw Cl. BB4 .... 105 A2
Swiss St. BB5 .... 102 F6
Swithemby St. BL6 .... 31 A4
Swollowfold. PR2 .... 138 D1
Sword Meanygate. PR4 .... 55 C6
Sycamore Ave. Blackpool FY4 109 F5
Sycamore Ave. Burnley BB12 126 B7
Sycamore Ave. Euxton PR7 ... 59 D3
Sycamore Ave. Garstang PR3 178 B8
Sycamore Bglws. BB7 .... 225 C3
Sycamore Cl. Blackburn BB1 100 F8
Sycamore Cl. Burnley BB12 . 126 C6
Sycamore Cl. Fulwood PR2 . 117 C6
Sycamore Cl. Mawdesley L40 . 39 C2
Sycamore Cl. Rishton BB1 .. 102 B8
Sycamore Cres. Caton LA2 . 231 C3
Sycamore Cres.
  Clayton-le-M BB5 .... 124 A5
Sycamore Cres. 1
  Rawtenstall BB4 .... 84 F1
Sycamore Ct. PR7 .... 42 B5
Sycamore Dr. Penwortham PR1 .. 95 E3
Sycamore Dr. Skelmersdale WN8 17 E2
Sycamore Gdns. Foulridge BB8 191 D1
Sycamore Gdns. Heysham LA3 208 E6
Sycamore Gr. Accrington BB5 . 103 E3
Sycamore Gr. Darwen BB3 .... 81 B2
Sycamore Gr. Formby L37 ...... 11 C1
Sycamore Gr. Lancaster LA1 210 D8
Sycamore Rd. Bilsborrow PR3 .. 157 A5
Sycamore Rd. Blackburn BB1 100 F8
Sycamore Rd. Caton LA2 ..... 231 C3
Sycamore Rd. Chorley PR6 .... 60 D2
Sycamore Rd. Fulwood PR2 . 117 E2
Sycamore Rise. BB8 .... 191 D1
Sycamore Trading Est. FY4 .. 109 F5
Sycamore Way. BB8 .... 200 A1
Sycamore Wlk. 1 BL6 .... 31 E1
Syd Brook La. PR5 & PR7 ...... 39 E7
Sydenham Terr. OL12 .... 51 D3
Sydney Ave. BB7 .... 143 D5
Sydney Ave. Accrington BB5 103 C6
Sydney St. 1
  Burnley BB11 & BB12 .... 126 F6
Sydney St. Darwen BB3 .... 64 B7
Sydney St. Enfield BB5 .... 124 A1
Sydney St. Hoddlesden BB3 .. 81 F1
Sydney St. Lytham St Anne's FY8 . 88 F6
Sydney Terr. BB8 .... 170 C3
Syke Hill. 14 PR1 .... 96 A7
Syke House La. PR3 .... 158 E4
Syke La. OL12 .... 51 F4
Syke Rd. OL12 .... 51 F4
Syke Side Dr. BB5 .... 124 E6
Syke St. Haslingden BB4 .... 84 C1
Syke St. Preston PR1 .... 96 A7
Sykelands Ave. LA2 .... 214 F7
Sykelands Gr. LA2 .... 214 F7
Sykes St. BL9 .... 32 A3
Sylvan Gr. PR5 .... 97 A2
Sylvan Pl. LA3 .... 208 E6
Sylvancroft. PR2 .... 116 A5
Sylvester St. LA1 .... 210 E7
Symonds Rd. PR2 .... 116 E3

Tabby Nook. PR4 .... 54 F2
Tabby's Nook. WN8 .... 26 A1
Taberner St. WN6 .... 28 F1
Tabley La. PR2 & PR4 .... 115 E7
Tabor St. BB12 .... 126 D6
Tadema Gr. BB11 .... 126 F2
Tadlow Cl. L37 .... 11 C1
Tag Croft. PR2 .... 115 F5
Tag Farm Ct. PR2 .... 115 F5
Tag La. PR2 .... 116 A4
Talaton Cl. PR9 .... 53 A5
Talbot Ave. 3 BB5 .... 123 F2
Talbot Cl. Clitheroe BB7 ...... 164 F7
Talbot Ct. Rawtenstall BB4 .... 67 B8
Talbot Ct. FY8 .... 89 A8
Talbot Dr. Brierfield BB10 ... 147 F2
Talbot Dr. Euxton PR7 .... 59 D2
Talbot Dr. Southport PR8 .... 34 B6
Talbot Gr. BL9 .... 32 A6
Talbot House. PR6 .... 60 C2
Talbot Liby. PR1 .... 95 D8
Talbot Mkt. FY1 .... 129 B1
Talbot Rd. Accrington BB5 .. 103 A8
Talbot Rd. Blackpool FY1 & FY3 . 129 C6
Talbot Rd. Leyland PR5 .... 75 C2
Talbot Rd. Lytham St Anne's FY8 . 90 C4
Talbot Rd. Penwortham PR1 .. 95 E5
Talbot Rd. Preston PR1 .... 95 D7
Talbot Row. PR7 .... 59 D1
Talbot Sq. FY1 .... 129 B5
Talbot St. Brierfield BB10 ... 147 F2
Talbot St. Burnley BB11 ...... 127 B6
Talbot St. Chipping PR3 ...... 182 E3
Talbot St. Chorley PR6 .... 60 D1
Talbot St. Colne BB8 .... 169 D6

Talbot St. Fulwood PR2 .... 116 D4
Talbot St. Rishton BB1 .... 123 C1
Talbot St. Southport PR8 .... 34 A6
Talbot Terr. FY8 .... 90 B3
Tamar Cl. PR5 .... 59 B7
Tamar St. PR1 .... 96 E8
Tamneys The. WN8 .... 17 F1
Tan Hill Dr. LA1 .... 213 F3
Tan House Cl. WN8 .... 26 C3
Tan House La. WN8 .... 26 C2
Tanfield Nook. WN8 .... 26 C2
Tanfields. WN8 .... 17 F1
Tanglewood. PR2 .... 117 B5
Tanhouse La. PR6 .... 60 F6
Tanhouse Rd. Skelmersdale WN8 . 9 C8
Tanhouse Rd. Skelmersdale WN8 9 C7
Tanner Barn. BB5 .... 84 B7
Tanner St. 8 BB11 .... 126 F6
Tanners Croft. 5 BL0 .... 49 B6
Tanners St. BL0 .... 49 B6
Tannersmith La. PR7 .... 39 F5
Tanpits La. LA6 .... 234 F7
Tanpits Rd. BB5 .... 102 F6
Tansley Ave. PR7 .... 41 D1
Tansy La. PR 203 F4
Tanterton Hall Rd. PR2 .... 116 A6
Tanyard Cl. PR7 .... 41 D1
Tape St. 2 BL0 .... 49 B6
Taper St. BL0 .... 49 B6
Tapestry St. BB2 .... 100 D1
Tarbert Cres. BB1 .... 101 D4
Tarbet St. LA1 .... 211 A7
Tardy Gate Trad Ctr. PR5 ...... 76 A8
Tarleswood. WN8 .... 17 F1
Tarleton Ave. BB5 .... 127 B4
Tarleton CE Prim Sch. PR4 ... 56 A5
Tarleton Cty High Sch. PR4 ... 56 A7
Tarleton Cty Prim Sch. PR4 .. 55 F8
Tarleton Mere Brow CE
  Prim Sch. PR9 .... 54 F2
Tarleton Rd. PR9 .... 35 A8
Tarleton St. BB11 .... 127 B4
Tarlscough La. L40 .... 37 D1
Tarn Ave. BB5 .... 123 F4
Tarn Brook Cl. BB5 .... 124 F1
Tarn Brow. L39 .... 15 C3
Tarn Cl. Penwortham PR1 ...... 94 F4
Tarn Cl. Storth LA7 .... 237 F5
Tarn Ct. FY7 .... 193 D1
Tarn Hows Cl. PR7 .... 42 B5
Tarn La. LA5 & LA6 .... 234 B6
Tarn Rd. Formby L37 .... 11 D3
Tarn Rd. Thornton FY5 .... 151 D7
Tarnacre La. PR3 .... 177 E2
Tarnacre View. PR3 .... 178 C6
Tarnbeck Dr. L40 .... 39 D2
Tarnbrick Ave. PR3 .... 92 C7
Tarnbrook Cl. Carnforth LA5 217 C1
Tarnbrook Cotts. PR3 .... 196 E5
Tarnbrook Dr. FY3 .... 130 A7
Tarnbrook Rd. 2
  Lancaster LA1 .... 213 D2
Tarnside. FY4 .... 130 B1
Tarnside Rd. WN5 .... 10 E6
Tarnsyke Rd. LA1 .... 213 D2
Tarnway Ave. FY5 .... 151 D8
Tarradale. PR4 .... 93 F1
Tarry Barn La. BB7 .... 165 A3
Tarvin Cl. Brierfield BB10 ... 147 F3
Tarvin Cl. Southport PR9 .... 53 D5
Tasker St. 12 BB5 .... 103 C6
Taskers Croft. BB7 .... 143 F8
Tatham Ct. FY7 .... 193 C1
Tatham Fells CE (VC)
  Prim Sch. LA2 .... 233 C4
Tattersall St. Blackburn BB2 100 E4
Tattersall St. Haslingden BB4 . 84 B6
Tattersall St. Oswaldtwistle BB5 102 D4
Tattersall St. 1 Padiham BB12 125 D8
Tattershall Sq. BB5 .... 85 F3
Tatton St. BB8 .... 169 B3
Tauheedul Islam Girls
  High Sch. 100 E6
Taunton Rd. BB2 .... 100 B5
Taunton St. 6 Blackpool FY4 129 D1
Taunton St. Preston PR1 ...... 117 D1
Tavistock Dr. PR2 .... 20 B6
Tavistock St. BB9 .... 168 F1
Tawd Rd. WN8 .... 9 C8
Tay St. Burnley BB11 .... 126 D5
Tay St. Preston PR1 .... 95 D6
Taybank Ave. FY4 .... 109 D7
Taylor Ave. Newchurch BB4 .. 85 F2
Taylor Ave. Ormskirk L39 ...... 16 A5
Taylor Cl. BB2 .... 100 C3
Taylor Gr. LA4 .... 213 B6
Taylor Holme Ind Est. OL13 .. 69 B8
Taylor St. Barnoldswick BB8 200 B2
Taylor St. Blackburn BB2 .... 100 D3
Taylor St. Brierfield BB9 ..... 147 B6
Taylor St. Burnley BB10 ...... 127 A8
Taylor St. Bury BL9 .... 32 A3
Taylor St. Chorley PR7 .... 42 B5
Taylor St. Clitheroe BB7 ...... 164 F6
Taylor St. Darwen BB3 .... 64 A8
Taylor St. Haslingden BB4 .... 84 B6
Taylor St. Horwich BL6 .... 31 B3
Taylor St. Preston PR1 .... 95 D6
Taylor St. 1 Rawtenstall BB4 . 85 A3
Taylor St. Rochdale OL12 ...... 51 F1
Taylor St. Skelmersdale WN8 17 C1
Taylor St. Whitworth OL12 ... 51 D8
Taylor St W. BB5 .... 103 B6
Taylor's Bldgs. BB6 .... 142 D1
Taylor's La. Fisher's Row PR3 . 196 B6

Stu – Thi 283

Taylor's La. Holmes PR4 .... 55 D3
Taylor's Meanygate. PR4 ...... 55 A7
Taylors Cl. FY6 .... 151 C5
Taylors Pl. 18 OL12 .... 51 F1
Taywood Cl. FY6 .... 151 F4
Taywood Rd. FY5 .... 173 A4
Teak St. BL9 .... 32 B2
Teal Cl. Blackburn BB1 .... 100 D8
Teal Cl. Ormskirk L39 .... 15 C2
Teal Pl. PR5 .... 58 D7
Teanlowe Ctr. FY6 .... 151 D3
Tears La. WN8 .... 17 F8
Teasel Wlk. LA3 .... 212 E2
Tebay Ave. Cleveleys FY5 .... 172 D4
Tebay Ave. Kirkham PR4 ..... 113 C5
Tebay Cl. L31 .... 5 F2
Tebay Ct. LA1 .... 213 E4
Tedder Ave. Burnley BB12 ... 126 B6
Tedder Ave. Southport PR9 ... 35 A7
Teenadore Ave. FY4 .... 109 E7
Tees Cl. FY7 .... 193 D2
Tees St. PR1 .... 117 C2
Teesdale Ave. FY3 .... 129 D8
Teil Gn. PR2 .... 117 E6
Telford St. Burnley BB12 ..... 126 C7
Telford St. Horwich BL6 .... 31 D2
Temperance St. 3 PR6 .... 42 E8
Temple Cl. 2 BB1 .... 101 B4
Temple Ct. PR1 .... 95 F7
Temple Dr. BB1 .... 101 B4
Temple St. Blackpool FY1 .... 129 B5
Temple St. Burnley BB11 ..... 127 B5
Temple St. Colne BB8 .... 169 E6
Temple St. Nelson BB9 .... 147 F8
Templegate Cl. WN6 .... 28 F2
Templemartin. WN8 .... 17 F2
Templeton Cl. BB3 .... 81 A2
Ten Row. LA2 .... 205 E5
Tenby. WN8 .... 17 E2
Tenby Cl. BB1 .... 100 E7
Tenby Gr. 6 OL12 .... 51 C1
Tenby Rd. PR1 .... 96 A6
Tenby St. OL12 .... 51 C1
Tennis St. BB10 .... 127 A8
Tennyson Ave. Chorley PR7 .. 42 C6
Tennyson Ave.
  Lytham St Anne's FY8 .... 90 D4
Tennyson Ave.
  Oswaldtwistle BB5 .... 102 C4
Tennyson Ave. Padiham BB12 .. 125 E7
Tennyson Ave. Read BB12 .. 144 D2
Tennyson Ave. Thornton FY5 173 A3
Tennyson Ave. Warton PR4 ... 91 E6
Tennyson Cl. LA5 .... 216 A5
Tennyson Dr. Longshaw WN5 10 D1
Tennyson Dr. Ormskirk L39 .. 15 D6
Tennyson Pl.
  Bamber Bridge PR5 .... 96 D2
Tennyson Pl.
  Great Harwood BB6 .... 123 B4
Tennyson Rd. Blackpool FY3 129 F7
Tennyson Rd. Colne BB8 ..... 169 D5
Tennyson Rd. Fleetwood FY7 194 A4
Tennyson Rd. Preston PR1 ... 117 D1
Tennyson St. Brierfield BB10 147 F3
Tennyson St. Burnley BB11 . 126 D5
Tennyson St. Hapton BB12 .. 125 C4
Tensing Ave. FY2 .... 150 D5
Tensing Rd. L31 .... 5 D1
Tenterfield St. 6
  Newchurch BB4 .... 68 F8
Tenterfield St. 26
  Preston PR0 & PR1 .... 95 F8
Tenterheads. BB4 .... 68 F7
Terance Rd. FY4 .... 109 E8
Terra Cotta Bldgs. BB4 .... 106 A1
Terrace Row. BB7 .... 143 C4
Terrace St. PR1 .... 117 C1
Terry St. BB9 .... 169 A2
Tetbury Cl. BB2 .... 79 E8
Teven St. 4 PR5 .... 96 E1
Teversham. WN8 .... 17 F2
Teviot Ave. FY7 .... 193 D3
Tevlot. WN8 .... 17 E2
Tewkesbury. WN8 .... 17 F2
Tewkesbury Ave. FY4 .... 109 D5
Tewkesbury Cl. BB5 .... 103 C3
Tewkesbury Dr. FY8 .... 90 D5
Tewksbury St. BB2 .... 100 B1
Thames Ave. BB10 .... 147 C3
Thames Dr. WN5 .... 10 F7
Thames House. 5 PR1 .... 96 D8
Thames Prim Sch. FY4 .... 109 B7
Thames Rd. PR4 .... 113 F2
Thames St. PR4 .... 113 F2
Thanet. WN8 .... 17 F2
Thanet Lee Cl. BB10 .... 127 E1
Thealby Cl. WN8 .... 17 E2
Theatre St. PR1 .... 95 F7
Thelma St. BL0 .... 49 B6
Thermdale Cl. PR3 .... 178 B7
Thetis Rd. LA1 .... 210 C8
Thickrash Brow. LA2 .... 233 D7
Third Ave. Blackpool FY4 .... 109 C7
Third Ave. Bury BL9 .... 32 D4
Thirlemere Ave. FY7 .... 193 C1
Thirlemere Ct. LA1 .... 214 B1
Thirlmere Ave. Burnley BB10 147 B4
Thirlmere Ave. Carleton FY6 151 C4
Thirlmere Ave. Colne BB8 ... 169 F6
Thirlmere Ave. Formby L37 .. 12 A4
Thirlmere Ave. Haslingden BB4 67 C8
Thirlmere Ave. Horwich BL6 . 31 C5
Thirlmere Ave. Orrell WN5 ... 10 F7
Thirlmere Ave. Padiham BB12 145 C2

Thirlmere Ave. Up Holland WN8 . **10** B7
Thirlmere Cl. Accrington BB5 .... **124** D1
Thirlmere Cl. Adlington PR6 ...... **30** B8
Thirlmere Cl. 6 Blackburn BB1 **100** F6
Thirlmere Cl.
  Knott End-on-S FY6 .... **194** F6
Thirlmere Cl. Longton PR4 .... **74** B8
Thirlmere Cl. Maghull L31 .... **5** E2
Thirlmere Dr. Ainsdale PR8 .... **20** B3
Thirlmere Dr. Darwen BB3 .... **81** C2
Thirlmere Dr. Longridge PR3 .... **138** F5
Thirlmere Dr. Morecambe LA4 . **212** D4
Thirlmere Dr. Withnell Fold PR6 . **78** D2
Thirlmere Gdns. LA4 .... **212** E4
Thirlmere Rd. Blackpool FY4 .... **109** C7
Thirlmere Rd. Blackrod BL6 ...... **30** C3
Thirlmere Rd. Burnley BB10 .... **127** E5
Thirlmere Rd. Chorley PR7 .... **42** B6
Thirlmere Rd. Hightown L38 .... **3** A4
Thirlmere Rd. Lancaster LA1 .... **214** B2
Thirlmere Rd. Preston PR1 .... **117** F1
Thirlmere Way. BB4 .... **105** A1
Thirnby Ct. LA6 .... **238** C2
Thirsk. WN8 .... **17** E2
Thirsk Ave. FY8 .... **89** B7
Thirsk Gr. FY1 .... **129** D2
Thirsk Rd. LA1 .... **211** B4
Thistle Cl. FY5 .... **172** F5
Thistle St. 15 OL13 .... **86** F2
Thistlecroft. PR2 .... **116** A5
Thistlemount Ave. BB4 .... **85** F1
Thistleton Rd. Preston PR2 ...... **94** E8
Thistleton Rd.
  Thistleton PR4 &FY6 .... **153** C1
Thomas Gr. LA4 .... **212** E5
Thomas St. Blackburn BB2 ...... **100** D4
Thomas St. Brierfield BB9 .... **147** A5
Thomas St. Burnley BB11 .... **127** A5
Thomas St. Colne BB8 .... **169** C4
Thomas St. Cornholme OL14 ... **108** C1
Thomas St. 4 Haslingden BB4 ... **84** A3
Thomas St. Nelson BB9 .... **147** E7
Thomas St. Oswaldtwistle BB5 . **102** D3
Thomas St. 3 Preston PR1 .... **96** B7
Thomas St. Whitworth OL12 ...... **70** D2
Thomason Fold. BL7 .... **47** D6
Thompson Ave. L39 .... **16** B5
Thompson Dr. BL9 .... **32** C3
Thompson St. Blackburn BB2 .. **100** C4
Thompson St. Darwen BB3 .... **64** B7
Thompson St. Horwich BL6 .... **31** A3
Thompson St. Kirkham PR4 ..... **112** F6
Thompson St. Padiham BB12 ... **125** D7
Thompson St. Preston PR1 ...... **117** D1
Thonock Rd. LA4 .... **212** G3
Thorburn Dr. OL12 .... **51** B7
Thorn Bank. OL13 .... **87** A2
Thorn Cl. OL13 .... **87** A2
Thorn Cres. OL13 .... **87** A2
Thorn Cty Prim Sch. OL13 .. **86** F3
Thorn Dr. OL13 .... **87** A2
Thorn Gdns. OL13 .... **87** A2
Thorn Gr. Blackpool FY1 .... **129** E2
Thorn Gr. Colne BB8 .... **169** F6
Thorn Hill Cl. BB1 .... **101** A5
Thorn La. PR3 .... **139** B2
Thorn St. Bacup OL13 .... **87** A2
Thorn St. Burnley BB10 .... **127** A8
Thorn St. Clitheroe BB7 .... **164** D8
Thorn St. Great Harwood BB6 . **123** D6
Thorn St. Preston PR1 .... **117** C1
Thorn St. Ramsbottom BL0 .... **49** C3
Thorn St. Rawtenstall BB4 .... **84** F5
Thorn St. Sabden BB7 .... **145** A7
Thorn View. BB9 .... **32** C3
Thornbank. FY3 .... **130** B7
Thornbank Dr. PR3 .... **178** D2
Thornbeck Ave. L38 .... **2** F3
Thornber. WN8 .... **17** F2
Thornber Gr. FY1 .... **129** D3
Thornber St. BB2 .... **100** C3
Thornbridge Ave. L40 .... **24** E3
Thornbury. WN8 .... **17** F2
Thornby. WN8 .... **17** F2
Thorncliffe Dr. BB3 .... **64** D8
Thorndale. WN8 .... **17** F2
Thorne St. BB9 .... **169** A2
Thorney Bank St. 4 BB11 .... **126** F5
Thorneybank Ind Est. BB11 .... **125** C2
Thorneycroft Cl. FY6 .... **151** B5
Thorneyholme Rd. BB5 .... **103** C8
Thorneyholme Sq. BB9 .... **167** E5
Thorneylea. OL12 .... **70** D1
Thornfield. Lancaster LA1 .... **210** F5
Thornfield. Much Hoole PR4 ..... **73** E4
Thornfield Ave. Fulwood PR2 .. **117** F3
Thornfield Ave. Longridge PR3 . **139** A8
Thornfield Ave. Newchurch BB4 . **85** E1
Thornfield Ave. Thornton FY5 . **151** D8
Thorngate. PR1 .... **95** B4
Thorngate Cl. PR1 .... **95** B4
Thornham Ct. FY3 .... **129** E5
Thornhill. L39 .... **6** B8
Thornhill Ave.
  Knott End-on-S FY6 .... **195** A5
Thornhill Ave. Rishton BB1 ..... **102** A8
Thornhill Cl. Blackpool FY4 .... **109** F5
Thornhill Cl. Ormskirk L39 .... **6** B8
Thornhill Rd. Chorley PR6 .... **60** E2
Thornhill Rd. Leyland PR5 .... **58** D8
Thornhill Rd. Ramsbottom BL0 .. **49** A1
Thornhill St. BB12 .... **126** E6
Thornlea Dr. OL12 .... **51** B2
Thornleigh Cl. FY5 .... **173** A2
Thornleigh Dr. LA6 .... **234** C7
Thornley Ave. BB1 .... **101** C6
Thornley Pl. PR2 .... **118** A3
Thornley Rd. PR2 & PR5 .... **118** A3
Thornpark Dr. PR2 .... **115** D1
Thorns Ave. LA2 .... **215** D1
Thorns The. L31 .... **5** B2
Thornton. WN8 .... **17** F2
Thornton Ave. Fulwood PR2 ... **116** B4
Thornton Ave.
  Lytham St Anne's FY8 .... **89** B8
Thornton Ave. Morecambe LA4 . **212** F6
Thornton Cl. Accrington BB5 ... **103** A8
Thornton Cl. Blackburn BB2 ..... **80** F8
Thornton Cl. Rufford L40 .... **38** C4
Thornton Cres. Burnley BB10 .. **127** E5
Thornton Cres. Morecambe LA4 **212** F5
Thornton Dr. FY5 .... **173** C1
Thornton Dr. Gregson Lane PR5 . **97** D4
Thornton Dr. Leyland PR5 .... **75** E4
Thornton Gate. LA4 .... **212** F5
Thornton La. Morecambe LA4 . **212** F5
Thornton La. Thornton in L LA6 . **236** F5
Thornton Manor Cl. BD23 ...... **201** A5
Thornton Rd. Burnley BB10 .... **127** E5
Thornton Rd. Morecambe LA4 . **212** F5
Thornton Rd. Southport PR9 .... **34** F7
Thornton-in-Craven Cty
  Prim Sch. BD23 .... **201** B6
Thorntrees Ave. Newsham PR3 **136** B5
Thorntrees Ave. Preston PR2 .. **115** D1
Thornway Ave. FY5 .... **151** D8
Thornwood. WN8 .... **17** F2
Thornwood Cl. Blackburn BB1 . **121** E1
Thornwood Cl.
  Lytham St Anne's FY8 .... **89** E4
Thorough Way. PR3 .... **198** E7
Thoroughfare The. LA5 .... **217** D5
Thoroughgood Cl. L40 .... **24** D2
Thorpe. WN8 .... **17** F2
Thorpe Ave. LA4 .... **213** B4
Thorpe Cl. PR1 .... **116** F1
Thorpe St. BL0 .... **49** B5
Thrang Brow La. LA5 .... **219** C6
Threagill La. LA5 & LA6 .... **217** F5
Three Lane Ends. PR6 .... **61** C4
Three Nooks. PR5 .... **77** C5
Three Oaks Cl. PR4 .... **25** B2
Three Pools. PR9 .... **53** C3
Three Tuns La. L37 .... **11** F3
Three Turns. PR3 .... **141** A8
Threefields. PR2 .... **116** A5
Threlfall. PR7 .... **59** F2
Threlfall Rd. FY1 .... **129** D1
Threlfall St. 1 PR1 .... **116** C1
Threlfall's La. PR9 .... **52** F2
Threlfalls Cl. PR9 .... **52** F3
Threshers Ct. PR3 .... **204** C2
Threshfield Ave. LA3 .... **208** F8
Thrimby Ct. LA4 .... **212** E4
Thrimby Pl. LA4 .... **212** E4
Thropps La. PR4 .... **74** D6
Throstle Cl. BB12 .... **127** A7
Throstle Gr. LA2 .... **213** F8
Throstle Nest La. PR3 .... **198** C4
Throstle St. Blackburn BB2 .... **100** C4
Throstle St. 7 Nelson BB9 ...... **168** E1
Throstle Way. 1 FY5 .... **172** F1
Throstle Wlk. LA4 .... **213** F8
Throughs La. LA7 .... **237** F5
Throup Pl. BB9 .... **168** E2
Thrum Fold. OL12 .... **51** D3
Thrum Hall La. Lower Fold OL12 . **51** D3
Thrum Hall La.
  Lower Healey OL12 .... **51** E3
Thrush Dr. BL9 .... **32** B4
Thrush St. OL12 .... **51** C1
Thrushgill Dr. LA2 .... **214** F7
Thurcroft Dr. WN8 .... **17** E2
Thurland Ct. LA4 .... **212** D3
Thurnham Rd. PR2 .... **94** E8
Thurnham St. LA1 .... **210** F7
Thursby Ave. FY4 .... **109** D6
Thursby Cl. PR8 .... **20** B3
Thursby Pl. 11 BB9 .... **168** F2
Thursby Rd. Burnley BB10 ..... **147** C1
Thursby Rd. Nelson BB9 .... **168** F2
Thursby Sq. BB10 .... **127** A8
Thursden Ave. BB10 .... **147** F3
Thursden Pl. BB9 .... **169** B1
Thursfield Ave. FY4 .... **109** E8
Thursfield Rd. BB10 .... **127** B5
Thursford Gr. BL6 .... **30** D1
Thursgill Ave. LA4 .... **212** F3
Thurston. WN8 .... **17** E2
Thurston Rd. PR5 .... **76** A1
Thurston St. BB10 & BB11 ...... **127** B6
Thwaite Brow La. LA5 .... **216** B6
Thwaite La. LA2 .... **233** C5
Thwaites Ave. BB2 .... **120** E2
Thwaites Rd. BB5 .... **102** C4
Thwaites St. BB5 .... **102** C3
Tib St. 16 BL0 .... **49** B5
Tiber Ave. BB11 .... **126** C4
Tiber Pl. PR1 .... **96** B7
Tibicar Dr E. LA3 .... **212** A1
Tibicar Dr W. LA3 .... **212** A1
Tilbury Gr. WN6 .... **19** D7
Tilcroft. WN8 .... **17** E2
Timber Brook. PR7 .... **60** A2
Timber St. Accrington BB5 ..... **103** C5
Timber St. Bacup OL13 .... **86** F1
Timber St. Brierfield BB9 .... **147** B6
Timberhurst. BL9 .... **32** D2
Timbrills Ave. BB7 .... **144** F8
Timms Cl. L37 .... **11** F5
Timms La. L37 .... **11** F5
Tincklers La. PR7 .... **40** A6
Tinedale View. BB12 .... **145** D1
Tinker's La. LA2 .... **220** B7
Tinkerfield. PR2 .... **116** E7
Tinklers La. BB7 .... **223** E7
Tinline St. BL9 .... **32** A2
Tinniswood. PR1 .... **116** B1
Tinsley Ave. PR8 .... **34** E3
Tinsley's La. Brown Edge PR8 ... **35** A1
Tinsley's La. Out Rawcliffe PR3 **175** D4
Tintagel. WN8 .... **17** E2
Tintagell Cl. BB2 .... **79** C7
Tintern Ave. Chorley PR7 .... **42** D5
Tintern Ave. Falinge Fold OL12 . **51** E2
Tintern Cl. Accrington BB5 ..... **103** E2
Tintern Cl. Read BB12 .... **144** D1
Tintern Cres. BB1 .... **101** B8
Tintern Dr. L37 .... **12** B2
Titan Way. PR5 .... **75** B2
Tithe Barn La. Knowley PR6 .... **61** A4
Tithe Barn La.
  Runshaw Moor PR5 & PR7 ...... **58** F5
Tithe Barn La. Scorton PR3 .... **199** E5
Tithebarn Hill. LA2 .... **205** E5
Tithebarn Pl. FY6 .... **151** D4
Tithebarn Rd. PR8 & PR9 .... **34** E6
Tithebarn St. 6 Preston PR1 ... **96** A7
Tithebarn St. Preston PR1 .... **96** A8
Tithebarn St. Thornton FY5 ... **151** D4
Tithebarn St. Up Holland WN8 . **10** B7
Tittrington Brow. BB7 .... **223** C2
Tiverton Ave. WN8 .... **17** E2
Tiverton Cl. PR2 .... **116** F8
Tiverton Dr. Blackburn BB2 ..... **80** C8
Tiverton Dr. Brierfield BB10 ... **147** F3
Tockholes CE Prim Sch. BB3 . **80** A3
Tockholes Rd.
  Darwen BB3 & PR7 .... **80** A3
Tockholes Rd. Darwen BB3 ...... **80** F2
Tod Holes La. BD23 .... **230** E4
Todd Carr Rd. BB4 .... **85** F1
Todd Hall Rd. BB4 .... **83** F4
Todd La N. PR5 .... **96** C2
Todd La S. PR5 .... **76** C8
Todd's La. PR5 .... **54** A6
Todmorden Old Rd. OL13 .... **87** B5
Todmorden Rd.
  Bacup OL13 & OL14 .... **87** B4
Todmorden Rd. Burnley BB11 .. **127** B3
Todmorden Rd. Cockden BB10 . **148** B1
Todmorden Rd.
  Lytham St Anne's FY8 .... **88** C8
Todmorden Road Prim Sch.
  BB11 .... **127** B5
Toll Bar Bsns Pk. OL13 .... **69** C8
Toll Bar Cres. LA1 .... **210** F3
Tollgate. PR1 .... **95** E4
Tollgate Rd. L40 .... **24** B3
Tolsey Dr. PR4 .... **94** D2
Tom Benson Way. PR2 & PR1 . **115** F4
Tom La. BB8 .... **85** F2
Tomlinson Rd. Heysham LA3 . **208** F6
Tomlinson Rd. Leyland PR5 ..... **75** F2
Tomlinson Rd. Preston PR1 ... **116** C2
Tomlinson St. BL6 .... **31** B3
Tonacliffe Cty Prim Sch. OL12 . **51** C6
Tonacliffe Rd. OL12 .... **51** C6
Tonacliffe Terr. OL12 .... **51** C7
Tonacliffe Way. OL12 .... **51** C6
Tong End. OL12 .... **70** C2
Tong La. Bacup OL13 .... **87** B2
Tong La. Whitworth OL12 .... **70** D1
Tongbarn. WN8 .... **17** E2
Tongues La. PR3 .... **195** C6
Tontine. WN5 .... **10** C5
Tontine Dr. WN5 & WN8 .... **10** C6
Tontine St. BB1 .... **100** E5
Toogood La. WN6 .... **27** F2
Tootell St. PR7 .... **42** B6
Tootle La. L40 .... **38** A3
Tootle Rd. PR3 .... **139** B8
Top o' th' Croft. BB2 .... **80** D8
Top Acre. PR4 .... **94** C1
Top Barn La. BB4 .... **85** E1
Top Locks. PR5 .... **25** A4
Top of Fawna Rd. PR3 .... **161** D1
Top of Heap. OL10 .... **32** F2
Top of Wallsuches. BL6 .... **31** F4
Top Row. BB7 .... **144** F8
Topaz St. BB1 .... **121** F2
Topham St. BL9 .... **32** A1
Topping Fold Rd. BL9 .... **32** C3
Topping St. Blackpool FY1 ..... **129** B5
Topping St. Bury BL9 .... **32** A3
Tor Ave. BL8 .... **48** F2
Tor End Rd. BB4 .... **66** F6
Tor Scar Rd. LA6 .... **236** F7
Tor View. Haslingden BB4 .... **84** C1
Tor View. Rawtenstall BB4 .... **85** A1
Tor View Rd. BB4 .... **84** C1
Tor View Sch Valley Site. BB4 . **67** D8
Torcross Rd. PR9 .... **53** A5
Torn Cotts. LA5 .... **216** C6
Toronto Ave. Blackpool FY2 .. **150** E3
Toronto Ave. Fleetwood FY7 .. **193** E2
Toronto Rd. BB2 .... **100** C8
Torquay Ave. Blackpool FY3 .. **130** A2
Torquay Ave. Brierfield BB10 . **147** D2
Torra Barn Cl. BL7 .... **46** E3
Torrentum Ct. PR7 .... **173** C1
Torrisholme Cty Prim Sch.
  LA4 .... **213** B5
Torrisholme Rd. LA1 .... **213** D3
Torrisholme Sq. LA4 .... **213** B4
Torsway Ave. FY3 .... **129** F6
Torver Cl. BB12 .... **126** B8
Totnes Cl. FY6 .... **151** C5
Totnes Dr. PR9 .... **53** A5
Tottenham Rd. BB3 .... **80** F6
Tottington Rd. BL7 & BL8 .... **47** F2
Tottleworth. BB6 .... **123** D3
Tottleworth Rd. BB6 .... **123** C2
Toulmin Cl. PR3 .... **178** D2
Tower Ave. BL0 .... **49** A5
Tower Ct. Chapeltown BL7 ...... **47** C4
Tower Ct. Lancaster LA1 .... **210** F7
Tower End. L37 .... **11** C5
Tower Gn. PR2 .... **116** F7
Tower Hill. Clitheroe BB7 .... **186** F1
Tower Hill. Ormskirk L39 .... **16** A5
Tower Hill Rd. WN8 .... **10** B6
Tower La. PR2 & PR3 .... **116** F7
Tower Nook. WN8 .... **10** A5
Tower Rd. Blackburn BB2 .... **99** E2
Tower Rd. Darwen BB3 .... **64** B8
Tower St. 13 Bacup OL13 .... **86** F2
Tower St. Blackpool FY1 .... **129** B5
Tower St. Chapeltown BL7 ...... **47** C4
Tower St. Cornholme OL14 .... **108** A1
Tower St. Oswaldtwistle BB5 .. **102** D3
Tower The. FY5 .... **129** B5
Tower View. Belthorn BB1 .... **82** A5
Tower View. Blackrod BL6 .... **30** C3
Tower View. Darwen BB3 .... **81** C1
Tower View. Penwortham PR1 .. **95** C7
Towers Ave. L31 .... **5** C2
Town Brook House. 4 PR1 .... **116** E1
Town Brow. PR6 .... **76** F2
Town End. Bolton-le-SA LA5 .. **216** A3
Town End. Kirkham PR4 .... **113** A5
Town End. Slaidburn BB7 ...... **223** C7
Town End. Thornton FY5 .... **173** A2
Town Green & Aughton Sta.
  L39 .... **6** C8
Town Green Ct. L39 .... **6** C8
Town Green La. L39 .... **6** C8
Town Hall Sq. 6 BB6 .... **123** C5
Town Hall St. 16
  Blackburn BB1 & BB2 .... **100** E5
Town Hall St. 7
  Great Harwood BB6 .... **123** C5
Town Hill Bank. BB12 .... **145** D1
Town House Rd. BB9 .... **148** B8
Town La. Coppull PR7 .... **41** C1
Town La. Heskin Green PR7 .... **40** C2
Town La. Much Hoole PR4 .... **73** D1
Town La. Southport PR8 .... **34** E3
Town La. Whittle-le-W PR6 ...... **60** D6
Town Lane (Kew). PR8 .... **34** E3
Town Rd. PR5 .... **57** B2
Towneley High Sch. BB11 ..... **127** C4
Towneley Rd. PR3 .... **139** A7
Towneley Rd W. PR3 .... **139** A7
Towneley St. BB10 .... **147** B1
Townely Ave. BB5 .... **124** F2
Townfield Ave. BB10 .... **127** F6
Townfield Cl. PR4 .... **73** F7
Townfield La. LA2 .... **213** E7
Towngate. Eccleston PR7 .... **40** B7
Towngate. Foulridge BB8 .... **191** D1
Towngate. Leyland PR5 .... **58** F7
Towngate. Leyland PR5 .... **59** A8
Townhouse Sch. BB9 .... **169** C1
Townley Ave. FY4 .... **109** E8
Townley Cl. LA1 .... **210** D7
Townley La. PR1 .... **94** D4
Townley St. Brierfield BB9 ..... **147** B5
Townley St. Chorley PR6 & PR7 . **42** D7
Townley St. Colne BB8 .... **169** E6
Townley St. Morecambe LA4 .. **212** E3
Townsend St. Haslingden BB4 . **84** A3
Townsend St. Newchurch BB4 . **68** F8
Townsfield. LA5 .... **218** C4
Townshill Wlk. PR4 .... **113** A6
Townsley St. BB9 .... **147** E6
Townsway. PR5 .... **76** C8
Towpath Wlk. LA5 .... **217** D1
Toxhead Cl. BL6 .... **31** A3
Tracks La. WN5 .... **10** D3
Trafalgar Cl. PR2 .... **116** D3
Trafalgar Rd. Blackpool FY1 .. **129** B2
Trafalgar Rd. Lancaster LA1 .. **211** A6
Trafalgar Rd. Southport PR8 ... **33** E3
Trafalgar St. Burnley BB11 .... **126** F5
Trafalgar St. Chorley PR6 .... **60** D1
Trafalgar St.
  Lytham St Anne's FY8 .... **88** F7
Trafford St. PR1 .... **116** E2
Tram La. LA6 .... **238** C2
Tramway La. PR5 .... **77** B6
Tranmere Ave. LA3 .... **212** A1
Tranmere Cres. LA3 .... **212** A1
Tranmere Rd. FY4 .... **129** E1
Tranmoor. PR4 .... **73** F6
Trans Brittania Enterprise Ctr.
  BB11 .... **126** A3
Trap Hill. L37 .... **11** C2
Trapp La. Sabden BB12 .... **144** F4
Trapp La. Simonstone BB12 ... **144** F2
Trash La. Darwen BB3 .... **80** B2
Trash La. Rimington BB7 .... **225** B1
Travers Pl. PR1 .... **95** C8
Travers St. BL6 .... **31** D1
Travis St. BB10 .... **127** A8
Trawden Cl. BB5 .... **103** C4
Trawden Cres. PR2 .... **117** E4
Trawden Cty Prim Sch. BB8 . **170** C2
Trawden Rd. BB8 .... **170** B5
Traylen Way. OL12 .... **51** A1
Treales CE Prim Sch. PR4 ..... **133** E2
Treales Rd. PR4 .... **114** B6
Trecastle Rd. OL13 .... **1** A4
Tredgold St. BL6 .... **31** C2
Treen Cl. PR9 .... **53** B6
Treesdale Rd. PR8 .... **33** F4
Treetops Ave. BL0 .... **49** A3
Trefoil Cl. FY5 .... **173** A5
Tremellen St. BB5 .... **103** A6
Trengrove St. 7 OL12 .... **51** C1
Trent Ave. Maghull L31 .... **5** F2
Trent Cl. Burscough Bridge L40 . **24** F5
Trent Cl. Lancaster LA1 .... **213** B2
Trent Rd. Blackpool FY4 .... **109** B7
Trent Rd. Nelson BB9 .... **148** A8
Trent St. Longridge PR3 .... **138** F7
Trent St. Lytham St Anne's FY8 . **90** D3
Tresco Cl. BB2 .... **100** B1
Trevarrick Ct. BL6 .... **31** E2
Trevelyan Dr. WN5 .... **10** D1
Trevor Cl. BB1 .... **100** F7
Trevor Rd. Ainsdale PR8 .... **20** C4
Trevor Rd. Burscough L40 .... **24** E4
Triangle The. PR2 .... **116** E4
Trigg La. PR6 & PR7 .... **61** D5
Trigge House. PR6 .... **60** C2
Trinity Cl. BB2 .... **125** D6
Trinity Ct. 3 BB1 .... **100** F6
Trinity Fold. 23 PR4 .... **95** F8
Trinity Gdns. Southport PR8 ... **34** A6
Trinity Gdns. Thornton FY5 ... **173** A3
Trinity Gn. BL0 .... **49** B2
Trinity Mews. PR9 .... **34** C7
Trinity Pl. 27 PR1 .... **95** F8
Trinity Prim Sch. WN8 .... **17** F1
Trinity Rd. PR7 .... **42** B7
Trinity St. 15 Bacup OL13 .... **69** C8
Trinity St. Blackburn BB1 ...... **100** F6
Trinity St. Oswaldtwistle BB5 . **102** D3
Trinity Towers. 6 BB11 .... **126** E6
Trinket La. LA2 .... **232** E6
Tristan Ave. PR4 .... **74** A5
Triumph House. BB11 .... **126** E5
Troon Ave. Blackburn BB1 ..... **101** C3
Troon Ave. Thornton FY5 .... **151** D8
Troon Ct. PR1 .... **95** A6
Trough Rd. BB7 .... **222** B5
Troughton Cres. FY4 .... **109** E8
Trout Beck. BB5 .... **123** F4
Trout St. 8 Blackpool BB10 ... **127** A8
Trout St. Preston PR1 .... **96** C7
Troutbeck Ave. Fleetwood FY7 **193** D2
Troutbeck Ave. Forton PR3 ... **204** B3
Troutbeck Ave. Maghull L31 ..... **5** E2
Troutbeck Cl. Burnley BB12 .. **126** B8
Troutbeck Cl. Hawkshaw BL8 . **48** B2
Troutbeck Cres. FY4 .... **110** D8
Troutbeck Dr. BL0 .... **49** C7
Troutbeck Pl. PR2 .... **117** E5
Troutbeck Rd. Chorley PR7 ..... **42** B5
Troutbeck Rd. Lancaster LA1 . **214** A1
Troutbeck Rd.
  Lytham St Anne's FY8 .... **109** D1
Trowbarrow Cotts. LA5 .... **218** F5
Trower St. PR1 .... **96** B6
Troy St. BB1 .... **100** F7
Trumacar Cty Prim Sch. LA3 . **208** E5
Trumacar La. LA3 .... **208** E5
Truman Ave. LA1 .... **210** C7
Trumley Ct. LA3 .... **212** D2
Trunnah Gdns. FY5 .... **173** B3
Trunnah Rd. FY5 .... **173** B3
Truro Ave. PR9 .... **53** B5
Truro Pl. 8 PR1 .... **117** D1
Truro St. 5 FY4 .... **129** D1
Truscott Rd. L40 .... **24** D4
Tucker Hill. BB7 .... **186** E1
Tucker's Hill Brow. WN2 .... **30** B1
Tudor Ave. Preston PR2 .... **115** D1
Tudor Ave. Preston PR1 .... **117** F1
Tudor Cl. Blackpool FY6 .... **151** A4
Tudor Cl. 1 Cleveleys FY5 .... **172** F1
Tudor Cl. Darwen BB3 .... **81** A2
Tudor Cl. Langho BB6 .... **142** D1
Tudor Cl. Preston PR2 .... **115** D1
Tudor Croft. PR5 .... **76** C7
Tudor Ct. L39 .... **15** F6
Tudor Dr. PR4 .... **113** B2
Tudor Gr. LA4 .... **213** A6
Tudor Mansions. PR8 .... **33** F6
Tudor Pl. FY4 .... **109** B6
Tudor Rd. Ainsdale PR8 .... **20** B6
Tudor Rd. Lytham St Anne's FY8 . **88** D8
Tuer St. PR5 .... **75** F2
Tulip Gr. OL12 .... **51** E2
Tulketh Ave. PR1 .... **116** B1
Tulketh Brow. PR1 .... **116** C1
Tulketh Cres. PR1 .... **116** C1
Tulketh High Sch. PR2 .... **116** B4
Tulketh Rd. PR1 & PR2 .... **116** B1
Tulketh St. PR8 .... **34** B7
Tullyallen Sch. BB3 .... **80** E3
Tunbridge Pl. 7 PR1 .... **117** D1
Tunbridge St. 4 PR0 & PR1 ... **117** D1
Tunbrook Ave. PR2 .... **138** E1
Tunley Holme. PR5 .... **77** C5
Tunley La. WN6 .... **27** E4
Tunley Moss. WN6 .... **27** E4
Tunnel St. Burnley BB12 .... **126** D6
Tunnel St. Darwen BB3 .... **64** C7
Tunstall Mill Terr. 4 OL13 ...... **69** B8
Tunstall St. LA4 .... **212** D5
Tunstead Ave. BB12 .... **124** F8
Tunstead Cres. OL13 .... **86** C5
Tunstead La. OL13 .... **86** B1
Tunstead Rd. OL13 .... **86** C5
Tunstill Fold. BB12 .... **167** F5
Tunstill St. BB10 .... **147** B1
Turbary Rd. LA6 .... **236** E7
Turbary The. PR2 .... **116** C3
Turf Moor Football Gd
  (Burnley AFC). BB10 .... **127** B6
Turf St. BB11 .... **127** B6

Turflands. PR5 .... 57 B1
Turkey St. Accrington BB5 .... 103 D7
Turkey St. Out Rawcliffe PR3 .... 175 A1
Turks Head Yd. 23 PR1 .... 96 A7
Turn La. BB3 .... 63 F8
Turn Rd. BL0 .... 49 E8
Turnacre. L37 .... 12 B6
Turnberry. WN8 .... 17 D2
Turnberry Ave. FY5 .... 151 D8
Turnberry Cl. Kirkham PR4 .... 113 A4
Turnberry Cl. Morecambe LA4 .... 212 G6
Turnberry Way. PR9 .... 53 D5
Turnbridge Rd. L31 .... 5 C3
Turncroft Rd. BB3 .... 64 B8
Turner Ave. PR5 .... 76 A7
Turner Rd. BB9 .... 147 B8
Turner St. 3 Bacup OL13 .... 69 C8
Turner St. Barnoldswick BB8 .... 200 C2
Turner St. Clitheroe BB7 .... 164 E7
Turner St. 2 Preston PR1 .... 117 A1
Turner St. Rochdale OL12 .... 51 E1
Turner's Place. OL12 .... 51 E3
Turnerford Cl. BL7 .... 46 E1
Turnfield. PR2 .... 115 F6
Turning La. PR8 .... 35 A1
Turnpike. BB4 .... 85 F1
Turnpike Rd. L39 .... 15 A2
Turnpike The. PR2 .... 116 D6
Turnpike Way. BB5 .... 102 C5
Turnstone. FY3 .... 130 B6
Turpin Green La. PR5 .... 76 B1
Turton Dr. PR6 .... 60 E1
Turton Golf Course. BL7 .... 47 A1
Turton Gr. BB10 .... 127 D6
Turton Hollow Rd. BB4 .... 85 A8
Turton Rd. BL8 .... 48 B1
Turton Tower. BL7 .... 47 C3
Tuscan Ave. BB11 .... 126 C5
Tuson Croft. PR4 .... 73 F8
Tuson Dr. PR1 .... 95 E8
Tuson House. PR1 .... 95 E2
Tuxbury Cl. FY5 .... 151 D8
Tuxford Rd. FY8 .... 89 C6
Tweed St. Blackburn BB2 .... 80 D8
Tweed St. 6 High Bentham LA2 .... 233 D8
Tweed St. Nelson BB9 .... 148 A8
Tweedy Ct. PR3 .... 182 C4
Twemlow Par. Heysham LA3 .... 208 F8
Twemlow Par. Morecambe LA3 .... 212 A1
Twenty Acre La. PR4 .... 74 B1
Twickenham Pl. FY8 .... 89 D6
Twig La. L31 .... 5 E1
Twin Lakes Ind Est. PR5 .... 57 A3
Twine Wlk. LA6 .... 236 C3
Twist Moor La. PR7 .... 62 B8
Twistfield Cl. PR8 .... 33 F5
Twiston La. BB7 .... 188 D5
Twitter La. BB7 .... 186 A3
Two Brooks La. BL8 .... 48 B2
Two Gates Dr. BB3 .... 81 B2
Two Gates Wlk. BB3 .... 81 B2
Twyford Cl. L31 .... 5 E1
Tyldesley Rd. FY1 .... 129 B3
Tyne Ave. FY3 .... 129 D4
Tyne Cl. FY5 .... 172 E5
Tyne St. 1 Bamber Bridge PR5 .... 96 F1
Tyne St. Preston PR1 .... 95 D6
Tynedale Rd. FY6 .... 151 B1
Tynwald Rd. BB2 .... 100 E1
Tyrer Rd. L39 .... 15 F7
Tyrer's Ave. L31 .... 5 B5
Tyrers Cl. L37 .... 11 F2
Tyrone Ave. FY2 .... 150 D2
Tyseley Gr. BB8 .... 201 A1
Tythebarn St. BB3 .... 81 B1

Udale Pl. LA1 .... 213 E2
Uggle La. LA1 .... 210 F3
Uldale Cl. Ainsdale PR8 .... 20 B3
Uldale Cl. Nelson BB9 .... 147 E6
Ulleswater Rd. LA1 .... 211 A8
Ullswater Ave. Accrington BB5 .... 124 D1
Ullswater Ave. Fleetwood FY7 .... 172 D8
Ullswater Ave. Morecambe LA4 .... 212 G4
Ullswater Ave. Orrell WN5 .... 10 F7
Ullswater Ave.
Spotland Fold OL12 .... 51 C1
Ullswater Ave. Thornton FY5 .... 173 B1
Ullswater Cl. Blackburn BB1 .... 100 F6
Ullswater Cl. Hambleton FY6 .... 174 C2
Ullswater Cl. 3 Rishton BB1 .... 123 A1
Ullswater Cres. Carnforth LA5 .... 216 E8
Ullswater Cres. Thornton FY5 .... 173 B1
Ullswater Rd. Blackpool FY4 .... 109 C7
Ullswater Rd. Burnley BB10 .... 127 F5
Ullswater Rd. Chorley PR7 .... 42 B6
Ullswater Rd. Fulwood PR2 .... 117 C4
Ullswater Way. BB4 .... 105 A1
Ulnes Walton La. PR5 .... 58 A6
Ulpha Cl. BB12 .... 126 B8
Ulster Rd. LA1 .... 211 B5
Ulster St. BB11 .... 126 D5
Ulverston Cl. Blackburn BB2 .... 101 A1
Ulverston Cl. Maghull L31 .... 5 E2
Ulverston Cres. FY8 .... 89 C7
Ulverston Dr. BB1 .... 123 A1
Under Billinge La. BB2 .... 99 F4
Underbank Cl. 3 OL13 .... 86 F3
Underbank House. 1 OL13 .... 86 F3
Underbank Rd. Haslingden BB4 .... 83 F3
Underbank Rd.
Rising Bridge BB5 .... 84 A7
Underbank Rd. Thornton FY5 .... 173 F1
Underbank Way. 1 BB4 .... 84 A3
Underley Hall Sch. LA6 .... 238 C5
Underley St. BB10 .... 147 C3
Underwood. PR2 .... 116 C3
Union Ct. 13 OL13 .... 69 C8
Union La. PR3 .... 175 C7
Union Pas. PR4 .... 113 A5
Union Rd. Oswaldtwistle BB5 .... 102 D3
Union Rd. Rawtenstall BB4 .... 84 D2
Union St. Accrington BB5 .... 103 B6
Union St. Bacup OL13 .... 69 C8
Union St. Bacup OL13 .... 86 F2
Union St. Blackburn BB2 .... 100 E3
Union St. Brierfield BB9 .... 147 B5
Union St. Chorley PR6 & PR7 .... 42 C8
Union St. Clitheroe BB7 .... 164 C8
Union St. Colne BB8 .... 169 E5
Union St. Darwen BB3 .... 81 A1
Union St. Egerton BL7 .... 46 D2
Union St. Haslingden BB4 .... 84 A3
Union St. Morecambe LA4 .... 212 D5
Union St. 11 Preston PR1 .... 95 F8
Union St. Ramsbottom BL0 .... 49 C6
Union St. Rawtenstall BB4 .... 85 A3
Union St. Southport PR9 .... 34 C8
Union St. Whittle-le-W PR6 .... 60 C8
Union St. Whitworth OL12 .... 51 C8
Union Terr. BB4 .... 85 B2
Unit Rd. PR8 .... 20 D5
Unity St. Barnoldswick BB8 .... 200 C2
Unity St. Blackburn BB2 .... 100 E2
Unity St. Kelbrook BB8 .... 192 A6
Unity Trad Est. BB2 .... 100 D4
Univ of Central Lancashire.
PR1 .... 95 E8
Univ of Central Lancashire
Avenham Annexe. PR1 .... 96 A6
Univ of Lancaster. LA1 .... 207 B7
Unsworth Ave. FY6 .... 195 A4
Unsworth St. OL13 .... 69 D7
Up Holland High Sch. WN5 .... 10 C4
Up-Brooks. BB7 .... 187 A1
Up-brooks Ind Est. BB7 .... 187 A1
Upholland Rd. WN5 .... 10 D2
Upholland Sta. WN8 .... 9 F4
Uplands Chase. PR2 .... 116 B6
Uplands Dr. BB12 .... 146 D7
Upper Ashmount. BB4 .... 85 C1
Upper Aughton Rd. PR8 .... 34 B4
Upper Cliffe. BB6 .... 123 C6
Upper George St. 23 OL12 .... 51 F1
Upper Lune St. FY7 .... 194 B5
Upper Mead. BL7 .... 46 F1
Upper Westby St. FY8 .... 90 A3
Upphall La. LA6 .... 234 C4
Uppingham. WN8 .... 17 D1
Uppingham Dr. BL0 .... 49 B7
Upton Ave. PR8 .... 20 B6
Upton Barn. L31 .... 5 C2
Upwood Cl. FY2 .... 150 E5
Urban View. PR6 .... 61 F8
Ushers Meadow. LA1 .... 210 E7

Vale Ave. BL6 .... 31 A3
Vale Cl. WN6 .... 19 E8
Vale Coppice. BL6 .... 31 A3
Vale Cotts. BL6 .... 30 F2
Vale Cres. PR8 .... 20 C2
Vale Ct. BB5 .... 124 F1
Vale House Cl. BB7 .... 143 C5
Vale La. L40 .... 17 F5
Vale Rd. LA1 .... 213 E3
Vale Royal. PR4 .... 113 C5
Vale St. Bacup OL13 .... 87 A3
Vale St. Blackburn BB2 .... 100 E2
Vale St. Darwen BB3 .... 80 F2
Vale St. Haslingden BB4 .... 84 B4
Vale St. Nelson BB9 .... 147 F8
Vale Terr. PR3 .... 179 E8
Vale The. Appley Bridge WN6 .... 19 D8
Vale The. Fulwood PR2 .... 116 F5
Valentia Rd. FY2 .... 150 D3
Valentines Meadow. PR4 .... 115 E4
Valeway Ave. FY5 .... 150 D8
Valley Cl. BB9 .... 169 A1
Valley Ctr The. 4 BB4 .... 85 A2
Valley Dr. Barnoldswick BB8 .... 200 D4
Valley Dr. Padiham BB12 .... 125 D8
Valley Gdns. Earby BB8 .... 201 B2
Valley Gdns. Padiham BB11 .... 125 F4
Valley Rd. Barnoldswick BB8 .... 200 C2
Valley Rd. Earby BB8 .... 201 B2
Valley Rd. Hoghton PR5 .... 98 F3
Valley Rd. Longridge PR3 .... 139 C7
Valley Rd. Penwortham PR1 .... 95 D5
Valley Rd. Wilpshire BB1 .... 121 F5
Valley St. BB11 .... 126 B4
Valley Terr. BB12 .... 144 E1
Valley View. Chorley PR7 .... 42 E7
Valley View. Fulwood PR2 .... 117 A4
Valley View. Whitworth OL12 .... 70 D4
Valley View Rd. PR1 .... 96 A3
Vance Rd. FY1 .... 129 B4
Vancouver Cres. BB2 .... 100 C8
Vanckyl Ave. BB11 .... 126 E2
Vanguard House. 8 BB11 .... 126 E5
Vardon Rd. BB2 .... 100 B2
Varley St. Colne BB8 .... 169 F6
Varley St. 2 Darwen BB3 .... 81 A1
Varley St. Preston PR1 .... 117 A2
Varlian Cl. L40 .... 16 C3
Vaughan Cl. L37 .... 11 D4
Vaughan Rd. PR8 .... 34 B4
Vaughan St. BB9 .... 147 F7
Vauxhall St. BB2 .... 100 B3
Vauze Ave. BL6 .... 30 D1
Vauze House Cl. BL6 .... 30 D2
Veevers St. Brierfield BB9 .... 147 A6
Veevers St. 5 Burnley BB11 .... 126 F6
Veevers St. Padiham BB12 .... 125 D8
Velvet St. BB2 .... 80 D8
Venables Ave. BB8 .... 169 F6
Venice Ave. BB11 .... 126 C4
Venice St. BB11 .... 126 D5
Ventnor Pl. PR2 .... 116 A4
Ventnor Rd. Blackpool FY4 .... 109 B6
Ventnor Rd. 1 Chorley PR7 .... 42 B6
Ventnor Rd. Haslingden BB4 .... 84 C1
Venture Ct. BB5 .... 124 D5
Venture Rd. FY5 .... 173 A6
Venture St. 18 OL13 .... 87 A3
Verax St. OL13 .... 86 F1
Vermont Gr. FY5 .... 150 E8
Vernon Ave. Blackpool FY3 .... 129 E3
Vernon Ave. Warton PR4 .... 91 E6
Vernon Cres. LA2 .... 207 A3
Vernon Ct. PR8 .... 34 D5
Vernon Lodge. FY8 .... 88 F5
Vernon Pk. LA2 .... 207 A4
Vernon Rd.
Laneshaw Bridge BB8 .... 170 D6
Vernon Rd.
Lytham St Anne's FY8 .... 109 E1
Vernon Rd. Ramsbottom BL8 .... 49 A1
Vernon Rd. Southport PR9 .... 35 A8
Vernon St. Blackburn BB2 .... 100 E4
Vernon St. Darwen BB3 .... 81 B1
Vernon St. Nelson BB9 .... 147 E7
Vernon St. Preston PR1 .... 116 F1
Verona Ave. BB11 .... 126 C5
Verona Ct. FY5 .... 173 A2
Veronica St. BB3 .... 80 E4
Verulam Rd. PR9 .... 53 B3
Vesta St. 6 BL0 .... 49 B6
Vevey St. PR5 .... 76 A1
Viaduct Rd. BB2 & PR5 .... 98 F2
Vicar St. Blackburn BB1 .... 100 F5
Vicar St. Great Harwood BB6 .... 123 C4
Vicarage Ave. Caton LA2 .... 231 C3
Vicarage Ave. Cleveleys FY5 .... 172 D3
Vicarage Ave. Padiham BB12 .... 125 B8
Vicarage Cl. Adlington PR6 .... 30 A8
Vicarage Cl. Burton-in-K LA6 .... 234 C7
Vicarage Cl. Euxton PR7 .... 59 D3
Vicarage Cl. Formby L37 .... 11 D4
Vicarage Cl. Fulwood PR2 .... 116 F4
Vicarage Cl.
Lytham St Anne's FY8 .... 88 F7
Vicarage Cl. Morecambe LA3 .... 212 F2
Vicarage Cl.
Scarth Hill L39 & L40 .... 16 B3
Vicarage Cl. Wrea Green PR4 .... 112 B4
Vicarage Dr. BB3 .... 64 C8
Vicarage Fold. BB7 .... 143 F7
Vicarage La. Accrington BB5 .... 103 E1
Vicarage La. Banks PR9 .... 53 F7
Vicarage La. Blackpool FY4 .... 129 E1
Vicarage La. Burton-in-K LA6 .... 234 C7
Vicarage La. Churchtown PR3 .... 178 A2
Vicarage La. Fulwood PR2 .... 116 F4
Vicarage La.
Kirkby Lonsdale LA6 .... 238 C2
Vicarage La.
Newton-with-S PR4 .... 114 A3
Vicarage La. Samlesbury PR5 .... 118 E1
Vicarage La.
Scarth Hill L39 & L40 .... 16 C3
Vicarage La. Wilpshire BB1 .... 121 F6
Vicarage Rd. Barnoldswick BB8 .... 200 C3
Vicarage Rd. Blackrod BL6 .... 30 D2
Vicarage Rd. Formby L37 .... 11 D4
Vicarage Rd. Kelbrook BB8 .... 192 A6
Vicarage Rd. Nelson BB9 .... 147 D7
Vicarage Rd. Orrell WN5 .... 10 D4
Vicarage Rd. Poulton-le-F FY6 .... 151 E3
Vicarage Rd W. BL6 .... 30 C2
Vicarage St. PR6 .... 60 D1
Vicarage Wlk. L39 .... 15 E5
Vicarsfields Rd. PR5 .... 59 A7
Viceroy Ct. PR8 .... 34 A6
Victor Ave. LA4 .... 213 A6
Victoria Ave. Accrington BB5 .... 103 D2
Victoria Ave. Blackburn BB2 .... 79 E8
Victoria Ave. Brierfield BB9 .... 147 B6
Victoria Ave. Chatburn BB7 .... 187 E5
Victoria Ave. Lancaster LA1 .... 210 F5
Victoria Bldgs. BB3 .... 81 E3
Victoria Bridge Rd. PR8 .... 34 C6
Victoria Bsns & Ind Ctr. BB5 .... 103 B4
Victoria Cross. 4 BB1 .... 100 E6
Victoria Ct. 6 Blackburn BB1 .... 100 E5
Victoria Ct. Broughton PR3 .... 136 C2
Victoria Ct. Chatburn BB7 .... 187 D5
Victoria Ct. Horwich BL6 .... 31 C3
Victoria Ct. Padiham BB12 .... 125 E7
Victoria Dr. BB4 .... 84 B2
Victoria Gdns. BB9 .... 168 C2
Victoria House. BB1 .... 101 B3
Victoria Lodge. BB12 .... 144 D2
Victoria Mansions. PR2 .... 95 A7
Victoria Mews. LA4 .... 212 F6
Victoria Par. Morecambe LA4 .... 212 F6
Victoria Par. Newchurch BB4 .... 68 E8
Victoria Par. Preston PR1 .... 116 B1
Victoria Park Ave. Leyland PR5 .... 58 D7
Victoria Park Ave. Preston PR2 .... 115 D1
Victoria Park Dr. PR2 .... 115 D1
Victoria Pk. WN8 .... 17 C1
Victoria Pl. 6 LA1 .... 210 F7
Victoria Quay. PR2 .... 95 A7
Victoria Rd. Barnoldswick BB8 .... 200 C2
Victoria Rd. Earby BB8 .... 201 B2
Victoria Rd. Formby L37 .... 11 D5
Victoria Rd. Fulwood PR2 .... 117 A4
Victoria Rd. Horwich BL6 .... 31 C2
Victoria Rd. Ince Blundell L38 .... 3 E3
Victoria Rd. Kirkham PR4 .... 112 F5
Victoria Rd.
Lytham St Anne's FY8 .... 88 F5
Victoria Rd. Ormskirk L39 .... 15 C2
Victoria Rd. Padiham BB12 .... 125 E7
Victoria Rd. Poulton-le-F FY6 .... 151 E4
Victoria Rd. Preston PR1 & PR5 .... 96 D5
Victoria Rd E. FY5 .... 173 B1
Victoria Rd W. Cleveleys FY5 .... 172 C2
Victoria Rd W. Cleveleys FY5 .... 172 E2
Victoria Sq. FY5 .... 172 D2
Victoria St. Accrington BB5 .... 103 B5
Victoria St. Bacup OL13 .... 69 D8
Victoria St. Bamber Bridge PR5 .... 76 B8
Victoria St. Barrowford BB9 .... 168 D3
Victoria St. 25 Blackburn BB1 .... 100 E5
Victoria St. Blackpool FY1 .... 129 B5
Victoria St. Blackrod BL6 .... 30 D2
Victoria St. 1 Burnley BB11 .... 126 F5
Victoria St.
Burscough Bridge L40 .... 24 E5
Victoria St. Carnforth LA5 .... 217 D1
Victoria St. Chorley PR6 .... 42 D7
Victoria St. Church BB5 .... 102 E6
Victoria St. Clayton-le-M BB5 .... 123 F2
Victoria St. Clayton-le-M BB5 .... 123 F3
Victoria St. Clitheroe BB7 .... 164 D7
Victoria St. Cornholme OL14 .... 108 C1
Victoria St. 21 Darwen BB3 .... 81 A1
Victoria St. Earby BB8 .... 201 B2
Victoria St. Fleetwood FY7 .... 194 B5
Victoria St. Great Harwood BB6 .... 123 D5
Victoria St. Haslingden BB4 .... 84 A3
Victoria St. Longridge PR3 .... 139 A7
Victoria St.
Lytham St Anne's FY8 .... 90 C3
Victoria St. Morecambe LA4 .... 212 D5
Victoria St. Nelson BB9 .... 147 D8
Victoria St. Newchurch BB4 .... 68 E8
Victoria St. Oswaldtwistle BB5 .... 102 D3
Victoria St. Preston PR1 .... 116 E1
Victoria St. Ramsbottom BL0 .... 49 B6
Victoria St. Rawtenstall BB4 .... 85 C1
Victoria St. Rishton BB1 .... 123 B1
Victoria St. 22 Rochdale OL12 .... 51 F1
Victoria St. Southport PR8 .... 34 B8
Victoria St. Wheelton PR6 .... 61 A7
Victoria St. Whitworth OL12 .... 51 C8
Victoria Terr. Abbey Village PR7 .... 79 B2
Victoria Terr. 3
Bamber Bridge PR5 .... 76 A8
Victoria Terr. Billington BB7 .... 143 A4
Victoria Terr. Calder Vale PR3 .... 179 E8
Victoria Terr. Chorley PR6 .... 60 D1
Victoria Terr. Glasson LA2 .... 205 F5
Victoria Terr. 6 Leyland PR5 .... 59 A8
Victoria Terr. Tockholes BB3 .... 79 F2
Victoria Terr. Wheelton PR6 .... 61 A7
Victoria Way. Formby L37 .... 11 D5
Victoria Way. Rawtenstall BB4 .... 85 C2
Victoria Way. Southport PR8 .... 33 F7
Victoria Wharf. LA1 .... 213 E1
Victory Ave. PR9 .... 35 A7
Victory Cl. BB9 .... 147 E8
Victory Ctr The. 1 BB9 .... 147 E8
Victory House. 5 BB11 .... 126 E5
Victory Rd. FY1 .... 129 C6
View Rd. BB3 .... 80 E5
View St. PR7 .... 40 C7
View Terr. BB4 .... 85 F3
Vihiers Cl. BB7 .... 143 C6
Villa Way. PR3 .... 178 C6
Village Croft. PR7 .... 59 D3
Village Dr. PR1 & PR2 .... 117 F2
Village Green La. PR2 .... 115 F6
Village Way. Blackpool FY2 .... 150 D5
Village Way. Hightown L38 .... 2 F4
Villas Rd. L31 .... 6 B2
Villiers Ct. PR1 .... 116 E2
Villiers St. Burnley BB11 .... 126 C5
Villiers St. Bury BL9 .... 32 A3
Villiers St. Padiham BB12 .... 125 D7
Villiers St. Preston PR1 .... 116 D2
Villiers St. Preston PR1 .... 116 E2
Vincent Ct. BB2 .... 80 D8
Vincent Rd. BB9 .... 147 F8
Vincent St. Blackburn BB2 .... 80 D8
Vincent St. Colne BB8 .... 169 F6
Vincent St. 8 Lancaster LA1 .... 211 A7
Vincit St. BB10 .... 127 C8
Vine Ct. FY2 .... 150 C1
Vine St. Accrington BB5 .... 103 A6
Vine St. Brierfield BB9 .... 147 B5
Vine St. Chorley PR6 .... 60 C1
Vine St. Lancaster LA1 .... 210 F6
Vine St. Oswaldtwistle BB5 .... 102 C3
Vine St. Preston PR1 .... 95 D8
Vine St. Ramsbottom BL0 .... 49 A4
Vinery The. PR4 .... 74 F8
Viola Cl. WN6 .... 28 D2
Violet St. BB10 .... 147 A1
Virginia Ave. L31 .... 5 D3
Virginia Gr. L31 .... 5 C3
Virginia St. PR8 .... 34 C6
Vivary Way. BB8 .... 169 B5
Vivian Dr. PR8 .... 34 A2
Vulcan Rd. PR4 .... 113 B1
Vulcan St. Burnley BB11 .... 126 F6
Vulcan St. 3 Nelson BB9 .... 168 F1
Vulcan St. Southport PR9 .... 34 C7

Wackersall Rd. BB8 .... 169 B3
Waddington Ave. BB10 .... 127 D6
Waddington Ct. FY8 .... 89 C6
Waddington Hospl
(Almshouses). BB7 .... 186 B5
Waddington Rd.
Accrington BB5 .... 103 D6
Waddington Rd. Clitheroe BB7 .... 186 E1
Waddington Rd.
Fulwood PR1 & PR2 .... 118 A2
Waddington Rd.
Lytham St Anne's FY8 .... 89 C7
Waddington Rd.
West Bradford BB7 .... 186 D5
Waddington St. Earby BB8 .... 201 B2
Waddington St. 2
Padiham BB12 .... 125 D8
Waddington & West Bradford
CE (VA) Sch. BB7 .... 186 C5
Waddow Gn. BB7 .... 164 C8
Waddow Gr. BB7 .... 186 C4
Waddow View. BB7 .... 186 B4
Wade Brook Rd. PR5 .... 57 F6
Wade St. BB12 .... 145 D1
Wades Croft. PR4 .... 92 C6
Wades Ct. FY3 .... 150 F1
Wadham Rd. PR1 .... 96 B6
Wagon Rd. LA2 & PR3 .... 220 B8
Waidshouse Cl. BB9 .... 147 E6
Waidshouse Rd. BB9 .... 147 E6
Wain Ct. BB2 .... 100 B4
Waingap Cres. OL12 .... 51 D8
Waingap Rise.
Lower Healey OL12 .... 51 F4
Waingap Rise. Whitworth OL12 .... 51 D7
Waingate. Grimsargh PR2 .... 138 C1
Waingate. Rawtenstall BB4 .... 85 B3
Waingate Cl. BB4 .... 85 B3
Waingate La. BB4 .... 85 B3
Waingate Rd. BB4 .... 85 B3
Waitholme La. LA5 .... 234 A7
Wakefield Ave. LA4 .... 212 G6
Wakefield Dr. LA1 .... 211 A4
Wakefield Rd. FY2 .... 150 E4
Walden Rd. BB1 .... 121 F4
Waldon St. PR1 .... 96 E8
Waldron. WN9 .... 8 D8
Wales Rd. BB4 .... 85 F1
Walesby Pl. FY8 .... 89 D5
Walgarth Dr. PR7 .... 42 B7
Walk Mill Pl. BB10 .... 127 E1
Walk The. Hesketh Bank PR4 .... 72 C4
Walk The. Southport PR8 .... 34 A5
Walkdale. PR4 .... 94 D2
Walker Ave. BB5 .... 103 A4
Walker Cl. L37 .... 11 F2
Walker Gr. LA3 .... 208 F7
Walker La. PR2 .... 116 B6
Walker Pl. PR1 .... 96 B7
Walker Rd. BB1 .... 81 C7
Walker St. Blackburn BB1 .... 100 F4
Walker St. Blackpool FY1 .... 129 B6
Walker St. Clitheroe BB7 .... 164 F8
Walker St. Preston PR0 & PR1 .... 95 F8
Walker Way. FY5 .... 173 B4
Walkers Hill. FY4 .... 110 A7
Wall La. PR3 .... 153 E5
Wall St. Blackpool FY1 .... 129 C7
Wall St. Newchurch BB4 .... 85 E2
Wallace La. LA2 & PR3 .... 204 C4
Wallbank Dr. OL12 .... 51 C7
Wallbrook Ave. WN5 .... 10 D1
Wallcroft St. WN8 .... 8 E8
Walled Garden The. PR7 .... 60 B6
Wallend Rd. PR2 .... 94 D7
Waller Ave. FY2 .... 150 C5
Waller Hill. BB8 .... 191 D1
Walletts Rd. PR7 .... 42 B6
Wallhurst Cl. BB10 .... 128 B5
Walling's La. LA5 .... 218 B4
Wallstreams La. BB10 .... 128 B5
Wallsuches. BL6 .... 31 F4
Walmer Ct. PR8 .... 33 F4
Walmer Gn. PR4 .... 73 F5
Walmer Rd.
Lytham St Anne's FY8 .... 88 F8
Walmer Rd. Southport PR8 .... 34 A3
Walmersley Golf Course. BL9 .... 32 B8
Walmersley Old Rd. BL9 .... 49 F2
Walmersley Rd. BL9 .... 49 F1
Walmesley Ave. BB1 .... 102 B8
Walmsgate. BB8 .... 200 B2
Walmsley Brow. BB7 .... 143 B4
Walmsley CE Prim Sch. BL7 .... 46 E1
Walmsley Cl. Church BB5 .... 102 E6
Walmsley Cl. Garstang PR3 .... 178 C7
Walmsley Ct. BB5 .... 123 F1
Walmsley St. Darwen BB3 .... 81 B2
Walmsley St. Fleetwood FY7 .... 194 A4
Walmsley St. 14
Great Harwood BB6 .... 123 C5
Walmsley St. Rishton BB1 .... 123 B1
Walney Pl. FY3 .... 130 A7
Walnut Ave. Bury BL9 .... 32 C3
Walnut Ave. Haslingden BB4 .... 84 C3
Walnut Cl. PR1 .... 95 B3
Walnut St. Bacup OL13 .... 86 F3
Walnut St. Blackburn BB1 .... 100 F7
Walnut St. Southport PR8 .... 34 C4
Walpole Ave. FY4 .... 109 B5
Walpole St. Blackburn BB1 .... 100 F4
Walpole St. 10 Burnley BB10 .... 147 B1
Walro Mews. PR9 .... 53 A3
Walsden Gr. BB10 .... 127 C6
Walsh Fold. BL7 .... 47 D2
Walsh St. Blackburn BB2 .... 100 E2
Walsh St. Horwich BL6 .... 31 B4
Walshaw High Sch. BB10 .... 147 D1
Walshaw La. BB10 .... 147 D2
Walshaw St. BB10 .... 127 B8
Walter Ave. FY8 .... 110 A2
Walter Robinson Ct. FY3 .... 129 D6
Walter St. Accrington BB5 .... 103 B6
Walter St. Blackburn BB1 .... 101 A4
Walter St. Blackburn BB1 .... 101 B4
Walter St. Brierfield BB10 & BB9 .... 147 B5
Walter St. Darwen BB3 .... 64 B5

Walter St. Huncoat BB5 .... 124 E2
Walter St. Oswaldtwistle BB5 .... 102 D3
Walter Street Prim Sch. BB9 . 147 B5
Waltham Ave. FY4 .... 109 D5
Waltham Cl. BB5 .... 103 E3
Waltham Ct. LA2 .... 214 E7
Waltho Ave. L31 .... 5 E1
Walton Ave. Morecambe LA4 .... 213 B6
Walton Ave. Penwortham PR1 .... 95 B3
Walton Cl. OL13 .... 87 A1
Walton Cottage Homes. BB9 . 169 A4
Walton Cres. BB2 .... 101 A1
Walton Gn. PR5 .... 96 C4
Walton Gr. LA4 .... 213 B5
Walton High Sch. BB9 .... 169 A2
Walton La. BB9 .... 169 A1
Walton St. Accrington BB5 .... 124 A1
Walton St. Adlington PR7 .... 30 A6
Walton St. Barrowford BB9 ...... 168 E4
Walton St. Colne BB8 .... 169 D4
Walton St. 8 Nelson BB9 .... 168 E1
Walton St. Southport PR9 .... 34 C8
Walton Summit Rd. PR5 .... 77 A7
Walton View. PR1 .... 96 D8
Walton's Par. PR1 .... 95 E7
Walton-le-Dale Cty Prim Sch.
PR5 .... 96 D2
Walton-le-Dale High Sch. PR5 96 F2
Walverden Ave. FY4 .... 109 D8
Walverden Cres. 3 BB9 .... 147 F8
Walverden Prim Sch. BB9 ...... 147 F8
Walverden Rd. Brierfield BB9 .. 147 D5
Walverden Rd.
Lane Bottom BB10 .... 148 B4
Walverden Terr. BB9 .... 147 F7
Wandales La. LA6 .... 238 F2
Wanes Blades Rd. L40 .... 25 E5
Wanishar La. L39 .... 14 A5
Wansbeck Ave. FY7 .... 193 D2
Wansbeck House. FY7 .... 193 D2
Wansfell Rd. BB7 .... 164 C7
Wanstead Cres. PR1 .... 129 E1
Wanstead St. PR1 .... 96 E8
Warbreck Cl. FY2 .... 150 B1
Warbreck Dr. FY2 .... 150 B2
Warbreck High Sch. FY2 .... 150 D1
Warbreck Hill Rd. FY2 .... 150 D1
Warburton Bldgs. BB4 .... 83 F1
Warburton St. BB4 .... 83 F1
Warcock La. OL13 .... 87 B3
Warbury St. PR1 .... 117 E1
Ward Ave. Cleveleys FY5 .... 172 D3
Ward Ave. Formby L37 .... 11 D2
Ward Ave. Oswaldtwistle BB5 .. 102 C3
Ward Green Cross. PR3 .... 140 A7
Ward Green La. PR3 .... 140 A7
Ward St. Bamber Bridge PR5 .... 76 B7
Ward St. Belmont BL7 .... 45 C5
Ward St. Blackpool FY1 .... 129 B1
Ward St. Burnley BB11 .... 126 E6
Ward St. Chorley PR6 .... 42 E7
Ward St. Great Harwood BB6 .... 123 C5
Ward St. Kirkham PR4 .... 113 A4
Ward's End. PR1 .... 96 A7
Warde St. 7 BB9 .... 147 E8
Wardle Dr. FY5 .... 172 F3
Wardle St. OL13 .... 69 D8
Wardley's La. FY6 .... 174 A3
Wareham Rd. FY3 .... 150 F1
Wareham St. BB1 .... 101 A7
Warehouse La. BB8 .... 191 D1
Waring Dr. FY3 .... 151 A3
Warings The. Heskin Green PR7 . 40 E4
Warings The. Nelson BB9 .... 147 E6
Warkworth Terr. 17 OL13 .... 87 A3
Warley Ave. LA3 & LA4 .... 213 A4
Warley Dr. LA3 & LA4 .... 213 A4
Warley Rd. FY1 & FY3 .... 129 C8
Warley Wise La. BB8 .... 192 F3
Warmden Ave. BB5 .... 103 E3
Warner Rd. PR1 .... 117 D1
Warner St. Accrington BB5 ...... 103 C5
Warner St. Haslingden BB4 ...... 84 B3
Warpers Moss Cl. L40 .... 24 F5
Warpers Moss La. L40 .... 25 A5
Warren Ave N. FY7 .... 193 F4
Warren Ave S. FY7 .... 193 F4
Warren Ct. LA2 .... 213 E8
Warren Ct. PR8 .... 33 E5
Warren Dr. Bacup OL13 .... 70 C8
Warren Dr. Barrowford BB9 ...... 168 C3
Warren Dr. Blackpool FY5 .... 150 E7
Warren Dr. Hest Bank LA2 .... 213 E8
Warren Fold. BB6 .... 141 F8
Warren Gn. L37 .... 11 D3
Warren Gr. LA3 .... 208 E5
Warren Rd. Heysham LA3 .... 208 E5
Warren Rd. Southport PR9 .... 35 A8
Warren St. FY7 .... 194 B4
Warren The. BB4 .... 100 A7
Warrenhouse Rd. L33 .... 1 B4
Warrenhurst Rd. FY7 .... 193 F3
Warrenhurst Rd. FY7 .... 194 A4
Warrenside Cl. BB1 .... 122 A4
Warrington St. BB1 .... 101 A8
Warrington Terr. BB6 .... 143 D8
Warsicks Cotts. FY6 .... 152 E1
Warth La. LA6 .... 236 F2
Warton Ave. LA3 .... 208 E6
Warton Crag
(Nature Reserve). LA5 .... 217 C6
Warton Pl. PR7 .... 42 A8
Warton Rd. LA5 .... 217 D2
Warton St. Lytham St Anne's FY8 . 90 C3
Warton St. Preston PR1 .... 95 E6

Wartonwood View. LA5 .... 217 D1
Warwick Ave. Accrington BB5 .. 103 B7
Warwick Ave. Clayton-le-M BB5 123 F4
Warwick Ave. Cleveleys FY5 .... 172 F4
Warwick Ave. Darwen BB3 .... 80 E3
Warwick Ave. Lancaster LA1 .... 211 A5
Warwick Ave. Morecambe LA4 .. 213 B6
Warwick Cl. Church BB5 .... 102 F7
Warwick Cl. Fulwood PR2 .... 116 E4
Warwick Cl. Ramsbottom BL8 .... 49 A1
Warwick Cl. Southport PR8 .... 34 B4
Warwick Cres. 3 BB4 .... 85 B2
Warwick Dr. Barnoldswick BB8 . 200 F1
Warwick Dr. Brierfield BB9 ...... 147 D5
Warwick Dr. Clitheroe BB7 ...... 186 F2
Warwick Dr. Padiham BB12 ...... 125 D7
Warwick House. PR1 .... 96 A6
Warwick Pl. Fleetwood FY7 .... 194 A5
Warwick Pl. Normoss FY3 ...... 130 B8
Warwick Rd. Bamber Bridge PR5 96 D4
Warwick Rd. Blackpool FY3 .... 129 D7
Warwick Rd. Eccleston PR7 ...... 40 C7
Warwick Rd. Leyland PR5 .... 58 E7
Warwick St.
Lytham St Anne's FY8 .... 88 F6
Warwick St. Adlington PR7 .... 29 F6
Warwick St. Church BB5 .... 102 F7
Warwick St. Haslingden BB4 ...... 84 B3
Warwick St. Longridge PR3 ...... 139 A8
Warwick St. Nelson BB9 .... 147 E7
Warwick St. Preston PR1 .... 95 F8
Warwick St. Southport PR8 .... 34 B4
Wasdale Ave. Blackburn BB1 .... 101 C3
Wasdale Ave. Maghull L31 .... 5 F2
Wasdale Cl. Leyland PR5 & PR7 . 59 B6
Wasdale Cl. Padiham BB12 ...... 145 C1
Wasdale Gr. PR3 .... 138 F5
Wasdale Rd. FY4 .... 110 A8
Wash La. BL9 .... 32 B2
Washbrook Cl. BB7 .... 164 D1
Washbrook Way. L39 .... 15 E4
Washburn Ct. LA1 .... 213 B2
Washington Ave. FY2 .... 150 E2
Washington Cl. LA1 .... 210 D7
Washington Ct. FY2 .... 150 E2
Washington Dr. LA5 .... 217 E6
Washington Hall Fire Brigade
Training Ctr. PR7 .... 59 F2
Washington La. PR7 .... 59 F2
Washington St. BB5 .... 103 C6
Waste La. LA2 .... 220 C7
Wastwater Dr. LA4 .... 213 A4
Watchyard La. L37 .... 12 A4
Water Fold. BB4 .... 86 A8
Water La. Edenfield BL0 .... 67 D2
Water La. Preston PR1 .... 116 D1
Water La. Southport PR9 .... 53 D5
Water Prim Sch. BB4 .... 86 A8
Water St. 10 Accrington BB5 .... 103 C6
Water St. Adlington PR6 .... 30 A6
Water St. Bamber Bridge PR5 .... 76 F2
Water St. Brindle PR6 .... 77 F5
Water St. Chorley PR6 & PR7 .... 60 C1
Water St. Clayton-le-M BB5 .... 123 F5
Water St. 1 Colne BB8 .... 169 E5
Water St. Earby BB8 .... 201 B2
Water St. Egerton BL7 .... 46 D2
Water St. Great Harwood BB6 .. 123 C4
Water St. Hapton BB12 .... 125 C4
Water St. Lancaster LA1 .... 213 F1
Water St. Nelson BB9 .... 147 E8
Water St. 8 Ramsbottom BL0 .... 49 B5
Water St. Rawtenstall BB4 .... 85 A8
Water St. Ribchester PR3 .... 140 E3
Water St. Whitworth OL12 .... 51 C8
Water St. Worsthorne BB10 .... 128 B5
Water's Edge. PR2 .... 115 F4
Waterbarn La. OL13 .... 69 B8
Waterbarn St. 2 BB10 .... 147 B1
Waterdale. FY2 .... 150 E5
Waterfall Terr. BL7 .... 45 C5
Waterfield Ave. BB3 .... 64 B6
Waterfold La. BL9 .... 32 C1
Waterfoot Ave. Ainsdale PR8 .... 20 B3
Waterfoot Ave. Rawtenstall BB4 123 F6
Waterfoot Cty Prim Sch. BB4 .. 68 F8
Waterford Cl. PR7 .... 117 C5
Waterford St. BB9 .... 168 F1
Waterfront Marine & Ind Est.
FY8 .... 90 E3
Waterhead Cres. FY5 .... 150 C6
Watering Pool La. PR1 & PR5 .... 96 B1
Waterloo Cl. BB2 .... 80 B8
Waterloo Rd. Blackpool FY4 .... 129 D1
Waterloo Rd. Burnley BB11 ...... 127 B4
Waterloo Rd. Burnley BB11 ...... 127 B5
Waterloo Rd. Clitheroe BB7 .... 164 F8
Waterloo Rd. Kelbrook BB8 .... 192 A6
Waterloo Rd.
Preston PR1 & PR2 .... 116 C1
Waterloo Rd. Southport PR8 .... 33 E2
Waterloo Sch (Prim & Inf).
FY1 .... 129 D1
Waterloo St. Chorley PR6 .... 60 D1
Waterloo St. Enfield BB5 .... 124 A1
Waterloo Terr. PR1 .... 116 C1
Watermans Cl. BL6 .... 31 C4
Watermede. WN5 .... 10 E3
Waters Edge. BB1 .... 100 F4
Waterside Cl. BB5 .... 178 B7
Waterside Ind Est. BB8 .... 169 E4
Waterside Mews. BB12 .... 125 D8
Waterside Rd. Colne BB8 .... 169 D4
Waterside Rd. Haslingden BB4 .. 84 A2
Waterside Rd.
Ramsbottom BL0 & BL8 & BL9 .. 49 C3
Waterside Terr. 11 Bacup OL13 .. 86 F3
Waterside Terr. Waterside BB3 . 81 E3

Waterslack Rd. LA5 .... 218 E6
Waterworks Rd. L39 .... 16 A6
Watery Gate La. PR3 & PR4 .... 154 D3
Watery La. Darwen BB3 .... 64 B6
Watery La. Garstang PR3 .... 199 E1
Watery La. Lancaster LA1 .... 213 D3
Watery La. Preston PR1 & PR2 .. 95 B8
Watery La. Preston PR1 .... 96 E7
Watford St. 5 BB1 .... 100 E6
Watkin La. PR5 .... 76 B7
Watkin Rd. PR6 .... 60 B8
Watkins Cl. BB10 .... 147 C4
Watling Cl. BB2 .... 81 A8
Watling St. BL8 .... 48 A1
Watling Street Rd.
Fulwood PR2 .... 117 B3
Watling Street Rd.
Fulwood PR2 .... 117 E5
Watson Gdns. OL12 .... 51 D2
Watson Rd. FY4 .... 109 C7
Watson St. Blackburn BB2 ...... 100 B2
Watson St. 8
Oswaldtwistle BB5 .... 102 E4
Watt St. Burnley BB12 .... 126 C7
Watt St. Sabden BB7 .... 144 F7
Watton Beck Cl. L31 .... 5 F2
Watts Cl. L33 .... 1 A4
Watts Cl. BL6 .... 31 C2
Watts St. BL6 .... 31 C2
Wavell Ave. PR9 .... 35 B7
Wavell Cl. Southport PR9 .... 35 B7
Wavell St. BB12 .... 126 C6
Waverledge Rd. BB6 .... 123 B4
Waverledge St. BB6 .... 123 C4
Waverley. Skelmersdale WN8 .... 17 D1
Waverley Ave. Blackpool FY1 .. 129 C8
Waverley Ave. Fleetwood FY7 .. 193 D3
Waverley Cl. Brierfield BB9 .... 147 D4
Waverley Cl. Read BB12 .... 144 D1
Waverley Dr. New Longton PR4 . 74 F7
Waverley Dr. Tarleton PR4 .... 56 A6
Waverley Gdns. PR2 .... 117 E2
Waverley Pl. BB2 .... 100 B5
Waverley Rd. Accrington BB5 .. 103 E3
Waverley Rd. Blackburn BB1 .. 101 F4
Waverley Rd. Preston PR1 ...... 117 D1
Waverley Rd. Wilpshire BB1 .... 121 C4
Waverley St. 1 Burnley BB11 .. 126 E6
Waverley St. Southport PR8 ...... 34 A7
Waxy La. PR4 .... 92 C7
Way Gate. FY5 .... 172 D5
Way The. LA4 .... 213 B3
Wayfarers Arc. PR8 .... 34 B7
Wayman Rd. FY3 .... 129 D6
Wayoh Croft. BL7 .... 47 D6
Wayside. FY6 .... 194 D5
Weasel La. BB3 .... 80 B2
Weatherhill Cres. BB9 .... 147 E5
Weaver Ave. L40 .... 24 F5
Weaver's Brow. PR7 .... 42 F5
Webb St. BL6 .... 31 C3
Webber Ct. BB11 .... 126 A3
Webber St. L33 .... 1 C1
Weber St. BB4 .... 85 D1
Webster Ave. FY4 .... 109 E7
Webster Gr. LA4 .... 213 C6
Webster St. PR1 .... 116 C1
Wedgewood Rd. BB5 .... 124 F1
Weeton Ave. Blackpool FY4 .... 109 E5
Weeton Ave. Cleveleys FY5 .... 172 D3
Weeton Ave.
Lytham St Anne's FY8 .... 89 A8
Weeton CE Prim Sch. PR4 .... 131 E1
Weeton Cty Prim Sch. PR4 .... 131 E6
Weeton Pl. PR2 .... 115 E1
Weeton Rd.
Great Plumpton PR4 .... 111 F7
Weeton Rd. Kirkham PR4 .... 112 C8
Weeton Rd. Kirkham PR4 .... 112 F7
Weeton Rd. Weeton PR4 .... 131 F2
Weeton Rd. Weeton Camp PR4 . 131 E7
Weets View. BB8 .... 200 C3
Weind The. PR3 .... 154 B5
Weir Ave. OL13 .... 87 A7
Weir St. BB2 .... 100 E4
Welbeck Ave. Blackburn BB1 .. 101 B8
Welbeck Ave. Blackpool FY4 .. 129 E1
Welbeck Ave. Fleetwood FY7 .. 193 F3
Welbeck Gdns. FY7 .... 193 F3
Welbeck Rd. PR8 .... 34 A4
Welbeck Terr. PR8 .... 34 A4
Welbourne. WN8 .... 17 D1
Welbury Cl. BB8 .... 201 C2
Weld Ave. PR7 .... 42 C5
Weld Blundell Ave. L31 .... 5 A5
Weld Par. PR8 .... 33 F4
Weld Rd. PR8 .... 33 F5
Weldbank La. PR7 .... 42 C5
Weldbank St. PR7 .... 42 C5
Weldon Dr. L39 .... 15 F4
Weldon St. BB11 .... 126 E5
Well Ct. WN6 .... 28 E1
Well Field. BB4 .... 124 A2
Well Fold. BB7 .... 164 F8
Well Head. BB8 .... 170 B4
Well Head Rd. BB12 .... 167 A3
Well La. Barton L39 .... 13 E6
Well La. Brinscall BB7 .... 61 F7
Well La. High Casterton LA6 .... 238 F2
Well La. Little Eccleston PR3 .... 153 D6
Well La. Southport PR8 .... 34 B7
Well La. Yealand Redmayne LA5 . 219 E3
Well Orch. PR5 .... 77 B5
Well St. Newchurch BB4 .... 85 F3
Well St. Padiham BB12 .... 125 B8
Well St. Rishton BB1 .... 123 B2

Well St N. BL0 .... 67 C2
Well St W. 6 BL0 .... 49 B5
Well Terr. BB7 .... 186 F1
Welland St. FY2 .... 150 E4
Wellbrow Dr. PR3 .... 139 B8
Wellbrow Terr. OL12 .... 51 D2
Wellcross Rd. WN8 .... 10 B6
Wellesley St. BB12 .... 125 F6
Wellfield. PR4 .... 93 F1
Wellfield Ave. PR5 .... 75 F1
Wellfield CE/Meth Sch. BB12 126 D8
Wellfield Dr. BB2 .... 126 D7
Wellfield High Sch. PR5 .... 75 F1
Wellfield La. L40 .... 16 C3
Wellfield Rd. Bamber Bridge PR5 76 A7
Wellfield Rd. Blackburn BB2 .. 100 C6
Wellfield Rd. Preston PR1 .... 95 D8
Wellgate. BB7 .... 164 F8
Wellhouse Rd. BB8 .... 200 B2
Wellhouse Sq. 15 BB8 .... 200 B2
Wellhouse St. BB8 .... 200 B2
Wellington Ave. PR5 .... 59 B8
Wellington Ct. 6
Accrington BB5 .... 103 C5
Wellington Ct. Burnley BB10 .. 127 B5
Wellington Fold. 3 BB3 .... 81 A1
Wellington Pl. Blackburn BB2 .. 100 C3
Wellington Rd. Blackpool FY1 .. 129 B2
Wellington Rd. Chapeltown BL7 . 47 D4
Wellington Rd. Lancaster LA1 .. 211 A5
Wellington Rd. Preston PR1 .... 116 C1
Wellington St. Accrington BB5 .. 103 C5
Wellington St.
Barnoldswick BB8 .... 200 B1
Wellington St.
Blackburn BB1 & BB2 .... 100 D6
Wellington St. Chorley PR6 ...... 60 C1
Wellington St. Clayton-le-M BB5 123 F2
Wellington St.
Great Harwood BB6 .... 123 C4
Wellington St. Kirkham PR4 .... 112 F5
Wellington St.
Lytham St Anne's FY8 .... 90 D3
Wellington St. 16 Nelson BB9 . 168 D1
Wellington St. Preston PR1 ...... 95 D8
Wellington St. 19 Rochdale OL12 51 F1
Wellington St. Southport PR8 .... 34 A6
Wellington Terr. LA4 .... 212 E5
Wellogate Gdns. FY4 .... 109 D6
Wellow Pl. FY8 .... 89 C5
Wells Cl. Morecambe LA3 .... 212 E2
Wells Cl. Thornton FY5 .... 173 A2
Wells St. Haslingden BB4 .... 84 B3
Wells St. 9 Preston PR1 .... 117 D1
Welsby Rd. PR5 .... 58 D8
Welwyn Ave. PR8 .... 20 E6
Welwyn Pl. FY5 .... 172 E1
Wembley Ave. Blackpool FY3 .. 129 E8
Wembley Ave. Penwortham PR1 . 95 B5
Wembley Ave. Poulton-le-F FY6 151 F3
Wembley Rd. FY5 .... 173 B4
Wemyss Cl. LA3 .... 208 E7
Wendover Rd. FY6 .... 151 A6
Wenlock Cl. BL6 .... 31 C6
Wenning Ave.
High Bentham LA2 .... 233 D7
Wenning Ave. Maghull L31 .... 5 E2
Wenning Pl. LA1 .... 213 E2
Wennington Hall Sch. LA2 .... 235 E1
Wennington Rd. Southport PR9 . 34 F7
Wennington Rd. Wray LA2 ...... 232 D6
Wennington Sta. LA2 .... 232 E8
Wensley Ave. FY7 .... 193 E1
Wensley Cl. BB11 .... 126 E3
Wensley Dr. Accrington BB5 .... 103 D5
Wensley Dr. Lancaster LA1 .... 213 F3
Wensley Fold CE Prim Sch.
BB2 .... 100 B5
Wensley Pl. PR2 .... 117 D4
Wensley Rd. BB2 .... 100 B4
Wensleydale Ave. FY3 .... 130 A7
Wensleydale Cl. Maghull L31 .... 5 B2
Wensleydale Cl. Thornton FY5 . 151 B8
Wentcliffe Dr. BB8 .... 201 B1
Wentworth Ave. Fleetwood FY7 172 D7
Wentworth Ave. Inskip PR4 .... 134 C8
Wentworth Cl. Ainsdale PR8 .... 20 C4
Wentworth Cl. Penwortham PR1 . 95 A6
Wentworth Cres. LA3 & LA4 .... 212 E2
Wentworth Dr. Broughton PR3 . 136 C3
Wentworth Dr. Thornton FY5 .. 151 B8
Werneth Cl. PR5 .... 95 F1
Wescoe Cl. WN5 .... 10 E5
Wesham Cross. PR4 .... 112 F7
Wesham Hall Cl. PR4 .... 113 A6
Wesham Hall Rd. PR4 .... 113 A6
Wesham Park Hosp. PR4 ...... 112 F7
Wesley Cl. LA2 .... 233 D8
Wesley St. FY7 .... 194 B5
Wesley Dr. LA3 .... 208 F7
Wesley Gr. BB12 .... 126 D7
Wesley Pl. OL13 .... 86 E1
Wesley St. Accrington BB5 ...... 102 F6
Wesley St. Bamber Bridge PR5 .. 76 F8
Wesley St. Blackburn BB1 ...... 100 F7
Wesley St. Oswaldtwistle BB5 .. 102 E4
Wesley St. 8 Padiham BB12 .. 125 D8
Wesley St. Sabden BB7 .... 144 D4
Wesley St. Southport PR8 .... 34 B7
Wesley Terr. BB4 .... 87 A1
Wesleyan Row. BB7 .... 164 D8
Wessex Cl. Huncoat BB5 .... 103 F8
Wessex Cl. Standish WN1 .... 29 B1
West Ave. Barnoldswick BB8 .. 200 B2
West Ave. Fulwood PR2 .... 116 A4

West Bank. PR7 .... 42 C8
West Bank Ave. FY8 .... 89 E3
West Beach. FY8 .... 90 A2
West Bradford Rd.
Waddington BB7 .... 186 C5
West Bradford Rd.
West Bradford BB7 .... 186 F4
West Cliff. PR1 .... 95 E6
West Cliff Terr. PR1 .... 95 E6
West Cliffe. PR8 .... 90 C3
West Close Ave. BB12 .... 145 F5
West Close Rd. BB8 .... 200 B3
West Craven High Sch. BB8 . 200 C1
West Cres. Accrington BB5 ...... 103 B8
West Cres. Broughton PR3 ...... 136 C3
West Cres. Lytham St Anne's FY8 88 E6
West Ct. FY5 .... 172 C5
West Dene. WN8 .... 26 B2
West Dr. Clayton-le-W PR5 .... 76 D3
West Dr. Cleveleys FY5 .... 172 E3
West Dr. Inskip PR4 .... 134 C8
West Dr. Kirkham PR4 .... 112 C7
West Dr. Lancaster LA1 .... 213 D2
West Dr. Whalley BB7 .... 143 A7
West Dr W. FY5 .... 172 D3
West End. Great Eccleston PR3 . 154 A5
West End. Penwortham PR1 ...... 95 B6
West End Cty Prim Sch.
Morecambe LA4 .... 212 C4
West End Cty Prim Sch.
Oswaldtwistle BB5 .... 102 C5
West End La. PR4 .... 91 B5
West End Rd. LA4 .... 212 D4
West Exchange St. 7 BB8 ...... 169 D4
West Field Rd. BB8 .... 200 A4
West Gate. FY7 .... 193 D4
West Gdns. 1 OL13 .... 69 B8
West Gillibrands Ind Est. WN9 .. 8 E1
West Hall La. LA6 .... 235 C6
West Hill. BB4 .... 168 D4
West Ing La. BD23 .... 225 D5
West La. Downham BB7 .... 188 A4
West La. Formby L37 .... 11 F6
West Leigh Rd. BB1 .... 100 C8
West Meade. L31 .... 5 B2
West Meadow. PR4 .... 115 E3
West Moss La. FY4 & FY8 ...... 110 E1
West Mount. WN5 .... 10 F6
West Paddock. PR5 .... 58 E8
West Park Ave. PR2 .... 115 F2
West Park Dr. FY3 .... 129 E4
West Park La. PR2 .... 116 A2
West Park Rd. BB2 .... 100 C6
West Rd. Fulwood PR2 .... 116 F3
West Rd. Lancaster LA1 .... 210 E5
West Sq. PR4 .... 74 A8
West St. Blackpool FY1 .... 129 B5
West St. Burnley BB10 .... 127 C8
West St. Chorley PR7 .... 42 C7
West St. Colne BB8 .... 169 E4
West St. Great Harwood BB6 .. 123 C4
West St. Lancaster LA1 .... 210 F5
West St. Morecambe LA3 .... 212 B4
West St. 6 Nelson BB9 .... 168 D1
West St. Newchurch BB4 .... 68 E8
West St. Padiham BB12 .... 125 B8
West St. 7 Ramsbottom BL0 .... 49 B5
West St. Southport PR8 .... 34 A7
West Strand. PR1 & PR2 .... 95 D8
West Street Cty Prim Sch.
BB8 .... 169 E4
West Terr. PR7 .... 59 D4
West View. Bacup OL13 .... 69 B8
West View. Bamber Bridge PR5 .. 76 E7
West View. Blackburn BB2 ...... 100 B4
West View. Blackpool FY1 ...... 129 C3
West View. Clitheroe BB7 ...... 164 D7
West View. Glasson LA2 .... 205 E5
West View. Haslingden BB4 ...... 84 B4
West View. Helmshore BB4 ...... 67 A7
West View. Hollins Lane PR3 .. 204 C2
West View. Kirkham PR4 .... 112 F7
West View. Longton PR4 .... 74 A8
West View. 4 Newchurch BB4 .. 85 F1
West View. Oswaldtwistle BB5 . 102 E4
West View. Parbold WN8 .... 26 C2
West View. Preston PR1 .... 117 C2
West View. Ramsbottom BL0 .... 67 C2
West View. Wheelton PR6 .... 61 A7
West View Ave. FY1 .... 129 B2
West View Pl. BB2 .... 100 B6
West View Rd. Morecambe LA4 212 D5
West View Rd.
Whitewell Bottom BB4 .... 85 F5
West View Terr. Darwen BB3 .... 80 A2
West View Terr. Padiham BB12 125 C7
West View Terr. Preston PR1 .... 95 C8
West Way. Chorley PR7 .... 60 A2
West Way. Fleetwood FY7 ...... 172 D8
West Wlk. BL7 .... 46 D2
Westbank Ave. FY4 .... 110 A7
Westbro Cl. LA3 .... 212 A1
Westbourne Ave. Blackpool FY1 129 C1
Westbourne Ave. Burnley BB11 126 D3
Westbourne Ave.
Wrea Green PR4 .... 112 B3
Westbourne Ave S. BB11 .... 126 E3
Westbourne Dr. LA1 .... 210 D7
Westbourne Gdns. PR8 .... 33 D4
Westbourne Pl. LA1 .... 210 D8
Westbourne Rd. Chorley PR7 .... 42 B6
Westbourne Rd. Cleveleys FY5 172 D5
Westbourne Rd.
Knott End-on-S FY6 .... 194 D5
Westbourne Rd. Lancaster LA1 210 D7
Westbourne Rd. Middleton LA3 209 A2
Westbourne Rd. Southport PR8 . 33 D4
Westbourne Rd. Warton LA5 .. 217 C4

Westbrook Cres. PR2 .... 116 A3
Westbury Cl. Blackpool FY5 .... 150 C7
Westbury Cl. Brierfield BB10 .... 147 E2
Westbury Gdns. BB1 .... 101 C4
Westby Ave. FY4 .... 109 E5
Westby Gr. FY7 .... 194 B5
Westby Pl. PR2 .... 115 F1
Westby Rd. Lytham St Anne's FY8 .... 88 E8
Westby Rd. Westby PR4 .... 111 E5
Westby St. FY8 .... 90 B3
Westby Way. FY6 .... 151 D2
Westcliff Inf Sch. FY5 .... 150 C5
Westcliffe. BB6 .... 123 B6
Westcliffe Dr. Blackpool FY3 .... 129 E8
Westcliffe Dr. Morecambe LA3 .... 212 D2
Westcliffe Rd. PR8 .... 33 F5
Westcliffe Wlk. BB9 .... 147 D7
Westcote Rd. BB3 .... 64 B6
Westcroft. PR4 .... 73 E3
Westend Ave. PR7 .... 41 D1
Westerlong. PR2 .... 115 D1
Western Ave. BB11 .... 126 E4
Western Ct. OL13 .... 69 B8
Western Dr. PR5 .... 75 D2
Western Rd. OL13 .... 69 C8
Westfield. Bamber Bridge PR5 .... 76 A8
Westfield. Nelson BB9 .... 168 D1
Westfield Ave. Blackpool FY3 .... 151 A1
Westfield Ave. Fleetwood FY7 .... 193 E2
Westfield Ave. Normoss FY3 .... 130 B7
Westfield Ave. Read BB12 .... 144 D1
Westfield Dr. Bolton-le-S LA5 .... 216 A6
Westfield Dr. Fulwood PR2 .... 117 E4
Westfield Dr. Gregson Lane PR5 .... 97 D1
Westfield Dr. Leyland PR5 .... 75 E1
Westfield Dr. Warton PR4 .... 91 F5
Westfield Dr.
  West Bradford BB7 .... 186 E6
Westfield Gr. LA4 .... 212 D4
Westfield Rd. FY1 .... 129 D1
Westfields. PR5 .... 57 A2
Westgate. Barnoldswick BB8 .... 200 A1
Westgate. Burnley BB11 .... 126 E6
Westgate. Fulwood PR2 .... 116 D5
Westgate. Leyland PR5 .... 76 B2
Westgate. Morecambe LA3 & LA4 .... 212 F3
Westgate. Read BB12 .... 144 C1
Westgate. Skelmersdale WN8 .... 8 D8
Westgate. Wallbank OL12 .... 51 B7
Westgate Ave.
  Morecambe LA3 & LA4 .... 212 E2
Westgate Ave. Ramsbottom BL0 .... 49 A2
Westgate Cl. OL12 .... 51 B7
Westgate Cty Prim Sch. LA4 .... 212 E3
Westgate Dr. WN5 .... 10 D5
Westgate La. LA6 .... 236 E5
Westgate Park Rd. LA4 .... 212 F3
Westgate Rd. FY8 .... 109 C4
Westgate Trad Est. 2 BB11 .... 126 F6
Westham St. LA1 .... 211 A7
Westhaven Cres. L39 .... 15 C1
Westhead Ave. L33 .... 1 A1
Westhead Cl. L32 & L33 .... 1 A1
Westhead Rd. PR5 .... 57 B2
Westhead Wlk. 1
  Fleetwood FY7 .... 193 F2
Westhead Wlk. Kirkby L32 & L33 .... 1 A1
Westholme Lower Sch. BB2 .... 100 B6
Westholme Sch. Blackburn BB2 .... 99 E6
Westholme Sch. Blackburn BB2 .... 100 A6
Westhoughton Rd. PR6 .... 42 F1
Westland Ave. BB3 .... 63 F8
Westlands. PR5 .... 58 C7
Westlands Ct. FY5 .... 151 B8
Westleigh Rd. PR2 .... 115 F1
Westminster Ave. LA4 .... 212 C4
Westminster Cl. Accrington BB5 .... 103 E3
Westminster Cl.
  Morecambe LA3 .... 212 E2
Westminster Cl. Read BB12 .... 144 D1
Westminster Dr. PR8 .... 20 A4
Westminster Pl. Eccleston PR7 .... 40 A8
Westminster Pl. Hutton PR4 .... 94 D1
Westminster Rd. Blackpool FY1 .... 129 C8
Westminster Rd. Chorley PR7 .... 42 C7
Westminster Rd. Darwen BB3 .... 80 E3
Westminster Rd.
  Morecambe LA3 & LA4 .... 212 B3
Westmoor Gr. LA3 .... 208 E5
Westmoreland Rd. PR8 .... 34 D5
Westmoreland St. BB9 .... 147 C8
Westmorland Ave.
  Blackpool FY1 .... 129 D3
Westmorland Ave.
  Cleveleys FY5 .... 172 D4
Westmorland Cl. Leyland PR5 .... 58 E7
Westmorland Cl.
  Penwortham PR1 .... 95 B4
Westmorland House. 15 PR4 .... 95 F8
Westmorland St. BB11 .... 126 D5
Weston La Heads. PR4 .... 131 F1
Weston Pl. FY1 .... 129 D1
Weston St. PR1 .... 95 D8
Westover Ave. LA5 .... 217 D5
Westover Cl. L31 .... 5 C1
Westover Gr. LA5 .... 217 E5
Westover Rd. Maghull L31 .... 5 C1
Westover Rd. Warton LA5 .... 217 E5
Westover St. LA4 .... 212 E5
Westside. FY4 .... 109 F8
Westway. Burnley BB11 .... 126 D6
Westway. Freckleton PR4 .... 92 A6
Westway. Fulwood PR2 .... 117 A4
Westway. Hightown L38 .... 2 F4
Westway. Maghull L31 .... 5 C2
Westway. PR2 .... 117 B4
Westway Sch. BB12 .... 126 F8
Westwell Gr. FY1 .... 129 C4

Westwell Rd. PR6 .... 60 D1
Westwell St. Darwen BB3 .... 80 E4
Westwell St. 11
  Great Harwood BB6 .... 123 C5
Westwood Ave. Blackpool FY3 .... 129 E4
Westwood Ave. Fleetwood FY7 .... 193 E3
Westwood Ave. Poulton-le-F FY6 .... 151 E3
Westwood Ave. Rishton BB1 .... 123 A1
Westwood Cl. PR8 .... 34 E3
Westwood Ct. BB1 .... 101 A6
Westwood Mews. FY8 .... 90 A3
Westwood Rd. Blackburn BB1 .... 101 B4
Westwood Rd. Burnley BB12 .... 126 C8
Westwood Rd.
  Clayton Brook PR5 & PR6 .... 77 C4
Westwood Rd. Leyland PR5 .... 76 B2
Westwood Rd.
  Lytham St Anne's FY8 .... 90 A3
Westwood St. BB5 .... 103 B7
Wetherall St. PR1 .... 116 D1
Wetherby Ave. FY4 .... 109 B5
Wetherfield Cl. LA1 .... 214 A4
Weymouth Rd. FY3 .... 129 F3
Weythorne Dr. BL9 .... 32 F4
Whalley Banks. BB2 .... 100 D4
Whalley CE Prim Sch. BB7 .... 143 C5
Whalley Cres. Darwen BB3 .... 81 B1
Whalley Cres. Staining FY3 .... 130 E5
Whalley Dr. Formby L37 .... 12 A2
Whalley Dr. Ormskirk L39 .... 6 D8
Whalley Dr. Rawtenstall BB4 .... 85 A4
Whalley Gdns. OL12 .... 51 B1
Whalley La. FY4 .... 110 A8
Whalley New Rd.
  Billington BB6 & BB7 .... 142 F3
Whalley New Rd.
  Blackburn BB1 .... 121 F1
Whalley New Rd.
  Langho BB6 & BB1 .... 142 D1
Whalley Old Rd.
  Billington BB6 & BB7 .... 143 B3
Whalley Old Rd. Blackburn BB1 .... 101 A7
Whalley Old Rd.
  Sunny Bower BB1 .... 122 B1
Whalley Pl. FY8 .... 89 B6
Whalley Range. BB1 .... 100 F6
Whalley Rd. Accrington BB5 .... 103 B7
Whalley Rd. Bank Lane BL0 .... 49 E7
Whalley Rd. Barrow BB7 .... 164 D2
Whalley Rd.
  Clayton-le-M BB5 & BB6 .... 123 F5
Whalley Rd. Clitheroe BB7 .... 164 D5
Whalley Rd. Heskin Green PR7 .... 40 D4
Whalley Rd. Hurst Green BB7 .... 163 B1
Whalley Rd. Lancaster LA1 .... 213 F4
Whalley Rd. Langho BB6 .... 142 D2
Whalley Rd. Mellor Brook BB2 .... 120 C3
Whalley Rd. Padiham BB12 .... 125 B8
Whalley Rd. Passmonds OL12 .... 51 B1
Whalley Rd. Read BB12 & BB7 .... 144 C1
Whalley Rd. Sabden BB7 .... 144 D6
Whalley Rd.
  Turner Green BB2 & PR5 .... 119 C2
Whalley Rd. Wilpshire BB1 .... 122 B7
Whalley St. Bamber Bridge PR5 .... 76 F2
Whalley St. Blackburn BB1 .... 100 E6
Whalley St. Blackburn BB10 .... 147 A1
Whalley St. 4 Chorley PR7 .... 42 C7
Whalley St. Clitheroe BB7 .... 164 D8
Whalley St. BB3 .... 143 B6
Whalley Terr. BB3 .... 80 B6
Whalleys Rd. WN8 .... 18 B5
Wham Bottom La. OL12 .... 51 D4
Wham Brook Cl. BB5 .... 102 B5
Wham Hey. PR4 .... 75 A7
Wham La. New Longton PR4 .... 75 A7
Wham La. Walmer Bridge PR4 .... 74 D4
Whams La. LA2 .... 204 D7
Wharf St. Blackburn BB1 .... 100 F5
Wharf St. Lytham St Anne's FY8 .... 90 C3
Wharf St. Rishton BB1 .... 123 C1
Wharfdale Ave. BB10 .... 147 B4
Wharfdale Ct. FY6 .... 151 C3
Wharfe Ct. LA1 .... 213 B3
Wharfedale. FY4 .... 109 F7
Wharfedale Ave. Fulwood PR2 .... 117 E5
Wharfedale Ave. Thornton FY5 .... 173 B3
Wharfedale Cl. Blackburn BB2 .... 79 D7
Wharfedale Cl. Leyland PR5 .... 59 A7
Wharfedale Rd. LA1 .... 210 D8
Wharton Ave. FY5 .... 173 D1
Whave's La. PR6 .... 78 D4
Wheat La. L40 .... 25 A4
Wheat St. Accrington BB5 .... 103 A6
Wheat St. Padiham BB12 .... 125 D7
Wheatacre. WN8 .... 8 E8
Wheatcroft Ave. BB12 .... 146 B8
Wheatfield. PR5 .... 58 A8
Wheatfield Ct. 5 LA1 .... 210 E8
Wheatfield St. Lancaster LA1 .... 210 E8
Wheatfield St. Rishton BB1 .... 123 B2
Wheathead La. BB9 .... 168 B8
Wheatholme St. BB4 .... 85 B2
Wheatlands Cres. FY3 .... 130 C2
Wheatley Cl. Burnley BB12 .... 126 D7
Wheatley Cl. Fence BB12 .... 146 D7
Wheatley Dr. PR3 .... 139 B8
Wheatley Gr. BB9 .... 168 C3
Wheatley Lane Prim Sch.
  BB12 .... 146 E8
Wheatley Lane Rd.
  Barrowford BB9 & BB9 .... 168 B2
Wheatley Lane Rd. Fence BB12 .... 146 E8
Wheatsheaf Ave. PR3 .... 139 A7
Wheatsheaf Wlk. L39 .... 15 E5
Wheel La. PR3 .... 196 A6
Wheelton La. PR5 .... 76 A3

Wheelwrights Cl. BB7 .... 225 C3
Wheelwrights Wharf. L40 .... 22 F4
Whernside. FY4 .... 109 F7
Whernside Cl. BB8 .... 200 A4
Whernside Cres. PR2 .... 117 D5
Whernside Gr. LA5 .... 217 E2
Whernside Rd. LA1 .... 213 D3
Whernside Way. PR5 .... 76 C1
Whimberry Cl. 1 PR6 .... 42 E8
Whimbrel Dr. FY5 .... 173 A4
Whin Ave. LA5 .... 216 B6
Whin Dr. LA5 .... 216 B6
Whin Gr. LA5 .... 216 B6
Whin La. PR3 .... 153 B8
Whinberry Ave. BB4 .... 85 A1
Whinfell Dr. LA1 .... 211 A3
Whinfield Ave. Chorley PR6 .... 60 D1
Whinfield Ave. Fleetwood FY7 .... 193 E2
Whinfield La. PR1 & PR2 .... 95 A8
Whinfield Pl. Blackburn BB2 .... 100 A6
Whinfield Pl. Preston PR2 .... 95 A8
Whinfield St. BB5 .... 124 A1
Whinney Brow. PR3 .... 204 C3
Whinney Heys Rd. FY3 .... 130 A6
Whinney Hill Rd. BB5 .... 124 C1
Whinney La.
  Blackburn BB1 & BB2 .... 100 C8
Whinney La. Langho BB6 .... 142 D1
Whinney La. Mellor BB2 .... 121 B2
Whinny La. Euxton PR7 .... 59 E3
Whinny La. Knott End-on-S FY6 .... 194 E4
Whinny La. Waddington BB7 .... 185 E6
Whinnyfield La. PR4 .... 135 D2
Whinnysty La. LA3 .... 212 A1
Whinpark Ave. FY3 .... 130 A6
Whins Ave. BB7 .... 144 E7
Whins La. Read BB12 .... 144 E3
Whins La. Wheelton PR6 .... 61 A8
Whinsands Cl. PR2 .... 117 D5
Whinsfell View. LA4 .... 212 E5
Whipp Ave. BB7 .... 164 D7
Whitaker St. BB5 .... 103 B7
Whitbarrow Sq. 8 LA1 .... 211 A8
Whitburn. WN8 .... 17 D1
Whitburn Rd. L33 .... 1 A4
Whitby Ave. Fulwood PR2 .... 115 F5
Whitby Ave. Southport PR9 .... 53 D6
Whitby Dr. BB2 .... 101 A1
Whitby Pl. PR2 .... 115 F5
Whitby Rd. Lytham St Anne's FY8 .... 110 A1
Whitby Rd. Morecambe LA4 .... 212 F5
White Acre Rd. BB5 .... 103 E2
White Ash Est. BB5 .... 102 D4
White Ash La. BB5 .... 102 D3
White Birk Cl. BL8 .... 48 F2
White Bull St. BB12 .... 126 C6
White Carr La. Baldingstone BL9 .... 50 A1
White Carr La. Cleveleys FY5 .... 151 A8
White Carr La. Hollins Lane PR3 .... 204 E4
White Carr La. Moor Side PR4 .... 133 C2
White Cross St. LA1 .... 210 F7
White Gate Fold. PR7 .... 41 E3
White Gr. BB8 .... 169 C6
White Hill Cl. OL12 .... 51 D4
White Horse Cl. BL6 .... 31 C5
White Horse La. PR3 .... 156 E1
White House La.
  Drummersdale L40 .... 36 C1
White House La.
  Lane Heads PR3 .... 154 E4
White Lea. PR3 .... 199 C1
White Lee Ave. BB8 .... 170 C2
White Lee La. PR3 .... 180 C2
White Lund Ave. LA3 .... 212 F2
White Lund Rd. LA3 .... 212 F2
White Lund Trad Est. LA3 .... 212 G2
White Meadow. PR4 .... 115 E3
White Moss La. FY6 .... 174 E4
White Moss Rd. WN8 .... 8 C7
White Moss Rd S. WN8 .... 8 D7
White Rd. BB2 .... 100 B6
White St. Burnley BB12 .... 126 B6
White St. Colne BB8 .... 169 B4
White Walls Cl. BB8 .... 169 A3
Whiteacre. WN6 .... 28 A2
Whiteacre La. BB6 .... 143 E8
Whitebeam Cl. Penwortham PR1 .... 95 B3
Whitebeam Cl. Thornton FY5 .... 172 F5
Whitebeck La. LA6 .... 234 B4
Whitebirk Cl. Blackburn BB1 .... 101 C8
Whitebirk Dr. Blackburn BB1 .... 101 D6
Whitebirk Ind Est. BB1 .... 122 C1
Whitebirk Rd. BB1 .... 101 D5
Whitechapel Prim Sch. PR3 .... 158 D7
Whitecotes Dr. FY8 .... 90 A4
Whitecrest Ave. FY5 .... 172 F4
Whitecroft Ave. 7 BB4 .... 84 B2
Whitecroft Cl. BB4 .... 84 B2
Whitecroft Ct. BB12 .... 120 C2
Whitecroft Meadows. BB4 .... 84 B2
Whitecroft View. BB5 .... 103 E2
Whitefield Cl. L38 .... 2 F2
Whitefield Cty Prim Sch. BB9 .... 147 C8
Whitefield La. L40 .... 38 C3
Whitefield Meadow. PR5 .... 96 F2
Whitefield Pl. LA3 .... 212 F2
Whitefield Prim Sch. PR1 .... 95 A4
Whitefield Rd. PR1 .... 95 A4
Whitefield Rd E. PR1 .... 95 B4
Whitefield Rd W. PR1 .... 95 A4
Whitefield St. BB12 .... 125 C4
Whitefriar Cl. PR2 .... 116 A5
Whitegate. LA3 .... 212 G3
Whitegate. BB12 .... 125 E7
Whitegate Dr. FY3 .... 129 E3
Whitegate Gdns. BB12 .... 125 C7
Whitehalgh La. BB6 .... 142 C1
Whitehall Ave. WN6 .... 19 E8

Whitehall La. Blackrod BL6 .... 30 D3
Whitehall La. Grindleton BB7 .... 224 A1
Whitehall Rd. Blackburn BB2 .... 100 B7
Whitehall Rd. Darwen BB3 .... 64 A5
Whitehall St. Darwen BB3 .... 64 B5
Whitehall St. Nelson BB9 .... 168 F1
Whitehall St. Rochdale OL12 .... 51 F1
Whitehaven Cl. Ainsdale PR8 .... 20 B3
Whitehaven Cl. Blackburn BB2 .... 101 A1
Whitehead Cl. FY3 .... 130 D5
Whitehead Cl. Blackburn BB2 .... 100 C5
Whitehead St. 11 BB11 .... 126 E5
Whitehead St. 10
  Rawtenstall BB4 .... 85 A3
Whitehey. WN9 .... 8 E8
Whitehey. WN8 .... 8 E8
Whitehill Rd. FY4 .... 110 E6
Whiteholme Dr. FY6 .... 151 B6
Whiteholme Pl. PR2 .... 115 E1
Whiteholme Rd. FY5 .... 150 E7
Whitehouse Ave. L37 .... 12 A3
Whitehouse La. L37 .... 12 A3
Whiteledge Rd. WN8 .... 9 B6
Whitelees Way. PR5 .... 151 B3
Whiteley Ave. BB2 .... 100 A1
Whiteley St. BB4 .... 84 C1
Whiteleys La. L40 .... 16 D2
Whitemoor Rd. BB8 .... 191 C2
Whitemoss. OL12 .... 51 B2
Whitemoss Ave. FY3 .... 130 B7
Whitendale. 8 LA1 .... 213 C2
Whitendale Cres. BB1 .... 101 A3
Whitendale Dr.
  Bamber Bridge PR5 .... 76 F8
Whitendale Dr. Hest Bank LA5 .... 215 F2
Whitendale Hall. PR1 .... 116 F1
Whitepits La. LA2 .... 233 D5
Whiterails Dr. L39 .... 15 D6
Whiterails Mews. L39 .... 15 D6
Whiteray Rd. 9 LA1 .... 213 D2
Whiteside Fold. OL12 .... 51 A1
Whiteside Way. FY5 .... 172 E3
Whitestock. WN8 .... 8 E8
Whitethorn Cl. PR6 .... 77 A2
Whitethorn Mews. FY8 .... 110 A2
Whitethorn Sq. PR2 .... 115 D1
Whitethorne Mews. FY5 .... 151 C8
Whitewalls Dr. BB8 .... 169 A4
Whitewalls Ind Est. BB8 .... 169 A3
Whitewell Cl. BB7 .... 178 D3
Whitewell Dr. BB7 .... 164 C7
Whitewell Pl. 11 BB1 .... 100 F6
Whitewell Rd. BB5 .... 103 D8
Whitewood Cl. FY8 .... 89 E4
Whitley Ave. Blackpool FY3 .... 129 D5
Whitley Ave. Cleveleys FY5 .... 172 E5
Whitley Rd. WN8 .... 19 D3
Whitmore Dr. PR1 & PR2 .... 118 A2
Whitmore Pl. PR1 .... 118 A2
Whitmore Pl. PR1 & PR2 .... 118 A2
Whitstone Dr. WN8 .... 9 D7
Whittaker Ave. FY3 .... 129 E7
Whittaker Cl. BB12 .... 126 B8
Whittaker St. BB2 .... 100 C5
Whittakers La. BB7 .... 186 F8
Whittam Ave. FY4 .... 129 E1
Whittam Cres. BB7 .... 143 B6
Whittam Rd. Chorley PR7 .... 42 B5
Whittam Rd. Whalley BB7 .... 143 B6
Whittam St. BB11 .... 126 F5
Whitters La. PR3 .... 198 D2
Whittingham Dr. BL0 .... 49 C3
Whittingham Hosp. PR3 .... 137 F4
Whittingham La.
  Goosnargh PR3 .... 137 C5
Whittingham La.
  Grimsargh PR2 .... 138 B2
Whittingham Rd. PR3 .... 138 F7
Whittle Brow. PR7 .... 41 C1
Whittle Cl. BB7 .... 186 F1
Whittle Dr. L39 .... 15 E7
Whittle Gn. PR4 .... 135 E3
Whittle Hill. BL7 .... 46 E3
Whittle St. WN6 & WN8 .... 26 F4
Whittle St. Haslingden BB4 .... 84 A2
Whittle St. Rawtenstall BB4 .... 85 A3
Whittle-le-Woods CE Sch. PR6 60 B8
Whittlefield Cty Prim Sch.
  BB12 .... 126 D7
Whittles St. OL13 .... 70 B8
Whitton Mews. 5 BL6 .... 31 B4
Whittycroft Ave. BB9 .... 168 E6
Whittycroft Dr. BB9 .... 168 E6
Whitwell Ave. 4 FY4 .... 109 C5
Whitwell St. WN6 .... 28 D2
Whitwell Gdns. BB6 .... 31 B5
Whitworth Ct. PR4 .... 113 B4
Whitworth Dr. PR7 .... 42 A7
Whitworth High Sch. OL12 .... 51 C8
Whitworth Rake. OL12 .... 51 F2
Whitworth Rd. OL12 .... 51 F2
Whitworth Sq. OL12 .... 51 F2
Whitworth St. Horwich BL6 .... 31 C2
Whitworth St. Kirkham PR4 .... 112 F6
Whitworth Way. BB8 .... 200 C4
Wholesome La.
  Drummersdale PR9 .... 36 C2
Wholesome La. New Longton PR4 74 E5
Whytha Rd. BB7 & BB9 .... 189 D6
Wicken Tree Row. BB12 .... 144 F3
Wickentree Holt. OL12 .... 51 A1
Wickliffe St. 7 BB9 .... 168 F1
Wicks Cres. L37 .... 11 C4
Wicks Gdns. L37 .... 11 D3
Wicks Gn. L37 .... 11 C3

Wicks Green Cl. L37 .... 11 C3
Wicks La. L37 .... 11 D3
Wickworth St. BB9 .... 148 A7
Widford Wlk. BL6 .... 30 E1
Widgeon Cl. 5 FY5 .... 172 F4
Widow Hill Rd. BB10 .... 147 D1
Wigan Golf Course. PR7 .... 29 D2
Wigan La. PR6 & PR7 .... 42 E2
Wigan La. Bamber Bridge PR5 .... 76 E7
Wigan Rd.
  Euxton PR6 & PR7 & PR5 .... 59 C5
Wigan Rd. Ormskirk L39 & L40 .... 16 A5
Wigan Rd. Skelmersdale WN8 .... 8 F8
Wigan Rd. Westhead L40 .... 16 E4
Wiggins La. L40 & PR4 .... 37 B6
Wignall St. 5 PR1 .... 117 C1
Wignalls Meadow. L38 .... 2 F3
Wigston Cl. PR8 .... 20 B4
Wigton Ave. PR5 .... 58 D7
Wilbraham St. PR0 & PR1 .... 117 C1
Wilcove. WN8 .... 17 F1
Wild La. FY4 .... 110 D4
Wilderswood Ave. BL6 .... 31 C4
Wilderswood Cl. PR6 .... 77 C2
Wilderswood Ct. BL6 .... 31 D4
Wilding's La. FY8 .... 89 B8
Wildman St. Blackpool FY3 .... 129 D7
Wildman St. Preston PR1 & PR2 .... 116 E2
Wildoaks Dr. FY5 .... 151 D8
Wilfield St. BB11 .... 126 E6
Wilford St. FY3 .... 129 E7
Wilfred Dr. BL9 .... 32 B4
Wilfred St. BB5 .... 103 C4
Wilfrid's Pl. WN6 .... 28 F1
Wilkie Ave. BB11 .... 126 E2
Wilkin Sq. 6 BB7 .... 164 E8
Wilkinson Ave. FY3 .... 129 E4
Wilkinson Mount. BB8 .... 201 B2
Wilkinson St.
  Bamber Bridge PR5 .... 76 B8
Wilkinson St. Barrowford BB9 .... 168 C2
Wilkinson St. Haslingden BB4 .... 84 B4
Wilkinson St. Higham BB12 .... 145 F5
Wilkinson St. Rawtenstall BB11 .... 105 B4
Wilkinson Way. FY6 .... 194 F5
Willacy La. PR4 .... 134 E2
Willacy Par. LA3 .... 212 B2
Willard Ave. WN5 .... 10 D3
Willaston Ave. BB9 .... 168 E8
William Henry St. 6 PR1 .... 96 C8
William Herbert St. 18 BB11 .... 100 F6
William Hopwood St. 8 BB11 .... 101 A4
William St. Accrington BB5 .... 103 C7
William St. Bacup OL13 .... 70 C8
William St. Blackburn BB2 .... 100 E2
William St. Blackpool FY3 .... 129 E7
William St. Brierfield BB9 .... 147 B6
William St. Carnforth LA5 .... 217 D3
William St. Colne BB8 .... 169 E4
William St. 11 Darwen BB3 .... 81 A1
William St. Earby BB18 .... 201 B1
William St. Enfield BB5 .... 124 A1
William St. 17 Nelson BB9 .... 168 E1
William St. Ramsbottom BL0 .... 67 C3
William St. Whitworth OL12 .... 70 C1
William Thompson Rec Ctr.
  BB11 .... 127 A5
Williams Ave. LA2 & LA4 .... 213 C6
Williams La. PR2 .... 117 C2
Williams Pl. 2 BB9 .... 147 F8
Williams Rd. BB10 .... 127 B8
Williamson Rd. LA1 .... 211 A8
Willis Rd. BB2 .... 100 A2
Willis St. BB11 .... 126 E5
Willoughby Ave. FY5 .... 172 D2
Willoughby St. 6 BB1 .... 100 E6
Willow Ave. BB4 .... 85 A4
Willow Bank. BB3 .... 64 A6
Willow Brook. BB5 .... 103 B6
Willow Cl. Adlington PR6 .... 30 B8
Willow Cl. Bamber Bridge PR5 .... 76 A8
Willow Cl. Barrowford BB9 .... 168 B1
Willow Cl. Clayton-le-M BB5 .... 123 E3
Willow Cl. Forton PR3 .... 204 B3
Willow Cl. Freckleton PR4 .... 92 A5
Willow Cl. Gregson Lane PR5 .... 97 E1
Willow Cl. Penwortham PR1 .... 95 A4
Willow Cl. Thornton FY5 .... 173 D4
Willow Coppice. PR4 .... 115 E3
Willow Cres.
  Burscough Bridge L40 .... 24 F6
Willow Cres. Clayton-le-W PR5 .... 76 D3
Willow Cres.
  Fulwood PR1 & PR2 .... 117 E2
Willow Dr. Barrow BB6 .... 143 D8
Willow Dr. Charnock Richard PR7 .... 41 D3
Willow Dr. Freckleton PR4 .... 92 A5
Willow Dr. Garstang PR3 .... 199 C1
Willow Dr. Poulton-le-F FY6 .... 130 D8
Willow Dr. Skelmersdale WN8 .... 17 E1
Willow Dr. Wrea Green PR4 .... 112 C4
Willow Field. PR6 .... 77 C3
Willow Field Chase. PR5 .... 98 B2
Willow Gn. Ormskirk L39 .... 15 F5
Willow Gn. Preston PR1 .... 95 A8
Willow Gr. Blackpool FY3 .... 151 A8
Willow Gr. Formby L37 .... 11 F4
Willow Gr. Goosnargh PR3 .... 137 D6
Willow Gr. Hambleton FY6 .... 174 B2
Willow Gr. Morecambe LA4 .... 213 B6
Willow Gr. Rufford L40 .... 38 A3
Willow Gr. Southport PR9 .... 34 E7
Willow Gr. West Bradford BB7 .... 186 D7

Willow Hey. Skelmersdale WN8 .. **17** F1
Willow Hey. Tarleton PR4 .... **56** A7
Willow La. LA1 .... **210** C2
Willow Lodge. FY8 .... **89** C7
Willow Mill. LA2 .... **231** C3
Willow Mount. BB1 .... **121** F3
Willow Pk. BB5 .... **102** C2
Willow Pl. PR4 .... **153** F1
Willow Rd. Chorley PR6 .... **60** E2
Willow Rd. Wymott PR5 .... **57** F6
Willow St. Accrington BB5 .... **103** B6
Willow St. Blackburn BB1 .... **101** A4
Willow St. Burnley BB12 .... **126** E6
Willow St. Bury BL9 .... **32** B3
Willow St. Clayton-le-M BB5 ..... **123** E3
Willow St. Darwen BB3 .... **80** F1
Willow St. Fleetwood FY7 .... **194** A4
Willow St. Great Harwood BB6 .. **123** C4
Willow St. Haslingden BB4 .... **84** B3
Willow St. Newchurch BB4 .... **68** E8
Willow Tree Ave.
  Broughton PR3 .... **136** D3
Willow Tree Ave.
  Rawtenstall BB4 .... **84** E2
Willow Tree Cres. PR5 .... **75** D1
Willow Tree Gdns. FY5 .... **173** D1
Willow Trees Dr. BB1 .... **121** C1
Willow Way. PR4 .... **74** F7
Willow Wlk. WN8 .... **18** B4
Willow-Dale. FY5 .... **173** D1
Willowbank Ave. FY4 .... **109** E6
Willowcroft Dr. FY6 .... **174** B1
Willowdene. FY5 .... **172** E1
Willowfield Rd. LA3 .... **209** A7
Willowhey. PR9 .... **52** F4
Willowmead Way. OL12 .... **51** A2
Willows Ave. Cleveleys FY5 .... **172** E1
Willows Ave.
  Lytham St Anne's FY8 .... **89** E3
Willows La. Accrington BB5 .... **103** A3
Willows La. Kirkham PR4 .... **112** F5
Willows Park La. PR3 .... **139** B8
Willows RC Prim Sch The.
  PR4 .... **112** F5
Willows The. Broadley OL12 .... **51** C5
Willows The. Coppull PR7 .... **28** E8
Willows The.
  Lytham St Anne's FY8 .... **89** E3
Willows The. Mawdesley L40 .... **39** C2
Willows The. Southport PR8 .... **33** F6
Wills Ave. L31 .... **5** C2
Willshaw Rd. FY2 .... **150** B1
Willy La. LA2 .... **203** D6
Wilmar Rd. FY2 .... **76** C2
Wilmcote Gr. PR8 .... **20** B4
Wilmore Cl. BB8 .... **169** C5
Wilmot Rd. PR2 .... **117** C3
Wilpshire Banks. BB1 .... **121** F4
Wilpshire Golf Course. BB1 ..... **122** A6
Wilpshire Rd. BB1 .... **122** E4
Wilson Cl. PR4 .... **56** A7
Wilson Dr. PR4 .... **153** F1
Wilson Fold Ave. BL6 .... **31** F1
Wilson Gr. LA3 .... **208** E8
Wilson Sq. FY5 .... **150** D7
Wilson St. Blackburn BB2 .... **100** D2
Wilson St. Bury BL9 .... **32** A1
Wilson St. Clitheroe BB7 .... **164** E7
Wilson St. Foulridge BB8 .... **191** E1
Wilson St. Horwich BL6 .... **31** A4
Wilson's Endowed CE Prim Sch.
  LA6 .... **231** B8
Wilton Cl. LA1 .... **214** A4
Wilton Gr. PR1 .... **95** A4
Wilton Par. FY1 .... **129** B7
Wilton Pl. PR5 .... **76** B1
Wilton St. Barrowford BB9 .... **168** D3
Wilton St. Brierfield BB9 .... **147** B5
Wilton St. Burnley BB10 .... **147** B1
Wiltshire Ave. BB12 .... **126** B7
Wiltshire Dr. BB4 .... **67** B8
Wilvere Dr. FY5 .... **150** C8
Wilworth Cres. BB1 .... **121** E2
Wimberley Banks. BB1 .... **100** F7
Wimberley Gdns. BB1 .... **100** E6
Wimberley Pl. BB1 .... **100** E6
Wimberley St. BB1 .... **100** E7
Wimbledon Ave. FY5 .... **150** D7
Wimbledon Cl. FY5 .... **150** D6
Wimborne Cl. BL6 .... **31** F1
Wimbourne Pl. FY4 .... **109** B6
Wimbrick Cres. L39 .... **15** D3
Winchcombe Rd. FY5 .... **150** E7
Winchester Ave.
  Accrington BB5 .... **103** C7
Winchester Ave.
  Blackpool FY4 .... **129** D1
Winchester Ave. Chorley PR7 ..... **42** E4
Winchester Ave. Lancaster LA1 **211** B6
Winchester Ave.
  Morecambe LA4 .... **212** G6
Winchester Cl.
  Morecambe LA3 .... **212** E2
Winchester Cl. Orrell WN5 .... **10** F7
Winchester Dr. FY6 .... **151** B6
Winchester Dr. Longshaw WN5 . **10** C2
Winchester Rd. Padiham BB12 **125** D6
Winchester St. BB1 .... **101** A3
Winckley Ct. PR4 .... **95** F7
Winckley Rd. Clayton-le-M BB5 **123** F2
Winckley Rd. Preston PR1 .... **95** E6
Winckley Sq. PR1 .... **95** F7
Winckley St. PR4 .... **95** F7
Winder Garth. LA6 .... **234** B1
Winder La. PR3 .... **204** B2

Windermere Ave.
  Accrington BB5 .... **124** D1
Windermere Ave. Burnley BB10 **147** A2
Windermere Ave. Clitheroe BB7 **164** C7
Windermere Ave. Colne BB8 ..... **169** F6
Windermere Ave.
  Fleetwood FY7 .... **172** D8
Windermere Ave. Leyland PR5 ... **76** A3
Windermere Cl.
  Morecambe LA4 .... **212** G4
Windermere Cl. BB1 .... **100** F6
Windermere Cres. PR8 .... **20** C3
Windermere Cl. BB1 .... **100** F6
Windermere Dr. Adlington PR6 ... **43** B1
Windermere Dr. Darwen BB3 ...... **81** C3
Windermere Dr. Maghull L31 .... **5** E2
Windermere Dr.
  Rainford Junction WA11 .... **8** F2
Windermere Dr. Ramsbottom BL0 **49** C7
Windermere Dr. Rishton BB1 ..... **123** A1
Windermere Rd. Bacup OL13 ..... **87** A3
Windermere Rd. Blackpool FY4 **109** C8
Windermere Rd.
  Bolton-le-S LA5 .... **216** A4
Windermere Rd. Carnforth LA5 **216** E8
Windermere Rd. Chorley PR7 ..... **42** E7
Windermere Rd. Fulwood PR2 .. **117** C4
Windermere Rd. Hightown L38 .... **3** A4
Windermere Rd. Lancaster LA1 **211** B8
Windermere Rd. Orrell WN5 .... **10** F8
Windermere Rd. Padiham BB12 **145** C2
Windermere Rd. Preston PR1 .... **118** A1
Windermere Sq. FY8 .... **109** F2
Windgate. Much Hoole PR4 .... **73** E2
Windgate. Skelmersdale WN8 ..... **17** F1
Windgate. Tarleton PR4 .... **56** A5
Windham Pl. LA1 .... **213** C3
Windholme. LA1 .... **213** C2
Windle Ash. L31 .... **5** C2
Windmill Ave. Kirkham PR4 .... **113** C4
Windmill Ave. Ormskirk L39 .... **15** F5
Windmill Cl. Blackpool FY4 .... **109** F6
Windmill Cl. Staining FY3 .... **130** E5
Windmill Ct. LA1 .... **211** A3
Windmill Hts. WN8 .... **10** A8
Windmill La. PR5 & PR6 .... **78** B7
Windmill Rd. WN8 .... **9** F7
Windmill St. LA1 .... **210** D8
Windmill View. PR4 .... **113** A6
Windrows. WN8 .... **17** F1
Windrush Ave. BL0 .... **49** A2
Windrush The. OL12 .... **51** C4
Windsor Ave. Adlington PR6 .... **29** F6
Windsor Ave. Blackpool FY4 .... **109** B8
Windsor Ave. Church BB5 .... **103** A8
Windsor Ave. Clitheroe BB7 ..... **164** C7
Windsor Ave. Fulwood PR2 .... **116** B2
Windsor Ave. Haslingden BB4 .... **84** A1
Windsor Ave. Lancaster LA1 .... **211** A8
Windsor Ave. Longridge PR3 .... **138** F7
Windsor Ave. Morecambe LA4 . **212** D3
Windsor Ave. New Longton PR4 **95** A1
Windsor Ave. Newchurch BB4 .... **85** E1
Windsor Ave. Penwortham PR1 .. **95** C3
Windsor Ave. Thornton FY5 ...... **173** B2
Windsor Cl. Blackburn BB1 ...... **101** B3
Windsor Cl. Burscough L40 .... **24** E3
Windsor Cl. Chorley PR7 .... **42** B7
Windsor Cl. Ramsbottom BL8 ..... **49** A1
Windsor Cl. Read BB12 .... **144** D2
Windsor Cl. Poulton-le-F FY6 ... **151** E3
Windsor Ct. Southport PR8 .... **33** E4
Windsor Dr. Brinscall PR6 .... **61** E8
Windsor Dr. Fulwood PR2 .... **116** D6
Windsor Dr. Horwich BL6 .... **31** E2
Windsor Gdns. BB3 .... **178** B7
Windsor Gr. LA4 .... **212** D4
Windsor Lodge. FY8 .... **89** D4
Windsor Pl. Barnoldswick BB8 .. **200** D3
Windsor Pl. Fleetwood FY7 .... **194** A4
Windsor Rd. Bamber Bridge PR5 **96** D3
Windsor Rd. Blackpool FY4 ...... **100** B6
Windsor Rd. Blackburn BB1 ...... **101** E4
Windsor Rd. Chorley PR7 .... **42** B7
Windsor Rd. Darwen BB3 .... **80** F3
Windsor Rd. Eccleston PR7 .... **40** C7
Windsor Rd. Formby L37 .... **11** F1
Windsor Rd. Garstang PR3 .... **178** B7
Windsor Rd. Great Harwood BB6 **123** D6
Windsor Rd. Hall Green WN8 ..... **10** A8
Windsor Rd. Lytham St Anne's FY8 **89** A5
Windsor Rd.
  Lytham St Anne's FY8 .... **89** D4
Windsor Rd. Maghull L31 .... **5** C1
Windsor Rd.
  Morecambe LA3 & LA4 .... **212** C3
Windsor Rd. Normoss FY3 .... **130** B7
Windsor Rd. Southport PR9 .... **34** D7
Windsor St. Accrington BB5 ..... **103** C6
Windsor St. Burnley BB12 .... **126** C6
Windsor St. Colne BB8 .... **169** E5
Windsor St. Nelson BB9 .... **148** A7
Windsor Terr. FY7 .... **194** B5
Windy Bank. BB8 .... **169** E5
Windy Harbour Rd.
  Singleton FY6 .... **153** A4
Windy Harbour Rd.
  Southport PR9 .... **20** E7
Windy Hill. LA2 .... **233** A8
Windy St. PR3 .... **182** B3
Windyhill. LA1 .... **210** F8
Winery La. PR1 & PR5 .... **96** C5
Winewall La. BB8 .... **170** C5
Winewall Rd. BB8 .... **170** B5
Wingate Ave. Cleveleys FY5 ...... **150** D7
Wingate Ave. Morecambe LA4 .. **212** F4
Wingate Pl. FY5 .... **150** D8
Wingate Rd. L33 .... **1** A3

Wingate Wlk. L33 .... **1** A3
Wingate-Saul Rd. LA1 .... **210** E7
Wingates. PR1 .... **95** C3
Wingrove Rd. FY7 .... **193** F2
Winifred Ave. BL9 .... **32** F4
Winifred La. L39 .... **6** B8
Winifred St. Blackpool FY1 .... **129** B4
Winifred St. Passmonds OL12 ... **51** B1
Winifred St. Ramsbottom BL0 .... **49** B5
Winmarleigh Rd. Lancaster LA1 **211** A2
Winmarleigh Rd. Preston PR1 .. **116** B1
Winmarleigh St. BB1 .... **101** C5
Winmarleigh Wlk. BB1 .... **101** C4
Winmorleigh CE Prim Sch.
  PR3 .... **198** E5
Winnipeg Cl. BB2 .... **100** B8
Winnipeg Rd. BB2 .... **150** E3
Winsford Cres. FY5 .... **150** C8
Winsford Wlk. BB11 .... **126** B5
Winslow Ave. FY6 .... **151** B5
Winslow Cl. PR1 .... **95** C2
Winsor Ave. PR5 .... **59** B8
Winstanley Coll. WN5 .... **10** F3
Winstanley Gr. FY1 .... **129** C5
Winstanley Rd. Orrell WN5 .... **10** F8
Winstanley Rd. Skelmersdale WN8 **8** F8
Winster Cl. PR5 .... **97** E4
Winster Ct. BB5 .... **123** E2
Winster Pk. LA1 .... **213** C2
Winster Pl. FY4 .... **130** D1
Winster Wlk. LA1 .... **213** C2
Winsters The. WN8 .... **17** F1
Winston Ave. Cleveleys FY5 ...... **172** F2
Winston Ave.
  Lytham St Anne's FY8 .... **89** B6
Winston Cres. PR8 .... **34** E2
Winston Rd. BB1 .... **100** D7
Winter Gdns. FY1 .... **129** B5
Winter Hey La. BL6 .... **31** B3
Winterburn Rd. BB2 .... **80** C7
Winterley Dr. BB5 .... **124** E1
Winterton Rd. BB3 .... **81** A2
Winthorpe Ave. LA4 .... **212** G3
Winton Ave. Blackpool FY4 ...... **130** A1
Winton Ave. Fulwood PR2 .... **116** F6
Winton Gn. BL6 .... **31** F1
Winton Rd. FY4 .... **130** A2
Wiseman St. BB11 .... **126** F6
Wisp Hill Gr. LA2 .... **214** F6
Wiswell Cl. Brierfield BB10 .... **147** E2
Wiswell Cl. Rawtenstall BB4 ...... **85** A4
Wiswell La. BB7 .... **143** D6
Wiswell Shay. BB7 .... **143** E7
Witham Cl. WN6 .... **28** D1
Witham Rd. WN8 .... **17** D1
Withens Rd. L31 .... **5** D3
Withers St. BB1 .... **100** F4
Witherslack Cl. LA4 .... **212** E3
Within Gr. BB5 .... **103** D8
Withington La. PR7 .... **40** E2
Withins Field. L38 .... **2** F3
Withins La. L38 .... **4** A7
Withnell Fold Old Rd. PR6 .... **78** L1
Withnell Fold Prim Sch. PR6 ..... **78** C3
Withnell Gr. PR7 .... **60** E1
Withnell Rd. FY4 .... **109** B8
Withy Ct. PR2 .... **116** E3
Withy Grove Cl. PR5 .... **96** F1
Withy Grove Cres. PR5 .... **96** F1
Withy Grove Rd. PR5 .... **96** F1
Withy Par. PR2 .... **116** E4
Withy Trees Ave. PR5 .... **96** F1
Withy Trees Cl. PR5 .... **96** F1
Witney Ave. BB2 .... **79** E8
Witton Ave. FY7 .... **193** E1
Witton Ctry Pk. BB2 .... **99** F4
Witton Gr. FY7 .... **193** E1
Witton Par. BB2 .... **100** C3
Witton Park High Sch. BB2 ...... **100** A4
Witton St. PR1 .... **96** B8
Woborrow Rd. LA3 .... **208** E8
Woburn Cl. BB5 .... **103** E3
Woburn Gn. PR5 .... **76** B2
Woburn Rd. FY1 .... **129** C7
Wolfenden Gn. BB4 .... **68** F8
Wollaton Dr. PR8 .... **34** F3
Wolseley Cl. PR5 .... **59** A8
Wolseley Pl. PR1 .... **96** A7
Wolseley Rd. PR1 .... **95** E5
Wolseley St. Blackburn BB2 .... **100** D1
Wolseley St. Lancaster LA1 ..... **211** A8
Wolsey Cl. FY5 .... **172** E3
Wolsley Rd. Blackpool FY1 ...... **129** B1
Wolsley Rd. Fleetwood FY7 ...... **193** F4
Wolverton. WN8 .... **8** F8
Wolverton Ave. FY2 .... **150** B2
Wood Bank. PR1 .... **95** C3
Wood Cl. BB9 .... **168** A5
Wood End. BB12 .... **146** F3
Wood End Rd. PR6 .... **77** B2
Wood Gn. Kirkham PR4 .... **113** B7
Wood Gn. Leyland PR5 .... **75** C2
Wood Green Dr. FY5 .... **150** F8
Wood Hey Gr. OL12 .... **51** F4
Wood House La. BB7 .... **223** A8
Wood La. Great Altcar L37 & L39 . **13** D1
Wood La. Heskin Green PR7 .... **40** E3
Wood La. Hoscar L40 .... **25** E5
Wood La. Mawdesley PR5 .... **39** D5
Wood La. Parbold WN8 .... **26** D2
Wood Lea Bank. BB4 .... **68** F8
Wood Lea Rd. BB4 .... **68** F8
Wood Nook. BB4 .... **85** A7
Wood Park Rd. FY1 .... **129** E1
Wood Road La. BL8 & BL9 .... **49** C1
Wood St. Blackpool FY1 .... **129** B5
Wood St. Brierfield BB9 .... **147** B5
Wood St. Burnley BB10 .... **127** A8

Wood St. Church BB5 .... **102** E5
Wood St. Colne BB8 .... **169** E4
Wood St. Darwen BB3 .... **80** F1
Wood St. Fleetwood FY7 .... **172** E8
Wood St. Great Harwood BB6 ... **123** E5
Wood St. Hapton BB12 .... **125** C4
Wood St. Horwich BL6 .... **31** C3
Wood St. Lancaster LA1 .... **210** F8
Wood St. Lytham St Anne's FY8 . **88** E6
Wood St. Poulton-le-F FY6 .... **152** A3
Wood St. Ramsbottom BL0 .... **49** B5
Wood Street Livesey Fold. BB3 . **80** F2
Wood View. Blackburn BB2 .... **99** F1
Wood View. Burton in L LA6 ...... **236** C3
Wood's Brow. PR3 .... **140** B6
Wood's La. PR3 .... **177** A6
Woodacre Rd. PR1 & PR2 .... **118** A2
Woodale Laithe. BB9 .... **168** C3
Woodbank Ave. BB3 .... **80** C2
Woodbine Rd. Blackburn BB2 .. **100** B6
Woodbine Rd. Burnley BB12 ..... **126** C6
Woodbine Terr. OL14 .... **108** B1
Woodbridge Gdns. OL12 .... **51** C2
Woodbury Ave. Blackburn BB2 **100** D2
Woodbury Ave. Fence BB12 ...... **146** D7
Woodcock Cl. FY5 .... **173** A5
Woodcock Est. PR5 .... **76** D5
Woodcock Fold. PR7 .... **40** C7
Woodcourt Ave. BB11 .... **126** D3
Woodcrest. BB1 .... **121** B1
Woodcroft. Appley Bridge WN6 .. **19** E6
Woodcroft. Skelmersdale WN8 .... **8** F8
Woodcroft Ave. BB4 .... **84** F5
Woodcroft Cl. PR1 .... **95** C2
Woodcroft St. BB4 .... **84** F5
Woodfall. PR7 .... **60** B2
Woodfield. PR5 .... **76** B3
Woodfield Ave. Accrington BB5 **103** D3
Woodfield Ave. Blackpool FY1 . **129** B2
Woodfield Ave.
  Falinge Fold OL12 .... **51** E2
Woodfield Rd. Blackpool FY1 ... **129** B2
Woodfield Rd. Chorley PR7 .... **60** C1
Woodfield Rd. Ormskirk L39 ...... **15** D3
Woodfield Rd. Thornton FY5 ..... **173** D1
Woodfield Terr. BB7 .... **147** C5
Woodfield View. BB7 .... **143** C5
Woodfields. BB7 .... **163** B3
Woodfold Cl. BB2 .... **120** C3
Woodfold La. PR3 .... **199** C5
Woodfold Pl. BB2 .... **100** B5
Woodford Copse. PR7 .... **42** A7
Woodgate. LA3 .... **213** B2
Woodgate Ave. BL9 .... **32** D4
Woodgate Hill Rd. Bury BL9 ...... **32** C4
Woodgate Hill Rd. Bury BL9 ...... **32** D4
Woodgates Rd. BB2 .... **99** F5
Woodgrove Rd. BB11 .... **127** B4
Woodhall Cres. PR5 .... **97** E4
Woodhall Gdns. FY6 .... **174** C2
Woodhart La. PR7 .... **40** C5
Woodhead Cl. Ramsbottom BL0 . **49** C4
Woodhead Cl. Rawtenstall BB4 .. **86** A2
Woodhead Rd. BB12 .... **144** D2
Woodhouse Rd. FY5 .... **151** E8
Woodhouse St. BB11 .... **127** B4
Woodhurst Dr. WN6 .... **28** D1
Woodland Ave. Bacup OL13 ...... **86** F5
Woodland Ave. Bescar L40 .... **22** F7
Woodland Ave. Thornton FY5 ... **173** B2
Woodland Cl. Hambleton FY6 .. **174** D1
Woodland Cl. Wrea Green PR4 .. **112** B3
Woodland Cres. FY6 .... **195** A6
Woodland Dr. Clayton-le-M BB5 **123** F5
Woodland Dr. Poulton-le-F FY6 **151** E1
Woodland Dr. Standish WN6 .... **28** E2
Woodland Gr. Blackpool FY3 ... **129** E4
Woodland Gr. Egerton BL7 .... **46** D2
Woodland Gr. Penwortham PR1 . **95** B5
Woodland Pk. BB7 .... **143** C5
Woodland Rd. OL12 .... **51** C2
Woodland Terr. OL13 .... **86** F4
Woodland View. Bacup OL13 ..... **86** F4
Woodland View. Brinscall PR7 ... **61** F7
Woodland View.
  Great Harwood BB6 .... **123** C6
Woodlands Ave.
  Bamber Bridge PR5 .... **97** A2
Woodlands Ave. Blackburn BB2 . **99** E1
Woodlands Ave. Fulwood PR2 .. **117** C2
Woodlands Ave. Kirkham PR4 .. **112** F5
Woodlands Ave.
  Penwortham PR1 .... **95** E2
Woodlands Cl.
  Newton-with-S PR4 .... **113** C3
Woodlands Cl. Ormskirk L39 ...... **16** A4
Woodlands Cl. Storth LA7 .... **237** F4
Woodlands Cl.
  West Bradford BB7 .... **186** D7
Woodlands Cl. Whalley BB7 ..... **143** B7
Woodlands Cres. PR3 .... **136** B5
Woodlands Dr. Fulwood PR2 .... **116** B8
Woodlands Dr. Leyland PR5 .... **75** F1
Woodlands Dr. Morecambe LA3 **212** B2
Woodlands Dr. Shevington WN6 . **19** F4

Woodlands Dr. Silverdale LA5 .. **218** C4
Woodlands Dr. Warton PR4 .... **91** C5
Woodlands Dr.
  West Bradford BB7 .... **186** D7
Woodlands Dr. Whalley BB7 ..... **143** C5
Woodlands Gr. Darwen BB3 .... **80** D2
Woodlands Gr. Grimsargh PR2 . **138** E1
Woodlands Gr. Morecambe LA3 **212** B2
Woodlands Gr. Padiham BB12 .. **145** B1
Woodlands Meadow. PR7 .... **42** C3
Woodlands Prim Sch. L37 .... **11** D3
Woodlands Rd. Edenfield BL0 ..... **67** D2
Woodlands Rd. Formby L37 .... **11** C3
Woodlands Rd. Lancaster LA1 .. **214** A4
Woodlands Rd.
  Lytham St Anne's FY8 .... **89** D4
Woodlands Rd. Nelson BB9 ...... **147** F8
Woodlands Sch. PR2 .... **117** E2
Woodlands Special Sch. FY3 ... **129** E4
Woodlands The. Ainsdale PR8 .... **20** C5
Woodlands The. Garstang PR3 . **178** B8
Woodlands The. Preston PR2 ... **115** E1
Woodlands View.
  Over Kellet LA6 .... **231** B8
Woodlands View.
  Ramsbottom BL0 .... **49** C6
Woodlands Way. Longton PR4 .... **73** F8
Woodlands Way. Newsham PR3 **136** B5
Woodlea Chase. BB3 .... **64** C3
Woodlea Cl. PR9 .... **53** D5
Woodlea Gdns. BB9 .... **147** D5
Woodlea Jun Sch. PR5 .... **58** F8
Woodlea Rd. Blackburn BB1 .... **101** B4
Woodlea Rd. Leyland PR5 .... **58** F8
Woodlee Rd. PR4 .... **72** F2
Woodleigh Cl. L31 .... **5** B5
Woodley Ave. Accrington BB5 .. **103** C4
Woodley Ave. Thornton FY5 ..... **173** D1
Woodley Park Rd. WN8 .... **18** B4
Woodman La. LA6 .... **235** F6
Woodmancote. PR7 .... **60** B2
Woodmoss La. PR9 & L40 .... **35** E2
Woodnook Cty Prim Sch. BB5 **103** C4
Woodnook Rd. WN6 .... **19** E8
Woodpecker Hill. BB11 .... **126** C5
Woodplumpton La. PR3 .... **136** C2
Woodplumpton Rd.
  Burnley BB11 .... **126** F1
Woodplumpton Rd.
  Fulwood PR2 .... **116** C3
Woodplumpton Rd.
  Moor Side PR4 .... **135** D4
Woodplumpton Rd.
  Preston PR1 & PR2 .... **116** C2
Woodplumpton Rd.
  Woodplumpton PR4 .... **135** E2
Woodridge Ave. FY5 .... **150** C8
Woodrow. WN8 .... **8** E8
Woodrow Dr. WN8 .... **26** A1
Woodroyd Dr. BL9 .... **32** C3
Woodruff Cl. FY5 .... **172** F5
Woodrush. LA4 .... **213** B6
Woods Brow. BB2 .... **119** D5
Woods Cl. L39 .... **14** A4
Woods Gn. PR1 .... **95** E6
Woods La. PR4 & PR3 .... **134** E8
Woodsend Cl. BB2 .... **81** A8
Woodside. Chorley PR7 .... **42** E4
Woodside. Euxton PR7 .... **59** C3
Woodside. Haslingden BB4 .... **84** C1
Woodside. Leyland PR5 .... **76** C4
Woodside Ave.
  Ainsdale PR8 .... **20** B3
Woodside Ave.
  Clayton Green PR6 .... **77** B1
Woodside Ave. Fulwood PR2 .... **116** E4
Woodside Ave.
  New Longton PR4 .... **74** F7
Woodside Ave. Ribbleton PR2 .. **117** E3
Woodside Ave. Rishton BB1 ..... **101** F8
Woodside Cl. Accrington BB5 .. **124** F1
Woodside Cl. Up Holland WN8 .. **10** C8
Woodside Cres. BB4 .... **85** D1
Woodside Dr. Blackpool FY3 ... **130** A5
Woodside Dr. Ramsbottom BL0 . **49** A5
Woodside Gr. BB2 .... **80** A8
Woodside Rd. Accrington BB5 .. **124** F1
Woodside Rd. Huncoat BB5 ..... **103** E8
Woodside Rd.
  Simonstone BB12 .... **144** E2
Woodside Terr. BB9 .... **147** C8
Woodsley St. BB11 .... **126** B5
Woodstock Ave. FY5 .... **151** C8
Woodstock Cl. PR5 .... **76** C8
Woodstock Cres. BB2 .... **79** E8
Woodstock Dr. PR8 .... **20** F8
Woodstock Gdns. FY4 .... **109** B7
Woodstock St. OL12 .... **51** C1
Woodtop CE Inf Sch. BB11 ...... **126** D5
Woodvale. Darwen BB3 .... **80** F1
Woodvale. Leyland PR5 .... **58** A8
Woodvale Airfield. PR8 .... **20** A2
Woodvale Prim Sch. PR8 .... **20** D3
Woodvale Rd. PR8 .... **20** E2
Woodville Rd. Adlington PR6 ..... **42** F1
Woodville Rd. Blackburn BB1 .. **101** A7
Woodville Rd. Brierfield BB9 ... **147** C6
Woodville Rd. Chorley PR7 .... **42** C8
Woodville Rd. Penwortham PR1 . **95** D2
Woodville Rd W. PR1 .... **95** C2
Woodville St. Lancaster LA1 .... **211** A8
Woodville St. Leyland PR5 .... **76** B2
Woodville Terr. Darwen BB3 ...... **64** B6
Woodville Terr.
  Lytham St Anne's FY8 .... **89** F3
Woodward Rd. L33 .... **1** D4
Woodway. PR2 .... **116** C4
Woodwell La. LA5 .... **218** C1
Wookey Cl. PR2 .... **117** D6

Wooley La. BB5 .... 103 F2
Woolman Rd. FY1 .... 129 C4
Woolpack. BB8 .... 169 E3
Woolwich St. BB1 .... 101 B5
Woone La. BB7 .... 164 D7
Worcester Ave. 4
  Accrington BB5 .... 103 A7
Worcester Ave. Garstang PR3 .. 178 B8
Worcester Ave. Lancaster LA1 .. 211 B5
Worcester Ave. Leyland PR5 ...... 59 B8
Worcester Pl. PR7 .... 42 E3
Worcester Rd. Blackburn BB1 .. 101 C5
Worcester Rd. Blackpool FY3 .. 130 A3
Worden Cl. PR5 .... 58 F7
Worden La. PR5 .... 59 A7
Worden Rd. PR2 .... 116 D3
Wordsworth Ave.
  Blackpool FY3 .... 130 B2
Wordsworth Ave.
  Bolton-le-S LA5 .... 216 A5
Wordsworth Ave.
  Longshaw WN5 .... 10 D1
Wordsworth Ave.
  Lytham St Anne's FY8 .... 90 D4
Wordsworth Ave. Orrell WN5 .... 10 F6
Wordsworth Ave.
  Padiham BB12 .... 125 E7
Wordsworth Ave.
  Thornton FY5 .... 173 A2
Wordsworth Ave. Warton PR4 ... 91 E6
Wordsworth Cl. Ormskirk L39 ... 15 D6
Wordsworth Cl.
  Oswaldtwistle BB5 .... 102 C4
Wordsworth Ct. FY8 .... 89 C4
Wordsworth Dr. BB6 .... 123 B4
Wordsworth Gdns. BB3 .... 81 B1
Wordsworth House. LA1 .... 213 E4
Wordsworth Pl. PR5 .... 96 D2
Wordsworth Rd.
  Accrington BB5 .... 103 A4
Wordsworth Rd. Colne BB8 ..... 169 D5
Wordsworth St.
  Brierfield BB10 .... 147 F2
Wordsworth St. Burnley BB12 .. 126 C6
Wordsworth St. Hapton BB12 ... 125 C4
Wordsworth Terr. PR6 .... 60 D2
Workshop Rd. LA3 .... 208 F2
Worrall St. OL12 .... 51 D2
Worsley Ave. FY4 .... 109 C7
Worsley Cl. PR5 .... 194 E5
Worsley Ct. 13 BB5 .... 102 E4
Worsley Rd. FY8 .... 89 C5
Worsley St. Accrington BB5 ..... 103 D4
Worsley St. Haslingden BB5 ...... 84 A8
Worsthorne Prim Sch. BB10 .. 128 A6
Worston Cl. Accrington BB5 ..... 102 F4
Worston Cl. Rawtenstall BB4 .... 85 A4
Worston La. BB6 .... 123 F6
Worston Pl. BB2 .... 100 C5
Worthing Cl. PR8 .... 33 F3

Worthing Rd. PR2 .... 116 A4
Worthington Rd. FY4 .... 110 B4
Worthy St. PR6 & PR7 .... 42 E7
Wraith St. BB3 .... 64 A8
Wray Cres. Wrea Green PR4 ..... 112 C4
Wray Cres. Wymott PR5 .... 57 F6
Wray Ct. LA1 .... 213 E4
Wray Gr. FY5 .... 150 D8
Wray-with-Botton
  Endowed Prim Sch. LA2 .... 232 D6
Wraywood Ct. FY7 .... 193 C1
Wren Ave. PR1 .... 95 E5
Wren Cl. Blackpool FY6 .... 151 A4
Wren Cl. Thornton FY5 .... 151 D8
Wren Dr. BL9 .... 32 B4
Wren Gr. FY3 .... 129 E2
Wren St. Burnley BB12 .... 126 C6
Wren St. Nelson BB9 .... 147 F8
Wren St. Preston PR1 .... 117 B2
Wrennalls La. PR7 .... 40 B5
Wright St. Chorley PR6 .... 42 E8
Wright St. Horwich BL6 .... 31 B4
Wright St. Kirkham PR4 .... 112 F6
Wright St. Southport PR9 .... 34 C7
Wright St. Weir OL13 .... 87 A7
Wright St W. 3 BL6 .... 31 B4
Wrightington Hospl. WN6 .... 27 D2
Wrights Fold. PR5 .... 59 C8
Wrights Terr. PR8 .... 34 B3
Wrigleys Cl. L37 .... 11 F5
Wrigleys La. L37 .... 11 F5
Written Stone La. PR3 .... 160 E1
Wroxham Cl. BB10 .... 147 D2
Wroxton Cl. FY5 .... 150 F7
Wycherley Rd. OL12 .... 51 B2
Wychnor. PR2 & PR4 .... 116 B7
Wycollar Cl. BB5 .... 103 C4
Wycollar Dr. BB2 .... 100 A6
Wycollar Rd. BB2 .... 100 B6
Wycoller Ave. BB10 .... 127 D5
Wycombe Ave. FY4 .... 109 B6
Wyfordby Ave. BB2 .... 100 A7
Wyke Cop Rd. PR8 & PR9 .... 35 D2
Wyke La. PR8 & PR9 .... 35 E6
Wyke Wood La. PR9 .... 35 F7
Wykeham Gr. OL12 .... 51 B1
Wykeham Rd. FY8 .... 90 B4
Wyllin Rd. L33 .... 1 A2
Wymundsley. PR7 .... 60 A2
Wyndene Cl. PR3 .... 139 C8
Wyndene Gr. PR4 .... 92 B6
Wyndham Gdns. FY4 .... 109 D6
Wyndham Pl. LA4 .... 213 B6
Wynfield. PR5 .... 96 F2
Wynnstay Ave. L31 .... 5 D3
Wynnwood Ave. FY1 .... 129 D8
Wynotham St. BB10 .... 147 C1
Wyre Ave. PR4 .... 113 B5
Wyre Bank. PR3 .... 155 B6
Wyre Cl. Great Eccleston PR3 .... 154 C5

Wyre Cl. Lancaster LA1 .... 213 B2
Wyre Cres. BB3 .... 80 D4
Wyre Ct. Fleetwood FY7 .... 193 E3
Wyre Ct. Poulton-le-F FY6 ...... 152 A3
Wyre Gr. FY1 .... 129 C3
Wyre House. LA1 .... 210 F7
Wyre La. PR3 .... 199 D1
Wyre Rd. FY6 .... 151 F6
Wyre St. Fleetwood FY7 .... 193 F3
Wyre St. Kirkham PR4 .... 112 F6
Wyre St. Padiham BB12 .... 125 D8
Wyre St. Preston PR1 .... 116 C1
Wyre View. FY6 .... 194 E5
Wyredale Ct. FY7 .... 193 F3
Wyredale Rd. FY8 .... 88 C8
Wyrefields. FY6 .... 152 A3
Wyresdale Ave.
  Accrington BB5 .... 103 A8
Wyresdale Ave. Blackpool FY2 . 150 D4
Wyresdale Ave.
  Morecambe LA3 .... 212 B1
Wyresdale Ave.
  Poulton-le-F FY6 .... 151 C3
Wyresdale Ave. Southport PR8 .. 34 D4
Wyresdale Cres. Fulwood PR2 . 117 D4
Wyresdale Cres. Glasson LA2 .. 205 E4
Wyresdale Cres. Scorton PR3 .. 199 E7
Wyresdale Ct. LA1 .... 211 B7
Wyresdale Dr. PR5 & PR7 .... 59 B6
Wyresdale Gdns. LA1 .... 211 B7
Wyresdale Rd.
  Knott End-on-S FY6 .... 194 D5
Wyresdale Rd. Lancaster LA1 .. 211 B6
Wyresdale Rd. Quernmore LA2 . 226 A6
Wyreside Cl. PR3 .... 178 C8
Wyreside Dr. FY6 .... 174 B2
Wytham St. 3 BB12 .... 125 D7
Wythburn Ave. BB2 .... 79 E8
Wythburn Cl. BB12 .... 126 B8
Wythorpe Croft. LA4 .... 212 E4
Wyvern Way. FY6 .... 151 C5

Yale St. BL7 .... 47 D4
Yans La. LA37 .... 237 F5
Yardley Ctr. L33 .... 1 C1
Yardley Rd. L33 .... 1 C1
Yare St. 7 BB4 .... 68 F8
Yarlside La. BD23 .... 225 E4
Yarm Pl. BB11 .... 127 A6
Yarmouth Ave. BB4 .... 84 C2
Yarraville St. BB4 .... 85 A2
Yarrow Ave. L31 .... 5 F2
Yarrow Cl. Croston PR5 .... 57 B2
Yarrow Cl. Withnell PR6 .... 79 A1
Yarrow Gate. PR7 .... 42 E6
Yarrow Gr. BL6 .... 31 B4
Yarrow Pl. PR5 .... 58 D8
Yarrow Pl. Chorley PR7 .... 42 E6
Yarrow Rd. Leyland PR5 .... 58 D8

Yarrow Wlk. LA3 .... 212 E2
Yarwood St. BL9 .... 32 A2
Yates Fold. BB2 .... 100 F2
Yates Rd. PR7 .... 42 B5
Yates St. FY1 .... 129 B6
Yeadon. WN8 .... 18 B1
Yeadon Gr. PR7 .... 42 A7
Yeadon Way. FY4 .... 109 D7
Yealand Ave. LA3 .... 208 F6
Yealand Conyers CE Prim Sch.
  LA5 .... 219 E3
Yealand Dr. LA1 .... 211 A4
Yealand Gr. LA5 .... 217 E2
Yealand Rd. LA5 .... 219 E2
Yeargate Ind Est. BL9 .... 32 D2
Yellow Hall. BB8 .... 192 A5
Yellow House La. PR8 .... 34 B6
Yenham La. LA3 .... 209 E1
Yerburgh Rd. BB2 .... 120 E2
Yew Ct. FY7 .... 193 C1
Yew Gn. PR4 .... 113 B7
Yew St. 7 Blackburn BB1 .... 101 A7
Yew St. 2 Bury BL9 .... 32 C3
Yew Tree Ave. Euxton PR7 .... 59 C4
Yew Tree Ave. Grimsargh PR2 . 138 C2
Yew Tree Cl. Garstang PR3 ..... 178 B8
Yew Tree Cl.
  Newton-with-S PR4 .... 113 F3
Yew Tree Dr. Blackburn BB2 ... 121 B1
Yew Tree Dr.
  Oswaldtwistle BB5 .... 102 F3
Yew Tree Gr. BB4 .... 67 F8
Yew Tree Rd. Blackpool FY6 ... 151 A1
Yew Tree Rd. Ormskirk L39 ...... 15 E7
Yewbarrow Cl. BB12 .... 146 C1
Yewdale. WN8 .... 18 A1
Yewdale Ave. LA3 .... 208 F6
Yewlands Ave. 4
  Bamber Bridge PR5 .... 96 F1
Yewlands Ave.
  Heskin Green PR7 .... 40 F3
Yewlands Ave. 3 Leyland PR5 .. 76 A1
Yewlands Cres. PR2 .... 116 E6
Yewlands Dr. Brierfield BB10 .. 147 B3
Yewlands Dr. Fulwood PR2 ..... 116 E6
Yewlands Dr. Garstang PR3 .... 199 C1
Yewlands Dr. 2 Leyland PR5 .... 76 A1
Yewtree Ave. PR2 .... 118 A4
Yewtree Cl. PR7 .... 42 C3
Yewtree Dr. LA2 .... 233 C8
Yewtree Gr. PR5 .... 76 A7
York Ave. Cleveleys FY5 .... 172 D2
York Ave. Fleetwood FY7 .... 193 E3
York Ave. Fulwood PR2 .... 116 E4
York Ave. Haslingden BB4 .... 67 B8
York Ave. Southport PR8 .... 34 A5
York Cl. Accrington BB5 .... 103 B7
York Cl. Bamber Bridge PR5 ..... 96 D3
York Cl. Clayton-le-M BB5 ...... 123 F3

York Cl. Formby L37 .... 11 F6
York Cl. Leyland PR5 .... 58 E7
York Cres. BB1 .... 121 F3
York Dr. Great Eccleston PR3 ... 154 C5
York Dr. Kirkham PR4 .... 113 B2
York Dr. Ramsbottom BL0 .... 49 A4
York Fields. BB8 .... 200 B1
York Gdns. PR8 .... 34 A5
York Gr. PR3 .... 178 B7
York House. 28 PR1 .... 96 A7
York La. BB6 .... 122 D8
York Pl. Morecambe LA4 .... 212 F5
York Rd. Blackpool FY2 .... 150 B4
York Rd. Formby L37 .... 12 A3
York Rd. Lancaster LA1 .... 211 A5
York Rd. Langho BB1 & BB6 ... 122 D6
York Rd. Lytham St Anne's FY8 .. 88 F5
York Rd. Southport PR8 .... 33 F4
York St. Accrington BB5 .... 103 B7
York St. Bacup OL13 .... 86 F5
York St. Barnoldswick BB8 ..... 200 B2
York St. Blackburn BB2 .... 100 E3
York St. Blackpool FY1 .... 129 B3
York St. Bury BL9 .... 32 A2
York St. Chorley PR7 .... 42 D7
York St. Church BB5 .... 102 E6
York St. Clitheroe BB7 .... 186 F1
York St. Colne BB8 .... 169 F5
York St. Great Harwood BB6 ... 123 D5
York St. Nelson BB9 .... 147 F8
York St. Oswaldtwistle BB5 ..... 102 C3
York St. Rawtenstall BB4 .... 85 A7
York St. Rishton BB1 .... 123 A1
York Terr. Blackburn BB2 .... 79 D8
York Terr. Southport PR9 .... 34 C8
Yorke St. 2 BB11 .... 126 F5
Yorkshire St. Accrington BB5 .. 103 C4
Yorkshire St. 3 Bacup OL13 .... 86 F3
Yorkshire St. Blackpool FY1 ... 129 B3
Yorkshire St. Burnley BB11 ..... 127 B6
Yorkshire St. Huncoat BB5 ..... 124 E2
Yorkshire St. 11 Nelson BB9 ... 147 E8
Yorkshire St E. LA4 .... 212 C4
Yorkshire St W. LA3 & LA4 ..... 212 B4
Young Ave. PR5 .... 76 C1
Young St. Blackburn BB2 .... 100 B2
Young St. Ramsbottom BL0 ...... 49 B6

Zama St. 9 BL0 .... 49 A4
Zebudah St. BB2 .... 100 C2
Zechariah Brow. BB1 & BB2 ... 121 B3
Zetland St. Preston PR1 .... 96 C7
Zetland St. Southport PR9 .... 34 D7
Zion Rd. BB1 .... 101 A8
Zion St. Bacup OL13 .... 87 A3
Zion St. Colne BB8 .... 169 D4

STREET ATLASES ORDER FORM

All Street Atlases contain Ordnance Survey mapping and provide the perfect solution for the driver who needs comprehensive, detailed regional mapping in a choice of compact and easy-to-use formats. They are indispensable and are ideal for use in the car, the home or the office.

The series is available from all good bookshops or by mail order direct from the publisher. Before placing your order, please check by telephone that the complete range of titles are available. Payment can be made in the following ways:

By phone Phone your order through on our special Credit Card Hotline on 01733 371999 (Fax: 01733 370585). Speak to our customer service team during office hours (9am to 5pm) or leave a message on the answering machine, quoting your full credit card number plus expiry date and your full name and address.

By post Simply fill out the order form (you may photocopy it) and send it to: **Reed Books Direct, 43 Stapledon Road, Orton Southgate, Peterborough** PE2 6TD.

NEW COLOUR EDITIONS

	HARDBACK	SPIRAL	POCKET	£ Total
	Quantity @ £10.99 each	Quantity @ £8.99 each	Quantity @ £4.99 each	£ Total
BERKSHIRE	☐ 0 540 06170 0	☐ 0 540 06172 7	☐ 0 540 06173 5	➤
	Quantity @ £10.99 each	Quantity @ £8.99 each	Quantity @ £3.99 each	£ Total
MERSEYSIDE	☐ 0 540 06480 7	☐ 0 540 06481 5	☐ 0 540 06482 3	➤
	Quantity @ £12.99 each	Quantity @ £8.99 each	Quantity @ £4.99 each	£ Total
SURREY	☐ 0 540 06435 1	☐ 0 540 06436 X	☐ 0 540 06438 6	➤
	Quantity @ £12.99 each	Quantity @ £9.99 each	Quantity @ £4.99 each	£ Total
DURHAM	☐ 0 540 06365 7	☐ 0 540 06366 5	☐ 0 540 06367 3	➤
GREATER MANCHESTER	☐ 0 540 06485 8	☐ 0 540 06486 6	☐ 0 540 06487 4	➤
HERTFORDSHIRE	☐ 0 540 06174 3	☐ 0 540 06175 1	☐ 0 540 06176 X	➤
TYNE AND WEAR	☐ 0 540 06370 3	☐ 0 540 06371 1	☐ 0 540 06372 X	➤
SOUTH YORKSHIRE	☐ 0 540 06330 4	☐ 0 540 06331 2	☐ 0 540 06332 0	➤
WEST YORKSHIRE	☐ 0 540 06329 0	☐ 0 540 06327 4	☐ 0 540 06328 2	➤
	Quantity @ £14.99 each	Quantity @ £9.99 each	Quantity @ £4.99 each	£ Total
LANCASHIRE	☐ 0 540 06440 8	☐ 0 540 06441 6	☐ 0 540 06443 2	➤

BLACK AND WHITE EDITIONS

	HARDBACK	SOFTBACK	POCKET	£ Total
	Quantity @ £12.99 each	Quantity @ £9.99 each	Quantity @ £4.99 each	£ Total
BRISTOL AND AVON	☐ 0 540 06140 9	☐ 0 540 06141 7	☐ 0 540 06142 5	➤
BUCKINGHAMSHIRE	☐ 0 540 05989 7	☐ 0 540 05990 0	☐ 0 540 05991 9	➤
CARDIFF, SWANSEA & GLAMORGAN	☐ 0 540 06186 7	☐ 0 540 06187 5	☐ 0 540 06207 3	➤

STREET ATLASES ORDER FORM

BLACK AND WHITE EDITIONS

	HARDBACK	SOFTBACK	POCKET	£ Total
	Quantity @ £12.99 each	Quantity @ £9.99 each	Quantity @ £4.99 each	
CHESHIRE	☐ 0 540 06143 3	☐ 0 540 06144 1	☐ 0 540 06145 X	➤ ☐
DERBYSHIRE	☐ 0 540 06137 9	☐ 0 540 06138 7	☐ 0 540 06139 5	➤ ☐
EDINBURGH & East Central Scotland	☐ 0 540 06180 8	☐ 0 540 06181 6	☐ 0 540 06182 4	➤ ☐
GLASGOW & West Central Scotland	☐ 0 540 06183 2	☐ 0 540 06184 0	☐ 0 540 06185 9	➤ ☐
SOUTH HAMPSHIRE	☐ 0 540 05855 6	☐ 0 540 05856 4	☐ 0 540 05857 2	➤ ☐
WEST KENT	☐ 0 540 06029 1	☐ 0 540 06031 3	☐ 0 540 06030 5	➤ ☐
STAFFORDSHIRE	☐ 0 540 06134 4	☐ 0 540 06135 2	☐ 0 540 06136 0	➤ ☐
WEST SUSSEX	☐ 0 540 05876 9	☐ 0 540 05877 7	☐ 0 540 05878 5	➤ ☐
	Quantity @ £10.99 each	Quantity @ £8.99 each	Quantity @ £4.99 each	£ Total
WARWICKSHIRE	☐ 0 540 05642 1	—	—	➤ ☐
	Quantity @ £12.99 each	Quantity @ £8.99 each	Quantity @ £4.99 each	£ Total
EAST ESSEX	☐ 0 540 05848 3	☐ 0 540 05866 1	☐ 0 540 05850 5	➤ ☐
WEST ESSEX	☐ 0 540 05849 1	☐ 0 540 05867 X	☐ 0 540 05851 3	➤ ☐
NORTH HAMPSHIRE	☐ 0 540 05852 1	☐ 0 540 05853 X	☐ 0 540 05854 8	➤ ☐
EAST KENT	☐ 0 540 06026 7	☐ 0 540 06027 5	☐ 0 540 06028 3	➤ ☐
NOTTINGHAMSHIRE	☐ 0 540 05858 0	☐ 0 540 05859 9	☐ 0 540 05860 2	➤ ☐
OXFORDSHIRE	☐ 0 540 05986 2	☐ 0 540 05987 0	☐ 0 540 05988 9	➤ ☐
EAST SUSSEX	☐ 0 540 05875 0	☐ 0 540 05874 2	☐ 0 540 05873 4	➤ ☐

Post to: Reed Books Direct, 43 Stapledon Road, Orton Southgate, Peterborough PE2 6TD

◆ Free postage and packing

◆ All available titles will normally be dispatched within 5 working days of receipt of order but please allow up to 28 days for delivery

☐ Please tick this box if you do not wish your name to be used by other carefully selected organisations that may wish to send you information about other products and services

Registered Office: Michelin House, 81 Fulham Road, London sw3 6rb. Registered in England number:1974080

I enclose a cheque / postal order, for a **total** of ☐

made payable to *Reed Book Services,* or please debit my

☐ Access ☐ American Express ☐ Visa ☐ Diners

account by ☐

Account no
☐☐☐☐ ☐☐☐☐ ☐☐☐☐ ☐☐☐☐

Expiry date ☐☐ ☐☐

Signature...

Name...

Address...

....

....

....POSTCODE